MEDICAL LAW

MEDICAL LAW

Text, Cases, and Materials

Emily Jackson

OXFORD

UNIVERSITY PRESS

OXFORD

UNIVERSITY PRESS

Great Clarendon Street, Oxford OX2 6DP

Oxford University Press is a department of the University of Oxford.
It furthers the University's objective of excellence in research, scholarship,
and education by publishing worldwide in

Oxford New York

Auckland Cape Town Dar es Salaam Hong Kong Karachi
Kuala Lumpur Madrid Melbourne Mexico City Nairobi
New Delhi Shanghai Taipei Toronto

With offices in

Argentina Austria Brazil Chile Czech Republic France Greece
Guatemala Hungary Italy Japan Poland Portugal Singapore
South Korea Switzerland Thailand Turkey Ukraine Vietnam

Oxford is a registered trade mark of Oxford University Press
in the UK and in certain other countries

Published in the United States
by Oxford University Press Inc., New York

First published 2006
Second edition 2010

British Library Cataloguing in Publication Data

Data available

Library of Congress Cataloging in Publication Data

Typeset by Newgen Imaging Systems Pvt Ltd., Chennai, India
Printed in Great Britain
on acid-free paper by
Ashford Colour Press Ltd, Gosport, Hants

ISBN 978–0–19–955192–7

1 3 5 7 9 10 8 6 4 2

To my father, Douglas Jackson.

PREFACE

My intention in writing this book has been to provide students of medical or health care law and ethics with both a textbook and a source of relevant materials. Medical law is extraordinarily fast-moving and newsworthy. This makes it exciting both to teach and to study, but it also means that there are likely to be many new developments during the lifetime of this book. Wherever possible, I have tried to draw attention to areas where change is likely, and to flag up sources of up-to-date information.

People often have strongly held views on medical law and ethics, and in this book I have included extracts which embody a number of diverse perspectives. My principal aim has been to explain and describe medical law, and provide a balanced analysis of the issues, rather than to offer my personal views. There are places where my own opinions will become evident, but I hope this is not too intrusive.

Despite including a new chapter on genetics, the second edition of this book is slightly shorter than the first. At first sight, this might suggest that I have had an easy time of it in the past year, and have simply been cutting a bit of 'fat' from the first edition. Nothing could be further from the truth. Parliament, the courts, the Department of Health, and a range of other bodies responsible for producing advice, guidance, and guidelines have been extremely busy since I completed the first edition of this book, in August 2005. The Mental Health Act 2007 and the Human Fertilisation and Embryology Act 2008 were both substantial amending pieces of legislation which have significantly altered the legal treatment of people suffering from mental disorders and the regulation of fertility treatment and embryo research. This book will be published just before the latter statute comes into force, and it therefore describes the law as of October 2009, rather than attempting to provide a full description of imminently irrelevant legislative detail.

While undertaking a task that resembles painting the Forth Road Bridge, only without the pleasant view, I have acquired a number of debts of gratitude. First of all, my thanks go to the students who have taken my medical law course over the years. I have learned a great deal from them, and from my co-teacher, Stuart Andrews. My colleagues in the Law Department and in the BIOS Institute at the LSE have provided a wonderfully stimulating intellectual environment, for which I am very grateful.

A few other individuals deserve specific thanks. Eleanor Williams at OUP has been a helpful and encouraging editor. Kristen Veblen proofread the whole manuscript, and made useful and constructive suggestions along the way. David Gomez provided invaluable comments on chapter 15, and I am very grateful for his feedback. In the past few years, I have learned a great deal from Sarah Franklin, and I understand some of the topics covered here much better as a result of discussing them with her.

Closer to home, Douglas, Sue, Emma, and Sophie Jackson have been the perfect dad, sister-in-law and nieces, and I have no idea how I would manage without them. My oldest friends—Alison Cox, Ciarán O'Meara, Duncan Paterson, Monica Thurnauer, and Matthew Weait—have, as ever, been extraordinarily supportive. They must be sick of me prefacing every sentence with 'when I've finished the second edition...' and I am very much looking forward to spending more time with them and less time with my computer. Finally, Robert Phillips deserves an extra special prize for patience and support beyond the call of duty.

ACKNOWLEDGEMENTS

Grateful acknowledgement is made to all the authors and publishers of copyright material which appears in this book, and in particular to the following for permission to reprint material from the sources indicated:

Crown copyright material is reproduced under Class Licence Number C2006010631 with the permission of the Controller of HMSO and the Queen's Printer for Scotland. Parliamentary copyright material is reproduced with the permission of the Controller of Her Majesty's Stationery Office on behalf of Parliament.

BMJ Publishing Group Ltd: extracts from *British Medical Journal* and *Journal of Medical Ethics*: Charles A Erin and John Harris: 'An ethical market in human organs' 29 *JME* 137 (2003), copyright © 2003; John Harris: 'Scientific research is a moral duty', 31 *JME* 242 (2005, copyright © 2005; D Kirklin: 'The role of medical imaging in the abortion debate', 30 *JME* 426 (2004), copyright © 2004; Linsey McGoey and Emily Jackson: 'Sexorat and the suppression of clinical trial data: regulatory failure and the uses of legal ambiguity', 35 *JME* 107 (2009), copyright © 2009; David Prayle and Margaret Brazier: 'Supply of medicines: paternalism, autonomy and reality', 24 *JME* 93 (1998), copyright © 1998; M P M Richards, M Ponder, P Pharoah, S Everest and J Mackay: 'Issues of consent and feedback in a genetic epidemiological study of women with breast cancer', 29 *JME* 93 (2003), copyright © 2003; and D Thomas: 'Laboratory animals and the art of empathy', 31 *JME* 197 (2005), copyright © 2005.

Cambridge University Press: extracts from John Keown: *Euthananasia, Ethics and Public Policy* (CUP, 2002), and Bernard Williams: *Making Sense of Humanity* (CUP, 1995); and extracts from *Cambridge Quarterly of Healthcare Studies*: John Harris: 'Stem Cells, Sex, and Procreation', 12 (04) CQHE 353 (2003), Soren Holm: 'The Ethical Case against Stem Cell Research', 12 CQHE 372 (2003), and Martin Smith and Heidi Foster: 'Morally Managing Medical Mistakes', 9 (01) CQHE 38 (2000).

General Medical Council: extracts from 'Withholding and Withdrawing Life-prolonging Treatments' (2002), 'Good Medical Practice' (2006), '0–18 Guidance for all doctors' (2007), 'Consent: Patients and doctors making decisions together' (2008), 'Personal beliefs and Medical Practice' (2008), 'Research: The Role and Responsibility of Doctors' (2008), 'Confidentiality: protecting and Providing Information' (2004), and Supplement to Confidentiality Guidance (2009), available at http://www.gmc-uk.org.uk.

HarperCollins Publishers and **Alfred A Knopf, a division of Random House Inc**: extract from R Dworkin: *Life's Dominion: An Argument About Abortion and Euthanasia* (HarperCollins, 1993)

Hart Publishing: extracts from N Eastman & J Peay (eds.): *Law Without Enforcement: Integrating Mental Health and Justice* (Hart, 1999): Fiona Caldicott, Edna Conlan and Anthony Zigmund: 'Client and Clinician - Law as an Intrusion?', Nigel Eastman and Jill Peay: 'Afterword: Integrating Mental Health and Justice', and Eric Matthews: 'Mental and Physical Illness - an Unsustainable Separation?'.

Harvard Law Review and the author: extracts from Frederick Schauer: 'Slippery Slopes', 99 *Harvard Law Review* 361.

Development Risk Defence: Knowledge, Discoverability and Creative Leaps', 4 JPIL 258 (2004); and *Law Quarterly Review*: Tony Honore: 'Causation and Disclosure of Medical Risks', 114 LQR 52 (1998; and extracts from the *European Human Rights Reports* (EHRR).

Taylor & Francis Group (http://www.informaworld.com) via Copyright Clearance Center: extracts from Trudo Lemmens and Carl Elliot: 'Justice for the Professional Guinea Pig', 1 *American Journal of Bioethics* 51 (2001), and Samantha Singer: 'Casenote: Rees v Darlington', 26 *Journal of Social Welfare and Family Law* 403 (2004).

Washington University in St Louis School of Law and the author: extract from *Washington University Law Quarterly*: Lori B Andrews: 'A Conceptual Framework for Genetic Policy: Comparing the Medical, Public Health and Fundamental Rights Models', 79 *Wash ULQ* 221 (2001).

Wiley-Blackwell Publishing Ltd: extracts from Ranaan Gillon: 'Confidentiality', Helga Kuhse and Peter Singer: 'What is bioethics? A historical introduction', Laura Purdy: 'Assisted Reproduction' and Mary Warnock: 'Experimentation on human embryos and fetuses, in H Kuhse and P Singer (Eds): *Companion to Bioethics* (Blackwell, 1998); and from *Bioethics*: Heather Draper and Tom Sorrell: 'Patients' Responsibilities in Medical Ethics', 16 *Bioethics* 335 (2002), Helga Kuhse: 'Clinical ethics and nursing: "yes" to caring, but "no" to a female ethics of care', 9 *Bioethics* 207 (1995); *Modern Law Review*: Laura Hoyano: 'Misconceptions about Wrongful Conception', 65 MLR 883 (2002), and Nigel Lowe and Satvinder Juss: 'Medical Treatment--Pragmatism and the Search for Principle', 56 MLR 865 (1993); and *Sociology of Health and Illness*: Peter Conrad & Deborah Potter: 'Human growth hormone and the temptations of biomedical enhancement', 26 Sociology of Health and Illness 184 (2004).

CONTENTS

1   AN INTRODUCTION TO BIOETHICS   1

2   RESOURCE ALLOCATION   32

3 | MEDICAL MALPRACTICE ... 100

8   GENETIC INFORMATION   391

9   CLINICAL RESEARCH   429

10   PRODUCT LIABILITY AND THE REGULATION OF MEDICINES   497

11 ORGAN TRANSPLANTATION   552

12 EMBRYO AND STEM CELL RESEARCH   620

TABLE OF CASES

Where cases are dealt with in detail the relevant page numbers are shown in **bold**.

TABLE OF STATUTES

Page references in **bold** indicate that the text is reproduced in full.

TABLE OF STATUTORY INSTRUMENTS

Page references in **bold** indicate that the text is reproduced in full.

TABLE OF TREATIES, CONVENTIONS, AND EUROPEAN LEGISLATION

1

AN INTRODUCTION
TO BIOETHICS

CENTRAL ISSUES

1 Conventional medical ethics focused on the individual doctor–patient encounter. Bioethics' remit is much broader, taking in the dilemmas new technologies raise for society as a whole.

2 Religious perspectives on bioethics tend to be less individualistic than secular approaches. Few now believe that modern medicine 'usurps God's will'. Instead, medical progress is, within limits, supported by most religious bioethicists.

3 There is an important difference between consequentialist and deontological reasoning. Consequentialists judge an action by its consequences, whereas deontological reasoning starts from the premise that respect for a person's rights is important for its own sake.

4 The 'principlist' approach lays out four key principles: autonomy, beneficence, non-maleficence, and justice,

which can be brought to bear on medical dilemmas. In contrast, casuistry involves reasoning by analogy from previous cases. Virtue ethics is concerned with working out what a 'virtuous' person would do in a particular situation. A feminist ethic of care rejects the individualistic model of patient autonomy, and places more emphasis upon interdependence and relationships.

5 Arguments from 'human dignity' or respect for the 'sanctity of human life' have particular resonance in the medical context, but their meaning, and the extent to which they are religiously inspired, is opaque.

6 Slippery slope claims are often essentially empirical claims, and effective regulation might be the best way to accommodate them.

1 INTRODUCTION

The purpose of this chapter is to provide an introduction to bioethical reasoning. The words 'ethics' and 'morality' derive from the Greek (*ethos*) and Latin (*mores*), meaning 'customs'. In their ordinary usage, the words have slightly different connotations. 'Morality' often implies a restrictive code of conduct, which sets out the difference between right and wrong. 'Ethics' tends to refer to the systematic analysis of what it might mean to lead a decent life. Medical ethics is a branch of applied ethics, and it is principally concerned with how we should go about resolving particularly difficult questions that arise from the practice of medicine.

As we shall see throughout this book, it is impossible to study medical law without confronting complex ethical dilemmas. For example:

- When is it acceptable for doctors to withhold lifesaving treatment from a profoundly disabled baby?
- Should parents be allowed to choose their children's sex?
- What, if anything, would be wrong with paying someone to 'donate' one of their kidneys?
- Should an anorexic teenager be force-fed?
- Should scientists be allowed to create animal–human hybrid embryos?
- What limits, if any, should be placed upon women's access to abortion?
- Should voluntary euthanasia be legalized?

It would be difficult to work out the appropriate *legal* response to such questions without also considering their ethical implications. While this is principally a book about medical law, it would be artificial to draw a sharp distinction between medical law and ethics. Rather, throughout this book we will be considering how law should respond to the ethical dilemmas thrown up by the practice of medicine.

This opening chapter attempts to summarize various ways in which we might go about resolving, or at least discussing, these ethical problems. We begin by looking at what we might mean by 'medical ethics' and the more recent term 'bioethics'. Next, we consider several different types of ethical reasoning: from religious bioethics to a feminist ethic of care.

When justifying a preference for a particular outcome in the field of medical law and ethics, it is common for people to appeal to the dangers of the 'slippery slope', or ground their argument in the need to respect 'human dignity', or to have respect for the 'sanctity of human life'. We briefly consider what these claims might involve. We conclude by looking at changing attitudes towards the human body within medical law and ethics.

2   BIOETHICS

While medical ethics has a long history, bioethics is a much newer discipline. Conventionally, medical ethics has been concerned with the ethics of good medical practice: that is, with what it means to be a good doctor. Ethical rules or codes of conduct were guidelines that the medical profession imposed upon itself in order to ensure that doctors' behaviour towards both their colleagues and their patients met appropriate standards of moral decency. Unsurprisingly, therefore, the vantage point was always that of the doctor himself: how the doctor should obtain consent; when a doctor can breach his duty of confidentiality; and so on. Medical practice was strongly paternalistic: doctors were under a duty to act in their patients' best interests, but it was doctors (as opposed to the patients themselves) who decided what those interests were.

In the next extract Susan Sherwin argues that conventional medical ethics tended to marginalize both the patient's perspective and the broader social causes of ill health.

Susan Sherwin[1]

Until very recently, conscientious physicians were actually trained to act paternalistically toward their patients, to treat patients according to the physician's own judgement about what would be best for their patients, with little regard for each patient's own perspectives or preferences. The problem with this arrangement, however, is that health care may involve such intimate and central aspects of a patient's life—including, for example, matters such as health, illness, reproduction, death, dying, bodily integrity, nutrition, lifestyle, self-image, disability, sexuality, and psychological well-being—that it is difficult for anyone other than the patient to make choices that will be compatible with that patient's personal value system...

A striking feature of most...discussions about patient autonomy is their exclusive focus on individual patients; this pattern mirrors medicine's consistent tendency to approach illness as primarily a problem of particular patients...Within the medical tradition, suffering is located and addressed in the individuals who experience it rather than in the social arrangements that may be responsible for causing the problem. Instead of exploring the cultural context that tolerates and even supports practices such as war, pollution, sexual violence, and systemic unemployment—practices that contribute to much of the illness that occupies modern medicine—physicians generally respond to the symptoms troubling particular patients in isolation from the context that produces these conditions.

Heather Draper and Tom Sorrell also argue that the focus of medical ethics has been too narrow, but in a different way. They maintain that by focussing upon the duties of doctors, the obligations of *patients* have been ignored.

Heather Draper and Tom Sorrell[2]

In comparison to what it asks of doctors, mainstream medical ethics makes very few demands of patients, and these usually begin and end with consent. Traditionally medical ethics has asserted that, as autonomous agents, competent patients must be allowed to decide for themselves the course of their medical treatment, and even whether to be treated at all....Little or nothing is said about what kinds of decisions patients *ought* to make. Nor is much said about their responsibilities for making good rather than bad decisions. Indeed...mainstream medical ethics implies that a competent patient's decision is good simply by virtue of having been made by the patient. At times it seems as though patients never make, or cannot make, bad decisions...

In welfare states, discussion about the use of limited resources extends naturally to a consideration of whether citizens have some sort of moral obligation, other things being equal, to limit their demands on these resources. If the answer is 'Yes', then there may be a civic obligation to follow preventive health measures recommended by one's doctor. If one

---

[1] 'A Relational Approach to Autonomy in Healthcare' in Susan Sherwin (ed.), *The Politics of Women's Health: Exploring Agency and Autonomy* (Temple UP: Philadelphia, 1998) 19–47, 21.

[2] 'Patients' Responsibilities in Medical Ethics' (2002) 16 Bioethics 335–51.

is advised to stop smoking or over-eating, and one disregards that advice, so that one's condition deteriorates to the point that expensive treatment is required to keep one alive, one may be doing something doubly wrong—breaking obligations to oneself and breaking civic obligations not to use public resources unnecessarily...

In short, there are duties not to use health services casually....Someone who indulges their hypochondria by frequent visits to the GP, or who summons an ambulance after getting sunburn; someone who knowingly presents himself at an emergency room with nothing more than severe indigestion; or who calls out a doctor because he needs a prescription that could be filled in office hours next day; all of these patients do something morally wrong, wrong primarily because they have taken away time and resources better spent on more urgent cases.

Bioethics' remit is generally assumed to be much wider than that of traditional medical ethics. It emerged as a distinctive discipline in the 1960s in response to a number of different factors. First, rapid technological progress was posing some complex dilemmas, particularly at the beginning and end of life, which went beyond ethical conduct within the doctor–patient encounter. For example, once it became possible to (a) perform organ transplants, and (b) keep a patient's heart beating after death, it was necessary to ask whether 'brain-dead' but still breathing patients could be a legitimate source of organs for transplantation.

Secondly, medical paternalism was beginning to be challenged, and the principle of patient autonomy was instead ascendant. Patients no longer automatically deferred to doctors' superior medical expertise, but were increasingly willing to insist upon their 'rights'.

In the next extract, Helga Kuhse and Peter Singer reflect upon the origins and remit of bioethics.

Helga Kuhse and Peter Singer[3]

Since the 1960s, ethical problems in health care and the biomedical sciences have gripped the public consciousness in unprecedented ways. In part, this is the result of new and sometimes revolutionary developments in the biomedical sciences and in clinical medicine... These technological breakthroughs, however, have not been the only factor in the increasing interest in ethical problems in this area. Another factor has been a growing concern about the power exercised by doctors and scientists, which shows itself in concern to assert 'patients' rights' and the rights of the community as a whole to be involved in decisions that affect them. This has meant greater public awareness of the value-laden nature of medical decision making, and a critical questioning of the basis on which such decisions are made...

It was in the climate of such new ethical issues and choices that the field of inquiry now known as 'bioethics' was born. The word was not originally used in this sense. Van Rensselaer Potter originally proposed the term for a 'science of survival' in the ecological sense—that is, an interdisciplinary study aimed at ensuring the preservation of the biosphere. This terminology never became widely established, however, and instead 'bioethics' came to refer to the growing interest in the ethical issues arising from health care and the biomedical sciences...

---

[3] 'What is Bioethics? A Historical Introduction' in Helga Kuhse and Peter Singer (eds), *A Companion to Bioethics* (Blackwell: Oxford, 1998) 3–11.

Traditionally, medical ethics has focused primarily on the doctor–patient relationship and on the virtues possessed by the good doctor. It has also been very much concerned with relations between colleagues within the profession...Bioethics, on the other hand, is a more overtly critical and reflective enterprise. Not limited to questioning the ethical dimensions of doctor–patient and doctor–doctor relationships, it goes well beyond the scope of traditional medical ethics in several ways. First, its goal is not the development of, or adherence to, a code or set of precepts, but a better understanding of the issues. Second, it is prepared to ask deep philosophical questions about the nature of ethics, the value of life, what it is to be a person, the significance of being human. Third, it embraces issues of public policy and the direction and control of science.

3 HOW SHOULD WE MAKE DIFFICULT ETHICAL DECISIONS?

Many people have 'gut feelings' or intuitive reactions to ethical dilemmas. It is very common for people to react to a controversial medical practice, such as the creation of animal–human hybrid embryos, by saying: 'I just think it's wrong.' These judgements are immediate, unreasoned responses, and while they will often inevitably form the starting point for moral judgement, on their own they do not offer a good reason for *anyone else* to be persuaded by them. In order to convince others, it is necessary to point to some coherent reasoning process, or moral principle, which explains or justifies one's position.

In short, we need to find some mechanism for resolving ethical dilemmas that goes beyond an appeal to our 'gut instincts'. As we will see in the following sections, bioethicists are principally concerned with trying to work out what this mechanism should be.

(a) RELIGIOUS BIOETHICS

There has always been an interesting relationship between religion and the practice of medicine. In the past, the belief that illness has a spiritual origin was commonplace. As a result, people sought cures through prayer, rather than from the medical profession. Indeed, there were those who believed that seeking medical intervention was an insult to God.

While the comprehensive rejection of medical expertise on religious grounds is now rare, there are still many people whose religious beliefs ground their anxiety about modern medicine's unprecedented power to create and to destroy life. Within a secular and culturally diverse society, however, religion tends to be regarded as a matter of private faith. As a result, while religious leaders' pronouncements on bioethics will obviously be of central importance to the adherents of particular religions, and will often determine how they approach their own personal medical dilemmas, it is less clear what role they should have in shaping public policy.

In the next extract Daniel Callahan regrets the 'secularisation' of bioethics and suggests that because all religions have a long and rich history of grappling with questions that are of central importance to medical law and ethics—such as the meaning of life and death—religious perspectives might be a particularly useful resource for the comparatively new secular discipline of bioethics.

Daniel Callahan[4]

> The net result of this narrowing of philosophy and the disappearance or denaturing of religion in public discourse is a triple threat. It leaves us, first of all, too heavily dependent upon the law as the working source of morality. The language of the courts and legislatures becomes our only shared means of discourse. That leaves a great number fearful of the law (as seems the case with many physicians) or dependent upon the law to determine the rightness of actions, which it can rarely do since it tells us better what is forbidden or acceptable, than what is commendable or right.
>
> It leaves us, secondly, bereft of the accumulated wisdom and knowledge that are the fruit of long-established religious traditions. I do not have to be a Jew to find it profitable and illuminating to see how the great rabbinical teachers have tried to understand moral problems over the centuries. Nor will Jews find it utterly useless to explore what the popes, or the leading Protestant divines, have had to say about ethics. . . .
>
> It leaves us, thirdly, forced to pretend that we are not creatures both of particular moral communities and the sprawling inchoate general community that we celebrate as an expression of our pluralism. Yet that pluralism becomes a form of oppression if, in its very name, we are told to shut up in public about our private lives and beliefs and talk a form of what Jeffrey Stout has called moral Esperanto. The rules of that language are that it deny the concreteness and irregularities of real communities, that it eschew vision and speculation about goals and meaning, and that it enshrine the discourse of wary strangers (especially that of rights) as the preferred mode of daily relations.

There are clearly important differences both between and within religions. Within Christianity, for example, views on the moral status of the embryo—and hence the acceptability of abortion and embryo research—differ markedly. Nevertheless, a number of similarities between religious approaches to bioethics might be identified. First, religious bioethics tend to emphasize the intrinsic rightness or wrongness of a particular course of action, and be less swayed by pragmatic or consequentialist arguments. In relation to euthanasia, for example, a religious perspective would concentrate upon the legitimacy or otherwise of bringing about another person's death, rather than any practical difficulties in policing doctors' behaviour.

Secondly, religions tend to share two principal moral concerns: (a) love for one's neighbour (almost every religion, for example, contains some version of the Golden Rule: that you should treat your neighbour as you would want to be treated yourself); and (b) a sense of awe and respect for 'God's creation', and most especially for human life, through what we might call the 'sanctity principle'.

In the next extract, Hazel Markwell and Barry Brown describe how a belief in the sanctity of life informs Roman Catholic responses to a wide variety of bioethical questions.

Hazel Markwell and Barry Brown[5]

> There is a long tradition of bioethical reasoning within the Roman Catholic faith, a tradition that extends from Augustine's writings on suicide in the early Middle Ages to recent papal

---

[4] 'Religion and the Secularization of Bioethics' (1990) 20 Hastings Center Report 2–4.
[5] 'Bioethics for Clinicians: Catholic Bioethics' (2001) 165 Canadian Medical Association Journal 189–92, 189.

teachings on euthanasia and reproductive technologies. Roman Catholic bioethics...comprises a complex set of positions that have their origins in scripture, the writings of the Doctors of the Church, papal encyclicals, and reflections by contemporary Catholic theologians and philosophers...

Fundamental to Catholic bioethics is a belief in the sanctity of life: the value of a human life, as a creation of God and a gift in trust, is beyond human evaluation and authority. God maintains dominion over it. In this view, we are stewards, not owners, of our own bodies and are accountable to God for the life that has been given to us.

Applied to medicine, then, religious perspectives tend to be less individualistic than secular bioethics and to start from the premise that life is a gift, which is not ours to destroy: taken together this means that less emphasis is placed on patient autonomy.

Thirdly, the idea that life is a gift raises the question of how far man should 'interfere' with the natural order. Answers have varied dramatically—from the idea that modern medicine is frustrating God's will, to the more progressive (and now much more common) view that man's quest for knowledge, and hence medical progress, is itself part of God's creation.

Paul Badham explains this shift, from a Christian perspective.

Paul Badham[6]

[M]edical ethics provides the largest number of instances where Christians today almost unanimously accept as good practices which their predecessors in the faith regarded as evil. For many centuries Christians forbade the giving of medicine, deeming it equivalent to the practice of sorcery. The practice of surgery, the study of anatomy and the dissection of corpses for medical research were all at one time firmly forbidden. Later the practices of inoculation and vaccination faced fierce theological opposition. Indeed in 1829 Pope Leo XII declared that whoever decided to be vaccinated was no longer a child of God; smallpox was a judgement of God, vaccination was a challenge to heaven. For similar reasons the initial use of quinine against malaria was denounced by many Christians. The introduction of anaesthesia and, above all, the use of chloroform in childbirth were seen as directly challenging the biblical judgement that, because of their inheritance of the guilt of Eve's original sin, all women must face the penalty that 'in pain you shall bring forth children'. Consequently the use of chloroform in childbirth was vigorously attacked from public pulpits throughout Britain and the United States...

The root objection to all the medical practices mentioned above was the belief that the duty of human beings was to submit in patience to what God had willed. All innovations in medical practice were initially seen as implying a lack of faith and trust in God's good purposes. Doctors were accused of 'playing God', of being unwilling to accept that God knows what is right for a particular person, of prying into sacred mysteries and areas of God's own prerogative. Yet gradually all mainstream Christian churches have modified their teaching, and the formerly criticized activity of the doctor has itself come to be seen as itself a channel of God's love and the vehicle of his providence...Christians today are happy to think of doctors as fulfilling the will of God in restoring to heath persons struck down by curable illness.

6 'Theological Examination of the Case for Euthanasia' in Paul Badham and Paul Ballard, *Facing Death: An Interdisciplinary Approach* (Cardiff University of Wales Press: Cardiff, 1996) 101–16, 103.

Judaism has a longer tradition of accepting medical interventions. The conviction that one's body belongs to God translates into a duty to care for it. Not only is there an emphasis on preventative medicine—such as an interest in hygiene and diet—but also, as Shimon Glick explains, within Judaism the treatment of illness is *obligatory*, on the part of both physicians and their patients.

Shimon Glick[7]

Consonant with the high priority given to life, the Jewish tradition, unlike Anglo-Saxon law, *requires* the physician to respond to any patient's call for help. . . . But just as the physician is obligated to render care, so too, the seeking of care by the patient is mandatory. The reason for this obligation is that, in our Jewish tradition, man does not possess title to his life or his body. Man is but the steward of the divine possession which he has been privileged to receive. The terms of that stewardship are not of man's choice, but are determined by God's commands. We forbid suicide and require man to take all reasonable steps to preserve life and health. When beneficence conflicts with autonomy, the former is given precedence by Judaism, a view clearly in conflict with the modern Western consensus. While such a violation of autonomy for the patient's good is not enforceable in our modern pluralistic societies, it has full sanction in the Jewish tradition, and Jewish courts may enforce medical treatment when unequivocally indicated.

In the deliberations as to permissibility of a given act, its being 'natural' or 'unnatural' plays little role. In our tradition, the world is regarded as a deliberately unfinished product placed in the trust of man—himself a finite and imperfect being. Man is expected, indeed commanded. . . to engage in completing. . . the work of the Creator. . .

Healing the ill . . . is therefore not only theologically acceptable, but is mandated. This eagerness to modify Nature, together with the great value placed on human life, contributed to the exalted place occupied by the healing profession in Jewish tradition.

Mainstream Muslim theologians agree that technological intervention in nature, so long as its purpose is to improve human welfare, does not contravene the prohibition against changing God's creation. Indeed, it has been argued that scientific research is protected by the *Shari'a*, and that medicine is a religious duty in every community. Preventative medicine—through the *Shari'a*'s rulings on hygiene and self-restraint—is encouraged. The Islamic Code of Medical Ethics, for example, states that:

The natural prophylaxis against some diseases rests in the revival of such religious values as chastity, purity, self-restraint, and refraining from advertently or inadvertently inflicting harm on self or others. To preach these values is preventative medicine and therefore lies within the jurisdiction and obligation of the medical profession.[8]

Fourthly, religious bioethics tend to adopt a normative approach to ethical dilemmas. Whereas secular bioethics might accept that there is no *right* answer to a particularly controversial ethical question, and might instead concentrate upon devising an acceptable procedure through which a compromise position might be reached, someone reasoning

---

[7] 'A View from Sinai: a Jewish Perspective on Biomedical Ethics' in E Pellegrino, P Mazzarella, and P Corsi (eds), *Transcultural Dimensions* (University Publishing Group: Frederick, MD, 1992) 73–82.

[8] Issued by the International Organisation of Islamic Medicine (later called the Islamic Organisation of Medical Sciences) in 1981.

from within a religious tradition would be more likely to come down firmly in favour of, or against a particular practice. Fifthly, religious perspectives on ethical dilemmas tend to consist in the interpretation of past authority, and are always to some extent constrained by the written or oral teachings or texts of the particular tradition.

(b) SECULAR BIOETHICS

While it would be a mistake to gloss over the internal disagreements that are common *within* the various religious traditions, the existence of a source of authority, or multiple sources, provides an obvious starting point for ethical reasoning on a particular issue, and the rich web of interpretative precedent should—in theory at least—lead religious scholars towards the *right* answer. In contrast, secular bioethics has no obvious starting point, and is much less certain about whether a right answer exists.

If secular bioethics is not looking for the right answer to a difficult ethical dilemma, what is it doing? One possibility might be that reasoned argument and deliberation is simply the most rational way to resolve difficult or controversial questions. In the next two extracts, Tim Dare and Dan Brock argue that the requirement to give reasons, or to justify one's moral views, is an especially important feature of ethical reasoning.

Tim Dare[9]

If a position of mine is to count as an ethical position I must produce reasons for it. This is not to say that I must articulate a complex moral theory or even state a moral principle that I am following for my position to count as moral. But in practice there are certain sorts of reasons or responses which will not do. Because a mere prejudice, for instance, is precisely a belief that is not supported by reasons, I cannot offer mere prejudices in support of my position. Similarly, mere emotional reactions will not count as reasons...This is not to say that ethical positions should be unemotional or dispassionate. On the contrary, we should care about our moral views. But emotional reactions should be prompted by or grounded in moral judgments and not vice versa.

Dan W Brock[10]

[M]oral judgments are unlike some judgments of taste and moral disagreements are unlike some disagreements over matters of taste, because moral judgments must be backed by reasons. If you like vanilla ice cream and I like chocolate, we can just accept this as a difference in taste—there is no correct preference about flavours of ice cream, and if asked why I prefer chocolate, I may be able to repeat only that it tastes better to me. Unlike matters of taste, moral judgments, for example, about whether voluntary euthanasia is wrong, must be backed with reasons...[T]he very process of having and offering reasons for our moral judgments is the principal feature distinguishing morality from mere expressions of simple taste or preference.

---

9 'Applied Ethics, Challenges to' in Ruth Chadwick (ed.), *Encyclopaedia of Applied Ethics* 1(1) (Academic Press: San Diego, 1997) 183–90.
10 'Public Moral Discourse' in LW Sumner and Joseph Boyle (eds), *Philosophical Perspectives on Bioethics* (University of Toronto Press: Toronto, 1996) 271–96.

> Because the principal role of moral judgments is to guide action…moral judgments are subject to a special worry. The worry is that they may be no more than a hodgepodge of thinly veiled rationalizations and biases reflecting our own self-interest, prejudices, and arbitrary preferences. General moral principles or theories can help allay this worry by explaining these judgments: they are shown to fit, and to be derivable and made from, a coherent, unified moral conception. We come to see that our particular moral judgments have a coherent identifiably moral source, heretofore likely only implicit, and are not merely a cover for our prejudices and self-interest.

(1) Moral Theories

The question of how we should go about resolving complex ethical dilemmas has formed the basis of moral philosophy for thousands of years. There is insufficient space here to fully describe the extensive and rich philosophical literature from which medical ethics has borrowed, but three different traditions are worth noting.

First, teleological (from the Greek *telos*: consequences) theories judge the rightness or wrongness of an action in terms of its *consequences*. So to argue that legalizing euthanasia might damage the doctor–patient relationship would be an example of consequentialist or teleological reasoning. Utilitarianism—or the idea that we should act so as to maximize the amount of pleasure or happiness within society—is the most well-known teleological theory.

Secondly, deontological (from the Greek *deontos*: duty) theories, in contrast, insist that the intrinsic rightness or wrongness of an action does not depend upon its consequences, but rather upon whether it is consistent with certain *basic moral principles*. An example might be basing an argument for the legalization of euthanasia upon the principle that we should respect the autonomous decisions of competent adults. The writings of the philosopher Immanuel Kant (1724–1804) are often used as an example of deontological moral theory.[11] In short, as Matti Häyry has argued, the utilitarian places the concepts of 'good and bad' before the ideas of 'right and wrong', whereas the Kantian does the opposite.[12]

Thirdly, virtue ethics are derived from Ancient Greek moral philosophy, and in particular the work of Aristotle, with its emphasis upon working out what it means to lead a good or flourishing human life. Virtue ethics are concerned not only with good outcomes, but also with the character or motivation of the individual: a person acts virtuously if they do the right thing for the right reason.

Let us consider each of these approaches in turn.

(a) Utilitarianism

Utilitarianism emerged as a secular alternative to Christian ethics in the late eighteenth and early nineteenth centuries through the work of Jeremy Bentham (1748–1832), and later John Stuart Mill (1806–73), whose father was one of Bentham's pupils. According to utilitarianism, morality lies not in religious obedience, but in the maximization of human welfare. Because the pleasure and wellbeing of each human being matters equally, utilitarianism is essentially egalitarian.

---

[11] I. Kant, *Groundwork of the Metaphysics of Morals* (1785).

[12] 'Utilitarianism and Bioethics' in RE Ashcroft, A Dawson, H Draper and JR McMillan (eds) *Principles of Health Care Ethics* 2nd edn (Wiley: Chichester, 2007) 57–64.

A utilitarian is interested in the *consequences* of an action, rather than whether it is intrinsically either right or wrong. An example might be the question of whether we should keep our promises. A utilitarian would have to say that there can be both good and bad consequences from keeping a promise. When the good consequences outweigh the bad consequences, it will be right to keep the promise; but when the reverse is true, the promise should be broken. The problem with this is that it ignores the fact that simply having made a promise to another person is itself a good reason to keep it.

A variation on utilitarianism, called 'rule utilitarianism', provides a partial solution to some of the defects of utilitarian moral reasoning. A rule utilitarian would ask not which *action* will maximize welfare, but rather which *general rules* will, on the whole, lead to the best consequences. When deciding whether doctors should respect patient confidentiality, for example, a strict utilitarian would answer: 'it depends'. Sometimes it might be good to keep patient information secret, but at other times it might not. This case-by-case approach would require doctors to predict the consequences of both revealing and not revealing information about each of their patients. This would clearly be an unmanageable task, which would itself have negative consequences because the provision of health care services would grind to a halt. So, a rule utilitarian might say that it is, *on the whole*, better to impose a duty on doctors to respect their patients' confidentiality, since this rule will tend to maximize wellbeing.

Another problem with utilitarianism is its *quantitative* approach to welfare. It is the total aggregate of wellbeing that matters, not any particular individual's welfare. If killing one healthy person would enable us to transfer her organs into five patients who would otherwise die, surely the utilitarian would be forced to conclude that this would be the right thing to do. Again, rule utilitarianism might offer a way to avoid this unpalatable conclusion: applying the principle that doctors should 'above all do no harm' will, in general, tend to have better consequences than allowing doctors to kill their patients in order to save other people's lives.

It is also necessary to work out what counts as 'utility'. While improved health is clearly a good outcome, it is not the only thing that matters. Indeed, many of us have dietary and other lifestyle preferences which may be positively harmful to health. Do we maximize utility by eating low-fat food and spending every evening at the gym, or by eating things we enjoy and going to the pub with friends?

Utilitarianism, as Kevin Wildes explains, depends upon the existence of a mechanism through which different outcomes can be ranked; otherwise it would be impossible to tell whether consequence A is preferable to consequence B.

Kevin Wildes[13]

The appeal to the consequences of one's decisions brings no more success [in resolving moral controversies], because it faces the problem of how to assess and evaluate different consequences. For example, some believe that living somewhat longer as a result of chemotherapy is a better consequence, even with the side-effects, than dying. Yet for others, living a life unimpaired by treatment is a more important outcome than extending the length of life. To make a judgment among consequences one needs an agreed-upon method by

---

[13] 'Particularism in Bioethics: Balancing Secular and Religious Concerns' (1994) 53 Maryland Law Review 1220, 1228.

which to rank the outcomes. Therefore a consequentialist must build in some presuppositions about the assessment and ranking of values, both to evaluate possible outcomes of ethical choices and to know which outcomes are more desirable and should be given priority....Consequentialist accounts therefore, are no better than those of intuitionists for purposes of demonstrating which set of outcomes is preferable because such a judgment requires an authoritative means of ranking benefits and harms. We are left in a position in which there is no way to judge between methods of valuing consequences except by appeal to our own moral sense.

(b) Kantianism

The aspect of Kant's philosophy that we are particularly interested in here is his 'Categorical Imperative'. Kant himself gives four formulations of the Categorical Imperative, two of which are worth singling out here:[14]

(a) Act only on that maxim whereby you can at the same time will that it should become a universal law.

(b) So act as to treat humanity, whether in your own person or in that of any other, never solely as a means but always also as an end.

The first imperative requires us to act *consistently* and *justly*. The latter (which is more commonly cited by medical ethicists) demands that we do not ever treat another person—or allow ourselves to be treated—purely in order to satisfy another's purposes.

Both are in some sense negative tests for actions: that is, they tell us what we must *not* do: one must not act inconsistently, and one must not use another person solely for one's own ends. They do not consist in positive prescriptions for action: not all acts that conform to the categorical imperative are ones that we ought to perform. Furthermore, as John Rawls has pointed out, it would be 'a serious misconception to think of the Categorical Imperative procedure as an algorithm intended to yield, more or less mechanically, a correct judgement'.[15] Rather, he suggests that the point of the categorical imperative may simply be to inculcate 'a form of moral reflection that could reasonably be used to check the purity of our motives'.[16]

In the next extract, Onora O'Neill argues that Kant was interested in 'principled autonomy', or the giving of reasons which others might understand.

Onora O'Neill[17]

Autonomy in thinking is no more—but also no less—than the attempt to conduct thinking (speaking, writing) on principles on which all others whom we address could also conduct their thinking (speaking, writing). Autonomy in action is also no more—but also no less—than the attempt to act on principles on which all others could act...

So 'self-legislation' is not a mysterious phrase for describing merely arbitrary ways in which a free individual might or might not act. It is the basic characteristic of ways of thinking or

---

[14] I. Kant, *Groundwork of the Metaphysics of Morals* (1785).

[15] John Rawls, *Lectures on the History of Moral Philosophy* (Barbara Herman (ed.)) (Harvard UP: Cambridge, MA, 2000) 166.

[16] Ibid, 148.   [17] *Autonomy and Trust in Bioethics* (CUP: Cambridge, 2002).

willing that are conducted with sufficient discipline to be followable or accessible to others. Such ways of thinking and acting must be lawlike rather than lawless, and will thereby be in principle intelligible to others, and open to their criticism, rebuttal or reasoned argument.

In contrast, Barbara Secker is concerned that Kantian autonomy, with its emphasis upon independence and rationality, asks too much of patients.

Barbara Secker[18]

[G]iven the nature of patienthood, the Kantian concept of autonomy demands too much of patients. This idealistic concept is of little practical relevance in health contexts where patients, on the whole, bear little resemblance to the Kantian free, independent, exclusively rational individual...

Moreover, the highly rationalistic, individualistic Kantian account appears to assume that all that patients need to qualify as autonomous, in addition to the requisite intrinsic capacities... is negative freedom. However, patients frequently are in vulnerable positions, are unable to act on their decisions, and require that positive measures be taken on their behalf....

If we appeal to the Kantian view (based on an ideal of the self as independent and exclusively rational), very few, if any, patients will be regarded as autonomous. Actual patients are likely to be dependent or interdependent, and their decision-making capacity is not always based (exclusively) on reason.

My second concern is that Kantian autonomy appears to place a premium on independence. The corresponding normative assumptions about the nature of human capacities and interaction may contribute to the devaluing of those patients who may be dependent and vulnerable... [I]f autonomy is morally valuable, and if autonomy is associated with independence, then dependence is regarded as morally inadequate and, consequently, those who are dependent are devalued.... The nature of patienthood, however, is partially characterized by dependency of one kind or another.

(c) Virtue Ethics

Recent interest in virtue ethics, which derives from Ancient Greek philosophy, emerged as a reaction to a number of perceived disadvantages with the theories discussed in the previous two sections. For example, virtue ethicists have drawn attention to the minimal ethical content of most moral theories. Both Kantianism and utilitarianism lead us to evaluate acts according to whether they are *permissible*, rather than whether they would be the *best* or the *right* thing to do. In contrast, a virtue ethicist would maintain that people should always try to do the right thing for the right reason.

One important feature of virtue ethics is its rejection of the idea that patient autonomy is an absolute or overriding virtue. This means that the fact that an individual wants to do something is not, in itself, a reason for thinking it would be the right thing to do. For example, in relation to euthanasia, Philippa Foot has argued that simply wanting to die is not enough to make death a good thing for a person.[19] Rather, causing a person's death could only be the right thing to do if her life now lacks the most basic human goods.

---

[18] 'The Appearance of Kant's Deontology in Contemporary Kantianism: Concepts of Patient Autonomy in Bioethics' (1999) 24 Journal of Medicine and Philosophy 43–66.
[19] 'Euthanasia' (1977) 6 Philosophy and Public Affairs 85–112.

Similarly, in Chapter 13, we will encounter Rosalind Hursthouse's argument that the morality of a woman's decision to have an abortion depends upon the character she manifests in electing to terminate a new human life.[20] According to Hursthouse, parenthood is intrinsically good and so a woman who fails to appreciate this, and wants an abortion because pregnancy would interfere with her holiday plans, has not reflected with due seriousness, and has therefore not made a virtuous decision. In contrast, a teenager who knows that she would be unable to provide her child with a decent life may have acted virtuously in terminating an unwanted pregnancy.

If acting purely out of self-interest is not virtuous, what is? According to virtue ethicists, the virtues are those character traits that are necessary for human flourishing: these will be things like honesty, compassion, kindness, justice, and courage. While compiling a list of virtuous motivations may be comparatively straightforward, it is clear that they will often point in different directions. For example, in the NHS, doctors often have to select which of the patients on their waiting list should have priority for an available bed. Should a non-urgent patient who has already waited for six months be given priority, or should the bed always go to the patient with the most immediately pressing need? The virtues of fairness and compassion are both relevant here, but they do not tell us who should get the vacant bed.

Or, let us imagine that a doctor who is advising a couple on the chance that their second child would have the same inherited condition as their first, discovers, as a result of genetic tests, that the husband could not be the first child's father. Does she act virtuously by being honest with the husband? Or would a virtuous person reveal this information only to the wife? Or not at all?

Just as with the principlist approach, virtue ethics will not tell us what to do, but may, on the contrary, sanction a number of responses to a particular dilemma, all of which are consistent with acting virtuously. It has also been pointed out that virtuous people will sometimes act wrongly despite having good intentions. Robert Veatch, for example, says that he is 'concerned about well-intentioned, bungling do-gooders'.[21] A doctor who withholds a diagnosis of terminal cancer from her patient may be acting out of compassion, but it still might be the wrong thing to do.

(2) Principlism and its Critics

While applying moral philosophy to medical dilemmas can undoubtedly enrich our reasoning process, it will seldom provide clear prescriptions for doctors faced with difficult moral dilemmas. For example, a doctor might be told that: 'A utilitarian would do X, and a Kantian would do Y', which might be interesting, but is not terribly helpful.

A more practical way to decide medical questions was set out in Tom Beauchamp and James Childress's groundbreaking book *Principles of Biomedical Ethics*, now in its sixth edition. Beauchamp and Childress distilled four basic principles—autonomy, non-maleficence, beneficence, and justice—from what Beauchamp has described as 'the most general and basic norms of the common morality'.

(a) The word *autonomy*—from the Greek *autos* (self) and *nomos* (rule)—initially referred to the self-rule of independent cities. It has since been extended to mean individual

---

[20] 'Virtue Theory and Abortion' (1991) 20 Philosophy and Public Affairs 223–46.
[21] R Veatch, 'The Danger of Virtue' (1988) 13 Journal of Medicine and Philosophy 13.

self-governance, and encompasses a cluster of interests such as liberty, privacy, and freedom of choice. In relation to medicine, respect for autonomy means giving competent adults the right to make decisions about their medical treatment.

(b) *Non-maleficence*, or the duty to 'above all do no harm' (*primum non nocere*) has its origins in the Hippocratic oath. This principle captures the idea that doctors should never use their medical training for immoral purposes, such as involvement in torture or execution.

While it would be difficult to find anyone who thought that it was acceptable for doctors to be involved in torture, in other cases there may be disagreement over what counts as 'harm'. For example, some would argue that it is this principle which proscribes medical participation in euthanasia, whereas others would argue that by bringing an end to a patient's suffering, a doctor who complies with a request for euthanasia has not harmed her, but rather has acted to avoid the *greater harm* of a protracted and distressing death.

(c) *Beneficence* refers to the obligation to act for the benefit of others. Since acting to benefit the patient is a primary goal of medicine, beneficence has been seen by some as its foundational value. It is, however, important to distinguish between what one might call the Hippocratic duty of beneficence: that is, the doctor's duty to act in their patient's interests, and 'social' beneficence, which might refer to the duty to benefit society as a whole. This distinction helps to illuminate the fact that some (socially) beneficent actions are discretionary: I do not have an obligation to donate my body to medical science after my death or to donate one of my healthy kidneys to a stranger with kidney failure. Other (Hippocratic) duties of beneficence are mandatory, such as the duty of care health care professionals owe to their patients.

(d) *Justice* is often interpreted to mean that we should treat like cases alike. But of course, this depends upon being able to tell when cases are either 'like' or 'unlike'. When allocating lungs for transplant, do we act justly by making non-smokers a lower priority than smokers (i.e. are these 'unlike' cases?), or should the only relevant criteria be clinical need, in which case the smoker and the non-smoker are 'like' cases? In relation to health care, it is seldom possible to give every patient immediate access to the best medical treatment, so justice instead demands that we ration scarce resources fairly and transparently.

These principles are more 'user-friendly' than abstract moral philosophy, but they nevertheless borrow from the traditions we considered in the previous sections. So, respect for patient autonomy might be described as a deontological principle because it is valuable regardless of the consequences of the patient's decision. Beneficence and non-maleficence are plainly consequentialist principles, which require us to take into account possible benefits and harms. Virtue ethicists would be principally concerned with the virtues of 'doing good' (beneficence) and acting justly.

While there are those who believe in 'single principle' approaches—a libertarian, for example, believes that actions are right if, and only if, they respect a person's autonomy—most people accept that all four of these principles may have a role to play in medical decision-making. In fact, commonly more than one principle will be relevant. Sometimes they will pull in the same direction: for example, respect for autonomy is generally good for patients: being told the truth, having their privacy respected, and making treatment decisions for themselves are also important aspects of beneficence.

At other times, the principles may come into conflict with each other. Indeed, almost every medical dilemma could be framed in terms of a tension between two or more of these basic principles. It might even be argued that the reason why some questions are difficult is precisely because they are cases in which principles that most of us accept are in conflict with each other. Consider assisted suicide: the principle of autonomy might suggest that a competent patient's wish to die should be respected. Against this, the principle of non-maleficence might be invoked to argue against doctors actively helping their patients take their own lives.

So, while the principlist approach might enable us to describe a moral dilemma as a conflict between competing principles, and work out what important values are at stake, it will seldom tell us what to do. Rather, when principles conflict there is no escaping the need to decide which factor is more important in the particular circumstances. One solution might be to rank the principles, but any hierarchy requires justification which cannot be provided by the principles themselves. If, for example, we want to say that autonomy should take priority over beneficence, either in general, or in a particular case, then we need to explain why.

In the next extract, Beauchamp and Childress admit that the principlist approach requires what they describe as further 'specification' and 'balancing'.

Tom L Beauchamp and James F Childress[22]

Our four clusters of principles do not constitute a general moral theory. They provide only a framework for identifying and reflecting on moral problems. The framework is spare, because prima facie principles do not contain sufficient content to address the nuances of many moral circumstances. We therefore need to examine how to specify and balance these abstract principles....

Specification is a process of reducing the indeterminateness of abstract norms and providing them with action guiding content. For example, without further specification, 'do no harm' is an all-too-bare starting point for thinking through problems, such as assisted suicide and euthanasia. It will not adequately guide action when norms conflict....

Principles, rules and rights require balancing no less than specification. We need both methods because each addresses a dimension of moral principles and rules range and scope, in the case of specification, and weight or strength, in the case of balancing. Specification entails a substantive refinement of the range of scope of norms, whereas balancing consists of deliberation and judgment about the relative weights or strength of norms. Balancing is especially important for reaching judgments in individual cases, and specification is especially useful for policy development.

While it has undoubtedly been hugely influential, Beauchamp and Childress's approach is not without its critics. In the next extract, K Danner Clouse and Bernard Gert argue that, rather than clarifying difficult questions, principlism may be unsystematic and misleading.

K Danner Clouse and Bernard Gert[23]

We believe that the 'principles of biomedical ethics' approach is mistaken and misleading. Principlism is mistaken about the nature of morality and is misleading as to the foundations

---

[22] *Principles of Biomedical Ethics*, 5th edn (OUP: Oxford, 2001).
[23] 'A Critique of Principlism' (1990) 15 Journal of Medicine and Philosophy 219–36.

of ethics...Our bottom line, starkly put, is that 'principle', as conceived by the proponents of Principlism, is a misnomer and that 'principles' so conceived cannot function as they are in fact claimed to be functioning by those who purport to employ them. At best, 'principles' operate primarily as checklists naming issues worth remembering when considering a bio-medical moral issue. At worst 'principles' obscure and confuse moral reasoning by their fail-ure to be guidelines and by their eclectic and unsystematic use of moral theory...

Taking what is properly the moral ideal of helping others (and hence not morally required), and lumping it under a 'principle' of beneficence along with genuine duties (which are required), eg, the duty of health care professionals to help their patients, leads to confusion and misunderstanding. The confusion basically results from treating beneficence as if it were morally required just as noninterference with the freedom of others is morally required.

The appeal of principlism is that it makes use of those features of each ethical theory that seems to have the most support. Thus, in proposing the principle of beneficence, it acknowledges that Mill was right in being concerned with consequences...In proposing the principle of autonomy, it acknowledges that Kant was right in emphasising the importance of the individual person...But there is no attempt to see how these different concerns can be blended together as integrated parts of a single adequate theory, rather than disparate concerns derived from several competing theories.

(3) Casuistry

While philosophers and ethicists are accustomed to discussing general and abstract prin-ciples, clinicians tend to be more interested in cases. For doctors, moral questions do not precede difficult cases, rather they emerge from them. This has contributed to renewed interest in casuistry, or case-based reasoning, a tradition which has its origins in Roman Catholic theology.

In casuistry, instead of starting with broad, abstract principles (a top-down approach), we instead begin with our response to concrete cases and reason by analogy (a bottom-up approach). This is, as John Arras points out, similar to the judiciary's incremental develop-ment of the common law.

John D Arras[24]

Developed in the early Middle-Ages as a method of bringing abstract and universal ethico-religious precepts to bear on particular moral situations, casuistry has had a chequered history. In the hands of expert practitioners during its salad days in the sixteenth and seven-teenth centuries, casuistry generated a rich and morally sensitive literature devoted to numer-ous real-life ethical problems, such as truth-telling, usury, and the limits of revenge. By the late seventeenth century, however, casuistical reasoning had degenerated into a notoriously sordid form of logic-chopping in the service of personal expediency. To this day, the very term 'casuistry' conjures up pejorative images of disingenuous argument and moral laxity.

In spite of casuistry's tarnished reputation, some philosophers have claimed that casuistry, shorn of its unfortunate excesses, has much to teach us about the resolution of moral prob-lems in medicine. Indeed through the work of Albert Jonsen and Stephen Toulmin this 'new

[24] 'Getting Down to Cases: The Revival of Casuistry in Bioethics' (1991) 16 Journal of Medicine and Philosophy 29–51.

Casuistry' has emerged as a definite alternative to the hegemony of the so-called 'applied ethics' method of moral analysis that has dominated most bioethical scholarship and teaching since the early 1970s.

Contrary to deductivist ethical theories, wherein principles are said to preexist the actual cases to which they apply, the new casuistry contends that ethical principles are 'discovered' in the cases themselves, just as common law legal principles are developed in and through judicial decisions on particular legal cases...Rather than stemming originally from some ethical theory, such as Utilitarianism, these principles are said to emerge gradually from reflection upon our responses to particular cases.

In the next extract, Albert Jonsen argues that no moral dilemma is entirely novel, and that it therefore makes sense to look at how analogous dilemmas have been resolved in the past.

Albert R Jonsen[25]

No ethical problem is completely unprecedented. Regardless how novel, it bears some resemblance to problems that are more familiar. The more familiar ones will often be ones for which resolutions have been offered and sometimes accepted. Thus, one compares the new case with the more familiar one. That comparison almost always involves seeking for the similarities and differences in circumstance. Occasionally, in the more novel cases, one will recognize that the topics under which the moral discussion proceeds are inadequate because the practice or institution has manifestly or subtly changed. In this view, ethical reasoning is primarily reasoning by analogy, seeking to identify cases similar to the one under scrutiny and to discern whether the changed circumstances justify a different judgement in the new case than they did in the former.

In essence, casuistry's starting point is the idea that moral certainty derives from our shared intuitive response to so-called paradigm cases, and that we can approach a new case by drawing analogies and disanalogies between the new case and cases which we have resolved in the past.

While it is obviously important to draw upon past experience when addressing novel dilemmas, a number of problems with casuistry have been identified. First, even if we do believe that our intuitions will sometimes embody universally valid moral judgements—an example might be condemnation of Nazi doctors' abuse of research subjects during the Second World War—these are the exception rather than the norm. Moreover, it is not clear that our intuitive response to 'easy' cases actually helps us very much when we are faced with much tougher moral choices. For example, we can all agree that it would be wrong to kill disabled children. But how does that assist us when we are faced with the much more finely balanced question of whether it could ever be right to withdraw life-sustaining medical treatment from a very severely disabled neonate? Some would say that the cases are the same and neither course of action should be permitted, while others would point to important differences between the two cases.

Secondly, case-based reasoning will only yield a definite answer if there is some consensus upon what counts as a relevant similarity. Is abortion relevantly similar to murder (the

---

[25] 'Casuistry: An Alternative or Complement to Principles' (1995) 5 Kennedy Institute of Ethics Journal 237–51.

killing of an innocent human being), or is it relevantly similar to contraception (allowing women to control their reproductive capacity)? Without underlying agreement on certain fundamental moral questions, casuistry provides us with little concrete guidance.

Thirdly, the analogy with the common law is imperfect. The common law contains a system of *binding* precedent, and identifies individuals (that is, judges) whose interpretation of previous cases is *authoritative*. In the field of bioethics, there are no clearly identifiable moral 'experts' to adjudicate on competing interpretations of previous authority.

Fourthly, it is not clear how we can be guided by decisions in previous cases unless those decisions are distilled into some sort of general principle. We could, for example, say that depriving someone of their liberty would normally be wrong, but we might also be able to think of exceptional circumstances in which detention might be justified, perhaps because someone suffers from such a serious mental illness that she would otherwise pose a serious risk of harm to herself, or others. So we distil from this reasoning process the *general principle* that compulsory detention will be legitimate only where there is a serious risk of harm.

On the other hand, even if casuistry—like principlism—cannot tell us what to do when faced with a difficult dilemma, it would be a mistake to downplay the important role cases play in modern bioethics. In the previous section, we saw that there will often be a conflict between, say, autonomy and non-maleficence. At a high level of abstraction, it is impossible for us to tell which should take priority. In the context of a real case, however, it may be possible to reason why, *in this particular case*, there are grounds for thinking that autonomy (or non-maleficence) is more important. So, for example, in chapter 5 we will encounter the case of a teenager E, who wanted to refuse a blood transfusion. Without greater detail than this, it is impossible to tell whether the priority should be to respect E's wishes or to act in his best interests. For example, we need to know more about E's age, and reasoning capacity, and it will be helpful to consider how similar cases were decided in the past. In practice, decision-making in a case like this will be guided not only by principles, but also by careful analysis of the facts in individual cases.

In addition to the use of 'real' cases, bioethicists tend to make extensive use of imagined cases, or thought experiments. Judith Jarvis Thomson's classic essay on abortion (extracted in chapter 13) asks the reader to imagine that they wake up to discover that a world famous violinist has been attached to their body and will be wholly dependent upon them for another nine months. In the context of the acts/omissions distinction, James Rachels has asked us whether there is a moral difference between Smith, who drowns his cousin, and Jones, who has the same intention, but finds that at the critical moment, the cousin bangs his head and drowns anyway.[26] Are these hypothetical examples useful? On the one hand, if they are too fantastical, their relevance to real cases may be tenuous, at best. On the other hand, they may offer a fresh lens from which to view a moral problem that has, as Adrian Walsh puts it, 'become stale'.[27] The point of Thomson's violinist analogy is not necessarily to claim that an unwanted pregnancy is exactly *the same as* waking up attached to a world famous violinist, but rather it is intended to prompt us to identify salient similarities and differences between these cases.

[26] J Rachels 'Active and Passive Euthanasia' (1975) 292 *New England Journal of Medicine* 78–80.

[27] A Walsh 'The Use of Thought Experiments in Health Care Ethics' in RE Ashcroft, A Dawson, H Draper and JR McMillan (eds) *Principles of Health Care Ethics* 2nd edn (Chichester: Wiley, 2007) 177–83.

(4) Feminism

There is no single 'feminist' approach to bioethics. At the risk of drastic over-simplification, three different approaches might be identified.

First, liberal feminists are concerned to redress inequalities between the sexes. In relation to health care, the drive towards equality has meant focussing upon ways in which women have been treated differently from men. One of the most important examples of a liberal feminist analysis is Judith Jarvis Thomson's classic essay on abortion, mentioned above. The point of Thomson's at first sight bizarre analogy between an unwanted pregnancy and finding that one's body is necessary to support the life of a famous violinist, is that the former is an experience which only women can experience, while the latter (hypothetical) experience is gender neutral. If, Thomson reasons, we can agree that it would clearly be unreasonable to expect a person to give up his body for nine months to support the violinist, then we ought to be able to agree that it is unreasonable to expect women to exercise a similar degree of self-sacrifice in relation to an unwanted pregnancy.

A different example of inequality, which we explore in more detail in chapter 9, is women's traditional exclusion from research trials, due both to their fluctuating hormonal profiles, and the possibility of pregnancy. Systematic exclusion of women from clinical trials means that medicines may not be as safe or as effective when taken by female patients. In a variety of contexts like this, liberal feminists are concerned to highlight and remedy instances of inequality.

A second feminist approach is concerned primarily with oppression, and how practices may (perhaps unwittingly) contribute to, or exacerbate, existing systems of oppression. As we see in chapter 15, feminists were initially among the fiercest critics of reproductive technologies, arguing that (male) scientists and doctors were essentially experimenting on women's bodies and exploiting women's desire for children by persuading them to consent to dangerously untested new treatments. Now that in vitro fertilization (IVF) has become a routine medical treatment, feminist criticism of it is more muted; however, this sort of feminist analysis is still evident in relation to stem cell research. Some feminists have criticized human embryonic stem cell research on the grounds that it relies upon a plentiful supply of eggs, which can only be obtained by asking women to undergo the uncomfortable and not entirely risk-free process of ovarian stimulation and egg collection.

Another example of an oppression-based feminist analysis might be opposition to paid surrogacy on the grounds that asking a woman to bear a child for money is inherently exploitative, in much the same way as prostitution.

The third feminist approach represents the most direct challenge to bioethics itself. What we might call the 'ethics of care' emerged as a result of some feminists' dissatisfaction with conventional medical ethics. First, medical ethics used to be principally concerned with the doctor–patient encounter, and the medical profession was, until comparatively recently, heavily male-dominated. Women, on the other hand, are disproportionately represented among patients. Their reproductive capacity, their role as principal carers for both children and the elderly, and their greater life expectancy combine to make women more frequent users of medical services than men. Women are also more likely to be employed in health services as *carers*, either as nurses (whose role, until fairly recently, was confined to carrying out doctors' orders) or as auxiliary staff.

When medical ethicists focus upon the dilemmas facing *doctors*, they are ignoring the equally important ethical issues that are encountered by carers, nurses, and patients. In the late 1990s, for example, anthropologist Rayna Rapp documented the moral dilemmas pregnant women faced in relation to the decision to use new prenatal testing techniques, such as amniocentesis. These patients were, she argued, 'moral pioneers ... forced to judge the quality of their own fetuses, making concrete and embodied decisions about the standards for entry into the human community'.[28]

Secondly, drawing on the influential and controversial work of psychologist Carol Gilligan, feminist theorists have argued that abstract moral reasoning, and in particular, an emphasis on individualistic values such as autonomy, are both distinctively 'male'. Women's existence, according to this analysis, is characterized by connections with others, especially through pregnancy and childrearing, and this makes them value relationships more highly than individual autonomy.

Carol Gilligan[29]

> The psychology of women that has consistently been described as distinctive in its greater orientation toward relationships and interdependence implies a more contextual mode of judgment and a different moral understanding. Given the differences in women's conceptions of self and morality, women bring to the life cycle a different point of view and order human experience in terms of different priorities.

A third and related point is that the dominant principle of medical ethics, namely patient autonomy, presupposes an independent, largely self-sufficient individual who is able to weigh information in order to reach a rational decision about his medical treatment. Yet, of course, few patients meet this exacting standard. Illness commonly creates dependency and vulnerability. And in any event, a model of moral reasoning which privileges the rational, self-directed individual relies on a partial and inaccurate understanding of what it is to be human. All of us were completely dependent on others at the beginning of our lives, and most of us will spend some time unable to function independently before we die.

Taken together, these three criticisms of conventional bioethics have led to interest in developing an ethic of care, which, in short, takes for granted the inevitability of dependency and requires us to treat others with sympathy and compassion. But what does this mean in practice? One important difference between an ethic of care and conventional medical ethics is that the patient is not seen as an atomized and free-floating individual, making entirely self-interested decisions in isolation from her relationships with others, most importantly her dependants and/or those who care for her.

In the next extract, Jonathan Herring explains that because 'caring' has traditionally been 'women's work', it has been systematically undervalued and largely ignored by medical ethicists. This is a mistake, not least because without informal and unpaid carers—whose care has been valued at £57.4 billion per year, as much as the entire NHS budget—the health service would undoubtedly grind to a halt.

Jonathan Herring[30]

> Caring is a gendered activity. It is seen as 'women's work' and as such is ignored in the 'male gaze'. I mentioned earlier the enormous economic value of care and yet it is not given the

---

[28] *Testing Women, Testing the Fetus: The Social Impact of Amniocentesis in America* (NY Routledge, 1999) 3.

[29] *In a Different Voice* (Harvard UP: London, MA, 1982) 22.

[30] 'Where are the Carers in Healthcare Law and Ethics?' (2007) 27 Legal Studies 51–73.

respect or recognition that other higher profile 'economically productive' activities have. By describing care work as 'voluntary' and 'informal' it is marginalised as unimportant. Hence, the professional doctor–patient relationship is subject to careful and extensive legal regulation and is dealt with at length in the court reports and the wider media. The carer–patient relationship, of greater significance to many patients, is ignored. This all has the impact of care work being unvalued and unnoticed. All of this is convenient to a society in which 'men's' work goes rewarded and valorised, while 'women's' work is invisible and unrecognised. The lack of respect owed to caring has played a significant role in the unequal economic position of women.

Under an ethic of care the practice of caring would be hugely valued within society. Carers would, far from being hidden, come to represent a norm. Social structures and attitudes would need to be set up to encourage and enable caring. This would require adequate remuneration of carers: not the payment of benefits of the kind paid to those 'unable to work', but payment acknowledging the key role they play. Work would need to be done to ensure that the burden of caring did not fall on the few but was shared across the community.

The feminist ethics of care has its critics, however. In the following extract, Helga Kuhse questions whether it can replace ethical principles and reasoned argument.

Helga Kuhse[31]

Is ethics gendered? Do women and men approach ethics differently? The answer of many thinkers has been 'yes'. Rousseau thought that abstract truths and general principles are 'beyond a woman's grasp...; woman observes, man reasons'. Schopenhauer bluntly proclaimed: 'the fundamental fault of the female character is that it has *no sense of justice*'. This 'weakness in their reasoning faculty', Schopenhauer continued, 'also explains why women show more sympathy for the unfortunate than men'... Freud believed that 'for women the level of what is ethically normal is different from what it is in men'. Women, he wrote, 'show less sense of justice than men'. On these views, then, men and women not only approach ethics differently, but insofar as women were thought to lack a head for abstract principles, and a sense of justice, their ethical approach was also regarded as somewhat defective and inferior to that of men...

There is [a] school of thought that holds that traditional male thinkers, while wrong on much else, were right...that women and men do approach ethics differently. This school of thought rejects the idea that women are *incapable* of abstract, principled thinking; rather, and much more fundamentally, it claims that principled ethical thinking is not the only valid (or best) approach to ethics. There is, according to this view, an alternative 'female' approach to ethics which is based not on abstract 'male' ethical principles or wide generalisations, but on 'care', that is, on receptivity and responsiveness to the needs of others...

[T]he assumption is that caring, in its sensitive attention to the particularities of the situation can give the right answer. But this is not so. Sensitivity and particularity alone can not guide action...

If women...excessively devalue reasoned argument, if they dismiss ethical principles and norms and hold that notions of impartiality and universalizability have no place in a female

[31] 'Clinical Ethics and Nursing: "Yes" to Caring, But "No" to a Female Ethics of Care' (1995) 9 Bioethics 207–19.

ethics of care, then they will be left without the theoretical tools necessary to condemn some actions or practices, and to defend others. Bereft of a universal ethical language, women will be unable to participate in ethical discourse.

Rather than seeing an ethic of care as an *alternative* to norms like justice and impartiality, perhaps it would be more useful to regard it as a necessary *supplement*. An ethic of care, just like the principlist approach discussed above, will rarely *dictate* a solution to a difficult dilemma, such as which patient should get the only available intensive care bed. Instead, it is useful as a reminder that patients are not, in fact, solitary autonomous individuals, making rational self-interested decisions; that their interests cannot, and perhaps should not, always be considered in isolation from the interests of their carers.

(c) COMMON JUSTIFICATORY STRATEGIES

(1) Human Dignity; The Sanctity of Human Life and Playing God

A common response to novel or controversial medical techniques—such as euthanasia, cloning and abortion—is to argue that they interfere with human dignity; or that they are at odds with the sanctity of human life; or that they would involve human beings 'playing God'. International agreements on biomedicine have also emphasized the importance of respect for human dignity: the preamble to the Council of Europe Convention on Human Rights and Biomedicine requires signatories 'to take such measures as are necessary to safeguard human dignity and the fundamental rights and freedoms of the individual with regard to the application of biology and medicine'.

But what do these phrases actually mean? In the next extract, Ruth Chadwick attempts to pin down what might be meant by the expression 'playing God'.

Ruth F Chadwick[32]

[I]t seems clear that the use of the term 'playing God' normally indicates moral disapproval on the part of the speaker, but it is not obvious what is supposed to be bad about taking the decision. Let us consider alternative ways of looking at the question.

(a) God's prerogative
   From a religious point of view the objection may be that it is for God to give life and for God to take it away. Such a view notoriously has the difficulty however that it seems to imply the rejection of medicine altogether...

(b) Letting nature take its course
   Here the playing-God objection is interpreted as a claim that human beings are interfering with the course of nature, and that this is wrong. As such it can be, and has been, fairly easily answered...John Stuart Mill points out that it is impossible for humans to let nature take its course because every human action has an impact, however slight, upon nature.

(c) Equality

---

[32] 'Playing God' (1989) 3 Cogito 186–93, 188.

A third possibility...is that the objection expresses an intuition about equality...The suggestion may be that human beings have lives that are of equal value and that it is therefore wrong for one set of people to judge that the lives of others are of less value....

(d) Omniscience

A further claim about equality may be involved here. The suggestion would be that one thing that human beings have in common is that their knowledge is limited. Those who take decisions about the quality of the lives of others are aspiring to the kind of omniscience that is simply not available to them...

The playing-God objection may be useful, then, in that it reminds us that certain things have unpredictable and possibly disastrous consequences. But it seems doubtful that it can provide a conclusive argument against a certain course of action.

In a secular society, what might it mean to say that human life is sacred? In the next extract, Ronald Dworkin suggests that there is a universal, and not necessarily religious, sense of awe at the 'miracle' of human creation.

Ronald Dworkin[33]

Something is sacred or inviolable when its deliberate destruction would dishonour what ought to be honoured....The idea that each individual human life is inviolable is...rooted, like our concern for the survival of our species as a whole, in two combined and intersecting bases of the sacred: natural *and* human creation. Any human creature, including the most immature embryo, is a triumph of divine or evolutionary creation, which produces a complex, reasoning being from, as it were, nothing, and also of what we often call the 'miracle' of human reproduction, which makes each new human being both different from and yet a continuation of the human beings who created it....

The life of a single human organism commands respect and protection, then, no matter in what form or shape, because of the complex creative investment it represents and because of our wonder at the divine or evolutionary processes that produce new lives from old ones, at the processes of nation and community and language through which a human being will come to absorb and continue hundreds of generations of cultures and forms of life and value, and, finally, when mental life has begun and flourishes, at the process of internal personal creation and judgement by which a person will make and remake himself, a mysterious, inescapable process in which we each participate, and which is therefore the most powerful and inevitable source of empathy and communion we have with every other creature who faces the same frightening challenge. The horror we feel in the wilful destruction of a human life reflects our shared inarticulate sense of the intrinsic importance of each of these dimensions of investment.

On the other hand, Peter Singer argues that the 'sanctity of human life', which he condemns as speciesist, derives from a specifically Christian moral tradition.

---

[33] *Life's Dominion: An Argument about Abortion and Euthanasia* (HarperCollins: London, 1993) 83–4.

Peter Singer[34]

People often say that life is sacred. They almost never mean what they say. They do not mean, as their words seem to imply, that *all* life is sacred. If they did, killing a pig or even pulling up a cabbage would be as contrary to their doctrine as infanticide. So when in the context of medical ethics people talk of the sanctity of life, it is the sanctity of *human* life that they really mean...

[W]hat is the position when we compare severely and irreparably retarded human infants with nonhuman animals like pigs and dogs, monkeys and apes? I think we are forced to conclude that in at least some cases the human infant does not possess any characteristics or capacities that are not also possessed, to an equal or higher degree, by many nonhuman animals. This is true of such capacities as the capacity to feel pain, to act intentionally, to solve problems, and to communicate with and relate to other beings; and it is also true of such characteristics as self-awareness, a sense of one's own existence over time, concern for other beings, and curiosity....

So when we decide to treat one being—the severely and irreparably retarded infant—in one way, and the other being—the pig or monkey—in another way, there seems to be no difference between the two that we can appeal to in defense of our discrimination...The doctrine of the sanctity of human life, as it is commonly understood, has at its core a discrimination on the basis of species and nothing else...

[T]he intuitions which lie behind [the doctrine of the sanctity of human life] are not insights of self-evident moral truths, but the historically conditioned product of doctrines about immortality, original sin and damnation which hardly anyone now accepts; doctrines so obnoxious, in fact, that if anyone did accept them, we should be inclined to discount any other moral views he held. Although advocates of the doctrine of the sanctity of human life now frequently try to give their position some secular justification, there can be no possible justification for making the boundary of sanctity run parallel with the boundary of our own species, unless we invoke some belief about immortal souls.

Human dignity is an especially vague and ambiguous concept. In particular, its scope is potentially wider than respect for persons or human rights. We might, for example, be required to treat an embryo or a corpse, neither of which is a person or rights' holder, with *dignity*. We might not have to behave as though an embryo or a corpse was a human person, but neither are we entitled to use and dispose of them as if they were *things*.

Deryck Beyleveld and Roger Brownsword have argued that the concept of human dignity has undergone a significant shift in meaning in recent years. Respect for human dignity used to mean promoting autonomous choice, which they describe as 'human dignity as empowerment'. According to Joseph Raz, for example:

Respecting human dignity entails treating humans as persons capable of planning and plotting their future. Thus, respecting people's dignity includes respecting their autonomy, their right to control their future....An insult offends a person's dignity if it consists of or implies a denial that he is an autonomous person or that he deserves to be treated as one.[35]

In recent years, however, Beyleveld and Brownsword suggest that human dignity is instead being invoked in order to *restrict* individual's choices, which they refer to as 'human dignity

34 H Kuhse (ed.), *Unsanctifying Human Life: Essays on Ethics* (Blackwell: Oxford, 2002).
35 J Raz, *The Authority of Law* (OUP: Oxford, 1979) 221.

as constraint'. This is commonly done by arguing that a controversial medical practice is 'against human nature'.

Deryck Beyleveld and Roger Brownsword[36]

Many persons feel that a number of scientific interventions are 'unnatural', and cite this as the reason why it is wrong to employ them. This reaction may be linked to the idea that such interventions are contrary to dignity by the following reasoning. Dignity is the property by virtue of which human beings have moral rights or moral standing. All human beings have dignity simply by virtue of being human. Dignity is thus an essential part of human nature. Therefore, to act contrary to human nature is to act contrary to human dignity, and it might, then, be alleged that, for example, assisted reproduction itself is against nature; or 70-year-old women bearing children is against nature; or lesbianism is against nature; or men bearing children is against nature....

An attempt to explicate respect for human dignity in terms of human nature is not without its problems even if couched within a framework that links having dignity to being human (in a biological sense)...Suppose that it is held that it is unnatural for a lesbian woman to bear a child, or for a man to bear a child. What is meant by saying that it is unnatural? Clearly, it cannot be meant that it goes against the laws of nature. If something is contrary to the laws of nature then it cannot (physically) happen. And, if it is not possible for it to happen then there is no need to prescribe that it ought not to happen or to take steps to prevent it from happening.

Perhaps, then, what is meant is that it cannot happen without human intervention. However, there are so many things that cannot happen without human intervention that this threatens to imply that human action itself is contrary to human nature. Certainly, anyone who adopts such a view must, it seems, hold that all medical intervention without which a person would die is contrary to human nature.

(2) The Slippery Slope

Another common objection to controversial medical practices is that they might represent the first step on a slippery slope. This is a consequentialist argument in that it does not appeal to the intrinsic wrongness of a particular technique; rather, as Frederick Schauer explains, the fear is that allowing something that may seem fairly innocuous in itself might have unforeseeable, uncontrollable, or dangerous consequences.

Frederick Schauer[37]

Sometimes the warning is of 'a foot in the door,' and the British often refer to 'the thin edge of the wedge'. Most commonly we are told to beware of the 'slippery slope'. Yet regardless of the term employed, the phenomenon referred to is the same. The single argumentative claim supported by each of these metaphors, as well as by many others, is that a particular act, seemingly innocuous when taken in isolation, may yet lead to a future host of similar but

---

[36] *Human Dignity in Bioethics and Biolaw* (OUP: Oxford, 2001).
[37] 'Slippery Slopes' (1985) 99 Harvard Law Review 361.

increasingly pernicious events. But why should this be? What induces people to believe that in some cases neither doctrinal limits nor judicial intervention can prevent the slide down the slippery slope?...

As a start we can say that a slippery slope argument necessarily contains the implicit concession that the proposed resolution of the instant case is not itself troublesome. By focusing on the consequences for future cases, we implicitly concede that this instance is itself innocuous, or perhaps even desirable. If we felt otherwise, then we would not employ the slippery slope argument, but would rather claim much more simply that this case, in itself, is impermissible. By implicitly conceding that the instant case is, by itself, unobjectionable, the slippery slope argument directs our attention and our fears to the danger case in the future. It is not permitting the instant case that worries us, but rather the possibility that permitting the instant case will lead to the danger case...

Thus, what can distinguish a slippery slope claim from other warnings about the future is the identification of factors increasing the likelihood not only of slippage, but of slippage in the particular direction that takes us from the instant case to the danger case. The task confronting one who makes a slippery slope argument is thus to identify possible sources of this skewed risk factor.

In the next extract, Bernard Williams contrasts two different types of slippery slope claims: the 'horrible result' argument and the 'arbitrary result' argument. He also explains that slippery slope arguments do not necessarily justify banning a practice; rather, a different response might be regulation, which draws a line between acceptable and unacceptable practices.

Bernard Williams[38]

First it is worth distinguishing two types of slippery slope argument. The first type—the *horrible result* argument—objects, roughly speaking, to what is at the bottom of the slope. The second type objects to the fact that it is a slope: this may be called the *arbitrary result* argument....

All of the arguments that I shall be considering use the idea that there is no point at which one can non-arbitrarily get off the slope once one has got onto it—that is what makes the slope slippery. Arguments that belong to the first type that I have distinguished involve, in addition, the further idea that there is a clearly objectionable practice to which the slope leads. The second type of argument, by contrast, relies merely on the point that after one has got on to the slope, subsequent discriminations will be arbitrary...

The first requirement is that it should be probable in actual social fact that such a process will occur. This requires that there should be some motive for people to move from one step to the next. Suppose it is plausible that there will be a slide, and that there will be, at each stage, pressure to take the next step. What follows from that? The slippery slope argument concludes that one should not start, and that the first case should not be allowed, on the ground that after the first step there is nowhere to stop...

But there is an obvious alternative. Granted that we are now considering cases in which a definite rule of practice is needed, we have the alternative of drawing a sharp line between cases that are allowed and cases that are not...Is drawing a line in this way reasonable? Can it be effective? The answer to both these questions seems to me evidently to be 'Yes, Sometimes'...

[38] *Making Sense of Humanity and Other Philosophical Papers* (CUP: Cambridge, 1995) 213–14, 220–1.

[T]he slippery slope argument should be properly understood as in good part an empirical, consequentialist argument...Seen in this light, it seems to me that the slippery-slope style of argument can carry weight, and is to be taken seriously; but that, equally, it need not necessarily carry the day, in the sense of proving that the first step should never be taken. We may, instead, take the path of drawing a line, and that is a perfectly reasonable reaction, in the right circumstances, to the challenge that is indeed posed by the slippery slope considerations.

4 THE BODY

In recent years, there has been a great deal of academic interest in 'the body'. For our purposes, two particular themes are worth highlighting. First, in the past medical knowledge about the body was believed to be scientific, and hence neutral and objective. In recent years, however, sociologists have argued that medicine *controls* our bodies, first, by defining illness and abnormality, and also by instilling us with a sense of responsibility for the state of our bodies. Secondly, our relationship with our bodies is difficult to classify according to conventional legal norms. Let us briefly mention both these themes in turn.

(a) THE SOCIAL CONSTRUCTION OF THE BODY

Medicine undoubtedly has the power to decide what counts as an illness. In the nineteenth century, for example, masturbation was believed to be a dangerous illness which produced a cluster of symptoms, including vertigo, headaches, loss of hearing and memory, and which had some very serious long-term consequences, such as heart disease, insanity, blindness, and even death. While this now seems like a comical example of Victorian ignorance and prudery, today other natural processes, such as the menopause, are increasingly treated as 'medical conditions', in need of professional intervention and control.

In the next extract Deborah Lupton fleshes out the claim that medical knowledge about the body is not neutral, but instead embodies a set of cultural and political assumptions.

Deborah Lupton[39]

Social theorists who are interested in the body and medicine deny that medical knowledge, or indeed any other type of knowledge, can be regarded as neutral, scientific or politically disinterested. Rather, like the body or any other phenomenon, medicine is socially constructed, is mediated through social understandings, and has political effects. For instance, while we may think that the version of the human body presented in a medical textbook is 'scientific truth' and therefore politically neutral, closer examination reveals conventions of representation that support wider sociocultural and political assumptions and objectives. The body in such textbooks is nearly always that of a young white male, suggesting that this type of body is the 'real' or 'normal' human body, against which other bodies (those of women, people of non-white ethnicity, or the elderly) are considered 'abnormal'...

---

[39] 'The Body, Medicine and Society' in John Germow (ed.), *Second Opinion: An Introduction to Health Sociology* (OUP: Oxford, 1998) 121–35.

Throughout the history of scientific medicine, medical and public health knowledges have been employed to distinguish and differentiate between 'normal', 'healthy' bodies and those that are regarded as 'abnormal', 'diseased' or 'deviant'. The male European body has been represented as the archetypical normal, healthy body...By way of contrast, the female body, the bodies of the working classes or the poor, non-white bodies, and homosexual bodies have been singled out as diseased, passive, contaminating, dirty and lacking self-control. There is a symbiotic relationship, therefore, between identifying the bodies of particular social groups (such as women, non-Whites, the working class, or homosexuals) as being uncontrolled, dirty, and as a result, more susceptible to illness, disease and early death, and the reproduction of the notion that such groups are inferior to the dominant social group (that is, well-off, white, heterosexual men)....

Compared with the male body, the female body has been represented as sickly, weak, and susceptible to illness. Women are typically described in the legal, medical and early social scientific literature as possessing problematic and unruly bodies, with their sexual and reproductive capacities requiring constant surveillance and regulation. Particularly in the nineteenth and twentieth centuries, medical assumptions about women—for example, that they were prone to uncontrolled emotional outbursts, which in turn were produced by the uterus, or that their natural place was in the home rather than participating in the public sphere—have contributed to the control of women and their confinement to the domestic sphere.

In the next extract, Bill Hughes argues that the ill and dependent body is increasingly seen as a reflection of the patient's weakness or failure. In part, this is because preventative medicine emphasizes the individual's responsibility for her own health, and may downplay some of the wider social causes of ill health, such as poverty and social inequality.

Bill Hughes[40]

As health maintenance—as opposed to curative—strategies emerge as the priority in contemporary patterns of health care, then responsibility for health shifts from the professional to the lay person...There can be no doubt that this apparent democratisation of the relationship between professional and patient suited western governments intent on reducing public expenditure and squeezing the welfare state. The ideas of self care and health maintenance as the responsibility of the lay person rather than the professional became, in the 1980s, important ideological tools in the privatisation of healthcare activities. In the contemporary, secular, deregulated world, a good deal of the policing of human behaviour—which is traditionally invested in the powers of religion and law—is carried out in the name of health...Medical knowledge, often in the form of behavioural prescriptions, challenges the population to be healthy, to adopt healthy behaviours and to choose healthy places to live and work.

Disease—in at least some of its manifestations—can now be regarded as a failure of health maintenance, a sign of an improper relationship to one's body and to what one does with it.

---

[40] 'Medicalized Bodies' in Philip Hancock, Bill Hughes, Elizabeth Jagger, Kevin Paterson, Rachel Russell, Emmanuelle Tulle-Winton, and Melissa Tyler (eds), *The Body, Culture and Society: An Introduction* (Open UP: Milton Keynes, 2000) 12–28.

(b) DO WE OWN OUR BODIES?

In contemporary bioethics, the question of whether we have rights in our bodies akin to ownership emerges in debates about surrogacy and payment for organ donation. Certainly, some of the rights that we have over our bodies look very like property rights: a right to use them, to exclude others, and to be compensated for negligently inflicted damage are all rights that also commonly exist in relation to things that we own. On the other hand, it is less clear whether we possess another right that we would normally associate with ownership, namely the right to transfer for value.

In the next extract Stephen Munzer argues that while it would not make sense to say that we have full ownership of our bodies, we do possess some limited property rights in them.

Stephen Munzer[41]

[S]ome hold that the body should be thought of as property and emphasize that each person owns or has title to himself or herself. Others maintain that the body ought not to be thought of as property at all, and indeed that it demeans human beings to think of them or their bodies as property. In contrast, the position advocated here is that, insofar as one takes an overall view, people do not own, but have some limited property rights in, their bodies....

It is unhelpful to say that no body rights are property rights. It is also unhelpful to say that all body rights are property rights...Since both extreme views should be rejected, one must provide a criterion for classifying some, but not all, body rights as property rights. The most useful criterion is transferability...

[O]ne can divide all body rights into personal rights and property rights. Personal rights are body rights that protect interests or choices other than the choice to transfer. Property rights are body rights that protect the choice to transfer...One can subdivide property rights in the body into weak and strong varieties. A weak property right involves only a choice to transfer gratuitously. A strong property right involves a choice to transfer for value...

[I]t is a mistake to characterize body rights, jointly or individually, as self-ownership. Taken jointly, the body rights of each person amount not to ownership but only to a weaker package of limited property rights. Considered individually, the body rights of each person are not all in the same boat. Most body rights are personal rather than property rights; examples are rights not to be murdered, not to be searched without a warrant or just cause...and to exclude others from sexual or other physical contact. Some body rights are property rights—whether weak, such as the right to donate an organ upon death, or strong, such as the right to sell semen; but these weak and strong property rights are neither so numerous nor so central as to establish that persons 'own' themselves.

5 CONCLUSION

In the remainder of this book, we will see that, in recent years, there has been a shift from a paternalistic model of medical decision-making, based upon the idea that 'doctor knows best', towards an autonomy model, which assumes that a competent adult patient should have an almost absolute right to refuse medical treatment. It would, however, be a mistake

---

[41] *A Theory of Property* (CUP: Cambridge, 1990).

to regard patient autonomy as the overriding value in *all* medical decision-making. The right to autonomy is a *negative* right to prevent unwanted intervention, and patients do not have the right to demand access to medical treatment when resources are unavailable; or when treatment would be against the doctors' clinical judgement; or when Parliament has decided that the treatment in question is ethically unacceptable and should be legally proscribed (examples currently include human reproductive cloning and female circumcision).

The problem for the law is that there will be very few cases when there is agreement over the legitimacy of controversial medical practices. There will never be any consensus over whether euthanasia should be legalized, for example, or whether it is legitimate to experiment on embryos. In this chapter, we have focused mainly upon how we might go about *discussing* these questions. We could, for example, look at the *consequences* of regulating in one way or another. So, in relation to euthanasia, we could ask whether legalization would, on balance, make life better or worse for sick and vulnerable patients. We could also think about what *principles* might be at stake, and how the tension between *autonomy* and *non-maleficence* should be resolved. It might be important to think about what arguments grounded in *human dignity* or respect for the *sanctity of human life* mean in this context, and whether there is a *slippery slope* that either could, or could not, be contained through regulation. None of these considerations can tell us what to do, however, and undoubtedly most of us will also bring our own values and experiences to bear on these questions. In relation to euthanasia, for example, someone with strong religious convictions will be influenced by their faith, and someone who has seen a relative die a protracted and painful death may find that that experience shapes their judgement. Our 'gut instincts' will inevitably often provide the starting point for our reasoning process, but it is important to remember that, on their own, there is no reason why anyone else should find them persuasive.

FURTHER READING

Ashcroft, RE, Dawson, A, Draper H, and McMillan JR (eds) *Principles of Health Care Ethics*, 2nd edn (Chichester: Wiley 2007) chapters 1, 3, 5, 6, 7, 11.

Beauchamp, Tom L and Childress, James F, *Principles of Biomedical Ethics*, 6th edn (OUP: Oxford, 2008).

Beyleveld, Deryck and Brownsword, Roger, *Human Dignity in Bioethics and Biolaw* (OUP: Oxford, 2001).

Harris, John (ed.), *Bioethics* (OUP: Oxford, 2001).

Kuhse, Helga and Singer, Peter (eds), *A Companion to Bioethics* (Blackwell: Oxford, 1998).

O'Neill, Onora, *Autonomy and Trust in Bioethics* (CUP: Cambridge, 2002).

2

RESOURCE ALLOCATION

CENTRAL ISSUES

1. Most people accept that rationing has become a fact of life in the modern NHS. There are a number of different possible rationing strategies; such as equal access to treatment; rationing according to clinical need; maximizing health gains, through the QALY approach; discriminating on the grounds of age; taking individual responsibility for ill health into account; rationing according to ability to pay; singling out certain types of excluded treatment; rationing by diluting the standard of care; and finally, random allocation of treatment.

2. In addition to working out how to make rationing decisions, it is also important to decide *who* should be charged with making these tough choices. Doctors and politicians would rather avoid taking direct responsibility for withholding treatment from patients on the grounds of cost, and in England and Wales, decision-making is increasingly delegated to the National Institute of Clinical Excellence (NICE). In Scotland, a similar task is performed by the Scottish Medicines Consortium (SMC).

3. Patients may want to challenge rationing decisions in the courts by applying for judicial review. Historically, the judiciary has been reluctant to interfere with decisions about the allocation of scarce resources. In recent years, there have been some important exceptions, but it is not yet clear whether they represent a decisive trend towards more pro-active judicial scrutiny.

4. Patients might want to seek treatment abroad, and within the EU their right to do so may now be protected by law. Non-EU citizens have attempted to resist deportation on the grounds that depriving them of needed treatment might amount to inhuman and degrading treatment, and hence violate their human rights. These claims have seldom succeeded.

1 INTRODUCTION

In this chapter we examine the complex and politically contentious question of resource allocation, or rationing. Our principal emphasis will be on the rationing of National Health Service (NHS) expenditure, rather than other scarce goods, such as organs (which we consider separately in chapter 11). While there are those who prefer to use the less pejorative term 'priority-setting', 'rationing' more honestly and bluntly captures the reality that when resources are scarce, it is impossible to provide everyone with immediate access to the best possible care.

At the outset, it is interesting to note a subtle shift in the meaning of the word 'rationing' over the course of the twentieth century. Rationing used to mean that people should be entitled to a fixed quota of resources: an obvious example would be the rationing of food and other goods during and immediately after the Second World War. This was conspicuously egalitarian: deprivation was to be shared equally across society as part of a collective commitment to the national good. Now, however, rationing refers to the discretionary allocation of scarce resources, with deprivation generally distributed *unevenly* across society.

Since the NHS first started treating patients in 1948, demand for health care services has far outstripped the NHS's capacity to supply them. In the first section of this chapter, we consider some of the reasons why NHS resources are overstretched, but we also examine the arguments of those who believe that rationing should be unnecessary. For example, some people argue that a fairer society would spend less money on going to war, or on footballers' salaries, and more on the NHS. Alternatively, it is claimed that reducing inefficiency and waste, by ensuring that treatments are only provided when they meet a threshold level of effectiveness, would again largely remove the need to make 'tragic choices' about the allocation of scarce NHS funds. While increasing public spending on the NHS and eliminating inappropriate use of resources are clearly worthwhile goals, for the foreseeable future it is unlikely that the NHS will be able to provide immediate access to optimum care for every citizen in the UK.

If some sort of rationing is inevitable, it is important to distinguish between the various different levels at which resource allocation decisions may be taken. At the **macro** level, political choices must be made about how much public money should be spent on the NHS: in the light of the other competing demands upon the nation's resources, and within the health budget, priorities must be set in order to determine how much money should be spent on different types of health care. Should priority be given to acute hospital services, or should we increase spending on local GP services? At the **micro** level, it might be necessary to choose between individual patients, perhaps in order to work out which one should be given the only available bed in an intensive care unit.

In an ideal world, these invidious choices would be unnecessary; but if such decisions are inevitable, it is important to ensure that they are taken fairly. In the second section, we consider how we might distinguish between fair and unfair ways to allocate scarce resources, at both the macro and the micro levels. While it is clear that certain patient characteristics, such as race, should be irrelevant, disagreement exists over whether it might be reasonable to take into account other factors, such as a person's age, or her responsibility for her own ill health.

In addition to working out the criteria that should inform a fair system of resource allocation, it is also important to decide who should be responsible for making these decisions. Ought responsibility to rest with central government or local health authorities? In England

and Wales, the National Institute for Health and Clinical Excellence (NICE), set up in 1999, judges the clinical and cost-effectiveness of treatments and makes recommendations about their provision within the NHS.

Finally, we look at the ways in which choices about the allocation of resources might be challenged, principally, of course, by dissatisfied patients who believe they have been unfairly denied access to appropriate treatment. NHS funding decisions may be subject to judicial review, but in practice, patients have seldom succeeded in proving that the NHS has acted irrationally, unreasonably or unlawfully, or that denial of treatment interferes with their human rights.

2 THE SCARCITY OF RESOURCES

After the end of the Second World War, a labour government was elected under Clement Attlee which promised to massively expand welfare provision, and in particular to introduce a national health service. Before the NHS was set up in 1948 (under the National Health Service Act, 1946), it had been thought that providing the whole population with free and comprehensive health care, in addition to the other social services which were to be provided through the welfare state, might improve the nation's health, and thus lead to a diminishing demand for health care services. David Hunter explains that:

> the NHS was founded on a fallacy: that there was a finite amount of ill-health in the population which, once removed, would result in the maintenance of health and the provision of health care becoming cheaper as the need for it dropped off. What has happened is that success in health care has resulted in people living longer potentially to be ill more often and therefore consume more resources.[1]

From the outset, it became obvious that the assumption that a national health service would lead to *reduced* expenditure on health was hopelessly naïve. It was immediately clear that the costs of providing care were going to exceed the available resources, and three years after the NHS was set up, prescription charges were introduced. This move led to the resignation of Aneurin Bevan, the chief architect of the NHS and the first Secretary of State for Health.

Over the past six decades, successive governments have increased spending on the NHS at above the rate of inflation, and the proportion of the UK's gross domestic product (GDP) spent on health has risen from 5 per cent in the 1980s to 9.4 per cent in 2006.[2] Yet, the NHS continues to face financial difficulties. Why is this?

First, the NHS may be a victim of its own success. Life expectancy has increased dramatically since the 1940s. Our need for medical care is concentrated at the end of our lives: indeed, more than 25 per cent of all acute health care costs are incurred in our last year of life.[3] If we were healthy throughout old age, and just made extensive use of NHS resources immediately before our deaths, increased life expectancy would not impose additional costs

---

[1] *Desperately Seeking Solutions: Rationing Health Care* (Longman: London, 1997) 20.

[2] Anne Griffin, 'UK Nears European Average in Proportion of GDP Spent on Health Care' (2007) 334 British Medical Journal 442.

[3] D Wanless, *Securing Our Future Health: Taking a Long-term View* (HM Treasury: London, 2002) para 9.16.

on the NHS. However, our success in extending the average life-span has not been accompanied by the same level of success in reducing the infirmity and morbidities associated with ageing. Hence extending the period of old age increases demand for health services. It is the very elderly sector of the population which is set to increase most rapidly in the future. By 2031 the proportion of the UK's population who are over 85 years old is predicted to grow from 1.9 per cent to 3.5 per cent.[4]

Secondly, technological and scientific progress has led to the availability of more sophisticated (and expensive) treatments for a wide variety of conditions. Not only are more options available, but the numbers of us who can be categorized as patients increases as treatments for conditions which were previously not treatable—such as the menopause or hypertension—emerge.

Thirdly, patients' expectations have risen dramatically. Most of the UK's population have been able to take the NHS's existence for granted throughout their lives, and, as a result, assume that they have a right to free and comprehensive health care. Patients are increasingly well informed about the availability of different treatments, and are more willing to insist upon access to them. This trend is undoubtedly assisted by the internet: in 2002 the Wanless report estimated that there were already around 10,000 health information websites and that this figure was increasing by about 300 per month in the EU alone.[5] There are also a growing number of patient groups, such as 'Woman Fighting for Herceptin', which are set up to put pressure on the NHS to fund expensive treatments.

Fourthly, when a service is provided free of charge, there are fewer constraints on demand than is the case when people have to pay. With no financial disincentives to seeking medical care, people visit their GP for minor complaints that are overwhelmingly likely to clear up by themselves within a few days. Demand—particularly for primary care services—is therefore especially elastic.

Fifthly, the proportion of the NHS budget spent on secondary care in hospitals has decreased, while more money has been diverted to primary care and preventative medicine. Although few would dispute the virtue of keeping as many patients as possible out of hospital, failures in hospital care—such as patients being kept on trolleys or dying from hospital-acquired infections like MRSA[6]—are often particularly newsworthy, adding to the public's perception of the NHS as a failing service.

Sixthly, more than half of all NHS resources is spent on salaries,[7] and, particularly for some health care professionals such as GPs, these have increased above the rate of inflation in recent years. Reductions in the hours worked by junior doctors have also increased pressure on the NHS budget.

Seventhly, as we shall see in the next chapter, clinical negligence claims represent a significant drain on NHS funds. In early 2009, it was reported that trusts faced an 80 per cent increase in the cost of claims, up from £400 million to £713 million.[8]

---

[4] Christopher Newdick, *Who Should we Treat? Rights, Rationing and Resources in the NHS*, 2nd edn (OUP: Oxford, 2005) 8.

[5] D Wanless, *Securing Our Future Health: Taking a Long-term View* (HM Treasury: London, 2002) para 9.16.

[6] Methicillin-resistant *Staphylococcus aureus*.

[7] Christopher Newdick, *Who Should We Treat? Rights, Rationing and Resources in the NHS*, 2nd edn (OUP: Oxford, 2005) 3.

[8] NHS facing £700 million negligence bill 5 February 2009 <www.bbc.co.uk>.

Finally, the problem of health care funding appears to be universal. The central problem, as Mark Hall explains, is that providing the whole population with optimum access to medical care would probably absorb all of a country's resources:

> When we are ill, we desperately want our doctors to do everything within their power to heal us, regardless of the costs involved. Medical technology has advanced so far, however, that literal adherence to this credo for everyone would consume the entire gross domestic product.[9]

In fact, one study estimated that providing all the health care that could be beneficial to each French citizen would cost five-and-a-half times France's gross national product.[10] Although we want money to be no object when we are patients, as taxpayers we are rather more cost conscious.

A variety of factors are therefore responsible for the NHS's persistent financial difficulties, but it would be a mistake to regard each of these sources of pressure on the NHS budget as 'problems'. On the contrary, longer life expectancy and the availability of more effective treatments are to be welcomed. If the additional demands placed on the NHS are always likely to outstrip the available resources, we then have to think about the best ways to minimize any negative impact on patient care. Many believe that rationing has become inevitable, and as Alan Maynard explains in the next extract, that the important task now facing the NHS is to ensure that resources are rationed as fairly and as openly as possible.

Alan Maynard[11]

> There are two certainties in life: death and scarcity. A long, good-quality life free of pain, disability and distress from birth to death is the exception rather than the rule. Most people confront morbidity over the life-cycle and demand cures and care which are expensive and often of unproven benefit. Principles and practices (mostly only implicit) determine who is left in pain and discomfort, who is treated and who is left to die. The policy issue is therefore not whether, but how, to ration access to health and social care. Society and its political representatives are, however, reluctant to confront this reality...A health service in 'political denial' stunts the development of socially agreed rationing principles, that are openly discussed and accountably applied, and creates a market of special pleading on both the demand—(for example, patient advocacy groups) and supply side (for example, the pharmaceutical industry). These are organisations with overlapping goals which result in a single demand: spend more!

Before we consider what a fair rationing system might look like, we should acknowledge the arguments of those who argue that this acceptance of the inevitability of rationing is either unnecessary or premature.

First, there are those who would dispute the premise that anyone other than the individual patient/consumer should be responsible for paying for health care services. Robert

---

[9] 'Rationing Health Care at the Bedside' (1994) 69 New York Universiy Law Review 693, 694.
[10] Cited in Richard D Lamm, 'Rationing of Health Care: Inevitable and Desirable' (1992) 140 University of Pennsylvania Law Review 1511, 1512.
[11] 'Ethics and Health Care "Underfunding" ' (2001) 27 Journal of Medical Ethics 223–7.

Nozick, for example, has argued against any sort of 'patterned' distribution of resources.[12] According to Nozick, provided everyone has acquired their resources justly, the way in which they choose to spend their wealth is none of the state's business. Taxation is, in Nozick's view, akin to forced labour, and hence illegitimate. If some people choose to spend their money on health care or medical insurance, and others do not, the distribution of health care that results will be just. As we see later in this chapter, however, the consequences of a completely free market in health care would be unedifying, to say the least.

Secondly, Donald Light argues that it is illegitimate to even contemplate rationing before attempts have been made to eliminate waste and inefficiency.[13] Evidence-based medicine, which is intended to reduce expenditure upon ineffective or inefficient treatments, is perceived to be a more appropriate solution to the NHS's funding crisis than rationing.

Donald W Light[14]

[T]o say that 'rationing is inevitable and therefore we should focus on how to ration reasonably' is like the medical profession deciding that 'death is inevitable and therefore we should focus on how to die reasonably'. Death is inevitable, but the conclusion denies the whole purpose of medicine. Likewise, our purpose should be to postpone and minimise rationing as much as possible...

What this means is that rationing by any reasonable definition is avoidable, and the British can have a healthcare system without widespread denial of care, waiting lists, run down facilities, and underservice ... If the government and the healthcare professions seriously want to minimise the rationing of care to sick patients, they need to address the sorts of waste that have been identified by the Anti-rationing Group—including overtesting, inappropriate prescribing, the organisation of follow up for new outpatients, and the provision of care by doctors that can be done by nurses. The Anti-rationing Group has concluded that if these sources are eliminated, the waiting lists 'would disappear within a year, never to return'.

It has also been suggested that demand for services could be managed more efficiently, by ensuring that people do not make inappropriate use of NHS resources, and finding new ways to meet people's need for advice about their health, through pharmacists, websites, and help lines (such as NHS Direct).

While it is undoubtedly true that the NHS could operate more efficiently, it is unlikely that this could wholly eliminate the need to ration services. The NHS spends more than half of its budget on salaries, and so huge gains in efficiency would only be possible if staff costs could be significantly reduced. For obvious reasons, it would be undesirable to expect health care professionals to work longer hours for smaller salaries.

Finally, it is sometimes argued that the UK could afford to spend far more of its GDP on health care, and that a massive increase in resources would remove the need for rationing. Devoting more public money to the NHS would mean either that less would be available to other public services, such as education or defence, or that tax rates would have to rise significantly. Both are, of course, possible. But we should remember that while health is undoubtedly very important, it is clearly not the only thing that matters to us, as is evident

---

[12] *Anarchy, State and Utopia* (Blackwell: Oxford, 1974).
[13] Donald W Light, 'The Real Ethics of Rationing' (1997) 315 British Medical Journal 112–15.
[14] Ibid.

from our lifestyles: few of us could claim that we *always* put our health first when deciding how to occupy our time, or what to eat and drink.

While the UK used to spend a much smaller proportion of its GDP on health than many other European countries, it is now close to the European average of approximately 10 per cent. It is true that the UK spends much less than the US, but increased spending does not necessarily lead to improved services. In 2000 the World Health Organization[15] attempted to rank national health systems' performance according to the extent to which they achieved three goals:

(1) good health;

(2) responsiveness to the population's expectations;

(3) fairness of financial contribution.

The results were interesting, not least because—as is evident from the extract reproduced below—there appears to be no correlation between the amount spent on health care per capita and a country's rank. Nor does the percentage of care provided privately appear to make any difference. France came first; the UK 18th; and the US was 37th (out of 191 countries).

WHO rank	Country	Expenditure per capita ($)	% private
1	France	2,077	23.6
2	Italy	1,783	32.0
7	Spain	1,218	23.2
10	Japan	1,822	21.7
11	Norway	2,425	17.2
18	United Kingdom	1,461	16.2
20	Switzerland	2,794	26.6
25	Germany	2,424	25.4
32	Australia	2,043	30.7
37	United States	4,178	55.3

3 DIFFERENT RATIONING STRATEGIES

The reality of rationed health care is that patients are deprived of beneficial treatment. If a treatment is withheld from a patient because it is not likely to do any good, then this would be a straightforward case of clinical judgement rather than rationing. Depriving individuals of care that might help them is radically at odds with the rule of rescue, which is 'the strong human proclivity to provide aid to identified victims of illness or accident'.[16]

The concept of triage (from the French verb *trier*: to sort) was developed on the battlefields of the First World War, when there were insufficient resources to treat every injured

---

[15] World Health Report 2000, *Health Systems: Improving Performance* (WHO, 2000).
[16] DC Hadorn, 'The Problem of Discrimination in Health Care Priority Setting' (1992) 268 Journal of the American Medical Association 1454–8, 1454.

soldier. 'Battlefield triage' involves deciding who to treat, based upon the severity of their injuries, and how quickly they could return to active service. Treatment might then be withheld from someone who is unlikely to recover, so that it can be given to someone who is more likely to benefit. Some people have suggested that pandemic flu—which could infect 50 per cent of the population—may present us with choices akin to 'battlefield triage': in the early stages, there will simply not be sufficient supplies of the right flu vaccine for the particular strain, and tough choices will have to be made about who should have priority. But while these decisions are always going to be difficult, Loren Lomasky argues that decisions taken *in extremis* may be less 'dreadful' than non-emergency choices to treat one patient rather than another.

Loren E Lomasky[17]

Two classic examples of triage are the dangerously overloaded lifeboat and the harried medic patching up the wounded on a battlefield. Whatever is done, some salvageable lives will be forfeited. The dreadfulness of these choices though is somewhat softened by the urgency of a crisis: action must be immediate and there is little luxury for reflective deliberation. If called upon to justify his actions, an agent could plead that he was reacting instinctively to the needs of the moment.

Contemporary medical technology is responsible for triage situations of a rather different character. A mechanism is devised that is effective against some previously untreatable condition. Unfortunately, only a small percentage of those afflicted can receive treatment. Who shall be allowed to live? Here decision-makers are dealing with a series of events predictable well in advance. Not enmeshed in a precipitously developing crisis, they are privileged to assume the role of detached administrator. There is, however, a price to be paid for this relative ease: whatever standards are developed and employed are subject to close scrutiny. Those disfavoured in the selection process are perfectly entitled to ask why...

Triage is never unproblematic, but on what basis could a creature of the state adopt any principle of selection? Whoever is excluded can justifiably complain that he is thereby being disadvantaged by the very institution whose special duty is to extend equal protection to all persons.

In the following sections, we examine different criteria that could plausibly be used to ration health care services. While we might agree that resources should be allocated fairly, this just begs the question: what do we mean by fair? Do we treat people fairly when we treat them equally? Or should priority always be given to those in the greatest need? Alternatively, should we ensure that resources are allocated where they will do most good, using some sort of cost-effectiveness calculation? We could choose to take an individual's responsibility for their own ill health into account; or their social value; or we could opt for a straightforward free market in health care, in which those who were prepared to spend the most would have access to the best treatment. Finally, we could abandon the search for defensible rationing criteria and instead distribute health care resources by some process of random selection.

It is important to remember that a perfectly fair and universally acceptable rationing system is an unrealistic goal. Rather, we may instead be looking for ways to allocate scarce

---

[17] 'Medical Progress and National Health Care' (1980) 10 Philosophy and Public Affairs 65–88.

resources which attempt to mediate fairly between competing claims on NHS resources. In practice, most people would probably advocate some sort of mixed rationing system, in which a number of different factors are taken into account when allocating resources. For example, an approach based upon the cost-effectiveness of treatment may have to be supplemented by additional criteria, such as the urgency of clinical need.

Before we assess potentially fair rationing criteria, it is worth pointing out that some very obviously unfair grounds for distinguishing between patients might nevertheless have an effect upon the ways in which resources are allocated in the NHS. First, while it would clearly be unethical for doctors to take a patient's personal appeal into account when deciding whether to offer them treatment, in practice health care professionals are human beings capable of feeling sympathy for one patient and exasperation with another. Of course, these emotions should not be allowed to colour their clinical judgement, but it would be impossible to guarantee that doctors will never be prompted to do more for a patient out of personal sympathy.

Secondly, some patients are simply more demanding and assertive than others, and this will undoubtedly affect their access to NHS resources. A patient who demands a second opinion, or who repeatedly telephones a consultant's secretary may receive care that other patients might not have the confidence or the knowledge to seek out. John Butler interviewed health care professionals about their attitudes to rationing, and as we see in the following extract, concern was expressed about patients' uneven ability to exert pressure upon health care resources.

John Butler[18]

> The health visitor was clear about the injustice that could result from rationing by inaccessibiliy, in which the astute and the persistent were rewarded at the expense of those who lacked the know-how to seek out what they wanted. Those who are put off, she said, will not be the better-educated middle-class families, they will be the poorer families who are under-educated and inarticulate...
>
> The surgeon, too, expressed his moral concern at the potential for social bias in the innate responsiveness of the service to the pressure exerted upon it by patients. Those who 'push and shove a bit' will often get the best treatment, but they will not be a cross-section of all those waiting to be seen. He recognized it as wrong (albeit, perhaps, unavoidable) that a class bias will ensue through which cases may not always be seen in the order of their clinical urgency. It was the replacement of need by pressure as the determinant of access to secondary care that he saw as wrong.

(a) EQUALITY

Equal distribution of health care resources does not, of course, mean that the NHS's total budget should be divided equally between all UK citizens. Rather, as Amy Gutmann explains, equality of access instead means that everyone with an equivalent health need should have equivalent access to appropriate care. Patients who are alike in relevant ways should be treated alike, and patients who are unlike each other should be treated differently.

---

[18] *The Ethics of Health Care Rationing: Principles and Practices* (Cassell: London, 1999) 230.

But of course, this just begs the question: what factors justify treating patients similarly and what factors justify differentiating between them? Is an alcoholic who needs a liver transplant 'like' a non-drinker with a history of liver disease who has a similarly urgent need for a transplant, or does the patient's alcoholism turn them into 'unlike' cases?

Amy Gutmann[19]

A principle of equal access to health care demands that every person who shares the same type and degree of health need must be given an equally effective chance of receiving appropriate treatment of equal quality so long as that treatment is available to anyone....The principle requires that if anyone within a society has an opportunity to receive a service or good that satisfies a health need, then everyone who shares the same type and degree of health need must be given an equally effective chance of receiving that service or good.

Equal access also places limits upon the market freedoms of some individuals, especially, but not exclusively, the richest members of society. The principle does not permit the purchase of health care to which other similarly needy people do not have effective access...Thus, the rigorous implementation of equal access to health care would prevent rich people from spending their extra income for preferred medical services, if those services were not equally accessible to the poor.

In practice, on its own, equality does not tell us very much about how to allocate scarce NHS resources. Instead, it supplements other rationing criteria, such as need or cost-effectiveness, by ensuring that these are employed consistently between patients in order to avoid arbitrary and unfair distribution of resources. As Ian Kennedy suggests, it might also lead us to give particular priority to the needs of the most disadvantaged and vulnerable members of society.

Ian Kennedy[20]

[I]f we are concerned with what constitutes a just allocation of resources, my prescription, at the very least, would call for policies aimed at ensuring, as far as possible, that everyone had an equal opportunity to enjoy an equal share of the total net welfare of society.

One ingredient of the net benefits that a society enjoys is health. It follows that a just society must set its policies and write its laws to ensure that everyone, beginning with the least advantaged and most vulnerable, has an equal opportunity to enjoy an equal share of the total net resources allocated to health.

Fairness in the distribution of health care resources might mean striving, as far as possible, to ensure that everyone has an *equal opportunity* to participate in society. Of course, there will always be people with very serious illnesses or disabilities who are so handicapped by their conditions that no amount of spending on healthcare will return them to a reasonable standard of health. Nevertheless, this approach to rationing might lead us to direct resources to those who are most disadvantaged by their ill health, perhaps to people with the greatest health *needs*.

[19] 'For and Against Equal Access to Health Care', Milbank Memorial Fund Quarterly/Health and Society 59(4) (1981) in *Classic Works in Medical Ethics*, Gregory Pence (ed.) (McGraw Hill: Boston, 1998) 367–8.
[20] *Treat Me Right: Essays in Medical Law and Ethics* (Clarendon Press: Oxford, 1998) 291.

(b) NEEDS

At first sight, distributing NHS resources according to need might appear attractively fair and simple. Needs, after all, have much greater moral force than wants or desires. But the concept of 'need' is remarkably elastic and culturally variable. New technologies will constantly expand our category of medical 'needs'. As Richard Lamm has argued: '[m]edical "need" is an infinitely expandable concept. We need what is available, and in a creative and inventive society such as our own, there is no end to what we can do to treat aging bodies.'[21]

Moreover, need could only operate as a rationing criteria if we were able to construct some sort of hierarchy of needs, so that we could tell whether one patient's need was greater or less than the need of other candidates for treatment. We would, for example, have to decide whether life-preserving needs are always more important that life-enhancing needs. Someone whose life is in danger clearly 'needs' treatment more than someone who will survive without treatment, and so it might be argued that life-saving treatment should always be our first priority. But this would disregard other relevant criteria, such as a person's capacity to benefit from treatment. The life of a patient who is in a permanent vegetative state can be preserved—at great cost—for many years using artificial nutrition and hydration. It is not clear that this sort of expenditure should necessarily take priority over treatment, such as palliative care, which is capable of alleviating a terminally ill patient's pain and discomfort, but which will not save her life.

Norman Daniels has applied John Rawls' theory of justice to the distribution of health care. Daniels argues that health care is of special importance, and should be regarded as a primary social good, because of its capacity to ensure fair equality of opportunity. Disease and infirmity interfere with the range of opportunities open to an individual. In order to rectify these inequalities, health care should be directed toward those needs which most interfere with 'normal species functioning'. When deciding between competing needs, Daniels argues that we can rank them according to the extent to which normal species function is impaired. Someone with a broken hip has their normal opportunity range restricted more than someone with a disfiguring scar, and hence, according to Daniels's analysis, hip replacement operations should take priority over cosmetic surgery.

Norman Daniels[22]

> What emerges here is the suggestion that we use impairment of the normal opportunity range as a fairly crude measure of the relative importance of health-care needs at the macro level. In general, it will be more important to prevent, cure, or compensate for those disease conditions which involve a greater curtailment of normal opportunity range....
>
> [W]e can characterize health-care needs as things we need to maintain, restore, or compensate for the loss of, normal species-functioning. Since serious impairments of normal functioning diminish our capacities and abilities, they impair individual opportunity range relative to the range normal for our society.

There are, however, several problems with the attempt to prioritize different health needs by the extent to which they interfere with normal species functioning. First, 'normal species

[21] Richard D Lamm, 'Rationing of Health Care: Inevitable and Desirable' (1992) 140 University of Pennsylvania Law Review 1511, 1512.

[22] 'Health-Care Needs and Distributive Justice' (1981) 10 Philosophy and Public Affairs 146–79.

functioning' may sound like an objective criterion, but it is in fact quite difficult to pin down. How much infirmity is 'normal' in old age, for example? It is 'normal' for human bodies to fail progressively in old age, yet we would not want to give a low priority to treatment of very elderly patients on the grounds that their ill health is 'normal'.

More worryingly, normal species functioning depends in part upon the availability of decent health services, leading to a degree of circularity in using 'normal functioning' as a criterion for the distribution of health care. Allan Buchanan, for example, has argued that:

> A principle which requires only that resources be allocated so as to assure that everyone attains the normal opportunity range would be inadequate in situations in which the normal opportunity range was unacceptably narrow due to a failure to allocate sufficient resources for health care.[23]

Secondly, in practice it would be extremely difficult to construct an objective, population-wide hierarchy of illnesses and disabilities according to their degree of interference with normal species functioning. For some people, such as surgeons or pilots, losing the sight in one eye will have disastrous consequences, for others its impact upon their quality of life may be comparatively slight.

Finally, there would have to be exceptions to Daniels's classification in order to accommodate valuable medical treatments which do not attempt to 'restore normal species functioning'. Contraception, for example, is intended to *disrupt* normal functioning, yet in the UK it is considered such a cost-effective public good that it is exempt from prescription charges.

(c) MAXIMIZING HEALTH GAINS

(1) Assessing Cost-Effectiveness: The QALY

Quality-Adjusted Life Years, known as QALYs, are an attempt to quantify the costs and health gains which can be expected from different treatments, in order to compare their relative cost-effectiveness.[24] The point of QALYs is that they do not only measure the amount of extra life that a particular treatment might generate, but also its quality; the assumption being that we should divert resources to treatments which are likely to offer people the longest periods of healthy and active life. Alan Williams explains them as follows:

Alan Williams[25]

> The essence of a QALY is that it takes a year of healthy life expectancy to be worth 1, but regards a year of unhealthy life expectancy as worth less than 1. Its precise value is lower the worse the quality of life of the unhealthy person (which is what the 'quality adjusted' bit is all about). If being dead is worth zero, it is, in principle, possible for a QALY to be negative, i.e. for the quality of someone's life to be judged worse than being dead.

[23] 'The Right to a Decent Minimum of Health Care' (1984) 13 Philosophy and Public Affairs 55–78, 64.

[24] The QALY scale was first developed in the work of Rosser *et al.* in the 1970s. See further R Rosser and VC Watts, 'The Measurement of Hospital Output' (1972) 1 International Journal of Epidemiology 361–8; R Rosser and P Kind, 'A Scale of Values of States of Illness: Is There a Social Consensus?' (1978) 7 International Journal of Epidemiology 347–58.

[25] 'The Value of QALYs' (1985) 94 Health and Social Service Journal.

> The general idea is that a beneficial health care activity is one that generates a positive amount of QALYs, and that an efficient health care activity is one where the cost per QALY is as low as it can be. A high priority health care activity is one where the cost-per-QALY is low, and a low priority activity is one where cost-per-QALY is high.

There are therefore various stages to a QALY assessment. First, a quality of life scale must be worked out ranging from 0 (death) to 1.0 (full health). Next, we multiply the patient's life expectancy and quality of life score, both before and after treatment. The difference between these will be the QALY score. Let us imagine that, without treatment, patient A has 2 years of life left, and her quality of life is judged to be 0.5. Before treatment, her life contains 1 QALY. If treatment X would give her 6 years with a quality of life of 1.0, post-treatment, her life contains 6 QALYs. The QALY value of treatment X is therefore 5. The next stage is to calculate the cost per QALY. So let us imagine that treatment X costs £5,000. Since it provides 5 QALYs, the cost per QALY is £1,000.

If QALY scores are worked out for a number of different treatments, it should be possible to draw up league tables of treatments in order to work out which offer the best value for money. In the following extract from one such table, we can see that GP advice to stop smoking has a low cost per QALY compared with heart transplantation, for example.

Alan M Maynard[26]

QALY of competing therapies: some tentative estimates	Cost/QALY £
Cholesterol testing and diet therapy (adults aged 40–69)	220
GP advice to stop smoking	270
Pacemaker insertion	1,100
Hip replacement	1,800
Kidney transplant	4,710
Breast cancer screening	5,780
Heart transplantation	7,840
Hospital haemodialysis	21,970
Neurosurgical intervention for malignant brain tumour	107,780

In short, QALYs are an attempt to objectively compare the cost-effectiveness of different treatments so that scarce NHS resources 'do as much good as possible'.[27]

While QALYs lend a degree of objectivity to the ranking of medical treatments, on their own they cannot tell us how much money should be allocated to health care, nor which treatments should be funded. Kidney transplants may cost more than cholesterol testing in the above QALY 'league table', but that does not mean that kidney transplants should not be performed within the NHS. Rather, QALY scores simply provide policymakers with a technical and supposedly objective method with which to assess and compare cost-effectiveness. Although QALYs provide relevant information, there will still be difficult choices to make.

[26] Alan Williams, 'Developing the Health Care Market' (1991) 101 The Economic Journal 1277–86.

[27] Alan Williams, 'Economics, QALYs and Medical Ethics: A Health Economist's Perspective' in Souzy Dracopoulou (Ed), *Ethics and Values in Health Care Management* (Routledge: London, 1998) 29–37.

It is also important to note that a number of commentators have challenged the usefulness and fairness of the QALY approach to resource allocation. First, according to the logic of QALYs, the purpose of a health service is to generate the maximum number of quality-adjusted life years at the lowest cost. QALYs therefore assume that society is neutral as to how these health benefits are distributed across society, and are concerned only with ensuring the maximization of health gains. It makes no difference, for example, whether the years of healthy life go to people who are already in good health or to those whose health is poor.

Thus, QALYs have a tendency to ignore the *fairness* of distribution in favour of an approach concerned only with the total aggregate health improvement. In practice, most of us would prefer the NHS to fund interventions for patients with serious conditions, such as cancer and heart disease, rather than offering treatments for more trivial complaints, such as hayfever or acne, even if these latter treatments are more cost-effective. Our concern is not simply to maximize the aggregate health gain in society at the lowest cost, but rather to ensure that the NHS responds appropriately to those in the greatest need.

Secondly, the emphasis upon maximizing health gains is explicitly utilitarian. QALYs measure units of lifetime, as if they are interchangeable, rather than treating patients as separate individuals who value their own lives, and those of people they love, especially highly. If spending £5,000 on treatment X will enable us to extend patient A's life for 5 years, while spending the same amount of money on treatment Y will only extend patient B's life for a year, QALYs would suggest that we get most value for money from treatment X. But as John Harris, one of QALYs most vigorous critics, explains, patient B who is thereby forced to sacrifice an additional year of life might not agree:

John Harris[28]

What matters is that the person is not prepared to agree that his interest in continued life is of less value than that of anyone else, nor that that interest necessarily varies with the quality of his life nor with his life expectancy. In short, if a person wants continued existence, then, in my view, his interest in continued existence is entitled to be treated as on a par with that of anyone else. All people who want to go on living have an interest in continued existence, the value of which can only be determined by themselves.

Simona Giardano explains that while QALYs appear to capture what matters for us—securing the longest life expectancy of the best quality—this is in fact an illusion because 'what matters to people is not "the number of healthy life years the world contains", but the number of healthy years that *they or people they care about* will have'.[29]

Thirdly, it has been suggested that using QALYs to ration treatment will tend to exacerbate existing discrimination against the elderly and the disabled, whose QALY scores are likely to be fairly low because of their reduced life expectancy and/or their lower pre-existing quality of life. People who are unlucky enough to suffer from conditions that are very expensive to treat—and this is usually people with very serious illnesses—will also be discriminated against, because the cost per QALY of treating them is always likely to be high. This is, in Harris's words, 'a sort of double jeopardy', whereby people who have already

[28] 'Double Jeopardy and the Veil of Ignorance—A Reply' (1995) 21 Journal of Medical Ethics 151–7, 151.
[29] 'Respect for Equality and the Treatment of the Elderly: Declarations of Human Rights and Age-Based Rationing' (2005) 14 Cambridge Quarterly of Healthcare Ethics 83–92.

been unlucky enough to be seriously ill or disabled will be further disadvantaged when competing for scarce resources.[30]

John Harris[31]

> The ageism of QALY is inescapable, for any calculation of the life-years generated for a particular patient by a particular therapy must be based on the life expectancy of that patient after treatment. The older the patient is when treated, the fewer the life-years that can be achieved by the therapy...[I]t will usually be more QALY efficient to concentrate on areas of medicine which will inevitably generate more QALYs, neonatal care or paediatrics, for example. And equally, to channel resources away from (or deny them altogether to) areas such as geriatric medicine or terminal care.

This argument has been contested by commentators, who argue that Harris has overlooked a crucial feature of QALYs, namely, that what is measured is the *change* in a person's health brought about by a particular intervention. In order to maximize QALYs, resources should not always be diverted to people whose post-treatment quality of life or life expectancy is greatest, but whose QALY gain per pound spent is higher. If I am already fit and healthy, a medical treatment may not alter my QALY score very much at all, whereas, if my existing quality of life is low, my QALY score post-treatment may be much higher. Michael Rawlins and Andrew Dillon—respectively, the Chair and CEO of NICE—give the example of a treatment for osteoporosis, which costs £32,936 per QALY for patients aged 50 years, and £12,191 per QALY at age 70: 'this occurs because older patients have a greater risk of complications of osteoporosis and thus benefit more'.[32]

Fourthly, the QALY approach is inconsistent with the principle that people with equal health needs should have equal access to appropriate medical treatment. Rather, maximizing QALYs means that people with equal need for treatment will not be treated equally. As Penelope Mullen and Peter Spurgeon explain, their access to treatment will depend upon the costs of treating them: 'Thus systematic discrimination could result against, say, those from ethnic minority groups who require interpreters, those living in poorer housing who might require inpatient stays rather than day surgery and those living in remote sparsely populated locations.'[33]

Fifthly, when a new treatment is introduced, at first it may be extremely expensive, but its cost may decrease as the technology becomes cheaper, or as the expense of additional staff training is eliminated. The QALY scale might then discourage innovation in favour of established and *currently* cheaper treatments, even where there might be cost-savings from adopting the new treatment over the longer term.

Sixthly, QALYs assume that it is possible to devise an objective and accurate mechanism for measuring the anticipated length and quality of a person's life. In fact, the medical profession's predictions of future life expectancy are notoriously unreliable, and speculating about the future quality of a person's life will also be inherently uncertain. Treatment outcomes

---

[30] 'QALYfying the Value of Life' (1987) 13 Journal of Medical Ethics 117–23, 120.

[31] 'More and Better Justice' in JM Bell and Susan Mendus (eds), *Philosophy and Medical Welfare* (CUP: Cambridge, 1988) 75–96, 80.

[32] 'NICE Discrimination' (2005) 31 Journal of Medical Ethics 683–4, 683.

[33] Penelope Mullen and Peter Spurgeon, *Priority Setting and the Public* (Radcliffe Medical Press: Abingdon, 2000).

depend upon a wide variety of factors, such as the doctor's skill and the quality of aftercare services, and since the QALY calculation is simply too crude to capture all of the relevant variables, its results will be imprecise and indeterminate.

It could also be argued that it is impossible to reduce such a complex concept as quality of life to a single numerical value between 0 and 1. Not only would devising a universally accepted quality of life scale be extremely difficult, but we would also need to work out who should be charged with making these assessments. Would it be people suffering from the particular illness or disability; or the medical profession; or members of the public? It could be argued that only people who live with a condition are in any position to judge its effect on their quality of life. But, of course, it is not easy for such people to make the sort of comparative assessments demanded by the QALY scale. Doctors and members of the public may be able to speculate about the relative inconvenience or distress caused by a range of disabilities, especially if they have experience of caring for people with disabling conditions, but they inevitably do so from a position of relative ignorance.

Moreover, not only is it very difficult for anyone to judge whether depression might be worse than losing sensation in one's right arm, say, but also quality of life judgements are necessarily subjective, and hence do not lend themselves to the sort of objective quantification which the QALY scales are supposed to provide. The QALY weightings may be inevitably arbitrary: how can we tell whether living for ten years with a quality of life score of 0.9 is equivalent to living for nine years in perfect health? They are also incapable of taking the individual patient's own preferences and needs into account. For some people, immobility may not greatly interfere with their ability to gain enjoyment from life; for others it will be devastating.

Using QALYs at the macro level is less objectionable because we would just be deciding that treatment X, in general, leads to better patient outcomes at lower cost than treatment Y. As John Harris explains, it is at the micro level, when choices have to be made between individual patients, that taking QALYs into account is especially invidious.

John Harris[34]

There are two ways in which QALYs might be used. One is unexceptionable and useful, and fully in line with the assumptions which give QALYs their plausibility. The other is none of these.

QALYs might be used to determine which of rival therapies to give to a particular patient or which procedure to use to treat a particular condition. Clearly the one generating the most QALYs will be the better bet, both for the patient and for a society with scarce resources. However, QALYs might also be used to determine not what treatment to give these patients, but which group of patients to treat, or which conditions to give priority in the allocation of health care resources.

But whereas it follows from the fact that given the choice a person would prefer a shorter, healthier life to a longer one of severe discomfort, that the best treatment for that person is the one yielding the most QALYs, it does not follow that treatments yielding more QALYs are preferable to treatments yielding fewer QALYs where different people are to receive the treatments. That is to say, while it follows from the fact (if it is a fact) that I and everyone else would prefer to have, say, one year of healthy life rather than three years of severe discomfort, that we value healthy existence more than uncomfortable existence for ourselves, it does not

---

[34] 'QALYfying the Value of Life' (1987) 13 Journal of Medical Ethics 117–23, 118.

follow that where the choice is between three years of discomfort for me or immediate death on the one hand, and one year of health for you or immediate death on the other, that I am somehow committed to the judgement that you ought to be saved rather than me.

(2) A Wide or Narrow Interpretation of Cost-Effectiveness?

When health economists engage in cost-effectiveness analysis of medical treatments, they tend to judge 'effectiveness' according to the extent to which a treatment produces a clinical benefit. It would, however, be possible to broaden the scope of these sorts of calculations in a number of ways. First, health is improved not only by direct medical intervention. In fact, health care is probably one of the least important factors behind the dramatic improvements in public health that occurred during the twentieth century. Better nutrition, sanitation, workplace safety, and a reduction in poverty levels almost certainly contributed more to the nation's health than medical treatment. It has been estimated that health services affect about 10 per cent of the principal indices for measuring health (such as infant mortality, absences through sickness, and life expectancy), while 90 per cent are determined by factors beyond the control of the NHS, such as environment, nutrition, and lifestyle.[35] Could it therefore be argued that the cost-effectiveness of new medical technologies should be judged not only against other medical treatments, as in the QALY league tables, but also against other social measures, which might in fact lead to greater improvements in health at lower cost? Reducing child poverty levels, for example, would be likely to have a dramatic—and quite possibly highly cost-effective—impact upon health; yet raising welfare payments to poor families does not have the same popular appeal as heroic medical interventions to cure the sick.

In order to engage in a cost–benefit calculation, it is also, of course, necessary to work out what counts as a benefit. Are we concerned only with the health benefit to the particular individual, or might it be legitimate to take into account other benefits that might result from her successful treatment? Enabling members of the workforce to return to paid employment has clear social benefits that, if included in the cost/benefit calculation, might lead us to give priority to the treatment of adults of working age, or to those in full-time employment, or even to sub-sections of society who do especially valuable jobs. Should we take into account whether a patient has dependent children who will also benefit from her recovery? In deciding what priority substance abuse treatment programmes should receive, is it relevant that successfully treating drug addiction will not only improve the individual addict's life, but also that of her family and the community in which she lives?

Jonathan Glover argues that it will sometimes be legitimate to take into account any benefit that might accrue to third parties, such as dependent children, when deciding which patient to treat.

Jonathan Glover[36]

If there are two people whose lives are in question and we have to choose to save only one, the number of people dependent on them should be regarded as very important. If other

---

[35] David J Hunter, *Desperately Seeking Solutions: Rationing Health Care* (Longman: London, 1997) 18.
[36] *Causing Death and Saving Lives* (Penguin: London, 1977) 222–3.

things are equal, but one has no family and the other is the mother of several young children, the case against deciding between them randomly is a strong one... Refusal to depart from random choice when knowledge about their dependants is available is to place no value on avoiding the additional misery caused to the children if the mother is not the one saved...

If we give some weight to the interests of dependants, should we take into account more generalized side-effects, such as the relative importance of the contributions to society made by different people? There are good grounds for rejecting this as a general policy. It is a truism that we have no agreed standard by which to measure people's relative contribution to society. How does a mother compare with a doctor or a research scientist or a coal-miner? Any list of jobs ranked in order of social value seems, at least at present, to be arbitrary and debatable. It also seems to introduce the offensive division of people into grades.

In contrast, John Harris argues that discriminating against childless or single people in the distribution of health care resources fails to treat them as individuals whose lives are intrinsically, as opposed to instrumentally, valuable and offends the basic egalitarian principle that all lives have equal moral worth.

John Harris[37]

[T]he feeling that it is somehow more important to rescue those with dependants, when elevated to the level of policy, amounts to a systematic preference of those with families over those without...Dependence...is not simply dependence on parents, and grief and misery are not confined to family relationships. But even if they were, it is unclear that they would constitute adequate reasons for preferring to save one person rather than another. We should not forget that while the bereaved deserve sympathy, by far the greatest loss is to the deceased, and the misfortune of her friends and relations pales into insignificance besides the tragedy to the individual who must die. It seems as obviously offensive systematically to inflict this loss on the childless, and perhaps the friendless, as it would be to grade people in any other way.

Finally, if systematic family preference became overt public policy, it might begin to seem that a relatively cheap form of insurance against a low-priority rating in the rescue stakes would be the acquisition of a family.

It could further be argued that it would in practice be impossible to calculate the non-health benefits of treating a particular individual with any accuracy or certainty. It is difficult enough for doctors to make predictions about their patients' future life expectancy; expecting them to accurately predict their likely contribution to society would be absurd. Even a fairly simple example of an indirect benefit, such as whether a patient has young children, has the capacity to operate unfairly. Not all parents actually support and love their children. Patient Z may be an estranged father who has not had any contact with his children since they were born; should he nevertheless take priority over Patient Y, who is childless but devotes all of her spare time to voluntary work with deprived teenagers? If we instead only want to reward people whose contribution to their children's lives is real and tangible, we would have to engage in an extremely intrusive investigative process.

---

[37] *The Value of Life* (Routledge: London, 1985) 104–6.

There is also, as Dan Brock argues, no obvious stopping point once we start to take into account the indirect non-health benefits of treating particular individuals, and an inevitable potential for bias, prejudice, and stereotyping would creep into these sorts of assessments.[38] Offering priority to people in high-skilled employment may benefit the country as a whole, but it would be indirectly discriminatory because the people most likely to receive treatment would be white, middle-class men.

On the other hand, where particular types of care, such as substance abuse treatment programmes, are likely to have enormously beneficial effects upon the wellbeing of others, it seems less obviously unjust to use this as an additional reason for diverting funds to this type of treatment. After all, the purpose of the NHS is not only to relieve individual suffering, but also to promote the welfare of the community as a whole. Taking these broader purposes into account when setting health care priorities does not involve claiming that certain people's lives are more valuable than others. As a result, Dan Brock argues below that taking into account indirect non-health benefits can be legitimate at a macro level, where the decisions do not involve discriminating against particular individuals on account of their relative usefulness, but rather choosing what proportion of public money should be allocated to a range of different health services.

Dan Brock[39]

As a rough generalization and all other things being equal, the higher level a macro health care resource allocation or prioritization decision, the more defensible it is to give weight to the indirect non health benefits and costs of alternative resource uses in health care. The closer to micro level choices by health professionals between the needs of their individual patients, the stronger the case that these indirect non health benefits and costs should be ignored on grounds of fairness.

While agreeing that social-utilitarian considerations should normally be disregarded, Beauchamp and Childress argue that in exceptional circumstances it may be legitimate to take an individual's social worth into account when rationing treatment.

Tom Beauchamp and James Childress[40]

[J]udgements of comparative social worth are inescapable and acceptable in some situations. For example, in an earthquake when some injured survivors are medical personnel who suffer only minor injuries, they justifiably receive priority of treatment if they are needed to help others. Similarly, in an outbreak of infectious disease, it is justifiable to inoculate physicians and nurses first to enable them to care for others. Under such conditions, a person may receive priority for treatment on grounds of social utility if and only if his or her contribution is indispensable to attaining a major social goal. As in analogous lifeboat cases, we should limit judgements of comparative social value to the specific qualities and skills that are essential to the community's immediate protection without assessing the general social worth of

---

[38] Dan Brock, 'Separate Spheres and Indirect Benefits' (2003) 1 Cost Effectiveness and Resource Allocation 4. Available online at <www.resource-allocation.com/content/1/1/4>.
[39] Ibid.   [40] *Principles of Biomedical Ethics*, 6th edn (OUP: Oxford, 2008).

persons. If we limit exceptions based on social utility to emergencies involving necessity, they do not threaten the ordinary moral universe or imply the general acceptability of social-utilitarian calculations in distributing health care.

(d) AGE

The question of whether it is acceptable to take into account a patient's age when rationing treatment is hotly contested. The principle argument in favour of age-based rationing is that an older person is more likely to have had what is often described as a 'fair innings':

> What the fair innings argument needs to do is capture and express in a workable form the truth that while it is always a misfortune to die when one wants to go on living, it is not a tragedy to die in old age; but it is on the other hand, both a tragedy and a misfortune to be cut off prematurely.[41]

It has also been suggested that treating the elderly may be less cost-effective, because they may take longer to recover, and are more likely to suffer from multiple morbidities.

Against age-based rationing, assumptions about older people's frailty are generalizations, and fail to take into account the fact that many elderly individuals are extremely fit. While age may be one variable that affects a person's prognosis, it is by no means the only or even the most important one, and to use sweeping generalizations about a large and diverse section of the population in order to ration services is arbitrary and unjust. The severity of a person's condition is, in fact, a much more accurate predictor of a person's chance of recovery than their age, but it would be unacceptable to exclude terminally ill people from health care services on the grounds that they do not have a long life ahead of them.

Secondly, concerns about the efficacy of treatment in older people may not be grounded in concrete evidence of ineffectiveness, but rather might arise from their underrepresentation in clinical research trials (considered in Chapter 9). By reducing clinicians' confidence in the effectiveness of treatment for older people, the unfairness of ageism in research might be magnified by its 'trickle down' effect upon their access to medical treatment.

Thirdly, enabling older people to live independently for as long as possible will in fact lead to cost savings in other parts of the health and social services budget by reducing their dependence upon social and residential care services.

Finally, in the next extract John Harris suggests that age discrimination in the distribution of health care resources amounts to 'the systematic disvaluing of the old', which would have a corrosive effect upon society as a whole.

John Harris[42]

> A society that accords lower priority in the allocation of resources for healthcare to the old or those with reduced life expectancy is saying, in effect, that their lives are less worth saving, in short, are less valuable. If the right or good done in saving or preserving a life is the less,

[41] John Harris, *The Value of Life* (Routledge: London, 1985) 93.
[42] 'The Age-Indifference Principle and Equality' (2005) 14 Cambridge Quarterly of Healthcare Ethics 93–9.

then so is the wrong done in taking it, which would make, for example, the crime of murder inevitably less serious when the victims are old or terminally ill...

The systematic disvaluing of the old or those with life-threatening illness might have a corrosive effect on social morality and community relations more generally. It might, for example, lead to an increasing tolerance of the idea that any and all resources, or even care, devoted to the old or those with life-threatening disease was a waste of time, money, and emotion....

Moreover, once the old, however defined, had been ruled out of account, the middle-aged would become the old. They would after all have greater elapsed time 'in the bank' and shorter life expectancy ahead than the rest of society and the cycle of argument and discrimination would have a tendency to extend indefinitely, a tendency moreover that would be difficult to restrain.

(e) INDIVIDUAL RESPONSIBILITY FOR ILL HEALTH

Many diseases and disabilities are caused or exacerbated by a patient's own behaviour. Should this be relevant when allocating scarce resources? If an individual is responsible for creating her own need for health care services, should she also bear the cost of her treatment, or perhaps be a lower priority for the expenditure of public money? On the one hand, it might be argued that making access to treatment depend upon whether someone has contributed to their own ill health could provide a powerful incentive towards healthy behaviour. On the other hand, if the prospect of ill health and premature death does not dissuade someone from engaging in unhealthy activities, it is hardly likely that being a low priority for NHS care will have this effect.

Nevertheless, regardless of its impact upon behaviour, some commentators, such as Robert Blank, have suggested that it is fair and just to take individual responsibility into account when rationing scarce resources:

[P]eople who try to take care of themselves are helping underwrite the costs incurred by those who fail to do so. Understandably, there is an increasingly vocal demand to shift the monetary burden to those individuals who knowingly take the health risks...Considerable initiative for these actions comes from distaste at having to pay for someone else's bad habits.[43]

In practice, however, it would probably be impossible to devise a fair system for accurately attributing responsibility for ill health. First, the obvious examples of smokers, alcoholics, and drug abusers may not attract much public sympathy, but these are not the only types of behaviour which may have an adverse effect upon an individual's health. Should we also penalize cyclists who are injured in road traffic accidents; skin cancer sufferers who sunbathed too much in their youth; athletes with sporting injuries; individuals who subject themselves to too much stress at work; people who eat a lot of junk food? The list of people who may have contributed to their own need for health care services is potentially endless.

---

[43] Robert Blank, *Rationing Medicine* (Columbia UP: New York, 1988) 199–200.

Secondly, it is also highly questionable whether all unhealthy behaviours are in fact the result of deliberate choice. Very few people actively choose to become alcoholics or drug addicts. Indeed, alcoholism is increasingly regarded as a disease, triggered at least in part by genetic factors which are outside of a person's control.[44]

Thirdly, smoking, drug use and poor diet tend to correlate with socioeconomic status, hence penalizing people with unhealthy lifestyles would in practice mean that priority for health care services is given to the richest and healthiest sections of society.

Fourthly, it is seldom possible to isolate a single causal factor for most diseases. The fact that a person likes fried food and beer may have contributed to his need for a heart bypass operation, but there are many other possible causes. Commonly, genetic predisposition and environmental and lifestyle factors interact with each other to increase someone's susceptibility to a particular disease.

Fifthly, accurately identifying voluntary risk-takers would necessarily involve substantial violations of privacy. Finally, as Beauchamp and Childress have pointed out, in practice, their shortened life expectancy means that a voluntary risk-taker will generally cost the NHS *less* over the course of her lifetime than a self-disciplined, fit, and abstemious individual, who might live into her nineties.

> Some risk-taking involves less rather than more medical care, because it results in earlier and quicker deaths than might occur if individuals lived longer and developed chronic debilitating conditions...'low-risk' non-smoking men with low blood pressure consistently generate far higher health care costs per year of life than 'high-risk' men who smoke and have high blood pressure.[45]

While penalizing people for unhealthy behaviour might be likely to operate unfairly or be impracticable, HM Evans has argued that someone who costs the NHS a great deal of money, because of their diet or lifestyle, should take responsibility for the fact that their behaviour will have an impact upon other patients' access to services. NHS resources are finite and if someone uses up more than their fair share, perhaps because they get very drunk every Friday night and frequently end up in Casualty, or because they eat so much junk food that they become morbidly obese, there is less left in the 'pot' for other people.

Evans admits that the duties he would impose on patients to take care of their own health in the interests of other patients who are in greater need may not be enforceable, but he maintains that a sense of social responsibility should persuade us not to selfishly squander public resources and recklessly disregard the needs of others.

HM Evans[46]

> Public provision of this sort involves mutual benefit and mutual participation: so my own medical treatment is, whatever else it is, liable to be an opportunity cost (however justifiable)

---

[44] DM Dick and LJ Bierut, 'The Genetics of Alcohol Dependency' (2006) 8 Current Psychiatric Reports 151–7.

[45] Tom L Beauchamp and James F Childress, *Principles of Biomedical Ethics*, 6th edn (OUP: Oxford, 2008).

[46] 'Do Patients have Duties?' (2007) 33 Journal of Medical Ethics 689–94.

in terms of the healthcare needs of others requiring comparable treatment at the time when I am treated. Both in general, and in the specific context of public healthcare provision, I have at least a prima facie moral responsibility to take other people's interests seriously; this implies that I ought not to incur opportunity costs to others avoidably, recklessly or excessively...

Second, and as a result, the interests of my 'competitor' co-patients produce in me not merely the negative duties of avoiding either uncivil behaviour or needless waste, but also, provocatively, positive duties to promote my own health and, in the case of illness, to recover as quickly as possible.

The NHS Constitution, published in January 2009 and discussed further below, adopts this approach. It falls short of suggesting that a failure to take care of one's health would be grounds for a denial of care, but rather lists taking care of one's own and one's family's health as one of the responsibilities patients acquire in return for their rights to NHS care.

You should recognise that you can make a significant contribution to your own, and your family's, good health and well-being, and take some personal responsibility for it.[47]

(f) RELEVANCE OF PUBLIC OPINION

What role should public opinion play in setting priorities within the NHS? On the one hand, the NHS is funded through taxation, and used by almost everyone in the country, and so as both taxpayers and health care consumers, perhaps the public should have some say over the distribution of NHS resources. Involving the public in setting health care priorities might help to ensure that services are appropriate and meet the population's needs and preferences. Moreover, since depriving individual citizens of beneficial medical treatment on the grounds that it costs too much is so controversial and potentially divisive, public consent to, or agreement with, the goals and principles of resource allocation might be important.

On the other hand, there may be disadvantages in relying too heavily on public opinion. Why should citizen A have any right to decide whether citizen B's need for treatment for schizophrenia is more or less important than citizen C's need for orthopaedic surgery? Members of the public are simply not qualified to judge the relative degree of clinical need in these cases. There is also evidence that the public tends to prioritize 'deserving' patients who elicit particular sympathy, such as very sick children, and be less keen on funding treatment for drug addicts or people with mental illnesses. By excluding whole categories of patients, 'rationing by opinion poll' might leave addiction and mental illness untreated, and this would have negative consequences for society, as well as for the individuals suffering from these conditions.

In the next extract, Bill New and Julian Le Grand point out that respondents to one-off public opinion surveys will seldom be well-informed about the competing demands upon the NHS budget, and will not generally have had time to reflect upon what are exceptionally complex decisions.

---

[47] The NHS Constitution (2009), available at <www.dh.gov.uk>.

Bill New and Julian Le Grand[48]

But even if perfectly representative samples of the public can be consulted, the legitimacy of their having a direct influence on resource allocation and rationing will still be deeply problematic. The outcome of such exercises will reflect majority opinion and, although it is hard to be sure what that opinion would be, it is likely that the interests of very old, infirm, mentally ill or disabled people will be neglected in favour of the concerns of the majority. High-technology rescue or repair medicine, for example, can easily be conceived as immediately relevant to us all. Furthermore, it is simply naïve to suppose that the lay public have the requisite knowledge to make many decisions which are of a complex, technical nature…

Political decision-making—and that is what rationing decisions are—must be open to challenge, scrutiny and debate, and those who make the decisions must bear the responsibility for and deal with the consequences of those decisions. If not, poor decision-making can result. Why, for example, should members of the public make considered judgements when they do not face the prospect of being challenged on them, nor of answering for any unfavourable consequences? Accountability would, under these circumstances, be weakened. Political decisions will always be a compromise, arbitrating between different groups in society, made by people who represent the whole community and not just one set of interests. The general 'public' are not accountable in this sense.

(g) ABILITY TO PAY

A free market in health care would replace rationing with market forces. Consumers would be free to purchase health care, either at the point of use or via insurance schemes, and services would be supplied to meet this demand. Treatment which nobody wished to purchase would simply not be available. Market forces might deter inappropriate use of health care services—many of us would make less profligate use of GP services if we were charged £50 per visit—but there are many reasons why a free market in medical treatment is an unattractive proposition.

Most importantly, there would always be people who were unable to afford treatment and insurance, and who would therefore die easily preventable deaths or experience unnecessary pain if society was not prepared to cover the costs of their care. Our consumption of health care resources is concentrated in our last years of life, when we will often be least able to pay for the health care that we need. Even allowing for the pooling of risk via insurance, there is an inverse correlation between socioeconomic status and good health. Insurance premiums are set according to risk rather than wealth, so in a free market the cost of insurance would generally be highest for those with the least resources. A society which had such little concern for the lives of its poorest and sickest members would be a depressing place to live.

Secondly, although charges might deter some people from approaching the doctor for trivial or minor conditions, evidence indicates that charges lower demand for all types of care. People often do not know in advance if their symptoms are trivial or significant, and discouraging them from seeking medical advice will in practice reduce the likelihood of early diagnosis, which in turn will reduce the clinical and cost-effectiveness of their treatment.

[48] *Rationing in the NHS: Principles and Pragmatism* (King's Fund: London, 1996).

Thirdly, in general patients do not choose medical treatment, in the same way as they might choose to purchase other goods and services. A free market is supposed to work because consumers are able to exercise choice over their spending: they will only buy those goods or services which they want, and they can select providers who best meet their needs. Patients are unlike purchasers of other consumer goods, however. Nobody wants medical treatment for its own sake: indeed, many clinical interventions are unpleasant, to say the least. (Of course, this is also true of some other 'goods', such as travelling on the London underground during rush-hour: we buy a ticket for the Northern line not in order to enjoy the ride, but because we want to get home as quickly and cheaply as possible.) Efficient markets also depend in part upon informed and discerning consumers. But there is a fundamental information imbalance in the doctor/patient relationship, and patients are unable to exercise much control (other than the straightforward right of refusal) over which treatments they receive.

Fourthly, because few people could afford to pay for acute medical treatment as they needed it, and no one would want to face the additional stress of borrowing money when they are seriously ill, a free market in health care would tend to operate through insurance schemes. And there are a number of additional specific problems that arise from using private insurance to cover the costs of health care:

- Some health risks will usually be considered uninsurable. Many insurance policies exclude certain conditions, such as self-inflicted injuries, drug abuse, HIV/AIDS, or major epidemics. Very elderly people, or those with serious pre-existing conditions may find it very difficult or even impossible to purchase health insurance. There would therefore always have to be a state-funded safety-net to cover the treatment of risks which private companies choose to exclude from their insurance policies. Thus, the problem of rationing publicly funded care remains.

- When risks are pooled through insurance, low-risk patients will often be charged premiums that appear to be higher than their anticipated benefits, and they may therefore decide that purchasing insurance is not worthwhile. As a result, high-risk individuals' premiums will be even higher, and may prove to be unaffordable, thus increasing the proportion of the population which is uninsured and dependent, again, on the publicly funded safety net.

- Because insurance insulates the patient from the real costs of care, it encourages people to make more use of medical services than they would in a straightforward free market.

- Insurance schemes will also tend to give health care providers an incentive to overtreat, and thus waste resources for no additional health gain.

- Finally, the administration costs of multiple private insurers are much higher than those of state-run systems. The US spends much more than any other developed country on health, yet 45 million Americans have no insurance, and Americans are not any healthier than residents of European countries which spend half as much on their national health services. In fact, as we saw from the table reproduced earlier, health care in the US ranked only 37th in the WHO 'league table'.

Rationing according to the patient's ability to pay might appear to be fundamentally incompatible with the NHS's core principle that health care should be free at the point of delivery, but there are already some health services, such as infertility treatment, which are routinely provided in the private sector. Very few adults receive free dental or optical care. Working adults must pay the prescription charge, and people who need long-term social care often have to contribute towards its cost. In 2006, the Health Select Committee looked at the issue of charging in the NHS, and their conclusion was that the current system 'is a mess'.

Health Select Committee[49]

The system of health charges in England is a mess. Charges for prescriptions and dentistry have been in place for over 50 years and sight tests for almost 20 years. They have not been introduced following detailed analysis of their likely consequences; rather they have come about piecemeal, often in response to the need to raise money. There are no comprehensible underlying principles. The charges remain largely for 'historical' reasons. In recent years, hospital patients and their visitors have also had to pay increasing sums for non-clinical services, such as car parking and bedside telecommunications.

International research has shown that health charges have a negative effect on health, and that patients with long-term illnesses suffer particularly when charges are in place... There are exemptions, which aim to mitigate the negative effects of charges... [But] the system of exemptions is full of anomalies. Age and income exempt some people, but this does not apply across the board...

The system of medical exemptions to the prescription charge is particularly confusing. People with diabetes who require insulin receive free medicines for all conditions while people with diabetes controlled by diet must pay for all their medication. The list of exemptions was compiled in 1968 and has not changed. Given the vast improvements in medical science since that time, this is unacceptable.

The current system of charges must change. However, even after over 50 years of operation, there is a woeful absence of evidence about the effects of charges in this country.

In addition to charges levied within the system, an increasing proportion of the services routinely provided by the NHS can be purchased privately, and private patients will usually be treated more quickly than those who have to wait for publicly funded care. Approximately 11 per cent of the UK population is now covered by private medical insurance, and the number of people paying directly for elective surgery continues to rise each year. This is clearly rationing according to ability to pay rather than need, and it has become a normal feature of health care provision in the UK. Later in this chapter, we consider the government's recent decision to permit what are known as 'top-up' payments, whereby NHS patients continue to receive NHS care while paying for expensive drugs which the NHS will not fund.

A mixture of public and private provision of health care services does then exist in the UK, but a reluctance to admit that one of the founding principles of the NHS has been compromised means that the relationship between the public and the private sector lacks clarity and transparency. The British Medical Association has advocated greater honesty about the inability of the NHS to provide both free and comprehensive health care. It argues that the NHS should continue to be publicly funded, and to provide care which is free at the point of use, but that it is unrealistic to expect such a service to be fully comprehensive.

---

[49] Third Report 2005/6, available at <www.publications.parliament.uk>.

British Medical Association[50]

> The BMA believes that while the NHS should provide a comprehensive range of services, priority setting and, hence, rationing is inevitable, if we are to retain an equitable approach within limited resources. This needs to be acknowledged by politicians so that the right environment will exist for politicians, health professionals and the public to debate and decide upon a process to define a list of 'core' services that will be nationally available. The approach should be national and explicit, setting priorities for the whole service. It should provide an ongoing mechanism to review and change priorities in the NHS, which must include an effective way of incorporating public and patient views...
>
> We need an admission from the government and politicians across the board that the NHS will not be able to provide all services. We already set criteria for who may access limited resources and on what grounds. There is a lack of openness on this fact, however, and a lack of transparency in how these are set locally.

It is also important to remember that a parallel private sector is not a simple 'add-on' to the NHS. Instead, the two interact with each other. The NHS subsidizes the private sector through allowing its employees to carry out private treatment within NHS hospitals, and by permitting NHS consultants to maintain private practices. In order to meet Government targets, it is increasingly common for NHS trusts to purchase private sector care for their patients.[51]

(h) DEFINING A PACKAGE OF CARE

This type of rationing involves setting limits upon the treatments that will be funded by the state. A core package of essential services would be provided free of charge, but other services would only be available privately. Rationing policies which exclude particular treatments clearly lend themselves to openness and transparency. Public expectations of the health service could then be based upon clearly defined limits. The NHS would continue to provide universal access to a basic health care package, but would no longer claim to offer every citizen every possible type of medical treatment.

In some other countries, most notably New Zealand, the Netherlands, and the US state of Oregon, there have been explicit attempts to devise packages of health care services. These have not proved to be overwhelmingly successful. In New Zealand, the Core Services Committee could not find any treatment or area of service within the current range of provision which could be completely excluded. So, 'in something of an anti-climax, the Committee recommended that "core" be defined as being what was already being provided prior to the reforms'.[52] Similarly, in the Netherlands, too many treatments satisfied the criteria which were intended to act as a filter, and waiting lists had to be used instead. In Oregon, conditions and treatments were ranked in order of priority, taking account of community views and the cost–benefit ratio.[53] At first, the rankings produced some bizarre results.

[50] A Rational Way Forward for the NHS in England (2007), available at <www.bma.org.uk/>.

[51] Christopher Newdick, *Who Should we Treat? Rights, Rationing and Resources in the NHS*, 2nd edn (OUP: Oxford, 2005) 233.

[52] M Cooper, 'Core Services and the New Zealand Health Reforms' in R Maxwell (ed.), *Rationing Health Care* (Churchill Livingstone: London, 1995) 799–807, 805.

[53] Newdick, *Who Should We Treat? Rights, Rationing and Resources in the NHS*, 2nd edn (OUP: Oxford, 2005) 33.

Cosmetic breast surgery, for example, ranked higher than treatment for open thigh fractures, and tooth capping higher than appendectomy. A revised list gave highest priority to treatment for pneumonia and TB. Oregon chose to fund the top 565 (out of 696) condition/treatment pairs.

Some health authorities in the UK have specified that they will not fund certain procedures such as tattoo removal, sterilization reversal, or gender reassignment surgery. The reason for identifying these low priority interventions and excluding them from NHS coverage is not that such treatments are ineffective, nor that they are a significant drain on NHS resources. Rather, the purpose of such restrictions is to reflect the judgement that it is not appropriate to provide certain procedures within a publicly funded health service. Because tattoo removal or sterilization reversal in fact cost very little compared with the maintenance of acute health services, a refusal to fund these procedures may help to clarify what it is reasonable to expect from the NHS, but it will not solve its funding crisis.

Moreover, as we see below, blanket exclusions may be unfair and unlawful. Tattoo removal may seem trivial, but what if a person was tattooed while he was a prisoner of war? Fairness demands that a ban on funding for marginal procedures is able to accommodate exceptional cases.

(i) RATIONING BY DILUTION

Rationing by dilution involves offering less care than is ideal; perhaps by carrying out fewer diagnostic tests, or by spending less time with patients. It has, for example, been estimated that extending the average GP consultation time to ten minutes would require a 30 per cent increase in the number of GPs, with obvious cost implications.[54] Rationing by delay means that patients have to wait to be treated, perhaps by waiting for an appointment with their GP, or by being put on a waiting list for hospital treatment. Delays in treating patients may reduce demand because some patients will get better while waiting to see a doctor, and others may die.

As Donald Light explains, health services in the UK continue to be available to everyone, but few get immediate access to the best possible treatment.

Donald Light[55]

The NHS already rations on a massive scale. The NHS rations by delay to get on waiting lists, and then on the waiting lists themselves, and then with the further wait after an appointment has been made. It rations by undersupply of staff, doctors, machines, facilities, etc; by undercapitalisation of run down facilities; by dilution of tests done and services received; by discharge earlier than desirable; and by outright denial to even the chance to wait or be undertreated.

McPake *et al.* argue that queueing should be regarded as a rationing device, whereby treatment is rationed 'on the basis of the patient's willingness to allocate time in order to receive a

---

[54] British Medical Association, Briefing note of the National Plan for the NHS, 18 July 2000.
[55] Donald W Light, 'The Real Ethics of Rationing' (1997) 315 British Medical Journal 112–15.

service', but it is, they argue, 'an inefficient and inappropriate rationing mechanism' because its true purpose will generally be to maximize 'the efficiency with which health profession-als' time is used', rather than to ensure fair distribution of health care.[56]

Alan Williams would go further and argues that a narrow focus on the *economic* costs of health care misses the fact that there are other costs, such as patients' time, which is cur-rently 'used profligately by the system, as any "free" resource would be'.[57] There is a 'cost' incurred when a patient has to wait for 3 hours in an Accident and Emergency department, but this cost is borne by the patient herself and hence is marginalized in debates about the rationing of NHS resources.

(j) LOTTERIES

As we saw earlier, rationing inevitably means that some patients will be deprived of poten-tially beneficial medical treatment. Because it is so hard to defend denying an identifiable individual appropriate health care on the grounds of cost, would it be preferable to opt for some sort of random selection process, such as a lottery, which would allow decision-makers to avoid choosing between equally deserving potential recipients? Avoiding what Jonathan Glover refers to as 'the unpleasantness of making non-random choices between people's lives'[58] is the principal merit of distribution by lottery.[59]

Lotteries are sometimes used when we cannot come up with rational and defensible reasons for choosing between people. Citizens are randomly allocated to jury service, for example. And in times of war, conscription to military service has been done on a random basis. Because most people believe that there *are* rational and defensible reasons for distin-guishing between different patients, random selection has few supporters. A lottery would not be capable of targeting resources where they are most needed, or where they are likely to do most good. Relatively fit and healthy individuals would have as much chance of getting treatment as patients whose lives are in danger.

4 RESOURCE ALLOCATION IN THE NHS

(a) GOVERNMENT POLICY

There continues to be strong public support for the idea of a health care system which is free at the point of use, and which provides everyone with access to the same standard of health care. Other former state-run enterprises, such as the transport system, are now largely run on free-market principles, but the public appears to be stubbornly resistant to the privatiza-tion of the NHS. The feared political implications of abandoning a commitment to a fully funded and comprehensive NHS have led successive governments to maintain the fiction that the NHS is currently providing such a service, when the reality is rather different.

Although the Treasury decides how much money the NHS should receive from pub-lic funds each year, the government does not generally become involved in resource

---

[56] B McPake, L Kumaranayake, and C. Normand, *Health Economics: An International Perspective* (London: Routledge, 2002) 204.

[57] Rudolf Klein and Alan Williams, 'Setting Priorities: What is Holding us Back—Inadequate Information or Inadequate Institutions?' in Coulter and Ham (eds), *The Global Challenge of Healthcare Rationing* (Open University Press, 2000) 15–26, 18.

[58] *Causing Death and Saving Lives* (Penguin: London, 1977) 219.   [59] Ibid.

allocation decisions within the NHS. Rather, it has delegated this task to Primary Care Trusts (PCTs) and to NICE, considered below. PCTs determine the allocation of 85 per cent of the total NHS budget, through the commissioning of local services. In England, there are currently 152 PCTs, each with an average population of 330,000. At an even more local level, GP practices are increasingly involved in practice-based commissioning, enabling them to direct resources to the particular needs of their patient population.

As we see later, when setting local priorities, PCTs are under a duty to fund NICE-approved treatments. While this should therefore lead to national consistency in the implementation of NICE guidelines, devolving priority setting to the local level inevitably means that there are regional differences, or what is sometimes called a 'postcode' lottery', in access to treatments which have not been appraised by NICE.

The principal ways in which central government policies influence spending priorities in the NHS is through the setting of targets, such as waiting-time initiatives, and through National Service Frameworks (NSFs), such as the Cancer Reform Strategy, which are designed to set national standards for the treatment of particular conditions. In order to meet these targets, health authorities must divert resources to the chosen area, inevitably leaving less money for other types of health care.

In January 2009, the government produced the first NHS Constitution, setting out patients' rights and responsibilities within the NHS. This is necessarily a high-level statement of principles, a handful of which are worth mentioning here.

The National Health Service Constitution[60]

Principles

1. The NHS provides a comprehensive service, available to all irrespective of gender, race, disability, age, sexual orientation, religion or belief. It has a duty to each and every individual that it serves and must respect their human rights. At the same time, it has a wider social duty to promote equality through the services it provides and to pay particular attention to groups or sections of society where improvements in health and life expectancy are not keeping pace with the rest of the population.

2. Access to NHS services is based on clinical need, not an individual's ability to pay....

6. The NHS is committed to providing best value for taxpayers' money and the most effective, fair and sustainable use of finite resources...

Rights

You have the right to drugs and treatments that have been recommended by NICE for use in the NHS, if your doctor says they are clinically appropriate for you.

You have the right to expect local decisions on funding of other drugs and treatments to be made rationally following a proper consideration of the evidence. If the local NHS decides not to fund a drug or treatment you and your doctor feel would be right for you, they will explain that decision to you.

On a few rare occasions, resource allocation decisions have been taken directly by the Secretary of State for Health. One notable example was his attempt to specify how

[60] (2009), available at <www.dh.gov.uk>.

sildenafil (Viagra) should be rationed within the NHS. Initially, a Department of Health circular was issued stating that 'doctors should not prescribe sildenafil. Health authorities are also advised not to support the provision of sildenafil at NHS expense...other than in exceptional circumstances.' The circular was successfully challenged by Pfizer, the manufacturer of Viagra. Collins J held that by stating 'in bald terms that Viagra should not be prescribed', the circular purported to override GPs' clinical judgement, which would place them in breach of their terms of service.

Subsequently, the Secretary of State issued Regulations which specified that NHS prescriptions could only be issued to certain categories of patients, such as those suffering from specified medical conditions. These restrictions were confirmed by the Secretary of State when he reviewed his policy a year later. The reason he gave was that unrestricted prescribing of sildenafil would cost the NHS £125 million per year. In contrast, restricted prescribing was costing £25 million. Pfizer again sought judicial review of this policy, arguing that it did not comply with Article 7.3 of the Council Directive (EEC 89/105), known as the Transparency Directive, which states that: 'Any decision to exclude an individual medicinal product from the coverage of the national health insurance system shall contain a statement of reasons based on objective and verifiable criteria.'

In *R (on the application of Pfizer Ltd) v Secretary of State for Health* the Court of Appeal rejected Pfizer's claim. The requirements of the Transparency Directive were, as Buxton LJ explained, easily satisfied.

R (on the application of Pfizer Ltd) v Secretary of State for Health[61]

Buxton LJ

For the criteria to be 'verifiable', all that is necessary is that they should be published and available, in particular to would-be importers, to satisfy themselves that they do not contain disguised restrictions on intra-Community trade. And the measures are 'objective'... if they are based on a legitimate aim, that of improving the economics of the state health system.

The criterion adopted by the Secretary of State in this case fully meets those requirements. And that is all that the directive requires, that the criteria used by the member state should meet its (fairly modest) objectives. What the directive plainly does not require, and what would be wholly inappropriate in view of its objectives, is that each decision applying the criteria should be subject to the detailed scrutiny and exposition of the merits and economics of particular medicinal products that the applicants seek to achieve in this case.

(b) CLINICAL DISCRETION

For a number of reasons, the medical profession may be ill-equipped to make rationing decisions. First, the doctor's primary ethical duty is do the best for her patient, rather than make broad policy decisions about competing priorities. Medical ethics has been dominated by individualistic values, such as beneficence and autonomy; in contrast, economic analysis tends to be broadly utilitarian. There may be an irreconcilable conflict between the goal of diverting health care resources where they will do most good, and acting in the best

---

[61] [2002] EWCA Civ 1566.

interests of a particular patient. Having conducted empirical research into the attitudes of physicians to rationing, van Delden *et al.* found that:

> Physicians tend to primarily look to the government for making allocation decisions. In their view, their primary concern should be the interests of their patients. They accept that their decisions influence the distribution of means and are willing to take this into account, but choosing between patients is not their job.[62]

Secondly, doctors are at the sharp end of rationing decisions, unlike politicians or health service managers. It is exceptionally difficult for a doctor to have to tell a patient that effective treatment exists, but that it is too expensive and will not be funded.

Thirdly, doctors fear that knowingly withholding potentially beneficial treatment from a patient will leave them open to litigation. As we see in the next chapter, the standard of care in negligence is objective, and insufficient resources do not necessarily offer a defence.

However admirable the professional ideal of complete devotion to each patient's best interests might be, doctors cannot avoid making rationing decisions because choosing to allocate money to one patient inevitably means that there is less money to spend on other people. If the NHS has finite resources, all clinical decisions are effectively choices about resource allocation.

Indeed, it could be argued that the 'gatekeeping' role played by GPs in the NHS is itself a form of rationing. The intention is that everyone in the UK should be registered with a GP who will be their first point of contact when they become ill. If the patient's condition is potentially serious, or requires expert attention, the GP will refer the patient to an appropriate specialist, usually in a local hospital. Specialist services are therefore only provided to those patients whose need for them has been vetted first by their GP, rather than being clogged up by anyone who thinks that they might benefit from seeing a consultant. But, as McPake *et al.* explain, 'the mechanism works imperfectly, general practitioners have widely varying rates of referral and large numbers of patients directly attend Accident and Emergency departments for minor complaints that could be dealt with by the GP'.[63]

In practice, doctors do recognize that they have obligations to others, which will sometimes override their duty towards an individual patient. Ranaan Gillon gives the example of a GP who is listening to a patient's account of his personal difficulties when a fifty-five-year-old man with chest pain collapses in the waiting room. Of course, he says, the doctor would choose to subordinate the interests of the patient in his consulting room in favour of the person outside.[64]

Indeed, the judiciary has acknowledged that it is legitimate for clinicians to take the resources available for other patients into account when making treatment decisions. For example, in *R v North Derbyshire Health Authority, ex parte Fisher*, Dyson J held that:

[62] JJM van Delden, AM Vrakking, A van der Heide, and PJ van der Maas, 'Medical Decision Making in Scarcity Situations' (2004) 30 Journal of Medical Ethics, 207–11.

[63] B McPake, L Kumaranayake, and C Normand *Health Economics: An International Perspective* (London: Routledge, 2002) 202.

[64] Raanan Gillon, 'Ethics, Economics and General Practice', in Gavin Mooney and Alistair McGuire (eds), *Medical Ethics and Economics in Health Care* (OUP: Oxford, 1988) 114–34, 116.

> When deciding whether to prescribe treatment to a patient, a clinician has to have regard to many factors, including the resources available for that treatment and the needs of and likely benefit to that patient, as compared with other patients who are likely to be suitable for that treatment during the financial year.[65]

In *Arthur J S Hall & Co (A Firm) v Simons*, a non-medical case, Lord Hoffmann drew an analogy between lawyers' and doctors' duties to third parties:

> The doctor, for example, owes a duty to the individual patient. But he also owes a duty to his other patients which may prevent him from giving one patient the treatment or resources he would ideally prefer.[66]

In the UK, doctors have seldom explicitly acknowledged that they are rationing medical treatment, and instead cost–benefit considerations have been absorbed within their clinical discretion. If a patient is suffering from symptoms which are very likely to be caused by a minor illness, but there is a remote chance that there is something much more serious wrong with them, doctors will often adopt a 'wait and see' approach: the patient will be asked to return in a week or two if their symptoms have not improved, even though there is a very small chance that they might benefit from undergoing expensive investigative procedures immediately. Few doctors would regard this as an example of rationing, but instead would view this as the sensible exercise of clinical discretion. As Ranaan Gillon explained:

> If one were to take thoroughly to heart the idea that as curative doctors we should never allow concern for cost to others to deflect us from doing whatever we could to benefit our patients, then diagnostic services would be overwhelmed as we tested for rare but possible problems.[67]

(c) FROM IMPLICIT TO EXPLICIT RATIONING

Until relatively recently, few patients were aware that the NHS rationed medical treatment. In part, this was because patients tended to have lower expectations, and to trust that decisions to give or not give treatment were dictated entirely by their doctors' benevolent view of their best interests. Rationing decisions were, as Keith Syrett explains, implicit rather than explicit.

Keith Syrett[68]

> [F]or many years, rationing in the NHS was not a matter of significant political or public debate. This was in part because lower expectations in the early years of the Service led to

---

[65] (1997) 38 BMLR 76 (QBD).   [66] [2002] 1 AC 615, 690.

[67] Raanan Gillon, 'Ethics, Economics and General Practice', in Gavin Mooney and Alistair McGuire (eds), *Medical Ethics and Economics in Health Care* (OUP: Oxford, 1988) 114–34, 128.

[68] 'Impotence or Importance? Judicial Review in an Era of Explicit NHS Rationing' (2004) 67 Modern Law Review 289–304.

acceptance that deficiencies in provision were simply a fact of life. More significantly, most rationing took place under cover of clinical judgment: that is, it was *implicit*, in that 'the reasoning involved [was] not clearly stated to anyone except…the person making the decision'. Medical professionals effectively 'converted' political decisions on resource allocation into clinical decisions about treatment by 'internalising' resource limits and providing justification for denial on medical grounds by portraying the decision as optimal or routine in the specific circumstances. Suspicion that such decisions were in reality dictated by resource considerations tended to be minimal because of the existence of high levels of trust between doctors and patients, premised upon the belief that physicians possessed both expertise and access to all medical resources necessary for effective care and that they would act as dedicated patient advocates in attempting to secure these.

Explicit rationing, in contrast, involves much greater honesty to patients who are denied care for cost reasons. Inevitably, explicit rationing will lead to more resentment among patients who realize that treatment has been withheld for cost reasons. This has led some to argue in favour of implicit rationing, on the grounds that it is 'more conducive to stable social relations and a lower level of conflict'.[69] Implicit rationing works, according to David Mechanic 'because patients trust that doctors are their agents and have their interests at heart'.[70]

Whatever its disadvantages—in terms of greater public dissatisfaction and social instability—most people now accept that the arguments in favour of explicit rationing trump the 'benign deceit' of the past.[71] One aspect of patient autonomy, which we consider in chapter 4, is that patients need access to relevant information in order to make informed choices about their treatment. The existence of an effective treatment which the NHS will not fund is, for many patients, a significant fact. If they know that treatment is available but has been withheld, they might decide to pay for it privately, or to challenge this decision in the courts.

Transparency is a pre-requisite for public accountability and it also facilitates consistency of decision-making.[72] Moreover, it could be argued that the public are now so well-informed about the availability of different treatment options, that 'camouflaging' rationing decisions as exercises of clinical judgement is no longer feasible. As James Sabin has put it: 'personal computers and the internet drive the nails into the coffin of implicit rationing'.[73]

It is also important to recognize that every patient who is denied treatment will believe that the *substantive* decision was the wrong one. Increasingly, then, emphasis has been placed upon ensuring that the *processes* through which tough choices are made are fair and transparent. This is what Norman Daniels and James Sabin have referred to as 'accountability for reasonableness'.[74] They set out four requirements relevant to an assessment of whether the process through which a decision was reached was reasonable:

- Publicity: decisions, and the grounds for making them, must be transparent and open.

- Relevance: decisions must be based upon relevant criteria.

---

[69] D Mechanic, 'Dilemmas in Rationing Health Care Services: The Case for Implicit Rationing' (1995) 310 British Medical Journal 1655–9.

[70] Ibid.

[71] Bill New and Julian LeGrand, *Rationing in the NHS* (Kings Fund: London, 1996) 24.

[72] Keith Syrett, *Law, Legitimacy and the Rationing of Health Care* (CUP: Cambridge, 2007) 62–3.

[73] 'Fairness as a Problem of Love and the Heart: A Clinician's Perspective on Priority Setting' in A Coulter and C Ham (eds), *The Global Challenge of Healthcare Rationing* (Taylor and Francis: London, 2000) 117–22, 120.

[74] N Daniels and J Sabin, *Setting Limits Fairly—Can we Learn to Share Medical Resources?* (OUP: 2000).

- Revision and appeals: there must be a process for challenging decisions, and the possibility of their subsequent revision.
- Enforcement: there must be regulation to ensure compliance with these criteria.[75]

If a rationing decision was based on relevant criteria and sound evidence, and if affected patients have a right of challenge, decisions which are always going to be unpopular may nevertheless secure some level of public legitimacy and social acceptability.

(d) NICE

The National Institute for Health and Clinical Excellence (NICE), is a special health authority which was set up by statutory instrument in 1999, in part to make resource allocation decisions in the NHS more explicit and transparent, and to address the problem of the 'postcode lottery'.

There are four types of NICE guidance:

- **Public health**—this is guidance on promoting good health and preventing ill health. An example would be NICE's 2008 guidance on effective smoking cessation services. These are not mandatory, but organizations such as PCTs should work towards their implementation.
- **Clinical practice**—this is guidance on appropriate treatment and care for people with specific diseases and conditions within the NHS. For example, in 2008 NICE issued a new guideline on the care and treatment of people with osteoarthritis which recommended a number of core lifestyle changes, such as exercise and weight loss, as well as pharmaceutical treatments. Again, these are not mandatory but organizations such as PCTs should take steps towards their implementation.
- **Interventional procedures**—this is guidance on the clinical efficacy and safety of interventional procedures: that is surgery and any tests or treatments that involve entering the body through skin or a vein. Cost-effectiveness is not relevant.
- **Health technologies (both single and multiple)**—this is guidance on the use of new and existing medicines, treatments, and procedures within the NHS. An example would be a 2007 multiple technology appraisal of inhaled corticosteroids for the treatment of chronic asthma in children under 12. The appraisal worked out which inhalers were most cost-effective, and made detailed recommendations for clinicians. PCTs have a legal obligation to implement these within three months.

As of December 2007, NICE had published 133 technology appraisals, 248 interventional procedure appraisals, 65 clinical guidelines and seven pieces of public health guidance.

In this chapter, we are principally concerned with NICE's appraisals of new and existing treatments, and its guidance about their provision within the NHS. Appraisals can recommend: (1) the treatment's unrestricted use in the NHS; (2) its restricted use confined to certain categories of patients; (3) its use to be confined to clinical trials (this option is very seldom used); or (4) that it should not be used in the NHS. Its decisions between 1999 and 2005 were:

- negative (a 'no' decision) in 19 per cent of cases;
- positive ('yes') in 23 per cent of appraisals;

---

[75] Ibid.

- 'yes with major restrictions' in 32 per cent of cases; and
- 'yes with minor restrictions' in 26 per cent of cases.

As we saw earlier, some commentators have suggested that reducing NHS expenditure upon ineffective or inefficient treatments would largely eliminate the need to ration services. In essence, NICE adopts a middle ground: it promotes evidence-based medicine, but does not regard it as a complete solution to the problem of scarce resources in the NHS. Even treatments which have been proved to be clinically effective may not reach some threshold level of cost-effectiveness, and NICE would then recommend that they are not offered within the NHS at all, or that their availability should be restricted to certain categories of patients. So, for example, the NICE appraisal of Aricept for sufferers of Alzheimer's Disease, discussed further below, initially recommended that it should only be available to sufferers in the advanced stages of the disease.

NICE's decision-making process is undoubtedly open and transparent: all of NICE's appraisals are available on its website, and before decisions are finalized, there is an opportunity for 'stakeholders'—such as patient groups and the medical profession—to comment upon its draft conclusions. There is also a right of appeal for interested groups who will be directly affected by NICE guidance, such as drugs manufacturers.

NICE has been open about its use of QALY scores. According to NICE, the general threshold for affordability in the NHS is approximately £20,000 per QALY. If treatments costing less than £20,000 are not to be recommended, reasons should be given; an example might be that there are significant limitations to the generalizability of the evidence for effectiveness. For treatments which cost between £20,000 and £30,000 per QALY, NICE will consider whether there are considerations which justify recommending the technology, such as the particular needs of the relevant patient group.

Costs of more than £30,000 per QALY are generally not acceptable, and so if a treatment is to be recommended above this threshold, a strong case for supporting the intervention as an effective use of NHS resources would have to be made.

NICE's QALY thresholds meant that many drugs which are capable of extending the life of cancer patients for a relatively short period of time were judged too expensive. Following a series of decisions in which cancer drugs which were widely available in Europe and the US were rejected by NICE, it became evident that many terminally ill patients were struggling to pay for these medicines themselves. In 2008, the Richards report made recommendations about permitting 'top-up' payments, and we consider this in the next section, but it also recommended that NICE rethink its approach to drugs capable of prolonging the lives of people with cancer.

In January 2009, NICE issued supplementary guidance, to apply to patients with less than two years to live, where the medicine is capable of extending life by at least three months. In such cases, and provided the estimates of life expectancy are robust, the Appraisals Committee is invited to give 'greater weight to QALYs achieved in the later stages of terminal diseases'.

National Institute for Health and Clinical Excellence[76]

2.1 This supplementary advice should be applied in the following circumstances and when all the criteria referred to below are satisfied:

---

[76] Appraising Life-extending, End of Life Treatments (2009), <www.nice.org.uk>.

2.1.1 The treatment is indicated for patients with a short life expectancy, normally less than 24 months and;

2.1.2 There is sufficient evidence to indicate that the treatment offers an extension to life, normally of at least an additional 3 months, compared to current NHS treatment, and;

2.1.3 No alternative treatment with comparable benefits is available through the NHS, and;

2.1.4 The treatment is licensed or otherwise indicated, for small patient populations.

Following the publication of this new guidance, James Raftery analysed NICE's decisions on cancer drugs in the previous nine years. He found that only two of the cancer drugs rejected by NICE would have met these criteria, so it is not clear whether the supplementary guidance will make much difference in practice. Raftery also points out that, while NICE has clearly responded to public concern about cancer patients being denied effective treatments, there may be risks in creating an exception to the universality of the QALY approach.

James Raftery[77]

The main attraction of the cost per QALY measure is its universal applicability. Making an exception for any group—such as, life-extending treatments for terminally ill patients—limits that universality and sets a precedent for other groups. In addition, setting the threshold higher for some groups within a fixed overall budget results in other patient groups being denied treatment.

NICE guidance against NHS use of cancer drugs is controversial when those drugs offer any prospect of increased life expectancy. Patients inevitably protest when an estimated average cost per QALY is used to deny them treatment. This valuing of what is essentially a statistical or abstract life is challenged by real patients, who attract publicity. Ethical, legal, and political dilemmas become high profile stories.

While NICE's appraisals are carried out by scientific and clinical experts, the views of the public are taken into account through its Citizen's Council. This is a representative sample of thirty UK citizens, to whom questions are referred by NICE. For example, in 2008, the Citizens Council was asked to consider whether the severity of a disease should be relevant to NICE's decisions, and if so, whether this should be part of the QALY calculation, or whether severity should be separately considered alongside clinical and cost-effectiveness.[78] They recommended that it should be taken into account as a separate value, because this would give appraisal panels more flexibility. In trying to define severity, they came up with the following factors:

- life expectancy;
- how far away you are from perfect health;
- your state of health prior to, during, and after diagnosis and treatment;

---

[77] 'NICE and the Challenge of Cancer Drugs' (2009) 338 British Medical Journal 67.
[78] Quality Adjusted Life Years (QALYs) and the Severity of Illness: Report on NICE Citizens Council meeting 2008 (available at <www.nice.org.uk>).

- the nature of the treatment and its impact (side-effects as well as benefits) on health;
- health states that incur social stigma, such as incontinence.

The Citizens Council also played an important part in the drawing up of *Social Value Judgements*, a document which sets out the social values which NICE adopts when making decisions. In the extract below, NICE sets out its approach to the questions of whether a person's age or their responsibility for their condition should be relevant.

NICE *Social Value Judgements,* 2nd edition[79]

NICE is committed to promoting equality, eliminating unlawful discrimination, and actively considering the implications of its guidance for human rights.

6.3 Age

There is much debate over whether, or how, age should be taken into account when allocating healthcare resources. The Citizens Council considered that health should not be valued more highly in some age groups than in others; and that social roles at different ages should not affect decisions about cost effectiveness. They said, though, that where age is an indicator of benefit or risk, it can be taken into account.

NICE's general principle is that patients should not be denied, or have restricted access to, NHS treatment simply because of their age. The Institute's guidance should refer to age only when one or more of the following apply.

- There is evidence that age is a good indicator for some aspect of patients' health status and/or the likelihood of adverse effects of the treatment.
- There is no practical way of identifying patients other than by their age (for example, there is no test available to measure their state of health in another way).
- There is good evidence, or good grounds for believing, that because of their age patients will respond differently to the treatment in question.

6.6 Behaviour-dependent conditions

The Citizens Council advised that NICE should not take into consideration whether or not a particular condition was self-induced. It was often impossible, in an individual, to decide whether the condition was dependent on their own behaviour or not; and receiving NHS care should not depend on whether people 'deserved' it or not.

NICE should not produce guidance that results in care being denied to patients with conditions that are, or may have been, dependent on their behaviour. However, if the behaviour is likely to continue and can make a treatment less clinically effective or cost effective, then it may be appropriate to take this into account.

So has NICE been a success? The answer would seem to be a qualified 'yes'. Delegating rationing decisions to a specialist, independent body has advantages over more direct governmental control, and over local, and hence variable, decision-making. NICE decisions about cost-effectiveness are open and transparent, and offer a right of challenge, thereby satisfying some of the criteria for procedural justice, or 'accountability for reasonableness', outlined above.

[79] NICE July 2008, available at <www.nice.org.uk>.

NICE has, however, been subject to a number of criticisms in its first decade of operation. First, the status of NICE guidance is slightly ambiguous. Directions issued in January 2002 instructed health authorities that any treatments which have been approved by NICE should normally be available to patients within three months,[80] and the government has explicitly stated that 'scarce resources is [sic] not a good reason for failure to implement NICE guidance'.[81] These Directions do not give patients a *right* to treatment which has been endorsed by NICE. There may be a duty on NHS trusts to fund NICE-recommended treatments, but there is no duty on doctors to use them. The question of what treatment is appropriate for a particular patient remains a matter of clinical discretion, although obviously in fulfilling their duty of care, doctors would be expected to have regard to authoritative guidance on a treatment's clinical effectiveness.

Secondly, despite the quasi-mandatory status of NICE technology appraisals, extra money is seldom put aside to fund their implementation, and so health authorities must find the resources to pay for NICE-approved technologies and treatments from elsewhere in their budgets. This has had two consequences. First, different health authorities will choose to make savings in different ways, resulting in a new 'postcode lottery', as the cuts in coverage necessary to implement NICE's recommendations are made unevenly throughout the country. Paradoxically, they might thereby restrict or deny access to treatments which are, in fact, *more* cost-effective, and could benefit *more* people, than those recommended by NICE, but which have not yet been appraised.

Thirdly, despite some signs of improvement in recent years, implementation of NICE guidance remains variable.[82] The Audit Commission, for example, found that only 25 per cent of PCTs could verify that implementation of NICE technology appraisals took place within three months.[83]

There is also some confusion between technology appraisals, which *must* be implemented by PCTs, and clinical guidelines, which PCTs are supposed to work towards but which are not mandatory. The House of Commons Health Select Committee drew attention to this problem.

House of Commons Health Select Committee[84]

It appears that patients and the public are sometimes not aware that only approved technology appraisals are mandatory and that the NHS is not under any obligation to implement other types of guidance within a specific timeframe. This is partly because of the terminology used by NICE: the term 'guidance' is commonly employed for all types of advice given by the Institute, and does not differentiate between that which is obligatory and that which is not.

This has led to confusion about the status of the different types of guidance issued by NICE, and elevated expectations among patients of the type of treatment that they will

[80] Directions to Health Authorities, Primary Care Trusts and NHS Trusts in England (DH: London, 11 Dec 2001).

[81] Government response to the Health Committee's 2nd report of session 2001–02 on National Institute for Clinical Excellence (2002) 9.

[82] Trevor A Sheldon, Nicky Cullum, Diane Dawson, Annette Lankshear, Karin Lowson, Ian Watt, Peter West, Dianne Wright, and John Wright, 'What's the Evidence that NICE Guidance has Been Implemented? Results from a National Evaluation Using Time Series Analysis, Audit of Patients' Notes, and Interviews' (2004) 329 British Medical Journal 999.

[83] Audit Commission, Managing the Implementation of NICE Guidance, 2005.

[84] National Institute for Health and Clinical Excellence: First Report of Session 2006–07, available at <www.publications.parliament.uk> paras 289–90.

receive. For example, in vitro fertilisation (IVF) is the subject of a clinical guideline. NICE recommended that PCTs should provide three cycles of IVF to eligible patients. Many patients therefore believe that the NICE guideline means that they should have access to three cycles of IVF through the NHS.[85]

The Committee called into question the logic of this differential status of guidelines and appraisals: 'it seems illogical that technology appraisals must be implemented while eminently sensible elements of clinical guidelines are not obligatory'.

Fourthly, NICE's 'topic selection' process is not random, but rather is intended to ensure that NICE issues guidance on particularly controversial or expensive treatments in a rolling programme of appraisals, decided upon by both the Institute and the Department of Health, in collaboration with the Horizon Scanning Centre at the University of Birmingham. It would, of course, be impossible to subject every available medical procedure to the sort of rigorous assessment carried out by NICE, and it is clearly sensible for NICE to ensure that it evaluates the cost-effectiveness of expensive new treatments. But when coupled with the duty to fund NICE recommendations, the result may be that few patients are able to benefit from this prioritized funding. It is important to note that most medicines and other technologies which are prescribed and used in the NHS have *not* been assessed by NICE. This skews funding towards new and expensive medicines for acute illness, and away from lower-tech interventions and preventative and primary care. It also means that NICE has spent more time evaluating new medicines, at the expense, perhaps, of promoting disinvestment from cost-ineffective existing medicines.

Taken together, the previous two points could even cast doubt on whether NICE is in fact capable of deciding upon priorities within the NHS, since this would require *all* treatments to be compared, so that only the most cost-effective are funded. NICE is not a budget holder and does not have to decide which treatments—of all those which are potentially available to patients—should be paid for by the NHS. Rather, it looks at different treatments in isolation, and decides whether they meet some threshold level of cost-effectiveness. It simply cannot tell whether the treatments it recommends are more or less cost-effective than the vast majority of treatments, which have not had their cost-effectiveness investigated.

Fifthly, giving 'interested parties'—such as patient groups and the pharmaceutical industry—a right to make representations and a right of appeal has led to the criticism that NICE might be too easily swayed by powerful lobbying organizations. Of its first 130 technology appraisals, 47 were subject to appeals. Keith Syrett explains how NICE's susceptibility to lobbying by interested parties may pose a threat to its legitimacy:

The campaigns mounted by Glaxo-Wellcome on zanamivir and by the Multiple Sclerosis Society on beta-interferon and glatiramer acetate demonstrate how 'evidence becomes an instrument of politics rather than a substitute for it', as lobby interests seek to infiltrate and manipulate the decision-making process in their favour.[86]

There is then the danger that certain diseases and treatments will receive preferential treatment over other conditions which may be just as deserving, but which lack skilled and

---

[85] Ibid.

[86] 'A Technocratic Fix to the "Legitimacy Problem"? The Blair Government and Health Care Rationing in the United Kingdom' (2003) 28 Journal of Health Politics, Policy and Law 715.

powerful advocates. Richard Cookson *et al.* go so far as to claim that NICE may have become the pharmaceutical industry's 'golden goose':

> NICE has effectively become an advocacy mechanism by which lobbies of specialists and their supporters in the pharmaceutical industry extract more public money from the NHS. Instead of challenging the pharmaceutical industry to show value for money, NICE has become their 'golden goose'.[87]

Sixthly, despite its commitment to open and transparent decision-making, in practice NICE routinely withholds the evidence upon which its appraisals are based because pharmaceutical companies have specified that the relevant information was supplied in confidence.

NICE has been the subject of a number of reviews since it was set up, most recently by the House of Commons Health Select Committee in 2008.[88] While it found that 'NICE does a vital job in difficult circumstances', and that 'reviews have shown its evaluation processes to be generally robust', the Select Committee also identified several problems with the evaluation process, including the following.

House of Commons Health Select Committee[89]

> • Topic selection. Only a few selected medical technologies are chosen as suitable for assessment as technology appraisals. There is also far too little emphasis on disinvestment. While few older treatments may do no good at all, many will not be cost-effective;
>
> • The wider benefits of treatment to society, for example to carers, are not included in NICE's economic evaluations;
>
> • NICE often does not have all the information it needs to make a full assessment. It does not have access to all the information the Medicines and Healthcare products Regulatory Agency (MHRA) uses and clinical trials are usually designed without NICE's work on cost-effectiveness in mind;
>
> • Experts are not sufficiently well used; and
>
> • Publication of guidance is slow; licensed medicines are often not prescribed while PCTs and clinicians wait for NICE to make a decision.

The Committee then made a number of recommendations:

House of Commons Health Select Committee[90]

> • Key among them is the need for a system whereby all medicines are assessed at launch. A shorter, less in-depth evaluation should be made between the time of licensing authorisation and marketing, so that clinicians can prescribe useful and cost-effective drugs as soon as they are launched.

[87] 'Wrong SIGN, NICE Mess: Is National Guidance Distorting Allocation of Resources?' (2001) 323 British Medical Journal 743–5.

[88] National Institute for Health and Clinical Excellence: First Report of Session 2006–07.

[89] Ibid.　　[90] Ibid.

- In order to ensure that NICE has the information it needs, NICE should have access to the same material used by the licensing body, clinical trials should be registered and there should be closer working between NICE and the pharmaceutical industry. This will be particularly important for the effective assessment of drugs in time for launch.
- We recommend that more be done to encourage disinvestment. No evaluation of older, possibly cost ineffective therapies has taken place to date; two are currently underway. Our predecessor committee made the same recommendation; it is not acceptable that NICE continues to ignore this recommendation.

Since 1999, NICE guidance has been the subject of one judicial review action: *Eisai Limited v The National Institute for Health and Clinical Excellence*. In this case Eisai, the manufacturer of a drug with the brand name Aricept, challenged the decision of NICE's appeal panel, and NICE's subsequent guidance—Aricept should not be funded for patients in the earlier stages of Alzheimer's disease (AD)—on the grounds of procedural unfairness, discriminatory effects, and irrationality.

The initial estimate of Aricept's cost per QALY was approximately £94,000. After further investigation, this was reduced to £54,000, and by limiting treatment to patients with moderately severe (as opposed to mild) AD, the estimates of cost per QALY ranged from £31,000 to £38,000.

At first instance, Eisai succeeded on only one ground: that of discrimination. This was because the NICE guidance relied on what are known as mini mental-state examination (MMSE) scores in order to judge the severity of a patient's Alzheimer's disease. Because MMSE tests are known to produce inaccurate results in certain populations, such as people whose first language is not English or those with learning difficulties, over-reliance upon them breached NICE's obligations under anti-discrimination legislation.

Eisai then appealed to the Court of Appeal on the grounds of procedural fairness. Their claim was that, by giving them access to 'read only' versions of NICE's economic modelling formulae, it was impossible for them to check or comment upon the reliability of NICE's calculations. Dobbs J had rejected this claim on the grounds that there was no right on the part of drugs manufacturers to 'quality assure' NICE's processes. The Court of Appeal, in contrast, unanimously found for Eisai.

Eisai Limited v The National Institute for Health and Clinical Excellence[91]

Richards LJ

The view I have come to is that, notwithstanding NICE's considered position to the contrary (to which in itself I am prepared to give some weight), procedural fairness does require release of the fully executable version of the model. It is true that there is already a remarkable degree of disclosure and of transparency in the consultation process; but that cuts both ways, because it also serves to underline the nature and importance of the exercise being carried out. The refusal to release the fully executable version of the model stands out as the one exception to the principle of openness and transparency that NICE has acknowledged as appropriate in this context. It does place consultees (or at least a sub-set of them, since it is mainly the pharmaceutical companies which are likely to be affected by this in practice) at

[91] [2008] EWCA Civ 438.

a significant disadvantage in challenging the reliability of the model. In that respect it limits their ability to make an intelligent response on something that is central to the appraisal process. The reasons put forward for refusal to release the fully executable version are in part unsound and are in any event of insufficient weight to justify NICE's position.

At first instance in this case, the interesting claim was made that NICE's evaluation had placed insufficient weight on the benefits of Arisept for the *carers* of AD sufferers, and on the cost savings through delaying the AD sufferer's need for institutional care. Dobbs J rejected this argument: given the inadequate evidence base for carer costs, NICE's approach could not be described as irrational.

While it may be difficult to place an accurate numerical figure on the benefits these drugs might have for carers, and benefits to carers are not relevant to the overtly individualistic QALY calculation, there is no doubt that the benefits to carers of delaying the onset of AD are real and substantial. This point is made forcefully by Jonathan Herring.

Jonathan Herring[92]

For carers of those suffering from Alzheimer's the distress of seeing an individual they love change their personality, memory and become, in a sense, a different person is hard to bear. This is particularly so where the disease manifests itself in aggression. Medication which may inhibit the progress of this condition is of huge benefit, not just to the individual patient, but for those caring for him or her. However, traditional use of QALY takes no account of such matters...

[C]osts to the NHS count, costs to carers do not. Yet the costs to the individual carer are costs to real people whose lives bear the blight of caring. By contrast, any costs to the NHS and society is spread across everyone. To count for nothing the sacrifices of carers and to consider only the monetary loss to the NHS in allocating health care resources is unjustifiable. Politically, of course, the approach is understandable. Costs to the NHS are in the public eye and impact on the sensitive issues of levels of taxation. Costs to carers go unnoticed in the public arena, although they are real enough to those who suffer them, and real enough in their effect on society as a whole.

In Scotland, the Scottish Medicines Consortium assesses and makes recommendations on the availability of *all* new drugs.[93] The process is much quicker—the whole process takes less than 4 months—but it is less in-depth and less transparent. The SMC can recommend one of the following:

- The new drug is unique: all NHS Boards should make these drugs available within three months.

- The new drug is an advance on the alternatives or the same: each Board can decide whether to allow the use of the drug in their area.

- The new drug is worse than the alternatives: Boards are advised not to use the medicine.

---

[92] 'The Place of Carers' in M Freeman (ed.), *Law and Bioethics* (Oxford UP, 2008) 390–408.
[93] More information is available at <www.scottishmedicines.org.uk>.

(e) 'TOP-UP' PAYMENTS

While a patient's decision to opt-out of NHS care altogether is straightforward, more complex issues arise when a patient wants to continue to receive NHS care, but also wants to pay 'top-up' fees for aspects of their care—an expensive cancer drug, for example—which NICE has decided does not represent good enough value for money. We can see examples of two patients who did just this in the *Rogers* and the *Otley* cases, which we consider later in this chapter.

Until recently, there was considerable variation in how PCTs approached the question of top-up fees. The general principle was that a patient could not be both an NHS patient and a private patient during the same course of treatment. This meant that some patients were told that if they wanted to pay for one part of their care privately, they must opt out altogether, and pay for the whole course of their treatment themselves. While some patients might be able to find a few thousand pounds for a new drug, very few could afford to pay for all of their nursing care, and the costs of staying in hospital. Other PCTs tried to find creative solutions to this problem, by permitting patients to buy drugs which would then be administered at home.

On the one hand, allowing patients to pay top-up fees seems fairer, since otherwise a patient who would like to pay for a medicine that the NHS will not fund cannot do so unless she can cover the full costs of all of the care that she receives, which is likely to be prohibitively expensive for all but the richest members of society. This could be said to discriminate against the majority of the population, who might be able to find some additional resources, but who cannot afford to opt out of NHS care altogether. On the other hand, allowing top-up fees means that the standard of care NHS patients receive may depend upon their ability to pay, which appears to contradict the NHS's utopian founding principles.

In 2008, the first National Clinical Director for Cancer, Mike Richards, produced a report on access to medicines in the NHS, which directly considered the question of top-up fees. These should be permitted, Richards recommended, but only if the privately purchased medicine is administered separately, in non-NHS premises.

Mike Richards[94]

The clearest way to ensure separation between NHS and private care is to force patients to make a choice from the outset whether they wish to be a private patient or an NHS patient for the duration of their treatment for that condition. I share the view of the large majority of stakeholders that this option is unfair, as it would deny patients NHS care they would have otherwise received.

Recommendation 8

The Department of Health should make clear that no patient should lose their entitlement to NHS care they would have otherwise received, simply because they opt to purchase additional treatment for their condition.

It is important to stress that every possible approach to implementing this recommendation has practical difficulties and I have tried to balance these considerations in recommending a way forward.

---

[94] Improving Access to Medicines for NHS Patients: A Report (2008), available at <www.dh.gov.uk>.

The most integrated solution would be to introduce a system of NHS top-ups whereby patients would pay a user charge to receive additional drugs. However, I believe that this approach presents significant practical challenges and is inequitable for those NHS patients who could not afford to top up. It would also place the NHS in the perverse position of charging for treatments that have not been deemed as cost-effective. For these reasons I believe that the option of NHS top-ups should be rejected. My preferred option for ensuring that patients do not lose their entitlement to NHS care because they purchase additional drugs is for the government to clarify that individuals may pay for these drugs while continuing to be treated as an NHS patient for other elements of care as long as the two elements of care are provided separately.

Not all NHS hospitals have private facilities or a private hospital nearby. In these circumstances there may be practical difficulties in implementing the parallel arrangements.

The Department of Health then issued a Consultation on implementation of new arrangements for top-up fees, accepting Richards' recommendation that purchasing additional private services should not exclude a patient from receiving NHS care, but that the private treatment must be delivered separately, in order to avoid the NHS subsidizing private treatment.

Department of Health[95]

3.3 As overriding rules, it is essential that:

- the NHS should never subsidise private care with public money, which would breach core NHS principles; and
- patients should never be charged for their NHS care, which would contravene the founding principles and legislation of the NHS.

3.4 To avoid these risks, there should be as clear a separation as possible between private and NHS care.

4.1 This guidance establishes that, where a patient opts to pay for private care, their entitlement to NHS services remains and may not be withdrawn.

4.2 Patients may pay for additional private healthcare while continuing to receive care from the NHS. However, in order to ensure that there is no risk of the NHS subsidising private care:

- It should always be clear whether an individual procedure or treatment is privately funded or NHS funded.
- Private and NHS care should be kept as clearly separate as possible.
- Private care should be carried out at a different time and place. A different place would include the facilities of a private healthcare provider, or part of an NHS organisation which has been designated for private care, including amenity beds.
- This guidance applies to additional private healthcare that patients receive over and above their NHS care. It does not permit a "pick and mix" approach where patients can pay to upgrade any individual elements of their NHS care.

[95] Guidance on NHS Patients Who Wish to Pay for Additional Private Care—A Consultation (2008), available at <www.dh.gov.uk>.

In addition to avoiding NHS cross-subsidy of private care, the 'separate delivery' requirement will also reduce the possibility that the standard of care received by NHS patients in adjoining beds will differ according to their ability to pay, which many people regard as fundamentally incompatible with the principles underpinning delivery of NHS treatment.

In practice, however, requiring the privately purchased medicine to be delivered in another location may prove problematic. Where an NHS hospital contains a private ward, it may be relatively easy to move an NHS patient there for delivery of the privately purchased medicine. But not all NHS hospitals do contain private facilities, and so for some patients, separate delivery may mean having to undertake a clinically unnecessary journey to another hospital. Not only will this be an avoidable upheaval for patients who may be very unwell, but also it compromises the clinical team's ability to provide continuity of care.

5 CHALLENGING RATIONING DECISIONS

(a) JUDICIAL REVIEW

As we saw earlier, one requirement of 'accountability for reasonableness' in rationing is that decisions should be open to challenge. Judicial review is available to scrutinize the legality but not the merits of decisions taken by public authorities. A patient who believes that a health authority has deprived them of appropriate treatment can apply for judicial review, but only on the grounds that the decision was taken unlawfully: that is, that the health authority acted outside of its statutory powers, or irrationally: that is, the decision is so unreasonable that no reasonable health authority could have come to the same decision (known as *Wednesbury*[96] unreasonableness). An action could also be brought for judicial review on the grounds that it infringed an applicant's rights under the Human Rights Act.

It is noteworthy that there were no challenges to NHS decisions in the first thirty years of the NHS's existence. We have explored some possible reasons for this already in this chapter: the comparatively recent move from implicit towards explicit rationing means that in the past patients were seldom aware that treatment may have been rationed. In addition, patients' expectations are now higher, and they are more willing to complain, to the courts if necessary.

Initially, however, the judiciary were what can only be described as extremely hostile to actions brought against struggling health authorities.

In *R v Central Birmingham Health Authority, ex parte Walker*,[97] a non-urgent operation required by a premature baby was postponed on a number of occasions due to a shortage of nurses. The baby's mother applied for judicial review of the decision to postpone, but the Court of Appeal refused her application. Having pointed out that 'resources are, and perhaps always will be, finite', Sir John Donaldson MR found that: 'It is not for this court, or indeed any court, to substitute its own judgment for the judgment of those who are responsible for the allocation of resources.'

A year later, in *R v Central Birmingham Health Authority, ex parte Collier*,[98] the Court of Appeal was faced with a similar issue. This time, a four-year-old boy had had a number of unsuccessful heart operations, and was in desperate need of open heart surgery. Despite

---

[96] *Associated Provincial Picture Houses v Wednesbury Corporation* [1948] 1 KB 223.
[97] (1987) 3 BMLR 32.
[98] Unreported, 6 Jan 1988.

being placed at the top of the waiting list, the operation was postponed several times because of a shortage of both beds and nurses in the intensive care unit. His father applied for judicial review, but the Court of Appeal rejected his application as 'wholly misconceived'.

R v Central Birmingham Health Authority, ex parte Collier[99]

Sir Stephen Brown

This is not the forum in which a court can properly express opinions upon the way in which national resources are allocated or distributed. They may be very good reasons why the resources in this case do not allow all the beds in the hospital to be used at this particular time...

From the legal point of view, in the absence of any evidence which could begin to show that there was a failure to allocate resources in this instance in circumstances which would make it unreasonable in the Wednesbury sense to make those resources available, there can be no arguable case. I am bound to say that, whilst I have for my part every sympathy with the position of Mr Collier and his family and can understand their pressing anxiety in the case of their little boy, it does seem to me unfortunate that this procedure has been adopted. It is wholly misconceived in my view. The courts of this country cannot arrange the lists in the hospital, and, if it [sic] is not evidence that they are not being arranged properly due to some unreasonableness in the Wednesbury sense on the part of the authority, the courts cannot, and should not, be asked to intervene.

The decision in *Collier* has been sharply criticized by Christopher Newdick as 'one of the most unsatisfactory cases ever to have emanated from the Court of Appeal in England'.

Christopher Newdick[100]

The case is unsettling because neither the applicant nor the court appeared to know how, or why, facilities could not be made available for this undeniably urgent operation. On any Hippocratic assessment of the case, its merits could hardly have been greater: the case was urgent, surgery was life-saving and well-understood, and the prospects of success were good. How could any reasonable system of priorities sensibly have abandoned such a deserving case?

The first judicial review case to attract intense media attention was the 'Child B' case, or *R v Cambridge Health Authority, ex parte B*.[101] Jaymee Bowen, whose name was initially concealed in order to protect her from the knowledge of the seriousness of her illness, was first diagnosed with acute lymphoblastic leukaemia when she was five years old. She recovered, but at the age of ten developed acute myeloid leukaemia. Consultants at Addenbrookes Hospital in Cambridge, and at the Royal Marsden Hospital in London agreed that the only possible treatment (intensive chemotherapy and a second bone marrow transplant) would be very unlikely to succeed and was not in her best interests. Her father sought opinions from

---

[99] Unreported, 6 Jan 1988.
[100] 'Public Health Ethics and Clinical Freedom' (1998) 14 Journal of Contemporary Health Law and Policy (1998) 335, 354.
[101] [1995] 1 WLR 898.

other doctors in the UK and in the US. Treatment in the US would have been prohibitively expensive, but he did find one doctor at the Hammersmith Hospital in London who was prepared to treat his daughter privately, and he sought an extracontractual referral from Cambridge and Huntingdon Health Authority to pay for the £75,000 treatment. His request was refused, and he applied for judicial review of this decision. At first instance, Laws J called upon the health authority to justify its decision by explaining the priorities which had led it to refuse to fund Child B's treatment.

Laws J

[W]here the question is whether the life of a ten year old child might be saved, by more than a slim chance, the responsible authority must in my judgment do more than toll the bell of tight resources. They must explain the priorities that have led them to decline to fund the treatment.

Later the same day, the Court of Appeal overturned his judgment on the grounds that the health authority had acted rationally and fairly, and that court intervention in such a case would be misguided.

R v Cambridge Health Authority, ex parte B[102]

Sir Thomas Bingham MR

I have no doubt that in a perfect world any treatment which a patient, or a patient's family, sought would be provided if doctors were willing to give it, no matter how much it cost, particularly when a life was potentially at stake. It would however, in my view, be shutting one's eyes to the real world if the court were to proceed on the basis that we do live in such a world. It is common knowledge that health authorities of all kinds are constantly pressed to make ends meet. They cannot pay their nurses as much as they would like; they cannot provide all the treatments they would like; they cannot purchase all the extremely expensive medical equipment they would like; they cannot carry out all the research they would like; they cannot build all the hospitals and specialist units they would like. Difficult and agonising judgments have to be made as to how a limited budget is best allocated to the maximum advantage of the maximum number of patients. That is not a judgment which the court can make. In my judgment, it is not something that a health authority such as this authority can be fairly criticised for not advancing before the court.

The case attracted lurid media interest—*The Sun*'s headline was 'Condemned by Bank Balance' and the *Daily Mail*'s was 'Sentenced to Death'. Some commentators condemned the health authority for effectively depriving a little girl of her only chance of survival, while others argued that such tough choices were now inevitable within the NHS. It was, however, generally agreed that the Child B case was an example of rationing. Interestingly though, the then Chief Executive of Cambridge and Huntingdon health authority has challenged this assumption, contending that the decision had been made solely on the basis of Jaymee Bowen's best interests: 'Our decision was not motivated by a shortage of money and in reality had little ever to do with the current debate about healthcare rationing.'[103]

102 [1995] 1 WLR 898.
103 Stephen Thornton, 'The Child B Case—Reflections of a Chief' (1997) 314 British Medical Journal 1838.

There had, he maintained, been no decision to withdraw funding for the treatment which her doctors had recommended; rather the consensus of expert opinion among the doctors who had been treating Jaymee Bowen was that the treatment requested by her father would be ineffective and inappropriate.

Following the intense publicity, an anonymous private benefactor came forward to pay for Jaymee Bowen's treatment. The consultant who had agreed to treat Jaymee privately decided against a second bone marrow transplant, and instead gave her an experimental treatment known as a donor lymphocyte infusion. Jaymee survived for a few more months and died in May 1996.

One of the reasons why the courts have proved reluctant to overturn a health authority's decision not to fund a particular patient's treatment is that they are not in a position to know about the other—possibly more compelling—claims upon its resources. If funds are diverted to patient A, there may not be enough to pay for the treatment of patients B, C, or D, none of whom has been represented before the court. This point was emphasized in *Re J (A Minor)*.

Lord Donaldson MR[104]

I would stress the absolute undesirability of the court making an order which may have the effect of compelling a doctor or health authority to make available scarce resources (both human and material) to a particular child, without knowing whether or not there are other patients to whom those resources might more advantageously be devoted.

More recently, there have been a few cases in which the courts have found that health authorities have acted unlawfully when deciding not to fund particular treatments. In *R v North Derbyshire Health Authority, ex parte Fisher*, Dyson J criticized a health authority's decision not to fund Beta-Interferon except in conjunction with clinical trials. Since no trials were scheduled to take place, this amounted to a blanket ban, which was inconsistent with a Department of Health circular which had asked health authorities: 'to develop and implement local arrangements to manage the entry of such drugs into the NHS...; and in particular, to initiate and continue prescribing of Beta-Interferon through hospitals'.

Although the circular had only issued guidance and not directions, the health authority was under a duty to take it into consideration.

Dyson J[105]

The respondents had to have regard to that national policy. They were not obliged to follow the policy, but if they decided to depart from it, they had to give clear reasons for so doing, and those reasons would have been susceptible to a Wednesbury challenge.

The health authority was held to have acted unreasonably by ignoring the Department of Health circular, and their policy on Beta Interferon therefore had to be reconsidered, taking proper account of NHS national policy.

In *R v North West Lancashire Health Authority, ex parte A and Others* a group of patients was successful in establishing that a health authority's rationing policy was unlawful. In 1995

---

[104] *Re J (A Minor)* [1992] 4 All ER 614.
[105] *R v North Derbyshire Health Authority, ex parte Fisher* (1997) 38 BMLR 76 (QBD).

the health authority had adopted a restrictive referral policy for transsexuals seeking gender reassignment surgery at the country's only specialist Gender Identity Clinic at the Charing Cross Hospital in London. Three applicants who had had their requests for extra-contractual referrals turned down applied for judicial review. Auld LJ agreed that health authorities were entitled to make lists of treatments which were and were not a priority, and he agreed that it would 'make sense' to give gender reassignment surgery a lower priority than treatment for cancer, heart disease, or kidney failure. But he found that the policy did not make adequate provision for an individual's exceptional circumstances to be taken into account, and that the policy should be reformulated in order to (a) properly acknowledge that transsexualism is an illness, and (b) make effective provision for exceptions in individual cases.

R v North West Lancashire Health Authority, ex parte A and Others[106]

Auld LJ

[I]t is an unhappy but unavoidable feature of state funded health care that regional health authorities have to establish certain priorities in funding different treatments from their finite resources. It is natural that each authority, in establishing its own priorities, will give greater priority to life-threatening and other grave illnesses than to others obviously less demanding of medical intervention. The precise allocation and weighting of priorities is clearly a matter of judgment for each authority, keeping well in mind its statutory obligations to meet the reasonable requirements of all those within its area for which it is responsible. It makes sense to have a policy for the purpose—indeed, it might well be irrational not to have one—and it makes sense too that, in settling on such a policy, an authority would normally place treatment of transsexualism lower in its scale of priorities than, say, cancer or heart disease or kidney failure. Authorities might reasonably differ as to precisely where in the scale transsexualism should be placed and as to the criteria for determining the appropriateness and need for treatment of it in individual cases. It is proper for an authority to adopt a general policy for the exercise of such an administrative discretion, to allow for exceptions from it in 'exceptional circumstances' and to leave those circumstances undefined. In my view, a policy to place transsexualism low in an order of priorities of illnesses for treatment and to deny it treatment save in exceptional circumstances such as overriding clinical need is not in principle irrational, provided that the policy genuinely recognises the possibility of there being an overriding clinical need and requires each request for treatment to be considered on its individual merits...

Accordingly, given the authority's acknowledgement that transsexualism is an illness, its policy, in my view, is flawed in two important respects. First, it does not in truth treat transsexualism as an illness, but as an attitude or state of mind which does not warrant medical treatment. Second, the ostensible provision that it makes for exceptions in individual cases and its manner of considering them amount effectively to the operation of a 'blanket policy' against funding treatment for the condition because it does not believe in such treatment...

The authority should reformulate its policy to give proper weight to its acknowledgement that transsexualism is an illness, apply that weighting when setting its level of priority for treatment and make effective provision for exceptions in individual cases from any general policy restricting the funding of treatment for it.

[106] [2000] 1 WLR 977.

In practice, of course, it is possible that the health authority could still refuse to fund these applicants' gender reassignment surgery, but satisfy the Court of Appeal that it was not operating a blanket ban by offering *reasons* for the decisions to refuse funding in each individual's case. Could it then be argued that the practical consequence of the decision in *NW Lancashire* is not to ensure that these patients actually received treatment, but to instead offer them a personalized justification for a refusal to treat them? In Derek Morgan's words: 'The right to health care becomes in fact a right to transparency about the tragic choices that are being negotiated.'[107]

But while the judgment in *NW Lancashire* did not necessarily force the Authority to pay for the patients' treatment, the duty to give reasons does at least force health authorities to examine the fairness and consistency of their decisions.

R v North and East Devon Health Authority, ex parte Coughlan is an even more exceptional case. Miss Coughlan had been seriously injured in a road traffic accident in 1971. She was tetraplegic and required constant care. In 1993, she and seven other seriously disabled patients were moved to Mardon House, a purpose-built unit, which they were assured would be their 'home for life'. In 1996, the health authority recommended that Mardon House should be closed, although it accepted that it had a continuing commitment to finance the care received by the residents to whom this promise had been made.

Miss Coughlan applied for judicial review. The Court of Appeal found that the patients had a legitimate expectation not only to be treated fairly and impartially by the health authority, but also to the *substantive benefit* of a home for life in Mardon House. Frustrating that expectation would be so unfair that it would amount to an abuse of power. Lord Woolf even suggested that a failure to honour the substantive promise made to the applicant was 'equivalent to a breach of contract in private law'.

R v North and East Devon Health Authority, ex parte Coughlan[108]

Lord Woolf MR

It is, however, clear from the health authority's evidence and submissions that it did not consider that it had a legal responsibility or commitment to provide a home, as distinct from care or funding of care, for the applicant and her fellow residents. It considered that...the provision of care services to the current residents had become 'excessively expensive', having regard to the needs of the majority of disabled people in the authority's area...

But the cheaper option favoured by the health authority misses the essential point of the promise which had been given. The fact is that the health authority has not offered to the applicant an equivalent facility to replace what was promised to her. The health authority's undertaking to fund her care for the remainder of her life is substantially different in nature and effect from the earlier promise that care for her would be provided at Mardon House. That place would be her home for as long as she chose to live there.

We have no hesitation in concluding that the decision to move Miss Coughlan against her will and in breach of the health authority's own promise was in the circumstances unfair. It was unfair because it frustrated her legitimate expectation of having a home for life in Mardon House. There was no overriding public interest which justified it.

It is, however, important to remember that one of the reasons for treating public law differently from private law is that public authorities have a duty to balance competing claims

---

[107] *Issues in Medical Law and Ethics* (Cavendish: London, 2001) 58.   [108] [2001] QB 213.

upon their resources. The health authority's evidence to the Court of Appeal stated that Mardon House had become:

> a prohibitively expensive white elephant. The unit was not financially viable. Its continued operation was dependent upon the Authority supporting it at an excessively high cost. This did not represent value for money and left fewer resources available for other services.[109]

While it is, of course, honourable to keep one's promises, maintaining Mardon House might jeopardize the health authority's ability to offer services to other patients, whose interests were not represented in this case. Could it be argued that in *Coughlan* the Court of Appeal was in fact judging the *merits*, as opposed to the *legality* of the authority's decision?

Against this, Paul Craig and Soren Schonberg suggest that the Court of Appeal in *Coughlan* rightly separated two different exercises of power by the health authority: the promise to Miss Coughlan and the policy decision to close Mardon House. They agree that the policy change was not irrational in the *Wednesbury* sense, but that the breach of promise amounted to an abuse of power.

Paul Craig and Soren Schonberg[110]

> [T]here were two lawful exercises of power in this type of case: the promise and the policy change. It was this consideration which led the Court of Appeal to distinguish between two standards of judicial review of discretion. There was, on the one hand, bare or intrinsic irrationality, which allowed the court to intervene to quash a decision which defied comprehension…Such cases were rare. Irrationality also embraced decisions made on the basis of flawed logic…. It was acknowledged that the present decision might well pass a rationality test cast in these terms.
>
> There was, on the other hand, the possibility of intervention on the ground of abuse of power. A power which had been abused had not been lawfully exercised.

In recent years, there have been a number of cases in which patients have sought to challenge funding decisions concerning expensive cancer drugs. Their unavailability within the NHS has, as we have already seen, been behind the Richards' review into top-up payments and NICE's decision to produce supplementary guidance on medicines capable of prolonging the life of terminally ill patients. In the following three cases, we see that patients have also had some success in persuading the courts that the 'exceptionality' review process has not operated fairly in their cases.

A patient's challenge to her PCT's decision not to fund Herceptin for early-stage breast cancer was successful in *R (Ann Marie Rogers) v Swindon Primary Care Trust and the Secretary of State*. Ms Rogers suffered from stage 1 breast cancer. She had had a mastectomy, and, following her son's research on the internet, she asked to be tested for HER2 breast cancer, which could apparently be treated with a new drug, Herceptin, which was as yet unlicensed for the early stages of breast cancer, and had not been appraised by NICE.

Ms Rogers tested positive for HER2. Her consultant, Dr Cole, asked Swindon PCT if Ms Rogers could pay for Herceptin, while remaining an NHS patient. Their response was that she could not. Dr Cole agreed to waive his fees, and Ms Rogers paid for two doses

---

[109] Ibid.   [110] 'Substantive Legitimate Expectations after *Coughlan*' (2000) Public Law, 684–701.

of Herceptin herself. She was unable to pay for the whole course of treatment, and sought legal advice. The PCT's policy was not to fund 'off-licence' drugs unless the patient's case was exceptional. It therefore conducted an 'exceptional case review' of Ms Rogers' circumstances, and decided that, because she was in the same position as other sufferers of stage 1 breast cancer, her case could not be considered exceptional.

Ms Rogers sought judicial review of this decision on the grounds that it was arbitrary and irrational. The Court of Appeal overturned the first instance judge's rejection of Ms Rogers case, and found that the PCT had acted irrationally. Because all women with stage 1 breast cancer were in the same situation as Ms Rogers, its 'exceptionality' review procedure was meaningless.

R (Ann Marie Rogers) v Swindon Primary Care Trust and the Secretary of State[111]

Sir Anthony Clarke MR

The essential question is whether the policy was rational; and, in deciding whether it is rational or not, the court must consider whether there are any relevant exceptional circumstances which could justify the PCT refusing treatment to one woman within the eligible group but granting it to another. And to anticipate, the difficulty that the PCT encounters in the present case is that while the policy is stated to be one of exceptionality, no persuasive grounds can be identified, at least in clinical terms, for treating one patient who fulfils the clinical requirements for Herceptin treatment differently from others in that cohort...

The non-medical personal situation of a particular patient cannot in these circumstances be relevant to the question whether Herceptin prescribed by the patient's clinician should be funded for the benefit of the patient. Where the clinical needs are equal, and resources are not an issue, discrimination between patients in the same eligible group cannot be justified on the basis of personal characteristics not based on healthcare.

All the clinical evidence is to the same effect. The PCT has not put any clinical or medical evidence before the court to suggest any such clinical distinction could be made. In these circumstances there is no rational basis for distinguishing between patients within the eligible group on the basis of exceptional clinical circumstances any more than on the basis of personal, let alone social, circumstances.

For these reasons we have reached the conclusion that the policy of the PCT is irrational. Here the evidence does not establish the possibility of there being relevant clinical circumstances relating to one patient and not another and, in the case of personal characteristics, there is no rational basis for preferring one patient to another.

Note that Sir Anthony Clarke specifically rules out using 'non-medical' or personal circumstances as a reason to distinguish between different patients. In deciding whether a woman's case was 'exceptional', non-clinical considerations—the example he gave was a patient who had to care for a disabled child—were irrelevant.

The PCT had said that its decision was not based upon cost. This was because the then Secretary of State for Health, Patricia Hewitt, had stated publicly that PCTs should not refuse to fund Herceptin on cost grounds. If the PCT *had* cited cost as a reason not to fund Herceptin for Ms Rogers, ironically the Court of Appeal found they would have been on stronger ground: 'If that policy had involved a balance of financial considerations against a general policy not to fund off-licence drugs not approved by NICE and the healthcare needs of the particular patient in an exceptional case, we do not think that such a policy would have been irrational.'

---

[111] [2006] EWCA Civ 392.

In the next extract, Keith Syrett argues that the *Rogers* case is not, as some commentators have suggested, 'a landmark victory for an individual over a health trust... [and] an important step forward for "patient power"', but rather it demonstrates that if PCTs are honest about the scarcity of resources, they will have a much wider discretion to fund, or not fund, particular treatments.

Keith Syrett[112]

[I]t is submitted that it is most useful to read the case as a judicial exhortation to PCTs to be transparent as to the part played by financial considerations in making difficult choices on the availability of treatments and services for the population which they serve.

Provided that cost plays a part in the decision-making of a PCT and it is acknowledged as pertinent, a court will allow the PCT considerable scope to do as it pleases, subject only to intervention where the policy adopted is egregious in the extreme (such as funding Herceptin only to women with red hair) or where it fails to admit of the possible relevance of exceptional individual circumstances (which need not be defined in advance, but which may embrace any of personal, social or clinical factors). However, if the PCT has sufficient funds available for treatment or if, like Swindon PCT, it purports as such, the court will scrutinise the decision-making process much more closely to ensure that any policy or decision to deny access to treatment can be *properly justified* to disappointed patients (and the wider public) *by reference to clinical factors*, since it is to be expected that the PCT will meet all clinical needs if it is operating under no resource constraints. In practice, it is likely to prove difficult for a PCT free of financial restrictions to justify provision of funding for a treatment to one patient for whom it has been recommended while denying access to another with the same condition on clinical grounds... Accordingly, in the absence of resource constraints, a policy of exceptionality is almost certain to be unlawful, as no rational explanation can be offered for discriminating between patients.

In the second case, *R on the Application of Otley v Barking and Dagenham NHS Primary Care Trust*,[113] the Health Authority again operated an 'exceptionality policy', which this time was held to be lawful. What was not lawful, however, was its application to Ms Otley, who was suffering from metastatic colorectal cancer, and tumours in her liver. Ms Otley had responded poorly to chemotherapy. Her sister discovered the existence of a new drug, Avastin, on the internet. Avastin is licensed in the US and in many European countries, but not in England and Wales. It costs between £1,000 and £1,500 per cycle.

Ms Otley had sufficient funds for five cycles of Avastin, which she took in combination with other drugs. Her response to Avastin was excellent: there were minimal side-effects; she felt much better and the tumours appeared to have shrunk. Ms Otley's doctor applied to the NHS Trust to fund a further five prescriptions of Avastin. The application was refused and Ms Otley applied for judicial review.

Mitting J found that the panel which made this decision had acted irrationally. This was not because the policy was irrational, as in *Rogers*. On the contrary, Mitting J found that 'the policy is entirely rational and sensible'. It was the application of this policy to Ms Otley's case which was irrational. The panel had failed to take into account the fact that there were

[112] 'Opening Eyes to the Reality of Scarce Health Care Resources? R. (on the application of Rogers) v Swindon NHS Primary Care Trust and Secretary of State for Health' (2006) Public Law 664–73.
[113] [2007] EWHC 1927 (Admin).

no other options available to Ms Otley. Ms Otley, he found, *should* be treated as an exceptional case. He found that 'on any fair minded view of the exceptionality criteria identified in the critical analysis document, her case was exceptional': she was young and fit, did not tolerate other drugs, had suffered no side-effects and had benefited from Avastin. Resource considerations could not be a decisive factor in her case because the expected outlay—of another five cycles of Avastin—would be relatively modest and certainly would not jeopardize the Trust's capacity to provide care for other patients.

More recently, in *R (Murphy) v Salford Primary Care Trust*, another case in which a patient challenged the refusal to pay for expensive renal cancer treatment, Burnett J set out the principles to be applied in these cases.

R (Murphy) v Salford Primary Care Trust[114]

Burnett J

The legal principles that are in play are not controversial:

a. When an NHS body makes a decision about whether to fund a treatment in an individual patient's case it is entitled to take into account the financial restraints on its budget as well as the patient's circumstances.

b. Decisions about how to allocate scarce resources between patients are ones with which the Courts will not usually intervene absent irrationality on the part of the decision-maker. There are severe limits on the ability of the Court to intervene.

c. The Court's role is not to express opinions as to the effectiveness of medical treatment or the merits of medical judgment.

d. It is lawful for an NHS body to decide to decline to fund treatment save in exceptional circumstances, provided that it is possible to envisage such circumstances.

Seven grounds were put forward as to why Ms Murphy's case should be treated as exceptional, such as the fact that she also suffered from breast cancer, which excluded her from a clinical trial of the new drug, and that she had had mental health problems. The panel considered each of these factors individually, and none was found to be sufficient to mark Ms Murphy out as an exceptional case. Burnett J decided that, in addition to their individual consideration, they should also have looked at Ms Murphy's case 'in the round':

As a matter of general principle when considering a series of factors which might inform the overall decision, it is of course necessary to look at them individually...But having looked at all factors individually, it seems to me that it is necessary to consider them in the round.

Burnett J therefore quashed the original decision and remitted it back to the Commissioning Panel, who could, of course, come to the same decision again, provided that before doing so they *had* considered Ms Murphy's circumstances 'in the round'.

---

[114] [2008] EWHC 1908 (Admin).

(b) THE HUMAN RIGHTS ACT 1998

A patient who is denied access to medical treatment might try to invoke the Human Rights Act 1998 in order to challenge the decision. If a patient is denied treatment which might save her life, for example, would it be possible to argue that her right to life, protected under Article 2, has been violated? Certainly, Article 2 does not only oblige public bodies to refrain from deliberately taking its citizens' lives, but can also require them to take adequate measures to protect life. However, patients will not generally be able to invoke Article 2 in order to force health authorities to fund treatment which has been refused on the grounds of cost or clinical judgement. The European Court of Human Rights has generally been slow to interfere with resource allocation decisions within public services. In the *Osman* case, it found that the right to life 'must be interpreted in a way which does not impose an impossible or disproportionate burden on the authorities'.[115]

Nevertheless, actions against public bodies for refusal to fund life-saving measures are possible, in exceptional circumstances. A failure to provide any treatment at all to a dying patient might violate Article 2. One exceptional case where an action brought under Article 2 succeeded was *Savage v South Essex Partnership NHS Foundation Trust*,[116] in which the House of Lords found that, where a mentally ill patient was a known suicide risk, there was an obligation, under Article 2, to do all that could reasonably be expected in order to prevent that risk materializing. The duty to provide services under Article 2 was triggered, according to Baroness Hale, by 'a "real and immediate risk to life" about which the authorities knew or ought to have known at the time'.

Might a refusal to fund treatment also be challenged under Article 8, the right to respect for one's private and family life? Or if sufficiently serious, could a denial of medical treatment ever amount to 'inhuman or degrading treatment' under Article 3? Furthermore, might a patient be able to claim that they were discriminated against in the exercise of their Convention rights under Article 14? All three claims were made by the applicants in questions in *NW Lancashire Health Authority v A, D and G*, discussed in the previous section, and were briskly dismissed by the Court of Appeal.

NW Lancashire Health Authority v A, D and G[117]

Buxton LJ

[I]t is plain that in this case there has occurred no interference with either the applicants' private life or with their sexuality...Such an interference could hardly be founded on a refusal to fund medical treatment.

It is impossible to see how the applicants have been the victims of discrimination on grounds of sex. True it is that they seek a particular treatment related to their sexuality; but that has been refused not because of that sexuality, but on grounds of allocation of resources.

At first instance in *R (on the application of Watts) v Bedford Primary Care Trust*, discussed further in the following section, Munby J rejected the claim that having to wait a year for a

---

[115] *Osman v UK* (Case 87/1997/871/1083) [1999] 1 FLR 193.   [116] [2008] UKHL 74.
[117] [2000] 1 WLR 977.

hip replacement operation, with all the pain and suffering to be endured in the meantime, might be in breach of Article 3.

R (on the application of Watts) v Bedford Primary Care Trust[118]

Munby J

Article 3 is not engaged unless the 'ill-treatment' in question attains a minimum level of severity and involves actual bodily injury or intense physical or mental suffering. However that is not this case. Making every allowance for the constant pain and suffering that the claimant was having to endure—and I do not seek in any way to minimise it—the simple fact in my judgment is that nothing she had to endure was so severe or so humiliating as to engage Article 3.

But while it would be difficult for a claimant to establish that a failure to provide medical treatment infringed on their rights under the Human Rights Act, 1998, it is certainly not impossible. In *Price v United Kingdom* the prison authorities could not cope with the special needs of a four-limb-deficient thalidomide victim with numerous health problems including defective kidneys. The Court found that there had been a breach of Article 3.

Price v United Kingdom[119]

Judgment of the ECtHR

There is no evidence in this case of any positive intention to humiliate or debase the applicant. However, the Court considers that to detain a severely disabled person in conditions where she is dangerously cold, risks developing sores because her bed is too hard or unreachable, and is unable to go to the toilet or keep clean without the greatest of difficulty, constitutes degrading treatment contrary to Article 3.[120]

Regardless of the Convention Rights' usefulness to patients who are upset by rationing decisions, the Human Rights Act 1998 has undoubtedly led to a greater emphasis upon the proportionality of decisions to restrict access to medical treatment. In the next extract, Keith Syrett explains how a shift from *Wednesbury* unreasonableness to proportionality, as the standard of scrutiny, makes it easier to successfully challenge the decisions of public bodies, because it necessarily requires the decision-maker to give reasons.

Keith Syrett[121]

[In *Collier*] the Court took the view that judicial intervention was only permissible if the decision was 'unreasonable' in the so-called *Wednesbury* sense, that is that it was 'so unreasonable that no reasonable authority could ever have come to it'. Under this test, a public body is

---

[118] [2003] EWHC 2228 (Admin).
[119] (2001) 34 EHRR 1285.   [120] [2003] EWHC 2228 (Admin).
[121] *Law, Legitimacy and the Rationing of Health Care* (CUP: Cambridge, 2007) 166–7.

under no obligation to explain the decision reached unless the applicant for judicial review can make a case for its irrationality. This represents a much less searching standard of scrutiny than other public law principles, notably proportionality, which requires a court to assess the balance struck between competing interests by the decision-maker and the relevant weight accorded to interests and considerations. Necessarily, in undertaking scrutiny according to this latter standard, a court will be required to examine the justifications put forward by the decision-maker as to why it has favoured one interest over another, so that it can establish that interference with the latter is not disproportionate.

(c) SEEKING TREATMENT ABROAD

Could a patient who has been denied treatment in the UK, or who wants to avoid UK waiting lists seek reimbursement for treatment abroad? Article 49 of the EC Treaty prohibits restrictions on the freedom to provide services which are 'normally provided for remuneration' within the EU. Unquestionably this covers private medical treatment, and the ECJ has also held that remuneration exists in some types of publicly funded treatment.[122] But while Article 49 may enable patients to seek treatment abroad, it confers no right to be reimbursed for such treatment.

As amended Article 22 of Council Regulation No 1408/71, which coordinates national social security systems, allows Member States to decide whether to authorize reimbursement for treatment abroad, but states that authorization:

> may not be refused where the treatment in question is among the benefits provided for by the legislation of the Member State on whose territory the person concerned resides and where he cannot be given such treatment within the time normally necessary for obtaining the treatment in question in the Member State of residence, taking account of his current state of health and the probable course of the disease.

This means that patients cannot claim financial support for treatment abroad where the treatment in question is unavailable within the NHS, perhaps because NICE has decided that it is not cost-effective. Whether or not the provision can be used to avoid NHS waiting lists depends upon how 'the time normally necessary for obtaining the treatment in question' is interpreted. It seems clear that patients cannot expect the NHS to pay for treatment abroad just because they will not be treated *immediately* in the UK. Instead, it is only where the waiting time in the UK amounts to 'undue delay' that it will be possible to invoke Article 22 to demand access to services in another country.

The question of whether or not European law entitles a patient on an NHS waiting list to be reimbursed for treatment in another Member State arose for the first time in the UK in *R (on the application of Watts) v Bedford Primary Care Trust and Another*. Yvonne Watts sought a hip replacement operation in France in order to avoid the NHS waiting time of approximately one year. Her local NHS Trust refused to fund the operation, and she challenged this decision, arguing that it was contrary to her free movement rights under EU law. The critical question was whether the waiting list meant that the Ms Watts would be subject to 'undue delay'. The Court of Appeal asked for further clarification from the European Court of Justice on a number of questions, among them:

---

[122] Case C-158/96, *Kohll v Union de Caisses de Maladie* [1998] ECR I-1931.

> Is the United Kingdom National Health Service entitled to refuse to authorise a patient's treatment in another Member State if it reasonably judges that to do so in the particular and similar cases would dislocate its system of administering priorities through waiting lists?[123]

There are, as Gareth Davies explains, good reasons why the NHS might fear the consequences of a wide-ranging right to be reimbursed for treatment abroad.

Gareth Davies[124]

> The Member States' central fear is that patients going abroad, usually to avoid waiting lists, will result in higher costs. Not only will the national authorities lose their control over the rate of treatment, and hence spending, but they will also be left with possibly half-empty institutions. These cannot simply be closed down, because maintaining the national medical infrastructure is a matter of strategic and public health importance. Therefore the state will be forced to operate an inefficient system, adding an extra burden to its budget.

In *R (on the application of Watts) v Bedford Primary Care Trust and another*[125] the ECJ decided that, while NHS patients are entitled to have treatment in another Member State, they cannot expect the NHS to pay for this treatment unless they have received prior authorization. Refusal to grant prior authorization for NHS-funded treatment abroad could not be based merely on the existence of waiting lists intended to enable the supply of hospital care to be planned and managed. Instead, it would be necessary to carry out an objective medical assessment of the patient's medical condition; the history and probable course of his illness; the degree of pain he was in and/or the nature of his disability. Where the delay arising from waiting lists appeared to exceed an acceptable time, having regard to an objective medical assessment of the patient's circumstances, the NHS should not refuse to pay for treatment abroad on the grounds that funding the patient's treatment abroad would distort the NHS's capacity to prioritize patients on the basis of the urgency of their treatment.

Hence, the question of whether the delay is 'undue' in the particular patient's circumstances depends principally upon their clinical needs. Budgetary constraints and the need for planning within the NHS will only be grounds to refuse prior authorization for NHS-funded treatment abroad where the delay is 'reasonable', based upon an objective assessment of the patient's circumstances. Although this may seem like a patient-friendly decision, as Christopher Newdick explains, only *certain* patients are likely to benefit:

> To introduce a European right to travel will do much to benefit the strong and articulate. But it ignores those who cannot travel, or inarticulate patients who do not press for their rights. A system which skews health care rights in this way has little to recommend it.

In 2008, the European Union issued a Directive to provide greater clarity on the question of access to cross-border health care provision within Europe. It does not mandate a

---

[123] *R (on the application of Watts) v Bedford Primary Care Trust and Another* [2004] EWCA CIV 166.

[124] 'Health and Efficiency: Community Law and National Health Systems in the Light of Müller-Fauré' (2004) 67 Modern Law Review 94–107.

[125] (Case C-372/04) [2006] All ER (D) 220 (May).

system of prior authorization, but suggests that it is legitimate for a State to determine that access to reimbursed hospital care abroad should depend upon prior authorization, where this is necessary to avoid disruption to the social security budget or to planning within the Health Sector. Where a prior authorization system is in place, the Directive requires it to be clear and accessible. The Directive is not expected to come into force until 2010, at the earliest.

Commission of the European Communities[126]

The right to reimbursement of the costs of healthcare provided in another Member State from the statutory social security scheme of patients as insured persons was recognised by the Court of Justice in several judgements. The Court of Justice has held that the Treaty provisions on the freedom to provide … Whilst Community law does not detract from the power of the Member States to organise their healthcare and social security systems, Member States must when exercising that power comply with Community law, in particular with the Treaty provisions on the freedom to provide services. Those provisions prohibit the Member States from introducing or maintaining unjustified restrictions on the exercise of that freedom in the healthcare sector.

In accordance with the principles established by the Court of Justice, and without endangering the financial balance of Member States' healthcare and social security systems, greater legal certainty as regards the reimbursement of healthcare costs should be provided for patients and for health professionals, healthcare providers and social security institutions.

(d) THE RIGHTS OF NON-RESIDENTS

While it is clear that other EU citizens have a right, similar to that of Yvonne Watts, to seek treatment in the UK, following prior authorization from their state health care provider, under the NHS Act, 2006, it is only those who can be described as 'ordinarily resident' in the UK who have the right to free health care. Section 175 provides that anyone who is not ordinarily resident may be charged for NHS services. This is the case even if they have British citizenship. Certain sorts of treatment are exempt from charges, including treatment given in an accident and emergency department and compulsory psychiatric treatment, as are certain sorts of visitors, such as students whose courses last more than six months or are substantially funded by the UK government.[127]

The question of whether a failed asylum seeker could nevertheless be 'ordinarily resident' came before the court in *R (on the application of A) v West Middlesex University Hospital NHS Trust*.[128] Mitting J held that until removal directions were set, a failed asylum seeker had the same immigration status as that of a person whose asylum claim has yet to be determined, they could be 'ordinarily resident in the UK', and hence that guidance advising NHS trusts to charge failed asylum seekers was unlawful. Mitting J did not decide that *all* failed asylum seekers would be ordinarily resident, but that such judgements should be made on

---

[126] Directive of the European Parliament and the Council on the application of patients' rights in cross-border healthcare (2008) 2008/0142, available at <http://ec.europa.eu>.

[127] Full details are available on the DH website: <www.dh.gov.uk>.

[128] [2008] EWHC 855 (Admin).

a case-by-case basis. At the time of writing, the Department of Health has been granted to leave to appeal against Mitting J's decision.

When a failed asylum seeker is desperately ill and facing deportation to a country where they will not receive the care that they need, the courts have, on a number of occasions, considered whether deportation in such cases could amount to a human rights violation.

In *D v United Kingdom*[129] D was due to be deported to St Kitts after his release from prison. He had been diagnosed as suffering from HIV/AIDS while in prison, and he requested leave to remain in the UK on compassionate grounds. D's illness was at a very advanced stage, and death was imminent. Deportation to St Kitts would mean that he would not have access to treatment and palliative care, meaning that he would be likely to die in extremely distressing circumstances. The ECtHR decided that 'in the very exceptional circumstances of this case and given the compelling humanitarian considerations at stake, it must be concluded that the implementation of the decision to remove the applicant would be a violation of Article 3'.

Subsequent cases have attempted to flesh out when a patient's circumstances will be sufficiently 'exceptional' to make deportation a breach of Article 3, and it is clear that this condition is very seldom be satisfied. The House of Lords considered the question in *N v Secretary of State for the Home Department*.[130] N was a Ugandan citizen whose application for asylum had been refused. After coming to the UK in order to seek asylum, N was diagnosed with advanced HIV/AIDS. After receiving medical treatment in the UK, her condition had stabilized. She had a good chance of surviving for decades if treatment continued, but without treatment, she would be unlikely to live for more than two years. N claimed that returning her to Uganda would breach her right under Article 3 not to be subjected to 'inhuman and degrading treatment'. The House of Lords dismissed her appeal on the grounds that her case was not sufficiently exceptional.

N then took her case to the European Court of Human Rights. A majority agreed with the House of Lords that deportation would only violate Article 3 in exceptional circumstances, and that N's case did not fit within the exceptionality test criteria established by *D v UK*.

D v United Kingdom[131]

Judgment of the ECtHR

The decision to remove an alien who is suffering from a serious mental or physical illness to a country where the facilities for the treatment of that illness are inferior to those available in the Contracting State may raise an issue under Article 3, but only in a very exceptional case, where the humanitarian grounds against the removal are compelling. In the *D.* case the very exceptional circumstances were that the applicant was critically ill and appeared to be close to death, could not be guaranteed any nursing or medical care in his country of origin and had no family there willing or able to care for him or provide him with even a basic level of food, shelter or social support.

The Court does not exclude that there may be other very exceptional cases where the humanitarian considerations are equally compelling. However, it considers that it should

---

[129] (1997) 24 E.H.R.R. 423.
[130] [2005] UKHL 31.
[131] (2008) (Application No. 26565/05).

maintain the high threshold set in *D. v the United Kingdom* and applied in its subsequent case-law, which it regards as correct in principle, given that in such cases the alleged future harm would emanate not from the intentional acts or omissions of public authorities or non-State bodies, but instead from a naturally occurring illness and the lack of sufficient resources to deal with it in the receiving country....

Advances in medical science, together with social and economic differences between countries, entail that the level of treatment available in the Contracting State and the country of origin may vary considerably. While it is necessary, given the fundamental importance of Article 3 in the Convention system, for the Court to retain a degree of flexibility to prevent expulsion in very exceptional cases, Article 3 does not place an obligation on the Contracting State to alleviate such disparities through the provision of free and unlimited health care to all aliens without a right to stay within its jurisdiction. A finding to the contrary would place too great a burden on the Contracting States.

There are two particular factual difficulties that affect asylum seekers suffering from HIV/AIDS. First, the disease is so common in certain parts of the world, and treatment so inadequate, that proving that anyone's circumstances are *exceptional* is, almost by definition, impossible. In *ZT v The Secretary of State for the Home Department*[132], a case involving a woman with HIV/AIDS facing deportation to Zimbabwe, the IAT had held that:

[T]he claimant's situation is far from exceptional. It is certainly not unique. On the contrary, it is estimated that one-third of the adult population of Zimbabwe is now infected with HIV and/or AIDS. Whilst the situation which would face the claimant on return to Zimbabwe is undoubtedly a grim and distressing one, it is not one which is exceptional.

In the Court of Appeal, Sedley LJ admitted that the ubiquity of suffering from HIV/AIDS makes the exceptionality requirement very difficult to satisfy.

Sedley LJ

If HIV were a rare affliction, readily treatable in the UK but not treatable except for the fortunate few in many other countries, the courts would have little hesitation in holding removal of sufferers to such countries to be inhuman treatment contrary to Article 3. It is the sheer volume of suffering now reaching these shores that has driven the Home Office, the Immigration Appellate Authority and the courts to find jurisprudential reasons for holding that neither Article 3 or Article 8 can ordinarily avail HIV sufferers who face removal.

Secondly, *D v United Kingdom* is treated as the paradigm example of an 'exceptional' case, and yet, as Stephanie Palmer points out, treatment options for HIV/AIDS have improved dramatically since D's case was decided. If the critical factor which marked D's case out was his imminent death, the existence of anti-retroviral drugs which enable HIV/AIDS sufferers to lead much longer and healthier lives again make it virtually impossible for someone currently receiving effective treatment to fit within the *D v UK* exception.

---

[132] [2005] EWCA Civ 1421. See also *BK (Zimbabwe) v The Secretary of State for the Home Department* [2008] EWCA Civ 510.

Stephanie Palmer[133]

The Strasbourg jurisprudence concerning the expulsion of aliens with HIV/AIDS has been shown to be unsatisfactory because of the medical advances in the treatment of this disease. The question in *D* concerned the particular circumstances of his inevitable death. In contrast, the seminal issue in N's case concerned the length and quality of her life and whether there is a positive obligation on the state to sustain her medical treatment on a long-term basis.

It is not just sufferers from HIV/AIDS who have sought to resist deportation on health grounds, and in other cases, the threshold for finding that deporting of them would breach their human rights is also very high indeed. In *Bensaid v United Kingdom*[134] B, an Algerian national, had been receiving NHS treatment for schizophrenia. He was due to be deported, on the grounds that his marriage to a UK citizen had been found to be a marriage of convenience. B claimed that his removal would violate his rights under Article 3 and Article 8. The ECtHR held that B failed to meet the high threshold required by Article 3, because treatment was available in Algeria, albeit not as conveniently as in the UK. His removal would not breach Article 8, because the disruption of relationships he had formed in the UK was found to be justifiable on the grounds of protecting the UK's economy and preventing crime.

This was followed by the House of Lords in *R (on the application of Razgar) v Secretary of State for the Home Department* (No. 2).[135] R was an Iraqi of Kurdish origin who had been refused asylum in Germany. R resisted removal from the UK on the ground that it would violate his human rights under Article 8, because he was receiving psychiatric treatment for depression and post-traumatic stress disorder. The House of Lords found that it would be possible to rely on Article 8 to resist removal if removal would damage a person's mental health, but that the threshold was again very high, amounting to, according to Lord Bingham, 'something very much more extreme than relative disadvantage'.

(e) NEGLIGENCE

Could an NHS trust's decision to offer care that is less than ideal on grounds of cost represent a breach of their primary duty of care to patients? As we see in the next chapter, NHS trusts do owe a duty to provide an acceptable standard of care. Because the standard of care in negligence is assessed objectively, lack of resources does not offer an excuse for providing negligent care. In *Bull v Devon Area Health Authority*, a case we consider again in the next chapter, Exeter City Hospital operated on two sites, and its resources were evidently severely stretched: Slade LJ suggested that 'in cases where multiple births were involved, the system in operation at the hospital in 1970 was obviously operating on a knife-edge'. During the delivery of Mrs Bull's twins, unsuccessful attempts were made to summon a registrar, and a consultant finally arrived to deliver the second twin over an hour later, during which time he had been deprived of oxygen and as a result was left profoundly mentally and physically disabled. The Court of Appeal was clear that limited resources was not necessarily a defence to an allegation of negligence; Mustill LJ, for example, said that:

---

[133] 'AIDS, Expulsion and Article 3 of the European Convention on Human Rights' (2005) 5 European Human Rights Law Review 533–40.
[134] (2001) 33 EHRR 10.   [135] [2004] UKHL 27.

> it is not necessarily an answer to allegations of unsafety that there were insufficient resources to enable the administrators to do everything which they would like to do.[136]

Nevertheless, the Court of Appeal accepted that less than ideal care will sometimes be inevitable. Here a delay of 15 to 20 minutes in summoning a registrar or consultant would have been acceptable, but the delay of 68 minutes amounted to negligence. The Hospital was not under a duty to have a system in place which would eliminate the possibility of any delay. Rather, the duty was to provide 'a staff *reasonably sufficient* for the foreseeable requirements of the patient' (my emphasis).

(f) BREACH OF STATUTORY DUTY

If a patient could argue that a health authority was under a statutory duty to provide her with a particular treatment, an action for breach of statutory duty may appear to offer a more positive avenue for redress. A statutory duty is not the same as a discretionary power, which means that a lack of resources cannot provide an excuse for a failure to fulfil the duty.

Clearly the National Health Service Act creates a duty on the part of the Secretary of State:

National Health Service Act 2006 sections 1 and 3

1 Secretary of State's duty to promote health service

(1) The Secretary of State must continue the promotion in England of a comprehensive health service designed to secure improvement—

(a) in the physical and mental health of the people of England, and

(b) in the prevention, diagnosis and treatment of illness.

(2) The Secretary of State must for that purpose provide or secure the provision of services in accordance with this Act.

(3) The services so provided must be free of charge except in so far as the making and recovery of charges is expressly provided for by or under any enactment, whenever passed.

3 Secretary of State's duty as to provision of certain services

(1) The Secretary of State must provide throughout England, to such extent as he considers necessary to meet all reasonable requirements—

(a) hospital accommodation,

(b) other accommodation for the purpose of any service provided under this Act,

(c) medical, dental, ophthalmic, nursing and ambulance services,

(d) such other services or facilities for the care of pregnant women, women who are breastfeeding and young children as he considers are appropriate as part of the health service,

---

[136] *Bull v Devon Area Health Authority* (1989) 22 BMLR 79 (CA).

> (e) such other services or facilities for the prevention of illness, the care of persons suffering from illness and the after-care of persons who have suffered from illness as he considers are appropriate as part of the health service,
>
> (f) such other services or facilities as are required for the diagnosis and treatment of illness.

Notice, however, that the Secretary of State's statutory duty under the Health Service Act is not to *provide* comprehensive access to all types of medical treatment, but rather to *promote* a comprehensive health service. In *Coughlan*, Lord Woolf admitted that the duty to promote a comprehensive NHS was very far from a duty to *ensure* that the service was comprehensive.

R v North and East Devon Health Authority, ex parte Coughlan[137]

Lord Woolf

When exercising his judgment [the Secretary of State] has to bear in mind the comprehensive service which he is under a duty to promote as set out in section 1 [of the National Health Service Act, 2006]. However, as long as he pays due regard to that duty, the fact that the service will not be comprehensive does not mean that he is necessarily contravening either section 1 or section 3. The truth is that, while he has the duty to continue to promote a comprehensive free health service and he must never, in making a decision under section 3, disregard that duty, a comprehensive health service may never, for human, financial and other resource reasons, be achievable. Recent history has demonstrated that the pace of developments as to what is possible by way of medical treatment, coupled with the ever increasing expectations of the public, mean that the resources of the NHS are and are likely to continue, at least in the foreseeable future, to be insufficient to meet demand.

It is generally accepted that there will always be types of medical care which the NHS simply cannot afford to offer free of charge: counsellors and psychotherapists often charge for their services and cosmetic surgery is seldom available on the NHS. The Secretary of State's duty is therefore to ensure that the NHS provides an *adequate* service, whatever that might mean. Because, as Rudolf Klein has explained, 'the frontiers of adequacy have never been defined',[138] and adequacy remains a rather 'fuzzy and elastic notion',[139] it would be very difficult to prove that the Secretary of State was ever actually in breach of the duty to 'continue the promotion' of a comprehensive NHS.

In *R v Secretary of State for Social Services, ex parte Hincks*, patients who had been on the waiting list for orthopaedic surgery for several years sought a declaration that the Secretary of State was in breach of his duty under the previous National Health Service Act 1977 to 'provide throughout England and Wales to such extent as he considers necessary to meet all reasonable requirements (a) hospital accommodation…[and] (c) medical services'. Their application was dismissed.

---

[137] [2001] QB 213.

[138] Rudolf Klein, 'Defining a Package of NHS Healthcare Services: The Case Against' in Bill New (ed), *Rationing: Talk and Action in Health Care* (BMJ: London, 1997) 85–94, 85.

[139] Ibid, 86.

R v Secretary of State for Social Services, ex parte Hincks[140]

Lord Denning MR

It cannot be supposed that the Secretary of State has to provide all the latest equipment....it cannot be supposed that the Secretary of State has to provide all the kidney machines which are asked for, or for all the new developments such as heart transplants in every case where people would benefit from them...It cannot be that the Secretary of State has a duty to provide everything that is asked for in the changed circumstances which have come about. That includes the numerous pills that people take nowadays: it cannot be said that he has to provide all these free for everybody.

The Secretary of State says that he is doing the best he can with the financial resources available to him: and I do not think that he can be faulted in the matter.

But even if it was possible to prove that there had in fact been a breach of the duty to promote a comprehensive health service, or to provide hospital accommodation or medical services, a patient would only be able to claim a remedy in tort if the court judged that parliament had intended that individuals should have a *private law* remedy for any breach of the duties in sections 1 and 3 of the Act.

Under the 2006 Act there is no penalty or remedy prescribed for breach of the duties imposed upon the Secretary of State. And in the context of other social services, the House of Lords has confirmed that the purpose of legislation is to benefit society as a whole, rather than to offer remedies to individual citizens.[141] In *Re HIV Haemophiliac Litigation*,[142] Rougier J had held that it was plain that Parliament did not intend there to be a cause of action for any member of the public affected by breach of the duties in the National Health Service Act, and this was upheld by the Court of Appeal. Ralph Gibson LJ said:

For my part, I share the judge's view of the apparent nature of the duties imposed by the 1977 Act. They do not clearly demonstrate the intention of Parliament to impose a duty which is to be enforced by individual civil action.

In contrast to the NHS Act, a rather more specific obligation is imposed on health authorities by section 117 of the Mental Health Act 1983:

117(2) it shall be the duty of the district health authority...to provide...after-care services for any person to whom this section applies until such time as the district health authority...are satisfied that the person concerned is no longer in need of such services.

This is not a vague duty to *promote* aftercare, instead it is clear that there is a duty to *provide* appropriate services for patients who have been discharged from mental hospitals. Nevertheless, the courts have been reluctant to find health authorities liable to individual

---

[140] (1980) 1 BMLR 93 (CA).

[141] See, for example, the comments of Lord Browne-Wilkinson in *X v Bedfordshire CC* [1995] 3 All ER 353.

[142] (1990) 41 BMLR 171.

patients for failing to make appropriate provision. In *Clunis v Camden and Islington HA*, the Court of Appeal rejected Clunis's claim that the health authority might be liable for breach of the statutory duty to provide appropriate aftercare services.

Beldam LJ[143]

The primary method of enforcement of the obligations under section 117 is by complaint to the Secretary of State. No doubt, too, a decision by the district health authority or the local social services authority under the section is liable to judicial review at the instance of a patient...[But] the wording of the section is not apposite to create a private law cause of action for failure to carry out the duties under the statute.

6 CONCLUSION

One thing is certain: there will never be sufficient funds devoted to the NHS to eliminate the need to make tough choices about the allocation of scarce resources. The important questions are therefore not *whether* to ration treatment within the NHS, but *how* to do this in the fairest possible way and *who* should be charged with making these difficult decisions.

Fairness also demands that people who are affected by a funding decision should be able to challenge it, and hold the decision-maker to account. Does judicial review adequately fulfil this function? As we have seen, there has been a tradition of judicial deference to health authorities' funding decisions, much like the judicial deference to clinical judgement embodied in the *Bolam* test (considered in the next chapter). In recent years, there appears to be evidence of a shift towards more proactive judicial scrutiny of funding choices within the NHS, but the judiciary exercises no control over the Treasury's decision about how much public money should be allocated to the NHS, which will ultimately dictate the extent to which trusts must ration their services.

In the UK, we are, as our politicians realize, very attached to the principle of universal access to free health care. But is this feasible? Certainly few of us are willing to pay much higher rates of income tax, and so rationing by dilution within the NHS has become inevitable. It also worth thinking about whether it would be preferable to confront more directly the possibility of a mixed health care system, in which patients sometimes have to contribute directly to the costs of their care. In relation to some treatments, such as dentistry, optometry and fertility treatment, such a system already exists, and the decision to permit top-up payments extends this mixed health economy into the area of life-saving as opposed to life-enhancing care. It remains to be seen whether a new insurance market to cover the costs of top-up payments will develop, and given that premiums are likely to be considerably lower than full private health coverage, whether this will mean that a growing proportion of the UK's population will purchase some form of health insurance. In the coming years, we may have to acknowledge that the utopian post-war dream of a completely comprehensive and entirely free NHS is no longer possible, and that the best we can hope for is transparency and fairness in the allocation of scarce resources.

---

[143] *Clunis v Camden and Islington HA* [1998] QB 978.

FURTHER READING

Craig, Paul and Schonberg, Soren, 'Substantive Legitimate Expectations after *Coughlan*' (2000) Public Law 684–701.

Daniels, N and Sabin, J, *Setting Limits Fairly—Can we Learn to Share Medical Resources?* (OUP: Oxford, 2000).

Davies, Gareth, 'Health and Efficiency: Community Law and National Health Systems in the Light of Müller-Fauré' (2004) 67 Modern Law Review 94–107.

Evans, HM, 'Do Patients have Duties?' (2007) 33 Journal of Medical Ethics 689–94.

Harris, John, 'Double Jeopardy and the Use of QALYs in Health Care Allocation' (1995) 21 Journal of Medical Ethics 144–50.

Harris, John, 'The Age-Indifference Principle and Equality' (2005) 14 Cambridge Quarterly of Healthcare Ethics 93–9.

Light, Donald W, 'The Real Ethics of Rationing' (1997) 315 British Medical Journal 112–15.

Maynard, Alan, 'Ethics and Health Care "Underfunding"' (2001) 27 Journal of Medical Ethics 223–7.

New, Bill and Grand, Julian Le, *Rationing in the NHS: Principles and Pragmatism* (King's Fund: London, 1996).

Newdick, Christopher, *Who Should We Treat? Rights, Rationing and Resources in the NHS* 2nd edn (OUP: Oxford, 2005).

Palmer, Stephanie, 'AIDS, Expulsion and Article 3 of the European Convention on Human Rights' (2005) 5 European Human Rights Law Review 533–40.

Syrett, Keith, 'Impotence or Importance? Judicial Review in an Era of Explicit NHS Rationing' (2004) 67 Modern Law Review 289–304.

Syrett, Keith, 'Opening Eyes to the Reality of Scarce Health Care Resources? *R (on the application of Rogers) v Swindon NHS Primary Care Trust and Secretary of State for Health*' (2006) Public Law 664–73.

3

MEDICAL MALPRACTICE

CENTRAL ISSUES

1. Actions for breach of contract are possible if a patient has paid for her medical treatment. In practice, however, contracts will generally contain an implied term that the doctor will exercise reasonable care and skill, and this is indistinguishable from the doctor's duty of care in the tort of negligence.

2. Establishing that a doctor owes her patient a duty of care will usually be straightforward. More complex issues arise if a third party wishes to sue a doctor, perhaps because the doctor had failed to ensure that her patient would not cause harm to others.

3. The standard of care expected of doctors has been dominated by the *Bolam* test, as modified by *Bolitho*: the doctor will not be found to have acted negligently if she has acted in accordance with a practice accepted as proper by a responsible body of medical opinion, provided that that opinion is capable of withstanding logical analysis.

4. Having established that the doctor has breached her duty of care, the claimant must prove that this breach caused her injuries. This is often difficult in medical negligence cases because, by definition, the patient is generally *already* ill, and so there may immediately be at least two possible causes of her poor health.

5. There is a great deal wrong with the clinical negligence system: it is costly and inefficient, and claimants are seldom successful. More importantly still, it fosters a 'blame culture', which makes learning from mistakes less likely.

---

1 INTRODUCTION

In this chapter, we consider the law's response to medical treatment that has gone wrong. Conventionally, it has been assumed that people who have been injured as a result of poor medical treatment will want financial compensation. In reality, evidence appears to suggest that an explanation, an apology, and reassurance that the incident will not be repeated are more important to patients. In one study of people affected by medical injuries, 60 per cent wanted an apology, explanation, or inquiry into the cause of the incident; only 11 per cent thought that financial compensation was the most appropriate remedy.[1]

Despite failing to offer patients their preferred remedies, the volume of clinical negligence cases has increased dramatically—by as much as 1,200 per cent—over the past thirty years.[2] Where treatment is provided privately, there will be a contract between the health care provider and the patient, and so an action for breach of contract may be possible. There is no contract between NHS patients and their doctors, and so in the public sector, injured patients will have to sue in tort. In practice, however, there is little difference between these two actions.

We begin this chapter by looking briefly at the possibility of an action for breach of contract, before exploring the different stages involved in a clinical negligence claim. Tort and contract are not the only possible responses to inadequate medical treatment, and mention is also made of the NHS complaints system; the possibility of disciplinary action by the General Medical Council (GMC); and the circumstances in which a doctor might be prosecuted for gross negligence.

In recent years, there has been a great deal of criticism of the way in which medical mishaps are handled. The clinical negligence system costs the NHS millions of pounds each year and arguably works to hamper rather than promote improved patient care. By fostering a 'blame culture' it offers a disincentive for health care workers to own up when something goes wrong, making learning from mistakes less likely. It also fails to provide patients with the apologies and explanations which are so important to them. In the last sections of this chapter, we look at these criticisms in detail, and evaluate whether the NHS Redress Act 2006 will make a difference.

In this chapter, our focus is mainly upon *doctor*'s mistakes, rather than those of other health care workers. This is partly because doctors are principally responsible for patient care, and are therefore also responsible for negligently caused bad outcomes, and partly because historically the bulk of litigation has been against the medical profession, and so there is comparatively little case law addressing nurses' duties of care.

It should also be noted that two 'special cases' in the tort of negligence are dealt with elsewhere in this book: the question of liability for failing to provide sufficient information to patients, and the possibility of liability for occurrences before birth, are covered in Chapters 4 and 14, respectively. Of course, the basic principles of negligence, which are the subject of this chapter, are equally applicable in these cases, but because each raises a number of distinctive questions, they warrant separate consideration.

2 BREACH OF CONTRACT

If health care is provided in the private sector, the patient will have a contract with her doctor and/or with the clinic or hospital where she receives treatment. The nature of these contracts varies. For example, a patient may make an agreement directly with a doctor, who

---

[1] Making Amends: A Consultation Paper Setting Out Proposals for Reforming the Approach to Clinical Negligence in the NHS (DH: London, 2003) 75.
[2] V Harpwood, *Medicine, Malpractice and Misapprehensions* (Routledge-Cavendish: Abingdon, 2007) 2.

will then arrange for the patient's admission, or alternatively the patient's agreement may be made with the hospital, which then employs a doctor to provide the necessary services. The terms of contracts for private health care will also differ. Some contracts contain terms naming a specific individual as the treating doctor. Breach of this sort of contractual term could give rise to an action for breach of contract.

Contracts for private health care will also contain terms that are implied by statute. An example might be the supply of medical devices, which must—under sections 4 and 9 of the Supply of Goods and Services Act 1982—be of satisfactory quality and fit for their purpose. Statutory limits on the use of exclusion clauses also apply; for example, it is not possible to exclude or restrict liability for death or personal injury caused by negligence.[3]

It is possible, if unlikely, that a contract could contain an express term guaranteeing the outcome of the procedure. Few doctors would ever choose to give such a warranty, however, and it has become clear that the courts will be very slow to imply such a term into a contract for health care services. In *Thake v Maurice*, a failed sterilization case, which we consider again in chapter 14, Neill LJ stated:

> I do not consider that a reasonable person would have expected a responsible medical man to be intending to give a guarantee. Medicine, though a highly skilled profession, is not, and is not generally regarded as being, an exact science. The reasonable man would have expected the defendant to exercise all the proper skill and care of a surgeon in that speciality; he would not in my view have expected the defendant to give a guarantee of 100% success.[4]

The Court of Appeal in *Thake v Maurice* did accept that there might be some circumstances in which a guarantee of success might reasonably be inferred. Nourse LJ gave the example of an operation to amputate a limb. A patient who goes into hospital to have her right leg amputated could reasonably expect that the operation will in fact remove her right leg. Such cases are likely to be rare, and more commonly, a reasonable person could not expect a doctor to guarantee a successful outcome.

In *Thake v Maurice* the Court of Appeal held that the contract contained an implied term guaranteeing that the doctor would exercise reasonable care and skill. In practice, this is indistinguishable from the duty to take reasonable care in the tort of negligence, owed by all doctors to their patients. Because the vast majority of malpractice claims are brought in negligence, rather than for breach of contract, it is within our discussion of clinical negligence actions that we flesh out what might be meant by 'reasonable care and skill'. Similar considerations apply where a private patient claims that there has been a breach of the implied contractual term warranting that the doctor will exercise reasonable care.

As private health care becomes more common, and as patients increasingly see themselves as consumers exercising choice, rather than as grateful recipients of the NHS's beneficence, might contract have a more central role to play in framing the doctor–patient relationship? In the next extract Harvey Teff suggests that the power imbalance between doctors and patients is an obstacle to the greater use of private contractual ordering in the medical context.

---

[3] Unfair Contract Terms Act 1977 section 2(1).   [4] *Thake v Maurice* [1986] QB 644.

Harvey Teff[5]

In certain respects, the relationship between doctor and patient does have more affinity with contract than with tort…To begin with, it is a *relationship*. Medical encounters differ from stock situations in tort in that the parties are seldom total strangers to one another prior to the event precipitating litigation. There is, in principle, scope for negotiation about the terms of the arrangements which they make; the doctor is paid for having undertaken to provide professional services to the patient…

[A]s the public service ethic of the NHS progressively gives way to a more commercial one, health care is more readily perceived as a commodity and its provision as a matter of private ordering. The more this altered perception takes root, the stronger might appear to be the case for a contractual framework, with terms designed by the parties, in place of externally imposed criteria, largely shaped by the medical profession via the *Bolam*…approach. If the doctor–patient relationship is truly envisaged as consensual and especially if patient autonomy is to be taken seriously, what could be more natural, mutually acceptable, and effective than for the parties to frame the terms of engagement to suit individual circumstances?…

The courts have so far held the line on familiar public policy grounds. Maintenance of high standards in health care is seen as an overriding need, not to be jeopardized by allowing providers to exercise their bargaining power to the detriment of relatively vulnerable and inadequately informed patients. Such a change of regime could, it is argued, easily lead to a widespread diminution of standards, contrary to the interests of patients and difficult to reconcile with the ethical obligations of doctors…

Freedom of contract is of little avail if the doctor nearly always has a better understanding of the medical indications and knows more about the nature and quality of proposed treatment and available options.

3 NEGLIGENCE

In order to succeed in an action in negligence, the claimant must establish:

(a) that she is owed a duty of care by the defendant (this will usually be the treating doctor, and her employer will be vicariously liable. GPs are a special case, and are sued personally, though they will be insured by a medical defence union); and

(b) that the defendant breached that duty by failing to exercise reasonable care; and

(c) that the breach of duty caused the claimant's injuries, and that those injuries are not too remote.

Finally, there are a number of defences which may be available to the defendant. Let us examine each of these stages in turn.

(a) THE EXISTENCE OF A DUTY OF CARE

The existence of a duty of care within the doctor–patient (or nurse–patient) relationship can generally be taken for granted. It is a well-established duty situation, and it is inconceivable

---

[5] *Reasonable Care: Legal Perspectives on the Doctor–Patient Relationship* (Clarendon Press: Oxford, 1994) 164–5, 169.

that a doctor, or other health care worker, who had made a mistake during medical treatment would attempt to argue that she did not owe her patient a duty of care. The duty will be to exercise reasonable care and skill in diagnosis, advice, and treatment. Provided that the doctor committed the tort in the course of her employment—which will invariably be the case in clinical negligence cases—her employer (the NHS Trust) will be vicariously liable for her negligence. In three situations, however, the question of the existence of a duty of care becomes slightly more complicated.

(1) When does the Doctor–Patient Relationship Come into Being?

Usually, of course, the existence of a doctor–patient relationship will be obvious. But there could be times when the question of whether a particular individual was in fact the doctor's patient at the relevant time is not straightforward. Because a doctor is under no obligation to treat a 'stranger', it is important to know when the transition from 'stranger' to 'patient' takes place. The common law position is that a duty of care is imposed upon the doctor once she has *assumed responsibility* for the patient's care.

The duty of care will generally arise only when the doctor knows of the patient's need for medical services. For some patients, such as those over the age of 75, who must be offered an annual consultation, a GP's duty of care might extend to seeking out the patient, but normally it is only when the patient requests the doctor's assistance that the duty of care comes into being.

In hospitals, the duty may arise as soon as the patient presents herself for treatment, before she is actually seen by a doctor. This was the case in *Barnett v Chelsea and Kensington Hospital Management Committee*. After drinking tea later discovered to have contained arsenic, three nightwatchmen had started vomiting and attended the casualty department of the defendant's hospital. The nurse telephoned the casualty officer, Dr Banerjee, who told her to tell them to go home and call their own doctors. He did not see the men, who died hours later from arsenic poisoning. One of the men's widows brought an action in negligence. Nield J held that Dr Banerjee had undertaken to exercise reasonable care and owed the men a duty of care, which he had breached by failing to examine them himself. (Later in this chapter we will see that her action failed on the question of causation.)

Barnett v Chelsea and Kensington Hospital Management Committee[6]

Nield J

In my judgment, there was here such a close and direct relationship between the hospital and the watchmen that there was imposed on the hospital a duty of care which they owed to the watchmen. Thus I have no doubt that Nurse Corbett and Dr. Banerjee were under a duty to the deceased to exercise that skill and care which is to be expected of persons in such positions acting reasonably...Without doubt Dr. Banerjee should have seen and examined the deceased. His failure to do either cannot be described as an excusable error as has been submitted, it was negligence. It is unfortunate that Dr. Banerjee was himself at the time a tired and unwell doctor, but there was no-one else to do that which it was his duty to do. Having examined the deceased I think that the first and provisional diagnosis would have been one of food poisoning.

[6] [1969] 1 QB 428.

(2) Who Else Might Owe Primary Duties of Care to Patients?

In addition to being vicariously liable for its employees' negligence, might the health authority or NHS Trust owe a primary duty of care to patients to ensure that they receive adequate treatment? In *Wilsher v Essex AHA*, a case we consider in more detail below, members of the Court of Appeal clearly thought it was possible for a health authority to owe patients a primary, non-delegable duty of care to provide properly skilled medical staff, and an adequately equipped hospital.

Wilsher v Essex AHA[7]

Sir Nicolas Browne-Wilkinson VC

In my judgment, a health authority which so conducts its hospital that it fails to provide doctors of sufficient skill and experience to give the treatment offered at the hospital may be directly liable in negligence to the patient...

Claims against a health authority that it has itself been directly negligent, as opposed to vicariously liable for the negligence of its doctors, will, of course, raise awkward questions. To what extent should the authority be held liable if (eg in the use of junior housemen) it is only adopting a practice hallowed by tradition? Should the authority be liable if it demonstrates that, due to the financial stringency under which it operates, it cannot afford to fill the posts with those possessing the necessary experience? But, in my judgment, the law should not be distorted by making findings of personal fault against individual doctors who are, in truth, not at fault in order to avoid such questions. To do so would be to cloud the real issues which arise.

One problem with the hospital's primary duty is that, as we saw in the previous chapter, NHS Trusts inevitably operate with scarce resources and there is probably always more that could be done to improve the standard of health care services. While courts may be prepared to impose some minimum standard of care, they are generally reluctant to interfere with policy decisions about the allocation of limited resources. In *Bull v Devon AHA* we can see the Court of Appeal attempting to draw a distinction between the hospital's duty to provide minimally adequate treatment, for which it could be liable in negligence, and its freedom to choose how to organize its services within the limited funds available to it.

Mrs Bull had brought an action against Devon Health Authority on behalf of her severely handicapped son, one of twins, who had been injured as a result of a delay in the registrar's arrival while she was in labour. The system for urgently summoning an obstetrician had broken down, and there was a delay of about an hour before the registrar arrived. The health authority argued that such a delay was unavoidable because the hospital operated on two sites. The Court of Appeal rejected this, and held that the system failed to provide an acceptable level of care.

Bull v Devon AHA[8]

Dillon LJ

We have had a certain amount of discussion in the course of the argument as to whether the law should impose, or a patient should have the right to expect, the same standard of care

---

[7] [1987] QB 730.   [8] [1993] 4 Med LR 117 (CA).

and treatment from a local district hospital such as the defendant's hospital in the present case as from a 'centre of excellence'—a major teaching hospital in London or Oxbridge or a large modern hospital in a large city. Obviously, there are highly specialised medical services which a district hospital does not have the equipment to provide and does not hold itself out as ready to provide. But this case is not about highly specialised services like that. The Exeter City Hospital provides a maternity service for expectant mothers, and any hospital which provides such a service ought to be able to cope with the not particularly out of the way case of a healthy young mother in somewhat premature labour with twins....

In my judgment, the plaintiff has succeeded in proving, by the ordinary civil standards of proof, that the failure to provide for Mrs Bull the prompt attendance she needed was attributable to the negligence of the defendants in implementing an unreliable and essentially unsatisfactory system for calling the registrar.

So while Mrs Bull was not entitled to expect that an obstetrician would be available immediately, waiting for an hour fell below the minimum standard of care that the hospital were under a duty to provide. If, say, the registrar had been bleeped and arrived within 15 minutes, Mrs Bull's action would probably have failed.

In *Garcia v St Mary's NHS Trust*, it had taken 30 minutes for the on-call cardio-thoracic register to arrive at Mr Garcia's bedside, after he lost consciousness following cardiac surgery, and this delay was held to be non-negligent.

Garcia v St Mary's NHS Trust[9]

Judge Shaun Spencer

I take into account that the presence on site of an on-call specialist registrar does not necessarily mean he would be available for Mr Garcia. He might be engaged with another patient in the fast track. He might be engaged with a medical emergency. If an accident came into Accident and Emergency requiring the care of a chest surgeon he might be required for that. Having the surgeon on site does not necessarily signify that he would be available for Mr Garcia.

I also have to bear in mind the rarity of the occurrence. Systems and resources obviously have to be designed in order to accommodate what is reasonably to be foreseen, always bearing in mind that the unexpected sometimes occurs and, therefore, should come within the range of the foreseeable. I bear in mind that the Trust, operated under the provisions of the National Health Service, has a duty to Mr Garcia to take reasonable care of him and that that duty co-exists together with the duty which is owed to other patients, and also the duty as employers to its own staff.

Despite the possibility of relying upon the Trust's non-delegable duty to provide adequate treatment, it will usually be more straightforward to find the Trust liable through its vicarious liability for an employee's negligence, where these difficult distinctions between operational and policy decisions do not arise.

The primary duty to provide adequate treatment might be more significant, however, when, as is increasingly common, a patient's NHS treatment has been contracted out to

[9] [2006] EWHC 2314 (QB).

a private hospital. In such cases, the NHS Trust will continue to be liable for a failure to arrange adequate care, even though it is *not* the doctors' employer. Of course, the NHS Trust will normally have made an arrangement with the private hospital to indemnify them against any liability, but the patient herself will be able to sue the NHS Trust.

It is not just health authorities who might owe primary duties of care to patients. In *Re HIV Haemophiliac Litigation* haemophiliac patients had had transfusions with HIV-contaminated blood products. They brought an action against the Secretary of State for Health for failing to warn patients of the risks of contamination. The Court of Appeal held that the case could proceed to trial because there was at least an arguable case.

Re HIV Haemophiliac Litigation[10]

Bingham LJ

[W]here, as here, foreseeability by a defendant of severe personal injury to a person such as the plaintiff is shown, and the existence of a proximate relationship between plaintiff and defendant is accepted, the plaintiff is well on his way to establishing the existence of a duty of care. He may still fail to do so if it is held that imposition of such a duty on the defendant would not in all the circumstances be just and reasonable, but it is by no means clear to me at this preliminary stage that the department's submissions on that aspect must prevail.

The case was then settled by the Government, and so did not proceed to a full hearing.

A relationship of proximity between the Secretary of State for Health and individual patients would be the exception rather than the norm, however. There are a small number of patients with haemophilia in the UK, each of whom may need at least one blood transfusion during their lifetime. In *Danns v Department of Health*, Mr and Mrs Danns unsuccessfully brought an action against the Department of Health for failure to take steps to disseminate new findings about the reversibility of vasectomy to the 1.5 million people estimated to be relying upon vasectomies as their only method of birth control. The Court of Appeal found that the Department of Health did not owe Mr and Mrs Danns a duty of care.

Danns v Department of Health[11]

Roch LJ

[T]he Department did not owe the plaintiff a duty at common law to take reasonable care, for the reason that there did not exist as between the plaintiffs and the defendants that degree of the proximity which the law requires. The plaintiffs were not the defendants' neighbours...I agree with the Judge when...he said:

Yet further, I would also hold that requirements of fairness, justice and reasonableness do not require the Department to give to the public at large the warnings contended for by the plaintiffs in this action.

---

[10] [1990] NLJR 1349 962.   [11] [1998] PIQR P226.

(3) Could Health Care Workers Ever Owe Non-Patients a Duty of Care?

Usually, of course, the only person likely to be injured or to suffer loss if a doctor or other health care worker makes a mistake is the patient herself. But could a third party ever be owed a duty of care by a health care professional? In the next sections, we consider four different scenarios in which this question might arise:

- wrongful pregnancy;
- psychiatric injury;
- failure to prevent the patient from causing harm;
- medical examinations.

(a) 'Wrongful pregnancy'

Where a sterilization operation has been carried out negligently, or a patient has been given negligent advice about its success, it is, as we see in Chapter 14, possible to recover damages in tort for the pain and discomfort associated with pregnancy and childbirth. These are, of course, suffered only by women. Where a man's sterilization has failed, the 'damage' is therefore suffered not by the patient himself, but by a third party. She will generally only be able to recover damages if she was within the doctor's contemplation at the time of the operation, because she was the patient's wife or partner.

In *McFarlane v Tayside Health Board*,[12] a case we consider in detail in Chapter 14, the patient was married, and not only was his wife's reliance upon the assurances that sterility had been achieved foreseeable, but also she was in a sufficiently proximate relationship with her husband's doctors. In contrast, in *Goodwill v BPAS*, the court decided that a doctor carrying out a vasectomy does not owe a duty to all of his patient's *future* sexual partners.

Goodwill v BPAS[13]

Peter Gibson LJ

The defendants were not in a sufficient or any special relationship with the plaintiff such as gives rise to a duty of care. I cannot see that it can properly be said of the defendants that they voluntarily assumed responsibility to the plaintiff when giving advice to Mr MacKinlay. At that time they had no knowledge of her, she was not an existing sexual partner of Mr MacKinlay but was merely, like any other woman in the world, a potential future sexual partner of his, that is to say a member of an indeterminately large class of females who might have sexual relations with Mr MacKinlay during his lifetime.

(b) Psychiatric injury

A different sort of case in which a non-patient might suffer injury is where a patient's relative suffers psychiatric injury, such as post-traumatic stress disorder (PTSD), as a result of witnessing her negligent medical treatment. In such cases, the third party is plainly a secondary victim, and so the limiting principles developed in cases like *Alcock v Chief*

---

[12] 2000 SC (HL) 1.   [13] [1996] 1 WLR 1397.

Constable of South Yorkshire[14] and *White v Chief Constable of South Yorkshire*[15] apply. In short, the claimant must have a close relationship with the victim; she must be close in time and space to the incident; she must witness it, or its immediate aftermath, with her unaided senses; and she must suffer a recognizable psychiatric illness as a result.[16]

In *Sion v Hampstead Health Authority*, a father had stayed in hospital with his son, who had been injured in a motor-cycle accident. His son lapsed into a coma and died fourteen days later. The father alleged that the hospital treating him had been negligent, and claimed damages for his own psychiatric illness. His claim was dismissed by the Court of Appeal on the grounds that, as Staughton LJ explained, there had been:

> no sudden appreciation by sight or sound of a horrifying event. On the contrary, the report describes a process continuing for some time, from first arrival at the hospital to the appreciation of medical negligence after the inquest. In particular, the son's death when it occurred was not surprising but expected.[17]

Similarly in *Taylor v Somerset Health Authority*, Auld J found that there had not been a sufficiently traumatic 'event' to bring the deceased's wife's visit to the mortuary within the 'immediate aftermath' of his death.

Taylor v Somerset Health Authority[18]

Auld J

Here, the main purpose of Mrs Taylor's visit to the mortuary was to confirm or otherwise the information that she had received from the doctor that her husband was dead. Apart from the obvious shock to her of the sight of his dead body, it bore no marks or signs to her of the sort that would have conjured up for her the circumstances of his fatal attack... In my view, the fact that Mrs Taylor's main purpose in viewing her husband's body in the mortuary was to settle her disbelief as to his reported death is not capable of being part of any possible immediate aftermath in the circumstances of this case.

In *North Glamorgan NHS Trust v Walters*, a mother whose newborn baby's death was the result of the defendant's negligence, and who witnessed his distressing final 36 hours, was said to have suffered the requisite 'shock'.

North Glamorgan NHS Trust v Walters[19]

Ward LJ

In my judgment on the facts of this case there was an inexorable progression from the moment when the fit occurred as a result of the failure of the hospital properly to diagnose and then to treat the baby, the fit causing the brain damage which shortly thereafter made

---

[14] 1992] 1 AC 310.   [15] [1999] 2 AC 455.

[16] Both *Alcock* and *White* arose out of the Hillsborough stadium disaster in 1989, and involved claims brought by friends or relatives (Alcock) and policemen (White).

[17] *Sion v Hampstead Health Authority*, The Times, 10 June 1994.

[18] (1993) 16 BMLR 63.   [19] [2002] EWCA Civ 1792.

termination of this child's life inevitable and the dreadful climax when the child died in her arms. It is a seamless tale with an obvious beginning and an equally obvious end. It was played out over a period of 36 hours, which for her both at the time and as subsequently recollected was undoubtedly one drawn-out experience . . . The necessary proximity in space and time is satisfied. The assault on her nervous system had begun and she reeled under successive blows as each was delivered. It comes as no surprise to me that when her new baby was ill she should suffer the flashbacks of 36 horrendous hours which wreaked havoc upon her mind.

One of the most strikingly 'claimant friendly' judgments is *Froggatt v Chesterfield and North Derbyshire Royal Hospital NHS Trust*, in which Forbes J allowed a patient's husband and son to recover damages for the psychiatric conditions they had developed after discovering that she had had an unnecessary mastectomy following negligent misdiagnosis of breast cancer: the shocking 'events' were (in the case of the husband) seeing his wife naked, and (in the case of the son) overhearing a telephone conversation.

Froggatt v Chesterfield and North Derbyshire Royal Hospital NHS Trust[20]

Forbes J

In Mr Froggatt's case, his sudden appreciation of the trauma that had been suffered by Mrs Froggatt as the result of the Defendant's negligence occurred when he saw her undressed for the first time after the mastectomy. He was quite unprepared for what he saw and he was profoundly and lastingly shocked by it. As a result, his sleep became fitful, he became generally agitated and he suffered an adjustment disorder that lasted for about one and a half years . . .

In Dane's case, the sudden appreciation came as a result of overhearing his mother's telephone conversation and his immediate belief, based on the negligent advice that had been given to his mother and that she felt obliged to repeat to him, that she had cancer and was likely to die. He was completely unprepared for such a shock and, as a result, he suffered a moderate Post Traumatic Stress Disorder.

In the next extract, Paula Case discusses some of the special problems facing relatives seeking to claim for psychiatric illnesses triggered by their relatives' negligent medical treatment.

Paula Case[21]

The relative is unlikely to witness at first hand the 'sudden shocking event' currently required by English law as, unlike the typical accident environment, the hospital is a highly controlled space where the family's view of tragedy is often occluded by the intervention of hospital personnel . . .

---

[20] 2002 WL 31676323.
[21] 'Secondary Iatrogenic Harm: Claims for Psychiatric Damage Following a Death Caused by Medical Error' (2004) 67 Modern Law Review 561–87.

> The claimant will generally not witness the moment of their relative's demise and may rely on viewing the deceased's body after death as the 'shocking event' which caused the harm. Where the relative is absent during the events which caused the death of the deceased, an attempt to rely on identification of the body after death as the 'shocking event' is likely to fail...In *Alcock*, their Lordships agreed that secondary victims must demonstrate that their injury be caused by a 'sudden appreciation by sight or sound of a horrifying event which violently agitates the mind'.
>
> The sudden shocking event requirement presents particular problems in hospital cases, because it might be argued by defendants that the 'suddenness' of the shocking event is negated by the reasons that brought the MAV [medical accident victim] to hospital. In other words, the probability of deterioration is known merely by the fact that the MAV was in hospital.

Psychiatric injury might also be caused to non-patients by the communication of traumatic information. It would be difficult to fit this within the *Alcock* criteria, on the grounds that the claimant is supposed to have witnessed the shocking event with her unaided senses, as opposed to just being told about it. Nevertheless, if information is communicated negligently, might it be possible for a relative to claim that she is a primary victim, and hence that the distinction between physical and psychiatric injury is less important?

At first sight, this might seem improbable, given that it has generally been assumed that primary victims must have been *physically* endangered by the defendant's negligence. In *Page v Smith*,[22] for example, Lord Lloyd said that to be a primary victim, the claimant had to be 'within the range of foreseeable physical injury'. A different approach was, however, adopted in *Farrell v Avon HA*.[23] When the claimant arrived at the hospital following the birth of his son, he was wrongly informed that his baby had died, and was given a dead baby to hold for 20 minutes. He was then told that there had been a mistake, and his son was in fact alive and well. Bursell J held that the claimant was a primary victim because he was directly involved in the traumatic incident, and he was therefore able to recover for his PTSD.

(c) Failure to prevent the patient from causing harm

There are a number of ways in which patients who are not offered proper advice or treatment might pose a risk to others. First, if a doctor discovers that her patient is unfit to drive, she is under a duty to tell her not to drive,[24] and should she fail to do so, it is foreseeable that a third party might be injured as a result. Secondly, patients with infectious or contagious diseases clearly pose a risk to third parties, hence a doctor's negligent failure to diagnose her patient's condition, or to offer her appropriate advice or treatment might put others at risk. Thirdly, if a doctor does not 'section' a psychiatric patient when she has reasonable grounds for believing that the patient is likely to harm someone else (see further Chapter 6), it is foreseeable that a third party might be attacked. In these situations, could a doctor owe foreseeably injured non-patients a duty of care?

It is important to remember that in such cases the doctor has not directly *caused* the third party's injury; rather, she would be being sued for an omission, or a failure to prevent

---

[22] [1996] AC 155.   [23] (2000) 2 LGLR 69.

[24] She is also under a duty to inform the Driver and Vehicle Licensing Agency (DVLA).

harm from occurring. As a result, the three stage test from *Caparo v Dickman*[25] applies: (1) the claimant's injury must be foreseeable; (2) there must be a proximate relationship between the claimant and the doctor; and (3) the imposition of a duty must be fair, just, and reasonable in all the circumstances. While it might be relatively straightforward to establish foreseeability, proving that there is a sufficient relationship of proximity and that imposing a duty of care would be fair, just, and reasonable will often be much more problematic.

The question of whether doctors might be under a duty to protect a member of the public from a dangerous psychiatric patient arose in *Palmer v Tees Health Authority*. A man called Armstrong, who had a long history of psychiatric problems, abducted, sexually assaulted and murdered Rosie Palmer, who was four years old. Her mother claimed that the defendant health authority's medical staff had failed to diagnose that there was a real, substantial, and foreseeable risk that this man would commit serious sexual offences against children, and that the defendants should therefore be liable for Rosie's death, and for her own post-traumatic stress disorder and pathological grief reaction. It was not disputed that the injuries to Rosie and her mother might have been foreseeable; but the judge held that there was not a relationship of sufficient proximity between the health authority and Rosie Palmer, and that it was not fair, just, and reasonable to impose a duty of care upon the defendants. Mrs Palmer's appeal was dismissed.

Palmer v Tees Health Authority[26]

Stuart-Smith LJ

An additional reason why in my judgment in this case it is at least necessary for the victim to be identifiable (though as I have indicated it may not be sufficient) to establish proximity, is that it seems to me that the most effective way of providing protection would be to give warning to the victim, his or her parents or social services so that some protective measure can be made…

It may be a somewhat novel approach to the question of proximity, but it seems to me to be a relevant consideration to ask what the defendant could have done to avoid the danger, if the suggested precautions ie committal under s.3 of the Mental Health Act or treatment are likely to be of doubtful effectiveness, and the most effective precaution cannot be taken because the defendant does not know who to warn. This consideration suggests to me that the Court would be unwise to hold that there is sufficient proximity.

For these reasons I would uphold the judge's conclusion that there is no proximity between the defendants and Rosie. The claim in respect of her injury and death must fail and so must the claimant's brought on her own behalf.

There have been no cases in which claimants have sued medical professionals or their employers for failure to prevent a patient from causing injuries through dangerous driving or infectious disease, but it seems likely that the courts would find that injuring other road users or infecting close contacts were foreseeable consequences of the failure to provide reasonable care to the patient. Where injuries are caused by dangerous driving, it is very unlikely that there would be a sufficient relationship of proximity between the doctor and the injured third party.

---

[25] [1990] 2 AC 605.
[26] [1999] Lloyd's Rep Med 351 CA.

In the case of infectious or contagious disease, unless both the claimant's existence and her risk of infection were known to the doctor, it would again be difficult to argue that there was a sufficiently proximate relationship. Even if the claimant was identifiable in advance as someone likely to be infected by the patient, perhaps because the doctor knew about their sexual relationship, other considerations, such as the duty to protect patient confidentiality (considered in Chapter 7), might mean that it would not be fair, just, or reasonable to impose a duty to protect the claimant from infection.

It should, however, be noted that in *Osman v UK*,[27] the European Court of Rights held that state authorities could be under a duty to take positive action to protect a third party whose life is in danger where they knew or ought to have known of the existence of a real and immediate risk to the person's life. *Osman* involved a case against the police, and so its implications in the health context are unclear, especially since the police are not bound by the same duty of confidentiality as doctors.

(d) Medical examinations

Finally, could a doctor who has been employed to carry out a medical examination on behalf of a third party, such as an employer or an insurer, owe a duty of care to the person who is examined?

In *D v East Berkshire Community Health NHS Trust*, the Court of Appeal held that a doctor examining a child where there is a suspicion that the child has been abused undoubtedly owes the child a duty of care.

Lord Phillips MR[28]

Where child abuse is suspected the interests of the child are paramount: Given the obligation of the local authority to respect a child's convention rights, the recognition of a duty of care to the child on the part of those involved should not have a significantly adverse effect on the manner in which they perform their duties.

The case then went to the House of Lords, on the question of whether the doctor in such circumstances might *also* owe a duty of care to the parents. In *JD v East Berkshire Community Health NHS Trust* the House of Lords decided that this would create an unacceptable conflict of interest, and so any duty of care would be owed to the child alone.

JD v East Berkshire Community Health NHS Trust[29]

Lord Rodger

In considering whether it would be fair, just and reasonable to impose such a duty, a court has to have regard, however, to all the circumstances and, in particular, to the doctors' admitted duty to the children. The duty to the children is simply to exercise reasonable care and skill in diagnosing and treating any condition from which they may be suffering. In carrying out that duty the doctors have regard only to the interests of the children. Suppose, however, that

---

[27] (Case 87/1997/871/1083) [1999] 1 FLR 193.
[28] *D v East Berkshire Community Health NHS Trust* [2003] EWCA Civ 1151.
[29] [2005] UKHL 23.

they were also under a duty to the parents not to cause them psychiatric harm by concluding that they might have abused their child. Then, in deciding how to proceed, the doctors would always have to take account of the risk that they might harm the parents in this way. There would be not one but two sets of interests to be considered. Acting on, or persisting in, a suspicion of abuse might well be reasonable when only the child's interests were engaged, but unreasonable if the interests of the parents had also to be taken into account. Of its very nature, therefore, this kind of duty of care to the parents would cut across the duty of care to the children.

(b) BREACH

(1) What is the Standard of Care?

Having established (usually very straightforwardly) that she was owed a duty of care, the next stage for a claimant in a negligence action is to prove that the doctor breached her duty of care. In the law of tort generally, when deciding whether some precaution should have been taken against a foreseeable risk, the courts will weigh a number of factors, including (i) the magnitude of the risk; (ii) the gravity of the consequences should the risk materialize; (iii) the difficulty and cost of taking the precaution in question; and (iv) the utility of the defendant's conduct.

Hence, if the likelihood of the harm materializing is low, it may be reasonable not to take precautions against it. On the other hand, if the risk is high; or if its consequences are likely to be grave; or if it could be very easily eliminated, then a reasonable person might take steps to prevent the risk materializing. The standard of care must be assessed in terms of the individual patient, so if the doctor knows that her patient is unusually susceptible to a particular risk, then a reasonable doctor would take that into account.

The standard of care will be assessed at the time when the alleged negligence occurred; so if the claimant was injured during childbirth twenty years ago but only now brings an action for her injuries, the obstetrician will be judged by the standards of reasonable and responsible obstetric care twenty years ago. In *Roe v Minister of Health*, heard in 1954, the defendants had administered contaminated anaesthetic to the claimant in 1947, but at that time the risk of contamination was unknown. The Court of Appeal found that there had been no negligence, Denning LJ, as he then was, famously saying 'We must not look at the 1947 accident with 1954 spectacles.' In 1951, a leading textbook had warned against the practice which led to the accident in *Roe*, and Denning LJ therefore went on to say:

If the hospitals were to continue the practice after this warning, they could not complain if they were found guilty of negligence. But the warning had not been given at the time of this accident. Indeed, it was the extraordinary accident to these two men which first disclosed the danger. Nowadays it would be negligence not to realise the danger, but it was not then.[30]

Of course, the standard of care which can be expected of doctors is not that of the reasonable man or woman on the street; rather, it is the standard of the reasonable medical practitioner. In a negligence action, this means it will be necessary to establish that the doctor did not act as a reasonable doctor, skilled in the particular speciality, would have done. A GP

---

[30] *Roe v Minister of Health* [1954] 2 QB 66.

must act as a reasonable GP; a neurosurgeon as a reasonable neurosurgeon, and so on. If a GP were to attempt a specialist procedure, such as anaesthesia, she would be judged by the standard of a reasonable anaesthetist. If the GP is unable to meet this standard, then she might be found negligent for undertaking treatment beyond her competence.

The central problem in judging the standard of care is that reasonable doctors within the same area of expertise may disagree about how best to treat an individual patient. If differences of medical opinion are inevitable, how can the court decide which view should be preferred? As many law students will recall, the answer to this question has been dominated by what has become known as the *Bolam* test.

(a) The Bolam *test*

In *Bolam v Friern Hospital Management Committee* Mr Bolam, who was suffering from mental illness, was advised by a consultant at the defendants' hospital to undergo electro-convulsive therapy (ECT). He was not warned of the very small risk of fracture. He was not given relaxant drugs, nor was he physically restrained. Mr Bolam sustained a fractured hip during treatment. At the time, medical opinion on the desirability of warning patients of the risk of fracture and the use of relaxant drugs and physical restraint varied.

Bolam v Friern Hospital Management Committee[31]

McNair J (in his direction to the jury)

But where you get a situation which involves the use of some special skill or competence, then the test whether there has been negligence or not is not the test of the man on the top of a Clapham omnibus, because he has not got this special skill. The test is the standard of the ordinary skilled man exercising and professing to have that special skill. A man need not possess the highest skill at the risk of being found negligent. It is well established law that it is sufficient if he exercises the ordinary skill of an ordinary competent man exercising that particular art....

A doctor is not guilty of negligence if he has acted in accordance with a practice accepted as proper by a responsible body of medical men skilled in that particular art... Putting it the other way round, a doctor is not negligent, if he is acting in accordance with such a practice, merely because there is a body of opinion that takes a contrary view. At the same time, that does not mean that a medical man can obstinately and pig-headedly carry on with some old technique if it has been proved to be contrary to what is really substantially the whole of informed medical opinion. Otherwise you might get men today saying: 'I don't believe in anaesthetics. I don't believe in antiseptics. I am going to continue to do my surgery in the way it was done in the eighteenth century.' That clearly would be wrong.

Although *Bolam v Friern Hospital Management Committee* was itself only a first instance decision, and one of the last medical negligence cases to come before a jury, McNair J's formula was subsequently approved by the House of Lords.[32]

The *Bolam* test appears to treat medical negligence differently from other negligence actions. When deciding whether an employer or a driver has been negligent, the standard

---

[31] [1957] WLR 582.
[32] In *Whitehouse v Jordan* [1981] 1 WLR 246; *Maynard v West Midlands* [1984] 1 WLR 634.

of care is set by the *court* using the device of the reasonable man. When the defendant is a doctor, however, the standard of care has historically been set by *other doctors*, via the *Bolam* test. This judicial deference to medical opinion may have been partly due to the complexity of medical evidence, but might also be explained by a sense of professional solidarity, and by the high regard in which the medical profession has conventionally been held.

Maynard v West Midlands RHA, a case in which a patient sought to challenge her doctor's decision to carry out an invasive test for Hodgkin's disease, offers a good example of the judiciary's obvious reluctance to question the evidence of a 'responsible' medical practitioner.

Maynard v West Midlands RHA[33]

Lord Scarman

I have to say that a judge's 'preference' for one body of distinguished professional opinion to another also professionally distinguished is not sufficient to establish negligence in a practitioner whose actions have received the seal of approval of those whose opinions, truthfully expressed, honestly held, were not preferred.... For in the realm of diagnosis and treatment negligence is not established by preferring one respectable body of professional opinion to another.

In *Maynard*, notice that Lord Scarman suggests that the courts should defer to the opinions of expert witnesses if they are 'truthfully expressed, honestly held', which implies that the court would scrutinize only the *credibility* of witnesses, rather than the content of their evidence. For many years doctors were therefore able to escape liability if they could find one or more respectable expert witnesses prepared to say that they would have acted in the same way.

There had, however, been one notable exception to the court's apparent reluctance to review the substance, as opposed to just the credibility, of expert evidence. In *Hucks v Cole*, a case decided in 1968 but not widely reported until 1994, the Court of Appeal rejected the evidence of the defendant's four expert witnesses, and found that the doctor who had failed to prescribe penicillin to a pregnant woman, who developed puerperal fever as a result, had been negligent.

Hucks v Cole[34]

Sachs LJ

When the evidence shows that a lacuna in professional practice exists by which risks of grave danger are knowingly taken, then, however small the risks, the court must anxiously examine that lacuna—particularly if the risks can be easily and inexpensively avoided. If the court finds, on an analysis of the reasons given for not taking those precautions that, in the light of current professional knowledge, there is no proper basis for the lacuna, and that it is definitely not reasonable that those risks should have been taken, its function is to state that fact and where necessary to state that it constitutes negligence. In such a case the practice will no doubt thereafter be altered to the benefit of patients.

---

[33] [1984] 1 WLR 634.   [34] [1993] 4 Med LR 393.

On such occasions the fact that other practitioners would have done the same thing as the defendant practitioner is a very weighty matter to be put on the scales on his behalf; but it is not...conclusive. The court must be vigilant to see whether the reasons given for putting a patient at risk are valid in the light of any well-known advance in medical knowledge, or whether they stem from a residual adherence to out-of-date ideas—a tendency which in the present case may well have affected the views of at any rate one of the defendant's witnesses, who, at a considerable age, seemed not to have any particular respect for laboratory results...

Despite the fact that the risk could have been avoided by adopting a course that was easy, efficient and inexpensive, and which would have entailed only minimal chances of disadvantages to the patient, the evidence of the four defence experts to the effect that they and other responsible members of the medical profession would have taken the same risk in the same circumstances has naturally caused me to hesitate considerably on two points. Firstly, whether the failure of the defendant to turn over to penicillin treatment during the relevant period was unreasonable. On this, however, I was in the end fully satisfied that...failure to do this was not merely wrong but clearly unreasonable. The reasons given by the four experts do not to my mind stand up to analysis....

Doctor Cole knowingly took an easily avoidable risk which elementary teaching had instructed him to avoid; and the fact that others say they would have done the same neither ought to nor can in the present case excuse him in an action for negligence however sympathetic one may be to him.

(b) Bolitho: *A less deferential approach?*

Then in 1997, in *Bolitho v City and Hackney HA*, the House of Lords adopted a more robust, and potentially less deferential version of the *Bolam* test. Patrick Bolitho, who was two years old, had been admitted to hospital suffering from breathing difficulties. His condition deteriorated, and he suffered a cardiac arrest, leading to brain damage and subsequently to his death. The on-duty paediatric registrar did not see him, but even if she had, she said that she would not have intubated him. Intubation was the only procedure which could have prevented respiratory failure, but it was not without risks. The expert witnesses for each side expressed diametrically opposed views about whether a failure to intubate would have been reasonable. On the facts, the House of Lords held that the registrar had not breached her duty of care, but the case is important for Lord Browne-Wilkinson's comments on the circumstances in which the court would decide that there had been negligence, despite expert evidence agreeing with the defendant's course of action.

Bolitho v City and Hackney HA[35]

Lord Browne-Wilkinson

[I]n my view, the court is not bound to hold that a defendant doctor escapes liability for negligent treatment or diagnosis just because he leads evidence from a number of medical experts who are genuinely of opinion that the defendant's treatment or diagnosis accorded with sound medical practice...

[35] [1998] AC 232.

> In the vast majority of cases the fact that distinguished experts in the field are of a particular opinion will demonstrate the reasonableness of that opinion. In particular, where there are questions of assessment of the relative risks and benefits of adopting a particular medical practice, a reasonable view necessarily presupposes that the relative risks and benefits have been weighed by the experts in forming their opinions. But if, in a rare case, it can be demonstrated that the professional opinion is not capable of withstanding logical analysis, the judge is entitled to hold that the body of opinion is not reasonable or responsible.
>
> I emphasise that, in my view, it will very seldom be right for a judge to reach the conclusion that views genuinely held by a competent medical expert are unreasonable. The assessment of medical risks and benefits is a matter of clinical judgment which a judge would not normally be able to make without expert evidence. As the quotation from Lord Scarman makes clear, it would be wrong to allow such assessment to deteriorate into seeking to persuade the judge to prefer one of two views both of which are capable of being logically supported. It is only where a judge can be satisfied that the body of expert opinion cannot be logically supported at all that such opinion will not provide the bench mark by reference to which the defendant's conduct falls to be assessed.
>
> I turn to consider whether this is one of those rare cases. Like the Court of Appeal, in my judgment it plainly is not.

Following *Bolitho*, the views of expert witnesses must not only be honestly and sincerely held, but must also be *defensible*, in the sense that they must be 'capable of withstanding logical analysis'. What does this mean in practice?

It is impossible to tell whether the decision in *Bolitho* has led to more cases being settled in the claimants' favour, but in those cases that have reached the courts, it is evident that is still by no means easy to prove that a doctor, whose conduct has been endorsed by other expert witnesses, was in fact negligent. In *Wisniewski v Central Manchester Health Authority*, there was disagreement between the expert witnesses over the reasonableness of the defendant's failure to carry out a procedure to detect whether the baby's umbilical cord was wrapped around his neck during childbirth. Brooke LJ explained that:

> *Hucks v Cole* itself was unquestionably one of the rare cases which Lord Browne-Wilkinson had in mind....In my judgment the present case falls unquestionably on the other side of the line, and it is quite impossible for a court to hold that the views sincerely held by Mr Macdonald (an eminent consultant and an impressive witness) and Professor Thomas cannot logically be supported at all.[36]

There have, however, been a few 'rare cases' in which the courts have been willing to challenge the logic or defensibility of medical evidence. In *Reynolds v North Tyneside Health Authority*, Gross J found that the failure to examine the claimant's mother properly during childbirth—which led to the claimant's asphyxia, and resulting cerebral palsy—was one of those 'rare cases' in which the court should be prepared to disregard expert witnesses who claimed that they would have acted in the same way as the treating doctor.

---

[36] *Wisniewski v Central Manchester Health Authority* [1998] Lloyd's Rep Med 223 CA.

Reynolds v North Tyneside Health Authority[37]

Gross J

In the circumstances, it was logical to conduct an immediate VE [vaginal examination] on admission... If, notwithstanding the above, there was a contrary body of opinion that would not have conducted VEs when the foetal head was 3/5 palpable (without other complications), then this was one of those rare cases where the Court could and should conclude that such body of opinion was unreasonable, irresponsible, illogical and indefensible...

In any event, even if there was any such contrary practice, or body of opinion, then the only reason articulated in its support for not conducting an immediate VE, namely the risk of infection, does not withstand scrutiny. Where the sole reason relied upon in support of a practice is untenable, it follows (at least absent very special circumstances) that the practice itself is not defensible and lacks a logical basis. That is the case here. The suggested contrary practice (or body of opinion) is neither defensible nor logical. Having carefully examined the evidence, this is one of those rare cases where it is appropriate to conclude that there is a lacuna in the practice for which there is no proper basis. Put another way, insofar as any such contrary practice turns on the risk of infection, I would be unable to accept that its proponents had (i) properly directed their minds to the comparative risks and benefits and (ii) reached a defensible conclusion.

In *Marriott v West Midlands RHA*, Mr Marriott had suffered a head injury and had been unconscious for 20–30 minutes. During the following week he had been lethargic, had suffered from headaches, and had had no appetite. His GP, Dr Patel, attended him but did not think there was anything wrong with him. Four days later Mr Marriott's condition deteriorated and he lost consciousness. He had to undergo surgery to remove a haematoma, and was left permanently disabled. One expert witness supported Dr Patel's judgment, while another claimed that it had been negligent not to refer Mr Marriott back to the hospital. The Court of Appeal decided that the evidence given by the expert witness who defended the doctor's conduct could not be logically supported.

Marriott v West Midlands RHA[38]

Beldam LJ

The judge then identified the area of disagreement which lay, she said, in the element of discretion which a reasonably prudent doctor would exercise whether or not to advise readmission to hospital.

'Furthermore, whilst a Court must plainly be reluctant to depart from the opinion of an apparently careful and prudent general practitioner, I have concluded that, if there is a body of professional opinion which supports the course of leaving a patient who has some 7 days previously sustained a severe head injury at home in circumstances where he continues to complain of headaches, drowsiness etc, and where there continues to be a risk of the existence of an intracranial lesion which could cause a sudden and disastrous collapse, then such approach is not reasonably prudent. It may well be that, if in the vast majority of cases, the risk is very small. Nevertheless, the consequence, if things go wrong, are disastrous to the patient. In such

---

[37] [2002] Lloyd's Rep Med 459.   [38] [1999] Lloyds Rep Med 23.

circumstances, it is my view that the only reasonably prudent course in any case where a general practitioner remains of the view that there is a risk of an intracranial lesion such as to warrant the carrying out of neurological testing and the giving of further head injury instructions, then the only prudent course judged from the point of view of the patient is to re-admit for further testing and observation.'...

It was open to the judge to hold that, in the circumstances as she found them to have been, it could not be a reasonable exercise of a general practitioner's discretion to leave a patient at home and not to refer him back to hospital. Accordingly, I would dismiss the appeal.

In the next extract, Lord Woolf (writing extra-judicially) suggests that there has, since *Bolitho*, been a trend away from the excessive deference of the past, and he explores some of the reasons for this shift.

Lord Woolf[39]

[U]ntil recently the courts treated the medical profession with excessive deference, but recently the position has changed. It is my judgment that it has changed for the better...

What is it that has caused the change? I would identify the following causes:

First, today the courts have a less deferential approach to those in authority. The growth in judicial review has resulted in the judiciary becoming accustomed to setting aside decisions of those engaged on behalf of the Crown in public affairs, from a Minister of the Crown downwards. By comparison the medical profession and the Health Service were small beer.

Secondly, while there has been the huge growth in the scale of litigation, including actions brought against hospital trusts and the medical profession, the proportion of successful medical negligence claims in England is put at only 17 per cent. The courts became increasingly conscious of the difficulties which bona fide claimants had in successfully establishing claims.

Thirdly, there had developed an increasing awareness of patients' rights. The public's expectations of what the profession should achieve have grown...The move to a rights-based society has fundamentally changed the behaviour of the courts.

Fourthly, the 'automatic presumption of beneficence' has been dented by a series of well-publicised scandals...Almost daily there are reports in the media suggesting that there is something amiss with our health treatment.

Fifthly, our courts were aware that courts at the highest level of other Commonwealth jurisdictions, particularly Canada and Australia, were rejecting the approach of the English courts. They were subjecting the actions of the medical profession to a closer scrutiny than the English courts...

Sixthly, medical negligence litigation was revealed as being a disaster area. The Health Service and the insurance industry had to be required to change their approach to handling litigation. They appeared to consider that every case was worth fighting...The annual cost of medical negligence litigation is estimated to be at least equivalent to building, running and staffing one new hospital annually. The litigation was particularly bitter and often singularly unproductive...

Seventhly, recently a series of cases have come before the courts that raised fundamental questions of medical ethics....The courts, having had to struggle with issues such as

---

[39] 'Are the Courts Excessively Deferential to the Medical Profession?' (2001) 9 Medical Law Review 1–16.

these, were prepared to adopt a more proactive approach to resolving conflicts as to more traditional medical issues.

Eighthly, a final influence that will be of increasing importance and probably played a part in the case of some of the factors I have already mention was first the proposal for and subsequently the incorporation into English domestic law of the European Convention of Human Rights.

Harvey Teff argues that the courts' increasing willingness to scrutinize the *content* of expert evidence is especially welcome, given lawyers' tendency to treat expert witnesses as 'hired hands'.

Harvey Teff[40]

Reassertion at the highest level of the court's role in scrutinizing professional practice is welcome, not least because of current concerns about the dynamics of providing expert evidence for the purposes of adversarial litigation....

A very recent survey of 500 expert witnesses revealed that 70% of them said that they had been asked by lawyers to modify their report or opinion in some way and that around one-third had done so. Most of the resulting amendments would have taken the form of innocent clarification and correction of factual errors in reports. However, about a quarter of the respondents' recorded comments are more equivocal, in some instances acknowledging the alteration of opinions...Despite the requirement 'that expert evidence presented to the court should be and should be seen to be the independent product of the expert uninfluenced as to form or content by the exigencies of litigation', it remains the case that 'expert witnesses instructed on behalf of parties to litigation often tend...to espouse the cause of those instructing them to a greater or lesser extent, on occasion becoming more partisan than the parties'...

One prominent medicolegal authority has bluntly declared that '*Bolam* will only work fairly if the use of hired hands as defence medical experts is eliminated. It would then be possible to talk of a responsible body of medical opinion.'

(c) The role of guidelines

In England, the NHS Litigation Authority (whose role we consider below) operates a Clinical Negligence Scheme for Trusts (CNST), which sets its own approved risk management standards, against which health care providers are assessed. The CNST operates as a quasi-insurance system for NHS Trusts, so there are obvious economic incentives for Trusts to ensure compliance with the NHSLA risk management standards.

In addition, the Royal Colleges of Medicine routinely issue best practice guidance, and the National Institute of Health and Clinical Excellence (whose role we considered in the previous chapter) has developed treatment protocols for a number of conditions. Unsurprisingly, given the wealth of evidence of best practice which now exists, courts increasingly rely on professional guidance when determining the standard of care.

---

[40] 'The Standard of Care in Medical Negligence—Moving on from Bolam?' (1998) 18 Oxford Journal of Legal Studies 473–84.

This does not necessarily mean that any doctor who deviates from clinical guidance will be found negligent if something goes wrong. Guidelines are, by definition, not mandatory. Nevertheless, although evidence of a departure from accepted practice is not necessarily determinative, as we can see from the comments of Field J in *Richards v Swansea NHS Trust*, it may help a claimant who is seeking to prove negligence.

Richards v Swansea NHS Trust[41]

Field J

In my judgement once the decision had been taken to deliver Jac by emergency Caesarean section, a decision which in the circumstances a reasonably competent obstetric registrar was entitled to make, the defendant owed a duty of care to Jac to deliver him as quickly as possible with the aim of trying to deliver him within 30 minutes... This is the approach in the NSCSAR and the NICE/RCOG Caesarean section guideline and I am satisfied that the guidance set out in these reports reflects the approach that was operative in 1996.

In the next extract, Margaret Brazier and José Miola argue that increased availability of professional guidance, coupled with the decision in *Bolitho*, indicate that the courts may be not only more willing to challenge medical evidence, but also will be better equipped to do so.

Margaret Brazier and José Miola[42]

Most importantly, *Bolitho* has been decided at a time when other developments also point to a revolution in the way medical malpractice is judged. Medicine itself is changing with practitioners increasingly evaluating their own practice and seeking to develop evidence-based medicine. The traditional guardians of clinical standards, the Royal Colleges of Medicine, have over the last decade become more and more proactive, issuing guidelines about good practice with reference to treatments and procedures... [T]he National Institute for Clinical Excellence (NICE) has been established to develop guidelines for good practice, not just in the context of new drug treatments, but in a much wider sphere of reviewing all forms of therapies and procedures.... The judge confronted by individual experts who disagree about good practice will in certain cases be able to refer to something approaching a 'gold standard'....

The judge will have access to material, independent of the particular dispute before him, enabling him to assess the logic of the parties' cases. *Bolitho*, plus more ready access to clinical guidelines, suggests a more proactive role for judges assessing expert evidence. Nor will clinical guidelines necessarily be the only source of judicial guidance on the logic of the evidence presented by the parties. The burgeoning literature on medical developments, often presented in a style comprehensible to lay people, may also be resorted to much more frequently in litigation. *Bolitho* demands that doctors explain their practice. Doctors themselves are developing tools which will enable judges to review those explanations.

---

[41] [2007] EWHC 487 (QB).
[42] 'Bye-Bye Bolam: A Medical Litigation Revolution?' (2000) 8 Medical Law Review 85–114.

In contrast, others have argued that guidelines are meant to have general application and might not take the particular patient's circumstances into account.[43] In the next extract, Harvey Teff expresses some reservations about the move towards a 'guideline mentality'.

Harvey Teff[44]

Yet as [clinical guidelines] do become more 'authoritative', the perceived epitome of 'best practice', they could, even without displacing *Bolam*, create pressure to reverse the onus of proof, requiring the doctor to establish that failure to adhere to guidelines was not negligent. Granting such a high level of putative authority to guidelines would, it is submitted, be undesirable. They are not designed *as* legal rules. Depending on their provenance, they may offer a counsel of perfection that is locally unattainable, or be too undemanding, perhaps unduly influenced by considerations of cost-containment. Equally, there are often reasonable grounds for arguing that seemingly controlling guidelines, derived from population studies, are either not meant to, or did not in fact, cover the particular clinical circumstances.

In view of such inevitable limitations, it would be inappropriate for guidelines to become the sole basis of liability, and imprudent to make them a key, or even, *prima facie*, determinant, especially if this would encourage more people to initiate misconceived claims when guidelines had not been followed...

If EBM [evidence based medicine] becomes the 'new deity in clinical medicine', it could herald the dominance of a new kind of medical paternalism—'*the guideline knows best'*.

Ash Samanta *et al.* agree, and suggest some further limitations with using guidelines to determine the standard of care.

Ash Samanta, Michelle M. Mello, Charles Foster, John Tingle, and Jo Samanta[45]

Guidelines have a number of inherent limitations. There is a danger in applying the generalised prescription of guidelines in a rigid fashion to every patient...There is always a need for flexibility in patient care, and although guidelines are designed to promote best practice, in any given clinical episode, the slavish adherence to guidelines may not be the best practice for that particular patient. In medical practice, many situations arise where the art of identifying patient problems and the application of clinical acumen to individual patients' needs remain removed from the science and technological advances of the discipline...Additionally, guidelines are only as good as the underlying empirical evidence and the appropriateness of the conclusions reached on the basis of synthesis of evidence. The validity of guidelines may be undermined by weak research data as well as confounding factors and biases emanating from misconceptions, personal experiences and beliefs of the developers....

Decisions reflected in some guidance might be motivated predominantly by economic considerations. NICE, for instance, has a specific remit to ensure the cost-effectiveness of treatment or interventional modalities, and its guidance is frequently against

---

[43] Brian Hurwitz, 'How does Evidence Based Guidance Influence Determinations of Medical Negligence?' (2004) 329 British Medical Journal 1024–28.

[44] 'Clinical Guidelines, Negligence and Medical Practice' in M Freeman and A Lewis (eds), *Current Legal Issues: Law and Medicine* vol 3 (OUP: Oxford, 2000) 67–8, 79.

[45] 'The Role of Clinical Guidelines in Medical Negligence Iitigation: A Shift from the Bolam Standard' (2006) Medical Law Review 321.

clinical interventions on the basis of cost.... If guidelines are perceived as a tool for rationing healthcare, it is less likely that they will be used by the court as a determinant of the legal standard.

Another inherent problem with guidelines is that they may be proven wrong over time.

(2) Is the Standard of Care Fixed?

It is normally said that the standard of care in tort law is objective. Many law students will recall the case of *Nettleship v Weston*,[46] in which a learner driver was found to be negligent for failing to meet the standard of care that would be expected of a reasonably experienced driver. Does this mean that the standard of care in medical negligence is fixed and objectively determined, or might it vary according to the circumstances? In the next sections we look at whether it would be reasonable to expect a lower standard of care in four different situations:

- if resources are scarce;
- if the doctor is treating the patient in an emergency;
- if the doctor is inexperienced; or
- if the doctor is practising alternative medicine.

(a) Scarce resources

In determining what standard of care would be reasonable, should the court take into account the scarcity of resources, discussed at length in the previous chapter? Clearly within the NHS, it is not always possible to provide the optimum standard of care to everybody. This political reality makes judging the standard of care in negligence especially difficult. If less than perfect care is inevitable, how do courts tell when treatment has failed to meet an acceptable standard?

In *Knight v Home Office*, insufficient resources did not offer a complete defence to an allegation of negligence, but were nonetheless relevant to the standard of care a mentally ill prisoner could expect in the hospital wing of Brixton prison. Failure to put him on continuous observation meant that he had the opportunity to hang himself. Pill J decided that the prison doctors had not been negligent.

Knight v Home Office[47]

Pill J

It is not a complete defence for a government department any more than it would be for a private individual or organisation to say that no funds are available for additional safety measures.

I cannot accept what was at one time submitted by counsel for the defendants that the plaintiffs' only remedy would be a political one. To take an extreme example, if the evidence was that no funds were available to provide any medical facilities in a large prison there would be a failure to achieve the standard of care appropriate for prisoners.

---

[46] [1971] 2 QB 691.   [47] [1990] 3 All ER 237.

> In making the decision as to the standard to be demanded the court must, however, bear in mind as one factor that resources available for the public service are limited and that the allocation of resources is a matter for Parliament.
>
> I am unable to accept the submission that the law requires the standard of care in a prison hospital to be as high as the standard of care for all purposes in a psychiatric hospital outside prison. I am unable to accept that the practices in a prison hospital are to be judged in all respects by the standard appropriate to a psychiatric hospital outside prison. There may be circumstances in which the standard of care in a prison falls below that which would be expected in a psychiatric hospital without the prison authority being negligent.

As Pill J makes clear, a prison is undoubtedly under a duty to provide a basic minimum level of medical care to prisoners. *Brooks v Home Office* was a case involving a remand prisoner with a high-risk pregnancy, and Garland J held that she was entitled to the same standard of care as any other pregnant woman. In this case, there had been a five-day delay in seeking specialist advice when a scan revealed that one of the prisoner's twins was not growing normally. Garland J held that this fell below the standard of care which could reasonably be expected. However, a two-day delay before admission to hospital would have been permissible and, as the baby had died within that period, the doctor's breach of his duty of care had not caused the baby's stillbirth.

Garland J[48]

> I cannot regard Knight as authority for the proposition that the plaintiff should not, while detained in Holloway, be entitled to expect the same level of antenatal care, both for herself and her unborn infants, as if she were at liberty, subject of course to the constraints of having to be escorted and, to some extent, movement being retarded by those requirements.

Similarly, in *Bull v Devon AHA*,[49] discussed earlier, the Court of Appeal held that a certain minimum standard of care should be met regardless of the hospital's financial constraints. It was no excuse to a failure to provide this *minimum* standard of care that the hospital had limited resources.

Let us take the common example of having to wait to be seen in a busy accident and emergency department. It would not be negligent to expect people with minor injuries to wait for a few hours, but a similar failure to attend to someone who had had a heart attack would fail to meet this basic minimum standard of care, and the fact that the hospital was operating with limited resources would offer no excuse.

(b) Emergencies

In an emergency, it might be difficult for doctors to provide the same standard of care as might normally be expected. Following a major disaster, such as a train crash or bomb blast, hospitals may be overwhelmed with casualties. A doctor who is off duty may stop at the roadside to assist the victims of a road traffic accident, when lack of equipment will inevitably compromise the standard of care that she can provide. In such circumstances, would it be reasonable to expect a lower standard of care than normal?

---

[48] *Brooks v Home Office* [1999] 2 FLR 33 QBD.   [49] [1993] 4 Med LR 117 (CA).

Off-duty doctors in the UK are not under a legal duty to offer assistance if they come upon a medical emergency, but a failure to assist in an emergency might prompt disciplinary action by the General Medical Council, whose guidance on the duties of a doctor states that: 'In an emergency, wherever it may arise, you must offer assistance, taking account of your own safety, your competence, and the availability of other options for care.'[50]

Once a doctor has undertaken to offer care to an injured person, she undoubtedly assumes a duty of care. But since what is expected of doctors is 'reasonable care', it is appropriate to take into account the situation in which the doctor is administering treatment. It would, for example, not be reasonable to expect a doctor who has been called out to the site of a train crash to provide the level of care that would be available in a well-equipped intensive care unit. Indeed, in *Wilsher v Essex Area Health Authority*, discussed below, Mustill LJ said:

> I accept that full allowance must be made for the fact that certain aspects of treatment may have to be carried out in what one witness...called 'battle conditions'. An emergency may overburden resources and, if an individual is forced by circumstances to do too many things at once, the fact that he does one of them incorrectly should not lightly be taken as negligence.[51]

(c) Inexperience

Should a doctor's inexperience affect the standard of care which can reasonably be expected of her? On the one hand, doctors have to learn by experience, and it would seem harsh for junior doctors to be potentially liable in negligence for their inability to reach the standard of care that would be expected from a more experienced doctor. But on the other hand, if the standard of care patients are entitled to expect fluctuates according to the doctor's experience, patients would be well advised to refuse to be treated by anyone who is not highly experienced, and the system through which junior doctors learn 'on the job' would break down.

This issue arose in *Wilsher v Essex AHA*, where a baby was deprived of oxygen after a junior doctor mistakenly inserted a catheter into a vein rather than an artery. Although the junior doctor was ultimately exonerated because he had taken the reasonable step of asking a registrar for assistance, a majority of the Court of Appeal held that the standard of care should not be lower for inexperienced doctors.[52]

Wilsher v Essex Area Health Authority[53]

Glidewell LJ

In my view, the law requires the trainee or learner to be judged by the same standard as his more experienced colleagues. If it did not, inexperience would frequently be urged as a defence to an action for professional negligence.

---

[50] Good Medical Practice (GMC: London, 2006) para 11.

[51] *Wilsher v Essex Area Health Authority* [1987] 1 QB 730.

[52] It was only on the issue of causation that appeal was made to the House of Lords, and this judgment is considered below. It is the Court of Appeal judgment in *Wilsher* which determined whether the junior doctor had breached his duty of care.

[53] [1987] 1 QB 730.

If this test appears unduly harsh in relation to the inexperienced, I should add that, in my view, the inexperienced doctor called on to exercise a specialist skill will, as part of that skill, seek the advice and help of his superiors when he does or may need it. If he does seek such help, he will often have satisfied the test, even though he may himself have made a mistake. It is for this reason that I agree that Dr Wiles was not negligent. He made a mistake in inserting the catheter into a vein, and a second mistake in not recognising the signs that he had done so on the X-ray. But, having done what he thought right, he asked Dr Kawa, the senior registrar, to check what he had done, and Dr Kawa did so.

(d) Complementary and alternative medicine

How should the courts determine the standard of care, which can reasonably be expected of practitioner of complementary or alternative medicine? Should a Chinese herbalist be judged against the reasonable practitioner of Chinese herbal medicine, or should he be expected to meet the same standard of care as an orthodox clinician? Interestingly, there have been virtually no reported cases brought by patients who claim that they have been injured as a result of alternative therapies. This is not necessarily because such treatments have a high level of safety; rather, it is possible that patients who believe that they have been left worse off after resorting to alternative medical treatments are less likely to complain, and in particular may be reluctant to consult a conventional doctor about their symptoms.

The issue has arisen only once in the UK, in *Shakoor v Situ*. Mr Situ, a practitioner of traditional Chinese herbal medicine (CHM), had been consulted by Abdul Shakoor about a skin condition for which the only orthodox medical treatment was surgery. After taking nine doses of the herbal remedy, Mr Shakoor suffered acute liver failure and died. It had been established that, on the balance of probabilities, his death was probably caused by the remedy, but Bernard Livesey QC rejected his widow's claim that Mr Situ had been negligent.

Shakoor v Situ[54]

Bernard Livesey QC

Is he to be judged by the standards of the reasonably careful practitioner of CHM or according to the standards applicable to orthodox medical practitioners in this country? There is not any authority on this point in this country or, so far as I am aware after appropriate searches, in other common law jurisdictions....

The Chinese herbalist, for example, does not hold himself out as a practitioner of orthodox medicine. More particularly, the patient has usually had the choice of going to an orthodox practitioner but has rejected him in favour of the alternative practitioner for reasons personal and best known to himself and almost certainly at some personal financial cost... The decision of the patient may be enlightened and informed or based on ignorance and superstition. Whatever the basis of his decision, it seems to me that the fact that the patient has chosen to reject the orthodox and prefer the alternative practitioner is something important which must be taken into account. Why should he later be able to complain that the alternative practitioner has not provided him with skill and care in accordance with the standards of those orthodox practitioners whom he has rejected?

[54] [2001] 1 WLR 410.

> On the other hand, it is of course obviously true to say that the alternative practitioner has chosen to practice in this country alongside a system of orthodox medicine and must abide by the laws and standards prevailing in this country...
>
> [W]here he prescribes a remedy which is taken by a patient it is not enough to say that the remedy is traditional and believed not to be harmful, he has a duty to ensure that the remedy is not actually or potentially harmful...An alternative practitioner who prescribes a remedy must take steps to satisfy himself that there has not been any adverse report in such journals on the remedy which ought to affect the use he makes of it. That is not to say that he must take a range of publications himself. It should be enough if he subscribes to an 'association' which arranges to search the relevant literature and promptly report any material publication to him. The relevant literature will be that which would be taken by an orthodox practitioner practising at the level of speciality at which the alternative practitioner holds himself out. If he does not subscribe to such an association the practitioner will not have discharged his duty to inform himself properly and may act at his peril.
>
> Accordingly, a claimant may succeed in an action against an alternative practitioner for negligently prescribing a remedy either by calling an expert in the speciality in question to assert and prove that the defendant has failed to exercise the skill and care appropriate to that art...Alternatively, the claimant may prove that the prevailing standard of skill and care 'in that art' is deficient in this country having regard to risks which were not and should have been taken into account....
>
> In these circumstances, I find that the defendant was not in breach of his duty to the deceased. I am satisfied that he acted in accordance with the standard of care appropriate to TCHM as properly practised in accordance with the standards required in this country. The fact that the deceased died in consequence of the medication, as the doctors have on a balance of probability agreed, is a tragic accident but not the fault of the defendant.

In short, there would seem to be two ways in which a claimant might establish negligence on the part of an alternative medical practitioner. First, she could attempt to prove that the defendant did not meet the standard of care for the reasonable practitioner of that particular 'art'. Secondly, even if the defendant did act as a reasonable alternative practitioner, it would still be open to the claimant to establish that the prevailing standard of care in that 'art' is itself deficient, on the grounds that it fails to take proper account of published evidence of toxicity.

(3) Proof of Breach

It is for the claimant to prove on the balance of probabilities that the defendant has breached her duty of care. The maxim *res ipsa loquitur* (the thing speaks for itself) allows the courts, in certain circumstances, to draw an inference that the defendant was negligent. There is some dispute over whether it reverses the burden of proof, such that it is for the defendant to prove that she was *not* negligent, or alternatively whether the burden of proof remains with the claimant, but the facts appear to give rise to an inference of negligence, which might be rebutted by evidence that the defendant had not in fact been negligent. The better view is that the burden of proof remains with the claimant, but there is, of course, little difference in practice between asking the defendant to justify actions, which have raised an inference of negligence, and reversing the burden of proof.

The maxim will apply where an accident would not normally happen unless someone had been negligent. An example might be if a surgical instrument is left inside the patient's body after surgery. It would be difficult to think of circumstances in which this had occurred, but no one had breached their duty of care towards the patient. Similarly, if a patient went into hospital in order to have her gangrenous right leg amputated, and her healthy left leg was amputated instead, again the inference might reasonably be drawn that the surgeon had been negligent.

Essentially then, *res ipsa loquitur* is just an elaborate way of saying that there will occasionally be circumstances in which a judge would be entitled to find that the defendant had been negligent without evidence from expert witnesses confirming that the defendant's actions fell below the appropriate standard of care. It will apply then only to very simple and unusual cases where negligence can readily be inferred by a lay person, from the facts themselves.

Hobhouse LJ's judgment in *Ratcliffe v Plymouth and Torbay Health Authority* offers a helpful explanation of the limited application *res ipsa loquitur* is likely to have in actions against doctors. Mr Ratcliffe had undergone an operation on his ankle, and had been given a spinal anaesthetic to relieve his post-operative pain. The operation itself was a success, but he was left with a serious neurological defect, causing severe pain, a total loss of sensation in his leg and penile numbness. He contended that this raised an inference that the spinal anaesthetic had been given negligently. His claim was dismissed by Mantell J, and the Court of Appeal dismissed his appeal.

Ratcliffe v Plymouth and Torbay Health Authority[55]

Hobhouse LJ

Res ipsa loquitur is no more than a convenient Latin phrase used to describe the proof of facts which are sufficient to support an inference that a defendant was negligent and therefore to establish a prima facie case against him. . . . The burden of proving the negligence of the defendant remains throughout upon the plaintiff. The burden is on the plaintiff at the start of the trial and, absent an admission by the defendant, is still upon the plaintiff at the conclusion of the trial . . . The plaintiff may or may not have needed to call evidence to establish a prima facie case. The admitted facts may suffice for that purpose . . .

If the facts of the present case had been that the plaintiff had gone into the operating theatre to have an arthrodesis to his right ankle and had come out of the theatre with his right ankle untouched and an arthrodesis to his left ankle, clearly no expert evidence would be required to support an inference of negligence on the part of the defendants. 'In the ordinary course of things', that does not happen if those conducting the operation have used proper care. . . . In practice, save in the most extreme cases of blatant negligence, the plaintiff will have to adduce at least some expert evidence to get his case upon its feet. . . .

Res ipsa loquitur is not a principle of law: it does not relate to, or raise, any presumption. It is merely a guide to help to identify when a prima facie case is being made out. Where expert and factual evidence has been called on both sides at a trial, its usefulness will normally have long since been exhausted.

In *Lillywhite v University College London Hospitals' NHS Trust*,[56] a case we consider again in chapter 14, a Professor of Obstetrics had viewed a scan and recorded the presence of brain structures which were not, in fact, there. While not formally applying the maxim of

[55] [1998] Lloyd's Rep Med 168.   [56] [2005] EWCA Civ 146.

res ipsa loquitur, Latham LJ held that the court was required 'to focus with some care on the explanation given by a defendant to displace that which would otherwise be the inevitable inference from the claimant's case that negligence has been established'.

(c) CAUSATION

Once a claimant has established that the doctor has breached her duty of care, she still has to prove that it was this breach of duty that caused her injuries. In practice, causation poses particular difficulties in medical negligence actions because there may be at least two possible causes of the patient's injury: the doctor's actions and the patient's pre-existing condition. Where there are multiple causes, proving causation on the balance of probabilities is especially problematic. The patient's health may have deteriorated even if the care she received was non-negligent, so often what has been lost is the *chance* of being restored to health. The courts are therefore often forced to speculate about what *might* have happened if the doctor had not in fact breached her duty of care.

(1) The 'but for' Test

The standard test for causation is often referred to as the 'but for' test: but for the defendant's negligence, would the claimant have suffered the injuries in question? In the medical context, this means that the claimant must show that their injury was caused by the doctor's negligence, rather than something that would have happened anyway. It is not enough to show both that the doctor breached her duty of care, and that the claimant's health has deteriorated; rather, there must be a *causal link* between these two facts.

A case where the application of the 'but for' test was straightforward was *Barnett v Chelsea and Kensington Hospital Management Committee*, the case involving a man who died of arsenic poisoning shortly after admission to hospital.

Barnett v Chelsea and Kensington Hospital Management Committee[57]

Nield J

It remains to consider whether it is shown that the deceased's death was caused by this negligence or whether, as the defendants have said, the deceased must have died in any event....

There has been put before me a timetable which, I think, is of much importance. The deceased attended at the casualty department at 8.05 or 8.10 a.m. If Dr Banerjee had got up and dressed and come to see the three men and examined them and decided to admit them, the deceased could not have been in bed in a ward before 11 a.m. I accept Dr. Goulding's evidence that an intravenous drip would not have been set up before 12 noon...Dr. Lockett, dealing with this, said 'If [the deceased] had not been treated until after 12 noon the chances of survival were not good'...

If the principal condition is one of enzyme disturbance—as I am of the view that it was here—then the only method of treatment which is likely to succeed is the use of the specific or antidote which is commonly called B.A.L. Dr. Gouding said this in the course of his evidence:

---

[57] [1969] 1 QB 428.

> The only way to deal with this is to use the specific B.A.L. I see no reasonable prospect of the deceased being given B.A.L. before the time at which he died...
>
> I regard that evidence as very moderate, and that it might be a true assessment of the situation to say that there was no chance of B.A.L. being administered before the death of the deceased.
>
> For these reasons, I find that the plaintiff has failed to establish, on the grounds of probability, that the defendants' negligence caused the death of the deceased.

Two different sorts of cases raise particularly difficult issues of causation in the medical context. The first is where there is some uncertainty about whether, as a matter of past fact, the claimant's injuries were caused by the defendant's negligence. The second are so-called 'loss of a chance' cases, where there is uncertainty about hypothetical future events.

Taking evidential uncertainty first, unlike the *Barnett* case, it is not always possible to be certain what would have happened to the claimant if they had, in fact, been properly treated. In medical cases there will often be multiple possible causes, which means that it will be particularly difficult to prove, on the balance of probabilities, which one caused the claimant's injuries. In *Wilsher v Essex Area Health Authority*,[58] there were five possible causes of Martin Wilsher's near blindness, one of which was the fact that he had negligently been given excess oxygen on two occasions. The House of Lords found that he had failed to prove that it was the excess oxygen that caused his injuries. Lord Bridge stated that:

> [W]hether we like it or not, the law, which only Parliament can change, requires proof of fault causing damage as the basis of liability in tort. We should do society nothing but disservice if we made the forensic process still more unpredictable and hazardous by distorting the law to accommodate the exigencies of what may seem hard cases.

Loss of a chance cases arise when the doctor's breach of duty deprives the patient of the opportunity of recovery. In *Hotson v East Berkshire AHA* the claimant had injured his hip in a fall when he was thirteen years old. He was taken to hospital, where his injury was not correctly diagnosed, and was sent home. After five days of severe pain, he was taken back to hospital, where a proper diagnosis was made and he was given emergency treatment. He was, however, left permanently disabled. At the trial, the judge found that even if the claimant's injury had been diagnosed and treated immediately, there was still a 75 per cent risk of his disability developing, but that the breach of duty had turned that risk into an inevitability, thus denying him a 25 per cent chance of a good recovery. The judge awarded the claimant 25 per cent of the full value of the damages awardable for the claimant's disability. The Court of Appeal affirmed the judge's decision, but the Health Authority successfully appealed to the House of Lords.

Hotson v East Berkshire AHA[59]

Lord Bridge

Unless the plaintiff proved on a balance of probabilities that the delayed treatment was at least a material contributory cause of the avascular necrosis he failed on the issue of causation and no question of quantification could arise....

---

[58] [1988] 1 AC 1074.   [59] [1987] 1 AC 750.

> The upshot is that the appeal must be allowed on the narrow ground that the plaintiff failed to establish a cause of action in respect of the avascular necrosis and its consequences.
>
> **Lord Ackner**
>
> I have sought to stress that this case was a relatively simple case concerned with the proof of causation, on which the plaintiff failed, because he was unable to prove, on the balance of probabilities, that his deformed hip was caused by the authority's breach of duty in delaying over a period of five days a proper diagnosis and treatment. Where causation is in issue, the judge decides that issue on the balance of the probabilities....
>
> Once liability is established, on the balance of probabilities, the loss which the plaintiff has sustained is payable in full. It is not discounted by reducing his claim by the extent to which he has failed to prove his case with 100% certainty.

According to *Hotson*, the courts must be satisfied that it is *more likely than not* that the claimant's injuries would have been avoided if the doctor had not been negligent. If there is a 55 per cent chance that the patient would have made a complete recovery if she had received non-negligent treatment, she can recover in full, whereas if there is a 45 per cent chance of recovery, her claim fails because she has not proved on the balance of probabilities that her injuries were caused by the defendant's negligence. The problem with framing the issue in this way is that the courts are engaged in an inevitably hypothetical inquiry about what *might have happened* if the doctor had not acted as she did, and this sort of speculation is not well suited to precise quantification in percentage terms.

In *Hutchinson v Epsom and St Helier NHS Trust*,[60] the question for the judge was whether a heavy drinker would have stopped drinking if he had been told he had end-stage liver disease. On the evidence of his wife, the judge found that he would have done. For obvious reasons, it is impossible to judge the truth or falsity of this finding.

In the non-medical case of *Fairchild v Glenhaven Funeral Services*,[61] the House of Lords adopted a rather more flexible approach to causation, and compensated employees for the lost chance of not contracting mesothelioma from exposure to asbestos. However, this is probably of limited relevance to claimants in clinical negligence actions. In *Fairchild*, the House of Lords expressly approved the more restrictive approach to causation in *Wilsher*.

Fairchild v Glenhaven Funeral Services[62]

> **Lord Bingham**
>
> It is plain, in my respectful opinion, that the House was right to allow the defendants' appeal in *Wilsher* for the reasons which the Vice-Chancellor had given and which the House approved. It is one thing to treat an increase of risk as equivalent to the making of a material contribution where a single noxious agent is involved, but quite another where any one of a number of noxious agents may equally probably have caused the damage.

---

[60] [2002] EWHC 2363.   [61] Applied in *Barker v Corus* [2006] UKHL 20.
[62] [2002] UKHL 22.

Lord Hoffmann

[T]he political and economic arguments involved in the massive increase in the liability of the National Health Service... are far more complicated than the reasons... for imposing liability upon an employer who has failed to take simple precautions.

Certainly in *Gregg v Scott*, a case in which a GP's failure to diagnose a lymphoma (a type of cancer) and refer Malcolm Gregg to a specialist, reduced his chance of survival from 42 per cent to 25 per cent, a majority of the House of Lords confirmed that *Fairchild* did not affect the requirement that the claimant must prove causation on the balance of probabilities.

Gregg v Scott[63]

Lord Hoffmann

In effect, the Appellant submits that the exceptional rule in Fairchild should be generalised and damages awarded in all cases in which the defendant may have caused an injury and has increased the likelihood of the injury being suffered....

It should first be noted that adopting such a rule would involve abandoning a good deal of authority. The rule which the House is asked to adopt is the very rule which it rejected in Wilsher's case. Yet Wilsher's case was expressly approved by the House in Fairchild. Hotson too would have to be overruled. Furthermore, the House would be dismantling all the qualifications and restrictions with which it so recently hedged the Fairchild exception. There seem to me to be no new arguments or change of circumstances which could justify such a radical departure from precedent...

[A] wholesale adoption of possible rather than probable causation as the criterion of liability would be so radical a change in our law as to amount to a legislative act. It would have enormous consequences for insurance companies and the National Health Service. In company with my noble and learned friends Lord Phillips of Worth Matravers and Baroness Hale of Richmond, I think that any such change should be left to Parliament.

Lord Phillips

My Lords, it seems to me that there is a danger, if special tests of causation are developed piecemeal to deal with perceived injustices in particular factual situations, that the coherence of our common law will be destroyed.

Under our law as it is at present, and subject to the exception in Fairchild, a claimant will only succeed if, on balance of probability the negligence is the cause of the injury. If there is a possibility, but not a probability, that the negligence caused the injury, the claimant will recover nothing in respect of the breach of duty....

The complications of this case have persuaded me that it is not a suitable vehicle for introducing into the law of clinical negligence the right to recover damages for the loss of a chance of a cure. Awarding damages for the reduction of the prospect of a cure, when the long term result of treatment is still uncertain, is not a satisfactory exercise. Where medical

---

[63] [2005] UKHL 2.

treatment has resulted in an adverse outcome and negligence has increased the chance of that outcome, there may be a case for permitting a recovery of damages that is proportionate to the increase in the chance of the adverse outcome. That is not a case that has been made out on the present appeal.

It is worth noting the final paragraph in the above extract from Lord Phillips' judgment. By the time the case reached the House of Lords, Mr Gregg's chance of survival looked rather better than 25 per cent, and in such circumstances, Lord Phillips thought that he should not be able to recover for the loss of a chance of a cure. On a different set of facts, Lord Phillips implies that he would not, in principle, be hostile to such claims. Given this, and the powerful speeches from the two dissenting judges, Lord Hope and Lord Nicholls (see below), it is possible that, in the future, the courts will revisit the question of whether the conventional approach to causation, set out in *Hotson* and *Wilsher*, works unfairly where the patient has lost a less than 50/50 chance of recovery.

Lord Nicholls (dissenting)

A patient is suffering from cancer. His prospects are uncertain. He has a 45% chance of recovery. Unfortunately his doctor negligently misdiagnoses his condition as benign. So the necessary treatment is delayed for months. As a result the patient's prospects of recovery become nil or almost nil. Has the patient a claim for damages against the doctor? No, the House was told. The patient could recover damages if his initial prospects of recovery had been more than 50%. But because they were less than 50% he can recover nothing.

This surely cannot be the state of the law today. It would be irrational and indefensible. The loss of a 45% prospect of recovery is just as much a real loss for a patient as the loss of a 55% prospect of recovery. In both cases the doctor was in breach of his duty to his patient. In both cases the patient was worse off. He lost something of importance and value. But, it is said, in one case the patient has a remedy, in the other he does not.

This would make no sort of sense. It would mean that in the 45% case the doctor's duty would be hollow. The duty would be empty of content. For the reasons which follow I reject this suggested distinction. The common law does not compel courts to proceed in such an unreal fashion. I would hold that a patient has a right to a remedy as much where his prospects of recovery were less than 50–50 as where they exceeded 50–50....

It cannot be right to adopt a procedure having the effect that, in law, a patient's prospects of recovery are treated as non-existent whenever they exist but fall short of 50%. If the law were to proceed in this way it would deserve to be likened to the proverbial ass...

The way ahead must surely be to recognise that where a patient is suffering from illness or injury and his prospects of recovery are attended with a significant degree of medical uncertainty, and he suffers a significant diminution of his prospects of recovery by reason of medical negligence whether of diagnosis or treatment, that diminution constitutes actionable damage. This is so whether the patient's prospects immediately before the negligence exceeded or fell short of 50%...

The present state of the law is crude to an extent bordering on arbitrariness. It means that a patient with a 60% chance of recovery reduced to a 40% prospect by medical negligence can obtain compensation. But he can obtain nothing if his prospects were reduced from 40% to nil. This is rough justice indeed. By way of contrast, the approach set out above meets the perceived need for an appropriate remedy in both these situations and does no more than reflect fairly and rationally the loss suffered by a patient in these situations.

The case of *Gouldsmith v Mid Staffordshire General Hospitals NHS Trust* raises another 'loss of a chance' question. At first instance, the judge found that it had been negligent not to refer the patient, who suffered from lesions on her left hand, to a specialist hospital. Mrs Gouldsmith had established that *most* but not all specialists would be likely to have operated on her hand, and that operating then would have avoided the subsequent amputation of her fingers. At first instance the judge found that she had not proved, on the balance of probabilities, that if she had been referred to a specialist hospital, she would have had this operation.

By a majority, the Court of Appeal disagreed. They found that having established that most specialists would have operated *prima facie* justified the conclusion that the specialist to whom the respondents should have referred her would be likely to have done so. It was not necessary for the claimant to prove that the specialist would have, in fact, operated, but just that it was more likely than not that she would have done.

Gouldsmith v Mid Staffordshire General Hospitals NHS Trust [64]

Pill LJ

[H]er establishment of the fact shifted the evidential burden of proof on to the respondents. It was open to them to have countered, had they had the material with which to do so, with evidence that the reference would be likely to have been to a particular specialist who would not have operated on the appellant. In the absence of credible evidence of that character the answer to the first question proffered on behalf of the appellant should have secured judgment for her.

In his dissenting judgment, Maurice Kay LJ argued that the claimant had not, in fact, proved on the balance of probabilities that referral would have been to a doctor who would have operated on her:

Maurice Kay LJ (dissenting)

In a case in which there is no established probability about where or by which consultant the decision to operate would have been considered, the first question (what would have happened?) has not been answered on a balance of probability because, on Professor McCollum's evidence, in some places and in the hands of some consultants, a decision not to operate could reasonably eventuate. Even where, on the accepted evidence, most consultants in most centres of excellence would have decided upon surgical intervention, a claimant has not discharged the burden of proof if he or she has failed to establish that the hospital to which and the consultant to whom the reference would have been made would probably have been one of the majority rather than one of the still Bolam-compliant minority.

(2) Remoteness

There is another hurdle to overcome once a claimant has succeeded in proving factual causation: it is also necessary to establish that the type of damage is not too remote. According

[64] [2007] EWCA Civ 397.

to the *Wagon Mound*[65] test for remoteness, the type of damage must be foreseeable, although its extent, and the manner in which it occurred, need not be. Normally in clinical negligence cases the *type* of damage will be some sort of physical injury, which is obviously a foreseeable consequence of negligent medical care. As a result, there are few medical cases where remoteness has been an issue.

One exception is *R v Croydon Health Authority*.[66] The claimant had undergone a pre-employment chest X-ray, and the radiographer failed to alert her to an abnormality (primary pulmonary hypertension or PPH), which would be exacerbated by pregnancy. She argued that if she had known that she had PPH, she would not have become pregnant. The Court of Appeal dismissed her claim for the costs arising from the birth of her child because, as Kennedy LJ held:

> The damage was, as is sometimes said, too remote. The chain of events had too many links.... We understand that the radiologist never actually saw the plaintiff, and he probably knew very little about her except her age. He would no doubt have accepted that, in so far as he failed to observe an abnormality which could have affected her fitness for work as an employee of the health authority in the immediate future, that was something for which he should be held accountable, but her domestic circumstances were not his affair.

In *Page v Smith*,[67] a non-medical case, the House of Lords held that provided physical injury was foreseeable, the defendant might also be liable if the claimant suffers psychiatric injury as a result of her negligence. Hence, if it is foreseeable that a doctor's negligence will physically injure her patient, then the doctor could be liable if the patient in fact suffers psychiatric injury, even if no physical injury in fact results. This issue arose in *The Creutzfeldt-Jakob Disease Litigation; Group B Plaintiffs v Medical Research Council*, where the claimants were children of short stature who had taken part in a clinical experimental trial with a type of human growth hormone (Hartree HGH). They subsequently learned that this may have infected them with Creutzfeldt-Jacob Disease (CJD), the human form of BSE or mad-cow disease. On a trial of the preliminary issues, Morland J held that it might be possible to recover damages for the psychiatric injury that had been caused by this knowledge.

The Creutzfeldt-Jakob Disease Litigation; Group B Plaintiffs v Medical Research Council[68]

Morland J

I am satisfied that when the defendants breached their duty of care to them by being responsible for injecting them with potentially lethal Hartree HGH they should have reasonably foreseen that, if deaths occurred from CJD caused by HGH contaminated with the CJD agent, some of the recipients of that HGH, including some of normal phlegm and ordinary fortitude, might well suffer psychiatric injury on becoming aware of the risk to them.... The defendants as tortfeasors committed a wrong upon the Group B plaintiffs by imperilling their lives from a terrible fatal disease. It was reasonably foreseeable that, if the worst fears were realised and deaths from CJD occurred, Hartree HGH recipients, both those of normal

---

[65] [1961] AC 388.   [66] (1997) 40 BMLR 40.   [67] [1996] AC 155.
[68] [2000] Lloyd's Rep Med 161.

> fortitude and those more vulnerable, might suffer psychiatric injury. I cannot see in the facts and circumstances of this litigation why public policy, including social and economic policy considerations, should exclude them from compensation.

A further dimension to remoteness is the question of whether an intervening act or decision has broken the chain of causation. If a psychiatric patient who was known to be a suicide risk succeeds in committing suicide as a result of a negligent failure to keep her under appropriate surveillance, has the chain of causation been broken by the patient's own action in deliberately taking her own life? In *Kirkham v Chief Constable of Greater Manchester*,[69] the court rejected the claim that the deceased's suicide had been a *novus actus* on the grounds that it was the very act that the defendants had been under a duty to prevent.

Where there was no prior indication that a patient was at risk of committing suicide, her actions would be much more likely to break the chain of causation. In *Hyde v Tameside AHA*,[70] the claimant was being treated in a general hospital for a physical disability. He became depressed and jumped out of a window, leaving him permanently disabled. The Court of Appeal held that the hospital staff were not on notice that he was a suicide risk, and hence were not under a duty to prevent him from attempting to commit suicide.

(d) DEFENCES

Various defences to an action in negligence are possible. A partial defence would exist if the patient had been contributorily negligent, perhaps because she discharged herself from hospital against medical advice. Under section 1 of the Law Reform (Contributory Negligence) Act 1945, damages can be reduced in proportion to the extent of the claimant's responsibility for her injuries. Hence if a patient completely ignores her doctor's advice, she might be found to bear some responsibility if her condition deteriorates.

Where the patient has been wholly responsible for her injuries, this may simply lead to a finding that the doctor had not been negligent at all. In *Venner v North East Essex Health Authority and Another*[71] a woman who was about to undergo a sterilization operation was advised to come off the contraceptive pill, but to take other contraceptive precautions prior to the operation. Before the operation she was asked whether there was any chance that she could be pregnant, to which she answered 'no', despite the fact that she and her husband had engaged in unprotected sexual intercourse. She was in fact pregnant when the operation took place, and subsequently gave birth to a healthy child. Tucker J found that there had been no negligence, and the patient herself—a mature woman who understood the likelihood of conception—was responsible for her pregnancy.

The defence of *volenti non fit injuria*[72] is extremely unlikely to affect clinical negligence claims. It is difficult to imagine a case in which the patient was said to have voluntarily assumed the risk of being injured by their doctor's negligence.

In contrast, there have been cases where the defence of illegality or *ex turpi causa non oritur actio*[73] has been raised. In *Clunis v Camden and Islington Health Authority*, a man

---

[69] [1990] 2 QB 283.   [70] The Times, 15 Apr 1981.   [71] The Times, 21 Feb 1987.

[72] This translates as 'to a willing person, no injury is done', and means that there is no liability when an injured person 'volunteered' to run the risk.

[73] This means 'from a dishonorable cause an action does not arise', and means that actions can be barred by the claimant's illegal behaviour.

with mental health problems who had killed a tube passenger argued that the health authority had failed to treat him with reasonable care and skill, and that if they had, he would have been detained and would not have killed Jonathan Zito. The Court of Appeal applied the defence of illegality to reject his claim.

Clunis v Camden and Islington Health Authority[74]

Beldam LJ

In our view, the plaintiff's claim does arise out of and depend upon proof of his commission of a criminal offence.... In the present case the plaintiff has been convicted of a serious criminal offence. In such a case, public policy would in our judgment preclude the court from entertaining the plaintiff's claim unless it could be said that he did not know the nature and quality of his act, or that what he was doing was wrong. The offence of murder was reduced to one of manslaughter by reason of the plaintiff's mental disorder but his mental state did not justify a verdict of not guilty by reason of insanity. Consequently, though his responsibility for killing Mr Zito is diminished, he must be taken to have known what he was doing and that it was wrong....

The court ought not to allow itself to be made an instrument to enforce obligations alleged to arise out of the plaintiff's own criminal act and we would therefore allow the appeal on this ground.

(e) LIMITATION PERIODS

Most personal injury cases must be brought within three years either of the date when the injury occurred, or the date when the patient realized, or should have realized, that she might be able to sue.[75] If the patient dies as a result of her injuries, her relatives have three years from the date of death, or from the date when they realize, or should have realized, that an action could be brought.[76] Section 14 of the Limitation Act sets out when the three year period starts to run:

Limitation Act 1980 section 14

14(1) ...references to a person's date of knowledge are references to the date on which he first had knowledge of the following facts—
  (a) that the injury in question was significant; and
  (b) that the injury was attributable in whole or in part to the act or omission which is alleged to constitute negligence...; and
  (c) the identity of the defendant; and
  (d) if it is alleged that the act or omission was that of a person other than the defendant, the identity of that person and the additional facts supporting the bringing of an action against the defendant....

[74] [1988] QB 978 CA. [75] Limitation Act 1980, ss 11(4) and 14(1).
[76] Ibid.

(2) For the purposes of this section an injury is significant if the person whose date of knowledge is in question would reasonably have considered it sufficiently serious to justify his instituting proceedings for damages...

(3) For the purposes of this section a person's knowledge includes knowledge which he might reasonably have been expected to acquire—

(a) from facts observable or ascertainable by him; or

(b) from facts ascertainable by him with the help of medical or other appropriate expert advice which it is reasonable for him to seek.

One of the problems section 14 presents in medical cases is that it may be particularly difficult for an individual to determine whether their injury was 'attributable in whole or in part to the act or omission which is alleged to constitute negligence'. Medical treatment is not always successful, and so an individual whose condition deteriorates may have just been unlucky. It is not necessary for the claimant to *know* that their injuries are due to negligence: rather, time starts to run when they could be said to have constructive knowledge of the *possibility* of litigation.

In *Forbes v Wandsworth Health Authority* Mr Forbes had had an unsuccessful operation on his left leg in October 1982. As a result, he had to have his leg amputated. In June 1991 he consulted a solicitor. Advice from a vascular surgeon obtained in October 1992 suggested that the amputation could have been avoided. In December 1992 Mr Forbes issued proceedings against the defendant health authority. At first instance, the judge held that his action was not time-barred because he had no reason to suspect or think that the removal of his leg was due to the act or omission of the defendant. Before the health authority's appeal was heard by the Court of Appeal, Mr Forbes died. By a majority, their appeal was allowed.

Forbes v Wandsworth Health Authority[77]

Stuart-Smith LJ

It seems to me that where, as here, the plaintiff expected or at least hoped that the operation would be successful and it manifestly was not, with the result that he sustained a major injury, a reasonable man of moderate intelligence, such as the deceased, if he thought about the matter, would say that the lack of success was 'either just one of those things, a risk of the operation or something may have gone wrong and there may have been a want of care; I do not know which, but if I am ever to make a claim, I must find out'.

In my judgment, any other construction would make the 1980 Act unworkable since a plaintiff could delay indefinitely before seeking expert advice and say, as the deceased did in this case, I had no occasion to seek it earlier. He would therefore be able, as of right, to bring the action, no matter how many years had elapsed. This is contrary to the whole purpose of the 1980 Act which is to prevent defendants being vexed by stale claims which it is no longer possible to contest....

I have come to the conclusion, therefore, that in the circumstances of this case the deceased did have constructive knowledge.

[77] [1997] QB 402 CA.

Section 33 of the Limitation Act 1980 gives the court discretion to extend the limitation period where it would be equitable to do so. In making this judgment, the court has to balance the degree to which the statutory limitation period prejudices the claimant, with the degree to which an extension of that period will prejudice the defendant. The court will have regard to a number of factors, such as the reasons for the delay and the conduct of both parties. In *Forbes v Wandsworth Health Authority*, the court declined to exercise its discretion.

Forbes v Wandsworth Health Authority[78]

Stuart Smith LJ

[I]t is necessary to consider the effect of s 33 of the 1980 Act.... This gives rise to the question whether in the circumstances this court must now exercise its discretion afresh.... But for one feature, this might prove to be a difficult and important question. That feature is the death of Mr Forbes between the trial of the preliminary point and the appeal. That is a new situation which to my mind undoubtedly affects the exercise of discretion under s 33, if for no other reason than that the potential damages recoverable for the benefit of the estate of the deceased are significantly less than they would have been if the deceased were still alive. No damages for pain, suffering and loss of amenity can be recovered for any period after the death, and the claim for future cost of care, aids and appliances... will not be recoverable....

There is a further aspect which is relevant to consideration of the exercise of discretion under s 33. That is the strength of the plaintiff's case.... Taking a broad view of the plaintiff's chances of success on the material available, I have to say that I can only regard them as modest. For all these reasons, I have come to the conclusion that the court should not exercise discretion in favour of the plaintiff.

In contrast, in *Smith v Leicestershire Health Authority* Mrs Smith, who was now aged fifty-four, had her condition misdiagnosed when she was a child, resulting in her having an operation which caused tetraplegia. The possibility of an action in negligence only became apparent twenty-five years later. In deciding whether it should exercise its discretion under section 33, the Court of Appeal found that to do so would be of tremendous importance to the claimant, while not unduly prejudicing the defendants.

Smith v Leicestershire Health Authority[79]

Roch LJ

The degree to which the provisions of s. 11 of the 1980 Act would prejudice the plaintiff far outweighs the prejudice to the defendants that a direction under s. 33 of the Act would create. The plaintiff has a terrible disability for which it has now been established that the defendants are tortiously liable. The extent to which the defendants themselves may be worse off because the claim was not brought prior to 1 April 1990 pales in comparison with the loss to the plaintiff if a court were not to exercise its discretion in her favour....

In this case, all the expert witnesses were agreed that the radiologist at the defendants hospitals had fallen below proper standards for a radiologist in the 1950s, and the judge unhesitatingly accepted that evidence. Causation does not change with the passage of time....

---

[78] [1997] QB 402 CA.   [79] [1998] Lloyd's Rep Med 77.

> This is not even a case where the defendants could complain that had the proceedings been brought in the 1960s or 1970s the plaintiff would have been unable to establish the causal connection, whereas advances in medical science between the 1970s and the 1990s had enabled her to do so. Causation was established by the acceptance of the defendant's expert evidence. For these reasons we would had it been necessary have exercised our discretion under s. 33 in the plaintiffs favour.

Richard Lewis explains that section 33 is an example of the balance the law on limitation strikes between the need for finality and the interests of justice.

Richard Lewis[80]

> There is general agreement over the aims of the law of limitation. First, it provides finality so that sooner or later an incident or transgression which might have led to a claim can be safely treated as closed by all concerned. Secondly, it gives defendants a degree of protection from stale claims which they can no longer properly contest. And thirdly it provides an incentive to plaintiffs to commence proceedings without delay. This is closely related to the need to protect defendants from old claims but goes further in that it also recognises that the trial of disputes on complete or unreliable evidence is prejudicial to the public interest in the proper administration of justice. These objectives must of course be balanced against the interests of plaintiffs and the law now attaches very great weight to the need to give injured persons a fair chance to commence proceedings; hence the date of knowledge provisions and the section 33 discretion.

For children or incompetent adults, the limitation period does not begin to run until or unless they become competent.[81] In such cases, it is obviously possible to sue many years after the alleged negligent act, when evidence as to the precise circumstances which led to the claimant's injuries may no longer be reliable.

4 THE NHS COMPLAINTS SYSTEM

Patients who are dissatisfied with their medical treatment will not necessarily either choose, or be eligible to pursue an action in negligence. Such patients may nevertheless want to complain about the care they received.

Every NHS Trust and Primary Care Trust has its own Patient Advice and Liaison Service (PALS) with staff available to listen to patients' concerns, and to offer information and support. These support staff will liaise with other staff and managers to help resolve problems before a formal complaint is made. There is then a two-stage process for formal complaints. Local resolution is the first stage, and it is usually successful—only 2 per cent of complaints progress beyond the local resolution stage. The Department of Health has produced a *Good Practice Toolkit* for local resolution, to ensure that it works consistently across the NHS. An Independent Complaints Advocacy Service (ICAS) has also been set up to ensure that

---

[80] 'The Limitation Period in Medical Negligence Claims' (1998) 6 Medical Law Review 62–98, 64.
[81] Limitation Act 1980, s 28.

complainants have access to support in articulating their concerns and in navigating the complaints system.

Until April 2009, if complainants were unsatisfied with the way the local Trust had dealt with their complaint, the next stage would be to complain to the Healthcare Commission. In its final annual report on complaints, the Healthcare Commission gave details of the sort of complaints it receives and how many are upheld. Approximately 380 million treatments are provided in the NHS each year, giving rise to about 135,000 complaints, 7,500 of which are referred to the Healthcare Commission for further consideration. In 2007–8, it upheld 30 per cent of complaints. In practice, this means that the Healthcare Commission would make recommendations to the NHS organization to resolve the complaint or improve services. Perhaps ironically, a significant proportion of complaints to the Healthcare Commission were about poor handling of the person's initial complaint.

In *Spotlight on Complaints*, the Commission explained what recommendations it might make when it upheld a complaint, and it went on to make twelve recommendations to Trusts on how to resolve complaints more effectively at the local level.

Healthcare Commission[82]

Typically, this would involve us recommending that the organisation should:

- Provide an apology to the complainant.
- Hold meetings with relevant staff.
- Offer a clearer explanation of the events leading to the complaint.
- Make improvements to a service to assure the complainant that lessons had been learned to prevent a recurrence of the problem for other patients.
- Provide redress, for example, expenses incurred by the complainant where it is apparent that administrative failings within the trust have unnecessarily prolonged the process of complaining.

Drawing on our experience as an independent reviewer of complaints, we have set out the following 12 key recommendations for NHS organisations on improving the way they resolve complaints locally.

1. Acknowledge the person's right to complain.
2. Ensure that the complaint is assessed upon receipt, so that any concerns about a risk to the safe care of other patients can be identified promptly.
3. Clarify what the person's concerns are and manage expectations about possible outcomes to the investigation of the complaint.
4. Consider the various options for resolving the complaint—for example, a meeting or reimbursement of costs.
5. Ensure that the person is kept informed of progress throughout the life of the complaint.
6. Confirm to the person what support is available to assist in making a complaint—for example, the Independent Complaints Advocacy Service (ICAS).

---

[82] Spotlight on Complaints 2009: A Report on Second-stage Complaints about the NHS in England (2009), available at <www.healthcarecommission.org.uk>.

7. Take statements from, and interview if necessary, those staff involved in the events leading up to the complaint. This should be done as soon as possible, so that events are still fresh in the memory.

8. Where necessary, obtain clinical advice on the matters raised. This advice must have a high degree of independence—for example, by obtaining advice from the trust's medical director or from a clinician at another trust.

9. Ensure that any letters to the person making the complaint are written in plain English and are as free as possible of clinical or other technical terminology.

10. Offer an apology if appropriate.

11. Ensure that general learning is taken from specific complaints and is embedded into the system of care for the future.

12. Ensure that the boards of trusts are satisfying themselves that all the above are happening.

From April 2009, the Healthcare Commission ceased to exist and its successor, the Care Quality Commission does not have a role in resolving complaints. The three-stage process has now been replaced by a two-stage one. If people are not satisfied with the way a local NHS body has dealt with their complaint they must now go directly to the Health Service Ombudsman, who used to provide the third and final stage in the NHS complaints system.

A complaint to the Ombudsman has to be made within a year from when the patient became aware of the events which are the subject of the complaint, and the patient must show that she has suffered some hardship or injustice. It is not usually possible to obtain damages, although in some rare circumstances, where the person involved can prove that they have suffered financial loss, the ombudsman can order some financial payment. This happens in fewer than ten cases each year.

The Ombudsman does not investigate cases where the complainant could bring an action for negligence, unless it would not be reasonable to expect her to pursue a legal remedy. However, in some circumstances the Ombudsman will take on complaints about negligent treatment, provided that the complainant undertakes not to start legal proceedings.

In 2007/8 the Parliamentary and Health Service Ombudsman received 4,257 complaints against the National Health Service.[83] Most of these were deemed to be premature because they had failed to exhaust local resolution. The Ombudsman accepted 703 cases for investigation and reported on 636 investigations. Forty-nine per cent of complaints were upheld in full or in part.

5 THE GENERAL MEDICAL COUNCIL

The General Medical Council (GMC) regulates the medical profession. Doctors can only practise medicine in the UK if they are registered with the GMC. In cases of seriously poor practice, a patient might report a doctor to the General Medical Council (GMC), and if she is found guilty of serious professional misconduct, the doctor can be struck off or suspended from the medical register, or conditions may be imposed upon her practice, such as a

[83] 2007/8 Annual Report, available at <www.ombudsman.org.uk>.

requirement that she refrains from carrying out a particular procedure. Since 2008, the civil rather than the criminal standard of proof has applied.

While doctors' mistakes will seldom amount to 'serious professional misconduct', serious cases of negligence can result in disciplinary action. In *McCandless v GMC*, the appellant had been struck off the medical register, and appealed to the Privy Council (which at that time was responsible for hearing appeals from GMC decisions), arguing that 'serious professional misconduct' implied that the conduct had to have been morally blameworthy. The appellant admitted that he had been negligent, but said that an honest mistake could not amount to serious professional misconduct. The Privy Council rejected his appeal.

McCandless v GMC[84]

Lord Hoffmann

[T]he possible penalties available to the committee, which used to be confined to the ultimate sanction of erasure, have been extended to include suspension and the imposition of conditions upon practise. This suggests that the offence was intended to include serious cases of negligence…[T]he public has higher expectations of doctors and members of other self-governing professions. Their governing bodies are under a corresponding duty to protect the public against the genially incompetent as well as the deliberate wrongdoers.

The Medical (Professional Performance) Act 1995 introduced a procedure for suspending a doctor from the register, or making registration conditional upon retraining or avoiding a particular procedure, where she is guilty of 'seriously deficient performance'. Seriously deficient performance is defined as 'a departure from good professional practice, whether or not it is covered by specific GMC guidance, sufficiently serious to call into question a doctor's registration'. Obviously, this definition is somewhat question-begging; nevertheless, it is clearly not necessary to prove that patients have been harmed by the doctor's 'seriously deficient performance'.

It is not only patients who might want to report the conduct of an incompetent doctor. Other health care workers will often be better placed than patients to spot unusually poor results, or inadequate care. The GMC's guide to good medical practice states that doctors must take steps to protect patients where they suspect a colleague may be unfit to practice.

General Medical Council[85]

43 You must protect patients from risk of harm posed by another colleague's conduct, performance or health. The safety of patients must come first at all times. If you have concerns that a colleague may not be fit to practise, you must take appropriate steps without delay, so that the concerns are investigated and patients protected where necessary.

A similar duty is placed on nurses by the Nursing and Midwifery Council.

In practice, however, it is often difficult for doctors and nurses to raise concerns about a colleague's poor performance. Stephen Bolsin, the 'whistleblower' who reported his doubts about the practice of paediatric cardiac surgery at the Bristol Royal Infirmary was ostracized

---

[84] [1996] 1 WLR 167.   [85] Good Medical Practice (2006), available at <www.gmc-uk.org.uk>.

by the medical establishment, and eventually emigrated to Australia. The Public Interest Disclosure Act 1998 protects employees who have disclosed information in the public interest from dismissal and victimization, and NHS Trusts are under a duty to investigate staff concerns, and to guarantee that staff who raise concerns responsibly and reasonably will be protected against victimization.[86] It remains to be seen whether this will remove some of the cultural and institutional barriers to open reporting. Certainly, Julia Burrows' empirical research found that comparatively few nurses would report concerns about risky GPs.

Julia Burrows[87]

Only 61 per cent of nurses said they would report a concern about 'risky' GP performance, 6 per cent said they would not, while 33 per cent were unsure. Only 37 per cent knew whom to report it to…The nurses were given options to choose regarding the reasons they might not report concerns. The two most likely reasons to stop them reporting anything was a feeling it might not make a difference anyway…and a lack of trust in the authority or manager to take appropriate action…Nearly one third of the nurses questioned said that during their career they had had concerns about GPs' performance to the extent they felt patients were at risk, yet over half of these did not report them. Of the 47 per cent who did report the concern, no action was taken in more than half of cases.…In my study, of the seven nurses who had raised their concern about specific GP performance, six of these (86 per cent) felt that the response they received was not adequate to protect patients.…It is suggested that the situation where more than a third of nurses are unsure whether or not they would report a GP even when they feel patients could be at risk, has worrying implications for patient safety. Even among those who feel they would report a concern, there was little clarity about the correct procedures for doing this.

The GMC also now has a role in the ongoing scrutiny of doctors' standard of care. Historically, doctors were admitted to the medical register on qualification, and no further checks were made unless the doctor's performance gave rise to serious concern. Since 2005, to retain their licence to practise, doctors have to 'revalidate', by demonstrating that they remain up-to-date and fit to practise. The purpose of revalidation is to shift the emphasis away from simply checking a doctor's initial qualifications towards regular assessment of the doctor's ability to provide appropriate care. Doctors must now *prove* that their own practice over the previous five years has been in line with the principles set out in the GMC's guide to the duties of a doctor, *Good Medical Practice*. This means routinely collecting and keeping data and information drawn from their day-to-day medical practice. The GMC also demands evidence of participation in an internal appraisal scheme.

This process became more formal in 2009, when a new licensing process came into being, whereby in addition to being registered, doctors will have to hold a licence to practise, which must be renewed annually.[88]

---

[86] *The Public Disclosure Act 1998: Whistleblowing in the NHS,* Health Service Circular 1999/198, available at <www.dh.gov.uk>.

[87] 'Telling Tales and Saving Lives: Whistleblowing—the Role of Professional Colleagues in Protecting Patients from Dangerous Doctors' (2001) 9 Medical Law Review 110–29.

[88] See further Draft General Medical Council (Licence to Practise) Regulations 2009 and Supporting Guidance for Doctors (2009) available at <www.gmc-uk.org>.

6 THE CRIMINAL LAW

In extreme cases, might a doctor's misconduct lead to criminal liability? If death is caused by gross negligence, a conviction for manslaughter is possible, making it important to be able to tell when negligence is 'gross'. In *R v Adomako* the House of Lords held that negligence is 'gross' when it is so bad that it should be criminal. The defendant had been the anaesthetist during an eye operation, and had failed to notice that the tube from the ventilator had become disconnected. The patient suffered a cardiac arrest and died.

R v Adomako[89]

Lord Mackay

The jury will have to consider whether the extent to which the defendant's conduct departed from the proper standard of care incumbent upon him, involving as it must have done a risk of death to the patient, was such that it should be judged criminal.

It is true that to a certain extent this involves an element of circularity, but in this branch of the law I do not believe that is fatal to its being correct as a test of how far conduct must depart from accepted standards to be characterised as criminal. This is necessarily a question of degree and an attempt to specify that degree more closely is I think likely to achieve only a spurious precision. The essence of the matter, which is supremely a jury question, is whether, having regard to the risk of death involved, the conduct of the defendant was so bad in all the circumstances as to amount in their judgment to a criminal act or omission.

The circularity of this definition was unsuccessfully challenged in *R v Misra*. Two junior doctors had failed to identify that a patient who had undergone routine surgery on his leg was very seriously ill, despite him showing the classic signs of infection. By the time the infection was diagnosed, the patient had suffered toxic shock syndrome and he died as a result. The two junior doctors were convicted of gross negligence manslaughter. They appealed against their convictions on the grounds that the definition of manslaughter by gross negligence lacks certainty: the judge's direction to the jury is that the defendant should be convicted if they are satisfied that his conduct was so bad as to be criminal. The Court of Appeal dismissed their appeals.

R v Misra[90]

Judge LJ

The decision of the House of Lords in Adomako clearly identified the ingredients of manslaughter by gross negligence. In very brief summary...the offence requires, first, death resulting from a negligent breach of the duty of care owed by the defendant to the deceased; second, that in negligent breach of that duty, the victim was exposed by the defendant to the risk of death; and third, that the circumstances were so reprehensible as to amount to gross negligence....

---

[89] [1995] 1 AC 1.   [90] [2004] EWCA Crim 2375.

> In our judgment the law is clear.... The jury concluded that the conduct of each appellant in the course of performing his professional obligations to his patient was 'truly exceptionally bad', and showed a high degree of indifference to an obvious and serious risk to the patient's life. Accordingly, along with the other ingredients of the offence, gross negligence too, was proved. In our judgment it is unrealistic to suggest that the basis for the jury's decision cannot readily be understood.

Despite judicial confidence in the clarity of the definition of gross negligence manslaughter, it has been suggested that the vagueness, circularity, and possible subjectivity of the need to establish that what the defendant did was 'so bad as to be criminal', or 'truly exceptionally bad' has the potential to operate unfairly. In the next extract Oliver Quick draws on his interviews with Crown Prosecutors to defend his claim that gross negligence manslaughter should be abolished.

Oliver Quick[91]

> [S]everal reasons for principle and practice point to its abolition. First, the offence is too broad for prosecutorial judgment to be consistently applied, and this translates into particular harshness for those operating in error-ridden activities who are exposed to risk of prosecution by virtue of their socially vital work, and often at the mercy of moral luck. An analysis of the interview responses suggests that no meaningful hierarchy of seriousness is adopted in relation to classifying errors as gross. Respondents struggled to pin down their understanding of the term gross, often initially relying on gut instinct...
>
> The statistics show that a disproportionate number of non-white practitioners figure in medical manslaughter prosecutions. This is a troubling finding and one that may be understood with reference to a number of sociological explanations, such as the training and language skills of overseas-trained practitioners, as well as their ability to gain employment and superior supervision in better performing hospitals. The high number may also be related to racist attitudes that creep into the decisions to complain about and consider investigating individuals in the first place.

In recent years, there has been a marked increase in the number of prosecutions against doctors for manslaughter. Ferner and McDowell's 2006 study found that there were seventeen prosecutions in 2005 alone,[92] compared with four in the whole of the 1970s and 1980s. This is almost certainly not because there has been a dramatic increase in instances of gross negligence. Rather, more plausible explanations are an increased tendency to involve the police, and greater willingness on the part of the Crown Prosecution Service to prosecute doctors, perhaps because it perceives that juries have become more likely to convict.[93]

In the next extract, Jon Holbrook argues that an increased willingness to prosecute doctors who have simply made mistakes points to a shift in our attitude towards accidents.

[91] 'Prosecuting 'Gross' Medical Negligence: Manslaughter, Discretion and the Crown Prosecution Service' (2006) 33 Journal of Law and Society 421–50, 449.
[92] RE Ferner and SE McDowell, 'Doctors Charged with Manslaughter in the Course of Medical Practice' (2006) 99 Journal of the Royal Society of Medicine 309–14.
[93] Ibid.

Jon Holbrook[94]

> This increase in prosecutions for medical manslaughter reflects society's changed attitude towards the notion of gross negligence. . . . Previous generations were concerned to ensure that doctors were not prosecuted for the sort of mistake that a reasonably competent doctor could make due to an error of judgment or by mischance or misadventure.
>
>   But social attitudes to accidents have changed. . . . Our modern day intolerance of accidents as innocent events has tended to turn medical mistakes resulting in death into tragedies calling for criminal investigation.

It is also now possible that NHS Trusts could be prosecuted under the Corporate Manslaughter and Homicide Act 2007, though as yet there have been no such prosecutions. There have, however, been prosecutions under the Health and Safety at Work Act 1974. In *R v Southampton University Hospital Trust*[95] the Trust pleaded guilty to failing to discharge the duty imposed on it by the Health and Safety at Work Act to people other than employees. This case followed the successful prosecution of two junior doctors in *R v Mirza*, above. In addition to their own gross negligence, there had also been serious failures in their supervision. Initially, the Trust was fined £100,000, but this was reduced on appeal to £40,000, in part to reflect the fact that rapid steps had been taken to put proper systems in place after these failures had been identified.

7 PROBLEMS WITH CLINICAL NEGLIGENCE

There is widespread dissatisfaction with the clinical negligence system for a number of different reasons, explored in the following sections.

(a) COSTS TO THE NHS

In 2007/8, Clinical negligence actions cost the NHS £550 million. Most of this is the cost of damages (£385 million), but approximately £166 million is spent on legal costs.

   Regardless of how deserving individual claimants' cases might be, it must be acknowledged that diverting NHS funds to the payment of damages and lawyers' fees inevitably reduces the amount of money available for patient care. As Alan Merry and Alexander McCall Smith explain:

> If damages become payable, then that means that there is a correspondingly reduced amount available for the maintenance of wards and equipment, the purchase of drugs or the provision of treatment. A medium-sized award, therefore, may be crudely translated into ten fewer hip replacements.[96]

---

94 'The Criminalization of Fatal Medical Mistakes' (2003) 327 British Medical Journal 1118–19.
95 [2006] EWCA Crim 2971.
96 *Errors, Medicine and the Law* (CUP: Cambridge, 2001) 212.

In the following extract, John Harris suggests that victims of medical negligence should compete for scarce NHS funds according to the same rationing criteria that exist throughout the NHS, rather than, as happens now, being given absolute priority.

John Harris[97]

In most healthcare systems the need to prioritise patients for care and to ration the resources available is now well recognised....However, one group of claimants for healthcare resources have been guaranteed top priority for receipt of funds available for health care—victims of medical accidents. This fact has been scarcely noted and its justice seldom questioned....

If people who need treatment to save their life can be told that scarcity of resources does not allow them to be treated, why, equally, should not people who need legal redress and compensation (out of the same limited pot of money) be told that the resources necessary to fund the professional help and compensation that they need are either exhausted or committed to those with a greater need?...

If public resources available for patient care are to be cash limited and patients forced to compete for priority within those limits, why should not the same be true of access to litigation and compensation? Why, in short, are some victims of medical accidents given priority over the victims of all other types of accidents, injuries, and illnesses?...

I think it plausible to insist that the health related needs of victims of medical accidents or negligence compete on at least an equal footing with other such needs rather than having automatic and absolute priority.

(b) FAILURE TO PROVIDE REMEDIES TO INJURED PATIENTS

As we have seen, proving breach of duty and causation are formidable obstacles, and most of those patients who do seek compensation will receive nothing. In 2006–7, the NHSLA estimated that, of the 113 clinical negligence claims, which had been litigated in court over the past three financial years, 29 per cent were settled in favour of the claimant and 67 per cent in favour of the NHS (four per cent were settled mid-trial).[98] For the majority of claimants, then, stressful and expensive litigation will end in disappointment. Research appears to indicate that even where claimants are awarded damages, many remain dissatisfied because they have not been given an explanation, an apology, or reassurance that the same thing will not happen again.[99]

Cases which get as far as the court are the exception. According to the NHSLA, 60–70 per cent of claims do not proceed beyond initial contact with a solicitor or disclosure of medical records and 30 per cent of claims which are formally pursued are abandoned by the claimant.[100] Moreover, many patients who have suffered injury as a result of their medical

---

[97] 'The Injustice of Compensation for Victims of Medical Accidents' (1997) 314 British Medical Journal 1821.

[98] NHSLA Claims Factsheet available at <www.nhsla.com>.

[99] L Mulcahy, *Disputing Doctors: The Socio-legal Dynamics of Complaints about Medical Care* (Open UP: Maidenhead, 2003) 96.

[100] Department of Health Full Regulatory Impact Assessment NHS Redress Act (2006), available at <www.dh.gov.uk/>.

treatment never even consider suing the NHS Trust where they were treated. Some patients may not realize that they are eligible to bring an action in negligence. Others, as Linda Mulcahy explains in the following extract, may simply decide that the difficulties of pursuing a legal claim outweigh the small chance of receiving compensation.

Linda Mulcahy[101]

Studies of the link between medical negligence claims and medical mishaps have also found that claiming is an atypical response to medical mishap....

It is also clear from empirical studies that many people do not express their grievance in a formal setting because they do not know how to, fear retribution and defensive responses or because they do not believe that it would make a difference to their lives or the lives of others... It has also been argued that a key reason why people do not complain about doctors is that they feel doubly vulnerable. If they are long-term sick or likely to need future care, they may feel that the risk of upsetting the doctor and jeopardizing their future care is too great. Patients may also *choose* not to make a complaint or clinical negligence claim... for some, avoiding disputes is a positive and rational choice. Asked why they had not voiced their dissatisfaction, this subset said they had other priorities, wished to put negative experiences behind them or avoid confrontation.

The fear that doctors might be advised not to apologize to patients in case it was later used against them in court, as an admission that they had made a mistake, was addressed in the Compensation Act 2006, section 2 of which provides that 'An apology, an offer of treatment or other redress, shall not of itself amount to an admission of negligence or breach of statutory duty.' Apologies are also encouraged in the latest version of the GMC's *Good Medical Practice*.

General Medical Council[102]

30. If a patient under your care has suffered harm or distress, you must act immediately to put matters right, if that is possible. You should offer an apology and explain fully and promptly to the patient what has happened, and the likely short-term and long-term effects.

31. Patients who complain about the care or treatment they have received have a right to expect a prompt, open, constructive and honest response including an explanation and, if appropriate, an apology. You must not allow a patient's complaint to affect adversely the care or treatment you provide or arrange.

While duties of candour are to be welcomed, it would, as Vivienne Harpwood explains, be over-optimistic to imagine that providing apologies and explanations will satisfy disgruntled patients and reduce the number of claims against the NHS.

---

[101] L Mulcahy, *Disputing Doctors: The Socio-legal Dynamics of Complaints about Medical Care* (Open UP Maidenhead, 2003) 64–6.

[102] (2006), available at <www.gmc-uk.org/>.

Vivienne Harpwood[103]

There is evidence that once a claimant has received information about the errors that were made, even coupled with a carefully framed apology, a claim may follow hard upon it, so that the complaints system becomes a route to litigation . . . . Unfortunately some patients are less than honest about their intentions, and use the system for 'fishing expeditions' in order to gather sufficient information to assist a decision as to whether it would be advisable to make or abandon a claim.

(c) A COMPENSATION CULTURE?

Despite the low chance of success and their apparent dissatisfaction with the available remedies, patients have been increasingly willing to sue when their medical treatment goes wrong. In the late 1970s, there were about 700 claims each year against doctors, dentists, and pharmacists; in 2006/7, the NHSLA received 5,426 claims of clinical negligence and 3,293 claims of non-clinical negligence against NHS bodies.[104] While this, in fact, represents a relatively small proportion of the number of medical mishaps which happen each year, this dramatic increase in the number of claims has raised the fear that the UK is moving towards a US-style 'compensation culture'.

This is thought to have two negative consequences for the NHS. First, as we have seen, it means that money that could be spent on patient care is diverted towards litigation, in which the principal beneficiaries are lawyers. Secondly, the threat of litigation may persuade doctors to practise what is known as 'defensive medicine'. This means that doctors will tend to choose treatment which is legally safest, rather than in the best interests of their patients. An example might be the excessively high caesarean delivery rates in the US, which are thought to be prompted by obstetricians' fear of litigation if something goes wrong during a natural delivery. Obstetricians in the US are, on average, sued three times in their careers, and insurance premiums are very high indeed.

It is not, however, clear that doctors *are* primarily motivated by a desire to avoid litigation. As Baroness Hale said in *Gregg v Scott*:[105] 'of course doctors and other health care professionals are not solely, or even mainly, motivated by the fear of adverse legal consequences. They are motivated by their natural desire and their professional duty to do their best for their patients.'

Furthermore, as Michael Jones points out in the next extract, the claim that fear of being sued might prompt doctors to practise defensive medicine is difficult to evaluate, because there will be times when the more cautious approach, which may result from the prospect of litigation if something goes wrong, will in fact lead to better patient care.

Michael Jones[106]

The increase in medical malpractice litigation over the last 15 or 20 years has been accompanied by claims that, in response to the threat of litigation, doctors now practise defensively.

---

[103] Harpwood, supra 169.

[104] *Making Amends*: A Consultation Paper Setting Out Proposals for Reforming the Approach to Clinical Negligence in the NHS (DH: London, 2003) 58.

[105] [2005] UKHL 2.

[106] 'Breach of Duty' in A Grubb with J Laing (eds), *Principles of Medical Law*, 2nd edn (OUP: Oxford, 2004) 369–441.

This involves undertaking procedures which are not medically justified but are designed to protect the doctor from a claim for negligence. The most commonly cited examples are unnecessary diagnostic tests, such as X-rays, and unnecessary caesarean deliveries. However, applying the *Bolam* test, a reasonable doctor would not undertake an *unnecessary* procedure and so a doctor could not avoid a finding of negligence by performing one. In fact, to the extent that the procedure carries some inherent risk, a practitioner acting in this way may increase his chances of being sued. Moreover, there is little clear understanding within the medical profession of what the term 'defensive medicine' means. 'Defensive' may mean simply treating patients conservatively or even 'more carefully', and this begs the question whether that treatment option is medically justified in the patient's interests. Nonetheless, the courts have apparently acknowledged the existence of the phenomenon of defensive medicine, despite the fact that there is virtually no empirical, as opposed to anecdotal evidence of such practices in this country.

Nevertheless, despite some doubts over whether defensive medicine exists and whether it is always necessarily a bad thing, the Compensation Act 2006 was in part directed at the perceived problem that certain people, including health care workers, might engage in excessively risk-averse behaviour for fear of being sued.

Compensation Act 2006 section 1

1. A court considering a claim in negligence or breach of statutory duty may, in determining whether the defendant should have taken particular steps to meet a standard of care (whether by taking precautions against a risk or otherwise), have regard to whether a requirement to take those steps might—

   (a) prevent a desirable activity from being undertaken at all, to a particular extent or in a particular way, or

   (b) discourage persons from undertaking functions in connection with a desirable activity.

In the next extract, Kevin Williams suggests that the 'problem' of defensive medicine, and other risk-averse practices arising from fear of litigation is a media-driven 'urban myth', and he argues that section 1 of the Compensation Act provides a 'phoney' solution to a non-existent problem.

Kevin Williams[107]

The fact that there may be no objective proof that we live in an increasingly 'blame and sue' society is beside the point when an 'urban myth' to the contrary is said to have taken hold...
   [T]he 'Explanatory Notes' which accompanied the Bill tersely state that it does no more than 'reflect the existing law' as expressed 'in recent judgments of the higher courts'. Repeating what lawyers already know about the common law is an unusual legislative strategy, and one which seems poorly suited to changing lay attitudes, especially those of public

---

[107] 'Politics, the Media and Refining the Notion of Fault: Section 1 of the Compensation Act' (2006) Journal of Personal Injury Law 347.

sector workers, such as teachers and healthcare professionals, who seem peculiarly prone to exaggerating their exposure to ruinous litigation…

Crucially, s.1 is unlikely to reduce fear of litigation, defensive practices or the number of frivolous claims; nor is it likely to cause socially valuable activities, such as volunteering, to increase. Unless it is read as a tacit invitation to judges to raise the height of the breach barrier, s.1 looks like a strongly media-driven phoney solution to a phoney problem.

The 'compensation culture' has also been blamed for the rise in what are known as Claims Management organizations, or more pejoratively 'ambulance chasers' or 'claims farmers'. These are organizations, such as 'Claims Direct', which encourage or pressurize people to bring personal injury claims, through aggressive advertising and high-pressure sales techniques. The Compensation Act 2006 attempts to regulate these bodies by controlling advertising. It set up a Claims Management Regulator (CMR) which, in its first year Impact Assessment, reported that it had largely dealt with the problem that these bodies would place leaflets, often containing the NHS logo, in hospitals: 'Vigorous action has been taken against unauthorized advertising in hospital. Such marketing has now largely been eliminated.'[108]

(d) INACCURACY OF AWARDS

Another criticism made of the clinical negligence system is that the cost of private care may be included in the award, even though the claimant may, in fact, receive her treatment within the NHS. Lump sum awards, which used to be the norm, raise the possibility of both over- and under- compensation because they are based upon predictions about the claimant's future needs and life expectancy. Periodical payments resolve many of these problems, but because they require ongoing contact between the claimant and the NHS Trust, there may be higher administration costs.

(e) WHAT ABOUT OTHER PEOPLE WITH DISABILITIES?

Finally, it is also worth remembering that most people who have to live with serious illness and disability will not receive any damages at all. Only those who can establish that another's negligence caused their ill health will receive generous financial assistance with the costs of their care. The needs of brain-damaged babies, for example, are identical regardless of whether their disabilities were caused by negligence during childbirth or a congenital condition. Is it fair that some brain-damaged infants receive millions of pounds to pay for private treatment for the rest of their lives, while other babies with identical practical needs receive nothing? A social security system, or welfare state, which allocates resources according to need might then be fairer than the tort of negligence.

It is not just the expense, inconvenience, and unfairness of negligence claims that has come under attack. Even more importantly, as we see in the next section, it is increasingly recognized that the clinical negligence system works to obstruct efforts to ensure that mistakes are not repeated.

---

[108] Ministry of Justice, *Claims Management Regulation Impact of Regulation One Year Assessment* (2008) para 16, available at <www.claimsregulation.gov.uk/>.

8 A NEW APPROACH: LEARNING FROM MISTAKES

If adverse events result from human error, the tort system is not necessarily an effective way to ensure that such errors are not repeated. Conventionally, negligence is supposed to raise standards of behaviour through the deterrent effect of the prospect of having to pay damages. Doctors, however, will very seldom pay damages themselves. Instead, these will be met by their employers, or in the case of GPs and some private doctors, by the Medical Defence Unions. Of course, doctors may fear being sued for the damage a finding of negligence could do to their reputation, but paradoxically the most egregious examples of negligence will tend to be settled quickly and quietly by the NHS Trust, and will attract little publicity.

Furthermore, as Alan Merry and Alexander McCall Smith point out: 'A point which is often misunderstood is that human error, being by definition unintentional, is not easily deterred.'[109] Most doctors will have prescribed or administered the wrong drug, or the wrong dose of a drug, to a patient at some point in their career. Usually, these mistakes are harmless, and may go unnoticed. If the patient dies or is injured as a result, the doctor (or in practice, her employer) may be sued for negligence. Alan Merry and Alexander McCall Smith describe this as 'outcome bias', whereby culpability depends on the *consequences* of an action, rather than upon its *blameworthiness*.[110] A system of deterrence built upon such haphazard foundations is unlikely to work. Instead, a more effective way to prevent human error is to anticipate likely mistakes, such as drug administration errors, and to design systems intended to minimize the risk materializing.

Merry and McCall Smith have also argued that the negative impact litigation has upon individual doctors is also unlikely to improve the standard of patient care:

Alan Merry and Alexander McCall Smith[111]

Working under a threat of litigation creates a climate of fear, which cannot be conducive to the best use of human resources within the medical system. Moreover, the impact on a doctor, once a complaint has been made, is likely to be deleterious to his or her subsequent discharge of professional duties. The adverse effect of excessive stress on performance is well known, and a person experiencing the trauma of litigation is therefore likely to be a greater safety risk than one who is not under such personal pressure.

Medical mishaps are common: it has been estimated that ten per cent of hospital inpatient admissions result in an adverse event.[112] Many of these have serious consequences: one study found that a third of adverse events led to moderate or great disability, or death.[113] Each year, nearly 10,000 serious adverse reactions to drugs are reported, and around 1,150 people who have been in recent contact with mental health service commit suicide. Research suggests that as many as 70 per cent of adverse incidents are preventable.[114] The National Audit Office has estimated that, at any one time, nine per cent of patients have an infection, such

---

[109] *Errors, Medicine and the Law* (CUP: Cambridge, 2001) 2.   [110] Ibid, 46–7.

[111] Ibid, 217.

[112] Department of Health Expert Group, *An Organisation with a Memory* (DH: London, 2000) viii.

[113] Charles Vincent *et al.*, 'Adverse Events in British hospitals: Preliminary Retrospective Record Review' (2001) 322 British Medical Journal 517–19.

[114] Department of Health Expert Group, *An Organisation with a Memory* (DH: London, 2000) 26.

as MRSA (methicillin-resistant Staphylococcus aureus) or *Clostridium difficile*, which has been acquired during their stay in hospital. The effects vary from extended length of stay, to permanent disability and, in nearly 5,500 patients each year, death.[115] These hospital-acquired infections are estimated to cost the NHS nearly £1 billion each year, and at least 15 per cent of them are preventable.[116]

Historically, there has been a difference between the NHS and other high-risk activities, such as the aviation industry,[117] where human error is anticipated, and non-punitive reporting systems are used to ensure that learning from mistakes is the norm. Open reporting of adverse incidents and 'near-misses' would ensure that medical staff are able to learn from them, but the adversarial negligence system has provided strong disincentives to admitting mistakes. An open reporting system depends upon moving away from a 'blame culture', which inevitably deters medical staff from being open about their mistakes. It might also be promoted by making reporting mandatory, confidential, and anonymous.

In *An Organisation with A Memory*, the Department of Health's Expert Group contrasted a person-centred approach to mistakes, such as that embodied by the clinical negligence system, where the emphasis is upon discovering who was at fault, and a systems approach, which assumes that humans are fallible and that errors are inevitable. The problem with the person-centred approach is that by trying to apportion individual blame, systemic reasons for adverse events may be missed, and effective learning hampered.

Department of Health Expert Group[118]

- When things go wrong whether in health care or in another environment, the response has often been an attempt to identify an individual or individuals who must carry the blame. The focus of incident analysis has tended to be on the events immediately surrounding an adverse event, and in particular on the human acts or omissions immediately preceding the event itself...

- Human error may sometimes be the factor that immediately precipitates a serious failure, but there are usually deeper, systemic factors at work which if addressed would have prevented the error or acted as a safety-net to mitigate its consequences...

- There is evidence that 'safety cultures', where open reporting and balanced analysis are encouraged in principle and by example, can have a positive and quantifiable impact on the performance of organisations. 'Blame cultures' on the other hand can encourage people to cover up errors for fear of retribution and act against the identification of the true causes of failure because they focus heavily on individual actions and largely ignore the role of underlying systems. The culture of the NHS still errs too much toward the latter.

- Reporting systems are vital in providing a core of sound representative information on which to base analysis and recommendations. Experience in other sectors demonstrates the value of systematic approaches to recording and reporting adverse events and the

---

[115] Harpwood, supra 38.

[116] *Improving Patient Care by Reducing the Risk of Hospital Acquired Infection: A Progress Report* (NAO: London, 2004) 1.

[117] Although compared with the NHS, the aviation industry is relatively low risk. The Chief Medical Officer, Sir Liam Donaldson, has estimated that the odds of dying as a result of hospital treatment is 33,000 times that of dying in an air crash (Harpwood, supra 38).

[118] *An Organisation with a Memory* (DH: London, 2000) viii–ix, 21, available at <www.dh.gov.uk>.

merits of quarrying information on 'near misses' as well as events which actually result in harm. The NHS does not compare well with best practice in either of these areas....

- When an adverse event occurs, the important issue is not who made the error but how and why did the defences fail and what factors helped to create the conditions in which the errors occurred...

- Human error is commonly blamed for failures because it is often the most readily identifiable factor operating in the period just prior to an adverse event. Yet two important facts about human error are often overlooked. First, the best people can make the worst mistakes. Second, far from being random, errors fall into recurrent patterns. The same set of circumstances can provoke similar mistakes, regardless of the people involved. Any attempt at risk management that focuses primarily upon the supposed mental processes underlying error (forgetfulness, inattention, carelessness, negligence, and the like) and does not seek out and remove these situational 'error traps' is sure to fail....

- The possibility of developing design solutions to specific hazards is under-explored in health care. In other sectors significant efforts are being made to design equipment and products in a way which helps to minimise potential hazards, yet despite one or two examples of good practice which demonstrate its applicability to health care this approach has not yet been applied extensively or systematically in the NHS.

A further recommendation from the Expert Group relates to the importance of reporting not only adverse events themselves, but also near misses. If data is only collected from incidents which in fact result in serious harm, this risks 'skewing learning towards a very small cross-section of accidents'.[119] In the aviation industry, for example, pilots are under a duty to report near misses since these are likely to yield useful information that might help to ensure that similar mistakes, which might cause serious accidents, are not made in the future: if only crashes were analysed, there would be much less opportunity to learn from mistakes.

The Final Report of the Bristol Royal Infirmary Inquiry began as a public inquiry into the abnormally high death rate for paediatric cardiac surgery at Bristol Royal Infirmary, but it culminated in some damning conclusions about the NHS's response to adverse events, and argued that clinical negligence should be abolished.

Bristol Royal Infirmary Inquiry[120]

Chapter 26

28 Clinical negligence litigation does not represent a systematic approach to accountability, far less to the proper analysis of error. Rather, it is an entirely haphazard process. Furthermore, any system of accountability, to be effective, requires that there be openness about who is accountable and for what. There is no such parallel in the system of clinical negligence litigation. Few cases ever actually see the light of day in court. Indeed in many of the more obvious cases of error, where it is clear to the trust, the NHS Litigation Authority, or a defence society, that a hospital or a particular professional was at fault, the claim is settled

---

[119] Ibid. 39.
[120] Learning from Bristol: The Report of the Public Inquiry into Children's Heart Surgery at the Bristol Royal Infirmary 1984–1995 Cm 5207 (2001), <www.bristol-inquiry.org.uk/>.

and no public airing of the issues ever takes place. What might be learned from such cases cannot thus be shared across the NHS. Other hospitals and healthcare professionals, indeed even those in the same institution, may not learn of, and thus from, the case. Paradoxically, those cases which are not settled, and thus become publicly known, tend to be those in which it is less certain that a hospital or a particular professional was at fault. Thus, at its extreme, we have the bizarre situation under the current system of clinical negligence litigation, in which the worst excesses rarely come into view, while the more borderline cases attract the attention of the press and public. This is a far cry from any system for holding the NHS to account for its conduct and its errors....

33 It is our view, therefore, that the culture and the practice of clinical negligence litigation work against the interests of patients' safety. The system is positively counter-productive, in that it provides a clear incentive not to report, or to cover up, an error or incident. And, once covered up, no one can learn from it and the next patient is exposed to the same or a similar risk....

35 Ultimately, we take the view that it will not be possible to achieve an environment of full, open reporting within the NHS when, outside it, there exists a litigation system the incentives of which press in the opposite direction. We believe that the way forward lies in the abolition of clinical negligence litigation, taking clinical error out of the courts and the tort system. It should be replaced by effective systems for identifying, analysing, learning from and preventing errors along with all other sentinel events. There must also be a new approach to compensating those patients harmed through such events.

The crucial point is that instead of expecting that medical staff will never make mistakes, it is more realistic to assume the inevitability of human error, and to try to build protections into the system to minimize their adverse effects. To take a mundane example, the designers of word-processing packages take it for granted that users are likely to close documents without remembering to save their work. As a result, prompting mechanisms are built into computer software to remind users that they might want to save documents before closing them, and back-up documents are generated automatically.

In relation to medical practice, a systems approach might involve practices such as ensuring that different drugs do not have confusingly similar packaging, or that drugs with similar names are not stored together, thus reducing the risk of confusing them. The Chief Pharmaceutical Officer's Report, *Building a Safer NHS for Patients: Improving Medication Safety*,[121] lays out a number of strategies for reducing medication errors, such as automatic double-checking by a second person in defined high-risk situations; discussing medication with patients and carers at the time of administration; and readily distinguishable wristbands for patients with known allergies.[122]

In the fertility sector, particular interest in avoiding adverse incidents was generated after the *Leeds* case, considered in Chapter 15, in which a woman's eggs were fertilized with the wrong man's sperm. Human fallibility means that the risk of this sort of mistake cannot be eliminated, but it can be reduced. As a result, there are now witnessing requirements to ensure that at least two people confirm the patients' identity. Rather than just relying upon the patient's name as an identifier, additional information such as their date of birth and hospital number must also be recorded, in order to reduce the likelihood of error when different patients with similar names are being treated at the same time.

---

[121] DH: London, 2004.
[122] *Building a Safer NHS for Patients: Improving Medication Safety* (DH: London, 2004) 9.

But while a 'systems' approach is widely endorsed, in the next extract Oliver Quick argues that entirely eliminating blame and individual accountability may have its dangers.

Oliver Quick[123]

The focus on systems also risks diluting the notion of individual professional responsibility that has been central to medical autonomy and accountability. As Dingwall reminds us, responsibility for risks becomes more elusive in modern society: 'the interdependence of productive forces characteristic of modern societies dissolves personal responsibility into that of a diffuse "system"'. Beck is also critical of the consequences of systems thinking arguing that:

> causes dribble away into a general amalgam of agents and conditions, reactions and counter-reactions, which brings social certainty and popularity to the concept of system. This reveals in exemplary fashion the ethical significance of the system concept: *one can do something and continue doing it without having to take personal responsibility for it.*

In the medical context, if blaming the system becomes the default response, to what extent will this shelter the incompetent or poor performer? Sir Donald Irvine, president of the GMC during the turbulent times of the Bristol affair, warned against this over-emphasis on the system which may mask individual failings. A recent example of this followed a surgeon's conviction for manslaughter with the judge remarking that:

> It was not your fault that you were allowed to go on operating, subject to restrictions, for another two years. Much of the evidence of these events was known at the time and the balance of the evidence was easily discoverable had it occurred to anyone making elementary inquiries.

As comments such as this become a more common reaction to error, it is worth questioning whether this drift towards blaming others and organisations risks underplaying the ethics of individual conscience.

Nevertheless all would agree that openness about mistakes is vital in order to identify 'error traps'—such as misleadingly similar drugs' packaging—and putting in place systems to ensure that the risk of human error is minimized.

Openness about mistakes is also important for patients who have been the victims of medical mishaps, who, as we have seen, are often more interested in obtaining an explanation and an apology than financial compensation. Indeed, litigation is more likely where patients believe that there has been a cover-up or that a mistake has gone unacknowledged. Vincent *et al.*'s study of the motivations of litigants found that the decision to take legal action was determined not only by the original injury, but also by insensitive handling and poor communication afterwards. Patients who had decided to sue were seeking greater honesty; an acknowledgement of the severity of the trauma they had suffered; and assurances that lessons had been learnt from their experiences: 'Communication assumes a special importance when things have gone wrong. Patients often blame doctors not so much for the original mistakes, as for a lack of openness or willingness to explain.'[124]

---

[123] 'Outing Medical Errors: Questions of Trust and Responsibility' (2006) Medical Law Review 22, 41–2.
[124] C Vincent 'Why do People Sue Doctors? A Study of Patients and Relatives Taking Legal Action' (1994) 343 The Lancet 1609–13, 1613.

In the next extract, Martin Smith and Heidi Foster argue that the disclosure of medical mistakes is justified by a variety of different types of ethical reasoning (which we considered in Chapter 1).

Martin Smith and Heidi Foster[125]

Pertaining to rights-based reasoning, honest and candid communication followed by apology are a sign and a support of patients' rights to respectful treatment and care, and to self-determination....

A consideration of professional virtues or character traits also supports the general principle of disclosing mistakes with forthrightness...The virtue of truthfulness is ultimately essential for an effective professional–patient relationship because relationships cannot endure failures of truthfulness for long....

Finally, in ethically evaluating disclosure of mistakes from a consequentialist perspective, consideration needs to be given to the harms and benefits to all 'parties' who stand to be harmed or benefited by disclosure and apology...On the harm side of the ledger, disclosure is not always a benign activity. Patients can be emotionally fragile or in the middle of life-threatening situations; a disclosure of a mistake at that moment, similar to the giving of 'bad news' in such situations, could be detrimental to patient welfare and best interests. If mistakes are disclosed, patients or families might worry unnecessarily about other aspects of their care, and such worry might cause stress, discourage patients from seeking necessary care, and lead them to reject beneficial interventions in the future...Also in the current climate of healthcare, professionals could have their reputations, careers, livelihoods, referrals, staff privileges, and future employment opportunities jeopardized if they disclose a serious mistake.

On the benefit side of disclosure, patients...who have greater clarity and understanding of the medical situation may make better healthcare decisions...Honest disclosure can provide them with explanations and understanding..., give consolation that lessons have been learned, promote acceptance and closure about what transpired, and eliminate lawsuits filed to find out what really happened....

Although the terms are paradoxical, mistakes can be viewed as 'gems' and 'treasures' because much can be learned from them for the betterment of future patients.

9 REFORMING CLINICAL NEGLIGENCE

Before the NHS Redress Act 2006 was passed, there had been a number of attempts to improve the functioning of the clinical negligence system. The NHS Litigation Authority (NHSLA) was set up in 1995, and it has encouraged the earlier admission of liability, and the provision of explanations and apologies. This led to reductions in the time taken to settle claims: new cases now take, on average, 1.19 years to settle, compared with 5.5 years in 1999/2000.[126] The NHSLA uses a specialized panel of solicitors, and has also promoted

---

[125] 'Morally Managing Medical Mistakes' (2000) 9 Cambridge Quarterly of Healthcare Ethics 38–53.

[126] Making Amends: A Consultation Paper Setting Out Proposals for Reforming the Approach to Clinical Negligence in the NHS (DH: London, 2003) 92.

wider use of mediation. Now fewer than 50 cases per year reach the courts, and 96 per cent are settled by some sort of alternative dispute resolution, such as mediation.

The reforms to the civil justice system, prompted by Lord Woolf's report *Access to Justice*, have also gone some way towards streamlining clinical negligence claims, which Lord Woolf identified as the area where civil justice was 'failing most conspicuously'.[127] In 1998 the *Pre-Action Protocol for the Resolution of Clinical Disputes* was issued. Its purpose is to encourage openness, and to reduce the need to resort to adversarial litigation. Parties are now given incentives to settle actions quickly, and to make use of mediation. Patients initially send letters of claim, which identify the alleged negligence, and the injuries and losses suffered as a result. The NHS Trust (or other defendant) must respond within three months, either admitting the claim or denying it, with specific answers to the allegations made by the patient.

Where a trial does go to court, pre-trial agreements to determine what the court will be asked to decide are now encouraged, and the Court has a more pro-active role in case management. The Civil Procedure Rules[128] emphasize that expert witnesses' primary duty is to assist the court to discover the truth, and not to offer partisan evidence to support one party's point of view, and in straightforward cases, the judge can appoint a single expert. Where more experts are used, they may be invited to submit a joint report. Alternative dispute resolution is encouraged. There is evidence that claims are being managed more effectively and that there has been greater use of mediation, but it does not seem to have reduced the total number of claims.

The Clinical Negligence Scheme for Trusts (CNST), administered by the NHSLA, was set up in 1995 in order to help NHS Trusts fund litigation by pooling resources, so that one high-value case does not threaten an NHS Trust's capacity to carry out its other responsibilities. As a condition for discounted premiums, it requires the development of clinical incident reporting systems and compliance with its risk management standards.

Set up in 2001, the National Patient Safety Agency (NPSA) runs a mandatory reporting system for logging all failures, mistakes, errors, and near-misses across the health service. It is intended to introduce a streamlined approach to dealing with errors and mistakes, and to ensure that lessons are learnt and spread throughout the health service. In 2004 the NPSA launched the national reporting and learning system (NRLS). In addition to extracting information from existing local risk management systems, NHS employees are also able to report patient safety incidents *anonymously* directly to the system through an online form. The NRLS encourages open reporting of 'all patient safety' incidents, including 'those that caused no harm or minimal harm to patients' and 'near misses'.

From its inception until November 2008, the NRLS had collected reports of 2,771,786 incidents. Between 1 July 2008 and 30 September 2008, it collected 234,825 reports in England alone. Having gathered information about incidents—an example might be a patient identification error resulting from two patients having the same hospital number— the NPSA issues alerts and workbooks to ensure that all other trusts are able to learn from them.[129]

In 2001 the National Clinical Assessment Authority, now the National Clinical Assessment Service (NCAS), was set up in England, Wales, and Northern Ireland to support

---

[127] Lord Woolf, *Access to Justice: Final Report to the Lord Chancellor on the Civil Justice System* (HMSO: London, 1996) 15.2.
[128] 1998/3132, pursuant to the Civil Procedure Act 1997.
[129] See further <www.npsa.nhs.uk/nrls/reporting/>.

the NHS in dealing with doctors and dentists whose performance gives cause for concern. It provides advice about the local handling of cases, and can carry out clinical performance assessments of individual practitioners. In 2006/7, it received 691 requests for advice about practitioners and carried out 36 clinical assessments.[130] Where the assessment reveals that the practitioner's performance could be improved, it will put in place an action plan. From 2008, the NCAS has operated in Scotland too.

As we saw earlier, the NHS complaints system has also been reformed recently. Unfortunately, however, the complaints and the claims systems still largely operate independently, with patients having to choose whether to lodge a complaint or to pursue a claim. It would perhaps make more sense to have a single-track system, providing all patients with an explanation, apology, and assurance that steps have been taken to avoid repetition.

In its review of clinical negligence, the government acknowledged that there had been significant recent improvements in the system, but it argued that fundamental reform remained necessary. It was not persuaded to move towards a no-fault compensation scheme, however. Although such schemes also exist in Denmark, Sweden, and Finland, and to a limited extent in France, the most well-known example is in New Zealand where a no-fault scheme has been in place since 1972.

Although removing the need to prove fault would undoubtedly simplify and speed up the process of compensation, the problem of establishing causation remains, and as we have seen, in medical cases this is a significant obstacle. It also means that arbitrary lines continue to be drawn between patients who are eligible for compensation because they can prove that their injuries were caused by a medical mishap, and those who cannot. As we have seen, the needs of a brain-damaged baby are the same, regardless of whether its injuries were caused by asphyxia at birth or a congenital disability. A no-fault compensation scheme would continue to distinguish between patients on grounds other than need.

No-fault schemes may be cheaper to administer, but they are also likely to attract higher numbers of claims, and may therefore end up costing more than the clinical negligence system. In New Zealand for example, the proportion of the population making claims each year is more than double that in England,[131] and the Chief Medical Officer estimated that a no-fault scheme would be unaffordable for the NHS:

> Estimates suggest that even with a 25% reduction in the current level of compensation the cost of a true no-fault compensation scheme would vary between £1.6 billion per year (if 19% of eligible claimants claimed) to almost £4 billion (if 28% of eligible claimants claimed). This compares with £400 million spent on clinical negligence in 2001.[132]

A no-fault scheme would also fail to address patients' desire for apologies and explanations, and would not necessarily promote learning from mistakes.

Having rejected both the status quo and a move towards a no-fault compensation system, the Government's preferred solution was the NHS Redress Act, which received Royal Assent in 2006.

The Act permits the Secretary of State to use regulation-making powers to set up an NHS Redress scheme in England and Wales. There is very little detail on the face of the legislation, much of which is left to be determined by regulations. Under section 1, a redress scheme only applies to 'qualifying liability':

---

[130] 2006–7 Medical Director's Report, available at <www.ncas.npsa.nhs.uk>.
[131] Ibid, 106.   [132] Ibid, 112.

NHS Redress Act 2006 section 1

> 1(4) The reference in subsection (2) to qualifying liability in tort is to liability in tort owed—
>
> (a) in respect of or consequent upon personal injury or loss arising out of or in connection with breach of a duty of care owed to any person in connection with the diagnosis of illness, or the care or treatment of any patient, and
>
> (b) in consequence of any act or omission by a health care professional.

The scheme will also be limited to qualifying services, which are, according to 1(5)(a) services provided in a hospital, or in other qualifying services which fall in the 'grey area' between primary and secondary care (examples might be pathology laboratory services or palliative care units—which may or may not be located in hospitals, and the ambulance service). Primary care services, such as GP practices and dental surgeries are not covered, although the government intends to review this three years after the Scheme comes into force.

According to section 3(2):

> 3(2) A scheme must provide for redress ordinarily to comprise—
>
> (a) the making of an offer of compensation in satisfaction of any right to bring civil proceedings in respect of the liability concerned,
>
> (b) the giving of an explanation,
>
> (c) the giving of an apology, and
>
> (d) the giving of a report on the action which has been, or will be, taken to prevent similar cases arising.

Under section 3(5) an upper limit on the amount of compensation payable may be set, and it is anticipated that this will be £20,000. The government's view is that it is in the context of low-value claims where the Redress Scheme will be most useful, because it is these claims where the legal costs frequently amount to more than any damages paid. Costs exceeded the damage awards in 78 per cent of claims valued between £10,000 and £15,000, compared to 18 per cent in claims valued over £50,000.[133]

It will also be possible, but not mandatory, for redress to consist in an offer of care and treatment.[134] To mean anything, this would have to involve the provision of services other than the normal NHS services to which any patient is entitled. It might, for example, cover the provision of private rehabilitation services.

Once an offer of redress has been made, free legal advice will be provided to help the patient determine whether the offer is reasonable, and how it might compare to a possible court order. Where an offer is accepted, the patient will have to sign a waiver of the right to bring civil proceedings in relation to the same matter. If the patient does not accept the offer, they retain the right to sue in negligence, although it is envisaged that the refusal of an offer of redress would be taken into account by the Legal Services Commission when deciding whether to grant legal aid. Under section 12, there is a general duty to have regard to the desirability of redress being provided without recourse to civil proceedings.

---

[133] Department of Health Full Regulatory Impact Assessment NHS Redress Act (2006), available at <www.dh.gov.uk/>.

[134] Section 3(3)(a).

At the time of writing, no NHS Redress Scheme has been set up, although the Welsh Assembly has issued its own NHS Redress (Wales) Measure, which set out regulation making powers for Welsh Ministers to enable them to outline in detail arrangements for the handling of lower-value clinical negligence claims outside of the Courts.

So, if it is ever implemented, will the NHS Redress Scheme solve the problems associated with clinical negligence? The lack of detail makes it difficult to answer this question, but a number of potential problems have been highlighted.

First, because the Act confines redress to cases of personal injury arising from a breach of duty, the need to prove both breach and causation remain intact. Both, as we saw earlier, pose considerable difficulties for claimants. In *Making Amends*, the Chief Medical Officer had suggested that a 'lower qualifying threshold' might be appropriate, and a charity which campaigns on patients' behalf had argued for an 'avoidability test': that is, there should be redress unless the patient's injuries were unavoidable. Because the test for negligence under the scheme is identical to that used in the courts, all of the difficulties which we have seen that claimants face in establishing liability in negligence will be reproduced under the NHS redress scheme.

Second, while *Making Amends* had advocated the setting up of an independent body to run the redress scheme, the Scheme will, in fact, be managed by the NHSLA. The NHSLA will have a wide discretion to decide whether to instruct medical experts, and it will be responsible for determining whether patients have established liability in tort, and if they have, what sort of redress they should be offered. Many commentators have questioned the NHSLA's capacity to act independently in these matters, given that it is also the protector of the NHS's interests in litigation, and if the offer is rejected, 'the NHSLA will in effect represent the opposing party in any subsequent litigation arising out of such claims in the courts'.[135] Harpwood puts it bluntly, 'the NHS will be investigator, judge and jury in its own cause',[136] and she wonders whether this arrangement might be challenged under Art 6 of the European Convention (denial of a fair trial).

Thirdly, the Act does not take forward the CMO's suggestion in *Making Amends* that the legislation should impose a duty of candour upon health care professionals to report any incidences of suspected negligence they had seen or participated in. An incentive was to have been provided in the form of exemption, where appropriate, from disciplinary action. The government has argued that the NHS Redress Scheme will promote a culture of openness, and thereby encourage disclosure. The Act's Regulatory Impact Assessment stated that:

> The reforms will assist to create a cultural shift within the NHS, moving the emphasis away (where appropriate) from attributing blame towards preventing harm, reducing risks and learning from mistakes. The expectation is that the new scheme will provide benefits for both patients (the individual harmed patient and patients generally), and provide impetus for wider NHS improvement. The Redress Scheme will take an active approach, and it is intended that it will be triggered both by patient applications and by service providers themselves identifying cases that are eligible.[137]

[135] Anne-Maree Farrell and Sarah Devaney, 'Making Amends or Making Things Worse? Clinical Negligence Reform and Patient Redress in England' (2007) 27 Legal Studies 27 630–48.

[136] Harpwood, supra, 202.

[137] Department of Health Full Regulatory Impact Assessment NHS Redress Act (2006) available at <www.dh.gov.uk/>.

The Act itself does nothing to encourage health care professionals to report eligible cases. Such a duty might be contained in regulations, but otherwise it will remain to be seen whether reporting by health care professionals will develop as a result of the anticipated 'cultural shift'.

Fourthly, will the NHS Redress Scheme in fact lead to cost savings? It is certainly possible that it will have the opposite effect. By making it easier to claim, it is likely to bring new claims into the system. The Department of Health has predicted that the increase in the number of cases may be as high as 43 per cent, although it also envisages that opportunistic claims will easily be rejected, and in the longer term, it expects to see substantial savings in legal costs.[138] Overall, Department of Health economists have estimated that, with a payout cap of £20,000, the financial effect of the Scheme will range from a saving of £7 million to a cost of £48 million.[139]

In many ways the NHS Redress Scheme will be indistinguishable from the Complaints procedure, aside from the possibility of fairly modest compensation payments. Harpwood describes the NHS Redress Scheme, as 'little more... than an enhanced complaints system'.

10 CONCLUSION

It is commonly said that tort law serves two purposes: compensation and deterrence. In the context of medical negligence, we have seen, first, that it does not offer an efficient compensation scheme for patients who suffer injury or damage as a result of negligent treatment, and second, that it does not effectively deter poor practices or encourage good ones. Worse still, not only is tort law costly and inefficient, but it may actually contribute towards the repetition of mistakes by fostering a 'blame culture' and inhibiting open reporting of errors, which is, of course, the best way to ensure that they are not repeated.

Whether or not an NHS Redress Scheme would improve matters is open to question. Lower administration costs and lower awards may be off-set by increases in the number of claims. The need to establish that there has been a serious shortcoming in NHS care means that it will still be necessary to *blame* an individual doctor, or other health care provider. As a result, the Scheme will not necessarily fulfil the Bristol Inquiry's recommendation that we 'treasure' mistakes, in order to learn effectively from them. The NHS Redress Scheme will also continue to distinguish between people whose illnesses or disabilities can be attributed to 'serious shortcomings' in NHS care, and those who have become unwell or disabled as a result of natural processes. In 1970, with the first publication of *Accidents, Compensation and the Law*, Patrick Atiyah drew attention to the unfairness of drawing a distinction between individuals with identical needs in this way, and his remarks undoubtedly remain pertinent today.

Patrick Atiyah[140]

Why, for example, should a child born disabled as a result of negligence on the part of the doctor who delivered the child be entitled to substantial compensation from the tort system, while the child born with similar congenital disabilities receives no common law

---

[138] Ibid.   [139] Ibid.

[140] Peter Cane, *Atiyah's Accidents, Compensation and the Law*, 5th edn (Butterworths: London, 1993) 331–2.

damages?...It has been suggested that the view that brain-damaged babies deserve more generous compensation than the congenitally disabled is rooted in the desire for account-ability, not compensation. More generally, it might be argued that compensating victims of human causes at a higher level than victims of natural causes is a way of giving effect to notions of personal responsibility: a person should be required to pay compensation for inju-ries if, but only if, that person was in some sense responsible for the disabilities...

Nevertheless, if compensation for disabilities was paid by individuals, the argument based on personal responsibility might have some force. However, we have seen that most tort compensation is not paid by individuals, but by insurers...and in this light it is less clear why tort-type benefits should only be available to those injured by human action. On the whole, those disabled people who can recover tort damages...are much better provided for than those disabled people who must rely on social security benefits alone. Can this be justified in the light of the fact that the tort system and the social security system are, in effect, both financed by the public at large?

FURTHER READING

Bristol Royal Infirmary Inquiry, *Learning from Bristol: The Report of the Public Inquiry into Children's Heart Surgery at the Bristol Royal Infirmary 1984–1995* <http://www.bristol-inquiry.org.uk/>.

Case, Paula, 'Secondary Iatrogenic Harm: Claims for Psychiatric Damage Following a Death Caused by Medical Error' (2004) 67 Modern Law Review 561–87.

Farrell, Anne-Maree and Devaney, Sarah, 'Making Amends or Making Things Worse? Clinical Negligence Reform and Patient Redress in England' (2007) 27 Legal Studies 27 630–48.

Harris, John, 'The Injustice of Compensation for Victims of Medical Accidents' (1997) 314 British Medical Journal 1821.

Making Amends: A Consultation Paper Setting Out Proposals for Reforming the Approach to Clinical Negligence in the NHS (DH: London, 2003), available at <http://www.dh.gov.uk>.

Merry, Alan, and McCall Smith, Alexander, *Errors, Medicine and the Law* (CUP: Cambridge, 2001).

Newdick, Christopher, 'NHS Governance after *Bristol*: Holding On, or Letting Go?' (2002) 10 Medical Law Review 111–13.

Quick, Oliver, 'Outing Medical Errors: Questions of Trust and Responsibility' (2006) Medical Law Review 22, 41–2.

Quick, Oliver, 'Prosecuting "Gross"' Medical Negligence: Manslaughter, Discretion and the Crown Prosecution Service' (2006) Journal of Law and Society 33 421–50.

Samanta, Ash *et al.*, 'The Role of Clinical Guidelines in Medical Negligence Litigation: a Shift from the Bolam Standard' (2006) Medical Law Review 321.

Witting, Christian, 'National Health Service Rationing: Implications For The Standard Of Care In Negligence' (2001) 21 Oxford Journal of Legal Studies 443.

Woolf, Lord, 'Are the Courts Excessively Deferential to the Medical Profession?' (2001) 9 Medical Law Review 1–16.

4

CONSENT I: UNDERSTANDING

CENTRAL ISSUES

1. It is increasingly recognized that the medical treatment of competent adults should be preceded by the patient's informed consent. The difficult question is working out exactly how much information patients need in order to be properly or adequately 'informed'.

2. If a patient was not informed 'in broad terms' about the nature of the medical treatment she has received, her consent was not real and an action in battery is possible. Such cases are rare.

3. More usually, a patient who claims not to have been adequately informed will bring an action in negligence, claiming that by failing to provide sufficient information, the doctor was in breach of her duty of care.

4. The question of how much information is necessary to avoid liability in negligence was traditionally governed by the *Bolam* test: that is, a doctor was judged by her conformity with responsible medical opinion. In contrast, the 'reasonable patient' test would ask whether the doctor had provided the information which a reasonable person, in the patient's position, would want to know.

5. Causation raises particular difficulties for patients who want to argue that their doctors failed to warn them about an adverse side-effect. This is because the patient has to prove that, if she had been told about a particular risk, she would have refused to consent to the treatment. This is a necessarily speculative inquiry, made more difficult by the fact that the patient now has the benefit of hindsight.

6. In practice, professional guidance appears to impose much more onerous duties of information disclosure upon doctors than tort law, but because a 'reasonable doctor' will follow professional guidelines, these more stringent standards might be indirectly incorporated into the doctor's duty of care.

1 INTRODUCTION

One of the first principles of medical law is that a competent adult patient must give their consent to medical treatment. Touching a person without their consent—however benevolently—is prima facie unlawful. For consent to be valid, it must be given voluntarily, by someone who has the capacity to consent, and who has been told what the treatment involves. We deal with the issues of capacity and voluntariness in the next chapter. Here we are concerned with the question of how much information must be provided to patients before they consent to medical treatment. This issue is often referred to as 'informed consent'. If a patient's consent to medical treatment has to be 'informed', this begs the question of how much information is needed to fulfil this requirement.

We begin by considering the ethical justifications for informing patients about their medical treatment. We then turn to explore the legal framework which is supposed to protect patients' interests in information disclosure. As we shall see, neither battery nor negligence has proved capable of capturing all of the interests which are at stake when patients are deprived of information that may be material to them when deciding whether to consent to a proposed treatment. In fact, both suffer from significant defects, leading some commentators to suggest that a wholly different approach might be appropriate. We then consider a few alternatives to the law of tort, and conclude by considering the difference between the case law on informed consent and the more rigorous guidance on informing patients produced by the medical profession itself.

2 WHY INFORM PATIENTS?

In the past, doctors were under no duty at all to provide their patients with information about their prognoses, or the advantages and disadvantages of different treatments. On the contrary, the assumption was that a doctor would exercise her customary care and skill in deciding upon the best course of action for a patient. Indeed, Hippocrates himself even enjoined physicians to take positive steps to conceal information from their patients:

> Perform [your duties] calmly and adroitly, concealing most things from the patient while you are attending to him . . . turning his attention away from what is being done to him; . . . revealing nothing of the patient's future or present condition.[1]

And the Hippocratic Oath itself assumes that treatment decisions are for the doctor alone:

> I swear by Apollo and Aesculapius that I will follow that system of regimen which according to my ability and judgment I consider for the benefit of my patients.[2]

Until relatively recently, it would not have occurred to doctors that patients too might have the ability or the judgement to make choices about their medical care. It was thought that informing patients about a poor prognosis, possible side-effects, or the availability of

---

[1] Hippocrates, *Decorum* (trans. W Jones) (Harvard UP: Cambridge, MA, 1967) 267.
[2] Hippocrates, 'Oath of Hippocrates', in *1 Hippocrates* 299–301 (WHS Jones trans., 1962).

alternative treatments would be likely to cause distress and confusion, and hence might jeopardize the possibility of recovery. Keeping patients in ignorance, and maintaining patients' trust and hope through the illusion of medical certainty was especially important given that most of the available treatments were in fact largely ineffective, and any reported improvements principally resulted from the placebo effect. Silence and, in certain circumstances, deception were themselves intended to achieve medical benefits by maintaining the patient's belief in the possibility of a cure.

There were times, however, when a doctor might judge the provision of information to be in a patient's best interests. When surgical procedures were carried out without anaesthetics, for example, it was important for patients to prepare themselves for the infliction of excruciating pain. In the 1767 case *Slater v Baker and Stapleton*[3] a surgeon had, without the patient's consent, refractured his leg and placed it in an experimental apparatus to stretch and strengthen it during healing. The court found that it was the normal practice of surgeons to seek consent before refracturing a patient's leg, and therefore there had been an improper breach of professional conduct. In addition, the court reasoned: 'It is reasonable that a patient should be told what is about to be done to him, that he may take courage and put himself in such a situation as to enable him to undergo the operation.'

Patients did not then have an autonomy-based *right* to be provided with information: rather, doctors might sometimes decide that telling patients what was going to happen to them would be in their best interests.

During the twentieth century, the idea that doctors might be under a duty to offer patients sufficient information to enable them to exercise some control over their medical care took hold. In part, this was a result of the growing importance of the principle of patient autonomy, which we considered in Chapter 1. It was also thought, as Michael Jones explains, that information-giving might help to redress the imbalance of knowledge and power within the doctor–patient relationship.

Michael Jones[4]

It is a trite observation that the doctor–patient relationship involves a major imbalance of power, some of which stems from social norms—patients expect to be at a disadvantage, because of their lack of knowledge, their lack of training, and sometimes because we want to believe desperately that the doctor is all knowing and all powerful and therefore will definitely make the correct diagnosis and provide a complete cure. Although some of this disparity is inherent in most professional–client relationships those relationships are not generally conducted when the client is ill (and on occasion when the client is at the disadvantage of being naked, apart from a flimsy robe). Part of the imbalance between doctor and patient is due to the patient's lack of information, and, on one view, it is the function of the law to redress the imbalance by providing patients with the 'right' to be given that information, or perhaps more accurately imposing a duty on doctors to provide it.... [A] patient with no rights is a citizen who is stripped of his or her individuality and autonomy, as well as her clothes, as soon as she walks into the surgery or the hospital.

---

[3] 2 Wils KB 359, 95 ER 850 (1767).
[4] 'Informed Consent and Other Fairy Stories' (1999) 7 Medical Law Review 103–34, 129.

In addition, advances in medical knowledge mean that there is now frequently more than one possible option for a patient diagnosed with a particular condition. Since few treatments are entirely without side-effects or possible adverse consequences, it is often necessary to choose between a number of therapeutic options, weighing up their relative advantages and disadvantages. While doctors' special skill qualify them both to diagnose a patient's condition and to carry out specialist medical procedures, it does not enable them to determine which treatment best accommodates the patient's own priorities. On the contrary, the patient herself is the only person with the expertise necessary to make a judgement about the tolerability of side-effects and possible adverse consequences. Following a diagnosis of breast cancer, the choice between chemotherapy and mastectomy may be one that is best made by the patient herself, in the light of her doctors' advice about each treatment's side-effects and likely success rates.

The Hippocratic principle that the doctor should decide which treatment the patient should receive has thus gradually been replaced by a *partnership* model of decision-making, in which both the doctor and the patient have specialist knowledge which must be shared in order to ensure that the patient makes the best possible decision *for herself*. The doctor is a source of information and expert advice, but on this model, the ultimate decision is for the patient.

Applying some of the concepts we explored in Chapter 1, it might be possible to detect both deontological and consequentialist justifications for the twin elements of informed consent: (a) to seek the patient's consent prior to treatment; and (b) to ensure that the patient has sufficient information about the proposed course of treatment. The deontological justification is obviously respect for patient self-determination and bodily autonomy. Respect for persons requires us to allow individuals to make their own decisions about their medical treatment, hence the need to gain the patient's consent. And, as we saw in Chapter 1, autonomous decision-making is only possible where an individual is free from external constraints, such as a lack of relevant information. The principle of patient self-determination therefore demands that patients have access to the information they need in order to choose whether to consent to medical treatment.

The consequentialist justification would instead emphasize the beneficial consequences that flow from involving patients in medical decision-making. Giving patients some control over the medical care that they receive will tend to lead to better outcomes. Patients might be more likely to comply with a treatment regime that they have chosen for themselves. Imposing a duty on doctors to communicate effectively might also improve the quality of care which patients receive.

But while there are sound ethical reasons for giving patients enough information to enable them to make informed decisions about their medical treatment, the concept of 'informed consent' has been subject to a number of criticisms.

The expression 'informed consent' itself may be both ambiguous and misleading. It is, for example, not entirely clear whether the word 'informed' refers to the doctor's conduct or the patient's state of mind. Has consent been 'informed' if information has simply been provided before consent is given, regardless of whether the patient has in fact read, listened to, or understood anything? Or must the consent itself have been 'informed' by the patient's prior consideration of all relevant material factors? Simply providing patients with information does not ensure that they have understood everything that they have been told. Not only are hypothetical predictions about risk inherently difficult to understand, but, as Onora O'Neill points out, illness can also undermine an individual's willingness and capacity to digest complex information.

Onora O'Neill[5]

A person who is ill or injured is highly vulnerable to others, and highly dependent on their action and competence. Robust conceptions of autonomy may seem a burden and even unachievable for patients; mere choosing may be hard enough. And, in fact, the choices that patients are required to make are typically quite limited. It is not as if doctors offer patients a smorgasbord of possible treatments and interventions, a variegated menu of care and cure. Typically a diagnosis is followed with an indication of prognosis and suggestions for treatment to be undertaken. Patients are typically asked to choose from a smallish menu—often a menu of one item—that others have composed and described in simplified terms. This may suit us well when ill, but it is a far cry from any demanding exercise of individual autonomy.

Moreover, the rather confusing implication of the phrase 'informed consent' is that consent is either informed or uninformed, when in fact a sharp boundary does not exist and instead the important issue is working out *how much* information patients might need in order to be adequately—though probably not fully—informed. PDG Skegg has suggested that:

It is regrettable, although entirely understandable, that it was not the expression 'sufficiently informed consent' which became so common. This would have alerted users to the fact that there is an issue of how informed it is necessary to be, in the context and for the purpose in question.[6]

To say that consent should be 'informed' does not tell us exactly how much information should be provided. On the contrary, as we shall see later, it is almost impossible for doctors to know prospectively how much disclosure will be necessary in order to avoid liability in negligence. As a result of this uncertainty, there is then a danger that doctors may feel compelled to disclose too much information to patients. Presenting patients with lengthy and complex consent forms may inhibit rather than promote genuine communication between doctors and their patients. There is, for example, some evidence that patients' understanding of consent forms is inversely related to their length. Information overload might also prompt patients to attach disproportionate importance to a very remote risk, and, as a result, refuse treatment which is overwhelmingly likely to be both safe and successful.

Giving patients detailed information about remote risks, and ensuring that they have understood it, takes time, and therefore costs money. Scarce NHS resources might then be diverted to lengthy consent procedures, which could be more effectively spent on providing medical treatment.

In practice, the process of obtaining patient consent is commonly limited to a single encounter before treatment begins, when the doctor recommends a particular procedure and offers the patient some information about its risks and benefits, before asking the patient to sign a consent form. Yet this model of decision-making is unsatisfactory for two reasons. First, it sits uneasily with the reality of medical treatment, which will rarely involve one single decision, but rather a series of decisions taken as more information becomes available about the patient's condition, and alternative treatment options are suggested.

Consent forms exacerbate the false perception that consent is an event, rather than a process which takes place over time. A doctor's duty to communicate effectively with her

---

[5] *Autonomy and Trust in Bioethics* (CUP: Cambridge, 2002) 38–9.

[6] 'English Medical Law and "Informed Consent": An Antipodean Assessment and Alternative' (1999) 7 Medical Law Review 135–65, 138.

patients may be especially important *during* treatment, and should not be confined to some brief bureaucratic ritual when the patient is first admitted to hospital.

Secondly, although patients are free to withdraw from treatment at any point, some may wrongly believe that signing a consent form binds them to its contents. In other contexts, a person who signs a document will usually have made a binding commitment to fulfil their side of the bargain, and it is therefore unsurprising that many patients do not understand that their right to refuse treatment persists throughout their care.

In their small empirical study of patients' perceptions of the consent process, Rob Heywood, Ann Macaskill, and Kevin Williams discovered that, while patients valued openness and good communication, and thought that this helped people to cope with bad news and to prepare themselves for treatment and its aftermath, they did not think this had anything to do with the consent process, which they instead regarded as a non-optional precondition for access to medical treatment.

Rob Heywood, Ann Macaskill, and Kevin Williams[7]

Few patients mentioned or even implied that consent was about their right to self-determination. Instead it seems to be viewed as a means to an end; something that is *necessary* and that they have to do in order to get to the next stage, treatment...

Despite patients looking favourably on openness and disclosure, there is evidence to suggest that any information provided is not used in the decision-making process and that patients make their decision long before they reach the 'consenting stage'. In other words, the patients in this study failed to make the link between the actual signing of the consent form and the information that was given to them in order that they could make an informed choice. The legal rules governing consent and information disclosure attempt to protect patient autonomy and redress the imbalance of power in the doctor–patient relationship. However, the patients in this study were not predominantly concerned with these factors, or at least they did not perceive them as the most important basis for disclosure. They failed to make the link between *information disclosure* and the *consent process* and did not relate consent to any notions of self-determination. Instead the importance they attached to pre-operative information was the way in which it enhanced coping mechanisms and the recovery process.

In their survey of 732 patients who had undergone obstetric surgery within the previous month, Akkad *et al.* found similar levels of confusion about the purpose of the consent forms that they had signed.

Andrea Akkad, Clare Jackson, Sara Kenyon, Mary Dixon-Woods, Nick Taub, and Marwan Habiba[8]

[M]ost participants (646, 88%) believed it was a legal requisite to sign a consent form before surgery. A fifth (20%) did not know whether they could change their mind after they had signed the form, and 118 (16%) incorrectly thought that signing a consent form removed their right to compensation.... One in 10 patients reported that they did not know what

[7] 'Patient Perceptions of the Consent Process: Qualitative Inquiry and Legal Reflection' (2008) 242 Professional Negligence 104–21.

[8] 'Patients' Perceptions of Written Consent: Questionnaire Study' (2006) 333 British Medical Journal 528.

they agreed to when they signed the consent form.... Almost half of all participants (46%) believed that the main function of signing the consent form was to protect the hospital from litigation, and two thirds (68%) thought it gave doctors control over what happened...

Many patients did not see written consent as functioning primarily in their interests nor as a way of making their wishes known. As suggested in previous work, many thought the primary function of the form was to protect the hospital.

Misunderstandings about the consent process are especially common in preventative screening programmes. When people are invited to participate in screening—such as the triannual cervical smear test or annual mammograms for women over the age of 50—there is evidence that many participants believe that they have been 'called in' for testing, rather than being asked if they wish to take part. Patients commonly believe that taking part in screening programmes is self-evidently beneficial, and that there is no need for them to weigh up any risks or benefits. While they appreciate the provision of leaflets to explain what is going to happen, they do not consider themselves to be evaluating the pros and cons of consenting to be screened.[9]

In their analysis of the leaflets provided to UK patients invited to take part in routine breast cancer screening Gøtzsche *et al.* point out that they over-emphasize the benefits of screening and downplay the existence of what they argue are, in fact, significant risks.

Peter C Gøtzsche, Ole J Hartling, Margrethe Nielsen, John Brodersen, and Karsten Juhl Jørgensen[10]

No mention is made of the major harm of screening—that is, unnecessary treatment of harmless lesions that would not have been identified without screening.... It is in violation of guidelines and laws for informed consent not to mention this common harm, especially when screening is aimed at healthy people...Another harm is false positive diagnoses....We now know that the psychosocial strain of a false alarm can be severe and may continue after women are declared free from cancer...A third harm is caused by radiotherapy of overdiagnosed women.

If 2000 women are screened regularly for 10 years, one will benefit from the screening, as she will avoid dying from breast cancer. At the same time, 10 healthy women will, as a consequence, become cancer patients and will be treated unnecessarily. These women will have either a part of their breast or the whole breast removed, and they will often receive radiotherapy and sometimes chemotherapy. Furthermore, about 200 healthy women will experience a false alarm. The psychological strain until one knows whether it was cancer, and even afterwards, can be severe.

3 LEGAL PROTECTION FOR PATIENTS' INTERESTS IN INFORMATION DISCLOSURE

In this section we tackle the central problem of what legal claim is appropriate when consent has *not* been properly informed. Does the lack of adequate information vitiate the patient's consent altogether, in which case the claim would lie in battery? Or is the provision

---

[9] W Osterlie, M Solbjor, J-A Skolbekken, S Hofvind, A R Saetnan, and S Forsmo, 'Challenges of Informed Choice in Organised Screening' (2008) 34 Journal of Medical Ethics e5.

[10] 'Breast Screening: The Facts—or Maybe Not' (2009) 338 British Medical Journal b86.

of information part of the doctor's ordinary duty of care, meaning that a failure to offer adequate information might ground an action in negligence? In the UK, the duty to obtain the patient's consent prior to treatment is protected by the tort of battery, while the duty to ensure that the patient has been given enough information (whatever that might mean) is normally treated as an aspect of the doctor's ordinary duty of care.

In short, an action in battery will only be successful if the patient did not in fact consent to the medical treatment that she received, and for a number of reasons the courts have been extremely reluctant to hold that a failure to give the patient information about risks or alternatives wholly invalidates the patient's consent. Most cases involving allegations of insufficient disclosure are therefore brought in negligence.

An action in negligence will only be successful if damage was caused by the doctor's breach of duty. Patients who have been inadequately informed prior to undergoing treatment can therefore only bring an action in negligence if they happen to have suffered injury as a result of the doctor's failure to disclose some relevant piece of information. As we see later, this requirement means that tort law will only provide a solution to a tiny sub-set of cases of inadequate information disclosure.

(a) BATTERY

Trespass to the person can be both a tort (battery) and a crime (assault). A patient's consent to medical treatment will only absolve the medical practitioner from liability in battery for unlawful touching if the consent is 'real': the patient must know what she is consenting to. If a patient consented to a different procedure from that which is in fact performed, her consent will not be effective, and the doctor might be found liable for unlawful touching. An example cited by Bristow J in *Chatterton v Gerson*[11] was a case from the 1940s in which a boy was admitted to hospital in Salford for a tonsillectomy. Due to an administrative error, he was circumcized instead. According to Bristow J, the appropriate cause of action here would have been trespass to the person.

Trespass to the person can be a criminal offence. In *R v Tabassum*,[12] T—who had no medical qualifications at all—was convicted of indecent assault after he persuaded the three complainants to consent to him showing them how to carry out a breast self-examination. Each complainant said they had only consented because they thought T had medical qualifications or relevant training. The Court of Appeal upheld his conviction on the grounds that 'consent was given because they mistakenly believed that the defendant was medically qualified…and that, in consequence, the touching was for a medical purpose. As this was not so, there was no true consent.'

In contrast, in *R v Richardson*,[13] a dentist continued to treat her patients after she had been suspended from practising. Her patients were not mistaken as to her identity, because she had treated them before, but as to her qualifications to practise. The Court of Appeal stated that 'either there is consent to actions on the part of a person in the mistaken belief that he or they are other than they truly are, in which case it is assault or, short of this, there is no assault'. Because 'the complainants were fully aware of the identity of the appellant', the Court of Appeal overturned her conviction.

The advantage of an action in battery is that it is not necessary to establish that any physical harm has been caused by the inadequate disclosure. As we see below, causation represents an almost insuperable obstacle to most claimants' actions in negligence because of the need to prove that proper disclosure would have prompted the patient to reject the

---

[11] [1981] QB 432.   [12] [2000] 2 Cr App Rep 328 (CA).   [13] 43 BMLR 21 (CA).

proposed course of treatment. Instead, a successful action in battery will lead to compensation for the dignitary harm of being treated without valid consent. This more accurately protects the patient's interest in self-determination because it is the violation of the patient's right to make an informed choice which is being compensated, rather than the materialization—through nobody's fault—of some small risk. Patients who are inadequately informed about an alternative treatment option will only be able to recover in negligence if the treatment that they received in fact goes wrong and they suffer physical injury as a result. Yet arguably, the patient's right to make an informed choice about which therapeutic option is best for them may have been infringed even if their treatment does not happen to cause them physical injury.

It is also no defence to a charge of battery that the doctor was acting in the best interests of her patient, or that she exercised all reasonable care and skill in carrying out the non-consensual treatment. Evidence of accepted medical practice is also irrelevant: if the failure to provide information to a patient vitiates an apparent consent, the fact that the defendant can point to other doctors who would have acted in the same way will not absolve her of responsibility.

There could also be no 'therapeutic privilege' (discussed below) if the cause of action is battery rather than negligence. If certain information is necessary for consent to be real, the doctor is not absolved from a failure to disclose it because she judges that disclosure might cause the patient severe distress or anxiety. Since the concept of therapeutic privilege is inherently paternalistic, its irrelevance to an action in battery further protects patient self-determination. The competent adult patient's right to be free from non-consensual touching is almost absolute, and the tort of battery appears to offer strong and uncompromising protection for a patient's right to make treatment decisions for herself.

Despite appearing to go more precisely to the infringement of patient autonomy involved in depriving patients of material information, judges have generally been hostile to the prospect of using battery to protect patients' interests in information disclosure. Provided that the patient agreed to the procedure which was in fact carried out, their consent will be effective and no action in battery will lie. The leading case is *Chatterton v Gerson*, in which Bristow J held that consent would be real as long as the patient had been informed 'in broad terms' about the nature of the procedure.

Miss Chatterton suffered from chronic and unendurable pain in a post-operative scar, and was sent for treatment to a pain clinic, where the defendant operated to block the sensory nerve. The defendant and Miss Chatterton's accounts of what information was provided differed. He said his normal practice was to explain to patients before the operation that it would result in numbness, and that it might involve temporary loss of muscle power. She claimed not to have been so warned. She lost sensation in her right leg, and claimed that her consent to operation was vitiated by the lack of explanation of the procedure's implications.

Chatterton v Gerson[14]

Bristow J

In my judgment what the court has to do in each case is to look at all the circumstances and say 'Was there a real consent?' I think justice requires that in order to vitiate the reality of

---

[14] [1981] QB 432 (QBD).

consent there must be a greater failure of communication between doctor and patient than that involved in a breach of duty if the claim is based on negligence. When the claim is based on negligence the plaintiff must prove not only the breach of duty to inform, but that had the duty not been broken she would not have chosen to have the operation. Where the claim is based on trespass to the person, once it is shown that the consent is unreal, then what the plaintiff would have decided if she had been given the information which would have prevented vitiation of the reality of her consent is irrelevant.

In my judgment once the patient is informed in broad terms of the nature of the procedure which is intended, and gives her consent, that consent is real, and the cause of the action on which to base a claim for failure to go into risks and implications is negligence, not trespass. Of course if information is withheld in bad faith, the consent will be vitiated by fraud. Of course if by some accident, as in a case in the 1940s in the Salford Hundred Court where a boy was admitted to hospital for tonsillectomy and due to administrative error was circumcised instead, trespass would be the appropriate cause of action against the doctor, though he was as much the victim of the error as the boy. But in my judgment it would be very much against the interests of justice if actions which are really based on a failure by the doctor to perform his duty adequately to inform were pleaded in trespass.

In *The Creutzfeldt-Jakob Disease Litigation*, the claimants had been treated with Human Growth Hormone (HGH), which had been extracted from pituitary glands that had been unlawfully harvested from dead bodies. They argued that their consent had been given on the understanding that the drug had been lawfully prepared, and that this ostensible consent was vitiated by the fact that the pituitaries had been unlawfully harvested. Their claim was dismissed by May J.

May J[15]

There is assault and battery when there is physical violation of a person's body without true consent. There is true consent when a person consents to the nature of the act done. There is no English law doctrine of informed consent and a person may succeed in a claim for failure to inform or warn only if the failure alleged amounts to negligence. To frame such a claim in battery is not only deplorable but insupportable in law.

In part, this judicial hostility to the use of battery in medical cases flows from the assumption that battery involves *deliberately* inflicted injury. A doctor who fails to tell a patient about a small inherent risk posed by a proposed course of treatment does not intend to injure her. Because a battery will also often be an assault, judges have been reluctant to criminalize by association a doctor's well-meaning but misguided decision to withhold information from a patient.

In *Wells v Surrey AHA*,[16] a sterilization operation was first suggested to the claimant after she had gone into labour, and the operation was performed at the same time as a caesarean section. The court found that the doctor had been negligent in failing to give the claimant 'proper advice' about the advisability of sterilization. Given the absence of adequate advice, and the circumstances in which her consent was obtained, it is hard to believe that this claimant had genuinely understood the implications of the operation to which she consented. Despite this, the court found that her consent had been real. Gerald Robertson suggests that

---

[15] *The Creutzfeldt-Jakob Disease Litigation* [1995] 54 BMLR 1 (QBD).

[16] The Times, 29 July 1978.

the only explanation for this is 'that the court was struggling to avoid the conclusion that the doctor was guilty of the tort of battery'.[17]

There have been a handful of successful cases, however. In *Appleton v Garrett* the dentist had deliberately carried out extensive and wholly unnecessary dental treatment for personal financial gain, and had been struck off the Dental Register as a result. It was almost certainly this element of intentional and fraudulent wrongdoing which persuaded the court to find him liable for battery rather than negligence.

Appleton v Garrett[18]

Dyson J

The evidence undoubtedly establishes that none of these eight plaintiffs was given any information on which to base a suitably informed consent. None was told why Mr Garrett was of the view that massive restorative treatment was required, often on perfect teeth. Typically, the plaintiff went for a normal routine check-up, and was subjected to the course of treatment without any explanation at all...I am quite satisfied that the failure to inform in these eight cases was not mere negligence and that Mr Garrett withheld information deliberately and in bad faith. The scale of the unnecessary treatment was so great that it must have been obvious to him that it was indeed unnecessary. The radiographs that he took before he embarked on the treatment showed in many cases that the teeth in these young plaintiffs were free from caries and were in what has been described as 'virgin condition'.

Much of the treatment on these teeth was considerable in its scope and extent. For example, several surfaces of virgin teeth were cut heavily and received large fillings, quite often supported by pins. Others received root canal treatment and crowns...

I conclude therefore that Mr Garrett deliberately embarked on large-scale treatment of these plaintiffs which he knew was unnecessary and that he deliberately withheld from them the information that the treatment was unnecessary because he knew that they would not have consented had they known the true position....I find, therefore, that none of the plaintiffs consented, at any rate to the treatment of those teeth that required no treatment, and that, at least in relation to those teeth, the tort of trespass to the person has been made out.

In the next extract, Ian Kennedy suggests that a broader application of the tort of battery might better protect patients' interests in information disclosure.

Ian Kennedy[19]

[P]atients' interests could well be better protected if the tort of battery were held to have a wider application. In particular, questions of what has come to be known as 'informed consent' could well be differently analysed and decided. A patient may have consented on the 'nature and purpose' test, but the information provided by the doctor may be so inadequate, in that it failed to respect the patient's right to know, so as to be able to choose, that the

[17] 'Informed Consent to Medical Treatment' (1981) 97 Law Quarterly Review 102–26, 123.
[18] 34 BMLR 23 (QBD).
[19] 'The Fiduciary Relationship and its Application to Doctors' in P Birks (ed.), *Wrongs and Remedies in the Twenty-first Century* (Clarendon Press: Oxford, 1986) 111–40.

consent should be regarded as entirely invalid. Such an extension of the tort of battery would restore the law's protection of the symbolic harm represented by the complaint that the patient's right to know was not respected. It would, in other words, reflect a legal response based upon rights.

But even if judges could be persuaded to carve out an extended role for the tort of battery, there are reasons why battery too might offer inadequate protection for patients' right to make informed medical decisions. Medical treatment can only amount to battery if there has been some sort of physical contact between doctor and patient. Hence, while an action in battery might be relatively straightforward if the treatment in question is surgery, there are many medical decisions which do not involve touching, and which would therefore be unaffected by a more robust application of the tort of battery. The prescription of drugs, for example, does not involve any physical contact, and so a patient who is inadequately informed about a medicine's side-effects could not bring an action in battery.

As Marjorie Maguire Shultz explains, a doctor's decision *not* to treat a patient could not form the basis of an action in battery, even where there was wholly inadequate disclosure of the risks of not being treated.

Marjorie Maguire Shultz[20]

Defining the scope of an autonomy interest in terms of physical contact with the body has intuitive appeal and offers a certain simplicity of administration. But ultimately, physical contact is too literal a demarcation for what is a much broader, non-tangible interest in patient choice. Health care choices of vast consequence can be made and implemented without such bodily contact as predictably triggers battery analysis. Most notably, this occurs when a doctor makes a decision not to act.

(b) NEGLIGENCE

If a patient's consent to a medical procedure has been sufficiently informed to be legally effective, and hence to avoid a charge of battery, the patient's only option is to argue that the doctor's failure to disclose information about their treatment amounted to negligence. As we saw in the previous chapter, there are three stages to an action in negligence. First, the defendant must owe the claimant a duty of care of the scope contended for; secondly, he must breach that duty; and thirdly, the breach must have caused the claimant's damage. Let us examine each stage in turn.

(1) The Duty of Care

At the outset, it is worth noting, as Andrew Grubb explains in the next extract, that imposing liability on a doctor for a failure to disclose information amounts to the creation of a duty to act positively rather than to simply refrain from causing harm. Such duties are exceptional in English law, and generally require special justification.

[20] 'From Informed Consent to Patient Choice: A New Protected Interest' (1985) 95 Yale Law Journal 219.

Andrew Grubb[21]

[I]t is immediately apparent that if the patient is entitled to be informed, the doctor is under a duty to provide the information. To so assert, however, is to place on the doctor a duty of affirmative action. It is trite law that English law regards such a duty as exceptional. While it is one thing to expect people to refrain from careless behaviour, English law, with its aversion to the 'officious intermeddler', will not ordinarily impose a duty to do something on behalf of another. The first step, therefore, is to examine the legal basis for the doctor's duty to inform a patient, so as to obtain valid consent to treatment.

One well-established ground on which a duty to inform could be based would be to find that, as between the doctor and the patient, there exists a 'special relationship', giving rise to a duty to act. The traditional example is the parent–child and, by extension, the teacher–child relationship. In effect, therefore, the duty is derived from the status of the parties. The common law has not, however, regarded the doctor–patient relationship as falling into the category of special relationships. . . .

So, where does the duty come from? Curiously, when the English courts very belatedly got round to examining whether a doctor is under a duty to inform a patient, the legal-technical difficulties involved in actually finding some juristic basis for a duty of affirmative action were largely ignored. Instead, the general duty of care owed by a doctor to a patient was interpreted as extending not only to acts but also omissions, in this case the failure properly to inform.

Despite some ambiguity about the origin of the duty to inform, it is now widely accepted that one aspect of the duty of care which doctors always owe to their patients is to provide them with information about any proposed treatment. The chief problem has then been working out when the doctor has breached this duty. How much information is required in order to fulfil the doctor's duty of care? As we see in the following sections, the law has struggled to devise a satisfactory test for assessing the adequacy of a doctor's disclosure.

(2) The Standard of Care

(a) From Sidaway to Chester

It is sometimes forgotten that the *Bolam*[22] case itself involved the doctor's failure to warn the patient about the risks involved in electroconvulsive therapy and to advise him that these could be minimized by the use of restraints or muscle relaxants. In a less famous passage from his direction to the jury, McNair J suggested that the doctor might act properly in withholding information about a risk which he considers to be 'minimal'.

Bolam v Friern Hospital Management Committee[23]

McNair J

You have to make up your minds whether it has been proved to your satisfaction that when the defendants adopted the practice they did (namely, the practice of saying very little and

---

[21] 'Consent to Treatment: The Competent Patient' 131–203 in A Grubb with J Laing (eds), *Principles of Medical Law*, 2nd edn (OUP: Oxford, 2004) 179–80.

[22] *Bolam v Friern Hospital Management Committee* [1957] WLR 582.

[23] [1957] WLR 582.

waiting for questions from the patient), they were falling below a proper standard of competent professional opinion on this question of whether or not it is right to warn. Members of the jury, though it is a matter entirely for you, you may well think that when dealing with a mentally sick man and having a strong belief that his only hope of cure is E.C.T. treatment, a doctor cannot be criticized if he does not stress the dangers which he believes to be minimal involved in that treatment.

The first House of Lords case to consider the question of how much information patients should be given before consenting to medical treatment was *Sidaway v Board of Governors of the Bethlem Royal Hospital and the Maudsley Hospital*. Mrs Sidaway complained that she had not been told about an operation's small risk—estimated to be between one and two per cent—of damage to her spinal column. She claimed that if she had been warned, she would not have had the operation. This risk had in fact materialized, and Mrs Sidaway was now seriously disabled. The House of Lords unanimously rejected Mrs Sidaway's claim that the failure to warn her of this risk had been negligent. They were also all agreed that the duty to disclose information is part of the doctor's ordinary duty of care. There were, however, very marked differences in their approaches to determining the relevant standard of care.

Sidaway v Board of Governors of the Bethlem Royal Hospital and the Maudsley Hospital[24]

Lord Scarman

The right of 'self-determination'—the description applied by some to what is no more and no less than the right of a patient to determine for himself whether he will or will not accept the doctor's advice—is vividly illustrated where the treatment recommended is surgery. A doctor who operates without the consent of his patient is, save in cases of emergency or mental disability, guilty of the civil wrong of trespass to the person: he is also guilty of the criminal offence of assault. The existence of the patient's right to make his own decision, which may be seen as a basic human right protected by the common law, is the reason why a doctrine embodying a right of the patient to be informed of the risks of surgical treatment has been developed in some jurisdictions in the USA and has found favour with the Supreme Court of Canada. Known as the 'doctrine of informed consent,' it amounts to this: where there is a 'real' or a 'material' risk inherent in the proposed operation (however competently and skilfully performed) the question whether and to what extent a patient should be warned before he gives his consent is to be answered not by reference to medical practice but by accepting as a matter of law that, subject to all proper exceptions (of which the court, not the profession, is the judge), a patient has a right to be informed of the risks inherent in the treatment which is proposed. The profession, it is said, should not be judge in its own cause: or, less emotively but more correctly, the courts should not allow medical opinion as to what is best for the patient to override the patient's right to decide for himself whether he will submit to the treatment offered him. . . .

Ideally, the court should ask itself whether in the particular circumstances the risk was such that this particular patient would think it significant if he was told it existed. I would think that, as a matter of ethics, this is the test of the doctor's duty. The law, however, operates not in Utopia but in the world as it is: and such an inquiry would prove in practice to be frustrated

24 [1985] AC 871.

by the subjectivity of its aim and purpose. The law can, however, do the next best thing, and require the court to answer the question, what would a reasonably prudent patient think significant if in the situation of this patient. . . .

My conclusion as to the law is therefore this. To the extent that I have indicated I think that English law must recognise a duty of the doctor to warn his patient of risk inherent in the treatment which he is proposing: and especially so, if the treatment be surgery. The critical limitation is that the duty is confined to material risk. The test of materiality is whether in the circumstances of the particular case the court is satisfied that a reasonable person in the patient's position would be likely to attach significance to the risk. Even if the risk be material, the doctor will not be liable if upon a reasonable assessment of his patient's condition he takes the view that a warning would be detrimental to his patient's health.

Lord Diplock

In English jurisprudence the doctor's relationship with his patient which gives rise to the normal duty of care to exercise his skill and judgment to improve the patient's health in any particular respect in which the patient has sought his aid, has hitherto been treated as single comprehensive duty covering all the ways in which a doctor is called upon to exercise his skill and judgment in the improvement of the physical or mental condition of the patient for which his services either as a general practitioner or specialist have been engaged. This general duty is not subject to dissection into a number of component parts to which different criteria of what satisfy the duty of care apply, such as diagnosis, treatment, advice (including warning of any risks of something going wrong however skilfully the treatment advised is carried out). The *Bolam* case itself embraced failure to advise the patient of the risk involved in the electric shock treatment as one of the allegations of negligence against the surgeon as well as negligence in the actual carrying out of treatment in which that risk did result in injury to the patient. . . .

In matters of diagnosis and the carrying out of treatment the court is not tempted to put itself in the surgeon's shoes; it has to rely upon and evaluate expert evidence, remembering that it is no part of its task of evaluation to give effect to any preference it may have for one responsible body of professional opinion over another, provided it is satisfied by the expert evidence that both qualify as responsible bodies of medical opinion. But when it comes to warning about risks, the kind of training and experience that a judge will have undergone at the Bar makes it natural for him to say (correctly) it is my right to decide whether any particular thing is done to my body, and I want to be fully informed of any risks there may be involved of which I am not already aware from my general knowledge as a highly educated man of experience, so that I may form my own judgment as to whether to refuse the advised treatment or not.

No doubt if the patient in fact manifested this attitude by means of questioning, the doctor would tell him whatever it was the patient wanted to know; but we are concerned here with volunteering unsought information about risks of the proposed treatment failing to achieve the result sought or making the patient's physical or mental condition worse rather than better. The only effect that mention of risks can have on the patient's mind, if it has any at all, can be in the direction of deterring the patient from undergoing the treatment which in the expert opinion of the doctor it is in the patient's interest to undergo. To decide what risks the existence of which a patient should be voluntarily warned and the terms in which such warning, if any, should be given, having regard to the effect that the warning may have, is as much an exercise of professional skill and judgment as any other part of the doctor's comprehensive duty of care to the individual patient, and expert medical evidence on this matter should be treated in just the same way. The *Bolam* test should be applied.

Lord Bridge (with whom Lord Keith agreed)

I should perhaps add at this point, although the issue does not strictly arise in this appeal, that, when questioned specifically by a patient of apparently sound mind about risks involved in a particular treatment proposed, the doctor's duty must, in my opinion be to answer both truthfully and as fully as the questioner requires.

I recognise the logical force of the *Canterbury* doctrine [see below p. 189], proceeding from the premise that the patient's right to make his own decision must at all costs be safeguarded against the kind of medical paternalism which assumes that 'doctor knows best'. But, with all respect, I regard the doctrine as quite impractical in application for three principal reasons. First, it gives insufficient weight to the realities of the doctor/patient relationship. A very wide variety of factors must enter into a doctor's clinical judgment not only as to what treatment is appropriate for a particular patient, but also as to how best to communicate to the patient the significant factors necessary to enable the patient to make an informed decision whether to undergo the treatment. The doctor cannot set out to educate the patient to his own standard of medical knowledge of all the relevant factors involved. He may take the view, certainly with some patients, that the very fact of his volunteering, without being asked, information of some remote risk involved in the treatment proposed, even though he describes it as remote, may lead to that risk assuming an undue significance in the patient's calculations. Secondly, it would seem to me quite unrealistic in any medical negligence action to confine the expert medical evidence to an explanation of the primary medical factors involved and to deny the court the benefit of evidence of medical opinion and practice on the particular issue of disclosure which is under consideration. Thirdly, the objective test which *Canterbury* propounds seems to me to be so imprecise as to be almost meaningless. If it is to be left to individual judges to decide for themselves what 'a reasonable person in the patient's position' would consider a risk of sufficient significance that he should be told about it, the outcome of litigation in this field is likely to be quite unpredictable...

[T]he issue whether non-disclosure in a particular case should be condemned as a breach of the doctor's duty of care is an issue to be decided primarily on the basis of expert medical evidence, applying the *Bolam* test. But I do not see that this approach involves the necessity 'to hand over to the medical profession the entire question of the scope of the duty of disclosure, including the question whether there has been a breach of that duty'...I am of opinion that the judge might in certain circumstances come to the conclusion that disclosure of a particular risk was so obviously necessary to an informed choice on the part of the patient that no reasonably prudent medical man would fail to make it. The kind of case I have in mind would be an operation involving a substantial risk of grave adverse consequences, as, for example, the ten per cent risk of a stroke from the operation which was the subject of the Canadian case of *Reibl v Hughes*.

Lord Templeman

There is no doubt that a doctor ought to draw the attention of a patient to a danger which may be special in kind or magnitude or special to the patient....

Whenever the occasion arises for the doctor to tell the patient the results of the doctor's diagnosis, the possible methods of treatment and the advantages and disadvantages of the recommended treatment, the doctor must decide in the light of his training and experience and in the light of his knowledge of the patient what should be said and how it should be said. At the same time the doctor is not entitled to make the final decision with regard to treatment which may have disadvantages or dangers. Where the patient's health and future are at stake, the patient must make the final decision. The patient is free to decide whether or not to submit to treatment recommended by the doctor and therefore the doctor impliedly

> contracts to provide information which is adequate to enable the patient to reach a balanced judgment, subject always to the doctor's own obligation to say and do nothing which the doctor is satisfied will be harmful to the patient....
>
> At the end of the day, the doctor, bearing in mind the best interests of the patient and bearing in mind the patient's right of information which will enable the patient to make a balanced judgment must decide what information should be given to the patient and in what terms that information should be couched.

Lord Diplock thought that the *Bolam* test applied to all aspects of a doctor's duty of care, and saw no reason to treat advice differently from diagnosis and treatment: the doctor's disclosure should therefore be judged by its conformity with responsible medical practice. At the other extreme, Lord Scarman argued that the doctor's duty of disclosure arose from the patient's 'basic human right' to make her own medical decisions. He was persuaded that the common law should follow the example set in cases from Canada and the US, and adopt a 'prudent patient' test: the doctor's duty should be to disclose that which a reasonable, prudent person in this patient's position would want to know, subject only to the 'therapeutic privilege' (discussed below).

Falling somewhere in between are the judgments of Lord Bridge, with whom Lord Keith agreed, and Lord Templeman. Lord Bridge 'recognized the logical force of the doctrine of informed consent', but regarded it as 'quite impractical'. First, he said it gave 'insufficient weight to the doctor–patient relationship', because doctors could not be expected to educate patients to their own level of understanding. This is of course true, but the prudent patient test demands *adequate*, not full disclosure. Secondly, he argued that it would be unrealistic to 'deny the court evidence of medical opinion and practice on disclosure'. It is not entirely clear what he means by this: the fact that evidence of medical practice exists does not necessarily mean that it should be decisive. Thirdly, he said that judging what the reasonable person in the patient's position would want to know is 'almost meaningless', and would lead to unpredictability in litigation. This criticism sits uneasily with the fact that the entire tort of negligence relies upon the judiciary's application, and greater specification of the 'reasonable man' test.

Having rejected the prudent patient test, Lord Bridge adopted a modified *Bolam* test. Disclosure, he argued, was 'primarily a matter of clinical judgment', but this did not mean that the profession was entirely free to set its own standards of disclosure. Rather, in certain circumstances, the judge might conclude that a risk ought to have been disclosed even if there was a body of responsible medical opinion which would not have warned the patient of it. The sort of risk he had in mind was 'an operation involving a substantial risk of grave adverse consequences', and the example he gave was a 10 per cent risk of a stroke. But while we know that Lord Bridge believed that a 1–2 per cent risk of spinal cord damage was not a substantial risk of grave adverse consequences, and a 10 per cent risk of a stroke was such a risk, his judgment begs the question of how to draw the line in between these two points of certainty. Is a 5 per cent risk of a stroke sufficient; or a 2 per cent risk of death?

Aside from the 'grey area' problem, Ian Kennedy points out that Lord Bridge's qualification to the *Bolam* test also 'beg[s] the central question: "substantial" and "grave" to whom?'[25] It cannot be to the doctor because otherwise this would simply restate the *Bolam* test which Lord Bridge instead intends to qualify. If it is 'substantial and grave' to *this* patient, then this

---

[25] *Treat Me Right* (OUP: Oxford, 1988) 200–1.

would introduce a subjective patient-orientated standard, which again would be inconsistent with Lord Bridge's rejection of the less radical prudent patient test. Instead, Ian Kennedy suggests that Lord Bridge must mean that the *court* should judge whether a particular risk is substantial and grave.[26] Ironically, in practice this assessment would not be very different from what the courts would have to do if they were to apply the prudent patient test, which Lord Bridge dismissed as unworkable.

Lord Templeman also advocated a modified *Bolam* test. There is, he argued, 'no doubt that a doctor ought to draw the attention of a patient to a danger which may be special in kind or magnitude or special to the patient'. When a risk is 'special', the *Bolam* test is not necessarily decisive, and a judge may decide that non-disclosure was negligent despite evidence of its conformity with responsible medical practice. But, of course, this again begs the question of what qualifies as a 'special' risk. It is notable that Lord Templeman expressly includes risks which are *special to the patient*, even though they are not special in kind or magnitude. This looks rather like a test which judges the reasonableness of disclosure from the *patient's* rather than the doctor's perspective.

Four years later, the Court of Appeal in *Gold v Haringey HA*—a case involving a failure to warn a patient about the failure rate of female sterilization—adopted a rather surprising interpretation of the judgments in *Sidaway*. Despite the views of Lords Bridge, Keith, and Templeman that it would be negligent not to warn a patient of a risk which was either 'substantial and grave' or 'special', the Court of Appeal in *Gold* simply stated that the House of Lords in *Sidaway* had applied the *Bolam* test. The only judgment referred to was that of Lord Diplock, whose straightforward application of *Bolam* did not represent the slightly more nuanced approach of the majority.

Gold v Haringey HA[27]

Lloyd LJ

In *Sidaway* the House of Lords applied the [*Bolam*] test to a case in which a doctor, before carrying out an operation, failed to warn his patient of a very small risk of very serious injury. . . . If there had been any doubt on the question, which I do not think there was, it was removed by the speech of Lord Diplock in the *Sidaway* case . . . It is clear from Lord Diplock's speech in *Sidaway* that a doctor's duty of care in relation to diagnosis, treatment and advice, whether the doctor be a specialist or general practitioner, is not to be dissected into its component parts.

Since *Sidaway*, the House of Lords judgment in *Bolitho v City and Hackney HA*[28] has modified the traditional *Bolam* test by emphasizing the need for the doctor's conduct to be logically supportable, as well as compliant with accepted medical practice. When a doctor seeks to rely upon the evidence of other doctors who say that they would have acted in the same way, the courts will nevertheless be prepared to make a finding of negligence where the professional opinion in question 'is not capable of withstanding logical analysis'. Indeed, it could be argued that this was the approach adopted in a pre-*Bolitho* case, *Smith v Tunbridge Wells Health Authority*,[29] in which Morland J found that while some surgeons in 1988 might

---

[26] Ibid, 201.   [27] [1988] QB 481.
[28] [1998] AC 232.
[29] [1994] 5 Med LR 334.

not have warned a 28-year-old man of the risk of impotence associated with an operation to repair a rectal prolapse, 'that omission was neither reasonable nor responsible'.

While Lord Browne-Wilkinson in *Bolitho* was careful to specify that his judgment applied to questions of diagnosis and treatment, and not to disclosure of risk, there does seem to be some evidence of a trend towards greater judicial willingness to challenge clinical judgment in informed consent cases.

In *Pearce v United Bristol Healthcare NHS Trust*, the Court of Appeal appeared to move closer to the 'reasonable patient' test in determining whether the 0.1–0.2 per cent risk of still-birth associated with waiting for a natural birth should have been disclosed to a pregnant woman whose baby was two weeks overdue, and who had begged to have an induced labour or a caesarean section. Tina Pearce accepted her consultant's advice to 'let nature take its course', and her baby died *in utero* a few days later.

Pearce v United Bristol Healthcare NHS Trust[30]

Lord Woolf MR

In a case where it is being alleged that a plaintiff has been deprived of the opportunity to make a proper decision as to what course he or she should take in relation to treatment, it seems to me to be the law, as indicated in the cases to which I have just referred, that if there is a significant risk which would affect the judgment of a reasonable patient, then in the nor-mal course it is the responsibility of a doctor to inform the patient of that significant risk, if the information is needed so that the patient can determine for him or herself as to what course he or she should adopt....

Turning to the facts of this case, the next question is, therefore, 'Was there a significant risk?...[O]n any basis, the increased risk of the stillbirth of Jacqueline, as a result of additional delay, was very small indeed...Even looked at comprehensively it comes to something like 0.1–0.2%. The doctors called on behalf of the defendants did not regard that risk as signifi-cant; nor do I...

Particularly when one bears in mind Mrs Pearce's distressed condition, one cannot criticise Mr Niven's decision not to inform Mrs Pearce of that very, very small additional risk....This is a case where, in my judgment, it would not be proper for the courts to interfere with the clinical opinion of the expert medical man responsible for treating Mrs Pearce.

As to what would have been the consequence if she had been told of this particularly small risk, it is difficult to envisage..., but my conclusion is that, in so far as it was possible for this court to make an assessment of this, the inference is that if Mrs Pearce had been able to understand what she had been told about the increased risk, her decision would still have been to follow, reluctantly, the advice of the doctor who was treating her.

Lord Woolf MR stated that 'a significant risk which would affect the judgment of the reasonable patient' should be disclosed. This would appear to be a more patient-centred approach to the question of how much information should be provided, but note that in deciding whether the doctors should have disclosed a 0.1–0.2 per cent risk of stillbirth, Lord Woolf said that '*the doctors* called on behalf of the defendants did not regard that risk as significant, nor do I' (my emphasis). Thus he appeared to rely upon the *doctors'* judgement of whether the risk was 'significant', and not on Tina Pearce's own assessment of whether

---

[30] (1998) 48 BMLR 118 [CA].

the risk was sufficiently material that it would have affected her decision to accept medical advice and proceed to a natural birth.

Despite this, in *Wyatt v Curtis*, a case in which a woman was not warned about the risk of abnormality as a result of contracting chicken pox during pregnancy, Sedley LJ suggested that Lord Woolf's approach in *Pearce* 'refines' Lord Bridge's judgment in *Sidaway* by explaining that whether a risk is 'substantial' or 'grave' should be assessed from the patient's and not the doctor's point of view.

Wyatt v Curtis[31]

Sedley LJ

Lord Woolf's formulation refines Lord Bridge's test by recognising that what is substantial and what is grave are questions on which the doctor's and the patient's perception may differ, and in relation to which the doctor must therefore have regard to what may be the patient's perception. To the doctor, a chance in a hundred that the patient's chickenpox may produce an abnormality in the foetus may well be an insubstantial chance, and an abnormality may in any case not be grave. To the patient, a new risk which (as I read the judge's appraisal of the expert evidence) doubles, or at least enhances, the background risk of a potentially catastrophic abnormality may well be both substantial and grave, or at least sufficiently real for her to want to make an informed decision about it.

In his judgment in the House of Lords in *Chester v Afshar*, a case we discuss in detail below, Lord Steyn also quoted with approval Lord Woolf's approach in *Pearce*, and said that patients have the *right* to be informed of 'small but well-established' risks of serious injury.

Chester v Afshar[32]

Lord Steyn

A surgeon owes a legal duty to a patient to warn him or her in general terms of possible serious risks involved in the procedure. The only qualification is that there may be wholly exceptional cases where objectively in the best interests of the patient the surgeon may be excused from giving a warning. This is, however, irrelevant in the present case. In modern law medical paternalism no longer rules and a patient has a prima facie right to be informed by a surgeon of a small, but well established, risk of serious injury as a result of surgery.

Again, notice that while Lord Steyn states that the duty is to warn the patient about 'serious' risks, it is not clear whether seriousness should be judged from the patient's or the doctor's perspective. Nevertheless, Lord Steyn's explicit rejection of 'medical paternalism' may offer some evidence of a shift towards the reasonable patient test.

This trend towards a more patient-centred evaluation of the content of the doctor's duty to provide information has been continued in the case of *Birch v UCL Hospital NHS Foundation Trust*. In this case, the patient had been warned that there was a 1 per cent risk of stroke associated with catheter angiography, but she was not told that there was an alternative,

[31] [2003] EWCA Civ 1779.   [32] [2004] UKHL 41.

albeit slightly less exact, diagnostic technique, namely an MRI scan, which carried no risk of stroke. Mrs Birch suffered a stroke and claimed that the doctor had breached his duty of care by failing to tell her about the *comparative* risks of angiography versus MRI. Despite the defendant's expert witnesses claiming that the doctor's duty was just to inform Mrs Birch of the risks associated with the catheter angiogram, which he had undoubtedly done, Cranston J agreed with Mrs Birch that this approach was not logically supportable.

Birch v UCL Hospital NHS Foundation Trust[33]

Cranston J

If patients must be informed of significant risks it is necessary to spell out what, in practice, that encompasses. In this case the defendant informed the patient of the probabilities, the one per cent, and the nature of the harm of this risk becoming manifest, the stroke. But these were the objectively significant risks associated with the procedure which was performed, the catheter angiogram. Was it necessary for the defendant to go further and to inform Mrs Birch of comparative risk, how this risk compared with that associated with other imaging procedures, in particular MRI? No authority was cited to this effect but in my judgment there will be circumstances where consistently with Lord Woolf MR's statement of the law in *Pearce v United Bristol Healthcare NHS Trust* the duty to inform a patient of the significant risks will not be discharged unless she is made aware that fewer, or no risks, are associated with another procedure. In other words, unless the patient is informed of the comparative risks of different procedures she will not be in a position to give her fully informed consent to one procedure rather than another.

I am convinced that in Mrs Birch's case no reasonable, prudent medical practitioner would have failed to discuss the respective modalities and risks with her along the lines outlined. In their absence she was denied the opportunity to make an informed choice. Even if I am wrong on this, the failure to discuss with Mrs Birch these matters could not be described in law as reasonable, responsible or logical. On either approach, therefore, the failure to provide her with this information was in breach of duty.

A further, but less frequently discussed practical problem in negligence cases lies in establishing what information was, in fact, disclosed to the patient. Patients are unlikely to have made notes during their encounter with the doctor, and many years later, may not be able to accurately recall what they were told. Doctors' notes seldom record every detail of the conversations they have had with patients, and it is often difficult for doctors to remember exactly what passed between them and an individual patient, particularly if the consultation happened some years ago. The courts will therefore often be faced with two contradictory accounts of the discussions that took place prior to treatment. Evidence of a doctor's usual practice will sometimes be relevant, though in many cases, the judge will simply have to decide who is the more credible witness. In *Chatterton v Gerson*, for example, Bristow J believed the doctors' account of the pre-operation discussions:

I have come to the conclusion that on the balance of probability Dr. Gerson did give his usual explanation about the intrathecal phenol solution nerve block and its implications of

---

[33] [2008] EWHC 2237 (QB).

> numbness instead of pain plus a possibility of slight muscle weakness, and that the plaintiff's recollection is wrong; and on the evidence before me I so find.[34]

In contrast, in the first instance decision in *Chester v Afshar*, the trial judge had preferred the claimant's account on the grounds that it had the 'ring of truth and [was] most unlikely to be the result of either invention or reconstruction'.[35]

While *Sidaway* itself has not been overruled, it seems clear that English law has, in the past twenty-five years, moved away from the strict *Bolam* approach adopted by Lord Diplock and applied by the Court of Appeal in *Gold*. There may be some doubt over whether the test in law is now better described as the prudent patient test rather than the reasonable doctor test—note that Cranston J explicitly evaluated the doctor's disclosure according to whether a *reasonable doctor* would have failed to disclose the comparative lack of risk associated with an MRI scan—but it is clear that the 'doctor knows best' approach is no longer dominant.

Let us now turn to critically evaluate the three possible options in setting the standard of care: (a) the reasonable doctor test; (b) the prudent patient test; and (c) the subjective standard, as well as the 'therapeutic privilege' exception.

(b) The reasonable doctor test

The reasonable doctor test suffers from a number of disadvantages. First, and most importantly, it does not protect the patient's right to self-determination. The central problem with employing a professional standard test in order to determine what information patients need in order to make informed choices about their medical treatment is that, unlike diagnosis and treatment, this is not a question which requires clinical expertise. On the contrary, if the patient has the right to decide whether to consent to a proposed treatment, she can only exercise meaningful choice over this decision if she has sufficient information to allow her to weigh the advantages and disadvantages of the treatment in question, in the light of her own values and priorities. Medical progress has expanded the range of available treatment options, and there is always the possibility of declining treatment altogether. As Harry Lesser explains in the next extract, most treatments will have side-effects, the acceptability of which can be judged only from the patient's own perspective. Cancer of the throat can be treated by surgery or by radiation. Surgery is more effective, but will deprive the patient of normal speech. Only the patient herself can determine whether the higher chance of prolonging life outweighs the reduction in the quality of her life.

Harry Lesser[36]

> [T]here is not always a medically best course of action, for two reasons. One is that medicine has at least three aims—to prolong life, to remove obstacles to a person's physical and mental functioning and to relieve suffering. Very often these three all come together…But this is not always so; if, for example, the choice is to relieve pain at the cost of leaving patients feeling 'woozy' and confused, or to help them to be mentally alert at the cost of appreciable

---

[34] *Chatterton v Gerson* [1981] QB 432.

[35] [2002] EWCA Civ 724.

[36] 'The Patient's Right to Information' in Margaret Brazier and Mary Lobjoit (eds), *Protecting the Vulnerable: Autonomy and Consent in Health Care* (Routledge: London, 1991) 150–60.

physical pain, then there is no 'better' course of action, even medically, except in terms of the individual patient's preference, whichever it may be: it is honourable to choose alertness and the price of physical suffering, but in no way dishonourable to choose the reverse...

Even where the aim is clear, and agreed on by doctor and patient—for example to cure a particular disease or malfunctioning—it may not be possible to produce a 'right' or 'correct' ordering of the possible lines of treatment. This is because types of treatment can differ in at least five ways: in the likelihood of success, the degree of success possible, the seriousness of the 'side-effects' (which are also not all of the same type), the seriousness of the harm if things go wrong and the degree of risk that things might go wrong....Once again, doctors' expertise enables them to know the possible consequences of various alternatives and to have some idea of their likelihood; but there is still no right answer to the question which alternative is best, which risks are worth taking and which are not, except in terms of what the patient chooses.

Secondly, the reasonable doctor test inevitably emphasizes the question of what the doctor actually said: would other doctors have said similar things to patients in these circumstances? But if the purpose of giving information to patients is to ensure informed decision-making, the question should instead be: does the patient have an adequate *understanding* of the relative advantages and disadvantages of treatment? Individual patients' capacity to understand complex information about risk will vary considerably. English is not every patient's first language. An emphasis upon what the patient understands, rather than on what the doctor said, would require doctors to become engaged in more direct communication and questioning of patients than is possible if information is conveyed using a standardized information sheet.

Thirdly, the emphasis on consent implies a paternalistic model of medical decision-making in which a doctor offers the patient a particular treatment, which she can then accept or decline. But there is rarely only one possible course of action, and so framing the issue in this way already implicitly accepts that the doctor should have the power to determine which treatment is appropriate, with the patient's only option being to agree with the doctor, or reject treatment altogether. Choice, on the other hand, is a much more patient-centred concept, which might involve greater emphasis upon the various alternative courses of action open to the patient.

Fourthly, the reasonable doctor test offers little prospective guidance for doctors faced with the question: 'What am I legally required to disclose to this patient?' The rather cryptic and unhelpful answer to this question must be that a doctor should tell the patient that which no reasonably prudent doctor would fail to disclose, as determined retrospectively by a court.

Finally, the reasonable doctor test largely ignores the role of other health care professionals who are not medical practitioners. Nurses, for example, may have more time to spend discussing treatment options, and might be better at communicating with patients than doctors.

The advantage of a reasonable doctor test for the standard of disclosure is its comparative ease of application. Should a doctor be sued in negligence, expert witnesses can offer evidence of whether other doctors would in fact have acted in the same way if faced with a similar patient. In contrast, if the test is instead what this patient would want to know, doctors will be forced to guess what might matter to this patient. It is increasingly rare for doctors—particularly those carrying out specialist treatments such as surgery—to have had any contact at all with the patient prior to their admittance to hospital. Without knowing anything about the patient's values and goals, the doctor has no way of knowing which pieces of information matter to her. If doctors were to be held to a subjective patient-specific standard of information disclosure, in order to avoid liability, the doctor might be tempted to give the patient more information than she could possibly digest, thereby reducing, rather than enhancing, her ability to make an informed choice.

(c) The prudent patient test

The prudent patient test—which, as Lord Scarman pointed out in *Sidaway* has replaced the reasonable doctor test in the US, Canada, Australia, and New Zealand—is intended to address some of the defects in the reasonable doctor test. Its most famous formulation is taken from the 1972 US case *Canterbury v Spence*:[37] 'a risk is thus material when a reasonable person, in what the physician knows or should know to be the patient's position, would be likely to attach significance to the risk or cluster of risks in deciding whether or not to forego the proposed therapy'.

While this test focuses on what the patient would want to know, rather than what other doctors would do, it is not without disadvantages. How are doctors supposed to know in advance what the abstract, hypothetical, reasonable patient would want to know? Since the standard of care in a particular case could only be conclusively determined *retrospectively* by the courts, the doctor will have to second-guess the court's assessment of what a reasonable patient would consider material. Since there are very few cases in this area, doctors facing a decision about how much information to provide to a particular patient will gain little practical assistance from consulting the law. Instead, they are likely to seek guidance from *other doctors* as to what patients generally want to know. It is easy to see how in practice this test could become indistinguishable from the reasonable doctor test.

Paul Appelbaum, Charles Lidz, and Alan Meisel suggest, perhaps a little optimistically, that this inherent difficulty in knowing what patients want to know will in practice encourage doctors to spend more time finding out what matters to their patients, thus improving patient care:

> The very difficulty in knowing and applying the patient-oriented standard turns out to be its virtue (though possibly not from physicians' perspective). To determine what a reasonable patient would find material to making a decision, physicians are compelled to engage in a discussion with each patient. In so doing, they act to implement one of the fundamental goals of the idea of informed consent: to inform patients in decision making about their own care.[38]

It is, however, important to remember that the 'reasonable' or 'prudent patient' test does not mean that the doctor should tell *this patient* all the information which *she* would like to know: rather, it is intended to deliver to *all* patients that which *most patients* would want to know. It might then be argued that, just like the reasonable doctor test, the prudent patient test cannot adequately protect patient self-determination, because individual patients' interests in information vary dramatically. People have different priorities, beliefs, and family histories, all of which will affect the relative importance they attach to the risks and benefits of medical treatment.

---

[37] 464 F 2d 772 (DC Cir 1972).
[38] Paul S Appelbaum, Charles W Lidz, and Alan Meisel, *Informed Consent: Legal Theory and Clinical Practice* (OUP: Oxford, 1987) 45–6.

While all patients want to know about risks that are very likely to materialize or which have potentially grave consequences, lesser risks may be significant only to a small number of patients. Telling every patient about risks or side-effects which the abstract reasonable patient would consider material might be preferable to the *Bolam* standard of disclosure, but it will result in some patients being deprived of information about a proposed treatment which is in fact of vital importance to them. As we shall see later, this problem may be exacerbated by the application of a quasi-objective 'reasonable patient' test for causation. If the claimant must prove not that she herself would have refused treatment if she had been properly informed, but rather that the reasonable patient would not have consented to the treatment in question, the right to act according to one's own preferences and priorities is not protected at all.

(d) The subjective standard

In the next extract, Alexander Capron argues that only a subjective standard of disclosure can adequately protect patient autonomy. A subjective standard acknowledges that people have highly variable information needs, and imposes a duty upon doctors to tailor their disclosures according to the individual patient's own priorities and concerns.

Alexander Morgan Capron[39]

The importance of a subjective rather than an objective standard of materiality can be seen by comparing how well each standard would serve the functions of informed consent. For example, a physician-investigator's self scrutiny is likely to be increased if he has to ask, 'Is this procedure right for this patient, based on what I actually know about him or her?' and not on what is known about the 'reasonable patient'. . . . The requirement that the physician-investigator individualize the informing process is consistent with the obligation to individualize the diagnostic and therapeutic processes. Similarly, the respect for the patient-subject as a full human being is better served by a subjective standard.

In practice, however, a subjective standard might prove almost impossible to enforce. Patients will rarely be able to articulate all of their relevant values and priorities during a brief consultation. Within the modern and increasingly impersonal health care system, doctors cannot be expected to know enough about their individual patients' values and experiences to accurately predict what factors will be material to their decision-making, and it would be unfair to hold doctors liable in negligence for their inability to anticipate all of their patients' idiosyncratic beliefs or fears. On the contrary, patients must rely on their doctors to make judgements about what factors are likely to be important to them. Of course, in making this assessment, doctors will inevitably rely on evidence both of what other doctors generally do in such circumstances, and of what patients generally appear to want to know.

This is not to say that the subjective standard should be completely dismissed as an impractical ideal. Rather, while practical considerations mean that it would be difficult for it to ground the test of liability in negligence, it might nevertheless be important for doctors to at least *try* to discover the individual patient's subjective priorities through appropriate

---

[39] 'Informed Consent in Catastrophic Disease Research and Treatment' (1974) 123 University of Pennsylvania Law Review 340, 416–17.

questioning. In the next extract, Ruth Faden *et al.* advocate a shift away from standards of disclosure towards a duty to enter into an 'informational exchange' with patients.

Ruth R Faden, Tom L Beauchamp, with Nancy MP King[40]

[T]he solution lies not in reformulations of conventional or proposed legal disclosure standards, but rather in the adoption of a different approach to understanding and informed consent—an approach that focuses more broadly on issues of communication....

From the perspective of informed consent..., disclosure standards requiring a specified quantum of information are not only insufficient, but present an entirely misleading approach to the issues. Such disclosure standards are not adequate to protect autonomous decision-making, because the emphasis on disclosure is the wrong emphasis. The central question is not merely, 'What facts should the professional provide?' but 'What should the professional ask and say?' and, as we see shortly, 'How should the professional act?' Traditional questions about adequate disclosures need to be reformulated as questions about effective communication....

Professionals would do well to end their traditional preoccupation with disclosure and instead ask questions, elicit the concerns and interests of the patient or subject, and establish a climate that encourages the patient or subject to ask questions. This is the most promising course to ensure that the patient or subject will receive information that is personally material—that is, the kind of description that will permit the subject or patient, on the basis of his or her personal values, desires, and beliefs, to act with substantial autonomy.

It seems clear that the latest GMC guidance on consent adopts this approach.

General Medical Council[41]

4. No single approach to discussions about treatment or care will suit every patient, or apply in all circumstances. Individual patients may want more or less information or involvement in making decisions depending on their circumstances or wishes...

28. The amount of information about risk that you should share with patients will depend on the individual patient and what they want or need to know. Your discussions with patients should focus on their individual situation and the risk to them....

31. You should do your best to understand the patient's views and preferences about any proposed investigation or treatment, and the adverse outcomes they are most concerned about. You must not make assumptions about a patient's understanding of risk or the importance they attach to different outcomes.

Finally, it could also be argued that there is a tension between the therapeutic privilege, discussed in the following section—which is subjectively assessed—and the standard of care. Why should doctors be entitled to take into account the patient's special sensibilities when deciding *not* to tell them about a particular risk, while their special sensibilities are irrelevant to the decision to positively disclose information?

[40] *A History and Theory of Informed Consent* (OUP: Oxford, 1986) 306–7.
[41] Consent: Patients and Doctors Making Decisions Together GMC (2008), available at <www.gmc-org.uk>.

(e) Therapeutic privilege

In *Sidaway*, Lord Scarman accepted that the 'prudent patient' test should, if it were adopted by English law, be subject to one exception, namely the doctor's therapeutic privilege, according to which there is no duty to disclose information which might be positively harmful to patients. If a doctor believes that a patient's reaction to a particular piece of information would cause a serious deterioration in her condition, then that information may reasonably be withheld. In the next extract, Len Doyal suggests that there may be circumstances in which selective non-communication will in fact protect the patient's capacity to exercise informed choice later on.

Len Doyal[42]

> [S]uppose that an oncologist is faced with a 'rational' (that is, non-psychiatrically ill) patient who is so anxious about possible bad news that any attempt at complete truth will probably meet with misunderstanding. In this case, a decision to be selective with information may well be taken in order to respect the right of the patient to make an *informed* choice later on. If one froze such a decision in time then no doubt it would appear to be paternalistic. Yet when the process of informing and understanding is seen as precisely that—a process over time involving complex intellectual and emotional interaction between clinician and patient—then accusations of paternalism may not be correct. Of course, there is still the question of how long to sequence the information and what to do if the anxiety does not abate. In practice, the answers to such questions are sometimes unclear because of the contingencies of patient competence and the difficulties of knowing what it means to respect autonomy when confronted with them. Clinicians must just do the best they can.

Because the therapeutic privilege exception allows the doctor's paternalistic concern for her patient's best interests to trump the principle of patient self-determination, its precise scope must be tightly circumscribed if it is not to undermine the patient's ability to make informed choices about her medical treatment. In particular, it is important that information is not withheld just because it might prompt the patient to refuse treatment which the doctor believes to be in her best interests. If this came within the therapeutic privilege exception, patients' right to refuse treatment would be substantially diminished by the indirect resurrection of the paternalistic assumption that it is doctors alone who should decide what treatment a patient should undergo. A better and narrower formulation would allow doctors to invoke the therapeutic privilege exception only if the patient would suffer physical or mental harm *other than that which the doctor believes would be caused by her decision to refuse to have the treatment in question.* This is enshrined in the GMC's guidance to doctors:

> 16 You should not withhold information necessary for making decisions for any other reason, including when a relative, partner, friend or carer asks you to, unless you believe that giving it would cause the patient serious harm. In this context 'serious harm' means more than that the patient might become upset or decide to refuse treatment.[43]

---

[42] 'Medical Ethics and Moral Indeterminacy' (1990) 17 Journal of Law and Society 1–16, 9.
[43] General Medical Council, Consent: Patients and Doctors Making Decisions Together GMC (2008), available at <www.gmc-uk.org>.

While the therapeutic privilege does allow beneficence (or the doctor's duty to act in her patient's best interests) to trump respect for patient self-determination in certain exceptional circumstances, the presumption is still in favour of disclosure. In order to invoke the therapeutic privilege exception, the burden of proof is on the doctor to establish that she had reasonable grounds for believing that this instance of non-disclosure was justifiable.

(f) When and how should information be provided

It is plainly not sufficient that doctors should simply give patients information about a proposed course of treatment without any attempt to ensure that the patient has understood what they have been told. Information must be comprehensible, and should be communicated in a way that facilitates understanding. It is therefore important for health care professionals to take reasonable steps to present information in a way that patients will be able to understand, and to ensure that the context in which disclosures are made is appropriate. If the patient cannot understand English, access to translated information, or to an interpreter might be necessary.

However comprehensive the disclosure, giving a patient information about the risks associated with surgery immediately before or after an operation might nevertheless be negligent. In *Lybert v Warrington HA*[44] the surgeon discussed the irreversibility of sterilization, and the risks of failing to achieve sterility immediately after the patient had undergone the operation. The court concluded that the surgeon had been negligent because the warning was not sufficiently emphatic and clear, and because the timing and the conditions in which it was given were inappropriate.

It is also important that the task of informing patients about the risks and benefits associated with the various treatment options is taken seriously, and not delegated to junior medical staff who may have little experience of communicating with patients, and whose ability to answer patients' questions may be limited. There is also a danger that obtaining patients' consent to medical treatment is perceived by some doctors to be a formal bureaucratic requirement, that offers protection against litigation, but which can be fulfilled by getting the patient to sign a standard consent form.

A central problem is that it is difficult to communicate effectively with patients. Research indicates that patients are seldom able to recall information that has been disclosed to them about their condition and its treatment. It is common for patients to sign consent forms without reading them. Perfect patient comprehension is an unrealistic goal. Nevertheless, health staff should do as much as is reasonable in the circumstances to promote their patients' understanding of relevant information. Again GMC guidance suggests that doctors should do their best to ensure that patients have understood the information which has been provided.

General Medical Council[45]

> 21. You should check whether the patient needs any additional support to understand information, to communicate their wishes, or to make a decision. You should bear in mind that some barriers to understanding and communication may not be obvious; for example,

---

[44] [1996] 7 Med LR 71.

[45] Consent: Patients and Doctors Making Decisions Together GMC (2008), available at <www.gmc-uk.org>.

a patient may have unspoken anxieties, or may be affected by pain or other underlying problems. You must make sure, wherever practical, that arrangements are made to give the patient any necessary support. This might include, for example: using an advocate or interpreter; asking those close to the patient about the patient's communication needs; or giving the patient a written or audio record of the discussion and any decisions that were made . . .

34. You must use clear, simple and consistent language when discussing risks with patients. You should be aware that patients may understand information about risk differently from you. You should check that the patient understands the terms that you use, particularly when describing the seriousness, frequency and likelihood of an adverse outcome. You should use simple and accurate written information or visual or other aids to explain risk, if they will help the patient to understand.

In *Al Hamwi v Johnston*, counsel for Mrs Al-Hamwi went further and argued that the clinician's duty of care incorporated a duty to *ensure* that the information given to the patient had been understood. In this case, despite evidence that Mrs Al-Hamwi had received the standard information about the risks of amniocentesis, which include a one per cent risk of miscarriage, Mrs Al-Hamwi claimed to have understood the risk to be about 75 per cent. Simon J held that to place doctors under a duty to ensure that the patient has, in fact, understood the information would 'place too onerous an obligation on the clinician'.

Al Hamwi v Johnston[46]

Simon J

It is difficult to see what steps could be devised to ensure that a patient has understood, short of a vigorous and inappropriate cross-examination. A patient may say she understands although she has not in fact done so, or has understood part of what has been said, or has a clear understanding of something other than what has been imparted. It is common experience that misunderstandings can arise despite reasonable steps to avoid them. Clinicians should take reasonable and appropriate steps to satisfy themselves that the patient has understood the information which has been provided; but the obligation does not extend to ensuring that the patient has understood.

In the next extract, José Miola is critical of the decision in *Al Hamwi*, suggesting that its emphasis on merely imparting information rather than communicating with patients is out of step with the House of Lords' judgment in *Chester*.

José Miola[47]

[T]he judge accepted the views of the expert witnesses that the leaflet was itself an 'appropriate way of conveying information'. Again, the impression given is that what is important is the *imparting* of the information and that its effective *communication* —actual understanding on the part of the patient—is less critical . . . .

---

[46] [2005] EWHC 206 (QB).
[47] 'Autonomy Rued Ok?' (2006) 14 Medical Law Review 108–114.

> If the purpose of the law in this area is to protect autonomy, then this approach is incompatible with that ideal. Although it is possible to sympathise with the views of Simon J. that doctors should not be required to 'cross-examine' their patients in a 'vigorous' manner, it may be argued that this judgment may be seen as going a little too far in the opposite direction—and certainly against the general direction of the law, as exemplified by the House of Lords in *Chester*.

(g) Is there a duty to answer questions?

Although the judgments in *Sidaway* were concerned with the voluntary disclosure of information, Lords Diplock, Bridge, and Templeman all appeared to agree that a doctor should be under a duty to answer their patient's questions. Lord Diplock contrasted the educated and inquiring patient (the example he used was a judge) for whom the *Bolam* test did not matter because 'the doctor would tell him whatever it was the patient wanted to know'.

Drawing a distinction between the patient who asks questions (who should receive full and truthful information), and the patient who does not (who may only receive the standardized information sheet) may be objectionable for a number of reasons. First, as Margaret Brazier points out, the educated, middle-class patient, who is not intimidated by a consultant's expertise, will have access to a subjectively defined, patient-orientated standard of information disclosure: they should be told whatever they want to know. In contrast, frightened, inarticulate patients will be offered a more minimal, standardized level of information.

Margaret Brazier[48]

> [I]t has to be doubted whether in any real sense a test which requires the patient to take the initiative can ever genuinely promote patient autonomy. The articulate middle-class patient, whether receiving private or NHS treatment, may well be in a position to initiate discussion of risks and benefits. The less articulate, the apprehensive, those who feel socially ill at ease with the consultant, or whose doctors are hard-pressed in inner city clinics, will be hesitant to initiate discussions. Not 'bothering' the doctor is a deeply entrenched tradition in many parts of Britain. It implies that the patient doubts the doctor's skill, raises fears of offending those who are going to care for you, and may just seem plain rude. It does not follow though that the tradition of patient silence implies lack of interest or desire to participate in decision-making if that opportunity is offered by the doctor.

Secondly, the three Law Lords in *Sidaway* do not explain *why* patients who ask questions should be entitled to full and truthful answers. Presumably, the justification is that a patient has the right to make an autonomous and meaningful choice in the light of information which her question indicates is clearly relevant and important to her. Yet surely there is no reason why this right should be confined to patients who *happen* to be sufficiently articulate and confident to know how to ask the right questions.

In *Poynter v Hillingdon Health Authority*, the trial judge took the view that the parents of a very ill child, who had religious objections to heart transplantation, had not asked sufficiently precise questions to place the medical team under a duty to tell them about a one per cent risk of serious permanent brain damage.

---

[48] 'Patient Autonomy and Consent to Treatment: The Role of the Law?' (1987) Legal Studies 169–93.

Poynter v Hillingdon Health Authority[49]

Sir Maurice Drake

Mr and Mrs Poynter say they wanted all information about the risks arising from the proposed heart transplant, but they do not say that at any time they specifically asked what were the risks of permanent serious disability to Matthew, nor that they asked any question about the risk of permanent brain damage. . .

My conclusion is that nothing that these parents asked made it known to any of the defendants' medical team that they were being asked to inform them about the risks of serious permanent brain damage or serious permanent disability. The hospital were of course aware of such a risk but assessed it as being only a very small one. They chose not to mention it to the parents.

Poynter may now be an historical oddity. In *Pearce v United Bristol Healthcare NHS Trust*[50] Lord Woolf stated that 'if a patient asks a doctor about the risk, then the doctor is required to give an honest answer', and again, this is the approach taken in the latest GMC guidance: 'You must answer patients' questions honestly and, as far as practical, answer as fully as they wish.'[51]

(h) Waiving the right to information?

While some patients may seek additional information by asking the doctor specific questions, a converse scenario is also possible, in which a patient manifests a desire *not* to be told detailed information about the risks and side-effects of treatment. People have different ways of coping with illness: some will seek out as much information as possible, and strive to become experts in their condition and the treatment options, while others would prefer not to think about it.

As we saw earlier, when we are ill and in pain, we may not feel able to digest and weigh complex information. It is common for a patient to ask her doctor what she would do if she were in the patient's shoes. Does the patient have the right to refuse to read or be told information about the treatment's advantages and disadvantages, and just ask the doctor to make a decision on her behalf? Where a patient has a high level of trust and confidence in her doctor, it might be argued that she exercises her own autonomous choice by expressing a preference for the doctor to make the decision for her.

U Khilbom[52]

A patient can take an autonomous decision to undergo a medical treatment without having (positive) knowledge of the treatment and risks. . . . Furthermore, if I, as the patient, choose to let you, as the physician, determine my treatment, and I have well founded beliefs that you will choose the treatment that best promote my values, and that the risks of the treatment you will choose, is in accordance with my attitudes towards different kinds of risks, I will exercise my autonomy, not waive my right to exercise it.

Against this, it might be argued that what Khilbom calls 'negative informed consent' could lead to problems if a patient subsequently wants to claim that, if they had been informed

---

[49] (1997) 37 BMLR 192.   [50] (1998) 48 BMLR 118 [CA].   [51] Para 12.
[52] 'Autonomy and Negatively Informed Consent' (2008) 34 Journal of Medical Ethics 146–9.

about a particular risk, they would not have consented to treatment. Kihlbom counters that it should be possible for the consent form to record that they gave their consent to treatment proceeding in the absence of any disclosure of risks or side-effects, hence absolving the doctor of future liability for non-disclosure.

(3) Causation

In order to succeed in an action in negligence, the claimant must not only prove the existence of a duty of care and its breach, but also that damage has been caused by the defendant's breach of duty. This means that a failure to disclose material information will only be actionable if the negligent non-disclosure caused the claimant to suffer some injury or loss. The claimant who has managed to establish that her doctor was in breach of the duty to give her sufficient information—itself by no means an easy task—therefore has three further obstacles to a successful claim in negligence. She must prove:

(1) that she has suffered an injury that has made her worse off than she would have been if the procedure had not been performed; *and*

(2) that her injury is the materialization of the negligently undisclosed risk; *and*

(3) that if she had been informed of this risk, she (or a reasonable patient) would not have consented to the procedure, and so the injury would not have occurred.

(a) Causation in practice

Applying the 'but for' test to disclosure cases means that we have to ask whether, but for the doctor's failure to disclose a particular piece of information to this patient, the patient would have suffered their injury. We need to know whether the injury would still have occurred if the patient had been properly informed. Causation will therefore be established if the claimant can prove that proper disclosure would have caused them to refuse the treatment which has resulted in their injury. But of course, this question is almost impossible to answer. Not only is it a speculative inquiry about what the patient might have done in different circumstances, but also by the time the case gets to court the claimant has the benefit of hindsight. She now *knows* that a particular remote risk *has* materialized. From her perspective, the one per cent risk of an adverse outcome has ceased to be a remote hypothetical possibility, and has become a 100 per cent certainty. It is therefore likely that the claimant's assertions of what she would have done had she known about the risk will be coloured by her knowledge that she has had the misfortune of being among the one per cent of patients whose treatment results in an adverse outcome.

The 'but for' test would ordinarily require us to ask whether *this patient* would have refused to be treated if she had been properly informed. If *she* would have had the treatment anyway, the doctor's breach of duty did not cause her loss. On the other hand, if *she* would have refused treatment, and hence avoided the risk which has now materialized, causation is established. Causation is thus normally judged subjectively—we ask whether this particular claimant would still have suffered the loss even if the defendant had not been negligent. But non-disclosure cases are exceptional in the sense that establishing factual causation is, strictly speaking, impossible because the court must instead resolve a purely hypothetical problem: what would the claimant have done in circumstances which, by definition, never existed?

Concern about relying too heavily on the patient's own testimony in disclosure cases has therefore led to the adoption of a hybrid subjective/objective test, such as that employed in *Smith v Barking, Havering, and Brentwood HA*. Hutchison J suggested that an objective test should be used to 'test' the truth of the patient's assertion from the witness box that she would not have consented if she had been told about a particular risk. If a reasonable patient would have agreed to the proposed treatment even if she had been told about the particular risk, then the onus would be on the patient to produce some evidence to back up her claim that she would have declined the treatment.

Smith v Barking, Havering and Brentwood HA[53]

Hutchison J

However, there is a peculiar difficulty involved in this sort of case—not least for the plaintiff herself—in giving, after the adverse outcome is known, reliable answers as to what she would have decided before the operation had she been given proper advice as to the risks inherent in it. Accordingly, it would, in my judgment, be right in the ordinary case to give particular weight to the objective assessment. If everything points to the fact that a reasonable patient, properly informed, would have assented to the operation, the assertion from the witness box, made after the adverse outcome is known, in a wholly artificial situation and in the knowledge that the outcome of the case depends upon the assertion being maintained, does not carry great weight unless there are extraneous or additional factors to substantiate it. By extraneous or additional factors I mean, and I am not doing more than giving examples, religious or some other firmly-held convictions; particular social or domestic considerations justifying a decision not in accordance with what, objectively, seems the right one; assertions in the immediate aftermath of the operation made in a context other than that of a possible claim for damages; in other words some particular factor which suggests that the plaintiff had grounds for not doing what a reasonable person in her situation might be expected to have done.

This passage was quoted by approval by His Honour Judge Peter Langan QC in *Sem v The Mid Yorkshire Hospitals NHS Trust*, a case in which it was admitted that the consultant had been negligent in not offering the patient alternatives to hysterectomy to treat her chronic pain and incontinence. Despite Mrs M's assertion that, if given a choice, she would have chosen the least invasive form of intervention, Peter Langan held that there were no external or objective factors to substantiate this assertion.

Sem v The Mid Yorkshire Hospitals NHS Trust[54]

Peter Langan

In my judgment, Mrs M, acting as a reasonable patient . . . would have been likely to follow the surgeon's advice. Patients do normally follow the advice of a consultant, and I cannot see in this case any factors which lead me to suppose that Mrs M would have done otherwise.

Indeed, in this case such extraneous factors as there were militated *against* the conclusion that Mrs M would have rejected surgery. She suffered from a somatoform disorder, which involves illness behaviour, exaggeration of symptoms and adopting the patient role, and one feature of these disorders is a tendency to seek out more dramatic interventions, than more conservative or non-invasive ones.

---

[53] (1988) reported [1994] 5 Med LR 285.   [54] [2005] EWHC 3469 (QB).

While a patient with unusual religious beliefs might be able to demonstrate that she would not have acted in the same way as a reasonable patient, it will usually be difficult for a claimant to produce evidence to support her assertion that she would have responded idiosyncratically to information about a remote risk. Furthermore, adopting an objective test for establishing causation will enable the doctor to rely on evidence that, even when they have been informed about the risk in question, patients in general very seldom refuse to consent, and this sort of solid, empirical evidence inevitably contrasts sharply with the claimant's easily discredited post hoc assertion that *she* would not have consented if she had known about this risk.

A further problem with adopting an objective approach to causation is that it confuses the question of the *credibility* of the claimant's evidence with its objective reasonableness. A patient is under no duty to make decisions which are consistent with those of an ordinarily prudent patient. On the contrary, as we see in the next chapter: 'A mentally competent patient has an absolute right to refuse to consent to medical treatment for any reason, rational or irrational, or for no reason at all, even where that decision may lead to his or her own death.'[55]

In the next extract, Alexander Capron argues that testing a claimant's evidence against what a hypothetical reasonable person in her situation would have done significantly undermines the patient's right to make foolish or idiosyncratic choices about her medical care. The credibility of evidence from a patient with peculiar priorities should be assessed in the ordinary way—does the judge believe her account?—rather than against a standard of objective reasonableness.

Alexander Morgan Capron[56]

[T]he patient owes no one a duty to decide prudently or to require for his decision only the facts that an ordinary person would want.... An 'individualized test of causation is indicated because informed consent seeks to assure patients the right to make even irrational decisions'. To deny recovery because...a reasonable person would not have cared about a certain factor (although...the factor did matter to the particular patient-plaintiff) undermines the fundamental purpose of the informed consent rule, the promotion of individual autonomy.

In contrast, in the next extract Tony Honoré suggests, in the context of discussion of a Canadian 'failure to warn' case, that the need for additional evidence to back up the claimant's hypothetical assertions of what she would have done if properly warned should instead be seen as a necessary buttress to evidence which is necessarily speculative.

Tony Honoré[57]

In *Arndt v Smith* a mother sued her physician, who had not warned her that her foetus might be injured as a result of the chickenpox she contracted during her pregnancy. When her

---

[55] *Re MB* (1997) 38 BMLR 175, per Butler-Sloss LJ.

[56] 'Informed Consent in Catastrophic Disease Research and Treatment' (1974) 123 University of Pennsylvania Law Review 340.

[57] 'Causation and Disclosure of Medical Risks' (1998) 114 Law Quarterly Review 52–5.

daughter was born with a congenital injury attributable to the chickenpox, she claimed the cost of raising the child, alleging that, had she been told of the risk, she would have sought an abortion. . . .

The causal issue in such cases turns on a hypothesis about events that did not happen. Did one non-event—the doctor's failure to warn—cause another non-event—the patient's not deciding to have an abortion? There may be little evidence available apart from that of the patient herself. She, after the event, is almost certain to say that, had she been warned, she would have reached a different decision. Otherwise she would not have sued. But her evidence, however honest, is speculative. We cannot know for certain what we would have done in circumstances with which we were never faced. . . .

Assertions about hypothetical conduct therefore need buttressing by more solid evidence about the plaintiff's temperament and beliefs (how keen was she to have a child? was she pro- or anti-abortion?), how great the risks really were and what medical advice would have been given in the light of them. Evidence of this sort may be termed objective, since it does not turn on the plaintiff's say-so. But to adduce it goes, surely, to the discharge of the evidential burden that lies on the plaintiff on the causal issue. . . : 'would a reasonable patient in her position have decided to opt for an abortion?'. . .

To show after the event that she would have refused or demanded certain treatment a patient must show that she would at the time have had a reason for doing so.

Some cases in the UK have appeared to adopt a more straightforwardly subjective test for causation, tempered only by the judge's assessment as to the witness's credibility, as opposed to its substantive reasonableness.[58] In *O'Keefe v Harvey-Kemble*, K claimed that she would not have undergone breast augmentation surgery if she had been properly informed of the risks, and the recorder believed her.

O'Keefe v Harvey-Kemble[59]

Neill LJ

[T]here were weighty arguments for the defendant . . . as to why the defendant's version of events should have been preferred; alternatively, that the plaintiff would have been likely to proceed with the operation whatever warnings she received from the defendant. However, in the event, the recorder preferred the recollection of the plaintiff and accepted her evidence as to whether she would have proceeded if she had been fully and properly advised of the attendant risks. Those were essentially findings of fact based on the recorder's assessment of the witnesses, of a kind with which this court will only interfere in rare cases.

Similarly, in *Birch v University College London Hospital NHS Foundation Trust*, a case we considered earlier, Cranston J accepted Mrs Birch's evidence that she would have opted for an MRI scan if she had been properly informed about the risk of stroke from catheter angiography.

---

[58] See also *Gowton v Wolverhampton HA* [1994] 5 Med LR 432.
[59] (1999) 45 BMLR 74 (CA).

Birch v University College London Hospital NHS Foundation Trust[60]

Cranston J

To establish liability on the defendant's part, Mrs Birch needs also to demonstrate, on the balance of probabilities, that had she been so informed she would have declined catheter angiography....In her evidence Mrs Birch said explicitly that if the comparative risks had been explained to her she would have chosen an MRI. I accept that evidence. Mrs Birch struck me as an intelligent and sensible individual, well able to have made that decision... It is clear to me that had she been given a fair and balanced account in the way I have held was necessary she would have rejected catheter angiography in favour of MRI. In other words, properly informed she would have declined the procedure leading to her stroke.

A further difficulty exists where the patient can establish that she would not have consented to have this particular treatment at this time if she had been properly informed, but cannot prove that she would never have undergone the procedure in the future. Here the question of causation becomes especially complicated. Applying the 'but for' test, it could be argued that the patient can prove that the doctor's inadequate disclosure caused her injury because she would not have undergone the operation when she did, and therefore the risk would not have materialized on this occasion. But on the other hand, she might have undergone the same operation—and been exposed to an identical risk of an adverse outcome—at a later date.

This issue first came before the English courts in *Chester v Afshar*, a case in which Mr Afshar, a neurosurgeon, did not warn Miss Chester, who was reluctant to undergo surgery to treat her chronic back pain, of a 0.9–2 per cent risk of cauda equine syndrome (a serious condition involving pain, loss of sensation, and bowel and bladder dysfunction) associated with an operation he proposed to carry out on her spine. Miss Chester's evidence was that, if she had been warned of this risk, she would not have consented to the operation when she did, but would have sought a second opinion, advice on alternatives, and taken more time to think it over. She admitted that she might, nevertheless, have consented to the operation at a later date.

By a 3:2 majority the House of Lords applied the reasoning adopted in an earlier Australian case, *Chappel v Hart*,[61] and found that it was not necessary for a patient to prove that she would have refused the operation for the rest of her life if she had been properly advised. Instead, the fact that 'but for' the defendant's negligence, she might nevertheless have been exposed to an identical risk at a later date would only be relevant when quantifying her loss. Normally, of course, the chance that the particular risk would materialize if she had the operation on another occasion will be very small and so any reduction in damages would be likely to be nominal. The only exception to this is if the claimant is especially susceptible to the risk, such that the chance of the same risk materializing on another occasion is much higher than average.

Chester v Afshar[62]

Lord Steyn

The starting point is that every individual of adult years and sound mind has a right to decide what may or may not be done with his or her body. Individuals have a right to make important

60 [2008] EWHC 2237 (QB).   61 (1998) 72 AJLR 1344.
62 [2004] UKHL 41.

medical decisions affecting their lives for themselves: they have the right to make decisions which doctors regard as ill advised. Surgery performed without the informed consent of the patient is unlawful. The court is the final arbiter of what constitutes informed consent. Usually, informed consent will presuppose a general warning by the surgeon of a significant risk of the surgery...

Secondly, not all rights are equally important. But a patient's right to an appropriate warning from a surgeon when faced with surgery ought normatively to be regarded as an important right which must be given effective protection whenever possible.

Thirdly, in the context of attributing legal responsibility, it is necessary to identify precisely the protected legal interests at stake. A rule requiring a doctor to abstain from performing an operation without the informed consent of a patient serves two purposes. It tends to avoid the occurrence of the particular physical injury the risk of which a patient is not prepared to accept. It also ensures that due respect is given to the autonomy and dignity of each patient....

Fourthly, it is a distinctive feature of the present case that but for the surgeon's negligent failure to warn the claimant of the small risk of serious injury the actual injury would not have occurred when it did and the chance of it occurring on a subsequent occasion was very small. It could therefore be said that the breach of the surgeon resulted in the very injury about which the claimant was entitled to be warned...

I have come to the conclusion that, as a result of the surgeon's failure to warn the patient, she cannot be said to have given informed consent to the surgery in the full legal sense. Her right of autonomy and dignity can and ought to be vindicated by a narrow and modest departure from traditional causation principles.

Lord Hope

I would prefer to approach the issue which has arisen here as raising an issue of legal policy which a judge must decide. It is whether, in the unusual circumstances of this case, justice requires the normal approach to causation to be modified.

I start with the proposition that the law which imposed the duty to warn on the doctor has at its heart the right of the patient to make an informed choice as to whether, and if so when and by whom, to be operated on. Patients may have, and are entitled to have, different views about these matters. All sorts of factors may be at work here—the patient's hopes and fears and personal circumstances, the nature of the condition that has to be treated and, above all, the patient's own views about whether the risk is worth running for the benefits that may come if the operation is carried out. For some the choice may be easy—simply to agree to or to decline the operation. But for many the choice will be a difficult one, requiring time to think, to take advice and to weigh up the alternatives. The duty is owed as much to the patient who, if warned, would find the decision difficult as to the patient who would find it simple and could give a clear answer to the doctor one way or the other immediately.

To leave the patient who would find the decision difficult without a remedy, as the normal approach to causation would indicate, would render the duty useless in the cases where it may be needed most. This would discriminate against those who cannot honestly say that they would have declined the operation once and for all if they had been warned. I would find that result unacceptable.

The majority in *Chester*, all of whom admitted to departing from traditional causation principles, focused upon the *purpose* of warning patients about risks, namely ensuring that 'due respect is given to the autonomy and dignity of each patient' (*per* Lord Steyn). The defendant's failure to give Miss Chester information about the risks associated with this operation had deprived her of the opportunity to make a fully informed choice. In a sense, then, it could be argued that the majority found for the claimant *not* because she had proved that the lack of proper information caused her to be exposed to a risk to which she would not have been exposed if she had been properly informed, but rather because she had been deprived of the right to weigh up the risks in order to make an informed choice.

Underlying the judgments of the majority of the House of Lords was a reluctance to penalize Miss Chester for her candour in admitting that she could not be certain that she would not have undergone the operation at some point in the future, even if properly warned. To require her to assert that she would never have undergone the operation would, according to Lord Hope, discriminate against patients who have found the decision difficult.

In contrast, in their vigorous dissenting judgments, Lords Bingham and Hoffmann followed the dissenting judgment of McHugh J in *Chappel v Hart*,[63] arguing that Miss Chester had in fact failed the 'but for' test, since the timing of the operation did not affect the risk of injury.

Lord Bingham (dissenting)

[I]n the ordinary run of cases, satisfying the 'but for' test is a necessary if not a sufficient condition of establishing causation. Here, in my opinion, it is not satisfied. Miss Chester has not established that but for the failure to warn she would not have undergone surgery. She has shown that but for the failure to warn she would not have consented to surgery on Monday 21 November 1994. But the timing of the operation is irrelevant to the injury she suffered, for which she claims to be compensated. That injury would have been as liable to occur whenever the surgery was performed and whoever performed it.

Thus the question arises whether Miss Chester should be entitled to recover even though she cannot show that the negligence proved against Mr Afshar was, in any ordinary sense, a cause of her loss...

A claimant is entitled to be compensated for the damage which the negligence of another has caused to him or her. A defendant is bound to compensate the claimant for the damage which his or her negligence has caused the claimant. But the corollaries are also true: a claimant is not entitled to be compensated, and a defendant is not bound to compensate the claimant, for damage not caused by the negligence complained of. The patient's right to be appropriately warned is an important right, which few doctors in the current legal and social climate would consciously or deliberately violate. I do not for my part think that the law should seek to reinforce that right by providing for the payment of potentially very large damages by a defendant whose violation of that right is not shown to have worsened the physical condition of the claimant.

Lord Hoffmann (dissenting)

The burden is on a claimant to prove that the defendant's breach of duty caused him damage. Where the breach of duty is a failure to warn of a risk, he must prove that he would have taken the opportunity to avoid or reduce that risk. In the context of the present case, that means proving that she would not have had the operation....

The claimant argued that as a matter of law it was sufficient that she would not have had the operation at that time or by that surgeon, even though the evidence was that the risk could have been precisely the same if she had it at another time or by another surgeon.

[63] Ibid.

> In my opinion this argument is about as logical as saying that if one had been told, on entering a casino, that the odds on no 7 coming up at roulette were only 1 in 37, one would have gone away and come back next week or gone to a different casino. The question is whether one would have taken the opportunity to avoid or reduce the risk, not whether one would have changed the scenario in some irrelevant detail. The judge found as a fact that the risk would have been precisely the same whether it was done then or later or by that competent surgeon or by another.
>
> It follows that the claimant failed to prove that the defendant's breach of duty caused her loss. On ordinary principles of tort law, the defendant is not liable. The remaining question is whether a special rule should be created by which doctors who fail to warn patients of risks should be made insurers against those risks.
>
> The argument for such a rule is that it vindicates the patient's right to choose for herself. Even though the failure to warn did not cause the patient any damage, it was an affront to her personality and leaves her feeling aggrieved.
>
> I can see that there might be a case for a modest solatium in such cases. But the risks which may eventuate will vary greatly in severity and I think there would be great difficulty in fixing a suitable figure. In any case, the cost of litigation over such cases would make the law of torts an unsuitable vehicle for distributing the modest compensation which might be payable.

Andrew Grubb argues that the majority in *Chester* made the right decision, while Charles Foster agrees with the dissenting judges, and argues that the majority judgments effectively abolish the need for claimants to prove causation.

Andrew Grubb[64]

> It is difficult to argue with [the majority's] reasoning. It would undermine the rule and be unjust for a doctor to require a patient to show that she would never have a particular procedure in the future. It is also counterintuitive to think that because the patient may run the risk in the future—by agreeing to and having the procedure—the negligence is not connected to her injury. At worst, she will be exposed to a small risk of injury which is unlikely *then* to eventuate. She had in a real and immediate sense suffered injury that she would not otherwise have suffered. That should be sufficient to establish a causal link.

Charles Foster[65]

> This is Alice in Wonderland stuff. Causation is not established but, since it should be, it will be deemed to be. Where a duty exists for some reason that can be described in terms of human rights (and what duty cannot be?) a breach will entitle the claimant to damages on policy grounds, even if causation cannot be proved. The House of Lords has stretched the rules of causation before—notably in *Fairchild v Glenhaven Funeral Services*. But *Chester* goes much further: it abolishes the requirement for causation in any meaningful sense....

---

[64] 'Consent to Treatment: The Competent Patient' 131–203 in A Grubb with J Laing (eds), *Principles of Medical Law*, 2nd edn (OUP: Oxford, 2004) 200.

[65] 'It Should Be, Therefore It Is' (2004) 154 New Law Journal 7151.

The reasoning was, basically: a human right has been breached. That is a bad thing because human rights are important. Therefore, although causation is not really established, we will say that it is. The claimant is therefore entitled, presumably, to damages identical to those that she would have received had she been able to prove that a proper warning would have led her to decline the operation. Surely a more logical thing to do would be to award her the fairly notional damages that she would have got under the European Convention on Human Rights for the article 8 breach she had suffered. Indeed, Lord Hoffmann conceded that 'there might be a case for a modest solatium'.

Causation in consent cases of the *Chester* type has always been difficult to prove. Now it will be easy. Claimants' witness statements will in future, no doubt, say: 'If I had been properly warned, I would have gone off and pondered.' That will be difficult to gainsay...

We have always thought of causation as a logical, almost mathematical business. To intrude policy into causation is like saying that two plus two does not equal four because, for policy reasons, it should not. After *Chester*, nothing seems unthinkable.

Kumaralingam Amirthalingam further argues that the decision in *Chester* reflects an increasing tendency to view causation as a matter of moral accountability rather than factual cause.

Kumaralingam Amirthalingam[66]

Causation is increasingly a proxy for moral accountability. While it was always meant to be a normative inquiry designed to fix liability on a responsible person, courts have been, for the most part, conscious of maintaining a causal link between breach and injury, whether through the traditional 'but for' test or the 'common sense' approach. Recently, causation has transcended its role in attributing causal responsibility and has been used instead to fix liability on a party who, in the court's eyes, ought to have been held accountable even if there were no evidence that that party actually caused the injury. The current mantra is that causation must be seen in the context of the purpose of the law and should not be separated from questions of liability. Effectively, this means that courts may find a defendant causally responsible if at the end of the day, despite the absence of actual evidence of a causal link, it is fair, just and reasonable that the defendant, rather than the plaintiff, should bear the loss. This confuses causation with the broader question of liability, more properly addressed at the duty or remoteness stage.

If Miss Chester's loss is better described as the loss of the right to make an informed choice, rather than exposure to a risk which she would have avoided with proper information, it could be argued that damages should be directed towards compensating her for this deprivation of autonomy, rather than for the physical injury she suffered. It is interesting that the majority in *Chester* did not consider the possibility of making a 'conventional award', as they had done in *Rees v Darlington Memorial NHS Trust*[67] (see chapter 14), for the patient's loss of autonomy. The majority awarded Miss Chester full damages for physical injury, despite the fact that their judgments describe the real loss in this case as the deprivation of

---

[66] 'Medical Non-Disclosure, Causation and Autonomy' (2002) 118 Law Quarterly Review 540–4, 542.
[67] [2003] UKHL 52.

the right to make an informed choice. As J Kenyon Mason and Douglas Brodie point out, this may mean that Miss Chester was overcompensated.

J Kenyon Mason and Douglas Brodie[68]

However, the measure of damages allowed does not, in truth, reflect the loss suffered because, at the end of the day, the loss lay in an invasion of autonomy per se, and an award of full damages can be said to over-compensate. What is, in some ways, surprising is that the solution adopted in *Rees v Darlington Memorial NHS Trust* was not applied here. There, the requirements of distributive justice meant that damages should not be awarded to compensate the plaintiff for the loss that had arisen as the result of a failed sterilisation operation...The solution adopted was to award a 'modest' conventional sum by way of general damages to acknowledge the infringement of the plaintiff's autonomy by the fault of the defendant.

The possibility of a conventional award was mentioned by Lord Hoffmann, in his dissenting judgment: 'I can see that there might be a case for a modest solatium.' In the end, he rejects this solution for two reasons: it would be difficult to settle on an appropriate amount, and, on the grounds of costs, the courts would be an unsuitable place to pursue what would always be a modest award.

Effectively, then, the consequence of *Chester* is that the autonomy-based right to make an informed choice is so important that doctors who fail to warn patients about material risks associated with treatment may have to indemnify patients should those risks materialize, despite the exercise of all proper care and skill in carrying out the operation, and, *critically*, despite the fact that the patient admits that they would have been prepared, in fact, to knowingly run this risk on another occasion.

(b) Additional problems with causation

The full impact of the House of Lords' relaxation of causation principles in *Chester v Afshar* remains to be seen. Will it be limited to cases where the patient can establish that she would not have been exposed to the risk at this time, but may have been at a later date? Or could it have wider application, through which deprivation of the autonomy-based right to make an informed choice, or even the right to have time for reflection before consenting to an operation, becomes the 'gist' of an action in negligence?

In addition to the uncertainty created by *Chester*, there are a number of further reasons why the causation requirement raises particular difficulties in actions for negligent non-disclosure of relevant information.

First, a successful claim in negligence for failure to disclose a material risk is in practice synonymous with strict liability for medical mishaps. Informed consent therefore becomes a route for patients to seek financial compensation for unfortunate but blameless medical outcomes. Doctors who exercised all reasonable care and skill in the performance of an operation will be found liable for the consequences of an accident which they could have done nothing to prevent just because their pre-operation disclosures were inadequate. As Peter Cane explains, 'whatever the ideological basis of the duty to warn (or, in other words,

---

[68] 'Bolam, Bolam—Wherefore Are Thou Bolam?' (2005) 9 Edinburgh Law Review 298–305.

the interest which it protects), its importance in practice lies in providing a basis for imposing liability for physical injury not caused by negligence'.[69]

Gerald Robertson[70]

It is beyond doubt that one effect of the recognition of the doctrine of informed consent is to expand the liability of the medical profession. The explanation for this is quite simple. Courts, particularly in this country, constantly stress the truism that things can go wrong in the course of medical treatment without that treatment having necessarily been performed negligently... This means that a large number of patients who suffer injury in the course of medical treatment will, under a fault-based system of compensation such as our own, go without compensation because they are the victims, not of negligent performance of the treatment, but rather of the risks incident thereto. One way in which to remedy this situation, within the present fault-based framework, is to expand liability by making the doctor answerable in damages for failing to warn the patient of these risks prior to undergoing treatment. In this way a greater number of medical accident victims receive compensation, by means of extending the liability of the medical profession beyond the bounds of actual negligent performance of treatment.

Secondly, because the claimant must prove that the inadequate disclosure caused her injury, cases only come before the courts where the patient has not been informed about the risk of an adverse outcome which has then materialized. Adequate information is not, however, confined to disclosure of risks. In order to exercise meaningful choice, it is important that patients are told about alternatives to the proposed treatment. As Marjorie Maguire Shultz explains, negligently depriving the patient of choices will rarely result in the sort of damage or injury which is recognized in tort law.

Marjorie Maguire Shultz[71]

[P]reemption of patients' authority by doctors may also give rise to injuries that are real but intangible, or to physical outcomes that are arguably not 'injurious' except from the individual's vantage point. These outcomes may be excluded from negligence doctrine's definitions of harm. Thus, a patient not told about a method of sterilization that is more reversible than the one performed may have difficulty convincing a court that nonreversibility is a cognizable physical injury. A patient who alleges that, properly informed, she would have chosen a lumpectomy rather than a radical mastectomy might find it hard, under existing negligence rules, to characterize the successful operation that removed her breast and eradicated her cancer as having 'injured' her. Similarly, the patient with a desire to go home or to a hospice to die, who is instead maintained alive by hospital machinery, might have difficulty establishing 'injury' under definitions of an interest in physical well-being rather than choice.

In addition to information about other treatment options, patients might also want to know whether their doctor will benefit financially from their decision to opt for a particular

---

[69] 'A Warning about Causation' (1999) 115 Law Quarterly Review 21–7, 23.
[70] 'Informed Consent to Medical Treatment' (1981) 97 Law Quarterly Review 102–26.
[71] 'From Informed Consent to Patient Choice: A New Protected Interest' (1985) 95 Yale Law Journal 219.

course of treatment. Patients may also regard information about who will carry out the procedure, how much experience they have, and their success rates as important. In the following extract, Frances Miller discusses a particular type of information which might be increasingly important for patients, but which is again marginalized within a negligence model. As we saw in Chapter 2, rationing of scarce medical resources has become inevitable, and it will not always be possible to provide every patient with the best available treatment. If treatment is withheld on the grounds of cost, are patients entitled to be told that a treatment exists which will not be available to them unless they pay for it privately?

Frances Miller[72]

If physicians withhold the information that potentially beneficial treatment is being denied their patients for economic reasons, they not only usurp the possibility of patient choice or self-help on the matter, but they assume a staggering moral burden. The traditional justification for silence under such circumstances is that it would be cruel and inhumane to tell patients that therapy might help them, but that they have no access to it. One can construct a powerful argument, however, that silence under such circumstances often is not only equally cruel and inhumane, but also morally unacceptable.

Physicians truly are 'playing God' in such circumstances, but they may not have all the facts. Some patients may have their own resources for obtaining medical care about which their doctors are unaware. Others may choose to invest their energies in trying to change rationing policies that affect them detrimentally, rather than passively accepting denial of care as their lot.

Certainly, the British Medical Association's advice to doctors is that they should normally be candid with their patients about unfunded treatment options, particularly since patients may well discover the existence of these for themselves on the internet. In the light of the decision to permit top-up payments within the NHS (considered in chapter 2), the need to be candid with patients about the existence of potentially beneficial treatments which are not funded by the NHS becomes even more important.

British Medical Association[73]

In the BMA's view, part of the role of doctors is to ensure that decision making is returned as much as possible to the patient rather than pre-empting the choice by withholding potentially important information....

Although it might be argued that patients should be protected from the distress of receiving information about treatment options which are not publicly funded, this undermines the increasingly accepted concept of a partnership in decision making between patients and health professionals. It must be recognised that knowing a possible, even if unproven, treatment exists may make some families feel pressured to incur debts to buy it. On the other hand, however, patients and their families increasingly want to have the choice of making

---

[72] 'Denial of Health Care and Informed Consent in English and American Law' (1992) 18 American Journal of Law and Medicine 37.

[73] Duty of Candour? Truth Telling and Rationing of Resources (July 1997 revised September 2000).

even difficult decisions of this type for themselves. They often seek out information from sources such as the internet and can lose trust in their medical advisers if they discover belatedly that information about potential options has been withheld.

Thirdly, 'cause' appears to have acquired a rather special meaning in failure to warn cases. As Peter Cane has explained, the doctors in these cases rarely 'caused' the injury in question 'in the central sense of the word "cause" as it is used outside the law', because 'failure to warn of a risk does not "cause" the materialization of the risk'.[74] Rather, the injury has usually been caused by an unfortunate and inherently unlikely combination of circumstances, and the doctor simply *created the situation* in which this extraordinary sequence of events could occur. The question of whether a doctor should be liable for a failure to disclose a risk is more accurately stated as whether she should be liable for creating the situation in which an accidental injury might or (much more likely) might not occur.

(c) MOVING AWAY FROM BATTERY AND NEGLIGENCE

The central problem, then, with the current legal mechanisms for protecting a patient's right to information about their treatment is that both battery and negligence possess significant defects. Battery is inadequate because it will only be relevant where the treatment involves unlawful touching, and in any event the courts have tightly circumscribed its application in non-disclosure cases. Negligence requires proof that the lack of information caused physical harm, which of course will seldom be the case when a patient is not given enough information. What alternatives might there be?

(1) The New Zealand Code

In the next extract Joanna Manning describes the system which exists in New Zealand. If a patient wishes to obtain compensation for a doctor's failure to warn her of a particular risk, under the no-fault compensation scheme it will still be necessary to establish a causal link between the failure to warn and physical injury. However, in addition a Code of Rights offers additional protection to patients' interests in information disclosure, since it is a breach of the Code not to disclose information which the reasonable patient would consider material. While the Code does not provide financial compensation to patients who have been inadequately informed—this is the function of the compensation scheme—it nevertheless places doctors under a robust duty to give patients sufficient information to enable them to make informed choices.

Joanna Manning[75]

One of the advantages of the Code is its recognition that a consumer is likely to want a wider range of information than about risks in making decisions about treatment. Right 6, in referring to 'the information that a reasonable consumer, in that consumer's circumstances,

---

[74] 'A Warning about Causation' (1999) 115 Law Quarterly Review 21–7, 23.
[75] 'Informed Consent To Medical Treatment: The Common Law And New Zealand's Code Of Patients' Rights' (2004) 12 Medical Law Review 181.

would expect to receive', recognises that the information patients might need is not confined to information about risks, but extends to other types of information that may be needed to enable them to make an informed decision about their care...

In New Zealand, separating compensation for injury from issues of professional account-ability has made possible one of the advantages of the Code for complainants—breach of the Code does not depend upon proof of injury, nor of a causal link between any injury suffered and a breach of a Code Right...It is not necessary to show that the patient suffered harm as a result of a failure to be sufficiently informed. So, it is strictly irrelevant to whether there has been a breach of Right 6 that the Commissioner finds it probable that, even if the health pro-vider had explained the risks of the procedure, the patient would have gone ahead with it in any event. The patient is entitled to appropriate information irrespective of whether it would have been a determinative factor in the decision to proceed...This properly reflects the para-mount interest that the duty of disclosure and the concept of informed consent is designed to secure—the individual's autonomy and right to decide in an informed manner, not just the interest in bodily safety.

(2) A Fiduciary Relationship?

If the doctor–patient relationship could be said to be fiduciary in nature, we might have an alternative basis for imposing an obligation on doctors to disclose material information. Since equitable duties of disclosure usually arise in relationships where one party is unusu-ally vulnerable to the other's ability to exercise some discretion or power over her interests, they might seem a promising basis for a more patient-orientated approach to informed con-sent. The case law, however, is not encouraging. In *Sidaway* in the Court of Appeal,[76] Dunn LJ said that the fiduciary relationship 'has been confined to cases involving the disposition of property, and has never been applied to the nature of the duty which lies upon a doc-tor in the performance of his professional treatment of his patient'. In the House of Lords, Lord Scarman was the only Law Lord to consider the possibility of a fiduciary relationship between doctor and patient, and he was similarly dismissive:

Sidaway v Board of Governors of the Bethlem Royal Hospital and the Maudsley Hospital[77]

Lord Scarman

Counsel for the appellant referred to *Nocton v Lord Ashburton* in an attempt to persuade your Lordships that the relationship between doctor and patient is of a fiduciary character entitling a patient to equitable relief in the event of a breach of fiduciary duty by the doctor. The attempt fails: there is no comparison to be made between the relationship of doctor and patient with that of solicitor and client, trustee and cestui qui trust or the other relationships treated in equity as of a fiduciary character.

It is, however, uncontroversial that the doctor–patient relationship is one of trust and con-fidence, and, in other contexts, the courts have recognized that it might be fiduciary in character. A presumption of the invalidity of gifts and bequests from patient to doctor, for

[76] [1984] QB 491.
[77] [1985] AC 871 at 884.

example, was established in the nineteenth century.[78] There are obligations which doctors owe to their patients—most obviously, the duty of confidentiality—which are plainly equitable in nature, and which arise because equity has acknowledged the special dependency which exists within the doctor–patient relationship. Conceding that fiduciary relationships normally arise only when property interests are at stake, Margaret Brazier has nevertheless argued that 'in a sense the patient does entrust his most precious property, his body and health to the doctor. Is equity too rigid...to expand to fill the inflexibility of tort within the common law?'[79]

In some other countries, the courts have suggested that while some aspects of the doctor–patient relationship might involve fiduciary obligations, these should be confined to situations in which neither contract nor tort already provides an adequate remedy. For example, Sopinka J in the Canadian Supreme Court case of *Norberg v Wynrib* suggested that '[f]iduciary duties should not be superimposed on these common law duties simply to improve the nature and extent of the remedy'.

In short, if the issue is the doctor's malpractice, equitable remedies would be inappropriate. The doctor's breach of her duty to use appropriate care and skill is not a breach of her fiduciary duty. But while the courts have become accustomed to regarding the duty to provide adequate pre-treatment disclosure as part of the doctor's ordinary duty of care, negligence's requirement that actionable damage should have been caused by the failure to give adequate information has, as we saw in the previous section, rendered the chance of a poorly advised patient succeeding in a negligence action virtually non-existent. Indeed, this point was made persuasively by MacLachlin J in her dissenting judgment in *Norberg v Wynrib*,[80] when she rejected her colleagues' 'closed commercial view of fiduciary obligations':

Recognising the fiduciary nature of the doctor–patient relationship provides the law with an analytical model by which physicians can be held to the highest standard of dealing with their patients which the trust accorded to them requires...The fact that society encourages us to trust our doctors, to believe that they will be persons worthy of our trust, cannot be ignored as a factor inducing a heightened degree of vulnerability.[81]

Moreover, other self-evidently fiduciary relationships, such as that between agent and principal, are also contractual in nature, so it is not necessarily true that fiduciary obligations can arise only when actions in contract and tort are unavailable.

There are some cases from other countries which have appeared to categorize the doctor's duty of disclosure as a fiduciary obligation. In *Miller v Kennedy*,[82] the State of Washington's Court of Appeals held that: 'The duty of the doctor to inform the patient is a fiduciary duty. The patient has the right to chart his own destiny, and the doctor must supply the patient with the material facts the patient will need in order to intelligently chart that destiny with dignity.'

But while an equitable basis for the duty of disclosure might initially appear attractive, as Ian Kennedy argues in the following section, there are good reasons to be sceptical about

---

[78] *Rhodes v Bate* (1866) 1 Ch App 252.
[79] 'Patient Autonomy and Consent to Treatment: The Role of the Law?' (1987) 7 Legal Studies 169–93, 191.
[80] (1992) 138 NR 81 at 176.   [81] At 128 and 137.
[82] 522 P.2d 852.

the extent to which recognizing a fiduciary relationship would in fact improve patients' access to adequate information. Since the fiduciary's principal obligation is to act in her client's best interests, a paternalistic 'doctor knows best' approach to information disclosure might be defensible within a fiduciary model. Ian Kennedy goes so far as to describe the 'best interests' test, which would define the fiduciary's duties, as 'the anti-principle, the means whereby courts have handed power to doctors by allowing them to determine what should be done',[83] and as a result he is sceptical about the progressive potential of fiduciary obligations. He also warns of the dangers of adopting an approach which defines the doctor–patient relationship in terms of the patient's vulnerability and dependence.

Ian Kennedy[84]

The whole tenor of the doctor as fiduciary approach is to perpetuate the notion of the patient as victim. This may seem an odd criticism when throughout this paper I have been trumpeting the power imbalance between doctor and patient. Surely, it can be said, all that the fiduciary relationship approach does is to recognise this imbalance and seek to take account of it. Well, my criticism stands. What the adoption of a fiduciary approach does, in fact, is to entrench the power imbalance, to make it part of the law. This is the last thing which the law should be doing. What we should be looking for is a framework which recognises the difference in power and tries to do something about it; tries in short to redress it.

In conclusion, therefore, my submission is that the fiduciary relationship as applied to doctors and patients is a false dawn. It does not provide nor should be seen as laying the foundations for a more appropriate legal framework governing them. It is confused jurisprudentially, it infantilises patients, it leaves doctors unsure. Most important it extends the *carte blanche* of 'best interests' when the 'best interests' approach is arguably one of medical law's most glaring weaknesses.

4 GOOD MEDICAL PRACTICE

In the rules governing disclosure of information to patients, there is a striking gap between tort law and the principles of good medical practice. As we have seen in this chapter, tort law has traditionally imposed fairly minimal requirements on doctors, whereas the codes of practice and guidelines promulgated by the General Medical Council, the British Medical Association,[85] the Royal Colleges, and the Department of Health[86] tend to be much more detailed and expansive. As we have seen at various points in this chapter, the GMC's guidance on obtaining patients' consent imposes considerably more onerous duties on the medical profession than the reasonable doctor standard in tort law. The GMC's guidance is explicitly based upon the 'partnership' model of medical decision-making, and advocates a *subjective patient-specific standard of information disclosure*:

---

[83] 'The Fiduciary Relationship and its Application to Doctors' in P Birks (ed.), *Wrongs and Remedies in the Twenty-first Century* (Clarendon Press: Oxford, 1986) 111–40, 138.

[84] Ibid, 139–40.

[85] British Medical Association, Consent Tool Kit, 3rd edn (August 2007), available at <www.bma.org.uk/>.

[86] Reference Guide to Consent for Examination or Treatment, (DH 2001, available at <www.dh.gov.uk>).

General Medical Council[87]

> 2 Whatever the context in which medical decisions are made, you must work in partnership with your patients to ensure good care. In so doing, you must:
>
> (a) listen to patients and respect their views about their health
>
> (b) discuss with patients what their diagnosis, prognosis, treatment and care involve
>
> (c) share with patients the information they want or need in order to make decisions
>
> (d) maximise patients' opportunities, and their ability, to make decisions for themselves
>
> (e) respect patients' decisions.
>
> 3 For a relationship between doctor and patient to be effective, it should be a partnership based on openness, trust and good communication...
>
> 7 The exchange of information between doctor and patient is central to good decision-making. How much information you share with patients will vary, depending on their individual circumstances. You should tailor your approach to discussions with patients according to:
>
> (a) their needs, wishes and priorities
>
> (b) their level of knowledge about, and understanding of, their condition, prognosis and the treatment options
>
> (c) the nature of their condition
>
> (d) the complexity of the treatment, and
>
> (e) the nature and level of risk associated with the investigation or treatment.
>
> 8 You should not make assumptions about:
>
> (a) the information a patient might want or need
>
> (b) the clinical or other factors a patient might consider significant, or
>
> (c) a patient's level of knowledge or understanding of what is proposed.

While every failure to follow the GMC's guidance does not automatically lead to disciplinary action, the latest guidance robustly states that 'Serious or persistent failure to follow this guidance will put your registration at risk.'[88]

So while the standard of care patients can expect according to the law of tort has been gradually moving away from 'the reasonable doctor' test towards a version of the 'reasonable patient' test, the GMC instructs doctors to tailor their disclosure of information to the *needs and interests of the particular patient*. Since the 'reasonable doctor' should undoubtedly be paying close attention to GMC guidance, and, as we saw in Chapter 3, the proliferation of professional guidelines gives the courts concrete guidance as to how a responsible doctor will behave, could this more onerous standard of care be gradually incorporated into tort law? Alasdair Maclean is doubtful:

> [I]t is by no means certain that the courts will insist that the GMC guidelines dictate the legal standard, as it would be open to them to say that, while the guidance reflects ethically good practice the legal standard is what it is reasonable to expect rather than what is ethically commendable.[89]

---

[87] Consent: Patients and Doctors Making Decisions Together, GMC (2008).   [88] Ibid. 5.

[89] 'The Doctrine of Informed Consent: Does it Exist and has it Crossed the Atlantic?' (2004) 24 Legal Studies 386–413, 411.

While GMC guidance, breach of which can result in disciplinary action, does more than lay out an 'ethically commendable' ideal, and instead should form the basis of *proper,* as opposed to *perfect,* medical treatment, it is certainly true that not every breach of GMC guidance would, or indeed should give rise to a finding of negligence. Even if tort law is becoming more concerned about the patient's right to make informed choices, there will almost certainly continue to be a gap between the high standards of disclosure contained in the GMC guidance and the less onerous requirements of the common law.

Of more practical importance, since tort law offers virtually no prospective guidance to doctors, and since law reports are not doctors' normal reading matter, doctors are more likely to consult professional guidance—which sets out a subjective patient-specific standard of disclosure—when working out how much information to provide to their patients. Happily then, the failings of tort may have little practical impact upon patients' access to information.

5 CONCLUSION

In this chapter, we have seen that there are significant problems with using tort law to protect patients' interests in informative disclosure, and that instead the profession's own good practice guidelines impose much more robust responsibilities upon doctors.

Emily Jackson[90]

[W]hile most doctors do attempt to find out what each individual patient wants to know, and try to provide this information in an accessible and straightforward way, this is certainly not because of the 'deterrent' effect of tort law. On the contrary, it is *despite* the complete absence of any effective deterrent to inadequate disclosure in the law of tort. Law students are usually told that tort law serves two principal functions: compensation and deterrence. In relation to information disclosure, it serves neither. As a result, I think there is an increasing need to think seriously about abandoning the pretence that tort law offers any protection at all to patients' interests in access to information about their medical treatment.

FURTHER READING

Brazier, Margaret, 'Patient Autonomy and Consent to Treatment: The Role of the Law?' (1987) Legal Studies 169–93.

Heywood, Rob, Macaskill, Ann and Williams, Kevin 'Patient Perceptions of the Consent Process: Qualitative Inquiry and Legal Reflection' (2008) 242 Professional Negligence 104–21.

Jackson, Emily, 'Informed Consent to Medical Treatment and the Impotence of Tort' in SAM McLean (ed.), *First Do No Harm* (Ashgate: Aldershot, 2006).

---

[90] 'Informed Consent to Medical Treatment and the Impotence of Tort' in SAM McLean (ed.), *First Do No Harm* (Ashgate: Aldershot, 2006).

Jones, Michael, 'Informed Consent and Other Fairy Stories' (1999) 7 Medical Law Review 103–34.

Kihlbom, U, 'Autonomy and Negatively Informed Consent' (2008) 34 Journal Of Medical Ethics 146–9.

Skegg, PDG, 'English Medical Law and "Informed Consent": An Antipodean Assessment and Alternative' (1999) 7 Medical Law Review 135–65, 138.

Stapleton, Jane, 'Cause in Fact and the Scope of Liability for Consequences' (2003) 119 Law Quarterly Review 388–425.

CONSENT II: CAPACITY AND VOLUNTARINESS

CENTRAL ISSUES

1. Without the patient's consent, invasive medical treatment could amount to both battery and assault.

2. The principle of patient autonomy means that every competent adult patient has the *right* to refuse medical treatment, even if her reasons are bizarre, irrational, or non-existent, and even if her refusal will result in her death.

3. Patients who lack capacity can be treated without consent, and different rules apply depending on whether the patient is a child or an adult.

4. The treatment of incompetent adults is governed by the Mental Capacity Act 2005, which replaced the common law and allows adults who lack capacity to be treated in their best interests. In Scotland the Adults with Incapacity (Scotland) Act 2000 applies.

5. Parents normally give consent to their children's medical treatment, unless there is a dispute or the treatment is especially controversial, when the court might be asked to exercise its wide powers to authorize the medical treatment of minors.

6. Mature minors can acquire the right to consent to treatment, but they do not necessarily have the same right to refuse treatment, especially if it is life-saving.

7. The patient's consent must have been given voluntarily: that is, it must not have been vitiated by undue influence or coercion.

1 INTRODUCTION

One of the first principles of medical law is that a competent adult patient must give her consent to medical treatment. As Cardozo J famously said in the US case, *Schloendorff v New York Hospital*:[1]

---

[1] 105 NE 92 (1914).

> Every human being of adult years and sound mind has a right to determine what shall be done with his own body; and a surgeon who performs an operation without his patient's consent, commits an assault.

Touching a person without her consent, however benevolently, is prima facie unlawful. For consent to be valid, first the patient must have the capacity to consent; secondly, her consent must be given voluntarily; and thirdly she must understand, in broad terms, the nature of the treatment to which she has consented. We consider the first two criteria in this chapter. The question of how much information should be provided to fulfil the third criterion was dealt with in the previous chapter.

We begin by noting that consent has a legal, a moral, and a clinical function. Legally, consent will sometimes convert what would otherwise be unlawful touching into a lawful practice. Morally, consent is required in order to respect the patient's right to self-determination. Clinically, a patient's consent will make it easier to treat her, and her cooperation may contribute towards the treatment's success.

Having established the necessity of obtaining the patient's consent to medical treatment, we go on to consider what happens when a patient *cannot* give consent. Different rules apply to adults and children, and we consider them separately. Finally, we turn to the requirement that the patient's consent must have been given voluntarily, and we briefly consider three factors that might undermine the patient's ability to freely consent to medical treatment: coercion, undue influence, and mistake.

2 THE CONSENT REQUIREMENT

(a) CRIMINAL LAW

It is commonly believed that it is the patient's consent to medical treatment which prevents it from being both a civil wrong and a criminal assault. This is only partially true, however, because consent does *not* offer a defence to the infliction of actual or grievous bodily harm. Some medical procedures, such taking a patient's blood pressure, will not cause 'bodily harm', meaning the patient's consent offers a defence to what might otherwise be unlawful touching. In contrast, surgery involves cutting the body in a way which could undoubtedly be described as 'grievous bodily harm', when consent cannot offer a defence.

Nevertheless, the legality of 'reasonable' and 'proper' surgical interventions does not seem to be in doubt. In *Attorney General's Reference (No 6 of 1980)*, the Court of Appeal refers to the accepted legality of, among other things, 'reasonable surgical interference . . . as needed in the public interest'.

Lord Lane CJ[2]

Nothing which we have said is intended to cast doubt upon the accepted legality of properly conducted games and sports, lawful chastisement or correction, reasonable surgical interference, dangerous exhibitions, etc. These apparent exceptions can be justified as involving the exercise of a legal right, in the case of chastisement or correction, or as needed in the public interest, in the other cases.

---

[2] *Attorney General's Reference (No. 6 of 1980)* [1981] QB 715.

In *R v Brown*, a case in which the House of Lords decided that occasioning actual bodily harm during consensual sado-masochistic practices was an offence, the Lords agreed that 'proper' medical treatment does not constitute a criminal offence, but as Lord Mustill explains, this exception cannot derive solely from the patient's consent.

R v Brown[3]

Lord Mustill

Many of the acts done by surgeons would be very serious crimes if done by anyone else, and yet the surgeons incur no liability. Actual consent, or the substitute for consent deemed by the law to exist where an emergency creates a need for action, is an essential element in this immunity; but it cannot be a direct explanation for it, since much of the bodily invasion involved in surgery lies well above any point at which consent could even arguably be regarded as furnishing a defence. Why is this so? The answer must in my opinion be that proper medical treatment, for which actual or deemed consent is a prerequisite, is in a category of its own.

Lord Mustill had made similar remarks a year earlier in *Airedale NHS Trust v Bland*:

Airedale NHS Trust v Bland[4]

Lord Mustill

[T]here is a point higher up the scale than common assault at which consent in general ceases to form a defence to a criminal charge.... If one person cuts off the hand of another it is no answer to say that the amputee consented to what was done.

How is it that, consistently with the proposition just stated, a doctor can with immunity perform on a consenting patient an act which would be a very serious crime if done by someone else? The answer must be that bodily invasions in the course of proper medical treatment stand completely outside the criminal law. The reason why the consent of the patient is so important is not that it furnishes a defence in itself, but because it is usually essential to the propriety of medical treatment.

So at common law, it seems to be well established that, for public interest reasons, rather than because the patient gave consent, 'reasonable' or 'proper' medical treatment stands completely outside the criminal law.

Of course, the use of words such as 'reasonable' and 'proper' means that not every surgical intervention will satisfy this public interest exception. Female circumcision is specifically proscribed by the Female Genital Mutilation Act 2003, but it is also possible that it could be an offence at common law, if it is judged not to be 'reasonable surgical interference'.

Amputating a person's healthy limbs in order to increase her income from begging could not be considered 'proper' medical treatment. More complicated, however, is the question of whether amputating a healthy limb when its presence appears to cause the patient considerable distress could ever be legitimate. In 2000 a great deal of media attention was generated when it was revealed that a surgeon in Scotland had performed

---

[3] [1994] 1 AC 212.   [4] [1993] AC 789.

elective single-leg amputations on two physically healthy individuals with psychiatric disorders. Both individuals were suffering from a rare sort of body dysmorphic disorder in which the patient wishes to be an amputee.[5] The surgeon involved said that 'at follow up, both patients remain delighted with their new state'.[6] On the one hand, operating in order to transform a non-disabled individual into a disabled one self-evidently causes grievous bodily harm, and seems manifestly 'unreasonable'. Yet, on the other hand, we now accept as 'reasonable' both gender reassignment surgery and cosmetic surgery, and, in both cases, the purpose is similarly to alter the patient's physical body so that it better fits her preferred body image.

(b) CIVIL LAW

Consent will prevent a doctor from being liable for the tort of battery. Provided that the patient consented to treatment, there could be no possibility of an action to recover damages in tort for unlawful touching. If a patient wishes to claim that their consent was not 'real', perhaps because they were not told what they were consenting to, or because they were coerced into agreeing to the treatment, then an action for battery might be possible. In practice, such actions are extremely rare. As we saw in the previous chapter, very few patients are able to persuade a court that their apparent consent was defective due to a lack of information, and later in this chapter, we see that coercion and undue influence are also unlikely to vitiate a patient's consent.

(c) THE FORM CONSENT SHOULD TAKE

There is no common law requirement that consent to medical treatment must be in writing. There are a few procedures, such as fertility treatment, where a statutory requirement to obtain written consent exists,[7] but this is exceptional. In most routine medical treatment the patient's consent can be inferred from her conduct. If I put out my arm to have a blood sample taken, the doctor or nurse can legitimately assume that I am consenting to having a needle stuck into my vein. In most patient encounters with health care professionals, formal consent procedures are non-existent. Rather, by seeking treatment and complying with instructions, the patient indicates her willingness to be treated.

Where the treatment involves surgery, it is good medical practice, albeit not a legal requirement, to obtain the patient's consent in writing, usually by the patient signing a standard consent form. It is, however, important to remember that the consent form does not amount to a contract between the doctor and her patient. Rather, the patient's consent must be ongoing throughout her treatment, and she is free to withdraw her consent at any time. Signing a consent form does not affect the patient's right to refuse to undergo the procedure.

(d) THE PRINCIPLE OF AUTONOMY

The principle that a competent adult must not be treated without her consent is clearly directed towards protecting both her autonomy and her bodily integrity. As we can see

---

[5] Sarah Ramsay, 'Controversy over UK Surgeon Who Amputated Healthy Limbs' (2000) 355 The Lancet 476.

[6] Ibid.   [7] See further, Chapter 15.

from the following judicial statements, every competent adult patient has the *right* to refuse medical treatment, even if her reasons are bizarre, irrational, or non-existent, and even if her refusal will result in her death.

The case of *Airedale NHS Trust v Bland* (which we consider in detail in Chapter 17) contains strong confirmation of the priority that must be given to the principle of patient self-determination:

Airedale NHS Trust v Bland[8]

Lord Mustill

If the patient is capable of making a decision on whether to permit treatment, ... his choice must be obeyed even if on any objective view it is contrary to his best interests.

Lord Goff

[T]he principle of self-determination requires that respect must be given to the wishes of the patient, so that if an adult patient of sound mind refuses, however unreasonably, to consent to treatment or care by which his life would or might be prolonged, the doctors responsible for his care must give effect to his wishes, even though they do not consider it to be in his best interests to do.

In *Re T*, all three judges in the Court of Appeal again articulated a robust commitment to patient autonomy:

Re T (Adult: Refusal of Treatment)[9]

Lord Donaldson MR

An adult patient who, like Miss T, suffers from no mental incapacity has an absolute right to choose whether to consent to medical treatment, to refuse it or to choose one rather than another of the treatments being offered.... This right of choice is not limited to decisions which others might regard as sensible. It exists notwithstanding that the reasons for making the choice are rational, irrational, unknown or even non-existent.

Butler-Sloss LJ

A man or woman of full age and sound understanding may choose to reject medical advice and medical or surgical treatment either partially or in its entirety. A decision to refuse medical treatment by a patient capable of making the decision does not have to be sensible, rational or well-considered.

Staughton LJ

An adult whose mental capacity is unimpaired has the right to decide for herself whether she will or will not receive medical or surgical treatment, even in circumstances where she is likely or even certain to die in the absence of treatment. Thus far the law is clear.

Of course, it is also now necessary to consider whether the patient's right to make her own medical decisions might be protected by the Human Rights Act 1998. A number of

---

[8] [1993] AC 789.   [9] [1993] Fam 95.

convention rights might be relevant here, such as Article 2 (the right to life); Article 3 (the right not to be subjected to inhuman or degrading treatment); Article 5 (the right to liberty); Article 8 (respect for private and family life); and Article 9 (respect for religious views). We will encounter cases in which mentally ill people have argued that compulsory treatment infringes their rights in the next chapter.

Respect for patient autonomy is also undoubtedly considered to be good medical practice. The British Medical Association, for example, advises doctors that: 'It is well established in law and ethics that competent adults have the right to refuse any medical treatment, even if that refusal results in their death.'[10]

It seems then to be settled law that competent adult patients have the right to make *irrational* and *life-threatening* decisions to refuse medical treatment, and we shall explore the implications of this in the context of end of life decisions in Chapter 17.

In Chapter 1, we looked at the principle of patient autonomy, and saw that some commentators have suggested that it is an excessively individualistic value. Giving the competent adult patient an absolute right to reject life-saving medical treatment ignores the impact that this might have upon other people, such as her dependent children. The principle of patient autonomy gives the individual a right to make decisions which may have a profoundly negative impact upon others' wellbeing. Here there may be a tension between a patient's *legal* right to determine what is done to her body, and her *moral* obligations to others.

In the next extract, Shimon Glick argues that there may also be dangers in respecting the short-term autonomy of a frightened and distressed patient.

Shimon Glick[11]

[O]ftentimes individuals under acute stress may make hasty tragic decisions which they subsequently, under more careful consideration, regret...I would hope that even the most devoted advocates of autonomy might accept the premise that a patient who is frightened and stressed, may not be fully autonomous; his/her refusal should therefore be assigned less weight. It is tragic to accept such a patient's refusal automatically at face value, even if a team of psychiatrists and lawyers judge that person legally competent...

In addition, autonomy is of no value to a dead person. By permitting a patient to die avoidably, when it is virtually certain that were he saved against his present protest he would be grateful, one is granting that person his short term 'autonomous' wish while depriving him of his long term autonomy.

(e) PREGNANT WOMEN'S AUTONOMY?

In *Re T*,[12] Lord Donaldson mooted one possible exception to the right to refuse treatment:

The only possible qualification is a case in which the choice may lead to the death of a viable foetus. That is not this case and, if and when it arises, the courts will be faced with a novel problem of considerable legal and ethical complexity.

---

[10] British Medical Association, *Withholding and Withdrawing Life-prolonging Medical Treatment: Guidance for Decision Making*, 3rd edn (BMA: London, 2007), para 25.5.
[11] 'The Morality of Coercion' (2000) 26 Journal of Medical Ethics 393–5.   [12] [1993] Fam 95.

Later the same year, just such a case arose. In *Re S (Adult: Refusal of Treatment)*,[13] Mrs S wanted to refuse a caesarean section on religious grounds (she was described as a 'born-again Christian'). Her competence was not in doubt. An emergency application was made, and after an *ex parte* hearing lasting less than two hours, Sir Stephen Brown granted a declaration that the operation would be lawful. He suggested that there was 'some American authority' which suggested that the US courts would be likely to grant a declaration in these circumstances. On this point, with respect, Sir Stephen Brown was mistaken. In the only case he mentions, *Re AC*,[14] the decision had in fact been that the caesarean which had been carried out on Angela Carder against her wishes had been unlawful, and should not have been performed.

In addition to being an unlawful infringement of the competent adult patient's right to refuse unwanted medical treatment, forcing women to have caesarean sections against their will is ultimately likely to result in poorer outcomes for fetuses in general, since women who object to surgical delivery might be deterred from seeking any medical attention during pregnancy and labour.

Re S is almost certainly now of historical interest only. In two subsequent cases, the Court of Appeal has confirmed that pregnancy does not diminish the competent adult patient's right to refuse unwanted medical intervention. In *Re MB (An Adult: Medical Treatment)*, although MB was judged temporarily incompetent on the grounds of her needle phobia, Butler-Sloss LJ referred to *Re S* as 'a decision the correctness of which we must now call in doubt'. Instead, she was emphatic that:

> A competent woman who has the capacity to decide may, for religious reasons, other reasons, for rational or irrational reasons or for no reason at all, choose not to have medical intervention, even though the consequence may be the death or serious handicap of the child she bears, or her own death.[15]

A year later, in *St George's NHS Trust v S* the emergency caesarean section which had been performed upon S against her wishes was held to be a trespass. Judge LJ defended the pregnant woman's right to refuse treatment which could save her fetus's life, even if her decision might appear to be 'morally repugnant'.

St George's NHS Trust v S[16]

Judge LJ

In our judgment while pregnancy increases the personal responsibilities of a woman it does not diminish her entitlement to decide whether or not to undergo medical treatment. Although human, and protected by the law in a number of different ways..., an unborn child is not a separate person from its mother. Its need for medical assistance does not prevail over her rights. She is entitled not to be forced to submit to an invasion of her body against her will, whether her own life or that of her unborn child depends on it. Her right is not reduced or diminished merely because her decision to exercise it may appear morally repugnant.

While the Court of Appeal's judgment in *St George's NHS Trust v S* undoubtedly represents an especially robust assertion of the principle of patient autonomy, Thorpe LJ, writing

---

[13] [1992] 4 All ER 671.   [14] [1990] 573 A 2d 1235.
[15] *Re MB (An Adult: Medical Treatment)* [1997] 2 FLR 426.   [16] [1999] Fam 26.

extra-judicially, suggests that it may be easier for an *appellate* court to extol the primacy of autonomy, after the operation has already been successfully carried out, than it was for the judge who made the decision in the 'heat of the moment', when the surgery was immediately necessary in order to prevent loss of life.

Matthew Thorpe[17]

It is, perhaps, easier for an appellate court to discern principle than it is for a trial court to apply it in the face of judicial instinct, training, and emotion…It is simply unrealistic to suppose that the preservation of each life will not be a matter of equal concern to the Family Division judge surveying the medical dilemma. Whatever emphasis legal principle may place upon adult autonomy with the consequent right to choose between treatments, at some level the judicial outcome will be influenced by the expert evidence as to which treatment affords the best chance of the happy announcement that both mother and baby are doing well.

3 INCAPACITY

As we have seen, if a patient is judged to be competent, their consent or refusal of medical treatment is decisive. In contrast, if a patient is incompetent, they may be treated without their consent. Clearly, it is therefore vitally important to be able to tell when a patient either is or is not competent.

Before we come to the rules governing the treatment of people without capacity, it is worth distinguishing two different possible approaches to the assessment of capacity: one based upon *status* and the other upon *function*.

- According to the status approach, certain categories of patients are treated as incompetent because of their status (an example would be age), regardless of their real decision-making ability. On this approach, all children would be treated as though they were incompetent, despite the fact that there is huge variation between different children's reasoning skills.

- The functional approach instead focuses on the individual's actual capabilities. A child would not automatically be disqualified from taking decisions on this approach: rather, her capacity to make the particular decision would have to be individually assessed.

Although the status approach benefits from ease of application—it is much more straightforward to discover a child's age than it is to judge her decision-making capacity—it is, as Ian Kennedy points out, the functional approach which better promotes the principle of patient self-determination:

Ian Kennedy[18]

The fundamental flaw in the status approach is that it takes no account of the individuality of each person. Respect for autonomy, however, involves respect for each person's individuality. It demands, therefore, that any criterion intended to determine when someone is

---

[17] 'The Caesarean Section Debate' [1997] 27 Family Law 663 at 663–4.
[18] *Treat Me Right* (OUP: Oxford, 1988) 57–8.

incapable of being autonomous should, equally, be respectful of that person's individuality. Merely placing him in a class is far too gross a test of incapacity. It denies respect to the individual as an individual, and must therefore be rejected.

As we shall see later, the law adopts a combination of the status and the functional approaches to capacity: all adults are presumed to be competent, and all children under the age of 16 are presumed to be incompetent. Although these twin presumptions are status-based, they are simply starting points, and they can be rebutted by evidence of the person's *actual* decision-making capacity. The difference between the two groups is therefore a shift in the burden of proof: evidence must be brought forward to establish that an eighteen year old *does not* have capacity, while, conversely, it would be for a fifteen year old to establish that she *does*, in fact, have the capacity to make a particular medical decision.

There appears to be one exception to this mixed approach, however. When children want to take life-threatening decisions, it is, as we see later, virtually impossible to for them to establish that they are competent, and so their 'status' as minors seems to be decisive.

It is important to remember that, in reality, capacity is a question of degree. Although patients at either end of the spectrum might be readily identified as either competent or incompetent, towards the middle it will be difficult to determine where the line should lie. As Michael Gunn explains:

Capacity/incapacity are not concepts with clear a priori boundaries. They appear on a continuum which ranges from full capacity at one end to full incapacity at the other end. There are, therefore, degrees of capacity. The challenge is to choose the right level to set as the gateway to decision-making and respect for persons and autonomy.[19]

Normally, as we all know from experience, the question of whether an adult patient has capacity does not arise. Few people reading this book will have undergone a specific capacity assessment before they were allowed to consent to medical treatment. Questioning a patient's decision-making capacity only tends to happen in two situations. First, if the patient belongs to a group whose members often or normally lack capacity, health care professionals may be alerted to the possibility that she may not be able to give a valid consent to treatment. A person suffering from Alzheimer's disease may or may not still have capacity, but the presence of this disease will make doctors more likely to question her ability to make decisions for herself. This may mean that people suffering from certain mental disorders are more likely to be judged incompetent, even though it is important to remember that mental illness and incapacity are not synonymous with each other, and mentally ill people too benefit from the presumption of competence.

Secondly, if the patient's doctors believe that her decision is seriously misguided or irrational, they are more likely to question her decision-making capacity. The irrationality of a patient's choice does not justify a finding of incompetence, however. On the contrary, if competent, a patient's decision must be respected regardless of how foolish or irrational it may seem. But it is probably inevitable that doctors will be more likely to question a patient's capacity when she refuses to consent to treatment that the doctor believes to be in her best interests, than when she expresses her agreement.

---

[19] 'The Meaning of Incapacity' (1994) 2 Medical Law Review 8.

Of course, if the medical profession is unlikely to challenge a patient's decision-making capacity when she has *consented* to a proposed treatment, the pool of patients who are currently labelled incompetent will be smaller than it would be if *all* patients' decision-making capacity was scrutinized and assessed. In the study discussed in the next extract, Raymont *et al.* assessed the decision-making capacity of acutely ill medical inpatients, and found that almost half of them lacked capacity, but since none of them had refused treatment, the treating doctors had treated their acquiescence as if it amounted to valid consent.

Vanessa Raymont, William Bingley, Alec Buchanan, Anthony S David, Peter Hayward, Simon Wessely, and Matthew Hotopf[20]

Our study suggests that in routine clinical practice, doctors most usually fail to identify that patients with significant cognitive impairment do not have capacity. If we accept that a high proportion of acutely ill medical inpatients do not have mental capacity to make decisions about current treatment, our findings have implications for clinical practice, legislation, and the doctor–patient relationship. The current position is to assume capacity unless there is strong evidence to the contrary. We suspect that a substantial proportion of patients with decisional difficulties place their trust in doctors, and passively acquiesce with treatment plans. Thus, incapacity is frequently overlooked....

However, to accept the passive acquiescence of such patients as evidence of true consent would be dangerous when important and irreversible decisions need to be made. Before making such decisions, the clinician should have considered the possibility that the patient is unable to give valid consent.

Let us now turn to consider how the law treats patients who lack capacity or whose capacity is in doubt. Despite some similarities, there are important differences between the treatment of adults and children, and so we consider the two groups separately.

(a) ADULTS

There were a number of reasons why statutory reform of the law relating to the treatment of adults who lack capacity was thought desirable. The common law framework was believed to be unclear, leaving medical professionals and carers uncertain how to act, and vulnerable to criticism and legal challenge. It was also thought that this legal uncertainty led to delays in people receiving treatment, and to some people being wrongly labelled incompetent.

Given the high proportion of patients who are likely to lack capacity at some point during their lives, set out here in the Mental Capacity Bill's Regulatory Impact Assessment, this lack of certainty could not be ignored.

---

[20] 'Prevalence of Mental Incapacity in Medical Inpatients and Associated Risk Factors: Cross-sectional Study' (2004) 364 The Lancet 1421–7.

Department for Constitutional Affairs[21]

The scale of...the risks...is reflected in the size of the population of people who may lack capacity. This includes a wide range of people:

(a) more than 700,000 people in the UK are estimated to suffer from dementia and, in an ageing population, this is projected to rise to around 840,000 by 2010;

(b) around 145,000 adults in England have severe and profound learning disabilities, and at least 1.2 million have a mild to moderate learning disability. In Wales, over 12,000 people were registered as having a learning disability in 2001;

(c) at some point in their lives, approximately 1% of the UK population will suffer from schizophrenia, 1% will be subject to bipolar disorder and 5% will have serious or clinical depression; and

(d) 10–15 people per 100,000 of the population will suffer a severe head injury each year, and there are currently an estimated 120,000 people in the UK suffering from the long-term effects of severe brain injury.

The Mental Capacity Act 2005 (MCA) came into force in 2007. The Act's scope is much broader than the *medical* treatment of people who lack capacity: it also covers questions about the management of their property and financial affairs and decisions about where they should live. These broader issues are outside the scope of this book, and so our discussion will be confined to the MCA's application to decisions about health care.

(1) The 'Principles'

Section 1 of the MCA sets out five statutory principles which capture the most basic and important assumptions underpinning the statutory scheme, namely that people who lack capacity should (a) be protected, and (b) be helped, as far as possible, to make or take part in decisions affecting them.

Mental Capacity Act 2005 section 1

1(1) The following principles apply for the purposes of this Act.

(2) A person must be assumed to have capacity unless it is established that he lacks capacity.

(3) A person is not to be treated as unable to make a decision unless all practicable steps to help him to do so have been taken without success.

(4) A person is not to be treated as unable to make a decision merely because he makes an unwise decision.

(5) An act done, or decision made, under this Act for or on behalf of a person who lacks capacity must be done, or made, in his best interests.

(6) Before the act is done, or the decision is made, regard must be had to whether the purpose for which it is needed can be as effectively achieved in a way that is less restrictive of the person's rights and freedom of action.

---

[21] The Mental Capacity Bill: Full Regulatory Impact Assessment, available at <www.dca.gov.uk>.

The Code of Practice, issued in 2007, sets out how these principles, and the legislative provisions described below, should apply in practice. The Act uses the shorthand 'P' to refer to the person lacking capacity, and this will be adopted here.

The Act only applies to people over the age of 16. As we see later in this chapter, young people aged 16 and 17 are in a slightly curious position. The Mental Capacity Act may apply to them, if they do not have capacity according to its definition, but, as we see later, the presumption of capacity which applies to them is slightly different from the more robust presumption which applies to over 18s.

(2) Definition of Incapacity

(a) What is incapacity?

The statutory principles, reproduced above, preserve the common law presumption of capacity, and the principle that patients have the right to make unwise or foolish decisions.

Unlike the common law, section 2 of the Mental Capacity Act 2005 then introduces a two-stage test for capacity.

Mental Capacity Act 2005 section 2

2 People who lack capacity

(1) For the purposes of this Act, a person lacks capacity in relation to a matter if at the material time he is unable to make a decision for himself in relation to the matter because of an impairment of, or a disturbance in the functioning of, the mind or brain.

(2) It does not matter whether the impairment or disturbance is permanent or temporary.

First, under section 2(1), it must be established that the person is suffering from 'an impairment of, or a disturbance in the functioning of, the mind or brain'. This 'diagnostic threshold' means that someone will not fall within the provisions of the Act unless they are suffering from some sort of mental impairment, which can be either temporary or permanent.

The Code of Practice suggests that a wide variety of conditions will be covered, such as alcohol or drug misuse, delirium and concussion, as well as the more obvious categories of learning difficulties and brain damage.

Mental Capacity Act Code of Practice para. 4.12

4.12 Examples of an impairment or disturbance in the functioning of the mind or brain may include the following:

- conditions associated with some forms of mental illness
- dementia
- significant learning disabilities
- the long-term effects of brain damage
- physical or medical conditions that cause confusion, drowsiness or loss of consciousness
- delirium

- concussion following a head injury, and
- the symptoms of alcohol or drug use.

It is also worth noting that the Mental Capacity Act Code of Practice attempts to address two problems mentioned above, namely underdiagnosis of incapacity (a) in patients suffering from chronic *physical* illness, and (b) among patients who agree with a doctor's proposed treatment plan:

Mental Capacity Act Code of Practice paras 4.26 and 4.45

4.26 Temporary factors may also affect someone's ability to make decisions. Examples include acute illness, severe pain, the effect of medication, or distress after a death or shock...

4.45 Be aware that the fact that a person agrees with you or assents to what is proposed does not necessarily mean that they have capacity to make the decision.

Secondly, once this diagnostic requirement has been satisfied, it is necessary to work out whether the person is able to make a decision for himself. Section 3(1) sets out what is meant by being 'unable to make a decision':

Mental Capacity Act 2005 section 3

3 Inability to make decisions

(1) For the purposes of section 2, a person is unable to make a decision for himself if he is unable—

(a) to understand the information relevant to the decision,

(b) to retain that information,

(c) to use or weigh that information as part of the process of making the decision, or

(d) to communicate his decision (whether by talking, using sign language or any other means).

(2) A person is not to be regarded as unable to understand the information relevant to a decision if he is able to understand an explanation of it given to him in a way that is appropriate to his circumstances (using simple language, visual aids or any other means).

(3) The fact that a person is able to retain the information relevant to a decision for a short period only does not prevent him from being regarded as able to make the decision.

This second stage is, essentially, a statutory version of the test at common law which governed decisions about capacity before 2007. This was first set out by Thorpe J in *Re C (Adult: Refusal of Treatment)*. C suffered from chronic paranoid schizophrenia. He had delusions that he had had an international career in medicine, during which he had never lost a patient. His consultant was of the view that, unless his gangrenous leg was amputated, he had an 85 per cent chance of death. C said that he would rather die with two feet than live with one. C's solicitor sought, and was granted, a declaration that no amputation should take place without C's written consent.

Re C (Adult: Refusal of Treatment)[22]

Thorpe J

I consider helpful Dr E's analysis of the decision-making process into three stages:

- first, comprehending and retaining treatment information,
- secondly, believing it and,
- thirdly, weighing it in the balance to arrive at choice.

Applying that test to my findings on the evidence, I am completely satisfied that the presumption that Mr C has the right of self-determination has not been displaced. Although his general capacity is impaired by schizophrenia, it has not been established that he does not sufficiently understand the nature, purpose and effects of the treatment he refuses. Indeed, I am satisfied that he has understood and retained the relevant treatment information, that in his own way he believes it, and that in the same fashion he has arrived at a clear choice.

Thorpe J's test was approved by the Court of Appeal a few years later in *Re MB (An Adult: Medical Treatment)*. Butler-Sloss LJ initially appeared to qualify the *Re C* test by missing out the second stage, namely the need for the person to 'believe' information.

Re MB (An Adult: Medical Treatment)[23]

Butler-Sloss LJ

A person lacks capacity if some impairment or disturbance of mental functioning renders the person unable to make a decision whether to consent to or to refuse treatment. That inability to make a decision will occur when:

(a) the patient is unable to comprehend and retain the information which is material to the decision, especially as to the likely consequences of having or not having the treatment in question.

(b) the patient is unable to use the information and weigh it in the balance as part of the process of arriving at the decision.

Butler Sloss's formulation is the one adopted in the MCA, but, as Munby J explains in *Local Authority X v MM*, the difference in wording is not significant.

Local Authority X v MM[24]

Munby J

It will have been noticed that in *Re C* Thorpe J identified, as the second of three ingredients of the test, the ability or capacity to 'believe' the relevant information, whereas that ingredient is seemingly missing both from the formulation of the test in *Re MB* and from section 3(1)

---

[22] [1994] 1 WLR 290.   [23] [1997] 2 FLR 426.   [24] [2007] EWHC 2003 (Fam).

of the Act. The answer to this seeming lack of correspondence...is to be found towards the end of the passage which I quoted above from Butler-Sloss LJ's judgment in *Re MB*. If one does not 'believe' a particular piece of information then one does not, in truth, 'comprehend' or 'understand' it, nor can it be said that one is able to 'use' or 'weigh' it. In other words, the specific requirement of belief is subsumed in the more general requirements of understanding and of ability to use and weigh information.

Importantly, someone only needs to be able to retain information temporarily in order to satisfy this limb of the test. Section 3(3) of the Act specifies that someone who can retain information only for short periods of time should nevertheless be entitled to make their own decisions. Hence people in the early stages of a degenerative condition like Alzheimer's disease may still have the capacity to exercise control over their medical treatment. Moreover, the Code of Practice suggests that efforts should be made to help people to retain information: 'Items such as notebooks, photographs, posters, videos and voice recorders can help people record and retain information.'[25]

A second difference between section 3(1) of the MCA and the *Re C* test is the addition of the fourth limb of the section 3(1) test: namely that P is not able to communicate his decision. This was not mentioned by Thorpe J because it was not an issue in C's case. It was, however, always the case at common law that, for patients who cannot express themselves *at all*, there is no option but to treat them as if they lack capacity. The MCA Code of Practice confirms that this applies only to the tiny number of patients, such as those suffering from conditions like locked-in syndrome, who cannot communicate by even the most minimal means, such as by squeezing an arm or blinking an eyelid.[26]

(b) The right to take irrational decisions?

While the statutory principles preserve the patient's right to take unwise decisions without having their capacity called into question, it is worth noting that, in relation to irrational decision-making, there was a degree of ambiguity in the *Re C* test which has been reproduced in the legislation. On the one hand, it seems clear that provided a patient satisfies the test for capacity, it does not matter whether the decision she wants to take is irrational, or based upon her own peculiar values or beliefs. As Lord Donaldson MR explained in *Re T*:[27] 'the patient's right of choice exists whether the reasons for making that choice are rational, irrational, unknown or even non-existent'.

On the other hand, it is sometimes difficult to draw the line between a person's bizarre and irrational wishes, which must nevertheless be respected, and a person's inability to use and weigh information in order to come to a decision, as demanded by section 3(1)(c).

The central tension is that while competent patients have the right to make illogical decisions, for irrational reasons or for no reasons at all, there are times when irrationality, or making a decision for no reasons at all, may offer *evidence* of incompetence. As Butler-Sloss LJ put it in *Re MB*,[28] 'panic, indecisiveness and irrationality in themselves do not as such amount to incompetence, but they may be symptoms or evidence of incompetence'.

We can see an irrational decision informing assessment of a patient's capacity in *NHS Trust v T (Adult Patient: Refusal of Medical Treatment)*. Ms T had attempted to execute an

---

[25] Mental Capacity Act 2005 Code of Practice para 4.20.   [26] Para 4.23.
[27] [1993] Fam 95.   [28] *Re MB* [1997] 1 FCR 274.

advance directive refusing the blood transfusions she needed regularly because of her tendency to self-harm through blood-letting. In her advance directive, she explained her reasons for refusing blood transfusions as follows:

> I believe my blood is evil, carrying evil around my body. Although the blood given in transfusions is perfectly healthy/clean once given to me it mixes with my own and also becomes evil. Contaminated by my own. Therefore the volume of evil blood in my body will have increased and likewise the danger of my committing acts of evil.[29]

Charles J stressed that while making a bizarre or irrational decision was not sufficient for a finding of incapacity, Ms T's belief that blood was evil amounted to a disorder of the mind.

NHS Trust v T (Adult Patient: Refusal of Medical Treatment)[30]

Charles J

If there are difficulties in deciding whether the patient has sufficient mental capacity, particularly if the refusal may have grave consequences for the patient, it is most important that those considering the issue should not confuse the question of mental capacity with the nature of the decision made by the patient, however grave the consequences. The view of the patient may reflect a difference in values rather than an absence of competence and the assessment of capacity should be approached with this firmly in mind. The doctors must not allow their emotional reaction to or strong disagreement with the decision of the patient to cloud their judgment in answering the primary question whether the patient has the mental capacity to make the decision....

Ms T's references to her blood being evil equate to the example given that 'the blood is poisoned because it is red'. From that it seems to me that this assertion and belief of Ms T is a misconception of reality which can more readily be accepted to be, and on the present evidence should be accepted to be, a disorder of the mind and further or alternatively symptoms or evidence of incompetence.

Drawing the line between irrational decisions which must be respected, and irrational decisions which amount to evidence of incompetence is difficult, not least because of the tendency to make assumptions about different people's capacity according to whether or not they suffer from a mental health problem or not. So, for example, an articulate, middle-class professional who decides to refuse conventional treatment for cancer and rely instead on 'Dr Simoncini's "bicarbonate of soda" treatment for cancer',[31] is making a decision which is bizarre and irrational, and yet her decision to reject conventional treatment would not necessarily mean that her capacity would be called into question. In contrast, Ms T suffered from borderline personality disorder, and so it was much easier to jump to conclusions about her decision-making capacity. The right to make eccentric decisions thus receives rather uneven protection. Someone with an existing mental health problem may find that she is more likely to have her capacity challenged if she wants to make an odd choice than a person whose capacity is not in doubt.

---

[29] *NHS Trust v T (Adult Patient: Refusal of Medical Treatment)* [2004] EWHC 1279 (Fam).
[30] [2004] EWHC 1279 (Fam).
[31] An Italian 'oncologist' who believes that cancer is a fungus which can be cured with bicarbonate of soda.

Cases involving anorexic patients are a particularly good example of the rather blurred line between the protection of the competent patient's right to make irrational *decisions*, and the questioning of capacity on the grounds of the patient's irrational *decision-making process*. The Mental Capacity Act 2005 Code of Practice suggests that anorexic patients often do understand information about their need for food, but they are unable to use or weigh this information because of their condition.

Mental Capacity Act Code of Practice paras 4.21 and 4.22

> 4.21 Sometimes people can understand information but an impairment or disturbance stops them using it....
> 4.22 For example, a person with the eating disorder anorexia nervosa may understand information about the consequences of not eating. But their compulsion not to eat might be too strong for them to ignore.

At common law, anorexics commonly failed the *Re C* test, on the grounds that they were incapable of weighing information in the balance in order to arrive at a decision, and hence, on a number of occasions, treatment (namely force-feeding) without consent was declared lawful.[32] The courts thus appeared to believe that a sharp distinction could be drawn between C's (irrational) delusions of grandeur—which did not cast doubt upon his competence—and an anorexic's (irrational) belief that she needed to lose weight, which demonstrated her inability to weigh information in order to arrive at a choice.

Heather Draper has also pointed out an interesting distinction between chronic undereating usually caused by psychological problems, where a finding of incapacity and the authorization of force-feeding is relatively straightforward, and chronic *overeating*, which might similarly be prompted by psychological problems such as low self-esteem, and which will sometimes be similarly life-threatening, but where compulsory treatment would be extremely unlikely.[33]

Of course, one explanation for this difference is that anorexia is classified as a mental illness in the International Classification of Diseases (ICD-10), whereas extreme gluttony is not, although it should be noted that this classification is not universally accepted, and that, in any event, having a mental illness is not synonymous with lacking capacity.[34] Draper has also contrasted an anorexic's refusal of food with a woman's rejection of radical mastectomy.

Heather Draper[35]

> Let us take a step back from the emotionally charged issue of anorexia and consider a parallel case—that of a woman who knows that with a radical mastectomy and chemotherapy she has a good chance of recovering from breast cancer but who refuses to have the operation because, in her opinion, living with only one breast or no breasts at all will be intolerable. She is *also* making a decision based on her perception of her body image and we might

---

[32] *Re W* [1993] Fam 64 CA; *South West Hertfordshire Health Authority v B* [1994] 2 FCR 1051.

[33] 'Anorexia Nervosa and Respecting a Refusal of Life-prolonging Therapy: a Limited Justification' (2000) 14 Bioethics 120–33, 131.

[34] Ibid, 130; Rebecca Dresser, 'Feeding the Hunger Artists: Legal Issues in Treating Anorexia Nervosa' (1984) Wisconsin Law Review 297.

[35] 'Treating Anorexics Without Consent: Some Reservations' (1998) 24 Journal of Medical Ethics 5–7.

think that this is an irrational perception. Nevertheless, operating without her consent is unthinkable.[36]

(c) Equal treatment

Buttressing the presumption of capacity, the Act spells out certain factors which must *not* be used to ground a finding of incapacity. As we have seen, the fourth principle specifies that: 'a person should not be assumed to lack capacity just because they make an unwise decision', and, according to section 2(3):

Mental Capacity Act 2005 section 2

2(3) A lack of capacity cannot be established merely by reference to—

(a) a person's age or appearance, or

(b) a condition of his, or an aspect of his behaviour, which might lead others to make unjustified assumptions about his capacity.

The intention of this section is clear: to remind health care professionals that they should not rely on stereotypes when judging capacity. The use of the word 'merely' is, however, rather odd, since the implication is that a lack of capacity *could* be established based upon a person's age or appearance, as long as there are other factors which *also justify this finding*. If assumptions about his condition are 'unjustified', as they would have to be to fit within section 2(3)(b), then they should not be relevant at all, rather than being relevant if buttressed by other factors.

This unfortunate form of words is repeated in section 4 when deciding what treatment to offer. When deciding what is in the person's best interests the Act again stresses that stereotypes about people are *not* relevant. Section 4(1)'s use of the word 'merely' is again regrettable, since it carries the implication that someone's appearance or behaviour *could* be relevant to the decision as to what is in their best interests, as long as it is not the only factor:

Mental Capacity Act 2005 section 4

4(1) In determining for the purposes of this Act what is in a person's best interests, the person making the determination must not make it merely on the basis of—

(a) the person's age or appearance, or

(b) a condition of his, or an aspect of his behaviour, which might lead others to make unjustified assumptions about what might be in his best interests.

(3) Assisting Decision-Making

The second statutory principle, in section 1(3) provides that 'a person is not to be treated as unable to make a decision unless all practicable steps to help him to do so have been taken without success'. This is bolstered by section 3(2):

---

[36] Ibid.

Mental Capacity Act 2005 section 3

3(2) A person is not to be regarded as unable to understand the information relevant to a decision if he is able to understand an explanation of it given to him in a way that is appropriate to his circumstances (using simple language, visual aids or any other means).

The Code of Practice gives more detail as to the kind of support people might need, and offers guidance on how to maximize their decision-making ability.

Mental Capacity Act Code of Practice paras 2.7, 3.10, 3.13 and 3.14

2.7 The kind of support people might need to help them make a decision varies. It depends on personal circumstances, the kind of decision that has to be made and the time available to make the decision. It might include:

- using a different form of communication (for example, non-verbal communication)
- providing information in a more accessible form (for example, photographs, drawings, or tapes)
- treating a medical condition which may be affecting the person's capacity or
- having a structured programme to improve a person's capacity to make particular decisions (for example, helping a person with learning disabilities to learn new skills)....

3.10 To help someone make a decision for themselves, all possible and appropriate means of communication should be tried.

- Ask people who know the person well about the best form of communication (try speaking to family members, carers, day centre staff or support workers). They may also know somebody the person can communicate with easily, or the time when it is best to communicate with them.
- Use simple language. Where appropriate, use pictures, objects or illustrations to demonstrate ideas.
- Speak at the right volume and speed, with appropriate words and sentence structure. It may be helpful to pause to check understanding or show that a choice is available.
- Break down difficult information into smaller points that are easy to understand. Allow the person time to consider and understand each point before continuing.
- It may be necessary to repeat information or go back over a point several times.
- Is help available from people the person trusts (relatives, friends, GP, social worker, religious or community leaders)?
- Be aware of cultural, ethnic or religious factors that shape a person's way of thinking, behaviour or communication.
- If necessary, consider using a professional language interpreter.
- Would an advocate (someone who can support and represent the person) improve communication in the current situation?

3.13 Where possible, choose a location where the person feels most at ease. For example, people are usually more comfortable in their own home than at a doctor's surgery.

3.14 Try to choose the time of day when the person is most alert—some people are better in the mornings, others are more lively in the afternoon or early evening. It may be necessary to try several times before a decision can be made.

Of course, in an emergency, these extensive steps to support the person to make their own decision may not be practicable. The Code suggests that when an urgent decision is required, 'the only practical and appropriate steps might be to keep a person informed of what is happening and why'.[37]

(4) How Should People Who Lack Capacity be Treated?

The statutory principles confirm the common law position that treatment of people who lack capacity is governed by a best interests test, and that the 'least restrictive alternative' principle applies.

Mental Capacity Act 2005 section 1

> 1(5) An act done, or decision made, under this Act for or on behalf of a person who lacks capacity must be done, or made, in his best interests.
>
> (6) Before the act is done, or the decision is made, regard must be had to whether the purpose for which it is needed can be as effectively achieved in a way that is less restrictive of the person's rights and freedom of action.

This means that when deciding between possible courses of action, there should be a presumption in favour of the least intrusive one, and it also means that consideration should be given as to whether it is necessary to act at all. So, for example, where a woman who lacks capacity cannot cope with her heavy periods, hysterectomy must be an option of last resort, and less intrusive methods of interfering with her menstrual cycle, such as injections or progesterone-only contraceptive pills should be tried first.

Section 4 fleshes out the factors to be considered when making a determination of what is in a person's best interests. It is not an exhaustive list of relevant factors. Rather, the Code makes it clear that the section 4 'checklist is only the starting point: in many cases, extra factors will need to be considered'.[38]

Mental Capacity Act 2005 section 4

> 4(2) The person making the determination must consider all the relevant circumstances and, in particular, take the following steps.
>
> (3) He must consider—
>
> (a) whether it is likely that the person will at some time have capacity in relation to the matter in question, and
>
> (b) if it appears likely that he will, when that is likely to be.
>
> (4) He must, so far as reasonably practicable, permit and encourage the person to participate, or to improve his ability to participate, as fully as possible in any act done for him and any decision affecting him . . .
>
> (6) He must consider, so far as is reasonably ascertainable—
>
> (a) the person's past and present wishes and feelings (and, in particular, any relevant written statement made by him when he had capacity),
>
> (b) the beliefs and values that would be likely to influence his decision if he had capacity, and
>
> (c) the other factors that he would be likely to consider if he were able to do so.

[37] Para 2.9.   [38] Para 5.6.

> (7) He must take into account, if it is practicable and appropriate to consult them, the views of—
>
> (a) anyone named by the person as someone to be consulted on the matter in question or on matters of that kind,
>
> (b) anyone engaged in caring for the person or interested in his welfare,
>
> (c) any donee of a lasting power of attorney granted by the person, and
>
> (d) any deputy appointed for the person by the court,
>
> as to what would be in the person's best interests and, in particular, as to the matters mentioned in subsection (6).

(a) Temporary incapacity

The 'best interests' test applies to *all* patients who have been found to lack capacity, and as we saw earlier, this is by no means a homogenous group. A patient who is temporarily incapacitated—for example, someone who is unconscious when they arrive at A&E or who has been anaesthetized—is in a very different position from a patient in a permanent vegetative state. Where a patient *temporarily* lacks capacity, a particularly important factor is that, under section 4(3), regard must be had to whether and when a person is likely to regain capacity. This means that if the person's incapacity is likely to be short-lived, decisions should only be taken where it would not be possible to wait until she regains capacity, and is able to decide for herself.

Again, this confirms the position at common law, explained here by Lord Goff in *F v West Berkshire*, which permitted incapacitated patients to be treated in their best interests in an emergency, but if they were expected to regain capacity, and the decision could wait, the doctors should only do that which was immediately necessary to prevent death or serious harm.

F v West Berkshire[39]

Lord Goff

Where, for example, a surgeon performs an operation without his consent on a patient temporarily rendered unconscious in an accident, he should do no more than is reasonably required, in the best interests of the patient, before he recovers consciousness. I can see no practical difficulty arising from this requirement, which derives from the fact that the patient is expected before long to regain consciousness and can then be consulted about longer term measures.

Section 4(3) does not just apply to emergency treatment, however, and is also intended to capture the idea that many sorts of treatment which might appear to be in a person's best interests might be able to wait until efforts have been made to treat the cause of their incapacity, or facilitate communication. If capacity might be regained, consideration must be given to the possibility of delaying making a decision in order to allow the patient to take the decision herself.

---

[39] [1990] 2 AC 1 HL.

(b) Relevance of the patient's views

One striking feature of the MCA's best interests checklist is the emphasis it places on the patient's own views and values. Of course, where a patient has never been competent or has never been able to express an opinion, it will be hard to take her 'values' into account, and the doctor's objective assessment of her clinical interests will inevitably take priority. But where there is any evidence at all of the factors that would matter to the patient herself, then their 'best interests' are not to be judged purely objectively, according to what the doctor believes to be clinically indicated. The Act recognizes that there may be a range of reasonable responses to the patient's condition, and that the patient's previously expressed views or values may be relevant to what is best for her.

In cases where the patient's views about treatment are in direct conflict with her doctor's views about what treatment would be in her best interests, it remains to be seen whether the MCA's patient-centred approach will, in practice, ever allow her wishes to trump her doctor's assessment of her clinical best interests. If it did, this would represent a radical break with the treatment of adults who lacked capacity at common law. Recall in *NHS Trust v T (Adult Patient: Refusal of Medical Treatment)*,[40] the patient had made her strong views about blood transfusions known, and yet, having decided that she lacked capacity, in part *because of* her bizarre views, Charles J did not consider that those views might nevertheless be relevant to a decision about whether a transfusion was in her best interests.

Mary Donnelly has argued that the new regime under the MCA should require more rigorous justification of the grounds for acting against such a strongly held preference.

Mary Donnelly[41]

At a practical level, the participation requirement should, at a minimum, necessitate the acknowledgement, if this is the case, that the person lacking capacity has an alternative preference. This in turn should lead to a rigorous scrutiny of the evidence presented in favour of the argument that the decision-maker should act against this preference. It cannot be enough for a decision-maker simply to acknowledge the views of the person lacking capacity before reaching a decision which takes no account of these views.

The patient's previous values and beliefs were certainly not irrelevant before the MCA came into force. In *Ahsan v University Hospitals Leicester NHS Trust*, the court had to decide between two different care regimes for a patient, Mrs Ahsan, who was in a permanent vegetative state as a result of the defendant trust's admitted negligence. While Mrs Ahsan would continue to be wholly unaware of the environment in which she was cared for, Hegarty J rejected the defendant's claim that, because nothing could affect her wellbeing, treatment at home could not benefit her. He found further support for this conclusion in the MCA scheme, which was not yet in force.

---

[40] [2004] EWHC 1279 (Fam).

[41] 'Best Interests, Patient Participation and the Mental Capacity Act 2005' (2009) Medical Law Review 1–29.

Ahsan v University Hospitals Leicester NHS Trust[42]

Hegarty J

I do not think for one moment that a reasonable member of the public would consider that the religious beliefs of an individual and her family should simply be disregarded in deciding how she should be cared for in the unhappy event of supervening mental incapacity. On the contrary, I would have thought that most reasonable people would expect, in the event of some catastrophe of that kind, that they would be cared for, as far as practicable, in such a way as to ensure that they were treated with due regard for their personal dignity and with proper respect for their religious beliefs....

[T]hat approach appears to be entirely consistent with the scheme intended to be established by the Mental Capacity Act, if and when it is brought into force....

I have no doubt whatever that if Mrs Ahsan had been asked her views before incapacity supervened, or if she had been able to form and express a view today as to her future treatment, she would have expressed a strong desire to be cared for at home once her condition had stabilised and, if possible, to die at home surrounded by her family. She would have wished, I am sure, to spend her remaining days in an environment where she would be confident that her spiritual needs were administered to and her physical requirements attended to in a manner compatible with the traditions of her culture.

In a post-MCA case, *Ealing LDC v KS*,[43] we can see that the fact that there had been a decision that KS lacked capacity, and that an operation to remove a cyst was in her best interests, did not mean doctors had *carte blanche* to carry out other procedures which they believed to be in her best interests. Here the doctors had proposed fitting an intra-uterine contraceptive device (IUD) when they carried out the operation to remove the cyst. KS had been pregnant on several occasions, giving birth only once to a child, who died shortly after birth. Given KS's vehement opposition to contraception, the fitting of an IUD was found not to be in her best interests.

It could be argued that the Act implicitly acknowledges that capacity exists on a spectrum. While law needs to be able to draw a bright line boundary between competent patients, who benefit from robust protection of their right to make 'irrational decisions', and incompetent patients, who can be treated in their best interests, in practice there may be patients who only just fail the section 1(3) test, and who may have strong views about where their best interests lie.

The Act specifically mentions the importance of consulting carers and family members in order to elicit information about the patient's values and beliefs. Here there is an obvious tension with the principle of patient confidentiality, considered in more detail in chapter 7, and the Code of Practice makes it clear that section 4(7) certainly does not suspend the incapacitated person's right to confidentiality, but rather that health care professionals need to balance the duty to consult with the duty to respect confidentiality:

Mental Capacity Act Code of Practice para 5.56

5.56 Decision-makers must balance the duty to consult other people with the right to confidentiality of the person who lacks capacity. So if confidential information is to be discussed, they should only seek the views of people who it is appropriate to consult, where their views are relevant to the decision to be made and the particular circumstances.

---

[42] [2006] EWHC 2624 (QB).   [43] [2008] EWHC 636 (Fam).

It is also possible that those who are consulted will disagree about what the patient would have wanted. The Code of Practice advocates trying to reach agreement, involving the person who lacks capacity as far as possible, but ultimately responsibility for deciding what treatment is in a patient's best interests lies with the decision-maker.[44]

Of course, there will be times when a patient's apparent wishes have to be viewed in the light of the influence others may have over them. This was the case in *A Primary Care Trust v P*, in which P's mother, AH, who was extremely close to her son, held eccentric views on the appropriate treatment of his uncontrolled epilepsy.

A Primary Care Trust v P[45]

Sir Mark Potter P

The real difficulty in this case has been, and continues to be, that, such is the closeness of the relationship between P and AH, his mother and carer, that...there is real and unresolved doubt as to how far P's expressed views as to where, by whom, and in what manner he wishes or is prepared to accept treatment, are his own, and how far they are no more than simple adoption and repetition of his mother's views in a situation where he would otherwise be malleable and co-operative with the attempts of the experts to understand the true aetiology and interrelationship of his various symptoms and to relieve P from what is now largely a wheelchair bound existence.

Mary Donnelly further argues that care must be taken to ensure that reports of a person's previously expressed views in fact represent their wishes. Elderly patients, for example, may have made vague and ambiguous statements about not wanting to be a burden, which may, in fact, reflect a desire for comfort and reassurance, rather than their considered view about their future medical treatment.

Mary Donnelly[46]

While the consultative model is a good one, it is important to remember that even close friends or family members cannot always know the past preferences or the relevant beliefs and values of the person lacking capacity. Statements such as 'I would rather die than be dependent' may reflect a desire for reassurance, or may be a result of temporary depression or fear, and may not represent the person's considered views on future care should they lose capacity.

For patients who do not have close friends or family, sections 35–7 provide for the appointment of an Independent Mental Capacity Advocate (IMCA) to support and represent them. Under section 37(3), an IMCA *must* be appointed when an NHS body is proposing to give 'serious medical treatment' to someone without capacity when no close family member or friend is available to consult about his wishes or feelings. The Mental Capacity Act 2005 (Independent Mental Capacity Advocate) (General) Regulations 2006 set out in detail

---

[44] Para 5.64.   [45] [2008] EWHC 1403 (Fam).
[46] 'Best Interests, Patient Participation and the Mental Capacity Act 2005' (2009) Medical Law Review 1–29.

how and when IMCAs should be appointed, their functions, and their role in challenging decisions.

The Regulations define 'serious medical treatment':

Mental Capacity Act 2005 (Independent Mental Capacity Advocate) (General) Regulations 2006 section 4

4(2) Serious medical treatment is treatment which involves providing, withdrawing or withholding treatment in circumstances where—

(a) in a case where a single treatment is being proposed, there is a fine balance between its benefits to the patient and the burdens and risks it is likely to entail for him,

(b) in a case where there is a choice of treatments, a decision as to which one to use is finely balanced, or

(c) what is proposed would be likely to involve serious consequences for the patient.

The Code of Practice gives some examples of serious medical treatment, including treatment for cancer, electroconvulsive therapy, major surgery, termination of pregnancy, and withholding artificial nutrition and hydration. If the treatment is needed urgently in an emergency, there is no need to appoint an IMCA, although this should be done for any follow-up serious treatment.

The IMCA is specifically charged with trying to elicit the person's wishes and values, and with ensuring that they have been given all the support they need to be involved in decision-making.

Mental Capacity Act 2005 (Independent Mental Capacity Advocate) (General) Regulations 2006 section 6

6(5) The IMCA must evaluate all the information he has obtained for the purpose of—

(a) ascertaining the extent of the support provided to P to enable him to participate in making any decision about the matter in relation to which the IMCA has been instructed;

(b) ascertaining what P's wishes and feelings would be likely to be, and the beliefs and values that would be likely to influence P, if he had capacity in relation to the proposed act or decision;

(c) ascertaining what alternative courses of action are available in relation to P;

(d) where medical treatment is proposed for P, ascertaining whether he would be likely to benefit from a further medical opinion.

(c) Not just medical best interests

By requiring the decision maker to consider factors which would have been relevant to the patient, it is evident that the best interests test accommodates factors other than the patient's immediate clinical needs, and can also take account of their emotional and welfare interests, or even, in some cases, the interests of others. The Code of Practice gives an example of taking a blood sample from someone who lacks capacity when investigating a familial genetic predisposition to cancer.

Non-clinical factors were also relevant to the best interests assessment at common law, as we can see from the following two cases. First, in *Re A (Medical Treatment: Male Sterilisation)*, the Court of Appeal had to consider an application to sterilize a mentally incapable man. There could be no clinical benefit to A from his sterilization. Although the Court of Appeal rejected the application, because his 63-year-old mother was providing him with constant care and supervision, it nevertheless left open the possibility that the decision might be reversed if A's circumstances changed. A's mother's health was poor and so it was likely he would have to be moved into local authority care in the future. If it became evident that his freedom of movement and association was being restricted in order to avoid the risk that he might engage in unprotected sexual intercourse, then a vasectomy might be in his best interests.

Re A (Medical Treatment: Male Sterilisation)[47]

Dame Elizabeth Butler-Sloss P

In the present appeal it is necessary to focus upon the best interests of A himself. It is clear from the evidence of his mother that, as long as she cares for him, he will continue to be subjected to the present regime of close supervision...When in due course he goes into local authority care, the degree of freedom might be affected by the fear that he might form a sexual relationship with another resident. It would however, in my view, be likely that the woman concerned would be the object of protection rather than A. If his quality of life were, however, to be diminished, that would be a reason to seek at that time a hearing before a High Court judge to grant a declaration that sterilisation would then be in A's best interests.

Secondly, in *Re Y (Mental Patient: Bone Marrow Donation)*, acting as a bone marrow donor to a desperately ill sibling was held to be in the best interests of an severely mentally handicapped adult. There could be no possible *medical* benefit to Y from undergoing an invasive and uncomfortable procedure in order to donate bone marrow to her sister. Rather, the donation was authorized on the grounds that it would be of immeasurable benefit to Y's *mother* (who was already in poor health), as well as to her sister, who might otherwise die. Because both her mother and sister would be profoundly grateful to Y, the operation was said to be for her 'emotional, psychological and social benefit'.

Re Y (Mental Patient: Bone Marrow Donation)[48]

Connell J

If the plaintiff [the sister] dies, this is bound to have an adverse effect upon her mother who already suffers from significant ill health. One lay witness took the gloomy view that this event would prove fatal to the mother, but in any event her ability to visit the defendant [Y] would be handicapped significantly, not only by a likely deterioration in her health, but also by the need which would then arise for her to look after her only grandchild.

　　In this situation, the defendant would clearly be harmed by the reduction in or loss of contact to her mother. Accordingly, it is to the benefit of the defendant that she should act as donor to her sister, because in this way her positive relationship with her mother is most likely to be prolonged. Further, if the transplant occurs, this is likely to improve the defendant's

47 [2000] 1 FLR 549.
48 [1996] 2 FLR 787.

> relationship with her mother who in her heart clearly wishes it to take place and also to improve her relationship with the plaintiff who will be eternally grateful to her.
>
> The disadvantages to the defendant of the harvesting procedure are very small...
>
> It is doubtful that this case would act as a useful precedent in cases where the surgery involved is more intrusive than in this case, where the evidence shows that the bone marrow harvested is speedily regenerated and that a healthy individual can donate as much as two pints with no long-term consequences at all. Thus, the bone marrow donated by the defendant will cause her no loss and she will suffer no real long-term risk.

Of course, cases where the proposed procedure would benefit *someone else* throw into particularly sharp relief the need to make sure that the family members whose views are sought under section 4(7)(b) are consulted about what the patient would have wanted, rather than their own wishes. The Code of Practice draws attention to this:

Mental Capacity Act Code of Practice para 4.49

> 4.49 ...Family members and close friends may be able to provide valuable background information...But their personal views and wishes about what *they* would want for the person must not influence the assessment.

(d) Exceptions to the best interests test

It is worth noting that there are two exceptions to the requirement that treatment given to a person who lacks capacity must be in their best interests. First, it is possible for someone who lacks capacity to participate in research, where the purpose is not necessarily to benefit the individual patient. We deal with this issue in chapter 9.

Secondly, as we see below, valid and applicable advance refusals of treatment are binding and must be complied with, even if they force a doctor to refrain from giving treatment which she believes to be in the patient's best interests. The Code of Practice spells this out:

Mental Capacity Act Code of Practice para 9.36

> 9.36 Where an advance decision is being followed, the best interests principle does not apply. This is because an advance decision reflects the decision of an adult with capacity who has made the decision for themselves. Healthcare professionals must follow a valid and applicable advance decision, even if they think it goes against a person's best interests.

(5) Advance Directives

Sections 24 and 25 of the MCA specifically deal with advance directives, referred to in the Act as advance decisions (ADs). Advance decisions are defined in section 24.

Mental Capacity Act 2005 section 24

> 24(1) 'Advance decision' is a decision made by a person ('P'), after he has reached 18 and when he has capacity to do so, that if—
>
> (a) at a later time and in such circumstances as he may specify, a specified treatment is proposed to be carried out or continued by a person providing health care for him, and

> (b) at that time he lacks capacity to consent to the carrying out or continuation of the treatment
>
> the specified treatment is not to be carried out or continued.

Section 24(1) specifies that advance decisions must have been made when an adult was competent, and must specify which treatment should not be carried out or continued when P lacks capacity. Hence section 24 only covers advance *refusals* of treatment. An advance *request* for treatment would be relevant under section 4(6)(a) when deciding what is in a person's best interests, but could not be decisive.

In line with the first statutory principle, the assumption should be, as the Code of Practice makes clear, that the person *did* have capacity when she made the advance decision:

Mental Capacity Act Code of Practice para 9.8

> 9.8 In line with principle 1 of the Act, that 'a person must be assumed to have capacity unless it is established that he lacks capacity', healthcare professionals should always start from the assumption that a person who has made an advance decision had capacity to make it, unless they are aware of reasonable grounds to doubt the person had the capacity to make the advance decision at the time they made it.

With one exception, there are no particular formalities that have to be satisfied for an advance decision to be valid. Under section 24(2), it is enough for the treatment which P wishes to refuse to be described in layman's terms, so a failure to use precise technical language will not defeat an advance directive.

For most advance decisions, with the exception of refusals of life-saving treatment, which must be signed and witnessed, there is no need for them to be in writing, so an oral refusal of non-life-sustaining treatment must be complied with. Under section 24(3), a person can withdraw or alter their advance decision at any time when he has capacity to do so, and under sections 24(4) and (5), withdrawals and alterations do not have to be in writing.

Section 25(1) specifies that, to be effective, an advance decision must be both *valid* and *applicable to the treatment*. If a decision is both valid and applicable, then under section 26(1) 'the decision has effect as if he had made it, and had had capacity to make it, at the time when the question arises whether the treatment should be carried out or continued'.

(a) Validity

Section 25(2) sets out when an AD will not be *valid*.

Mental Capacity Act 2005 section 25

> 25(2) An advance decision is not valid if P—
>
> (a) has withdrawn the decision at a time when he had capacity to do so,
>
> (b) has, under a lasting power of attorney created after the advance decision was made, conferred authority on the donee (or, if more than one, any of them) to give or refuse consent to the treatment to which the advance decision relates, or

> (c) has done anything else clearly inconsistent with the advance decision remaining his fixed decision.

Hence, to be valid, there must be no evidence that the P has either withdrawn the decision or conferred authority in relation to the relevant treatment on a donee via a lasting power of attorney.

Under section 25(2)(c) the decision is not valid if the P has acted in a way which is 'clearly inconsistent' with the decision. What does this mean? One obvious example might be if someone has explicitly renounced the religious beliefs upon which their decision was based. In *HE v A Hospital NHS Trust*—a pre-MCA case—doubt was cast on the validity of an advance directive, drawn up when the patient was a Jehovah's Witness, because of her decision to abandon her faith. Munby J found that given the existence of this doubt, the burden of proof was on those who sought to uphold the advance directive to establish that it was still valid.

HE v A Hospital NHS Trust[49]

Munby J

No doubt there is a practical—what lawyers would call an evidential—burden on those who assert that an undisputed advance directive is for some reason no longer operative, a burden requiring them to point to something indicating that this is or may be so. It may be words said to have been written or spoken by the patient. It may be the patient's actions—for sometimes actions speak louder than words. It may be some change in circumstances. Thus, it may be alleged that the patient no longer professes the faith which underlay the advance directive; it may be said that the patient executed the advance directive because he was suffering from an illness which has since been cured; it may be said that medical science has now moved on; it may be said that the patient, having since married or had children, now finds himself with more compelling reasons to choose to live even a severely disadvantaged life. It may be suggested that the advance directive has been revoked, whether by express words or by conduct on the part of the patient inconsistent with its continued validity. It may be suggested that, even though not revoked, the advance directive has not survived some material change of circumstances. But whatever the reasons may be, once the issue is properly raised, once there is some real reason for doubt, then it is for those who assert the continuing validity and applicability of the advance directive to prove that it is still operative. The burden of proof is on them. And, as I have said, what is required is clear and convincing proof. If there is doubt that doubt falls to be resolved in favour of the preservation of life. So, if there is doubt the advance directive cannot be relied on and the doctor must treat the patient in such way as his best interests require . . .

There is simply no clear and convincing proof that the advance directive is still valid and applicable. The father's evidence having raised doubts—real doubts, not fanciful doubts or mere speculations—those doubts must be resolved in favour of the preservation of life.

---

[49] [2003] EWHC 1017 (Fam).

It is, of course, possible to imagine situations where it will be difficult to tell whether a person's subsequent actions are 'clearly inconsistent' with their AD. For example, the Act does not specify whether the actions which serve to invalidate the AD under section 25(2)(c) must have occurred while the P was still competent, or whether the now incompetent P's conduct could also invalidate their AD. On the one hand, the failure to specify when the 'clearly inconsistent' actions should take place would seem to lead to the conclusion that *any* inconsistent conduct will invalidate the decision. Yet on the other hand, section 24(3) specifies that P may withdraw or alter an AD only 'when he has capacity to do so', so it might seem odd that someone who lacks capacity could invalidate their previous AD *indirectly* by acting inconsistently with it.

The Code of Practice recommends that patients should be advised to regularly review and update their advance decisions because a recently reviewed decision is more likely to be found valid than if considerable time has elapsed since it was made.

(b) Applicability

Section 25(3)–(6) specify when an advance decision will not be *applicable*.

Mental Capacity Act 2005 section 25

25(3) An advance decision is not applicable to the treatment in question if at the material time P has capacity to give or refuse consent to it.

(4) An advance decision is not applicable to the treatment in question if—

(a) that treatment is not the treatment specified in the advance decision,

(b) any circumstances specified in the advance decision are absent, or

(c) there are reasonable grounds for believing that circumstances exist which P did not anticipate at the time of the advance decision and which would have affected his decision had he anticipated them.

An advance decision will therefore lapse if the person who executed it regains capacity. Just as at common law, it is also necessary that the advance decision precisely covers the situation in which the P now finds himself, and that there are no reasonable grounds for believing that there has been a change of circumstances which casts doubt upon whether the advance decision would continue to reflect the P's views. An example might be where a patient executes an advance refusal of a particular medication because she finds its side-effects intolerable. If, in the meantime, a new formulation has been developed which does not have those side-effects, there may be reasonable grounds for believing that the patient might not have wanted to refuse medication for her condition.

When deciding whether an advance decision is applicable, the Code of Practice recommends that health care professions consider a number of factors.

Mental Capacity Act Code of Practice para 9.43

9.43 So when deciding whether an advance decision applies to the proposed treatment, healthcare professionals must consider:

- how long ago the advance decision was made, and
- whether there have been changes in the patient's personal life (for example, the person is pregnant, and this was not anticipated when they made the advance decision) that might affect the validity of the advance decision, and
- whether there have been developments in medical treatment that the person did not foresee (for example, new medications, treatment or therapies).

The Code of Practice recommends that, when drawing up an advance decision, it is important to try to anticipate possible future circumstances, in order to avoid doubt as to whether it applies in the circumstances that have arisen.

Mental Capacity Act Code of Practice para 9.16

9.16 It is a good idea to try to include possible future circumstances in the advance decision. For example, a woman may want to state in the advance decision whether or not it should still apply if she later becomes pregnant. If the document does not anticipate a change in circumstance, healthcare professionals may decide that it is not applicable if those particular circumstances arise.

The Code of Practice again suggests that people should be advised to regularly update and review their advance decisions, in order to minimize the chance that the decision will be found inapplicable on the grounds either that the patient's own circumstances have changed, or that the patient was not aware of some new medical development, which might have changed his attitude towards treatment.

Mental Capacity Act Code of Practice para 9.29

9.29 Anyone who has made an advance decision is advised to regularly review and update it as necessary. Decisions made a long time in advance are not automatically invalid or inapplicable, but they may raise doubts when deciding whether they are valid and applicable. A written decision that is regularly reviewed is more likely to be valid and applicable to current circumstances—particularly for progressive illnesses. This is because it is more likely to have taken on board changes that have occurred in a person's life since they made their decision.

It is unclear whether section 25(4)(c) could apply to a scenario which we consider in more detail in chapter 17, in which a now demented individual appears to be contented and does not want to die, despite have issued an otherwise binding advance directive refusing life-sustaining treatment. Is the fact that he appears to be happy despite his dementia a circumstance 'which P did not anticipate at the time of the advance decision and which would have affected his decision'? If interpreted in this way, the scope of section 25(4)(c) is potentially extremely broad since it would almost always be possible to argue that the patient issued their advance decision in a state of relative ignorance about what it would actually be like to be incapacitated.

In the next extract, Sabine Michalowski argues that advance directives should not be subject to a 'present best interests' exception, otherwise their value in preserving patient autonomy would be massively reduced.

Sabine Michalowski[50]

To disregard the decision made by the competent patient because it violates the general (or one person's) perception of the patient's present interests would mean that the validity of an advance directive is subjected to a 'present best interests' assessment exercised by a third party at the time a treatment decision needs to be made. Advance directives would then no longer be a means by which a patient can ensure that his/her own subjective values govern his/her medical treatment towards the end of life.

(c) Advance refusals of life-saving treatment

Section 25(5) and (6) lay down special rules for advance refusals of life-sustaining treatment. The P must specifically acknowledge that he intends to refuse treatment even if this puts his life at risk; the decision must be in writing and signed by P or a representative in P's presence, and the signature must be witnessed. This is more exacting than the common law, under which there was no requirement for an advance refusal to be in writing, regardless of the gravity of its consequences. It is therefore possible that patients who had made binding oral advance refusals of life-sustaining treatment before the Act came into force, and have subsequently lost capacity, will find that their previously valid advance refusal has been invalidated. This would mean that they would be given treatment which they had competently refused before the Act came into force.

(d) Effects of advance decisions

Where there is doubt about the validity or applicability of an advance decision, under section 26(4) an application can be made to the court for a declaration as to whether it is valid and applicable. If it is, the court has no power to overrule it. While the court's advice is being sought, under 26(5) nothing in the advance decision should prevent the provision of life-sustaining treatment or steps to prevent a deterioration in the P's condition.

An advance decision which fails to meet the above criteria does not become completely irrelevant, however. The doctor will, in such circumstances, have to decide what treatment is in the patient's best interests, and if the advance decision expresses the person's wishes or feelings, it is explicitly relevant to this assessment under section 4(6)(a). The Code of Practice reiterates that a finding that an advance decision does not apply, does not therefore mean that doctors are entitled to provide the treatment it purported to refuse.

Mental Capacity Act Code of Practice para 9.45

9.45 If an advance decision is not valid or applicable to current circumstances:

- healthcare professionals must consider the advance decision as part of their assessment of the person's best interests if they have reasonable grounds to think it is a true expression of the person's wishes, and

---

[50] 'Advance Refusals of Life Sustaining Treatment' (2005) 68 Modern Law Review 958.

> • they must not assume that because an advance decision is either invalid or not applic-
> able, they should always provide the specified treatment (including life-sustaining
> treatment)—they must base this decision on what is in the person's best interests.

It remains to be seen whether the MCA will make it more likely that advance refusals will
be found to be binding. Certainly, as we see in the next section, doctors who ignore advance
decisions on the grounds of doubt about their validity are very unlikely to face liability for
treating a patient without consent.

At common law, while ADs were not always ineffective, the courts appeared to approach
any lack of 'fit' between the advance refusal and the patient's current predicament with a
strong predilection in favour of preserving life. In *W Healthcare NHS Trust v H*, for example,
there was considerable evidence from H's friends and family members that she had said
repeatedly that if the time came when she could no longer recognize her daughters, she did
not want to be kept alive. That was now the case, but the Court of Appeal found that this was
insufficiently precise to qualify as a binding advance directive.

W Health Care NHS Trust v H[51]

Brooke LJ

I am of the clear view that the judge was correct in finding that there was not an advance
directive which was sufficiently clear to amount to a direction that she preferred to be deprived
of food and drink for a period of time which would lead to her death in all circumstances.
There is no evidence that she was aware of the nature of this choice, or the unpleasantness
or otherwise of death by starvation, and it would be departing from established principles of
English law if one was to hold that there was an advance directive which was established and
relevant in the circumstances in the present case, despite the very strong expression of her
wishes which came through in the evidence.

(6) Avoiding Liability

Normally it will be doctors who decide whether a person lacks capacity in relation to a particular decision, and, if they do, what treatment would be in their best interests. It is, of
course, possible that these decisions might subsequently be challenged, and found to be
mistaken. If it turns out that the patient did, in fact, have capacity, has a doctor who mistakenly treated her as if she lacked capacity—i.e. without seeking her consent—committed
an assault or battery?

According to section 5 of the Act, in order to be protected from a charge of battery or
assault, a doctor needs (a) to take 'reasonable steps' to establish whether the P has capacity;
(b) have a 'reasonable belief' that the person lacks capacity; and (c) 'reasonably believe' that
the treatment is in P's best interests.

---

[51] [2004] EWCA Civ 1324.

Mental Capacity Act 2005 section 5

5 Acts in connection with care or treatment

(1) If a person ('D') does an act in connection with the care or treatment of another person ('P'), the act is one to which this section applies if—

(a) before doing the act, D takes reasonable steps to establish whether P lacks capacity in relation to the matter in question, and

(b) when doing the act, D reasonably believes—

(i) that P lacks capacity in relation to the matter, and

(ii) that it will be in P's best interests for the act to be done.

(2) D does not incur any liability in relation to the act that he would not have incurred if P—

(a) had had capacity to consent in relation to the matter, and

(b) had consented to D's doing the act.

In order to establish that reasonable steps were taken to establish whether the P lacks capacity, and that the doctor had a reasonable belief in the patient's incapacity and in the fact that the treatment was in her best interests test, it is important that decision-makers record the fact that they have applied the statutory test for incapacity, and gone through the section 4 checklist. The Mental Capacity Act 2005 Code of Practice makes clear that health care staff will be assumed to be more skilled in assessing capacity than other people who are also bound by the Act, such as informal carers.

Mental Capacity Act Code of Practice para 6.33

6.33 If healthcare and social care staff are involved, their skills and knowledge will affect what is classed as 'reasonable'. For example, a doctor assessing somebody's capacity to consent to treatment must demonstrate more skill than someone without medical training. They should also record in the person's healthcare record the steps they took and the reasons for the finding.

A doctor might also make a mistake in relation to an advance refusal of treatment. As we saw earlier, a valid and applicable advance refusal of treatment has the same effect as a contemporaneous one. This means that if a doctor treats a patient contrary to the terms of the advance decision (AD), the possibility of liability—either for wrongly relying on an invalid AD, or wrongly treating in the face of a valid AD—arises. Section 26(2) and (3) provide for exemption from liability in certain circumstances:

Mental Capacity Act 2005 section 26

26(2) A person does not incur liability for carrying out or continuing the treatment unless, at the time, he is satisfied that an advance decision exists which is valid and applicable to the treatment.

(3) A person does not incur liability for the consequences of withholding or withdrawing a treatment from P if, at the time, he reasonably believes that an advance decision exists which is valid and applicable to the treatment.

There is a significant difference between the test for avoiding liability depending upon whether the doctor has wrongly treated despite the existence of a valid AD, or not treated because he was relying on an invalid AD.

If the doctor wrongly fails to comply with a valid AD, the doctor will not be liable for giving treatment in the face of a valid refusal unless at the time he was 'satisfied' that there was a valid AD in existence. This means that only doctors who blatantly disregard what they know to be a valid AD will face the possibility of liability. Hence, doctors can ignore a valid AD with relative impunity: as long as they have doubts about its validity, it will be relatively straightforward to establish that they were not 'satisfied' that a valid AD existed.

If a doctor thinks that there *might* be a valid AD, he may but does not have to, refer the question to the court for a declaration. There would therefore appear to be no penalty for a doctor who treats a patient because he does not think their AD is valid, even if that belief was not objectively reasonable.

In contrast, under section 26(3), if a doctor does not treat a patient because he wrongly believes their AD was valid, he will avoid liability provided that he reasonably believes that a valid AD exists. Taken together, these provisions suggest that doctors should be wary of complying with ADs where they have any 'genuine doubts' about an AD's validity. This would appear to be confirmed by the Code of Practice.

Mental Capacity Act Code of Practice paras 9.57–9.59

9.57 Healthcare professionals must follow an advance decision if they are satisfied that it exists, is valid and is applicable to their circumstances. Failure to follow an advance decision in this situation could lead to a claim for damages for battery or a criminal charge of assault.

9.58 But they are protected from liability if they are not:

- aware of an advance decision, or

- satisfied that an advance decision exists, is valid and is applicable to the particular treatment and the current circumstances.

- If healthcare professionals have genuine doubts, and are therefore not 'satisfied', about the existence, validity or applicability of the advance decision, treatment can be provided without incurring liability.

9.59 Healthcare professionals will be protected from liability for failing to provide treatment if they 'reasonably believe' that a valid and applicable advance decision to refuse that treatment exists. But they must be able to demonstrate that their belief was reasonable (section 26(3)) and point to reasonable grounds showing why they believe this.

In the next extract, Alasdair Maclean argues that giving this protection to doctors who treat a patient despite the existence of a valid AD shows that the MCA's protection of patients' precedent autonomy is trumped by its protection of clinical discretion.

Alasdair Maclean[52]

The statute tries to balance four things: respect for the patient's self-determination, facilitation of healthcare provision, protection of the incompetent adult's welfare and protection

---

[52] 'Advance Directives and the Rocky Waters of Anticipatory Decision-making' (2008) 16 Medical Law Review 1–22.

of the treating physician. In trying to achieve this balance, the Government has arguably tipped the scale towards protection and facilitation and away from individual autonomy. If the provisions were intended to protect the competent patient's precedent autonomy, then the Act is open to criticism for the resulting vulnerability of advance directives. The Act is arguably most successful in facilitating the provision of healthcare by supporting clinical discretion and protecting the physician who acts in good faith. Thus, the Act provides patients with a trump that only works when healthcare professionals and/or the courts are comfortable with the patient's decision.

(7) The Use of Restraint

Just like at common law, there are times when it is legitimate to use force or restraint under the 2005 Act. The use of force will not attract liability provided the conditions in section 6(2) and (3) are met:

Mental Capacity Act 2005 section 6

6(2) The first condition is that D reasonably believes that it is necessary to do the act in order to prevent harm to P.

(3) The second is that the act is a proportionate response to—

(a) the likelihood of P's suffering harm, and

(b) the seriousness of that harm.

The Code of Practice makes clear that the onus will be on D to prove that restraint is *necessary* and not just convenient.

Mental Capacity Act Code of Practice para 6.44

6.44 Anybody considering using restraint must have objective reasons to justify that restraint is necessary. They must be able to show that the person being cared for is likely to suffer harm unless proportionate restraint is used. A carer or professional must not use restraint just so that they can do something more easily. If restraint is necessary to prevent harm to the person who lacks capacity, it must be the minimum amount of force for the shortest time possible.

The use of force or restraint must also not interfere with the patient's right, under Article 3 of the Human Rights Act 1998, to be free from inhuman and degrading treatment. In the *Herczelgfalvy* case, which we consider again in the next chapter, force and restraint had been used on a mentally ill patient. The ECtHR found that this did not breach Article 3 because it was 'a therapeutic necessity'. The Court held that: 'a measure which is a therapeutic necessity cannot be regarded as inhuman or degrading. The Court must nevertheless satisfy itself that the medical necessity has been convincingly shown to exist.' It follows that where treatment is *not* a therapeutic necessity, the use of force might amount to a violation of Article 3.

It will seldom be in the best interests of incompetent patients to undergo forced treatment. Where the patient's cooperation is important, the harm that might be done by imposing treatment on an unwilling patient might sometimes outweigh the clinical benefits of treatment. This situation arose in *Re D*,[53] where an incompetent adult with end-stage renal failure refused to undergo dialysis. Since he would not keep still, dialysis (which he needed four times a week) could only be provided under general anaesthetic. Given the patient's condition, this would be both impracticable and dangerous. The doctors therefore sought a declaration from the court that it would be lawful not to impose dialysis upon him. Sir Stephen Brown P granted the declaration, finding that it would be in the best interests of the patient, and hence lawful 'not to impose haemodialysis upon him in circumstances in which, in the opinion of the medical practitioners responsible for such treatment, it is not reasonably practicable to do so'.

(8) Proxy Decision-Making

One of the principal changes the Act makes to the common law is the introduction, for the first time, of the possibility of formal proxy medical decision-making for incapacitated adults. This involves P nominating one or more people, referred to as 'donees', with lasting power of attorney (LPA) who, under section 9(1)(a) will have the authority to make decisions about, among other things, P's personal welfare, or specified matters concerning his personal welfare, when/if he loses capacity. This power undoubtedly extends to taking medical decisions. A donee is only permitted to take decisions about life-sustaining treatment if P has included a clear statement to this effect in the LPA document.

An LPA must be registered with the Office of the Public Guardian before it can be used. Donees do not have a right to take decisions if the P regains capacity, or if she has made an advance decision to refuse a proposed treatment.

If more than one donee is appointed, the donor can specify, under section 10(4), whether they should act 'jointly' or 'severally' in relation to different decisions. If they are to act jointly, the donees must agree on all decisions; if they can act 'severally', the decision of one donee is sufficient. An LPA could specify that the donees must agree where serious medical decisions have to be made, but that they could act independently in relation to more trivial decisions. If the LPA does not specify which applies, and more than one donee is appointed, they will have to act jointly.

The power of the donee of LPA is, under section 9(4), subject to the provisions of the Act, and in particular to the principles set out in section 1, and the best interests checklist in section 4. This means that the donee is not empowered to take decisions which are not in the incapacitated person's best interests. It also means that section 4(3) applies, and the donee must take into account whether P is likely to regain capacity in the near future, and, under section 4(6), that the person's past and present wishes and feelings must be considered.

If someone has not nominated a 'donee', their close friends or relatives might be consulted under section 4(7)(e) when assessing their best interests, although their views will not be decisive.

There are two potential problems with proxy consent under the MCA, highlighted in the next extract. First, empirical studies suggest that we are, in fact, not very good at guessing what others would decide, even when we know them very well indeed. Secondly, because proxies do not have the same freedom as the patient to take decisions which conflict with the doctors' assessment of her best interests, they are not really substituting for the patient's own decision. Anthony Wrigley therefore suggests that a proxy is better described as an adviser, rather than a substitute decision-maker.

---

[53] (1997) 41 BMLR 81.

Anthony Wrigley[54]

> There is evidence to indicate that we are simply not very good at making substituted judge-
> ments for other people, not even for close relatives...This empirical evidence suggests that
> as a practical means of extending the autonomous wishes and desires of a patient who now
> lacks capacity, substituted judgement is an extremely poor method, as it is likely to be unrep-
> resentative and could lead to errors....
>
> The MCA places fairly obvious restrictions on what a proxy can and can't consent
> to...Upon analysis, the MCA has created a situation where lip service is paid to the notion of
> a proxy consenter, but when the matter is pursued, the ethical and, ultimately, legal status of
> such a proxy seems diminished to that of an advisor. This should not be taken in a negative
> light, however, because this role of advisor to a professional medical team is the most use-
> ful and morally authoritative role a proxy can take....Ultimately, 'proxy consent' should not
> be seen as consent at all, but rather 'assistance' to those best placed to judge the patient's
> best interests.

Under section 16, it is also open to the court to appoint a deputy to make decisions on
behalf of an incapacitated person. Section 17(d) specifies that the deputy's powers extend
to 'giving or refusing consent to the carrying out or continuation of a treatment by a person
providing health care for P', with one important exception: deputies are not able to refuse
consent to life-sustaining treatment. The appointment of deputies will be unusual in relation to health care decisions. Section 16(4)(a) provides that 'a decision by the court is to be
preferred to the appointment of a deputy to make a decision', and the Code of Practice suggests that the appointment of a deputy will only be appropriate in 'the most difficult cases',
perhaps because of a history of serious family disputes.[55]

(9) The Court of Protection

Section 45 of the Act sets up the Court of Protection. The Court has the same power as
the High Court, but is intended to build up specialist expertise in matters involving incapacitated individuals, and is charged with resolving disputes and uncertainties over, for
example, whether a person lacks capacity; whether proposed treatment is in his best interests and whether an advance decision is valid and applicable.

Section 15 sets out the powers the Court of Protection has to make declarations.

Mental Capacity Act 2005 section 15

> 15 Power to make declarations
>
> (1) The court may make declarations as to—
>
>   (a) whether a person has or lacks capacity to make a decision specified in the
>   declaration;
>
>   (b) whether a person has or lacks capacity to make decisions on such matters as are
>   described in the declaration;

[54] 'Proxy Consent: Moral Authority Misconceived' (2007) 33 Journal of Medical Ethics 527–31.
[55] Para 8.39.

(c) the lawfulness or otherwise of any act done, or yet to be done, in relation to that person.

(2) 'Act' includes an omission and a course of conduct.

Court involvement in decisions about the medical treatment of people who lack capacity is unusual, and in the vast majority of cases, decisions are taken by their doctors, in consultation with their close relatives or friends. There are, however, a handful of especially controversial medical procedures where court involvement should be routine, regardless of whether the doctors and patient's family agree.

Continuing the position at common law, the Code of Practice sets out a non-exhaustive list of decisions which should be brought before a court.

Mental Capacity Act Code of Practice paras 8.18 and 8.23

8.18 …Cases involving any of the following decisions should therefore be brought before a court:

- decisions about the proposed withholding or withdrawal of artificial nutrition and hydration (ANH) from patients in a permanent vegetative state (PVS)

- cases involving organ or bone marrow donation by a person who lacks capacity to consent

- cases involving the proposed non-therapeutic sterilisation of a person who lacks capacity to consent to this (e.g. for contraceptive purposes) and

- all other cases where there is a doubt or dispute about whether a particular treatment will be in a person's best interests.…

8.23 Other cases likely to be referred to the court include those involving ethical dilemmas in untested areas (such as innovative treatments for variant CJD), or where there are otherwise irresolvable conflicts between healthcare staff, or between staff and family members.

The Code of Practice suggests that where there is a dispute or uncertainty over medical treatment, the application to the Court of Protection should normally be made by the NHS trust, or other body responsible for the patient's care. Where there is a dispute between family members, one of them may wish to apply to the court. Any person who is alleged to lack capacity will also be able to make an application, though more usually he will be made a party to the proceedings, and the Official Solicitor will be appointed to protect his interests.

(b) CHILDREN

Childhood covers the period in a person's life from birth to the age of 18. It is, however, worth remembering that the law adopts a number of different cut-off points for different activities. A ten-year-old can, in some circumstances, be held criminally responsible for her actions; when she reaches the age of 16 she can have lawful sexual intercourse and marry; at 17, she can learn to drive, but she cannot vote until she is 18.

So when is a child able to consent to medical treatment? As we will see in the following sections, this will depend upon the child's age and the nature of the medical treatment in question, as well as the individual child's decision-making capacity.

(1) Parental Consent

Anyone with parental responsibility for a child undoubtedly has the power to consent to her medical treatment. Provided that both parents have parental responsibility, each would normally be able to give a valid consent to their child's medical treatment without consulting the other. The consent of both parents is only necessary for certain treatments, such as non-therapeutic circumcision.

Re J (Specific Issue Orders: Child's Religious Upbringing and Circumcision)[56]

Dame Elizabeth Butler-Sloss P

There is, in my view, a small group of important decisions made on behalf of a child which, in the absence of agreement of those with parental responsibility, ought not to be carried out or arranged by one parent carer although she has parental responsibility under s 2(7) of the Children Act 1989. Such a decision ought not to be made without the specific approval of the court.... The issue of circumcision has not, to my knowledge, previously been considered by this court, but in my view it comes within that group. The decision to circumcise a child on grounds other than medical necessity is a very important one; the operation is irreversible, and should only be carried out where the parents together approve of it or, in the absence of parental agreement, where a court decides that the operation is in the best interests of the child.

In *Re C (Welfare of Child: Immunisation)*,[57] a case in which the mother and the father disagreed over whether their child should receive the MMR vaccine, Thorpe LJ said that: 'In my opinion this appeal demonstrates that hotly contested issues of immunization are to be added to that "small group of important decisions".'

Hence, where the parents agree with each other, consent to circumcision and vaccination lies within a zone of parental discretion, and the court will not impose its own view of whether the procedure is in the child's best interests. Where the parents cannot agree, the court can make the decision instead, according to *its* view of where the child's best interests lie.

If they are married, both parents automatically have parental responsibility. If they are unmarried, the father acquires parental responsibility by being registered on the child's birth certificate. Non-parents may also have parental responsibility (perhaps because the child is living with them and they have a residence order), in which case they too would be able to give a valid consent to medical treatment. Non-parents who have care of the child— such as teachers and child-minders—are entitled to do what is reasonable in all the circumstances to safeguard or promote the child's welfare.[58]

In an emergency, if there is no-one with parental responsibility who is either able or willing to consent to a child's medical treatment, the doctors would be entitled to treat in the

---

[56] [2000] 1 FLR 571.   [57] [2003] EWCA Civ 1148.
[58] Children Act 1989, s 3(5)(b).

absence of consent. See, for example, the comments of Lord Templeman and Lord Scarman in *Gillick v West Norfolk and Wisbech AHA*, a case we consider in detail below.

Gillick v West Norfolk and Wisbech AHA[59]

Lord Templeman

I accept that if there is no time to obtain a decision from the court, a doctor may safely carry out treatment in an emergency if the doctor believes the treatment to be vital to the survival or health of an infant and notwithstanding the opposition of a parent or the impossibility of alerting the parent before the treatment is carried out.

Lord Scarman

Emergency, parental neglect, abandonment of the child, or inability to find the parent are examples of exceptional situations justifying the doctor proceeding to treat the child without parental knowledge and consent.

Where treatment could reasonably be delayed until the parents can be found or a court order obtained, the doctors should not proceed with treatment.

Parents clearly have the ability to consent to medical treatment, but do they also have the right to *refuse*? Parents have the authority to act for the benefit of their children, so their right to consent or to refuse to consent to treatment is abrogated where they seek to make a decision which might harm the child. Hence, if one or both of the parents withhold consent to treatment which the doctors believe to be in the child's best interests, the doctors can seek approval from another source, namely the courts.

(2) Court Involvement

The court's power to authorize the medical treatment of children derives from wardship, its inherent jurisdiction, and more recently from statute. Wardship differs slightly from the inherent jurisdiction—if a child is made a ward of court, the court must make *all* important decisions about her upbringing until the wardship comes to an end, whereas the inherent jurisdiction can apply to a one-off decision. In practice, however, the two processes are largely indistinguishable. Both derive from the Crown's prerogative power as *parens patriae*, exercised by judges of the High Court, and both give the courts more sweeping powers than are possessed either by parents or by mature minors.

Usually, if a child's parents refuse to consent to treatment which her doctors believe to be necessary, it is the doctors who will apply to the court using wardship or the inherent jurisdiction. It is also possible that another concerned individual might apply if, for example, both the doctors and the parents were proposing to take a step which appeared not to be in the child's best interests. This was the case in *Re D (A Minor) (Wardship: Sterilisation)*. D was an 11-year-old girl who suffered from Sotos syndrome and 'had a dull, normal intelligence'. Her behavioural problems, academic skills, and social competence were all improving. As yet, D had shown no interest in the opposite sex, and in any event, she had no opportunity to engage in sexual intercourse because her mother never left her side. Nevertheless, D's parents, her paediatrician, and a consultant obstetrician had all agreed that D should be

---

[59] [1984] QB 581.

sterilized. It was D's educational psychologist who applied to have D made a ward of court, and the question of whether sterilization was in D's best interests was then considered by the court, which made a declaration that the operation should not go ahead.

Re D (A Minor) (Wardship: Sterilisation)[60]

Heilbron J

A review of the whole of the evidence leads me to the conclusion that in a case of a child of 11 years of age, where the evidence shows that her mental and physical condition and attainments have already improved, and where her future prospects are as yet unpredictable, where the evidence also shows that she is unable as yet to understand and appreciate the implications of this operation and could not give a valid or informed consent, but the likelihood is that in later years she will be able to make her own choice, where, I believe, the frustration and resentment of realising (as she would one day) what had happened, could be devastating, an operation of this nature is, in my view, contra-indicated.

For these, and for the other reasons to which I have adverted, I have come to the conclusion that this operation is neither medically indicated nor necessary, and that it would not be in D's best interests for it to be performed.

In addition to wardship and the inherent jurisdiction, under the Children Act 1989, the court can issue either a specific issue order, or a prohibited steps order to determine what treatment a child should receive.[61] In *Re C (Welfare of Child: Immunisation)*,[62] the fathers of two children who were living with their mothers sought specific issue orders to enable their children, who had received none of the recommended childhood vaccines, to be immunized. The judge ordered each mother to have her child immunized, and the Court of Appeal upheld his decision.

Regardless of the route taken to bring the question of a child's medical treatment before the courts, the decision will be governed by the welfare principle. Under section 1 of the Children Act, in any question affecting a child's upbringing, her welfare must be the 'paramount consideration'.[63] What does this mean in practice?

It is clear from the GMC's guidance on the treatment of under-18s, that best interests is not confined to the child's clinical best interests. As with the MCA checklist, if the child is able to express her own feelings and wishes, or was able to do so previously, these are relevant, regardless of whether she is *Gillick* competent (see below). The GMC guidance also embodies the 'least restrictive alternative' principle.

General Medical Council[64]

12. An assessment of best interests will include what is clinically indicated in a particular case. You should also consider:

a. the views of the child or young person, so far as they can express them, including any previously expressed preferences

b. the views of parents

---

[60] [1976] 2 WLR 279.   [61] Section 8(1).   [62] [2003] EWCA Civ 1148.
[63] Children Act 1989, s 1(1).
[64] 0–18 Years: Guidance for all Doctors (2007), available at <www.gmc-uk.org>.

c. the views of others close to the child or young person

d. the cultural, religious or other beliefs and values of the child or parents

e. the views of other healthcare professionals involved in providing care to the child or young person, and of any other professionals who have an interest in their welfare

f. which choice, if there is more than one, will least restrict the child or young person's future options.

(a) Controversial medical treatments

Most types of medical treatment will self-evidently be therapeutic, and in the best interests of a sick child. For a few procedures, however, there may be less certainty. Blood tests for the purposes of establishing paternity will generally be allowed: the test itself causes only slight discomfort, and the child might in fact benefit from knowing the truth about her origins.[65] Bone marrow, blood, or organ donation (see further Chapter 11) are not in a child's best *clinical* interests, although just like *Re Y*, above, it might be possible to argue that saving a sibling's life by donating bone marrow is overwhelmingly in the child's emotional best interests. It is less likely that the courts would judge the removal of a solid organ from a child donor to be in her best interests, and as yet no cases have come before the English courts.

There have also been no cases in which the courts have had to determine whether cosmetic surgery is in a child's best interests. Cosmetic surgery for a burns victim would be easy to justify, but what if the parents want their child with Down's syndrome to have facial reconstructive surgery in order to look more 'normal', so that she will be less likely to be teased and/or discriminated against? [66]

Just as with adults, sterilization carried out in order to avoid pregnancy, rather than because of some medical disorder, has also been treated as a special case, where court involvement is necessary, and the Official Solicitor will represent the child's interests. In *Re B (A Minor)*, Lord Templeman was clear that only the court could authorize such a 'drastic step':

In my opinion sterilisation of a girl under 18 should only be carried out with the leave of a High Court judge. A doctor performing a sterilisation operation with the consent of the parents might still be liable in criminal, civil or professional proceedings. A court exercising the wardship jurisdiction emanating from the Crown is the only authority which is empowered to authorise such a drastic step as sterilisation after a full and informed investigation.[67]

Improvements in contraceptive techniques mean that requests to perform sterilization operations on girls in order to avoid the risk of pregnancy should now be rare. Because long-acting contraceptives, such as injections or implants, can achieve the same effect, an irreversible operation under general anaesthetic would not be a proportionate response to the need to avoid pregnancy.

In the past few years, however, a new question has arisen, namely whether surgical and other interventions could ever be appropriate where the purpose is not to avoid

---

[65] *Re F (A Minor) (Blood Tests: Parental Rights)* [1993] 3 All ER 596; *Re H (A Minor) (Blood Tests: Parental Rights)* [1996] 4 All ER 28.

[66] See further RB Jones, 'Parental Consent to Cosmetic Facial Surgery in Down's Syndrome' (2000) 26 Journal of Medical Ethics 101–2.

[67] *Re B (A Minor)* [1988] AC 199.

pregnancy, but instead to stop a disabled child 'growing up'. The issue first arose in the US. In January 2007, the parents of a nine-year-old girl called Ashley decided to publish a 'blog' explaining their controversial decision to stunt her growth. Unsurprisingly, there was an explosion of media interest around the world in what the parents described as 'the Ashley treatment'.

Ashley X was nine years old, but had, and would continue to have, a mental age of about three months. Ashley suffers from static encephalopathy, which means she cannot move around, or sit up unaided. Her parents' fear was that, as Ashley got bigger, they would cease to be able to care for her on their own. It would, they reasoned, improve Ashley's quality of life if she remained small enough to be cuddled and carried easily by her parents.

When Ashley began to display early signs of puberty, her parents asked doctors to remove her uterus, appendix, and breast buds, and give her oestrogen to stunt her growth. Before going ahead with this treatment, the doctors obtained approval from the hospital's ethics committee, which agreed that this treatment could be said to be in Ashley's best interests. The removal of Ashley's uterus meant that she would never have periods, and it would also remove the risk of uterine cancer. Removing Ashley's breasts would, they argued, prevent discomfort and protect her from the elevated risk of breast cancer which she faced.

A year later, there were reports that a British mother was seeking a hysterectomy for her daughter, Katie Thorpe, in order to avoid what she called the 'pain, discomfort and indignity of menstruation'. The hospital refused to agree to the operation, and so the case did not come before a court.

If a doctor in the UK agreed to perform a hysterectomy on a girl like Katie Thorpe, or to carry out the full 'Ashley treatment', there is no doubt that, before proceeding, the case would have to come before the Court for a declaration as to whether or not it would be lawful. The basis for the Court's decision would be the best interests test.

It is evident that best interests is not confined to clinical best interests, and also takes into account emotional and psychological best interests. It might therefore be possible to argue that this treatment would improve Ashley's (or Katie's) quality of life. On the other hand, the 'least restrictive alternative' principle, would mean that the least invasive way to achieve one's ends should always be preferred. Long-acting contraceptives, for example, might be preferable to a hysterectomy, and, perhaps more importantly, better equipment and access to professional carers and other resources might be a less invasive way than surgery and growth restriction to ensure that Ashley's parents continue to be able to care for her at home.

(b) Disagreements between parents and doctors

Most of the cases in which the courts have had to make decisions about a child's medical treatment have involved parents (or, as we see below, the child herself) disagreeing with the doctors about what treatment should, or should not be provided. The difficult question that arises is whether parents can ever legitimately take a different view from the doctors about where a child's best interests lie. In general, the answer to this question is 'no': the courts have been willing to override parental refusals, and as we see below, refusals by the child too, whenever a child's life or health might be endangered.

In *Re A (Children) (Conjoined Twins: Separation),*[68] a case we consider in more detail in Chapter 17, the Court of Appeal ordered the separation of conjoined twins in order to save the stronger twin's life, despite the parents' refusal to consent to the operation. In *Re*

---

[68] [2001] Fam 147 CA.

C (A Child) (HIV Test) the mother, who was HIV-positive, rejected conventional medical thinking on the causes and treatment of HIV, and refused to allow her child to be tested. At first instance, Wilson J overruled her objections on the grounds that it was overwhelmingly in the child's best interests to be tested for HIV, and the Court of Appeal refused permission to appeal.

Re C (A Child) (HIV Test) [69]

Butler-Sloss LJ

I have no doubt at all, for my part, that it is right that this child should have the test done...In my view, the child is clearly at risk if there is ignorance of the child's medical condition. The degree of intrusion into the child of a medical test is slight...It does not matter whether the parents are responsible or irresponsible. It matters whether the welfare of the child demands that such a course should be taken...This child has the right to have sensible and responsible people find out whether she is or is not HIV positive...What seems to me to be crucial is that someone should find out so that one knows how she should be looked after...Either way this child has her own rights. Those rights seem to me to be met at this stage by her being tested to see what her state of health is for the question of knowledge.

There is one exceptional case which appears to point in a different direction. In *Re T (A Minor) (Wardship: Medical Treatment)*, the Court of Appeal refused to authorize a liver transplant against the parents' wishes, despite the likelihood that the child would not live beyond the age of two-and-a-half without a transplant. The Court of Appeal found that this was a case in which there was 'genuine scope for a difference of view between parent and judge', and that the mother's objection to the transplant surgery should therefore be respected.

The parents were both health care professionals, who had sensibly framed their objection in terms of the distress and discomfort the surgery might cause their son. The Court of Appeal held that their refusal to give consent to the transplant operation was not based upon 'scruple or dogma', and in such cases, it was in the best interests of the child that important decisions about his upbringing be taken by his parents.

Re T (A Minor) (Wardship: Medical Treatment) [70]

Waite LJ

It can only be said safely that there is a scale, at one end of which lies the clear case where parental opposition to medical intervention is prompted by scruple or dogma of a kind which is patently irreconcilable with principles of child health and welfare widely accepted by the generality of mankind; and that at the other end lie highly problematic cases where there is genuine scope for a difference of view between parent and judge...[T]here must be a likelihood (though never of course a certainty) that the greater the scope for genuine debate between one view and another the stronger will be the inclination of the court to be influenced by a reflection that in the last analysis the best interests of every child include an expectation that difficult decisions affecting the length and quality of its life will be taken for it by the parent to whom its care has been entrusted by nature.

---

[69] [2000] Fam 48.
[70] [1997] 1 WLR 242.

The case is, however, probably best regarded as a rather idiosyncratic and anomalous judgment. In *Re C (Welfare of Child: Immunisation)*,[71] for example, Thorpe LJ said of *Re T*: 'the outcome of that appeal, denying a child life-prolonging surgery, is unique in our jurisprudence and is explained by the trial judge's erroneous focus on the reasonableness of the mother's rejection of medical opinion'.

The court in *Re T* appeared to be swayed by the fact that the child would need to be cared for by his mother after the operation, and that her ability to provide proper care would somehow be compromised if the operation had been carried out without her agreement. The family were living abroad at the time, and the court also took into account the difficulties returning to England for the operation would pose for the family. Since the prognosis was that the child would be likely to die within the next two years without the operation, these factors were perhaps given undue prominence, and most commentators have suggested that this was not in fact a case where there could reasonably be any disagreement about where the child's best interests lay.

Furthermore, the Court of Appeal appeared to be asking themselves whether the mother's refusal was prompted by her love and concern for her son, whereas, as Marie Fox and Jean McHale point out in the next extract, the proper question is not whether the parents care for their child, but whether the proposed treatment is in the child's best interests. For Jehovah's Witness parents, a refusal to consent to their child's blood transfusion would also be prompted by their love for their child, whom they genuinely believe will be seriously disadvantaged by receiving blood products, and yet the courts would not hesitate to override such refusals.

Marie Fox and Jean McHale[72]

> In the first place, we would question whether the downplaying of [Jehovah's Witness] beliefs is legitimate. Furthermore, it is debatable whether the Court of Appeal judges were right to be more receptive to the parents' objections in *Re T*, which were rooted in factors other than religious or ethical conviction, including the location of the parties and the nature of the treatment. Although parents may legitimately object to proposed treatment where it is deemed 'heroic' in nature and parental opposition is rooted in the experimental, invasive and/or prolonged nature of the procedure, it would seem that this is not such a case ... [I]t was a recognised clinical procedure, and one with a high success rate according to some experts ...
>
> We are given little evidence to support the Court's opinion that this mother was exceptionally devoted. Furthermore, even assuming that this representation is accurate, two troublesome issues arise. First, if we accept the Court's depiction of her as especially caring, it was surely incumbent upon the judges to examine why she was so reluctant to undertake the care of her son following a procedure which could save his life, particularly in view of her professional expertise in this area. Secondly, there is no exploration of the relationship between caring and reasonableness. It must be doubted whether the decisions of an exceptionally caring parent, even one who is a health professional herself, may automatically be deemed reasonable ones.

Of course, it is possible that the courts might become involved because of a different sort of disagreement between the child's parents and her doctors. In *Re J (A Minor) (Child in Care: Medical*

---

[71] [2003] EWCA Civ 1148.
[72] 'In Whose Best Interests?' (1996) 60 Modern Law Review 700–9.

Treatment), a case we will consider again in Chapter 17, the doctors caring for J believed that 'it would not be medically appropriate to intervene with intensive therapeutic measures' such as artificial ventilation, if J were to suffer a life-threatening event. J's mother, however, wanted J to be ventilated if he was no longer able to breathe spontaneously. Lord Donaldson MR was clear that the courts would never force doctors to act contrary to their clinical judgment.

Re J (A Minor) (Child in Care: Medical Treatment)[73]

Lord Donaldson MR

The fundamental issue in this appeal is whether the court in the exercise of its inherent power to protect the interests of minors should ever require a medical practitioner or health authority acting by a medical practitioner to adopt a course of treatment which in the bona fide clinical judgment of the practitioner concerned is contra-indicated as not being in the best interests of the patient. I have to say that I cannot at present conceive of any circumstances in which this would be other than an abuse of power as directly or indirectly requiring the practitioner to act contrary to the fundamental duty which he owes to his patient. This, subject to obtaining any necessary consent, is to treat the patient in accordance with his own best clinical judgment.

Hence, when the court becomes involved in disputes over a child's medical treatment, it can *authorize* the doctors to take such steps as they believe to be in the child's best interests, and it can *overrule* both a parent's and a child's refusal, but it cannot *compel* doctors to do something which is contrary to their clinical judgment.

(3) The Use of Force

It seems clear that the inherent jurisdiction gives courts the power to authorize the use of reasonable force and detention, in order to ensure that the child receives the treatment in question. It is, however, important to remember that, as with adults, force should be used only when treatment is a 'therapeutic necessity', otherwise it might amount to inhuman and degrading treatment, and be prohibited by Article 3 of the Human Rights Act (HRA) 1998.

This test would almost certainly have been satisfied in a pre-HRA case—*A Metropolitan Borough Council v DB*[74]—in which the health of a 17-year-old crack cocaine addict who had just given birth was seriously at risk. Cazalet J authorized the use of force, but confined it to 'such reasonable force may be authorized by the local authority to be used to implement such medical treatment to DB as may be considered necessary by the doctors concerned for her to prevent her death or serious deterioration in her health'.

While the use of force against children might be capable of surviving an Article 3 challenge, in the next extract, Jane Fortin suggests that it may be harder for it to survive a challenge under Article 5 (the right to liberty and security). While the detention of persons of 'unsound mind' can be justified under Article 5(1)(e), Fortin suggests that some of the adolescents whose refusals of life-saving treatment have been overridden, such as the boy in *Re E* discussed below, were certainly not of 'unsound mind'. Fortin therefore argues that the use of force could only be justified if Article 2 (the right to life) is given priority.

---

[73] [1991] 2 WLR 140.
[74] [1997] 1 FLR 767.

Jane Fortin[75]

> The courts might now find it difficult to justify employing the wardship jurisdiction to force an intelligent 16-year-old to undergo treatment against his will, as the High Court did in *Re E (A Minor) (Wardship: Medical Treatment)*. According to Ward J, the boy in that case was not *Gillick*-competent because he was unable to grasp the implications of a range of decisions. In particular, he did not have a full understanding of the implication of refusing treatment and choosing to die. But that, surely, is a very far cry from describing him as of 'unsound mind' within Article 5(1)(e) of the Convention. How then is the court to gain its authority to force such a patient to undergo medical treatment without itself infringing Article 5? In such circumstances, it might survive an Article 5 challenge by turning to Article 2 for a solution, when confronted by a teenager refusing life-saving treatment. It might argue that since a minor's rights under the Convention sometimes inevitably conflict, notably his rights under Articles 2 and 5, it must find an appropriate balance between those rights. Although a minor patient is entitled to freedom from restraint under Article 5, this right may be outweighed by the patient's right to life itself, particularly if he lacks the capacity to comprehend the implications of refusing life-saving treatment. Furthermore, Article 2 imposes a positive obligation on all public authorities, including the courts, to take all reasonable steps to preserve life. A court, when exercising its inherent jurisdiction, might therefore argue that it cannot ignore its duty to save the life of a desperately ill adolescent.

4 THE COMPETENT MINOR

(a) AT COMMON LAW (*GILLICK* COMPETENCE)

Until 1986, it was not clear whether doctors could ever lawfully treat a minor without her parent's consent. Mrs Victoria Gillick's unsuccessful battle to prevent her daughters from receiving contraceptive advice without her consent established that a doctor could provide contraceptive advice to a minor without consulting her parents.

Mrs Gillick had challenged a Memorandum of Guidance, from the Department of Health and Social Security (DHSS), as it then was, which stated that, in exceptional cases it was for a doctor, exercising his clinical judgment, to decide whether contraceptive advice or treatment should be provided to under-16s without parental consent. Mrs Gillick, who was the mother of five girls under the age of 16, wrote to her local health authority seeking an assurance from them that no contraceptive advice or treatment would be given to any of her children while under 16 without her knowledge and consent. The health authority refused, and Mrs Gillick sought a declaration that the Memorandum was unlawful. The Court of Appeal overturned Woolf J's rejection of her claim, and then by a 3:2 majority, the House of Lords allowed the DHSS's Appeal.

Gillick v West Norfolk and Wisbech AHA[76]

Lord Fraser

Nobody doubts, certainly I do not doubt, that in the overwhelming majority of cases the best judges of a child's welfare are his or her parents. Nor do I doubt that any important medical

---

[75] 'Children's Rights and the Use of Physical Force' (2001) 13 Child and Family Law Quarterly 243.
[76] [1984] QB 581.

treatment of a child under 16 would normally only be carried out with the parents' approval. That is why it would and should be 'most unusual' for a doctor to advise a child without the knowledge and consent of the parents on contraceptive matters....But there may be circumstances in which a doctor is a better judge of the medical advice and treatment which will conduce to a girl's welfare than her parents. It is notorious that children of both sexes are often reluctant to confide in their parents about sexual matters, and the DHSS guidance under consideration shows that to abandon the principle of confidentiality for contraceptive advice to girls under 16 might cause some of them not to seek professional advice at all, with the consequence of exposing them to 'the immediate risks of pregnancy and of sexually-transmitted diseases.'...

There may well be other cases where the doctor feels that because the girl is under the influence of her sexual partner or for some other reason there is no realistic prospect of her abstaining from intercourse. If that is right it points strongly to the desirability of the doctor being entitled in some cases, in the girl's best interest, to give her contraceptive advice and treatment if necessary without the consent or even the knowledge of her parents. The only practicable course is to entrust the doctor with a discretion to act in accordance with his view of what is best in the interests of the girl who is his patient. He should, of course, always seek to persuade her to tell her parents that she is seeking contraceptive advice, and the nature of the advice that she receives. At least he should seek to persuade her to agree to the doctor's informing the parents. But there may well be cases, and I think there will be some cases, where the girl refuses either to tell the parents herself or to permit the doctor to do so and in such cases, the doctor will, in my opinion, be justified in proceeding without the parents' consent or even knowledge provided he is satisfied on the following matters: (1) that the girl (although under 16 years of age) will understand his advice; (2) that he cannot persuade her to inform her parents or to allow him to inform the parents that she is seeking contraceptive advice; (3) that she is very likely to begin or to continue having sexual intercourse with or without contraceptive treatment; (4) that unless she receives contraceptive advice or treatment her physical or mental health or both are likely to suffer; (5) that her best interests require him to give her contraceptive advice, treatment or both without the parental consent.

Lord Scarman

I would hold that as a matter of law the parental right to determine whether or not their minor child below the age of 16 will have medical treatment terminates if and when the child achieves a sufficient understanding and intelligence to enable him or her to understand fully what is proposed. It will be a question of fact whether a child seeking advice has sufficient understanding of what is involved to give a consent valid in law. Until the child achieves the capacity to consent, the parental right to make the decision continues save only in exceptional circumstances....

When applying these conclusions to contraceptive advice and treatment it has to be borne in mind that there is much that has to be understood by a girl under the age of 16 if she is to have legal capacity to consent to such treatment. It is not enough that she should understand the nature of the advice which is being given: she must also have a sufficient maturity to understand what is involved. There are moral and family questions, especially her relationship with her parents; long-term problems associated with the emotional impact of pregnancy and its termination; and there are the risks to health of sexual intercourse at her age, risks which contraception may diminish but cannot eliminate. It follows that a doctor will have to satisfy himself that she is able to appraise these factors before he can safely proceed upon the basis that she has at law capacity to consent to contraceptive treatment. And it further follows that ordinarily the proper course will be for him, as the guidance lays down, first to

seek to persuade the girl to bring her parents into consultation, and if she refuses, not to prescribe contraceptive treatment unless he is satisfied that her circumstances are such that he
ought to proceed without parental knowledge and consent.

Lord Fraser laid out several conditions that should be satisfied before a doctor should offer
contraceptive advice to a minor without her parents' knowledge. These conditions are principally directed to ensuring that it is in the minor's best medical interests that she is given
contraceptive advice or treatment in the absence of parental consent. In effect, the parents'
right to consent to their child's treatment cedes to the doctor's judgment about where the
child's best interests lie. This is not especially radical.

In contrast, part of Lord Scarman's judgment appears to be much more far-reaching. He
suggests that when the child achieves sufficient maturity and understanding, her parents'
right to consent to her medical treatment *terminates*, and is *replaced by* the minor's right to
make her own decisions.

For three reasons, however, it could be argued that Lord Scarman's judgment is not
quite as radical as this. First, Lord Fraser's was the first judgment to be delivered, and Lord
Scarman began his judgment by agreeing with him, without qualification. Secondly, given
that the third Law Lord in the 3:2 majority, Lord Bridge, said 'I fully agree with the reasons
expressed by both my noble and learned friends', it would appear that Lord Bridge at least
believed that Lords Fraser and Scarman were essentially saying similar things.

Thirdly, Lord Scarman suggests that the purpose of establishing that the child has capacity is 'to enable him or her to exercise a *wise* choice in his or her own interests', recognizing
the social reality 'which is that many girls are fully able to make *sensible* decisions about
many matters before they reach the age of 16' (my emphasis). Permitting a child to make
'wise choices' and 'sensible decisions' is plainly not the same thing as a child acquiring an
absolute right to make mistakes once she has reached a sufficient level of maturity.

In 2006, it was established that the *Gillick* principle that under-16s could receive contraceptive advice and treatment without parental knowledge or consent also applied to abortion.
In *R (on the application of Axon) v Secretary of State for Health* a mother applied for judicial
review of the Department of Health's Best Practice Guidance on sexual and reproductive
health for under-16s,[77] which made it clear that people under the age of 16 could expect
confidentiality when seeking advice about contraception and abortion. Mrs Axon, who had
five children, claimed that this 2004 guidance was unlawful, since it would permit a doctor
to perform an abortion on one of her daughters without her knowledge. This, she claimed,
misrepresented *Gillick*, by making confidentiality the default position. By excluding parents
from involvement in important decisions, she claimed the guidance also amounted to a
breach of her Article 8 right to respect for her family life.

Silber J rejected her application. While he recognized that abortion was more intrusive
than contraception, and raised serious and complex issues, he nevertheless thought that
there was no reason why Lord Fraser's guidelines and Lord Scarman's criteria from the
Gillick case should not be adapted and applied to advice and treatment for abortion.

---

[77] Best Practice Guidance for Doctors and other Health Professionals on the Provision of Advice
and Treatment to Young People under 16 on Contraception, Sexual and Reproductive Health (2004), <www.
dh.gov.uk>.

R (on the application of Axon) v Secretary of State for Health[78]

Silber J

[T]he reasoning of the majority [in *Gillick*] was that the parental right to determine whether a young person will have medical treatment terminates if and when the young person achieves a sufficient understanding and intelligence to understand fully what is proposed, with the result that the doctor was entitled in cases in which it was appropriate to do so, to provide advice and treatment to a young person on sexual matters without parental knowledge'.

He said he was 'fortified' in coming to this conclusion by the fact that young women would be deterred from seeking advice and treatment on sexual matters without the assurance of confidentiality, which would have 'very undesirable and far-reaching consequences'.

Silber J agreed that all attempts should be made to persuade the young person to notify and consult their parents, but if these efforts failed, medical advice and treatment can be given on matters concerning contraception and sexually transmitted diseases without parental knowledge or consent if the following criteria are met:

Silber J

(1) That the young person, although under 16 years of age, understands all aspects of the advice.

(2) That the medical professional cannot persuade the young person to inform his or her parents or to allow the medical professional to inform the parents that their child is seeking advice and/or treatment on sexual matters.

(3) That (in any case in which the issue is whether the medical professional should advise on or treat in respect of contraception and sexually transmissible illnesses) the young person is very likely to begin or to continue having sexual intercourse with or without contraceptive treatment or treatment for a sexually transmissible illness.

(4) That unless the young person receives advice and treatment on the relevant sexual matters, his or her physical or mental health or both are likely to suffer.

(5) That the best interests of the young person require him or her to receive advice and treatment on sexual matters without parental consent or notification.

Silber J gave short shrift to Mrs Axon's Article 8 claim:

Silber J

As Lord Scarman explained, a parental right yields to the young person's right to make his own decisions when the young person reaches a sufficient understanding and intelligence to be capable of making up his or her own mind in relation to a matter requiring decision, and this autonomy of a young person must undermine any Article 8 rights of a parent to family life.

Interestingly, Silber J appears to suggest that when a child becomes *Gillick*-competent, their parents' Article 8 rights disappear. It would have been possible, as Rachel Taylor indicates in the next extract, for him to make the same decision without rejecting the idea that parents' Article 8 rights survive their children's maturity. He could have decided that

---

[78] [2006] EWHC 37 (Admin).

there was interference with Mrs Axon's Article 8 rights, but this could be justified under Article 8(2) because, for a *Gillick*-competent child, any Article 8 right that parents normally have to be involved in important decisions about their child's upbringing is trumped by the *child's* Article 8 right to have her privacy respected.

While this may seem like a technical point, there might be other contexts in which a parent might want to claim Article 8 rights in relation to their mature teenage children—an example might be challenging a deportation order—and it would be unfortunate if Silber J's judgment were to rule out the possibility of parents having a right to family life with a *Gillick*-competent child.

Rachel Taylor[79]

Silber J bases his analysis of Article 8 on the view that 'family life' will terminate once the child reaches maturity. This is an unusual approach to the term 'family life'. It is clear that 'family life' depends on 'the real existence in practice of close personal ties' and that parents are usually regarded as sharing family life with their dependent, minor children....As those seeking advice under the Guidance will be minors aged under 16, it is likely that they will be dependent on their parents and living with them. On the conventional approach to Article 8, it would therefore seem that they would enjoy family life together.

A finding that Ms Axon did enjoy family life with her dependent children would not necessarily mean that her submission would succeed: she would also need to show that 'respect' for her family life included recognition of parental control, and that any interference with her rights was unjustified.

(b) LIFE-THREATENING DECISIONS

While *Axon* confirms the *Gillick*-competent child's right to receive medical treatment which her doctor believes to be in her best interests, in the cases which followed *Gillick*, we can see that the courts' respect for the mature minor's autonomy has not always extended to giving them the same *right* as competent adults to make foolish or irrational decisions, especially when those choices might be life-threatening. This has happened in two ways.

First, it has proved relatively easy to establish that children who are very seriously ill are not *Gillick*-competent. In part, this is because the courts have suggested that capacity is not a free-standing concept, but rather that it has to be judged in the context of the particular decision that the child wishes to take: the more serious the decision, the greater the capacity needed to make it. So a child might be able to consent to having a leg X-rayed, but might not be capable of refusing a life-saving blood transfusion.

In *Re S (A Minor)(Consent to Medical Treatment)*,[80] Johnson J found that a 15-year-old girl suffering from thalassaemia who no longer wanted to undergo monthly blood transfusions, was not competent to make this decision:

---

[79] 'Reversing the Retreat from Gillick? *R (Axon) v Secretary of State for Health*' (2007) 19 Child and Family Law Quarterly 81.

[80] [1994] 2 FLR 1065.

> It does not seem to me that her capacity is commensurate with the gravity of the decision which she has made. It seems to me that an understanding that she will die is not enough. For her decision to carry weight she should have a greater understanding of the manner of the death and pain and the distress.

Indeed, it sometimes seems that the test for capacity when the child wishes to make a life and death decision is set so high that no child could ever be deemed sufficiently competent. In *Re E (A Minor) (Wardship: Medical Treatment)*, a 15-year-old boy, A, who was suffering from leukaemia, wished to refuse a blood transfusion because of his Jehovah's Witness beliefs. Ward J found that to be *Gillick*-competent it was not enough that A, who was 'obviously intelligent', knew he would die, but also that he would have to understand the manner of his death and the extent of his and his family's suffering.

Re E (A Minor) (Wardship: Medical Treatment)[81]

Ward J

I find that A is a boy of sufficient intelligence to be able to take decisions about his own well-being, but I also find that there is a range of decisions of which some are outside his ability fully to grasp their implications. Impressed though I was by his obvious intelligence, by his calm discussion of the implications, by his assertion even that he would refuse well knowing that he may die as a result, in my judgment A does not have a full understanding of the whole implication of what the refusal of that treatment involves...

I am quite satisfied that A does not have any sufficient comprehension of the pain he has yet to suffer, of the fear that he will be undergoing, of the distress not only occasioned by that fear but also—and importantly—the distress he will inevitably suffer as he, a loving son, helplessly watches his parents' and his family's distress. They are a close family, and they are a brave family, but I find that he has no realisation of the full implications which lie before him as to the process of dying. He may have some concept of the fact that he will die, but as to the manner of his death and to the extent of his and his family's suffering I find he has not the ability to turn his mind to it nor the will to do so.

If, therefore, this case depended upon my finding of whether or not A is of sufficient understanding and intelligence and maturity to give full and informed consent, I find that he is not...

There is compelling and overwhelming force in the submission of the Official Solicitor that this court, exercising its prerogative of protection, should be very slow to allow an infant to martyr himself.

In my judgment, A has by the stand he has taken thus far already been and become a martyr for his faith. One has to admire—indeed one is almost baffled by—the courage of the conviction that he expresses. He is, he says, prepared to die for his faith. That makes him a martyr by itself. But I regret that I find it essential for his well-being to protect him from himself and his parents, and so I override his and his parents' decision.

Of course, it is not clear that most adults are capable of fully grasping what it is like to die, and so it could be argued that children are being held to a test for capacity which is more difficult to satisfy than the comparatively undemanding test for adults which we considered

---

[81] [1993] 1 FLR 386.

earlier. Recall *Re C*, which formed the basis of the MCA test for capacity. C said he would rather die with two feet than live with one, but he nevertheless was found to have capacity to make a life and death decision. The durability of A's beliefs was confirmed when he continued to refuse blood after his 18th birthday, and died as a result.

In *Re L (Medical Treatment: Gillick Competency)*,[82] Sir Stephen Brown P again found that a 14-year-old girl who wanted to refuse a life-saving blood transfusion on religious grounds was not *Gillick*-competent. In part this was because she lacked vital information about the likely nature of her predicted death, but this had in fact been deliberately withheld from her. This seems, with respect, to be a misreading of the *Gillick* test for competence, which is supposed to judge whether the child is *capable* of understanding information, not whether she has been given sufficient information to enable her to make an informed choice. Since the patient's doctors will largely control her access to information about her condition and her treatment, as Andrew Grubb points out, it would be regrettable if an absence of information automatically led to a finding of incompetence:

> The fact that L was ignorant of the detail that the court required her to understand was hardly her fault. Of itself, this did not render her incompetent; rather, it left her uninformed. It cannot be right that a doctor may manipulate a patient's capacity to make a decision by failing to provide relevant information.[83]

In *Re S*, *Re L*, and *Re E*, the standard of competence demanded of children who wanted to refuse treatment was extremely high, and perhaps even unattainable. It is interesting to consider whether these cases would have been brought before the courts, and identical findings of incompetence made, if these children had instead wanted to *consent* to receive blood products.

The judgment of Johnson J in *Re P (A Minor)*, another case involving a teenager wishing to refuse blood products on religious grounds, is rather curious. On the one hand, Johnson J approaches the case with a strong predilection to respect John's decision. Johnson J says that there may be cases in which a mature child's refusal 'would be determinative', and that John's wishes had to be at the forefront of his consideration. Indeed, he says that there are 'weighty and compelling reasons' to respect John's refusal and reject the doctors' application for a declaration that it would be lawful to give him blood products without consent.

Yet despite his reluctance to grant the order, and without a finding that John lacked capacity (he was sixteen years and 10 months old, and so benefits from the Family Law Reform Act's presumption of competence, considered below), Johnson J found that it would be in John's best interests to receive treatment with blood without consent.

Re P (A Minor)[84]

Johnson J

[T]here may be cases as a child approaches the age of eighteen when his refusal would be determinative. A court will have to consider whether to override the wishes of a child approaching the age of majority when the likelihood is that all that will have been achieved will have been deferment of an inevitable death and for a matter only of months....

---

[82] [1998] 2 FLR 810.

[83] 'Commentary on *Re L (Medical Treatment: Gillick-Competency)*' (1999) 7 Medical Law Review 58–61, 60.

[84] [2003] EWHC 2327 (Fam).

I have to seek to achieve what is best for John and I put at the forefront of my consideration his wishes. He is nearly seventeen. He is a young man with established convictions. He is undoubtedly a young man whose religious faith must surely demand the respect of all about him. In a world in which religious or indeed any other convictions are not commonly held, John is a young man to be respected...

So I find there to be weighty and compelling reasons why this order should not be made. In the words of Mr Stevens, a solicitor who has come to act for John..., John said to him: 'I am my own person. I have a separate mind. It makes no difference what my parents think. I make my own decision.' John's instructions to Mr. Stevens are that he does not consent to receiving a blood transfusion in any circumstances. To overrule the wishes of John seems to me to be an order that I should be (as indeed I am) reluctant to make for the reasons which I have stated.

Nonetheless, looking at the interests of John in the widest possible sense—medical, religious, social, whatever they be—my decision is that John's best interests in those widest senses will be met if I make an order in the terms sought by the NHS Trust with the addition of those extra words, 'unless no other form of treatment is available'.

An additional difference between the test for capacity in children and adults is that, unlike adults' decision-making capacity, *Gillick* competence is a status which cannot fluctuate on a day-to-day basis, so that an individual is competent on one day and not on another. In *Re R*, a case we consider in detail below, Lord Donaldson appeared to hold that *Gillick* competence is a developmental stage, rather than a functional and hence potentially variable test for capacity.

Re R (A Minor) (Wardship: Consent to Treatment)[85]

Lord Donaldson MR

[E]ven if [R] was capable on a good day of a sufficient degree of understanding to meet the *Gillick* criteria, her mental disability, to the cure or amelioration of which the proposed treatment was directed, was such that on other days she was not only 'Gillick incompetent', but actually sectionable. No child in that situation can be regarded as 'Gillick competent'...'Gillick competence' is a developmental concept and will not be lost or acquired on a day to day or week to week basis.

A test which accommodates fluctuations in a person's ability to make decisions is plainly more protective of patient autonomy than a test which defines someone as competent only where their decision-making capacity is unwavering. Under the MCA, an adult is entitled to make choices about her medical treatment while she is competent, even if it is known that there will be times when she will lack capacity. Yet a child with fluctuating capacity is deemed to be incompetent, even though there will be times when she is clearly competent. Again, it appears that children are being held to a more exacting test of capacity than adults.

The second and more controversial way in which the courts have ignored teenagers' decisions is by drawing a curious distinction between consent to treatment and refusal.

---

[85] [1992] Fam 11 CA.

Gillick, on this view, endows mature minors with the right to consent, but does not give them a corresponding right to refuse. It was Lord Donaldson MR in his judgments in *Re R* and *Re W*,[86] discussed below, who first proposed this distinction between consent and refusal, and as we see later, he has come under sustained academic criticism ever since.

In *Re R (A Minor) (Wardship: Consent to Treatment)* R, who was 15, had been admitted to an adolescent psychiatric unit. In a lucid interval, R indicated that she would refuse compulsory administration of anti-pyschotic medication. The local authority began wardship proceedings, requesting court approval for the administration of the proposed medication without R's consent.

Re R (A Minor) (Wardship: Consent to Treatment)[87]

Lord Donaldson MR

In a case in which the 'Gillick competent' child refuses treatment, but the parents consent, that consent enables treatment to be undertaken lawfully, but in no way determines that the child shall be so treated. In a case in which the positions are reversed, it is the child's consent which is the enabling factor and again the parents' refusal of consent is not determinative. If Lord Scarman intended to go further than this and to say that in the case of a 'Gillick competent' child, a parent has no right either to consent or to refuse consent, his remarks were obiter, because the only question in issue was Mrs. Gillick's alleged right of veto. Furthermore I consider that they would have been wrong...

The... refusal of the 'Gillick competent' child is a very important factor in the doctor's decision whether or not to treat, but does not prevent the necessary consent being obtained from another competent source.

Because of the similarities between the decision in *Re R* and that in *Re W* (where the Family Law Reform Act 1969 applied) we examine the implications of Lord Donaldson's distinction between consent and refusal after mention has been made of the statute which applies to children aged 16 and 17.

(c) BY STATUTE (THE FAMILY LAW REFORM ACT 1969)

Children aged 16 or 17 are in a curious position. They may be incapacitated within the terms of the MCA, considered above, and hence treatment in their best interests is possible. More usually, teenagers of 16 and 17 are likely to be *Gillick*-competent, but in addition the Family Law Reform Act 1969 provides that their consent to medical treatment shall be as effective as it would be if they were an adult.

Family Law Reform Act 1969 section 8

8(1) The consent of a minor who has attained the age of sixteen years to any surgical, medical or dental treatment which, in the absence of consent, would constitute a trespass to his person, shall be as effective as it would be if he were of full age; and where a minor

---

[86] [1993] Fam 64 CA.   [87] [1992] Fam 11 CA.

has by virtue of this section given an effective consent to any treatment it shall not be necessary to obtain any consent for it from his parent or guardian.

(6) In this section 'surgical, medical or dental treatment' includes any procedure undertaken for the purposes of diagnosis, and this section applies to any procedure (including, in particular, the administration of an anaesthetic) which is ancillary to any treatment as it applies to that treatment.

(7) Nothing in this section shall be construed as making ineffective any consent which would have been effective if this section had not been enacted.

It is worth noting that section 8 only applies to *diagnosis* and *treatment*. Bone marrow or organ donation, and non-therapeutic research are therefore excluded, and the validity of a 16- or 17-year-old's consent to such procedures would be governed by the common law. It is also important to remember that the section merely creates a *presumption* in favour of capacity, which can be rebutted in the same way as the presumption that an adult is competent, namely by evidence that the child is *not*, in fact, able to believe, retain, and weigh information in the balance in order to arrive at a choice, and if this is the case, the MCA applies.

The most controversial question raised by section 8 is, as above, whether it applies only to consent, or whether it also gives 16- and 17-year-old children the same right as adults to *refuse* medical treatment. On the one hand, it might be argued that the right to refuse must complement the right to consent, otherwise this becomes a rather thin 'right' merely to agree with the doctor's recommended treatment. A right to agree, unless accompanied by the parallel right to disagree, could hardly be said to protect patient autonomy.

On the other hand, the section itself refers only to the minor's 'consent' being effective, and states that it displaces the *need* to obtain parental consent. Not only is it silent as to refusal, but also section 8(3) specifically states that although the 16- or 17-year-old has become capable of giving an effective consent, this does not render ineffective any consent, such as that of the parents, which existed before the statute was passed. It might then be argued that this section's principal purpose was simply to protect doctors, by enabling them to act lawfully when a 16- or 17-year-old gives consent, rather than to remove the parental right to consent in favour of older children's right to make autonomous decisions.

Certainly this was the preferred interpretation of the Court of Appeal in *Re W (A Minor) (Medical Treatment: Court's Jurisdiction)*, the only case to have considered section 8 in any detail. W, a sixteen-year-old girl suffering from anorexia, wanted to refuse treatment for her anorexia, and claimed, unsuccessfully, that section 8 conferred on her the same right as an adult to refuse medical treatment.

Re W (A Minor) (Medical Treatment: Court's Jurisdiction)[88]

Lord Donaldson MR

On reflection I regret my use in *In Re R (A Minor) (Wardship: Consent to Treatment)* of the key-holder analogy because keys can lock as well as unlock. I now prefer the analogy of the legal 'flak jacket' which protects the doctor from claims by the litigious whether he acquires it from his patient who may be a minor over the age of 16, or a 'Gillick competent' child under that

---

[88] [1993] Fam 64 CA.

age or from another person having parental responsibilities which include a right to consent to treatment of the minor. Anyone who gives him a flak jacket (that is, consent) may take it back, but the doctor only needs one and so long as he continues to have one he has the legal right to proceed....

[I]t is a feature of anorexia nervosa that it is capable of destroying the ability to make an informed choice. It creates a compulsion to refuse treatment or only to accept treatment which is likely to be ineffective. This attitude is part and parcel of the disease and the more advanced the illness, the more compelling it may become. Where the wishes of the minor are themselves something which the doctors reasonably consider need to be treated in the minor's own best interests, those wishes clearly have a much reduced significance.

There is ample authority for the proposition that the inherent powers of the court under its parens patriae jurisdiction are theoretically limitless and that they certainly extend beyond the powers of a natural parent. There can therefore be no doubt that it has power to override the refusal of a minor, whether over the age of 16 or under that age but 'Gillick competent'. It does not do so by ordering the doctors to treat which, even if within the court's powers, would be an abuse of them or by ordering the minor to accept treatment, but by authoris- ing the doctors to treat the minor in accordance with their clinical judgment, subject to any restrictions which the court may impose.

(d) THE CHILD'S 'RIGHT' TO REFUSE TREATMENT: *RE R* AND *RE W*

The argument advanced in both *Re R* and *Re W* can be simply stated. Doctors must have an effective consent before they can lawfully provide medical treatment. *Gillick* and the Family Law Reform Act 1969 endow certain older children with the right to give a valid consent to medical treatment, and hence allow doctors to proceed without seeking an additional con- sent from the child's parents. But the parental right to consent is not thereby extinguished: rather, it co-exists both with the child's right to consent, and with the court's even broader right to authorize medical treatment through the inherent jurisdiction. Because doctors need only one effective consent, once a child is *Gillick*-competent (or 16 or 17 years old), there are three possible sources of this consent: the parents, the courts, and the mature minor. Consent from any one of these three sources will suffice to protect the doctor from prosecution or liability in tort. That means the parents' or the court's consent will be effective *even if the mature minor refuses to give her consent.* The mature minor therefore has no right to have her refusal respected.

This distinction has subsequently been confirmed in a number of cases. According to Thorpe J in *Re K, W and H (Minors) (Medical Treatment)*:[89] 'The decision of the Court of Appeal in *Re R* made it plain that a child with *Gillick* competence can consent to treatment, but that if he or she declines to do so, consent can be given by someone else who has parental rights or responsibilities.'

In *Re W*, Lord Donaldson MR did not qualify the courts' right to overrule the mature minor, but both Balcombe and Nolan LJJ attempted to confine the courts' and parents' power to overrule the mature minor's refusal to cases in which the treatment is necessary to prevent death or severe permanent injury.

[89] [1993] 1 FLR 854.

Re W (A Minor) (Medical Treatment: Court's Jurisdiction) [90]

Lord Balcombe

It will normally be in the best interests of a child of sufficient age and understanding to make an informed decision that the court should respect its integrity as a human being and not lightly override its decision on such a personal matter as medical treatment, all the more so if that treatment is invasive. In my judgment, therefore, the court exercising the inherent jurisdiction in relation to a 16- or 17-year-old child who is not mentally incompetent will, as a matter of course, ascertain the wishes of the child and will approach its decision with a strong predilection to give effect to the child's wishes. . . . Nevertheless, if the court's powers are to be meaningful, there must come a point at which the court, while not disregarding the child's wishes, can override them in the child's own best interests, objectively considered. Clearly such a point will have come if the child is seeking to refuse treatment in circumstances which will in all probability lead to the death of the child or to severe permanent injury.

The courts' underlying presumption here seems to be that, while respecting a mature teenager's decision-making autonomy is important, it is trumped by the principle that society should not permit children to make decisions which might lead to their deaths. It seems that the English courts are applying an unstated principle that the right to make life-ending decisions is governed by a *status* approach to competence: all individuals under the age of eighteen are prevented from choosing to die. Caroline Bridge and Andrew Grubb argue that it would be better if the courts were explicit about this.

Caroline Bridge[91]

[J]udges should not go through the pretence of applying a functional test of capacity when the outcome of the young person's decision is not one that they, or probably society, would countenance. The law should openly declare that welfare reigns when grave decisions with momentous outcomes are considered and recognise that adolescent autonomy is, inevitably, circumscribed.

Andrew Grubb[92]

Clearly, the court is striving to act on its 'hunch' that society should not let children make a decision to die. In truth, it comes down to no more than the court (as society's instrument) acknowledging that at some point citizens must be allowed to make their own decisions, even ones which others might perceive as harmful to them. That point is the age of majority, which for us is 18. . . Once that point is reached, the state does not have a compelling interest to prevent rational citizens from reaching (most) decisions. Until that point, however, the protective duty of society permits intervention. If this is the public policy of this country, it would be far better for the courts . . . simply to say so rather than to obfuscate matters by distorting the legal concept of competence.

The case of *Re E* offers a particularly compelling illustration of the fact that the courts in fact employ a status test for competency to make life-threatening decisions. A was, it seems,

---

[90] [1993] 1 FLR 854.

[91] 'Religious Beliefs and Teenage Refusal of Medical Treatment' (1999) 62 Modern Law Review 585–94, 594.

[92] 'Commentary on *Re L (Medical Treatment: Gillick Competency)*,' (1999) 7 Medical Law Review 58–61.

incompetent the day before his eighteenth birthday but competent a day later when he was entitled to, and subsequently did, refuse a blood transfusion. It is very unlikely that A's reasoning abilities underwent a dramatic change on the day he became eighteen, so that he was unable to grasp what it was like to die when he was 17 years and 364 days old, but miraculously achieved this higher level of understanding within the next twenty-four hours.

In contrast, Nigel Lowe and Satvinder Juss argue that paternalism is justified where a child's decision would cause irreparable harm.

Nigel Lowe and Satvinder Juss[93]

We would support the decisions on either basis because it seems to us wrong for the court to allow a child to refuse treatment that would do him or her irreparable harm. After all, it is perhaps all too easily forgotten that, in the final analysis, a child is still only a child...

Balcombe LJ recognised that if W's refusal not to take solid food was not shortly reversed 'she would be likely to suffer permanent damage to her brain and reproductive organs' and not be able to bear children. Can it humanely be argued, in these circumstances, that the court ought not to have intervened? We agree with Ward J that a court should be slow to let a child martyr himself. To those who question how a child can be held able to give a valid consent yet be unable to exercise a power of veto, we would reply that there is a rational difference to be made between giving consent and withholding it. We must start with the assumption that a doctor will act in the best interests of his patient. Hence, if the doctor believes that a particular treatment is necessary for his patient, it is perfectly rational for the law to facilitate this as easily as possible and hence allow a 'Gillick competent' child to give a valid consent, and also to protect the child against parents opposed to what is professionally considered to be in his best interests. In contrast, it is surely right for the law to be reluctant to allow a *child* of whatever age to be able to veto treatment designed for his or her benefit, particularly if a refusal would lead to the child's death or permanent damage. In other words, the clear and consistent policy of the law is to protect the child against wrong-headed parents and against itself.

In their support for Donaldson's approach, Lowe and Juss are, however, in the minority. Many commentators, such as Ian Kennedy in the next extract, believe that Lord Donaldson's 'gloss' on the House of Lords' judgment in *Gillick* was illegitimate.[94]

Ian Kennedy[95]

But enter now Lord Donaldson. He had clearly taken against *Gillick* and decided that he was going to provide a gloss to it. The gloss he provided is such that if it were accepted as law, the House of Lords would have been overruled by a lower court—a rare legal phenomenon indeed...

---

[93] 'Medical Treatment—Pragmatism and the Search for Principle' (1993) 56 Modern Law Review 865–72.

[94] See also Gillian Douglas, 'The Retreat from *Gillick*' (1992) 55 Modern Law Review 569–76.

[95] 'Consent to Treatment: The Capable Person' in C Dyer (ed.), *Doctors, Patients and the Law* (Blackwell: Oxford, 1992) 44–71.

> The significance of this view cannot be overstated. A party under the age of 18, even though legally competent, would lose the most critical element of the right to self-determination, the right to refuse...
>
> In my respectful view, Lord Donaldson is wrong. His interpretation of *Gillick* is unique, which is an achievement given the buckets of ink spilt in analyzing that case. His failure to accept that the power to refuse is no more than the obverse of the power to consent and that they are simply twin aspects of the single right to self-determination borders on the perverse.

Certainly, none of the judgments in *Gillick* distinguished between consent and refusal, and instead their focus was upon the rights of mature minors to have their wishes about their medical treatment respected, which would appear to encompass a right of refusal as well as a right to consent. The distinction between consent and refusal is also inconsistent with sections 38(6) and 44(7) of the Children Act 1989, which provide children with 'sufficient understanding' with a right to refuse to be examined or assessed: 'if the child is of sufficient understanding to make an informed decision he may refuse to submit to the examination or other assessment'.

In the next extract, John Harris argues that the right to refuse is the necessary corollary of a right to consent, and without it, the right to consent becomes simply a right to acquiesce in a decision which has already been taken.

John Harris[96]

> The idea that a child (or anyone) might competently consent to a treatment but not be competent to refuse it is a palpable nonsense, the reasons for which are revealed by a moment's reflection on what a competent consent involves. To give an informed consent you need to understand the nature of the course of action to which you are consenting, which, in medical contexts, will include its probable and possible consequences and side effects and the nature of any alternative measures which might be taken and the consequences of doing nothing.
>
> So, to understand a proposed treatment well enough to consent to it is to understand the consequences of a refusal. And if the consequences of a refusal are understood well enough to consent to the alternative then the refusal must also be competent.

Similarly, Sarah Elliston suggests that Lord Donaldson's 'gloss' means that children's medical decisions will be respected only if 'they know what is good for them'.

Sarah Elliston[97]

> The establishment of competence of a minor... appears to be a meaningless exercise.…
>
> The situation we are faced with now is that the most that a competent child can expect is that their consent to medical intervention will be determinative. Therefore it may be seriously

---

[96] 'Consent and End of Life Decisions' (2003) 29 Journal of Medical Ethics 10–15, 12.
[97] 'If You Know What's Good for You: Refusal of Consent to Medical Treatment by Children' in S McLean (ed.), *Contemporary Issues in Law, Medicine and Ethics* (Ashgate: Dartmouth, 1996) 29–55.

doubted whether any real question of autonomous decision making by them arises. Their consent is a mere acceptance or endorsement of a procedure that may be authorised to be carried out anyway....

At present, the law in England permits those under 18 to have their medical decisions respected if, but only if, they know what is good for them and accept the treatment that is proposed. Such a situation is both illogical and unjust and may have wider implications for the way in which children are viewed in our society, in that it suggests that children are in some way less entitled to full respect as members of our society by virtue of their status.

It could even be argued that the right to refuse unwanted medical treatment is of more fundamental importance than the right to consent. For example, Jane Fortin draws attention to the practical consequences of ordering a fully grown adolescent to have treatment that she does not want: 'the case-law is surprisingly reticent over the practical details. Indeed, the courts have barely mentioned that the implication of authorizing treatment against the wishes of a fully grown adolescent is that he may have to be held down physically to undergo it.'[98]

Imagine a 15-year-old girl who is pregnant and does not wish to have an abortion. The logical consequence of Lord Donaldson MR's judgments is that even if the girl is *Gillick*-competent, both her parents and the courts would retain the right to consent to the abortion, and the operation could therefore proceed despite her refusal. In *Re W* Lord Donaldson MR and Balcombe LJ were undeterred by this 'hair-raising' possibility, on the grounds that it would be unlikely to happen in practice:

Re W (A Minor) (Medical Treatment: Court's Jurisdiction)[99]

Lord Donaldson MR

Hair-raising possibilities were canvassed of abortions being carried out by doctors in reliance upon the consent of parents and despite the refusal of consent by 16- and 17-year-olds. Whilst this may be possible as a matter of law, I do not see any likelihood taking account of medical ethics, unless the abortion was truly in the best interests of the child.

Balcombe LJ

In the course of the arguments before us it was suggested that a construction of section 8 of the Act of 1969 which denies a 16- or 17-year-old girl an absolute right to refuse medical treatment, but leaves it open to her parents to consent to such treatment, could in theory lead to a case where a pregnant 16-year-old refuses an abortion, but her parents consent to her pregnancy being terminated. So it could in theory, but I cannot conceive of a case where a doctor, faced with the refusal of a mentally competent 16-year-old to having an abortion, would terminate the pregnancy merely upon the consent of the girl's parents. Leaving aside all questions of medical ethics, it seems to me inevitable that in such highly unlikely circumstances the matter would have to come before the court. I find it equally difficult to conceive of a case where the court, faced with this problem and applying the approach I have indicated above, would authorise an abortion against the wishes of a mentally competent 16-year-old. The dilemma is therefore more apparent than real.

---

[98] 'Children's Rights and the Use of Physical Force' (2001) 13 Child and Family Law Quarterly 243.
[99] [1993] Fam 64 CA.

It is perhaps regrettable that we should have to rely upon doctors' good sense, rather than the law, to ensure that these 'hair-raising possibilities' do not take place.

Recall that at the beginning of this chapter, we noted that consent is widely believed to be necessary both to provide the doctor with a defence to a charge of assault or to liability in damages for trespass, and to protect the patient's autonomy. In relation to children, as John Eekelaar points out in the next extract, on Lord Donaldson's view, it appears that the former purpose of consent is the more important one: doctors need only one effective consent in order to lawfully treat a child, whereas respect for autonomy would involve offering equal protection to the child's right to refuse treatment.

John Eekelaar[100]

Lord Donaldson said that there were two reasons for requiring that a patient consents to medical treatment. The 'clinical' reason was that it made treatment easier. The 'legal' reason was 'to provide those concerned in the treatment with a defence to a criminal charge of assault or battery or a civil claim for damages for trespass to the person'. This is an astonishingly narrow view of the requirement, which…is surely rooted in the fundamental civil rights of all citizens that their personal integrity should not be infringed without their consent or lawful justification. Lord Donaldson is not unaware of this, for in a later case involving an adult, he relates it to the right 'to choose whether to consent to medical treatment, to refuse it or to choose one rather than another of the treatments being offered…notwithstanding that the reasons for making the choice are rational, irrational, unknown or even non-existent': *Re T (An Adult: Refusal of Medical Treatment)*….

Lord Donaldson seems to be reluctant to accept that the law should protect minors, even if competent, in the same manner. Rather, his primary concern is to fashion the law so as to minimise the risk of legal action against doctors.

5 VOLUNTARINESS

The next necessary ingredient of a valid consent to medical treatment is that it should have been given voluntarily. It will, of course, be rare for patients to be coerced by direct threats into consenting to medical treatment, but more subtle forms of pressure are possible. The important question is whether the external pressure was such as to overbear the patient's will.

To begin with, it is important to note that the experience of illness, and the offer of treatment, will often leave a patient feeling that she has no option but to consent. Particularly when the patient's condition is life-threatening, and there is only one possible way in which death might be avoided, the patient will be under considerable pressure to agree to the proposed treatment. Yet the pressurized context in which health care choices often have to be made does not mean that patients are incapable of consenting to medical treatment. As PDG Skegg has explained: 'Consent is no less effective when it is unwillingly or reluctantly given; few patients would consent to major surgery if it were not for the force of surrounding

---

[100] 'White Coats or Flak Jackets? Children and the Courts Again' (1993) 109 Law Quarterly Review 182–7.

circumstances, and the knowledge that health or even life may be in jeopardy if they do not consent.'[101]

But where there has been coercion, undue influence, or a fundamental mistake as to the nature of the procedure, it may be possible to argue that the patient's consent is not real.

(a) COERCION

Coercion may vitiate consent to treatment. If a patient was coerced into consenting to treatment, then her apparent consent will be invalid, and any medical treatment which was carried out may be both an assault and a battery. So what do we mean by coercion?

Ruth R Faden, Tom L Beauchamp, with Nancy MP King[102]

Coercion occurs if one party intentionally and successfully influences another by presenting a credible threat of unwanted and avoidable harm so severe that the person is unable to resist acting to avoid it. The three critical features in this definition . . . are that

1. the agent of influence must *intend* to influence the other person by presenting a severe threat,
2. there must be a credible *threat*, and
3. the threat must be *irresistible*.

On this definition, coercion will very seldom vitiate a patient's consent to medical treatment. In fact, when people talk about coercion in the context of consent to medical treatment, they are usually referring to *persuasion* or *manipulation* or *exploitation*, rather than coercion.

Offering someone a large sum of money to become a research subject, or to agree to become a living organ donor is often said to be coercive. Yet it is hard to see how someone is *coerced* by an attractive offer. We certainly would not want to say that someone who receives a very generous job offer has been *coerced*. As Bonnie Steinbock explains in the next extract, an offer might be exploitative, in that it takes advantage of someone's straitened circumstances, but this is not the same thing as coercion.

Bonnie Steinbock[103]

The mere existence of external pressure or influence does not establish coercion. The influence or pressure must be of a kind and an amount that diminishes free choice. The central question for understanding the concept of coercion, then, is how much, and what kind of influence or pressure deprives actions and decisions of their autonomous character. As we will see, the question does not have a simple or straightforward answer. Moreover,

[101] *Law, Ethics and Medicine: Studies in Medical Law* (Clarendon Press: Oxford, 1984) 97.
[102] *A History and Theory of Informed Consent* (OUP: Oxford, 1986) 339.
[103] 'The Concept of Coercion and Long-Term Contraceptives' in Ellen Moskowitz and Bruce Jennings, *Coerced Contraception? Moral and Policy Challenges of Long-Acting Birth Control* (Georgetown UP: Washington DC, 1996) 53–78.

pressure or influence that does not qualify as coercive may also be morally objectionable if, for example, it exploits a person's desperate situation...

Incentives, like threats, are ways of trying to get people to do things. Unlike threats, incentives are typically welcome offers that seem morally unobjectionable. Yet sometimes inducements and incentives are alleged to be coercive...Offering a poor person money for a body part exploits him or takes advantage of his poverty, but it is not clear that it forces or coerces him.

Incentives to do things that people ordinarily would not consider doing appear to be in the same category as exploitative offers. Whether they are coercive is unclear. However, even if they are not coercive, they may be morally impermissible.

While crude threats are unusual in health care settings, mentally ill patients, as Philip Bean explains, may be particularly susceptible to coercive treatment.

Philip Bean[104]

In an obvious sense there can be no consent if coercion is used: X cannot be said to be consenting if agreement is extracted with Y's gun...Coercion neutralises consent. The problem with coercion, as it affects mental patients..., is that it is never as naked as that but may involve more subtle threats of punishments, loss of privileges, threats of further detention etc. Where psychiatric staff say 'we shall do this or that to you unless you consent to this treatment', they are involved in coercion. Similarly, when they say 'we shall keep you in hospital unless you consent to this treatment' they are also involved in coercion...

So where consent is extracted with threats of punishment, loss of privileges and threats of further detention this is coercion for it takes unfair advantage of the patient's vulnerability.

In *Freeman v Home Office (No. 2)*, a prisoner serving a life sentence claimed that he had received medical treatment which had been administered against his will. He argued that where the doctor is also a prison officer, a patient's consent could never be truly voluntary. The Court of Appeal rejected this argument. Whether or not consent had been given voluntarily was a question of fact, and that although the patient's imprisonment might alert the court to the danger that the patient's apparent consent was not a real consent, the voluntariness of the patient's consent would have to be assessed on a case-by-case basis.

Freeman v Home Office (No. 2)[105]

Stephen Brown LJ

I find myself in complete agreement with the trial judge that the sole issue raised at the trial, that is to say whether the plaintiff had consented to the administration of the drugs injected into his body, was essentially one of fact: ...'The right approach, in my judgment, is to say that where, in a prison setting, a doctor has the power to influence a prisoner's situation and prospects a court must be alive to the risk that what may appear, on the face of it, to be real consent is not in fact so.'

---

[104] *Mental Disorder and Legal Control* (CUP: Cambridge, 1986) 138–9.
[105] [1984] 1 All ER 1036.

(b) UNDUE INFLUENCE

In *Re T*,[106] the court recognized that pressure to consent to, or to refuse medical treatment is unlikely to consist in physical force or duress, and much more likely to take the form of persuasion. Of course, many forms of persuasion are wholly legitimate. Doctors and relatives will often try to persuade patients of the merits of undergoing a procedure which they believe will benefit the patient. In *Re T*, Staughton LJ recognized that 'every decision is made as a result of some influence: a patient's decision to consent to an operation will normally be influenced by the surgeon's advice as to what will happen if the operation does not take place'.

Indeed, as Ruth Faden *et al.* explain, trying to persuade someone to undergo beneficial treatment may be a good thing:

> Frequently in clinical situations, professionals would be morally blameworthy if they did not attempt to persuade their patients to consent to interventions that are medically necessitated. Reasoned argument in defense of an option is itself information, and as such is no less important in ensuring understanding that disclosure of facts...Paradigmatically, persuasion succeeds by *improving*, and not by undermining, a person's understanding of his or her situation.[107]

Whether or not the persuasion amounts to undue influence would have to be established on the facts of each case. One obviously relevant factor, as pointed out in *Re T (Adult: Refusal of Treatment)*, is the relationship between the persuader and the patient: the closer the relationship, the harder it may be for the patient to resist complying with their views.

T had refused a blood transfusion, following discussions with her mother, a Jehovah's Witness. Since that refusal T's condition had deteriorated, and her baby had been stillborn. Her father, supported by her boyfriend, applied for a declaration that it would be lawful to give her a blood transfusion, The declaration was granted.

Re T (Adult: Refusal of Treatment)[108]

Lord Donaldson MR

When considering the effect of outside influences, two aspects can be of crucial importance. First, the strength of the will of the patient. One who is very tired, in pain or depressed will be much less able to resist having his will overborne than one who is rested, free from pain and cheerful. Second, the relationship of the 'persuader' to the patient may be of crucial importance. The influence of parents on their children or of one spouse on the other can be, but is by no means necessarily, much stronger than would be the case in other relationships. Persuasion based upon religious belief can also be much more compelling and the fact that arguments based upon religious beliefs are being deployed by someone in a very close relationship with the patient will give them added force and should alert the doctors to the possibility—no more—that the patient's capacity or will to decide has been overborne. In other words the patient may not mean what he says.

---

[106] [1993] Fam 95 CA.

[107] Ruth Faden, Tom Beauchamp, with Nancy King, *A History and Theory of Informed Consent* (OUP: Oxford, 1986).

[108] [1993] Fam 95 CA.

It is worth noting that in *Re T*, the decision which the court decided had been undermined by undue influence was a *refusal* of treatment, rather than consent. It might be predicted that if T's mother had in contrast persuaded her to *consent* to a life-saving blood transfusion, it is highly unlikely that the doctors would have sought a court declaration that T's apparent consent had been vitiated by her mother's undue influence.

(c) MISTAKE

A decision may not genuinely reflect the patient's wishes if it is based upon a misunderstanding about the seriousness of the patient's condition, or about the need for treatment. This was again an issue in *Re T*, where the patient had been reassured that a blood transfusion might not be necessary, and that equally effective alternatives existed. Her condition had, however, deteriorated since these assurances had been given, thus casting doubt upon the authenticity of her continuing refusal. If the patient's claim is that their apparent consent was vitiated by a mistake, they will generally be arguing that they were inadequately informed about the nature of the treatment, and in particular about its risks or side-effects. We considered this sort of claim in more detail in the previous chapter.

6 CONCLUSION

In this chapter we have principally been concerned with the medical treatment of vulnerable patients, such as children and adults who lack capacity. We have seen that a great deal turns on whether a patient has, or does not have, capacity to make a medical decision. If a patient is competent, then the principle of autonomy dominates, and the patient is entitled to refuse treatment, including life-saving treatment, for irrational reasons or even for no reason at all. If, on the other hand, the patient lacks capacity, doctors are entitled to act paternalistically and to carry out (almost) any treatment which they believe to be in the patient's best interests. Since the consequences of being classified as 'incompetent' or 'lacking capacity' are that one's wishes can legitimately be ignored, it is vitally important both that a clear definition of incapacity exists, and that it is applied objectively and consistently.

For some patients, such as very young children and permanently comatose adults, it will be self-evident that they lack the capacity to make decisions about their medical treatment. However, while the law demands a binary either/or categorization of a patient as either competent or incompetent, the reality is that decision-making capacity exists on a spectrum. Towards either end of this spectrum, decisions about whether a patient has capacity will be so obvious as to barely need stating. Towards the middle, however, the decision may be much more difficult. The patient in *Re C* was entitled to refuse amputation, despite his bizarre delusions, whereas an anorexic patient, who is deluded about her need to lose weight, might be deemed incompetent, and force-fed against her wishes. Deciding when a patient's unusual or misguided decision-making process amounts to incapacity is clearly a complicated and difficult task, and factors other than the patient's innate reasoning abilities sometimes come into play. For children, we have seen that the test for capacity is set so high in relation to potentially life-threatening decisions that it would be extraordinary if any child were able to satisfy it.

6

MENTAL HEALTH LAW

CENTRAL ISSUES

1. Mental health law is distinctive because it authorizes involuntary detention and compulsory treatment.

2. Most mentally ill patients are not, however, subject to compulsory powers. Among hospital inpatients, a minority have been 'sectioned', and most are admitted informally.

3. Usually patients are detained because they pose a risk to themselves or others, and/or because this is the only way to ensure that they receive appropriate treatment.

4. In a significant exception to the principle of patient autonomy, it is possible to treat a mentally disordered patient even if she is competent and refusing treatment. To be lawful, compulsory treatment must be treatment

for her mental disorder, and must not amount to 'inhuman and degrading treatment'.

5. The patient's right to challenge her detention is protected by Article 5 (the right to liberty) of the European Convention, as incorporated by the Human Rights Act.

6. The process of reforming mental health law began over ten years ago, culminating in a reforming statute, the Mental Health Act 2007, which has made a number of significant changes to the Mental Health Act 1983. During this process, mental health professionals in particular were critical of the emphasis the government placed upon the risk mentally ill people pose to others.

---

1 INTRODUCTION

In this chapter we attempt a broad overview of mental health law in the UK. There are arguments for and against including a chapter on mental health law in a medical law textbook. On the one hand, mental health law is a subject in its own right, and a single chapter is undoubtedly incapable of doing full justice to its breadth and complexity. Yet on the other hand, for a medical law textbook to exclude any discussion of the regime which governs the treatment of mentally ill patients would appear to mirror the misguided belief, described

Since the capacity/incapacity line is so critical, it is also important to consider *who* should be charged with making this assessment. While independent review by the courts is possible, usually the decision will be taken by the patient's doctors. Two important points follow from this. First, doctors are undoubtedly much less likely to question a patient's decision-making capacity when she has agreed to a proposed treatment. This means that uncooperative patients are more likely to be categorized as incompetent, and treated against their wishes. Secondly, once the doctor has determined that a patient lacks capacity, she is then entitled to treat the patient according to *her* assessment of the patient's best interests, as structured by the section 4(6) checklist. In most cases, then, doctors are responsible for applying both the test for incapacity *and* the best interests test, and therefore exercise considerable control over the treatment of incompetent patients.

Of course, all these choices can be brought before the courts, and in the case of especially controversial treatments such as sterilization, court involvement is routine. But in the ordinary run of things, it is important to acknowledge that it is not judges, but rather doctors, who must interpret and apply both the test for capacity and the best interests test.

FURTHER READING

Bridge, Caroline, 'Religious Beliefs and Teenage Refusal of Medical Treatment' (1999) 62 Modern Law Review 585–94.

Donnelly, Mary 'Best Interests, Patient Participation and the Mental Capacity Act 2005' (2009) Medical Law Review 1–29.

Douglas, Gillian, 'The Retreat from *Gillick*' (1992) 55 Modern Law Review 569–76.

Draper, Heather, 'Anorexia Nervosa and Respecting a Refusal of Life-prolonging Therapy: A Limited Justification' (2000) 14 Bioethics 120–33.

Fox, Marie and McHale, Jean, 'In Whose Best Interests?' (1996) 60 Modern Law Review 700–9.

Gunn, MJ *et al.*, 'Decision-Making Capacity' (1999) 7 Medical Law Review 269–306.

Jones, RB, 'Parental Consent to Cosmetic Facial Surgery in Down's Syndrome' (2000) 26 Journal of Medical Ethics 101–2.

Lowe, Nigel and Juss, Satvinder, 'Medical Treatment—Pragmatism and the Search for Principle' (1993) 56 Modern Law Review 865–72.

Maclean, Alasdair, 'Advance Directives and the Rocky Waters of Anticipatory Decision-making' (2008) 16 Medical Law Review 1–22.

McLean, Sheila, *Old Law, New Medicine* (Pandora: London, 1999) ch 5.

Michalowski, Sabine, 'Advance Refusals of Life Sustaining Treatment' (2005) Modern Law Review 958.

Sheldon, Sally and Wilkinson, Stephen, 'Female Genital Mutilation and Cosmetic Surgery: Regulating Non-therapeutic Body Modification' (1998) 12 Bioethics 263–85.

Taylor, Rachel, 'Reversing the Retreat from Gillick? *R (Axon) v Secretary of State for Health*' (2007) Child and Family Law Quarterly 81.

Wrigley, Anthony 'Proxy Consent: Moral Authority Misconceived' (2007) 33 Journal of Medical Ethics 527–31.

by Tom Campbell and Chris Heginbotham in the next extract, that the mentally ill are not really like other patients. In my view, the risks of oversimplification and omission are probably outweighed by this latter concern.

Tom Campbell and Chris Heginbotham[1]

Persons with mental illnesses are made to suffer a range of unnecessary deprivations which result from crude and erroneous assumptions about mental illnesses which lead us to lump their victims together in a pariah class of sub-humans. People with a history of mental illness repeatedly experience the frustration and insult caused by a lack of respect for them as individuals and the absence of humane consideration for their situation.

While a mental illness can happen to any member of society, its natural effects are such that its victims rarely achieve or sustain economic security or social influence. Social attitudes accelerate and reinforce this downward spiral through social and economic exclusion. Mental illness thus routinely brings with it membership of a wronged, insulted and excessively deprived class of persons...

[U]nreasonable hostile reactions to people with mental illnesses bring deprivations and disadvantages that would not be tolerated if they were inflicted on other citizens. The result is that mental illness discrimination exacerbates the often already unfortunate plight of those with mental illnesses.

We begin with a short history of mental health policy, tracing the rise and fall of asylums and the more recent emphasis, first, upon care in the community, and more recently still, upon risk-avoidance. Next we consider the various stages involved in the treatment of mental illness, starting with a definition of mental disorder and a description of how patients are admitted to the mental health system.

In the previous chapter, we looked at the concept of mental incapacity, and it is critically important to remember that mentally ill people are not necessarily incapable of making medical decisions. Recall the patient in *Re C*,[2] who suffered from paranoid schizophrenia, and yet was found to be capable of deciding that he did not want his gangrenous leg amputated. Competent mentally ill patients have the same right to refuse medical treatment as other competent adults, but the Mental Health Act creates important exceptions to this, and we consider when mentally ill patients can be treated without consent. Finally, we look at discharge from the mental health system, and the realities of care in the community.

The fundamental legal difference between mental health law and other areas of medical law is that it authorizes the detention and compulsory treatment of people suffering from mental illness. The Twelfth Biennial Report of the Mental Health Act Commission (MHAC)—a body set up to monitor the working of the Act—draws attention to what this means in practice.

Mental Health Act Commission[3]

Patients who are detained under Mental Health Act powers are placed in a quite different situation from many other NHS funded inpatients. They have not agreed to come into hospital

---

[1] *Mental Illness: Prejudice, Discrimination and the Law* (Dartmouth: Aldershot, 1991).

[2] [1994] 1 WLR 290.

[3] Twelfth Biennial Report, available at <www.mhac.org.uk/>. In 2009, the MHAC was subsumed within the overarching Care Quality Commission, <www.cqc.org.uk/>.

and in some cases do not accept that need for admission, yet they may not discharge them-selves from a ward that they find insupportable. They may experience no physical disability through their illness, and yet be confined, even by force, within a building with little access to exercise or fresh air....

We have found wards that are unventilated and hot in summer but cold in winter; wards where there is little natural light; noisy and smoky wards; and broken, worn and stained furni-ture, sticky floors and bad smells; peeling paint and graffiti; and non-existent or broken lock-able storage for patient's belongings. We have had cause to comment on broken and dirty toilet facilities, and even on inadequate numbers of toilet and bathroom facilities provided for certain wards.

Detention and treatment without consent are radically out of line with the principle of patient autonomy which, as we have seen, now dominates medical law. The Public Health (Control of Diseases) Act 1984 permits the detention of people suffering from notifiable diseases, such as cholera and plague, but even for these conditions, it is not possible to *give treatment* without a competent patient's consent. Why should people with mental health problems be treated differently?

Three possible justifications have been given:

(1) It might enable them to gain access to treatment. If a mentally ill patient is also incap-able of giving valid consent to treatment, the only way for her to obtain the treatment she may need is to treat her without consent. For competent mentally ill patients, how-ever, other justifications are necessary.

(2) It could be argued that detention and treatment without consent are sometimes necessary to protect the patient from herself. Someone who is depressed and feeling suicidal, for example, might subsequently be glad that she was prevented from taking her own life.

(3) Finally, it has been argued that detention and compulsory treatment are necessary to protect the public from dangerous mentally ill patients.

As we shall see throughout this chapter, this latter idea, that the public needs protection from people with mental health problems, has been in the ascendancy in recent years. It is, however, extremely controversial because it has been invoked to justify what is essentially *preventative detention*: that is, detaining someone not because they have been found guilty of a criminal offence, but because there is perceived to be a *risk* that they *might* cause harm to others. Not only does this create an exception to some basic principles of criminal justice, but it rests upon the mistaken assumption that a diagnosis of mental illness is an accurate predictor of future violent tendencies. We do not detain men who regularly binge drink on the grounds that they might, in the future, get involved in a pub brawl or hit their partner. Rather, detention is possible only after they have, in fact, broken the law.

There is always considerable media interest in cases in which mentally ill people have committed very serious offences, perhaps the most infamous of which is the Michael Stone case. Stone—who had mental health problems, as well as being a drug addict—was con-victed of the gruesome murders of Lin and Megan Russell, who were beaten to death in 1996 while on a country walk with Megan's surviving sister Josie. In cases like this, the press tends to take the view that a horrific crime committed by someone who has previously had contact with mental health services must be evidence of a *failure* on the part of those services. Of course, just as with ordinary criminals, it is not necessarily possible to predict in advance that someone is going to break the law. Nevertheless, the assumption seems to have taken root that mental health services should always be able to prevent mentally ill people from harming others.

Interestingly, despite the received wisdom appearing to be that Michael Stone was 'free to kill' as a result of failures on the part of mental health services, the inquiry into the circumstances leading up to the Russell murders found that at no point was Stone refused help by mental health care services. He had been refused inpatient care for detoxification by addiction services, but this finding received little publicity.[4]

In addition to the misguided tendency to blame mental health services, this sort of press coverage undoubtedly also has an influence on public attitudes towards the mentally ill. While most people who are mentally ill are completely harmless, and, if anything, pose a risk to themselves rather than to others, there seems to be evidence that the public is becoming more fearful and less accepting of people with mental health problems. According to a survey carried out by the Department of Health in 2007, more than half of respondents defined a person who is mentally ill as someone who 'has to be kept in a psychiatric or mental hospital'. The survey found evidence of greater intolerance towards people with mental health problems than there had been in the previous survey in the mid-nineties. Young people, in particular, were more likely to be frightened of the mentally ill, and to not want to live next door to someone with a mental disorder.

As Nancy Wolff explains in the next extract, the erroneous public perception that *all* mentally ill people pose a risk of harm to others leads to public support for their detention.

Nancy Wolff[5]

Implicit in the public's perception of severe mental illness is the notion that not only are persons with these disorders more likely to engage in violent acts, but also that the higher relative risk is evenly distributed across the entire group of disordered individuals. Evidence suggests, however, that the distribution of risk within this population is bimodal forming two subgroups: low risk and high risk.... The high risk group is comparatively small... Evidence on homicides in England and Wales suggests that 0.05 per cent of persons with severe mental illness pose the greatest risk of homicidal violence. The low risk group is the larger of the two, comprising roughly 90 per cent of persons with severe mental illness. While individuals in the low-risk group have violence profiles that are more like the general population, they may still engage in non-violent criminal or social deviance that arouses the concern of the public and brings them to the attention of law enforcement agencies. Behaviours that deviate from social norms, such as dishevelled and unkempt appearance, talking to oneself, sleeping on public sidewalks, may be interpreted by the public as evidence of menace potential. Guided by fear, the public may misinterpret and overreact to the behaviour or appearance of persons with mental illness, if such indicators of social nuisance confirm stereotypical beliefs...

If the public remains committed to the perfectability expectation, each violent act committed by a person with a mental illness will be interpreted as potentially avoidable, which could motivate the public to rightfully (a) demand that the government allocate more money to reduce future events through more secure care and supervision of high-risk individuals or (b) support legal reforms that constrain the civil liberties of persons with mental illness.

[4] Robert Francis, 'The Michael Stone Inquiry: A Reflection' (2007) Journal of Mental Health Law 85–96.
[5] 'Risk, Response and Mental Health Policy: Learning from the Experience of the United Kingdom' (2002) 27 Journal of Health Politics, Policy and Law 801–32.

This emphasis upon the risk mentally ill people might pose to others dominated the government's approach to the process of reforming the Mental Health Act 1983. It had been apparent for some time that the 1983 Act, which essentially simply updated and in parts reproduced the Mental Health Act 1959, was in need of reform, and this need became more pressing in the light of the incorporation of the European Convention on Human Rights through the Human Rights Act 1998. The Mental Health Act 1983 was the subject of the first declaration of incompatibility with the Human Rights Act, and the lack of fit between the two pieces of legislation proved to be a rich source of litigation.

While a number of convention rights might be invoked to challenge the treatment of the mentally ill, the most significant are probably Article 3, the prohibition of inhuman and degrading treatment, and Article 5, which provides that:

> (1) Everyone has the right to liberty and security of person. No one shall be deprived of his liberty save in the following cases and in accordance with a procedure prescribed by law:....
>
> (e) the lawful detention of persons for the prevention of the spreading of infectious diseases, of persons of unsound mind, alcoholics or drug addicts or vagrants.

Article 5 does not mention mental disorder as a legitimate ground for detention, but this is how 'unsound mind' has been interpreted and applied. While, as we shall see later, mentally ill people have been able to rely upon other requirements in Article 5, such as the right to challenge their detention, it could be argued that Article 5 itself is problematic, in so far as it suggests that one of the most basic human rights—the right to liberty—is not shared equally by people who are 'of unsound mind'.

An Expert Committee, chaired by Genevra Richardson, was established in 1998, and its review of the Mental Health Act was submitted to the Department of Health the following year.[6] There then followed two green papers, one white paper, and two substantial draft Bills, in 2002 and 2004, both of which were subjected to overwhelming and near-universal criticism. The British Medical Association and the Royal College of Psychiatrists, for example, argued that the first draft Bill was completely unworkable. Eventually, and after some passionately argued parliamentary debates, a shorter amending statute—the Mental Health Act 2007—received Royal Assent. Most of the changes this made to the 1983 Act came into force towards the end of 2008.

It is worth noting that reform of the law on mental incapacity proceeded almost entirely separately from these troubled mental health law reforms, and culminated in the Mental Capacity Act (MCA) 2005, discussed in the previous chapter. While mental incapacity and mental illness are not synonymous with each other, there are obvious areas of overlap. In the next extract, Aisling Boyle describes how the inclusive and 'patient-friendly' MCA is in stark opposition to new mental health legislation.

Aisling Boyle[7]

The Mental Capacity Act accords considerable respect for patients' treatment decisions. The prominence attached to maximising the number of patients who can exercise autonomy places the interests of the individual at the centre of the decision-making process....

---

[6] *Review of the Mental Health Act: Report of the Expert Committee* (DH: London, 1999).

[7] 'The Law and Incapacity Determinations: A Conflict of Governance?' (2008) 71 Modern Law Review 433–63.

The above approach contrasts markedly with the Mental Health Act, which makes no distinction between individuals who have capacity to make decisions and those who do not. Whilst the Mental Capacity Act seeks to minimise interference with patients' rights, new mental health legislation is likely to result in unwarranted stigmatisation of mentally disordered individuals....

In substantial opposition to the approach [in the MCA], under mental health legislation patients' best interests do not need to be taken into account....For confined patients, this approach is inherently discriminatory as an individual's competent refusal to consent to treatment may be trumped by the existence of 'mental disorder' or the 'threat of harm'.

This difference in approach is especially striking given that a substantial proportion of the group of patients who are covered by the Mental Health Act will also be subject to the Mental Capacity Act. Owen *et al.*'s 2008 study revealed that 60 per cent of all patients who were admitted to psychiatric hospitals lacked capacity, and the percentage was even higher for compulsorily detained patients (86 per cent).[8] For these patients, the MCA's patient-centred 'best interests checklist', which we considered in the previous chapter, applies unless they are receiving treatment for their mental disorder, when the more draconian Mental Health Act provisions take priority.

One principal difference between the Mental Capacity Act and the reforming Mental Health Act is that the former contains a set of statutory principles—such as the presumption of capacity and the 'least restrictive alternative' principle. In Scotland, the Mental Health (Care and Treatment)(Scotland) Act 2003 also includes a set of guiding principles, such as respect for the past and present wishes of the patient, and encouragement of equal opportunities. In contrast, and contrary to the recommendations of the Richardson Committee, the Mental Health Act does not contain any statutory principles. A set of principles does exist in the Code of Practice, but these do not have the same force as principles on the face of the statute. It is also noteworthy that the 'purpose' principle in the English Mental Health Act Code of Practice mentions 'protecting others from harm' as a justification for the use of compulsory powers, whereas the Scottish legislation's statutory principles are much more patient-focused and make no mention of public safety.

Mental Health Act Code of Practice paras 1.2–1.6[9]

Purpose principle

1.2 Decisions under the Act must be taken with a view to minimising the undesirable effects of mental disorder, by maximising the safety and wellbeing (mental and physical) of patients, promoting their recovery and protecting other people from harm.

Least restriction principle

1.3 People taking action without a patient's consent must attempt to keep to a minimum the restrictions they impose on the patient's liberty, having regard to the purpose for which the restrictions are imposed.

---

[8] Gareth S Owen, Genevra Richardson, Anthony S David, George Szmukler, Peter Hayward, and Matthew Hotopf, 'Mental Capacity to Make Decisions on Treatment in People Admitted to Psychiatric Hospitals: Cross sectional Study' (2008) 337 British Medical Journal 448.

[9] (2008), available at <www.dh.gov.uk>.

Respect principle

1.4   People taking decisions under the Act must recognise and respect the diverse needs, values and circumstances of each patient, including their race, religion, culture, gender, age, sexual orientation and any disability. They must consider the patient's views, wishes and feelings (whether expressed at the time or in advance), so far as they are reasonably ascertainable, and follow those wishes wherever practicable and consistent with the purpose of the decision. There must be no unlawful discrimination.

Participation principle

1.5 Patients must be given the opportunity to be involved, as far as is practicable in the circumstances, in planning, developing and reviewing their own treatment and care to help ensure that it is delivered in a way that is as appropriate and effective for them as possible. The involvement of carers, family members and other people who have an interest in the patient's welfare should be encouraged (unless there are particular reasons to the contrary) and their views taken seriously.

Effectiveness, efficiency and equity principle

1.6 People taking decisions under the Act must seek to use the resources available to them and to patients in the most effective, efficient and equitable way, to meet the needs of patients and achieve the purpose for which the decision was taken.

At the outset, it should be noted that the very existence of 'mental illness' is doubted by some commentators in what is often referred to as the 'anti-psychiatry' movement. These critics, including Thomas Szasz and Erving Goffman, have argued that psychiatry is not concerned with treating the sick, but instead with controlling and coercing strange or inconvenient behaviour. And, of course, as Szasz explains in the next extract, if there is no such thing as mental illness, a special set of laws governing the treatment of the mentally ill would also be unnecessary.

Thomas Szasz[10]

The term 'mental illness' is a metaphor. More particularly, as this term is used in mental hygiene legislation, 'mental illness' is not the name of a medical disease or disorder, but is a quasi-medical label whose purpose is to conceal conflict as illness and to justify coercion as treatment.

If 'mental illness' is a bona fide illness—as official medical, psychiatric, and mental health organizations, such as the World Health Organization, the American and British Medical Associations, and the American Psychiatric Association, maintain—then it follows, logically and linguistically, that it must be treated like any other illness. Hence, mental hygiene laws must be repealed. There are no special laws for patients with a peptic ulcer or pneumonia; why, then, should there be special laws for patients with depression or schizophrenia?

If, on the other hand, 'mental illness' is, as I contend, a myth, then, also, it follows that mental hygiene laws should be repealed...When I assert that mental illness is a myth, I am not saying that personal unhappiness and socially deviant behaviour do not exist; but I am saying that we categorize them as diseases at our peril.

The expression 'mental illness' is a metaphor which we have come to mistake for a fact. We call people physically ill when their body-functioning violates certain anatomical and physiological norms; similarly, we call people mentally ill when their personal conduct violates certain ethical, political, and social norms....

We should guard against...the discomfort that the mental patient's behaviour may cause us. Labeling conduct as sick merely because it differs from our own may be nothing more than discrimination disguised as medical judgment.

2 A SHORT HISTORY OF MENTAL HEALTH LAW AND POLICY

There is a very long history of subjecting people who have been classified as 'mad' to special treatment. Compulsory detention has been possible for hundreds of years, although it used to be the preserve of poor law officers, and Justices of the Peace, rather than doctors. The Vagrancy Act 1744, for example, enabled two or more Justices of the Peace to direct a constable, church-warden or overseer of the poor to apprehend and detain 'persons of little or no estates, who, by lunacy, or otherwise, are furiously mad, and dangerous to be permitted to go abroad'.

While private asylums existed, the vast majority of those who were considered insane were classified as paupers, and kept in poorhouses. Conditions were appalling. Beatings, whippings, and rape were common, and prolonged restraint was the norm. A select committee established in 1877 proposed a number of reforms, such as the provision of a system of asylums at public expense; a requirement that two medical certificates accompany an application to detain an individual; and a system of independent inspection of asylums. From the Lunacy Act 1890 onwards, a series of statutes brought such a system into being.

The Mental Treatment Act 1930 was intended to reduce the stigma associated with mental illness, a move that had its origins in the changing attitudes to people with mental health problems which were prompted by the return of 'shell-shocked' soldiers from the First World War. It also represented a shift towards 'medicalism', with admission decisions taken by psychiatrists. As treatments for mental illnesses became available, psychiatrists' social standing had improved because their role was increasingly like that of conventional doctors, and less like that of jailers.

The Percy Commission was set up to consider further reform in the 1950s, and its report culminated in the passage of the Mental Health Act 1959. This emphasized voluntary rather than compulsory admission to hospital, and short-term rather than permanent detention. Although based upon the 1959 Act, the Mental Health Act 1983 attempted to offer more legal safeguards, in order to protect the rights of mentally ill patients. The 2007 Act made a number of significant changes, but the Act's basic structure remains intact.

Many commentators have analysed mental health law as if it were a pendulum swinging between legalism—with an emphasis upon legal protection—and medicalism—where the medical profession is left to determine how individual patients should be treated. This distinction is described by Phil Fennell in the following extract.

Phil Fennell[11]

Nowhere is the tension between autonomy and paternalism more evident than in relation to the treatment of mentally disordered patients. Debate about these questions in the mental health sphere has, until comparatively recently, revolved around two organizing concepts. On the one hand has been legalism, which has emphasized the need to put limits on the power of mental health professionals and the rights of patients to respect for their autonomously expressed wishes. On the other has been that of medicalism which stresses that the safeguards for the individual rights of patients are not so cumbersome as to impede medical interventions aimed at serving those same patients' best interests.

As Nicola Glover-Thomas explains, legal constraints not only protect patients' rights, but also help to legitimate psychiatric practice.

Nicola Glover-Thomas[12]

Psychiatric practice must be seen to be subject to social, moral and political control. Legal scrutiny provides the final opportunity to protect patient rights. Clearly, the law acts as a mechanism of control because it establishes a framework in which care decisions are made and incorporates legal safeguards surrounding detention, treatment and other coercive aspects of the legislation. The formation of these safeguards protects both the patient and those working within the psychiatric field. They legitimate psychiatric practices because they ensure the decisions are made in a procedurally sound way.... The existence of a formal legal framework allows the public to accept decisions, which overtly remove rights from individuals. The need for psychiatrists to seek second medical opinions and to obtain opinions from other professionals allows psychiatric practice to be seen as accountable and legitimate.

Before we look at the law in detail, it is worth highlighting two particularly significant recent trends in mental health policy.

(a) DECARCERATION

The twentieth century saw a dramatic shift in attitudes towards institutionalizing people with mental illnesses. In 1850, there were 7,140 inpatients; by 1930 there were nearly 120,000 inpatients, and by 1954 this figure had risen to 148,000. Asylums were believed to offer humane and decent surroundings for some of the most marginal members of society. They also undoubtedly facilitated greater social control and surveillance of the insane.[13]

Then in the second half of the twentieth century there was a turn away from the incarceration of people suffering from mental illnesses. Even for those patients who are not capable of living independently, inpatient treatment is provided in psychiatric wards in general

---

[11] 'Inscribing Paternalism in the Law: Consent to Treatment and Mental Disorder' (1990) 17 Journal of Law and Society 29–51.

[12] *Reconstructing Mental Health Law and Policy* (Butterworths: London, 2002).

[13] See further, Michel Foucault, *The Birth of the Clinic: An Archaeology of Clinical Perception* (Penguin: London, 1973).

hospitals or in care homes, rather than in asylums. The number of psychiatric hospital beds is now around 33,000.[14]

Several reasons are commonly given for this move towards decarceration. First, it might be part of a broader trend in social policy away from institutional solutions to social problems; financial support for the poor, for example, is increasingly supposed to be a temporary measure to facilitate independence, rather than encouraging permanent dependency. Secondly, community care is often perceived to be cheaper than keeping a patient in an institution, and in an overburdened NHS, the pressure to save money is considerable. Thirdly, the discovery of widespread abuse of mentally ill people within institutions meant that asylums were no longer seen as places of safety. Fourthly, the development of drugs, such as tranquillizers, contributed to an increasingly *medical* model of mental disorders, where they are regarded as illnesses that can be effectively managed, if not cured, and sufferers thereby enabled to lead relatively normal lives. Finally, the discovery that mental illness is in fact much more common than had been previously realized contributed to the view that a diagnosis of mental disorder did not justify locking someone up.

A growing emphasis on community care is evident in mental health policy from the 1960s onwards, but while the number of hospital beds declined, other services were not put in place to replace inpatient care. It had been assumed that mentally ill people would be cared for at home, and readily reintegrated into the community, but this assumption proved to be hopelessly over-optimistic. It has not been easy for people with mental illnesses to find jobs and accommodation, and their families are not always able or willing to provide the care that they need.

High-quality community care is expensive, perhaps even more so than treatment which can be provided in a hospital setting, where patients stay in one place, making assessment of their needs and delivery of care relatively straightforward. The principal failing of community care is not, perhaps, the move towards decarceration. No-one would want to see a return to the days when people with mental disorders were kept in vast asylums, effectively 'out of sight and out of mind' of the rest of society. Rather, the mistake has been to underestimate the costs of providing high-quality care and other services—such as housing and help with finding employment—which mentally disordered individuals may need in order to live functioning lives in the community.

Jill Stavert suggests that we have tended to think about mental health patients' rights as the right to be free from unwarranted detention and the right to proper processes through which to challenge detention. In the community, what are often referred to as socio-economic rights to services and resources may be of much greater importance.

Jill Stavert[15]

> Over the last two decades we have come some way in Europe towards recognising that those suffering from mental illness require enforceable rights so that they are not subjected to abuse and neglect. These rights are, however, mainly civil rights which are applicable to the patient–institution relationship. If care takes place outside institutions, a far greater

[14] Patrick Keown, Gavin Mercer, and Jan Scott, 'Retrospective Analysis of Hospital Episode Statistics, Iinvoluntary Admissions Under the Mental Health Act 1983, and Number of Psychiatric Beds in England 1996–2006' (2008) 337 British Medical Journal 1837.

[15] 'Mental Health, Community Care and Human Rights in Europe: Still an Incomplete Picture?' (2007) Journal of Mental Health Law 182.

emphasis on socio-economic rights is required. This will enable those with mental illness to access and receive those services and that support which is necessary for them to function as effectively as possible within the communities in which they live.

(b) DETENTION FOR DANGEROUSNESS

As we have already seen, there has been increasing emphasis upon the use of mental health law powers, not in order to facilitate treatment, but in order to prevent harm to others. In reforming the 1983 Act, the government focused on a tiny number of patients who suffer from what it described as dangerous and severe personality disorders (DSPD).

The government was worried that the 1983 legislation placed obstacles in the way of the detention of DSPD patients, in part because it is not clear that their conditions are treatable. In the next extract, Eric Matthews argues that this is because personality disorders are not really illnesses at all, and that it is a mistake to deal with personality-disordered individuals as if they were suffering from mental illness.

Eric Matthews[16]

[T]here are some conditions classified as mental disorders...in which the harm caused by the disorder is not, or at least not primarily, to the disordered person, but to others. The various sorts of sexual deviation called 'paraphilias', such as paedophilia, represent good examples. These disorders seem to have no parallel among physical illnesses: someone who is physically ill suffers him- or herself, and any harm caused to others (eg through infection) is contingent. But a paedophile does not himself suffer from his paedophilia (except indirectly, in that he suffers social disapproval): those who suffer are the children he abuses...

Paedophiles are often said to be 'untreatable': but that is rather misleading. They do not *require* treatment in the medical sense, since their condition is not an illness, not something which causes them suffering contrary to their own wishes. It is their personality itself, and the wishes which emanate from it, which are said to be disordered. The treatment which they require is that which would prevent this disordered personality causing harm to others....

This suggests that what is legally required to deal with such cases is, again, not a 'Mental Health Act', which among other things has the unfortunate effect of reinforcing popular prejudices about the allegedly violent and dangerous character of all mentally ill people...Rather we need to address the difficult issues involved in the containment of people who behave in anti-social ways, but who are not what might be called 'rational criminals'.

So is 'personality disorder' a disease? The World Health Organizations' *International Statistical Classification of Diseases and Related Health Problems*, tenth revision (known as ICD-10), contains a definition of 'dissocial personality disorder',[17] and the Diagnostic and Statistical Manual, now known as DSM-IV, which is published by the American Psychiatric Association, and sets out diagnostic criteria for all recognized mental disorders suggests that a diagnosis of antisocial personality disorder is appropriate if three or more of the following criteria apply:

[16] 'Mental and Physical Illness—An Unsustainable Separation?' in N Eastman and J Peay (eds), *Law Without Enforcement: Integrating Mental Health and Justice* (Hart Publishing: Oxford, 1999) 47–58.

[17] ICD-10 F60.2 (WHO, 2007), available at <www.who.int>.

American Psychiatric Association DSM-IV

1. Failure to conform to social norms with respect to lawful behaviors as indicated by repeatedly performing acts that are grounds for arrest;

2. Deceitfulness, as indicated by repeatedly lying, use of aliases, or conning others for personal profit or pleasure;

3. Impulsivity or failure to plan ahead;

4. Irritability and aggressiveness, as indicated by repeated physical fights or assaults;

5. Reckless disregard for safety of self or others;

6. Consistent irresponsibility, as indicated by repeated failure to sustain consistent work behavior or honor financial obligations;

7. Lack of remorse, as indicated by being indifferent to or rationalizing having hurt, mistreated, or stolen from another.

While its inclusion in the DSM might appear to be prima facie evidence that personality disorder should be classified as a mental illness, it is worth bearing in mind that this diagnostic manual is not without its critics. Roy Porter, for example, describes how, in 1974, by a slim majority and following a threat to 'out' closet gay members, the American Psychiatric Association voted to delete homosexuality from its list of mental disorders:

Roy Porter

This notorious affair so utterly smacks of pantomime—the nullification of a major psychiatric disorder by ballot—that it is tempting to assume it must have been a one-off event, uniquely scandalous. But the whole history of the *Diagnostic and Statistical Manual* has been one of non-stop wheeling and dealing, the only difference being that the diagnostic horse-trading has usually taken place behind closed doors.[18]

Regardless of whether personality disorders are mental illnesses or not, the shift in emphasis in mental health policy towards detaining dangerous people has been heavily criticized. Psychiatrists, for example, fear that they will be forced to detain people where there is no *clinical* reason for keeping them in hospital, thus undermining their status as doctors, whose first priority is to care for the sick. Indeed, the Royal College of Psychiatrists, in their written evidence to a Joint Scrutiny Committee of an earlier draft Mental Health Bill, argued that the emphasis on public safety could cause 'significant damage' to the profession.

Royal College of Psychiatrists[19]

The draft Mental Health Bill suggests that a psychiatrist's primary role relates to public safety rather than the treatment of individual patients. This contrasts with the rest of medicine

---

[18] 'Is Mental Illness Inevitably Stigmatizing' in A Crisp (ed.), *Every Family in the Land: Understanding Prejudice and Discrimination against People with Mental Illness* (Royal Society of Medicine Press: London, 2004) 3–13.

[19] *Evidence Submitted to the Joint Committee on the Draft Mental Health Bill* (RCP: London, 2004) 31–4.

> where the General Medical Council is quite clear about the role of a doctor: 'Make the care of your patient your first concern' and 'Listen to patients and respect their views.' Surveys undertaken amongst trainees demonstrate that if there is a perception of a new law being increasingly coercive, or the role of the psychiatrist moving from that of a doctor (with roles and responsibilities similar to doctors in other branches of medicine) to a role primarily of social control this will exacerbate the recruitment difficulty....It is the College's view that significant damage will be done to the morale of the profession, the esteem in which the profession is held and, consequently, to patient care.

The Joint Scrutiny Committee was itself critical of the government's approach to reform of the Mental Health Act. Here the Chair of that committee, Lord Carlile, argues that psychiatrists should not be put in the position of 'least worst jailers'.

Alex Carlile[20]

> Naturally there is a desire at large to anticipate and limit the damage DSPD cases may cause. The stories make good news copy, lend themselves to exaggeration in terms of the mental health treatment potential available, and worst of all excite all too easily demands by elected politicians that 'something should be done', usually equated with the assumption that something can be done.
>
> The Committee was firmly of the view that where there is treatment available and a degree of therapeutic benefit, compulsory powers may well have a part to play in DSPD....However, the Committee was always clear that the Bill was fundamentally flawed and too focused on addressing public misconception about violence and mental illness, in effect creating mental health ASBOs. We had no doubt that hospitals and their clinical staff should not be placed in the position of least worst jailers without any realistic medical intervention taking place.

There are two further practical and empirical problems with the assumption that mental health law can help to reduce the risk posed by dangerous individuals. First, it presupposes that it is, in fact possible to accurately predict which patients pose a risk to others, whereas the evidence points in the opposite direction, and suggests that it is extremely difficult to accurately predict dangerousness.

The MacArthur project in the US involved 939 people, who were divided into five categories of risk and whose behaviour was monitored for the next twelve months.[21] Sixty-three individuals were categorized as high risk, of whom 48 were violent in the subsequent year. It is therefore important to remember that almost a quarter of these 'high risk' individuals were not violent, and if they had been detained under a dangerousness standard, the deprivation of their liberty would not have prevented any violence at all. In total 176 individuals in the study committed violent acts in the year following assessment, only 48 of whom would have been captured by a dangerousness standard which detained only those in risk category five.[22] To prevent the other 128 violent individuals from harming other people, individuals

---

[20] 'Legislation to Law: Rubicon or Styx?' (2005) Journal of Mental Health Law 107.

[21] J Monahan, HJ Steadman, E Silver, P Appelbaum, P Clark Robbins, EP Mulvey, LH Roth, T Grisson and S Banks, *Rethinking Risk Assessment: The MacArthur Study of Mental Disorder and Violence* (OUP: Oxford, 2001).

[22] Ibid.

who fell into the lower risk categories would have to be detained, and in these the predictions of violent behaviour were extremely unreliable. In risk category three, for example, 74 per cent of individuals were not violent in the year following assessment. If people in this risk category had been compulsorily detained in order to prevent harm to others, in most cases, the detention would have been wholly unwarranted.

Secondly, this 'public safety' approach to mental disorder presupposes that there is, in fact, a correlation between mental illness and dangerousness. Again, the evidence does not bear this out. It is also perhaps interesting that other factors that are implicated in the homicide statistics, such as alcohol use, do not lead to the same levels of public anxiety and desire for greater surveillance and control of alcohol users. In commenting on a previous draft Bill the Royal College of Psychiatrists further pointed out that not only is the emphasis on risk misguided, but that, by deterring potentially violent individuals from seeking help, this approach may in fact *increase* the danger they pose to the public.

Royal College of Psychiatrists[23]

Every death is a tragedy, for the victim, perpetrator, their family and friends and any professionals involved. The percentage of homicides committed each year by the mentally ill, as a percentage of the total is falling. The following figures are not intended to minimize the importance of each death but may help to put the matter into perspective.

For each citizen killed by a mentally ill person:

- 10 are killed by corporate manslaughter
- 20 by people who are not mentally ill
- 25 by passive smoking
- 125 by NHS hospital acquired infection.

The proposed legislation is extremely unlikely to have any impact on suicide or homicide rates. With reference to suicide, recent research demonstrated that even within the high-risk group of in-patients there would need to be 100 patients detained unnecessarily in order to prevent one suicide. With regard to homicide, [Crawford] has shown that with a predictive test with a sensitivity and specificity of 0.8 (far better than anything available currently) 5000 people would need to be detained to prevent one homicide. Szmukler has shown that if the predictive test became even better (0.9) this would still require the detention of 2000 people to prevent each homicide. This emphasises that prevention of homicide and suicide can only ever arise as a secondary benefit from improved mental health care for a population and never via prediction per se of such events.

The starting point in risk reduction is encouraging patients to seek help and talk about their thoughts and feelings... It is hard to believe that potential patients will not be deterred from the services if they know that psychiatrists will have a duty to enforce treatment on them, not only in hospital but also in the community, even when they are perfectly able to make decisions for themselves. Patient avoidance will certainly limit effective intervention.

Although, note that Peter Bartlett argues that compulsory psychiatric treatment is always inevitably about social control.

---

23 *Evidence Submitted to the Joint Committee on the Draft Mental Health Bill* (RCP: London, 2004) 31–4.

Peter Bartlett[24]

> The reality is that psychiatric treatment in any situation other than by free and competent consent of the patient is by its nature about social control. The vast bulk of people currently confined in psychiatric facilities are categorised as 'mentally ill', and for them there is no requirement of treatability. Most of them are treatable of course, but that does not remove the social control function. They tend to be admitted when their behaviour becomes socially unacceptable; and they are treated until it is no longer unacceptable. Alternatively, they are admitted when they are perceived to be unable to cope or function in society, and treated until they can be discharged, able to do so. When such behavioural features are significant factors in clinical decision-making, doctors are acting as agents of social control...
>
> The proper question is therefore not how psychiatrists can cease to be agents of social control: they cannot. The better question, to be asked bluntly, is when the social control is justified.

3   WHAT IS MENTAL ILLNESS?

Mental health problems are common: it is estimated than one in six adults in the UK will suffer from some sort of mental disorder each year. Some mental disorders are mild and relatively easy to live with, whereas others can be fatal. Mental illness is often more difficult to diagnose than physical illness. Unlike the X-rays, blood tests, and CT scans that are used to diagnose physical conditions like broken bones, HIV, and cancer, it can be much harder to establish precisely what is wrong with a person's mental health. While there are some who believe that brain imaging techniques may lead to more accurate and objective diagnoses, commonly psychiatrists still attempt to diagnose mental disorders by listening to the patient's description of her symptoms and observing her behaviour.

Insofar as illness means 'abnormal functioning', in order to define mental illness it might first be necessary to have some idea of what we consider to be *normal* mental wellbeing. Yet as we all know, this would be incredibly difficult to pin down. Feeling sad from time to time is normal, and is certainly not evidence of mental illness. On the other hand, depression can be an extremely debilitating condition which is capable of interfering with its sufferers' ability to lead a normal life at least as much as any physical illness.

Because mental health law can sanction involuntary detention and compulsory treatment, including treatment with powerful mind-altering chemicals, it is obviously crucial that there should be clear criteria defining the conditions that may trigger these draconian measures. It is also important to remember that labelling someone as mentally disordered will often carry more stigma, and result in more discriminatory treatment, than the diagnosis of a physical condition, so again a clear definition and accurate diagnosis are especially important.

(a)   DEFINING MENTAL DISORDER

Under the 1983 Act, as amended, the statutory definition of mental disorder is contained in section 1(2):

---

[24] 'The Test of Compulsion in Mental Health Law: Capacity, Therapeutic Benefit and Dangerousness as Possible Criteria' (2003) 11 Medical Law Review 326–52.

Mental Health Act 1983 section 1

1(2) In this Act—

'mental disorder' means any disorder or disability of the mind;

(2A) But a person with learning disability shall not be considered by reason of that disability to be–

(a) suffering from mental disorder...

(b) requiring treatment in hospital for mental disorder....

unless that disability is associated with abnormally aggressive or seriously irresponsible conduct on his part.

(3) Dependence on alcohol or drugs is not considered to be a disorder or disability of the mind for the purposes of subsection (2) above.

(4) In subsection (2A) above, 'learning disability' means a state of arrested or incomplete development of the mind which includes significant impairment of intelligence and social functioning.

The 2007 reforms substantially broadened section 1(2)'s definition of mental disorder. Any disorder or disability of the mind, other than dependence on alcohol or drugs, is covered.

Originally, the legislation specifically stated that no one should be treated as mentally disordered by reason only of 'promiscuity or other immoral conduct' or 'sexual deviancy'. The reason for this was that in the past people who did not conform to accepted moral standards were commonly confined to asylums: the Mental Deficiency Act 1913, for example, permitted the detention of unmarried women who gave birth while on poor relief, on the grounds that becoming pregnant outside of marriage amounted to evidence of moral depravity and mental defectiveness.

This exception was removed by the 2007 reforms because the government believed it placed an obstacle in the way of detaining sex offenders with personality disorders, since the implication was that someone should not be treated as mentally disodered where the principal manifestation of their personality disorder was their sexual deviancy. If paedophiles were believed to be at high risk of re-offending after their release from prison, the government thought that mental health legislation should facilitate rather than prevent their continued detention.

It is important to remember that simply being defined as mentally disordered does not necessarily mean that someone will be subject to the formal powers contained in the Bill: rather, it is a necessary but certainly not a sufficient condition. The other conditions are described in the next section.

4 ADMISSION TO THE MENTAL HEALTH SYSTEM

Over 180,000 people are admitted to NHS hospitals for mental disorders each year. While the proportion of these who are compulsorily detained or 'sectioned' has increased in recent years, it continues to be a minority. Because compulsory detention poses a greater threat to a patient's civil liberties than informal admission, both academic commentary and litigation has tended to focus upon the relatively small group of formally admitted patients. When we take into account the fact that most people who suffer from mental illness do not receive inpatient treatment in hospital, it becomes clear that compulsorily detained patients represent a tiny percentage of people living with mental health problems. Interestingly, then, 'mental health law' has little application to the vast majority of mentally ill individuals in society.

There are now three routes to admission to the mental health system (previously there were two): informal admission; detention under the *Bournewood* 'deprivation of liberty' procedure, and formal detention.

(a) VOLUNTARY ADMISSION UNDER THE 1983 ACT

Under section 131 of the 1983 Act, anyone who 'requires treatment for mental disorder' (defined in section 1(2) considered above) may be admitted informally.

Mental Health Act 1983 section 131

131(1) Nothing in this Act shall be construed as preventing a patient who requires treatment for mental disorder from being admitted to any hospital or [registered establishment] in pursuance of arrangements made in that behalf and without any application, order or direction rendering him liable to be detained under this Act, or from remaining in any hospital or [registered establishment] in pursuance of such arrangements after he has ceased to be so liable to be detained.

(2) In the case of a minor who has attained the age of 16 years and is capable of expressing his own wishes, any such arrangements as are mentioned in subsection (1) above may be made, carried out and determined even though there are one or more persons who have parental responsibility for him (within the meaning of the Children Act 1989).

Usually, informal admission is possible because the patient herself is willingly seeking treatment, and, where this is the case, there are clear advantages in avoiding the use of formal powers. If a patient's liberty is not restricted, it is less likely that her relationship with her doctors will be compromised. Voluntarily admitted patients may be more likely than detained patients to cooperate with their treatment plan, and may find the experience of admission to hospital less distressing.

Of course, it is possible that the patient will come under pressure, perhaps from her family, to agree to informal admission, and, in practice, she may not have anywhere else to go. It is also possible for an informally admitted patient to subsequently be formally detained under section 5 of the 1983 Act. Once in hospital, as Phil Fennell explains in the next extract, informally admitted patients are not, therefore, necessarily free to leave.

Phil Fennell[25]

Even if there were an unlimited right for informal patients to leave hospital, to speak of mentally incapacitated patients having it makes little sense. There may be nowhere else capable of providing the care which the patient needs, he may have no home to go to and be too dependent to survive in sheltered accommodation. Any hospital or nursing home accepting responsibility for looking after mentally incapacitated informal patients thereby

[25] 'Doctor Knows Best? Therapeutic Detention under Common Law, the Mental Health Act and the European Convention' (1998) 6 Medical Law Review 322–53.

assumes a duty of care towards them. That duty of care extends to preventing them from leaving when to do so would put them at risk. Not being detained does not make an informal patient 'freer'.

In the next extract, Michael Cavadino draws upon his interviews with patients at an NHS psychiatric hospital, which he calls 'Fardale', in order to examine whether informal patients' stays in hospital are genuinely voluntary.

Michael Cavadino[26]

[T]here is little empirical evidence that patients are typically or routinely coerced into *entering* hospital in the first place against their express wishes, although it does happen sometimes. But what about after admission? It is possible for patients to enter hospital voluntarily or acquiescently but at some later stage to be prevented from leaving, or be subjected to some other forcible control, which would normally be incompatible with informal admission. This can happen if patients are restrained from leaving hospital by force or threat of force; or led to believe that they are not free to leave; or locked in a side-room; or denied access to their clothes; or given medical treatment such as drugs by force or threat of force; or if the patient demands discharge and is not allowed to take it. Such occurrences were by no means uncommon in Fardale...

On the question of whether they would like to leave hospital, a substantial minority of the informal patients (38 per cent) said that they would... So why were so many patients still in hospital informally who would rather leave?... Of the informal patients who expressed a desire to leave, 14 per cent did indeed believe that they were not free to leave hospital... But in most cases, patients perceived other constraints as being more important. Foremost among these other constraints was lack of accommodation, or suitable accommodation, outside the hospital...

It seems, then, that although there are indeed *some* informal patients who stay in hospital because they feel coerced to do so, factors such as lack of accommodation are of much greater importance than the fear of legal or extra-legal force—certainly in the eyes of the patients themselves.

There are other times when patients are informally admitted to hospital not because they have willingly gone into hospital, but because they are too incapacitated to express a preference. The Percy Commission, whose Report formed the basis of the Mental Heath Act 1959, had recommended that compulsory powers should not be used for such patients:

We consider compulsion and detention quite unnecessary for a large number, probably the great majority, of the patients at present cared for in mental deficiency hospitals, most of whom are childlike and prepared to accept whatever arrangements are made for them. There is no more need to have power to detain these patients in hospital than in their own homes or any other place which they have no wish to leave.[27]

[26] *Mental Health Law in Context* (Dartmouth: Aldershot, 1989).
[27] *Report of the Royal Commission on the Law Relating to Mental Illness and Mental Deficiency 1954–1957* (1957) (Cmnd 169) 100–1, paras 289–91.

Notice that section 131 states that nothing in the Act prevents a patient from '*being admitted*' (my emphasis) to hospital, implying that there is no need for informal patients to actively and voluntarily admit themselves. Rather, the decision to admit the patient to hospital can be taken by others, but the patient's compliance means that compulsory detention is unnecessary.

While informal admission in such circumstances might be convenient for the hospital staff, it potentially leaves the patient without any of the formal protections which apply to compulsorily detained patients. This issue arose in the *Bournewood* case.

In *Bournewood*, the patient, HL, was a 48-year-old man, who was autistic and profoundly mentally retarded. He had been living with paid carers for a number of years, but on a visit to a day centre, had become agitated and been admitted to hospital informally. His carers were denied access to him, on the grounds that he might want to leave if he saw them.

If HL had tried to leave, it was admitted that he would have been compulsorily detained, but the NHS trust argued that, so long as HL was not trying to leave, he could continue to be kept in hospital informally under section 131. A majority (3:2) in the House of Lords agreed with them,[28] but the ECtHR took a different view and found that HL had been detained, and that the lack of protections in place for people in his position did not satisfy the requirements of Article 5(4), Right to Liberty and Security:

Article 5(4) Everyone who is deprived of his liberty by arrest or detention shall be entitled to take proceedings by which the lawfulness of his detention shall be decided speedily by a court and his release ordered if the detention is not lawful.

HL v United Kingdom[29]

Judgment of the ECtHR

[T]he concrete situation was that the applicant was under continuous supervision and control and was not free to leave. Any suggestion to the contrary was, in the Court's view, fairly described by Lord Steyn [dissenting] as 'stretching credulity to breaking point' and as a 'fairy tale'...The Court therefore concludes that the applicant was 'deprived of his liberty' within the meaning of Article 5 § 1 of the Convention....

It is recalled that an individual cannot be deprived of his liberty on the basis of unsoundness of mind unless three minimum conditions are satisfied: he must reliably be shown to be of unsound mind; the mental disorder must be of a kind or degree warranting compulsory confinement; and the validity of continued confinement depends upon the persistence of such a disorder...

[T]he Court finds striking the lack of any fixed procedural rules by which the admission and detention of compliant incapacitated persons is conducted. The contrast between this dearth of regulation and the extensive network of safeguards applicable to psychiatric committals covered by the 1983 Act is, in the Court's view, significant.

In particular and most obviously, the Court notes the lack of any formalised admission procedures which indicate who can propose admission, for what reasons and on the basis of

---

[28] *R v Bournewood Community and Mental Health NHS Trust, ex parte L* [1998] 3 WLR 107.
[29] *(Application no 45508/99)* 5 Oct 2004.

what kind of medical and other assessments and conclusions. There is no requirement to fix the exact purpose of admission (for example, for assessment or for treatment) and, consistently, no limits in terms of time, treatment or care attach to that admission. Nor is there any specific provision requiring a continuing clinical assessment of the persistence of a disorder warranting detention. The nomination of a representative of a patient who could make certain objections and applications on his or her behalf is a procedural protection accorded to those committed involuntarily under the 1983 Act and which would be of equal importance for patients who are legally incapacitated and have, as in the present case, extremely limited communication abilities.

As a result of the lack of procedural regulation and limits, the Court observes that the hospital's health care professionals assumed full control of the liberty and treatment of a vulnerable incapacitated individual solely on the basis of their own clinical assessments completed as and when they considered fit: as Lord Steyn remarked, this left 'effective and unqualified control' in their hands. While the Court does not question the good faith of those professionals or that they acted in what they considered to be the applicant's best interests, the very purpose of procedural safeguards is to protect individuals against any 'misjudgments and professional lapses'....

The Court therefore finds that this absence of procedural safeguards fails to protect against arbitrary deprivations of liberty on grounds of necessity and, consequently, to comply with the essential purpose of Article 5 § 1 of the Convention. On this basis, the Court finds that there has been a violation of Article 5 § 1 of the Convention.

As a result of this decision, the government had to put measures in place in order to fill what was known as the 'Bournewood gap': namely the lack of any process for challenging the de facto detention of patients who are compliant and incapacitated. It did not do so especially speedily, however. Three years after the ECtHR's judgment in the Bournewood case, provisions to amend the Mental Capacity Act, to provide a mechanism by which deprivation of liberty could be authorized, were included in the Mental Health Act 2007.

It is also worth noting that during the Bournewood litigation the Department of Health had warned that a finding that there had been a deprivation of liberty would affect approximately 48,000 individuals, with obvious cost implications if formal measures had to be put in place to sanction their detention. However, in the years following the ECtHR's judgment, there was not a significant increase in the number of applications to detain involuntary patients under section 3. There are several possible explanations for this: first, that the Department of Health's estimate was wildly inaccurate, and in fact there were hardly any patients who were detained *de facto* in the same way as HL (this seems unlikely); secondly, that following the ECtHR's judgment, the living conditions of people like HL were modified to ensure that their freedom to leave was real rather than illusory. Since the view was that patients in HL's position should *not* be free to leave hospital, again this seems improbable. Lucy Scott-Moncrieff has argued that a third explanation is more likely: namely that tens of thousands of compliant incapacitated patients continued to be unlawfully detained in nursing homes, without any of the protections necessary to satisfy Article 5(4).[30]

---

[30] Lucy Scott-Moncrieff, 'Two Steps Forward, One Step Back' (2007) Journal of Mental Health Law 107.

(b) MCA 'DEPRIVATION OF LIBERTY' PROCEDURE

The Mental Capacity Act (MCA) deprivation of liberty procedure only applies when someone is deprived of their liberty. As we saw in the previous chapter, the restraint of a patient who lacks capacity is possible under the MCA and will not necessarily amount to a deprivation of liberty, such that an authorization needs to be sought. The difference between a restriction and deprivation of liberty is therefore important, but it may be a fine one, and a question of degree.

In *JE v DE* Munby J had to decide whether DE had been deprived of his liberty. He said that the essential question was not whether DE had been locked up or restrained *within* the care homes X and Y, but whether he was, in fact, free to leave them in order to return to live with his wife, JE, who herself had some mental health problems and had at one point left him partially dressed on a chair on the pavement and called the police.

JE v DE[31]

Munby J

I accept that DE had within the X home, and has had and has within the Y home, a very substantial degree of freedom, just as he had and has a very substantial degree of contact with the outside world.... DE has never been subjected to the same invasive degree of control within the X home and the Y home, let alone the same complete and effective control within the two homes, to which HL was apparently subjected....

But the crucial question in this case, as it seems to me, is not so much whether (and, if so, to what extent) DE's freedom or liberty was or is curtailed *within* the institutional setting. The fundamental issue in this case, in my judgment, is whether DE was deprived of his liberty to leave the X home and whether DE has been and is deprived of his liberty to leave the Y home. And when I refer to leaving the X home and the Y home I do not mean leaving for the purpose of some trip or outing approved by SCC or by those managing the institution; I mean leaving in the sense of removing himself permanently in order to live where and with whom he chooses, specifically removing himself to live at home with JE...

I agree, therefore, with [counsel] when they identify the crucial issue here as being, just as it was in *HL v United Kingdom*, whether DE was or was not, is or is not, 'free to leave'. And I agree with them when they submit that DE was not and is not 'free to leave', and was and is, in that sense, completely under the control of SCC [Surrey County Council], because...it was and is SCC who decides the essential matters of where DE can live, whether he can leave and whether he can be with JE....

SCC's motives may be of the purest, but in my judgment, SCC has been and is continuing to deprive DE of his liberty.

In contrast, in *LLBC v TG* Munby J decided that the decision to obtain a court order to deliver a 78-year-old man, with dementia and cognititve impairment, to a residential care home did not amount to a deprivation of liberty.

---

[31] [2006] EWHC 3459 (Fam).

LLBC v TG[32]

Munby J

- Towerbridge was an ordinary care home where only ordinary restrictions of liberty applied;
- The family were able to visit TG on a largely unrestricted basis and were entitled to remove him from the home for outings;
- TG was personally compliant and expressed himself as happy at Towerbridge. He had lived in a local authority care home for over three years and was objectively content with his situation there;
- There was no occasion when he was objectively deprived of his liberty.

Whilst I agree that the circumstances of the present case may be near the borderline between mere restriction of liberty and Art 5 detention, I have come to the conclusion that, looked at as a whole and having regard to all the relevant circumstances, the placement of TG in Towerbridge falls short of engaging Art 5.

Guidance on what the deprivation of liberty entails is now contained in an addendum to the Mental Capacity Act Code of Practice:

Mental Capacity Act Code of Practice para 2.5[33]

Deprivation of liberty safeguards

2.5 The ECtHR and UK courts have determined a number of cases about deprivation of liberty. Their judgments indicate that the following factors can be relevant to identifying whether steps taken involve more than restraint and amount to a deprivation of liberty. It is ivmportant to remember that this list is not exclusive; other factors may arise in future in particular cases.

- Restraint is used, including sedation, to admit a person to an institution where that person is resisting admission.
- Staff exercise complete and effective control over the care and movement of a person for a significant period.
- Staff exercise control over assessments, treatment, contacts and residence.
- A decision has been taken by the institution that the person will not be released into the care of others, or permitted to live elsewhere, unless the staff in the institution consider it appropriate.
- A request by carers for a person to be discharged to their care is refused.
- The person is unable to maintain social contacts because of restrictions placed on their access to other people.
- The person loses autonomy because they are under continuous supervision and control.

---

[32] [2007] EWHC 2640 (Fam).

[33] (2008) Code of Practice to supplement the main Mental Capacity Act 2005 Code of Practice, available at <www.dh.gov.uk>.

The 2007 Mental Health Act amended the MCA to make provision for the lawful deprivation of liberty for people with mental disorders who lack capacity, where detention is in their best interests. The new Schedule 1A fleshes out six requirements, which must be met before an authorization for deprivation of liberty may be given:

Mental Capacity Act 2005 Schedule 1A Part 3

(a) the age requirement: the patient must be at least 18 years old.

(b) the mental health requirement: the patient must be suffering from a mental disorder within the meaning of the MHA.

(c) the mental capacity requirement: the patient must lack capacity.

(d) the best interests requirement;

- it is in the best interests of the relevant person to be deprived of liberty

- it is necessary for them to be deprived of liberty in order to prevent harm to themselves, and

- deprivation of liberty is a proportionate response to the likelihood of the relevant person suffering harm and the seriousness of that harm.

(e) the eligibility requirement: they must not be detained under the Act or subject to restrictions on their freedom in the community.

(f) the no refusals requirement: there must not be a valid and applicable advance refusal of the treatment for which the deprivation of liberty authorization of liberty is sought.

Deprivation of liberty, thus, has to be (a) necessary to protect P from harm, (b) proportionate, and (c) in P's best interests. There is a duty to appoint a representative, who must be someone that the P trusts and feels comfortable with. If there is no-one to act as their representative, an IMCA (see Chapter 5) must be appointed 'to represent and support the relevant person in all matters relating to the deprivation of liberty safeguards, including, if appropriate, triggering a review, using an organization's complaints procedure on the person's behalf or making an application to the Court of Protection'.[34]

Authorization of the deprivation of liberty is done by 'the supervisory' body, which will normally be the relevant PCT. Applications will be made by the NHS body responsible for the running of the hospital where P is being treated, and will last for twelve months. Under section 21A of the Mental Capacity Act, the authorization is then subject to review by the Court of Protection, which can vary or terminate the authorization. It is also possible for applications to be made to the Court of Protection by the patient or someone acting on their behalf.

As the Kings Fund point out, the provisions that have been incorporated into the MCA are extremely complex. This may also prove to be extraordinarily burdensome, if tens of thousands of incapacitated patients have to be assessed to determine whether they have been deprived of their liberty, and if they have, authorizations sought:

The Deprivation of Liberty Safeguards (DOLS) requirements will involve the assessment of possibly tens of thousands of people currently living in care homes and in hospital, and the

---

[34] Ibid.

assessment process is complicated, particularly if the person has fluctuating capacity. It may require test cases in the courts before a consistent approach to assessments is achieved.[35]

It would be a mistake to assume that this MCA process applies to all incapacitated patients who need to be detained in hospital. Incapacitated patients can also be detained under the normal Mental Health Act powers of detention, described in the next section. The MCA Code of Practice gives a number of examples of times when MHA powers will be more appropriate.

Mental Capacity Act Code of Practice para 13.12[36]

13.12 It might be necessary to consider using the MHA rather than the MCA if:

- it is not possible to give the person the care or treatment they need without carrying out an action that might deprive them of their liberty
- the person needs treatment that cannot be given under the MCA (for example, because the person has made a valid and applicable advance decision to refuse all or part of that treatment)
- the person may need to be restrained in a way that is not allowed under the MCA
- it is not possible to assess or treat the person safely or effectively without treatment being compulsory (perhaps because the person is expected to regain capacity to consent, but might then refuse to give consent)
- the person lacks capacity to decide on some elements of the treatment but has capacity to refuse a vital part of it—and they have done so, or
- there is some other reason why the person might not get the treatment they need, and they or somebody else might suffer harm as a result.

(c) INVOLUNTARY ADMISSION UNDER THE 1983 ACT

The 1983 Act provides for the compulsory admission of patients for assessment under section 2, and for treatment under section 3. At any one time approximately 15,000 patients are detained for treatment in hospital.

Mental Health Act 1983 sections 2 and 3

2(2) An application for admission for assessment may be made in respect of a patient on the grounds that—

(a) he is suffering from mental disorder of a nature or degree which warrants the detention of the patient in a hospital for assessment (or for assessment followed by medical treatment) for at least a limited period; and

(b) he ought to be so detained in the interests of his own health or safety or with a view to the protection of other persons.

---

[35] Kings Fund Briefing *Mental Health Act 2007* (2008), available at <www.kingsfund.org.uk/>.
[36] (2007), available at <www.dca.gov.uk>.

(3) An application for admission for assessment shall be founded on the written recommendations in the prescribed form of two registered medical practitioners, including in each case a statement that in the opinion of the practitioner the conditions set out in subsection (2) above are complied with.

(4) . . . a patient admitted to hospital in pursuance of an application for admission for assessment may be detained for a period not exceeding 28 days beginning with the day on which he is admitted, but shall not be detained after the expiration of that period unless before it has expired he has become liable to be detained by virtue of a subsequent application, order or direction under the following provisions of this Act.

3(2) An application for admission for treatment may be made in respect of a patient on the grounds that—

(a) he is suffering from [mental disorder] of a nature or degree which makes it appropriate for him to receive medical treatment in a hospital; and

(b) it is necessary for the health or safety of the patient or for the protection of other persons that he should receive such treatment and it cannot be provided unless he is detained under this section [and]

(c) appropriate medical treatment is available for him.

(3) An application for admission for treatment shall be founded on the written recommendations in the prescribed form of two registered medical practitioners, including in each case a statement that in the opinion of the practitioner the conditions set out in subsection (2) above are complied with; and each such recommendation shall include—...

(b) a statement of the reasons for that opinion so far as it relates to the conditions set out in paragraph (c) of that subsection, specifying whether other methods of dealing with the patient are available and, if so, why they are not appropriate.

(4) In this Act, references to appropriate medical treatment, in relation to a person suffering from mental disorder, are references to medical treatment which is appropriate in his case, taking into account the nature and degree of the mental disorder and all other circumstances of his case.

Before we flesh out the meaning of sections 2 and 3, it is worth noting that there are a few other routes into the mental health system. In an emergency, a patient can be admitted under section 4 on the basis of one medical recommendation that 'it is of urgent necessity for the patient to be admitted and detained under section 2'.

Under section 136, if a police officer finds 'a person who appears to him to be suffering from mental disorder and to be in immediate need of care or control' in a public place, he can be removed to a place of safety for 72 hours 'for the purpose of enabling him to be examined by a registered medical practitioner and to be interviewed by an Approved Mental Health Professional (AMHP) and of making any necessary arrangements for his treatment or care'.

If the person's behaviour poses 'an unmanageably high risk to other patients, staff or users of a healthcare setting', a police station may be used as a place of safety, but para 10.21 of the Mental Health Act Code of Practice suggests that this should be exceptional, and that 'it is preferable for a person thought to be suffering from a mental disorder to be detained in a hospital or other healthcare setting where mental health services are provided'. Despite this, it is clear that police cells are, in fact, used as places of safety more often than hospitals. A recent study found that 11,500 people per year were detained in police custody under section 136, compared with 5900 in hospital. This has been criticized by Ian Bynoe, an Independent Police Complaints Commissioner.

Ian Bynoe[37]

Police custody is an unsuitable environment for someone with mental illness and may make their condition worse, particularly if they are not dealt with quickly and appropriately and don't receive the care they need. The continued use of cells not only diverts police resources from fighting crime but criminalises behaviour that is not a crime. A police cell should only be used when absolutely necessary, for example, when someone is violent and not as a convenience.

Finally, under section 5 a voluntarily admitted patient can subsequently be compulsorily detained for up to 72 hours in order to prevent him from leaving hospital, after which continued detention is possible only if the formal powers in section 3 are invoked.

(1) The Process of Applying for Formal Powers

While applications for section 2 and 3 orders can be made by the patient's nearest relative, most are made by an AMHP, usually a social worker, and the application must be supported by two medical practitioners, one of whom must be approved under section 12(2) of the Act, 'as having special experience in the diagnosis or treatment of mental disorder', and one of whom must have 'previous acquaintance with the patient'.

Under section 2, an individual can be detained for assessment for up to 28 days, after which the patient must either be: (a) discharged; (b) admitted as an informal patient; or (c) detained under section 3. Under section 3, individuals can be admitted for treatment, initially for up to six months, and this can then be renewed for a further six months. Thereafter, the individual can be detained for up to a year, with the further possibility of annual renewal.

Because the compulsory detention of an individual represents a fundamental violation of her freedom of movement, it must be justified according to clear and defensible criteria. These have tended to consist of a combination of preventing the individual from harming herself and/or others, and enabling her to receive treatment.

For example, under sections 2 and 3, the person must be suffering from a mental disorder of, 'a nature or degree which warrants admission to hospital' (section 2), or, 'which makes it appropriate for him to receive medical treatment in a hospital' (section 3), both of which have a therapeutic intent. But under section 2, detention is permissible if the patient 'ought to be detained' to protect the health or safety of the patient, or to protect other persons, or under section 3, detention must be 'necessary for the health or safety of the patient or for the protection of other persons'.

---

[37] Quoted in Andrew Cole, 'Overuse of Police Cells for Detaining People with Mental Health Problems "Intolerable"' (2008) 337 British Medical Journal 1635.

The need to be in hospital means that these powers should only be used where the intention is that the patient will actually become an inpatient. It would not be possible to use section 3 where the intention is, in fact, to immediately discharge the patient under a Community Treatment Order (see below). It is also necessary to prove that the treatment cannot be provided *unless* the patient is detained, so where it might be possible to provide treatment in the community, section 3 is not satisfied. This is sometimes referred to as the 'least restrictive alternative' principle.

In the next extract, Jill Peay further suggests that the patient's 'need' to be in hospital may arise not because of the nature of her illness, but as a result of her *attitude* towards treatment.

Jill Peay[38]

> Curiously, in clinical terms, 'the need to be in hospital' may not arise. This is not because the illness *can only* be treated in hospital, but because the patient will not *accept* treatment where he is (in the community). Since the only route by which *compulsory* treatment can be legally achieved is via the Act, and since the Act only allows compulsory treatment *in hospital*, such treatment can only be achieved via admission to hospital. Hence, the person is perceived as needing to be in hospital because of his/her attitude to treatment, which may or may not be determined by the illness itself.

(2) The 'Treatability' Requirement

The at first sight innocuous condition for detention in section 3(d), namely that 'appropriate medical treatment is available' in fact represents one of the most contested aspects of the 2007 reforms. Under the original legislation, which contained some special rules for patients with personality disorders (then described as psychopathy), detention was only possible if there was treatment which was 'likely to alleviate or prevent a deterioration of his condition'.

This was known as the 'treatability' requirement, and was, in the eyes of some, problematic because, as we saw earlier, it is not clear that personality disorders are, in fact, treatable. If someone is suffering from an untreatable personality disorder, then, under the old law, it would be difficult to detain them under section 3. Making it easier to detain people with 'dangerous and severe personality disorders' (DSPD) was a primary focus of the government's reform agenda, which meant abandoning or modifying the treatability requirement.

In the next extract, Robert Francis QC, who chaired the inquiry into the circumstances leading up to murders of Lin and Megan Russell, queries the logic behind this move. He suggests first that there is no evidence that Michael Stone was, in fact, denied treatment on the basis of his disorder being untreatable, and, secondly, that powers of indefinite detention under the Criminal Justice Act would be a better response to fears about an individual's dangerousness than detention under the Mental Health Act. Admittedly, the powers of indefinite detention under the Criminal Justice Act only arise for individuals who have previously been convicted of offences, but Francis suggests that this will, in practice, rarely present a difficulty.

---

[38] *Decisions and Dilemmas: Working with Mental Health Law* (Hart Publishing: Oxford, 2003).

Robert Francis[39]

> [G]overnmental thinking still appears to be informed by a belief that persons with person-
> ality disorders are denied treatment which is available and effective and is more than mere
> detention. It is not within the expertise of the writer to say whether or not such a state of
> affairs exists, but the facts of Mr Stone's case may be instructive. He was not denied such
> treatment as was available, apart from, for a time, in-patient drug detoxification. In any event
> this was treatment which he appeared to be seeking: therefore detention to give it would not
> have been appropriate. Further, not only was he offered this in the end, drug misuse is not a
> ground on which to diagnose mental disorder....
>
> The perceived difficulty in relation to dangerous individuals who have not been convicted
> of offences is a somewhat artificial construct. It is difficult to believe that there are many
> persons who are known to the statutory agencies to be so dangerous that they would war-
> rant detention to protect the public, but who have not been convicted of at least one serious
> offence. Mr Stone was certainly not such a person: he had more than one conviction for a
> serious offence and was regarded within the criminal justice system as being dangerous. In
> regard to such cases the sentencing powers and obligations under the Criminal Justice Act
> 2003 provide a more fruitful means of reassuring the public...
>
> A risk of using the mental health legislation for non-clinical purposes is that the hospitals
> will become as full as the prisons are now, with the consequent adverse effect on the care
> and supervision of those already within that system, to the detriment not only of the patients
> themselves, but to the public who deserve properly focussed and informed protection.

During the protracted battles over its previous draft Bills, the government's intention to
remove or significantly dilute the treatability requirement was the subject of sustained criticism by psychiatrists, and the Mental Health Alliance, an umbrella group of mental health
professionals and patients, set up to campaign for better mental health legislation. The reason this issue is so important is that detaining people who cannot be treated, just in order to
protect others, is preventative detention, and psychiatrists argued that their role is to *treat
people who are unwell*, and not to lock up antisocial people.

Section 3(d) was not the government's preferred formulation. A previous draft Bill contained an even weaker requirement that 'appropriate treatment is available'. Critics of this
provision pointed out that it did not specify that there has to be any therapeutic element to
the treatment. There were concerns that simply locking someone up might be 'appropriate
treatment'. The government's proposal was defeated in the House of Lords, and the compromise, which was finally agreed is that appropriate *medical* treatment has to be available.
This receives a further definition in section 145(4).

Mental Health Act 1983 section 145

> 145(4) Any reference in this Act to medical treatment, in relation to mental disorder, shall be
> construed as a reference to medical treatment the purpose of which is to alleviate, or prevent
> a worsening of, the disorder or one or more of its symptoms or manifestations.

The key difference introduced by the 2007 reforms is that while the *purpose* of treatment must be to alleviate or prevent a deterioration, it no longer needs to be *likely* to actually

[39] 'The Michael Stone Inquiry—A Reflection' (2007) Journal of Mental Health Law 41.

have this effect. Also new is the requirement that appropriate treatment is actually available to a patient, and if it is not, detention cannot be justified.

The Code of Practice gives more detailed guidance on what appropriate treatment means. It specifically spells out that locking someone up is not appropriate medical treatment, but note that it also indicates that the test will be satisfied if treatment like cognitive behavioural therapy (for personality disorders) is available, even if the patient in fact refuses to engage with it. 'Talking cures', by definition, will not work without the patient's cooperation, and so the Code clearly envisages that the 'availability of treatment' criterion for detention will be satisfied, even if there is, in practice, no chance that the patient will actually receive any treatment at all.

Mental Health Act Code of Practice paras 6.6–6.7, 6.15–6.17, and 6.19 [40]

6.6 It should never be assumed that any disorders, or any patients, are inherently or inevitably untreatable. Nor should it be assumed that likely difficulties in achieving long-term and sustainable change in a person's underlying disorder make medical treatment to help manage their condition and the behaviours arising from it either inappropriate or unnecessary.

6.7 The purpose of the appropriate medical treatment test is to ensure that no-one is detained (or remains detained) for treatment, or is an SCT patient, unless they are actually to be offered medical treatment for their mental disorder....

6.15 Medical treatment which aims merely to prevent a disorder worsening is unlikely, in general, to be appropriate in cases where normal treatment approaches would aim (and be expected) to alleviate the patient's condition significantly. For some patients with persistent mental disorders, however, management of the undesirable effects of their disorder may be all that can realistically be hoped for.

6.16 Appropriate medical treatment does not have to involve medication or individual or group psychological therapy—although it very often will. There may be patients whose particular circumstances mean that treatment may be appropriate even though it consists only of nursing and specialist day-to-day care under the clinical supervision of an approved clinician, in a safe and secure therapeutic environment with a structured regime.

6.17 Simply detaining someone—even in a hospital—does not constitute medical treatment....

6.19 ...[P]sychological therapies and other forms of medical treatments which, to be effective, require the patient's co-operation are not automatically inappropriate simply because a patient does not currently wish to engage with them. Such treatments can potentially remain appropriate and available as long as it continues to be clinically suitable to offer them and they would be provided if the patient agreed to engage.

(3) The Use of Compulsory Powers in Practice

There is evidence that the proportion of patients who are admitted compulsorily is increasing. In their survey of admissions from 1996–2006, Keown *et al.* found a number of significant trends. While admission of people with depression and dementia had decreased, involuntary admissions of people with psychotic and substance abuse disorders

---

[40] (2008), available at <www.dh.gov.uk>.

had increased, and there was an increasing tendency for PCTs to pay for patients to be admitted to private care facilities.

Patrick Keown, Gavin Mercer, and Jan Scott[41]

The number of involuntary admissions for mental disorders in England per annum increased by 20% from 1996 to 2006, whereas the total number of admissions and number of NHS psychiatric beds decreased. Reductions in admissions have largely been confined to patients with depression, learning disability, or dementia....Psychiatric inpatient care changed considerably from 1996 to 2006, with more involuntary patients admitted to fewer NHS beds and increasing proportions of involuntary patients admitted to private facilities. The decrease in acute general adult admissions has been confined to voluntary patients with depression. The inpatient case mix has shifted further towards psychotic and substance misuse disorders, which has changed the milieu on inpatient psychiatric wards.

This latter point is reinforced in the Twelfth Biennial Report of the Mental Health Act Commission (MHAC):

The busy acute wards that we visit appear to be tougher and scarier places than we saw a decade ago. Something needs to be done about this. It is scandalous that we are forcing vulnerable people onto mental health wards that are frightening and dangerous places.[42]

A further and consistent trend in the use of powers under the Mental Health Act has been the over-representation of black people, both in mental health admissions, and in the use of compulsory powers. In Flannigan *et al.*'s study of admissions in Southwark, 23 per cent of the hospital psychiatric population was African-Caribbean, which represented twice the proportion in the general population.[43] Moreover, this minority ethnic group was also much more likely to be compulsorily admitted to the mental health system. White people were admitted informally in 80 per cent of cases; admitted under compulsory powers in 17 per cent of cases, and in an emergency in three per cent of cases.[44] In contrast, black people from the Caribbean were admitted informally in 55 per cent of cases; were compulsorily admitted in 35 per cent of cases, and were admitted using emergency powers in 10 per cent of cases.[45] These findings have been confirmed by many other studies. In 2002, for example, Audini and Lelliott found that African-Caribbean black people were six times more likely to be sectioned than white people.[46]

There is considerable debate over whether the reasons for this are patient-related or service related. Patient-related explanations suggest that there may be higher incidence of

---

[41] 'Retrospective Analysis of Hospital Episode Statistics, Involuntary Admissions under the Mental Health Act 1983, and Number of Psychiatric Beds in England 1996–2006' (2008) 337 British Medical Journal 1837.

[42] Twelfth Biennial Report, available at <www.mhac.org.uk/>. In 2009, the MHAC was subsumed within the overarching Care Quality Commission, <www.cqc.org.uk/>.

[43] C Flannigan, G Glover, S Feeney, J Wing, P Bebbington, and S Lewis, 'Inner London Collaborative Audit of Admissions in Two Health Districts' (1994) 165 British Journal of Psychiatry 734.

[44] Ibid.   [45] Ibid.

[46] 'Age, Gender and Ethnicity of Those Detained under Part II of the Mental Health Act 1983' (2002) 180 British Journal of Psychiatry 222.

mental health problems within these groups, perhaps as a result of some of the pressures experienced by people who are members of particular minority ethnic groups. Service-related explanations suggest these statistics represent institutional racism or unwarranted assumptions about different racial groups within the mental health system. A greater lack of trust in the system among certain groups may also make it more likely that compulsory powers will be used.

In 2002 the Sainsbury Centre conducted a review of the relationship between mental health services and African and Caribbean communities, and concluded that there was a vicious circle at play, as a result of what they described as 'circles of fear'. Partly as a result of poor and discriminatory service provision, and partly due to the particular stigma attached to mental illness in some communities, black people did not access treatment services in the early stages of mental illness, and were therefore more likely to reach a crisis point, when detention might be needed. This would then reinforce the perception of mental health care as coercive, thus further deterring early access to treatment.

The Sainsbury Centre for Mental Health[47]

There is a profound paradox at the centre of Black people's experience of mental health services in England. Young Black men, in particular, are heavily over-represented in the most restrictive parts of the service, including secure services. And Black people generally have an overwhelmingly negative experience of mental health services. Yet these same communities are not accessing the primary care, mental health promotion and specialist community services which might prevent or lessen their mental health problems. They are getting the mental health services they don't want but not the ones they do or might want....

Black people with potential mental health problems are not engaging with services at an early point in the cycle when they could receive less coercive and more appropriate services. Instead they tend only to come to services in crisis when they face a range of risks including over- and mis-diagnosis, police intervention and use of the Mental Health Act. In order to break this cycle, it is necessary to address the issue both from the perspective of services—by making primary care and other services more welcoming, accessible and relevant—and from the perspective of the Black community—by increasing understanding and knowledge and reducing the stigma associated with mental illness.

In 2005, the Department of Health issued *Delivering Race Equality in Mental Health Care*, an action plan intended to reduce differential experience of mental health services among black and minority ethnic (BME) groups.[48] It has three main 'building blocks':

- **more appropriate and responsive services**—achieved through action to develop organisations and the workforce, to improve clinical services and to improve services for specific groups, such as older people, asylum seekers and refugees, and children;

- **community engagement**—delivered through healthier communities and by action to engage communities in planning services, supported by 500 new Community Development Workers; and

---

[47] Breaking the Circles of Fear: A Review of the Relationship Between Mental Health Services and African and Caribbean Communities (2002), available at <www.scmh.org.uk>.
[48] More information is available at <www.actiondre.org.uk/>.

- **better information**—from improved monitoring of ethnicity, better dissemination of information and good practice, and improved knowledge about effective services. This will include a new regular census of mental health patients.

One aspect of the DRE plan is the publication each year of a national census of inpatients in mental health and learning disability services. Three years later, the 2008 *Count Me In* census was still showing considerable over-representation of minority ethnic groups within mental health services—23 per cent of inpatients in 2008 were from minority ethnic groups. Rates of admission were especially high for black and white/black mixed race people.[49] While one of the goals of the DRE is to reduce detention rates among black and minority ethnic groups, the 2008 census found patterns of over-representation were 'broadly similar to those reported in previous censuses, with no evidence of a decline'.[50] It also found that, 'as in previous years, patients from the Black Caribbean, White/Black Caribbean Mixed and Other Black groups were more likely than average to be on a medium or high secure ward'.[51]

(d) CRIMINALS AND RESTRICTED PATIENTS

It is possible for people who are convicted in criminal courts to be diverted to the mental health system if they suffer from a mental disorder. Under section 37 of the Act, a court can make a hospital order where someone has been found guilty of an offence which is punishable by imprisonment. Before making such an order the court has to be satisfied that the section 3 grounds for admission are satisfied, and, under section 27(2)(b), the court must be 'of the opinion, having regard to all the circumstances including the nature of the offence and the character and antecedents of the offender, and to the other available methods of dealing with him, that the most suitable method of disposing of the case is by means of an order under this section'.

The effect of a hospital order is that the person will be detained in one of the three high security special hospitals (Ashworth, Broadmoor, and Rampton) or, where appropriate, in a medium secure ward.

It should, however, be remembered that a significant proportion of the ordinary prison population suffers from mental health problems. It has been estimated that over half of all female and three-quarters of all male prisoners suffer from personality disorders. Six per cent of male prisoners and 13 per cent of female prisoners suffer from schizophrenia.[52]

In July 2006, the ECtHR found that containing mentally disordered offenders in prison could constitute a breach of Article 3. In *Jean-Luc Riviere v France*,[53] the continued detention in prison of a seriously mentally disordered person, without medical supervision appropriate to his condition, 'entailed particularly acute hardship and caused him distress or adversity of an intensity exceeding the unavoidable level of suffering inherent in detention'. Detention in these circumstances was found to amount to inhuman and degrading treatment. It would not be possible to empty UK prisons of all prisoners with mental health provles, but appropriate medical services should nevertheless be available to them.

---

[49] Count Me in 2008: Results of the 2008 National Census of Inpatients in Mental Health and Learning Disability Services in England and Wales (Healthcare Commission: London, 2008), available at <www.healthcarecommission.org.uk>.

[50] Ibid.   [51] Ibid.

[52] Phil Fennell, *Mental Health: The New Law* (Jordan: Bristol, 2007) 162.

[53] Application no. 33834/03.

In addition to being detained at the outset in a special hospital, there is also some movement between the prison system and the mental health system. This is especially marked when prisoners are nearing the end of their sentences, but are perceived to pose a continuing risk to the public. Detention under section 3 of the Mental Health Act has been used to prevent the release of people who can no longer be detained within the criminal justice system, because they have completed their sentences. This has been the subject of sustained criticism by the Mental Health Act Commission:

Mental Health Act Commission[54]

We continue to find cases of patients who are transferred at the end of their prison sentences, especially in the case of patients deemed to be suffering from personality disorder. Some complain that they were given neither notice nor explanation of the reasons for their transfer, and all understandably are shocked and disturbed to find themselves facing indeterminate detention in a psychiatric hospital when they had been expecting release from prison. At Broadmoor hospital in June 2007, we noted a number of such patients who were refusing to engage in therapy and otherwise proving to be a severe management problem due to their resentment at such late transfers. One patient told us that he had been assessed several times in prison and told that he did not have a mental disorder, before his sudden transfer towards the end of his sentence.... If transfers from prison are to serve a therapeutic purpose as well as that of containment, we feel that they should be managed much better than this and that transfer at the end of a sentence should be very much an exception.

Under section 41 of the Act, patients who have committed criminal offences can be made subject to indefinite restriction orders. This means, first, that the medical staff lose the right to determine the patient's movements, and secondly, that patients are subject to additional control and security. In deciding whether to make a restriction order, the court must take into account the nature of the offence; the offender's past history; the likelihood of re-offending, and of any risk to the public. While subject to a restriction order, it is not possible for the patient/prisoner to be given leave of absence, or be transferred or discharged without the Secretary of State's consent. It is, however, now possible for the MHRT to order the discharge of a restriction order if the criteria for detention are no longer met.

5 TREATMENT OF THE MENTALLY ILL

At the outset, it is important to remember that the normal rules which cover consent to medical treatment (considered in the previous chapter) apply to mentally disordered individuals. In short, competent adults have the right to refuse medical treatment, regardless of whether they are suffering from a mental disorder, and those who lack capacity may be treated in their best interests. There are, however, a number of important exceptions which apply only to those who have been formally admitted to the mental health system. Some of these create special protections for compulsorily admitted individuals, while others permit treatment without consent, regardless of the patient's competence.

---

[54] Twelfth Biennial Report, available at <www.mhac.org.uk/>. In 2009, the MHAC was subsumed within the overarching Care Quality Commission, <www.cqc.org.uk/>.

(a) TREATMENT UNDER SECTION 57 OF THE MENTAL HEALTH ACT 1983

Under section 57 of the Act, certain types of treatment cannot be given without both the patient's consent *and* the agreement of a doctor appointed to give a second opinion (known as a SOAD). The SOAD must consult two other people who have been involved in the patient's medical treatment, at least one of whom must be a nurse.

Section 57 applies to psychosurgery ('any surgical operation for destroying brain tissue or for destroying the functioning of brain tissue') and 'the surgical implantation of hormones for the purpose of reducing male sex drive', otherwise known as chemical castration. Under section 57, these treatments cannot be given without the patient's consent, so it would not be lawful to carry out psychosurgery or chemical castration on patients who lack capacity unless such treatment would fit within the emergency exception in section 62 (see below).

Section 57 is seldom used. One reason for this is that the surgical implantation of hormones would be unusual: most treatments to suppress a male patient's sex drive take the form of pills, given orally, or injections, neither of which are covered by this section. Such drugs can therefore be given under section 63 (see below) for up to three months, after which they would fall within section 58. Moreover, patients would normally be given what are known as synthetic hormones, known as hormone analogues, and the Court of Appeal has held that these are not covered by section 57.[55]

(b) TREATMENT UNDER SECTION 58 OF THE MENTAL HEALTH ACT 1983

Under section 58, the administration of psychiatric medicines for periods longer than three months require the informed consent of a competent patient *or* a second opinion from an independent doctor that *either* the patient is not capable of consenting *or* the patient is capable, and has not consented but it is nevertheless appropriate for them to receive the treatment.

Mental Health Act 1983 section 58

58(3) Subject to section 62 below, a patient shall not be given any form of treatment to which this section applies unless—

(a) he has consented to that treatment and either the approved clinician in charge of it or a registered medical practitioner appointed for the purposes of this Part of this Act by the Secretary of State has certified in writing that the patient is capable of understanding its nature, purpose and likely effects and has consented to it; or

(b) a registered medical practitioner appointed as aforesaid (not being the responsible clinician or the approved clinician in charge of the treatment in question) has certified in writing that the patient is not capable of understanding the nature, purpose and likely effects of that treatment or being so capable has not consented to it but that it is appropriate for the treatment to be given.

---

[55] *R v Mental Health Act Commission, ex parte X* (1988) 9 BMLR 77.

This provision means that there is no need for a second opinion of compulsory medication for up to three months (this will simply fall within section 63, below). During the law reform process, there were calls for this three-month period to be reduced, in order to give patients the benefit of a SOAD's assessment earlier in their treatment programme. Under section 58(2), the Secretary of State has the power to reduce this period, but he has not chosen to exercise it. Of course, as the Mental Health Act Commission explains, some patients will be discharged within this three-month period, and hence will never have their medication regime reviewed.

Mental Health Act Commission[56]

We are sympathetic to calls for the reduction of the three-month period. Many detained patients will never have their treatment subjected to the scrutiny of a statutory Second Opinion, because they are discharged within three months of treatment commencing... [S]ome such patients may have repeated admissions to hospital which cumulatively amount to long periods of treatment under the Act without this safeguard applying to them. Others who remain in hospital and go on to see a Second Opinion doctor may quite justifiably wonder where that safeguard has been for the initial period of their detention.

ECT used to be subject to the same provision, and hence could be given without consent to a competent refusing patient provided that it was authorized by a SOAD. Following pressure from patient groups and others, it is now dealt with separately in section 58A, and cannot be given without consent, unless section 62 applies in an emergency (see below). Under section 58A, ECT can only be given if the patient has consented or, if the patient lacks capacity, it is appropriate for it to be given and the patient did not refuse it in an advance directive.

It is important to note that the power, under the Mental Capacity Act 2005, to treat patients who lack capacity does not apply if the patient is detained under the Mental Health Act. This has two principal consequences. First, the 'best interests' checklist, which we considered in the previous chapter, with its emphasis upon the wishes and feelings of the incapacitated adult, does not apply where they have been detained, and the much lower threshold, namely that the doctor simply has to believe treatment is 'appropriate' governs whether long-term medication for mental disorder or ECT is given to patients who lack capacity. Secondly, the bar on giving the 'special treatments' covered by section 57 to patients who lack capacity is an absolute one, and cannot be avoided by relying on the best interests test in the MCA.

The need for a second opinion under sections 57 and 58 was intended to protect the interests of detained patients. It is, however, interesting to note that the presence of a second opinion may, in practice, *deprive* psychiatric patients of the opportunity to challenge treatment through tort law.

Peter Bartlett[57]

As for medication, the very protections provided by section 58 make a negligence action effectively impossible. How can a claim be made that the psychiatrist is negligent under Bolam when an SOAD, an officially selected and trained expert in the field, has signed off the treatment?

---

[56] Twelfth Biennial Report, available at <www.mhac.org.uk/>. In 2009, the MHAC was subsumed within the overarching Care Quality Commission, <www.cqc.org.uk/>.
[57] 'Psychiatric Treatment in the Absence of Law?' (2006) 14 Medical Law Review 124–31.

In the past, there was undoubtedly a tendency for the SOAD to simply rubber stamp the first clinician's judgment. In the 1990s Phil Fennell found that the SOAD approved the treatment plan in 96 per cent of cases.[58] In *Regina (Wilkinson) v Broadmoor Special Hospital Authority*, the Court of Appeal was critical of the tendency to regard the SOAD's role as one of review, rather than independent assessment, and held that a less deferential approach was needed.

Regina (Wilkinson) v Broadmoor Special Hospital Authority[59]

Simon Brown LJ

Whilst, of course, it is proper for the SOAD to pay regard to the views of the RMO [responsible medical officer] who has, after all, the most intimate knowledge of the patient's case, that does not relieve him of the responsibility of forming his own independent judgment as to whether or not 'the treatment should be given'. And certainly, if the SOAD's certificate and evidence is to carry any real weight in cases where, as here, the treatment plan is challenged, it will be necessary to demonstrate a less deferential approach than appears to be the norm.

It is also now clear that SOADs are under a duty to provide reasons for their decisions. In *Regina (Wooder) v Feggetter*, the claimant's clinician decided that he should receive antipsychotic medication, despite his refusal to consent. The SOAD had provided the necessary certificate under section 58(3)(b), but the claimant, who wanted his delusional condition to be treated without drugs, argued that the SOAD should provide reasons for granting the certificate. The Court of Appeal agreed.

Regina (Wooder) v Feggetter[60]

Brooke LJ

With the coming into force of the Human Rights Act 1998 the time has come, in my judgment, for this court to declare that fairness requires that a decision by a SOAD which sanctions the violation of the autonomy of a competent adult patient should also be accompanied by reasons... I would be disposed to grant a declaration that fairness demands that a SOAD should give in writing the reasons for his opinion when certifying under section 58 of the Mental Health Act 1983 that a detained patient should be given medication against his will, and that these reasons should be disclosed to the patient unless the SOAD or the RMO considers that such disclosure would be likely to cause serious harm to the physical or mental health of the patient or any other person.

(c) TREATMENT UNDER SECTION 62 OF THE MENTAL HEALTH ACT 1983

An exception to sections 57 and 58 is created by section 62:

---

[58] P. Fennell, *Treatment without Consent* (Routledge: London, 1996) 211.
[59] [2001] EWCA Civ 1545.   [60] [2002] EWCA Civ 554.

Mental Health Act 1983 section 62

62(1) Sections 57 and 58 above shall not apply to any treatment—

(a) which is immediately necessary to save the patient's life; or

(b) which (not being irreversible) is immediately necessary to prevent a serious deterioration of his condition; or

(c) which (not being irreversible or hazardous) is immediately necessary to alleviate serious suffering by the patient; or

(d) which (not being irreversible or hazardous) is immediately necessary and represents the minimum interference necessary to prevent the patient from behaving violently or being a danger to himself or to others....

(3) For the purposes of this section treatment is irreversible if it has unfavorable irreversible physical or psychological consequences and hazardous if it entails significant physical hazard.

This means that, in an emergency, all treatments covered by sections 57 and 58 can be given without a second opinion or the patient's consent. Given that the treatments covered by section 57 are rarely used, and will even more seldom be 'immediately necessary', section 62's suspension of the protection contained in section 57 is of little practical importance. Instead, section 62 is mainly used to suspend the second opinion requirements in section 58 and 58A, in relation to medication and ECT.[61] Although used comparatively infrequently, the principal effect of section 62's suspension of section 58 is that emergency ECT can be administered to a competent, refusing patient without her consent.

(d) TREATMENT UNDER SECTION 63 OF THE MENTAL HEALTH ACT 1983

Of more practical importance is section 63, which enables any treatment for mental disorder to be provided without consent:

Mental Health Act 1983 section 63

63 The consent of a patient shall not be required for any medical treatment given to him for the mental disorder from which he is suffering, not being a form of treatment to which section 57, 58 or 58A above applies, if the treatment is given by or under the direction of the approved clinician in charge of the treatment.

It is important to remember that section 63 applies to *competent* adults, and that, if a competent adult patient is consenting to treatment, there would be no need to resort to the power contained in section 63. In practice, then, this section enables treatment for mental disorder to be given to a competent adult who has refused to consent to treatment, without the need for a second opinion.

---

[61] P Fennell, *Treatment Without Consent: Law, Psychiatry and the Treatment of Mentally Disordered People since 1845* (Routledge: London, 1996) 199. Andy Bickle, Tarek Abdelrazek, Anne Aboaja, and Kim Page, 'Audit of Statutory Urgent Treatment at a High Security Hospital' (2007) Journal of Mental Health Law 66.

As Genevra Richardson explains in the next extract, this is radically out of step with the increasingly dominant principle of patient autonomy.

Genevra Richardson[62]

At present the law in England and Wales is unusually inconsistent and discriminatory in the way it deals with questions of competence and patient autonomy with regard to mental disorder. The Mental Health Act 1983 permits a person suffering from a mental disorder of the necessary degree to be detained in hospital and treated for that disorder against her competent wishes. No assessment of competence is required. Although the wishes of the patient may be relevant to the treatment decision taken on her behalf, statute allows that decision to be driven by beneficence and social protection; patient autonomy is only one of a number of factors to be considered. Thus, while the common law grants patient autonomy a central role in relation to both physical and mental disorder, in relation to treatment of mental disorder of sufficient severity statute requires patient autonomy to cede to the values of paternalism and social protection. It was suggested above that the paternalist justification for this statutory approach originated in the now contested belief that mental disorder equates to loss of judgment. It is therefore interesting to note that the statutory powers of compulsion are limited to treatment for mental disorder; compulsory patients can still refuse treatment for physical disorder: judgment, it seems, is lost in relation to treatment for *mental* disorder only...

Much, therefore, turns on the meaning given to mental disorder and if it is interpreted too generously there is a danger that a competent patient could be forced to accept treatment for a condition which has little or no bearing on his or her mental state.

Although not specifically mentioned, it has been assumed that if it is necessary to use force to administer treatment under section 63, then this is also permissible. In *R v Broadmoor Special Hospital Authority, ex parte S, H and D*, Auld LJ suggested that the power to detain and treat without consent was, by implication, accompanied by 'the necessary incidents of control'.

R v Broadmoor Special Hospital Authority, ex parte S, H and D[63]

Auld LJ

Sections 3 and 37 of the 1983 Act provide for detention, not just for its own sake, but for treatment. Detention for treatment necessarily implies control for that purpose....Both statutes leave unspoken many of the necessary incidents of control flowing from a power of detention for treatment, including: the power to restrain patients, to keep them in seclusion..., to deprive them of their personal possessions for their own safety and to regulate the frequency and manner of visits to them.

Obviously the scope of section 63 depends upon the meaning given to treatment 'for the mental disorder from which he is suffering'. In practice, a number of medical procedures,

---

[62] 'Autonomy, Guardianship and Mental Disorder: One Problem, Two Solutions' (2002) 65 Modern Law Review 702–23.

[63] The Times, 17 Feb 1998.

which are not straightforwardly directed towards curing the patient's mental illness, have been authorized under this section on the grounds that alleviating the symptoms of the disorder, or enabling the patient to receive treatment for her disorder, are all in fact intended to prevent a deterioration in the patient's condition.

In *Re KB (Adult) (Mental Patient: Medical Treatment)* Ewbank J held that force-feeding an anorexic patient was treatment for her mental disorder.

Re KB (Adult) (Mental Patient: Medical Treatment)[64]

Ewbank J

[A]norexia nervosa...is an eating disorder and relieving symptoms is just as much a part of treatment as relieving the underlying cause. If the symptoms are exacerbated by the patient's refusal to eat and drink, the mental disorder becomes progressively more and more difficult to treat and so the treatment by naso-gastric tube is an integral part of the treatment of the mental disorder itself. It is also said that the treatment is necessary in order to make psychiatric treatment of the underlying cause possible at all...feeding by naso-gastric tube in the circumstances of this type of case is treatment envisaged under s 63 and does not require the consent of the patient.

It is, however, clear that force-feeding does not cure anorexia, and, as Penney Lewis explains in the next extract, repeated episodes of force-feeding can make recovery from anorexia less likely.

Penney Lewis[65]

The anorexic's holy grail is control...Force-feeding crushes the patient's will, destroying who the patient is. This is the antithesis of what a successful, therapeutic treatment must be...The patient may be force-fed up to a more healthy weight and then discharged from hospital, free to return to her previous eating pattern and to lose the weight she has been forced to gain. As her trust has been violated, she may be less likely to seek medical help for her anorexia or for any other medical problem. The gain has been short-term, rather than long-term. The immediate crisis has been averted, but long term damage has been done. Forcing treatment upon a young sufferer of anorexia merely reinforces her lack of self-confidence by taking this decision out of her control, and denies her the capacity for self-directed action which must be developed if she is to recover from this illness. Anorexics who have been force-fed may turn to the more life-threatening behaviour associated with bulimia, including vomiting and laxative abuse. They may be more likely to commit suicide, or to become entrenched in their refusal to eat and thereby become chronic sufferers.

Kirsty Keywood points out that the courts have also been surprisingly disinterested in whether clinicians would characterize force-feeding as 'treatment' for anorexia.

---

[64] [1994] 2 FCR 1051.
[65] 'Feeding Anorexic Patients Who Refuse Food' (1999) 7 Medical Law Review 21–37.

Kirsty Keywood[66]

A number of clinicians perceive involuntary treatment as being necessary in a small number of cases in order to preserve life, restore weight, and restore patients' cognitive abilities to a sufficient degree that they may engage meaningfully in psychotherapy, without necessarily damaging the therapeutic alliance between doctor and patient. Others observe that compulsory treatment, with its higher mortality rate at follow up, may well compromise the relationship between doctor and patient and erode further the patient's self-esteem. Indeed, the courts' assessment of the appropriateness of involuntary treatment pays little regard to the consequences of overriding the expressed wishes of the patient diagnosed with anorexia nervosa. Notwithstanding the paucity of evidence that involuntary treatment of anorexia nervosa yields significant benefits to the patient in the long term, it is perhaps surprising that the courts have not given greater consideration to the appropriateness of interventions such as non-consensual nasogastric feeding... The courts have traditionally premised their judgments on a set of assumptions about the appropriateness of involuntary intervention in the treatment of anorexia nervosa which find (as yet) no firm empirical support within the domains of evidence-based medicine.

In *B v Croydon HA* the patient's compulsion to self-harm was said to be a symptom of her mental disorder, and hence the Court of Appeal again authorized force-feeding under section 63.

B v Croydon HA[67]

Neill LJ

I am satisfied that the words in section 63 of the Mental Health Act 1983 'any medical treatment given to him for the mental disorder from which he is suffering' include treatment given to alleviate the symptoms of the disorder as well as treatment to remedy its underlying cause. In the first place it seems to me that it would often be difficult in practice for those treating a patient to draw a clear distinction between procedures or parts of procedures which were designed to treat the disorder itself and those procedures or parts which were designed to treat its symptoms and sequelae. In my view the medical treatment has to be looked at as a whole, and this approach is reinforced by the wide definition of 'medical treatment' in section 145(1) as including 'nursing' and also 'care, habilitation and rehabilitation under medical supervision'.

In the next extract, Sameer Sarkar and Gwen Adshead highlight the 'striking' anomaly this case reveals between the treatment of those with and without mental disorder.

Sameer Sarkar and Gwen Adshead[68]

Such decisions reveal striking anomalies in the way that English courts have dealt with treatment refusal in relation to mental and physical disorder. Consider tube-feeding as an

---

[66] 'Rethinking the Anorexic Body: How English Law and Psychiatry 'Think' '(2003) 26 International Journal of Law and Psychiatry 599–616.

[67] [1995] Fam 133.

[68] 'Treatment over Objection: Minds, Bodies and Beneficence' (2002) Journal of Mental Health Law 105–18.

example. An ordinary person who decides to starve themselves to death (for example, a prisoner), or a terminally ill person who is not eating during the final stages of life, cannot be force fed against their will....

If, however, food-refusing individuals can be deemed to be suffering from a mental disorder, then they can be force fed, even if they are deemed to be competent. The 'not eating' is understood as a symptom, which is secondary to the mental disorder, and forced feeding is the appropriate treatment for that symptom. This was the case in *B v Croydon Health Authority* where, although B's treatment refusal was deemed to be competent, she could be force fed in the face of her refusal because she was detained for treatment of a mental disorder...

In the case of suspected mental disorder, the judiciary appears to abandon autonomy as the overriding value in relation to consent, and instead favour beneficence in the form of treatment intervention.

In *R v Collins, ex parte Brady*,[69] Ian Brady, one of the Moors murderers who was detained under the Mental Health Act 1983, had gone on hunger strike in order to protest at his perceived ill-treatment. Maurice Kay J held that force-feeding was justified under section 63 as treatment for the mental disorder from which he was suffering, because 'the hunger strike is a manifestation or symptom of the personality disorder'.

Using section 63 to give controversial treatments such as force-feeding to patients sits rather oddly with the special protections given to other sorts of treatment in section 58 and 58A of the Act. Neither ECT nor long-term medication can be given to a refusing patient without the approval of a SOAD. Forcibly inserting a nasogastric tube, against a patient's wishes, is arguably at least as intrusive as ECT or the long-term use of medication.

Nevertheless, if categorizing force-feeding as treatment for mental disorder is controversial, in *Tameside and Glossop v CH* Wall J gave section 63 an extraordinarily expansive interpretation, holding that a caesarean section could be authorized as treatment for CH's schizophrenia.

Tameside and Glossop v CH[70]

Wall J

At first blush, it might appear difficult to say that performance of a Caesarian [sic] section is medical treatment for the Defendant's mental disorder:

I am, however, satisfied that on the facts of this case so to hold would be 'too atomistic a view'... There are several strands in the evidence which, in my judgment, bring the proposed treatment within s 63 of the Act. Firstly, there is the proposition that an ancillary reason for the induction and, if necessary the birth by Caesarian [sic] section is to prevent a deterioration in the Defendant's mental state. Secondly, there is the clear evidence of Dr M that in order for the treatment of her schizophrenia to be effective, it is necessary for her to give birth to a live baby. Thirdly, the overall structure of her treatment requires her to receive strong antipsychotic medication. The administration of that treatment has been necessarily interrupted by her pregnancy and cannot be resumed until her child is born. It is not, therefore, I think stretching language unduly to say that achievement of a successful outcome of her pregnancy is a necessary part of the overall treatment of her mental disorder....

[69] [2000] Lloyd's Rep Med 355.   [70] [1996] 1 FCR 753.

> I am therefore satisfied that the treatment of the Defendant's pregnancy proposed by Dr G is within the broad interpretation of s 63 of the Mental Health Act approved by the Court of Appeal in *B v Croydon Health Authority*.

The judgment in *Tameside* has been widely criticized for what Andrew Grubb describes as its 'sheer breadth'.[71] While it has not been overruled, a few years later, in *St George's Hospital v S*—another case involving a woman with mental health problems who was refusing to consent to a caesarean section—the Court of Appeal took a more restrictive approach to section 63.

St George's Hospital v S[72]

Judge LJ

Section 63 of the Act may apply to the treatment of any condition which is integral to the mental disorder provided the treatment is given by or under the direction of the responsible medical officer. The treatment administered to MS was not so ordered: she was neither offered nor did she refuse treatment for mental disorder....

In the final analysis a woman detained under the Act for mental disorder cannot be forced into medical procedures unconnected with her mental condition unless her capacity to consent to such treatment is diminished.

In *R (on the application of B) v Ashworth Hospital Authority*, a slightly different question arose. The House of Lords had to consider whether section 63 only applied to treatment for the particular type of mental disorder which initially justified the patient's detention. B had been detained on the grounds of mental illness, namely schizophrenia, but while he was in hospital, he was also found to be suffering from a psychopathic disorder. B argued that the decision to place him on a ward for patients with psychopathic disorders was unlawful because this was not the type of mental disorder that had justified his detention. The House of Lords rejected this argument.

R (on the application of B) v Ashworth Hospital Authority[73]

Baroness Hale

I conclude that the words of section 63 mean what they say. They authorise a patient to be treated for any mental disorder from which he is suffering, irrespective of whether this falls within the form of disorder from which he is classified as suffering in the application, order or direction justifying his detention.

As I said earlier, compulsory patients are a vulnerable group who deserve protection from being forced to accept inappropriate treatment. But restricting their treatment to that which is designed for their 'classified' disorder is so haphazard as to be scarcely any protection at all....[P]sychiatry is not an exact science. Diagnosis is not easy or clear cut. As this and many

---

[71] 'Commentary: Treatment without Consent (Pregnancy) Adult' (1996) 4 Medical Law Review 193–8.
[72] [1998] 3 WLR 936.   [73] [2005] UKHL 20.

other cases show, a number of different diagnoses may be reached by the same or different clinicians over the years. As this case also shows, co-morbidity is very common...

It is not easy to disentangle which features of the patient's presentation stem from a disease of the mind and which stem from his underlying personality traits. The psychiatrist's aim should be to treat the whole patient....Once the state has taken away a person's liberty and detained him in a hospital with a view to medical treatment, the state should be able (some would say obliged) to provide him with the treatment which he needs. It would be absurd if a patient could be detained in hospital but had to be denied the treatment which his doctor thought he needed for an indefinite period while some largely irrelevant classification was rectified.

This latter point is an interesting one. In *R on the Application of B v SS* the Court of Appeal agreed with Baroness Hale, that once the criteria for detention for treatment are satisfied, it would be absurd if doctors then had to satisfy a higher evidential threshold in order to actually give that treatment:

R (on the application of B) v SS [74]

Lord Phillips CJ

If detention of a patient for treatment pursuant to s.3 is justified on the ground that the treatment is necessary for the protection of others, it is illogical to contend that a higher standard has to be applied to justify the administration of the treatment itself.

Peter Bartlett disagrees, arguing that Baroness Hale's conflation of detention and forcible treatment is not necessarily appropriate, given that forcibly introducing drugs into a person may be more intrusive than deprivation of liberty, and hence should require further justification.

Peter Bartlett [75]

From a human rights perspective, this is not as clear as this quotation suggests. Forced physical confinement is quite a different intervention into liberty from the introduction of drugs into an individual's body. While many certainly find the beneficial effects of the drug treatments outweigh the adverse effects, this does not change the fact that they act within the body, and are as such extraordinarily intrusive.

Kris Gledhill further comments that the consequence of the Lords decision in *B* is 'that a person can be detained for treatment in relation to one form of disorder but also treated for a form of disorder, which would not have justified his or her detention in the first place'. [76]

(e) THE IMPACT OF THE HUMAN RIGHTS ACT ON TREATMENT OF PEOPLE WITH MENTAL DISORDERS

(1) Article 3

Of course, since the Human Rights Act 1998 came into force, the courts have had to consider whether treatment without consent might violate a patient's convention rights. Article 3

---

[74] [2006] EWCA Civ 28.

[75] 'A Matter of Necessity? Enforced Treatment under the Mental Health Act' (2007) 15 Medical Law Review 86–98.

[76] Kris Gledhill, 'The House of Lords and the Unimportance of Classification: A Retrograde Step' (2005) Journal of Mental Health Law 174.

states that 'no-one shall be subjected to torture or to inhuman or degrading treatment or punishment'. This is supposed to be an absolute right, with no qualification, and yet it might be argued that the test which the courts use when applying Article 3 to treatment of the mentally ill introduces, by the back door, a qualification which applies only to the mentally disordered. The source of this is the ECtHR's judgment in *Herczegfalvy v Austria*:

Herczegfalvy v Austria[77]

Judgment of the ECtHR

The court considers that the position of inferiority and powerlessness which is typical of patients confined in psychiatric hospitals calls for increased vigilance in reviewing whether the Convention has been complied with. While it is for the medical authorities to decide, on the basis of recognised rules of medical science, on the therapeutic methods to be used, if necessary by force, to preserve the physical and mental health of patients who are entirely incapable of deciding for themselves and for whom they are therefore responsible, such patients nevertheless remain under the protection of art 3, the requirements of which permit of no derogation.

The established principles of medicine are admittedly in principle decisive in such cases; as a general rule, a measure which is a therapeutic necessity cannot be regarded as inhuman or degrading. The court must nevertheless satisfy itself that the medical necessity has been convincingly shown to exist.

It should, however, be noted that *Herczegfalvy* itself concerned a detained patient who was handcuffed and strapped to his bed, and these measures were said to be a therapeutic necessity:

In this case, according to the psychiatric principles generally accepted at that time, medical necessity justified the treatment in issue, including forcibly administered food and neuroleptics, isolation, and attaching handcuffs to a security bed. Thus, there was no violation of Article 3.[78]

It is also worth noting that *Herczegfalvy* involved a patient who lacked capacity, where a 'therapeutic necessity' test may not be very different from a judgement about whether treatment is in their best interests. Its 'therapeutic necessity' test has, nevertheless, been invoked in order to justify treatment without consent of patients *who are competent and refusing treatment*. This approach appears to create an exception to the absolute prohibition in Article 3, where the inhuman treatment could be said to *be medically necessary treatment for a patient's mental disorder*.

In *R (on the application of Munjaz) v Ashworth Hospital Authority*,[79] by a majority, the House of Lords held that a hospital authority's policy on seclusion, which provided for more infrequent review than that set out in the MHA Code of Practice, did not amount to inhuman or degrading treatment. The principal reason for this judgment was that, in practice, the risk of ill-treatment was very low, and hence it would be disproportionate to require the hospital to change its policy. Stephanie Palmer has argued that this reasoning is problematic

---

[77] (1992) 15 EHRR 437. [78] Ibid.
[79] [2005] UKHL 58.

in so far as it introduces a proportionality *balancing exercise* into what is supposed to be an unqualified convention right: 'The unconditional wording of Article 3 renders the motivation for the alleged treatment irrelevant: the ends can never justify the means.'[80]

The introduction of qualifications to the Article 3 prohibition is contrary to the absolute approach advocated by the Committee for the Prevention of Torture, Inhuman or Degrading Treatment or Punishment.

Committee for the Prevention of Torture, Inhuman or Degrading Treatment or Punishment[81]

Patients should, as a matter of principle, be placed in a position to give their free and informed consent to treatment. The admission of a person to a psychiatric establishment on an involuntary basis should not be construed as authorising treatment without his consent. It follows that every competent patient, whether voluntary or involuntary, should be given the opportunity to refuse treatment or other medical intervention. Any derogation from this fundamental principle should be based upon law and only relate to clearly and strictly defined exceptional circumstances.

Peter Bartlett suggests that the courts interpretation of section 63 does not meet this standard:

The interpretation afforded to the section...allows unfettered treatment of any mental disorder with which the confined patient is affected without the patient's consent, no matter how small or great and whether or not the patient has capacity to consent to it. This throws to the wind any concept of autonomy for the civilly or criminally confined psychiatric patient.[82]

Herczegfalvy v Austria was applied by the Court of Appeal in *Regina (Wilkinson) v Broadmoor Special Hospital Authority*. The claimant was a convicted mental health patient, who had been compulsorily detained at a secure hospital. He sought judicial review of a decision to administer anti-psychotic medication despite his refusal to consent, contending that it infringed his right to life (Art. 2); his right not to be subject to degrading treatment (Art. 3) and his right to privacy (Art. 8).

Regina (Wilkinson) v Broadmoor Special Hospital Authority[83]

Simon Brown LJ

If in truth this appellant has the capacity to refuse consent to the treatment proposed here, it is difficult to suppose that he should nevertheless be forcibly subjected to it. [I]ts impact on the appellant's rights above all to autonomy and bodily inviolability is immense and its

---

[80] Stephanie Palmer, 'A Wrong Turning: Article 3 ECHR and Proportionality' (2006) 65 Cambridge Law Journal 438–52.

[81] Council of Europe, Report of the Committee for the Prevention of Torture, Inhuman or Degrading Treatment or Punishment, Council of Europe 2000, para. 41.

[82] 'Psychiatric Treatment in the Absence of Law?'(2006) 14 Medical Law Review 124–31.

[83] [2001] EWCA Civ 1545.

prospective benefits (not least given his extreme opposition) appear decidedly speculative. Even, moreover, if the appellant is incompetent, the court will need to be satisfied (in the language of the ECtHR in *Herczegfalvy*) 'that the medical necessity has been convincingly shown to exist...according to the psychiatric principles generally accepted at the time'.

Non-consensual treatment, and any associated use of force or restraint, can therefore only avoid being categorized as inhuman or degrading treatment if it is 'convincingly shown' to be a medical or therapeutic necessity. What does this mean in practice, and how high is the standard of proof? These questions arose in *R (on the application of N) v M and Others*, another case in which a patient wanted to refuse anti-psychotic medication. Because the claimant had obtained an independent opinion that she should not be given anti-psychotic medication, she argued, unsuccessfully, that it could not have been convincingly shown that a medical necessity existed.

R (on the application of N) v M and Others[84]

Dyson LJ

In the light of [*Herczegfalvy v Austria*], it is common ground that the standard of proof required is that the court should be satisfied that medical necessity has been 'convincingly' shown....

Mr Kelly [for the claimant] submitted that this test is, in effect, the same as the criminal standard of proof. We disagree. It seems to us that no useful purpose is served by importing the language of the criminal law. The phrase 'convincingly shown' is easily understood. The standard is a high one. But it does not need elaboration or further explanation....

Mr Kelly's submission on analysis involves the proposition that, in a case where there is a responsible body of opinion that a patient is not suffering from a treatable condition, then it cannot be convincingly shown that the treatment proposed is medically necessary. We reject this submission.... In our judgment, the fact that there is a responsible body of opinion against the proposed treatment is relevant to the question whether it is in the patient's best interests or medically necessary, but it is no more than that. The court has to decide in the light of all the evidence in the case whether the treatment should be permitted.

In *R (On the Application of JB) v Haddock (Responsible Medical Officer)*, the Court of Appeal decided that it was not necessary to show that the treatment, which was found to be a medical necessity, would actually work. While the Court of Appeal resisted expressing the burden of proof in forensic terms, they suggested that it probably amounted to no more than that it was more likely than not that the treatment was necessary.

R (On the Application of JB) v Haddock (Responsible Medical Officer)[85]

Auld LJ

The s.58(3) power to treat a patient capable of consent against his will or a patient incapable of consent is potentially a violation of his Art.3 right not to be subjected to degrading

84 [2002] EWCA Civ 1789.
85 [2006] EWCA Civ 961.

treatment and/or his Art.8 right to respect for his private life. However, it is common ground that, while the risk of infringement of those rights may be greater when the patient is capable of giving or refusing consent, it is not necessarily an infringement to treat him against his will where such treatment can be convincingly shown to be medically or therapeutically necessary. . . .

To require of psychiatrists a state of mind of precision and sureness in matters of diagnosis akin to that required of a jury in a criminal case, even in this fraught context of forcible treatment potentially violating detained patients' human rights, is not sensible or feasible. . . . And, as to whether the treatment will do any good, it is unreal to require psychiatrists, under the umbrella of a requirement of medical or therapeutic necessity, to demonstrate sureness or near sureness of success, especially when the Act itself, in s.58(3)(b) hinges the SOAD's certificate on his conclusion as to 'the likelihood' of it benefiting him.

Accordingly I do not consider that the requirement on a court to be convinced, in this context, of medical necessity in the light of the medical evidence and other evidence, is capable of being expressed in terms of a standard of evidential proof. It is rather a value judgement as to the future—a forecast—to be made by a court in reliance on medical evidence according to a standard of persuasion. If it is to be expressed in forensic terms at all, it is doubtful whether it amounts to more than satisfaction of medical necessity on a balance of probabilities, or as a 'likelihood' of therapeutic benefit.

Peter Bartlett is critical of the decision in *Haddock*, suggesting that it invokes professional uncertainty as grounds for *weakening*, rather than strengthening, the protection of patients' human rights.

Peter Bartlett[86]

This is an odd argument from a human rights standpoint, as it suggests that the fact that an area is fraught with uncertainty is a justification for restricting human rights protection within that area. If we are serious that treatment without consent constitutes an 'invasion', to use Auld LJ's word, it would instead seem that enforced interventions in such uncertain circumstances ought to be approached with particular caution. If we accept that enforced treatment is a constitutional question, it is far from clear that the state is more justified in restricting an individual's rights in cases where the knowledge base of the intervention is so fluid. . . .

B's expert witness had called into question the appropriateness of treatment with antipsychotic medication for personality disorder. He acknowledged that such treatment was used by some clinicians, but stated that the evidence base for its efficacy was weak. Evidence-based practice is not a new concept in medicine; it seems not unreasonable to insist that practitioners wishing to treat persons without consent should at the very least be able to demonstrate a solid and objective foundation for their belief that the treatment would be beneficial to the patient. . . .

The outcome of the *Haddock* case would appear to be that any rights under Articles 3 or 8 of the ECHR to be free from involuntary treatment are to be subject to the professional practice of the psychiatric profession: that is not to be subject to significant scrutiny.

---

[86] 'A Matter of Necessity? Enforced Treatment under the Mental Health Act' (2007) 15 Medical Law Review 86–98.

While section 63 can be used to justify the compulsory treatment of *competent* patients, the protection that is superimposed upon it by the Human Rights Act applies equally to *incompetent* patients. Hence if a patient who lacks capacity nevertheless manifests a desire not to be treated, treating her against her wishes could amount to inhuman or degrading treatment, and thus would be acceptable only if it could be convincingly shown to be a therapeutic necessity. In *Keenan v United Kingdom* the solitary confinement of an incapacitated patient, who hanged himself within 24 hours, was held to have been a violation of Article 3.

Keenan v United Kingdom [87]

Judgment of the ECtHR

The Court recalls that ill-treatment must attain a minimum level of severity if it is to fall within the scope of Article 3. The assessment of this minimum is relative: it depends on all the circumstances of the case, such as the duration of the treatment, its physical and/or mental effects and, in some cases, the sex, age and state of health of the victim...

It is relevant in the context of the present application to recall also that the authorities are under an obligation to protect the health of persons deprived of liberty...In particular, the assessment of whether the treatment or punishment concerned is incompatible with the standard of Article 3 has, in the case of mentally ill persons, to take into consideration their vulnerability and their inability, in some cases, to complain coherently or at all about how they are being affected by any particular treatment....

The lack of effective monitoring of Mark Keenan's condition and the lack of informed psychiatric input into his assessment and treatment disclose significant defects in the medical care provided to a mentally ill person known to be a suicide risk. The belated imposition on him in those circumstances of a serious disciplinary punishment—seven days' segregation in the punishment block and an additional twenty-eight days to his sentence imposed two weeks after the event and only nine days before his expected date of release—which may well have threatened his physical and moral resistance, is not compatible with the standard of treatment required in respect of a mentally ill person. It must be regarded as constituting inhuman and degrading treatment and punishment within the meaning of Article 3 of the Convention.

Accordingly, the Court finds a violation of this provision.

(2) Article 2

In *Keenan* the ECtHR also considered whether the failure to protect Mark Keenan might also amount to a breach of the state's positive obligations under Article 2, to protect his right to life. The Court asked itself 'whether the authorities knew or ought to have known that Mark Keenan posed a real and immediate risk of suicide and, if so, whether they did all that reasonably could have been expected of them to prevent that risk?' It held that while the risk was real, the authorities' response to the risk of suicide was sufficient to discharge their duties under Article 2.

More recently, in *Savage v South Essex Partnership NHS Foundation Trust*, the House of Lords found that, where a mentally ill patient was a suicide risk, doing all that could reasonably be expected in order to prevent that risk involved balancing the need to prevent suicide with the need to provide the patient with proper therapeutic care.

---

[87] (27229/95) 10 BHRC 319.

Savage v South Essex Partnership NHS Foundation Trust[88]

Baroness Hale

The trigger is a 'real and immediate risk to life' about which the authorities knew or ought to have known at the time. That has rarely been shown. If the duty is triggered, it is, as it was put in Keenan's case to do 'all that reasonably could have been expected of them to prevent that risk'. In judging what can reasonably be expected, the court has shown itself aware of the need to take account of competing values in the Convention, in particular the liberty and autonomy rights protected by articles 5 and 8. The steps taken must be proportionate. If this is so in prison, it must be even more so in hospital, where the objectives of detention are therapeutic and protective rather than penal. Developing a patient's capacity to make sensible choices for herself, and providing her with as good a quality of life as possible, are important components in protecting her mental health. Keeping her absolutely safe from physical harm, by secluding or restraining her, or even by keeping her on a locked ward, may do more harm to her mental health.

(3) Article 8

The right to be free from non-consensual medical treatment might also be protected by Article 8, the right to respect for private and family life. In *X v Austria*,[89] for example, the European Commission explicitly stated that 'compulsory medical intervention, even if it is of minor importance, must be considered an interference with this right'. In practice, however, the protection offered by Article 8 is qualified insofar as an interference can be shown to be 'necessary in a democratic society' for, among other things, 'the protection of health'. This, as the Court of Appeal explained in *R (on the application of N) v M and Others*,[90] means that if the treatment has been convincingly shown to be medically necessary, neither Article 3 nor Article 8 will have been violated, since the interference with the right to respect for private life would be proportionate, and justified within the terms of Article 8(2).

Article 8 has also been invoked in order to challenge other sorts of restrictions on mental health patients' freedom. Recently, for example, in *R (on the Application of G) v Nottinghamshire Healthcare NHS Trust*, patients who were detained at Rampton high security hospital challenged the smoking ban on the grounds that Rampton was their home, and that they should therefore be permitted to smoke inside, like other people can in their homes (for security reasons, smoking outside was not possible). The administrative court rejected the claim that Article 8 required protection of a 'right to smoke'.

R (On the Application of G) v Nottinghamshire Healthcare NHS Trust[91]

Pill LJ

Preventing a person smoking does not, at any rate in the culture of the United Kingdom, generally involve such adverse effect upon the person's 'physical or moral integrity'...as would amount to an interference with the right to respect for private or home life within the meaning of Art.8...

---

[88] [2008] UKHL 74.   [89] (1980) 18 DR 154, 156.   [90] [2002] EWCA Civ 1789.
[91] [2008] EWHC 1096 (Admin).

> We are not persuaded that the requirement to respect private life and home in Art.8 imposes a general obligation on those responsible for the care of detained people to make arrangements enabling them to smoke. Whether it is put in terms of moral integrity, identity or personal autonomy, no general right for mental patients to smoke, or general obligation to permit smoking, arises…
>
> The legislative intention of reg.10 and the Trust policy was not merely to reduce smoking but also to increase the number of smoke-free enclosed public places and work places, thereby reducing levels of exposure to second hand smoke….
>
> We…are satisfied that the legislative objectives are sufficiently important to justify limiting any rights the claimants have under Art.8.

6 DISCHARGE

Once a patient has been detained, it is important to remember that her detention must continue to be justified by her condition. The exception to the right to liberty in Article 5 (1)(e), which permits the lawful detention of persons of unsound mind, exists only when detention is in accordance with procedure prescribed by law, and where it is possible to challenge the lawfulness of detention speedily in a court.

In *Winterwerp v The Netherlands* the European Court of Human Rights fleshed out three conditions that apply to the 'unsound mind' exception in Article 5(1)(e):

> In the court's opinion, except in emergency cases, the individual concerned should not be deprived of his liberty unless he has been reliably shown to be of 'unsound mind'. The very nature of what has to be established before the competent national authority—that is, a true mental disorder—calls for objective medical expertise. Further, the mental disorder must be of a kind or degree warranting compulsory confinement. What is more, the validity of continued confinement depends upon the persistence of such a disorder.[92]

The validity of continued confinement is therefore contingent upon the mental disorder's persistence. The responsible clinician (RC) has an ongoing duty to consider whether the conditions which justified the patient's original detention continue to be satisfied. Because the extent to which a patient is affected by their mental disorders will often fluctuate, Article 5(4) requires that there is a formal mechanism to review or challenge the lawfulness of continued detention at reasonable intervals.

(a) REVIEW OF DETENTION

Detentions under section 2 will automatically lapse after 28 days, and unless the patient is formally detained under section 3, the patient must be discharged. For patients detained under section 3, section 68 provides that hospital managers have a duty to refer their case to the Mental Health Review Tribunal (MHRT) after six months, and thereafter every three years. Each MHRT must have at least one legal, medical, and lay member, and most will contain just these three individuals.

---

[92] ECHR series A vol 33 (1979).

Under section 66 of the 1983 Act, a patient who has been admitted to hospital compulsorily under sections 2 or 3 of the 1983 Act has a right to request that the MHRT considers whether they should be discharged. Of course, not all patients will have the capacity to exercise this right, and in *R (on the application of H) v Secretary of State for Health* the question of whether this might lead to differential access to the MHRT, and be incompatible with the Human Rights Act, arose. MH, a 32-year-old woman with Down's syndrome, had been admitted under section 2. She lacked the capacity to appeal to the MHRT herself. Reversing the Court of Appeal's declaration of incompatibility, the House of Lords unanimously held that there had been no breach of Article 5(4).

R (on the application of H) v Secretary of State for Health[93]

Baroness Hale

The short answer to this question is that Article 5(4) does not require that every case be considered by a court. It requires that the person detained should have the right to 'take proceedings'.... The difference between a right to 'take proceedings' and a right to 'be brought promptly before a [court]' must be deliberate. It stops short of requiring judicial authorisation in every case. It leaves to the person detained the choice of whether or not to put the matter before a court...

Patients and nearest relatives have to be told how to apply to a tribunal, how to contact a suitably qualified solicitor, that free legal aid may be available, and how to contact any other organisation which may be able to help them make an application. In other words, the hospital managers have to do the best they can to make the patient's rights practical and effective.

(b) CRITERIA FOR REVIEW

In its original form, the Mental Health Act 1983 required the patient applying to the MHRT to prove that their continued detention was no longer justified. In effect, this amounted to a presumption against discharge: if the patient could not prove that her detention was unjustified, the default position would be that detention continues. This was found to be incompatible with Article 5 of the Convention, insofar as it imposed the burden of proof on the patient to establish that detention was unjustified, rather than requiring discharge if it cannot be proved that the criteria for admission continue to be satisfied. Now it is for those who are arguing against the patient's discharge to prove that the patient *does* meet the criteria for detention, and not for the patient to prove that she *does not*.

The criteria for the MHRT's decision-making are contained in section 72.

Mental Health Act 1983 section 72

72(a) the tribunal shall direct the discharge of a patient liable to be detained under section 2 above if [it is] not satisfied—

(i) that he is then suffering from mental disorder of a nature or degree which warrants his detention in a hospital for assessment (or for assessment followed by medical treatment) for at least a limited period; or

---

[93] [2005] UKHL 60.

(ii) that his detention as aforesaid is justified in the interests of his own health or safety or with a view to the protection of other persons;

(b) the tribunal shall direct the discharge of a patient liable to be detained otherwise than under section 2 above if [it is] not satisfied—

(i) that he is then suffering from mental disorder of a nature or degree which makes it appropriate for him to be liable to be detained in a hospital for medical treatment; or

(ii) that it is necessary for the health or safety of the patient or for the protection of other persons that he should receive such treatment; or

(iia) that appropriate medical treatment is available for him; or

(iii) in the case of an application by virtue of paragraph (g) of section 66(1) above, that the patient, if released, would be likely to act in a manner dangerous to other persons or to himself.

Notice that for continued detention to be justified, the patient has to be suffering from a mental disorder of a *nature or degree* which warrants detention in hospital. An important word here is 'or': a patient might be suffering from a disorder whose *nature* warrants detention in hospital, but to a *degree* which does not. In *R v Mental Health Review Tribunal for the South Thames Region, ex parte Smith*,[94] the court held that this means that someone might be detained on the grounds that the condition from which they are suffering generally justifies detention, even if at the time of the application, they are not affected to a 'degree' which warrants detention in hospital. Unsurprisingly, this wording has been criticized:

Peter Bartlett and Ralph Sandland[95]

[T]he requirement in *Winterwerp* is for unsound mind sufficient to 'justify' detention, and we would want to argue, as has not been done to date before the European Court, that a test which allows nature 'or' degree permits detention when a person's disorder is of a nature but *not* of a degree to justify compulsory hospitalisation, which is outside of the spirit of the Convention. In our, perhaps optimistic, view, the preferable and Convention-compliant wording must be that the mental disorder in question is of both a nature *and* a degree to warrant detention.

As Collins J explains in *R (on the application of Care Principles Ltd) v Mental Health Review Tribunal*, tribunals do not assess the lawfulness of the initial detention, but rather, on the balance of probabilities, whether grounds for detention exist at the time of the hearing.

R (on the application of Care Principles Ltd) v Mental Health Review Tribunal[96]

Collins J

[T]he Tribunal is concerned with the condition of the patient when the Tribunal considers the matter. Whether or not he was properly taken into hospital is not material for that consideration. When I say 'properly', I mean whether there was indeed material which justified the

---

[94] The Times, 9 Dec 1998.
[95] *Mental Health Law: Policy and Practice*, 3rd edn (OUP: Oxford, 2007) 403.
[96] [2006] EWHC 3194 (Admin).

admission, or indeed the other way round, whether at the time it was clearly justified. The question before the Tribunal is: is the detention proper now? The burden is upon the hospital, or those who seek his continued detention, to establish that that detention is necessary and within the terms of the Act.

It is always necessary for any such detention to be justified. The standard required is the balance of probabilities. The Tribunal has to be persuaded that it is more probable than not that the detention is needed. It has been said in another context that there needs to be some cogent evidence before the Tribunal to establish that the detention is necessary.

If the MHRT decides that the criteria for detention are not made out, it must order the patient's discharge. Discharge can, however, be deferred, if arrangements have to be made for the patient's accommodation and/or care.

The MHRT must give reasons for its decision. Where there is conflicting evidence, the MHRT must explain, in language that can be understood by the patient herself, why one witness's evidence was preferred. In *R v Ashworth Hospital Authority, ex parte H*,[97] the MHRT ordered the immediate discharge of a patient, despite the fact that five out of six medical reports had been against discharge. The Court of Appeal found that this decision was *Wednesbury*[98] unreasonable, since no reasonable tribunal could have come to this decision in the light of the evidence before it, and furthermore that the tribunal's reasons— namely that it simply preferred the evidence of the one doctor who believed discharge to be appropriate—were insufficient.

In practice, orders for the discharge of patients are comparatively rare. In 2006, of over 22,000 applications and referrals, 56 per cent proceeded to a full hearing, and only 11 per cent of these hearings resulted in an order for discharge.[99]

It is possible to appeal against an MHRT decision on a point of law under section 78 of the Mental Health Act 1983. But, because it will allow broader consideration of the issues, tribunals' decisions are more commonly challenged through applications for judicial review, usually on the grounds of illegality.

(c) THE NEED FOR SPEEDY REVIEW

Recall that under Article 5(4) of the European Convention, incorporated into the Human Rights Act, 'Everyone who is deprived of his liberty by arrest or detention shall be entitled to take proceedings by which the lawfulness of his detention shall be decided speedily by a court and his release ordered if the detention is not lawful.'

The question of how 'speedy' the legal challenge must be to satisfy Article 5(4) arose in *R (on the application of C) v Mental Health Review Tribunal*. C had been detained in hospital under section 3 of the Mental Health Act 1983 and immediately applied to the MHRT for discharge. It was the practice of the MHRT to list hearings of applications for discharge eight weeks after the application had been made. C submitted that the practice was arbitrary, and insufficiently 'speedy'. The Court of Appeal agreed.

---

[97] [2003] 1 WLR 127.
[98] *Associated Provincial Picture Houses v Wednesbury Corporation* [1948] 1 KB 223.
[99] MHAC Twelfth Biennial Report.

R (on the application of C) v Mental Health Review Tribunal[100]

Lord Phillips MR

I do not consider lawful a practice which makes no effort to see that the individual application is heard as soon as reasonably practicable, having regard to the relevant circumstances of the case. Such a practice will inevitably result in some applications not leading to the speedy decision required by article 5(4). The present case is an instance of this result.

Similarly, in *R v Mental Health Review Tribunal, ex parte KB* a conjoined application was brought by a number of patients who had waited between 4 and 27 weeks for a hearing. The reasons for the delays included difficulties in preparing reports and in timetabling tribunal hearings. Stanley Burton J found that lack of resources did not offer a defence to the breach of Article 5(4):

R v Mental Health Review Tribunal, ex parte KB[101]

Stanley Burton J

Under Article 5(4), it is for the state to ensure speedy hearings of detained patients' applications. The state must establish such Tribunals or courts and provide such resources, as will provide speedy hearings. It is therefore irrelevant to the question whether there has been an infringement of Article 5(4) which government department or other public authority was at fault.

In *R v MHRT, ex parte B* effective case management would have avoided the delay of nine months for a tribunal hearing, and Scott Baker J found that this amounted to a breach of Article 5(4).

R v MHRT, ex parte B[102]

Scott Baker J

A delay does not of itself give rise to a breach of Article 5(4), but it does give rise to the need for an explanation.... The delay in this case of eight and a half months is so long as to call for an explanation by the state (represented in this instance by the Tribunal). No adequate explanation has been forthcoming, albeit it is plain that with effective case management the substantive hearing would have taken place a great deal earlier without in any way prejudicing B's right to a fair hearing. I have come to the conclusion that the lawfulness of B's detention was not decided speedily in this case and that therefore there is a breach of Article 5(4) of the ECHR.

(d) STATUS OF THE MHRT DECISION

If the responsible clinician (RC) in charge of treatment disagrees with the tribunal's decision to order a patient's discharge, is there anything to stop her simply re-admitting the patient under section 3? Of course, if circumstances have changed dramatically between the time of the tribunal hearing and the time of re-admission, then this might be legitimate. But where there has not been a substantial change of circumstances, RCs should not attempt to override the tribunal's decision through a new admission.

---

[100] [2002] 1 WLR 176.
[101] [2002] EWHC 639 (Admin).   [102] [2002] All ER (D) 304 (Jul).

In *R v East London and the City Mental Health NHS Trust, ex p Von Brandenburg* the patient's discharge had been ordered by an MHRT, but had been deferred for seven days so that suitable accommodation could be found. Six days later, the patient's clinician (then referred to as a responsible medical officer, or RMO) arranged for his re-admission under section 3 of the Mental Health Act 1983. The patient sought judicial review of the decision to re-admit him. The House of Lords found that there might be circumstances when it would be lawful to re-admit a patient despite a tribunal's decision to discharge her, but that these would depend upon the Approved Mental Health Practitioner (AMHP) (which used to be known as an approved social worker, or ASW) forming the reasonable and bona fide belief that she had information not known by the tribunal which put a different complexion on the case. Re-sectioning is therefore only appropriate where material facts have subsequently come to light, and must not be used to trump tribunal decisions with which the AMHP disagrees.

R v East London and the City Mental Health NHS Trust, ex p Von Brandenburg[103]

Lord Bingham

[A]n ASW may not lawfully apply for the admission of a patient whose discharge has been ordered by the decision of a mental health review Tribunal of which the ASW is aware unless the ASW has formed the reasonable and bona fide opinion that he has information not known to the Tribunal which puts a significantly different complexion on the case as compared with that which was before the Tribunal. It is impossible and undesirable to attempt to describe in advance the information which might justify such an opinion. I give three hypothetical examples by way of illustration only:

The issue at the Tribunal is whether the patient, if discharged, might cause harm to himself. The Tribunal, on the evidence presented, discounts that possibility and directs the discharge of the patient. After the hearing, the ASW learns of a fact previously unknown to him, the doctors attending the patient and the Tribunal: that the patient had at an earlier date made a determined attempt on his life. Having taken medical advice, the ASW judges that this information significantly alters the risk as assessed by the Tribunal.

At the Tribunal hearing the patient's mental condition is said to have been stabilised by the taking of appropriate medication. The continuing stability of the patient's mental condition is said to depend on his continuing to take that medication. The patient assures the Tribunal of his willingness to continue to take medication and, on the basis of that assurance, the Tribunal directs the discharge of the patient. Before or after discharge the patient refuses to take the medication or communicates his intention to refuse. Having taken medical advice, the ASW perceives a real risk to the patient or others if the medication is not taken.

After the Tribunal hearing, and whether before or after discharge, the patient's mental condition significantly deteriorates so as to present a degree of risk or require treatment or supervision not evident at the hearing.

In cases such as these the ASW may properly apply for the admission of a patient, subject of course to obtaining the required medical support, notwithstanding a Tribunal decision directing discharge.

[103] [2003] UKHL 58.

7 COMMUNITY CARE

As we have seen, there has been a marked trend away from inpatient care towards what is euphemistically known as 'care in the community'. There are two types of community care: first, primary care services are supposed to ensure that mentally disordered individuals living in the community have access to appropriate treatment. Secondly, in recent years there has been interest in how a degree of control and supervision might be exercised over people who are not ill enough to be detained in hospital. In *R (on the application of H) v Mental Health Review Tribunal* a patient who had been discharged conditionally from a hospital order was subject to a condition that he should receive fortnightly injections. He sought absolute discharge, and the status of this condition was considered by the court. Holman J reiterated that the special exceptions to the need for the consent of a competent person contained in the Mental Health Act 1983 do not have wider application, and could not be used to force the patient to submit to treatment in the community.

R (on the application of H) v Mental Health Review Tribunal[104]

Holman J

The law with regard to consent to treatment is clear. . . An adult of full capacity has an absolute right to choose whether to consent to medical treatment. . . . Thus in this case, on each occasion that SH attends, or should attend, for his fortnightly depot injection he has an absolute right to choose whether to consent to it or not. The treating doctor or nurse must, on each occasion, satisfy himself that the apparent consent is a real consent and that the independence of the patient's decision or his will has not been overborne . . .

It thus follows, in my view, that condition 1 should clearly be read as importing and subject to the absolute right of SH to choose whether to consent. . . . In deciding whether actually to consent SH may take into account the imperative of the condition, just as he might take into account strong medical advice or the persuasion of a relative. But the condition must be read as respecting and being subject to his own final choice, which must be his real or true choice.

(a) AFTERCARE SERVICES

Section 117 of the Mental Health Act 1983 requires primary care trusts (PCTs) and social service departments, in cooperation with voluntary agencies, to provide aftercare services to those who have been discharged from detention under the Act. Usually, aftercare services involve medical treatment, help with accommodation, and assist with education and training. Although initially there was some confusion over whether local authorities were entitled to charge patients for services provided under section 117, the House of Lords in *R v Manchester City Council, ex parte Stennett*[105] agreed with the Court of Appeal that the exceptional vulnerability of compulsorily detained patients meant that aftercare services for these ex-patients must be provided free of charge.

---

[104] [2007] EWHC 884 (Admin).
[105] [2002] UKHL 34.

It is clear that there is a *duty* to provide aftercare services. In *R v Ealing District Health Authority, ex parte Fox* Otton J held that once a tribunal has ordered a conditional discharge, the health authority must ensure that the appropriate arrangements are in place:

R v Ealing District Health Authority, ex parte Fox[106]

Otton J

[A] district health authority is under a duty under s 117 of the Mental Health Act 1983 to provide after-care services when a patient leaves hospital, and acts unlawfully in failing to seek to make practical arrangements for after-care prior to that patient's discharge from hospital where such arrangements are required by a mental health review Tribunal in order to enable the patient to be conditionally discharged from hospital.

But what if a health authority cannot find healthcare professionals who are prepared to take responsibility for a patient's treatment after discharge? This was the issue in *Camden and Islington Health Authority, ex parte K*, where it proved impossible to find a psychiatrist willing to supervise the applicant's care in the community. The House of Lords held that section 117 should not be taken to impose an absolute and unworkable obligation on health authorities:

Camden and Islington Health Authority, ex parte K[107]

Lord Phillips

[S]ection 117 imposes on health authorities a duty to provide aftercare facilities for the benefit of patients who are discharged from mental hospitals. The nature and extent of those facilities must, to a degree, fall within the discretion of the health authority, which must have regard to other demands on its budget....

I can see no justification for interpreting section 117 so as to impose on health authorities an absolute obligation to satisfy any conditions that a Tribunal may specify as prerequisites to the discharge of a patient....An interpretation of section 117 which imposed on health authorities absolute duties which they would not necessarily be able to perform would be manifestly unreasonable.

Of course, if a patient is no longer sufficiently mentally disordered to justify detention in hospital, then the failure to facilitate her release might amount to a breach of Article 5(4). However, where a patient's release is conditional upon the provision of services, Lord Phillips suggests that, in the absence of those services, she may continue to be sufficiently mentally disordered to justify detention under Article 5:

Lord Phillips

If a health authority is unable, despite the exercise of all reasonable endeavours, to procure for a patient the level of care and treatment in the community that a Tribunal considers to be a prerequisite to the discharge of the patient from hospital, I do not consider that the continued detention of the patient in hospital will violate the right to liberty conferred by article 5.

---

[106] [1993] 1 WLR 373.   [107] [2001] EWCA Civ 240.

K then appealed to the European Court of Human Rights, which confirmed that there had been no violation of Article 5(1)(e).

Judgment of the ECtHR[108]

As events in the present case showed, the treatment considered necessary for such conditional discharge may not prove available, in which circumstances there can be no question of interpreting Article 5 § 1(e) as requiring the applicant's discharge without the conditions necessary for protecting herself and the public or as imposing an absolute obligation on the authorities to ensure that the conditions are fulfilled.

A similar result was reached in *R v Secretary of State for the Home Department, ex parte IH*.[109] Because it was impossible to find a psychiatrist willing to supervise IH in the community, the conditions attached to his discharge could not be met. In these circumstances, the House of Lords found that there had been no violation of Article 5(1)(e) and continued detention remained lawful, despite the tribunal's order.

(b) SUPERVISED COMMUNITY TREATMENT

One of the most significant changes introduced by 2007 reforms is the possibility of community treatment orders (CTOs). CTOs are intended to ensure that patients receive treatment in the least restrictive environment, so that an individual judged to be in need of some supervision does not necessarily have to be detained in hospital for that treatment to be provided. They are also intended to resolve what is known as the 'revolving door' problem: a patient is admitted to hospital, their condition is stabilized, and they are discharged into the community, only to stop taking their medication, resulting in deterioration and re-admission to hospital, where the pattern repeats itself.

The government's initial plans for CTOs undoubtedly posed a much greater threat to liberty than the provisions which were eventually incorporated into the Act—they could, for example, have applied to *anyone*, not just people who had already been detained.

Under section 17A, an RC can only make a community treatment order with the written agreement of an AHMP, and if the criteria in section 17A(5) are satisfied.

Mental Health Act 1983 section 17A

17A(5)(a) the patient is suffering from mental disorder of a nature or degree which makes it appropriate for him to receive medical treatment;

(b) it is necessary for his health or safety or for the protection of other persons that he should receive such treatment;

(c) subject to his being liable to be recalled as mentioned in paragraph (d) below, such treatment can be provided without his continuing to be detained in a hospital;

(d) it is necessary that the responsible clinician should be able to exercise the power under section 17E(1) below to recall the patient to hospital; and

(e) appropriate medical treatment is available for him.

---

[108] Judgment of the ECtHR, *Kolanis v United Kingdom* (APP NO 517/02) [2005] All ER (D) 227 (Jun).
[109] [2003] UKHL 59.

Essentially, CTOs do not allow treatment with compulsion in the community, but they provide for immediate recall, under section 17E, if the patient becomes in need of compulsory treatment:

Mental Health Act 1983 section 17E

17E(1) The responsible clinician may recall a community patient to hospital if in his opinion—

(a) the patient requires medical treatment in hospital for his mental disorder; and

(b) there would be a risk of harm to the health or safety of the patient or to other persons if the patient were not recalled to hospital for that purpose.

If a patient is recalled, she can be detained for up to 72 hours, after which time she can be discharged, and continue to be subject to the CTO, or if she refuses to comply with a condition in the CTO or continues to refuse treatment, the CTO can be revoked and she will become a detained patient once again.

Because treatment without consent can be given as soon as the patient is recalled, the power of recall could simply be used temporarily for this purpose, even if the clinician has no intention of revoking the CTO. It is therefore possible that a patient could 'yo-yo' between recall and living in the community with a CTO, in order to periodically facilitate treatment without consent. Furthermore, in the House of Lords debates over the Bill, Lord Patel drew attention to the fact that it might be possible to use CTOs routinely when discharging patients in order to continue to retain control over them:

Lord Patel[110]

They could even become part of the normal discharge process for detained patients generally, as a kind of safety net for risk-averse mental health service staff and managers. If this happens, Parliament will not have produced a measure that enables a less restrictive alternative for the effective management of this small group of patients, but instead will have increased massively the legal coercion of psychiatric patients generally.

The Act provides that the power to recall someone to hospital must be 'necessary', before a CTO can be made, but it remains to be seen how this will be interpreted.

In addition to giving the power of recall to hospital, a CTO can be used to impose conditions—such as that the patient make himself available for treatment or desist from certain conduct—if those conditions are necessary or appropriate for one of three purposes, set out in section 17B(2):

Mental Health Act 1983 section 17B

17B(2)(a) ensuring that the patient receives medical treatment;

(b) preventing risk of harm to the patient's health or safety;

(c) protecting other persons.

---

[110] Hansard HL 2 July 2007, Col 844.

There is no list of the sort of conditions that might be imposed: rather, this decision lies within the RC's discretion, subject only to the need for the condition to be 'necessary or appropriate' for one of three rather broad purposes. The use of the word 'or' makes this criterion especially broad—or 'lax indeed', according to Phil Fennell.[111] Necessary *and* appropriate would have forced the RC to consider whether the condition was necessary to fulfil a purpose *and* appropriate in these particular circumstances. 'Necessary *or* appropriate' instead suggests that a condition could be attached because it was thought appropriate, even if it is not, in fact, necessary.

While the Code of Practice does state that the conditions should be kept to a minimum and restrict freedom as little as possible, CTOs undoubtedly have the potential to interfere substantially with a person's freedom. An RC might decide that a patient should not be allowed to associate with certain individuals, for example, if seeing them might make it more likely that the patient will resume their previous drug habit.

Mental Health Act Code of Practice para 25.33

25.33 The conditions should:

- be kept to a minimum number consistent with achieving their purpose;
- restrict the patient's liberty as little as possible while being consistent with achieving their purpose;
- have a clear rationale, linked to one or more of the purposes; and
- be clearly and precisely expressed, so that the patient can readily understand what is expected.

25.34 The nature of the conditions will depend on the patient's individual circumstances..., they might cover matters such as where and when the patient is to receive treatment in the community; where the patient is to live; and avoidance of known risk factors or high-risk situations relevant to the patient's mental disorder.

In addition to the conditions that may be attached to CTOs, the 2007 reforms inserted new sections, 64A–K, into the Act, which authorize the giving of 'relevant treatment' to community patients. 'Relevant treatment' is defined as medicines for mental disorder and ECT, and can be provided to competent patients in the community only if they consent and there is, within a month of the CTO being issued, a certificate from a SOAD authorizing treatment. For patients who lack capacity, treatment in the community without consent is possible under section 64D.

While the government's initial proposals for supervised community treatment suggested that there would be a power to force competent individuals to receive treatment in the community, the Act does not go this far and hence avoids what has been graphically described as the 'injection over a kitchen table' scenario.[112] Instead, compulsion can only be exercised over community patients who are refusing to comply with their treatment regimes or failing to comply with conditions imposed upon their lifestyle, by exercising the power to recall them to hospital.

Patients have the right to apply to the MHRT if one of more of the conditions for making a CTO are not satisfied, and the MHRT must order discharge if, for example, the power of recall to hospital is not necessary.

111 Phil Fennell, *Mental Health: The New Law* (Jordan: Bristol, 2007) 212.
112 Kings Fund Briefing *Mental Health Act 2007* (2008), available at <www.kingsfund.org.uk/>.

CTOs have been subject to a number of criticisms. First, it has been suggested that patient trust, and in particular a patient's willingness to seek out psychiatric services, will be compromised by the prospect of compulsion in the community. In the next extract Fiona Caldicott *et al.* point out that compulsion in the community is rejected for physical illnesses on the grounds that patients might avoid contact with health services, and they question why similar arguments are not accepted in the context of mental illness.

Fiona Caldicott, Edna Conlan, and Anthony Zigmund[113]

Patients ask why it is that any prospective deterioration in their condition through failure to follow medical advice should be subject to compulsion? If the answer seeks justification in the risk that such failure poses a danger to the well-being of others, why is it that diabetics or epileptics who fail adequately to follow a prescribed medical regime should nonetheless still be able, for example, to drive their cars (until such time as their licence is removed based on a report from their doctor), without them being removed to hospital for forcible administration of a sticky bun or insulin (as appropriate) or of an anti-convulsant? Were this the case, is it not likely that even more patients suffering from disorders that might bring them within the ambit of state control would find ways to avoid contact with the medical profession in order never to risk being subject to such coercive care? In summary, such a response runs a high risk of being anti-therapeutic. If the argument is so readily understood in respect of HIV and sexually transmitted diseases (ie that we need confidentiality if patients are to volunteer themselves for treatment and thereby reduce the aggregate risk and extent of suffering) why is it seemingly so hard to understand that marking out those with mental disorders as suitable for subjection to a coercive regime is likely, in the short term in respect of that patient and in the long term in respect of the body of patients, to reduce overall patient compliance?

Secondly, Judith Laing queries whether community treatment orders will genuinely represent the least restrictive alternative.

Judith Laing[114]

The government's assertion that the community treatment order is justified on the basis of providing a less restrictive alternative is also debatable and somewhat 'illusory'. Opponents of compulsory community treatment allege that it is a controlling mechanism and will not be the least restrictive alternative due to the fact that it actually increases the potential for monitoring and controlling people's lives...It is also argued that compulsory community orders could act as a 'hazard' and a disincentive for patients to seek help...Indeed, compulsory community orders may well exacerbate the problems faced by the mentally ill by increasing the stigma directed towards them as well as the discrimination and social exclusion experienced by them.

Thirdly, in the next extract, Patricia Walton, writing from the perspective of an Approved Social Worker (ASW), suggests that, in any event, a patient's refusal to take psychotropic drugs may not be a decision that needs to be treated by compulsion: rather, it may be a rational response to the unpleasant side-effects of these drugs.

---

[113] 'Client and Clinician—Law as an Intrusion' in N Eastman and J Peay (eds), *Law Without Enforcement: Integrating Mental Health and Justice* (Hart Publishing: Oxford, 1999) 75–88.
[114] 'Rights Versus Risk? Reform of the Mental Health Act 1983' (2000) 8 Medical Law Review 210–50, 240.

Patricia Walton[115]

ASWs are strongly opposed to compulsion in the community on social and human rights grounds: some people find the drug effects intolerable; some people find relentless awareness of their circumstances intolerable; the risks of suicide and other effects of unwanted long term drug treatment have not been considered; psychiatric treatments can be harmful; the impact of forcible treatment on the family and within the community have not been considered; a person's home should be a safe haven; people ultimately have the right to choose ill health...In the experience of ASWs, when people stop taking medication there is often complex interplay of reasons and the thinking around compulsory community treatment takes a simplistic view of this...In their experience many, possibly most, people on long-term medication choose to come off it from time to time, to be free of side-effects or to achieve a feeling of autonomy.

Finally, it could be argued that CTOs disproportionately emphasize the administration of medication, at the expense of other services, such as psychotherapy, and help with housing and employment, which may be equally or perhaps more important in helping patients to function in the community.

(c) GUARDIANSHIP

Compulsory powers over patients in the community can also be exercised via the appointment of a guardian under section 7 of the Act. A guardianship application can be made by an AMHP or the patient's nearest relative. The patient must be over the age of 16, and two medical practitioners must certify that she is suffering from mental disorder of a nature or degree that warrants reception into guardianship, and that it is necessary in the interests of the welfare of the patient or for the protection of others.[116] The intention is to ensure that the individual has a safe and secure environment, rather than to provide treatment for her disorder; as a result there is no 'treatability' requirement. The nearest relative has a right of veto, so no guardianship application can succeed in the face of their objection. It is, however, possible to apply to replace the nearest relative, if, for example, the AHMP believes that the relative is exercising the right of veto unreasonably.

Under section 8, the guardian has certain powers, such as the power to decide where the patient should live; to require access to the patient's place of residence; and to ensure the patient attends hospital for treatment. There is no power to compel the patient to actually receive treatment, however, and no sanctions are available to the guardian if she is unable to exercise her powers. As a result, guardianship orders are effective only where the patient is relatively compliant, when the order is, in practice, probably unnecessary. Unsurprisingly, therefore, guardianship is used comparatively infrequently. Nicola Glover-Thomas explains that:

The guardian's lack of powers has created despondency and led to the growing debate about community treatment orders and the future of community care...In practice guardianship has failed to live up to expectations and has not provided a workable community care measure.[117]

---

[115] 'Reforming the Mental Health Act 1983: An Approved Social Worker Perspective' (2000) 22 Journal of Social Welfare and Family Law 410–14.

[116] Section 7(2).

[117] *Reconstructing Mental Health Law and Policy* (Butterworths: London, 2002) 79–80.

8 CONCLUSION

As should be evident, there is much dissatisfaction among academic commentators and those working in the mental health field with the reform agenda which led to the 2007 amending Act. While the changes that were eventually incorporated by the 2007 Act were not as draconian as some of the measures in earlier draft Bills, community treatment orders and the measures designed to make it easier to detain people with personality disorders are still the subject of much criticism.

If the 2007 reforms were not the best way forward, what alternative approaches might there be? In the next extract, Nigel Eastman and Jill Peay argue that detention and treatment without consent should only be possible (a) if the patient lacks capacity, or (b) under some dangerousness criterion, and that the two routes to admission should be clearly separated in order to avoid stigmatizing those who suffer from mental illness.

Nigel Eastman and Jill Peay[118]

We are not alone in suggesting that thought ought to be given to replacing our current structure of mental health law, possibly with generic legislation separately covering incapacity and dangerousness, and certainly by legislation which puts on an equal footing the treatment of mental and physical disorders. Whilst it has been argued that the discriminatory locus is in attitudes towards those with mental disorders and not in the law *per se*, we would argue that the special presence of the law underpins these discriminatory attitudes and sustains discriminatory treatment...

Generic dangerousness legislation with tightly drawn criteria based on established behaviour and a clear and present threat is attractive if only because it is likely to make us think seriously abvout the need for protection of the rights of offenders, rather than confusing the advantages of dangerousness legislation with a therapeutic justification. Moreover, since most dangerous people are not mentally ill the balance of any generic legislation would immediately shift the focus of attention away from those suffering from mental disorder...Where the evidence is that mentally disordered people are in the aggregate little more dangerous...than other citizens and that it is substance abuse that most significantly raises the rate of violence in both patient and comparison groups, it is wrong that the mentally disordered in general should be tainted with an association with these high risk offenders.

In Scotland, under the Mental Health (Care and Treatment) (Scotland) Act 2003 compulsory powers can be used only where the patient is suffering from 'significantly impaired ability to make decisions' about treatment. The Scottish Code of Practice spells out that 'impaired decision-making is not simply disagreeing with the doctors'. The government in Westminster had opposed similar suggestions on the grounds that it would prevent people from being detained, however much others were at risk a a result.

For patients who lack capacity, treatment without consent, and a degree of paternalism, is clearly justifiable. But for the sub-group of mentally ill patients who are competent, paternalism needs some further justification than that they need treatment, or pose a risk to themselves. As we saw in the previous chapter, competent patients who want to refuse life-

---

[118] 'Afterword: Integrating Mental Health and Justice' in N Eastman and J Peay (eds), *Law Without Enforcement: Integrating Mental Health and Justice* (Hart Publishing: Oxford, 1999) 197–218.

saving treatment undoubtedly pose a risk to themselves, but this does not justify treating them without consent. The 'risk to others' exception is also problematic insofar as it would be unthinkable to detain and treat without consent someone with whooping cough or gonorrhea. Is there something special about mental illness which justifies riding roughshod over the principle of patient autonomy in a way that would be unthinkable if a competent patient wanted to refuse treatment for a physical illness?

On the one hand, it is clear that some mental disorders create self-destructive desires, such as the desire to end one's life, which can sometimes be effectively treated by medication or therapy. On the other hand, the dependency and helplessness which result from *physical* illness can also lead to the desire to end one's life, and yet provided the patient remains competent, forcing them to undergo life-saving treatment against their wishes would plainly be unlawful. Permitting *competent* mentally ill people to be treated without consent for their mental disorders discriminates between identically situated patients on the grounds of mental illness, and on that basis alone, is seriously problematic. Also, as Earl Howe explained in the House of Lords, it may be counterproductive by acting as a powerful disincentive to seeking help.

Earl Howe[119]

The Government say that every limitation on the ability of doctors to detain patients against their will has the effect of preventing those patients receiving the treatment that they need. To put the matter in those terms, however, presupposes that compulsion is the only means by which effective treatment can be delivered. Of course, it is not: good treatment is available without compulsion, and the fear of some of us is that the wider the gateway to compulsion and the easier the law makes it to get people through it, the less likely it is that those who need help will come forward to ask for it. Never let us forget the anguish, trauma and humiliation involved in subjecting a patient to compulsion—and never let us forget…that compulsion should never be seen as a substitute for good healthcare.

Finally, it is undoubtedly true that there is a very small sub-set of mentally disordered people who are likely to be violent, but this is, of course, equally true of the population as a whole. A tiny minority of people, whether they are mentally ill or not, are simply more likely to commit violent offences than the rest of us. But our capacity to predict in advance who these people are is not sufficiently accurate to justify the deprivation of their liberty. In any event, the propensity to violence appears to correlate at least as much with substance abuse and drunkenness than it does with mental illness.

FURTHER READING

Bartlett, Peter, 'The Test of Compulsion in Mental Health Law: Capacity, Therapeutic Benefit and Dangerousness as Possible Criteria' (2003) 11 Medical Law Review 326–52.

Bartlett, Peter, 'A Matter of Necessity? Enforced Treatment Under the Mental Health Act' (2007) 15 Medical Law Review 86–98.

---

[119] Hansard HL 2 July 2007, Col 826.

Bartlett, P and Sandland, R, *Mental Health Law: Policy and Practice*, 3rd edn (OUP: Oxford, 2007).

Eastman, N and Peay, J (eds), *Law Without Enforcement: Integrating Mental Health and Justice* (Hart Publishing: Oxford, 1999).

Fennell, Phil, *Treatment Without Consent: Law, Psychiatry and the Treatment of Mentally Disordered People since 1845* (Routledge: London, 1996).

Fennell, Phil, *Mental Health: The New Law* (Jordans: Bristol, 2007).

Francis, Robert, 'The Michael Stone Inquiry: A Reflection' (2007) Journal of Mental Health Law 85–96.

Glover-Thomas, Nicola, *Reconstructing Mental Health Law and Policy* (Butterworths: London, 2002).

Laing, Judith, 'Rights Versus Risk? Reform of the Mental Health Act 1983' (2000) 8 Medical Law Review 210–50.

Lewis, Penney, 'Feeding Anorexic Patients Who Refuse Food' (1999) 7 Medical Law Review 21–37.

Palmer, Stephanie, 'A Wrong Turning: Article 3 ECHR and Proportionality' (2006) 65 *Cambridge Law Journal* 438–52.

Peay, Jill, *Decisions and Dilemmas: Working with Mental Health Law* (Hart Publishing: Oxford, 2003).

Richardson, Genevra, 'Autonomy, Guardianship and Mental Disorder: One Problem, Two Solutions' (2002) 65 Modern Law Review 702–23.

7

CONFIDENTIALITY

CENTRAL ISSUES

1. Doctors are under a duty to respect their patients' confidentiality for two principal reasons. First, information about a person's health is paradigmatically private. Secondly, without a guarantee of confidentiality, patients may be unwilling to provide information which might be vitally important in diagnosing and treating them.

2. The Data Protection Act 1998 provides that sensitive personal data must be processed fairly and lawfully. Normally the patient's consent is necessary, but there are a number of exceptions to this, such as the need to protect a person's 'vital interests' and the use of data for research and audit.

3. The legal duty of confidentiality is not absolute. The reality of modern medical treatment is that patient information will be shared between a number of health care professionals. Information can also be disclosed where the public interest in disclosure outweighs the public interest in respecting confidentiality, perhaps because there is a risk of serious harm to others.

4. Genetic information raises a number of complex issues in relation to confidentiality; these are dealt with in Chapter 8.

1 INTRODUCTION

Unlike patient autonomy, which is a relatively recent preoccupation of medical law and ethics, a doctor's duty to respect her patients' confidentiality has its origins in the first codes of medical ethics. The Hippocratic Oath, for example, states that:

whatsoever things I see or hear concerning the life of men, in my attendance on the sick or even apart therefrom, which ought not to be noised abroad, I will keep silence thereon, counting such things to be as sacred secrets, and patient confidentiality also receives unqualified protection in the modern version of the Oath, the Declaration of Geneva:

> I will respect the secrets which are confided in me, even after the patient has died.

In this chapter, we begin by examining the ethical justifications for protecting patient confidentiality. We then consider various different legal sources of the duty of confidence. Next, we flesh out the exceptions to the duty of confidence, and the remedies available for its breach. Finally, we briefly look at patients' rights to gain access to their medical records.

2 WHY RESPECT CONFIDENTIALITY?

Both deontological (duty-based) and teleological (consequentialist) reasoning (see chapter 1) can be used to justify the existence of a duty of confidence between patients and doctors. Deontological arguments would emphasize the patients' right to privacy, and their interest in controlling access to what will often be extremely sensitive and personal information. For example, the Medical Research Council's guidance on confidentiality states:

> Respect for private life is a human right, and the ability to discuss information in confidence with others is rightly valued. Keeping control over facts about one's self can have an important role in a person's sense of security, freedom of action, and self-respect.[1]

The consequentialist argument for respecting patient confidentiality is that optimum medical care can be provided only if a patient feels able to be honest with her doctor, and this will be dependent upon the patient believing that her doctor is under a duty not to disclose personal, and perhaps embarrassing information. As Raanan Gillon points out, confidentiality is beneficial for individual patients and for society as a whole.

Raanan Gillon[2]

> [I]n order to do a good job for their patients doctors often need to have information of a sort that people generally regard as private, even secret. Some of the information is merely embarrassing to discuss, some may be positively harmful to the patients or others if it is divulged. Doctors routinely ask a series of questions about bodily functions that people would not dream of discussing with anyone else. When a patient's medical problems may relate to genitourinary functions a doctor may need to know about that patient's sexual activities, sometimes in detail. When a patient's problems are psychological a doctor may need to know in great detail about the patient's experiences, ideas and feelings, relationships past and present, even in some contexts about the person's imaginings and fantasies. In genetics contexts investigations may demonstrate non-paternity—that is, that the putative father of a patient's child is not the genetic father.

[1] Personal Information in Medical Research (MRC: London, 2000).
[2] 'Confidentiality' in Helga Kuhse and Peter Singer (eds), *A Companion to Bioethics* (Blackwell: Oxford, 1998) 425–31.

Such intrusive medical inquiries are based not on prurience or mere inquisitiveness but on the pursuit of information that is of potential assistance to the doctor in treating and helping the patient. Nonetheless many patients are unlikely to pass on this information unless they have some assurances of confidentiality.

Quite apart from the medical benefits to the patient, maintenance of confidentiality may in some circumstances benefit the health of others. In the context of transmissible diseases, especially sexually transmissible diseases, so long as the patient continues to trust his or her doctor the doctor is left in a position of being able to educate and influence the patient in ways that can reduce the likelihood of the disease being passed on. As soon as confidentiality is broken the trusting relationship is likely to be undermined and the opportunity to help reduce the spread of disease is lost.

Of course, whether or not it is true that patients would be reluctant to be candid with their doctors, if their confidentiality was not protected, is essentially an *empirical* question. Interestingly, Chris Jones points out that few people have attempted to find out whether patient trust is, in fact, contingent upon respect for confidentiality. Jones's own study did, however, confirm the generally untested assumption that patients might be deterred from seeking treatment if their confidentiality was not respected.

Chris Jones[3]

The utilitarian justification for maintaining medical confidentiality rests ultimately on a calculation of the effects of confidentiality or disclosure on the behaviour of current and potential future patients. This calculation is often based upon theoretical views of how patients are likely to behave, but in principle it is also open to empirical study: how does the behaviour of patients alter when presented with different standards of confidentiality? Only if there is good reason, grounded in empirical evidence, to believe that patients will be reluctant to disclose potential [sic] damaging information in situations where subsequent disclosure is anticipated, could we be confident that the utilitarian basis for confidentiality is justified....

The utilitarian position receives considerable support from the views expressed in this study by patients. They clearly value confidentiality, see it as important in a medical consultation, and recognise that disclosure without consent would be likely to deter some patients from seeking treatment. To this extent it seems that the generally accepted view of the benefits of confidentiality can be justified. However for many people the utility of confidentiality appears to be outweighed by the benefits of disclosure in order to protect third parties. They were prepared to endorse disclosure of information at the same time as recognising that treatment might be impaired as a result.

Although important, confidentiality is clearly not an absolute obligation. The Hippocratic Oath only instructs doctors to keep secret that 'which ought not to be noised abroad', the implication being that there *are* circumstances in which information *should* be 'noised abroad'. The Declaration of Geneva does not appear to be qualified in this way, but the existence of exceptions to the duty of confidence is so well established that it would probably be a mistake to read too much into this.

[3] 'The Utilitarian Argument for Medical Confidentiality: A Pilot Study of Patients' Views' (2003) 29 Journal of Medical Ethics 348–52.

Most obviously, an absolute duty of confidentiality would make it impossible to provide effective medical treatment. The provision of appropriate diagnostic and therapeutic care is often dependent upon a number of health care professionals having access to a patient's records. Medical care is generally provided by teams of doctors and nurses. Patients may be referred to specialist consultants, or for additional diagnostic procedures, such as blood tests, X-rays, and scans. If information about the patient's condition could never be shared with others, the provision of health care would grind to a halt.

While the belief that what one tells one's doctor 'will go no further' has probably always been an illusion, in the next extract, Lawrence Gostin points out that, as a result of new technologies, patients' notes now contain a great deal of information that can very easily be shared and transferred.

Lawrence Gostin[4]

Only a few generations ago, physicians kept minimal written records about their patients. Physicians usually knew their patients and did not see a need to maintain extensive written reminders of patients' clinical histories. Today, the quantity of health records and the nature of the data they contain have increased substantially. The health records of patients, therefore, contain significant amounts of sensitive information that are available for inspection by many others....

The combination of emerging computer and genetic technologies poses particularly compelling privacy concerns. Science has the capacity to store a million fragments of DNA on a silicon microchip...This technology can markedly facilitate research, screening, and treatment of genetic conditions. But it may also permit a significant reduction in privacy through its capacity to inexpensively store and decipher unimaginable quantities of highly sensitive data.

Aside from sharing information within the health service, other exceptions to the duty of confidentiality exist, often justified by the 'public interest'. Because the principal justification for *respecting* patient confidentiality is also the public interest, working out whether disclosure is justified in a particular case will often involve a complex balancing exercise between competing interests. If a patient confides in his doctor that he has committed a very serious crime, such as child abuse, should the doctor inform the police? What if the offence is recreational drug use? On the one hand, there is a clear public interest in the prevention and detection of crime, but on the other, it is also in the public interest for paedophiles and drug users to willingly come forward to seek help.

Given the number of variables, it is difficult to draw hard and fast rules about the circumstances that would justify disclosure of confidential information. The lack of clarity that results from this sort of case-by-case balancing exercise undoubtedly makes it difficult for doctors to know exactly when their primary duty of confidentiality will be trumped by competing considerations. To make an already confusing situation worse, the law in this area is especially difficult to understand. This is largely because there are several possible sources of the legal duty of confidentiality. A legal duty of confidence exists in vastly different situations, from duties under the Official Secrets Act to the protection of commercially sensitive information. It is difficult to extrapolate principles which will be applicable in the context

---

[4] 'Health Informational Privacy' (1995) 80 Cornell Law Review 451.

of medical information from cases involving government secrets or patented information. Some statutes, most notably the Data Protection Act 1998, clearly have an impact upon medical records, and yet because this was never their principal focus, their application to the doctor–patient relationship can be ambiguous and confusing.

At the outset, it should be remembered that not all patient information is equally sensitive. A patient might be very anxious to keep her HIV status private, but be much less concerned about whether a consultant has used an X-ray of her broken foot in a lecture to junior doctors.

Furthermore, it could be argued that the priority given to patient confidentiality rests upon an unrealistically individualistic model of medical decision-making. In practice, most patients do not want to keep information about their health secret *from the whole world*. Rather, while people might not want their employers or insurers to have access to their medical records, they are generally happy to discuss their health with people who are close to them. Patients facing difficult medical choices or the diagnosis of serious illness often want someone close to them to be present during discussions with their doctors. In the next extract, Roy Gilbar argues that, in the context of familial relationships, the strict rule of confidentiality should be reconsidered.

Roy Gilbar[5]

While the relationship between patients and employers or insurers is primarily confrontational, with patients anxious to protect their rights and not be discriminated against, the relationship with family members is generally based on care, commitment and mutual responsibility. Consequently, information is in most cases communicated more freely within the family than with other third parties....

[P]atients often consider the interests of their relatives and the implications of their decision on their familial relationship, while doctors are willing to involve family members more than the law currently permits to help the patient cope with the bad news. In other words, doctors and patients value the patient's familial relationship as a separate and significant component in this area. Thus, the strict legal rule of medical confidentiality, which is adopted by many lawyers and policy-makers, should be re-considered....

If it is accepted that the gaps between law and practice should be bridged, then it can be argued that a doctor's duty of confidentiality must be qualified when it concerns the family. It must reflect awareness of familial solidarity and mutual responsibility and the reality that family members are inherently involved in the patient's well-being and medical care....

Doctors in various areas of medicine have learned to accept that the support and comfort that family members provide to the patient during all the stages of his/her illness is important, and that the family rather than the individual patient, should be considered as the unit of medical care. This, in many cases, leads to the conclusion that adhering to a strict rule of confidentiality may compromise the interests of the patient instead of promoting them.

Even if we were to accept that people do not always want to keep information about their health secret from their closest friends or relatives, disclosure should still lie within the patient's control. Not all intimate and familial relationships are harmonious and supportive, and a person might have very good reasons for wanting to keep information from her partner or her relatives.

5 'Medical Confidentiality Within the Family: The Doctor's Duty Reconsidered' (2004) 18 International Journal of Law, Policy and the Family 195.

3 A DUTY OF CONFIDENTIALITY

In the following sections we examine a number of different sources of the legal duty of confidence.

(a) AT COMMON LAW

The origins of the legal duty of confidence lie in the equitable jurisdiction of the Chancery Division to grant injunctions in order to prevent the infringement of legal and equitable rights. So what gives rise to an enforceable duty of confidentiality? In *AG v Guardian Newspapers (No. 2)*, known as the *Spycatcher* case, Lord Bingham explained that the duty of confidence arises from an obligation of conscience, and Lord Goff laid out the necessary conditions for the existence of a duty of confidence.

AG v Guardian Newspapers (No. 2)[6]

Lord Bingham

The cases show that the duty of confidence does not depend on any contract, express or implied, between the parties. If it did, it would follow on ordinary principles that strangers to the contract would not be bound. But the duty 'depends on the broad principle of equity that he who has received information in confidence shall not take unfair advantage of it'...A third party coming into possession of confidential information is accordingly liable to be restrained from publishing it if he knows the information to be confidential and the circumstances are such as to impose upon him an obligation in good conscience not to publish.

Lord Goff

[A] duty of confidence arises when confidential information comes to the knowledge of a person (the confidant) in circumstances where he has notice, or is held to have agreed, that the information is confidential, with the effect that it would be just in all the circumstances that he should be precluded from disclosing the information to others.

Lord Goff went on to suggest three limiting principles: first, that the information must itself be confidential, and must not already be in the public domain; secondly, there is no duty of confidentiality in relation to useless information or trivial; and thirdly, the duty to respect confidentiality is not an absolute one, and can sometimes be trumped where there is a weightier public interest in disclosure.

The factors that give rise to a duty of confidentiality are thus both vague and somewhat question-begging; effectively a duty of confidence arises when someone knows, or ought to know, that the information she has acquired is confidential. It is both the *nature* of the information and the *circumstances in which it was disclosed* that create the duty of confidentiality.

For our purposes, however, the position is relatively clear. Medical information will generally be the sort of information which is treated as confidential, and the doctor–patient relationship is plainly one in which a duty of confidence exists. As Boreham J stated in

---

[6] [1990] AC 109.

Hunter v Mann:[7] 'in common with other professional men, for instance a priest and there are of course others, the doctor is under a duty not to disclose, without the consent of his patient, information which he, the doctor, has gained in his professional capacity, save...in very exceptional circumstances'.

In *W v Egdell*, a case which we consider in more detail below, the existence of a duty of confidence between Dr Egdell and the patient was not in doubt.

W v Egdell[8]

Bingham LJ

It has never been doubted that the circumstances here were such as to impose on Dr Egdell a duty of confidence owed to W. He could not lawfully sell the contents of his report to a newspaper, as the judge held. Nor could he, without a breach of the law as well as professional etiquette, discuss the case in a learned article or in his memoirs or in gossiping with friends, unless he took appropriate steps to conceal the identity of W. It is not in issue here that a duty of confidence existed.

An alternative basis for the duty of confidentiality at common law would be to characterize it as an aspect of the doctor's duty of care. A doctor who discloses information which should have been kept private may not have acted as a reasonable doctor, and the patient might therefore be able to bring an action in negligence. This will only be possible, however, if the patient has suffered some sort of damage as a result of the negligent disclosure: an example might be being turned down for insurance coverage. More commonly, the 'harm' that results from a breach of confidentiality will be less tangible, and an action in tort much less promising.

It is usually assumed that the duty of confidentiality is owed to the patient, rather than to the hospital treating her. However, the hospital too might have an important interest in ensuring the confidentiality of its patient records. In *Ashworth Hospital Authority v Mirror Group Newspapers (MGN) Ltd*, the *Mirror* newspaper had published information about the medical treatment of Ian Brady, one of the Moors murderers. Ian Brady had been keen to publicize what he perceived to be his ill treatment, and had himself attempted to put information about his treatment into the public domain. The hospital obtained an order requiring the newspaper to identify the employee who had 'leaked' Brady's medical notes. On appeal, the House of Lords decided that the security of medical records was of such overriding importance that it was essential that the person who had disclosed them to the newspaper was identified and punished, even if the patient himself did not object to the disclosure.

Ashworth Hospital Authority v Mirror Group Newspapers (MGN) Ltd[9]

Lord Woolf

[W]hile Ian Brady's conduct in putting similar information into the public domain could well mean that he would not be in a position to complain about the publication, this did not destroy the authority's independent interest in retaining the confidentiality of the medical records

---

[7] [1974] QB 767.   [8] [1990] Ch 359.   [9] [2002] 1 WLR 2033.

> contained in Ashworth's files....The care of patients at Ashworth is fraught with difficulty and danger. The disclosure of the patients' records increases that difficulty and danger and to deter the same or similar wrongdoing in the future it was essential that the source should be identified and punished. This was what made the orders to disclose necessary and proportionate and justified. The fact that Ian Brady had himself disclosed his medical history did not detract from the need to prevent staff from revealing medical records of patients. Ian Brady's conduct did not damage the integrity of Ashworth's patients' records. The source's disclosure was wholly inconsistent with the security of the records and the disclosure was made worse because it was purchased by a cash payment.

The decision in *Ashworth* was not the end of the story, however. Instead of disclosing the name of the staff member who had leaked Brady's records, MGN only disclosed the name of the investigative journalist, Ackroyd. Ashworth, which had by this time been subsumed within the Mersey Care NHS Trust then brought an action against Ackroyd, requiring him to reveal his sources (he had admitted there was more than one).

The case reached the Court of Appeal, which had to engage in a fresh balancing act between the public interest in disclosure and the public interest in protecting the confidentiality of medical records. By this time, more facts had emerged about the circumstances of the leak: first, the motivation had not, in fact, been financial greed, as had previously been assumed; secondly, only part of Brady's notes had been disclosed; and, thirdly, it was by no means clear that the source had been a member of the hospital's staff. In *Mersey Care NHS Trust v Ackroyd (No. 2)*[10] the Court of Appeal decided that the journalist did not have to disclose his sources.

This case demonstrates that the confidentiality of medical records has to be put in the balance with other important interests, such as press freedom. Ralph Sandland suggests that *Ackroyd* tipped the balance in favour of journalistic freedom.

Ralph Sandland[11]

> From the perspective of Mersey NHS Trust and Ashworth Hospital, *Ackroyd* is bad news. The hospital's victory in *Ashworth* has been rendered pyrrhic; all that effort, over seven years of litigation, including three visits to the Court of Appeal and one to the House of Lords, has been for nothing. The hospital still does not know—but does now know that it will probably never know—the identities of the sources of the leak. From the perspective of journalists, the effective legal protection of sources, seen as having been damaged by *Ashworth*, has been largely restored.

(b) THE HUMAN RIGHTS ACT 1998

A patient's interest in confidentiality also receives protection from Article 8 of the Human Rights Act 1998: the 'right to respect for private and family life'. Article 8 is not an absolute right, however, and is qualified by 8(2):

---

[10] [2007] EWCA Civ 101.

[11] 'Freedom of the Press and the Confidentiality of Medical Records' (2007) 15 Medical Law Review 400–409.

Human Rights Act 1998 Schedule 1 Article 8

8(1) Everyone has the right to respect for his private and family life, his home and his correspondence.

(2) There shall be no interference by a public authority with the exercise of this right except such as is in accordance with the law and is necessary in a democratic society in the interests of national security, public safety or the economic well-being of the country, for the prevention of disorder or crime, for the protection of health or morals, or for the protection of the rights and freedoms of others.

There have been a number of cases in which patients have relied upon Article 8 when complaining about the disclosure of medical information. It has not proved especially difficult for individuals to establish that any disclosure of their medical records constitutes a prima facie violation of Article 8. The principal obstacle to a successful claim is that it has often been possible for public authorities to establish that disclosure is justifiable under Article 8(2).

In *Z v Finland*, for example, Z was married to someone who had been charged with a number of sexual offences. He was HIV positive, and in order to find out when he became aware of his HIV status, the police sought and gained access to Z's medical records. The ECtHR held that seizing Z's medical records and ordering her doctors to give evidence did not amount to a violation of Article 8 because there were good reasons for requiring this information: a legitimate aim was being pursued and the measures taken were not disproportionate.

Z v Finland[12]

Judgment of the ECtHR

In view of the highly intimate and sensitive nature of information concerning a person's HIV status, any state measures compelling communication or disclosure of such information without the consent of the patient call for the most careful scrutiny on the part of the court, as do the safeguards designed to secure an effective protection...

At the same time, the court accepts that the interests of a patient and the community as a whole in protecting the confidentiality of medical data may be outweighed by the interest in investigation and prosecution of crime and in the publicity of court proceedings, where such interests are shown to be of even greater importance.

In *Stone v South East Coast SHA*, the convicted murderer Michael Stone sought to suppress publication of a homicide inquiry, which contained considerable detail about his medical treatment. While Davis J acknowledged his right to privacy, and the argument that publication might deter patients from being frank with their doctors and with inquiry panel members, this was outweighed by the public interest in knowing more about the treatment which Mr Stone had, and perhaps more importantly had not received. Also relevant was the fact that the need for this inquiry arose from Mr Stone's own criminal acts, and that a great deal of information about his treatment was already in the public domain. Davis J also decided that a redacted or summarized version of the report would not work and, further, 'might be viewed with scepticism by the public, who might even suspect a cover-up'.

---

[12] (1997) 25 EHRR 371.

Stone v South East Coast SHA[13]

Davis J

So far as Mr Stone is concerned, much the most weighty point in his favour, as it seems to me, is his very entitlement to claim a right of privacy: in respect moreover of an aspect of private information (medical information) which—as the jurisprudence from Europe shows—is regarded as a vital and central element of that which should be protected under Article 8. Further, that is reinforced by other and wider considerations of the public interest: first, that persons may talk freely with their doctors, probation officers and other such persons without being deterred by risk of subsequent disclosure...; second, that such persons may give access to such information for the purposes of an inquiry without being deterred from doing so through fear of such matters later being released into the public domain.

But it seems to me that the force of those points is significantly outweighed by a number of other considerations...

[T]here is a true public interest in the public at large knowing of the actual care and treatment supplied (or, as the case may be, not supplied) to Mr Stone: and knowing, and being able to reach an informed assessment of, the failures identified and steps that may be recommended to be taken to address identified deficiencies....

[I]t is, I think, of importance as a justification for restricting Mr Stone's right to privacy in this context that this inquiry, and all this publicity, have arisen out of Mr Stone's own acts—acts found to have been criminal. He has, as it were, put himself in the public domain by reason of those criminal acts, which inevitably created great publicity. Of course that is not to say that a convicted murderer forfeits all his rights under Article 8; of course he does not. But here the information sought to be disclosed relates—and relates solely—to the investigation foreseeably arising out of the very murders which he himself committed.

I also think it a point of considerable importance as a justification for restricting Mr Stone's right to privacy in this context that a great deal of information relating to the background, treatment and mental health of Mr Stone has already been put in the public domain, and at a significant level of detail.... [P]revious publication of private information in the public domain does not mean that an individual necessarily loses his right to privacy in respect of a proposal to put yet more such material in the public domain. But, as it seems to me, it must be relevant to the balancing exercise and to the issue of proportionality: and here the previous disclosure in the public domain has already been very extensive indeed. That must tell against the asserted detrimental impact of publication of further, albeit more detailed, information.

In addition to Article 8(2)'s qualification of the right to privacy, Article 8 has to be put into the balance with Article 10, the right to freedom of expression, and section 12 of the Human Rights Act, which specifies that, 'The court must have particular regard to the importance of the Convention right to freedom of expression.'

The need to balance the interests protected by Articles 8 and 10 in the context of patient information arose in *Campbell v MGN Ltd*. The House of Lords had to determine whether the press's freedom to publish information about the model Naomi Campbell's treatment for drug addiction should take priority over her right to privacy. Ms Campbell accepted that the newspaper had been entitled, in the public interest, to disclose the information that she was a drug addict and that she was receiving treatment for her addiction, because she had previously falsely and publicly stated that she was not a drug addict. But she claimed that

---

13 [2006] EWHC 1668 (Admin).

the details of her attendance at Narcotics Anonymous, and accompanying photographs, amounted to a breach of her privacy.

Campbell v MGN Ltd[14]

Baroness Hale

I start, therefore, from the fact—indeed, it is common ground—that all of the information about Miss Campbell's addiction and attendance at NA which was revealed in the *Mirror* article was both private and confidential, because it related to an important aspect of Miss Campbell's physical and mental health and the treatment she was receiving for it. It had also been received from an insider in breach of confidence....

What was the nature of the freedom of expression which was being asserted on the other side? There are undoubtedly different types of speech, just as there are different types of private information, some of which are more deserving of protection in a democratic society than others. Top of the list is political speech. The free exchange of information and ideas on matters relevant to the organisation of the economic, social and political life of the country is crucial to any democracy....Artistic speech and expression is important for similar reasons...

But it is difficult to make such claims on behalf of the publication with which we are concerned here. The political and social life of the community, and the intellectual, artistic or personal development of individuals, are not obviously assisted by pouring over the intimate details of a fashion model's private life....

The weight to be attached to these various considerations is a matter of fact and degree. Not every statement about a person's health will carry the badge of confidentiality or risk doing harm to that person's physical or moral integrity. The privacy interest in the fact that a public figure has a cold or a broken leg is unlikely to be strong enough to justify restricting the press's freedom to report it. What harm could it possibly do? Sometimes there will be other justifications for publishing, especially where the information is relevant to the capacity of a public figure to do the job. But that is not this case and in this case there was, as the judge found, a risk that publication would do harm. The risk of harm is what matters at this stage, rather than the proof that actual harm has occurred. People trying to recover from drug addiction need considerable dedication and commitment, along with constant reinforcement from those around them. That is why organisations like NA were set up and why they can do so much good. Blundering in when matters are acknowledged to be at a 'fragile' stage may do great harm.

Notice that the House of Lords found that an obligation of confidence existed because of the *nature* of the information about Ms Campbell's treatment for drug addiction, rather than because of any pre-existing relationship between her and the *Mirror* newspaper. Unlike the cases on breach of confidence which we considered in the previous section, the right to *privacy* attaches to *any* private information, regardless of the circumstances in which that information is acquired.

In *R (on the application of B) v Stafford Combined Court* there was a conflict between two different competing interests: the need for a fair trial and a patient's right to confidentiality. B was a 14-year-old girl who was the main prosecution witness in the trial of a defendant, W, who was accused and subsequently convicted of sexually abusing her. His legal team had sought access to her psychiatric records, on the grounds that they were relevant to her

---

[14] [2004] UKHL 22.

credibility as a witness. At first instance, the judge had held that the interest in a fair trial was more important than the patient's interests in the confidentiality of her medical records, and ordered disclosure.

After an intervention by the Official Solicitor, the Judge, who was anxious not to delay the trial, invited B to attend court. There was no arrangement or opportunity for her to be represented, and she agreed reluctantly to disclosure, because she could not face the prospect of the trial being delayed. May LJ was sharply critical of the Judge's conduct, and found that the Court itself had breached B's Article 8 rights.

R (on the application of B) v Stafford Combined Court[15]

May LJ

I strongly deprecate what happened on 6 December 2005. It seems to me to be quite unacceptable for a vulnerable 14-year-old school girl known to have attempted suicide, the victim of alleged sexual abuse and a prosecution witness in the impending trial, to be brought to court at short notice, without representation or support, to be faced personally with an apparent choice between agreeing to the disclosure of her psychiatric records or delaying a trial which was bound to cause her concern and stress.

In my judgment, procedural fairness in the light of article 8 undoubtedly required in the present case that B should have been given notice of the application for the witness summons, and given the opportunity to make representations before the order was made. Since the rules did not require this of the person applying for the summons, the requirement was on the court as a public authority, not on W, the defendant. B was not given due notice or that opportunity, so the interference with her rights was not capable of being necessary within article 8(2). Her rights were infringed and the court acted unlawfully in a way which was incompatible with her Convention rights. This in substance is what the requested declarations seek and I would grant them.

(c) THE DATA PROTECTION ACT 1998

The Data Protection Act 1998 was passed in order to implement a European directive.[16] Schedule 1 of the Act contains eight Data Protection Principles. The first Data Protection Principle states that all personal data must be processed 'fairly and lawfully'. Processing essentially means doing anything at all with information, so obtaining, storing, disclosing, or using information will all be covered by the Act.

What does it mean to process data *fairly* and *lawfully*? Obviously to be lawful, processing must meet common law obligations of confidentiality, but the Act itself further defines 'fairness' and 'legality' in a way which is, to say the least, rather confusing. For sensitive personal data, which under section 2(e) includes information about a person's 'physical or mental health or condition', processing will have been fair and lawful provided that (in addition to meeting common law obligations of confidentiality) at least one condition from Schedule 2 of the Act and one from Schedule 3 are satisfied.

---

[15] [2006] EWHC 1645 (Admin).

[16] European Directive 95/46/EC on the Protection of Individuals with Regard to the Processing of Personal Data and on the Free Movement of Such Data (known as the Data Protection Directive).

Data Protection Act 1998 schedules 1–3

Schedule 1

1. Personal data shall be processed fairly and lawfully and, in particular, shall not be processed unless—

(a) at least one of the conditions in Schedule 2 is met, and

(b) in the case of sensitive personal data, at least one of the conditions in Schedule 3 is also met.

Schedule 2

CONDITIONS RELEVANT FOR PURPOSES OF THE FIRST PRINCIPLE: PROCESSING OF ANY PERSONAL DATA

1. The data subject has given his consent to the processing....
4. The processing is necessary in order to protect the vital interests of the data subject.
5. The processing is necessary—

(a) for the administration of justice,

(b) for the exercise of any functions conferred on any person by or under any enactment,

(c) for the exercise of any functions of the Crown, a Minister of the Crown or a government department, or

(d) for the exercise of any other functions of a public nature exercised in the public interest by any person.

6. (1) The processing is necessary for the purposes of legitimate interests pursued by the data controller or by the third party or parties to whom the data are disclosed, except where the processing is unwarranted in any particular case by reason of prejudice to the rights and freedoms or legitimate interests of the data subject.

(2) The Secretary of State may by order specify particular circumstances in which this condition is, or is not, to be taken to be satisfied.

Schedule 3

CONDITIONS RELEVANT FOR PURPOSES OF THE FIRST PRINCIPLE: PROCESSING OF SENSITIVE PERSONAL DATA

1. The data subject has given his explicit consent to the processing of the personal data....
3. The processing is necessary—

(a) in order to protect the vital interests of the data subject or another person, in a case where—

(i) consent cannot be given by or on behalf of the data subject, or

(ii) the data controller cannot reasonably be expected to obtain the consent of the data subject, or

(c) in order to protect the vital interests of another person, in a case where consent by or on behalf of the data subject has been unreasonably withheld....

8. (1) The processing is necessary for medical purposes and is undertaken by—

(a) a health professional, or

(b) a person who in the circumstances owes a duty of confidentiality which is equivalent to that which would arise if that person were a health professional.

(2) In this paragraph 'medical purposes' includes the purposes of preventative medicine, medical diagnosis, medical research, the provision of care and treatment and the management of healthcare services.

Under Schedule 2, either the data subject must consent to the 'processing' of personal data, or disclosure must fit within one of the six exceptions to the need to obtain consent contained in Schedule 2, three of which are worth highlighting here. First, data may be processed without consent if it is necessary to protect the vital interests of the data subject. This exception is not confined to situations where the patient's life is in danger: rather, it could simply mean that sharing the information is necessary in order to protect her health. It is, however, only justifiable if the processing is *necessary* as opposed to merely convenient.

Secondly, processing without consent might be justifiable under Schedule 2 if it is 'necessary' for functions of a public nature exercised in the public interest, or for the exercise of functions of government departments, or a Secretary of State. As we saw in Chapter 2, the Secretary of State for Health is under a duty to 'continue the promotion of a comprehensive health service'. Provided that the processing of patient information was *necessary* for him to fulfil this function, it would appear lawful to use patient records without consent. Here, of course, the problem is what might be meant by 'necessary'. For example, is the maintenance of nationwide cancer registries *necessary* for the promotion of a comprehensive health service?

Thirdly, processing without consent is legitimate if it is necessary for the purposes of the data controller's legitimate interests. This might allow disclosure for the purposes of training or audit, and again the crucial question is whether the use of data is *necessary* for these purposes.

Once a condition from Schedule 2 has been satisfied, it is then necessary to turn to Schedule 3, which contains ten exceptions to the need to obtain the data subject's 'explicit consent' to the processing of sensitive personal data. Here things become slightly clearer because the eighth condition in Schedule 3 is that processing without consent is justifiable if it 'is necessary for medical purposes', and is undertaken by a health professional or a person who owes an equivalent duty of confidentiality. Medical purposes are not confined to treatment, but include 'preventative medicine, medical diagnosis, medical research, the provision of care and treatment and the management of health care services'. Given this expansive list, the only limiting criterion here is again that the processing should be *necessary* for one of these purposes.

A further exception to the explicit consent requirement is contained in paragraph 3 of Schedule 3, which provides that processing will be fair and lawful if it is in the vital interests of the data subject or another person. Hence, information can be disclosed without consent to protect the health of a third party.

The Data Protection (Processing of Sensitive Personal Data) Order 2000 added a further condition to Schedule 3. This allows for processing which is in the 'substantial public interest' where necessary for the discharge of certain public functions, such as protecting the public against malpractice, or other seriously improper conduct, unfitness, or incompetence. Hence disclosure to the General Medical Council (GMC) in relation to an allegation of professional misconduct would be permissible without consent. The limiting factors are that the processing must be in the substantial public interest, and, again, that it must be necessary for discharging the particular public function.

The second Data Protection Principle specifies that information must be obtained only for one or more specified and lawful purposes, and must not be further processed in a way that is incompatible with those purposes. Section 33 contains an exception where the further processing is for the purposes of research. The final Data Protection Principle which is relevant for our purposes is the fifth one, which specifies that information must be kept no longer than necessary for the purposes for which it is processed. Again, there is an exception for information that is processed for research purposes, which can be kept indefinitely.

If any of these provisions are breached, the Data Protection Act provides for three different remedies. First, under section 10 a data subject can serve a notice requiring the data controller to cease or refrain from processing his personal data. The data subject must establish that the processing is causing, or would be likely to cause substantial damage, either to her or to a third party. Secondly, it is possible to seek compensation under section 13 where the data subject or another has suffered damage and consequent distress as a result of the disclosure. The data controller will, however, have a defence if he can show that he took reasonable care to comply with the Act. Thirdly, under section 14 the court can order the data controller to rectify or destroy inaccurate data.

(d) OTHER STATUTORY PROVISIONS

In certain situations, additional obligations to respect confidentiality are created by statute. For example, section 33 of the Human Fertilisation and Embryology Act 1990 imposes additional restrictions upon the disclosure of information held in confidence by the Human Fertilisation and Embryology Authority or by people working in licensed centres. Under the Abortion Regulations 1991[17] there is a duty to report each termination of pregnancy to the Chief Medical Office, but there are also a number of restrictions upon any further disclosure of this information.

(e) GOOD MEDICAL PRACTICE

As we saw at the outset of this chapter, the duty of confidentiality has been a fundamental ethical obligation since the first attempts to codify medical ethics in Ancient Greece. More modern guidance to doctors, most notably from the GMC, reinforces the importance of respecting patient confidentiality.

At the time of writing, the GMC has consulted on new guidance on confidentiality, but the final version has not been published. Extracts from the 2004 guidance are therefore reproduced here, but readers are advised to consult the latest GMC guidance, which will be available on its website.[18]

General Medical Council[19]

1 Patients have a right to expect that information about them will be held in confidence by their doctors. Confidentiality is central to trust between doctors and patients. Without

---

[17] SI 1991/499. [18] <www.gmc-uk.org>.
[19] Confidentiality: Protecting and Providing Information (GMC: London, 2004) <www.gmc-uk.org/>.

assurances about confidentiality, patients may be reluctant to give doctors the information they need in order to provide good care. If you are asked to provide information about patients you must:

- inform patients about the disclosure, or check that they have already received information about it;

- anonymise data where unidentifiable data will serve the purpose;

- be satisfied that patients know about disclosures necessary to provide their care, or for local clinical audit of that care, that they can object to these disclosures but have not done so;

- seek patients' express consent to disclosure of information, where identifiable data is needed for any purpose other than the provision of care or for clinical audit—save in the exceptional circumstances described in this booklet;

- keep disclosures to the minimum necessary; and

- keep up to date with and observe the requirements of statute and common law, including data protection legislation.

Although this guidance does not have the status of law, it is certainly not without teeth. First, given the confusion evident in the legal sources of the duty of confidentiality, in practice it is the GMC's guidance which will be most useful to doctors faced with a dilemma about whether breaching patient confidentiality would be justifiable. Secondly, breach of GMC guidance may lead to disciplinary proceedings, and if found guilty of 'serious professional misconduct', the doctor can be struck off the medical register. The United Kingdom Central Council for Nursing, Midwifery and Health Visiting's *Code of Professional Conduct* sets out similar duties and penalties for nurses, midwives, and health visitors.

Thirdly, a failure to follow GMC guidance might offer evidence that the doctor had not acted as a responsible medical practitioner and was therefore in breach of his duty of care. Proving that a doctor has been negligent should be relatively straightforward where there has been a clear breach of the GMC's rules. As noted earlier, however, the patient will only be able to bring an action in negligence if some sort of damage was caused by the breach of confidence.

In 1997 a review of the use of patient-identifiable information in the NHS, chaired by Fiona Caldicott, was published by the Department of Health. The Caldicott Committee's report advocated greater awareness of the need to respect patient confidentiality, and the introduction of security measures to limit unauthorized disclosures. It laid out six principles:

(1) justify the purpose(s) for which the information is required

(2) do not use patient-identifiable information unless it is absolutely necessary

(3) use the minimum necessary patient-identifiable information

(4) access to patient-identifiable information should be on a strict need-to-know basis

(5) everyone with access to patient-identifiable information should be aware of their responsibilities

(6) understand and comply with the law.

The Report made sixteen recommendations on the use of information in the NHS. These emphasized the need to develop techniques and systems to ensure the confidentiality of patient-identifiable data. It suggested that each health organization should nominate a senior health professional to be responsible for safeguarding the confidentiality of patient information. The Committee's recommendations were accepted, and so-called 'Caldicott Guardians' have been in existence since 1999. In 2003 the Department of Health issued a Code of Practice on Confidentiality for NHS Staff which embodies the Caldicott Principles, and lays out detailed guidance on the use of identifiable patient information.[20]

4 PATIENTS WHO LACK CAPACITY

If the legal basis for the general duty of confidence is unclear, its application to children and adults who lack capacity is even more obscure. On the one hand, it seems clear that this fundamental aspect of a doctor's duty towards her patients should be universal. A sweeping exception for all children and adults who lack capacity would be unacceptably discriminatory. Medical records self-evidently contain confidential information, and if the duty of confidentiality arises from the very nature of the information itself, then it must apply equally to the records of those who lack capacity. In *Venables v News Group Newspapers*,[21] Dame Elizabeth Butler-Sloss P stated that 'Children, like adults, are entitled to confidentiality in respect of certain areas of information. Medical records are the obvious example.'

On the other hand, for young children or mentally incapacitated adults, it may be necessary to involve others in decisions about their treatment, and so a strict duty of confidentiality would not make sense. Obviously, a very young child's right to confidentiality does not involve keeping treatment information from her parents. On the contrary, a child's parents are under a duty to take decisions about her medical treatment, and they can only do this if they are properly informed. The doctor's duty of confidentiality is therefore owed to the family unit of parent(s) *and* child, rather than just to the child herself.

The House of Lords decision in the *Gilllick* case (which we considered in detail in Chapter 5) clearly established that children who have reached an age of sufficient maturity will in certain circumstances have the right to keep information about their medical treatment from their parents, and this was confirmed more recently in the case of *R (on the application of Axon) v Secretary of State for Health*, which we also considered in Chapter 5. Following *Gillick*, Silber J confirmed that 2004 DH guidance, which stated that children had a right to confidentiality in relation to treatment for abortion, was lawful.

R (on the application of Axon) v Secretary of State for Health[22]

Silber J

This application raises a tension between two important principles of which the first is that a competent young person under sixteen years of age (who is able to understand all aspects of any advice, including its consequences) is an autonomous person, who first should be allowed to make decisions about his or her own health and second is entitled to confidentiality about such decisions even vis-à-vis his or her parents. The second principle is that a parent of a young person has a responsibility for that young person's health and moral welfare with the consequence that he or she should be informed if a medical professional is considering providing advice and treatment on sexual matters to that young person so that the parent

---

[20] Available at <www.dh.gov.uk/>.   [21] [2001] 2 WLR 1038.   [22] [2006] EWHC 37 (Admin).

could then advise and assist the young person. There is also a significant public policy dimension because there is evidence that without the guarantee of confidentiality, some of these young people might not seek advice or treatment from medical professionals on sexual matters with potentially disturbing consequences....

[T]he very basis and nature of the information which a doctor or a medical professional receives relating to the sexual and reproductive health of any patient of whatever age deserves the highest degree of confidentiality and this factor undermines the existence of a limitation on the duty of disclosure...

[I]n the period between the decision of the Court of Appeal in *Gillick* and that of the House of Lords during which medical professionals were required to pass on information to children's parents, the number of young women aged under 16 who sought advice on contraception fell from 1.7 per resident thousand to 1.2 per resident thousand, which was a striking and disturbing reduction of just under one-third. In addition, the rates of attendance at places where contraception advice and treatment were given did not return until 1988–89 to their previous levels prior to the Court of Appeal decision in December 1984. These statistics provide clear and powerful evidence of what happens when young people are not assured of confidentiality when they are considering obtaining advice and treatment on sexual matters.

Interestingly, the 2004 guidance which was challenged in *Axon* did not confine a child's right of confidentiality to children who are *Gillick*-competent:

The duty of confidentiality owed to a person under 16, in any setting, is the same as that owed to any other person. This is enshrined in professional codes.

All services providing advice and treatment on contraception, sexual and reproductive health should produce an explicit confidentiality policy which reflects this guidance and makes clear that young people under 16 have the same right to confidentiality as adults.[23]

However, if only *Gillick*-competent children can consent to treatment without parental knowledge, then the right to have the details of that treatment kept from their parents, in practice, only arises for children who are competent to give consent. Under-16s who are *not Gillick*-competent are therefore in a rather curious position. They are *prima facie* owed a duty of confidentiality, which may not arise in practice, because their inability to give consent means that their parents will usually be involved in decisions about their medical treatment.

Adults who lack capacity are undoubtedly also owed a duty of confidentiality, but as we saw in Chapter 5, section 4(7) of the Mental Capacity Act 2005 specifically states that people who are involved in their care should be consulted about their wishes and any relevant values and beliefs. The Code of Practice 5.56–7 insists that the duty of confidence still applies, and that discussions with carers must be strictly limited. The GMC guidance further suggests that doctors should seek the incompetent adult's agreement to sharing information with others, and should disclose information against their wishes only where disclosure is 'essential in their medical interests'.

---

[23] Department of Health, *Best Practice Guidance for Doctors and other Health Professionals on the Provision of Advice and Treatment to Young People under 16 on Contraception, Sexual and Reproductive Health* (2004), available at <www.dh.gov.uk>.

General Medical Council[24]

> 28 Problems may arise if you consider that a patient lacks capacity to give consent to treatment or disclosure. If such patients ask you not to disclose information about their condition or treatment to a third party, you should try to persuade them to allow an appropriate person to be involved in the consultation. If they refuse and you are convinced that it is essential, in their medical interests, you may disclose relevant information to an appropriate person or authority. In such cases you should tell the patient before disclosing any information, and where appropriate, seek and carefully consider the views of an advocate or carer. You should document in the patient's record your discussions with the patient and the reasons for deciding to disclose information.

In a case decided before the Mental Capacity Act was passed, *R (on the application of S) v Plymouth City Council*, Hale LJ explained that while C, a 27-year-old man with serious learning and behavioural difficulties, did have an interest, albeit 'purely theoretical', in the confidentiality of his medical records, disclosure to his mother who wished to challenge a local social services authority's recommendation, was both necessary and proportionate.

R (on the application of S) v Plymouth City Council[25]

Hale LJ

C's interest in protecting the confidentiality of personal information about himself must not be underestimated. It is all too easy for professionals and parents to regard children and incapacitated adults as having no independent interests of their own: as objects rather than subjects. But we are not concerned here with the publication of information to the whole wide world. There is a clear distinction between disclosure to the media with a view to publication to all and sundry and disclosure in confidence to those with a proper interest in having the information in question. . . .

There is no suggestion that C has any objection to his mother and her advisers being properly informed about his health and welfare. There is no suggestion of any risk to his health and welfare arising from this. The mother and her advisers have sought access to the information which her own psychiatric and social work experts need in order properly to advise her. That limits both the context and the content of disclosure in a way which strikes a proper balance between the competing interests.

Degenerative brain diseases, such as Alzheimer's, raise particularly interesting questions in relation to patient confidentiality. Patients who are suspected of having Alzheimer's disease are often first referred for diagnosis following a request from a partner or relative, rather than because the patient herself is concerned about her symptoms. The clinical assessment will often be based upon descriptions of behaviour given by others, and the diagnosis of Alzheimer's is, in practice, usually given to the patient's principal carer, rather than to the patient herself. As Pucci *et al.* point out,

---

[24] Confidentiality: Protecting and Providing Information (GMC: London, 2004), available at <www.gmc-uk.org/ standards/default.htm>.

[25] [2002] EWCA Civ 388.

> At a certain stage of the disease, the patient is completely dependent on a caregiver who, in most cases, is a close relative. The physician cannot do without the interaction with the relative. Thus, it is mandatory to recognise a relationship between the physician and the relative/patient dyad rather than a simple physician/patient one.[26]

Clearly, absolute respect for patient confidentiality in such circumstances is impractical. The reality of certain degenerative diseases is that the duty of confidentiality is in practice owed to the patient's primary carer. Indeed, Pucci *et al.*'s research indicated that most relatives of patients suffering from Alzheimer's disease believe that the patient should not be told about the diagnosis, for fear of provoking or aggravating depressive symptoms.[27]

5 DECEASED PATIENTS

Does the duty of confidentiality survive a patient's death? The Department of Health's Code of Practice and the GMC Guidance are both clear that the *ethical* duty to respect patient confidentiality continues to exist after the patient has died.

Department of Health[28]

> 28. ...[T]he Department of Health and the General Medical Council are in agreement that, whilst there are no clear legal obligations of confidentiality that apply to the deceased, there is an ethical basis for requiring that confidentiality obligations, as outlined in this document, must continue to apply.

General Medical Council[29]

> 30. You still have an obligation to keep personal information confidential after a patient dies. The extent to which confidential information may be disclosed after a patient's death will depend on the circumstances. If the patient had asked for information to remain confidential, his or her views should be respected. Where you are unaware of any directions from the patient, you should consider requests for information taking into account:
>
> - whether the disclosure of information may cause distress to, or be of benefit to, the patient's partner or family;
> - whether disclosure of information about the patient will in effect disclose information about the patient's family or other people;
> - whether the information is already public knowledge or can be anonymised;
> - the purpose of the disclosure.
>
> If you decide to disclose confidential information you must be prepared to explain and justify your decision.

---

[26] E Pucci *et al.*, 'Relatives' Attitudes Towards Informing Patients about the Diagnosis of Alzheimer's disease' (2003) 29 Journal of Medical Ethics 51–4.

[27] Ibid 51.   [28] Confidentiality: NHS Code of Practice (DH: London, 2003).

[29] Confidentiality: Protecting and Providing Information (GMC: London, 2004), available at <www.gmc-uk.org/>.

Until recently, it was unclear whether the legal duty of confidence survived death, and the assumption had been that it probably did not. In two recent decisions, the Information Tribunal and a court have taken a different view.

In *Bluck v The Information Commissioner* the mother of a woman who had died as a result of admittedly negligent treatment sought access to her medical records. No authority was found by any of the parties' legal teams either in support or against the proposition that the duty of confidence had survived Karen Davies's death. The Tribunal therefore considered the question from first principles, and concluded that it had.

Bluck v The Information Commissioner[30]

Information Tribunal

The Appellant's case was that a duty of confidence has to be owed to someone and that, once that person has died, there is no one capable of enforcing it. It was accepted that there might be continuing ethical, moral or professional duties requiring a doctor to maintain confidentiality... but that no legal obligation survived. The Information Commissioner and the Trust argued that the basis of the equitable obligation of confidence, in the circumstances of this case, stemmed from the purpose of the doctor's obligation of confidence. It was said that this was to create the trust that is needed to ensure that a patient makes full disclosure to his doctor of all matters that the doctor may require in order to diagnose and treat the patient....

[D]octor/patient trust might be undermined if a patient believed that information might be disseminated to the public after his death.... It was suggested that it would remain unconscionable to do so after the death of the person to whom the information related and that the duty must therefore survive death. It should not come to an end simply because it could be said that there was no one able to enforce it or capable of demonstrating harm resulting from its breach.

The Information Commissioner also invited us to consider the unacceptable practical consequence if the duty did come to an end on death. Any medical practitioner would then be legally entitled to publish information from the records of a deceased patient, possibly for financial gain. We think that this is a powerful point.

We also agree with the Trust and the Information Commissioner that, as a matter of principle, the basis of the duty in respect of private information lies in conscience.... In these circumstances we conclude that a duty of confidence is capable of surviving the death of the confider and that in the circumstances of this case it does survive.... We have concluded, therefore, that the Trust would breach the duty of confidence owed to Karen Davies if it disclosed the Medical Records.

While not binding upon a court, the Information Tribunal's decision was subsequently quoted with approval in *Lewis v Secretary of State for Health*, a case in which a doctor had been reluctant to disclose patient records, after the patients' deaths, to the *Redfern Inquiry*, which was investigating the removal and retention of tissue samples from individuals who had worked at Sellafield nuclear plant. The first question for Foskett J was whether it was at least arguable that the duty of confidentiality applied after these patients' deaths. Having concluded that it was, he decided that disclosure could nevertheless be justified in the public interest.

---

[30] 2007 WL 4266111.

Lewis v Secretary of State for Health[31]

Foskett J

There is no doubt that it is the view of those who administer the medical profession, both in the United Kingdom and worldwide, that the professional obligation of the doctor is to maintain the medical confidences of the patient after the patient's death. The Hippocratic oath, the Declaration of Geneva ('I will respect the secrets that are confided in me, even after the patient has died') and guidance given by the General Medical Council all point to this professional obligation. The content of an obligation imposed upon a professional by his profession is not, of course, necessarily coterminous with the obligation imposed by law in similar circumstances although it may be a useful indicator of the perceived values by which the relationship of the professional to his client (in this case, patient) are to be judged.

In the course of argument, I ventured the proposition that if anyone is asked whether they thought that something said in confidence to their doctor would remain confidential after their death, the answer would almost certainly be 'yes'. That seems to me to accord with contemporary notions of what is accepted practice and indeed it might even reflect notions of what the law, not merely professional ethics, may require....

[T]he period for which the obligation can be expected to continue will depend on many circumstances. On the assumption that I make for this purpose that this is an accurate statement of the law, one such circumstance, in my judgment, would be the nature and result of any examination that the patient has undergone. The more intimate and sensitive the type of examination, and the more sensitive the kind of results obtained, the more onerous and prolonged would be the obligation to maintain confidence....

I have not the slightest doubt that this is an appropriate case in which to hold that the public interest in disclosure of the material sought outweighs the other public interest, namely, that of maintaining the confidentiality of medical records and information, provided, of course, proper safeguards are put in place to ensure that no inappropriate information becomes public.

In support of this conclusion I would merely say that there is plainly a public interest (and by that I mean not just 'the interest of the public') in determining what happened and why in connection with the very difficult and sensitive issues that arise from these matters. Those families that know broadly what happened are entitled to fuller answers to the questions raised if they wish to have them and there is a wider public interest in maintaining confidence in the NHS and the nuclear industry, a confidence that may be fortified either by the results of the investigation of The Inquiry or by the recommendations of The Inquiry if past practices are found to have been wanting and improvements are suggested.

In the next extract, Jessica Berg explains why it might be important to maintain confidentiality after a patient's death.

Jessica Berg[32]

Whether or not one accepts the argument that there are interests that survive death, there are clearly interests of the living that must be considered. In fact, these interests seem to

---

[31] [2008] EWHC 2196 (QB).
[32] 'Grave Secrets: Legal and Ethical Analysis of Postmorten Confidentiality' (2001) 34 Connecticut Law Review 81.

form a stronger basis for understanding confidentiality protections in the postmortem context. First, there are the interests of current and future patients in assuming that information they disclose to their physicians will remain confidential.

The practical concern in the context of confidentiality is whether people will be less likely to confide sensitive information to their physician (lawyer, mental health professional, etc.) knowing the possibility of disclosure postmortem. The ethical rule to maintain confidentiality, even postmortem, is premised, at least in part, on the notion that such rule will result in the best consequences...

Moreover, there is yet another group of interests that must be considered in this context—those of people now living and their interests in preserving the confidentiality of the specific person who has died. First, blood relatives of the deceased have an interest in controlling information that has implications for their own health (and thus identity). Although the interests of blood relatives in maintaining confidentiality may not supersede the individual's right to control his or her medical information during life, they may well be given greater weight (or at least be less likely to be outweighed) after that person has died.

Second, there are more nebulous interests of third parties in preventing the disclosure of confidential information. The dead live on in the memories of the living. Harms to the memory of the deceased may entail very real harms to people now living who have an interest in preserving the original memory, such as relatives or close friends of the deceased.

6 EXCEPTIONS TO THE DUTY OF CONFIDENTIALITY

As was noted earlier, the duty of confidentiality is not absolute, and a number of exceptions exist which we flesh out in the following sections. At the outset, it is worth noting that breaches of confidentiality do not necessarily involve a doctor *deliberately* deciding to share information about a patient with other people. Rather, inadvertent breaches of confidentiality may be more common. NHS inpatients spend most of their time on wards, and as a result any conversations they have with their doctors may be overheard by other patients or health care workers. Patients' physical privacy can be protected to some extent by curtains, but it is probably impossible to guarantee the confidentiality of discussions which take place at the patient's bedside. Where there is particularly sensitive information to impart, it might therefore be important to ensure that the patient is given the opportunity to receive it in private.

Another way in which patient data may be inadvertently shared is if there are breaches of IT security. The government has engaged in an extraordinarily expensive and ambitious exercise, known as Connecting for Health, which will eventually ensure that there is a national electronic patient record. The sensitivity of the data means that considerable lengths will be gone to in order to ensure data security through sophisticated encryption systems. It is, however, impossible to eliminate human error. In recent years, civil servants have been criticized for leaving lap-tops on trains or sending CDs containing sensitive material through the post, but in NHS hospitals, more mundane errors—such as leaving a computer logged on—could have devastating implications for patients whose data is visible to others.

(a) CONSENT

If the patient explicitly consents to the disclosure of information, then plainly the doctor is no longer under a duty of non-disclosure. This is not strictly speaking an exception to the duty of confidence: rather, the patient's agreement to disclosure simply means that no duty of confidence exists. In *C v C*,[33] both parties to divorce proceedings had requested the respondent's doctor to disclose information about his venereal disease, and it was held that disclosure in such circumstances could not amount to a breach of confidence.

More complicated is the question of when a patient could be said to have *impliedly* consented to disclosure. The British Medical Association's *Confidentiality Toolkit* suggests that:

> In the absence of evidence to the contrary, patients are normally considered to have given implied consent for the use of their information by health professionals for the purpose of the care they receive. Information sharing in this context is acceptable to the extent that health professionals share what is necessary and relevant for patient care on a 'need to know' basis.[34]

In order to establish that there was implied consent to disclosure, it would, as the General Medical Council's guidance to doctors, and the Department of Health's Code of Practice make clear, be necessary to prove that the patient was aware of the practice of disclosure and given an opportunity to object to it.

General Medical Council[35]

> 10 Most people understand and accept that information must be shared within the health care team in order to provide their care. You should make sure that patients are aware that personal information about them will be shared within the health care team, unless they object, and of the reasons for this. It is particularly important to check that patients understand what will be disclosed if you need to share identifiable information with anyone employed by another organisation or agency who is contributing to their care. You must respect the wishes of any patient who objects to particular information being shared with others providing care, except where this would put others at risk of death or serious harm.

Department of Health[36]

> 14 Patients generally have the right to object to the use and disclosure of confidential information that identifies them, and need to be made aware of this right. Sometimes, if patients choose to prohibit information being disclosed to other health professionals involved in providing care, it might mean that the care that can be provided is limited and, in extremely rare circumstances, that it is not possible to provide certain treatment options. Patients must be informed if their decisions about disclosure have implications for the provision of care or treatment...
>
> 15 Where patients have been informed of
>
> (a) the use and disclosure of their information associated with their healthcare; and

---

[33] [1946] 1 All ER 562.

[34] Confidentiality and Disclosure of Health Information Tool Kit (BMA, 2008), available at <www.bma.org.uk>.

[35] Confidentiality: Protecting and Providing Information (GMC: London, 2004), available at <www.gmc-uk.org/ standards/default.htm>.

[36] Confidentiality: NHS Code of Practice (DH: London, 2003).

(b) the choices that they have and the implications of choosing to limit how information may be used or shared;

then explicit consent is not usually required for information disclosures needed to provide that healthcare. Even so, opportunities to check that patients understand what may happen and are content should be taken.

If a patient undergoes a medical examination requested by a third party, such as an employer, could it be said that she impliedly consents to the disclosure of the medical report to that third party? *Obiter dicta* in the Court of Appeal decision in *Kapadia v London Borough of Lambeth* suggested that the patient's consent to disclosure can be implied from her agreement to undergo the examination. This was a case in which an employee who was claiming that he had been discriminated against on the grounds of disability had refused to consent to the disclosure of a medical report to his employer, without first seeing the report. However, according to Pill LJ, having agreed to the examination, the employee's further consent to the report's disclosure was not required.

Kapadia v London Borough of Lambeth [37]

Pill LJ

On the facts the court knows, the report should, in my judgment, have been disclosed by the doctor to the employers. No further consent was required from the claimant. By consenting to being examined on behalf of the employers the claimant was consenting to the disclosure to the employers of a report resulting from that examination. A practice under which a person who has agreed to be examined in circumstances such as these, but then claims a veto upon disclosure of the report to those who obtained it is not, in my view, a good practice. Indeed it is an impediment to the fair and expeditious conduct of litigation.

(b) PUBLIC INTEREST

Probably the most important exception to the duty of confidentiality is where the public interest in disclosure of information outweighs the public interest in protecting patient confidentiality, as in the following case:

A-G v Guardian Newspapers Ltd (No. 2) [38]

Lord Goff

The third limiting principle is of far greater importance. It is that, although the basis of the law's protection of confidence is that there is a public interest that confidences should be preserved and protected by the law, nevertheless that public interest may be outweighed by some other countervailing public interest which favours disclosure. This limitation may apply, as the judge pointed out, to all types of confidential information. It is this limiting principle which may require a court to carry out a balancing operation, weighing the public interest in maintaining confidence against a countervailing public interest favouring disclosure.

---

[37] (2000) 57 BMLR 170.   [38] [1988] 3 WLR 776 at 807.

Because the public interest in protecting confidentiality is considerable, only weighty countervailing considerations should be allowed to override the doctor's prima facie duty of confidence, and disclosures should always be kept to the minimum. In the following sections we consider a number of different, though overlapping, public interest justifications for the disclosure of confidential information.

(1) Preventing Harm to Others

Where the possibility of harm to others is used to justify disclosure, there should, as the BMA and the GMC guidance makes clear, be a *real* risk of *serious* harm.

British Medical Association[39]

Ultimately, the public interest can only be determined by the courts. However, when considering disclosing information to protect the public interest, health professionals must:

- consider how the benefits of making the disclosure balance against the harms associated with breaching the patient's confidentiality both to the individual clinical relationship and to maintaining public trust in a confidential service;

- assess the urgency of the need for disclosure;

- persuade the patient to disclose voluntarily;

- inform the patient before making the disclosure and seek his or her consent, unless to do so would increase the risk of harm or inhibit effective investigation;

- disclose the information promptly to the appropriate body;

- reveal only the minimum information necessary to achieve the objective;

- seek assurance that the information will be used only for the purpose for which it is disclosed;

- document the steps taken to seek or obtain consent, and the reasons for disclosing the information without consent;

- be able to justify the decision; and

- document both the extent of and grounds for the disclosure.

General Medical Council[40]

27 Disclosure of personal information without consent may be justified in the public interest where failure to do so may expose the patient or others to risk of death or serious harm. Where the patient or others are exposed to a risk so serious that it outweighs the patient's privacy interest, you should seek consent to disclosure where practicable. If it is not practicable to seek consent, you should disclose information promptly to an appropriate person or authority. You should generally inform the patient before disclosing the information. If you seek consent and the patient withholds it you should consider the reasons for this, if

[39] Confidentiality and Disclosure of Health Information Tool Kit (BMA, 2008) card 10, available at <www.bma.org.uk>.
[40] Confidentiality: Protecting and Providing Information (GMC: London, 2004), available at <www.gmc-uk.org/>.

> any are provided by the patient. If you remain of the view that disclosure is necessary to protect a third party from death or serious harm, you should disclose information promptly to an appropriate person or authority. Such situations arise, for example, where a disclosure may assist in the prevention, detection or prosecution of a serious crime, especially crimes against the person, such as abuse of children.

W v Egdell is a relatively straightforward example of the public interest in disclosure trumping the public interest in protecting confidentiality. W had killed five people and wounded two others, and had been detained in a secure hospital. His application for release was turned down. His solicitors commissioned an independent psychiatrist's report from Dr Edgell, which indicated that he continued to pose a risk to the public. Dr Edgell disclosed this information both to the hospital and to the Secretary of State. W was unsuccessful in his application for an injunction to stop them from using the report, and damages for breach of confidence.

W v Egdell[41]

Bingham LJ

The decided cases very clearly establish (1) that the law recognises an important public interest in maintaining professional duties of confidence but (2) that the law treats such duties not as absolute but as liable to be overridden where there is held to be a stronger public interest in disclosure.

The parties were agreed, as I think rightly, that the crucial question in the present case was how, on the special facts of the case, the balance should be struck between the public interest in maintaining professional confidences and the public interest in protecting the public against possible violence.

There is one consideration which in my judgment, as in that of the judge, weighs the balance of public interest decisively in favour of disclosure. It may be shortly put. Where a man has committed multiple killings under the disability of serious mental illness, decisions which may lead directly or indirectly to his release from hospital should not be made unless a responsible authority is properly able to make an informed judgment that the risk of repetition is so small as to be acceptable. A consultant psychiatrist who becomes aware, even in the course of a confidential relationship, of information which leads him, in the exercise of what the court considers a sound professional judgment, to fear that such decisions may be made on the basis of inadequate information and with a real risk of consequent danger to the public is entitled to take such steps as are reasonable in all the circumstances to communicate the grounds of his concern to the responsible authorities.

While the balancing exercise in *W v Egdell* was relatively straightforward, other situations may be less clear-cut. What if the patient has never actually harmed anyone, but has violent thoughts or fantasies? In the US case *Tarasoff v Regents of the University of California*, the patient, Poddar, had confided in a university psychotherapist, Dr Moore, that he intended to harm T, a fellow student who had rejected his advances. The therapist informed the University police, but did not inform T herself, whom the patient subsequently murdered. The California Supreme Court held that the University's employee was under a duty to protect T by disclosing these threats to her.

---

[41] [1990] Ch 359.

Tarasoff v Regents of the University of California[42]

Justice Trobriner

When a therapist determines, or pursuant to the standards of his profession should determine, that his patient presents a serious danger of violence to another, he incurs an obligation to use reasonable care to protect the intended victim against such danger.... We conclude that the public policy favoring protection of the confidential character of patient-psychotherapist communications must yield to the extent to which disclosure is essential to avert danger to others. The protective privilege ends where the public peril begins.

Commenting on the likely response to a *Tarasoff*-type case in the UK, Sheila McLean and John Kenyon Mason have suggested that 'the probability is that there would be no legal obligation to warn the person at risk but that, should the doctor do so, the breach of confidentiality would be regarded as justified'.[43] Doctors are therefore in the difficult position of having to make a judgement about whether disclosure of information acquired in confidence is justified in any particular case.

While there is plainly a public interest in preventing a patient harming someone, routine disclosure in such circumstances might make patients reluctant to share information about their fantasies with their psychiatrists, which in turn makes it more likely that their underlying problems will remain untreated. Paradoxically then routinely breaching the confidentiality of potentially dangerous patients might *increase* the risks such patients pose to others. This point was made forcefully by Clark J in his dissenting judgment in *Tarasoff*.

Justice Clark

Assurance of confidentiality is important for three reasons. First, without substantial assurance of confidentiality, those requiring treatment will be deterred from seeking assistance....Second, the guarantee of confidentiality is essential in eliciting the full disclosure necessary for effective treatment...Third, even if the patient fully discloses his thoughts, assurance that the confidential relationship will not be breached is necessary to maintain his trust in his psychiatrist—the very means by which treatment is effected....

By imposing a duty to warn, the majority contributes to the danger to society of violence by the mentally ill and greatly increases the risk of civil commitment—the total deprivation of liberty—of those who should not be confined. Although...only a relatively few receiving treatment will ever present a risk of violence, the number making threats is huge, and it is the latter group—not just the former—whose treatment will be impaired and whose risk of commitment will be increased.

Here there is a clear overlap with an issue we considered in more detail in the previous chapter, namely the increased focus in mental health law upon reducing the risk mentally ill individuals might pose to the community. This emphasis upon risk-avoidance necessarily

---

[42] 551 P 2d 334 (Cal 1976).
[43] *Legal and Ethical Aspects of Healthcare* (Greenwich Medical Media: London, 2003) 42.

involves sharing information about potentially dangerous patients with a number of different people, such as potential employers, or housing and social service authorities. If patients realize that they can no longer expect their medical records to be confidential, there is a real danger that they might be deterred from seeking treatment, thus actually *increasing* the risk they might pose to the public.

Similar difficulties arise in relation to communicable diseases, such as HIV/AIDS. If a doctor knows that an HIV-positive individual has not informed her sexual partner of her HIV status, does the public interest in disclosure trump the public interest in protecting confidentiality? Although alerting the sexual partner of an HIV-positive individual may enable one individual to take steps to avoid infection, there is also a strong public interest in encouraging people to come forward for HIV testing and treatment, which might be hampered if disclosure of a positive result was routine. Nevertheless, the GMC suggest that non-consensual disclosure to a sexual partner will sometimes be justifiable.

General Medical Council[44]

8. You may disclose information to a known sexual contact of a patient with a serious sexually transmitted disease if you have reason to think that the patient has not informed that person, and cannot be persuaded to do so. In such circumstances you should tell the patient before you make the disclosure, whenever it is practicable and safe to do so. You must be prepared to justify a decision to disclose personal information without consent.

9. You must not disclose information to anyone, including relatives who have not been, and are not, at risk of infection.

What if the HIV-positive patient refuses to permit the doctor to inform other health care workers? Again, GMC advice appears to indicate that in exceptional circumstances, disclosure without consent may be legitimate.

A further difficult balancing exercise arises where the HIV-positive patient is also a health care worker. The risk of HIV transmission by health care workers is almost non-existent—in 2003 it was estimated that there had only ever been three reported cases worldwide.[45] Both the Department of Health and the GMC suggest that only in exceptional circumstances will the public interest in disclosure trump the normally overwhelming public interest in encouraging individuals to be tested and treated for the HIV virus.

Department of Health[46]

10.2 Every effort should be made to avoid disclosure of the infected worker's identity, or information which would allow deductive disclosure. This should include the use of a media injunction as necessary to prevent disclosure of a health care worker's identity. The use of personal identifiers in correspondence and requests for laboratory tests should be avoided

---

[44] This used to be contained in specific guidance on Serious Communicable Diseases, but will be contained instead in a supplement to the new Confidentiality guidance on serious communicable diseases (2009), available at <www.gmc-uk.org>.

[45] Department of Health, *AIDS/HIV Infected Health Care Workers Guidance on the Management of Infected Health Care Workers and Patient Notification* (DH: London, 2003) para 2.2.

[46] Ibid.

and care taken to ensure that the number of people who know the worker's identity is kept
to a minimum. Any unauthorised disclosure about the HIV status of an employee or patient
constitutes a breach of confidence and may lead to disciplinary action or legal proceedings.
Employers should make this known to staff to deter open speculation about the identity of
an infected health care worker.

10.3 The duty of confidentiality, however, is not absolute. Legally, the identity of infected
individuals may be disclosed with their consent or without consent in exceptional circumstances where it is considered necessary for the purpose of treatment, or prevention of
spread of infection. Any such disclosure may need to be justified.

In *X v Y*, a newspaper had discovered the identity of two general practitioners who were
living with AIDS, and were continuing to practise. The newspaper had already published
an article with the headline 'Scandal of Docs with AIDS'; and it intended to publish further
information which would enable the doctors to be identified. The health authority sought,
and was granted, an injunction restraining the defendants from publishing the identity of
the two doctors. Rose J took into account the fact that the risk of a GP transmitting the HIV
virus to his patients is negligible.

X v Y[47]

Rose J

In the long run, preservation of confidentiality is the only way of securing public health otherwise doctors will be discredited as a source of education, for future individual patients 'will
not come forward if doctors are going to squeal on them'. Consequently, confidentiality is
vital to secure public as well as private health, for unless those infected come forward they
cannot be counselled and self-treatment does not provide the best care....

I keep in the forefront of my mind the very important public interest in freedom of the
press. And I accept that there is some public interest in knowing that which the defendants
seek to publish (in whichever version). But in my judgment those public interests are substantially outweighed when measured against the public interests in relation to loyalty and confidentiality both generally and with particular reference to AIDS patients' hospital records.

A conflict between the freedom of the press and patients' interest in confidentiality also
arose in *H (A Healthcare Worker) v Associated Newspapers Ltd*. H was a health care worker,
who had been diagnosed as HIV-positive, and notified his employers, N Health Authority.
N proposed to carry out a 'lookback' exercise: that is, to notify H's patients and offer them
advice and an HIV test. Citing evidence that no infected patient had ever been identified
by one of these lookback exercises, H claimed that it would be unlawful.

Meanwhile, the *Mail on Sunday* wanted to publish a story about H's action against N.
H obtained an injunction restraining the soliciting or publication of any information which
might directly or indirectly lead to the disclosure of his identity, or his whereabouts, or
his speciality. The Court of Appeal stressed the importance of maintaining patient confidentiality, and granted orders restraining the publication of information of H's and N's
identity. It refused to order that his speciality too should be kept secret. The risk that this

---

47 [1988] 2 All ER 648.

would reveal H's identity was too small to justify inhibiting debate 'on what is a matter of public interest'.

H (A Healthcare Worker) v Associated Newspapers Ltd[48]

Lord Phillips MR

The consequences to H if his identity were to be disclosed would be likely to be distressing on a personal level. More than this, there is an obvious public interest in preserving the confidentiality of victims of the AIDS epidemic and, in particular, of healthcare workers who report the fact that they are HIV positive. Where a lookback exercise follows, it may prove impossible to preserve the identification of the worker but, if healthcare workers are not to be discouraged from reporting that they are HIV positive, it is essential that all possible steps are taken to preserve the confidentiality of such reports.

(2) Preventing or Detecting Crime

Both GMC guidance and the Department of Health Code of Practice specifically mention that disclosure of confidential information may be justified where it would assist in the prevention or detection of a serious crime.

Department of Health[49]

30 Under common law, staff are permitted to disclose personal information in order to prevent and support detection, investigation and punishment of serious crime and/or to prevent abuse or serious harm to others where they judge, on a case by case basis, that the public good that would be achieved by disclosure outweighs both the obligation of confidentiality to the individual patient concerned and the broader public interest in the provision of a confidential service.

31 Whoever authorizes disclosure must make a record of any such circumstances, so that there is clear evidence of the reasoning used and the circumstances prevailing. Disclosures in the public interest should also be proportionate and be limited to relevant details...

32 Wherever possible the issue of disclosure should be discussed with the individual concerned and consent sought. Where this is not forthcoming, the individual should be told of any decision to disclose against his/her wishes. This will not be possible in certain circumstances, e.g. where the likelihood of a violent response is significant or where informing a potential suspect in a criminal investigation might allow them to evade custody, destroy evidence or disrupt an investigation.

Section 11 of the Police and Criminal Evidence Act 1984 classifies medical records as 'excluded material' to which the police will not usually be allowed access. An exception exists if the police are investigating a 'serious arrestable offence'.[50] In such cases, the police may obtain a special procedure warrant which will require the disclosure of medical records. During a trial, the judge has discretion to excuse a witness from answering a question when

---

[48] [2002] EWCA Civ 195.   [49] Confidentiality: NHS Code of Practice (DH: London, 2003).
[50] Schedule 1.

it would involve a breach of confidence, but equally he can order a breach of confidentiality if it is necessary in the interests of justice.

Under section 172 of the Road Traffic Act 1988, a person can be required to give information which may lead to the identification of a driver who is alleged to have committed certain offences. In *Hunter v Mann*, a doctor had treated two people who had been involved in a road accident on the same day as a hit-and-run accident had occurred. A police officer asked the doctor to disclose the names and addresses of the two people he had treated, but he refused on the grounds that he would be breaching his duty of confidentiality. He was convicted under the Road Traffic Act 1972 (which preceded the 1988 Act), and this was upheld on appeal.

Hunter v Mann[51]

Boreham J

May I say, before leaving this case, that I appreciate the concern of a responsible medical practitioner who feels that he is faced with a conflict of duty. That the appellant in this case was conscious of a conflict and realised his duty both to society and to his patient is clear from the finding of the justices, but he may find comfort, although the decision goes against him, from the following. First that he has only to disclose information which may lead to identification and not other confidential matters; secondly that the result, in my judgment, is entirely consistent with the rules that the British Medical Association have laid down.

Often, of course, disclosure justified by the need to prevent serious crime could also be justified by the 'harm to others' exception we have just considered. But the two are not necessarily synonymous. There is a public interest in the detection of crime even when there is no immediate risk of re-offending, and even when the crime itself did not involve physical injury, though obviously, the less serious the criminal offence, the less likely that the public interest in protecting confidentiality will be trumped by the public interest in facilitating the prevention and detection of crime.

The Department of Health Code of Practice gives some guidance on the meaning of serious crime.

Department of Health[52]

The definition of serious crime is not entirely clear. Murder, manslaughter, rape, treason, kidnapping, child abuse or other cases where individuals have suffered serious harm may all warrant breaching confidentiality. Serious harm to the security of the state or to public order and crimes that involve substantial financial gain and loss will also generally fall within this category. In contrast, theft, fraud or damage to property where loss or damage is less substantial would generally not warrant breach of confidence.

It is worth noting that disclosure has also been justified in non-criminal proceedings. In *A Health Authority v X*,[53] the Court of Appeal held that disclosure, subject to conditions, would be justified on the grounds that the administration of disciplinary proceedings was

---

[51] [1974] QB 767.
[52] Confidentiality: NHS Code of Practice (DH: London, 2003) 35.
[53] [2001] EWCA Civ 2014.

analogous to the administration of criminal justice. According to Thorpe LJ: 'There is obviously a high public interest, analogous to the public interest in the due administration of criminal justice, in the proper administration of professional disciplinary hearings, particularly in the field of medicine.'

Similarly, in *Woolgar v Chief Constable of the Sussex Police* the Court of Appeal agreed that the police were entitled to disclose information to a professional regulatory body on public interest grounds, even though, in this case, no charges had been brought against the individual whom the police had interviewed.

Woolgar v Chief Constable of the Sussex Police[54]

Kennedy LJ

However, in my judgment, where a regulatory body . . , operating in the field of public health and safety, seeks access to confidential material in the possession of the police, being material which the police are reasonably persuaded is of some relevance to the subject matter of an inquiry being conducted by the regulatory body, then a countervailing public interest is shown to exist which, as in this case, entitles the police to release the material to the regulatory body on the basis that save in so far as it may be used by the regulatory body for the purposes of its own inquiry, the confidentiality which already attaches to the material will be maintained. . . . Putting the matter in convention terms . . . disclosure is 'necessary in a democratic society in the interests of . . . public safety or . . . for the protection of health or morals, or for the protection of the rights and freedoms of others'.

Even if there is no request from the regulatory body, it seems to me that if the police come into possession of confidential information which, in their reasonable view, in the interests of public health or safety, should be considered by a professional or regulatory body, then the police are free to pass that information to the relevant regulatory body for its consideration.

(3) Teaching, Research, and Audit

Without access to patient information, it would be impossible to train medical staff, conduct clinical research, and carry out audits of patient care. Usually, of course, the patient's consent to the use of their medical notes should be sought. But in certain circumstances, disclosure without consent may be legitimate. Initially fitting this within the 'harm to others' exception that we considered earlier might seem unpromising, since the benefits to patients from well-trained staff, and properly tested and regulated treatments, although substantial, are not sufficiently direct or immediate to establish that any particular instance of disclosure will avert an immediate risk of death or serious injury.

Remember, however, that the balancing exercise does not just involve looking at the harm that might be averted by disclosure, but also involves taking into account the relative importance of respecting patient confidentiality in the particular case. As we saw, where the identification of someone with HIV might result from disclosure, the public interest in keeping that information private is considerable, but where the disclosure involves the use of medical records in an epidemiological study, with no intention to disclose the patient's identity, or to feed any information back to her, the public interest in maintaining secrecy is reduced, and perhaps will be more readily outweighed by the public interest in improved health care provision.

---

[54] [1999] 3 All ER 604.

For research purposes, it will often be possible to anonymize data, and in *R v Department of Health, ex parte Source Informatics*, the Court of Appeal decided that disclosing anonymized information cannot amount to a breach of confidence. The applicants had paid GPs and pharmacists for information from prescription forms, aside from the patients' names. This anonymized information was then sold to pharmaceutical companies, who used it for marketing purposes. The Department of Health had issued advice that the anonymization of this information did not remove the duty of confidence, and that general practitioners and pharmacists should not participate in the scheme. The applicants applied for judicial review, seeking a declaration that the Department of Health's policy guidance was wrong. Latham J dismissed their application, but their appeal to the Court of Appeal was successful.

R v Department of Health, ex parte Source Informatics[55]

Simon Brown LJ

To my mind the one clear and consistent theme emerging from all these authorities is this: the confidant is placed under a duty of good faith to the confider and the touchstone by which to judge the scope of his duty and whether or not it has been fulfilled or breached is his own conscience, no more and no less. One asks, therefore, on the facts of this case: would a reasonable pharmacist's conscience be troubled by the proposed use to be made of patients' prescriptions? Would he think that by entering Source's scheme he was breaking his customers' confidence, making unconscientious use of the information they provide?...

In my judgment the answer is plain. The concern of the law here is to protect the confider's personal privacy. That and that alone is the right at issue in this case. The patient has no proprietorial claim to the prescription form or to the information it contains....

If, as I conclude, his only legitimate interest is in the protection of his privacy and, if that is safeguarded, I fail to see how his will could be thought thwarted or his personal integrity undermined.... [I]n a case involving personal confidences I would hold... that the confidence is not breached where the confider's identity is protected...

I would... hold simply that pharmacists' consciences ought not reasonably to be troubled by co-operation with Source's proposed scheme. The patient's privacy will have been safeguarded, not invaded. The pharmacist's duty of confidence will not have been breached.

The Data Protection Act 1998 raises another question in relation to anonymization of records. While completely anonymized data is not covered by the legislation, it will often be difficult to ensure that there is no possibility of linking the individual and the information about them. If it remains possible to link the individual and the information, then the Data Protection Act applies to any processing of that information.

Even if the law is clear that the disclosure of anonymized records is not a breach of confidence, the process of anonymization itself undoubtedly involves the 'processing' of sensitive personal data, and will therefore be subject to the Data Protection Act. Under the First Data Protection Principle, this must be done fairly and lawfully. If the patient has not specifically consented to the anonymization, it would have to be established that it was 'necessary' under Schedule 2, and done for 'medical purposes' under Schedule 3.

It is not clear that either requirement is easily satisfied in the *Source Informatics* case. Certainly it would be hard to argue that anonymizing data so that it could be sold to pharmaceutical companies who wanted to use it to increase their profits is 'necessary' for the exercise of public functions under Schedule 2. While it might be possible to argue that it was done for 'medical purposes' under Schedule 3, it could equally plausibly be argued that the *marketing* of medicines is not itself a medical purpose. Moreover, it was not the pharmaceutical companies who were carrying out the anonymization. Rather, Source Informatics were doing this purely for financial gain, and it would be very difficult to argue that increasing their profits was a medical purpose.

There is a further problem with the application of the Second Data Protection Principle to the *Source Informatics* case. The Second Principle is that data should be obtained for specific purposes, and not used for others. Here patient information was obtained for the purposes of treatment, and then used for commercial purposes by Source Informatics. The Second Data Protection Principle is qualified by section 33, which provides that it will not be breached where the further processing is done for 'research purposes'. Again, it might be possible to argue that Source Informatics were anonymizing the prescription forms for research purposes, but it is also at least arguable that Source Informatic's principal interest in the anonymized data was in fact commercial, and not strictly a 'research purpose'.

In order to trace the progression of disease, it is sometimes necessary to use coded data, where the patient is not named, but where the code, which might be the patient's NHS number, would make it possible to identify the patient. If information is completely anonymized (and so usable without consent), it would be impossible to validate and update data, and eliminate duplication.

The need to obtain the patient's consent to the use of her records in this sort of epidemiological research is potentially a significant obstacle to the generation of useful data. Cancer registries, for example, hold an enormous amount of information about past patients, and if these historical records could not be used without tracing every patient and retrospectively asking for consent, invaluable research into the causes of cancer would grind to a halt. Moreover, as Michael Ferriter and Martin Butwell explain in the next extract, there would be a danger of 'consent bias' since some people (perhaps those suffering from diseases which attract some sort of stigma) might be less likely than others to give consent, and the data would therefore no longer be representative of the UK population as a whole. Patients who have died or become incompetent would also be excluded, again skewing results. Seeking consent could also cause wholly unnecessary alarm to patients who might fear that a request to re-examine their medical records has been prompted by concern for their health.

Michael Ferriter and Martin Butwell[56]

There are whole areas of observational research—epidemiological research using case notes, case registers and disease registers—which do not require direct contact with the patient and where gaining consent may be impractical, impossible or undesirable: impractical because of dealing with such large numbers; impossible because of tracing all the participants; undesirable because in seeking consent the sample may be biased; or in gaining consent, needless anxiety may be caused to participants....

---

[56] 'Confidentiality and Research in Mental Health' in Christopher Cordess (ed.), *Confidentiality and Mental Health* (Jessica Kingsley Publishers: London, 2001) 159–69.

> [C]onsent can fundamentally damage research by introducing bias. On a technical level, one of the strengths of carrying out research where hitherto consent has not been needed is its freedom from many such biases. It is acknowledged that certain groups of people are more likely to consent to take part in research than others. For whatever reasons, younger patients, men and members of ethnic minorities are all less likely to consent to participate in health research. This leads to a consequent bias in research carried out, problems in generalisation to the wider population as a whole and, ultimately, to the disadvantage of people in less compliant groups....
>
> The crucial question that needs to be asked is: Has anyone ever been harmed by the use of their healthcare data in a case or disease register?

Of course, it is possible that identifiable data could be used without consent if it meets one of the criteria in Schedule 2 and one in Schedule 3 of the Data Protection Act 1998. For example, it is possible that epidemiological research could be said to be 'necessary for medical purposes', under Schedule 3 para. 8. Nevertheless, when the Data Protection Act 1998 came into force in 2000, there were fears that meeting the burden of establishing the 'necessity' of any particular research project might prove to be a significant obstacle to epidemiological research. These fears led to the passage of Section 60 of the Health and Social Care Act 2001, which has now been replaced by section 251 of the NHS Act 2006.

NHS Act 2006 section 251

Control of patient information

251(1) The Secretary of State may by regulations make such provision for and in connection with requiring or regulating the processing of prescribed patient information for medical purposes as he considers necessary or expedient—

(a) in the interests of improving patient care, or

(b) in the public interest....

(4) Regulations under subsection (1) may not make provision requiring the processing of confidential patient information for any purpose if it would be reasonably practicable to achieve that purpose otherwise than pursuant to such regulations, having regard to the cost of and the technology available for achieving that purpose.

Section 251 allows the Secretary of State to make regulations which authorize the disclosure of confidential patient information without consent where it is needed to support essential NHS activity. This power can only be used to support medical purposes that are, first, in the interests of patients or the wider public; secondly, where consent is not a practicable alternative; and, thirdly, where anonymized information will not suffice. This was originally intended to be a transitional arrangement, while the NHS developed mechanisms to seek and record consent and put more sophisticated anonymization techniques into place, but it is now acknowledged that section 251 powers will be necessary in the longer term.

The Patient Information Advisory Group (PIAG) was set up to advise the Secretary of State on whether bypassing consent would be appropriate. In 2009, its functions were taken over by the Ethics and Confidentiality Committee (ECC) of the National Information Governance Board for Health and Social Care (NIGB). When deciding whether confidential patient information can be used within the NHS, PIAG, and now the ECC take a number of factors into account.

PIAG Guidance Notes[57]

Is there a clear and acceptable description of how the activity may improve patient care or be in the public interest?

Is there an acceptable justification why data cannot be anonymised or pseudonymised?

Is there an acceptable justification why consent cannot or should not be obtained by either your organisation or the holder of the information you require?

Is it clear why the purpose cannot be satisfied in another reasonably practicable way which does not require patient-identifiable data?

Is there clear evidence that the organisation seeking support is following best practice in terms of confidentiality (e.g. Caldicott Guardian in place, adherence to national guidelines)?

Is there clear evidence that the organisation seeking support is complying with the Data Protection Act 1998? (Satisfies fair processing, subject access provisions, notification/registration, etc.)

In the next extract, PIAG explains why it advised permitting UK Biobank to use identifiable information without consent.

Patient Information Advisory Group[58]

UK Biobank sought approval to obtain name, address, date of birth, NHS number and GP practice registration. The reasons for seeking this information were to contact people in the right age group (40–65) and to inform all the relevant GPs in a recruitment area that patients in their practice were being invited to participate in UK Biobank (though not identifying which individuals). NHS number was requested to check whether patients were still alive (vital status) just before the invitations were sent out, to minimise the number of letters sent to recently bereaved families and thus causing them unnecessary distress. It was for these reasons that PIAG gave approval.

The reason it was agreed that consent for the disclosure of information was not feasible relates to the very large scale of this project. UK Biobank will need to contact something approaching 5 million people in order to obtain 500,000 participants. It is estimated the recruitment phase will take approximately five years. The NHS also continues to face significant workload pressures, particularly in primary care and PIAG felt it was impractical to ask GP practices to obtain consent from such a large number of patients to disclose their address so that they can be invited to take part in the study.

If individuals do not want to be approached about taking part in research studies they should inform their GP practice and each NHS organisation with which they have contact so that this can be recorded locally and should be respected.

In the next extract, Paula Case criticizes the original section 60 provision in the 2001 Act—now reproduced in section 251—arguing that the exception it creates to the principle of patient confidentiality is likely to undermine patient trust.

---

[57] Available at <www.advisorybodies.doh.gov.uk/piag>.

[58] PIAG Section 60 Approval UK Biobank, available at <www.advisorybodies.doh.gov.uk/piag/UKBiobankletterjul07.pdf>.

Paula Case[59]

The implications of the new Act for patient trust and the therapeutic relationship will be felt at two levels. First of all, it has been widely anticipated that the therapeutic relationship between doctors and patients will be scarred. Patients apprised of the possibility of disclosure of their records to 'government departments' may be less frank with their doctors with implications for the quality of their health care. That discretion may be exercised so as to protect confidence and to withdraw from the information supply chain as much as possible. Trust in health care institutions is also implicated by the provision in the 2001 Act. Not only might hospitals and relevant government departments be regarded by some as part of the conspiracy to deprive patients of informational autonomy, but the whole system of government and legislation are coloured by these reforms. The fact that Parliament has passed ostensibly contradictory legislation—protecting individual rights with the much applauded Human Rights Act and Data Protection Act, and biting chunks out of those protections in the next legislative breath, might be regarded as damning evidence of untrustworthiness.

But do patients in fact mind if their records are used in research and audit? In the next extract, MPM Richards *et al.* explain that patients in a breast cancer study seemed relatively unconcerned about the use of their medical notes for the purposes of research.

MPM Richards, M Ponder, P Pharoah, S Everest, and J Mackay[60]

None of those we interviewed had any concerns about confidentiality in relation to the ABC study. We asked if they knew how they had been selected for the study. None did; most simply assumed the researchers would have been told by their GPs or the cancer clinic of their breast cancer. Such possible passing on of information did not cause any concerns. In fact, the sample had been identified through the regional cancer registry but this was not stated in the information given at recruitment. The existence of such a registry was unknown to all but one of the interviewees, who included two nurses and a GP's secretary. The woman who knew of the registry had a close relative who worked in cancer research.

Women were asked how they would feel if their blood sample was passed to other medical researchers for work on other diseases 'such as heart disease or mental illness'. All said they would be quite happy for this to be done. They were further asked what they would feel about their samples going to a commercial company or a drug company for research. Most were also content with this though a couple were a little hesitant. One had concerns over patenting and said she would only agree if it was for a drug that would be available to everyone. She said she thought that cancer research should be done by the government, not private companies....

Our interviews suggest that those who have had breast cancer are pleased to take part in genetic epidemiological research and do not perceive any particular issues related to confidentiality. Furthermore, participants said they were content for their blood samples to be used for other medical research. Most, but not all women, included commercial or drug company research in this.

[59] 'Confidence Matters: The Rise and Fall of Informational Autonomy in Medical Law' (2003) 11 Medical Law Review 208–36.
[60] 'Issues of Consent and Feedback in a Genetic Epidemiological Study of Women with Breast Cancer' (2003) 29 Journal of Medical Ethics 93–6.

(4) Statutory Exceptions

A number of statutes create specific exceptions to the duty of confidentiality. The Public Health (Control of Disease) Act 1984 permits a registered medical practitioner who suspects or has become aware that a patient is suffering from a notifiable disease or food poisoning, to disclose the patient's name, age, sex, and address to the 'proper officer of the local authority'. Under section 10, notifiable diseases means, cholera, plague, relapsing fever, smallpox, and typhus. This is supplemented by the Public Health (Infectious Diseases) Regulations 1988,[61] which set out further infectious diseases which must be reported, such as tuberculosis, viral hepatitis, whooping cough, and yellow fever.

7 REMEDIES

If a patient discovers an impending breach of confidence, she can apply for an injunction to prevent disclosure. But what if the disclosure has already taken place? If it were possible to bring an action in negligence because the breach of confidence also amounted to a breach of the doctor's ordinary duty of care, then it might be possible to recover damages if, for example, the disclosure has caused economic loss or psychiatric illness. But what if the only 'harm' is the patient's distress? Usually, it is not possible to recover damages for injury to feelings or reputation, but there are exceptions to this rule, such as damages for defamation. It is not entirely clear whether the courts would be willing to award damages for the injured feelings caused by a breach of confidentiality. At first instance in *W v Egdell*, Scott J stated that he thought this was 'open to question':

> I think [it] open to question whether shock and distress caused by the unauthorised disclosure of confidential information can...properly be reflected in an award of damages...In my judgment, W would not, even if I had found Dr Edgell to be liable, have been entitled to damages. He would have had to be content with a declaration and an injunction.[62]

This point was not considered when the case reached the Court of Appeal.

In *Cornelius v De Taranto*, a psychiatric report, which contained certain potentially defamatory statements had been circulated without the subject's consent. At first instance, Morland J awarded the claimant £3,750 damages, which included £3,000 'for the injury to the claimants feelings caused by the unauthorized disclosure of the confidential information'.

Cornelius v De Taranto[63]

Morland J

Under art 8 of the Convention for the Protection of Human Rights and Fundamental Freedoms 1950 'everyone has the right to respect for his private and family life' and '(there) shall be no

---

[61] SI 1988/1546.
[62] *W v Egdell* [1989] 2 WLR 689.
[63] (2001) 68 BMLR 62.

interference by a public authority with the exercise of this right except such as is in accordance with the law and is necessary in a democratic society...for the protection of health'...

In my judgment, it would be a hollow protection of that right if in a particular case in breach of confidence without consent details of the confider's private and family life were disclosed by the confidant to others and the only remedy that the law of England allowed was nominal damages. In this case an injunction or order for delivery up of all copies of the medico-legal report against the defendant will be of little use to the claimant. The damage has been done. The details of the claimant's private and family life are within the archives of the National Health Service and she has been unable to retrieve them....

In the present case, in my judgment, recovery of damages for mental distress caused by breach of confidence, when no other substantial remedy is available, would not be inimical to 'considerations of policy' but indeed to refuse such recovery would illustrate that something was wrong with the law....

My conclusion is that I am entitled to award damages for injury to feelings caused by breach of confidence. Although it is a novel instance of such a remedy, it is in accord with the movement of current legal thinking.

On appeal, the Court of Appeal did not specifically discuss the question of compensation for breach of confidence, but they left the damages award intact. The Law Commission has recommended that damages should be available for the mental stress caused by a breach of confidence, but their proposals have not been implemented.[64]

As we saw earlier, there is a right to compensation for distress under section 13 of the Data Protection Act 1998, although the scope of this right is limited. The claimant must prove that she has suffered physical, financial, or psychiatric damage, and the data controller has a defence if she took all reasonable care to comply with the Act.

8 ACCESS TO MEDICAL RECORDS

Patients have a right of access to personal data, which includes their health records, under section 7 of the Data Protection Act 1998. In order to claim access to information, the data subject must make a request in writing; pay the specified fee (of up to £10); and supply information which confirms his identity and helps to locate the particular information. Information must then be supplied promptly, within 40 days or less. If the data controller fails to supply the relevant information, a court can order him to do so.

Exactly what are 'data subjects' entitled to under the Act? First, they can ask whether their personal data is being processed by the data controller; secondly, they can ask for a description of the data and the purposes for which it is being processed and the identity of its recipients; and thirdly, where possible, for a copy of any information held.

The right of access to health records under the Data Protection Act is not absolute, however. Under the Data Protection (Subject Access Modification) (Health) Order 2000,[65] data which might otherwise have to be disclosed can be withheld if it would be likely to cause serious harm to the physical or mental health of the data subject or any other person, or would lead the data subject to identify another person (other than a health professional who

---

[64] Breach of Confidence Report No. 110, 1981 Cmnd 838.
[65] SI 2000/413.

has been involved in the care of the data subject) who has not consented to the disclosure of his or her identity.

Personal data which is processed only for research purposes is also exempt from the right of access provided that the data is not processed to support measures or decisions with respect to particular individuals, is not done in such a way as would be likely to cause the patient substantial damage or distress, and the results do not identify the patient. Under section 31, regulatory agencies, such as the Care Quality Commission (formerly the Healthcare Commission) and bodies that protect the public against malpractice, such as the GMC, can also claim exemption.

Of course, the Data Protection Act 1998 must now be read in the light of the Freedom of Information Act 2000 which provides another route for access to information held by public bodies. Personal information is, however, exempt from the Freedom of Information Act's provisions both in relation to the patient's own access to her health records and to third parties seeking access to them. It is only non-personal health information, such as an NHS trust's policy decisions, which might be subject to requests under the Freedom of Information Act.

Clearly, one situation in which a patient might want access to her medical records is if she is contemplating an action in negligence. Under section 33 of the Supreme Court Act 1981, she can apply for a court order which will require the relevant doctor or hospital to disclose her records or notes. There must be a real prospect of litigation before disclosure will be ordered. A patient cannot use section 33 in order to engage in a 'fishing expedition' in the hope that some evidence of negligence might emerge. In addition, limitations can be imposed upon disclosure. The patient herself has no right to see her records: rather, the court may restrict disclosure to the patient's legal and/or medical advisers.

9 CONCLUSION

Despite the origins of the legal duty of confidence being somewhat opaque, doctors are unquestionably under a duty to respect their patients' confidentiality. The duty is not an absolute one, however. On the contrary, in a wide range of situations, the duty to respect confidentiality is suspended or modified. For example, patient notes have to be shared among health care professionals; information can be disclosed where there is a serious risk of harm to others; and patient records can be used for epidemiological research and clinical audit. Most exceptions to the duty of confidentiality could be justified on 'public interest' grounds, but it must be admitted that the existence of a 'public interest' exception to the duty of confidence does not offer very clear guidance to doctors about when disclosure of patient information is justifiable. Essentially, the public interest exception requires the merits of disclosure in a particular case to be weighed against the general public interest in the maintenance of patient confidentiality.

Not only is the 'public interest' exception both vague and potentially extremely broad, but also the legal rules that govern the duty of confidentiality are rather confusing. For example, the Human Rights Act protects privacy, and while privacy and confidentiality are clearly similar, they are not synonymous. The duty of confidentiality does not offer general protection for all personal information; instead it simply prevents the *redisclosure* of information that was originally disclosed within a confidential relationship. Hence viewing the question of confidentiality through the lens of the Human Rights Act may have a distorting effect upon the basic legal principles that underpin the duty of confidence.

Finally, at the time of writing, the Coroners and Justice Bill was making its way through Parliament. While principally a Bill designed to change aspects of the coroners' service, clause 152 would have permitted government ministers to share personal data in order to achieve any 'relevant policy objectives'. If enacted, this would mean that a data-sharing order could be made provided that it is proportionate to the relevant policy objective, and that it strikes a fair balance between the public interest and the interest of any person affected by it. Of critical importance for our purposes is that data-sharing orders would be able to remove or modify any legal barrier to data sharing, including both the common law duty of confidentiality and the Data Protection Act. In relation to medical information, the Bill's explanatory notes made clear that the Secretary of State for Health would be able to authorize the sharing of patient information for research purposes, but of course, data sharing would not be limited to research and could be authorized for any relevant policy objective. Following sustained pressure from, among others, the BMA, clause 152 was dropped but interest in the possibility of data-sharing orders remains. It is therefore possible that a modified version of clause 152 might be introduced in the future. If this happens, the implications for patient confidentiality could be profound.

FURTHER READING

Case, Paula, 'Confidence Matters: The Rise and Fall of Informational Autonomy in Medical Law' (2003) 11 Medical Law Review 208–36.

Gilbar, Roy, 'Medical Confidentiality Within the Family: The Doctor's Duty Reconsidered' (2004) 18 International Journal of Law, Policy and the Family 195.

Jones, C, 'The Utilitarian Argument for Medical Confidentiality: A Pilot Study of Patients' Views' (2003) 29 Journal of Medical Ethics 348–52.

McLean, Sheila and Mason, John Kenyon, *Legal and Ethical Aspects of Healthcare* (Greenwich Medical Media: London, 2003) ch 3.

Sandland, Ralph, 'Freedom of the Press and the Confidentiality of Medical Records' (2007) 15 Medical Law Review 400–409.

8

GENETIC INFORMATION

CENTRAL ISSUES

1. Genetic information raises a number of complex issues in relation to the duty of confidentiality that we considered in the previous chapter:

   (a) First, the inherently shared nature of genetic information poses particular challenges for a model of confidentiality which has stressed the privacy of an individual's health records. One person's diagnosis may reveal information about her close family members.

   (b) Secondly, genetic tests are often predictive rather than diagnostic. Their results provide information about a person's risk of *future* ill health, which might be of particular interest to third parties, such as employers and insurers.

   (c) Thirdly, DNA databases might be useful for the police, for research and resource planning within the NHS, and for the pharmaceutical industry, but they raise a number of important ethical issues.

2. In some other countries—but not in the UK—genetic discrimination is prohibited by law in the same way as discrimination on the grounds of sex, race, and disability.

3. Genetic testing used to take place only within the NHS's Regional Genetics Services. In recent years, there has been a rapid growth in direct-to-consumer testing, allowing the 'worried well' to discover whether they are at increased risk of a growing number of common conditions.

4. In the future, pharmacogenetics is likely to transform the way in which medicines are prescribed, by enabling doctors to know *in advance* whether a drug is likely to be safe and effective for a particular patient.

1 INTRODUCTION: WHAT IS GENETIC INFORMATION?

All of the cells in our bodies, aside from our reproductive cells (sperm and eggs) contain 23 pairs of chromosomes (one set from our mother and one from our father). Within each chromosome, genes are arranged in specific sequences. These genes are made up of DNA, which contains a code directing the production of different proteins, which in turn determines how our cells will function.

Progress in the field of genetics has been especially rapid in recent decades. The mapping of the human genome—which was completed in 2003—informed us that we have fewer genes than had previously been assumed: only twice as many as the roundworm. The sequence of most of our 20–25,000 genes is identical (99.9 per cent), and indeed we share a surprising proportion of our DNA with chimpanzees (96 per cent), and, perhaps even more surprisingly, with fruit flies (60 per cent).

In this chapter, we are principally concerned with questions about the regulation of access to genetic information. One reason why this is especially important is that faulty genes, or mutations, can increase one's chances of developing a condition in later life, and so access to information about someone's genetic make-up may amount to access to predictive information about their future health prospects.

There are a number of different sorts of genetic disease. Unifactorial genetic conditions were the first to be identified. They are conditions which are, in very simple terms, *caused by* a particular genetic mutation. These can be further divided into two groups. First, if the gene is *dominant*, a single gene inherited from either parent will cause the disease. An example is Huntington's disease, a neurological degenerative disease, which people usually develop between the ages of 30 and 50, and which causes progressive deterioration of bodily functions and cognitive abilities, leading to death within about 15–20 years. If someone with Huntington's disease reproduces, there is a 50 per cent chance that any child will inherit the disease. Huntington's disease has a penetrance of 100 per cent, which means that if a person

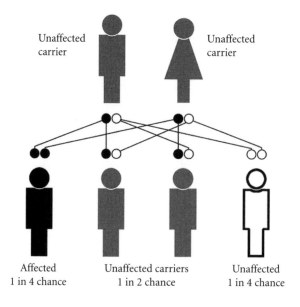

Unaffected carrier

Unaffected carrier

Affected
1 in 4 chance

Unaffected carriers
1 in 2 chance

Unaffected
1 in 4 chance

inherits the gene, then, provided they do not die first from another cause, they know that they will definitely develop Huntington's.

The second type of unifactorial condition is one where the gene is *recessive*. As the diagram opposite shows, this means that a person will only develop the disease if they inherit the gene from both parents. People who have only one copy of the gene are carriers. They will not develop the disease themselves, but if they reproduce with another carrier, there is a one-in-four chance that any child they might have will have a double dose of the relevant gene and will therefore suffer from the disease in question. There is a one-in-four chance that the child will be completely unaffected and not carry the gene at all, and a one-in-two chance that the child will herself be a carrier.

Examples of recessive genetic conditions are cystic fibrosis, a lung condition with a life expectancy of 20–40 years, and sickle cell disease, a serious blood disorder, again with considerably shortened life expectancy. Within some population groups, being a carrier for either of these conditions is fairly common. Among people of European descent, one in twenty-five are carriers of the cystic fibrosis gene. Families are often completely unaware that they are passing on this gene until one member happens to reproduce with another carrier. Sickle-cell trait (being a carrier of the sickle-cell gene) is much more common among people of African and Caribbean descent.

A further group of genetic diseases are X-linked disorders, which are triggered by a mutation on the X chromosome. Women have two X chromosomes, and so they will usually have a second normal X chromosome to compensate for the defective one. Women will usually therefore only be carriers of these diseases, and pose a risk of passing on the disease to their male offspring. Men have an X and a Y chromosome, and so if they inherit a mutation on the X chromosome from their mother, they will develop the disease. Boys always inherit the Y chromosome from their father, and hence cannot inherit an X-linked condition from their fathers. Examples of X-linked disorders are Duchenne Muscular Dystrophy and haemophilia.

Chromosomal disorders arise when a person has an abnormality in their chromosomes, perhaps because they have too many copies of a particular chromosome. Examples are Down's syndrome and Turner syndrome.

Unifactorial genetic diseases are unusual. Most conditions are, instead, complex and multifactorial: that is, they result from the interaction of several genes, and from the interaction between a person's genes and their environment. Some people will have genes that predispose them to heart disease, for example, but whether or not they develop heart disease, and at what age, may be influenced principally by lifestyle factors, such as diet, exercise, alcohol consumption, and smoking.

In recent years, there has been particularly rapid progress in identifying what we might call *susceptibility* genes: that is, genes which increase a person's risk of developing a condition, but where there is no guarantee that they will in fact do so. This means their penetrance, unlike Huntington's, is less than 100 per cent. Certain types of cancer are triggered by genetic mutations. Approximately 5 per cent of breast cancers are the result of faulty BRCA1 and BRCA2 genes, which increase the lifetime risk of developing breast cancer to the range of 60–80 per cent, and the lifetime risk of ovarian cancer to around 60 per cent.[1]

Finding out that someone has a genetic mutation associated with a genetic condition raises a number of specific issues. First, it is undoubtedly true that our capacity to understand and

---

[1] For more information on cancer genetics, see <www.cancerbackup.org.uk>.

identify the genetic component of a number of diseases currently massively outstrips our capacity to treat them. We have been able to identify the gene which causes Huntington's disease for some time now, but there is still no cure. This means that the decision to be tested is different from being tested for conditions like cancer or HIV, where treatment may not always succeed, but there is usually something that can be done in response to a positive test result.

In contrast, a positive test for the Huntington's gene involves the discovery that, in the absence of a scientific breakthrough or one's premature death from an unrelated cause, something extremely nasty will start happening to one's body in the fairly near future. Research appears to indicate that suicide rates in people who receive positive Huntington's test results are higher than normal,[2] and it is not surprising that many people have opted not to be tested (we return to this point below).

The only way in which 'something can be done' when one knows that an untreatable genetic condition runs in one's family, is to undergo pre-implantation (or prenatal) genetic diagnosis in order to ensure that future generations are not born with the condition in question. Because the special regulatory regime covering assisted conception also covers pre-implantation genetic diagnosis, we deal with this separately in Chapter 15. Prenatal diagnosis, unless carried out in order to help the parents prepare for the birth of an affected child, is generally done so that affected fetuses can be aborted. The law covering abortion for abnormality is dealt with in Chapter 13.

A second important difference is that genetic test results may be predictive, rather than diagnostic. If I discover that I have the BRCA1 mutation, I may be healthy now and for decades to come. Indeed, it is possible that I will never develop breast or ovarian cancer. But I have found out that I am much more likely than most women to develop both cancers, and at a younger age than normal. This information might be useful to others, such as insurance companies, who base their calculations of premiums upon actuarial tables that predict a person's life expectancy.

Another important issue is that if I find out that I have the BRCA1 mutation, I must have inherited this from one of my parents. Discovering this information about myself means that I also know that other family members may have the same elevated risk of breast and ovarian cancer. As Lori Andrews explains in the next extract, this means that genetic test results raise particularly interesting questions about confidentiality. The problem is obviously most acute for identical twins, who share the same DNA. If one twin is diagnosed with a genetic disorder, she cannot avoid knowing that her twin sister has the same genetic mutation. For other relatives, the implications of a relative's positive diagnosis may be less certain, but nonetheless significant.

Lori B Andrews[3]

Genetics shares many features with other medical fields, but it also has several unique features that raise concerns about its impact on people's lives. First, genetics often plays a central role in people's lives. Because genes are usually viewed as immutable and essential to the determination of a person's identity, information about genetic predispositions may

---

[2] T. Bird, 'Outrageous Fortune: The Risk of Suicide in Genetic Testing for Huntington's Disease' (1999) 64 American Journal of Human Genetics 1289.

[3] 'A Conceptual Framework for Genetic Policy: Comparing the Medical, Public Health and Fundamental Rights Models' (2001) 79 Washington University Law Quarterly 221.

cause a person to change his or her self-perception and may cause others to treat that person differently. Second, people may undergo genetic testing or therapy without sufficient advance consideration of its potential effects. In most instances, people seek medical services because they are already ill. However, ...healthy people undergoing testing may not consider the psychological, social, and financial impact of learning genetic information about themselves before they agree to genetic testing...

Genetics has another unique feature. Genetic testing of a particular individual also reveals genetic risk information about his or her relatives. A parent and a child have half their genes in common, as do siblings. Cousins share one-quarter of their genes, as do grandparents and grandchildren. The acquisition and disclosure of genetic information raise new and profound questions of 'gen-etiquette', questions about the moral obligations owed to relatives. If a woman learns she has a genetic mutation predisposing her to breast cancer, does she have a moral or even a legal duty to share that information with her sister? What about an estranged cousin?...

Genetic information influences people's relationships with third parties, such as insurers and employers. While individuals might want to know their own genetic makeup in order to make important life decisions, such information can also be used against them....The chilling irony of genetic testing is that, even in rare cases where a treatment exists, people may be afraid to get tested for the disorder because their insurer might drop them entirely or an employer may refuse to hire them based on their test results.

In addition to providing information about future ill health, DNA test results might also be exceptionally useful to the police by enabling them to maintain a DNA database that could be searched rapidly as soon as evidence is found at a crime scene. Of course, the public interest in the identification and prosecution of criminals is substantial, but difficult questions arise about whose DNA should be placed on a database, and how long it should be kept. DNA databases might also be useful for research purposes, and to assist the management and planning of health care provision.

One of the most important issues that arises in relation to genetic test information is therefore confidentiality, and we begin this chapter with a discussion of various third parties' interests in genetic test results and DNA profiles, and the extent to which genetic privacy is protected by the law.

The second important issue raised by genetic information is to the possibility of discrimination against those found to have genetic disorders. Adam Moore recounts an extreme example of genetic discrimination in Orchemenos, Greece, where sickle-cell anaemia is common.[4] Researchers tested everyone in the village so that carriers could ensure they did not marry each other. It was assumed that carriers would choose to marry non-carriers, in order to avoid having children with sickle-cell disease. The problem was that the non-carriers refused to cooperate. Carriers became a stigmatized subclass, who were forced to marry among themselves, thereby making the situation worse than before.

The potential for genetic discrimination may be exacerbated by the fact that certain genetic traits are particularly associated with different ethnic groups. Ashkenazi Jews, for example, are disproportionately likely to have the BRCA1 or BRCA2 mutations and to carry the gene associated with Tay-Sachs disease.

[4] 'Owning Genetic Information and Gene Enhancement Techniques: Why Privacy and Property Rights May Undermine Social Control of the Human Genome' (2000) 14 Bioethics 97–119, 107.

In 2008, the United States passed the Genetic Information Non-discrimination Act, which prevents discrimination by employers and health insurers. In contrast in the UK, the government decided against including 'genetic discrimination' within the cluster of categories of unlawful discrimination, now brought together in the Single Equality Act 2009. We therefore follow our discussion of confidentiality issues with a brief discussion of the arguments for and against specifically outlawing discrimination against people on the basis of their genetic test results.

A third issue which is of growing importance is the massive expansion of genetic testing, and in particular in the growth of direct-to-consumer tests. There is already a market in paternity testing 'kits', which enable suspicious men to test their children's DNA in order to confirm or rebut paternity. Now companies are increasingly interested in selling genetic screening kits to the 'worried well'. Advertised as 'personal DNA analysis', for as little as $399 companies will ship a kit direct to a consumer, who returns a tube containing their saliva. Eight to ten weeks later, the customer will receive a read-out of their susceptibility to a growing number of common diseases (at the time of writing, around 90). Consumers can also purchase recreational genealogy and ancestry testing kits in order to discover where their ancestors came from.

Clearly, a host of difficult practical and legal issues arise from direct-to-consumer testing. If I could send back a vial containing someone else's saliva, could I therefore find out information about them that is none of my business? Is it a good idea to receive complicated and potentially alarming news through the post or via email, rather than in the course of a consultation with a trained professional?

Finally, we consider the move towards pharmacogenetics, and the possibility that a genetic test could reveal whether a medicine is likely to work for a patient, and whether that patient is likely to suffer adverse side-effects. If our genetic make-up affects the way we metabolize medicines, pharmacogenetics could reduce the 'trial and error' approach to prescribing, and lead to more accurate, personalized medication regimes.

2 GENETIC PRIVACY

Let us now turn to consider in more detail the various third parties who might have an interest in acquiring a patient's genetic test results.

(a) INSURERS

In the UK, a minority of the population purchases health insurance, but other sorts of insurance—such as life insurance for the purposes of obtaining a mortgage—are common. Many people take out insurance to ensure that their families do not suffer financially if they die prematurely, and insurance to cover the costs of care in old age is becoming increasingly popular.

On the one hand, it instinctively seems unfair if a genetic test result, which is plainly not within her control, prevents someone from obtaining insurance, or means that she faces vastly increased premiums. On the other hand, insurance contracts rely on the duty of 'utmost good faith' (*uberimmae fides*) in the disclosure of risk. Insurance companies already take a person's health status, family history, and lifestyle risks such as smoking, into account when setting premiums. Someone who has just been diagnosed with cancer would be under a duty to disclose that fact when seeking health insurance.

Moreover, forbidding insurance companies from taking genetic information into account might also have adverse consequences. If individuals discover that they are very likely to suffer from a serious disease, they might purchase a great deal of insurance, whereas other individuals with no known elevated risk of future ill health might not bother buying insurance at all. This phenomenon is known as adverse selection. Plainly, it would be very difficult to maintain a functioning market in insurance if only those people who are 'bad' risks choose to insure themselves.

In the next extract, the Human Genetics Commission—the UK Government's advisory body on new developments in human genetics—explains how genetic information might be used and misused by insurance companies.

Human Genetics Commission[5]

7.37 There has been much written about the possible harmful consequences in using genetic information in insurance. It appears to us from our survey of the People's Panel and our consultation that there is a widely held public view that those who are affected by genetic conditions should not feel excluded from the normal benefits of society (employment, participation in public life, and, it might be argued, access to insurance). Over recent decades, the position of disabled people has been steadily improved by legislation designed to enhance their opportunities in society. It would run counter to this commitment were society to allow new classes of persons to grow up which would be subjected to improper discrimination....

7.40 Where insurance is linked to important public goods like house ownership or life insurance, the consequences of failure to obtain cover are immediately apparent. Here applicants or potential applicants cannot join the 'housing ladder' and cannot protect their families from financial disaster if they die prematurely. In such a case it is not unreasonable to balance the moral and social costs to individuals and society against the costs to the insurance industry. We are familiar with the idea that both individuals and corporations should be prepared (if not willing) to pay something in order to secure important moral or social goals....

7.65 Our overall conclusion is that there is now an opportunity for a reasoned dialogue on a long-term approach to the use of personal genetic information in life and health insurance. This needs to be informed by appropriate independent research and analysis. There also needs to be in our view, a more fundamental debate about the merits of moving towards socially-inclusive insurance pooling arrangements which can provide those with an adverse genetic test result with access to affordable insurance. We believe...that such measures will be necessary to ensure those individuals, and society, can benefit from advances in genetic testing for healthcare.

In 2001, insurance companies in the UK agreed to impose a voluntary five-year ban on the use of positive genetic test results to set insurance premiums. This moratorium was extended in 2005 and will now run until November 2014, with a review planned in 2011. The latest

---

[5] Inside Information: Balancing Interests in the Use of Personal Genetic Data (HGC: London, 2002), available at <www.hgc.gov.uk/>.

version of the Association of British Insurer's Code of Practice sets out a set of principles, four of which are reproduced below.

Association of British Insurers[6]

Principles on which the Code is based

1 Applicants will not be asked to, nor be put under any pressure to, undergo a predictive genetic test in order to obtain insurance.

2 Insurers may only take into account adverse results of those predictive genetic tests that the government's advisory body, GAIC [Genetics and Insurance Committee] has decided are technically, clinically and actuarially relevant.

3 There must be no increase in the premium or worsening in the terms an insurer offers, arising from such a test, unless GAIC has decided that an adverse predictive genetic test result is technically, clinically and actuarially relevant for insurance purposes.

4 A predictive genetic test result, indicating the absence or mitigation of a genetic risk factor, may alter the effects of a family history of a genetic condition, and so avoid the need for a loading. Insurers should publish their policy in respect of normal (negative) or mitigating genetic test results.

The only exceptions to the ban on the use of genetic test results in setting premiums, which are intended to limit the problem of adverse selection, are for income protection insurance of more than £30,000 per year; life insurance cover greater than £500,000, and health insurance (critical illness, income protection, or long-term care insurance) cover greater than £300,000. Ninety-seven per cent of insurance policies are below these limits. For policies above these amounts, positive genetic test results may be used provided that the Genetics and Insurance Committee (GAIC) has approved the test in question. The only test approved so far is for Huntington's Disease for life insurance of more than £500,000. The Association of British Insurers (ABI) has not applied to GAIC for the approval of a genetic test since 2000, and at the time of writing says it has no plans to do so.

The moratorium on the use of genetic tests applies only to positive results. Negative test results *can* be taken into account. So a person with a family history of early onset Alzheimer's Disease who has found out that she does *not* carry the relevant gene, can ask an insurer to take *this fact* into account, rather than her family history, in order to reflect her reduced risk of premature morbidity.

It is impossible to know the extent of adverse selection under the current moratorium. Zick *et al.* studied the insurance-purchasing behaviour of people following testing for a variation on the ApoE gene, which appears to correlate with an increased risk of late onset Alzheimer's disease,. They found that those who received a positive test result were 5.76 times more likely to have altered their long-term care insurance arrangements than those whose results were negative.[7] With the growth in direct-to-consumer genetic screening, considered below, more individuals may be likely to find out that they are at increased risk of developing a wide range of conditions, including Parkinson's disease or heart attacks, and be prompted to take out critical illness cover that they might not otherwise have purchased.

---

[6] ABI Code of Practice for Genetic Tests (2008), available at <www.abi.org.uk>.
[7] Cathleen D. Zick *et al.*, 'Genetic Testing for Alzheimer's Disease and its Impact on Insurance Purchasing Behavior' (2005) Health Affairs 483.

(b) EMPLOYERS

For a number of reasons, employers also might find genetic test results useful when planning recruitment and promotion.

Alexander Capron[8]

> First, an employee who is prone to get sick will generate expenses: medical treatment costs, sick days, and potentially even disability benefits. Second, if the problem might be described as job-related, then the genetic condition could lead directly to workers compensation payments—for instance, a genetic predisposition to a bad back in an employee who has to do a lot of lifting. Finally, employers generally want to avoid hiring persons who are going to be sick a great deal because such persons cannot be relied upon to be present when needed and the expense of training them may thus be wasted if they become totally disabled.

Employers might also be interested in genetic test results that reveal whether an individual might pose a risk to fellow workers or to its customers. For example, an airline might want to know if any of its pilots are at risk of epilepsy.

Genetic test results might reveal that a person is particularly susceptible to a workplace hazard, such as a chemical used in an industrial process. The employer might want to know this in order to reduce the risk that the employee will suffer a workplace injury, both for benevolent reasons and in order to reduce the risk of having to pay compensation.

While reducing risk to the individual worker by excluding people with a genetic predisposition to a work-related condition may initially appear to be a sensible precautionary step, it could be argued that this approach looks at the problem of dangers in the workplace from the wrong direction. Striving to employ individuals who are more resistant to dangerous workplaces assumes that the environment could not be made any safer. Yet this will seldom be true. Rather than attempting to exclude those who are particularly susceptible to toxic substances, might it not be preferable to provide a safe working environment for *all* workers?

It could also be argued that this apparently benevolent concern for employees' health is unduly paternalistic. An individual might rationally choose to engage in work that poses a small risk to her health in preference to unemployment, which itself carries a significant risk to health and wellbeing. It also seems rather disingenuous for employers to cite the long-term impact a particular hazard might have upon an individual's future participation in the workforce as grounds for refusing to employ her on a short-term contract. Few employees now stay in the same job for more than a few years, and short-term contracts are increasingly common.

In the US, employers' interest in their employees' health status is intensified by the fact that most people's health insurance is provided by their employers, thus providing a double disincentive to employ anyone with a genetic predisposition to ill health. Not only might a high-risk employee have a shorter or less productive working life, but also their insurance premiums will generally be higher, and so they will be more costly to employ even while they are healthy.

---

[8] 'Which Ills to Bear? Reevaluating the "Threat" of Modern Genetics' (1990) 39 Emory Law Journal 665, 692.

In the next extract, Richard Epstein argues that full disclosure should be the norm where there are informational asymmetries between, for example, people who know that they have the gene for Huntington's disease and their employers or insurers. Epstein would even extend this duty of disclosure to potential spouses who, he argues, have a right to know that the person they are marrying will develop a terminal degenerative disease in middle age.

Richard A Epstein[9]

I think that in the case of Huntington's disease it is immoral for a person to marry (or even take a job) and conceal the condition from the potential spouse or employer. This conclusion is valid in commercial settings as well as in marital ones so long as it results in selective knowledge to one side that is denied to the other. When an individual has knowledge that he is at risk of incapacitation, perhaps from family history, then full disclosure should be the norm. . . .

At this point it is critical to note that the plea for privacy is often a plea for the right to mis-represent one's self to the rest of the world . . . No doubt the individual who engages in this type of deception has much to gain. But equally there can be no doubt that this gain exists in all garden variety cases of fraud as well. To show the advantage of the fraud to the party who commits it is hardly to excuse or to justify it, for the same can be said of all cases of success-ful wrongs. On the other side of the transaction, there is a pronounced loss from not knowing the information when key decisions have to be made. For example, a woman may choose the wrong husband; an employer may pass up a good employee with a strong medical record and a clear upward path in favor of a worker who will, in the end, be the source of enormous personal and financial costs.

(c) FAMILY MEMBERS

Genetic disease is generally transmitted through procreation, and so the results of genetic tests will often reveal information (albeit often quite imprecise and uncertain) about other family members. If a person finds out that she has a particular genetic condition, she will inevitably also have found out that one or both of her parents passed on the relevant gene(s), and that her siblings may have the same increased risk of developing the same condition.

In addition, genetic diagnoses will often rely upon information about other family members. Indeed, the principal reason for having a genetic test in the first place will usually be the existence of a shared family history of a particular condition. One of the most important initial diagnostic tools is often to construct a family tree showing which other members of a family had, or might have had, the disease in question.

There is then an inevitable tension between an individualistic model of confidentiality, in which a person's health information is regarded as paradigmatically private, and the in-herently shared nature of genetic information. As a result, there are those who have argued that genetic information is, in some sense 'communal', and that sharing it between family

---

[9] 'The Legal Regulation of Genetic Discrimination: Old Responses to New Technology' (1994) 74 Boston University Law Review.

members is therefore legitimate. As Alastair Kent points out, this tends to be the view of members of families who are at risk of genetic disease:

> Among those living in families where there is a diagnosis of a substantial risk of genetic disease, there is a strongly held view that such information should not be seen as the private property of the individual. Rather it should be seen as family information held in common by all those to whom it applies.[10]

In the next extract, Katherine O'Donovan and Roy Gilbar argue that while a *legal* duty to share genetic information may not exist, people generally feel under a *moral* obligation to tell other family members about any increased risks they may face.

Katherine O'Donovan and Roy Gilbar[11]

> [W]hen individuals enter into close relationship and become members of family, they realise that their membership entails some responsibilities. This recognition emerges from the empirical data regarding patients' views about disclosure of genetic information to family members. These studies indicate that patients who receive genetic information from their doctors feel morally responsible for communicating the information to their family members...
>
> The argument that intimate relationship implies responsibility is reflected in another study conducted by Lehmann et al. This study reports that 85% of the respondents believe that patients should disclose genetic information to relatives even when the disease is unavoidable and incurable. This suggests that the underlying reason for sharing information within the family does not derive solely from the desire to prevent harm to others, as lawyers argue, but from a strong sense of moral responsibility and from the recognition that medical information has implications in various aspects of family members' lives.

Most people who are given genetic diagnoses that may be relevant to family members do feel morally obliged to inform relatives who might also be at risk, and most do so, at least with their first-degree relatives. While most genetic counselling is non-directive, genetic counsellors tend to encourage disclosure, with some taking a more directive approach.[12]

What if the person who has been tested refuses to tell her relatives? Could disclosure without her consent ever be justifiable? Alissa Brownrigg has suggests that five factors should be taken into account when deciding whether to disclose a person's positive genetic test result to other family members:

> (1) the severity of the disease identified by testing;
>
> (2) the availability of preventive or curative options for that disease;
>
> (3) the accuracy and reliability of the test performed;

---

[10] 'Consent and Confidentiality in Genetics: Whose Information Is It Anyway?' (2003) 29 Journal of Medical Ethics 16–18, 17.

[11] 'The Loved Ones: Families, Intimates and Patient Autonomy' (2003) 23 Legal Studies 353.

[12] Laura E Forrest, Martin B Delatycki, Loane Skene, and MaryAnne Aitken, 'Communicating Genetic Information in Families—A Review of Guidelines and Position Papers' (2007) 15 European Journal of Human Genetics 612–18.

(4) the ability of the physician or health care provider to interpret and address issues relevant to the test performed; and lastly,

(5) the protections afforded to the tested individual against discrimination.[13]

First, the severity of the disease is important because breach of confidentiality should be a last resort, and justifiable only if a threatened harm is imminent or serious. Secondly, if there are no available means of treating the disease or preventing its onset, knowing that one faces an increased risk of developing a serious disease may cause significant distress but without any prospect of averting the risk in question. Moreover, knowing about a genetic predisposition to ill health might have adverse financial consequences, such as increased insurance premiums. Of course, there may be some steps that individuals can take to reduce the risk of serious adverse consequences, even if a complete cure does not exist. Women who discover that they have the BRCA1 gene will be offered routine mammograms, which might enable the disease to be diagnosed in its early stages, thus increasing the prospect of a cure. Some women have even chosen to have prophylactic double mastectomies in order to eliminate the risk of developing breast cancer.

Genetic information might also be useful for people who are planning to have children. As we shall see in Chapter 15, a couple who know that they are at risk of passing on a serious genetic condition may be able to undergo pre-implantation genetic diagnosis in order to ensure that any child they have will not have the particular disease.

Thirdly, the risk of false positives and false negatives should be taken into account. Both can cause significant harm: a false negative result may mean that an individual does not receive the care that she needs, and a false positive result will cause unnecessary distress. Fourthly, genetic test results are complex and difficult to interpret. Disclosure without a proper explanation of the result's significance would be inappropriate. Finally, where a genetic test might reveal a person's susceptibility to debilitating illness, it may make it difficult to obtain insurance or employment, and unless anti-discriminatory measures are in place, again this may militate against disclosure.

In essence, these factors are relevant to whether disclosure to a family member fits within the 'public interest' exception to the duty of confidentiality which we considered in the previous chapter: that is, there must be a real risk of serious harm to others which could be averted by non-consensual disclosure. In the next extract, Dean Bell and Belinda Bennett argue that genetic information should not be treated as a special case, and that a doctor should divulge an individual's genetic test results only where it would 'prevent or lessen a serious or imminent threat to the life or health of a relative'.[14]

Dean Bell and Belinda Bennett[15]

It is not clear that genetic information is sufficiently different from other medical information to justify the development of an alternative legal framework for that information. As this article has shown, the law protects confidentiality with exceptions provided for certain circumstances. Furthermore, where a patient poses a risk to another individual the courts have

---

[13] Alissa Brownrigg, 'Mother Still Knows Best: Cancer-related Gene Mutations, Familial Privacy and a Physician's Duty to Warn' (1999) 26 Fordham Urban Law Journal 247, 273.
[14] 'Genetic Secrets and the Family' (2001) 9 Medical Law Review 130–61, 132.   [15] Ibid.

accepted that limited disclosures of confidential information may be justified in order to avert that harm. In other words, if the concern is that patients might not advise their relatives of their genetic risk, and that relatives may suffer as a result, the existing law of confidentiality arguably already provides a framework for disclosure to be permitted if the health of another is at risk.

Because one family member's genetic test results will usually just reveal that their relatives have an elevated risk of being predisposed to a particular condition, the 'public interest' exception will very rarely be satisfied. Not only is the risk of suffering the particular disease uncertain, for many genetic conditions there is currently no known cure, and so disclosure would seldom enable a risk to health to be averted. As a result, Loane Skene disagrees with Bell and Bennett, arguing that genetic information *is* a special case and that disclosure of familial risk will sometimes be justifiable even where it would not fit within the normal 'public interest' exception.

Loane Skene[16]

Bell and Bennett suggest that the common law is adequate to protect a doctor who feels compelled to disclose a genetic risk to a relative of the patient without the patient's consent. They base this on the 'public interest' exception to the general confidentiality requirement, which will justify disclosure where there is a serious and imminent risk to the person or a third party (I would add: and the risk is capable of being averted by a warning).

I have some doubts about the adequacy of this little-tested principle in relation to genetic testing...The law requires the risk to be serious and imminent. It is difficult to imagine a situation in which a genetic risk would be of this type. Take FAP [Familial Adenematous Polyposis, a type of colorectal cancer], for example, where in my view disclosure is most arguably justified. The risk is serious; it is a potentially lethal condition. The diagnosis is certain. And there is an effective intervention (monitoring and surgery if needed). Yet the risk could not be described as imminent. For these reasons I do not believe the common law exception is sufficient.

Our capacity to diagnose genetic disease currently far outstrips our capacity to treat it, so at present, breaching confidentiality by disclosing genetic information to relatives would seldom fit within the public interest exception to the duty of confidentiality which we considered in the previous chapter, Disclosing genetic information to relatives would not be able to prevent serious harm to others. In the future, however, as it becomes possible to successfully treat more genetic diseases, there will be increasing pressure on the principle of confidentiality in the context of genetic disease, and the balancing exercise between the public interest in disclosure and the public interest in confidentiality will become even more finely balanced and complicated.

In the next extract, Allen Buchanan cautions against treating all genetic tests in the same way. There are genetic conditions, such as hereditary hemochromatosis, which are serious, but for which a safe, relatively non-invasive, cheap, and fully effective treatment exists. Here the potential to avert serious harm by non-consensual disclosure is strong. In contrast,

---

[16] 'Genetic Secrets and the Family: A Response to Bell and Bennett' (2001) 9 Medical Law Review 162–9.

hereditary Alzheimer's disease is untreatable, and there is considerable stigma attached to its diagnosis. Buchanan argues that genetic conditions thus exist upon a spectrum, with conditions like hemochromatosis at one end and Alzheimer's at the other. Furthermore, where a condition lies on this spectrum is, of course, subject to change as more genetic diseases become treatable, thus steadily increasing the number of cases in which doctors will face difficult dilemmas about whether to breach patient confidentiality.

Allen Buchanan[17]

At present, with a few exceptions, diagnosis for genetic diseases outstrips treatment. This is especially true for the genetic tests that currently receive the most extensive media coverage and public discussion, including tests for the BRCA1 and BRCA2 genes, the APO E4 Alzheimer's gene test, and the test for the Huntington's gene. In each of these cases, the medical benefit of testing is very dubious at present because there is no effective treatment for the condition....

The situation is quite different if there is an effective treatment for a potentially lethal disease that can be detected by a genetic test. In this case, the clinician will reasonably believe that there is a single right course of action, and that the ethical responsibilities of the patient are clear from the perspective of widely accepted and easily defended values.

At present there are few such conditions. Perhaps the clearest case of a lethal late-onset disease that meets this description is hereditary hemochromatosis. If detected early enough, hereditary hemochromatosis has a simple, inexpensive, virtually riskless, and fully effective treatment; yet this disease has devastating effects on the liver, heart, and endocrine system if left untreated... It is reasonable to expect that in the future there will be more cases where those who test positive for a serious genetic condition will have the option of a successful treatment...

The fundamental point here is that it is necessary to think in terms of a continuum of tests for genetic disorders, with hereditary hemochromatosis at one end of the spectrum and Huntington's disease and Alzheimer's disease at the opposite extreme.

It is also important to recognize that disclosure might jeopardize the relatives' right *not* to know about any predisposition they might have to genetic disease. Where test results cannot lead to a cure, but might instead cause depression and despair, and make it difficult for an individual to purchase insurance, an individual may have very good reasons for preferring to remain in ignorance. Although testing may reveal that an individual is unaffected, and hence remove a huge source of anxiety, it is equally likely that she will discover that she is destined for a short, painful, and distressing future. We should not perhaps be surprised that take-up of genetic tests within families who know that there is a risk that they may have the gene which causes Huntington's Disease has been extremely low: fewer than 15 per cent of at-risk individuals have opted to take the test.[18] There is also some evidence that both positive *and negative* test results may be difficult to come to terms with within families at risk of Huntington's. Gargiulo *et al.*'s study found that 58 per cent of asymptomatic carriers and

---

[17] 'Ethical Responsibilities of Patients and Clinical Geneticists' (1998) 1 Journal of Health Care Law and Policy 391, 395–7.

[18] David Craufurd *et al.*, 'Uptake of Presymptomatic Predictive Testing for Huntington's Disease' (1989) 334 Lancet 603, 604.

24 per cent of non-carriers were depressed in the months after being tested.[19] Tibben *et al.* report that some of those who tested negative for the gene found themselves rejected by their families, once it became apparent that they no longer shared a bond which had previously brought the family closer.[20]

It is also important to note that it is not only direct disclosure that might threaten the right not to know. Simply alerting relatives to the existence of information, and asking them whether they wish to receive it, reveals to them that there is something to worry about.

The right 'not to know' is enshrined in a number of international documents. Article 10.2 of the European Convention on Human Rights and Biomedicine states:

> Everyone is entitled to know any information collected about his or her health. However, the wishes of individuals not to be so informed shall be observed.

And Article 5c of the UNESCO Declaration on the Human Genome similarly provides that:

> The right of every individual to decide whether or not to be informed of the results of genetic examination and the resulting consequences should be respected.

Is a right to ignorance in tension with the duty of doctors to be honest and frank with their patients, which we considered in the previous chapter? Graeme Laurie thinks not, and argues instead that a right not to know is an important aspect of personal autonomy.

Graeme Laurie[21]

> To disclose genetic information to someone who has not expressed a desire to know can be disrespectful in two ways.
>
> First, furnishing an individual with information that she has actually said she does not want to receive disrespects her wishes and is an affront to her as an autonomous person. The pivotal ethical principle of respect for autonomy surely requires that we respect her wishes.
>
> Second, even if no wish has been expressed, we cannot ignore the spatial privacy interests which are also compromised.... Control of information about ourselves must be an essential part of any concept of ourselves as autonomous persons, but 'control' should not be limited merely to control of who has access to that information. It should also include the facility not to accept the information ab initio....
>
> The precise content of the 'right' not to know will be context specific. For example, in the familial milieu, it might include a right not to be given information about a relative's diagnosis or a right not to be required to take part in linkage studies in order to build up an overall family profile. In the context of insurers and employers, it would certainly include a right not to be required to undergo testing and would probably also include a right to resist disclosure of test results if these were required simply to further the interests of third parties....

[19] Marcela Gargiulo *et al.*, 'Long-term Outcome of Presymptomatic Testing in Huntington Disease' (2009) 17 European Journal of Human Genetics 165–71.

[20] A Tibben *et al.*, 'Testing for Huntington's Disease with Support for All Parties' (1990) 335 Lancet 553.

[21] 'In Defence of Ignorance: Genetic Information and the Right not to Know' (1999) 6 European Journal of Health Law 119–32.

> Yet irrespective of context—and in each case—the kernel of the right not to know is the concept of respect for an individual privacy interest in not being subjected to unwarranted information about themselves.

The need to protect the right 'not to know' is one reason why parents can only consent to the genetic testing of their children where this will enable to child to receive treatment, ie the testing must be done for therapeutic reasons rather than in order to find out information about future risk.

In addition to ensuring the child herself can exercise her right not to know, there has been some concern over the motives of parents seeking to test their children for adult-onset diseases. It has, for example, been suggested that parents might want this information in order to decide whether to bother investing in a child's future. Wexler gives the extreme example of a woman in the US who requested genetic testing for Huntington's disease for her two children, on the grounds that she could only afford to send one of them to Harvard.[22] In the next extract, however, PJ Malpas argues that it is unfair to impute malevolent motivations to parents. She argues that parents are overwhelmingly likely to have their child's best interests at heart when making any decisions about genetic testing.

P J Malpas[23]

> A parent may comment that they would not save for their affected child's college education, intending instead to use that money to ensure that the child had a very positive and memorable childhood. One can imagine the parents who, knowing the child may only live until his or her early adulthood, devote their energies and resources into supporting and enabling the child's self esteem and confidence, and providing the child with opportunities they may otherwise not have had. For instance, travelling the world, regularly spending more time with older extended family members, actively pursuing a child's passions and hobbies, deciding not to send the child to boarding school, doing more together as a family, or simply spending more time with the child by limiting work hours.

(d) THE POLICE

If the DNA of every citizen were recorded and stored on a central police database, the identification of criminals from biological traces left at a crime scene would be much more straightforward. While a central record of every citizen's DNA, which could be scanned quickly and accurately, would undoubtedly be useful, it is almost certainly both impractical and ethically dubious. Universal testing would be expensive. Clearly, a population-wide database would be useful only if people could be compelled to give samples. A police database which contained only DNA profiles from samples given voluntarily would, for obvious

---

[22] N Wexler, 'Clairvoyance and Caution: Repercussions from the Human Genome Project' in DJ Kevles and L Hood (eds), *The Code of Codes: Scientific and Social Issues in the Human Genome Project* (Harvard UP: Cambridge, MA, 1992) 211–43, 233.

[23] 'Predictive Genetic Testing of Children for Adult-onset Diseases and Psychological Harm' (2008) 34 Journal of Medical Ethics 275–8.

reasons, be of limited use. However, forcing individuals to give samples without consent might be said to violate their rights to privacy and bodily autonomy.

More plausible are databases of DNA profiles made from biological samples taken from people who have been arrested or convicted of offences. Samples are regularly taken from both groups, and the costs of retaining the DNA profiles and the samples for future use would be relatively low. But should a distinction be drawn between those who have been convicted, and those who have been acquitted or released without charge? Should we distinguish between serious and trivial offences?

Until the end of 2008, the position in England and Wales was fairly clear. The Police and Criminal Evidence Act 1984 section 64(1A) was amended in 2001 to provide that DNA samples can be retained from all suspects, regardless of whether they have been convicted of an offence provided that they are used only for purposes related to the prevention and detection of crime.

Police and Criminal Evidence Act 1984 section 64

64(1A) Where—(a) fingerprints or samples are taken from a person in connection with the investigation of an offence, and (b) subsection (3) below does not require them to be destroyed, the fingerprints or samples may be retained after they have fulfilled the purposes for which they were taken but shall not be used by any person except for purposes related to the prevention or detection of crime, the investigation of an offence or the conduct of a prosecution.

Samples taken from volunteers, who supply them in order to eliminate themselves from suspicion have also been routinely retained, ostensibly with the volunteers' consent. Unsurprisingly, given the wide range of people whose profiles could find their way onto the database, the UK's National DNA Database (NDNAD) became one of the largest in the world, containing the DNA profiles of approximately six per cent of the population. For certain minority ethnic groups, a much higher proportion of the population is on the database. This is because any over-representation of people from minority ethnic groups in police arrest practices automatically translates in their over-representation on the database. In London, 55 per cent of the unconvicted people on the database in London were black or Asian.[24]

Interestingly, a different approach was taken in Scotland, where the parliament voted that the retention of the DNA of unconvicted persons should be possible only in the case of adults charged with violent or sexual offences, and then only for three years, with the possibility of an extension for a further two years if authorized by a court.

In 2007, the Nuffield Council on Bioethics issued a report which was critical of the NDNAD, and argued that England and Wales should adopt the Scottish model.

Nuffield Council on Bioethics[25]

We recommend that the law in England, Wales and Northern Ireland should be brought into line with that in Scotland. Fingerprints, DNA profiles and subject biological samples should

---

[24] Nuffield Council on Bioethics, The Forensic Use of Bioinformation: Ethical Issues (2008), available at <www.nuffieldbioethics.org.uk>.

[25] Ibid.

be retained indefinitely only for those convicted of a recordable offence. At present, the retention of profiles and samples can be justified as proportionate only for those who have been convicted. In all other cases, samples should be destroyed and the resulting profiles deleted from the NDNAD.

It is our view that consent given by a volunteer to retain their biological samples and resulting profile on the NDNAD must be revocable at any time and without any requirement to give a reason. This is a basic principle in all medical research and should equally apply to the voluntary component of the NDNAD, as it already does to the Scottish DNA Database. In view of the importance of this principle, we recommend that as a matter of policy, volunteers should not be asked to consent to the permanent storage of elimination biological samples and retention of DNA profiles derived from these samples beyond the conclusion of the relevant case...

In our view, the disproportionate over-representation of black ethnic minorities on the NDNAD is a matter of considerable concern, even if this arises from policing practice in making arrests rather than a fault with the NDNAD. Such disparities increase the risk of stigmatisation attendant on being known to have a profile on the NDNAD and can potentially lead to further alienation of whole minority ethnic communities.

Whether or not retaining samples from the unconvicted is compatible with the Human Rights Act 1998 came before the House of Lords in *R (on the application of S) v Chief Constable of South Yorkshire*, a case concerning two individuals who, in separate cases, had had their DNA samples retained, despite not being convicted of the crimes for which they had been arrested. By a 4:1 majority the House of Lords rejected their claim. Lord Brown found it difficult to understand why anyone should object to the retention of their samples.

R (on the application of S) v Chief Constable of South Yorkshire [26]

Lord Brown

I find it difficult to understand why anyone should object to the retention of their profile (and sample) on the database once it has lawfully been placed there. The only logical basis I can think of for such an objection is that it will serve to increase the risk of the person's detection in the event of his offending in future. But that could hardly be a legitimate objection, nor, indeed, is it advanced as such. Such objections as were suggested, however, seem to be entirely chimerical. First, the fear of an Orwellian future in which retained samples will be reanalysed by a mischievous state in the light of scientific advances and the results improperly used against the person's interest....

The second suggested objection is to the retention of profiles obtained from those at one time reasonably suspected of crime but subsequently acquitted or not proceeded against, the objection being that they are thereby stigmatised as properly belonging to the same group as the convicted. This to my mind is an equally unrealistic objection.

The applicants then took their case to the ECtHR. Towards the end of 2008, in *Marper v UK* the ECtHR unanimously held that retaining samples and DNA profiles from people who had been acquitted or never charged was incompatible with their Article 8 rights, and that,

---

[26] [2004] UKHL 39.

while it served a legitimate aim, namely the detection of crime, it was disproportionate and could not be regarded as necessary in a democratic society.

Marper v UK [27]

Judgment of the ECtHR

Given the nature and the amount of personal information contained in cellular samples, their retention *per se* must be regarded as interfering with the right to respect for the private lives of the individuals concerned....

In the Court's view, the DNA profiles' capacity to provide a means of identifying genetic relationships between individuals is in itself sufficient to conclude that their retention interferes with the right to the private life of the individuals concerned....

The Court further notes that it is not disputed by the Government that the processing of DNA profiles allows the authorities to assess the likely ethnic origin of the donor and that such techniques are in fact used in police investigations. The possibility the DNA profiles create for inferences to be drawn as to ethnic origin makes their retention all the more sensitive and susceptible of affecting the right to private life....

In view of the foregoing, the Court concludes that the retention of both cellular samples and DNA profiles discloses an interference with the applicants' right to respect for their private lives, within the meaning of Article 8 § 1 of the Convention....

The question, however, remains whether such retention is proportionate and strikes a fair balance between the competing public and private interests.

In this respect, the Court is struck by the blanket and indiscriminate nature of the power of retention in England and Wales. The material may be retained irrespective of the nature or gravity of the offence with which the individual was originally suspected or of the age of the suspected offender; fingerprints and samples may be taken—and retained—from a person of any age, arrested in connection with a recordable offence, which includes minor or non-imprisonable offences. The retention is not time-limited; the material is retained indefinitely whatever the nature or seriousness of the offence of which the person was suspected.

In conclusion, the Court finds that the blanket and indiscriminate nature of the powers of retention of the fingerprints, cellular samples and DNA profiles of persons suspected but not convicted of offences, as applied in the case of the present applicants, fails to strike a fair balance between the competing public and private interests and that the respondent State has overstepped any acceptable margin of appreciation in this regard. Accordingly, the retention at issue constitutes a disproportionate interference with the applicants' right to respect for private life and cannot be regarded as necessary in a democratic society.

Following this judgment, the government announced their intention to consult further on retention arrangements for DNA profiles and samples, including the possibility of varying the timescale of retaining DNA evidence based on the seriousness of the offence, and the age of and risk posed by the individual. DNA samples taken from children under the age of 10 were immediately removed.

In the next extract, Stephen Sedley, writing extra-judicially, argues for a different solution to the inequity of storing samples from people who have come into contact with the police but who have not actually been convicted.

---

[27] (Applications Nos 30562/04 and 30566/04) (2008).

Stephen Sedley[28]

> My argument is that the case is growing for a national database holding the DNA profile of everyone living in or entering the country.
>
> The present system, sanctioned by legislation, is that the police may take and keep a DNA sample from everyone they arrest, whether or not the person is charged or convicted. This has the unfortunate effect of putting the innocent on a par with the guilty. It draws a not very logical line between innocent people who have and have not passed through the hands of the police. But it does not follow that the law should be moved back to what it once was, so as to require the police to destroy their DNA records of everyone not eventually convicted. What follows no less logically is that the taking and retention of an individual's DNA profile should not depend at all on whether he or she happens to have come into the hands of the police. . . .
>
> It can be, in fact, something rather worse than a fortuity. We know that there is an ethnic imbalance in arrests for certain types of offence, as well as in the use of stop and search powers. This . . . has the unacceptable consequence that members of some ethnic minorities face a disproportionately high chance of getting on to the police DNA database without being convicted of anything. A universal and uniform database will at least resolve this problem.

In 2007, an Ethics Group was set up to monitor the operation and uses of the NDNAD. It is perhaps noteworthy that this happened after the NDNAD had been in operation for several years, rather than at the outset. The Group met for the first time in 2008, and considered a number of issues, such as the need for greater clarity about the status of the profiles of people who give samples voluntarily to exclude themselves from suspicion. The Ethics Group believed that there should be a presumption that these profiles would not be loaded on to the NDNAD. The decision in *Marper* makes their non-inclusion mandatory, in any event. The Group also considered, and rejected, the possibility of a population-wide database.

NDNAD Ethics Group[29]

> - A database containing the DNA profiles of all the supposed inhabitants of the United Kingdom at any one time would in fact never absolutely do so in practical terms. There would for example, be those who would avoid profiling (by illegal means or on the grounds of human rights), temporary visitors, migrant workers, and the deliberate submission of false identities;
>
> - Despite the existing legislative controls, there are unknown and unpredictable social consequences of being potentially able to identify the parentage and sibling status of all individuals. The ramifications extend beyond the discovery of unexpected birth relationships to inheritance rights and the penetration of genetic traits.
>
> - Consequently, it is inappropriate without public debate and fraught with ethical and social problems and questions of personal freedom, to allow a criminal intelligence database to convert into a national repository of the nation's DNA characteristics. Arguing that the

---

[28] An extract from a lecture, ' "Rarely Pure and Never Simple": The Law and the Truth', delivered in 2004 at Leicester University and published under the title 'Short Cuts' (2005) 27 London Review of Books.

[29] 1st Annual Report (2008), available at <www.policehomeoffice.gov.uk>.

database should be expanded to include all the population, (the majority of whom will never commit a crime), to prevent inequality and discrimination is, on balance, unsustainable when issues of proportionality and personal privacy are taken into account.

A further issue that arises in relation to the forensic use of genetic information is its use in the courtroom, where a match between the DNA profile of an individual and samples found at a crime scene is often assumed to offer irrefutable, scientific evidence of guilt. This is misleading, however, for a number of reasons. First, the fact that DNA evidence proves that person X was in a location where a crime was committed does not establish that person X committed that crime, merely that person X has been at that location at some point in the past. Secondly, there is always the possibility of human error or contamination or degradation of samples: crime scenes, almost by definition, are often the antithesis of ideal laboratory conditions.

Thirdly, let us imagine that there is a match between the DNA of an individual suspect and that of the person who committed the crime, and that the chance of this happening randomly is put at one in a million. While that sounds like fairly conclusive evidence of guilt, in a country with a population of sixty million, there will be fifty-nine other individuals with the same DNA profile who might also have been responsible for leaving their DNA at the crime scene. If one takes into account people from other countries who might also be a match, there may be many hundreds of people worldwide who could have left this DNA at this crime scene.

Even if we confine ourselves to the UK population, rather than establishing that there is a one in a million chance that the defendant is not guilty, this 'one in a million' match in fact establishes that there is a one in sixty chance that the defendant is the person whose DNA was left at the crime scene, which sounds rather different. Of course, there may be other evidence that points to the defendant being the criminal, rather than one of these other fifty-nine people, but DNA evidence alone does not establish their guilt.

The Human Genetics Commission carried out a citizen's inquiry into the NDNAD, with the Commission expected to produce a full report in 2009. The Citizen's Inquiry produced a number of unanimous recommendations, some of which focused on the need for greater public understanding of DNA evidence.

HGC Citizen's Inquiry on the NDNAD[30]

Unanimous recommendations

1. There is a need for a nationwide public awareness campaign about the NDNAD that will reach all sections of the population.

2. Information about the police powers to take a DNA sample should be given to people from whom DNA samples are taken.

3. There should be an independent body with broad membership, constituted by statue specifically to oversee the NDNAD.

4. Independent guidance should be provided to juries in trials that involve DNA evidence before they hear from expert witnesses.

[30] (2008), available at <www.hgc.gov.uk>.

5. Education at school level should include learning about DNA and its potential uses.

6. Where DNA is taken from children, a full explanation should be given in age-appropriate terms.

(e) OTHER DNA DATABASES

In 1998 Iceland granted a US biotechnology company called deCODE an exclusive licence to build a database of all Icelanders' medical records, including genetic test results, and the right to commercial exploitation of the database for 12 years. Although participation is not compulsory, the database operates on an 'opt out' basis, so unless Icelanders specifically object, their medical records and genetic test results will be held in the database. Consent can be presumed, it was argued, because coding techniques are in place to minimize the chances of individuals being identifiable. Critics have argued that it will be difficult to ensure that individuals cannot be identified from genetic data and medical records in a country with fewer than 300,000 inhabitants.[31] The intention is in part to provide information that will help to improve prediction, diagnosis, and treatment of disease, and to manage health services more cost-efficiently, but as Merz *et al.* point out in the following extract, it is principally a commercial venture, which has made some Icelanders suspicious about the use of their personal data.

Jon F Merz, Glenn E McGee, and Pamela Sankar[32]

The reasons why 20,000 Icelanders have opted out of the HSD [Health Service Database] are not known, but we can imagine several. For example, citizens might be concerned about violations of their medical privacy. The retrospective data collection will be performed by an estimated 300 trained medical transcriptionists, who will be assigned to sites throughout the country to access, abstract, and encode hundreds of thousands of medical records. While these transcriptionists may be contractually bound to maintain confidentiality of what they see, this systematic, comprehensive exposure and coding of 15 years of past medical records of nearly all citizens will nonetheless comprise an unparalleled invasion of privacy. In a nation of only 270,000 inhabitants, all of whom use the same medical care system, half of whom live in the capital Reykjavik, and most of whom are related to one another, the likelihood of a transcriptionist encountering information of personal interest is high....

While consent for legitimate centralized governmental collection and use for public health purposes would globally be deemed unnecessary, the fundamental, exclusive, and principal commercial research purpose of the HSD suggests that failure to secure express permission from citizens to collect and use their data for exclusive commercial research purposes violates international ethical standards...

In conclusion, we believe that the major ethical concerns posed by the HSD arise because its primary purpose is commercial, and only secondarily does it support legitimate governmental operations.

---

[31] Vilhjálmur Árnason, 'Coding and Consent: Moral Challenges of the Database Project in Iceland' (2004) 18 Bioethics 27–49.

[32] '"Iceland Inc?" On the Ethics of Commercial Population Genomics' (2004) 58 Social Science and Medicine 1201–9.

In the UK, the Biobank is a research initiative which will track the health of a representative sample of the population from the time at which they sign up until their deaths.[33] UK Biobank will involve half a million volunteers aged between 40 and 69, recruited by letter using details obtained from GP practices. Recruits will give a blood sample, answer questions about their lifestyle and medical history, and perhaps most significantly, prospectively grant full access to their past and future medical records. Data is encrypted with a code that has no external meaning, ie it will not be a person's NHS number. The intention is to generate data that will be useful for research into the causes of common diseases, such as cancer, heart disease, and stroke, and for public health purposes.

Participants in the project give generic consent at the outset to any future project for which the data is used, and to being recontacted in the future by UK Biobank itself or other researchers. While Biobank admits that it may have to give the police access to its database if they have a court order, it has committed itself to 'vigorously resisting' such access 'in all circumstances'.[34]

There is no payment for volunteering, and participants are specifically told that the initial consultation is not a 'health screening' opportunity. While measurements such as height and weight, obtained at the initial consultation, will obviously be available to participants at the time, any results obtained from their samples, which have implications for their own health, will not be fed back to them. This is because it is regarded as inappropriate to reveal health information outside of a clinical setting.

The consent form reads:

UK Biobank[35]

- I give permission for access to my medical and other health-related records, and for long-term storage and use of this and other information about me, for health-related research purposes (even after my incapacity or death).
- I give permission for long-term storage and use of my blood and urine samples for health-related research purposes (even after my incapacity or death), and relinquish all rights to these samples which I am donating to UK Biobank.
- I understand that none of my results will be given to me (except for some measurements during this visit) and that I will not benefit financially from taking part (e.g. if research leads to commercial development of a new treatment).

People are free to withdraw from UK Biobank at any time. In order to try to ensure that as much information as possible remains on the database if someone develops reservations about continued participation, there are three different levels of withdrawal:

---

[33] See further JV McHale, 'Regulating Genetic Databases: Some Legal and Ethical Issues' (2004) 12 Medical Law Review 70–96.

[34] UK Biobank Ethics and Governance Framework version 3.0 (2007), available at <www.ukbiobank.ac.uk>.

[35] 'Public Attitudes to Third Party Access and Benefit Sharing: Their Application to UK Biobank' (2008), available at <www.egcukbiobank.org.uk>.

UK Biobank[36]

> *"No further contact"*: UK Biobank would no longer contact the person directly, but would still have permission to retain and use information and samples provided previously and to obtain and use further information from your health records.
>
> *"No further access"*: UK Biobank would no longer contact the person or obtain additional information from their health records, but would still have permission to use the information and samples provided previously.
>
> *"No further use"*: in addition to no further contact or access, information and samples collected previously would no longer be available to researchers, and samples would be destroyed.

Unlike the NDNAD, from the outset UK Biobank has had to operate within an ethics and governance framework (EGF), a 'living document', currently in its third version.[37] It has an independent Ethics and Governance Council, which monitors compliance with the EGF, oversees the Biobank's activities, and advises on ethical and legal issues which arise during the different phases of the project. At the time of writing, over 260,000 people had been recruited. The expectation is that recruitment of all 500,000 participants will be completed by 2010.

3   GENETIC DISCRIMINATION

It has been suggested that genetic discrimination in the workplace or in the supply of goods and services should be treated in the same way as other illegitimate discriminatory practices. It has been illegal to discriminate on the grounds of disability in the UK since 1995, and so where someone has a genetic condition 'which has a substantial and long-term adverse effect on his ability to carry out normal day-to-day activities', unjustified discrimination is unlawful. This clearly excludes people with genetic conditions who are not yet symptomatic.

In the next extract, Larry Gostin advocates the specific prohibition of genetic discrimination.

Larry Gostin[38]

> Discrimination based upon actual or perceived genetic characteristics denies an individual equal opportunity because of a status over which she has no control. Discrimination based on genetic factors can be as unjust as that based on race, gender or disability. In each case, people are treated inequitably, not because of their inherent abilities, but solely because of pre-determined characteristics. The right to be treated equally and according to one's abilities in all the diverse aspects of human endeavor is a core social value.

---

[36] UK Biobank Ethics and Governance Framework version 3.0 (2007), available at <www.ukbiobank.ac.uk>.

[37] Ibid.

[38] 'Genetic Discrimination: The Use of Genetically Based Diagnostic and Prognostic Tests by Employers and Insurers' (1991) 17 American Journal of Law and Medicine 109.

> Genetic discrimination is harmful not merely because it violates core social values, but also because it thwarts the creativity and productivity of human beings, perhaps more than the disability itself. By excluding qualified individuals from education, employment, government service or insurance, the marketplace is robbed of skills, energy and imagination. Such exclusion promotes physical and economic dependency, draining rather than enriching social institutions. Finally, genetic discrimination also undercuts the Human Genome Initiative's fundamental purpose of promoting the public health..... If fear of discrimination deters people from genetic diagnosis and prognosis, renders them less willing to confide in physicians and genetic counselors, and makes them more concerned with loss of a job or insurance than with care and treatment, the benefits of genetic data collection will not be fully achieved.

In the US, the Genetic Information Nondiscrimination Act (GINA) was passed in 2008. It prohibits providers of health insurance and employers from discriminating against individuals on the basis of their genetic test results, and forbids them from requesting or demanding that a person undergoes a genetic test. Certain sorts of insurance are not covered. An insurer is allowed to ask for genetic test results before providing life insurance, disability insurance, and long-term care insurance. This means that, despite the existence of GINA, people may continue to be deterred from undergoing genetic testing in case it increases their insurance premiums for these excluded types of insurance.

Furthermore, GINA does not protect people who are symptomatic, and hence once the genetic condition manifests itself discrimination is not prohibited under the Act. As in the UK, discrimination on the grounds of disability is outlawed in the US. Nevertheless, people with genetic disorders may find themselves in a legal limbo in the period after first experiencing symptoms of the disorder, when GINA will cease to apply, but before they become seriously disabled and are covered by anti-disability discrimination legislation.

In addition to these exclusions, the *Harvard Law Review*'s commentary on GINA criticizes its promotion of 'genetic exceptionalism'. The consequence of GINA is that people with other sorts of knowledge about their likelihood of future ill-health are treated less favourably than those whose predictive diagnoses *happen* to be genetic.

Harvard Law Review[39]

> Although superficially appealing, GINA suffers from significant flaws. It implies and promotes genetic exceptionalism—the idea that genetic information needs special treatment—despite lacking a sound basis for separating genetic conditions from nongenetic ones that people did not knowingly cause and cannot change....
>
> Though instinctively accepted by most people outside the bioethics community, genetic exceptionalism produces unsettling results. Consider three women who have the same increased probability of breast cancer: one who carries the BRCA1 gene, a second who has unknown environmental hazards in her neighborhood, and a third who was exposed to diethylstilbestrol as a fetus. None of these women deserves blame for her predisposition to cancer, but under GINA an insurer could deny coverage or raise premiums based on the exposure-based conditions but not the genetic one. Discomfort with this result probably stems from the intuition that well-being should depend not on pure luck but rather on what we think of as conscious choices. The blamelessness of all three women makes it difficult

[39] (2009) 122 Harvard Law Review 1038.

to support giving benefits to the first woman but denying them to the others. The apparent equivalence of this genetic and nongenetic information makes separate genetic antidiscrimination legislation questionable—why should we care less about those with nongenetic health risks?...

Passing antidiscrimination legislation for genes, but not for uncontrollable nongenetic factors, seems at best an unfinished job.

James Mittra agrees. He asks why genetic information that bears on a person's future health and life expectancy should receive special protection, when other sorts of diagnoses—a positive HIV test, for example—must be disclosed.

James Mittra[40]

The practice of fair discrimination, as an underlying commercial philosophy, dictates that individuals pay a premium for life assurance that is commensurate with the risks they bring to the insurance pool. If a genetic test with demonstrable predictive efficacy predisposes an individual to a particular disease that is actuarially relevant, fairness demands that they are charged a higher premium for commercial insurance or are denied coverage. Those who argue that we should privilege such individuals, and bestow on them a specific right of non-disclosure, appear to permit inequity within the market. The implicit logic of their argument is that those individuals whose risk status has been discovered through a specific genetic test are more deserving of protection, and therefore have a greater moral claim to access a particular insurance product, than those individuals denied cover because an uninsurable risk has been identified by a clinical test not deemed sufficiently novel or problematic to justify unique treatment.

Hoyweghen et al. contrast faulty genes with lifestyle factors, such as smoking and being overweight, which, just like genetic tests, tell us something about a person's risk of future health. They argue that treating genetic risk factors differently from lifestyle risk factors reflects a normative judgement about whether a person deserves the solidarity of mutual insurance.

Ine Hoyweghen, Klasien Horstman and Rita Schepers[41]

The legal prohibition of genetics in insurance then seems to introduce a kind of fault-based labelling in insurance..... [A] good lifestyle has become decisive in offering cover and at what cost. By using lifestyle risk factors, insurers focus on the applicants' self-control over their risk..... Individual control over health is thus translated as selection criterion for taking out insurance....

Although both lifestyle and family history can be identified as asymptomatic risks and as predictors for an individual's future health status, lifestyle has gained ascendancy in the

[40] 'Predictive Genetic Information and Access to Life Assurance: The Poverty of "Genetic Exceptionalism"' (2007) 2 BioSocieties 349–73.

[41] 'Genetic "Risk Carriers" and Lifestyle "Risk Takers". Which Risks Deserve our Legal Protection in Insurance?' (2007) 15 Health Care Analysis 179.

> risk calculation process. Both sections of the group share the fact that the illness is not yet developed, and will possibly never do so, but the legal and moral evaluation of these risks in insurance is completely different. Implicitly insurers thus draw on the argument that our biological fate outweighs our social fate, and therefore deserves more solidarity. This underscores again how insurance is a normative technology. Risk selection is neither a purely technical procedure nor simply the application of insurance principles—but much more of a social and normative undertaking. In the selection of risks, insurance expresses normative claims...of who does or who does not *deserve* solidarity.

In bringing equality legislation together through the Single Equality Act, the government decided against specifically prohibiting genetic discrimination. Interestingly, in making this decision, it chose not to follow the advice of its advisory body, the Human Genetics Commission (HGC). According to the government, there is currently no evidence that people are, in fact, discriminated against as a result of genetic test results, but if this changes, the issue will be revisited.

Department for Communities and Local Government[42]

> 8.29 At present, there is little, if any, evidence of discrimination against those who have a genetic predisposition, or that genetic testing is being used in a way which would give rise to such discrimination in the UK. We therefore do not believe there is currently a need to legislate to prohibit discrimination on grounds of genetic predisposition.
>
> 8.30 However, we wholeheartedly endorse the Human Genetics Commission's view that no-one should be unfairly discriminated against on the basis of their genetic characteristics and we are committed to the continued monitoring of the use of genetic testing in the UK. There is a need to ensure that individuals are able to take medically recommended genetic tests secure in the knowledge that the results will not be used unfairly, while recognising the needs of employers to protect the public and their workforce and the need of insurers to be able to assess risk.
>
> 8.31 If necessary, the option of further non-legislative measures (e.g. guidance, moratoriums or voluntary industry codes or schemes) and legislative measures should be debated and considered carefully in the future, as and when justified by the emergence of any discriminatory practices in this area.

The HGC disputes the government's assumption that there is no evidence of discrimination occurring at present.

HGC statement on Government response to Single Equality Bill Consultation[43]

> Moves in other countries, such as the United States' Genetic Information Nondiscrimination Act, indicate a growing recognition that information about an individual's genetic status can be used in a way that divides people in socially unacceptable ways. Whilst evidence of actual harms resulting from genetic discrimination has not been collected systematically, in

---

[42] Discrimination Law Review: A Framework for Fairness: Proposals for a Single Equality Bill for Great Britain (2007), available at <www.communities.gov.uk>.

[43] August 2008, available at <www.hgc.gov.uk>.

part because it is difficult to gather, the HGC was able to cite anecdotal evidence of serious and distressing discrimination against those with genetic conditions. Moreover, there is evidence that people with genetic conditions, and those considering whether to take a genetic test, are concerned about the potential for genetic discrimination, for example, in insurance and employment, and that this can influence their decision-making and may prevent them from taking medically useful tests. This concern is amplified by uncertainty over how genetic information will be used in insurance after the end of the current moratorium period, in 2014. In this context, it is important to take account of continuing developments in genome technology, and the accompanying increase in genetic information, which may lead to an increase in opportunities for genetic discrimination.

4 DIRECT-TO-CONSUMER GENETIC TESTING

Until relatively recently, genetic testing had no relevance for the vast majority of the population. Only where a particular mutation was known to exist in an individual's family, or where there was clear evidence of familial susceptibility to a particular condition, would it be possible to carry out a genetic test to discover whether an individual had inherited the relevant genetic mutation.

Within the past few years there has been very rapid progress in identifying markers associated with an increasingly wide range of common diseases. This information does not have the predictive accuracy of a test for the gene that causes Huntington's disease: rather, it may show that a person is slightly more at risk than the rest of the population of developing a particular condition.

One consequence of these developments is that it is now plausible to offer screening to healthy, asymptomatic individuals with no obvious family history of a particular disease. This sort of 'personal genome analysis' is performed by looking at up to a million genetic variations known as single nucleotide polymorphisms (SNPs). A number of commercial companies now market these screening tests direct to the public. Most are based in the US, but with the advent of the internet, their websites are accessible to UK consumers, and testing kits—which as we saw earlier cost a few hundred dollars—can be shipped to customers in the UK.

As Peter Donnelly explains in the next extract, genome-wide analysis is likely to show that each of us is in a high-risk group for one or more conditions.

Peter Donnelly[44]

For a particular disease, most individuals will have inherited some sequence variants that confer risk and some variants that provide protection, and they will therefore have an overall risk around the average....Across 50 diseases, making the simplifying assumption that susceptibility to each disease is independent of susceptibility to every other disease, almost everyone will be in the top 5% of risk for at least one disease, and nearly half of all people will be in the top 1% for at least one disease. So, for example, I will be at particularly high risk of developing some diseases because of common variants that I inherited. At present, it is unclear which diseases these are, but with the advent of personal genomics, I can find out.

---

[44] 'Progress and Challenges in Genome-wide Association Studies in Humans' (2008) 456 Nature 728–31.

The value of results which show that there is a slight increase in risk compared with the population as a whole has, however, been questioned.[45] For example, Gert van Ommen and Martine Cornel explain what predictive genetic tests in relation to type II diabetes might reveal.

Gert Jan B van Ommen and Martina C Cornel[46]

Although the average inhabitant of Netherlands now has a lifetime risk of developing type II diabetes of 13%, for some people this might be 10 or 17% after testing. Whether this makes any difference to people is not known. Effective interventions to reduce a risk of 17% to the population average of 13% are not yet available. Whether paying US$300 or even $1000 helps to motivate people to follow-up their individual lifestyle advice is not known either.

When evaluating the results of a 'personal genome analysis', it is also important not to confuse absolute and relative risk. If the risk of developing stomach cancer in the population as a whole is 1 per cent, and a predictive test suggests that my risk is double that of the general population, that sounds serious, and as though it is something that I should be concerned about. In fact it means that I now know that I have a 2 per cent chance of developing stomach cancer, and a 98 per cent chance of being free from stomach cancer. Without specialist genetic counselling to help people make sense of this sort of complex predictive information, people who in fact are at very low risk of developing conditions may become unnecessarily anxious.

Part of the sales 'pitch' of direct-to-consumer testing is that information about elevated risk can enable people to take steps to reduce their lifetime risk by adopting appropriate lifestyle measures. As the DeCodeMe website explains:

Armed with knowledge from your unique genetic risk profile, you can start making the right lifestyle choices. With the help of a physician to monitor your health where it is most vulnerable, you can begin to take steps that will minimize the impact of your inherited risk of disease.[47]

Of course, it could be argued that we all already know what lifestyle changes are likely to reduce our risk of developing common conditions, such as cancer and heart disease. One does not need to know one's 'genetic risk profile' in order to know that the 'right lifestyle choices' involve more exercise, less fatty food, not smoking, and only drinking alcohol in moderation. It has been argued that one danger of these new tests is that people who receive results that suggest they do *not* face an elevated risk of these common conditions will wrongly believe that it is less important for them to give up smoking or do more exercise. If this sort of false reassurance makes people less likely to do anything about their unhealthy lifestyles, it may, paradoxically, increase the chance of them developing conditions like coronary heart disease, diabetes, and cancer.

[45] AC Janssens *et al.*, 'A Critical Appraisal of the Scientific Basis of Commercial Genomic Profiles Used to Assess Health Risks and Personalize Health Interventions' (2008) 82 American Journal of Human Genetics 593–9 (2008).

[46] 'Recreational Genomics? Dreams and Fears on Genetic Susceptibility Screening' (2008) 16 European Journal of Human Genetics 403–4.

[47] More information available at <www.decodeme.com>. Other companies providing a similar service are <htt://www.23andme.com>, <www.navigenics.com> and <www.seqwright.com>.

It is also possible that people's reactions to learning that they face an elevated risk of ill health—particularly where it suggests that alcoholism[48] or addiction to smoking may be 'in their genes'—could be fatalism rather than behavioural modification.

Theresa M Marteau and Caryn Lerman[49]

[G]iven a common perception that genetic risks are immutable, it might decrease motivation by weakening beliefs that changing behaviour will reduce risks. Genetic risk information may also weaken belief in the ability to change behaviour or example, among people who learn that they have a genetic vulnerability to nicotine addiction.....

The current evidence suggests that providing people with DNA derived information about risks to their health does not increase motivation to change behaviour beyond that achieved with non-genetic information. For some people, genetic information may even reduce motivation to change behaviour.

Cheryl Berg and Kelly Fryer-Edwards make a similar point, highlighting that, by over-emphasizing the role of genetics in the causation of common diseases, these tests will tend to exacerbate genetic determinism.

Cheryl Berg and Kelly Fryer Edwards[50]

Many genetic tests offered directly to the public look for predisposition to diseases and disorders that are far more heavily influenced by environmental factors than by genes. If biotech companies fail to adequately explain the role that gene–environment interactions play in disease development when advertising directly to consumers, they promote genetic determinism, the false notion that a person's fate (including future health outcomes) is determined solely by their genetic makeup.

In addition, as Melzer *et al.* point out, the risks from both false negatives and false positives may be considerable.

David Melzer, Stuart Hogarth, Katherine Liddell, Tom Ling, Simon Sanderson, and Ron L Zimmern[51]

Onlookers may view most of this activity as genetic astrology, producing entertaining horoscopes. Unfortunately,...misleading results could trigger erroneous treatment and involve major hazards. Recent reports that false negative... testing in breast cancer led to women being denied specific treatment indicates the high stakes involved. On the other hand, direct

---

[48] Christian Hopfer, 'Alcoholism: Study Boosts Evidence on Linkage Regions Associated with Alcoholism' (2006) 14 European Journal of Human Genetics 1231–2.

[49] 'Genetic Risk and Behavioural Change' (2001) 322 British Medical Journal 1056–9.

[50] 'The Ethical Challenges of Direct-to-Consumer Genetic Testing' (2007) 77 Journal of Business Ethics 17.

[51] 'Genetic Tests for Common Diseases: New Insights, Old Concerns' (2008) 336 British Medical Journal 590–93.

marketing of the BRCA1 and 2 familial breast cancer tests to women at low risk (for whom evidence of utility is lacking) was criticised for risking unfounded anxiety and unnecessary prophylactic surgery. False reassurance from tests for common diseases could result in effective prevention measures, such as controlling weight and exercising, being ignored.

A balance has to be struck between people's freedom to access information about themselves and the need to protect people from some of the dangers that might be posed by an expansion in direct-to-consumer testing. The Human Genetics Commission (HGC) has considered the issue on two occasions. In *Genes Direct*, published in 2003, it highlighted three principal concerns raised by direct-to-consumer genetic testing:

- the danger of consumers receiving misleading advice as a result of companies overstating the role of genetics in common diseases;
- the difficulty of ensuring informed consent when tests are offered direct to the public;
- the impact on NHS resources if patients seek advice from GPs, or the regional genetics services, before or after testing, and if patients seek confirmatory testing within the NHS.[52]

The report recommended that predictive genetic tests should only be available through consultation with a doctor and should be treated like prescription medicines, and not be advertised directly to the public. At this time, however, very few companies were offering predictive genetic tests direct to consumers, and most direct-to-consumer tests were for the purposes of paternity testing.

Four years later, there had been a marked increase in the number of companies offering predictive genetic testing over the internet, and the HGC decided to revisit the issue, arguing in favour of greater restrictions on direct-to-consumer genetic testing and public education.

Human Genetics Commission[53]

5.2 We recommend stricter controls on direct genetic testing, but we do not believe that there should be statutory prohibition of some, or all, direct genetic tests...

5.3 We feel strongly that there should be a well-funded NHS genetics service supported by a genetically literate primary care workforce, which can properly manage and allow access to new predictive genetic tests that are being developed...

5.4 In view of this, we conclude that most genetic tests that provide predictive health information should not be offered as direct genetic tests...

5.5 If a company wants to provide a direct genetic test then it should have to convince a regulator that the test is suitable and that anyone involved in providing the test has the right training and expertise to give good-quality advice to the consumer.

5.6 Renewed consideration should be given to the original recommendation in *Genes Direct* that certain genetic tests should only be offered by a suitably qualified health professional.

[52] Genes Direct: Ensuring the Effective Oversight of Genetic Tests Supplied Directly to the Public (2003), available at <www.hgc.org.uk>.

[53] More Genes Direct: A Report on Developments in the Availability, Marketing and Regulation of Genetic Tests Supplied Directly to the Public (2007), available at <www.hgc.org.uk>.

> 5.7 We have concerns about predictive genetic tests that are done at home ('direct-to-consumer')…This is because of the problems of providing full information so that the implications of the test can be properly understood. There is also a danger that children may be tested without proper lawful consent on behalf of the child. We have recommended a new offence of the misuse of genetic information that we feel must be introduced before such testing is acceptable…
>
> • Depending on the establishment of a system for classifying genetic tests according to their seriousness, advertisements for tests which it is deemed should only be available via a suitably qualified health professional should be restricted—i.e. no direct-to-public advertising…
>
> • We think that consumer education about genetic testing will play an important role in minimising the potential harms that may follow from direct genetic tests. We would like to see a broader Government effort to inform the public about all forms of predictive genetic testing and about which tests may be suitable for them…
>
> • The use of existing web-based information sources to provide comprehensive and independent information for consumers should be explored, and test developers/providers should be encouraged to facilitate consumer access to this information.
>
> • We have concluded that we cannot easily control genetic tests that are available overseas via the Internet. However, we want to promote high standards of regulation in the UK and to liaise with regulators in other countries to achieve effective and harmonised national and international controls.

One of the issues that concerns the HGC is the question of consent. There are two potential problems here. First, where a sample is taken at home, there is no guarantee that the person whose DNA is sent for analysis is, in fact, the person who has purchased the test. If I could persuade you to let me have some of your saliva, could I then find out extremely personal information about you, without your knowledge? Could parents send in their children's saliva in order to obtain information about their child's risk of future ill health?

The Human Tissue Act 2004 has attempted in section 45 to address the possibility of 'DNA theft' by making it an offence to analyse someone's DNA without consent:

> (1) A person commits an offence if—
>
> (a) he has any bodily material intending—
>
> (i) that any human DNA in the material be analysed without qualifying consent, and
>
> (ii) that the results of the analysis be used otherwise than for an excepted purpose,

Qualifying consent means the person's own consent, or, in the case of a child who is not competent to give consent themselves, consent from someone with parental responsibility. Under Schedule 4, excepted purposes include 'the medical diagnosis or treatment of the person whose body manufactured the DNA'. That means that a parent could use a child's sample for diagnostic purposes, but predictive genetic testing would probably not be permissible. In practice, however, it would be very difficult to prevent parents purchasing kits from the US and sending their children's samples back for testing.

The second concern is whether or not consent could be said to be properly informed. The only information people receive about these tests is from the companies' websites, the principal purpose of which is to persuade potential customers to buy their kits, rather than to offer unbiased, objective information about the value or otherwise of predictive testing.

This is in sharp contrast with non-directive genetic counselling, which is routinely provided in the UK via the Regional Genetics Services. People with a family history of a condition receive non-directive counselling in order to help them decide whether or not to be tested. Genetics counsellors will talk through the possible benefits and disadvantages of being tested, and ask the person to think about how they would feel about the result if it was positive, negative or inconclusive. Following genetic counselling, an individual may decide that they would rather not be tested. In contrast, it may be much less likely that someone will decide not to go ahead with testing once they have purchased a testing kit, for which they will have had to pay up front.

In addition to the range of practical problems raised by purchasing genetic test results from an internet-based company, rather than receiving proper advice from a clinical geneticist or specialist counsellor, Nikolas Rose situates the growth of genome-wide association studies within broader social trend towards the individualization both of risk and of responsibility for ill health.

Nikolas Rose[54]

This growing empire of risk management tries to bring our medical future into the present, making it calculable and obliging us to act in the light of such calculations in the name of a new kind of biological prudence. Such risk assessments partake of the apparently unquestionable logic of preventive medicine. This is not so much *'discipline and punish'* as *'screen and intervene'*—to identify risks before they become apparent in frank illness, and intervene early and preventively by a combination of therapeutic measures and lifestyle changes. It is in this context that we can locate the growing use of screening tests—whether from genomics or neuroscience—and the belief that these novel medical technologies can make the invisible seeds of future health or illness visible. And the promise of these tests is to move from risks assessed epidemiologically to susceptibilities assessed individually—that is to say, to the individualization of risk.

5 PHARMACOGENETICS

Pharmacogenetics is another relatively recent development in the field of genetics, and has the potential to transform the way in which medicines are prescribed. Currently, drugs are developed and prescribed for the whole population, even though we know that patients respond to drugs in different ways. A medicine which is effective for some patients may not work for others. Treatments for conditions such as diabetes, depression, and asthma may be effective in only 60 per cent of patients, and for some treatments for cancer, the figure is as

---

[54] 'Race Risk and Medicine in the Age of "Your Own Personal Genome"' (2008) 3 Biosocieties 423–39.

low as 25 per cent.[55] In addition, some patients will suffer adverse reactions, and others may need a higher or lower dose than normal. This means that doctors often have to engage in a 'trial-and-error' process, until a medication programme which works effectively for the individual patient is discovered. The delays this causes are particularly significant in relation to antidepressants, which often have to be taken for up to six weeks before any therapeutic effect becomes noticeable. The 'trial-and-error' approach to the prescription of antidepressants may then mean that patients spend many months in a depressed state waiting to find a medicine that will relieve their symptoms. Obviously, if it were possible for doctors to know in advance whether or not a medicine would be likely to suit a particular patient, it would be possible to ensure that patients receive effective medication immediately, and do not undergo useless or dangerous treatment.

Part of the variation in different patients' responses to the same medicine is thought to be due to genetic differences between them, which affect the way in which drugs are absorbed and metabolized. Pharmacogenetics means that prescribing would be preceded by a genetic test, which would reveal whether the drug would be likely to work, what dose would be appropriate, and whether the patient would be likely to suffer any adverse reactions. In practice, pharmacogenetics would be likely to identify genotype *groups* for whom particular medicines would be effective, or for whom they pose unacceptable risks of adverse side-effects.

While there are currently few drugs which must be preceded by a diagnostic test, pharmacogenetics is not entirely new, and a good example of how it works comes from a drug, Trastuzumab, commonly known as Herceptin. Trastuzumab is only effective for the 25–30 per cent of patients with breast cancer in whom the oncogene, HER2, is present at abnormally high levels. It is therefore only prescribed to this subset of breast cancer patients, and prescription is always preceded by a diagnostic test analysing the patients' HER2-status.

More recently, success has been reported in using a pharmacogenetic algorithm to predict the correct dose of Warfarin, an anti-blood-clotting drug used in patients who are at risk of stroke or heart attack. Currently, the standard dose has to be adjusted for each patient through a trial-and-error process. Some patients can only tolerate lower levels, and some need as much as ten times the standard dose. The consequences of giving a patient too much or too little Warfarin can be catastrophic, and it appears that this could be avoided by using a genetic test, along with other clinical information, in order to determine what dose would be likely to suit each patient.[56]

In their report into the ethical issues raised by pharmacogenetics, the Nuffield Council on Bioethics suggested that in the future the licensing body might be likely to require the use of a pharmacogenetic test as a condition of issuing a licence for a medicine's use.[57] Drugs which have been withdrawn from circulation because of adverse reactions might be re-instated for use only in population subgroups for whom they may be effective without posing a risk of unacceptable side-effects. As well as improving patient care, reducing prescribing errors has the potential to save NHS resources. Pharmacogenetics could also transform the clinical trial process. It has been estimated that within the near future, at least 50 per cent of clinical trials will be preceded by the genetic testing of participants.[58]

---

[55] Nuffield Council on Bioethics, *Pharmacogenetics: Ethical Issues* (Nuffield Council on Bioethics: London, 2003) 18.

[56] The International Warfarin Pharmacogenetics Consortium, 'Estimation of the Warfarin Dose with Clinical and Pharmacogenetic Data' (2009) 360 New England Journal of Medicine 753–64.

[57] Ibid, xvi.   [58] Ibid, 22.

Nevertheless, pharmacogenetics raises a number of important questions. First, if clinical trials were redesigned so that a drug was only tested on a genetically selected subgroup, there could be no guarantee that it would be safe for a patient with a different genotype, thus potentially increasing the risk of prescription errors.

Secondly, as OP Corrigan points out in the next extract, although genes undoubtedly affect the metabolism of medicines, other factors—such as the patient's age, sex, diet, or exposure to other drugs—will also have an impact. Genetic tests alone cannot establish exactly what medicine will work effectively, in what dose, and with what side-effects, leading Corrigan to argue that more effort should be put into identifying non-genetic reasons for variable responses to medicines.

OP Corrigan[59]

[T]he likelihood that pharmacogenetics can make a substantial impact on the reduction of the incidence of serious adverse drug reactions is also highly debatable. The [Nuffield] report accepts the premise that pharmacogenetics will be an effective mechanism for reducing the incidence of adverse drug reactions, a claim about benefit that has underpinned much of the ethical impetus for pharmacogenetics research. Although the report acknowledges that ADRs can be caused by various factors other than genetic variation, it fails to mention the importance of other variables such as age or sex, to name only two. A recent study of ADRs in the elderly has shown that serious ADRs are predictable, and that more than two thirds of ADRs are therefore preventable. In other words, the problem of ADRs could be radically reduced if other non-genetic based prescribing interventions were adopted.

Thirdly, the test results, which might reveal whether a drug would be likely to work for a particular patient, will rarely come in the form of a 'yes/no' answer, but rather are more likely to suggest the *probability* of success and safety. This means it will be necessary to decide what probability of effectiveness justifies treatment. If a genetic test reveals that the only available treatment for a patient's condition has a 30 per cent chance of working, does this justify prescribing it? And should the choice lie with the patient or the doctor?

Fourthly, pharmacogenetics will involve a massive expansion of genetic testing, which raises all the issues we considered earlier in this chapter, namely confidentiality, discrimination, and the patient's right 'not to know' information which may be inadvertently discovered during testing.

Fifthly, the ability to target drugs more effectively will not necessarily reduce NHS expenditure on drugs. Rather, if there is a dramatic reduction in the quantity of drugs prescribed, pharmaceutical companies will face a corresponding reduction in their profits, unless, as seems likely, they respond by increasing the price of drugs in order to cover both the reduction in demand, and the costs associated with developing new pharmacogenetic tests. If the cost of medicines rises, there would not necessarily be any net reduction in prescribing costs.

Sixthly, if pharmacogenetics reveals that a particular drug is only likely to be effective in a very small proportion of patients, then there may be little incentive for pharmaceutical companies to invest resources in developing it. Instead, drug companies might concentrate

---

[59] 'Pharmacogenetics, Ethical Issues: Review of the Nuffield Council on Bioethics Report' (2005) 31 Journal of Medical Ethics, 144–8.

their research and development budgets on drugs which will work for the majority of patients, leaving others with unusual diseases or unusual genetic reactions—which incidentally might correspond with membership of minority ethnic groups—with no effective treatment.

It is possible that population differences in metabolizing medicines may be drawn along racial lines. If this is the case—and there seems to be some evidence that it might be—it suggests that race might *matter* at the molecular level, while being an irrelevant difference, or a political construct, at the level of social policy. The symbolic significance of this leads many US commentators to resist what they have described as a move towards 'race-based medicine'.[60]

Finally, as Johannes Van Delden *et al.* point out in the next extract, there is, of course, the danger that genetic tests will reveal that there is no effective treatment for a particular patient. As well as being extremely upsetting, to say the least, being identified as hard, or even impossible to treat might have negative practical consequences for an individual, such as difficulties in obtaining insurance. This in turn, as Van Delden *et al.* suggest, might prompt people to refuse genetic testing, with the result that the doctor cannot know whether the patient is in the subgroup for whom a medicine is unsuitable or dangerous. By exposing the patient to the possibility of a serious adverse reaction, would the doctor be in breach of her duty of care, or should the patient herself be considered responsible for her resulting injuries?

Johannes Van Delden, Ineke Bolt, Annemarie Kalis, Jeroen Derijks and Hubert Leufkens[61]

The first problem that might occur in genotyping is that by testing the patient it might be revealed that the patient is a non-responder for all available drug options. The patient turns out to be an 'orphan' for whom genotyping provided no advantage, but only the knowledge that he probably cannot be treated....[S]omeone might turn out to be a non-responder for multiple drugs, which might give him the label 'hard to treat'. Therefore, some patients might not want to be tested for pharmacogenetic profiles, as they do not want to gain knowledge that might put them in a disadvantageous position.

This leads to the question of what a physician should do if a patient refuses to be genotyped. He could give the patient the 'bulk drug', but by doing so he in fact gives the patient a suboptimal treatment. Besides, he knowingly increases the risk of potentially dangerous side-effects by not testing the patient. If such side-effects emerge, who can then be considered to be responsible for them, the physician or the patient?

The Nuffield Council on Bioethics' report considered this problem, and argued that the way in which pharmacogenetics are presented to the public will inevitably affect people's willingness to undergo pre-treatment genetic testing.

[60] Dorothy E Roberts, 'Is Race-based Medicine Good for Us? African American Approaches to Race, Biomedicine and Equality' (2008) 36 Journal of Law, Medicine and Ethics 537.

[61] 'Tailor-Made Pharmacotherapy: Future Developments and Ethical Challenges in the Field of Pharmacogenomics' (2004) 18 Bioethics 303–21.

Nuffield Council on Bioethics[62]

A question arises regarding whether patients will have the option to receive treatment without taking an associated test. It cannot be assumed that patients will be keen to take a pharmacogenetic test, even if it will improve the likelihood of their receiving a safe and effective treatment. Such an aversion may be irrational, but may be based on a legitimate fear that information produced by the test could make it difficult to obtain insurance, or that it might indirectly reveal information about a medical condition which cannot be effectively treated....

The public perceptions of pharmacogenetics are important in part because resistance to pharmacogenetic testing could lead to patients not receiving the best care. Patients might not be given the most beneficial medicines if these may only be prescribed with a genetic test they refuse to take. Even more serious is the possibility that a medicine may be administered without an associated pharmacogenetic test, and result in a serious, predictable and avoidable adverse reaction. We think it likely that the acceptance of pharmacogenetics will depend not only on which tests are introduced and for which purposes they are used, but also on the way they are presented to the public at large and to individual patients.

6 CONCLUSION

This chapter has necessarily provided only a very brief snapshot of some issues raised by rapid developments in human genetics. In conclusion, one thread that connects the various issues we have considered here is that we are currently witnessing a move from genetic testing being relevant only to the relatively small proportion of the population with a family history of a unifactorial genetic condition towards it having much wider application, and potentially being relevant to all of us.

Each of us has a number of faulty genes, some of which might mean that we are at higher than average chance of developing a range of conditions in later life. If we can find this information out increasingly easily, questions of genetic privacy and discrimination become relevant to an increasing proportion of the population. If the prescription of a growing number of medicines must be preceded by a genetic test, again, issues of confidentiality and discrimination have much wider significance than has previously been the case.

While new developments in genetics are undeniably exciting and now incredibly fast-moving, it is also important to bear in mind that there are other fairly accurate predictors of future ill health which we should not ignore just because they seem more prosaic. We know, for example, that child poverty has a dramatic impact upon a child's health prospects in later life. Having an unhealthy diet—which often correlates with relative poverty—increases one's chance of developing heart disease and cancer. It is easy to be seduced into imagining that my 'personal genome analysis' holds the key to my future life chances, when in fact, how much I exercise, and what I eat and drink may be at least as important.

---

[62] Nuffield Council on Bioethics, *Pharmacogenetics: Ethical Issues* (Nuffield Council on Bioethics: London, 2003) xxii, 7.

FURTHER READING

Bell, Dean and Bennett, Belinda, 'Genetic Secrets and the Family' (2001) 9 Medical Law Review 130–61.

Forrest, Laura *et al.*, 'Communicating Genetic Information in Families—A Review of Guidelines and Position Papers' (2007) 15 European Journal of Human Genetics 612–18.

Human Genetics Commission, More Genes Direct: A Report on Developments in the Availability, Marketing and Regulation of Genetic Tests Supplied Directly to the Public (2007), available at <www.hgc.org.uk>.

Laurie, Graeme, 'In Defence of Ignorance: Genetic Information and the Right not to Know' (1999) 6 European Journal of Health Law 119–32.

Laurie, Graeme, *Genetic Privacy: A Challenge to Medico-Legal Norms* (CUP: Cambridge, 2002).

McHale, JV, 'Regulating Genetic Databases: Some Legal and Ethical Issues' (2004) 12 Medical Law Review 70–96.

Mittra, James 'Predictive Genetic Information and Access to Life Assurance: The Poverty of Genetic Exceptionalism' (2007) 2 BioSocieties 349–73.

Nuffield Council on Bioethics, The Forensic Use of Bioinformation: Ethical Issues (2008), available at <www.nuffieldbioethics.org.uk>.

Rose, Nikolas, 'Race Risk and Medicine in the Age of Your Own Personal Genome' (2008) 3 Biosocieties 423–39.

Skene, Loane, 'Genetic Secrets and the Family' (2001) 9 Medical Law Review 162–9.

Van Ommen, Gert Jan B, and Cornel, Martina C, 'Recreational genomics? Dreams and Fears on Genetic Susceptibility Screening' (2008) 16 European Journal of Human Genetics (2008) 403–4.

9

CLINICAL RESEARCH

CENTRAL ISSUES

1. Animal experiments usually precede trials involving human subjects. To obtain a licence from the Home Office, researchers have to establish that the use of animals is necessary, and animal suffering must be minimized.

2. International codes of research ethics, most importantly the Helsinki Declaration, have established universally applicable principles of good research practice, which have been incorporated into UK law by the Medicines for Human Use (Clinical Trials) Regulations 2004.

3. All research protocols must first be approved by an ethics committee.

4. Consent to participation in research must be both informed and voluntary. In particular, it is important to ensure that when patients are enrolled in clinical trials, they understand that they are taking part in an experiment, rather than receiving treatment which their doctor believes to be in their best interests.

5. For subjects who lack capacity, consent must be sought from their 'representative', and researchers must only use people who lack capacity when the research could not be conducted on competent adults.

6. Some groups have routinely been excluded from clinical trials, and while this may have been prompted by paternalistic concern for their welfare, the consequence is that it is impossible to be sure that treatments are safe or effective for members of excluded groups.

7. While it is vitally important that medicines are developed to treat diseases which are prevalent in the poorest nations in the world, carrying out research in developing countries raises a number of distinctive and complex ethical issues.

1 INTRODUCTION

Without research, medical progress would be impossible. New treatments can be tested on animals, but animal experiments will not always be able to predict what impact a treatment will have on human beings. As we shall see later, the compound, known as TGN1412, which caused multiple organ failure in the six men who took part in its 'first in man' trials at Northwick Park Hospital, had not caused adverse effects in animals, and was believed to be safe. Research on human subjects is the only way in which we can satisfactorily establish the effectiveness and safety of medical treatment. But while we all want the medical care that we receive to have been rigorously tested, serving as a research subject may pose risks to an individual's health.

The principal question raised by the regulation of experiments involving human subjects is how to balance the competing interests of society (which wants all of its medical treatment to have been proved safe and effective), and the individual research subject (who does not want to be exposed to increased health risks). Although research on human subjects is not the only time when medical law has to weigh the interests of society against the welfare of individuals, this balancing exercise offers a particularly good example of the conflict between deontological (duty-based) and teleological (consequentialist) reasoning that we considered in Chapter 1.

If we adopt a strict utilitarian perspective, conducting research on a comparatively small number of people—with or without their consent—in order to benefit the rest of society might be justifiable, even if it posed a considerable risk to their health. Take the example of Edward Jenner's discovery of the smallpox vaccine, described here by Margaret Brazier:

Margaret Brazier[1]

> Edward Jenner, injected an eight year old boy, James Phipps, with cowpox. Months later, he injected the boy with smallpox. The vaccination 'took' and the boy survived. Jenner's experiment has saved millions of lives and led to the virtual eradication of smallpox. . . . [I]t has often been said no modern ethics committee would have sanctioned such an experiment. Consider the case—the experiment used a child subject, who was too young to consent for himself, in non-therapeutic research where there was a high risk of death or disfigurement. The 'exploitation' of James Phipps undoubtedly saved the lives of some of us reading this.

In contrast, a deontological approach, such as that adopted by Hans Jonas in the next extract, would condemn any course of action that disregarded the rights, dignity, and integrity of the individual research subject, regardless of the benefits to the rest of society. Ignoring the research subject's welfare would offend Kant's categorical imperative (see further Chapter 1), because we would be treating these individuals as a means to an end, and not as ends in themselves. Indeed, Jonas would go further and say the subjects of experiments are treated as 'things'.

Hans Jonas[2]

> What is wrong with making a person an experimental subject is not so much that we make him thereby a means (which happens in social contexts of all kinds), as that we make him a thing . . .

---

[1] 'Exploitation and Enrichment: The Paradox of Medical Experimentation' (2008) 34 Journal of Medical Ethics 180–83.

[2] 'Philosophical Reflections on Experimenting with Human Subjects' (1969) 98 Daedalus 219–47.

Let me say only in conclusion that if some of the practical implications of my reasonings are felt to work out toward a slower rate of progress, this should not cause too great dismay. Let us not forget that progress is an optional goal, not an unconditional commitment, and that its tempo in particular, compulsive as it may become, has nothing sacred about it. Let us also remember that a slower progress in the conquest of disease would not threaten society, grievous as it is to those who have to deplore that their particular disease be not yet conquered, but that society would indeed be threatened by the erosion of those moral values whose loss, possibly caused by too ruthless a pursuit of scientific progress, would make its most dazzling triumphs not worth having.

Both extreme utilitarianism and its opposite are unattractive and caricatured moral positions. In practice, most people adopt a mixed approach, which takes into account both individual rights *and* the common good. We do not want to sacrifice some human beings' lives for the benefit of others, but at the same time we do not want to stifle medical progress by refusing to allow any experiments on human subjects.

Aside from the very small number of people in society who choose to reject all medical interventions, we all benefit from living in a society in which drugs and other treatments have been properly tested. It might therefore be argued that we are under a *moral* obligation to incur some inconvenience or slightly increased risk to our health by participating in medical research. If we wish to benefit from experiments on humans, but are not actually willing to take part in them ourselves, could we be said to be 'free-riding' on the sacrifices of others?

When thinking about how research on humans should be regulated, it is also important to remember that there are more interests at stake than just the individual research subject's concern for her own health, and society's interest in medical progress. The researcher will have considerable *self-interest* in devising, carrying out, and publishing significant research. Her reputation, career progression, and ability to secure funding in the future will largely depend upon whether she has conducted experiments which have yielded interesting and publishable results. In the next extract, Paul McNeill suggests that the desire for self-advancement creates a powerful incentive towards 'cutting corners'.

Paul M McNeill[3]

While society, or at least some individuals within it, *may* benefit from research, there are very direct and tangible benefits for the researcher. [Paul] Ramsey wrote that 'it is not only that medical benefits are attained by research but also that a man rises to the top in medicine by the success and significance of his research'. For this reason the scientist cannot be regarded as a disinterested party. The researcher's interest in his or her own advancement and standing may be an added pressure to cut corners and act in ways that are unsafe...

Instances of blatant disregard for subjects' welfare have understandably gained the most attention. However, it is likely that more harm has been caused (in total) by researchers who mean no harm but are unaware of the extent of risk to their patients. Their bias towards achieving the goals of their research may lead them to minimise, in their own thinking, the risks inherent in their research and give a disproportionate value to the research enterprise...

[3] *The Ethics and Politics of Human Experimentation* (CUP: Cambridge, 1993).

> Scientists are as capable as any other group of pursuing their own interests to the exclusion of the interests of others.

Not only is the reputation of the researcher at stake, but, as Solomon Benatar points out, sponsors of research—such as pharmaceutical companies—have considerable financial interests in producing profitable medicines.

Solomon Benatar[4]

> Clinical research has become a burgeoning activity in recent years, largely stimulated by the pharmaceutical industry's interest in new drugs with high marketing profiles...In industrialised countries...the major interest in large profitable markets for drugs has led to the proliferation of research on 'me too' drugs (with only marginal potential advantages [over existing drugs]) that may allow market niches to be captured. There is also a drive to develop 'lifestyle drugs' for improving the quality of life and alleviating the symptoms of old age. The desire to make vast sums of money from medicinal drugs can be viewed as a modern version of the gold rush. Why make drugs for sick people who cannot afford them when one can make drugs for people with resources who seek marginal improvements or those who are well and will pay for the possibility of a healthier old age. Proliferation of clinical research, much of it promotional and of dubious scientific value, follows.

The World Trade Organization's TRIPS[5] Agreement imposes a minimum 20-year period of patent protection, allowing pharmaceutical companies a monopoly over the production and marketing of new drugs for at least 20 years. If a new medicine has been proved to be safe and effective, as we see in the next chapter the profit which can be made may be phenomenal. 'Big pharma' has become one of Britain's principal manufacturing industries, spending around £4 billion each year on research and development.[6]

In the UK, clinical trials involving human subjects are regulated by the Medicines for Human Use (Clinical Trials) Regulations 2004, which incorporate the principles of good research practice that have been developed and refined over the past forty-five years in the World Health Organisation's Helsinki Declaration. Detailed guidance for researchers and ethics committees is also contained in various sets of guidelines issued by professional bodies, such as the General Medical Council and the Royal College of Physicians.

In addition to the existence of international codes of ethics, it is also important to remember that regulations in one country may exert indirect, but nevertheless significant control over research carried out in other countries. For example, the US licensing authority (the Food and Drug Administration, or FDA) insists that all drugs, except those used to treat life-threatening conditions, must have been subjected to placebo-controlled trials. As a result, pharmaceutical companies who wish to market their products in the exceptionally lucrative US market will have to comply with US regulations, even if the research in fact takes place elsewhere.

---

[4] 'Avoiding Exploitation in Clinical Research' (2000) 9 Cambridge Quarterly of Healthcare Ethics 562–5.
[5] Trade Related Aspects of Intellectual Property Rights.
[6] See further <www.abpi.org.uk>.

In this chapter, we begin with a brief summary of the rules governing experiments on animals, which will usually precede trials involving human subjects. Next we look at what is meant by 'research'. It is important to remember that not all medical research consists in the testing of new treatments or drugs. Epidemiological research, for example, may just involve tracking the incidence of a particular condition in the population, and thus raises different, and perhaps fewer ethical issues.

We then turn to examine the various international ethical codes, and the UK's regulatory system, and we examine the role of ethics committees in authorizing and monitoring research. The subject's voluntary and informed consent to participation is widely believed to be what justifies exposing her to the risks inherent in a research trial, and we consider what qualifies as sufficiently 'voluntary' and 'informed' consent. If consent is a necessary precondition of ethical research, we also investigate whether, and in what circumstances, it would be legitimate to carry out research on those who *cannot* give consent.

We then examine whether the benefits and burdens of research participation are evenly distributed, drawing particular attention to the special issues raised when research is conducted in developing countries. Next, we review the question of publication ethics—could there be a duty to disseminate one's research findings, and should unethical research ever be published? Finally, we look at the arrangements for compensation when individuals sustain injuries as a result of their participation in research.

2 ANIMAL EXPERIMENTS

In the UK, research involving laboratory animals is regulated by the Animals (Scientific Procedures) Act 1986. The Act defines 'protected animals' as all non-human vertebrates and the common octopus. Insects such as fruit flies are also commonly used in research but are not protected by the Act.

Before any experiment can be carried out on a protected animal, a licence must first have been obtained from the Home Office. Licences will be issued only when the scientific objectives cannot be achieved without using animals; and experiments must minimize animal suffering. The Home Office employs an inspectorate, consisting of doctors and veterinarians, to advise on applications for licences.

Under section 3 of the Act, the laboratory, the individual researcher and the project itself must each be separately approved.

Animals (Scientific Procedures) Act 1986 section 3

3. No person shall apply a regulated procedure to an animal unless—

(a) he holds a personal licence qualifying him to apply a regulated procedure of that description to an animal of that description;

(b) the procedure is applied as part of a programme of work specified in a project licence authorising the application, as part of that programme, of a regulated procedure of that description to an animal of that description; and

(c) the place where the procedure is carried out is a place specified in the personal licence and the project licence.

These three authorizations will be granted only if:

- the individual researcher has the necessary skills and training (Personal Licence); and
- the object of the research cannot be achieved in other ways and the likely benefits of the research justify any likely distress to the animals (Project Licence); and
- the laboratory has the necessary facilities and staff to house and care for the animals properly (Certificate of Designation).

To obtain a Personal Licence, the individual researcher must have been on an approved training course covering the law and ethics of animal research, the basics of caring for animals, and ways of recognizing symptoms of illness or distress. The Personal Licence will specify both the techniques and the species of animal which the individual is entitled to use.

To obtain a Certificate of Designation, a laboratory must meet strict Home Office criteria on staffing, veterinary care, and the quality of housing, lighting, ventilation, and temperature control. Each laboratory must have a 'Named Veterinary Surgeon' and a 'Named Animal Care and Welfare Officer', both of whom are responsible for protecting the health and welfare of animals within the laboratory.

Before applying for a Project Licence, the researchers must first have been subject to a local ethical review process. Once the project has been approved locally, an application can be made to the Home Office. Under section 4(3) of the Act, the Secretary of State can only issue licences for certain research purposes—such as 'the prevention or the diagnosis or treatment of disease, ill-health or abnormality, or their effects, in man, animals or plants'.

In determining whether to grant a project licence, under section 5(4) 'the Secretary of State shall weigh the likely adverse effects on the animals concerned against the benefit likely to accrue as a result of the programme to be specified in the licence'. The need to use protected animals must be justified under section 5(5), and a licence must not be issued if there is any other reasonably practicable method which does not entail the use of protected animals.

Section 5(6) provides that the project must use the smallest number of animals necessary to meet the objectives of the research, and use animals with the lowest possible degree of neurophysiological sensitivity, and cause them the minimum amount of pain, suffering, distress, or lasting harm necessary to produce satisfactory results. Most of the animals used in experiments in the UK are rodents (83 per cent); birds and fish are used in 4 per cent and 10 per cent of experiments, respectively.[7]

Under section 5(6) of the Act, specific justification is required for the use of cats, dogs, horses, and non-human primates. In practice, these animals are used in fewer than 1 per cent of all experiments. In 2007, 4000 non-human primates were used in research. Regulations prohibit the use of great apes, such as gorillas and chimpanzees. Almost all animals used in experiments are bred especially for the purposes of research in order to ensure that they are free from any infection or disease. Increasingly, animals used in research have been genetically modified: in 2007, 36 per cent of all procedures involved genetically modified animals.[8]

For complex licence applications, such as those involving primates, the Home Office may refer the project to the Animal Procedures Committee (APC), a committee of scientific,

---

[7] <www.homeoffice.gov.uk/docs/animalstats.html>.
[8] Available at <www.scienceandresearch.homeoffice.gov.uk>.

legal and ethical experts set up by section 19 of the Act to provide advice on especially controversial legal and ethical issues.[9] As well as advising on individual applications, the APC also publishes guidance on more general ethical issues, such as appropriate methods for humane killing.

The Home Office issues detailed statistics each year on the use of animals in experiments in the UK.[10] Although the number of animals used for research has halved in the past twenty-five years, in 2007 over 3.2 million procedures involving animals took place, a rise of about 6 per cent on 2006.

In what circumstances, if any, is it acceptable to use animals in research? Opinion on this question is, as Lyle Munro explains, very deeply divided.

Lyle Munro[11]

Experimentalists claim that as there is no satisfactory alternative, the use of animals is essential to human health. The antivivisectionists maintain that the researcher's case is deeply flawed and that the availability of cruelty free alternatives renders animal experimentation morally reprehensible. Neither side is willing to compromise since each perceives the other's position as evil. That it is no exaggeration to use the term 'evil' is borne out by the language of vilification that continues to be used by some of the protagonists in the controversy.

The Nuffield Council on Bioethics report on *The Ethics of Research Involving Animals* suggests that instead of thinking in terms of two diametrically opposed positions on whether animal experiments are justifiable, it would be more accurate to divide opinion into four camps.[12] They describe these as follows:

Nuffield Council on Bioethics[13]

The *'anything goes' view*—if humans see value in research involving animals, then it requires no further ethical justification.

The *'on balance justification' view*—although research involving animals has costs to animals, which must be taken seriously in moral reasoning, the benefits to human beings very often outweigh those costs in moral terms.

The *'moral dilemma' view*—however one decides to act, one acts wrongly, either by neglecting human health or by harming animals.

The *'abolitionist' view*—since any research that causes pain, suffering and distress is wrong, there is no moral justification for harmful research on sentient animals that is not to the benefit of the animal concerned.

In the next extract, Richard Ryder suggests that few scientists in fact hold the 'anything goes' view of animal research.

---

[9] See further <www.apc.gov.uk/>.
[10] Available at <www.scienceandresearch.homeoffice.gov.uk>.
[11] 'From Vilification to Accommodation: Making a Common Cause Movement' (1999) 8 Cambridge Quarterly of Healthcare Ethics 46–57.
[12] <www.nuffieldbioethics.org/>.
[13] The Ethics of Research Involving Animals (2005), available at <www.nuffieldbioethics.org.uk>.

Richard D Ryder[14]

As scientists we acknowledge that the human species is but one of many species. We know that other animals often behave as we do when in pain and that their nervous systems and their biochemistry are similar to our own. We know that nonhumans are related to us through evolution and that, therefore, it is inconsistent to put our own species on a moral pedestal entirely separate from all the others. How can it be moral to cause pain or misery to monkeys, dogs, or rats, if it is immoral to do this to humans? There are no *rational* grounds for asserting this. If it is wrong to experiment painfully upon unconsenting humans, it must, logically speaking, be wrong to do likewise to nonhumans. We cannot, with consistency argue that nonhumans are so like us that they produce valid experimental results and then claim that they are morally different. We should remember simply this: pain is pain regardless of species.

I have said that the trade-off problem is central to ethics. The work of the animal experimenter whose research is strictly therapeutic in its objectives and aimed specifically and sincerely at the alleviation of painful illness is a striking example of this problem. Such scientists are caught on the horns of this dilemma; in their quest to reduce pain are they justified in causing pain?

The critical issue is whether humans are entitled to use animals for their own ends, and one obvious point of comparison is with the food industry. If killing animals for food is morally acceptable (and obviously not everyone agrees that it is), then surely it must also be legitimate to use animals in potentially valuable scientific experiments? Of course, many opponents of animal experiments are also vegetarians or vegans, but there are those who would argue that laboratory animals suffer more than those bred for food, and that the two should therefore be treated differently. This claim is hard to sustain, however, given the nature of intensive factory farming and the strict controls that govern the treatment of animals used in experiments. Battery chickens, or veal calves lead restricted and distressing lives, whereas Home Office guidance states that animal experiments must not inflict prolonged distress on animals. It is also no longer lawful to use animals for 'trivial' research, such as the testing of cosmetics or tobacco products.[15]

In the next extract, David Thomas argues that, because animals can feel pain and cannot give consent, it would be more accurate to draw an analogy between animal experiments and research involving people who lack capacity.

D Thomas[16]

[W]hy should the fact (if this is what it is) that A has more value than B mean that A is at liberty to cause pain to B for A's benefit? This is the crucial gap in logic which pro-vivisectionists rarely address. Let us accept for the sake of argument that it was provable that the human species was more important than other species—whether because people generally (though not always) have greater capacity for rational thought, may have greater self awareness, are better able to empathise, or have more sophisticated culture. It is not explained why

---

[14] 'Painism: Some Moral Rules for the Civilized Experimenter' (1999) 8 Cambridge Quarterly of Healthcare Ethics 35–42.

[15] *Guidelines on the Operation of the Animals (Scientific Procedures) Act 1986* (Home Office: London, 2000).

[16] 'Laboratory Animals and the Art of Empathy' (2005) 31 Journal of Medical Ethics 197–202.

those attributes mean that we can cause pain to those we relegate further down the hierarchy of value. And, if cruel exploitation of *other* species is justified on a relative value basis, then, logically, so must cruel exploitation *within* our species. Some people, indisputably, have greater capacity for rational thought, have greater self awareness, are better able to empathise, or have a deeper cultural appreciation than other people. However, most people do not conclude that the more endowed are for that reason entitled to cause pain to the less endowed for their own benefit....

Experiments on animals and non-consensual experiments on people are obvious comparators because both involve physical and psychological suffering for an unwilling, sentient victim. In each case consent is neither sought nor presumed and the victim is not the intended beneficiary.

However, society treats the two cases very differently. This is because ethical sleight of hand is deployed. Different ethical principles are applied to the two types of experiment.

With non-consensual experiments on people, a *deontological* approach is taken. The prevailing view is that such experiments are *inherently* wrong, whatever the potential benefits to others...With animals, by contrast, the approach is a kind of *utilitarianism*. The law allows scientists to cause pain to animals if *others* might benefit.

In 2006, the Academy of Medical Sciences, the Medical Research Council, the Royal Society, and the Wellcome Trust commissioned a working group report into the use of non-human primates in research, chaired by Sir David Weatherall. In the following extract it adopts an explicitly quantitative utilitarian approach to animal suffering in research.

Weatherall Working Group Report[17]

One issue often neglected here is the fact that the numbers of non-human primates used in any medical experiment are very small, and the number of humans whose suffering is ameliorated is often very large. So the equation to be made is not simply between suffering caused and benefits to humans: both sides must be multiplied by the number of individuals involved. In the case of AIDS research, for instance, the number of macaques used may be measured in dozens, the number of humans who stand to benefit could be measured in millions. Suffering or harm caused in animal experiments, both in terms of numbers and in terms of degree, is likely to be less than the benefits to humankind from properly licensed research carried out with meticulous care.

Muireann Quigley is critical of this approach, suggesting that non-human primates should instead be regarded as a particularly vulnerable group of potential research subjects, and hence should receive *more* protection than competent adults.

Muireann Quigley[18]

It seems to me that most non-human primates are of a level of capacity that, if they were human, would fall into this category of vulnerable persons and would therefore be protected.

[17] The Use of Non-human Primates in Research (2006), available at <www.acmedsci.ac.uk/>.
[18] 'Non-human Primates: The Appropriate Subjects of Biomedical Research?' (2007) 33 Journal of Medical Ethics: 655–8.

> If, as argued previously, we cannot differentiate between non-human primates and humans merely on the grounds of species membership, and if there is no difference in capacity between non-human primates and some humans, then surely these guidelines ought to protect both.

In the next extract, RG Frey goes further and suggests that it may be preferable to carry out experiments on non-sentient human subjects than on sentient rodents.

RG Frey [19]

> The truth is, I think, that some human lives have fallen so far in value, quality, richness, and scope for enrichment that some animal lives exceed in value those human lives. Anencephalic infants and people in permanently vegetative states are cases in point. It was comforting in the past to think that all human lives were more valuable than any animal life, but the quality of life of a perfectly healthy dog or cat must vastly exceed the quality of any human life that has ceased to have experiences of any sort, that has ceased to have in essence any sort of content...
>
> If we have to experiment..., then which life do we use? We use that life of lower quality, and we have a non-speciesist way of determining which life that is... How can we justify an experiment on a perfectly healthy rodent with an experiential life as opposed to an anencephalic infant with, so far as we know, no experiential life at all?

In 2002 the House of Lords Animals in Scientific Procedures Select Committee published a report which lays out the arguments for and against animal experimentation.

House of Lords Animals in Scientific Procedures Select Committee [20]

> 4.4 The main criticisms levelled against the use of animals in research are:
>
> - research on animals is unethical. Harm should not be caused to any animal unless it is for the ultimate benefit of that particular animal;
>
> - research on animals is ineffective. Diseases manifest themselves in different ways in animals than in humans. New compounds (for example, new pharmaceutical products) may be beneficial to certain animals, but have no effect on humans. Similarly, compounds which might have been beneficial to humans have in the past been ruled out because they have produced negative results in animals;
>
> - animal research is harmful to human health, because it diverts money away from non-animal research, and some drugs have serious side-effects which are not discovered until the drug is administered to patients. A number of witnesses argued that animal research provides misleading information, and is responsible for the growing trend in drug-related doctor-induced illness ('iatrogenesis');
>
> - there is a record of failure in modelling disease. Induced conditions, such as artificially induced Parkinson's Disease caused by chemical or physical lesions in the brains of mice,

---

[19] 'Pain, Vivisection, and the Value of Life' (2005) 31 Journal of Medical Ethics 202–4.
[20] <www.publications.parliament.uk/pa/ld200102/ldselect/ldanimal/150/150.pdf>.

are not good models of naturally occurring conditions. Equally, drugs which have been effective in combating stroke in animals have been ineffective in humans;

- some animal research is trivial; some is used to develop products which duplicate existing ones; and some is of little relevance—retrospective analyses show that some animal research is never cited in the literature;

- animal use continues largely through habit, scientific inertia, and the availability of funding from pharmaceutical companies and research councils. If the same amount of money and intellectual effort had been invested in non-animal methods over the years, scientists would have discovered similarly effective drugs.

4.5 Scientists and industry have countered that animal research is effective. The Department of Health, which spends approximately £6 billion each year on pharmaceuticals, asserts unequivocally that: 'Properly regulated animal research is absolutely essential to the discovery of new treatments as well as to the assessment of safety and efficacy of medicines.'

4.6 In particular those in favour of animal research argue that:

- animals are used to develop an understanding of normal, healthy biological systems;

- animals are used as models for humans. Animal research helps scientists to understand the mechanisms of diseases and compounds, as well as their specific effects. Humans would of course be better models and human volunteers are always used in later stages during clinical trials. Experimenting on humans at the early stages of drug development is unacceptable, so the best available models—animals—should be used instead;

- many mammals are physiologically very similar to humans: they have similar vital organs—brain, heart, lungs, liver, kidneys—and process toxins in the liver in similar, though not identical, ways....

- the usefulness of animal models is illustrated by the similarity of the veterinary and human pharmacopoeias, and the same drugs are often used to treat the same diseases;

- research on animals is often carried out for the overall benefit of other animals;...

- animal experiments continue to be used because they have produced, and continue to produce, extensive and beneficial advances in science: 'Virtually every medical achievement of the last century has depended directly or indirectly on research in animals.'

Having weighed the advantages and disadvantages, the House of Lords Select Committee concluded by endorsing the use of animals *where necessary*:

On balance, we are convinced that experiments on animals have contributed greatly to scientific advances, both for human medicine and for animal health. Animal experimentation is a valuable research method which has proved itself over time.[21]

It also specifically endorsed what has become known as the 3Rs approach, explained in the following extract:

House of Lords Animal in Scientific Procedures Select Committee[22]

1.12 In 1959, two British scientists, the zoologist William Russell and the microbiologist Rex Burch, published *The principles of humane experimental technique*, a study of the ethical

[21] Ibid.   [22] Ibid.

aspects of animal research commissioned by the Universities Federation for Animal Welfare (UFAW). They said that all animal experiments should incorporate, so far as is possible, the Three Rs: replacement, reduction and refinement. They have been defined as:

- Replacement of conscious, living vertebrates by non-sentient alternatives;
- Reduction in the number of animals needed to obtain information of a given amount and precision; and
- Refinement of procedures to reduce to a minimum the incidence or severity of suffering experienced by those animals which have to be used.

1.13 The Three Rs are widely accepted by the international scientific community—almost all those who use animals have said in evidence that they agree with the principle that reduction, refinement, and replacement should take place wherever possible. Many of those who disagree with the use of animals in scientific procedures also agree with the principle of the Three Rs, but are concerned that they are not always implemented. Some anti-vivisectionists dispute the Three Rs concept on the basis that both reduction and refinement tacitly acknowledge that animals should continue to be used.

3   WHAT IS RESEARCH?

(a) USE OF ANONYMOUS DATA OR SAMPLES

A great deal of medical research is carried out without making direct contact with individual patients. Epidemiology, for example, is 'the study of the occurrence and distribution of diseases and other health-related conditions in populations'. Originally it just referred to the study of epidemics, but now it involves analysis of the prevalence and distribution of medical conditions, in order to test hypotheses about suspected causes of disease and relevant risk factors.

Major difficulties would be posed if patients had to give informed consent to the use of information from their medical notes. The process of tracking down every patient and asking their permission would be so time-consuming that this sort of research would not be viable. Ideally, the patient's agreement to the use of information gathered during her treatment should be sought, but if it would be impossible to obtain consent, then provided the information has been adequately anonymized, and there is no intention to feed the results back to individual patients, researchers do not have to seek consent. In Chapter 7, when we considered confidentiality, we saw that it is also sometimes possible for researchers to gain access to patient-identifiable data for research purposes.

(b) INNOVATIVE THERAPY

It is not always easy to tell the difference between treatment and research. Much medical knowledge is tentative: very few treatments have been proved to be 100 per cent effective in all patients. Given that almost all medical treatment is conducted under conditions of uncertainty, and that doctors are continuously learning from the outcomes of their patients' treatment, what justification could there be for treating 'research' as though it were wholly separate from the normal combination of treatment and information gathering?

Ordinary medical treatment, as we saw in Chapter 3, must satisfy the *Bolam* test, as modified by *Bolitho*: that is, it must reach a standard of care which is both accepted as proper by a responsible body of medical opinion, and capable of withstanding logical analysis. In general this means that doctors should only give their patients treatments that have been properly tested and are known to be effective. In certain circumstances, however, a doctor might act reasonably by offering a patient treatment which has not yet been tested on humans. For example, if all orthodox treatments have been exhausted, and the patient's condition is extremely serious, it might be acceptable to try a treatment which has not yet been licensed for use in humans. Certainly, the Helsinki Declaration endorses the use of unproven treatment where no other options exist:

Helsinki Declaration[23]

35 In the treatment of a patient, where proven interventions do not exist or have been ineffective, the physician, after seeking expert advice, with informed consent from the patient or a legally authorized representative, may use an unproven intervention if in the physician's judgement it offers hope of saving life, re-establishing health or alleviating suffering. Where possible, this intervention should be made the object of research, designed to evaluate its safety and efficacy. In all cases, new information should be recorded and, where appropriate, made publicly available.

Research is different from innovative therapy in one crucial respect: namely that the primary purpose of research is to generate new scientific knowledge by testing a hypothesis, rather than to offer the patient individualized care. But while innovative therapy is not, strictly speaking, research, it might nevertheless be important to ensure that extra care is taken when obtaining consent to treatment that has not been fully tested on humans. Applying the principles which govern the provision of information prior to medical treatment (considered in full in Chapter 4), we could say that the fact that treatment is experimental is a 'material fact', non-disclosure of which would be negligent. If the patient lacks capacity, other additional safeguards—such as the court declaration, which was sought and granted in the following case—might be necessary.

Simms v Simms involved an eighteen-year-old boy and a sixteen-year-old girl, who were in the advanced stages of vCJD (variant Creutzfeldt-Jakob disease—the human form of BSE—a rare, fatal, and incurable neurodegenerative disorder). Researchers had identified a treatment (PPS) which appeared to inhibit the progress of a similar disease in mice, but this had not yet been tested on humans. The patients' parents wanted their children to receive PPS, and applied for a declaration that the treatment would be in their best interests, and hence lawful.

Simms v Simms[24]

Dame Elizabeth Butler-Sloss P

To the question 'Is there a responsible body of medical opinion which would support the PPS treatment within the United Kingdom?' the answer in one sense is unclear. This is untried

[23] World Medical Association, Declaration of Helsinki: Ethical Principles for Medical Research Involving Human Subjects (6th version adopted at the 59th WMA General Assembly, Seoul, South Korea Oct 2008), available at <www.wma.net>.
[24] [2002] EWHC 2734 (Fam).

treatment and there is so far no validation of the experimental work done in Japan. The 'Bolam test' ought not to be allowed to inhibit medical progress. And it is clear that if one waited for the 'Bolam test' to be complied with to its fullest extent, no innovative work such as the use of penicillin or performing heart transplant surgery would ever be attempted. I do however have evidence from responsible medical opinion which does not reject the research...

Where there is no alternative treatment available and the disease is progressive and fatal, it seems to me to be reasonable to consider experimental treatment with unknown benefits and risks, but without significant risks of increased suffering to the patient, in cases where there is some chance of benefit to the patient. A patient who is not able to consent to pioneering treatment ought not to be deprived of the chance in circumstances where he would have been likely to consent if he had been competent...

The chance of improvement is slight but not non-existent. The families ought to regard that possibility as unlikely but not impossible, since no one knows the outcome. There is, from the medical evidence, a possibility of arresting the disease temporarily, and the possibility of prolonging the life of these two patients to some extent, although whether that be in weeks, months or years is impossible to tell...

I think it is reasonable, at this stage of my judgment, to put into the balance that, if there is a possibility of continuation of a life which has value to the patient and the patient is bound to die sooner rather than later without the treatment, these two young people have very little to lose in the treatment going ahead. I am satisfied it is a reasonable risk to take on their behalf...

Although this cannot be a research project, there would be an opportunity to learn, for the first time, the possible effect of PPS on patients with vCJD and to have the opportunity to compare it with the treatment about to be given to patients in Japan.

Jonathan Simms showed remarkable signs of recovery after receiving PPS, and became the longest surviving vCJD victim.

(c) NON-THERAPEUTIC AND THERAPEUTIC RESEARCH: PHASES I, II, AND III

Medicines can only be licensed for use after extensive clinical trials. First, animal trials must have shown that there is a reasonable likelihood that the new drug will work, and that it is unlikely to have unacceptable side-effects. After satisfactory evidence from animal trials has been gathered, there are usually then three phases of trials on humans. Phase I trials commonly involve a small number of healthy volunteers, who are given the drug so that researchers can study its toxicity, and the way in which it is absorbed. Next, in a phase II trial, the drug is given to a group of people suffering from the condition which it is intended to treat in order to evaluate its effectiveness, and the existence of any side-effects. Finally, phase III trials will involve monitoring a larger group of subjects who take the medicine under supervision for a longer period of time.

After licensing, the drug will continue to be monitored before it can be categorized as an 'established' medicine, and although no longer strictly research, because the intention is now to treat patients rather than to generate knowledge, this is sometimes referred to as a phase IV trial. Phase IV trials involve looking at how drugs work 'in the real world', and will therefore include patients who are routinely excluded from clinical trials, such as pregnant women and children.

Normally, phase I trials are non-therapeutic, whereas the subjects recruited for phase II and III trials will often be patients who may hope to receive some health benefit from participation. For certain new treatments, it would plainly be unethical to begin trials in healthy volunteers. An obvious example would be the use of very toxic drugs, such as chemotherapeutic agents, in cancer treatment. While the risks associated with these drugs may outweigh the benefits for patients with cancer, there could be no justification for imposing them upon healthy volunteers. Hence, some trials will have to involve patients from the outset.

The possible dangers of non-therapeutic phase I trials exploded into the public consciousness in 2006, when eight healthy male volunteers were enrolled in a Phase I drugs trial (of monoclonal antibody TGN 1412—thought to have potential uses in the treatment of arthritis, leukaemia, and multiple sclerosis) at Northwick Park Hospital. Primate toxicology studies had not shown any adverse effects, and it was anticipated that, at the proposed doses, TGN 1412 would be well tolerated in humans. This expectation of safety was misplaced. Six of the men immediately suffered life-threatening multiple organ failure. The other two had been given a placebo. None of the six men died, but in August 2006, it was reported that the most seriously affected volunteer had been diagnosed with the early stages of an aggressive lymphoma.

A report into the incident was commissioned by the Secretary of State for Health from an expert scientific group (ESG) chaired by Gordon Duff. *The Expert Group on Phase One Clinical Trials: Final report* made a number of findings about the proper conduct of 'first in man' studies.[25] It recommended that when deciding on the dose to be given, or about any increase in dosage, investigators should always err on the side of caution. Careful consideration should also be given to the route and rate of administration: the Expert Group recommended that slow infusion may be preferable, so that it can be stopped immediately if there are any signs of adverse effects. The Report was also critical of the decision in the TGN1412 trial to give all six men the active dose at the same time: 'New agents in first-in-man trials should be administered sequentially to subjects with an appropriate period of observation between dosing of individual subjects.'[26]

The TGN1412 trial was self-evidently non-therapeutic, whereas other projects which test new cancer drugs on desperately ill volunteers are plainly done with the hope that they might actually benefit the research subjects. While there may then seem to be a clear distinction between therapeutic research, which could also benefit the subject, and non-therapeutic research, where there could be no possible benefit to the volunteers, a number of commentators, such as Robert Levine, have questioned whether it is appropriate to treat therapeutic and non-therapeutic research completely differently. Even therapeutic trials will generally involve some non-therapeutic procedures, such as additional blood tests.

Robert J Levine[27]

Every clinical trial has some components that are non-therapeutic. When we evaluate entire protocols as either therapeutic or non-therapeutic...we end up with what I call the 'fallacy of the package deal'. Those who use this distinction typically classify as 'therapeutic research' any protocol that includes one or more components that are intended to be therapeutic;

---

[25] Available at <www.dh.gov.uk> (2006).   [26] Ibid.
[27] 'International Codes of Research Ethics: Current Controversies and the Future' (2002) 35 Indiana Law Review (2002) 557.

therefore, the non-therapeutic components of the protocol are justified improperly according to the more permissive standards developed for therapeutic research.

Practical difficulties in drawing a bright-line boundary between therapeutic and non-therapeutic research are particularly important given that, as Simon Verdun-Jones and David Weisstub explain, the principal legal consequence of labelling research 'therapeutic' is to weaken the protection available to vulnerable subjects. Patients who lack capacity can be enrolled in a research trial relatively easily if the trial can be described as 'therapeutic', even if it contains elements that are quite obviously non-therapeutic. If the research is instead categorized as non-therapeutic, it must pose no more than minimal risk. There is then a danger that researchers might exaggerate the likelihood of a direct benefit to research subjects— what Lars Noah refers to as 'benefit creep'[28]—in order to avoid the more restrictive rules which govern non-therapeutic research. Given that research which is described as 'therapeutic' can legitimately expose subjects who lack capacity to *more than minimal risk*, Simon Verdun-Jones and David Weisstub argue that it is critically important that a researcher's claim that an experiment is 'therapeutic' should be rigorously investigated.

Simon Verdun-Jones and David Weisstub[29]

Since the classification of an experiment as either therapeutic or non-therapeutic will profoundly affect the legal and ethical restrictions that apply, a high standard must be met before an experiment should be classified as *therapeutic*...[A]n element of uncertainty is, by definition, inherent in all experiments. However, 'possible', 'hypothetical', or 'speculative' benefits should not be sufficient in the present context. Rather, a therapeutic benefit must be 'likely', 'probable' or 'reasonably foreseeable'. If this standard cannot be achieved, then the experiment must be classified as *non-therapeutic*.

A further problem with the therapeutic/non-therapeutic distinction is that the whole point of doing the trial in the first place is that no-one actually *knows* whether the treatment which is under investigation will be effective, there is just a good *chance* that it might. To say that a trial is therapeutic implies that it is known in advance that participants will benefit, when any potential benefits are instead necessarily speculative.

Randomized controlled trials (RCTs), discussed in the next section, produce a further difficulty in categorizing research as either therapeutic or non-therapeutic. In a placebo-controlled RCT, there is a 50 per cent chance that the patient will receive no treatment at all. Could such a trial be properly described as 'therapeutic'? On the one hand, there is a chance that the patient will be in the active arm of the study and will receive a treatment which has some chance of working, but it is equally likely that the patient will receive no direct health benefit at all.

[28] 'Informed Consent and the Elusive Dichotomy between Standard and Experimental Therapy' (2002) 28 American Journal of Law and Medicine 361.

[29] 'Drawing the Distinction between Therapeutic Research and Non-therapeutic Experimentation: Clearing a Way Through the Definitional Thicket', 88–110 in David N Weisstub (ed.), *Research on Human Subjects: Ethics, Law and Social Policy* (Elsevier: Oxford, 1998).

(d) RANDOMIZED CONTROLLED TRIALS

While it is worth noting that some of the most important medical breakthroughs—such as the discovery of penicillin—were the result of luck, rather than well-planned clinical trials, randomized controlled trials (RCTs) are considered to be the 'gold standard' in medical research.

The purpose of research is to discover whether a new treatment works, and while this might sound straightforward, researchers have to ensure that their results are not distorted by positive results which are caused by factors other than the treatment which is being studied. For example, a proportion of patients would probably have recovered anyway, regardless of whether they received effective treatment.

In an RCT, the research participants are randomly allocated, usually by computer, to the control or the active arm of the study. Those in the active arm are given the new treatment, while those in the control group are given either an inert placebo or, as we see later, the best available treatment. In both groups, it can be anticipated that some of patients' conditions will improve regardless of whether they have received any treatment, so researchers will be interested in whether the extent of improvement in the patients in the active arm is greater than in the control group.

An RCT is also supposed to minimize what is known as the 'placebo effect'. Many people report an improvement in their condition after receiving a new 'treatment', even if they have in fact been given an inert substance, such as a sugar pill. If—say—1000 patients are allocated to each arm of the study, and 600 in the active arm experience some improvement, while 300 in the control group also appear to have been helped, it has been suggested that this tells us that the new treatment has actually worked in 300 subjects.

Two central ethical dilemmas are posed by RCTs. First, while they offer the best way to establish whether a new treatment actually works, randomly allocating a patient to the active or control arm of the study is in conflict with the doctor's normal duty to decide what treatment would be best for her patient. If a doctor believes that drug X is the optimum treatment for a patient's condition, enrolling that patient in an RCT—in which she may be given a placebo instead—clearly breaches the doctor's duty to place the interests of the research subject above the interests of science. As a result, an RCT will only be ethical if there is what is known as 'equipoise': that is, as Alex John London explains, there must genuine uncertainty about which treatment is best.

Alex John London[30]

In its most basic formulation equipoise represents a state of genuine and credible doubt about the relative therapeutic merits of some set of interventions that target a specific medical condition. The requirement that equipoise exist as a necessary condition for the moral acceptability of a clinical trial comparing these interventions is motivated by two interlocking ideas. First, when equipoise obtains it is morally permissible to allow an individual's medical treatment to be assigned by a random process because there is no sufficiently credible evidence to warrant a judgment that one intervention is superior to the other(s). Second, clinical trials that are designed to break or disturb equipoise provide information that will enable the medical community to improve its existing clinical practices. The requirement is thus seen as

---

[30] 'Equipoise and International Human Subjects Research' (2001) 15 Bioethics 312–32.

> a way to reconcile the need to improve the state of medical knowledge and clinical practice with the duty to ensure that the welfare of individual subjects is not knowingly sacrificed for the welfare of future patients of greater scientific understanding.

This conflict between the duty to protect participants' wellbeing and the need to obtain scientifically valuable results is thrown into particularly sharp focus when working out when a trial should be stopped. Preliminary results may appear to show that subjects receiving the new treatment are doing better than those in the control group. At this point, there are two good reasons for stopping the trial. First, it might be in the best interests of the individual subjects for the trial to be halted so that all patients can receive the new treatment. Secondly, the state of equipoise which justifies research on human subjects may have been lost, because the researcher now has *some* evidence that the new treatment works.

Stopping the trial in the early stages will, however, reduce the scientific validity of the results. There is a higher risk of error, and treatment which has been inadequately tested may endanger the health of future patients. The interests of science and society are therefore served by continuing the research until statistically significant results have been obtained.

The dilemma here, as FG Miller and D Wendler explain, is that the point at which interim results become relevant to the *individual's* decision whether to continue to participate will be sooner than when they become sufficiently compelling to justify stopping the trial:

> The point of becoming relevant to individual treatment decisions is reached when findings provide evidence indicating the comparative superiority of one treatment; the point necessary for stopping a trial is not reached until this evidence becomes sufficiently compelling to support a change in treatment guidelines, including evidence that will convince clinicians to adopt the preferred treatment.[31]

The second ethical dilemma raised by RCTs is whether it is ever possible to give informed consent to participation. A patient cannot be told whether they have been allocated to the active or the control arm of the test, because this would invalidate the results. Since an RCT is dependent upon the patients in the control group not knowing what treatment they will receive, their consent could never be *fully* informed. Against this, it could be argued that the patient gives informed consent to *random allocation*, and to taking part in an experiment in which they know they will not be told the results of that random allocation until after the trial has ended. As we see later, however, there is some evidence that patients find the concept of randomization difficult to understand, perhaps because it is radically at odds with the way they normally expect their doctors to behave.

(e) THE USE OF PLACEBOS

Giving the control group a placebo is relatively uncontroversial where there is no known treatment for the condition which the new medicine is supposed to treat: in such cases there is, in fact, equipoise between the new treatment and no treatment at all. As Claire Foster explains in the next extract, more difficult questions arise where effective

---

[31] Is it Ethical to Keep Interim Findings of Randomised Controlled Trials Confidential? (2008) 34 Journal of Medical Ethics 198–201.

treatment already exists, and the researcher instead wants to find out whether a new treatment might be better.

Claire Foster[32]

[T]o decide whether or not a trial should be placebo controlled rests on whether we tend to be more goal-based or duty-based in our thinking. The goal-based approach is to conduct placebo controlled trials wherever possible, only avoiding them when there is likelihood of real harm. The assumption is that the placebo controlled trial is the better trial scientifically. Arguments which have been raised against that view are (i) that this entails a too-simplistic interpretation of the placebo effect; and (ii) that a placebo controlled trial only shows a treatment's efficacy against nothing, it does not show its merits relative to other treatments. The latter problem can be overcome by including active arms in a placebo-controlled trial.

The duty-based approach, which will more often conclude that a trial should not be placebo controlled, would not do so for scientific reasons. Rather, the view is that it is simply wrong to deny treatments, if there are any, to patients who after all expect to be treated. For it is one thing to establish that, for scientific reasons, a trial needs a placebo arm. It is another for an individual researcher to be in equipoise about that placebo arm. For the duty-based approach to be satisfied, the researcher needs to be entirely happy that her patient will receive a placebo instead of an active treatment.

Because a placebo-controlled trial may deprive research subjects of appropriate treatment, it would appear to offend the founding principle of the Helsinki Declaration, incorporated into UK law by the Medicines for Human Use (Clinical Trials) Regulations 2004, Schedule 1 Part 2 para 3:

The rights, safety and wellbeing of the trial subjects are the most important considerations and shall prevail over the interests of science and society.

The Helsinki Declaration's solution to this problem is, in most cases, to ensure that patients in the control group are given the 'best current proven intervention' for the particular condition. Not only does this protect the wellbeing of research subjects, but it has also been suggested that it will often lead to more useful results: researchers will be able to establish whether or not the new treatment is better than existing treatments, rather than just proving that it is better than nothing.

Helsinki Declaration[33]

32. The benefits, risks, burdens and effectiveness of a new intervention must be tested against those of the best current proven intervention, except in the following circumstances:

---

[32] *The Ethics of Medical Research on Humans* (CUP: London, 2001).

[33] World Medical Association, Declaration of Helsinki: Ethical Principles for Medical Research Involving Human Subjects (6th version adopted at the 59th WMA General Assembly, Seoul, South Korea Oct 2008), available at <www.wma.net>.

> • The use of placebo, or no treatment, is acceptable in studies where no current proven intervention exists; or
>
> • Where for compelling and scientifically sound methodological reasons the use of placebo is necessary to determine the efficacy or safety of an intervention and the patients who receive placebo or no treatment will not be subject to any risk of serious or irreversible harm. Extreme care must be taken to avoid abuse of this option.

The second bullet point in paragraph 32 captures the idea that a blanket prohibition on placebo-controlled trials, where treatment already exists, may be inappropriate. The reason for this is that, particularly for conditions where the placebo effect is especially marked, statistically significant proof of efficacy can be obtained more quickly, using fewer research participants, when a placebo is used. Because approximately 75 per cent of participants in research into pain relief for headaches display a placebo response,[34] a trial that just compares the new treatment with an existing treatment will be difficult to interpret, since a large proportion of the apparent therapeutic effect in both groups will be due to the placebo effect. The Helsinki Declaration therefore now permits placebo-controlled trials where effective treatment exists if (a) there are compelling scientific reasons, and (b) the subjects would not be exposed to a risk of serious harm.

Particularly when testing new treatments for relatively minor conditions, such as headaches or hayfever, it would seem unduly paternalistic to insist that the control group should receive 'the best current proven intervention'. In their *Guidelines on the Practice of Ethics Committees in Medical Research with Human Participants*, the Royal College of Physicians explain why placebo controls are acceptable in headache research.

Royal College of Physicians[35]

> A protocol that required patient to wait two hours after the study medication before taking their usual medication if needed would expose the patient to, at worst, two hours of unrelieved headache. This constitutes inconvenience and discomfort but is unlikely to cause serious or irreversible harm. Participation would, of course, be consensual, with freedom to withdraw at any point. We believe that this would be an ethical use of placebo in a condition for which effective treatments are available.

(f) SHAM SURGERY

So far we have assumed that the most invasive experiments involving human subjects are trials of new medicines. In a placebo-controlled drugs trial, patients in the active arm may be exposed to the risks and benefits of the new treatment, while those in the control arm are deprived of the opportunity of receiving the new treatment, but are subjected to no extra risk. Where a course of medical treatment, such as surgery, is more intrusive, conducting a randomized controlled trial would involve carrying out a sham procedure on patients in the control group, which *does* expose them to some additional risks. Could this ever be ethical?

---

[34] RCP guidelines, 4th edn (2007) para 6.13.   [35] Ibid.

The issue has arisen in the context of trials of fetal tissue grafting for patients suffering from Parkinson's disease. Experiments in animals, and preliminary trials on 300 human subjects appeared to indicate that inter-cerebral transplants of fetal tissue could substantially improve the condition of sufferers of Parkinson's disease. Because these initial trials involving humans had not been RCTs, it was impossible to tell how much of this improvement was due to the placebo effect. This is an acute problem for a disease such as Parkinson's where patients' subjective accounts of their symptoms are particularly important. The only way to eliminate the distortions caused by the placebo effect would be to carry out sham surgery on a control group, and compare their results with those of patients who had been given fetal tissue grafts.

Patients receiving the sham surgery have a hole drilled in their skull, and are therefore exposed to the risks inherent in undergoing any surgical procedure, with no expectation of any benefit at all. Because the sole purpose of sham surgery is to generate useful information, some commentators have condemned these trials for putting the interests of science above the welfare of individual research subjects.

On the other hand, it might be argued that unless surgical techniques are properly tested on humans, future patients are likely to be exposed to potentially ineffective and/or unsafe treatment. Carrying out sham surgery on a small number of patients might then benefit thousands of people in the future, and prevent the NHS from wasting resources on inadequately tested and potentially useless or dangerous procedures. While this argument makes good sense from a utilitarian perspective, does it involve sacrificing the interests of a few individuals in order to benefit society as a whole?

The preferred solution to this problem has not been a blanket prohibition of sham surgery. Rather, as RL Albin explains in the next extract, their use has to be rigorously justified, and the risks to subjects must be minimized. In particular, extra care should be taken when obtaining informed consent to ensure that the research subjects actually understand what is meant by randomization, and are fully aware that they may be about to undergo a surgical procedure which will expose them to some risks, with no chance of improving their condition. Because sham neurosurgery obviously exposes subjects to more than minimal risk, it should be particularly difficult to justify carrying out such experiments on incompetent patients.

RL Albin [36]

[I]t is common for surgical techniques to be introduced into clinical practice without rigorous evaluation. The result can be exposure of substantial numbers of patients to procedures that incur significant risks and have no benefit. In addition to becoming a public health hazard, inadequately evaluated surgical methods can consume valuable societal resources...This is not a theoretical concern. There are abundant examples of widely adopted surgeries that were abandoned subsequently for lack of efficacy...

Use of sham surgery is unattractive because the increased risk to control subjects is not accompanied by any possibility of benefit. In some cases, however, sham surgery controls are strongly preferred on scientific grounds and may be necessary to answer the key questions. Sham surgery controls cannot be prohibited absolutely but their use must be balanced carefully against the safety of research subjects.

[36] 'Sham Surgery Controls: Intercerebral Grafting of Fetal Tissue for Parkinson's Disease and Proposed Criteria for Use of Sham Surgery Controls' (2002) 28 Journal of Medical Ethics 322–5.

> Because of the necessity of minimising risk for research subjects, sham surgery controls should not be the default method of constructing human clinical trials involving surgical interventions. Sham surgery controls should be used only with careful justification and I believe that these circumstances will be rare.

The first placebo-controlled study of fetal tissue grafts in Parkinson's patients took place in the US. Forty patients were recruited, and all of them had four tiny holes drilled into their foreheads. Half of them received fetal tissue grafts, and half received nothing. Three patients in the control group said their symptoms had improved. In two-thirds of the patients who received transplants, the fetal tissue took hold and started to produce the missing neurochemical, dopamine, which is necessary for the brain to generate both walking and speaking functions.[37]

4 INTERNATIONAL ETHICAL CODES

The first national code of research ethics was promulgated in Germany in 1900, when the Prussian Minister of Religious, Educational and Medical Affairs issued a directive which provided that research should only be carried out on competent adults, who had given consent after a proper explanation of the possible adverse consequences. Further rules were issued in Germany in 1931 which prohibited risky experiments involving children, and specified that research on humans was only legitimate where there had been previous tests on animals, and where informed consent had been given. Ironically, it was the grotesque corruption of some members of the German medical profession under the Nazis that led to the first *international* code of research ethics.

(a) THE NUREMBERG TRIALS

The discovery of what had been done in the name of medical research during the Second World War resulted in the prosecution of twenty German doctors and three scientists at Nuremberg.[38] Some of the defendants were eminent and internationally renowned physicians. Others, according to the prosecutor Telford Taylor, were 'the dregs of the German medical profession'.[39] The trial was conducted by the Allied Forces, and the judges were American lawyers appointed by the Military Governor of the American zone. Sixteen defendants were found guilty; seven, including Karl Brandt who was Hitler's physician, were hanged.

Many of the experiments carried out in the concentration camps were directed towards the 'war effort'. In Dachau, victims were forced to remain outdoors without clothing for 9–14 hours, or were kept in tanks of iced water for three hours at a time, in order to find out the best way to re-warm German pilots who had parachuted into the North Sea. Also at Dachau, 1,200 inmates were deliberately infected with malaria in order to test new immunization and treatment options. At Ravensbrueck, battle conditions were simulated by making incisions which were then contaminated with glass, woodshavings, or bacteria. Russian prisoners of war at Buchenwald were given poisons and their reactions were observed. Some

---

[37] Peter A Clark, 'Placebo Surgery for Parkinson's Disease: Do the Benefits Outweigh the Risks?' (2002) 30 Journal of Law, Medicine and Ethics 58.

[38] *Trials of War Criminals before the Nuremberg Military Tribunals, United States v Karl Brandt,* US Government Printing Office (Washington, DC, 1949).

[39] Telford Taylor, *Opening Statement of the Prosecution* 9 Dec 1946, US Government Printing Office (Washington, DC, 1949).

died immediately, others were killed so that autopsies could be performed. Vaccines for diseases such as typhus, smallpox, and cholera were tested by deliberately infecting a group of prisoners who had been given the vaccine, and members of a control group who had not been immunized, and who were obviously likely to develop fatal diseases as a result. Because mass surgical sterilization would be costly and time-consuming, the Nazis were keen to develop techniques which could sterilize large numbers of people, ideally without them noticing. Several thousand women were sterilized by injection, and men were castrated using X-rays.

In the next extract, Telford Taylor lays out some of the accusations against the Nazi scientists.

Telford Taylor[40]

A sort of rough pattern is apparent on the face of the indictment. Experiments concerning high altitude, the effect of cold, and potability of processed sea water have an obvious relation to aeronautical and naval combat and rescue problems. The mustard gas and phosphorus burn experiments, as well as those relating to the healing value of sulfanilamide for wounds, can be related to air-raid and battlefield medical problems. It is well known that malaria, epidemic jaundice and typhus were among the principal diseases which had to be combated by the German Armed Forces and by German authorities in occupied territories. To some degree, the therapeutic pattern outlined above is undoubtedly a valid one, and explains why the Wehrmacht, and especially the German Air Force, participated in these experiments. Fanatically bent upon conquest, utterly ruthless as to the means or instruments to be used in achieving victory, and callous to the sufferings of people whom they regarded as inferior, the German militarists were willing to gather whatever scientific fruit these experiments might yield.

But our proof will show that a quite different and even more sinister objective runs like a red thread through these hideous researches. We will show that in some instances, the true object of these experiments was not how to rescue or to cure, but how to destroy and kill. The sterilization experiments were, it is clear, purely destructive in purpose. The prisoners at Buchenwald who were shot with poisoned bullets were not guinea pigs to test an antidote for the poison; their murderers really wanted to know how quickly the poison would kill...

The thanatological knowledge, derived in part from these experiments, supplied the techniques for genocide, a policy of the Third Reich, exemplified in the 'euthanasia' program, and in the widespread slaughter of Jews, Gypsies, Poles, and Russians. This policy of mass extermination could not have been so effectively carried out without the active participation of German medical scientists.

While in no sense justifying these appalling crimes, Arthur Caplan points out an interesting comparison between the Nazis' willingness to sacrifice some individuals' lives in order to save others and the Allies' similar preparedness to knowingly sacrifice some conscripts' lives for the greater good.

Arthur Caplan[41]

Many who conducted lethal experiments or actively engaged in genocide argued that it was reasonable to sacrifice the interests of the few in order to benefit the majority. The most

---

[40] Ibid.
[41] 'How did Medicine Go so Wrong?' in Arthur L Caplan (ed.), *When Medicine went Mad: Bioethics and the Holocaust* (Human Press: Totowa NJ, 1992) 53–92.

distinguished of the scientists who was put on trial, Gerhard Rose, the head of the Koch Institute of Tropical Medicine in Berlin, said that he initially opposed performing potentially lethal experiments to create a vaccine for typhus on camp inmates. But he came to believe that it made no sense not to risk the lives of 100 or 200 men in pursuit of a vaccine when 1000 men a day were dying of typhus on the Eastern front. What, he asked, were the deaths of 100 men compared to the possible benefit of getting a prophylactic vaccine capable of saving tens of thousands? Rose, because he admitted that he had anguished about his own moral duty when asked by the Wehrmacht to perform the typhus experiments in a concentration camp, raises the most difficult and most plausible moral argument in defense of lethal experimentation.

The prosecution encountered some difficulty with Rose's argument. The defense team for Rose noted that the Allies themselves justified the compulsory drafting of men for military service throughout the war, knowing many would certainly die, on the grounds that the sacrifice of the few to save the many was morally just.

It is also worth noting that the United States' enthusiasm for prosecuting German doctors and scientists who had carried out brutal and inhuman experiments on concentration camp inmates did not extend to similarly abusive behaviour by Japan in the 1930s and 1940s. Between 1930 and 1945, Japan conducted extensive trials of biological warfare in a site in China known as Unit 731.[42] It has been estimated that over 3,000 people died through deliberate exposure to germs such as anthrax, cholera, and typhoid, and as a result of experiments involving being dehydrated, frozen, or given transfusions of horse blood. At the end of the war, the US gave Japanese experimenters immunity from prosecution in return for information about biological warfare.

In addition to judging the conduct of the defendants, the Court at Nuremberg set out a Code to govern the future conduct of medical research in order to protect the subjects' interest.

Nuremberg Code[43]

1. The voluntary consent of the human subject is absolutely essential.

2. The experiment should be such as to yield fruitful results for the good of society, unprocurable by other methods or means of study, and not random and unnecessary in nature.

3. The experiment should be so designed and based on the results of animal experimentation and a knowledge of the natural history of the disease or other problem under study that the anticipated results will justify the performance of the experiment.

4. The experiment should be so conducted as to avoid all unnecessary physical and mental suffering and injury.

5. No experiment should be conducted where there is an a priori reason to believe that death or disabling injury will occur; except, perhaps, in those experiments where the experimental physicians also serve as subjects.

6. The degree of risk to be taken should never exceed that determined by the humanitarian importance of the problem to be solved by the experiment.

---

[42] See further SH Harris, *Factories of Death: Japanese Biological Warfare 1932–45 and the American Cover-Up* (Routledge: London, 1994).

[43] 'Trials of War Criminals before the Nuremberg Military Tribunals under Control Council Law No. 10', vol 2, 181–2. US Government Printing Office (Washington, DC, 1949).

7. Proper preparations should be made and adequate facilities provided to protect the experimental subject against even remote possibilities of injury, disability, or death.

8. The experiment should be conducted only by scientifically qualified persons. The highest degree of skill and care should be required through all stages of the experiment of those who conduct or engage in the experiment.

9. During the course of the experiment the human subject should be at liberty to bring the experiment to an end if he has reached the physical or mental state where continuation of the experiment seems to him to be impossible.

10. During the course of the experiment the scientist in charge must be prepared to terminate the experiment at any stage, if he has probable cause to believe, in the exercise of the good faith, superior skill and careful judgment required of him that a continuation of the experiment is likely to result in injury, disability, or death to the experimental subject.

Although the publication of the Nuremberg Code had tremendous symbolic resonance, its impact upon medical practice was limited. In part, this is because many assumed that it was specifically addressing the abuses of Nazism, and, as a result, that it had limited relevance for the medical profession in general. Most of the defendants at Nuremberg were guilty of murder, and if the Code was simply directed towards ensuring that doctors did not kill their patients in the interests of science, its impact upon the conduct of ordinary clinical research would clearly be minimal.

The Code's scope is, however, wider than this: the permissible limits of medical research were also on trial. For example, the first principle in the Nuremberg Code—that the voluntary consent of the human subject is absolutely essential—would be redundant if the defendants' only crimes had been murder, where the consent of the victim is never a defence. Rather, the Code lays out the conditions under which *any* clinical research involving human subjects is acceptable.

Although there have not been research abuses on the scale of those conducted in the Nazi concentration camps since the Nuremberg trials, exploitative medical research did not start and stop with the Nazis. On the contrary, there were plenty of examples of unethical research prior to the Second World War. In the eighteenth and nineteenth centuries, for example, experiments would often be carried out on orphans, prostitutes, and other 'expendable' social groups. There have also been many incidences of exploitation since the end of the Second World War. Henry Beecher's article 'Ethics and Clinical Research', which appeared in the *New England Journal of Medicine* in 1966,[44] and Maurice Pappworth's book *Human Guinea Pigs*, published in 1967,[45] both gave details of extensive violations of the principles encapsulated in the Nuremberg Code. For example, in the US, between 1932 and 1972 the United States Public Health Services carried out the now infamous Tuskegee study, in which effective treatment for syphilis was withheld from 400 poor and uneducated black men without their knowledge or consent, so that the disease's progression could be observed.

(b) THE HELSINKI DECLARATION

In 1954, the Eighth General Assembly of the World Medical Association drafted a set of principles to be followed in research involving human subjects. This document was

---

[44] 'Ethics and Clinical Research' (1966) 274 New England Journal of Medicine 1354–60.
[45] *Human Guinea Pigs: Experimentation on Man* (Beacon Press: Boston, 1967).

redrafted in the early 1960s and adopted at the Eighteenth World Medical Association assembly in Helsinki in 1964. The Helsinki Declaration has since been revised eight times, most recently in Seoul in 2008.[46]

The Helsinki declaration goes into much greater detail than the Nuremburg Code as to the circumstances in which research on human subjects is legitimate. Through regular updating the Declaration has been able to respond to new concerns: for example, note that para 13 draws attention to the question of a trial's effects on the environment.

Helsinki Declaration[47]

3. It is the duty of the physician to promote and safeguard the health of patients, including those who are involved in medical research. The physician's knowledge and conscience are dedicated to the fulfilment of this duty...

6. In medical research involving human subjects, the well-being of the individual research subject must take precedence over all other interests....

11. It is the duty of physicians who participate in medical research to protect the life, health, dignity, integrity, right to self-determination, privacy, and confidentiality of personal information of research subjects.

12. Medical research involving human subjects must conform to generally accepted scientific principles, be based on a thorough knowledge of the scientific literature, other relevant sources of information, and adequate laboratory and, as appropriate, animal experimentation. The welfare of animals used for research must be respected.

13. Appropriate caution must be exercised in the conduct of medical research that may harm the environment.

14. The design and performance of each research study involving human subjects must be clearly described in a research protocol....

15. The research protocol must be submitted for consideration, comment, guidance and approval to a research ethics committee before the study begins. This committee must be independent of the researcher, the sponsor and any other undue influence...

16. Medical research involving human subjects must be conducted only by individuals with the appropriate scientific training and qualifications....

18. Every medical research study involving human subjects must be preceded by careful assessment of predictable risks and burdens to the individuals and communities involved in the research in comparison with foreseeable benefits to them and to other individuals or communities affected by the condition under investigation...

20. Physicians may not participate in a research study involving human subjects unless they are confident that the risks involved have been adequately assessed and can be satisfactorily managed. Physicians must immediately stop a study when the risks are found to outweigh the potential benefits or when there is conclusive proof of positive and beneficial results.

21. Medical research involving human subjects may only be conducted if the importance of the objective outweighs the inherent risks and burdens to the research subjects....

23. Every precaution must be taken to protect the privacy of research subjects and the confidentiality of their personal information and to minimize the impact of the study on their physical, mental and social integrity.

[46] World Medical Association, Declaration of Helsinki: Ethical Principles for Medical Research Involving Human Subjects (6th version adopted at the 59th WMA General Assembly, Seoul, South Korea Oct 2008), available at <www.wma.net>.
[47] Ibid.

(c) THE CIOMS GUIDELINES

In 1982, in response to the concern that research was being carried out in developing countries in order to save money and to avoid restrictive regulations, the World Health Organization (WHO) and the Council for International Organizations of Medical Sciences (CIOMS) published their *International Ethical Guidelines for Biomedical Research Involving Human Subjects*. These have since been updated twice, most recently in 2002. Their purpose is:

> to indicate how the ethical principles that should guide the conduct of biomedical research involving human subjects, as set forth in the Declaration of Helsinki, could be effectively applied, particularly in developing countries, given their socioeconomic circumstances, laws and regulations, and executive and administrative arrangements.

In short, they are designed to address the practical difficulties in implementing universally applicable ethical standards in countries with vastly different standards of health care provision. At the heart of the CIOMS Guidelines are three basic ethical principles: respect for persons, beneficence, and justice:

Council for International Organizations of Medical Sciences (CIOMS)[48]

> In general, the research project should leave low-resource countries or communities better off than previously or, at least, no worse off. It should be responsive to their health needs and priorities in that any product developed is made reasonably available to them, and as far as possible leave the population in a better position to obtain effective health care and protect its own health.
>   Justice requires also that the research be responsive to the health conditions or needs of vulnerable subjects. The subjects selected should be the least vulnerable necessary to accomplish the purposes of the research.

As we shall see later, the Guidelines advocate the universal applicability of certain basic ethical standards, while recognizing that there may be times when superficial aspects of these general principles may need to be modified in order to take account of different social and cultural values.

(d) THE INTERNATIONAL CONFERENCE ON HARMONISATION OF TECHNICAL REQUIREMENTS FOR REGISTRATION OF PHARMACEUTICALS FOR HUMAN USE

The International Conference on Harmonisation of Technical Requirements for Registration of Pharmaceuticals for Human Use (ICH) brings together the regulatory authorities of Europe, Japan, and the United States, as well as experts from the pharmaceutical industry. Its purpose is to make recommendations on ways to achieve greater harmonization of regulations in order to reduce the need to duplicate trials of new medicines.

---

[48] International Ethical Guidelines for Biomedical Research Involving Human Subjects, available at <www.cioms.ch/>.

To facilitate the mutual acceptance of data generated during clinical trials by regulatory authorities in the three regions, the ICH has published a number of guidelines on the conduct of clinical trials, including a general *Guideline for Good Clinical Practice*, which forms the basis of Schedule I Part 2 of the Medicines for Human Use (Clinical Trials) Regulations, and some specific guidance on trials involving geriatric and paediatric populations.

(e) IMPACT OF INTERNATIONAL CODES

Certain principles are common to all of these international documents, and the practical requirements that emerge from them could, perhaps, be summarized as follows:

1. Before the research starts:
   - it must be established that the research is scientifically valid;
   - the risks must be proportionate to the benefits;
   - the research protocol should have been approved by an ethics committee;
   - if competent, the subject must give informed consent;
   - if incompetent, other protections must be in place.
2. During the research:
   - the experiment must be stopped if there is a risk of injury or death;
   - the experiment must be stopped once equipoise has been lost;
   - the subject must be free to withdraw from the trial at any time.
3. After the research has finished:
   - the subject should have access to information about the trial, and to treatment which has been proved to be effective as a result of the trial;
   - research findings should be disseminated;
   - subjects who have been injured as a result of the trial should be appropriately compensated.

To be ethical, research must satisfy the requirements of good scientific practice. Unless research will produce valid and accurate results, there could be no justification for imposing its risks upon research subjects. Risks to participants must also be reasonable in relation to the anticipated benefits from the research. For a number of reasons, however, this principle is rather imprecise. First, the word 'reasonable' is itself ambiguous. If a strict utilitarian interpretation is adopted, would it be reasonable for a small group of subjects to incur considerable risk if the potential benefits are likely to be very great indeed? Recall that this was the justification given by some of the Nazi doctors for conducting research directed towards saving thousands of German soldiers' lives.

Secondly, because the outcome of the research is necessarily unknown, the researcher will rarely be in a position to *know* exactly what risks and benefits might flow from the research. If she already knows the answer to this question, then carrying out further experiments on humans would be scientifically pointless, and hence unethical. The rule that the risks must be proportionate to the anticipated benefits therefore relies on informed *guesswork*.

There is also a danger that invoking a risk/benefit calculation in order to justify research on human subjects may be dangerously misleading. If told that the risks of participation in a research trial are outweighed by its benefits, subjects might not appreciate that this calculation is necessarily speculative. Since we know that most people volunteer to participate in research as a result of perceived self-interest, unwittingly exaggerating the probability that the subject will benefit from participation may mean that her consent is less than fully informed. Even if participation in research *might* benefit the individual subject, it is important to remember that this will never be the trial's principal purpose. On the contrary, any anticipated benefit to individual research subjects will be incidental to its primary aim, which is to produce generalizable knowledge.

5 REGULATION OF RESEARCH IN THE UK

(a) MEDICINES FOR HUMAN USE (CLINICAL TRIALS) REGULATIONS 2004

The Medicines for Human Use (Clinical Trials) Regulations 2004, which implemented a European Directive, came into force in May 2004. A clinical trial is defined in Regulation 2(1).

Medicines for Human Use (Clinical Trials) Regulations 2004 Regulation 2

2(1) In these regulations…'clinical trial' means any investigation in human subjects, other than a non-interventional trial, intended—

(a) to discover or verify the clinical, pharmacological or other pharmacodynamic effects of one or more medicinal products,

(b) to identify any adverse reactions to one or more such products, or

(c) to study absorption, distribution, metabolism and excretion of one or more such products.

Regulation 28 states that 'No person shall conduct a clinical trial or carry out the functions of the sponsor of a trial…otherwise than in accordance with the conditions and principles of good clinical practice.' Good clinical practice (GCP) is fleshed out in Schedule 1, Part II, which confirms that the principles which have been developed in the Helsinki Declaration apply.

Medicines for Human Use (Clinical Trials) Regulations 2004 Schedule 1 Part 2

1. Clinical trials shall be conducted in accordance with the ethical principles that have their origin in the Declaration of Helsinki, and that are consistent with good clinical practice and the requirements of these Regulations.

2. Before the trial is initiated, foreseeable risks and inconveniences have been weighed against the anticipated benefit for the individual trial subject and other present and future patients. A trial should be initiated and continued only if the anticipated benefits justify the risks.

3. The rights, safety, and well-being of the trial subjects are the most important considerations and shall prevail over interests of science and society.

4. The available non-clinical and clinical information on an investigational medicinal product shall be adequate to support the clinical trial.

5. Clinical trials shall be scientifically sound, and described in a clear, detailed protocol.

6. A trial shall be conducted in compliance with the protocol that has a favourable opinion from an ethics committee.

7. The medical care given to, and medical decisions made on behalf of, subjects shall always be the responsibility of an appropriately qualified doctor or, when appropriate, of a qualified dentist.

8. Each individual involved in conducting a trial shall be qualified by education, training, and experience to perform his or her respective task(s).

9. Subject to the other provisions of this Schedule relating to consent, freely given informed consent shall be obtained from every subject prior to clinical trial participation.

10. All clinical trial information shall be recorded, handled, and stored in a way that allows its accurate reporting, interpretation and verification.

11. The confidentiality of records that could identify subjects shall be protected, respecting the privacy and confidentiality rules in accordance with the requirements of the Data Protection Act 1998 and the law relating to confidentiality.

12. Investigational medicinal products used in the trial shall be—

(a) manufactured or imported, and handled and stored, in accordance with the principles and guidelines of good manufacturing practice, and

(b) used in accordance with the approved protocol.

13. Systems with procedures that assure the quality of every aspect of the trial shall be implemented.

Under Regulation 17, in addition to the need for ethics committee approval, every clinical trial must now have a clinical trial authorization issued by the licensing authority, which in the UK is the Medicines and Healthcare products Regulatory Agency or MHRA (we consider the work of the MHRA in more detail in the next chapter, when we look at the licensing of medicines). The MHRA has the power to suspend or prohibit a clinical trial either generally, or at a particular site, if it has grounds for believing that the conditions set out in the original request for authorization are no longer satisfied, or if it receives information raising doubts about the conduct, safety, or scientific validity of the trial. Regulations 32–35 provide for notification, within strict time limits, of actual and suspected serious adverse events. Sponsors are required to provide an annual list of all serious adverse events, and a report on the safety of the trial's subjects. Regulations 49 and 50 create a number of criminal offences, punishable by up to two years' imprisonment. It is, for example, now an offence to start a clinical trial without a favourable ethics committee opinion.

The Regulations also contain detailed provisions on obtaining informed consent from competent patients and the circumstances in which research on incompetent subjects is legitimate. We consider these below in the context of a more detailed discussion of the role of consent in research.

(b) GUIDELINES

In the UK, a variety of bodies have issued guidance on good practice in research. The first was the Medical Research Council (MRC), which issued a statement in 1963 entitled

Responsibility in Investigations on Human Subjects. Its latest general set of guidance *Good Research Practice* was published in 2005, and is accompanied by a variety of other documents which are intended to offer guidance and advice on the conduct of high-quality and ethically sound research.[49] Detailed guidelines have also been issued by, among others, the Department of Health, the Royal College of Physicians, the Royal College of Psychiatrists, the Royal College of Paediatrics, and the General Medical Council, all of whom restate the fundamental principle that the interests of the subject must take precedence over the furthering of knowledge.

General Medical Council[50]

5. Because the benefits of the research are not always certain and may not be experienced by the participants, you must be satisfied that the research is not contrary to their interests. In particular:

- you must be satisfied that, in therapeutic research, the foreseeable risks will not outweigh the potential benefits to the patients. The development of treatments and furthering of knowledge should never take precedence over the patients' best interests;

- in non-therapeutic research, you must keep the foreseeable risks to participants as low as possible. In addition the potential benefits from the development of treatments and furthering of knowledge must far outweigh any such risks;

- before starting any research you must ensure that ethical approval has been obtained from a properly constituted and relevant research ethics committee...

- you must conduct research in an ethical manner and one that accords with best practice;

- you must ensure that patients or volunteers understand that they are being asked to participate in research and that the results are not predictable;

- you must obtain and record the participants' consent; save in exceptional circumstances where specific approval not to obtain consent must have been given by the research ethics committee;

- respect participants' right to confidentiality;

- you must complete research projects involving patients or volunteers, or do your best to ensure that they are completed by others, except where results indicate a risk that participants may be harmed or no benefit can be expected;

- you must record and report results accurately.

(c) ETHICS COMMITTEES

In 1967 the Royal College of Physicians (RCP) issued a report which stated that hospitals' responsibility for the safety and ethical acceptability of research could be discharged if projects had first been approved by a group of doctors. A year later, the then Ministry of

---

[49] Available at <www.mrc.ac.uk/>.

[50] *Research: The Role and Responsibilities of Doctors* (GMC: London, 2002), available at <www.gmc-uk.org/>.

Health sent a notice to regional and area health authorities, and to boards of governors of hospitals, asking them to set up research ethics committees (RECs).

A centralized system of local research ethics committees (LRECs) was instituted by the Department of Health in 1991, and in 1997 these were supplemented by a small number of multi-centre research ethics committees (MRECs), which were intended to eliminate duplication by granting one authorization to trials which would take place in several centres. In 2000 the Central Office for Research Ethics Committees (COREC) was established, and in 2005 the whole system was reviewed by Lord Warner's *Ad Hoc Advisory Group on the Operations of NHS Research Ethics Committee*.[51] The National Research Ethics Service (NRES) replaced COREC in 2007, and has implemented many of the Warner report's recommendations.

One of the most significant changes is the introduction of a 'triage' system. All applications are submitted centrally on a national REC application form. Applications which raise no material ethical issues can then be fast-tracked by a virtual sub-committee of two experienced national research ethics advisers. This means that only applications which *do* raise material ethical issues will receive full REC review. Of course, this system depends upon a clear and consistent definition of what counts as a 'material ethical issue'. Any invasive study will almost certainly raise material ethical issues, and so only research which does not involve any physical intervention is likely to be fast-tracked. An example might be research which consists in surveys or questionnaires, rather than the testing of new medicines. But a blanket rule that survey-based research does not require full REC review would be inappropriate because some surveys covering sensitive issues, such as exposure to sexually transmitted diseases, may not be entirely 'risk-free' for participants. Poorly designed questionnaires could cause distress, and if sensitive data is collected, breaches of confidentiality could have serious adverse consequences for the individual.

Regulation 12 of the Medicines for Human Use (Clinical Trials) Regulations 2004 specifies that the favourable opinion of an ethics committee is a precondition of any clinical trial. Under Regulation 15(5), an ethics committee is required to take into account various matters, including:

(a) the relevance of the clinical trial and its design;

(b) whether the evaluation of the anticipated benefits and risks is satisfactory and whether the conclusions are justified;

(c) the protocol;

(d) the suitability of the investigator and supporting staff; . . .

(e) the quality of the facilities for the trial;

(f) the adequacy and completeness of the written information to be given, and the procedure to be followed, for the purpose of obtaining informed consent to the subjects' participation in the trial;

(g) if the subjects are to include persons incapable of giving informed consent, whether the research is justified having regard to the conditions and principles specified in Part 5 of Schedule 1;

(h) provision for indemnity or compensation in the event of injury or death attributable to the clinical trial;

---

[51] DH, 2005, available at <www.dh.gov.uk/>.

> (i) any insurance or indemnity to cover the liability of the investigator or sponsor;
>
> (j) the amounts, and, where appropriate, the arrangements, for rewarding or compensating investigators and subjects; ...
>
> (k) the arrangements for the recruitment of subjects.

Regulation 15(10) sets a time limit of 60 days between receipt of a valid application and the issuing of the REC's opinion, unless the trial involves gene therapy, somatic cell therapy, or a medicinal product containing a genetically modified organism, in which case longer time limits (of up to 180 days) apply.

RECs—of which there are now 120 in the UK—will commonly have between 12 and 18 members, about a third of whom should be 'lay' members who should, according to the RCP guidelines, 'be persons of responsibility with relevant life experience, who will not be overawed by medical members'.[52]

The responsibility of RECs is to ensure that research involving human subjects meets certain ethical standards. There has been some debate over whether they have any role in judging the scientific validity of research. On the one hand, RECs may not have the expertise to ascertain whether the proposed project has any scientific merit, and the question of whether research is ethical is different from whether it is good science. Yet on the other, it will generally be unethical to expect volunteers to expose themselves to risk where there is no possibility of useful results being generated. As the second edition of the *Research Governance Framework for Health and Social Care*[53] makes clear: 'research which duplicates other work unnecessarily, or which is not of sufficient quality to contribute something useful to existing knowledge, is unethical'. The Framework states that RECs should be 'adequately reassured' that the scientific methods are appropriate, and the RCP guidelines suggest that this responsibility will be discharged by ensuring that proper scientific review has taken place, perhaps as a result of the peer-review process imposed by funding bodies. Research appears to indicate that RECs often go beyond this requirement and that it is not uncommon for unfavourable REC opinions to raise concerns about the scientific merit of proposals.[54]

Because of their access to the original protocol, RECs are particularly well placed to monitor researchers' adherence to the ethical standards upon which the REC's approval was based. In practice, however, RECs exercise comparatively little ongoing scrutiny of research once the initial protocol has been approved. While progress reports must be submitted, the committee's role is largely confined to collecting information volunteered by the researchers, rather than investigating the extent to which there has been compliance with the original protocol. NRES's Standard Operating Procedures for RECs make clear that monitoring compliance is the job of the trial sponsor (which may be the pharmaceutical company whose drugs are being tested), rather than the REC:

> The main REC is not required to monitor the conduct of the research proactively but should keep the ethical opinion under review in the light of progress and safety reports submit-

---

[52] RCP (2007) supra.   [53] (2005), available at <www.dh.gov.uk>.

[54] E L Angell *et al.*, 'An Analysis of Decision Letters by Research Ethics Committees: The Ethics/Scientific Quality Boundary Examined' (2008) 17 *Quality and Safety in Health Care* 131–6.

ted by the sponsor or Chief Investigator, and any other developments in the study. Primary responsibility for monitoring lies with sponsors and employing organisations.[55]

If deviations from the protocol are likely to go unnoticed, researchers do not have an incentive to ensure scrupulous compliance. Perhaps unsurprisingly, studies have indicated that there are divergences from the research plan in as many as a quarter of all projects.[56]

6 CONSENT TO PARTICIPATION IN RESEARCH

(a) THE COMPETENT SUBJECT

(1) Voluntariness

Because the research subject will commonly be exposing herself to some increased risk, without necessarily gaining any benefit in return, it has been suggested that we should be particularly concerned to ensure that her consent has been given voluntarily. It might, for example, be important to ensure that external factors had not exerted so much pressure on her that she felt she had no other option but to agree to take part. Choosing to 'volunteer' for research is only truly voluntary if it would have been possible for the subject to refuse.

In this section, we begin by looking at whether offering to pay research subjects might unduly influence their decisions. Next we consider the special vulnerability of patients. Finally, we look at other 'vulnerable' groups, such as prisoners and medical students.

(a) Payments

Paying people to participate in research has been criticized for a number of reasons. First, in the next extract, Paul McNeill argues that the offer of money may prove irresistible, especially for the poorest sections of society.

Paul McNeill[57]

The reason that inducement is particularly of concern is that those most susceptible to inducement may be the least able to assess the aims and technical information relating to the research and to decide on whether or not the risk is worth taking. It is already the poor and socially disadvantaged who volunteer for most research yet it is typically the better off members of society who benefit from research. The offering of financial inducement simply exacerbates this inequity and adds further to the risks for those disadvantaged people...

The basis of my argument against inducement is that it encourages people to expose themselves to risk of harm. This encouragement is greater for the impecunious....

There is something repugnant about offering money to relatively poor people, impecunious students, travellers and others, to take part in research, which, by its nature, exposes

---

[55] Standard Operating Procedures for RECs in the UK (NRES, 2008), available at <www.nres.npsa.nhs.uk>.

[56] T Smith, EJH Moore, and H Tunstall-Pedoe, 'Review by a Local Medical Research Ethics Committee of the Conduct of Approved Research Projects, by Examination of Patients' Case Notes, Consent Forms, and Research Records and by Interview' (1997) 314 British Medical Journal 1588.

[57] 'Paying People to Participate in Research: Why Not?' (1997) 11 Bioethics 391–6.

them to risks of harm. The poor in our societies already have higher risks of poor health and other adverse life events. Inducement to take part in experimentation should not be allowed when it adds to those risks.

Not only could the lure of money persuade poor people to volunteer for research, but it might also offer an incentive to misrepresent characteristics—such as depression or drug use—which would otherwise disqualify them from participation, thus increasing the health risks to which they are exposed, as well as potentially invalidating the trial's results. In the next extract, JP Bentley and PG Thacker draw on empirical research which suggests that while payments do not 'blind' individuals to risk, they do increase subjects' willingness both to participate in research, and to conceal information about 'restricted activities'.

JP Bentley and PG Thacker[58]

This study suggests that monetary payment increases respondents' willingness to participate in research regardless of the level of risk; higher levels of payment make respondents more willing to participate, even if the study is relatively risky....

Monetary payments appeared to influence respondents' propensity to neglect to tell researchers about restricted activities they have engaged in either before or during a study, with higher payment levels leading to a higher propensity to neglect to tell.

This study also showed that higher levels of monetary payment may influence subjects' behaviours regarding concealing information about restricted activities. If such activities were actually engaged in, the results of the hypothetical studies may have been distorted (that is, alcohol, caffeine, medications, herbal products may all affect the pharmacokinetics of a study drug).

Secondly, the 'taint' of money is thought by some to contaminate the ethical virtue of altruistic participation. Tod Chambers, for example, argues that 'the gift of one's own health should not be thought of as a commodity'.[59]

Thirdly, it is sometimes argued that payments will skew subject selection, and thereby undermine the validity of research findings. Poorer sections of society, such as students, are often overrepresented in research projects, while richer groups, such as wealthy, middle-aged men tend to be underrepresented. In an empirical study of Phase I participants in Tayside, Pamela Ferguson found that they 'conform[ed] to the stereotype of the typical Phase I volunteer;...they were predominantly male (74 per cent), aged between 18 and 45 (73 per cent), with a minority (23 per cent) in full-time employment'; 25 per cent were students, and half of these were medical students.[60]

The advertisement for recruitment to the TGN 1412 trial, described above, would clearly be likely to appeal to people who are not in full-time employment: 'You'll be paid for your time...Free food...digital TV, pool table, video games, DVD player and now FREE internet access!' The payment the volunteers received for participating in this trial was about £2,000.

---

[58] 'The Influence of Risk and Monetary Payment on the Research Participation Decision Making Process' (2004) 30 Journal of Medical Ethics 293–8.

[59] 'Participation as Commodity, Participation as Gift' (2001) 1 American Journal of Bioethics 48.

[60] Pamela R Ferguson, 'Clinical Trials and Healthy Volunteers' (2008) 16 Medical Law Review 23–51.

Following the publicity surrounding the adverse side-effects suffered by the six men who had received a dose of TGN 1412, agencies which recruit volunteers for clinical trials reported an *increase* in enquiries from the public. As Pamela Ferguson explains: 'Paradoxically, the case helped to advertise the high fees that could be earned by taking part, and the rarity of adverse events.'[61]

In favour of payments, it could be argued, first, that since participation in medical research will often be time-consuming, inconvenient, and uncomfortable, without payments it might be difficult to recruit sufficient numbers of subjects. Secondly, it is not clear why being paid to assume the burdens of research participation is necessarily more problematic than paying people to do other unskilled and unpleasant jobs which may pose some risk to their health.

In the next extract, Martin Wilkinson and Andrew Moore argue that inducements are not necessarily coercive.

Martin Wilkinson and Andrew Moore[62]

Consider the following argument for allowing inducements. Some researchers would find it worthwhile to pay inducements in order to attract enough subjects. Those who would accept this reward would not do so unless it were worth while to them. As a result of offering the reward, the researchers get the subjects they want. As a result of participating, the subjects get the reward they want. Both are better off. No one is worse off. Inducement is thus a good thing.

This seems to us to be a good argument, which at least makes a *prima facie* case for inducement. It has the same structure as an argument justifying wages for work, or any other market transactions. Many people would not work if they were not paid; in that sense wages are inducements. Few people think that, as a result, it is wrong to offer wages. Those that do have concerns about the existing wage system usually object that wages are too *low*, not that they are too high, or that they are offered at all . . .

If badly off people were in some way coerced into participating as subjects, then their autonomy would be infringed upon and their consent invalidated. Coercion is paradigmatically a case of the denial of autonomy, since it consists in the deliberate imposition of one person's will on another. However, coercion usually takes the form of threats, which restrict people's options. Inducements are offers, not threats, and they expand people's options.

Thirdly, the offer of experimental treatment to desperately ill patients, and the 'therapeutic misconception' (considered in the next section), will often offer a much more powerful incentive than money for agreeing to participate in research, and for misrepresenting one's disqualifying characteristics. A research subject who has been paid is probably *more* likely to have given fully informed consent to her participation in a research trial than a patient who is mistakenly under the assumption that her doctor is treating her in her best interests.

The compromise position adopted in the various ethical guidelines is that payment is acceptable provided it is at a fairly modest level, and hence unlikely to overbear an individual's will.

---

[61] Ibid.   [62] 'Inducement in Research' (1997) 11 Bioethics 373–89.

General Medical Council [63]

> 14 You must not offer payments at a level which could induce research participants to take risks that they would otherwise not take, or to volunteer more frequently than is advisable or against their better interests or judgement;

In the next extract, Christine Grady defends this idea that modest payments to research subjects compensate for the inconvenience and discomfort to which they will be exposed, without interfering with the voluntariness of their decision to participate.

Christine Grady[64]

> Commentators and common wisdom have argued that limiting the amount of payment offered for research participation minimizes the possibility that money will distort judgment and push people towards deception. Payment as recognition of the research participant's contribution and calculated according to some regularly applied and locally acceptable standard (per day, visit, or procedure) is likely to be more modest and less likely to distort judgement than amounts designed solely to attract subjects and outperform the competition in terms of recruitment.

In contrast, writing from a Canadian perspective, Trudo Lemmens and Carl Elliott suggest that the compromise position in which subjects are paid, but not much, is disingenuous. They argue that it would be better to straightforwardly admit that the researcher is *employing* the research subject. This would enable these 'employees' to benefit from protective legislation—such as health and safety rules—which would prevent them from being exposed to unreasonable risks.

Trudo Lemmens and Carl Elliott[65]

> In the world that regulatory bodies have created, healthy subjects take part in studies because of the money, yet researchers have to pretend that the subjects are motivated by something other than money. Research subjects cannot negotiate payment, since payment is not supposed to be the focus of the transaction...
>
> It is time to stop pretending that the relationship between for-profit, multibillion-dollar corporate entities and healthy volunteers is the same as the relationship between an academic physician-investigator and sick patients. We have argued that research studies on healthy subjects—unlike research on sick patients—are best characterized as a kind of labor relation. If regulatory bodies realized this, they would be in a far better position to protect these subjects from exploitation. Labor-type legislation could give research agencies the clout of occupational health and safety agencies by giving them the power to conduct inspections and ensure that 'working' conditions are safe. Collective negotiations and unionization could give research participants a stronger voice in arguing for good working conditions. Research

---

[63] Research: The Role and Responsibilities of Doctors (GMC: London, 2002), available at <www.gmc-uk.org/>.

[64] 'Money for Research Participation: Does it Jeopardize Informed Consent' (2001) 1 American Journal of Bioethics 40–4.

[65] 'Justice for the Professional Guinea Pig' (2001) 1 American Journal of Bioethics 51–3.

participants could negotiate standards of payment based on the level of discomfort they are asked to undergo, the number and types of procedures, the duration of the studies and other factors...

Are there dangers to this kind of shift? Yes, absolutely. The most serious danger is that the payment argument could be hijacked to defend even more commercialization of the research enterprise and even more exploitation of vulnerable subjects... The current regulatory system is even more dangerous. Ethical guidelines and regulations ought to protect healthy research subjects from exploitation. But instead, the current regulatory scheme prohibits subjects from receiving a fair wage and denies them the legal resources available to other high-risk workers.

(b) Patients

One of the principal problems faced when enrolling patients into clinical research trials is the 'therapeutic misconception'. This is the problem that individuals might not understand that they are taking part in research which is designed to yield generalizable knowledge, and not to meet their individual health needs. Of course, the danger that research subjects will wrongly assume that they are receiving treatment, which their doctor believes to be in their best interests, exists only when a new medicine is being tested on people who suffer from the condition it is designed to treat. For obvious reasons, healthy volunteers are much more likely to realize that they have consented to take part in an experiment.

Standard consent forms may exacerbate this problem by setting out what the study is hoping to achieve for future patients. Confusion between the goals of the research and what patients hope for themselves is then inevitable. Nancy King advocates a much blunter approach: 'When benefit cannot reasonably be expected, the consent form should say, "You will not benefit".'[66]

Terminally ill patients are an especially vulnerable group, particularly if none of the standard treatments have worked, and they have been told that no more can be done for them. In such circumstances, enrolling in a trial of an experimental new drug may appear to offer their best hope of recovery. Of course, their desperation to try anything does not necessarily vitiate their consent, but it does suggest that researchers should be careful not to overstate the likelihood that the patient will receive a direct health benefit.

The doctor–patient relationship is based upon trust, and it is often difficult for patients to understand that their doctor might be suggesting a course of action which may not be in their best interests. In the next extract, A Charuvastra and SR Marder explain that unconscious evaluations of a doctor's familiarity and trustworthiness are at least as important as the facts given during the informed consent process to a person's decision to agree to take part in research.

A Charuvastra and SR Marder[67]

[W]hen a patient is reading an informed consent document, he is also seeing a person in a white coat and appreciating that he is in a hospital or medical centre, and his evaluation of the

---

[66] 'Defining and Describing Benefit Appropriately in Clinical Trials' (2000) 28 Journal of Law, Medicine and Ethics (2000) 332, 334.

[67] 'Unconscious Emotional Reasoning and the Therapeutic Misconception' (2008) 34 Journal of Medical Ethics 193–7.

intention of the researcher and the benefits and risks of his relationship with this researcher will reflect to some degree all his prior social encounters with similar people in similar white coats in similar settings. A therapeutic misconception is even more likely to take place if the person proposing the research is someone the patient already knows, and especially if it is someone the patient already receives care from.

Certainly, there is evidence that some research subjects do not realize that they have taken part in an experiment, even when they have apparently given informed consent. In the next extract, Katie Featherstone and Jenny L Donovan describe interviews with participants in a research trial who clearly found it very hard to believe that the treatment they received had really been randomly allocated.

Katie Featherstone and Jenny L Donovan[68]

There were a number of factors that contributed to the men's struggle to under-stand...Allocation according to randomisation appeared to some to be very haphazard. It was difficult for these men to believe that such a haphazard procedure was reasonable, particularly when they had completed so many questionnaires about their symptoms and undergone clinical tests, some of which were very invasive. The men reasoned that the data from the questionnaires and clinical tests must be useful, not just for research purposes, but also for clinicians to make individualised treatment decisions—hence the unacceptability of randomisation....

[E]ven when trials adhere to strict informed consent procedures and ensure that 'simple language' is used, this does not guarantee that subjects will fully understand the implications of participation and that they may still have unrealistic treatment expectations....It has been suggested that potential trial participants should be informed specifically about the components of research that constitute a change from the standard doctor–patient relationship—randomisation and blinding.

It is common for patients to feel grateful to the medical team involved in their care, and so if asked to participate in a research trial, refusal may not feel like a realistic option. Patients have ongoing relationships with their doctors, and as a result, they may be concerned that a refusal might jeopardize their future care.

In the next extract, Franz J Ingelfinger further draws attention to the fact that illness often increases patients' vulnerability and dependency, and hence makes it even harder for them to object to participation in research.

Franz J Ingelfinger[69]

Incapacitated and hospitalized because of the illness, frightened by strange and impersonal routines, and fearful for his health and perhaps life, he is far from exercising a free power of choice when the person to whom he anchors all his hopes asks, 'Say, you wouldn't mind, would you, if you joined some of the other patients on this floor and helped us to carry out

---

[68] 'Why Don't They Just Tell Me Straight, Why Allocate It?' The Struggle to Make Sense of Participating in a Randomized Controlled Trial (2002) 55 Social Science and Medicine 709–19.

[69] 'Informed (But Uneducated) Consent' (1972) 287 New England Journal of Medicine 466.

some very important research we're doing?' When 'informed consent' is obtained, it is not the student, the destitute bum, or the prisoner to whom, by virtue of his condition, the thumb screws of coercion are most relentlessly applied; it is the most used and useful of all experimental subjects, the patient with disease.

(c) Other vulnerable groups

It is worth noting that the category of people who are considered vulnerable when obtaining consent to participation in research extends far beyond those who are unable to give a valid consent to medical treatment. Medical students or junior employees, for example, may feel pressure to agree to participate in their teachers' or employers' research projects. The Helsinki Declaration requires researchers to be particularly cautious if the subject is in a dependent relationship, and to ensure that consent is taken by an independent physician.

Helsinki Declaration[70]

26. When seeking informed consent for participation in a research study the physician should be particularly cautious if the potential subject is in a dependent relationship with the physician or may consent under duress. In such situations the informed consent should be sought by an appropriately qualified individual who is completely independent of this relationship.

Similarly, the General Medical Council guidance instructs doctors that they must:

[E]nsure that no real or implied coercion is used on participants who are in a dependent relationship to you, for example, medical students, a junior colleague, nurse in your practice or employee in your company.[71]

In the eighteenth and nineteenth centuries, prisoners were often used as research subjects. This was partly done because of their low social status, and partly for reasons of convenience: follow-up studies are obviously facilitated if the research subjects can be guaranteed to remain in the same place for many years. Now, however, for a number of reasons prisoners are categorized as a particularly vulnerable group for the purposes of obtaining consent to participation in research.

Small financial rewards may be disproportionately attractive in prison, where the opportunities for earning money are limited. Boredom too might encourage prisoners to enrol in scientific studies. It is not, however, clear that a prisoner who is willing to take part in research in order to relieve the monotony of prison life, or to earn a small amount of extra money, has necessarily been coerced. More importantly, prisoners may wrongly believe that agreeing to take part in research might lead to early parole or other privileges, and as a result may not feel that refusal is a realistic option. Because of their special vulnerability, as the RCP guidelines make clear, it is difficult to justify carrying out any research on prisoners unless the fact of a person's incarceration was directly relevant to the research. An example might be psychological studies involving the impact of imprisonment on depression.

---

[70] World Medical Association, Declaration of Helsinki: Ethical Principles for Medical Research Involving Human Subjects (6th version adopted at the 59th WMA General Assembly, Seoul, South Korea Oct 2008), available at <www.wma.net>.

[71] Research: The Role and Responsibilities of Doctors (GMC: London, 2002) para 8, available at <www.gmc-uk.org/>.

Royal College of Physicians[72]

8.47 Research that can be conducted on patients or healthy volunteers who are not in prison should not be conducted on prisoners. Incarceration in prison creates a constraint which could affect the ability of prisoners to make truly voluntary decisions without coercion to participate in research.

8.48 Research studies in prison should normally be limited to:

- Studies of the possible causes, effects and processes of incarceration and of criminal behaviour, provided the study presents no more than minimal risk.
- Research on conditions particularly affecting prisoners as a class.
- Research on practices which have the intent and reasonable probability of improving the health or well-being of a prisoner.
- Studies of prisons as institutional structures or of prisoners as incarcerated persons, provided the study presents no more than minimal risk.

(2) Information

As we saw in Chapter 4, treating someone without their consent may constitute battery. For consent to ordinary medical treatment to be valid, the patient must have been informed 'in broad terms' about the nature of the medical procedure.[73] So if someone has not been told that they are participating in a research trial, any apparent consent might be invalid, either because there has been fraud which vitiates their consent, or because they have agreed to a procedure which is materially different from that which is actually carried out.

The rule that competent subjects must give their fully informed consent to participation in research is common to all of the various guidelines and codes governing experiments on human subjects from Nuremberg onwards. Indeed, it is widely believed that the informed consent of the subject is what justifies imposing the risks of research participation upon individuals.

Schedule 1 Part 3 of the Medicines for Human Use (Clinical Trials) Regulations 2004 specify that the competent adult research subject must have given 'informed consent'.

Medicines for Human Use (Clinical Trials) Regulations 2004 Schedule 1 Part 3

Conditions Which Apply In Relation To An Adult Able To Consent Or Who Has Given Consent Prior To The Onset Of Incapacity

1. The subject has had an interview with the investigator, or another member of the investigating team, in which he has been given the opportunity to understand the objectives, risks and inconveniences of the trial and the conditions under which it is to be conducted.
2. The subject has been informed of his right to withdraw from the trial at any time.
3. The subject has given his informed consent to taking part in the trial.

---

[72] *Guidelines on the Practice of Ethics Committees in Medical Research with Human Participants*, 4th edn (RCP, 2007).
[73] *Chatterton v Gerson* [1981] QB 432.

> 4. The subject may, without being subject to any resulting detriment, withdraw from the clinical trial at any time by revoking his informed consent.
> 5. The subject has been provided with a contact point where he may obtain further information about the trial.

But what does it mean to give 'informed consent'? How much information does an individual have to be given before their consent can be considered 'informed'? The GMC guidance fleshes out this requirement.

General Medical Council[74]

> 19 You must ensure that any individuals whom you invite to take part in research are given the information which they want or ought to know, and that is presented in terms and a form that they ca understand. You must bear in mind that it may be difficult for participants to identify and assess the risks involved. Giving the information will usually include an initial discussion supported by a leaflet or sound recording, where possible taking into account any particular communication or language needs of the participants. You must give participants an opportunity to ask questions and to express any concerns they may have.

Although we might agree that researchers must tell subjects about the risks involved in participation before their consent can be considered fully informed, there will inevitably be grey areas, where the relevance of particular sorts of information is less clear. Do participants need to know about any personal or financial benefit that the researcher hopes to receive as a result of this trial, for example? Should they be told if the researcher has been paid to recruit subjects? How much should the researcher disclose about their own motivation in carrying out the research, or their qualifications for doing so?

Because gaining the subject's informed consent is a necessary precondition of participation in a research trial, there is also a danger that researchers will assume that the provision of information only has to happen at one fixed moment before the trial begins. But to be valid, the subject's consent to participation must be fully informed *throughout* the trial, and researchers may therefore be under a duty to ensure that subjects are provided with information that emerges after the trial has begun, so that their decision to *continue* to participate is also properly informed. As we saw earlier, however, this raises an obvious problem—if researchers must disclose their preliminary findings about the risks and benefits of a new treatment, subjects may exercise their right to withdraw from the trial before statistically significant data have been gathered.

Under Schedule 1 of the Medicines for Human Use (Clinical Trials) Regulations 2004 the subject's informed consent should normally be formally recorded on a signed, written consent form, or if the subject is unable to write, consent should be given orally in the presence of at least one witness and recorded in writing. It is important to remember that a signed consent form is not the same thing as a binding contract between the subject and the researcher. The existence of a signature on a consent form does not guarantee that the subject has given informed consent to participation. Nor does it force the subject to keep

---

[74] Research: The Role and Responsibilities of Doctors (GMC: London, 2002), available at <www.gmc-uk.org/>.

her side of the 'bargain': subjects must always be free to withdraw from the research project, without being subject to any penalty at all.

It is also worth noting that there is an important difference between providing information and ensuring that patients fully *understand* the information that they have been given. Evidence that patients are sometimes unaware that they have taken part in research, despite their signature on a written consent form which unambiguously states that the procedures are part of a research project, shows that simply providing information will not always be sufficient to ensure that the subject's consent has been properly informed.

As Jay Katz explains in the following extract, the need to dispel the therapeutic misconception, in particular, will take time, and will not be achieved by simply offering research subjects a printed sheet of information.

Jay Katz[75]

The investigators who appear before patient-subjects as physicians in white coats create confusion. Patients come to hospitals with the trusting expectation that their doctors will care for them. They will view an invitation to participate in research as a professional recommendation that is intended to serve their individual treatment interests. It is that belief, that trust, which physician-investigators must vigorously challenge so that patient-subjects appreciate that in research, unlike therapy, the research question comes first. This takes time and is difficult to convey. It can be conveyed to patient-subjects only if physician-investigators are willing to challenge the misperceptions that many patients bring to the invitation.

Thus, recruitment of subjects will prove to be more time consuming. Completion of research may also be delayed.

(b) THE INCOMPETENT SUBJECT

If the consent of the subject is what makes research morally acceptable, where does this leave individuals who are unable to give legally valid consent to treatment? As we saw in Chapter 5, there are several categories of patients who are unable to consent to medical treatment: children, mentally incapacitated adults, and unconscious patients.

Recall that parents usually give consent to their child's treatment, subject to the courts' power to overrule parental decision-making in order to protect the child's best interests. The treatment of adults who lack capacity is governed by the Mental Capacity Act 2005, which specifies that, unless the patient has a binding advance decision in place, incompetent patients should be given treatment which is in their best interests. An unconscious patient may be given treatment that is immediately necessary to preserve their life or health.

None of this would appear to facilitate incompetent patients' participation in medical research. Since taking part in an experiment involves being exposed to a procedure whose effect is, by definition, uncertain, it may not be in the best interests of a patient. It is, however, important to remember that a blanket ban on research involving patients who lack capacity might also be inappropriate. If no trials can ever take place involving children and mentally incapacitated or unconscious adults, members of these groups will have access only to inadequately tested treatments. Children absorb drugs differently from adults, and so simply giving them a reduced dose of a medicine which has been tested on adults is

---

[75] 'Human Experimentation and Human Rights' (1993) 38 Saint Louis University Law Journal 7.

likely to be either ineffective or unsafe. In the next extract, Paul Miller and Nuala Kenny explain that shielding children from the dangers of research might itself cause children significant harm.

Paul B Miller and Nuala P Kenny[76]

Ironically, the protective impulse to shield children entirely from the harms of research participation has the potential to cause them significant harm. History tells of the dangerous consequences of presuming treatments tested on adults to be safe and efficacious for children... For scientific and ethical reasons, children should receive wherever possible only those treatments that have been adequately evaluated on children.... Reliance on the results of research involving adults as the knowledge base from which to develop the care of children may make the provision of such care unnecessarily dangerous.

Moreover, as Lainie Friedman Ross points out, we allow parents to subject their children to other sorts of risks, such as being a passenger in a car or taking part in sporting activities.

Lainie Friedman Ross[77]

Parental authorization of a child's participation in research of minimal risk and harm does not necessarily treat the child solely as a means. Rather, parents who value participation in social projects will try to inculcate similar values into their child....

Many activities in a typical child's life, in fact, will present greater risks and harms, including such routine activities as participation in contact sports and traveling as a passenger in the family car... Parents are morally and legally authorized to decide which risks their child can take and in what settings. Parental authorization or prohibition of a child's participation in this type of research, then, is not abusive or neglectful....

Given the minimal amount of risk which the proposed research entails, the child's participation will not interfere with the child's developing personhood even if she is forced to participate against her will. Their decision to override their child's dissent is not abusive; parents legitimately override their child's decisions in many daily activities. This is one way in which parents steer their child's development into the person she will become...

Although parents should always consider their child's opinion in their decisionmaking, parents ought to have final decisionmaking authority about whether their child participates in such research.

Since some mental illnesses impede their sufferers' decision-making capacity, it will only be possible to test drugs which might improve the lives of people with these sorts of conditions if research is carried out upon patients who cannot give consent. Emergency medicine often involves treating patients who have lost consciousness, and are therefore unable to consent to treatment. Again, excluding such patients from research would inhibit the development of new techniques to address severe, life-threatening conditions.

---

[76] 'Walking the Moral Tightrope: Respecting and Protecting Children in Health-Related Research' (2002) 11 Cambridge Quarterly of Healthcare Ethics 217–29.

[77] 'Children as Research Subjects: A Proposal to Review the Current Federal Regulations Using a Moral Framework' (1997) 8 Stanford Law and Policy Review 159.

If a blanket ban on incompetent subjects' participation in research is not justified, when might it be permissible to carry out research on individuals who cannot give consent? Although slightly different rules apply depending upon the reason for a person's inability to consent, some common principles can be detected:

- It must be impossible to do the research on individuals who *are* able to consent to participation.
- The research must be likely to benefit either the individual subject, or other members of the group to which the subject belongs.
- Efforts should be made to gain the subject's assent to participation, and any evidence that the subject does not wish to participate should be taken into account.

Because the benefits from non-therapeutic research accrue to society, rather than to the individual subject, in the absence of the subject's freely given consent, such research might appear to contradict the basic principle that the wellbeing of the subject should take precedence over the interests of science and society. To expose incompetent subjects to risks *solely* in order to advance scientific knowledge might be to treat such individuals as means, rather than as ends in themselves. If non-therapeutic research on those who cannot give consent does offend the Kantian imperative (see Chapter 1), it will do so regardless of whether the risk to the subject is minimal or substantial.

In the following extract Penney Lewis argues that non-therapeutic research on incompetent patients can only be justified by engaging in a utilitarian calculation in which the gains to society are allowed to justify infringing the rights and dignity of the individual subject. The conditions laid out in the various guidelines may appear to reduce the practical impact of this violation, by ensuring that incompetent subjects are only used as 'a means to an end' in certain tightly circumscribed circumstances, but it would seem difficult to square carrying out non-therapeutic research on incompetent adults with the fundamental principle governing codes of research ethics, namely that concern for the interests of the subject should always prevail over the interests of science and society.

Penney Lewis[78]

In the context of non-therapeutic research, the existence of an international 'consensus', supporting the participation of incompetent persons, is used to avoid providing a justification for a utilitarian calculation that allows the use of vulnerable members of society in order to benefit others...

Judicial approval is generally considered desirable for organ and tissue donation from incompetents and for their non-therapeutic sterilization. It is not, however, encouraged for the approval of non-therapeutic research with incompetent subjects. To obtain judicial approval for all research projects would be overly burdensome on both the judiciary and the research community. A separate system has evolved of research ethics committees, which approve research projects. These committees may be more willing than judges to engage in utilitarian balancing of the interests of society against the interests of the incompetent prospective research subject.

[78] 'Procedures that are Against the Medical Interests of Incompetent Adults' (2002) 22 Oxford Journal of Legal Studies 575–618.

> Regardless of the means, if we are willing to encroach on the interests of incompetents for reasons related to societal good, then there is no principled reason why this should be the case solely for non-therapeutic research.

Let us now turn to the rules contained in the Medicines for Human Use (Clinical Trials) Regulations 2004 Schedule 1. There are some differences between the rules covering children, adults, and emergencies, but before we consider these separately, let us first consider the need to obtain consent from the incompetent person's 'legal' representative, which is common to all three situations.

(a) Seeking a representative's consent

Under Schedule 1, Parts 4 and 5 of Medicines for Human Use (Clinical Trials) Regulations 2004, where a person cannot give consent to participation, consent must be obtained from their 'legal representative'. Usually, it is envisaged that someone will act as a potential research subject's legal representative by virtue of their relationship with her. For a child, the personal legal representative should be a person with parental responsibility. The personal legal representative of an adult should be a person who is herself capable of giving consent, and who has a close personal relationship with the potential subject.

There will, however, be situations in which finding a suitable personal legal representative will be impossible, either because there is no-one who is sufficiently close to the patient able or willing to take on this role; or in an emergency, identifying and contacting a close friend or relative in time may not be feasible. In such circumstances, the regulations stipulate that the patient's doctor should fulfil the role of the 'professional legal representative', unless she is 'connected with the conduct of the trial'. This will disqualify not only the principal researcher and those on her team, but also anyone who provides health care under the direction or control of members of the investigating team. If the patient's doctor has any connection with the trial, the health care trust must nominate someone else.

Once a personal or professional legal representative has been identified, her consent to the subject's participation in the clinical trial should be sought. She is expected to base her decision on the subject's 'presumed will', hence the desirability of finding a personal legal representative who has a good understanding of the subject's values and preferences. The legal representative should be given an opportunity to understand the objectives, risks, and inconveniences of the trial, and the conditions under which it is to be conducted. They should be informed that their decision should be based on what the potential subject would have wanted herself, and that they can withdraw consent to the subject's participation at any time. Independent advice about their role should be made available. Where a professional legal representative has been appointed, subject to the duty to respect patient confidentiality, she may consult anyone who might be able to help her determine the potential subject's presumed will.

The legal representative is also responsible for ensuring that the subject's continued participation remains appropriate. This will be comparatively straightforward where the personal legal representative is a close friend or relative, who will be aware of any changes in the subject's circumstances. Where a professional legal representative has been appointed, this sort of informal review will not be possible and specific arrangements should be in place to ensure that the legal representative regularly re-evaluates the subject's continued participation.

(b) Children

If a child is ill, and there is no standard treatment available for her condition, enrolling her in a research trial in which she might receive an experimental new treatment could be consistent with her doctor's ordinary duty of care. But where the research is purely non-therapeutic, and by definition, *not* in the child's best interests, should children ever be used as research subjects? According to the Medicines for Human Use (Clinical Trials) Regulations 2004, the answer would appear to be 'no'. In addition to it being impossible to use adults in the research, the Regulations provide that minors should only be involved where there will be some 'direct benefit' to the research participants. This aspect of the Regulations is in conflict with the Royal College of Paediatrics guidelines, which would instead endorse the 'minimal risk' criterion for non-therapeutic research:

Royal College of Paediatrics[79]

A research procedure which is not intended directly to benefit the child subject is not necessarily either unethical or illegal...

[P]arents can consent to research procedures that are intended directly to benefit the child, but that research that does not come into this category can only be validly consented to if the risks are sufficiently small to mean that the research can be reasonably said not to go against the child's interests.

Medicines for Human Use (Clinical Trials) Regulations 2004 Schedule 1 Part 4

Conditions And Principles Which Apply In Relation To A Minor

... 6. The minor has received information according to his capacity of understanding, from staff with experience with minors, regarding the trial, its risks and its benefits.

7. The explicit wish of a minor who is capable of forming an opinion and assessing the information referred to in the previous paragraph to refuse participation in, or to be withdrawn from, the clinical trial at any time is considered by the investigator.

8. No incentives or financial inducements are given—

(a) to the minor; or

(b) to a person with parental responsibility for that minor or, as the case may be, the minor's legal representative, except provision for compensation in the event of injury or loss.

9. The clinical trial relates directly to a clinical condition from which the minor suffers or is of such a nature that it can only be carried out on minors.

10. Some direct benefit for the group of patients involved in the clinical trial is to be obtained from that trial.

Clearly, there might be a conflict of interest if parents could be paid to enrol their children in research trials. As a result, any incentives or financial inducements to the child, or to anyone with parental responsibility, are ruled out by the Medicines for Human Use (Clinical Trials) Regulations 2004.

[79] 'Child Health: Ethics Advisory Committee Guidelines for the Ethical Conduct of Medical Research Involving Children' (2000) 82 Archives of Disease in Childhood 177–82.

If the potential child subject is over the age of 16, or *Gillick*-competent, as we saw in Chapter 5, she may be able to give a valid consent to medical treatment. Regulation 2 of the Medicines for Human Use (Clinical Trials) Regulations 2004 defines 'minor' as 'a person under the age of 16 years' and 'adult' as 'a person who has attained the age of 16 years'. For *Gillick*-competent children under the age of 16, both their consent *and* that of their parents should be sought.

Note that the Regulations provide that the wishes of the minor simply have to be 'considered' by the investigator. It is hard to imagine many researchers would ignore clear evidence that the child objected to taking part, but the Regulations fall short of making such evidence decisive. More recently, however, the European Commission's Ad Hoc Working Group on the implementation of the Directive issued further recommendations for research on children: *Ethical Considerations for Clinical Trials on Medicinal Products Conducted with the Paediatric Population.*[80] While reiterating the need for the informed consent of the minor's legal representative, the document recommends that, in addition, the child's 'assent' should be sought. If the child wishes to withdraw from the trial, the recommendation is that their 'will should be respected'.

In a separate development, the Regulation on Medicinal Products for Paediatric Use[81] creates a system of incentives for carrying out paediatric trials, and sets up a European database of paediatric, including the publication of both favourable and unfavourable results, in order to ensure that trials in children are not unnecessarily duplicated.

(c) Adults

Again, in addition to the consent of their personal or legal representative, a number of additional conditions and principles are laid out in the 2004 Regulations.

Medicines for Human Use (Clinical Trials) Regulations 2004 Schedule 1 Part 4

Conditions And Principles Which Apply In Relation To An Incapacitated Adult

. . . 6. The subject has received information according to his capacity of understanding regarding the trial, its risks and its benefits.

7. The explicit wish of a subject who is capable of forming an opinion and assessing the information referred to in the previous paragraph to refuse participation in, or to be withdrawn from, the clinical trial at any time is considered by the investigator.

8. No incentives or financial inducements are given to the subject or their legal representative, except provision for compensation in the event of injury or loss.

9. There are grounds for expecting that administering the medicinal product to be tested in the trial will produce a benefit to the subject outweighing the risks or produce no risk at all.

11. The clinical trial relates directly to a life-threatening or debilitating clinical condition from which the subject suffers.

Note that the Medicines for Human Use (Clinical Trials) Regulations 2004 specify that research involving incapacitated adults will be acceptable only if 'the clinical trial relates directly to a life-threatening or debilitating clinical condition from which the subject suffers'. This limiting criterion is clearly directed towards ensuring that incompetent individuals are not used

---

[80] http://ec.europa.eu/enterprise/pharmaceuticals/eudralex/vol-10/ethical_considerations.pdf (2008).
[81] EC No 1901/2006.

where it would be possible to recruit competent subjects. However, it could be argued that the requirement that the study must be concerned with the disorder from which the patient suffers pays too little attention to the preferences and wishes of incompetent adults. An adult who lacks capacity might wish to take part in non-therapeutic research to investigate a condition from which a number of close family members suffer, in preference to research which is only likely to benefit unknown individuals who share her own mental disorder.

A further limiting criterion is that there must be reason to believe that the medicinal product 'will produce a benefit to the subject outweighing the risks or produce no risk at all'. This provision raises two difficulties. First, it may be at odds with the principle of clinical equipoise, considered above, according to which research is ethical only if there is *genuine uncertainty* as to whether the treatment to be tested is better than the alternative. Secondly, by requiring research which is not likely to benefit the incapacitated adult to 'produce *no risk at all*', it would be very difficult to justify carrying out *any* non-therapeutic procedures on incapacitated adults. Additional blood tests or X-rays would satisfy a 'minimal risk' condition, but it would not be true to say they are absolutely risk-free.

It is important to remember that adults who lack the capacity to consent to medical treatment exist on a spectrum from those who are permanently insensate and wholly unaware of their own existence (such as patients in a permanent vegetative state), to those whose cognitive impairments are only slightly more severe than those of adults who fall on the other side of the legal 'cut-off' point for decision-making capacity. Individuals in this latter group, while unable to give a valid consent to medical treatment, are nevertheless able to express their desire or unwillingness to participate in research. Just as with minors, the Medicines for Human Use (Clinical Trials) Regulations 2004 provide that the subject's desire not to participate must be considered. The GMC guidance goes further and suggests that their wishes should be decisive.

General Medical Council[82]

> 49. You must also ensure that participants' right to withdraw from the research is respected at all times. Any sign of distress, pain or indication of refusal irrespective of whether or not it is given in a verbal form should be considered as implied refusal.

It is, however, important to remember that patients who lack capacity will generally be familiar with limitations upon their capacity to make decisions for themselves. If an incompetent person is used to being treated or detained without consent, she may have no reason to believe that her reluctance to take part in research would be respected. As we saw earlier, it is difficult for *all* patients to understand the difference between treatment and research, and this problem may be even more acute for mentally incapacitated individuals. Simply stating that research should not be carried out *against* the wishes of an incompetent adult presupposes both that such patients will understand that they have more robust rights to refuse to participate in research than they do for treatment, and that they will be both able and willing to make their feelings known.

The Mental Capacity Act 2005 (MCA) applies to all 'intrusive' research, which is not covered by the 2004 Regulations. Research is 'intrusive' if it would be unlawful if carried out on a competent adult without consent. Such research will be unlawful unless it has been approved by an appropriate body (this will be an REC), and the conditions in sections 31–33 are satisfied. These include that it must not be possible to carry out the research on people who could give consent, and that

[82] Research: The Role and Responsibilities of Doctors (GMC: London, 2002), available at <www.gmc-uk.org/>.

31(5) The research must—

(a) have the potential to benefit P without imposing on P a burden that is disproportionate to the potential benefit to P, or

(b) be intended to provide knowledge of the causes or treatment of, or of the care of persons affected by, the same or a similar condition.

If the research does not have the potential to benefit P him or herself, the risk to P must be likely to be negligible; it must not significantly interfere with P's freedom of action or be unduly invasive or restrictive. There is a tension here with the Regulations, since the MCA clearly envisages that it would be legitimate to carry out research which has no potential to benefit the P provided the risk is negligible, as opposed to non-existent.

Under section 32 of the MCA, the researcher must identify someone who is caring for or interested in the welfare of P (other than in a professional capacity), for advice on whether P should take part in the project, and what P's wishes and feelings about taking part in the project would be likely to be if P had capacity. If this person advises that P's wishes and feelings would mean he would not want to take part, or would want to withdraw, he must not participate in the research project.

Section 33 further bolsters the need to take account of the P's views.

Mental Capacity Act 2005, section 33

33(2) Nothing may be done to, or in relation to, him in the course of the research—

(a) to which he appears to object (whether by showing signs of resistance or otherwise) except where what is being done is intended to protect him from harm or to reduce or prevent pain or discomfort, or

(b) which would be contrary to—

(i) an advance decision of his which has effect, or

(ii) any other form of statement made by him and not subsequently withdrawn…

(4) If he indicates (in any way) that he wishes to be withdrawn from the project he must be withdrawn without delay.

Because the definition of 'clinical trial' in regulation 2 is broad—all research involving medicinal products is covered—the 2005 Act's scope is rather limited. This is a pity, because in many ways the protection the MCA offers patients is more robust than the 2004 Regulations. Under the Regulations, the subject's unwillingness to participate must simply be 'taken into account', whereas the 2005 Act provides that any indication that a person objects must be decisive.

(d) Emergencies

In an emergency, the requirement to obtain a third party's consent will normally involve seeking the views of a professional legal representative. Even if a personal legal representative is available, she may be severely traumatized. In such trials, it might be appropriate for suitable professional legal representatives to be nominated at the outset of the trial.

Where a professional legal representative has been appointed in an emergency, review of the appropriateness of continued participation is especially important. It might also be appropriate for the role of legal representative to be transferred subsequently to an individual who is closely connected with the subject. Alternatively, if the subject recovers competence, she has the right to decide whether or not to continue participation in the trial, and the legal representative will have no further role. After the 2004 Regulations came into force it became apparent, following the experience of researchers involved in a large international trial investigating cardiac arrest—who had found it impossible to include UK patients—that the process of appointing and consulting a legal representative is unworkable in the context of emergency medicine.[83]

This led to the Medicines for Human Use (Clinical Trials) (Amendment No. 2) Regulations 2006, which allow patients to be entered into a trial prior to consent being obtained from a legal representative provided that:

- having regard to the nature of the trial and the particular circumstances of the case, it is necessary to take action for the purpose of the trial as a matter of urgency; and

- it is not reasonably practicable to obtain informed consent from a legal representative, and

- the action to be taken is carried out in accordance with a procedure approved by the ethics committee, and

- steps must be taken to seek informed consent either from the subject (if capacity has been recovered) or from a legal representative as soon as practicable after the initial emergency has passed. If consent is withheld, the subject must be withdrawn from the trial.

Research involving emergency medicine is obviously important if treatments are to improve. However, as we saw in Chapter 5, patients who have been temporarily incapacitated in an emergency can be given medical treatment only if it is necessary to save their lives, or to prevent grave permanent injury. Hence, unless participation in a particular research trial offers the best chance of saving a person's life, or averting serious injury, it would be very difficult to justify enrolling them in a trial without their consent.

Certainly, the GMC guidance makes clear that research into emergency medicine can only be justified where it is clearly therapeutic. The doctor must genuinely believe that participation in the trial offers her patient a chance of receiving potentially life-saving treatment, which is at least as good, or better than that offered by other available treatments.

General Medical Council[84]

51. In an emergency where consent cannot be obtained, treatment can be given only if it is limited to what is immediately necessary to save life or avoid significant deterioration in the patient's health. This may include treatment that is part of a therapeutic research project, where the risks of the new treatment are not believed to exceed the known risks of standard treatment. If, during treatment, the patient regains capacity, the patient should be told about the research as soon as possible and their consent to continue should be sought.

---

[83] Hansard 18 Jan 2005: Column 32WS.
[84] Research: The Role and Responsibilities of Doctors (GMC: London, 2002), available at <www.gmc-uk.org/>.

7 FACILITATING PARTICIPATION IN RESEARCH

(a) THE BENEFITS OF PARTICIPATION

So far, we have concentrated on the special vulnerability of research subjects, and discussed the sort of safeguards that should be in place in order to protect people from being pressurized into taking part in research. Because the outcome of research is, by definition, uncertain, our assumption has been that research participants are exposed to some risks without necessarily receiving any health benefits in return. But this view of participation in clinical trials as a burden has been challenged in recent years as a result of the recognition that being a research subject might sometimes hold out the possibility of very great benefits.

The catalyst for this has been the AIDS pandemic. Before the first anti-retroviral drugs were licensed for use in humans, anyone diagnosed as HIV-positive could expect to die from an AIDS-related illness within a comparatively short space of time. People living with HIV knew that research into drugs which might be capable of delaying the onset of AIDS was ongoing. Unsurprisingly, there was no shortage of volunteers for these studies. For some cancer patients too, access to 'cutting-edge' treatment may only be available to participants in clinical trials. If the important issue for individuals becomes access to the benefits of taking part in clinical research, rather than protection from its dangers, rather different ethical issues are raised. We might, for example, need to ensure that there is fair and equitable distribution of places in research trials.

In the next extract, Rebecca Dresser explains the role of patient advocacy groups in promoting research participation, and draws attention to the danger that they may overestimate the benefits of research participation.

Rebecca Dresser[85]

During the 1980s, HIV/AIDS activists became major figures in biomedical research... [Patient] advocates tend to stress the positive dimensions of biomedical research. In much advocacy communication, there is a failure to clearly distinguish between partially tested experimental interventions and proven medical care. Consistent with this approach, advocates often portray study participation as the way to obtain cutting-edge therapy...

Patient advocates may also promote the therapeutic misconception at a broader level. For example, patient advocates often suggest that research can end the suffering and deprivation inflicted by illness. The general message is that with more funding for research, cures are destined to emerge. Although this feel-good message may lift the spirits of people coping with disease and injury, and aid with fundraising, it may also promote public misunderstanding of the research process. There is no question that research can lead to health care improvements. Almost always, however, it takes many years and many false starts before effective practical applications become available. But advocates too often downplay this part of research; instead, they equate support for research with support for imminent improvements in treatment.

---

[85] 'Patient Advocates in Research: New Possibilities, New Problems' (2003) 11 Washington University Journal of Law and Policy 237.

(b) EXCLUSION FROM RESEARCH

A number of different groups within society have traditionally been underrepresented among research subjects. Most notable, perhaps, has been the exclusion of women. Obviously, if a disease (such as prostate cancer) occurs only in men, it would be inappropriate to recruit female subjects. But, for a number of reasons, women have also been excluded from research into conditions which affect both sexes.

First, it has been suggested that women's physiology is different from that of men, and that this might complicate results, and lead to less 'clean' data. Because women's monthly hormonal profiles fluctuate, more women would have to be recruited, thus increasing the costs of the research. Of course, women's reproductive physiognomy is only a complicating factor if the male body is regarded as the norm.

Of more practical importance, there is also a central paradox in this justification for women's exclusion. If the female body reacts differently to treatment, and hence might distort a study's results, then dosages of a treatment which have only been tested on men are likely to be either ineffective or unsafe for female patients. Despite being under-tested in women, most drugs are prescribed to both sexes, and it is therefore unsurprising that there is evidence that women are more likely than men to report adverse drug reactions.

A second reason for excluding women is the possibility that they might become pregnant during the trial, thus exposing their fetus to the unknown toxicity of the treatment in question, and the researchers to the possibility of liability for prenatal injury. Of course, there might be good reasons for not recruiting women who are trying to conceive onto trials of experimental drugs, but a blanket ban on *all* women's participation is unwarranted. Not all women of reproductive age are heterosexually active, or fertile, and so a more appropriate and less paternalistic approach would be to ask women whether there is a chance that they might become pregnant during the trial, and to believe them if they say that there is no risk of conception.

While it is understandable that few pregnant women would volunteer to take part in clinical trials, if no drugs are ever tested on pregnant women, it will never be possible to find out if they can safely be taken during pregnancy. This is why so many medicinal products contain a warning that they should not be used by pregnant woman. Most of these warnings are not designed to protect women and their fetuses from drugs which are known to be harmful: rather, they simply indicate that they have not been proved to be safe, because no studies have been carried out. It is important to remember that abstaining from using any medicines during pregnancy is not necessarily an option for some pregnant women. A woman who suffers from severe depression, for example, and might be likely to harm herself if she stops taking anti-depressants is faced with an invidious dilemma. She must either carry on taking a medicine which has not been proved safe during pregnancy, or risk the potentially serious consequences of stopping her medication.

In the next extract, Marie Fox criticizes the neglect of women's health needs which results from gender bias in research design.

Marie Fox[86]

> Although the justifications for explicit exclusions are generally couched in the rhetoric of protecting women and their unborn children, the issue which looms largest for those sponsoring

[86] 'Research Bodies: Feminist Perspectives on Clinical Research' in S Sheldon and M Thomson (eds), *Feminist Perspectives on Health Care Law* (Cavendish: London, 1998) 115–34.

or conducting trials is likely to be fear of liability for any teratogenic impact...Again feminist lawyers have challenged this rationale, arguing that there is potentially greater liability if
unsafe products are marketed, since pharmaceutical companies do not bar women, including
women of child-bearing capacity, from purchasing or being prescribed such drugs...

The relative neglect of women's health needs raises issues of justice, as well as calling
into question the scientifically dubious practice of marketing drugs and procedures which
have been inadequately tested for their impact on women. Since the choice and definition
of problems for research is influenced by the under-representation of women at all stages of
the research process, research on conditions specific to females receives low priority, funding and prestige. Even breast cancer is not a major research priority, despite being the most
prevalent form of cancer. Less politicised diseases, such as dysmenorrhoea or incontinence
in older women, fare much worse in funding terms.

Other groups have also tended to be underrepresented in research, with obvious implications for their access to safe and effective medical treatment. Elderly people, for example,
have often been excluded. Researchers have been concerned, first, that it would be difficult
to ensure that elderly subjects rigorously adhered to the research protocol; secondly, that
long-term follow-up might be impeded by the subjects' deaths; and thirdly, that subjects
might suffer from multiple disorders which could distort the results. But not only is research
on older subjects essential in order to improve the quality of care available to the elderly,
it is also a mistake to assume that all elderly people are equally infirm or close to death. On
the contrary, many old people are healthier and more independent than younger adults.
Moreover, elderly subjects are less likely to have work and family commitments which could
interfere with participation in research.

Exclusionary tendencies in research are increasingly regarded as illegitimate. And
according to the UK's Research Governance Framework, researchers must now justify any
recruitment restrictions in their protocols.

2.2.7 Research and those pursuing it should respect the diversity of human culture and
conditions and take full account of ethnicity, gender, disability, age and sexual orientation in
its design, undertaking, and reporting. Researchers should take account of the multi-cultural
nature of society. It is particularly important that the body of research evidence available to
policy makers reflects the diversity of the population.[87]

(c) A DUTY TO PARTICIPATE?

A further issue missed by the prevailing emphasis on protecting research subjects from
exploitation is the question of whether users of health care services might in fact be under a
duty to share in the burdens of research participation. It is certainly true that these burdens
are not distributed evenly across society. Most experiments are carried out on people who
are ill. Among healthy volunteers, certain groups—in particular students, junior medical
staff and the unemployed—are overrepresented, while others—such as wealthy individuals
in full-time employment—will very seldom participate.

---

[87] Research Governance Framework For Health And Social Care (DH: London, 2001), available at <www.
dh.gov.uk>.

Uneven recruitment of research subjects gives rise to two distinct problems. First, the de facto exclusion of certain groups from medical trials mean that we cannot be sure that medical treatment will be either safe or effective when given to members of the excluded group. Research which only proves that a medical treatment works in a small subset of the population to which it will eventually be provided is perhaps *methodologically* unsound.

Secondly, it might be argued that the risks associated with participation in research should be distributed fairly across society, and that it is unjust for certain sections of society to bear a disproportionate burden. Since the sort of financial rewards which persuade students or the unemployed to volunteer are unlikely to act as an incentive to those who do not currently participate in research, we might have to think in terms of some sort of *duty* to enrol as a research subject. We could, for example, view serving as a research subject as one of the duties we assume under the 'social contract', in which we accept some restrictions upon our freedom in return for the benefits of living in a safe and cohesive community.

In the UK, there is no *legal* duty to participate in research, but it could be argued that anyone who wants to have access to well-tested medical treatments is under a *moral* duty to serve as a research subject. Indeed, the Research Governance Framework suggests that all those using health and social care services should give serious consideration to invitations to become involved in the development or undertaking of research.[88]

Arthur Caplan would go further, arguing that, in certain circumstances, it might be appropriate for a hospital to refuse to treat those who are unwilling to take part in clinical research.

Arthur L Caplan[89]

Modern medicine is a vast social enterprise in which certain benefits are produced at the cost of various burdens, which include the need to conduct medical research. If individuals consciously, knowingly, and continuously accept the benefits of medical care by seeking out physicians and hospital personnel when they are ill, then they would seem to meet the conditions for being bound by the principle of fair play. If the only way the knowledge and skills utilized in modern medicine can be generated is through research involving human subjects, then those who accept the fruits of such research would appear to be under a duty to bear the burdens of research when called upon by the group to do so…

Medical institutions which clearly and forthrightly identify themselves to patients as research institutions would be within their rights to exclude persons who refuse to participate in any form of research.

John Harris also believes that we have an obligation to participate in research. According to Harris, whether or not a research subject stands to benefit from participation should not be confined to the narrow question of whether her health will be directly improved. Instead, he argues that we all benefit from living in a society in which medical research is ongoing, and that participation should no longer be regarded as a supererogatory act, but, like jury

[88] Ibid.
[89] 'Is There an Obligation to Participate in Biomedical Research' in Stuart F Spicker, Ilai Alon, Andre de Vries, and H Tristram Engelhardt (eds), *The Use of Human Beings in Research* (Kluwer Dordrecht NL) 1988 229–48.

service and taxation, as one of a number of mandatory contributions to the public good which we accept as the price of living in a civilized society.

John Harris[90]

> We all benefit from the existence of the social practice of medical research. Many of us would not be here if infant mortality had not been brought under control, or antibiotics had not been invented. Most of us will continue to benefit from these and other medical advances.... Since we accept these benefits, we have an obligation in justice to contribute to the social practice which produces them....
>
> We all also benefit from the knowledge that research is ongoing into diseases or conditions from which we do not currently suffer but to which we may succumb. It makes us feel more secure and gives us hope for the future, for ourselves and our descendants, and for others for whom we care. If this is right, then I have a strong general interest that there be research, and in all well founded research; not excluding but not exclusively, research on me and on my condition or on conditions which are likely to affect me and mine. All such research is also of clear benefit to me. A narrow interpretation of the requirement that research be of benefit to the subject of the research is therefore perverse....
>
> If it is right to claim that there is a general obligation to act in the public interest, then there is less reason to challenge consent and little reason to regard participation as actually or potentially exploitative. We do not usually say: 'are you quite sure you want to' when people fulfil their moral and civic obligations. We do not usually insist on informed consent in such cases, we are usually content that they *merely* consent or simply acquiesce. When—for example, I am called for jury service no one says: 'only attend if you fully understand the role of trial by jury, due process, etc in our constitution and the civil liberties that fair trials guarantee'.

8 PUBLICATION ETHICS

(a) SHOULD UNETHICAL RESEARCH BE PUBLISHED?

If unethical research has yielded useful information, should it be published, or used by future researchers? Data generated by the Dachau hypothermia experiments, for example, has been cited in subsequent research, but its use remains extremely controversial. On the one hand it might be argued that once unethical research has actually taken place, and produced results which might save lives, a refusal to disseminate this information will lead to even more suffering than has already occurred. Precautions could be taken to ensure that the researcher does not benefit from publication: names could be withheld, for example, and the results could be accompanied by an indictment of the researcher and her methods.

On the other hand, allowing unethical research to be published sends a rather confusing message to researchers. If it is impossible to disseminate research unless it has met certain ethical standards, researchers have a powerful incentive to ensure that they comply with them.

---

[90] 'Scientific Research is a Moral Duty' (2005) 31 Journal of Medical Ethics 242–8.

The various international codes contain a presumption against the publication of unethical research, but they all fall short of imposing an absolute prohibition. Paragraph 30 of the Helsinki Declaration, for example, states that 'Reports of research not in accordance with the principles of this Declaration should not be accepted for publication' (note the use of the word *should* as opposed to *must*).[91] The CIOMS Guidelines suggest that although unethical research should not normally be published, 'careful consideration' may be necessary where publication could have wider health benefits.

CIOMS[92]

Commentary on Guideline 2: Ethical Review Committees

Unless there are persuasive reasons to do otherwise, editors should refuse to publish the results of research conducted unethically, and retract any articles that are subsequently found to contain falsified or fabricated data or to have been based on unethical research. Drug regulatory authorities should consider refusal to accept unethically obtained data submitted in support of an application for authorization to market a product. Such sanctions, however, may deprive of benefit not only the errant researcher or sponsor but also that segment of society intended to benefit from the research; such possible consequences merit careful consideration.

(b) THE DUTY TO PUBLISH

If information gathered during research is not published, research subjects will have been exposed to some risks without any corresponding benefits to scientific knowledge. Any information produced will have no social value, and the original justification for carrying out the research will have been lost. It could also be argued that a failure to publish materially alters the basis upon which the subjects' informed consent was given. When asked why they agreed to take part in research, subjects commonly cite the prospect of helping future patients. If the participants knew that a trial's results would not be published, and would therefore have no practical benefit, few of them would have agreed to take part.

It is also important that both negative and positive results are published. While positive results (which prove that a new treatment works) may be more interesting and newsworthy than negative results (which show that a new treatment is ineffective or harmful), unless negative results are also published, there is a danger that other researchers may instigate identical and futile trials, thereby exposing a new set of research subjects to wholly avoidable risks. Researchers may therefore be under a duty to ensure that a trial's results are properly disseminated, regardless of whether they are positive or negative, and indeed principle 30 of the Helsinki Declaration confirms that 'negative and inconclusive as well as positive results should be published or otherwise made publicly available'.[93]

---

[91] World Medical Association, Declaration of Helsinki: Ethical Principles for Medical Research Involving Human Subjects (6th version adopted at the 59th WMA General Assembly, Seoul, South Korea Oct 2008), available at <www.wma.net>.

[92] International Ethical Guidelines for Biomedical Research Involving Human Subjects, available at <www.cioms.ch/>.

[93] World Medical Association, Declaration of Helsinki: Ethical Principles for Medical Research Involving Human Subjects (6th version adopted at the 59th WMA General Assembly, Seoul, South Korea Oct 2008), available at <www.wma.net>.

But while unpublished research may fail to fulfil the moral requirement that researchers only carry out research where there is a realistic prospect of obtaining valuable information, this is not translated into an enforceable legal duty to disseminate one's findings. On the contrary, research ethics committees cannot force researchers to publish their results. Alarmingly, studies appear to indicate that the *majority* of clinical trials do not result in published papers.[94]

One partial solution to this problem would be to require pre-trial registration of all clinical trials, so that unfortunate results cannot be 'buried'. To this end, the Royal College of Physicians (RCP) has argued that registration should become a precondition of REC approval.

Royal College of Physicians[95]

There have been major concerns about bias in the publication of drug trial results. There have been instances of trials showing negligible benefit of an active drug against a control, or greater than expected adverse effects, being concealed by the pharmaceutical industry 'burying' results to protect its own interests or by editorial choice. This distorts the medical literature, impairs meta-analyses and undermines the confidence of doctors and patients alike. It is important that the REC does all it can to ensure that the publication of negative results is not precluded in advance or otherwise impeded by the sponsors. The RCP wholeheartedly supports the registration of all clinical trials to help to ensure their eventual publication, irrespective of results and would like to see approval of applications conditional upon such registration. Registration of trials and publication of all results is the way to prevent publication bias—the tendency whereby favourable results are published more frequently and more rapidly.

And it is worth noting that, for the first time, the 2008 revision of the Helsinki Declaration states that 'Every clinical trial must be registered in a publicly accessible database before recruitment of the first subject.'[96]

9 RESEARCH IN DEVELOPING COUNTRIES

At the outset, it is important to acknowledge that drawing a distinction between 'developed' and 'developing' countries is itself controversial. Not only does it overemphasize economic development, at the expense of other social and political factors which are relevant to the provision of health care, it also implies that nations can easily be divided into two categories, when in fact economic prosperity exists on a spectrum. Moreover, within many poorer countries there are often vast differences between the quality of medical care available in cities and that which exists in rural areas. The terms 'developed' and 'developing' are commonly used in the relevant literature, but they should be regarded as simply a convenient shorthand, and the important distinction is between richer countries, which

---

[94] Judit Pich, Xavier Carné, Joan-Albert Arnaiz, Begoña Gómez, Antoni Trilla, and Juan Rodés, 'Role of a Research Ethics Committee in Follow-up and Publication of Results' (2003) 361 The Lancet 1015–16.

[95] *Guidelines on the Practice of Ethics Committees in Medical Research with Human Participants*, 4th edn (RCP: London, 2007).

[96] Para 19.

have well-developed systems for testing and providing high-quality health care to their populations, and poorer countries, where the system for delivering medical care is inadequate to meet the whole population's health needs.

Inadequate health care, and the resulting high rates of disease, disability, and premature mortality, are a major problem in the world's poorest nations. Less than 10 per cent of the $100+ billion spent on medical research each year is devoted to diseases which account for 90 per cent of the global disease burden: this is commonly referred to as the '10/90 gap'. Research into low-cost treatments for diseases, such as malaria and tuberculosis, which principally affect the populations of poorer nations, is desperately needed. It would therefore be a mistake to ban all externally sponsored research which addresses those countries' distinctive health needs. In some poorer countries, 'western' diseases such as type II diabetes and heart disease, are becoming more common, and so affordable treatments for these conditions are also desperately needed.

However, the adverse publicity and potentially crippling legal actions that sponsors of research may face when trials go wrong in developed countries offer a compelling incentive for companies to conduct research in places where they are much less likely to be held to account for engaging in dangerous research practices. In the next extract, Benjamin Mason Meier explains how the governments of poor countries are themselves sometimes complicit in ensuring that researchers face comparatively few obstacles when planning clinical trials.

Benjamin Mason Meier[97]

National regulation of human experimentation differs dramatically between developed and developing, particularly African, nations. Many African nations lack any legislative protections for subjects of medical research. To a large degree, this legislative vacuum is intentional. While governments of these nations are desperate to bring medical research to their dying populations, their nations cannot afford such research without subsidies from multinational pharmaceutical corporations. To court these pharmaceutical corporations, African nations vie to minimize regulation on the conduct of medical research. They fear that legislation, and resulting lawsuits, could have a chilling effect on beneficial research efforts. As a result, African nations have shown great reluctance to impose any restrictions on human research, thereby creating a medical 'race to the bottom' at the expense of human rights and human life.

Because the risk of exploitation is undoubtedly real, the principal task for regulations must therefore be to ensure that high-quality research capable of improving the lives of people in the world's poorest nations is encouraged, while also ensuring that these countries do not become the pharmaceutical industry's 'sweat shop'.

Most codes of ethics suggest that western companies should only carry out research in poorer countries where that research is likely to benefit the host nation. The Helsinki Declaration provides that:

Medical research involving a disadvantaged or vulnerable population or community is only justified if the research is responsive to the health needs and priorities of this population or

---

[97] 'International Protection of Persons Undergoing Medical Experimentation: Protecting the Right of Informed Consent' (2001) 20 Berkeley Journal of International Law 513.

> community and if there is a reasonable likelihood that this population or community stands to benefit from the results of the research.[98]

Similarly, the Nuffield Council on Bioethics' report on *The Ethics of Research Related to Healthcare in Developing Countries* suggested that externally sponsored research should 'fall within the ambit of the national priorities for research related to health care in developing countries'.[99]

It is also important to recognize that incentives to participation in research may work differently in extremely poor countries. Not only might comparatively small sums of money be disproportionately attractive, but also simply taking part in a research trial holds out the possibility of receiving medical care that might not otherwise be available. Regular contact with a team of health care professionals will enable any unrelated medical condition to be diagnosed and treated more speedily than normal. The offer of any medical care at all, as the Nuffield Council on Bioethics explains, offers a considerable incentive to participation.

Nuffield Council on Bioethics[100]

> 6.30 Guaranteed healthcare or a payment offered to individuals on condition that they take part in a research project could be considered to be exploitative if otherwise there is a very low probability of receiving such a benefit. This contrast in benefits, depending on whether an individual enrols in research is particularly important in developing countries...Research ethics committees should bear this in mind when assessing whether it is acceptable to conduct research projects which may involve more than minimal risk. In such circumstances special care should be taken when determining the nature of additional healthcare to be offered to participants as an inducement.

In some developing countries, it may be usual practice for decisions—such as whether to participate in research—to be taken by the leader of the community, or a senior family member, rather than by the individual herself. Does respect for cultural difference demand that consent should be sought from this authority figure, or is the duty to obtain the individual subject's free and informed consent a universal moral requirement?

The CIOMS Guidelines recommend that seeking consent from someone other than the research subject may sometimes be advisable in order to show appropriate respect for a community's cultural traditions, but that it could never replace the additional need to obtain the subject's own consent.

Commentary on Guideline 4: Individual informed consent

> In some cultures an investigator may enter a community to conduct research or approach prospective subjects for their individual consent only after obtaining permission from a community leader, a council of elders, or another designated authority. Such customs must be

---

[98] World Medical Association, Declaration of Helsinki: Ethical Principles for Medical Research Involving Human Subjects, para 17 (6th version adopted at the 59th WMA General Assembly, Seoul, South Korea Oct 2008), available at <www.wma.net>.

[99] Nuffield Council on Bioethics, The Ethics of Research Related to Healthcare in Developing Countries, Apr 2002, available at <www.nuffieldbioethics.org.uk>.

[100] Ibid.

respected. In no case, however, may the permission of a community leader or other authority substitute for individual informed consent.[101]

The Nuffield Council on Bioethics further recommends that where an individual does not wish to participate in research, despite the community leader's agreement, researchers have a duty to facilitate their non-participation.

Nuffield Council on Bioethics[102]

6.22 We recommend that, in circumstances where consent to research is required, genuine consent to participate in research must be obtained from each participant. In some cultural contexts it may be appropriate to obtain agreement from the community or assent from a senior family member before a prospective participant is approached. If a prospective participant does not wish to take part in research this must be respected. Researchers must not enrol such individuals and have a duty to facilitate their non-participation.

Another ethical problem that arises when research is carried out in developing countries is the extent of the researchers' obligations towards the community after the trial is over. Should researchers be under a duty to make treatments which have been proved effective available to all of the participants in the trial, or to the wider community as well? If the research subjects have benefited from better general health care during the trial, is there an obligation to continue to provide this level of care once the trial has ended?

It would be difficult to compel drugs companies to assume responsibility for *all* of the future health needs of developing countries, but providing post-trial access to the participants themselves is a different matter. Of course, not all trials result in beneficial medicines, and many participants do not need continuing access to drugs. In Phase I studies, for example, volunteers do not suffer from the condition which the medicine is supposed to treat, and so it makes no sense to suggest that the pharmaceutical companies should pay for them to have access to the medicine in question. However, where the trial has led to the development of a new intervention, which benefited the research participants, and where those people would not be able to access that intervention through their national health system, post-trial provision is increasingly regarded as an ethical requirement.

The Helsinki Declaration provides that post-trial access arrangements should be set out in advance, and subjects themselves are entitled to access to interventions which have been proved beneficial. Para 17 states that 'medical research involving a disadvantaged or vulnerable population or community is only justified if the research is responsive to the health needs and priorities of this population or community and *if there is a reasonable likelihood that this population or community stands to benefit from the results of the research.*' Furthermore, under para 14 'the protocol should *describe arrangements for post-study access* by study subjects to interventions identified as beneficial in the study or access to other appropriate care or benefits', and para 33 provides that 'At the conclusion of the study, patients entered into the study are entitled to be informed about the outcome of the study

---

[101] International Ethical Guidelines for Biomedical Research Involving Human Subjects, Commentary on Guideline 4: Individual Informed Consent, available at <www.cioms.ch/>.

[102] The Ethics of Research Related to Healthcare in Developing Countries, Apr 2002, available at <www. nuffieldbioethics.org.uk>.

and to share any benefits that result from it, for example, access to interventions identified as beneficial in the study or to other appropriate care or benefits.'

Another important issue raised by conducting trials in poorer countries is the use of placebo controls when their use would not be permitted in the West. In 1997 an article by Peter Lurie and Sidney Wolfe was published in the *New England Journal of Medicine* in which they criticized fifteen placebo-controlled clinical trials, involving 12,000 HIV-positive women in nine countries, which were designed to test whether low-cost treatments might be effective in reducing perinatal (ie mother-to-baby) transmission of the HIV virus.[103] These studies had been designed by, among others, the World Health Organization and UNAIDS, a United Nations agency which coordinates efforts to combat the spread of AIDS.

In developing countries, perinatal transmission of the HIV virus is a major public health problem. UNAIDS estimates that over 1,400 children become infected with HIV every day; 90 per cent of them acquire the virus from their mothers, during pregnancy. And this is despite the existence of an effective means of preventing transmission during pregnancy, which is now standard treatment in the West. The treatment, which is known as the 076 protocol, involves oral and intravenous doses of antiretroviral therapy (Zidovudine, generally known as AZT) to pregnant women throughout pregnancy, and during childbirth; abstaining from breastfeeding; and the provision of AZT to babies for six weeks after birth. On its own, the 076 protocol reduces transmission rates from 25 per cent to 8 per cent, and delivery by caesarean section can further reduce the risk of infection. When all possible precautions are taken, only about 1 per cent of infants born to HIV-positive mothers will themselves be infected.

Despite HIV infection in infancy being a largely preventable disease in the West, there are several reasons why it is impossible to offer the 076 protocol in most developing countries. First, it is prohibitively expensive, costing approximately one hundred times more than the average *per capita* health expenditure in many of the world's poorest countries. Secondly, it requires the intensive provision of health services throughout pregnancy and after childbirth. Such services will often simply be unavailable in poor countries. For example, early pregnancy testing is essential, and it must be possible to provide AZT intravenously during childbirth. Thirdly, in countries without clean water supplies, abstaining from breastfeeding will in fact represent a greater threat to infant health than that posed by HIV transmission.

The controversial trials that were the subject of the *New England Journal of Medicine* article were directed towards addressing this problem by testing whether a simpler and cheaper course of treatment could nevertheless reduce transmission rates. The studies were randomized-controlled trials, in which one group of HIV-positive pregnant women received a short course of AZT during the last four weeks of pregnancy, and a control group received a placebo. Following positive preliminary results from a trial in Thailand, in which perinatal transmission rates among breastfeeding women were halved (19 per cent of babies in the control group were infected, compared with 9 per cent of the babies whose mothers received the short course of AZT), the research was halted. Controversy continues, however, over whether these trials should ever have taken place.

In short, the problem was that the control group was given a placebo despite the existence, in the West, of effective treatment to prevent perinatal HIV transmission. And it has been estimated that before the trials were stopped, over 1,000 babies in the control group became infected with the HIV virus. This would appear to conflict with two basic ethical principles.

[103] 'Unethical Trials of Interventions to Reduce Perinatal Transmission of the Human Immunodeficiency Virus in Developing Countries' (1997) 337 New England Journal of Medicine 853–6.

First, Principle II(3) of the version of the Helsinki Declaration which applied in 1997 appeared to permit placebo controlled trials only where no treatment exists.

> In any medical study, every patient—including those of a control group, if any—should be assured of the *best proven* diagnostic and therapeutic method. This does not exclude the use of an inert placebo where no proven diagnostic or therapeutic method exists. (my emphasis)

Using a placebo control in these HIV trials deprived the patients in the control group of the 'best proven' treatment to prevent the perinatal transmission of the HIV virus, namely the 076 protocol.

Secondly, could it really be said that a state of equipoise existed over which treatment was best for the patients? Because the 076 protocol had already been *proved* to be extremely effective, it might be argued that the requisite uncertainty in the scientific community which justifies imposing risks on research subjects was absent.

Lurie and Wolfe accused researchers of exploiting subjects by withholding treatment which is provided as standard in developed nations. Deviating from the duty to provide a control group with the 'best proven' treatment was criticized on the grounds that it introduces a double standard in research, whereby subjects in rich countries are guaranteed a higher level of care than those from poorer nations. Not only does this offend basic egalitarian principles, it also offers a compelling incentive for sponsors of research trials to locate them in countries where subjects can legitimately be offered a lower standard of care.

P Lurie and SM Wolfe[104]

> What are the potential implications of accepting such a double standard? Researchers might inject live malaria parasites into HIV-positive subjects in China in order to study the effect on the progression of HIV infection, even though the study protocol had been rejected in the United States and Mexico. Or researchers might randomly assign malnourished San (bushmen) to receive vitamin-fortified or standard bread. One might also justify trials of HIV vaccines in which the subjects were not provided with condoms or state-of-the-art counseling about safe sex by arguing that they are not customarily provided in the developing countries in question. These are not simply hypothetical worst-case scenarios; the first two studies have already been performed, and the third has been proposed and criticized...
>
> Residents of impoverished, postcolonial countries, the majority of whom are people of color, must be protected from potential exploitation in research. Otherwise, the abominable state of health care in these countries can be used to justify studies that could never pass ethical muster in the sponsoring country.... It is time to develop standards of research that preclude the kinds of double standards evident in these trials.... Tragically, for the hundreds of infants who have needlessly contracted HIV infection in the perinatal-transmission studies that have already been completed, any such protection will have come too late.

In contrast, supporters of the trials argued that local solutions to the burden of disease should be sought, and that research capable of having practical application in poor countries

---

[104] Ibid.

should not be stopped in order to ease Western consciences. No woman in the control group was actually any worse off than she would have been if she had not enrolled in the trial, and using a placebo control meant that statistically significant results could be obtained quickly. It was further argued that the 076 protocol had only been proved effective in well-nourished populations with a low incidence of anaemia. Since AZT can exacerbate anaemia, it was necessary to test it against a placebo in order to ascertain its effectiveness in populations in which anaemia and malnutrition are common. Because this requirement that a control group must be given the 'best proven' treatment appeared to hamper research into cheaper alternatives, several commentators suggested that it should be replaced by a duty to give the control group the 'best attainable' or 'best current' treatment.

The Helsinki Declaration has since been revised, and rather than providing that subjects must receive the best proven treatment, para 32 now states that 'The benefits, risks, burdens and effectiveness of a new intervention must be tested against those of the *best current proven intervention.*'[105] The CIOMS Guidelines more specifically address the use of placebo or other controls in research into low-cost interventions in poorer countries.

CIOMS[106]

Commentary on Guideline 11: Choice of control in clinical trials

An exception to the general rule is applicable in some studies designed to develop a therapeutic, preventive or diagnostic intervention for use in a country or community in which an established effective intervention is not available and unlikely in the foreseeable future to become available, usually for economic or logistic reasons. The purpose of such a study is to make available to the population of the country or community an effective alternative to an established effective intervention that is locally unavailable. . . . [T]he scientific and ethical review committees must be satisfied that the established effective intervention cannot be used as comparator because its use would not yield scientifically reliable results that would be relevant to the health needs of the study population. In these circumstances an ethical review committee can approve a clinical trial in which the comparator is other than an established effective intervention, such as placebo or no treatment or a local remedy.

In the debates over the ethical legitimacy of these trials, the prohibitive cost of optimum treatment was often taken for granted. It is, however, important to remember that, while it may have cost a lot to develop, AZT is not, in fact, expensive to manufacture, and could have been made cheaply by pharmaceutical companies in poor countries, particularly because the R&D costs will already have been recouped from sales in richer countries. One reason why developing countries could not afford to provide the 076 protocol is that the TRIPS Agreement allowed one company to hold the global patent on AZT for twenty years, during which time no generic equivalent could be produced. Permitting poor countries to manufacture generic versions of expensive patented drugs within this 20-year period might offer

[105] World Medical Association, Declaration of Helsinki: Ethical Principles for Medical Research Involving Human Subjects (6th version adopted at the 59th WMA General Assembly, Seoul, South Korea Oct 2008), available at <www.wma.net>.

[106] International Ethical Guidelines for Biomedical Research Involving Human Subjects, available at <www.cioms.ch/>.

a more ethically defensible solution to the problem of unaffordable medicines than permitting a double standard in research ethics.

In response to pressure from African countries, in 2001 the World Trade Organization issued a *Declaration on the TRIPS Agreement and Public Health* at Doha, which allows developing countries to seek a waiver on public health grounds from the TRIPS Agreement. The new agreement states that the TRIPS Agreement:

> [C]an and should be interpreted and implemented in a manner supportive of WTO members' right to protect public health and, in particular, to promote access to medicines for all.

This means that public health concerns, particularly in an emergency, can, in certain circumstances, override intellectual property rights. Shortly after the Doha agreement, GlaxoSmithKline granted a voluntary licence to a South African manufacturer to produce generic versions of AZT and 3TC (another antiretroviral drug) to be sold only to the South African government and NGOs. AZT came out of patent protection in 2007.

While the perinatal transmission HIV trials may have been especially controversial, the ethical dilemmas raised by conducting AIDS-related research in developing countries extend far beyond this one example. HIV vaccine trials, for example, must be conducted in populations that are particularly at risk from contracting all the various forms of the HIV virus. Not only do most new infections now occur in developing countries, but there are also different strains of the HIV virus, some of which are prevalent only in certain parts of the world.

Trials of HIV vaccines raise exceptionally difficult ethical questions. For a new vaccine to be proved effective, it is necessary to test it in a population in which new infections are likely to be occurring, and to establish that the rate of infection in the vaccinated group is lower than that of the control group. This immediately introduces a conflict of interest for researchers, since it is in the interests of their study that members of the control group are not universally successful in preventing HIV infection through behaviour modification. It would, however, clearly be unethical to withhold information about preventative measures from the control group.

There is also the danger that participants in a vaccine trial may wrongly believe themselves to be protected against the HIV virus, and as a result may engage in riskier behaviour than they would otherwise, thus *increasing* their risk of infection. As we saw earlier, people taking part in research trials do not always understand the concept of randomization, so they may not fully grasp that being allocated to the control group will mean that they receive no protection at all against transmission. Furthermore, participants may not realize that even if they are in the 'active' arm of the trial, the vaccine has not yet been proved effective in preventing transmission of the HIV virus, and so should not be relied upon as a precautionary measure.

10 COMPENSATION FOR INJURIES

If a subject did not consent to her participation in a research trial, she could—in theory—bring an action in battery (see further Chapter 4). However, because a person who takes part in a research project will usually have signed a consent form, it will be difficult for her to establish that she was not informed 'in broad terms'[107] about the nature of the trial.

---

[107] *Chatterton v Gerson* [1981] QB 432.

If a subject suffers injury during a research trial, she might be able to claim that the researcher, who would undoubtedly owe her a duty of care, was in breach of that duty. This might happen in two ways. First, a person could be injured as a result of negligence in the design or execution of the research project. Secondly, the information provided to the subject, although sufficient to avoid a charge of battery, may have been inadequate, and amount to a breach of the researcher's duty of care. In this latter situation, the research subject will have to establish that she would not have consented to take part in the research trial if she had been provided with the relevant information, and hence would not have suffered whatever injury has materialized as a result of her participation.

Where it is the design of the research project that caused the subject's injuries, could the members of the REC also be liable for failing to notice that the protocol itself was defective? It could be argued that it is foreseeable that negligent approval of a dangerous research project will cause injury, and that there is a relationship of proximity between the REC and the research subjects. But would it be fair, just, and reasonable to impose liability on the members of the REC? There have been no cases in which injured research subjects have sued REC members, and such actions are improbable given the much deeper pockets of other potential defendants, such as an NHS trust and/or a pharmaceutical company. The Department of Health did address this concern in its 1991 *Guidelines on Local Research Ethics Committees*, and its advice then was that there would be little chance of a successful claim against an REC member:

> Legal advice available to the Department of Health is that there is little prospect of a successful claim against an LREC member for a mishap arising from research approved as ethical by the LREC. Any such claim would lie principally against the researcher concerned and against the NHS body under the auspices of which the research took place.[108]

As we saw in Chapter 3, victims of medical mishaps face numerous obstacles when bringing actions in negligence, and this will be equally true for individuals who have been injured during research rather than treatment. It has, however, been argued that people injured during research trials should not have to overcome all of the hurdles that the tort of negligence places in the path of those seeking compensation for injuries sustained during ordinary medical treatment. The Pearson Commission, for example, had advocated a 'no fault' compensation scheme for people injured during medical research, drawing an analogy with the statutory compensation offered to people injured by vaccination programmes. The community as a whole benefits from both vaccination and research, and should therefore offer adequate compensation for the small proportion of the population who will suffer injuries as a result. Their proposal was never implemented.

Regulation 15(5) of the Medicines for Human Use (Clinical Trials) Regulations 2004 provides that RECs should take into account the provision for indemnity or compensation in the event of injury or death attributable to the clinical trial, and the existence of any insurance or indemnity to cover liability of the investigator or sponsor.

It might also be thought that the adverse publicity, which would result from a court action in which a pharmaceutical company was sued for injuries inflicted on a research subject, represents a powerful incentive towards the making of *ex gratia* payments. Certainly, the Association of the British Pharmaceutical Industry (ABPI)'s guidelines recommend that

---

[108] Department of Health, Guidelines on Local Research Ethics Committees (DH: London, 1991) para 2.11, available at <www.dh.gov.uk>.

compensation should be paid, even if the victim cannot establish negligence. Not having to prove fault will undoubtedly make it easier to obtain compensation, but it should be remembered that the subject still has to establish causation, which will sometimes—as we saw in Chapter 3—be a significant obstacle, particularly where the subject is a patient whose pre-existing condition offers another plausible explanation for any deterioration in their condition.

The assumption that the pharmaceutical industry would be unlikely to leave those injured in drugs trials undercompensated, for fear of adverse publicity, has been challenged in the UK by the aftermath of the TGN1412 trials at Northwick Park Hospital. The injured men were offered an interim payment of £5,000 in return for an agreement not to sue, but they rejected this. It has emerged that the German company TeGenero, which manufactured TGN 1412 and was subsequently declared insolvent, only had insurance coverage of £2 million. The men involved have instituted legal proceedings against Parexel, the company which ran the trial, in order to force them to reveal data about the men's health which their lawyers argue is vital in order to calculate appropriate levels of compensation.

11 CONCLUSION

Throughout this chapter, we have seen that there is generally assumed to be a sharp distinction between research and ordinary medical treatment. In particular, in relation to research, there is undoubtedly a duty to obtain 'informed consent', whereas, as we saw in Chapter 4, the judiciary has been slow to introduce the 'doctrine of informed consent' for routine medical treatment. People who volunteer to take part in research are regarded as more vulnerable and dependent, and in greater need of clear and frank information than patients. But is this special concern for research subjects justified?

On the one hand, the long history of the abuse of research subjects should undoubtedly alert us to the need to have protective mechanisms in place to ensure that vulnerable individuals do not end up taking part in research without knowing that this is what they are doing, or without being given the option of refusal. Yet on the other hand, it is worth remembering that the decision to consent to treatment will also sometimes be a difficult decision, which requires an individual to balance risks and benefits, some of which may be uncertain and speculative. Rather than viewing research subjects as uniquely vulnerable and in need of a great deal of sensitively provided information, perhaps we should acknowledge that patients too are often faced with complex decisions, and with information which may be difficult for them to understand and evaluate.

A final interesting distinction between patients and research subjects is the insistence, in the Helsinki Declaration, that any control group should be assured of the 'best current treatment'. Again, this draws a sharp distinction between participants in research and patients. Within the NHS at least, patients are indubitably *not* assured of the best current treatment. Rather, it is generally accepted that limited resources mean that sometimes less than optimal treatment may have to be provided in order to ensure that the NHS can continue to run a comprehensive health service. As we saw in Chapter 2, the reality of rationed health care is that patients are deprived of beneficial treatment. If it is absolutely clear that patients do not have the right to demand the 'best current' treatment, is it anomalous that participating in research, in theory at least, gives subjects precisely this right?

FURTHER READING

Ferguson, Pamela, 'Clinical Trials and Healthy Volunteers' (2008) 16 Medical Law Review 23–51.

Foster, Claire, *The Ethics of Medical Research on Humans* (CUP: Cambridge, 2001).

Fox, Marie, 'Research Bodies: Feminist Perspectives on Clinical Research' in S Sheldon and M Thomson (eds), *Feminist Perspectives on Health Care Law* (Cavendish: London, 1998) 115–34.

Harris, John, 'Scientific Research is a Moral Duty' (2005) 31 Journal of Medical Ethics 242–8.

Lewis, Penny, 'Procedures that are Against the Medical Interests of Incompetent Adults' (2002) 22(4) Oxford Journal of Legal Studies 575–618.

Liddell, K *et al.*, 'Medical Research Involving Incapacitated Adults: Implications of the EU Clinical Trials Directive 2001/20/EC' (2006) 14 Medical Law Review 367–417.

Weisstub, David N (ed.), *Research on Human Subjects: Ethics, Law and Social Policy* (Elsevier: Oxford, 1998).

10

PRODUCT LIABILITY AND THE REGULATION OF MEDICINES

CENTRAL ISSUES

1. Before any new medicine can be put into circulation, it must have a marketing authorization.

2. European regulation is increasingly important in relation to the licensing and marketing of medicines, and it has two aims: to harmonize consumer protection regimes and to facilitate the free movement of goods.

3. The difficulty in using negligence to compensate patients for drug-related injuries is demonstrated by the case of thalidomide. Thalidomide had caused disabling and sometimes fatal injuries, but it would have been difficult to prove that its manufacturer had been negligent.

4. The Consumer Protection Act 1987 implemented a European directive and introduced strict liability for injuries caused by defective products. There has been less litigation than was initially anticipated, and hardly any cases involving medicines.

5. Causation represents a significant obstacle to recovery for drug-related injuries, in part because patients who take medicines are already ill, and in part because injuries may only manifest themselves many years later, when it might be difficult to identify which manufacturer's drug caused the injuries.

1 INTRODUCTION

In this chapter, we consider the regulation of medicines. Although the availability of safe and effective pharmaceutical drugs is not the only factor that has contributed to increased life expectancy in the past hundred years—better sanitation and nutrition have also been vitally important—there is no doubt that the increasing availability of effective medicines has significantly improved public health.[1] The development of penicillin, antibiotics, and

[1] Jasper Woodcock, 'Medicines—The Interested Parties' in R Blum *et al.* (eds) *Pharmaceuticals and Health Policy: International Perspectives on Provision and Control of Medicines* (Croom Helm: London, 1981) 27–35.

vaccines against diseases such as tuberculosis (TB) and polio, means that it is now comparatively rare for people living in the world's richest countries to die from infectious diseases,
and it is the degenerative diseases of old age, such as cancer and heart disease, which have
become the most common causes of death. But while medicines have undoubtedly helped
to transform the health of people living in the West, their availability in poorer countries
continues to be inadequate.

In the West huge profits can be made from successful drugs. In 2006, Pfizer earned
$12.9 billion from one drug alone, Lipitor (an anti-cholesteral drug, or statin). An effective
treatment for depression or obesity is likely to generate much higher profits than a cure for a
'neglected disease', like malaria or sleeping sickness. A 2002 *British Medical Journal* editorial spelled out the problem.

British Medical Journal[2]

[O]ut of 1393 new drugs marketed between 1975 and 1999, only 16 were for neglected diseases, yet these diseases accounted for over 10% of the global disease burden. In contrast,
over two thirds of new drugs were 'me too drugs' (modified versions of existing drugs),
which do little or nothing to change the disease burden...

When it comes to the world's most neglected diseases, however, these present absolutely no market opportunities. Without such opportunities, there is no incentive for the
pharmaceutical industry to invest in drug research and development. The patients have no
purchasing power, no vocal advocacy group is pleading for their needs, and no strategic
interests—military or security—are driving concern about these conditions.

For example, sleeping sickness, which claims thousands of lives annually in Africa, can be
considered as a most neglected disease. Current drug treatments are in scarce supply, difficult to administer, and often toxic. Melarsoprol, which was developed over 50 years ago, kills
up to 10% of people who are given the drug, and in some regions drug resistance means it
is ineffective in a third of patients. An effective, less toxic drug, has been developed—eflornithine—but the company that developed it stopped its production in 1995, citing commercial failure. African patients could not afford to buy the drug. Eflornithine became available
again five years later in the United States, when it was found to reduce unwanted facial hair
in women.

The drive to provide a pharmacological solution to an ever-increasing number of problems is sometimes referred to as 'medicalization'. The menopause can be 'treated' with
hormone replacement therapy; medication exists for behavioural difficulties in children;
and drugs can be used to combat conditions such as baldness, obesity, anxiety, and sexual
impotence.

The research and development of new drugs involves enormous financial investment. On
average it takes between ten and twelve years to develop a new medicine.[3] For every 10,000
compounds which are synthesized, tested, and developed, only one or two will ultimately reach the market,[4] and 90 per cent of compounds which get as far as the preclinical

---

2 'The World's Most Neglected Diseases' (2002) 325 British Medical Journal 176–7.
3 Zosia Kmietowicz, 'Regulations are Stifling Development of New Drugs' (2004) 328 British Medical
Journal 600.
4 Richard Sykes, *New Medicines, The Practice of Medicine, and Public Policy* (Nuffield Trust: London,
2000) 65.

development stage will fail before launch.[5] The money invested in these failures, which runs into hundreds of millions of pounds, inevitably increases the price of successful drugs.

In order to recoup their investment, pharmaceutical companies are allowed to hold the patent on any new drug for twenty years, during which time they have the right to prevent others from making or selling an identical product.[6] Of course, some of this patent term will expire while the drug is being tested, and so in reality firms may enjoy only ten years of 'on the market' patent protection. Nevertheless, generic versions of drugs, which are much more affordable, cannot be produced until this period is over. A good example of the impact of patent protection was AZT, an antiretroviral drug capable of substantially delaying the onset of AIDS. During its period of patent protection, many of the world's poorest countries simply could not afford to provide it to their HIV-positive populations.

There is some evidence that pharmaceutical companies attempt to delay or block competition from generic manufacturers. One strategy, described by the House of Commons Health Select Committee, is to make a number of minor modifications to the patented drug, known as 'evergreening'.

House of Commons Health Select Committee[7]

Evergreening involves extending the patented life of a branded product, typically by reformulating the drug, for instance by using a different drug delivery system, changing a dosage form, or presentation (e.g. from tablet to capsule)....

The significance of evergreening is underlined by the increased range of drug attributes eligible for patent protection....In the 1990s, the list extended protection in relation to range of use, methods of treatment, mechanism of action, packaging, delivery profiles, dosing route, regimen and range, drug combinations, screening and analytical methods, biological targets and field of use.

The British Generic Manufacturers Association (BGMA) listed five examples in which the originating company had employed evergreening methods, resulting in little or no therapeutic gain, but at a cost to the NHS estimated between £164 and £369 million.

A particularly audacious example of 'evergreening' happened in the US when Prozac, an anti-depressant, was about to lose its patent protection. Prozac's manufacturer, Eli Lilly, rebranded the active ingredient—fluoxetine—by producing pink and lavender pills (Prozac was green and white), naming it Sarafem, and marketing it for the treatment of premenstrual dysphoric disorder.

Although intellectual property rights undoubtedly raise the price of medicines, and hence might not appear to be in the interests of consumers, the counter argument is that, without them, investing in research and development would be so risky that the development of innovative medicines would be stifled, and ultimately public health would suffer. This claim is disputed in the next extract by MN Graham Dukes, who argues that the pharmaceutical industry's commercial accountability to shareholders takes priority over its accountability to communities.

---

[5] Ibid.

[6] Patent Act 1977 s 25(1). World Trade Organization (WTO) Agreement on Trade-Related Intellectual Property Rights (TRIPS), Art 33.

[7] The Influence of the Pharmaceutical Industry Fourth Report of Session 2004–05, available at <www.publications.parliament.uk>.

MN Graham Dukes[8]

> Two definitions of industry accountability predominate: commercial duty to shareholders; and duty to the community.
>
> In the commercial sense, a pharmaceutical company is obliged to deliver a sound return on investment for shareholders. That return must be adequate to reward investors but also be sufficient to attract new capital when needed. From this point of view, the pharmaceutical industry has done very well. Throughout periods of economic stagnation and even recession over the past 30 years, it has remained highly and increasingly profitable....
>
> From the broad social point of view, the pharmaceutical industry has a duty to supply communities with good drugs at an affordable price, and to provide reliable information on them...The much-repeated argument from pharmaceutical companies, that high drug prices are mainly attributable to research costs, merits cautious scrutiny. With publicly available data, we can ascertain that costs of advertising and promotion generally much exceed research expenditure. Furthermore, industrial research usually benefits from public support, either in the form of tax breaks or as direct scientific input.

A good example of the point Graham Dukes is making here comes from so-called 'orphan' drugs, which are defined by the European Medicines Agency as:

> • intended for the diagnosis, prevention or treatment of a life-threatening or chronically debilitating condition affecting no more than five in 10,000 persons in the European Union, or
>
> • intended for the diagnosis, prevention or treatment of a life-threatening, seriously debilitating or serious and chronic condition and without incentives it is unlikely that expected sales of the medicinal product would cover the investment in its development.[9]

Because it is recognized that developing such drugs is unlikely to be profitable, and hence will be a low priority for companies who have to maintain shareholder value, a system of tax breaks and incentives is in place to ensure that people with rare diseases are not 'abandoned' by the pharmaceutical industry. Within Europe, six million Euros of public money are set aside each per year to provide drug manufacturers with incentives to produce orphan drugs.

For a number of reasons, medicines are unlike other products. First, in the case of prescribed drugs, purchase decisions are generally not taken by the consumers themselves, but by their professional advisers, neither of whom will actually be paying the market rate for the medicine.

Secondly, any medicine which is powerful enough to cure disease or alleviate symptoms will also be strong enough to cause adverse side-effects in at least some consumers, and these can sometimes be extremely serious. If complete safety is unattainable, deciding when a medicine is safe *enough* involves a complex risk/benefit calculation. For example, chemotherapy has extremely unpleasant side-effects, which would not be worth putting up with in a medicine which treated a comparatively trivial condition, such as hayfever, but which might be outweighed by the possible benefit of curing cancer.

Thirdly, the cultural and symbolic significance of medicines is amply demonstrated by the placebo effect, which we considered in the previous chapter. The placebo effect is also at

---

[8] 'Accountability of the Pharmaceutical Industry' (2002) 260 The Lancet 1682–4.
[9] Orphan Drugs and Rare Diseases at a Glance, EMEA (2007).

work, as Jacky Law explains, when the same active ingredient is marketed, often under different names, for a range of different purposes.

Jacky Law[10]

The drugs work according to what the label says, what the doctor says, and what we believe. Our minds and bodies respond, in other words, to what the label says, to what we are told the drug will do. GlaxoSmithKline's Zyban for smoking cessation, for example, is a long-acting form of Wellbutin for depression, by another name. And Organon's antidepressant, Zispin is also marketed for sleeping disorders…Many lifestyle drugs are prescribed under a number of different names. Different studies are done to get different licensing data to get them known as different drugs so they can operate in different markets.

The active ingredient, however, remains the same. As such, the various effects the drugs have can be put down to the response elicited from expectation. What makes a smoker more likely to kick their habit on Zyban than on the identical drug posing as an antidepressant is the fact that this is what the doctor says, what the label says, and what the data from clinical studies corroborate.

Such drugs are a triumph of branding.

The role of regulation in this area is complex. First, since the rules only apply to medicines, a clear definition of what counts as a medicine is necessary. Secondly, it is important to ensure that drugs are both safe and effective, and next we examine the licensing process in the UK. Thirdly, we consider the increasing standardization of the regulation of medicines within the European Union. Finally, we consider the law's response to defective medicines, examining in turn the role of contract, negligence, and statute, most notably the Consumer Protection Act 1987.

At the outset it is worth noting that government policy in this area will be influenced by a number of competing factors, which may pull in different directions. On the one hand, the government has an interest in containing costs within the NHS, which might lead it to consider restricting access to new and expensive drugs. Yet the government will also be concerned to improve patient care, and in contrast that might mean expanding access to effective medicines. Because the pharmaceutical industry is phenomenally profitable, and a major employer—it invests around £4 billion each year on R&D in the UK[11]—the government has a further clear interest in ensuring that the UK is an attractive location for the industry, by, for example, making sure that its licensing processes are not overly cumbersome and that its product liability regime does not stifle innovation. At the same time, however, the government's interest in promoting patient safety might be best served by onerous licensing requirements and strict liability for drug-related injuries.

2 WHAT IS A MEDICINE?

(a) DEFINING MEDICINAL PRODUCTS

In practice, it will sometimes be difficult to determine whether something, such as a food supplement or an herbal remedy, is a medicine. Because the Medicines Act 1968 applies

---

[10] *Big Pharma: Exposing the Global Healthcare Agenda* (Carrol and Graf: NY, 2006) 63–4.
[11] See further <www.abpi.org.uk>.

only to medicinal products, it is obviously important to be able to tell whether a particular product needs a marketing authorization. This is a job for the Medicines and Healthcare products Regulatory Agency (MHRA), previously the Medicines Control Agency (MCA). As we can see from *R v Medicines Control Agency, ex parte Pharma Nord*, the courts will be slow to interfere with the Agency's determination of whether or not something is a medicinal product. In this case, the applicants had marketed melatonin tablets in the UK. The MCA informed manufacturers, importers, distributors, and retailers of unlicensed melatonin that, in its view, melatonin was a medicinal product and should only be supplied on prescription. The applicants argued that melatonin was similar to vitamin pills, which are freely on sale in the UK, without the need for a licence. The applicants applied for judicial review, arguing that the MCA's reasons for classifying melatonin as a medicinal product were inadequate and not in accordance with EC Directive 65/65. Recognizing that they were unlikely to succeed in proving *Wednesbury*[12] unreasonableness, they sought a full trial on the merits of whether melatonin should be considered a medicinal product. Collins J refused to exercise his discretion to transfer the case to the civil courts, and the Court of Appeal dismissed the applicant's appeal.

R v Medicines Control Agency, ex parte Pharma Nord[13]

Lord Woolf MR

1. Under European and domestic law it is the MCA which has the initial heavy responsibility of protecting the public against the dangers to health which can result from the unlicensed marketing of medicinal products. It is also the MCA's equally important initial responsibility to decide what is or is not a medicinal product. Unless it determines that a substance is a medicinal product there is no action which it can lawfully take to control its use....

4. The determination of the facts and the application of the policy in a case such as this are not ideally suited to the adversarial processes of the courts. If the case was one where the MCA could not reasonably have come to the decision which it did so that the outcome was one which is conventionally determined on applications for judicial review, the position would be different. However, in this case the MCA is in a better position to evaluate the evidence than a judge. It has accumulated experience in relation to other products which a court lacks. It is an expert body. The MCA has to develop a consistent policy between similar products. The issues are...ones in relation to which the court should be wary of becoming involved...

6. ...[W]here what is involved is reasonably regarded by the MCA as a medicinal product, I do not consider that, as a matter of discretion, the civil courts should readily exercise their discretionary declaratory jurisdiction to reinvestigate the facts in civil proceedings against the wishes of the MCA.

So how does the Agency decide whether a product is a medicine? 'Medicinal products' are defined in the Codified Pharmaceutical Directive, as amended,[14] as follows:

(a) Any substance or combination of substances presented as having properties for treating or preventing disease in human beings;

---

[12] That is, that the decision was so unreasonable that no reasonable regulator could have taken it. *Associated Provincial Picture Houses v Wednesbury Corporation* [1948] 1 KB 223.
[13] (1998) 44 BMLR 41.   [14] 2001/83/EEC.

> (b) Any substance or combination of substances which may be used in or administered to human beings either with a view to restoring, correcting or modifying physiological functions by exerting a pharmacological, immunological or metabolic action, or to making a medical diagnosis.

The two limbs of this test refer to *presentation* and *function*. In short, if a product is marketed for the treatment or prevention of disease, or used for diagnostic purposes, or to alter physiological function, it is a medicinal product.

When determining whether a product has been *presented* for the treatment of disease, the MHRA will consider any claims—both explicit and implicit—made for it, and will look at the presentation of the product as a whole, including its labelling, packaging, and advertising.[15] Also relevant will be the form the product takes and the way it is to be used: in effect, does it *look like* a medicine? Claims that a product relieves symptoms, such as stress or anxiety, will be regarded as medicinal claims.[16] The reference to 'prevention' means that products which claim to 'protect against' disease will similarly be treated as medicinal products.[17] Claims that a product 'helps to maintain a healthy lifestyle', in contrast, have not been regarded by the MHRA as medicinal claims.[18]

The second limb refers to the medicinal *purpose* of the product. Here it is enough that the product contains active ingredients which are known to have a physiological effect. It is not necessary for the product to also be presented as a medicine. Hence, an herbal remedy, which has an active ingredient in a therapeutic dose, will fall within the definition even if it does not claim to be a medicine.

(b) LIFESTYLE DRUGS AND THE PROBLEM OF ENHANCEMENT

When we think about medicines, we generally assume that people take them when they are unwell, in order to restore their health or alleviate their symptoms. Yet in recent years there has been increasing interest in biomedical enhancements which might be taken not to restore normal functioning, but rather to improve upon it. It is by no means easy to draw a line between enhancements and ordinary medical treatment. Many modern medicines are intended to reverse some of the symptoms of ageing, such as forgetfulness, baldness, and sexual dysfunction. Are these 'enhancements', or attempts to restore 'normal' functioning?

Treatments for recognized disorders can often also be used by people who want to feel 'better than well'.[19] Viagra is used to treat impotence, but it could also be taken by people who want to enhance their sexual performance. An effective treatment for memory loss might be regarded as necessary medical treatment for patients with Alzheimer's Disease, but what if it was prescribed to students to improve their performance in examinations, or obtained by professional chess players in order to gain a competitive advantage?[20] In all three cases, the drug *enhances* memory function, but its social acceptability depends upon the context in which it is taken. In the next extract, Peter Conrad and Deborah Potter discuss how difficult it can be to draw a distinction between therapy and enhancement.

---

[15] MHRA, A Guide to What is a Medicinal Product (MHRA Guidance Note 8, revised 2007).
[16] Ibid.   [17] Ibid.   [18] Ibid.
[19] Carl Elliott, *Better than Well: American Medicine meets the American Dream* (Norton: New York, 2003); Peter Kramer, *Listening to Prozac* (Penguin: New York, 1994).
[20] Peter Conrad and Deborah Potter, 'Human Growth Hormone and the Temptations of Biomedical Enhancement' (2004) 26 Sociology of Health and Illness 184–215.

Peter Conrad and Deborah Potter[21]

[T]he therapy–enhancement line is a thin one…Medical definitions can change; new medical diagnoses can be developed which will justify certain types of enhancement as therapy. In the US in recent years the diagnosis of Adult ADHD [Attention Deficit Hyperactivity Disorder] has become popular, for which Ritalin is often prescribed. Many 'successful' adults have approached their physicians with problems of personal disorganisation, inability to finish projects and difficulty with concentration or focus. Some have diagnosed themselves as having ADHD and sought treatment from physicians…, we have termed this the 'medicalization of underperformance' and raised the issue of whether Ritalin for adults is a treatment or an enhancement…

In a sense, we can see biomedical enhancement as a double temptation: the object itself is tempting (eg several inches of height, younger features or improved performance) *and* the biomedical route to the enhancement is a temptation as well (eg a rapid road to improvement, a technological strategy, a medical solution)….The key to enhancement, however, is that only some are enhanced. There is no edge if it is universal…

Biomedical enhancements do not involve hard work, in fact they are something of a technological fix. It seems likely most people do not…consider runners who raise their aerobic ability and run marathons in under three hours unnatural. Indeed we admire such individuals for their fortitude. They have achieved their enhancement through diligence and hard work, exemplary characteristics in our culture. If women could enhance their breasts at the gym or children increase their height by working out, would unnaturalness be an issue at all?…

[W]e might note that our society has adopted a sort of 'pharmaceutical Calvinism' when it comes to taking medications. This entails a belief that it is better to achieve an objective naturally than with drugs or medications; this includes pleasure, sexual satisfaction, mental stability and bodily fitness. Using drugs is an inferior and even suspect way of reaching a goal.

It is important to recognize that what we consider to be 'normal functioning' is itself socially constructed and culturally variable. As Carl Elliott explains, the pharmaceutical industry has learned that to sell new drugs successfully, it is sometimes first necessary to 'sell' the existence of the disease which they are intended to treat.

Carl Elliott[22]

The pharmaceutical industry…has learned that the key to selling psychiatric drugs is to sell the illnesses they treat. Antidepressants are a case in point. Before the 1960s, clinical depression was thought to be an extremely rare problem. Drug companies stayed away from depression because there was no money to be made in antidepressants. So when Merck started to produce amytriptaline, a tricyclic antidepressant, in the early 1960s, it realised that in order to sell the antidepressant it needed to sell depression.

Forty years later, of course, it is now clear to everyone that the market for antidepressants was not a shallow one at all: that it was, in fact, a tremendously lucrative market, as the remarkable success of Prozac and its sister drugs have demonstrated. The notion of 'clinical depression' has expanded tremendously to include many people who might once have been called melancholic, anxious, or alienated.…

---

[21] Ibid.
[22] *Better than Well: American Medicine meets the American Dream* (Norton: New York, 2003) 123–4.

This does not mean that drug companies are simply making up diseases out of thin air, or that psychiatrists are being gulled into diagnosing well people as sick. No one doubts that some people genuinely suffer from, say, depression, or attention-deficit/hyperactivity disorder, or that the right medications make these disorders better. But surrounding the core of many of these disorders is a wide zone of ambiguity that can be chiseled out and expanded. Pharmaceutical companies have a powerful financial interest in expanding categories of mental disease, because it is only when a certain condition is recognized as a disease that it can be treated with the products the companies produce.

In the next extract, L McHenry goes further and suggests that the whole basis of the 'chemical imbalance' explanation of depression—upon which Selective Serotonin Reuptake Inhibitors depend—is 'probably false'. If depression is 'caused by' serotonin deficiency, a pill to remedy this (which is what SSRIs are supposed to do) would work as a cure for depression. McHenry points out that the evidence that this is the case is weak, and perhaps even non-existent. SSRIs 'work' largely because of the placebo effect. If a sugar pill, suitably packaged, is almost as effective in treating depression, SSRIs may be a colossal waste of money.

L McHenry[23]

Although there seems to be no question about the fact that SSRIs act on the serotonin system, what has not been established is an abnormality of serotonin metabolism in depression or that SSRIs correct a chemical imbalance. Instead of going back to the proverbial drawing board…, however, the pharmaceutical company marketing departments revived the serotonin theory in the late 1980s and channelled all their financial might into promoting the SSRIs. It was a triumph of marketing over science…

The clinical trials that form the basis of Food and Drug Administration (FDA) approval of SSRIs demonstrate repeatedly that these drugs show a clinically negligible advantage over inert placebo (sugar pills) in the treatment of depression….FDA approval, however, only requires that the drugs are better than nothing. According to the best data available, there is a less than 10% difference in the effect of FDA approved antidepressants versus placebo…

The idea of selling us depression, whether we are truly ill or not, has become an immensely lucrative strategy for selling SSRIs, a large part of which succeeds on the basis of the idea of chemical imbalance…. The marketing strategy plays on the public's desire for a quick fix for all the vicissitudes of life and the power of the suggestion contained in the easy to understand model of chemical imbalance…. Approximately 50 to 100 people per million were thought to be depressed before the creation of antidepressants; today our best estimates put the figure at 100,000 to 200,000 people per million.

In the next extract, Ray Moynihan *et al.* use the example of anti-baldness medication to offer another example of industry-sponsored medicalization.

[23] 'Ethical Issues in Psychopharmacology' (2006) 32 Journal of Medical Ethics 405–10.

Ray Moynihan, Iona Heath, David Henry, and Peter C Gøtzsche[24]

There's a lot of money to be made from telling healthy people they're sick. Some forms of medicalising ordinary life may now be better described as disease mongering: widening the boundaries of treatable illness in order to expand markets for those who sell and deliver treatments. Pharmaceutical companies are actively involved in sponsoring the definition of diseases and promoting them to both prescribers and consumers. The social construction of illness is being replaced by the corporate construction of disease...

The medicalisation of baldness shows clearly the transformation of the ordinary processes of life into medical phenomena. Around the time that Merck's hair growth drug finasteride (Propecia) was first approved in Australia, leading newspapers featured new information about the emotional trauma associated with hair loss. The global public relations firm Edelman orchestrated some of the coverage but largely left its fingerprints off the resulting stories. An article...in the *Australian* newspaper featured a new 'study' suggesting that a third of all men experienced some degree of hair loss, along with comments by concerned experts and news that an International Hair Study Institute had been established. It suggested that losing hair could lead to panic and other emotional difficulties, and even have an impact on job prospects and mental wellbeing. The article did not reveal that the study and the institute were both funded by Merck and that the experts quoted had been supplied by Edelman.

So how should doctors respond to patients' requests for so-called 'lifestyle' drugs? In the next extract, the British Medical Association (BMA) suggests that improving a person's quality of life can sometimes be a legitimate use of NHS resources. The contraceptive pill, for example, which is available free of charge on prescription, does not treat any sort of disease, but rather enhances women's quality of life by enabling them to control their fertility.[25] However, the BMA also advises that patients do not have the right to be provided with any drug that they believe will improve their quality of life, especially since all medicines carry some risks, and these may be less acceptable where there is no clinical indication for prescribing the drug in question.

British Medical Association[26]

It is generally accepted that doctors should prescribe medication only if they consider it necessary for the patient, but views of what is 'necessary' differ. More frequent request from patients for what have been termed 'lifestyle drugs', such as antiobesity drugs, antidepressants, and hair loss treatments, illustrate the way in which perceptions of 'clinical need' have changed. Although there are certainly those for whom antidepressants and appetite suppressants are clinically indicated and cannot be considered as lifestyle drugs, for many others they are seen as a quick and easy solution. When in search of a quick fix, it is easier to take medication than to spend time and energy on diet and exercise, or to spend time exploring, through counselling, the root of anxiety or depression...

---

[24] 'Selling Sickness: The Pharmaceutical Industry and Disease Mongering' (2002) 324 British Medical Journal 886–91.

[25] See further, Silvia Pezzini, 'The Effect of Women's Rights on Women's Welfare: Evidence from a Natural Experiment' (2005) 115 The Economic Journal C208.

[26] *Medical Ethics Today: The BMA's Handbook of Ethics and Law*, 2nd edn (BMA: London, 2004) 458–9.

Improving quality of life is, however, a legitimate aim of the health service, so the fact that oral contraceptives fall within this definition does not mean they should not be prescribed within the NHS. Where the boundary lies between what is and what is not acceptable to prescribe with NHS funding, however, is a matter for debate. Until clear guidance is issued, cases should be considered on an individual basis....In addition to the financial considerations, there are also questions of safety. There are inherent risks with virtually all medication and part of the doctor's role is to balance those risks against the anticipated benefits for the patient. When the drug is not clinically indicated, the benefits the patient will, or believes he or she will, derive need to be weighed against the risks. Doctors must be willing to justify their decisions to prescribe in these circumstances; patient demand or preference, on its own, is unlikely to provide sufficient justification.

It is not always easy to tell whether a medicine is being used therapeutically or as an enhancement. A good example comes from Shakespeare *et al.*'s study of prescribing practices of Norethisterone, a drug which is prescribed for menorrhagia (abnormally heavy periods) and the menopause, but which can also be used simply to delay menstruation.[27] They found that there were peaks of prescribing during the summer holidays. Women, they concluded, were being prescribed Norethisterone because they did not want to get their periods when they went on holiday. Is this 'lifestyle or convenience prescribing'? In responding to Shakespeare *et al.*'s study, Bryant *et al.* argued that it is not.[28] Women suffering from menorrhagia often decide to put up with their problem periods—thus saving the NHS as much as £100 per year for the standard treatment. Using Norethisterone to delay menstruation once a year costs about £5. Bryant *et al.* therefore argue that 'women who tolerate their symptoms for most of the year but who take a period holiday make efficient use of NHS resources'.[29]

3 LICENSING

Thalidomide was marketed in the late 1950s as a remedy for morning sickness in pregnancy. Clinical trials gave no indication of its propensity to cause birth defects, and its UK manufacturers, Distillers, claimed that it could 'be given with complete safety to pregnant women and nursing mothers without adverse effect on mother or child'.[30] Unfortunately, this claim proved to be false, and between 1956 and 1961 12,000 children were born in over thirty countries with very severe limb defects. One-third of these 'Thalidomide' babies died within a month.

Before the 1960s, there had been remarkably few restrictions upon the marketing of medicines. There was, for example, no legal requirement upon pharmaceutical companies to prove the safety and efficacy of new medicines before putting them into circulation. Unsurprisingly, the Thalidomide tragedy led to increased interest in regulating the safety of medicines, resulting in the Medicines Act 1968, which was intended to provide an effective system for the licensing and monitoring of drugs.

---

[27] Judy Shakespeare, Elizabeth Neve, and Karen Hodder, 'Is Norethisterone a Lifestyle Drug? Results of Database Analysis' (2000) 320 British Medical Journal 291.

[28] Gerry Bryant, Ian Scott, and Anne Worrall, 'Is Norethisterone a Lifestyle Drug?: Health is Not Merely the Absence of Disease' (2000) 320 British Medical Journal 1605.

[29] Ibid.

[30] Pamela Ferguson, *Drug Injuries and the Pursuit of Compensation* (Sweet & Maxwell: London, 1996) 5.

The 1968 Act set up the Medicines Control Agency (MCA) which, in 2003, was merged with Medical Devices Agency to form the Medical and Healthcare products Regulatory Agency (MHRA).

(a) MARKETING AUTHORIZATION

Under regulations 17–21 of the Medicines for Human Use (Clinical Trials) Regulations 2004, authorization must be sought from the MHRA before a new medicine can be tested in a clinical trial. Schedule 3 of the Regulations sets out the information which must be submitted before a clinical trial can be authorized, such as summaries of the chemical, pharmaceutical, and biological data on the active substance and the finished product, and summaries of the non-clinical pharmacology and toxicology data on that product, if available.

Only when trials have indicated that the drug is reasonably safe and effective can a drug company apply for what used to be known as a product licence, and is now referred to as a marketing authorization. Before any medicinal product (including generic equivalents of established drugs) can be made available for public use, under section 7(2) of the Medicines Act, it must have a marketing authorization.

Medicines Act 1968 section 7

7(2) Except in accordance with a licence granted for the purposes of this section (in this Act referred to as a 'product licence') no person shall, in the course of a business carried on by him, and in circumstances to which this subsection applies,

(a) sell, supply or export any medicinal product, or

(b) procure the sale, supply or exportation of any medicinal product, or

(c) procure the manufacture or assembly of any medicinal product for sale, supply or exportation.

Although the Secretary of State for Health is formally responsible for the licensing of medicines, in practice this role is undertaken by the MHRA, with advice from the Commission on Human Medicines, formerly the Committee on the Safety of Medicines (CSM). Section 19 specifies a number of factors that it should take into account when deciding whether to grant a marketing authorization.

Medicines Act 1968 section 19

19(1) ... in dealing with an application for a product licence the licensing authority shall in particular take into consideration—

(a) the safety of medicinal products of each description to which the application relates;

(b) the efficacy of medicinal products of each such description for the purposes for which the products are proposed to be administered; and

(c) the quality of medicinal products of each such description, according to the specification and the method or proposed method of manufacture of the products, and the provisions proposed for securing that the products as sold or supplied will be of that quality.

(2) In taking into consideration the efficacy for a particular purpose of medicinal products of a description to which such an application relates, the licensing authority shall leave out of account any question whether medicinal products of another description would or might be equally or more efficacious for that purpose.

Notice that one factor which is *not* relevant is the price of the medicinal product. So the fact that a medicine is prohibitively expensive is not a good reason to deny it a marketing authorization. Of course, NICE (see chapter 2) might subsequently decide that an expensive new medicine should not be prescribed within the NHS, but provided that it meets the threshold levels of safety, effectiveness, and quality, it should be granted a marketing authorization.

Also irrelevant to the basic assessment of a drug's safety is the comparative question of whether other medicines are equally or more effective than this new one. This point is important because it facilitates the licensing of what are known as 'me too' drugs: that is, drugs that are versions of medicines which are already on the market. A similar provision exists in the US, and is criticized here by Marcia Angell.

Marcia Angell[31]

[I]n the five years 1998 through 2002, 415 new drugs were approved by the Food and Drug Administration (FDA), of which only 14% were truly innovative. A further 9% were old drugs that had been changed in some way that made them, in the FDA's view, significant improvements. And the remaining 77%? Incredibly, they were all me-too drugs—classified by the agency as being no better than drugs already on the market to treat the same condition. Some of these had different chemical compositions from the originals; most did not. But none were considered improvements.

This travesty is made possible by one crucial weakness in the law—namely, drug companies have to show...only that new drugs are 'effective'. They do not have to show that they are *more effective than* (or even as effective as) what is already being used for the same condition. They just have to show that they are better than nothing....If companies had to show their drugs were better than older treatments, there would be far fewer me-too drugs, because not many of them would pass that test. The companies would have no choice but to look for important new drugs, instead of taking the easier and cheaper route of spinning out old ones.

When applying for a marketing authorization, the pharmaceutical company must submit full details of the research that has been carried out and the results obtained, including any adverse reactions. The manufacturer must also provide information about the manufacturing process and quality control mechanisms, and must indicate how the drug will be marketed by, for example, submitting any leaflets to be supplied with the product. All this information will then be analysed by the Commission on Human Medicines. It is worth noting that the Commission on Human Medicines bases its advice to the MHRA principally upon information submitted by the manufacturer.

---

[31] *The Truth about the Drug Companies* (Random House: London, 2005) 75–6.

Once granted, a marketing authorization lasts for five years, after which a manufacturer must apply for its renewal. The House of Commons Select Committee criticized the renewal process for being, in practice, a bureaucratic formality rather than a fresh opportunity for rigorous review of the evidence: 'the 5-year renewal procedure has not been used to good effect, and appears to have become an automatic process focusing on safety issues rather than an opportunity to review both efficacy and safety data rigorously'.[32]

If a manufacturer is applying for a marketing authorization for a generic medicine, it is not necessary to supply the MHRA with such full information if it can be demonstrated that the product is 'essentially similar' to a product which has been in circulation for ten years.[33] In *In Re Smith Kline*[34] the applicant company, which had held the patent on a drug called 'Cimetidine' for nearly 20 years, did not want the MCA to rely upon its research when considering other companies' applications to manufacture generic versions of its product. Smith Kline argued that this was confidential information. The House of Lords held that the MCA was under a duty to protect the public, and that when considering applications for product licences for generic versions of a drug, it was necessary to compare the information supplied in the later application with that in the original application, in order to ensure that both products were similarly safe, effective, and reliable. The MCA therefore had a right and a duty to make use of all the information obtained by it under the Act.

A different issue arose in *R (on the application of Merck Sharp & Dohme Ltd) v Licensing Authority*. Merck Sharp and Dohme Limited (MSD) held marketing authorizations for Fosamax 5mg, 10mg (product A) and Fosamax Once Weekly, 70mg (product B), both of which were used to treat osteoporosis. A generics company wished to rely on their data in order to obtain a marketing authorization for a drug (product C) which was identical to product B. Product B (which was essentially seven times the dose of the daily version, to be taken weekly) had not yet been in circulation for the requisite 10 years. MSD therefore claimed that the generics company was not entitled to rely on the data for product A, which had been in circulation for more than ten years, because product C's dosage was not 'essentially similar' to product A, only to product B.

Moses J gave this argument short shrift. There were no new safety or efficacy questions in relation to product C, and so requiring the generics company to submit new data would result in unnecessary additional testing, without any benefit to public health. The only purpose of this exercise would be to grant additional protection to innovators' ten-year right to keep their data confidential, and this was not within the spirit of the Directive.

R (on the application of Merck Sharp & Dohme Ltd) v Licensing Authority[35]

Moses J

The right to cross-refer stems from the notion of one medicinal product being 'essentially similar' to another. Public health is safeguarded by ensuring that . . . a medicinal product is only authorised without reliance on further data if it is essentially similar to a product which has already been authorised. The absence of any need for further data, in circumstances where product C is essentially similar to A or B, also achieves the objective identified in Recital 10 of avoiding unnecessarily repetitive tests on humans or animals. . . .

---

[32] Para 301.   [33] Article 10 of Directive 2001/83/EC, as amended by Directive 2004/27/EC.
[34] [1990] 1 AC 64.   [35] [2005] EWHC 710 (Admin).

Thus the only justification for requiring generic companies to produce further data, would be to extend the period of protection for an innovator.... the suggestion that the generic companies should be compelled to produce their own data, from their own tests, in relation to a product which is identical to Fosamax Once Weekly 70mg has nothing whatever to do with safety or efficacy.... Since it is agreed that the product generic companies wish to develop is identical to Fosamax Once Weekly, any further data the generic companies were required to produce would involve unnecessary testing....

Product C is no less safe or efficacious because it is essentially similar to B rather than A. The only purpose to be achieved is to give a further period of protection to innovators.

In *Organon v Department of Health and Social Security*, the Court of Appeal had to consider whether it was appropriate to take into account not only a drug's safety when taken in the recommended dose for its intended purpose, but also its toxicity following overdose. Organon wanted to submit evidence that Mianserin was less toxic than other antidepressants, and hence less likely to be fatal if a patient took an overdose. Initially, the CSM ruled that it was only entitled to take account of the drug's safety when taken for the purposes indicated in the licence, and hence evidence of toxicity following the drug's misuse was not relevant. The Divisional Court disagreed and held that the risks a drug posed if it was misused should be relevant to an assessment of its safety, and this decision was upheld by the Court of Appeal.

Organon v Department of Health and Social Security[36]

Mustill LJ

It strikes me as plain, and this much was virtually conceded, that however sympathetically paragraph (g) is read, administering the drug for the purposes of alleviating the symptoms of depression cannot be stretched to include the taking of the drug for the purpose of suicide...

I do not, however, believe that this is the right approach to the Medicines Act, the object of which is to promote public health and safety, and which should, if at all possible, be construed in a way favourable to the attainment of that object. To read paragraph (g) in the narrow sense for which the Authority contends, and which the words at first sight themselves seem to indicate, would work in the opposite direction. This would entail that if the Authority discovered, after the grant of a licence, that although in the intended dosage the drug remained acceptably safe, nevertheless if taken in even moderate excess it was potentially lethal, it would be beyond the Authority's jurisdiction even to consider whether the original risk/benefit analysis should be reconsidered, with a view to variation, suspension or cancellation of the licence. This result strikes me as so absurd that it cannot have been within the contemplation of Parliament. It must therefore be taken that the references to 'administered' and 'purposes' extend beyond circumstances which involve strict compliance with the intended use of the drug, and that the risks attaching to misuse can properly be brought into account.

A special exception from the need to obtain a marketing authorization exists for herbal remedies. Under section 12 of the Medicines Act 1968, herbal remedies which contain only plant materials are exempt from the requirement to obtain a marketing authorization if

[36] The Times, 6 Feb 1990.

either the herbal remedy was made up on the premises from which it was supplied and prescribed after a one-to-one consultation (s 12(1)); or, if it is a pre-prepared over-the-counter remedy, it is not sold under any brand name, and does not make any written therapeutic claims (s 12(2)). Over-the-counter herbal remedies which *do* make therapeutic claims must have a marketing authorization.

A registration scheme for authorizing manufactured over-the-counter traditional herbal medicines (known as the Traditional Herbal Medicines Registration Scheme) was set up in 2005.[37] The scheme applies to traditional herbal remedies, which do not meet the criteria for a marketing authorization under the Medicines Act. By October 2008, the MHRA had granted 21 Traditional Health Registrations (THR).

Under the terms of the scheme, manufacturers have to demonstrate safety and quality, but not efficacy. Evidence of efficacy is seldom available for herbal medicines because randomized-controlled trials, which as we saw in the previous chapter are the 'gold standard' in clinical research, are seldom carried out. Applicants must submit a review of safety data and an expert report on quality, in addition to evidence of at least thirty years of traditional use, fifteen of which should have been in the EU. The assumption is that some level of efficacy will exist if the remedy has been used for this length of time. In exceptional circumstances, registration will be possible even if the product has not been in use in the EU for fifteen years, but it will still be necessary to prove that it has been used elsewhere for at least thirty years. The product label must inform the consumer that the basis for registration is traditional use, rather than clinical trial data, with the following warning:

> The safety and efficacy of the product rely exclusively on information obtained from its long-term use and experience.

In order to avoid the submission of duplicate evidence, the Committee for Herbal Medicinal Products (CHMP), which is part of the European Medicines Evaluation Agency (EMEA), has developed a European positive list of ingredients. Establishing that a product contains an ingredient which is on the indicative list does not necessarily mean that an application for registration will be successful, but it will mean that applicants do not need to submit detailed evidence of safety or traditional use. Evidence of quality will still be necessary. Section 12(1) of the Medicines Act continues to offer an exemption for herbal medicines that are made up on the premises and sold after a one-to-one consultation.

(b) CLASSIFICATION OF MEDICINES

In addition to deciding whether to grant a marketing authorization, the MHRA also classifies medicines into one of three categories:

(a) prescription-only medicines (POM);

(b) suppliable by a pharmacist without prescription (P);

(c) general sale list medicines, which can be sold over the counter and do not need to be dispensed by a pharmacist (GSL).

---

[37] The Traditional Herbal Medicinal Products Directive (2004/24/EC), Official Journal of the European Union L136/85. Details of the scheme are available at <www.mhra.gov.uk>.

A European directive specified the factors which should be taken into account when deciding whether a medicine should be prescription-only, and these were inserted into section 58A(2) of the Medicines Act 1968. The MHRA must consider whether the medicine:

(a) is likely to present a direct or indirect danger to human health, even when used correctly, if used without the supervision of a doctor or dentist; or

(b) is frequently and to a very wide extent used incorrectly, and as a result is likely to present a direct or indirect danger to human health; or

(c) contains substances or preparations of substances of which the activity requires, or the side-effects require, further investigation;

(d) is normally prescribed by a doctor or dentist for parenteral administration [that is, intravenously or by injection].

Section 58A(3) also specifies that the Secretary of State should take into account whether a medicine is likely, if incorrectly used, to present a substantial risk of medicinal abuse, lead to addiction, or be used for illegal purposes.

Medicines can be reclassified, if they no longer appear to pose the requisite danger to human health. Where self-medication is safe, as is the case in relation to treatments for colds or hayfever, for example, there are obvious advantages in enabling individuals to purchase medicines for themselves. This will save the NHS money, both through the costs of the medicine itself and by eliminating the need to make an appointment with a GP in order to obtain a prescription, and will often be more convenient for patients.

In recent years, partly in response to an EU directive,[38] an increasing number of prescription-only medicines have been reclassified in the UK. Of course, one consequence of this is that the leaflets supplied with medicines become even more important, since they may represent the only information the patient receives about how to take the medicine safely. One of the most high-profile reclassifications of a medicine was for the post-coital contraceptive pill, known colloquially as the 'morning after pill'. In 2000 the MCA and the CSM agreed that the risks posed by post-coital contraception did not justify its prescription-only status, so it was re-classified as a pharmacy-available medicine.[39] In the following extract, David Prayle and Margaret Brazier evaluate this trend towards the reclassification of medicines.

David Prayle and Margaret Brazier[40]

Three principal motivations for change can be identified. First, the Pharmaceutical Society, representing and regulating pharmacists, pressed for greater availability of medicines in pharmacies, ie changes from POM to P status. Making more medicines available over the counter in pharmacies was perceived as an extension of the pharmacist's professional role ... Second, the government has sought to promote change, partly as an integral element in its general policy of deregulation but also to drive down costs in the NHS drug budget. When a medicine moves to P status it is hoped more and more patients will simply purchase the product themselves, saving the cost to the NHS of certain prescriptions and saving expensive general practitioner (GP) time.

---

[38] Council Directive 92/26/EEC, Classification for the supply of medicinal products for human use.

[39] The Prescription Only Medicines (Human Use) Order was laid before Parliament on 11 Dec 2000.

[40] 'Supply of Medicines: Paternalism, Autonomy and Reality' (1998) 24 Journal of Medical Ethics 93–8.

Third, the pharmaceutical industry has an obvious and powerful interest in reclassification. Increased sales of P and GSL medicines can be expected, particularly as such medicines, unlike POM medicines, can be advertised to the general public. As a number of previously profitable POM medicines reach the stage when patent protection expires, the manufacturer must seek means of combating competition from generic copies. Altering the medicine's status to P and enthusiastically advertising the product under its tried and tested brand name is a useful strategy to maintain, if not increase sales figures.

A brave new world of more open access to medicines beckons. Should it be applauded?

A restrictive approach to access to medicines restricts individual autonomy. The longer the list of POM medicines, the less able individuals are to control their own health status via self-diagnosis and self-medication...Reducing the list of POM medicines might be seen as enhancing autonomy. The flaw in this approach derives from the anomalous P category of medicines. They can be purchased, but only from a pharmacy under the supervision and control of a pharmacist. Persons seeking a P medicine must in theory submit to an interrogation from the pharmacist (or his assistant) about their familiarity with the drug, their medical history and their potential use of the product. This 'consultation' may well take place before an audience of other customers.

(c) POST-LICENSING REGULATION

Regulation does not cease once a product has been licensed. Regulations specify the information that must be provided with a medicine, such as instructions for use, contra-indications and warnings about side-effects.[41] Leaflets supplied with medicines must contain information about its active ingredients; indications for its use; warnings about the product's interaction with other substances, such as alcohol, and about any effect it might have on the user's capacity to drive or operate machinery. Dosage instructions, such as how the medicine should be taken, and how frequently, must also be included, and if appropriate, what should be done in the event of an overdose.[42]

The advertising of medicines is also controlled. Prescription-only medicines cannot be marketed directly to the public (unlike in the US),[43] but the pharmaceutical industry spends enormous sums of money advertising drugs to health care professionals, and paying for conference attendance and continuing professional development. In 2009, the Royal College of Physicians issued a report which proposed a range of measure in order to 'restore patient confidence in medical independence'.

Royal College of Physicians[44]

Decoupling the pharmaceutical industry from continuing professional development

The industry presently pays for about half of all postgraduate medical education. In order to address widespread suspicions that drug promotion is carried out through continuing

---

[41] Medicines (Labelling) Regulations 1976 SI 1976/1726, as amended.

[42] Medicines (Leaflets) Regulations 1977 SI 1977/1055, as amended.

[43] Medicines (Advertising) Regulations 1994, SI 1994/1932, as amended.

[44] *Innovating for Health: Patients, Physicians, the Pharmaceutical Industry and the NHS* (RCP: London, 2009), executive summary available at <www.rcplondon.ac.uk>.

professional development, the working party recommends weaning postgraduate training off individual pharmaceutical company sponsorship over a time bound period while alternative sources of sustainable funding are organised through for example the royal colleges and the Department of Health.

As well as marketing their products to doctors, the pharmaceutical industry sponsors 'disease awareness' campaigns, which can involve briefing journalists or providing web-based resources. These can be effective ways of drawing the public's attention to the possibility that they might have a condition, such as depression or 'restless legs syndrome', and to the existence of effective drugs. The aim of these initiatives is to persuade people, who may not have realized that their symptoms might be caused by a medical condition, to visit their GP and ask for treatment. Where there is only one medicine to treat a condition, promoting that condition to the public comes very close to direct promotion of that product.

The House of Commons Select Committee found that the ban on direct advertising to consumers does not stop the pharmaceutical industry from thinking creatively about how to persuade more people to go to their GPs and either ask for, or be given, prescription drugs.

House of Commons Select Committee[45]

There is clear evidence that the industry is concerned with identifying populations who are not currently presenting for diagnosis. In one document relating to the 'strategic planning process,' these patients, who, 'do not currently present to their GP or take prescription medications,' are referred to as 'the missing millions' and are estimated to comprise almost 2 million people in the UK. This population is viewed as providing a 'significant opportunity' for the company.

Research is then conducted on behalf of the company that aims to understand what barriers exist to prevent these people from presenting and to identify factors, both rational and emotional, that will overcome these barriers and encourage patients to seek professional advice.

The pharmaceutical industry also attempts to influence prescribing practices by funding and supporting patient groups, as explained by Tim Kendall, a psychiatrist who gave evidence to the Select Committee:

I am aware that there are some . . . like Depression Alliance, which have very substantial funding at times from drug companies. They do lobby for an increased accessibility to drugs which the drug companies are selling to these patient organisations. They are persuading them that these are the drugs they must have, with very little evidence to support it.[46]

The Select Committee was critical of this process:

This leads to a situation in which, instead of representing the interests of patients, groups 'become marketing tools for the pharmaceutical companies'. Referral by the pharmaceutical

---

[45] Paras 253–4.   [46] Para 265.

industry to patient organisations as 'ground troops' for lobbying Government to increase access to new drugs is further evidence of this....The pharmaceutical industry's promotional efforts are relentless and pervasive. The evidence presented showed the lengths to which the industry goes to ensure that promotional messages reach their targets, and that these targets include not only prescribing groups, but patients and the general public.[47]

Because clinical trials are, by necessity, carried out on a relatively small number of patients, compared with the number of eventual users, they will inevitably only detect common adverse reactions. It is therefore important to monitor adverse reactions which emerge when the drug is taken by larger groups of patients, including people who are often excluded from clinical trials, such as pregnant women or people with multiple co-morbidities. As a result, manufacturers are under a duty to keep a record of all reported adverse drug reactions (ADRs) and to report these to the MHRA.

The 'yellow card scheme' enables GPs, nurses, midwives, health visitors, and patients to report ADRs electronically.[48] Drugs are divided into two groups for the purposes of the yellow card scheme: new drugs (denoted by a black triangle) are monitored closely for a minimum of two years, during which time *all* suspected ADRs should be reported. For established drugs, only serious suspected ADRs must be reported. Other areas of special interest have been identified, for which all suspected ADRs should be reported, such as reactions in children and the elderly. In 1996, following the identification of serious cases of liver toxicity associated with a traditional Chinese medicine, the yellow card scheme was extended to include unlicensed herbal products. Monitoring ADRs from herbal remedies has proved particularly difficult, however, since patients appear to be less likely to consult their doctor if they suspect an adverse reaction.

In 2007 21,875 ADRS were reported, 83 per cent of which were classified as 'serious'.[49] This is almost certainly an underestimate: the MHRA acknowledges that there is considerable underreporting of ADRs. The purpose of the scheme is not, however, to provide accurate data on the extent of ADRs, but rather to signal the existence of potential problems, which should be investigated further. Very few products are withdrawn as a result of safety concerns. According to the House of Commons Select Committee, twenty-four prescription drugs were withdrawn due to safety concerns in the UK between 1971 and 1992, inclusive (1.1 per year) and 19 were withdrawn between 1993 and 2004 (1.6 per year).[50]

It is certainly true that the mere existence of an adverse reaction does not mean that a medicine has become unacceptably unsafe. As we see later, aspirin is now known to be unsafe for use in children, but that does not mean that it should not be available to other patients, who benefit enormously from it. It is necessary to balance the risks to a minority of patients against the benefits the drug may have for the majority, and so, rather than withdrawing a product which causes adverse reactions in some users, a more appropriate response might be to give a more specific warning about contra-indications for its use.

As we see in the next section, there has been substantial criticism of the MHRA's post-licensing surveillance system. The House of Commons Select Committee found that it concentrated its efforts on scrutiny of pre-marketing data, and gave too little attention to post-marketing surveillance. Witnesses had suggested to the Committee that this may

---

[47] Paras 267, 271.   [48] <www.yellowcard.gov.uk/>.
[49] Medicines Act Advisory Bodies Annual Report 2007, available at <www.MHRA.gov.uk>.
[50] Para 106.

be because it is not in the MHRA's interests to discover that its initial findings on safety were mistaken.

> Several witnesses expressed concerns not only about the relatively weak emphasis on post-marketing investigations, but also about possible conflicts of interest that might arise when the same Agency is responsible for both pre- and post-marketing drug evaluation: if problems arise once a drug is on the market, it might indicate flaws in the original assessment and require the regulators to examine their own earlier failings.[51]

(d) THE IMPACT OF REGULATION

Obviously, the stricter the licensing requirements, the more difficult it is to introduce new medicines to the market. A stringent regulatory framework might then increase patient safety, but at the cost of stifling innovation, which in turn may mean that future patients are denied access to beneficial medicines. In the next extract, Harvey Teff claims that regulators are likely be risk-averse, since the damage to their reputation should they license another Thalidomide would be catastrophic, whereas any risk to public health through *not* licensing a potentially beneficial medicine will be much less visible.

> [T]he regulator tends to be unduly risk averse. In the context of pharmaceuticals, he has little or nothing to lose by refusing, or at least delaying, the grant of a licence; everything to lose if he approves a thalidomide. Thus where guidelines are bound to be arbitrary to some extent— how many species of animals should be tested, over what period of time, for what risks—the regulator is prone to err on the side of caution, to indulge in a kind of 'defensive licensing'.[52]

Teff's is, however, an unusual view. In the next extract, John Abraham argues that the pharmaceutical industry has too much influence over the licensing authority, leading to what he describes as 'regulatory capture'.

John Abraham[53]

> Pharmaceutical firms have well-oiled lobbying strategies to capture regulatory agencies: more subtly, industry can penetrate into the heart of regulatory political subculture via the so-called revolving door... In the UK, a large proportion of scientists in the British drug regulatory authority started their careers in industry, and many move back there...
>
> Regulatory capture is especially important because the risk–benefit assessment of drugs has a high degree of technical uncertainty, which is inherent in toxicology, clinical trials, and epidemiology. Therefore, it is crucial to know how far regulators are willing to give the manufacturer the benefit of scientific doubt about safety and efficacy of their product. Indeed, regulators too often consistently award industry the benefit of scientific doubt when reviewing products.

[51] House of Commons Health Select Committee, Para 302.
[52] 'Regulation under the Medicines Act 1968: A Continuing Prescription for Health' (1984) 47 Modern Law Review 303–23.
[53] 'The Pharmaceutical Industry as a Political Player' (2002) 360 The Lancet 1498–502.

> For the past 50 years, industry has been quick to ward off regulation it perceives to be contrary to its interests by threatening that such regulation will have damaging results for the nation's export trade, balance of payments, or employment. Too often, regulatory agencies have accepted these threats uncritically.

A number of substantive criticisms have been made of the UK's licensing system. First, the MHRA is funded entirely by the pharmaceutical industry, through licensing and other fees. This undoubtedly leads to pressure on the MHRA to provide a speedy licensing service.

House of Commons Select Committee[54]

> In return for the licensing and service fees paid by the industry, companies expect an efficient and rapid service...The speed at which the UK regulatory authority has historically processed licence applications has been one of the fastest in the world, which means that its services are much in demand from EU applications. In 2003, time from application to the granting of a licence of a new chemical entity, if no further information was needed, was approximately 70 working days, whereas a response may now usually be expected in approximately 30 working days.

Secondly, the MHRA relies on company data, presented as a series of detailed assessment reports, in its decision whether or not to license a drug. Raw data is very rarely analysed, leading the House of Commons Select Committee to suggest that the MHRA may be too 'trusting'.

House of Commons Select Committee[55]

> Trust is critical in the relationship between regulators and industry. However, at the heart of this inquiry are the concerns of those who believe that the MHRA is too trusting. Trust should be based on robust evidence; it should be earned rather than presupposed. The evidence indicated that the MHRA examined primary (raw) data on drug effects only if it suspected some misrepresentation in the summary data supplied. It was argued that such trust in regulated companies goes too far: reliance on company summaries is neither sufficient nor appropriate, in the absence of effective audit and verification of data that companies provide. The secrecy surrounding this information is also unacceptable.

The Select Committee's conclusions on the regulator's performance were damning:

House of Commons Health Select Committee[56]

> The regulatory authority, which is responsible for controlling much of the behaviour of the industry has significant failings. Lack of transparency has played a major part in allowing failings to continue. The traditional secrecy in the drug regulatory process has insulated regulators from the feedback that would otherwise check, test and stimulate their policies and

---

[54] Paras 99, 100.   [55] Para 284.
[56] Paras 340, 342–3, 349.

performance. Failure can be measured by the MHRA's poor history in recognising drug risks, poor communication and lack of public trust. Regulatory secrecy also underpins publication bias, and other unacceptable practices. The closeness that has developed between regulators and companies has deprived the industry of rigorous quality control and audit....

Unfortunately, a number of drugs which have been licensed and widely prescribed, have produced severe adverse reactions, and in some cases death, in large numbers of people. In this report we have highlighted the problems with SSRIs antidepressants, notably Seroxat, and the COX-2 inhibitors, Vioxx and Celebrex [drugs for arthritis which were withdrawn in 2004 after it emerged that they had probably caused many thousands of heart attacks and strokes].

Problems with these and other drugs have revealed major failings not just in the pharmaceutical industry relating to the design and presentation of clinical trials and the supply of data to the regulator, but also in the regulatory system. The regulator's analysis of trial data and advice to prescribers and patients have been inadequate and its responses to indications of adverse reactions slow....

Such problems are compounded by an excessive reliance on results from premarketing clinical trials, together with a failing system of pharmacovigilance. The lack of pro-active and systematic monitoring of drug effects and health outcomes in normal clinical use is worrying. Improvements in post-marketing surveillance are clearly needed and would, no doubt, have led to the earlier detection of problems with SSRI antidepressants, COX-2 inhibitors and other drugs.

A particularly striking example of failures in the system of pharmacovigilance emerged in March 2008, when the MHRA announced that there would be no prosecution of GlaxoSmithKline (GSK), for withholding trial data and meta-analyses, which demonstrated conclusively that Seroxat should not be prescribed to under-18s.

GSK had carried out two trials, Studies 329 and 377, which tested the efficacy of paroxetine (known as Seroxat in the UK and Paxil in the US) in children and adolescents in the mid-1990s in eleven countries. The trials were concluded by October 1998. The data, and a meta-analysis carried out on the data in 2002, were not submitted to the MHRA until May 2003, as part of an application to extend the licensable uses of Seroxat. As soon as it was received, this information was analysed by the Committee on the Safety of Medicines (CSM), which found that it provided clear evidence (a) that 'there is no good evidence of efficacy in major depressive disorder in the population studied';[57] and (b) that there was 'a clear increase in suicidal behaviour versus placebo'.[58] The MHRA immediately published a 'Dear Doctor' letter, informing doctors that Seroxat should not be prescribed to under-18s. A few months later, a criminal investigation into GSK's failure to submit this data was launched.

In early 2004, a leaked internal GSK document suggested that the decision to withhold Studies 329 and 377 had been intentional. The document, dated October 1998, stated that it would be 'commercially unacceptable to include a statement that efficacy had not been demonstrated, as this would undermine the profile of paroxetine'.[59]

---

[57] MHRA Assessment Report: Paroxetine (Seroxat) 4 June 2003, available at <www.mhra.gov.uk/Howweregulate/Medicines/Medicinesregulatorynews/CON014153>.

[58] Ibid.

[59] GSK Seroxat/Paxil Adolescent Depression: Position Piece on the Phase III Clinical Studies, available at <www.ahrp.org/risks/SSRI0204/GSKpaxil/index.php>.

Following a four-and-a-half year criminal investigation, the conclusion was reached that GSK could not be prosecuted for withholding this data, not because GSK had acted properly, but because the law was insufficiently clear to give a reasonable prospect of successful prosecution. This was because the relevant pharmacovigilance provisions, which placed pharmaceutical companies under a duty to provide '*any* information relevant to the evaluation of benefits and risks', could be read as applying only to information which emerged during 'normal conditions of use'.

Seroxat had not been specifically licensed for use in children, because at the time carrying out paediatric clinical trials was not encouraged, and so its widespread use by under-18s was effectively 'off label'. Perhaps ironically, GSK *had* carried out paediatric trials, but again because these adverse reactions had emerged during trials, and not during 'normal conditions of use', they were not captured by the relevant provisions. The duty to report adverse reactions in clinical trials, in section 31 of the Medicines Act, at the relevant time only applied to UK trials, and so again did not bite on this withheld data.

In the next extract, Linsey McGoey and I critically evaluate the MHRA's March 2008 announcement.

Linsey McGoey and Emily Jackson[60]

This conclusion prompts a number of questions, the first and most obvious of which is that if it is indeed true that the law was insufficiently clear in March 2008, then it must also have been insufficiently clear in October 2003, when the decision was taken to launch a criminal investigation. . . .

The existence of so many qualifications to what initially looks like a clear and comprehensive duty to submit '*any* other information relevant to the evaluation of the benefits and risks afforded by a medicinal product' is perhaps surprising. Certainly, two ordinary rules of statutory interpretation would militate against this conclusion. First, the words used in legislation are normally assumed to have their 'ordinary language meaning', unless otherwise specified. Use of the word 'any', according to the Oxford English Dictionary, captures the idea of 'indifference as to the particular one or ones that may be selected', which would suggest that 'any relevant information' should not, without a clear indication to the contrary, be qualified to mean 'only information gathered in a particular setting'.

The second rule of statutory interpretation which is at odds with the existence of these legal loopholes is that, in the event of statutory ambiguity, it is legitimate to ask what the legislator's intention was in drafting the provision in question. Here the intention was evidently to create a duty to report all relevant data, and in particular, to disclose suspected adverse reactions and other information relevant to the regulator's evaluation of risks and benefits.

The interpretation of the law which has led to the decision not to prosecute would seem to subvert the intention of the creators of the regulatory regime, which was indubitably not to provide a series of 'get-out' clauses for drugs companies who withhold, deliberately, evidence of lack of efficacy and serious side-effects for a group of patients who are routinely being prescribed the drug in question.

Following the collapse of this criminal investigation, the MHRA pressed for an immediate change in the law, and the Regulations now contain a provision which attempts to

---

[60] 'Seroxat and the Suppression of Clinical Trial Data: Regulatory Failure and the Uses of Legal Ambiguity' (2009) 35 Journal of Medical Ethics 107–12.

properly capture the need for a comprehensive, rather than a selective, duty of candour on the part of drugs' manufacturers.

The Medicines for Human Use (Marketing Authorisations etc.) Amendment Regulations 2008

The information that must be provided…includes information arising from use of the product—

    (a) in a country or territory outside the European Economic Area;

    (b) outside the terms of the marketing authorization,

Including use in clinical trials.

4 EUROPEAN REGULATION

European regulation of the pharmaceutical industry has become increasingly important in recent years. Its two principal aims are to protect consumer safety, and to harmonize the regulatory regimes throughout Europe in order to facilitate the free movement of goods. We look at the impact of the European directive on product liability later in this chapter, but other Europe-wide regulations apply to licensing, marketing, and advertising.

There has been progressive harmonization of rules on labelling and package leaflets,[61] advertising,[62] and the reporting of adverse side-effects.[63] These directives have amended the UK's regulations. The European Medicines Agency (formerly the European Agency for the Evaluation of Medicinal Products), known as EMEA, was established in 1993, and a new European system for the authorization of medicinal products was set up in January 1995. It offers two routes for the licensing of medicinal products, both with strict timetables:

(a) A centralized procedure with applications made directly to EMEA.[64] Assessments are carried out by a sub-committee, the Committee for Medicinal Products for Human Use (CHMP). Use of this procedure is compulsory for products derived from biotechnology and other high-technology processes. Its compulsory remit has been extended to cover all human medicines intended for the treatment of HIV/AIDS, cancer, diabetes, neurodegenerative diseases, autoimmune and other immune dysfunctions, and viral diseases, as well as so-called 'orphan medicines' for the treatment of rare diseases.

    For products authorized under the centralized procedure, national licensing authorities must report all adverse reactions to EMEA, which will then notify other states' licensing authorities.

(b) The decentralized procedure involves an application to one member state's national licensing authority, but all other EU countries agree to the 'mutual recognition' of these national marketing authorizations. Member states are entitled to object to the mutual recognition of another country's marketing authorization on the grounds that the product poses a risk to public health, although they do not have the final say, and following arbitration, the decision is taken centrally.

---

[61] Directive 92/27/EEC.   [62] Directive 92/28/EEC.   [63] Directive 75/319/EEC.
[64] Directive 93/41/EEC Council Regulation (EEC) No 2309/93.

Under the decentralized procedure, European regulatory agencies are effectively in competition with each other for regulatory business, which is especially significant given that the pharmaceutical company has to pay a fee to the regulator. A drug company seeking to market a new drug throughout Europe can obtain marketing authorization in any EU country, and so it will tend to choose the one that appears to have the speediest and least demanding licensing regime. Unsurprisingly, approval times for new medicines have been dropping throughout Europe. While this is good news for the pharmaceutical industry, many commentators have argued that there is, in effect, a 'race to the bottom' towards increasingly and perhaps dangerously light-touch regulation.[65]

In their study of industry and regulators' attitudes towards the EU's system of drug approval, one of Abraham and Lewis's respondents drew attention to a further downside of the mutual recognition procedure.[66] Under the 'old' system, several EU regulators would assess the same product. If they all adopted the same process, this would clearly be a waste of resources, but because there were differences between countries' approaches, a second or third opinion would sometimes flag up a safety issue which had not been spotted by the first regulator, thus offering an additional safety check.

Govin Permanand has argued that EU regulation is dominated by the interests of the pharmaceutical industry, rather than by patient safety considerations. There is, for example, no indication that patients have benefited from EMEA's faster approval times.[67] In part, this may be because EU-wide regulation of commercial markets and industry is familiar, whereas health policy issues have not generally been subject to EU regulation.

Govin Permanand[68]

Recent murmuring by several of the larger European multinationals about relocating their R&D elsewhere (specifically to the US where the research environment is said to be more conducive) has seen not just the member states, but so too the Commission, seek to placate the industry on a number of levels e.g. intellectual property rights and preferential tax arrangements.... The reason for the Commission's supportive approach to the industry in general is clear. The pharmaceutical industry is a major contributor to the European economy....

In the case of the EMEA 'policy',...industry was heavily involved throughout the policy-process. The Commission's first point of contact was the industry—to ascertain its views and requirements...Consequently, industry's demands helped to ensure an agency remit which, in many respects, is limited to speeding market approval rather than quality of assessment.

Efforts to harmonize the regulation of medicines also exist outside of the EU. Mutual recognition arrangements, akin to the EU's decentralized procedure, also exist between the EU and Switzerland, Canada, Australia, and New Zealand, and are intended to facilitate trade by eliminating the need to undergo duplicate testing and scrutiny of new products.

---

[65] J Abraham and G Lewis, 'Harmonising and Competing for Medicines Regulation: How Healthy are the EU's Systems of Drug Approval?' (1999) 48 Social Science and Medicine 1655–67.

[66] Ibid.

[67] P Edmonds, D Dermot, and C Oglialoro, 'Access to Important New Medicines' (2000) 13 European Business Journal 146–58.

[68] *EU Pharmaceutical Regulation* (Manchester University Press: Manchester, 2006).

The International Conference on Harmonisation (ICH), launched in 1990, attempts to harmonize certain technical requirements imposed upon the pharmaceutical industry in US, Europe and Japan.[69] The first ICH steering committee re-affirmed its:

> [C]ommitment to increased international harmonisation, aimed at ensuring that good quality, safe and effective medicines are developed and registered in the most efficient and cost-effective manner. These activities are pursued in the interest of the consumer and public health, to prevent unnecessary duplication of clinical trials in humans and to minimise the use of animal testing without compromising the regulatory obligations of safety and effectiveness.

Again, the question arises whether international harmonization can possibly achieve the twin goals of speeding up the licensing of medicines and improving safety standards. Abraham and Reed's study suggests that it cannot, and they claim that the former has taken priority.

John Abraham and Tim Reed[70]

> [W]e conclude that, in the field of carcinogenicity testing, the ICH management of international harmonisation of medicines regulation is not achieving the simultaneous improvements in safety standards and acceleration of drug development.... Rather, our research supports the more sceptical view that the latter is being achieved *at the expense of* the former....Reductions in drug testing requirements and increased flexibility in interpretations of what counts as evidence of carcinogenic risk make it easier for regulators to approve drugs—and approve them more quickly.

5 PRODUCT LIABILITY

No drug is 100 per cent safe; most will occasionally produce adverse drug reactions (ADRs). Some of these are common and fairly minor, and will generally have been discovered during clinical trials. Consumers can then be warned about potential side-effects when the drug is marketed. As we have seen, rare adverse reactions will usually only be discovered *after* a drug is put into circulation. During clinical trials, a new drug may be tested on between one and five thousand people. If a particular side-effect occurs in one patient in a thousand, it is unlikely that the connection between the medicine and these symptoms will have been picked up during the trial. If the reaction is rarer still, it may not come to light until many years after the drug is first used in patients. Furthermore, as we saw in the previous chapter, certain groups—such as the elderly—are routinely excluded from clinical trials, even though they may be among the ultimate consumers of the medicine being tested. As a result, ADRs, which particularly affect these excluded groups, will not be detected during clinical trials.

---

[69] See further <www.ich.org>.

[70] 'Reshaping the Carcinogenic Risk Assessment of Medicines: International Harmonisation for Drug Safety, Industry/Regulator Efficiency or Both?' (2003) 57 Social Science & Medicine 195–204.

A patient will only have a remedy if she can establish that the medicine was unacceptably unsafe, such that it should not have been marketed, or that it was unsafe *for her*, and should not have been prescribed, or should have been marketed with an appropriate warning. In the following sections, we consider the various options open to a patient who believes that she has been injured by a medicinal product.

(a) CONTRACT

Contractual remedies are of limited relevance to consumers who suffer drug-related injuries. It would be very unusual for a contract to exist directly between the consumer of a medicine and its manufacturer. And when a drug is prescribed under an NHS prescription, there will be no contract with either the pharmacist or the doctor who wrote the prescription.

In *Pfizer Corporation v Minister of Health* the House of Lords had to consider whether there had been a sale when outpatients were provided with prescription drugs on payment of the charge, then 2s (2 shillings or approximately 10 pence):

Pfizer Corporation v Minister of Health[71]

Lord Reid

[I]n my opinion there is no sale in this case. Sale is a consensual contract requiring agreement expressed or implied. In the present case there appears to me to be no need for any agreement. The patient has a statutory right to demand the drug on payment of 2s. The hospital has a statutory obligation to supply it on such payment. And if the prescription is presented to a chemist he appears to be bound by his contract with the appropriate authority to supply the drug on receipt of such payment. There is no need for any agreement between the patient and either the hospital or the chemist, and there is certainly no room for bargaining. Moreover the 2s. is not in any true sense the price: the drug may cost much more and the chemist has a right under his contract with the authority to receive the balance from them. It appears to me that any resemblance between this transaction and a true sale is only superficial.

It is only when drugs are supplied privately, or when medicines are bought over the counter, that a contractual remedy for a defective medicine is possible.

If the consumer does have a contract, either with the pharmacist or with a doctor dispensing a private prescription, then the ordinary rules of contract law apply. If the product does not correspond with its description, or is not of satisfactory quality, there might be a breach of the Sale of Goods Act 1979.[72] Liability does not require proof of fault on the part of the supplier. It would be relatively straightforward to establish a breach of one of these sections for what are known as manufacturing defects, such as the contamination of a particular batch of medicines. But since most drugs have some side-effects, it will be difficult to establish that a medicine which has caused an adverse reaction has breached the implied condition of satisfactory quality.

---

[71] [1965] 2 WLR 387.
[72] Sections 14(2) and 14(3), as amended.

One complicated question raised by the application of contract law to the sale of medicines relates to sections 14(2B) and 14(3) of the Sale of Goods Act, under which goods must either be fit for the purpose for which they are commonly supplied, or if the buyer makes known the particular purpose for which they are being bought, that they are reasonably fit for that purpose. How much information about the consumer's condition must the pharmacist obtain in order to assess whether the medicine is fit for its purpose? If a consumer has a contraindication for taking a particular over-the-counter medicine, such as high blood pressure or diabetes, then arguably that medicine is not fit for the purpose for which she has bought it. Pharmacists who fail to inquire whether a medicine is fit for the purpose for which the particular consumer has purchased it might then find themselves strictly liable for any consequent injuries.

(b) NEGLIGENCE

The manufacturer of a medicine could be liable in negligence if the consumer can prove that she was owed a duty of care, and that the manufacturer's breach of that duty caused her injury. Since *Donoghue v Stevenson*,[73] it is uncontroversial that manufacturers owe the ultimate consumers of their products a duty to take reasonable care to ensure that the product is safe, so establishing the existence of a duty of care will invariably be straightforward. Difficulties might arise for the consumer in proving first, that there was a breach of that duty, and, secondly, that the breach caused her injury.

In order to determine whether the manufacturer has breached its duty, it is necessary to work out what standard of care the pharmaceutical industry owes to the consumers of its products. The manufacturer's duty is simply to exercise such care as is reasonable in all the circumstances. Factors relevant to this assessment include the magnitude of risk, the probability of harm, the burden of taking precautions to prevent the risk materializing, and the utility of the defendant's conduct. Manufacturers are certainly not under a duty to ensure that every drug is completely safe for every potential consumer. All medicines present some risks: penicillin, for example, is generally considered safe and effective, even though it causes very serious allergic reactions in some consumers.

Three different types of product defect might be identified: manufacturing defects, design defects, and the failure to give adequate warnings. It will be relatively straightforward to prove that there has been a breach of duty when the patient's injury was caused by a manufacturing defect: an example might be where an error during the manufacturing process massively increased the quantity of the active ingredient in each pill. A manufacturer which does not take reasonable care to ensure that medicines leave its premises in a fit state for human ingestion would be in breach of its duty to consumers.

Design defects are rather more complicated. Plainly, manufacturers have a duty to design medicines safely, but particular difficulties arise if an unforeseen adverse side-effect subsequently emerges, as happened with Thalidomide. The claimants would have to prove that the risk of injury was foreseeable, and that supplying the product in the light of this risk was unreasonable. Not only will it be very difficult for claimants to gain access to the information necessary to prove this, but also clinical trials cannot be expected to discover every possible side-effect in every possible consumer. The benefits of new medicines mean that it will generally be reasonable to put them into circulation once experiments indicate that they meet an acceptable threshold level of safety.

[73] [1932] AC 562.

It would not be reasonable to expect manufacturers to have identified all potential ADRs before marketing a new drug: this would stifle innovation, unreasonably delay the availability of potentially valuable new medicines, and require vastly increased rates of participation in clinical trials. If, as was the case with Thalidomide, the pharmaceutical company could not reasonably have been expected to know that it would cause devastating birth defects if taken at a particular time in pregnancy, it would not be in breach of its duty of care.

Manufacturers might also be liable for defective warnings. No drug is completely safe for all possible users, and a manufacturer will generally have acted reasonably if he took reasonable steps to alert consumers to the risk of some side-effect, or to contra-indications for taking the medicine in question. Prescription drugs are a rather special case in that it is not necessary for them to be made safe for *anybody* who might use them. Unlike products which can be bought over the counter, it should be possible to ensure that a drug is not prescribed to those individuals for whom it would be unsafe. If, for example, the manufacturer categorically states in the information it has provided to doctors that medicine X should never be taken by anyone with high blood pressure, the manufacturer would be able to avoid liability if someone with high blood pressure subsequently suffers injuries after being wrongly prescribed medicine X.

In the US, this is known as the 'learned intermediary' rule: that is, it is for the doctor to determine whether to prescribe a particular drug to her patient, and to give appropriate warnings. A patient will generally rely upon her doctor's advice, and a manufacturer's package insert is unlikely to override assurance from her GP that she can safely take a medicine which she has been prescribed. Of course, doctors might make prescribing errors or fail to explain how to take the medicine safely. If a patient then wanted to sue her GP, this would be a straightforward clinical negligence action, and the principles which we considered in Chapter 3 would apply.

If the patient's claim is that a manufacturer's failure to warn her of possible side-effects caused her injury, then even if she succeeds in establishing a breach of its duty of care, she will come up against the vexed problem of proving causation in 'failure to warn' cases, which we considered in detail in Chapter 4. In short, the problem is that she must prove that she would not have been injured if she had been properly informed, and in this context, this means that she must establish that she would not have taken the drug in question if she had been warned of the particular side-effect. Let us imagine that a patient was not warned about a 0.1 per cent risk of hair loss associated with taking a particular anti-depressant. Even if she had in fact been warned, she might have judged that the benefits of alleviating her depression outweighed this very small risk of losing her hair. But after this risk has materialized, and with the benefit of hindsight, she now knows for certain that she is the one of the unfortunate minority who will suffer hair loss. In these circumstances, how reliable is her evidence that, if she had known about this tiny risk, she would have chosen not to take the drug?

As we saw earlier, there is no contract between a pharmacist and a patient receiving an NHS prescription. The pharmacist will, however, owe the patient a duty of care. If she negligently dispenses the wrong drug, or the wrong dosage, she could be liable for any resulting injury. In *Prendergast v Sam and Dee Ltd*,[74] a doctor had written a prescription for Mr Prendergast, an asthmatic suffering from a chest infection, which included Amoxil tablets. The pharmacist misread the doctor's unclear handwriting, and dispensed Daonil instead, a drug used in the treatment of diabetes. As a result of taking an excessive dose of

---

[74] The Times, 14 Mar 1989.

Daonil, Mr Prendergast suffered permanent brain damage. He sued both the doctor and the pharmacist, and both were found to have been negligent. Despite the unclear handwriting, the pharmacist should have realized that it was extremely unlikely that the doctor had meant to write Daonil on the prescription. The prescription was for a short course of Amoxil, to be taken three times a day. Diabetics would usually be on continuous courses of Daonil, which is taken only once a day. The dosage would also have been unusually high for Daonil, and since Mr Prendergast paid for his prescription, the pharmacist should have realized that he was not diabetic (people with diabetes do not pay the prescription charge). The Court of Appeal refused to overturn the judge's apportionment of liability: the pharmacist was liable to pay 75 per cent of Mr Prendergast's damages, and the doctor 25 per cent.

Might it also be possible for an injured patient to bring an action against the regulatory authorities for their failure to ensure that a drug was safe enough? Liability for breach of statutory duty is extremely unlikely, since it seems implausible that Parliament intended to create a private law action for damages for any breach of the Medicines Act 1968, which was clearly passed in order to protect public health, and not to provide redress to individual patients. In a negligence action, it would be necessary for the claimant to establish that there was a relationship of proximity between the regulatory agency and the injured patient, and that it would be fair, just and reasonable to impose a duty in these circumstances. Proving the existence of a proximate relationship between the MHRA or the CSM and the person who has been injured would be difficult.

Two cases can be contrasted here. In *Re HIV Haemophiliac Litigation*, the Court of Appeal refused to strike out a claim in negligence against the Department of Health by haemophiliacs who had been infected with the HIV virus following blood transfusions, while admitting that such actions will seldom succeed.

Re HIV Haemophiliac Litigation[75]

Bingham LJ

[W]here, as here, foreseeability by a defendant of severe personal injury to a person such as the plaintiff is shown, and the existence of a proximate relationship between plaintiff and defendant is accepted, the plaintiff is well on his way to establishing the existence of a duty of care. He may still fail to do so if it is held that imposition of such a duty on the defendant would not in all the circumstances be just and reasonable, but it is by no means clear to me at this preliminary stage that the department's submissions on that aspect must prevail.[76]

The case was settled before a full consideration of whether a duty existed or not took place. But in any event, the relationship between the relatively small number of haemophiliacs in the UK and the authorities responsible for the safety of blood transfusions is perhaps distinguishable from a case in which a patient claims that the MHRA or the Commission on Human Medicines owed them a duty of care, as we can see from *Smith v Secretary of State for Health (on behalf of the Committee on Safety of Medicines)*.

Amanda Smith had contracted chickenpox when she was six years old, and was given an aspirin tablet on two consecutive days. Her condition worsened, and she was diagnosed with Reye's syndrome. A month later, her parents discovered that the CSM had advised that

---

[75] (1990) 41 BMLR 171.   [76] Per Bingham LJ.

aspirin should not be given to children under the age of twelve, except on medical advice. The status of warnings on aspirin was to be changed, and junior aspirin was going to be reclassified as a Pharmacy Medicine. Amanda became permanently disabled with spastic tetraplegia, frequent epileptic convulsions, lack of speech, and had to be carried or pushed everywhere. She brought an action for negligence, arguing that the Secretary of State for Health or the Committee on Safety of Medicines was liable for failure to issue public warnings *immediately* after it had decided to change its advice on aspirin.

Smith v Secretary of State for Health (on behalf of the Committee on Safety of Medicines)[77]

Morland J

In my judgment, no common law duty was owed by the CSM or the Secretary of State in respect of the decisions allegedly negligent, even if there was fault in failing to stick to the original timetable. In my judgment, the reasons for that were discretionary/policy and not justiciable.

I wish to make it clear that I am not asserting that the Secretary of State or the CSM could never be liable at common law for breach of duty of care to an individual member of the public from a failure to exercise or a improper exercise of statutory powers and duties: for example, if the Secretary of State had delayed implementation of the CSM 29/30 May decision until after a bye-election in a marginal constituency where there was a large aspirin factory; or if the CSM had postponed its May meeting until the end of June because it clashed with the Epsom Derby meeting.

Even if a claimant were to succeed in establishing that a regulatory authority owed her a duty of care, proving that it had breached its duty would not be straightforward. If the CSM's duty is to act in accordance with a responsible body of medical opinion, given that it is composed of medical experts, proving that their collective judgment represented a breach of their duty of care would be exceptionally difficult.

(c) CONSUMER PROTECTION ACT 1987

In 1985 the European Union adopted a directive[78] which was intended to harmonize European product liability regimes, both in order to remove the distorting impact differing standards of legal liability within the EU were having upon competition, and to ensure that consumers throughout Europe enjoy equal protection against dangerous products. For a number of reasons, the directive has been only partially successful in achieving harmonization. First, certain aspects of the directive, most notably the controversial development risks defence (considered below), were optional, and their take-up has varied across Europe. Secondly, because it does not *replace* liability under member states' domestic tort systems, similar strict liability statutes throughout Europe co-exist with very different systems of tort liability for personal injuries. As Jane Stapleton explains:

---

[77] [2002] EWHC 200 (QB).   [78] Products Liability 85/374/EEC.

> despite the vaunted claim that the Directive was aimed at the approximation of product regimes across Member States, in a real sense, it has merely added onto existing regimes a further level of disparate rules varying, for example, according to which options in the Directive were implemented and what local rules exist in relation to non-pecuniary loss.[79]

Thirdly, the implementing legislation has to be applied by national courts, whose interpretations of the provisions in the directive may vary. For example, if there are national variations in consumer expectations, the directive's definition of defect (which relies upon what consumers generally are entitled to expect) may lead to varying levels of consumer protection.[80]

Of course, harmonization does not necessarily dictate the introduction of strict liability. It would have been possible to introduce an EU-wide fault-based system instead. So why did the Commission favour a strict liability regime? First, as Hans Claudius Taschner points out in the next extract, the Commission argued that strict liability promotes loss-spreading: rather than the costs of injuries falling on individual consumers, they will be borne by manufacturers, who are better able to spread the cost by insurance, and by raising prices, so the costs are ultimately borne by all consumers. Secondly, it was argued that justice demands that consumers should not have to bear their own losses if they cannot discharge the onerous burden of proving negligence.

Hans Claudius Taschner[81]

> The question of product liability is therefore who should bear the consequences of damage resulting from unavoidable defects: the victim, society at large, or the relatively small group of product users, one of whom unfortunately used a defective product. There are only three available solutions to the problem of product liability: first is liability for fault, or negligence, which is regarded as the classical solution; second is a no-fault system or compensation by the state as established in New Zealand; or third is liability independent of fault. The classical solution leads to the conclusion that the consequences of defective products must be borne by the victim like an Act of God. According to the New Zealand no-fault system, neither the victim nor the producer, but society at large should absorb the cost of damages....
>
> The Commission developed the third- and last-mentioned solution whereby the economic loss suffered by the victim, his damage, is transferred to the producer, at least provisionally. The producer insures himself and passes on the cost of the insurance premiums to all users of his products, one of which, having a manufacturing defect, has caused damage. The producer does this by including those costs in his general production costs which leads to a slight increase in the final product price. This so-called 'insurance solution' avoids the arbitrary character of the classical solution, as well as the collectivist aspect of the no-fault scheme. The only way to transfer the economic loss of the victim to all non-damaged users of non-defective products easily is to provide for liability independent of fault.

---

[79] 'Products Liability in the United Kingdom: The Myths of Reform' (1999) 34 Texas International Law Journal 45.

[80] Geraint Howells, *Comparative Product Liability* (Dartmouth: Aldershot, 1993) 196.

[81] 'Harmonization of Product Liability Law in the European Community' (1999) 34 Texas International Law Journal 21.

As we see later, the directive includes a number of 'defences', which inevitably limits its capacity to protect consumers. Jane Stapleton argues that by trying to protect both consumers *and businesses*, the directive is a classic example of 'Euro-fudge'.

Jane Stapleton[82]

The Directive did not result from some perceived bottom-up forensic pressure from claims. Rather, the engine of this reform was social and political. In particular, the concern of the public in these countries had been galvanized by the disaster caused by the unforeseen side effects of the Thalidomide pregnancy drug. Meanwhile, by the late 1970s, the European Commission was keen to promote consumer protection measures to show Europeans that the 'common market' was not there simply to serve big business. It proposed very pro-consumer draft Directives in 1976 and 1979. Yet there remained intense concern within the European Parliament and the Council that substantial exculpatory provisions be included in any future Directive.

As a result, the Directive is one of the high-water marks of Euro-fudge and textual vagueness. The point is that the Directive tries to square a circle: it uses the rhetoric of 'strict liability,' and yet, in Articles 6(2) and 7(e), it seems to provide solid protection for reasonable businesses, a compromise demanded by the UK Government of Margaret Thatcher.

The directive was given effect in the UK by the Consumer Protection Act 1987 (CPA). There are some differences in wording between the directive and the CPA, but in *Commission v UK*,[83] the European Court of Justice (ECJ) found that there was no evidence that the UK courts were interpreting the Act in a way that was inconsistent with the directive, though this may have been because there had been virtually no cases. Moreover, the ECJ was influenced by the fact that section 1 of the CPA specifically states that the provisions in the relevant part of the Act were passed in order to comply with the directive, and should be construed accordingly.

In *A v National Blood Authority*,[84] a case we consider in detail later, Burton J relied upon the judgment in *Commission v UK*[85] and section 1 of the CPA as evidence that the Act must be interpreted consistently with the directive. In the spirit of consistency, he decided to go straight to the directive and apply it directly:

[I]n so far as the wording of the CPA, in relation to matters which have been the subject matter of particular issue in this case, differs from the equivalent articles in the directive, it should not be construed differently from the directive; and consequently the practical course was to go straight to the fount, the directive itself.

The Act imposes strict liability on manufacturers and, in certain circumstances, suppliers for defective products which cause physical injury, or property damage greater than €500. Pure economic loss is not covered. Any claim must be brought within three years of the discovery of the damage or injury, with a long-stop of ten years from when the product was first put into circulation. This ten-year time limit is intended to make it easier for manufacturers to insure against liability, because no claims are possible more than ten years after a

---

[82] 'Bugs in Anglo-American Products Liability' (2002) 53 South Carolina Law Review 1225.
[83] [1997] AER (EC) 481.   [84] [2001] 3 All ER 289.   [85] [1997] AER (EC) 481.

product is first marketed. Some adverse reactions take many years to manifest themselves, and a claimant will have to bring an action in negligence if this happens outside the ten-year long-stop (see further chapter 3).

The Act only applies to products put into circulation *after* it came into force on 1 March 1988. Because it applies only to *new* products, it might have been expected that there would be comparatively little litigation immediately following the Act's introduction. The paucity of litigation in the past twenty years has, however, been surprising—certainly the evidence does not bear out Lord Griffiths (writing extra-judicially) *et al.*'s prediction in 1988: 'We have little doubt that, once it is no longer necessary to prove negligence, there will be a significant increase in product liability litigation in England.'[86]

In the next extract Jane Stapleton analyses possible explanations for the Act's more limited impact.

Jane Stapleton[87]

> But even sceptics have been surprised at how very little effect this new cause of action has had in practice....In short, the findings have been that there has been no perceptible, or at least no reported, impact on insurance premiums, research and development activity, product innovation in general, or product-caused injury rates...The truth is that the revolution in the products field that manufacturers feared and consumer advocates hoped the Directive would produce has simply not happened. What is the reason for this lack of impact?...
>
> In my view, the most convincing explanation for this no-significant-impact phenomenon is simply that the new law scarcely advances the position of the consumer at all...Save in a few peripheral contexts, no greater liability is imposed by the Directive than already exists under the other two main causes of action available to victims of defective products.

In the past twenty or so years, there have been hardly any reported cases involving medicines. *XYZ and Others v Schering Health Care Ltd* involved a group action by claimants who had taken different brands of the Combined Oral Contraceptive (COC), and who claimed to have suffered various cardio-vascular injuries (which come under the collective description of Venous-thromboembolism, VTE). They argued that the pills they took were defective under the Consumer Protection Act 1987 and/or the Product Liability Directive. Their claims followed a 'pill scare' in 1995. The CSM had written to doctors stating that three unpublished studies into the safety of COCs had indicated 'around a twofold increase in the risk' of VTE. The defendants claimed that there is no increased risk and that the CSM's warning was misjudged.

Both the defendants and the claimants agreed that the action under the CPA could only proceed if there was in fact a twofold increase in the risk of VTE. After an extraordinarily lengthy analysis of the evidence, Mackay J concluded that:

> [T]here is not as a matter of probability any increased relative risk of VTE carried by any of the third generation oral contraceptives supplied to these Claimants by the Defendants as compared with second generation products containing Levonorgesterel.[88]

---

[86] Lord Griffiths, Peter De Val, and RJ Dormer, 'Developments in English Product Liability Law: A Comparison with the American System' (1988) 62 Tulane Law Review 353, 375.

[87] 'Products Liability in the United Kingdom: The Myths of Reform' (1999) 34 Texas International Law Journal 45.

[88] *XYZ and Others v Schering Health Care Ltd* [2002] EWHC 1420 (QB).

Because the claimants' case had failed on this preliminary issue, it was not necessary for Mackay J to consider the application of the Consumer Protection Act.

In a more recent medicines case, and another one involving a class action, *Multiple Claimants v Sanifo-Synthelabo*,[89] Andrew Smith J was asked to resolve a number of questions, including whether Epilim, an anti-epileptic drug, was defective within the meaning of the Act. The claimants in this case are all children whose mothers who took Epilim during pregnancy. Their claim is that Epilim is a known teratogen (ie that it damages the fetus in utero), but for some women it is the only effective treatment for epilepsy. This clearly places pregnant women with epilepsy in an impossible dilemma, but does it mean that the product is 'defective' under the CPA? Andrew Smith J declined to make preliminary findings on this point, and hence this case will, unless settled or dropped, proceed to a full trial.

One of the difficult issues for claimants is that, in the absence of legal aid, litigation is prohibitively expensive. Because the factual issues are complex, trials involving injuries caused by medicinal products are likely to be lengthy, and so the Legal Services Commission's decision not to grant legal aid will almost inevitably mean that the action has to be dropped. This happened in relation to a class action against the manufacturer of the MMR vaccine after the Legal Services Commission decided that there was insufficient chance of success to justify continued funding. Andrew Wakefield's claim, in 1998, that there was a link between the MMR vaccine and autism has subsequently been almost universally discredited, and so there would almost certainly be no chance of succeeding on the question of causation.

Legal aid was also refused, perhaps more surprisingly, to claimants who wished to sue Merck, the manufacturer of Vioxx, which was withdrawn after evidence emerged that it caused strokes and heart attacks. In the US, actions against Merck, the manufacturer of Vioxx, have been successful, and Merck set aside $4.85bn for legal claims from US citizens. After legal aid was refused in the UK, the UK victims attempted to bring actions in the US courts, but these were rejected on the grounds that US juries could not be expected to understand another country's system of drug regulation.[90] Following this decision, one of the lawyers responsible for bringing the claims, Martyn Day, has commented: 'We are in a total quandary. I am totally stumped as to how we can get these cases into the courts anywhere.... [The Vioxx case was] the strongest drug-related case we've seen in the UK for a long time.'[91]

(1) Who Can be Liable?

Under section 2, a number of actors may be jointly and severally liable under the Act. This means that an injured consumer can choose to sue any of the various possible defendants, each of whom may be liable for the total loss. It would then be up to the losing defendant to recoup his losses from the other possible defendants. By increasing the number of potential defendants, the likelihood that a consumer will be able to find a solvent one is thereby increased.

Those who can be strictly liable for defective products include producers, importers into the European Union, and 'own-brand' suppliers (in relation to medicines, this might mean *Boots* could be liable for defects in their own-brand cold remedies). Under section 2(3) suppliers will be liable if they are unable to identify the producer.

---

[89] [2007] EWHC 1860 (QB).

[90] Clare Dyer and Sarah Boseley, 'US Court Ruling Shuts Door on Drug Claimants' Compensation Hopes' (2006) *The Guardian*, 7 October.

[91] Ibid.

It is clear that a pharmacist is a supplier. Doctors might also be suppliers if they actually provided the medicine, as commonly happens in hospitals. To absolve themselves of responsibility, both supplying doctors and pharmacists should therefore keep detailed records of the manufacturers of the drugs which they supply. Furthermore, as a result of the Act's limitation period, these records must be kept for ten years.

(2) What is a Product?

Medicines and medical devices are unquestionably 'products', for the purposes of the Act, but until fairly recently, it was unclear whether human tissues or fluids would be covered. In *A v National Blood Authority*,[92] it was accepted by both parties that blood was a product under the Act. While calling them 'products' seems counter-intuitive, it is possible that gametes (that is, sperm and eggs) might also be subject to the Act's provisions.

(3) What is a Defect?

An action can only lie if the product is 'defective', and the definition of defect under section 3 of the Act is, to say the least, rather confusing.

Consumer Protection Act 1987 section 3

3(1) Subject to the following provisions of this subsection, there is a defect in a product for the purposes of this Part if the safety of the product is not such as persons generally are entitled to expect; and for those purposes 'safety', in relation to a product, shall include safety with respect to products comprised in that product and safety in the context of risks of damage to property, as well as in the context of risks of death or personal injury.

(2) In determining for the purposes of subsection (1) above what persons generally are entitled to expect in relation to a product all the circumstances shall be taken into account, including—

(a) the manner in which, and purposes for which, the product has been marketed, its get-up, the use of any mark in relation to the product and any instructions for, or warnings with respect to, doing or refraining from doing anything with or in relation to the product;

(b) what might reasonably be expected to be done with or in relation to the product; and

(c) the time when the product was supplied by its producer to another; and nothing in this section shall require a defect to be inferred from the fact alone that the safety of a product which is supplied after that time is greater than the safety of the product in question.

The Act does not distinguish between manufacturing, design, or failure to warn of, defects. It simply states that a product is defective if its safety is not such as persons generally are entitled to expect. This definition of defect will apply easily and straightforwardly to manufacturing defects, where the product is less safe than it should have been because of a mistake in the production process.

---

[92] [2001] 3 All ER 289.

Manufacturing defects in medicinal products are, however, unusual. Usually patients who have been injured by a medicine will want to allege either that its design was defective, or that they were inadequately warned about a particular risk, and in both cases, working out what level of safety persons generally are entitled to expect becomes much more complicated. Indeed, Jane Stapleton has argued that a consumer expectation test is inherently unhelpful: 'The core theoretical problem with the definition, however, is that it is circular. This is because what a person is entitled to expect is the very question a definition of defect should be answering.'[93]

In relation to new or complex products, such as medicines, consumers may have no clear expectations about the level of safety they are entitled to expect. Of course, it could be argued that consumers never actually *expect* to be injured by something they have bought or ingested,[94] so that *any* product which causes injury is defective. The test is an objective one, however: it is what consumers are *entitled* to expect, and people are *not* entitled to expect that medicines will never cause any unwanted side-effects. On the contrary, it is to be expected that medicines which are powerful enough to alter physiological function will occasionally cause adverse reactions.

Section 3(2) sets out a number of factors which are relevant to what consumers generally are entitled to expect, such as, under section 3(2)(a), any warnings provided with the product. Of course, the existence of a warning does not necessarily mean that a product is not defective. If it did, then, given the relatively low cost of warnings, manufacturers would simply warn of every conceivable risk in the hope of avoiding liability. This would be undesirable, because the danger signal imparted by warnings is diluted if they become ubiquitous and over-inclusive. Moreover, it should not be possible for manufacturers of manifestly unsafe products, which could have been made safer, to avoid liability by warning of the risk the product presents. Rather, warnings should only absolve a manufacturer of liability if avoiding the existence of the risk was not a realistic option.

Also relevant under section 3(2)(b) is what might reasonably be expected to be done with the product. Plainly, this means that injuries caused by taking an overdose will not be covered by the Act. A more difficult question is the extent to which it is reasonable to expect consumers to take medicines *exactly* according to the manufacturer's instructions. Studies suggest that as many as sixty per cent of patients fail to comply with directions for the use of medicines.[95] Because it can reasonably be expected that a patient will forget to take a pill, for example, or leave too short a time between doses, a medicine should be safe enough even if there is some slight deviation from the product's instructions.

Section 3(2)(c) specifies that a product is not to be considered defective simply because a better product is subsequently put into circulation. So a product's defectiveness must be judged according to prevailing safety standards at the time when it was supplied, rather than at the time of the court hearing (as we saw in Chapter 3, an analogous rule applies in negligence actions).

A different sort of approach to the question of whether a product is defective would be to adopt a straightforward risk/benefit calculation: are the risks which the product presents justified by its benefits? So, for example, aspirin and penicillin both cause adverse side-effects in a small minority of patients, but given their overwhelming health benefits for other

---

[93] *Product Liability* (Butterworths: London, 1994) 234.   [94] Ibid, 235.
[95] Richard Sykes, *New Medicines, The Practice of Medicine, and Public Policy* (Nuffield Trust: London, 2000).

patients, persons generally are not entitled to expect that aspirin or penicillin can safely be taken by every possible consumer. In contrast, Thalidomide might have alleviated morning sickness, but the risks of premature death and severe disability are far too grave to justify its use in relieving nausea in early pregnancy, and adopting a risk/benefit approach, it would therefore be categorized as a defective product. Interestingly, there has been some interest in using Thalidomide to slow the rate at which brain tumours grow. Gravely ill patients, suffering from advanced brain tumours, are very unlikely to object to the condition that they do not become pregnant while taking Thalidomide, and hence for them the benefits may outweigh its risks.

The availability of alternative products would also be relevant to a risk/benefit safety assessment. Let us imagine that a new contraceptive pill will cause a very undesirable side-effect, such as blindness, in 0.01 per cent of consumers. Not only might we want to weigh the risk of blindness against the benefit of effective contraceptive protection, but it would also be relevant that other contraceptive pills exist which do not have this undesirable side-effect. If, however, a drug which carried a similar risk was the *only* cure for AIDS, a 0.01 per cent risk of blindness might be acceptable.

So how has the consumer expectation test worked in practice? Before Burton J's judgment in *A v National Blood*, considered below, in a handful of cases the courts appeared to suggest that what consumers were entitled to expect depended upon the *reasonableness* of the defendant's conduct. This looked very like an assessment of whether the defendant had been *negligent*.

In *Richardson v LRC*,[96] a condom had failed inexplicably. Ian Kennedy J held that although users did not expect condoms to fail, persons generally were not entitled to expect any contraceptive to be 100 per cent effective. He reached this conclusion after extensive discussion of the testing procedures adopted by the defendants. But if the level of safety people are entitled to expect cannot be measured without reference to the *reasonableness* of the defendant's conduct, 'strict liability' may be indistinguishable from negligence.[97]

In *Abouzaid v Mothercare*, a case involving a child injured by an elasticated strap on a baby's fleece sleeping bag, the Court of Appeal specifically stated that what the defendant could have done differently was relevant to what consumers generally were entitled to expect. Pill LJ stated:

> I have come to the conclusion that, though the case is close to the borderline, the product was defective within the meaning of the Act....Members of the public were entitled to expect better from the appellants....It is not necessary for the Court to determine precisely what more should have been done. It is clear that more could have been done.[98]

This trend towards a negligence-based interpretation of defect was interrupted by the decision of Burton J in *A v National Blood Authority*. The claimants had become infected with Hepatitis C from blood transfusions at a time when it was known that there was a strain of Hepatitis known only as non-A non-B Hepatitis, with which a small percentage of blood was infected. At the time, while the risk was known, reliable tests to identify this new strain of Hepatitis had not yet been devised. In deciding whether the infected blood was

[96] [2000] PIQR P164.
[97] See also *Worsley v Tambrands* [2000] PIQR P95 and *Foster v Biosil* (2000) 59 BMLR 178.
[98] The Times, February 20, 2001.

defective, Burton J asked himself what consumers were entitled to expect, and explicitly declined to take into account whether the defendants had acted reasonably.

A v National Blood Authority[99]

Burton J

It is quite plain to me that the directive was intended to eliminate proof of fault or negligence. I am satisfied that this was not simply a legal consequence, but that it was also intended to make it easier for claimants to prove their case, such that not only would a consumer not have to prove that the producer did not take reasonable steps, or all reasonable steps, to comply with his duty of care, but also that the producer did not take all legitimately expectable steps either....

I conclude therefore that avoidability is not one of the circumstances to be taken into account within article 6. I am satisfied that it is not a relevant circumstance, because it is outwith the purpose of the directive, and indeed that, had it been intended that it would be included as a derogation from, or at any rate a palliation of, its purpose, then it would certainly have been mentioned; for it would have been an important circumstance.

Crucially then, Burton J found that whether or not the risk of harm could be avoided was not relevant to what consumers might reasonably expect. Also irrelevant were the costs, difficulty or impracticability of taking precautionary measures, and the benefit to society or the utility of the product. The public, Burton J found, expected blood to be free from infection.

[The blood products in this case] were defective because I am satisfied that the public at large was entitled to expect that the blood transfused to them would be free from infection. There were no warnings and no material publicity, certainly none officially initiated by or for the benefit of the defendants, and the knowledge of the medical profession, not materially or at all shared with the consumer, is of no relevance. It is not material to consider whether any steps or any further steps could have been taken to avoid or palliate the risk that the blood would be infected.

So whether or not ensuring all blood was infection-free was in practice attainable did not affect the consumer's expectation that blood products would be safe. The consequence of his judgment is that consumers may legitimately expect 100 per cent safety, even if this is an unreasonable and wholly impractical expectation. In the context of HIV-infected blood, Andrew Grubb and David Pearl have, however, argued that consumers *do* take into account what might reasonably be done to avoid the risk of infection: 'If a reasonable person has any expectation about the safety of blood, it will be that the blood has been tested to the usual extent currently employed.'[100]

The central problem is that a consumer expectation test which excludes considerations of what the defendant could reasonably have done to avoid the risk has an air of

---

[99] [2001] 3 All ER 289.
[100] *Blood Testing, AIDS and DNA Profiling* (Jordan: Bristol, 1990) 144.

artificiality about it, particularly when the test is what people generally are *entitled* to expect. Are consumers really entitled to expect a wholly unattainable level of safety? Yet once we start to take into account the *reasonableness* of the defendant's actions, the inquiry begins to look indistinguishable from the sort of reasoning the court might adopt in a negligence action.

One way out of this apparent impasse would be to categorize blood as an unavoidably unsafe product. In *A v National Blood Authority* Burton J accepted that unavoidably unsafe products, such as knives or alcohol, would not be defective under the Act.

> There are some products, which have harmful characteristics in whole or in part, about which no complaint can be made. The examples that were used of products which have obviously dangerous characteristics by virtue of their very nature or intended use, were, on the one hand knives, guns and poisons and on the other hand alcohol, tobacco, perhaps foie gras....Drugs with advertised side-effects may fall within this category.

Where a product is unavoidably unsafe, and the danger is generally known, consumers are not entitled to expect 100 per cent safety. Burton J rejected this solution to the problem of infected blood, however, in part because consumers had not been warned about the risk of infection, and so the danger was not generally known.

In his judgment Burton J adopted a rather curious distinction between standard products, which are as the producer intended, and non-standard products, which differ from the standard product. This is analogous to the distinction between manufacturing defects, where the product is not as the producer intended, perhaps because it was contaminated during the manufacturing process, and design defects, where the product is as the producer intended, but because of some intrinsic problem in its design, it turns out to be defective. Of course, the language of manufacturing and design defects applies rather awkwardly to blood, which is neither manufactured nor designed, and this may be why Burton J chose to talk instead about standard and non-standard products.

> Thus a standard product is one which is and performs as the producer intends. A nonstandard product is one which is different, obviously because it is deficient or inferior in terms of safety, from the standard product: and where it is the harmful characteristic or characteristics present in the non-standard product, but not in the standard product, which has or have caused the material injury or damage.

Infected blood was, in his view, a non-standard product. He then had to ask himself:

> [W]hether the public at large accepted the non-standard nature of the product i.e., they accept that a proportion of the products is defective (as I have concluded they do not in this case).

In the next extract, Richard Goldberg argues that a risk/benefit approach might have made sense in *A v National Blood Authority,* since it would have allowed the utility of blood to be weighed against the unavoidable risk of infection.

Richard Goldberg[101]

It is arguable that all medicinal products carry a risk of adverse reactions, even in a minority of consumers, and that these consumers are not necessarily entitled to expect that the products will be risk free. Despite the emphasis on consumer expectation in Burton J's judgment, there is an inherent logic in addressing the problems of defective medicinal products by weighing the risks against the anticipated benefits and against the 'costs' of not using the product, such as the risk of disease.

In the US, what are known as 'blood shield statutes' have generally been adopted to exempt blood products from strict liability regimes. In part, this is because a risk/benefit analysis suggests that where the utility of a product is great, and is not achievable by a substitute product, and where the risk of infection is known and unavoidable, strict liability for infection would be unreasonable. Writing before the judgment in *A v National Blood*, Andrew Grubb and David Pearl assumed that a similar outcome would be likely under the Consumer Protection Act.

Andrew Grubb and David Pearl[102]

The utility of blood, ie the obvious benefits to patients coupled with the absence of any less dangerous alternative to blood which could be substituted for it, are likely to lead a court to the conclusion that blood is not defective....

The inapplicability of the 1987 Act to the transmission of HIV through blood or blood products should come as no surprise since, even in the jurisdictions where strict liability originates, the US courts usually do not impose strict liability where infection is transmitted through blood. The great utility of blood or blood products in the treatment of patients has led almost all courts not to apply strict liability in this area.

(4) Defences

Section 4 of the Consumer Protection Act provides a number of defences. First, it is a defence if the defect is attributable to compliance with a statutory obligation. This does not amount to a 'regulatory compliance' defence, which would offer a defence simply because the defective product had obtained a marketing authorization from the appropriate regulator: rather, it offers a defence only if the *defect itself* could be attributed to compliance with a regulatory requirement. This will be unusual, whereas clearly regulatory compliance is not.

Perhaps unsurprisingly, many manufacturers have argued that there should be a regulatory compliance defence, and this has not fallen on completely deaf ears. In the European Commission's third five-yearly report on the application of the product liability Directive, one of the issues which the Commission said it would continue to monitor closely is whether there should be a defence of regulatory compliance.[103]

In the next extract, however, Mark Mildred suggests that the inclusion of a regulatory compliance defence should be resisted.

---

[101] 'Paying for Bad Blood: Strict Product Liability after the Hepatitis C Litigation' (2002) 10 Medical Law Review 165–200, 174.

[102] *Blood Testing, AIDS and DNA Profiling* (Jordan: Bristol, 1990) 151–4.

[103] European Commission Third Report on the Application of the Directive (2006).

Mark Mildred[104]

There are objections to the introduction of the defence, however, of far more fundamental force than the mere financial balancing of cost against profits. First, a defence based on the existence of a marketing authorisation would fairly require that the judgement of the regulator was sound. Under the defence the consumer would be without remedy against the manufacturer but, in the current state of the law, highly unlikely to have any recourse against the regulatory authority itself....

There is little compelling evidence from the reviews by the Commission of the working of the PL Directive over nearly twenty years that innovation or competitiveness is being stifled or the pharmaceutical industry unfairly burdened with the costs of (or insuring against) an oppressive liability regime. In those circumstances the introduction of a preferential impunity for it in the form of a regulatory compliance defence would be incompatible with the fair apportionment of risk that is the primary intention of the PL Directive.

Secondly, a defence exists if the defendant can prove that the product was never supplied to another, or was not supplied in the course of a business.

Thirdly, there is a defence if the defect was not present when the product was supplied. This defence was applied in *Piper v JRI Ltd*. The claimant, Terence Piper had undergone a hip replacement operation, which involved the insertion of a prosthetic hip, manufactured by the defendant company. Eighteen months later, the hip fractured, and Mr Piper had to undergo a further operation, and was left with significantly impaired movement and mobility. He brought an action against the defendants, claiming that the hip had been defective within the meaning of section 3 of the Act.

By the time of the trial, expert examination had established that the prosthesis fractured as a result of fatigue failure initiating from a defect in the titanium alloy from which it was made. The question then was whether the defect was present at the time that the defendant supplied the hip to the hospital, in which case they would be liable, or whether it occurred subsequently, perhaps during implantation.

At first instance, the judge found that the defendant manufacturer had subjected this product to a 'vigorous and meticulous process of work and inspection of the highest quality'. Because the defect would have been visible, and hence easily detectable in the defendant's factory, given his finding as to the rigorousness of the defendant's processes, he said: 'I am simply not prepared to accept that such a mistake was made with the product.'

The Court of Appeal refused to overturn this finding.

Piper v JRI Ltd[105]

Thomas LJ

As the system was capable of detecting the only type of surface point defect capable of initiating the fatigue failure, given the view taken of those operating the system, it could be inferred that any such defect would have been detected had it been present prior to delivery to the hospital and that in the case of the prosthesis implanted into the claimant that the inspection system had not failed.

---

[104] 'Pharmaceutical Products: The Relationship between Regulatory Approval and the Existence of a Defect' (2007) European Business Law Review 1276–82.
[105] [2006] EWCA Civ 1344 CA.

> It seems to me that on an analysis of the evidence before the judge and on the way the case was presented to him, the judge was therefore correct in making the finding of fact made by him that the prosthesis was not defective at the time it was supplied to the hospital.

In essence, the Court of Appeal found for the manufacturer because the claimant had been unable to prove that it had made a mistake. This appears to re-introduce a negligence-type inquiry into the question of whether the manufacturer could rely upon the statutory defence that the product was not defective when it left its premises.

Interestingly, in the Court of Appeal Mr Piper did not pursue an alternative argument, namely that even if the hip had been in perfect condition when it left the factory, there must have been something wrong with it if it fractured as a result of the stress to which it was subject during implantation or during normal use.

Fourthly, contributory negligence applies, and so a patient who takes the wrong dose of a drug which subsequently causes injury may be responsible in whole or in part for her own injuries. It should perhaps be noted that the application of contributory negligence to a strict liability regime is rather complicated. If damages are to be apportioned according to the degree of fault of the parties, how might this work when the defendant might not have been at fault at all? Where the claimant has behaved irresponsibly, but the defendant is blameless, does apportionment mean that the claimant's damages must be reduced by 100 per cent? In practice, the application of contributory negligence just means that the claimant's damages will be reduced according to the extent to which their injury was caused by their blameworthy conduct.

The most important and controversial defence is known as the development risks or 'state of the art' defence and is contained in section 4(1)(e).

Consumer Protection Act 1987 section 4

> 4(1)(e) [I]t shall be a defence...that the state of scientific and technical knowledge at the relevant time was not such that a producer of products of the same description as the product in question might be expected to have discovered the defect if it had existed in his products while they were under his control.

The UK Act's version of the development risks defence is slightly different from that in Article 7(e) of the directive:

> The producer shall not be liable as a result of this Directive if he proves:...that the state of scientific and technical knowledge at the time when he put the product into circulation was not such as to enable the existence of the defect to be discovered.

The UK's defence thus appears to be broader in scope than that of the directive since the relevant state of knowledge is that of 'producer[s] of products of the same description', rather than the state of scientific knowledge. Hence a manufacturer could have a defence under the CPA if other producers were equally ignorant of the way to detect the defect in question, even if the defect was in fact discoverable. In contrast, under the directive, there would only be a defence if the defect was, in the light of contemporary scientific knowledge, *undiscoverable*.

It was this inconsistency which prompted the European Commission to bring infringement proceedings against the UK. As we saw earlier, the European Court of Justice found that section 4(1)(e) was capable of being interpreted in accordance with Article 7(e), and this is precisely what Burton J did in *A v National Blood*:

Although the United Kingdom Government has not amended s 4(1)(e) of the CPA so as to bring it in line with the wording of the directive, there is thus binding authority of the Court of Justice that it must be so construed.

This defence was included in order to accommodate the fear that liability for undiscoverable defects would be likely to impede innovation within the pharmaceutical industry. In particular, it was thought that strict liability for undiscoverable risks would make it impossible to obtain liability insurance. The defence is optional, and although most countries have chosen to include it, some, such as Luxembourg and Finland, have not. In Spain and Germany it does not apply to medicines, and in France it does not apply to products derived from the human body. This uneven take-up of the defence means that manufacturers who wish to market drugs throughout the EU will, in any event, have to insure against liability for undiscoverable risks in countries where the defence is unavailable.

Clearly, the development risks defence has little impact upon manufacturing defects. Rather, it is in relation to design defects, and failures to warn, that a manufacturer might seek to rely upon evidence that the risk in question was not discoverable when the product was put into circulation. The question of discoverability is, as Charles Pugh and Marcus Pilgerstorfer point out, of critical importance.

Charles Pugh and Marcus Pilgerstorfer[106]

A more difficult situation is where the defect is not known but is arguably discoverable. The strictness of liability imposed by the Directive as a whole is dependent upon whether, on a proper construction of Art. 7(e), the focus is on the simple ability to discover the defect, or whether the Court enquires into how reasonable it was for the defect to have been discovered....

There is an additional limit on what knowledge is relevant for the purposes of Article 7(e). Knowledge must be accessible in what has become known as the 'Manchurian' sense. [In *Commission v UK*] the ECJ held that it was 'implicit in the wording of article 7(e) that the relevant scientific and technical knowledge must have been accessible at the time when the product in question was put into circulation'. The much debated example given by the Advocate General is of an academic in Manchuria publishing in a local scientific journal in Chinese which does not go outside the boundaries of the region. In such cases the defence will remain available notwithstanding that the total world body of scientific and technical knowledge might have enabled the defect to be discovered. The relevant body of knowledge on which to focus is 'accessible knowledge'....

Once the relevant knowledge has been ascertained, the next stage in the Court's enquiry into the availability of the Article 7(e) defence is to consider the discoverability of the defect. The presence of this second criterion puts it beyond doubt that it is insufficient for the producer to show simply that the defect was not 'known' at the time the product was put into circulation. A producer must go further and show that the relevant knowledge was not such as to 'enable the existence of the defect to be discovered'.

As we can see from the next two extracts, the development risks defence has been extremely controversial. As Christopher Newdick explains, unforeseen risks are precisely

---

[106] 'The Development Risk Defence: Knowledge, Discoverability and Creative Leaps' (2004) 4 Journal of Personal Injury Law 258–69.

the sort of defects which are most likely to occur in medicines. If manufacturers have a defence for such risks, the impact of strict liability on the pharmaceutical industry will be minimal. Jane Stapleton further questions why we should treat unforeseeable design errors more leniently than equally blameless manufacturing errors.

Christopher Newdick[107]

It will be recalled that it was the tragedy of thalidomide that gave rise to the debate concerning strict liability in this country. Ironically, however, it is the future victims of an accident of precisely this form that would most seriously be prejudiced by a state of the art defence. The pharmaceutical industry in this country has not generally been accused of irresponsible or unreasonable behaviour. By its very nature it works in an area in which unforeseeable accidents are inevitable, where fault is usually absent and known risks frequently judged acceptable as regards the few, in the interests of the many. In addition, their actions have the approval of an official licensing body. These factors would effectively be sufficient to guarantee that, unless a special exception were made to such a defence, the pharmaceutical industry would be its principal beneficiary.

Jane Stapleton[108]

We still have no principled explanation of why, for example, it is fair to hold a manufacturer strictly liable for some product flaws he could not discover (for example, some manufacturing errors), but not fair to do so in relation to a different set of product flaws he could not discover (namely, unforeseeable design dangers).

The development risks defence does have its supporters, however. Christopher Hodges, for example, points out that the defence's positive impact upon innovative practices is, in the long run, likely to serve the interests of patients as well as manufacturers.

Christopher Hodges[109]

It is the essence of innovation that the risks which may be encountered in the use of a product cannot reasonably be identified or quantified at the time at which it is marketed—either fully or, in some cases, at all. Of course, one approach might be to require producers to test products fully before marketing them. But that would be unrealistic. First, testing usually includes testing in use by real humans in real life situations...there must be a limit to the duration and cost of such an exercise. With medicines, the limit is effectively prescribed by regulation, taking into account ethical constraints on repetitive or excessive testing. If testing were required to continue until all possible risks which might occur with use of a product had now been identified, few producers could afford to innovate and consumers would not benefit

---

[107] 'Strict Liability for Defective Drugs in the Pharmaceutical Industry' (1985) 101 Law Quarterly Review 405–31.

[108] 'Bugs in Anglo-American Products Liability' (2002) 53 South Carolina Law Review 1225, 1241.

[109] 'Development Risks: Unanswered Questions' (1998) 61 Modern Law Review 560–70.

from advances in science and technology. Research would stagnate if denied practical application and commercial advantage...

The basic problem with the defence is that a literal concept of *undiscoverability* is an unworkable test. The truth is that *any* defect can be discovered prior to marketing given sufficient testing. Such testing simply requires time and money....The issue, however, is how
much testing it is reasonable to expect the producer of an innovative product to undertake
pre-marketing. Community policy recognises ethical, commercial and social limitations on
the extent of pre-market testing.

Burton J's judgment in *A v National Blood Authority* may have come as a surprise to academic commentators. Most people had assumed that the development risks defence meant
that liability under the Act would in practice be indistinguishable from negligence, in that
manufacturers who had acted reasonably in attempting to discover possible risks would be
able to avoid liability for defective products. In *A v National Blood Authority*, the defendants knew about the existence of the risk of infection, but they did not know how to detect
it in individual bags of blood. The only way in which it would have been possible to ensure
that no recipients of blood transfusions became infected with the Hepatitis C virus would
have been to stop carrying out blood transfusions, which would have breached the National
Blood Authority's obligation to supply blood, and would lead to a much greater risk to public health than the comparatively small risk of Hepatitis C infection. In short, the National
Blood Authority almost certainly *had* exercised reasonable care.

Nevertheless, Burton J held that once the manufacturer knew of the existence of a defect,
it was a known risk and the development risks defence could not apply, even if there was no
known way of avoiding the risk in question. If the development risks defence is confined to
unknown risks, and has no application to *known but unavoidable* risks, its scope is significantly more restrictive than most people had assumed.

A v National Blood Authority[110]

Burton J

[I]t is common ground here that the existence of the defect in blood generally, ie of the infection of blood in some cases by Hepatitis virus notwithstanding screening, was known, and
indeed known to the defendants....

Conclusions on Article 7(e) (development risks defence)

[T]he risk ceases to be a development risk and becomes a known risk not if and when the
producer in question...had the requisite knowledge, but if and when such knowledge were
accessible anywhere in the world outside Manchuria. Hence it protects the producer in
respect of the unknown....

[O]nce the problem is known by virtue of accessible information, then the non-standard
product can no longer qualify for protection under art 7(e).

In the light of my construction of art 7(e), and the conclusion that the risk of Hepatitis C
infection was known, the art 7(e) defence does not arise.

---

[110] [2001] 3 All ER 289.

Geraint Howells and Mark Mildred point out that Burton J 'certainly did not fit the stereotype of a judge intoxicated by a negligence-based world view. Rather, he displayed a reformist zeal to show that he appreciated that the Directive was intended to make a break with the past and introduce a new form of civil liability.'[111] In the next extract Jane Stapleton argues that this 'reformist zeal' was misplaced.

Jane Stapleton[112]

> In short, the court in the Hepatitis C case was determined to give the Directive 'work to do' in the United Kingdom; that is to give it a wider ambit of entitlement than existed elsewhere in the English law of obligations. It was eager to avoid a construction that would 'not only be toothless but pointless'. The trial judge seems to have thought this required an adoption of the construction urged by the claimants. In my view, this was mistaken. . . . In my view, the 'reformist zeal' of the trial judge in the Hepatitis C case simply preferred the heroic rhetoric of the claimants' cause.

A v National Blood is a difficult case. On the one hand, it is hard not to feel sympathy for the claimants, who had already had the misfortune to be in need of blood transfusions, from which they were then unlucky enough to contract a potentially life-threatening illness. Yet on the other hand, the National Blood Authority was also in a difficult position. In two important respects, the National Blood Authority is unlike a manufacturer of a defective product, and so an Act which was designed to apply to manufacturers who have deliberately chosen to put defective products into circulation may apply somewhat awkwardly to this sort of public body.

First, the manufacturer of a product, such as a medicine, is not under a *legal duty* to supply that medicine. If the manufacturer has any doubts about a product's safety, on the contrary, its duty would be to ensure that it is not put into circulation. The National Blood Authority, in contrast, is under a *duty* to supply blood. It was not open to them to stop all blood transfusions in the UK while they worked out how to identify this new strain of Hepatitis.

Secondly, as we saw earlier, a principal purpose of the CPA was to facilitate loss-spreading. Rather than the loss falling on the unlucky victim, it would be transferred to the manufacturer, and the assumption was that manufacturers would be able to spread the loss among all consumers by raising the prices of its product. This is not an option for the National Blood Authority. People who need blood transfusions do not pay for blood, and so the Authority cannot spread the costs of damages among all consumers.

Even if, on balance, it is thought fair for the National Blood Authority to bear the costs of the claimant's injuries, it is perhaps ironic that, in the field of medical law, the only successful action under the CPA has not been against the deep pockets of the pharmaceutical industry, but rather against an integral part of the financially overstretched NHS.

(5) Causation

Regardless of whether or not it is necessary to prove fault in relation to a defective drug, the problem of establishing causation will remain. (In Chapter 3 we looked at causation in negligence actions in detail.)

---

[111] 'Infected Blood: Defect and Discoverability. A First Exposition of the EC Product Liability Directive' (2002) 65 Modern Law Review 95–106.

[112] 'Bugs in Anglo-American Products Liability' (2002) 53 South Carolina Law Review 1225.

In short, the 'but for' test applies, and the claimant must prove that 'but for' the defendant's negligence, she would not have suffered her injuries. As we can see from *Loveday v Renton*, this is by no means straightforward. This case involved a child claiming that she had suffered permanent brain damage after being vaccinated against whooping cough (pertussis). She sued the doctor who had administered the vaccine. Stuart-Smith LJ split the question of causation into two parts. First, there was the general question about whether the whooping cough vaccine *could ever cause* brain damage, and second, there was the question of whether it *had in fact caused* the specific injury to this plaintiff. Following a four-month trial, and having heard evidence from nineteen expert witnesses, Stuart-Smith LJ was not satisfied that the vaccine could in fact ever cause permanent brain damage.

Loveday v Renton[113]

Stuart-Smith LJ

[W]hen I embarked on the consideration of the preliminary issue, I was impressed by the case reports and what was evidently a widely held belief that the vaccine could, albeit rarely, cause brain damage...But...I have become more and more doubtful that this is so. I have now come to the clear conclusion that the Plaintiff fails to satisfy me on the balance of probability that pertussis vaccine can cause permanent brain damage in young children. It is possible that it does; the contrary cannot be proved. But in any event the Plaintiff's claim must fail.

There are a number of reasons why causation causes particular difficulties in product liability cases. People who take medicines are generally ill, and it may therefore be difficult to prove that any deterioration in their condition is caused by the drug they took, and not by their pre-existing illness. Many adverse drug reactions are indistinguishable from conditions which occur spontaneously, and it will be very difficult to *prove* that the patient's symptoms were caused by a particular medicine, rather than having some other organic cause.

In addition, patients will often take a number of different medicines, either simultaneously or over a period of time. Pinpointing which drug was responsible for their adverse reaction is therefore difficult, and exacerbated by the fact that it might be a combination of drugs which triggered the reaction. If each taken singly would be safe, could any manufacturer be said to be responsible for a reaction caused by several drugs' interaction with each other?

In the next extract, Pamela Ferguson discusses some practical difficulties which a claimant may face in trying to prove causation.

Pamela Ferguson[114]

Studies have shown that many people who are neither ill nor taking any medication perceive that they are suffering from 'symptoms'. Had such people been receiving drug therapy, they might have attributed their symptoms to the treatment.

A person who is injured by a car which has faulty brakes or by an exploding kettle is at least aware that the car or the kettle was 'involved' in causing the injury...This is in contrast to the position with pharmaceutical drugs which may leave little or no trace once consumed...

---

[113] [1990] 1 Med LR 117.
[114] *Drug Injuries and the Pursuit of Compensation* (Sweet & Maxwell: London, 1996).

> [W]hile some people do suffer from immediate allergic reactions to drugs, in the majority of cases..., the injuries which are alleged to have been caused by these drugs took several months, or in some cases years, to become manifest.

It should also be remembered that, as we have seen, patients often fail to follow prescribing instructions. Proving that the patient's deterioration was caused by taking the medicine, when there is a significant chance that the patient did not take it in the recommended way, may be difficult.

Even if it is clear that the patient's injuries were caused by taking a particular drug, a further problem is that it might be difficult to prove which manufacturer produced the drug in question. Once a drug can be produced generically, many different manufacturers will be producing an identical product, and by the time the patient's injury materializes, it may be impossible to prove which company manufactured the drug that was in fact taken by this patient. Additionally, patients may have taken the same drug, manufactured by a number of different companies, for several years, in which case it will be virtually impossible to identify which manufacturer's medicine actually caused the patient's injury.

In the US, a number of novel strategies have been adopted by the courts in order to assist claimants who might be defeated by evidential difficulties in identifying the correct defendant. Probably the most well known emerged from the case of *Sindell v Abbott Laboratories*,[115] and is referred to as 'market-share liability'. It is explained by Pamela Ferguson in the following extract:

Pamela Ferguson[116]

> The market share theory requires a plaintiff to demonstrate that the defendants were responsible for a substantial share of the drug market. Each defendant must then show that it did not produce the particular drug which was responsible for the plaintiff's injury ... Each manufacturer which fails to demonstrate this is liable to pay a percentage of the compensation awarded to the plaintiff, and this percentage is dependant on the share of the market for which the company was responsible at the relevant time (that is, at the time when the plaintiff's injury or loss occurred). A defendant may bring other producers of the drug into the action as co-defendants.

In essence, market share liability means that the defendants are held liable for creating a *risk of harm*. Would the English courts be likely to adopt such an approach? Until *Fairchild v Glenhaven Funeral Services*,[117] the short answer would almost certainly have been 'no'. As we saw in Chapter 3, in cases such as *Hotson v East Berkshire Area Health Authority*,[118] the courts have been adamant that the claimant must prove on the balance of probabilities that her injuries were caused by *this* defendant's actions.

In *Fairchild*, the House of Lords took a more flexible approach to causation. The claimants had suffered mesothelioma as a result of exposure to asbestos in the workplace, but they had worked for a number of companies during their lifetimes, and none could prove which employer had caused their illness. The House of Lords found that each of the employers had increased the risk to the workers, and causation was established against all of them.

---

[115] (1980) 607 P 2d 924.
[116] *Drug Injuries and the Pursuit of Compensation* (Sweet & Maxwell: London, 1996) 140–1.
[117] [2002] UKHL 22.   [118] [1987] AC 750.

It is not clear whether *Fairchild* would help people who suffer injuries after taking a drug, which is manufactured by several companies. As we saw in Chapter 3, in *Gregg v Scott*,[119] the House of Lords endorsed the traditional approach to causation in medical cases, and seemed reluctant to extend the *Fairchild* exception. And in *Fairchild* itself, Lord Hoffmann distinguished the market share approach adopted in *Sindell*:

> The case bears some resemblance to the present but the problem is not the same. For one thing, the existence of the additional manufacturers did not materially increase the risk of injury. The risk from consuming a drug bought in one shop is not increased by the fact that it can also be bought in another shop.

Nevertheless, he described the market share approach adopted in *Sindell* as 'imaginative', and suggested that such cases should 'be left for consideration when they arise'.

Although holding defendants liable in the absence of proof that their product actually caused the claimant's injuries might initially appear to be a measure which protects consumers' interests, it is important to remember that pharmaceutical companies will have to insure against the possibility of market share liability. Inevitably, this means their premiums will increase and that the costs of medicines will rise.

(6) Vaccine Damage

Special state compensation exists for patients who are disabled as a result of population-wide vaccination programmes. Vaccines are different from ordinary medicines in that the intention is not just to benefit the individual child who is immunized, but also to contribute towards the public health goal of eliminating certain diseases through population-wide immunization. Indeed, it has been argued that vaccination programmes are ethically problematic because the intervention is performed on an asymptomatic individual, who bears the risk associated with the vaccine, but who may not actually benefit from it.[120] Peter Cane explains the problem:

Peter Cane[121]

> [V]accination is a classic case of the 'free-rider' problem much discussed by economists. The benefit to each individual child of being vaccinated may not be very great in view of the fact that most other children are likely to be vaccinated, and that the risk of infection has been thus greatly reduced; yet if the parents of all children reasoned in this way, vaccination would decline and the diseases in question would spread more widely again, with greater risk to all. Further, the main beneficiary from vaccination is often not the vaccinated child but other younger children with whom he or she comes into contact: whooping cough is most dangerous for very young babies, prior to the normal age for vaccination; by the time a child is vaccinated it is normally past the age at which the disease could prove fatal. There is thus a case for arguing that young children who are vaccinated before they are old enough to understand the issues are being used for the benefit of others.

---

[119] [2005] UKHL 2.

[120] P Skrabanek, 'Why is Preventive Medicine Exempted from Ethical Constraints?' (1990) 16 Journal of Medical Ethics 187–90.

[121] *Atiyah's Accidents Compensation and the Law*, 6th edn (Butterworths: London, 1999) 89–90.

Although childhood vaccination is not compulsory in the UK, there are a number of vaccinations that are recommended. Before they start school, most children in the UK have received twenty-seven doses of vaccine.[122] Because vaccination involves the injection of small quantities of active, infectious agents in order to trigger the body's immune response, the existence of rare but serious adverse reactions is unsurprising. While the existence of a causal link between vaccination and some side-effects has been widely accepted, others—in particular, the widely discredited connection between the MMR vaccine and autism—are extremely controversial.

It would be very difficult for an individual who suffers a severe adverse reaction following routine vaccination to establish that either the doctor who performed the vaccination or the manufacturer of the vaccine had been negligent. To establish that the doctor who performed the vaccination had been negligent, it would be necessary to prove that doing so was not supported by a responsible body of medical opinion. Since almost all doctors strongly support all of the recommended vaccinations, this will be impossible, unless the child has some special characteristics which make vaccination unwise. Similar difficulties would be present in an action against the vaccine's manufacturer, who will be able to argue that it is impossible to ensure absolute safety from a vaccination programme. As we saw in *Loveday v Renton*, proving causation might also be exceptionally difficult.

Yet if vaccination programmes pose a risk of injury to a small number of people, which is believed to be outweighed by the enormous public health benefits of universal immunization, it would seem fair to offer some compensation to the small group of individuals whose health is compromised for the greater good. Of course, the cost/benefit calculation will not always favour vaccination. The chance of being exposed to the smallpox virus, for example, is now so small that the risk of harm from vaccination is no longer justified.

In the 1970s, the Pearson Commission recommended that a special strict liability scheme should be set up to compensate those who suffer injuries following vaccination. This proposal was never implemented, and instead an 'interim' scheme was introduced by the Vaccine Damage Payments Act 1979. As amended, the Act continues to apply today.

Under section 1, a person who has been severely disabled as a result of vaccination against diphtheria, tetanus, whooping cough, poliomyelitis, measles, rubella, tuberculosis, smallpox, mumps, Haemophilus type b infection (hib), or meningitis C, is entitled to a sum of £120,000 for claims made since July 2007 (reduced amounts are payable for claims made before this date).[123]

Applicants must have been vaccinated in the UK since 1948 (and in the case of smallpox, before 1971). Under section 3(1), claims must be made before the claimant's twenty-first birthday (this was increased from a six-year time limit in 2000). 'Severe disability' is defined in section 1(4) as 60 per cent disablement (this was reduced in 2000 from 80 per cent). And under section 3(5), the causal link between the vaccine and the disability has to be proved, on the balance of probabilities.

The Scheme is funded from the Social Security budget, and claims are made initially to the Department of Work and Pensions. If the claim is rejected, under section 4 the claimant can appeal to an independent tribunal. There is no further appeal to a court, although the Secretary of State is empowered to reverse the tribunal's decision.[124]

---

[122] Stephanie Pywell, 'A Critical Review of the Recent and Impending Changes to the Law of Statutory Compensation for Vaccine Damage' (2000) 4 Journal of Personal Injury Law 246–56.

[123] Written Ministerial Statement, 3 May 2007. Details at <www.dwp.gov.uk>.

[124] SI 1999/2677.

The scheme has not been an overwhelming success, and there have been comparatively few successful claims. As might have been expected, the majority of claims were made in the first few years after the scheme was set up. Between 1989 and 1999, only forty-four awards were made, thirty-two of which were made after appeals.[125] Rates of success vary between different vaccines: a high proportion of claims resulting from the single measles vaccine are successful, compared with low rates for the MMR vaccine.[126] Success rates also appear to vary considerably in different parts of the country.

The reduction in the disability threshold in 2000 might have marginally increased the number of eligible claimants, but it could plausibly be argued that setting any threshold level of disablement is unfair, regardless of the level at which it is set. Leaving aside the question of whether it is, in fact, possible to evaluate the extent of a child's disablement with this sort of precision, why should a child who suffers 59 per cent disablement receive nothing, while a child with 60 per cent disablement might be entitled to £120,000? A sliding scale which compensated a child according to the extent of her disabilities, without any minimum threshold level, might be fairer.

Moreover, the sum of £120,000, while undoubtedly substantial, will not necessarily be sufficient to meet all of the child's needs throughout his life, especially if the vaccine caused severe brain damage. It is certainly much less than an award in tort, where full compensatory damages are the norm, and brain-damaged children can receive many millions of pounds. On the other hand, as is pointed out in the following extract, children who receive lump sum payments under the Act are treated more generously than most disabled children.

Peter Cane[127]

Why should children disabled in this particular way be treated so generously in a financial sense, as compared with other disabled children? The OPCS Disability Survey estimated that there were some 136,000 children under 16 in the four most serious disability categories; and the Pearson Commission estimated that 90% of severely disabled children were suffering from congenital defects. Why does a very small number of vaccine-disabled children have a better claim to financial support than other disabled children? It appears that in this case, as in some others, preferential treatment for a small group was the result of a well conducted political campaign which played on public sympathy for particularly heart-rending cases.

6 CONCLUSION

The regulation of medicines, once they are ready to be marketed, cannot be viewed in isolation from the rules that govern the stages before medicines can be licensed for general use. It is worth noting that when we considered the regulation of clinical research in the previous chapter, it was similarly apparent that European law is playing an increasingly dominant role. This is interesting, because in many of the other areas of medical law that we consider in this book, European law is of comparatively little importance. In relation to issues such as

---

[125] Stephanie Pywell, 'The Vaccine Damage Payment Scheme: A Proposal for Radical Reform' (2002) 9 Journal of Social Security Law 73–93, 81.

[126] Ibid, 83.

[127] *Atiyah's Accidents Compensation and the Law*, 6th edn (Butterworths: London, 1999) 89–90.

abortion, euthanasia, organ transplantation, and stem cell research, for example, there are vast differences between the laws in different European countries. Of course, the European Convention on Human Rights has Europe-wide application, but member states often have a wide margin of appreciation in their interpretation.

When regulating the pharmaceutical industry and access to medicines, however, there is increasing European harmonization. Why is this? One obvious answer is that here we have been concerned with the regulation of a *market*, rather than with *sensitive ethical issues*. Protecting consumers and promoting economic growth are familiar aims for European regulation, whereas balancing the rights and wrongs of complex ethical dilemmas has usually been left to individual nation states.

In this chapter, one of the recurring themes has been the existence of a tension between the pharmaceutical industry's profit motive—where increasing shareholder value is a primary goal—and the needs of patients and the NHS, not to mention people in developing countries, who want access to effective and affordable medicines. Regulating the pharmaceutical industry is difficult, not least because a systematic pattern of takeovers means that there are now only a handful of companies supplying medicines within a global market. The economic and political power these companies wield is considerable, and time-limited patent protection means that they are under continual pressure to bring new and profitable medicines to the marketplace. The consequences of this pressure are, as we have seen in this chapter, not necessarily always in the best interests of patients.

In February 2009, the new CEO of one of the largest companies, GlaxoSmithKline announced a major change of strategy, chiefly in relation to providing drugs to the world's poorest nations and stimulating research into neglected diseases.[128] Andrew Witty pledged that GSK would cut its prices for all drugs in the 50 least developed countries to a maximum of 25 per cent of the costs of those drugs in the UK and US. Witty also committed GSK to putting currently patent-protected chemicals or processes which might be relevant to finding drugs for neglected diseases into a 'patent pool', so they are available to other researchers. In an interview with *The Guardian* he suggested that it will be possible to persuade shareholders that corporate responsibility should, in some cases, trump the pursuit of profit:

> I think the shareholders understand this and it's my job to make sure I can explain it. I think we can. I think it's absolutely the kind of thing large global companies need to be demonstrating, that they've got a more balanced view of the world than short-term returns.[129]

FURTHER READING

Elliott, Carl, *Better than Well: American Medicine meets the American Dream* (Norton: New York, 2003).

Ferguson, Pamela, *Drug Injuries and the Pursuit of Compensation* (Sweet & Maxwell: London, 1996).

Goldberg, Richard, 'Paying for Bad Blood: Strict Product Liability after the Hepatitis C Litigation' (2002) 10 Medical Law Review 165–200.

---

[128] Sarah Boseley 'Drug Giant GlaxoSmithKline Pledges Cheap Medicine for World's Poor', The Guardian, 13 February 2009.
[129] Ibid.

House of Commons Health Select Committee, The Influence of the Pharmaceutical Industry Fourth Report of Session 2004–05, available at <www.publications.parliament.uk>.

Howells, Geraint and Mildred, Mark, 'Infected Blood: Defect and Discoverability. A First Exposition of the EC Product Liability Directive' (2002) 65 Modern Law Review 95–106.

McGoey, Lindsey and Jackson, Emily, 'Seroxat and the Suppression of Clinical Trial Data: Regulatory Failure and the Uses of Legal Ambiguity' (2009) 35 Journal of Medical Ethics 107–12.

Mildred, Mark, 'Pharmaceutical Products: The Relationship between Regulatory Approval and the Existence of a Defect, European Business Law Review' (2007) European Business Law Review 1276–82.

Prayle, David and Brazier, Margaret, 'Supply of Medicines: Paternalism, Autonomy and Reality' (1998) 24 Journal of Medical Ethics 93–8.

Sykes, Richard, New Medicines, The Practice of Medicine, and Public Policy (Nuffield Trust: London, 2000).

11

ORGAN TRANSPLANTATION

CENTRAL ISSUES

1. Organ transplantation is successful and cost-effective, but there is an acute shortage of organs available for transplant, and the gap between supply and demand is widening. The UK currently has one of the lowest organ donation rates in the developed world.

2. Under the Human Tissue Act 2004, consent to cadaveric donation is necessary, either from the deceased person, her nominee, or from the highest ranking qualified relative.

3. In 2008, the Organ Donation Taskforce recommended no change to this consent-based model, but it did advocate a number of operational changes to improve the coordination and effectiveness of organ procurement. Many commentators have advocated more significant legal reform: examples include the introduction of an 'opt-out' system; requiring people to make a decision about organ donation; offering financial or non-financial incentives; and, most drastically, simply treating the organs of the dead as a public resource.

4. In recent years, the number of living organ donors has increased. Regulation of living organ donation is directed towards ensuring that the donor has given fully informed consent, and that no money has changed hands.

5. Xenotransplantation (animal-to-human transplantation) could potentially solve the organ shortage, but it raises a number of difficult ethical and practical issues. Currently, the most compelling objection to xenotransplantation is the unknown and possibly unknowable risk of cross-species infection, not only for individual recipients, but also for society as a whole.

1   INTRODUCTION

For two reasons, the first attempts to transplant organs from one person's body into another were inevitably unsuccessful. First, before it became possible to suppress the recipient's immune system, any foreign tissue would automatically be rejected. Secondly, because organs deteriorate rapidly as soon as a person's cardio-respiratory system stops working, it was also very difficult to ensure that organs taken from cadavers 'survived' the transplant process. The first recipients of transplanted organs were usually selected because they were in the final stages of acute organ failure, and they generally died within a matter of days or weeks.

The first successful organ transplant was a live kidney transplant, between identical twins, which took place in Boston in 1954. In the UK, the first successful transplant involved a similar operation six years later in Edinburgh. Since the 1960s, techniques for maintaining the quality of organs before and during transplantation have improved dramatically, and immunosuppressant therapy can minimize the problem of rejection. The prognosis for transplant patients is now extremely good. After one year, 81 per cent of heart transplants, 97 per cent of living donor kidney transplants, and 96 per cent of cadaveric kidney transplants will still be functioning well.[1] Of course, transplant surgery sometimes fails, and immunosuppressant drugs have negative side-effects, such as increasing the lifetime risk of developing certain cancers. But, from the point of view of patients, a transplant will commonly represent the optimum treatment for organ failure. Heart and liver transplants are often life-saving. The availability of dialysis[2] means that kidney failure is not necessarily life-threatening. Being dependent on dialysis is a miserable experience, however, and kidney transplant patients commonly benefit from a much improved quality of life.

Because alternative treatments for patients with organ failure are expensive, transplantation will also often represent a net gain for the NHS. Successful kidney transplantation is much cheaper than providing dialysis to a patient with renal failure. The average cost of dialysis is £30,800 per patient per year.[3] The cost of a kidney transplant is £17,000 per patient per transplant, and the immunosuppression required by a patient with a transplant costs around £5,000 per patient per year.[4] After the first year, each kidney transplant therefore saves the NHS £25,800 per year. Over a period of ten years (the median graft survival time) a successful kidney transplant saves the NHS £241,000.[5] The 1,914 kidney transplants that took place in 2005–6 collectively saved the NHS £46.1m in dialysis costs.[6] Restoring otherwise sick and dependent patients to better health clearly also has advantages for their families, and for society as a whole.

In short, transplantation surgery is a successful and cost-effective therapeutic option. The chief problem, as is well known, is that there are insufficient organs available for transplant, and this problem is exacerbated by improvements in transplant technology which expand the pool of potential recipients to include older patients, as well as those previously thought too ill to undergo such a major operation. Ironically, artificial organs have in fact exacerbated the organ shortage because, while not yet effective enough to offer permanent replacements, they allow transplant teams to temporarily 'bridge' patients who would otherwise die, enabling them to be put on the organ donor waiting list until a human organ becomes available. The pool of possible recipients therefore continues to grow steadily, while the pool of potential organ donors remains too small to satisfy this demand. Indeed, the number of cadaveric organs available for transplant has actually declined in recent years, due in part to a reduction in mortality rates from road traffic accidents.

---

[1] UK Transplant Transplant Activity in the UK 2007–8 (2008), available at <www.uktransplant.org.uk>.
[2] Renal replacement therapy.
[3] UK Transplant The Cost Effectiveness of Transplantation (UK Transplant, 2007), available at <www.uktransplant.org.uk>.
[4] Ibid.   [5] Ibid.   [6] Ibid.

Given waiting times of well over a year, it is not surprising that mortality rates on the organ donor waiting list are high: the Chief Medical Officer (CMO) estimates that 1,000 patients on the transplant waiting list die every year because of the lack of a transplant.[7] This understates the scale of the problem, however, because many patients are never put on the waiting list, even though they might benefit from an organ transplant, because the doctors involved in their care recognize that it is unlikely that they would become eligible for a transplant in time. These patients are, as the CMO put it, 'dying silently'.[8]

The most important issue raised by organ transplantation is therefore how to increase the number of organs, either from dead donors, or from alternative sources of supply, such as live donors or animals. An Organ Donation Taskforce was appointed in 2006 to investigate how this might best be achieved. In 2008, they issued two separate reports: the first looked at ways to increase donation rates without the need for legislative change, and the second considered whether law reform—specifically a move towards so-called 'presumed consent'—would be desirable. We consider both reports below.

In 2007, the European Commission issued a Communication which suggested a number of actions that could be taken at Community and Member State level, in order to increase the supply of donor organs across the EU. In April 2008, the European Parliament adopted a resolution on organ donation and transplantation, advocating that Member States share expertise in order to increase donor rates and equalize access to transplantation across the EU.[9]

There is, it seems, widespread public support for organ transplantation. Opinion polls consistently indicate that at least 70 per cent of the population would want their organs to be used to save others in the event of their death; some studies estimate the figure to be as high as 90 per cent. Yet despite broad public approval of transplantation, only 26 per cent of the population is registered on the organ donor register. The paradox of this situation is pointed out by Sheila McLean:

> We have the doctors ready, willing and able to undertake the surgery, we have people dying with usable organs and we apparently have a compliant public. Why then is the programme so strapped?[10]

It should, however, be noted that there are some voices of dissent who would contest the widespread assumption that increasing the number of organ transplants would be a self-evidently desirable end.[11] Although transplant surgery is often cost-effective, heart transplants continue to be extremely expensive, and this raises some of the questions about the appropriate allocation of scarce NHS resources, which we considered in Chapter 2. Discussions of the ethical issues arising from organ transplantation often leave out the costs of surgery, and instead appear to assume that a shortage of organs is the only barrier to a

---

[7] House of Lords European Union Committee 17th Report of Session 2007–08, Increasing the Supply of Donor Organs Within the European Union Volume I: Report (2008), available at <www.publications. parliament.uk>.

[8] Ibid.   [9] Ibid.

[10] 'Transplantation and the "Nearly Dead"; The Case of Elective Ventilation' in S Mclean (ed.), Contemporary Issues in Law, Medicine and Ethics (Dartmouth: Aldershot, 1996) 143–61, 146.

[11] Barbara Koenig, 'Dead Donors and the "Shortage" of Human Organs: Are We Missing the Point?' (2003) 3 American Journal of Bioethics 26–7; RC Fox and J Swazey, Spare Parts: Organ Replacement in American Society (OUP: Oxford, 1992).

hugely increased transplant programme, as if the NHS has a bottomless capacity to perform complex and expensive transplant surgery.

Although some people claim to have religious objections to organ donation, scholars from all the major religions have endorsed transplantation on the grounds that the imperatives of healing and saving life trump other considerations, such as a proscription of the mutilation of corpses. A 1995 Fatwa, for example, stated that giving and receiving organs is compatible with Islam.[12] Nevertheless, the Organ Donation taskforce highlighted a study which suggests that attempts to publicize religious acceptance of donation, via leaflets, have been unsuccessful.

Organ Donation Taskforce[13]

There was little prior awareness among the interviewees of the leaflets published some years ago setting out the views of some prominent faiths on organ donation. This was underlined by a recent study carried out in Birmingham, in which 60% of Muslims, from a wide variety of ethnic backgrounds, said that organ donation was contrary to their faith, when it is not. This suggests that written leaflets alone may be ineffective and that other methods of engagement need to be found.

Mary Jiang Bresnahan and Kevin Mahler studied what information relatives wavering about organ donation would find if they 'googled' a major religious faith (Christianity, Islam, Judaism, Buddhism, and Hinduism) and brain death. They found that the position described on the websites which people would be most likely to access is considerably more complex than the simple 'all religions approve of transplantation' message communicated by organ procurement agencies.

Mary Jiang Bresnahan and Kevin Mahler[14]

The claim of organ procurement agencies, promoted on their websites, that all major world religions approve of organ donation, doesn't tell the whole story of the ethical debate in many religions on the meaning of brain death and organ donation and the difficulty that such decisions pose for many families confronted with the request to donate organs of a loved one. This analysis of five major world religious organizations about brain death and organ donation shows that the situation has greater ambiguity and complexity than the simple religious endorsement suggested by organ procurement websites. The websites included in this study are sites that people would be likely to see first if they seek information online. . . . The ethics of organ donation in the context of brain death is not as clear as organ procurement agencies' claim about approval would suggest. This is an important issue for procurement agencies

---

[12] For discussion of Muslim attitudes towards organ donation, see Clare Hayward and Anna Madill, 'The Meaning of Organ Donation: Muslims of Pakistani Origin and White English Nationals Living in North England' (2003) 57 Social Science and Medicine 389–401; and Sahin Aksoy, 'A Critical Approach to the Current Understanding of Islamic Scholars on Using Cadaver Organs Without Permission' (2001) 15 Bioethics 461–72.

[13] The Potential Impact of an Opt Out System for Organ Donation in the UK: An Independent Report from the Organ Donation Taskforce (DH: London, 2008), available at <www.dh.gov.uk>.

[14] 'Ethical Debate over Organ Donation in the Context of Brain Death' (2008) Bioethics December 'early view'.

because the discrepancy between the need for organs and their availability has continued to increase.

In the UK, relatives from minority ethnic groups are much more likely to refuse to agree to transplantation: consent rates were 67 per cent for white potential donors, and 24 per cent for non-white potential donors. This discrepancy is especially significant because rates of renal failure are, in fact, higher in non-white populations, due in part to the increased frequency of type 2 diabetes. Given a greater need for organs among this group, and fewer tissue-matched donors, the shortage is particularly acute among minority groups. According to UK Transplant, people of Asian or African-Caribbean descent are three to four times more likely to develop end-stage renal disease. They make up 23 per cent of the kidney waiting list, but represent only 3 per cent of donors. Waiting times for a kidney in the UK are a median of 719 days for white patients, 1,368 days for Asian patients, and 1,419 days for black patients.[15]

The law relating to organ donation in England, Wales, and Northern Ireland is contained in the Human Tissue Act 2004, which came into force in 2006. In Scotland, although there are some provisions of the 2004 Act which have UK-wide application, most of the law is contained in the Human Tissue (Scotland) Act 2006.

In order to understand the form the Human Tissue Act 2004 takes it is important to bear in mind a principal factor behind the perceived need for legislative change: namely the retained organs scandals at Bristol Royal Infirmary and Alder Hey Children's Hospital. In the late 1990s, it became apparent that, at both institutions, children's organs had been retained without parental knowledge, let alone consent.[16] The Human Tissue Act covers the storage and use of almost all human tissue (sperm and eggs are not included, as we shall see in Chapter 15), and the need for specific consent is the Act's central organizing principle. Its remit is much broader than transplantation—it covers research, post-mortems, anatomy, and public display—but in this chapter, we will concentrate upon the Act's application to organ transplantation.

The Act set up the Human Tissue Authority (HTA), which issues licences for the storage and use of tissues. Most organs that are used in transplantation cannot be stored for any length of time, and so it is only when tissue, such as bone marrow, is banked for future use in transplantation that the licensing regime becomes relevant. Because we concentrate on solid organ donation in this chapter, the licensing process will not be discussed in any detail. Of more importance are the Codes of Practice which the HTA issues, one of which deals specifically with consent, and one with the donation of solid organs for transplantation.

At the time of writing, the HTA has consulted on new versions of these Codes, but the final versions have not yet been published. The original versions of these Codes will therefore be used here, but readers are advised that the latest versions will be published in 2009, and be available on the HTA's website.[17]

In this chapter, we first consider cadaveric donation, looking first at who may become a donor, and which organs may be taken. We then turn to the definition of 'brain death',

---

[15] Organs for Transplants: A report from the Organ Donation Taskforce (DH: London, 2008), available at <www.dh.gov.uk> para 4.48.

[16] See further, M Brazier, 'Organ Retention and Return: Problems of Consent' (2003) 29 Journal of Medical Ethics 30–3; Brazier, 'Human Tissue Retention' (2004) 72 Medico-Legal Journal 39; John Harris, 'Law and Regulation of Retained Organs: The Ethical Issues' (2002) 22 Legal Studies 527–49; M Brazier 'Retained Organs: Ethics and Humanity' (2002) 22 Legal Studies 550–69.

[17] <www.hta.gov.uk>.

which has enabled organs to be taken from donors whose hearts are still beating. The system of organ retrieval in the UK is then summarized, and we look at the consent-based model adopted in the Human Tissue Act 2004. Because of the shortage of organs from cadavers, a number of possible strategies to increase the number of cadaveric donors have been canvassed, including the 'presumed consent' model recently rejected by the Organ Donation Taskforce. We evaluate each of these in turn.

Next we look at living organ donation. We consider the legitimacy of performing such a serious operation on someone solely in order to benefit a third party. Could a person give valid consent in such circumstances, and could it ever be appropriate to take an organ from a child or an adult who lacks capacity? We discuss the restrictions placed on living organ donation in the Human Tissue Act, and we look at the controversial question of whether offering financial incentives to living donors would be an acceptable way to increase the number of volunteers. Finally, we consider the ethical, practical, and legal obstacles to transplanting animal organs into human recipients.

2 DEAD DONORS

(a) WHO CAN BE A DONOR?

It is important to remember that comparatively few people die in circumstances where it will be possible to use their organs for transplantation. A person's organs must be healthy, which will generally rule out people who die from degenerative diseases such as cancer. Potential donors will often be people who have suffered massive head injuries but whose other organs are unlikely to have been damaged. In order to reduce damage to the organs, it is preferable to remove them from a person who has died while on an artificial ventilator.

As part of its information-gathering role, each year UK Transplant carries out an audit of all potential donors. In 2007–8, of the 28,137 patients who died while connected to an artificial ventilator, only 2,383 (eight per cent) had been diagnosed as brain-stem dead with no medical contraindications to organ donation.[18] Of these 2,383 patients, only 809 go on to become solid organ donors. An average of 3.5 organs can be taken from each cadaver, so obtaining organs from the 1,574 unused but suitable potential donors undoubtedly has the potential to massively increase the number of transplants.

Obviously, the transplant team must try to ensure that the potential donor does not have any genetic condition or infectious disease which could jeopardize the recipient's health. It will, for example, be important to obtain as full a family and social history as possible, and to carry out such tests as are practicable. Guidance is provided by the Department of Health's *Guidance on the Microbiological Safety of Human Organs, Tissues and Cells used in Transplantation*.[19] Because organs must be transplanted quickly, however, there are limits on how thorough such investigations can be, and this means that some risk of disease transmission is probably inevitable. In seeking the recipient's consent to transplantation it is, of course, necessary to ensure that she is properly informed about this small residual risk.

While diagnostic tests can be carried out before transplantation to test for the HIV virus, an HIV test only shows that a person did not have the virus between 3 and 6 months

---

[18] UK Transplant *Transplant Activity in the UK 2007–8* (2008), available at <www.uktransplant.org.uk>.

[19] Department of Health 2000 <www.dh.gov.uk>.

previously. This means that there will always be a chance that the donor might have been in the 'window period' before seroconversion when he or she died. The Department of Health's guidance suggests that efforts should be made to ensure that there has been no evidence of high-risk activity, such as being paid for sex, injecting drugs, having homosexual sex, or sex with someone from a list of specified countries in Africa.[20]

(b) DEFINITION OF DEATH

If organs can only be removed once someone has died, and if they must be removed as soon as possible after death, accurately pinpointing the moment of death is vitally important. The problem, however, is that death is usually a process which takes place over a period of time. A person's organs do not all stop functioning at the same moment, rather they fail progressively once the brain has irreversibly died. Brain death itself involves two distinct changes, which do not always happen simultaneously. One is the permanent loss of consciousness (caused by death of the upper brain), and the other is the loss of the brain's ability to regulate other bodily functions, such as breathing (caused by death of the lower brain).

Throughout history, definitions of death have attempted to designate some point at which a person's loss of bodily functions becomes irreversible. In the distant past, a body could not be conclusively considered dead until putrefaction had begun. This changed in the nineteenth century, when death started to be diagnosed once a person had stopped breathing and their heart had stopped beating. During the twentieth century, medical progress undermined these tests because it became possible, in certain circumstances, to revive someone whose heart had stopped beating. If someone is successfully resuscitated, then plainly they were not dead, despite their temporary absence of heart function.

The invention of the artificial ventilator also made it necessary to decide whether a diagnosis of death could ever be made while someone's heartbeat was being maintained artificially. If such patients are alive, removing them from a ventilator would kill them, and hence be much more difficult to justify than if they have already been diagnosed as dead.

Pressure to rethink the definition of death also came from developments in transplant surgery. Loss of cardio-respiratory function soon causes irreversible damage to a person's organs. While there has been some recent success in perfusing organs taken from people whose hearts have stopped beating, it is generally agreed that it is preferable to obtain organs for transplantation following a diagnosis of irreversible brain death, instead of waiting for the donor's heart to stop beating. Although cardio-respiratory function cannot be maintained indefinitely once someone's brain has died, continuing to ventilate a person who has been diagnosed as brain dead enables doctors to remove organs while the heart is still beating. It is, of course, essential that these 'heart beating donors' must have been satisfactorily diagnosed as dead before their organs are taken: in Hans Jonas's words, 'the patient must be absolutely sure that his doctor does not become his executioner'.[21]

The first attempt to define death using cessation of brain function took place in France in 1959, when a group of neurosurgeons described a condition in which there was no detectable brain activity. They called this 'death of the central nervous system', and although they did not address the question of whether this was the same as death, they concluded

---

[20] Guidance on the Microbiological Safety of Human Organs, Tissues and Cells used in Transplantation. Department of Health 2000, available at <www.dh.gov.uk>.

[21] *Philosophical Essays: From Ancient Creed to Technological Man* (Prentice Hall: Englewood Cliffs, NJ, 1974) 131.

that removing a patient whose central nervous system had died from a ventilator would be justified, despite their artificially maintained heartbeat.

Debate over the need for a new definition of death continued during the 1960s, and brain death was formally defined in 1968 by an Ad Hoc Committee of the Harvard Medical School, whose report, *A Definition of Irreversible Coma*, opened with the following statement:

Ad Hoc Committee of the Harvard Medical School[22]

Our primary purpose is to define irreversible coma as a new criterion for death. There are two reasons why there is a need for a definition: (1) Improvements in resuscitative and supportive measures have led to increased efforts to save those who are desperately injured. Sometimes these efforts have only partial success, so that the result is an individual whose heart continues to beat but whose brain is irreversibly damaged. The burden is great on patients who suffer permanent loss of intellect, on their families, on the hospitals, and on those in need of hospital beds already occupied by these comatose patients. (2) Obsolete criteria for the definition of death can lead to controversy in obtaining organs for transplantation.

The concept of brain death has now been adopted by most Western countries. In Japan, however, brain-stem death has proved exceptionally controversial, in part because of cultural attitudes towards death and the special relationship that is believed to exist between ancestral spirits and the living, and in part because there is simply less trust in the medical profession. Indeed, the surgeon who performed the first heart transplant in Japan in 1968 was charged with murder.

In 1997, brain death was recognized in Japan, but only when the patient has specified in writing that she wishes to donate her organs after death, and her family does not wish to overrule her wishes. Unless both these conditions are satisfied, brain-dead patients are not considered legally dead. In the first three years following this change in the law, organs were procured from only nine brain-dead donors.[23]

In the UK there is no statutory definition of death. Rather, the diagnosis of death is regarded as a matter of clinical judgement. Since the late 1970s, brain-stem death, or the irreversible loss of brain-stem function has been treated as the definitive criterion for diagnosing death. The Department of Health issued a *Code of Practice for the Diagnosis of Brain Stem Death* in 1998,[24] and this was superseded in 2008 by a Code issued by the Academy of Medical Royal Colleges.

Academy of Medical Royal Colleges[25]

Death entails the irreversible loss of those essential characteristics which are necessary to the existence of a living human person and, thus, the definition of death should be regarded as the irreversible loss of the capacity for consciousness, combined with irreversible loss of the capacity to breathe. This may be secondary to a wide range of underlying problems in the body, for example, cardiac arrest.

[22] Ad Hoc Committee of the Harvard Medical School to Examine the Definition of Death (1968) 205 Journal of the American Medical Association 85–8, 85.

[23] See further Margaret Lock, *Twice Dead: Organ Transplants and the Reinvention of Death* (University of California Press: Berkeley, 2002).

[24] Department of Health, *Code of Practice for the Diagnosis of Brain Stem Death* (HSC 1998/035).

[25] A Code of Practice for the Diagnosis and Confirmation of Death (2008), available at <www.aomrc.org.uk>.

> The irreversible cessation of brain-stem function whether induced by intra-cranial events or the result of extra-cranial phenomena, such as hypoxia, will produce this clinical state and therefore irreversible cessation of the integrative function of the brain-stem equates with the death of the individual and allows the medical practitioner to diagnose death....
>
> [T]here are some ways in which parts of the body may continue to show signs of biological activity after a diagnosis of irreversible cessation of brain-stem function; these have no moral relevance to the declaration of death for the purpose of the immediate withdrawal of all forms of supportive therapy.

The Code of Practice states that the diagnosis of brain-stem death must be made by at least two senior registered medical practitioners, and to avoid conflicts of interest, neither of these should be a member of the transplant team.[26] Although death can only be pronounced following two sets of brain-stem tests, the legal time of death is when the first test indicates brain-stem death.[27]

Because organ transplantation depends so heavily upon public goodwill, it is especially important that the public accepts that brain-stem death is not an especially 'early' diagnosis of death. In 1980, a Panorama TV programme questioned the validity of brain-death criteria, leading to an immediate and sharp reduction in the number of organs becoming available for transplant. It took 15 months for organ procurement rates to recover.

It has been difficult for the public to accept that a person whose heart is still beating, and who appears to be breathing, albeit with mechanical assistance, is really dead. This confusion is exacerbated by the fact that the person will still be connected to what is commonly known as a *life*-support machine. A warm, pink, breathing body certainly does not look dead, and relatives often find it difficult to contemplate organ retrieval prior to cessation of heart and lung function.

In the next extract, Robert Truog points to a further possible reason for confusion. Some people have argued that brain-dead patients should be anaesthetized before organ retrieval, while others are concerned that this would raise further doubts over the question of whether such patients are really dead.

Robert D Truog[28]

> Most interesting is a debate that has occurred in the European anesthesia literature regarding the question of whether brain dead patients should receive an anesthetic during organ procurement. Some argue that the brain death criterion is insufficient to be absolutely sure that patients are incapable of experiencing pain, even if only at a rudimentary level, and so should receive 'the benefit of the doubt' and be given an anesthetic. Others respond, not by defending the criterion itself, but by arguing that administration of anesthesia to these patients will send a message to society that we are uncertain whether brain death is truly a state of permanent unconsciousness. As such, they argue, administration of an anesthetic to these patients will undermine the trust of the public and jeopardize the organ transplantation enterprise.

---

[26] Ibid, para 3.3.   [27] Ibid. See also *Re A* [1992] 3 Med LR 303.
[28] 'Brain Death—Too Flawed to Endure, Too Ingrained to Abandon' (2007) Journal of Law, Medicine & Ethics 273–81.

Critics of brain death have argued that death has been redefined in order to serve the needs of transplant surgeons.

> [W]e have identified a group of severely injured and dying persons who are so 'beyond harm' that we feel justified in killing them in order to obtain their organs. Since we would rather not think that we are killing them, we simply gerrymander the line between life and death to include them in the latter category. [29]

Peter Singer argues that the concept of brain death is a 'convenient fiction' and, in the next extract, explains why it has nevertheless proved to be relatively uncontroversial.

Peter Singer[30]

> Human beings are not the only living things in the world. All living things eventually die, and we can generally tell when they are alive and when they are dead. Isn't the distinction between life and death so basic that what counts as dead for a human being also counts as dead for a dog, a parrot, a prawn, an oyster, an oak, or a cabbage?...'Brain death' is only for humans. Isn't it odd that for a human being to die requires a different concept of death from that which we apply to other living beings?
>
> The question is a vital one, in every sense of the term. When warm, breathing, pulsating human beings are declared to be dead, they lose their basic human rights. They are not given life support. If their relatives consent..., their hearts and other organs can be cut out of their bodies and given to strangers. The change in our conception of death that excluded these human beings from the moral community was one of the first in a series of dramatic changes in our view of life and death. Yet, in sharp contrast to other changes in this area, it met with virtually no opposition? How did this happen?...
>
> In summary, the redefinition of death in terms of brain death went through so smoothly because it did not harm the brain-dead patients and it benefited everyone else: the families of brain-dead patients, the hospitals, the transplant surgeons, people needing transplants, people who worried that they might one day need a transplant, people who feared that they might one day be kept on a respirator after their brain had died, taxpayers and the government.

Further evidence that we cannot disassociate brain death from the needs of transplantation services comes from Robert Truog's prediction that if xenotransplantation were perfected, and the need for cadaveric donors disappeared, we would revert to pre-transplantation definitions of death:

> Without the need to obtain organs from other humans, the raison d'être of brain death will disappear. The concept, and the philosophical debate that has surrounded it, will become historical footnotes, and the term will no longer be found in the indices of medical textbooks. The concept will have died a natural death of its own.[31]

---

[29] Stuart Youngner, 'Some Must Die' in SJ Youngner, RC Fox, and LJ O'Connell (eds), *Organ Transplantation: Meanings and Realities* (University of Wisconsin Press: Madison, 1996) 50.

[30] *Rethinking Life and Death: The Collapse of our Traditional Ethics* (OUP: Oxford, 1994).

[31] 'Brain Death—Too Flawed to Endure, Too Ingrained to Abandon' (2007) Journal of Law, Medicine & Ethics 273–81.

It has also been suggested that medical techniques which might enable brain-stem function to be maintained artificially cast doubt upon the continued validity of brain-stem death. As Kerridge *et al.* suggest in the following extract, people who have been diagnosed as brain dead can have some bodily functions maintained artificially for increasingly long periods of time. If brain-dead patients can 'survive' on a ventilator for several months, are they really dead?

IH Kerridge, P Saul, M Lowe, J McPhee, and D Williams[32]

When the concept of brain death was first introduced it was argued that death of the brain stem inevitably implied the imminent death of the whole body...This argument is no longer tenable as medical therapy and intensive care have become increasingly sophisticated at replacing brain stem function, and we now know that bodies with a dead brain stem may be kept alive for prolonged periods of time. Brain dead pregnant women have been maintained for months and later given birth to healthy infants and brain dead children have been reported to survive for up to 14 years with ventilatory and nutritional support....

Suggestions that the brain stem is the supreme regulator of the body seem both biologically and philosophically simplistic...Furthermore the heart, the liver, the kidneys, and other organs are all required to maintain bodily integrity, and loss of the functions of any of these organs will result in eventual disintegration of the organism without artificial support. Many individuals who are clearly alive depend upon technology such as pacemakers, dialysis machines or even ventilators to live. Whether there is a 'supreme regulator' therefore seems open to question. This argument may also be confused by the fact that the functions of the kidneys, heart, and lungs can be replaced by technological means, whereas that of the brain stem cannot. This is, however, very dependent upon technology; indeed aspects of brain stem function can now be replaced and it seems likely that more progress might be made in this area.

Perhaps it should be admitted that it is impossible to define the moment of death with complete certainty and precision, and that the important task therefore is to determine at what point *in the process of dying* organ retrieval becomes legitimate. The rule that organs may only be taken once a person is dead is intended to foster public trust in the transplantation system. It is, however, at least arguable that the certainty implied by this 'dead donor' rule misrepresents the ambiguity of death.[33] Indeed, the authors of the next extracts suggest that we should straightforwardly admit that it is legitimate to retrieve organs from the 'imminently dying', with their consent.

RE Truog and WM Robinson[34]

[I]n some circumstances we believe that the harm of dying is sufficiently small that patients or surrogates should be allowed to voluntarily accept it to be able to donate organs. For

---

[32] 'Death, Dying and Donation: Organ Transplantation and the Diagnosis of Death' (2002) 28 Journal of Medical Ethics 89–94.

[33] Elyssa R Koppelman, 'The Dead Donor Rule and the Concept of Death: Severing the Ties That Bind Them' (2003) 3(1) American Journal of Bioethics 1–9, 4.

[34] 'Role of Brain Death and the Dead-donor Rule in the Ethics of Organ Ttransplantation' (2003) 31 Critical Care Medicine 2391–6.

example, some might say that if they were ever diagnosed as being permanently uncon-scious they would accept the harm of dying if this would make it possible for them to donate their organs to others. Similarly, some patients who are imminently dying might be willing to have their life shortened by a few minutes or hours if this would make organ donation possible...

Proposals similar to ours have been suggested by others over the years. All involve shift-ing the key ethical question from Is the patient dead? to Are the harms of removing life-sustaining organs sufficiently small that patients or surrogates should be allowed to consent to donation?

Julian Savulescu[35]

Since I believe we die when our meaningful mental life ceases, organs should be available from that point, which may significantly predate brain death. At the very least, people should be allowed to complete advance directives that direct that their organs be removed when their brain is severely damaged or they are permanently unconscious.

In the next extract, M Potts and DW Evans criticize these sorts of argument on the grounds that taking organs from living patients, even if they have given consent and are close to death, would involve doctors killing their patients.

M Potts and DW Evans[36]

Truog and Robinson's proposals that unpaired vital organs be removed from 'brain dead' and other classes of patients can be seen as the endorsement of killing people for their organs. One difficulty with this is that once utilitarian considerations are used to justify killing ven-tilator/dependent patients who are dying, those same considerations could also be used to justify killing non-ventilator/dependent patients or patients who are not dying...

Currently, the statement on organ donor cards asserts that organs may be taken 'after my death'. We believe that such wording should be changed to reflect the fact that 'brain dead' individuals are not dead in the usual understanding of what death is. Explanatory literature accompanying organ donor cards should be frank that a 'brain dead' donor's heart is beating during part of the organ removal surgery.

In an attempt to sidestep debates over whether brain-stem death is really death, Torbjörn Tännsjö suggests that the search for *one* definition of death is futile. The circulatory and respiratory criterion makes sense in some circumstances, because the logical conclusion of accepting brain death as the definitive and *only* diagnosis of death is that we should be prepared to bury a person who is still breathing and whose heart is still beating. For prac-tical reasons, people have to be disconnected from life-support before burial or cremation, and hence the question of whether we would bury a warm, breathing body does not arise. However, in theory at least, the brain-stem criterion would appear to permit this.

---

[35] 'Death, Us and Our Bodies: Personal Reflections' (2003) 29 Journal of Medical Ethics 127–30.

[36] 'Does it Matter that Organ Donors are Not Dead? Ethical and Policy Implications' (2005) 31 Journal of Medical Ethics 406–9.

In contrast, the brain-stem criterion seems more appropriate in the context of organ donation, when most organs have to be removed before heart and lung function ceases. Tännsjö's argument is therefore that we should admit that there are *two* separate criteria for defining death: one for death of the person and one for death of the body. Brain death means that the *person* has died, whereas the *body* is only dead when it has ceased to function as a unified organism.

Torbjörn Tännsjö[37]

We can now define death of a person as the point at which the person in question ceases to exist. This happens when there is too little psychological continuity and connectedness left over. If there is no consciousness at all, then there is no person at all. And we can define the death of the body as the point at which the body ceases to function as a unified organism. This means that bodies, in contradistinction to persons, often continue to exist after their death....

But could it not be objected that to have a beating heart is to be a person? I do not think that this is a plausible move. First of all, it could simply be rejected on linguistic grounds. Most of us would not call someone without a working brain, someone whose brain had irreversibly ceased to exist, a 'person'.

Secondly, and more importantly, even if some would do so, they would still have to admit that something of importance was gone once someone's brain had ceased to exist. In particular, even those who reject the brain-death criterion do typically accept that we stop ventilating people whose brains have irreversibly ceased to function. What they object to as manipulative is merely the saying that these people are 'dead'.

Patients in a permanent vegetative state, or anencephalic infants, have permanently lost the capacity for consciousness: that is, their upper brain is dead, but their lower brain continues to function. Because a person is only categorized as brain dead when the *whole* brain has stopped functioning, such patients are undoubtedly still alive. There are therefore those who argue that the current definition of death is too restrictive, and that certain categories of patients whom we now treat as alive—such as patients in a persistent vegetative state, or anencephalic infants—should instead be regarded as dead.

Anencephalic babies are born with the congenital absence of the cerebral cortex and major parts of the skull. Most are stillborn, and of those who are born alive, 95 per cent will die within a week. Anencephalic babies will never achieve consciousness, but they do have a functioning brain stem. For an anencephalic infant's organs to be suitable for use in transplantation, she must first have been placed on a ventilator. Would this be lawful? Because there is no chance that an anencephalic baby will recover, it will not be in *her* best interests to be connected to an artificial ventilator. Since ventilation is started only to benefit a third party, does it involve using the baby as a means to an end? There may be some emotional value to the parents from the knowledge that their inevitably doomed child was able to save another baby's life, but again, the benefit here is to a third party, and not to the anencephalic infant herself.

A further problem is that it is impossible to diagnose death using brain-stem tests in anencephalic newborn babies. The Academy of Royal Medical Colleges have confirmed that

---

[37] 'Two Concepts of Death Reconciled' (1999) 2 Medicine, Health Care and Philosophy 41–6.

'Organs for transplantation can be removed from anencephalic infants when two doctors who are not members of the transplant team agree that spontaneous respiration has ceased.'[38] Because cessation of cardiorespiratory function causes rapid deterioration of the organs, the organs of anencephalic babies may therefore be unsuitable for use for transplantation.

The solution advocated by John Robertson is to suggest that when the capacity for sentience is irrevocably absent, an anencephalic baby or a patient in an irreversible coma cannot be harmed by organ retrieval.

John Robertson[39]

A major reason for the requirement that the organ donor be dead is to protect the donor from being harmed by organ removal. If the donor is dead, taking his organs will not harm him. In contrast, if he or she is alive, it is assumed that removing organs will kill or otherwise injure the donor.

This view of the dead donor rule, however, assumes that the live donor has interests in continued living and in not being physically injured. Whereas this assumption is true in most instances and thus should be strictly followed, it may not apply to situations of irreversible coma, near-dead pediatric patients and anencephalics...Such patients, though legally still alive, may no longer have interests in living or in avoiding physical harm that should be respected.

Treating the destruction or absence of the cerebral cortex as evidence of death would increase the pool of potential organ donors, but not everyone would agree that this is a sufficient reason to redefine death. WF May, for example, warns of the dangers of the slippery slope (see further Chapter 1).

WF May[40]

To invoke the need for organs as a reason for declaring a specific class of people dead creates a runaway, imperial argument, difficult to limit. Under the press of one kind of exigency or another, one could redefine death to include anencephalics, and then perhaps the next time, hydrocephalics, microcephalics, and so on, denying any independent and firm boundaries to mark off the dead from the dying or the vegetative....

An opportunistic redefinition of death would eventually produce other unfortunate results. It would lead patients to distrust doctors and hospitals, and would weaken the readiness of families to donate the organs of truly dead patients. Convenience and utility should not justify enlarging the kingdom of the dead. While, historically the need for organs and the development of the technology for perfusing and successfully transplanting them supplied the *occasion* for reflection on the criteria for determining death, the need for healthy organs should not influence the standards for determining that a patient or a class of patient is dead. That decision should rest solely on the patient's condition.

[38] Conference of Medical Colleges and Faculties of the United Kingdom, Working party on Organ Transplantation in Neonates (DHSS: London, 1988).

[39] 'Relaxing the Death Standard for Organ Donation in Pediatric Situations' in Deborah Mathieu (ed.), *Organ Substitution Technology: Ethical, Legal and Public Policy Issues* (Westview Press: Boulder Colorado, 1988) 69–76.

[40] *The Patient's Ordeal* (Indiana UP: Bloomington and Indianapolis, 1991).

(c) TYPE OF TRANSPLANT

Donor cards allow people to specify which organs they are prepared to donate for use: it is judged preferable to allow people to 'opt out' of donating certain organs (commonly hearts or corneas), if this will increase the probability that they will volunteer to donate other organs, such as kidneys or lungs.

In recent years, the possibility of new types of transplant—most notably limbs and faces—has raised a number of fresh ethical dilemmas. First, while the side-effects and health risks of taking immunosuppressant drugs for the rest of one's life will often be worth assuming when the alternative to transplantation is death, or very severely impaired existence, the risk/benefit calculation may be less clear when the alternative is an otherwise normal and healthy life without the use of a hand, or with a disfigured face. Indeed, it has been argued that hand or face transplants convert a healthy person with an amputated hand or facial disfigurement 'into a morbidly ill individual who must endure a toxic regime of drugs for the remainder of their life'.[41] On the other hand, there are serious disadvantages in having only one functioning hand, and living with facial disfigurement can be extremely difficult, and lead to serious psychological problems. There is even some evidence that people might be willing to incur *more* risk in order to have a new face than a new kidney.[42]

Secondly, the long-term impact, both physiological and psychological, of receiving another person's hand, limb, or face remain unknown. People may feel less comfortable about receiving a visible part of another person's body than they do in relation to invisible internal organs. For the same reason, it is also likely that fewer people would be willing to donate their face or their limbs after death, and there is the further concern that consent to donation of other organs may be affected if people are put off donation in general because of some vague, albeit unsubstantiated fear that their face might be used as well.

While we only discuss limb and face transplants briefly here, it is worth noting that other novel transplantation techniques are being considered. In 2009, for example, the Royal College of Surgeons set up a working party to consider the possibility of voice box transplantation.

(1) Limbs and Hands

The first human hand transplant took place in 1998. The recipient regretted the operation and could not cope with his new hand. He failed to comply with the drug regime, and, following chronic rejection, his new hand had to be amputated. Other hand and limb transplants have been successful and enabled amputees to live more normal lives. Despite this, Donna Dickenson and Guy Widdershoven argue that our intimate relationships with our hands, and those of others, makes hand transplants more complex than transplants of 'invisible' internal organs.

---

[41] Richard Huxtable and Julie Woodley, 'Gaining Face or Losing Face? Framing the Debate on Face Transplants' (2005) 19 Bioethics 505–22.

[42] M Cunningham *et al.*, 'Risk Acceptance in Composite Tissue Allotransplantation Reconstructive Procedures—Instrument Design and Validation' (2004) 30 European Journal of Trauma 12–16.

Donna Dickenson and Guy Widdershoven[43]

It might be argued that hand allografts entail the transposition of an organ with personal qualities from one person to another. This goes beyond the issue of the hand's visibility, though that too is an issue.... Likewise, it may be conceivable that the intimacy which the hand can express is transformed as a result of transplantation, necessarily having an emotional impact on those who are intimately related to both donor and recipient...

The hand, as an expression of both agency and intimacy, occupies a different place in our moral sensibility than internal organs. Again, this is not a reason for absolutely prohibiting hand transplants, if those intimate with both donor and recipient consent, but it is a reason for thinking that the decision is not down to the individual donor or recipient alone.

(2) Faces

The first face transplant took place in France in 2005. The recipient, Isabelle Dinoire, had been attacked by her dog and had suffered very severe facial injuries. The operation was a success, and while long-term impact cannot be judged, at the time of writing, her new face still appears to be functioning well. The second face transplant happened in China, and again appeared to be successful.

While similar issues to those mentioned above in relation to visibility of the transplanted tissue, and identification with it arise with faces and hands/limbs, there are also important differences. In the event of transplant failure, removal of a face is not as straightforward as the amputation of a failed hand transplant. On the contrary, the failure of a face transplant would leave the recipient in a much worse position than they were before the operation.

A second significant difference is that the loss of the use of a hand or a limb is disabling, and so the transplant would be done in order to improve function, rather than purely for aesthetic reasons. While some facial disfigurement may also have an effect on function, the main hardship from having a seriously disfigured face is the reaction of others. Clarke describes what this can involve: 'visual and verbal assaults, and a level of familiarity from strangers, naked stares, startled reactions, double takes, whispering, remarks, furtive looks, curiosity, personal questions, advice, manifestations of pity or aversion, laughter, ridicule and outright avoidance'.[44]

Richard Huxtable and Julie Woodley have therefore argued that face transplant surgery is done because of *society's* inability to adapt itself to the interests of disfigured people.

Richard Huxtable and Julie Woodley[45]

In an important sense, one must query whether the 'patient' is actually society, and in particular image-conscious Western society... This apparent obsession with beauty is probably one of the strongest reasons for permitting this procedure and also ironically one of the main reasons why it gives cause for concern. Ideally, of course, society would celebrate, rather than alienate, such diversity. There nevertheless lingers the suspicion that the influence of societal norms amounts to a form of coercion, which might again threaten the validity of any

---

[43] 'Ethical Issues in Limb Transplants' (2001) 15 Bioethics 110–24.

[44] A Clarke, 'Psychosocial Aspects of Facial Disfigurement' (1999) 4 Psychology, Health and Medicine 127–42.

[45] 'Gaining Face or Losing Face? Framing the Debate on Face Transplants' (2005) 19 Bioethics 505–22.

> consent. Furthermore, we wonder whether alternative responses to disfigurement, such as counselling, would suffer once the transplantation doors are opened. As Strauss has pointed out, 'when something is correctable, our willingness to accept it as untouched is reduced'.

While it is, of course, true that disfigured people should not have to endure discriminatory attitudes and hostility, if someone who experiences disfigurement as extremely disabling and distressing gives voluntary and informed consent to facial transplantation, it is not clear why their autonomous choice should not be respected just because we might wish that society was a more tolerant place.

In the UK, the Royal College of Surgeons' Working Party initially suggested that more research was necessary before going ahead with facial transplantation, but in its second report, in 2006, it adopted a more permissive, although still cautious approach. The Working Party report lays out the special considerations which apply to facial transplantation and the questions which must have been answered satisfactorily before an REC should give approval.[46] With proper safeguards in place, the Royal College of Surgeons concluded that 'there is no a priori reason why prospective patients who have been shown to be sufficiently autonomous cannot be accurately informed about both known and unknown risks of transplantation—assuming that the REC has agreed the risk benefit ratio to be acceptable'.[47]

One of the matters which particularly concerned the Working Party was the need to protect patient's psychological wellbeing in the event of graft failure or rejection. They also emphasized the importance of the psychological challenges facing not only recipients, but their families and the families of face donors.

Royal College of Surgeons[48]

> All stages of the face transplantation process will present psychological challenges for recipients, their families and donor families....
>
> The prospective patient should be sufficiently resilient to cope with the considerable stress associated with the transplant, including the 'unknowns' associated with a new procedure of this nature, the complex immunological and behavioural post-operative regimen, the risks of rejection and intrusive media interest....
>
> Teams should be vigilant for signs of psychological rejection of the donor face, for example, lack of interest in looking at the face in a mirror, or indications that the patient feels the new face is 'not the real me'...The recipient may need assistance to resolve complex feelings about the donor (for example, curiosity about the sort of person, guilt about the donor's death, gratitude to the family)...
>
> Post-operatively, family members should be monitored for signs of excessive stress and anxiety.... Strategies may be needed to encourage acceptance of the new face.

In the next extract, Michael Freeman and Pauline Abou Jaoudé speculate about some more alarming (and perhaps alarmist) psychological consequences.

---

[46] Royal College of Surgeons of England, Facial Transplantation. Working Party Report (2003; 2nd edn 2006), available at <www.rcseng.ac.uk>.
[47] Ibid.   [48] Ibid.

Michael Freeman and Pauline Abou Jaoudé[49]

> The donor will die and in a disembodied form live on. What was the stuff of drama to earlier generations (Hamlet's father's ghost reappearing or the Commendatore returning in Mozart's *Don Giovanni*) is set for contemporary realisation.
>
> Should we therefore question a donor's motivation? Should it matter what this is? Should offers to donate be ruled out if the motivation is less altruistic than, literally, face saving? A form of 'life after death', a 'second coming', self-aggrandisement? Perhaps even a desire to haunt family, friends and colleagues? . . .
>
> The deceased's family is likely to think of him or her in terms of his or her face. This may be especially so where the deceased is a child or a young person. In such cases there may even be a desire for a continuing a quasi-relationship by means of contact. . . . It is most unlikely, indeed, undesirable, that any right to contact will develop. But denial could lead to frustration, anger and trauma, in extreme cases perhaps even to a macabre form of stalking.

While both face and limb transplants almost certainly do raise slightly different issues from the transplant of internal organs, intuitive distaste or discomfort does not offer a good reason to prohibit these sorts of transplants. In particular, it is worth reminding ourselves that people reacted similarly to the first organ transplants. There was, for example, widespread concern that having another person's heart would be psychologically disturbing.

(d) AUTHORIZATION OF REMOVAL

(1) The Human Tissue Act 2004

The Human Tissue Act clarifies and simplifies the process of authorizing removal of organs for transplantation. Under section 1, no organ can be taken without 'appropriate consent'.

(a) Adults

For adults appropriate consent can, under section 3, be obtained in three different ways.

Human Tissue Act 2004 section 3

> 3(6) Where the person concerned has died . . . 'appropriate consent' means—
>
> (a) if a decision of his to consent to the activity, or a decision of his not to consent to it, was in force immediately before he died, his consent;
>
> (b) if—
>
> (i) paragraph (a) does not apply, and
>
> (ii) he has appointed a person or persons under section 4 to deal after his death with the issue of consent in relation to the activity,
>
> (c) consent given under the appointment;
>
> (d) if neither paragraph (a) nor paragraph (b) applies, the consent of a person who stood in a qualifying relationship to him immediately before he died.

[49] 'Justifying Surgery's Last Taboo: The Ethics of Face Transplants' (2007) 33 Journal of Medical Ethics 76–81.

So if the deceased consented to organ transplantation, by being registered on the organ donor register or carrying an organ donor card, the doctors would act lawfully in retrieving her organs. Of course, some would argue that the process of giving consent when signing up to be on the register is very far removed from the normal consent process, which we considered in Chapters 4 and 5. People can fill in a brief registration form online, or they can sign up by ticking the relevant box on an application form for a driving licence or for a *Boots* advantage card.[50] This 'tick box' exercise gives no opportunity to assess their capacity to make the decision, and there is no formal information-giving process.

Organ Donation Taskforce[51]

Amongst clinicians there is a certain amount of concern that the carrying of a donor card, or even registration with the donor register, falls short of what would usually be defined as consent in a medical setting. Furthermore, in the absence of independent evidence of a persisting wish, the passage of time between registration and death is seen by some to weaken the ethical force of the action.

Of course, agreeing to become a donor after death is different from giving informed consent to medical treatment. But because 'consent' has such a specific meaning in medical law, it might be worth thinking about using a different term. The Human Tissue (Scotland) Act 2004, for example, refers to 'authorization', rather than consent.

The deceased's consent (or authorization) does not have to be in writing, and if there is no donor card, or the deceased is not on the organ donor register, other efforts should be made to find out whether the deceased had expressed her wishes about organ donation.

HTA Code of Practice[52]

39 If no records are held, an approach should be made to the deceased person's relatives or close friends by a transplant coordinator or a member of the team who cared for the person, or both together, to establish any known wishes of the deceased person.

If the deceased's wishes are not known, but she has appointed someone under section 4 to deal with consent, then the appointed person's consent will be sufficient. A person might want to nominate a representative, or more than one, to give consent in order to ensure that the decision is taken by someone who knows her wishes, rather than leaving it to whoever turns out to be the highest-ranking qualified relative at the time of her death. This might be particularly important for someone who knows that members of their family disagree about transplantation, so that they can be sure that the decision will be taken by a person who shares their views. An appointment can be made orally, if witnessed by two people, or in writing, with one witness.

Where the deceased person had not given consent and had either not nominated someone to give proxy consent, or under sections 3(7) and 3(8) their nominee is unable to consent, or 'it is not reasonably practicable to communicate with [him or her] within the time available', then consent can be sought from someone in a qualifying relationship.

---

[50] A loyalty card from the UK's largest chain of pharmacists.
[51] Organs for Transplants: A Report from the Organ Donation Taskforce (DH: London, 2008), available at <www.dh.gov.uk>.
[52] Code of Practice 2 (Donation of Solid Organs for Transplantation), available at <www.hta.gov.uk>.

Qualifying relationships are defined in section 27(4) and are ranked, so that the consent of a spouse or partner should be sought first, and that of a parent or child only if no spouse or partner is available to consent, and that of a brother or sister only if no spouse, partner, parent or child can give consent, and so on. The full hierarchy is as follows:

(a) spouse or partner;[53]

(b) parent or child;

(c) brother or sister;

(d) grandparent or grandchild;

(e) child of a brother or sister;

(f) stepfather or stepmother;

(g) half-brother or half-sister;

(h) friend of long standing.

Of course, because organs must be retrieved as quickly as possible after death, it may not always be feasible to contact the person highest in the hierarchy of qualifying relatives, or they may not wish to make the decision, or may lack the capacity to do so. In such circumstances, the HTA Code of Practice provides that a person can be omitted from the hierarchy, and the next person down becomes the appropriate person to give consent.[54]

Section 27(5) states that 'Relationships in the same paragraph of subsection (4) should be accorded equal ranking', so where there is both a parent and a child, either is able to give consent. And under section 27(7): 'If the relationship of each of two or more persons to the person concerned is accorded equal highest ranking…it is sufficient to obtain the consent of any of them.' This means that if the deceased has both an estranged spouse and a new partner, the consent of the estranged spouse would be sufficient, even if the current partner objects. Similarly, where the deceased has no spouse or partner, but several children, any one of them can give consent, even if all of the other children are opposed to organ retrieval.

It is important to remember that under the Human Tissue Act 2004, it is *lawful* to take organs where an appropriate consent exists, but not *obligatory*. In practice, the relatives' views will be taken into account even if the deceased has made her wishes known. The Code of Practice suggests that, in such circumstances, health professionals should try to encourage the family to respect the deceased's wishes, but in the face of continued objection, it may not be appropriate to proceed:

HTA Code of Practice[55]

56 Obtaining appropriate consent only makes the activity lawful if it goes ahead—it does not mean that it is obligatory.

57 …Great care should be taken to assess whether ignoring the family's strongly held objections might outweigh the benefits of proceeding.

So, while the deceased's family do not have a legal right of veto, in practice doctors may be reluctant to retrieve organs where relatives object, both for compassionate reasons and from

---

[53] Partner is defined in s 54(9): 'For the purposes of this Act,…a person is another's partner if the two of them (whether of different sexes or the same sex) live as partners in an enduring family relationship.'

[54] Code of Practice 2, para 52.

[55] Code of Practice 2.

the more pragmatic desire to avoid the bad publicity which might result from ignoring the wishes of recently bereaved and distraught relatives.

It could, however, be argued that giving relatives any say over what happens to a person's body after her death is inconsistent with the now-dominant principle of patient autonomy: why should a family member who has absolutely no say over my medical treatment during my life be permitted, in practice, to *overrule* my decision to donate my organs after my death?

On the other hand, Margaret Lock suggests that it is families, rather than donors, who make the greatest sacrifice when organs are taken from a dead body.

Margaret Lock[56]

[W]e encourage the idea that donation is a selfless act, but it can also be thought of as the giving away of something no longer of any use: it takes virtually no effort to sign a donor card. But donor families make a much greater emotional sacrifice. They must usually come to terms with the fact that someone dear to them has been transformed, in the space of a few hours, and often through a violent encounter, from a healthy individual into an irrevocably damaged entity, suspended between life and death. To give selflessly under these circumstances requires courage, as well as faith in the ICU staff and in the truth of their assessments.

In practice, when asked, about 40 per cent of relatives object to transplantation.[57] Where the deceased has registered on the organ donor register, this figure decreases to 10 per cent. UK Transplant's 2005 analysis of the reasons for relatives' refusal found that the most common reasons given are religious beliefs and wanting to be with the deceased when the ventilator is switched off (both 23 per cent); that the family do not know what the individual would have wanted (20 per cent); that they do not want surgery to the body (20 per cent); and that they feel the deceased has suffered enough (19 per cent).[58]

(b) Children

Where the deceased is a child, organ retrieval will be lawful if there is appropriate consent under section 2(7):

Human Tissue Act 2004 section 2

2(7) Where the child concerned has died...'appropriate consent' means—

    (a) if a decision of his to consent to the activity, or a decision of his not to consent to it, was in force immediately before he died, his consent;

    (b) if paragraph (a) does not apply—

---

[56] *Twice Dead: Organ Transplants and the Reinvention of Death* (University of California Press: Berkeley, 2002) 373.

[57] UK Transplant Transplant Activity in the UK 2007–8 (2008), available at <www.uktransplant.org.uk>.

[58] Potential Donor Audit (UK Transplant, 2005), available at <www.uktransplant.org.uk/>.

> (i) the consent of a person who had parental responsibility for him immediately before he died, or
>
> (ii) where no person had parental responsibility for him immediately before he died, the consent of a person who stood in a qualifying relationship to him at that time.

Hence a *Gillick*-competent minor's consent will be sufficient for organ retrieval to be lawful (see Chapter 5 for a description of *Gillick* competence). The problem here is that the child is now dead, and so establishing that they were, in fact, *Gillick*-competent will be difficult. Even where the child's wishes are known, retrieval should not go ahead without discussion with someone with parental responsibility, whose wishes must also be taken into account.[59]

Where the child has not made her views about organ donation known, or lacks capacity, consent can be obtained from anyone with parental responsibility, or if no-one has parental responsibility, someone in the highest-ranking qualifying relationship (using the above list) can give consent.

(2) Liability for Unlawful Removal

Section 5 of the Human Tissue Act 2004 provides that anyone who takes organs without appropriate consent commits an offence, unless he reasonably believes that he did in fact have appropriate consent. The maximum penalty is three years' imprisonment.

(e) SYSTEM FOR REMOVAL AND ALLOCATION

UK Transplant oversees transplantation arrangements in the UK. Its responsibilities include maintaining the national transplant waiting list; matching and allocating organs; transporting organs to recipient centres; and maintaining the organ donor register. It also promotes organ donation and transplantation, and maintains transplant coordination services.

Once a patient is identified as a potential organ donor, the local donor coordinator should be contacted. Donor coordinators are responsible for ascertaining the views of the potential donor's relatives or carers, and may contact UK Blood and Transplant in order to find out whether the donor is on the organ donor register. Once agreement to organ donation has been obtained, the donor coordinator will notify UK Blood and Transplant, which maintains a national database of all potential organ recipients. When the appropriate recipient has been identified, the donor coordinator liaises between the surgical teams responsible for both the donor and the recipient's care. Specialist recipient coordinators then oversee the recipients' care, both pre- and post-transplant.

In the UK, there are different systems of allocation for different organs. For livers, hearts, and lungs, the UK is divided into seven or eight zones, depending upon the organ. Once an organ becomes available, first priority is given to any patient in the UK whose need is categorized as 'super-urgent' because they are in imminent danger of death (ie, they will die within three days without a transplant). If there are none of these, the organ will then be offered within the zone in which the donor has died. If there are no appropriate local recipients, the organ will become available nationally, at which point there is a rota between the different

---

[59] Code of Practice 2, para 33.

zones. If, for example, zone A gets an organ on one occasion, it will then go to the bottom of the list for the next available organ.

Kidneys are allocated in a different way, because of the importance of tissue matching. This is especially important for children who may need more than one kidney transplant during their lifetime, when a good match the first time will make it less difficult to find a suitable donor in the future. Children are therefore given the highest priority for well-matched kidneys. After that, there is a points system, which takes account of a range of other factors, such as the time spent on the waiting list, the age gap between donor and recipient (which affects success rates) and geographical distance (to avoid having to transport the kidney a long distance). The process is done automatically by computer, and the kidney will be offered to the recipient who has the most 'points'.

Cadaveric organ donation is usually anonymous. It is, however, possible for the donor's family to be given some information, such as the age and sex of the people who have benefited from the donation. Patients who receive organs can obtain similar details about their donors.

(f) THE SHORTAGE OF ORGANS

UK Transplant issues detailed statistics on transplant activity in the UK.[60]

Year	Cadaveric donors	Cadaveric transplants	Waiting list	Living donors
1992	876	2,591	5,124	126
2007/8	809	2,381	7,655	854

As is clear from the above table, there are more people on the waiting list for transplants than there are available organs, and the gap between the supply of cadaveric organs and demand is widening. When it reformed the law on transplantation in 2004, the government opted to stick closely to a consent model for transplantation. The Organ Donation Taskforce has not recommended a change to this system, arguing instead that it should be possible to increase donation rates without changing the law.

In what follows, we evaluate the Taskforce's recommendations, as well as a number of other strategies that might be employed in order to increase donation rates.

(1) Improved Coordination

It has been suggested that many potential cadaveric donations are lost because the organ procurement system is inefficient. Transplant coordinators tend to be based in the few large transplant centres in the UK, and it is the responsibility of medical teams working in other hospitals to contact them should a potential organ donor be identified.

In contrast in Spain, following the introduction of a new transplant coordinator network in 1990, every major hospital with an intensive care unit, not just those which also have a

---

[60] UK Transplant Transplant Activity in the UK 2007–8 (2008), available at <www.uktransplant. org.uk>.

transplant unit, has a coordinating transplant team consisting of medical staff who also work in intensive care. This means that organ procurement and intensive care are much more effectively integrated, and health care professionals working in intensive care units are very well informed about the procedures involved in obtaining organs for transplant. While improving coordination could not eliminate the organ shortage, the effect on procurement rates seems to be extremely positive. In Spain, there are, on average, 35.1 donors per million population, although seven regions have around 40 donors per million, and one, La Rioja, has a rate of 72 per million. In the UK the equivalent figure is 12.8 per million, which is one of the lowest rates in the developed world. In the US, there are 26.9 donors per million, and in France 23.2.[61]

Of course, there might be other reasons—such as increased publicity—why Spain's transplant rates have increased over this period. And although the integration of organ procurement and intensive care may have advantages, there might be dangers in blurring the roles of carer and organ procurer. Intensive care unit (ICU) staff should always have the treatment of patients, rather than the procuring of organs, as their first priority. As Sheila McLean points out, 'medical ethics require that the doctors seeking to harvest organs should be different from those involved in the care of the patient'.[62]

Nevertheless, there would seem to be obvious benefits in ensuring that hospitals have closer links with transplant units. It is also crucially important that the first discussion with relatives in an intensive care unit—which, by definition, has to take place at a moment of extreme stress—is made sympathetically, by an experienced and well-informed health care professional.

The first report from the Organ Donation Taskforce, published in January 2008, made 14 recommendations, which are intended to improve the system of organ retrieval and donation. All of these were immediately accepted by the government. As is evident from the following extract, the intention is to make the preparatory steps for donation routine. At present the Trust where the donor dies must organize and pay for the retrieval surgery, even though the benefit may be to a patient in another part of the UK. The taskforce recommended appropriate reimbursement, and the development of specialist retrieval teams. They also recommended greater public recognition of donors.

Organ Donation Taskforce[63]

Recommendations

R4. All parts of the NHS must embrace organ donation as a usual, not an unusual event. Discussions about donation should be part of all end-of-life care when appropriate. Each Trust should have an identified clinical donation champion and a Trust donation committee to help achieve this....

R7. Brain Stem Death (BSD) testing should be carried out in all patients where BSD is a likely diagnosis, even if organ donation is an unlikely outcome.

---

[61] Organs for Transplants: A Report from the Organ Donation Taskforce (DH: London, 2008), available at <www.dh.gov.uk>.

[62] 'Transplantation and the "Nearly Dead"; The Case of Elective Ventilation' in S Mclean (ed.), *Contemporary Issues in Law, Medicine and Ethics* (Dartmouth: Aldershot, 1996) 143–61, 149.

[63] Organs for Transplants: A Report from the Organ Donation Taskforce (DH: London, 2008), available at <www.dh.gov.uk>.

R8. Financial disincentives to Trusts facilitating donation should be removed through the development and introduction of appropriate reimbursement....

R9. Additional coordinators, embedded within critical care areas, should be employed to ensure a comprehensive, highly skilled, specialised and robust service.

R10. A UK-wide network of dedicated organ retrieval teams should be established to ensure timely, high-quality organ removal from all heart beating and non heart beating donors...

R12. Appropriate ways should be identified of personally and publicly recognising individual organ donors, where desired. These approaches may include national memorials, local initiatives and personal follow-up to donor families.

R13. There is an urgent requirement to identify and implement the most effective methods through which organ donation and the 'gift of life' can be promoted to the general public, and specifically to the BME (black and minority ethnic) population.

The taskforce 'strongly believes that successful implementation will deliver a 50 per cent increase in organ donor numbers within five years (ie by 2013)', although it admits that initial progress will be slow while improved training and other new systems are put in place.

Clearly, the taskforce's suggestions are sensible and should help both to make organ donation more routine, and to ensure that the transplantation system has the capacity to cope with increased donation rates. There are, however, some who would argue for more radical reforms in order to address the gap between supply and demand.

(2) Elective Ventilation

In May 1988, the Royal Devon and Exeter Hospital introduced a new protocol designed to enable organs to be taken from potential donors who were dying outside of intensive care units (ICUs). Once identified, and with the agreement of the relatives, such patients would be transferred to an ICU and 'electively ventilated' to ensure that their organs would be suitable for transplant. The relatives were told that the patient was not going to recover, and were asked to agree both to organ donation and to the patient's transfer to an ICU to enable organ donation to proceed after the patient's death. During the next 19 months, the number of organs available for transplant increased by more than 50 per cent. Obtaining organs from people who would otherwise be unsuitable donors has clear health benefits for patients on the transplant waiting list, but for a number of reasons, there is some doubt over whether elective ventilation is legally or ethically justifiable.

First, beds in ICUs are scarce and expensive. Is it acceptable to transfer a dying patient to a high-dependency unit when this is done not for her own good, but in order to ensure that her organs will be capable of benefiting others? There are often not enough beds in an ICU for every patient who might need one, and it would seem unreasonable to deprive a patient who might recover of treatment in order to ventilate someone who will die in any event. Of course, this argument only rules out elective ventilation if the potential organ donor would *always* be depriving another patient of access to an intensive care bed. While this might often be the case, there could be circumstances in which a dying patient could be placed in a bed that would otherwise be unused in order to ensure that her organs would be available to others after her death. Might it in fact be unethical to leave a bed empty when its use might save several lives?

Moreover, because transplantation is more cost-effective than, say, dialysis, a substantial increase in the number of organs available for transplant would *save* the NHS money, and thus might offset the costs of elective ventilation, and enable more intensive care beds to be provided.

Secondly, elective ventilation is arguably unlawful. As we saw in Chapter 5, because unconscious patients lack capacity, doctors are under a duty to treat them in their best interests. Placing a patient who is not expected to recover on a ventilator in order to ensure that her organs are suitable for transplant is not done to benefit her, but rather to benefit third parties on the organ transplant waiting list. Indeed, as JK Mason points out in the next extract, ventilating a patient where there is no intention to benefit her could be an assault. Moreover, it is thought that there is a small risk that once placed on a ventilator, the patient who would have died might instead lapse into a coma or a permanent vegetative state.

JK Mason[64]

The practice of 'elective ventilation' is a far more controversial way of extending the source of organs beyond the intensive care unit (ICU) and into the medical and geriatric wards.... There is no way in which invasive non-consensual treatment of a dying and incurable patient can be regarded as being in his or her best interests; it follows that elective ventilation must involve an assault or trespass to the person...

The 'best interests' test must also apply to the ethical parameters. It cannot be in the patient's best interest to prolong his dying by invasive medicine. We can be doing him no good—and we *may* be doing him harm. Looked at in this way, there can be no starker example of using a patient as a means and offending a basic Kantian imperative...

It is prognosis, however, that raises the gravest doubts as to the validity of the process... [There are] three possible untoward outcomes: the patient may develop some other condition while under intensive care, such as sepsis, which invalidates him as a donor; the patient may recover sufficiently to be discharged from hospital; or the patient may stabilise in the persistent vegetative state. It is this last possibility which raises the greatest fears and it is, probably, the least unlikely of the three scenarios to develop. The production of a persistent vegetative state in a person who was close to a peaceful natural death could only be described as a clinical disaster which, if publicised, could be catastrophically detrimental to the whole transplantation programme.

While it would be difficult to argue that treatment which prolongs the process of dying is in the best interests of the patient, it might be possible to establish that the patient was so strongly committed to being an organ donor during her lifetime that elective ventilation would allow her final wishes about the fate of her body to be fulfilled. Might it then be possible to argue that elective ventilation would be lawful if the patient had executed an advance directive requesting that all steps, including elective ventilation, are carried out in order to enable her organs to be donated after death? The problem here is that, as we saw in Chapter 5, it is only advance *refusals* which are binding upon doctors. An advance request might be indicative of the patient's wishes, but would have no legal force.

A final possible justification for elective ventilation would be to argue that the patient is in fact already dead when ventilation is begun. If brain-stem tests are confirmatory, the patient will have died sometime before the tests confirm that she is now, in fact, dead. In

---

[64] 'Contemporary Issues in Organ Transplantation' in S Mclean (ed.), *Contemporary Issues in Law, Medicine and Ethics* (Dartmouth: Aldershot, 1996) 117–41.

the Exeter Protocol, ventilation was begun only *after* spontaneous respiratory arrest, and the doctors therefore argued that they ventilated the patient *at the moment of death*, even though death would be confirmed later once brain-stem tests had been carried out. If the patient is already dead, then there is no duty to act in her best interests, and procedures designed to maximize the chance that her organs could be used successfully would not necessarily be unlawful. This argument is, however, extremely controversial. If elective ventilation sometimes induces the permanent vegetative state (in which patients are plainly still alive), it would be difficult to argue that such patients were dead when ventilation began.

The Academy of Medical Royal Colleges' Code of Practice is clear that ventilation should only be initiated and maintained if it is in the patient's best interests, and not to ensure their organs can be used in transplantation.

Academy of Medical Royal Colleges[65]

7.3 If further intensive care is not considered appropriate because it can be of no benefit, nor in the patient's best interests, then neither is a continuation of the respiratory support being provided.

Endotracheal intubation and artificial ventilation of the patient should only be initiated and maintained to further the patient's benefit and not as a means of preserving organ function.

(3) Non-heartbeating Donors

In recent years there has been a substantial increase in the number of non-heartbeating donors (NHBDs). In 2003/4, there were 73 NHBDs; in 2007/8, there were 200.[66] Using NHBDs means that patients who die of cardiac arrest on general wards, or in accident and emergency departments, or those who are declared dead on arrival at hospital, might still be potential donors. It is only kidneys and livers that can be taken from non-heartbeating donors. Death is diagnosed using cardiac criteria, rather than brain-stem tests, and after death has been confirmed, the organs are cooled using an in situ perfusion technique. The Human Tissue Act 2004 confirms the legality of cold perfusion techniques: under section 43, if part of a body is or may be suitable for use for transplantation, it is lawful to take the minimum necessary steps for the purpose of preserving the part for use for transplantation, until it has been established that consent for transplantation has not been, and will not be, given.

More complex is the question of whether steps to ensure that the organs will be suitable for transplantation may be taken *before the patient has died*, such as giving the dying patient anti-coagulant drugs. This raises similar issues to those of elective ventilation, since the treatment would not be intended to benefit the patient, but rather to increase the likelihood of successful transplantation after death. The Organ Donation Taskforce discussed this concern.

---

[65] Academy of Medical Royal Colleges, A Code of Practice for the Diagnosis and Confirmation of Death (2008), available at <www.aomrc.org.uk>.

[66] UK Transplant Transplant Activity in the UK 2007–8 (2008), available at <www.uktransplant.org.uk>.

Organ Donation Taskforce[67]

> [I]n the case of non-heartbeating donors one could ask whether it is justified to carry out tests and procedures prior to death, in the interests of avoiding deterioration of the organ or organs. These are difficult ethical questions which genuinely trouble staff working with this group of patients.
>
> If we take registration as a donor to be a valid instance of consent, and further interpret it as a clear statement of an important wish on the part of the patient, we might argue that anything we do to facilitate the patient having that wish fulfilled is in his or her best interests. However, if we are unclear about the value of the consent, or where no wishes have been stated, we would have to concede that some of the actions taken to facilitate donation may not necessarily be in the interests of the donor.

Zeiler *et al.* argue that measures to preserve organs for transplantation should be considered acceptable 'after the patient has passed the point of no return': that is, it is clear that they are not going to recover and so treatment has become futile.[68]

While at first, success rates using organs taken from NHBDs were considerably lower than when organs were retrieved from deceased heart-beating donors, this is no longer the case. It is therefore important that staff in accident and emergency departments, and on ordinary medical wards, who will be less familiar with the process of organ transplantation than those working in intensive care units, are aware of the possibility of using kidneys or livers from such patients.

(4) Allowing Conditional Donation

In July 1998, a man who was unconscious and in a critical condition was admitted to an ICU in the North of England. His relatives agreed to organ donation in the event of his death, but only on condition that the organs went to white recipients. In this instance, the person on the waiting list who was most urgently in need of a liver transplant was white, and without the organ he would have died within 24 hours. The two people who came top in the kidney transplant points system also happened to be white. Because the condition would have made no difference in this case, the organs were accepted and two kidneys and a liver were successfully transplanted into three different individuals.

Unsurprisingly, the case received a great deal of publicity, and the Department of Health set up an investigation.[69] The panel established that the three organs went to the same people who would have received them if no condition had been attached, so no one was in fact disadvantaged. But the panel also concluded that it had been wrong for the organs to have been accepted in the first place. The panel recommended that organs must not be accepted if the donor or the family wish to attach conditions. This guidance has since been formalized by the Department of Health, and it is clear that the prohibition on conditional donation applies to *all* conditions, and not just those grounded in racism or any another sort of prejudice.

---

[67] Organs for Transplants: A Report from the Organ Donation Taskforce (DH: London, 2008) paras 4.11–4.12, available at <www.dh.gov.uk>.

[68] K Zeiler, E Furberg, G Tufveson, and S Welin, 'The Ethics of Non-heart-Beating Donation: How New Technology can Change the Ethical Landscape' (2008) 34 Journal of Medical Ethics 526–9.

[69] An Investigation into Conditional Organ Donation: The Report (2000), available at <www.dh. gov.uk>.

Although conditional donation in a case such as this is plainly morally objectionable, the issue is made more complicated by the presence of identifiable individuals on a waiting list who will die if a suitable organ is turned down on moral grounds. The liver recipient in this case would have died within 24 hours if this organ was not accepted, making it extremely unlikely that an alternative non-conditional organ would have become available in time to save his life. It would surely be understandable if he was prepared to put his interest in continued life over society's preference for unconditional altruism.

It is also worth remembering that cadaveric donation is anonymous. In practice then, the organ could be accepted with the condition attached, and the condition could then be ignored. Because the organs do not *belong* to the family, it is certainly very difficult to imagine what sort of remedy they might have if they discovered that the organ had in fact been given to someone who did not satisfy their condition. The argument that ignoring relatives' wishes might have an adverse impact upon donation rates also seems comparatively weak in this sort of case.

It might further be argued that there is an inconsistency between the rules on living organ donation, where donation is almost always to a specified individual, and cadaveric donation, which must be unconditional. As TM Wilkinson points out in then next extract, it is hard to see what would be wrong with allowing directed donation to a close friend or relative after death. Of course, it would rarely be possible for cadaveric donation to be directed to a specific individual because most organ donors are not aware of their impending and often sudden death. But it is possible to imagine circumstances in which a person knows that she is going to die, and in which she expresses a preference that one of her organs should be used to treat a close relative with acute organ failure.

TM Wilkinson[70]

Is it really so bad to attach a condition to an organ donation? Of course it was bad in the case of the racist. The motive there was some mix of hatred and contempt and there is nothing to be said for it. But what about the condition that an organ go to a relative? There seems nothing morally wrong about agreeing to donate a kidney, say, on condition that it go to a sibling, whether the donation is to be from a living person or a dead one . . .

Setting aside a special concern for one's nearest and dearest, let us consider the panel's explanation of what is wrong with attaching a condition to a donation. The panel claims that conditional donation 'offends against the fundamental principle that organs are donated altruistically and should go to patients in the greatest need'. Altruism in its normal sense refers roughly to a non-self-interested concern for the interests of others. Importantly, a wide variety of other-regarding motives can be regarded as altruistic, such as a special concern for children, or the deaf, or the poor. 'Altruism'. . . does not require, for example, that actions be motivated out of adherence to a greatest happiness principle or, saliently here, a greatest needs principle. Consequently, there need be nothing non-altruistic about conditional donation. Wanting organs to go to a child—although also apparently opposed by the panel—is not a violation of altruism any more than donating to a children's charity is.

In 2008 the Human Tissue Authority was criticized for not permitting conditional donation in the case of Laura Ashworth, who had apparently expressed an interest in becoming a living kidney donor for her mother, Rachel Leake. Laura then died from an acute attack of asthma before having taken any formal steps towards living donation. Because she was

---

[70] 'What's Not Wrong with Conditional Organ Donation?' (2003) 29 Journal of Medical Ethics 163–4.

registered on the organ donor register, her organs were retrieved for transplantation, and her kidneys went to two strangers. In response to public and media criticism of their decision to allocate Laura's organs in the normal way, and not to prioritize her mother, the CEO of the Human Tissue Authority, Adrian McNeil, told the press:

> The central principle of matching and allocating organs from the deceased is that they are allocated to the person on the UK Transplant waiting list who is most in need and who is the best match with the donor. In line with this central principle, a person cannot choose to whom their organ can be given when they die; nor can their family.[71]

Of course, if Laura Ashworth had been a living, rather than a deceased donor, there would have been no question of her donated kidney being given to a stranger rather than to her mother. In 2009, the Department of Health announced that it would allow consideration of requests for 'preferential donation', but only where there are no others in urgent clinical need.

(5) Required Request

It has been suggested that some doctors find it difficult to ask distressed relatives about organ donation. If doctors do not mention the possibility of donation, potentially life-saving organs may be lost, and individuals who could have benefited from those organs may die. To try to eliminate this risk, most US states have introduced a system called 'required request'. Rather than leaving the question of whether or not to ask distressed relatives about donation to the discretion of individual doctors, medical practitioners are instead under a *duty* to bring up the question of organ donation.

The chief ethical problem with required request legislation is its interference with clinical discretion. If we can imagine circumstances in which asking the relatives to consent to organ donation might cause grave harm or distress, we should have to include a 'professional privilege' exception. And indeed, it seems clear that even where required request legislation exists, some relatives are still not asked about donation because the medical team judges that such a request would be inappropriate in the circumstances.

Of course, the counter-argument might be that where a balance has to be struck between causing distress to the relatives of a dying person, and saving the lives of patients waiting for organ transplants, avoiding death should *always* take priority over upsetting grieving relatives. Wherever the balance lies, it is not in fact clear that a shift towards required request would actually make much difference in practice. Studies appear to indicate that most potential organ donors *are* identified and that their relatives *are* asked about organ donation.[72] Certainly, UK Transplant has found that there are very few cases in which solid organ donation is possible, but not mentioned to relatives.[73]

(6) Presumed Consent or an 'Opt-Out' System

Organ donation in the UK is an 'opt-in' system, where individuals are able to volunteer to become organ donors, and if they have not done so, under the Human Tissue Act 2004, their

---

[71] HTA Press release, 12 April 2008.

[72] D Gentleman, J Easton, and B Jennett, 'Brain Death and Organ Donation in a Neurosurgical Unit: Audit of Recent Practice' (1990) 301 British Medical Journal 1203.

[73] Potential Donor Audit (UK Transplant, 2005), available at <www.uktransplant.org.uk/ukt/statistics/potential_ donor_audit/potential_donor_audit.jsp>.

nominated representative or a qualifying relative may give appropriate consent. Opt-in systems are commonly contrasted with 'opt-out' systems, sometimes also referred to as 'presumed consent', where it is assumed that every potential donor is willing to donate their organs, but people who object to donation are able to 'opt out' by formally registering their unwillingness to donate. Certainly, on the basis of the evidence, this assumption seems warranted: when asked, most people say that they would be willing to donate. There are those who argue that we should be cautious about accepting the results of these sorts of public opinion surveys, on the grounds that people may respond in a way that they believe will show them in a good light, even if, in practice, they would not want to donate their organs. Nevertheless, even if opinion polls may overstate the percentage of those who wish to donate organs after death, there seems to be no question that donation is supported by a majority of the population.

While not necessarily insurmountable, there are a number of practical and ethical issues that would have to be addressed before moving towards an 'opt-out' system.

First, the assumption behind an opt-out system is that the public is sufficiently well-informed about the organ transplantation system that any failure to register an objection in fact reflects someone's willingness to donate, rather than lethargy or ignorance. It has been predicted that fewer people would register an objection than actually have reservations about donation, and that less educated or more marginal population groups will be both less likely to consent to donation and less likely to understand how to opt out. It is, however, interesting to note that when a presumed consent system was introduced in Brazil in 1997, people from all socio-economic groups opted out in such huge numbers that the law had to be repealed the following year.[74]

Secondly, it has been argued that the term 'presumed consent' is misleading. As we saw in Chapters 4 and 5, consent in medical law is generally assumed to active and positive, rather than something which can be assumed from inaction. The reality, in an 'opt-out' system, is that organs could be taken *without* consent.[75] In practice, then, presumed consent may simply be a more sympathetic way to describe a system in which organs are, in the absence of a recorded objection, treated as a public resource (see below). Thirdly, it would be necessary to maintain a large, centralized database on which objections could be recorded, and amended if people changed their minds. It would further be necessary to ensure that this database could be rapidly and accurately accessed as soon as a potential donor is identified.

A number of countries have adopted presumed consent laws, but in most of these relatives continue to be consulted about organ transplantation. Taking organs in the face of a relative's vigorous objection would probably be counter-productive because of the adverse publicity it would generate. In France, for example, doctors always ask for familial consent to organ donation, and the pre sumed consent policy exists only on paper.[76] Nevertheless, as English and Somerville suggest in the following extract, changing the default position may subtly influence relatives' attitudes towards donation, and lessen the decision-making burden.

[74] Marie-Andrée Jacob, 'Another Look at the Presumed-versus-informed Consent Dichotomy in Postmortem Organ Procurement' (2006) 20 Bioethics 293–300.

[75] CA Erin and J Harris, 'Presumed Consent or Contracting Out' (1999) 25 Journal of Medial Ethics 365–6.

[76] Bernard Teo, 'Is the Adoption of More Efficient Strategies of Organ Procurement the Answer to Persistent Organ Shortage in Transplantation?' (1992) 6 Bioethics 113–29, 127.

V English and A Sommerville[77]

> Arguably, simply changing the default position could have huge benefits. Not least for rela-
> tives themselves who, at a time of emotional upheaval and bereavement, may not relish
> being asked to decide in the absence of any indication of the wishes of the deceased. One of
> the advantages of a presumed consent system is that the main burden of making this deci-
> sion is lessened for the relatives although they would still be involved...
>
> The possibility of relatives refusing donation when the deceased person actually wished
> to donate has already been mentioned. The opposite can also happen. Currently, individuals
> who strongly object to donation lack any formal mechanism for registering that objection and
> the decision to donate may ultimately be made by distant relatives. Under the opt in system,
> there are no guarantees that relatives will not act contrary to the strongly held views of a
> deceased person, either through lack of knowledge or lack of agreement with them. In this
> way, an opt out system where objections can be registered and must be respected, would
> enhance individual autonomy for those who do not want to be donors.

In contrast, the Organ Donation Taskforce was persuaded that, rather than lessening the
burden for families, an opt-out system might erode trust.

Organ Donation Taskforce[78]

> 8.2 The clinical Working group heard from a number of clinicians from intensive care
> (where the majority of deaths leading to donation occur) who were persuasive in articulating
> the view that a presumption of consent might make families feel that they were being pres-
> sured and erode the relationship of trust between clinician and family...
>
> 8.6 ...An opt out system has the potential to erode the trust between clinicians and fam-
> ilies at a distressing time. The concept of a gift freely given is an important one to both donor
> families and transplant recipients. The Taskforce feels that an opt out system of consent has
> the potential to undermine this concept.

The main reason for moving towards an opt-out system is the possibility of increasing the
supply of organs for transplantation. In the next extract, Kennedy *et al.* discuss the increase
in the number of kidneys available for transplant which followed the introduction of a presumed consent system in Belgium.[79]

I Kennedy, RA Sells, AS Daar, RD Guttmann, R Hoffenberg, M Lock, J Radcliffe-Richards, N Tilney, and the International Forum for Transplant Ethics[80]

> Staff at the organ-transplantation centre in Antwerp were strongly opposed to the new
> law and retained a contracting-in policy accompanied by enhanced public and professional

---

[77] 'Presumed Consent for Transplantation: A Dead Issue after Alder Hey?' (2003) 29 Journal of Medical
Ethics 147–52.

[78] The Potential Impact of an Opt Out System for Organ Donation in the UK: An Independent Report
from the Organ Donation Taskforce (DH: London, 2008), available at <www.dh.gov.uk>.

[79] See also Kenneth Gundle, 'Presumed Consent: An International Comparison and Possibilities for
Change in the United States' (2005) 14 Cambridge Quarterly of Healthcare Ethics, 113–18.

[80] 'The Case for "Presumed Consent" in Organ Donation' (1998) 351 The Lancet, 1650–2.

education; by contrast, at Leuven the new law was adopted. In Antwerp, organ donation rates remained unchanged; in Leuven they rose from 15 to 40 donors per year over a 3-year period. In the whole country organ donation rose by 55% within 5 years despite a concurrent decrease in the number of organs available from road-traffic accidents. Citizens who wish to opt out of the scheme may register their objection at any Town Hall; since 1986 less than 2% of the population have done so. Use of a computerised register has simplified ascertaining the existence of any objection. In Belgium, despite the existence of this law, doctors are encouraged to approach the relatives in all cases and practitioners may decide against removing the organs if in their opinion this would cause undue distress or for any other valid reason. Less than 10% of families do object compared with 20–30% elsewhere in Europe.... It would seem from the Belgian experience that relatives may be reluctant to take a personal decision about the removal of organs, but they find it easier to agree if they are simply confirming the intention of the dead person. If this is so, a contracting out system has a moral benefit of relieving grieving relatives of the burden of deciding about donation at a time of great psychological stress. A change in the law thus achieves the dual effect of increasing the supply of organs and lessening the distress of relatives.

Interestingly, the Taskforce was not persuaded that an opt-out system would increase donations, and thought it possible that numbers might instead *decrease*:

Organ Donation Taskforce[81]

11.4 It is worth noting that presumed consent legislation was passed in Spain in 1979 but it was only a decade later, in 1989, when their national transplant organisation was founded, putting a new infrastructure in place, that donor rates began to rise.

11.5 ...The Taskforce is not confident that the introduction of opt out legislation would increase organ donor numbers, and there is evidence that donor numbers may go down.

The BMA has been one of the most consistent supporters of legislative change towards an opt-out system, and advocates 'soft' presumed consent. This would allow organs to be removed after the individual's death if consent can be presumed because there is no evidence from the non-donor register, or volunteered by the family, that the individual objected to his or her body, or any specific part of the body, being used for transplantation after death. If, however, the individual has not expressed any views about donation while alive but it is apparent that to proceed with the donation would cause major distress to a first-degree relative or long-term partner, the donation should not proceed.

Close relatives would thus retain a right of veto, but the difference would be in the nature of the approach to the relatives. Family members would not be asked to give permission for organ donation. Rather, they would be told that the individual had not registered an objection to donation while alive and that unless they object—either because they are aware of an unregistered objection by the individual or because it would cause a close relative or long-term partner major distress—the donation will proceed.

[81] The Potential Impact of an Opt Out System for Organ Donation in the UK: An Independent Report from the Organ Donation Taskforce (DH: London, 2008) Available at <www.dh.gov.uk>.

British Medical Association[82]

The BMA's reasons for supporting presumed consent are set out below.

- It is reasonable and appropriate to assume that most people would wish to act in an altruistic manner and to help others by donating their organs after death.
- Studies show that the majority of people would be willing to donate but only a small number of these are on the NHS Organ Donor Register or carry a donor card. While this level of apathy exists, people will continue to die while waiting for donor organs.
- Given that the majority of people would be willing to donate, there are good reasons for presuming consent and requiring those who object to donation to register their views.
- A shift to presumed consent would prompt more discussion within families about organ donation.
- It is more efficient and cost-effective to maintain a register of the small number who wish to opt out of donation than of the majority who are willing to be donors.
- With such a shift, organ donation becomes the default position. This represents a more positive view of organ donation which is to be encouraged.
- Despite the acknowledged difficulties of obtaining meaningful data about the success of presumed consent in other countries, the BMA believes that, as one part of a broader strategy, a shift to presumed consent is likely to have a positive effect on donation rates.

Most countries which have introduced opt-out systems have 'soft' versions like this, in which the relatives' wishes continue to be relevant. It would be possible to have a 'hard' version, where the failure to register an opt-out would be decisive, and the organs taken even if relatives object. This happens in Austria, where donation rates rose from 4.6 donors per million population to 27.2 within five years,[83] and the total number of kidney donations each year now almost equals the number of people on the waiting list.[84]

(7) Mandated Choice

Would it instead be possible to require every individual to decide whether or not they want their organs to be available for transplantation after their death? Mandated choice would allow people to opt in or opt out; what it would not allow them to do is not to make a decision. This could then avoid the problems faced by both opt-in and opt-out, namely that they may both allow organs to be either taken, or not taken, against the wishes of the donor. In an opt-out system, organs might be taken from people who do not wish to donate but have not got around to opting out, and the reverse problem exists with opt-in systems: as we have seen, more people wish to donate than have registered on the organ donor register.

Mandated choice would be analogous to other non-optional public duties, such as filling in the electoral register or paying taxes. Like a presumed consent system, it would require

---

[82] Organ Donation in the 21st Century: Time for a Consolidated Approach (BMA: London, 2007), available at <www.bma.org.uk>.

[83] Organ Donation Taskforce Annex E.

[84] Kenneth Gundle, 'Presumed Consent: An International Comparison and Possibilities for Change in the United States' (2005) 14 Cambridge Quarterly of Healthcare Ethics 113–18.

the maintenance and updating of an easily accessible database. As P Chouhan and H Draper explain in the next extract, it would also require extensive public education.

P Chouhan and H Draper[85]

Mandated choice requires competent adults to decide whether they wish to donate their organs after their deaths. Individuals are free to choose whether to donate, and even which organs they would like to donate: what they are not permitted to do is to fail to register their wishes. Individuals can also choose to let their relatives have the final say. Unless they are granted this right, however, the relatives have neither power nor opportunity to veto an individual's decision, whether it was for or against decision...

A move to mandated choice would also have to be accompanied by extensive public education so that when making their choices, people are sufficiently informed about both the need for choice and the implications of their decision. Finally, choices, though binding would also be revocable: indeed, people could change their minds as often as they wish, and the most recent choice would prevail....To avoid coercion, registered choices would be confidential and no privileges would accrue from the particular choice made.

A number of other practical difficulties would have to be resolved. For example, what penalty would there be for failing to make a decision? There would also be questions about what to do in the case of children or adults who lack the capacity to make a choice. While acknowledging that it was a popular option among their focus groups, the Organ Donation Taskforce decided against mandated choice, citing enforcement difficulties.

Organ Donation Taskforce[86]

6.7 In general in the UK, we do not require people to make choices. for example, we do not make voting mandatory as it is in Australia. We encourage UK citizens to make choices but also allow them the right not to make choices. A system of mandated choice on organ donation would be a significant departure from established UK norms.

6.8 It is debatable whether such a system would be effective in practice, since it would be difficult to force people to make a decision if they do not want to. The Taskforce was uncomfortable with the idea of a legal sanction if people did not make a choice. If sanctions were imposed, enforcement would raise difficult issues, especially for clinical staff. Moreover, the Taskforce was concerned that if people were forced to choose, this might cause resentment and have a negative impact on organ donation rates.

While it certainly did not go as far as mandating choice, it is interesting to note that when the government produced the first NHS Constitution in 2009, setting out patients' rights and responsibilities within the NHS, the need to discuss wishes about organ donation with others is listed as one of the responsibilities patients should take on in return for the rights

---

[85] 'Modified Mandated Choice for Organ Procurement' (2003) 29 Journal of Medical Ethics 157–62, 158.
[86] The potential Impact of an Opt Out System for Organ Donation in the UK: An Independent Report from the Organ Donation Taskforce (DH: London, 2008), available at <www.dh.gov.uk>.

they have to NHS care. The Constitution states: 'You should ensure that those closest to you are aware of your wishes about organ donation.'[87]

(8) Incentives

(a) Financial incentives

Financial incentives to cadaveric donation could not operate as a straightforward sale, in the same way as payments to living donors (considered below). When the organs are retrieved, the donor is dead and is therefore unable to receive money in return for their donation. Instead, there are a number of other possibilities.

First, people could receive a payment in return for their *agreement* to donate their organs after death. However, since very few of us are ever likely to be suitable organ donors, money would generally be paid to non-donors. Moreover, in order to protect patient autonomy it would have to be possible for people to change their minds about donation after they had been paid, which would obviously leave the system open to abuse. A second possibility is that the payment could be made to a nominated individual after donation has taken place. Thirdly, money could be offered directly to the relatives in return for their agreement to the donation. An example might be an offer of financial assistance with funeral expenses.

It is, however, unclear whether financial incentives would persuade potential donors or the families of people who have just died to agree to organ donation. Gill Haddow carried out empirical research and found that the reaction to financial incentives among potential donors was 'tepid', but for donor families, it was overwhelmingly negative.

G Haddow[88]

Offering a payment of £20 to register proved to be the least popular of all options. Approximately 40% of respondents reacted positively to the grants after death of a £2000 payment per organ to the family, to a favourite charity, or toward funeral costs. (We found certain groups to be more favourable toward incentives, especially the 16–24 age cohort and men.)...Importantly, there is a prominent level of 'would make no difference' response to all options—even the favoured 'cash to relatives' option. Therefore, the overall reaction to any of the financial options was decidedly tepid.

[Among donor families] the reaction to the general issue of financial incentives was unambiguous: sixteen of seventeen donor relatives asked were opposed. Others suggested that the introduction of financial incentives would produce the effect of non-donation...The response to financial incentives was it was 'immoral'.

Of course, any financial incentives to organ donation will come up against the arguments against commodification of the human body, which we consider in more detail below in relation to living donors. In the next extract, AL Caplan explains why he finds the offer of cash for body parts offensive.

---

[87] (2009), available at <www.dh.gov.uk>.

[88] '"Because You're Worth It?" The Taking and Selling of Transplantable Organs' (2006) 32 Journal of Medical Ethics 324–8.

AL Caplan[89]

There is no empirical evidence that families raise the issue of money or compensation at the time when they are faced with requests or decisions about making organs and tissues available for transplantation. What factual evidence there is lends support to the opposite conclusion—that significant numbers of Americans would be angered, offended and insulted by offers of money or financial rewards for the organs and tissues of their deceased loved ones....

If the only way US society, or any other, can find to pay for the uncompensated costs of medical care or funerals for the indigent is to offer cash for their body parts, such a society has no right to call itself humane, decent, or fair...Calls for markets, compensation, bounties, or rewards should be rejected because they convert human beings into products, a metaphysical transformation that cheapens the respect for life and corrodes our ability to maintain the stance that human beings are special, unique, and valuable for their own sake, not for what others can mine, extract, or manufacture from them. Nor will markets do what their proponents hope. The inevitable opposition such proposals will encounter from many religious leaders means any increase in lives saved attributable to cash prizes will be swamped by the number of lives lost when those who refuse to see the human body as available for sale decline to participate in anything having to do with transplants.

(b) Non-financial incentives

A different sort of incentive would be to give those who have indicated their willingness to donate priority if they ever need an organ themselves. If signing up to the organ donor register might have future health benefits for the potential donor, then 'opting-in' rates might be expected to increase, or, in an opt-out system, people might be less likely to opt out if this might adversely affect their chance of receiving an organ. Insofar as apathy rather than disapproval of transplantation is the principal reason why people do not take steps to register their agreement to donation, and given that the steps necessary to indicate one's willingness to donate are clearly not arduous, Rupert Jarvis argues that an appeal to the reciprocity of organ donation might be a cheap and effective way to increase donation rates.

Rupert Jarvis[90]

I suggest that legislation governing organ donation be amended such that all and only those who identify themselves as potential donors (perhaps by a card similar to the one currently in use, or by registration on a central computer) are eligible themselves to receive transplant organs...

This contract...trades a—if not *the*—central interest in remaining alive, against one's *post mortem* interest in not having one's organs removed. This latter is at best *de minimis*: my interests in my organs after death can hardly be said to be enormous. We are presented, then, with what appears to be a thoroughly attractive option: by sacrificing our minimal *post*

---

[89] *Am I my Brother's Keeper? The Ethical Frontiers of Biomedicine* (Indiana UP: Bloomington and Indianapolis, 1997) 96–8, 100.

[90] 'Join the Club: A Modest Proposal to Increase Availability of Donor Organs' (1995) 21 Journal of Medical Ethics 199–204.

mortem interests we guarantee our inclusion on the waiting list for the donor organ which might save or vastly improve the quality of our own life . . . .

It hardly seems fanciful to suggest that the vast majority of people would elect to join the scheme, since it is so clearly in their interests to do so, with the potential gain (life) being infinite and the potential loss (*post mortem* dissection which, depending on the manner of their death, they might well have to undergo anyway) being zero.

It is also worth noting that we are more likely to need an organ than we are to die in circumstances in which our organs would be suitable for transplantation, so most people who sign up to Jarvis's scheme will not, in fact, ever become organ donors, but they would benefit from knowing that they would be able to receive an organ if they suffer organ failure in the future.

Of course, as Ranaan Gillon explains, it would almost certainly be unethical and impracticable to make willingness to donate the *only* relevant factor when allocating organs to potential transplant recipients. Rather, a points system for allocation, like that used by UK Transplant, which takes into account a range of factors such as immediacy of clinical need and time spent on the waiting list, could be weighted such that willing donors received a slightly higher ranking than similar candidates who would not be prepared to have their own organs used for transplantation.

Ranaan Gillon[91]

Here seems to be the Achilles heel of Mr Jarvis's proposal. For even if such non-volunteers can properly be said to have only themselves to blame for their predicament; even if they can properly be said to have deliberately and autonomously made their choice and rejected the opportunity to give themselves priority for receipt of transplanted organs; even if they can properly be said to have been selfish, and/or inconsiderate and/or foolish, even immoral, in refusing to pre-volunteer their own organs, nonetheless there is an important countervailing moral tradition in medicine. It is that patients should be given treatment in relation to their medical need, and that scarce medical resources should not be prioritised on the basis of a patient's blameworthiness . . .

If the fault and/or inconsiderateness of not previously volunteering his or her organs for transplantation were to justify withholding scarce life-saving resources from a patient, then all other prior faults and inconsiderateness of equal or greater weight could, logically, also be regarded as morally relevant and potentially justificatory for withholding scarce life-saving medical resources from patients. Such a prospect hardly bears contemplation.

It should, however, be remembered that people are notoriously reluctant to contemplate the prospect of their own death. For many of us, the prospect of suffering acute organ failure seems both remote and difficult to contemplate, and hence concerns about future eligibility for transplantation may not seem sufficiently pressing to prompt people to take steps to register their willingness to donate.

Instead, a more effective way to penalize 'free-riders' would be to incorporate priority for willing donors as part of a presumed consent system. As Stephanie Eaton argues below,

[91] 'On Giving Preference to Prior Volunteers When Allocating Organs for Transplantation' (1995) 21 Journal of Medical Ethics 195–6, 196.

the presumption would be (a) that the deceased person had consented to donation; and (b) that she was not a free-rider. It would be for those who did not want their organs to be used after their death to register their objection, and they would be warned that 'opting out' might reduce their likelihood of being allocated an organ if they ever needed one.

Stephanie Eaton[92]

If it is agreed that most people would consent to benefiting from transplant technology and that free-riding is a morally precarious position to hold, it is possible to arouse people's awareness to the moral consequences of the stance which they are taking when they choose to opt-out. Where people still choose to opt-out knowing that this constitutes free-riding, they should be made aware that they may be disadvantaged in the future if they should ever become potential recipients of organs...

Publicity that promotes the idea that an opted-out person may be less likely to receive a transplant if he or she ever needs one, forces opters-out to reconsider their own moral standards. It is hoped that the unease that will be felt when opting-out is acknowledged as being a form of free-riding will have the consequence that few people will choose to opt out.

(9) A Duty to Donate? Organs as a Public Resource?

If it were possible to take organs from any dead body without the need for consent, many lives could be saved. In the next extract, HE Emson argues that, once dead, a person's organs should be treated as a public resource, to be distributed to those in need of them.

HE Emson[93]

In my opinion any concept of property in the human body either during life or after death is biologically inaccurate and morally wrong. The body should be regarded morally as on loan to the individual from the biomass, to which the cadaver will inevitably return...

I am deeply concerned with the right of the person to govern disposal of their body after death, when separation of body and soul is irrevocably complete and the individual is incapable of reconstitution. The person no longer exists, the soul has departed, and the individual who was but is no longer has no further use for the body which has been part of him or her during life. The concept of the right of a person to determine before death, the disposal of their body after death, made sense only when there was no continuing use for that body. It makes neither practical nor moral sense now, when the body for which the dead person no longer has any use, is quite literally a vital resource, a potential source of life for others...

If this argument is correct, then it is even more morally unacceptable for the relatives of the deceased to deny utilisation of the cadaver as a source of transplantable organs. Their only claim upon it is as a temporary memorial of a loved one, inevitably destined to decay or be burned in a very short time. To me, any such claim cannot morally be sustained in the face of what I regard as the overwhelming and pre-emptive need of the potential recipient...

In my opinion, the human cadaver, at the point at which life departs, should become a resource for those who may benefit from donation of its organs.

---

[92] 'The Subtle Politics of Organ Donation: A Proposal' (1998) 24 Journal of Medical Ethics 166–70, 168.
[93] 'It is Immoral to Require Consent for Cadaver Organ Donation' (2003) 29 Journal of Medical Ethics 125–7.

Alternatively, it could be argued that we are under a *duty* to donate our organs after death, equivalent to the duty of easy rescue, explained by JL Nelson in the next extract.

JL Nelson[94]

[T]here is a strong presumption that refusing to save another person's life when doing so is virtually costless to the person in a position to act, is seriously wrong....

I think that people typically have duties to provide organs to others, should the opportunity arise, and indeed, duties to reconsider and possibly refigure their attitudes about themselves and others insofar as those attitudes threaten their inclinations to be organ providers. Or, to put it a bit more carefully, since it seems a bit strained to think of dead people having duties, I think that removing organs from the dead typically neither harms nor wrongs them, and that therefore we the living have a prima facie duty to support the retrieval of useful organs, both from our own dead bodies, and from those of others. If we find ourselves repulsed or otherwise distressed by this prospect, we have a derivative duty: to seek to revamp our attitudes.

John Harris further points out that since the human body never remains intact for very long after death, objections to organ donation are intrinsically irrational, and, in any event, must be of less importance than the interest of potential recipients who might die without replacement organs.

John Harris[95]

All the moral concern of our society has so far been focused on the dead and their friends and relatives. But there are two separate sets of individuals who have moral claims upon us, not just one. There is the deceased individual and her friends and relatives on the one hand, and the potential organ or tissue recipient and her friends and relatives on the other. Both have claims upon us, the claims of neither have obvious priority. If we weigh the damage to the interests of the deceased and her friends, and relatives if their wishes are overriden against the damage done to would be recipients and their friends and relatives if they fail to get the organs they need to keep them alive, where should the balance of our moral concern lie?...

My point is that it is surely implausible to think that having one's body remain whole after their death is an objective anyone is entitled to pursue at the cost of other people's lives! It is implausible to the point of wickedness, not least because the objective is irrational and impossible of achievement...No dead body remains intact; the worms...or the fire and eventually dust claim it...The alternatives are not burial intact or disintegration. There is no alternative which does not involve disintegration.

Given the irrationality of the aim, it is difficult to defend a right to pursue such an aim when it is clear that doing so costs lives.

In the next extract, Sheelagh McGuinness and Margaret Brazier are critical of Harris's brisk dismissal of the views of those who find organ donation difficult.

[94] *Hippocrates' Maze: Ethical Explorations of the Medical Labyrinth* (Rowman & Littlefield: NY, 2003) 119.
[95] 'Organ Procurement: Dead Interests, Living Needs' (2003) 29 Journal of Medical Ethics 130–4, 130, 133.

Sheelagh McGuinness and Margaret Brazier[96]

Death is not akin to a switch that once 'off' means that the dead person ceases to matter at all. Death is described by some as, and can traditionally be seen to be, a socially constructed event. Death rituals have formed an important part of the grieving process. Throughout history there has been an expectation that in death the body will be respected as a symbol of the living person. Death of someone close to you is difficult to accept. We struggle to adjust to an understanding that the person is gone. Identifying with the dead is so hard that we think of the dead body as a symbol of the pre-mortem person.

The dead infant, the wife succumbing to breast cancer at 35, the elderly father dying suddenly of a heart attack, do not change their nature for their mother, husband or daughter. They remain Susannah, Lucy and Dad. They are not simply things.

Walter Glannon goes further and contends that our interest in what is done to our bodies after our death outweighs the interests of those in need of organs.

W Glannon[97]

Because the body is so closely associated with who we are, we can have an interest in what is done to it even after we cease to exist. The fact that my body is mine and is essential to my life plan means that I have a deep interest in what is done to it. If it is treated in a way that does not accord with my wishes or interests, then in an important respect this can be bad for me and I can be harmed. The special relation between humans and their bodies can make it wrong for others to ignore the expressed wish that one's organs not be harvested at death, despite their viability for transplantation...

Given the special relation between humans and their bodies, the moral importance of individual autonomy in having a life plan, and that what happens to one's body after death is part of such a plan, the negative right to bodily integrity after death outweighs any presumed positive right of the sick to receive organs from those who did not consent to cadaver donation.

It is, however, worth noting that we do not allow relatives to object to forensic post-mortems. This is certainly not because they are less invasive than transplantation. Rather, the public interest in the detection of serious crime trumps any concern about the family's feelings about what happens during a post-mortem investigation. It is perhaps interesting that the death of identifiable people on the transplant waiting list is not regarded as of comparable public importance.

3 LIVE DONORS

(a) THE ETHICAL ACCEPTABILITY OF LIVING ORGAN DONATION

As a response to the continuing shortage of cadaveric organs, there has been increasing interest in obtaining certain non-vital organs from living donors. The health risks to living

---

[96] 'Respecting the Living Means Respecting the Dead Too' (2008) 28 Oxford Journal of Legal Studies 297–316.

[97] 'Do the Sick Have a Right to Cadaveric Organs?' (2003) 29 Journal of Medical Ethics 153–6, 154.

donors are, in the case of kidney donation, comparatively small. It has been estimated that the increased risk of mortality from living with only one kidney is 0.03 per cent, which is 'equivalent to driving back and forth to work 16 miles a day'.[98] The risk of morbidity (ill health) is greater, with 2 per cent of kidney donors experiencing major morbidity, and 10–20 per cent experiencing minor morbidity. Risks from living liver donation are higher, with mortality rates of 0.5–0.1 per cent, and morbidity rates of 40–60 per cent.[99]

Success rates in living organ donation are higher than when cadaveric organs are used. In part, this may be because the organ is taken from a healthy, living person, rather than from someone who has died. Perhaps more importantly, the timing of the transplant can be controlled. When a cadaveric organ becomes available, the operation has to take place as soon as possible after the donor's (usually sudden) death. From the recipient's point of view, this may be less than ideal: she will have virtually no opportunity to prepare for the operation, and it may have to take place when she is unwell. When an organ is taken from a living donor, however, the transplant team can ensure the operation is carried out when the recipient is in the best possible health.

Despite the obvious advantages in increasing the pool of potential organ donors to include living persons, the practice remains controversial. Unlike cadaveric donation, living organ donation does pose real, albeit small, health risks to the donor. One study found that 15 per cent of live donors believed that donation had had a negative impact upon their health.[100] Another study found that approximately 4 per cent of live donors regretted their decision to donate.[101] Of course, this means that the vast majority of donors did not regret their decision, and that most did not believe that there had been any negative impact upon their health. Most studies appear to show that donors more commonly experience increased self-esteem and feelings of wellbeing.[102] Watching someone one loves suffer is itself a miserable experience, and being able to alleviate their suffering, or save their life, is likely to have substantial non-clinical benefits for the donor herself.

Interestingly, there appears to be a gender imbalance both among living organ donors, who are more likely to be female, and among recipients, the majority of whom are male.[103] A German study found that mothers were the most frequent donors (27 per cent), followed by wives (19 per cent), fathers (13 per cent), sisters (12 per cent), and husbands (11 per cent).[104] It is not clear why this difference exists, although possible explanations have included men's greater capacity to resist family pressure, and their higher wage-earning capacity, which may mean that sparing time for donation and recuperation is perceived to be easier for female family members.

---

[98] James F Blumstein, 'The Use of Financial Incentives in Medical Care: The Case of Commerce in Transplantable Organs' in A Grubb and MJ Mehlman (eds), *Justice and Health Care: Comparative Perspectives* (John Wiley & Sons: Chichester, 1995) 9–39, 34.

[99] James Neuberger and David Price, 'Role of Living Liver Donation in the United Kingdom' (2003) 327 British Medical Journal 676–9.

[100] LR Schover, SB Streem, N Boparai, K Duriak, and AC Novick, 'The Psychosocial Impact of Donating a Kidney: Long Term Follow-up from a Urology Based Center' (1997) 157 Journal of Urology 1596–601. See also the study by M Walter *et al.*, 'Quality of Life of Living Donors Before and After Living Donor Liver Transplantation' (2003) 35 Transplantation Proceedings 2961–3, which indicated that 10 per cent of living liver donors were having difficulty coping with psychological symptoms.

[101] EM Johnson, MJ Remucal, and AJ Matas, 'Living Kidney Donation: Donor Risks and Quality of Life' (1997) Clinical Transplantation 231–40.

[102] RG Simmons, SD Klein, and RL Simmons, *Gift of Life: the Social and Psychological Impact of Organ Transplantation* (Wiley: New York, 1977).

[103] N Biller-Andorno, 'Gender Imbalance in Living Organ Donation' (2002) 5 Medicine, Health Care and Philosophy 199–204, 201.

[104] Ibid.

While the altruistic act of the *donor* might be laudable, in the next extract Carl Elliott argues that both *recipients* of live organs and *doctors* who perform living organ retrieval are encouraging the donor's self-sacrifice, and that this is more problematic.

Carl Elliott[105]

[W]hile it is admirable to risk harm to oneself, it is not admirable to encourage another person to risk harm to himself for one's own benefit...

Accepting a sacrifice of great magnitude is not mere passive acquiescence, devoid of any moral import. If I allow someone else to risk his life or health for my sake, I am endorsing his self-sacrifice and agreeing to profit by it...If an ailing patient were to take advantage of a healthy donor's self-sacrifice, it might well be understandable, but it would not be morally admirable. It would not be the sort of behaviour that we would aspire to and want to encourage.

Finally, it is important to realize that the doctor is not a mere instrument of the patient's wishes. Analyses of living organ donation...are often simplified needlessly by a failure to acknowledge outright that the doctor is also a moral agent who should be held accountable for his actions....This shifts the moral balance of the problem in an important way, because while we admire the person who *undergoes* harm to himself for the sake of another, we do not necessarily admire the person who *inflicts* harm on one person for the sake of another. And the latter is what the doctor must do.

It has been argued that concern about the possibility of harm to living donors should lead us to be reluctant to encourage living donation until we have *exhausted* all possible means of increasing the number of cadaveric organs available for transplant. In addition to avoiding unnecessary health risks to living donors, there may also be concerns, as Arthur Caplan explains, about the genuineness of a live donor's consent to donation.

Arthur L Caplan[106]

In order to provide valid consent a person must have all relevant information and the opportunity to reflect upon and ask questions about the information from those who will provide objective answers. Transplant centers and other transplant personnel may face problems in providing 'objective' information to prospective donors because those involved in seeking donors have an inherent conflict of interest. They cannot both advocate for the best interests of patients who need transplants and simultaneously protect the best interests of prospective donors....

Finally, many critics of live donation worry that the environment in which live donation takes place makes it impossible for anyone to give free and voluntary consent. Family members will ordinarily feel extraordinary pressures to 'volunteer'. The realization that one could be blamed for the failure to help a spouse, a sibling, or a child may be so frightening that potential donors see themselves as having no choice.

---

[105] 'Doing Harm: Living Organ Donors, Clinical Research and The Tenth Man' (1995) 21 Journal of Medical Ethics 91–6, 93.
[106] 'Am I My Brother's Keeper ?' (1993) 27 Suffolk University Law Review 1195.

While it is almost certainly preferable to use cadaveric organs, as we have seen, demand massively outstrips supply, and will probably continue to do so. Two conclusions follow from this. First, we should probably bear in mind that there are good reasons for looking closely at mechanisms, such as an opt-out system, which might increase the pool of potential cadaveric donors. By reducing the need to resort to living organ donation, increased rates of cadaveric donation would have health benefits not only for the recipients of the organs, *but also for potential live donors*, whose services would no longer be needed.

Secondly, if it is almost certainly inevitable that we will continue to have to pursue alternatives to cadaveric donation, we will need to think about the circumstances in which live organ donation should be permitted.

(b) TYPE OF TRANSPLANT

Obviously, it is only possible for living organ donors to donate non-vital organs, such as kidneys, lobes of the lung, or liver segments. Most living organ donation involves kidneys (in 2007/8, there were 829 living donor kidney transplants; 24 living donor liver transplants, and there was one living lung transplant).[107] A difficult ethical question about the limits of autonomous decision-making arose in the US in 1998 when a man sought to donate his *second* kidney to his daughter after the first transplant had failed.[108] The operation would not have killed Mr Patterson, but it would have left him dependent upon dialysis for the rest of his life, unless, of course, he himself was able to obtain a kidney transplant. Unlike ordinary living kidney transplants, the donor in this situation faces a dramatic and substantial deterioration in his own health. It might therefore be argued that carrying out this operation conflicts with the doctor's duty to do no harm, and it is very unlikely that a doctor would be prepared to carry out this sort of operation purely in order to benefit a third party.

(c) LIVE TRANSPLANTATION IN THE UK

In the UK, there has been a steady increase in the use of living donors, particularly for kidney transplants: now approximately 36 per cent of all kidney transplants involve living donors. The Human Tissue Act covers consent to the *use* and *storage* of tissue taken from the living, but its *removal* continues to be dealt with at common law and under the Mental Capacity Act 2005.

(1) Consent to the Removal of Tissue

The criminal law places limits upon the extent to which an adult can consent to the infliction of harm. Although the increased risk of morbidity from living with only one kidney is low, nephrectomy (kidney removal) is a serious operation done under general anaesthetic, and as a result, carries with it a small risk of death or irreversible harm. It would undoubtedly qualify as grievous bodily harm, for which consent is no defence.

As we saw in Chapter 5, the courts have held that 'proper medical treatment' stands outside the normal criminal law, and, living organ donation has been assumed to come within

---

[107] <www.uktransplant.org.uk/ukt/statistics/transplant_activity_report/current_activity_reports. jsp/ ukt/tx_activity_report_2004_uk_pp6–10.pdf>.

[108] Ryan Sauder and Lisa S Parker, 'Autonomy's Limits: Living Donation and Health-Related Harm' (2001) 10 Cambridge Quarterly of Healthcare Ethics 399–401.

this category. According to the Law Commission: 'there is no doubt that once a valid consent has been forthcoming, English law now treats as lawful donation of regenerative tissue, and also non-regenerative tissue that is not essential to life'.[109]

Because the living organ donor is undergoing non-therapeutic surgery, it is especially important that their consent is fully informed and voluntary. This will sometimes be difficult. In the next extract, Ryan Sauder and Lisa Parker point out that many living donors feel that they have no choice but to offer to donate an organ to a desperately sick relative.

Ryan Sauder and Lisa S Parker[110]

Frequently, a prospective donor, particularly a parent or sibling of the prospective recipient, will experience the decision to donate as automatic. They frequently report feeling that they had no choice but to donate, and proceed to offer their organs willingly and without hesitation, sometimes even before hearing of the risks involved in such a donation. Disclosure of risks frequently has no effect on the decision to donate. These decisions hardly seem to meet the traditional requirements of informed consent. Failing to take risks of an intervention into account when deciding whether to consent to it, and feeling compelled to consent, are typically hallmarks of a failure of the informed-consent process. Yet we are reluctant to suggest that these prospective donors are not making autonomous decisions to donate and, consequently, that their decisions (and organs) should not be accepted.

In practice, clinicians recognize the existence of these sorts of pressures and will commonly provide a 'contrived medical excuse' for potential donors, if they not want to donate, but are fearful of their families' reaction.[111]

In addition to full disclosure of the risks to their own health, potential living organ donors should also be given frank information about the possibility that the transplant might not work, and the emotional impact of an unsuccessful donation. If the recipient's need for a transplant results from a genetic condition, more than one family member may require the same transplant, and donors should therefore be advised that they may be able to act as a donor only once.

Given the emphasis on informed consent, could organs ever be taken from those who lack the capacity to consent?

(a) Children

In the case of children, although parents normally consent to their minor children's medical treatment, sibling-to-sibling organ donation would present parents with a particularly difficult conflict of interest. How could they separate their responsibility for the interests of the potential donor from their equally compelling concern for the interests of the potential recipient, and for their own interests? As with other especially controversial procedures, court approval should be sought. While bone marrow donation between child

---

[109] Law Commission Consultation Paper No 139, *Consent in the Criminal Law* (HMSO: London, 1995) para 8.32.

[110] 'Autonomy's Limits: Living Donation and Health-Related Harm' (2001) 10 Cambridge Quarterly of Healthcare Ethics 399–401, 403.

[111] M Simmerling *et al.*, 'When Duties Collide: Beneficence and Veracity in the Evaluation of Living Organ Donors' (2007) 12 Current Opinions in Organ Transplantation 188–92.

siblings could be said to be in the donor's best interests, given that it is a relatively minor and risk-free procedure, with the potential to save a loved older sibling's life, whether a court would ever be prepared to authorize the removal of a non-regenerative organ, such as a kidney, is another matter.

There were some *obiter* comments about organ donation in *Re W (A Minor)*.[112] The Court of Appeal suggested that the Family Law Reform Act 1969, which gives minors of 16 and 17 years of age the right to consent to medical treatment, would not apply to organ donation because, 'so far as the donor is concerned, these do not constitute either treatment or diagnosis'.[113] Instead, until the age of 18, 'the jurisdiction of the court should always be invoked'.[114] Until such a case arises, it is not clear whether the courts would ever be prepared to authorize such an operation.

There have been instances of child organ donation in the US. In *Hart v Brown*,[115] for example, the court was satisfied that the psychological benefit to the donor from her identical twin sister's survival and continued companionship, justified the risks of donation.

(b) Adults who lack capacity

Under the Mental Capacity Act 2005, the position of adults who lack capacity is similar. The Mental Capacity Act Code of Practice makes it clear that court approval would be required for organ donation.

Mental Capacity Act Code of Practice para 6.16[116]

6.16 The Court of Protection must be asked to make decisions relating to . . .

- cases where it is proposed that a person who lacks capacity to consent should donate an organ or bone marrow to another person.

The court would then have to decide whether organ donation was in the incompetent adult's best interests, being guided by the checklist of factors in section 4 which, as we saw in Chapter 5, place particular emphasis upon the values and previously expressed wishes of the incompetent person.

In *Re Y (Mental Patient: Bone Marrow Donation)*—a pre-MCA case—bone marrow donation was authorized, on the grounds that this would also be in the donor's social or emotional interests. However, Connell J doubted whether similar reasoning could justify organ donation.

It is doubtful that this case would act as a useful precedent in cases where the surgery involved is more intrusive than in this case, where the evidence shows that the bone marrow harvested is speedily regenerated and that a healthy individual can donate as much as two pints with no long term consequences at all.[117]

As yet, no cases have arisen and so, as with children, it is unclear whether there could ever be circumstances in which a court would be satisfied that solid organ donation was in the best interests of an incompetent adult. Again, this has happened in the US. In *Strunk v Strunk*,[118]

---

[112] [1993] Fam 64.   [113] Per Lord Donaldson.   [114] Per Nolan LJ.
[115] (1972) 289 A 2d 386 (Conn Sup Ct).   [116] Para 6.16, available at <www.dca.gov.uk>.
[117] [1997] Fam 110.   [118] (1969) 445 SW 2d 145.

the court approved kidney donation from an incompetent adult on the grounds that his brother's death would have caused him psychological and emotional injury greater than any risk associated with the removal of one of his kidneys.

(2) The Human Tissue Act 2004

Under section 33(1) and (2), taking an organ from a living person for the purposes of transplantation (regardless of whether they are related to each other or not) is an offence, unless the requirements in sections 33(3) and 33(5) are satisfied. These are, under section 33(3), that no payment for reward has been given in contravention of section 32 (see below), and that such other conditions and requirements as may be specified in regulations are satisfied (see below). Section 33(5) offers a defence if the person who takes an organ reasonably believes that the transplant satisfies the section 33(3) requirements.

(a) Consent

Under section 1 of the Act, there must be 'appropriate consent' to the use of human tissue for transplantation. For competent adults, under section 3(2) 'appropriate consent' means 'his consent'. The HTA Code of Practice contains detailed guidance on the information which should be provided as part of the consent process:

HTA Code of Practice para 62[119]

62 Potential donors should be provided with sufficient information for them to reach an informed decision and give their consent. They should be advised about:

- the surgical procedures and medical treatments to which a donor may be subjected and the risks involved in both the short and long term;
- the potential advantages for the recipient and the fact that a positive outcome for the recipient cannot be guaranteed; and that if there is an adverse outcome, it is not their fault;
- the risks involved with the procedures, the chances of success and any possible side-effects;
- the tests for transmissible microbiological diseases, such as HIV, hepatitis B and C;
- Human T-cell Lymphotropic Virus (HTLV) and other such diseases and the implications of any positive tests;
- the requirement for anonymity in nondirected and paired/pooled donations;
- the process of tissue typing for transplants that can sometimes reveal an unrecognised discrepancy between the biological and legal/recognised parents;
- the counselling services that are available;
- the right to withdraw consent at any time;
- the consequences of the withdrawal of consent, especially if it is withdrawn late in the process;

---

[119] Code of Practice 2 (Donation of Solid Organs for Tranplantation), available at <www.hta.gov.uk>.

- their right to be free of any kind of coercion or threat against them or anyone else (for example, family or friends) and that consent deemed to be given under any such pressure will not be validated by the Independent Assessor;
- the fact that it is an offence to seek or receive payment or any other benefit for providing controlled material for transplantation and will attract a penalty;
- the need to check with their insurance companies that their existing policies remain valid; or that they might wish to make arrangements for life insurance if they have not already done so.

As with the common law on organ retrieval, the Act does not rule out the possibility of using organs taken from adults who lack capacity, but any such transplants would have to be approved by a panel of at least three members of the HTA and comply with regulations,[120] which effectively duplicate the assessment that the court would carry out in deciding whether retrieval would be lawful, namely that the donation must be in the incompetent child or adult's best interests.

Section 3(2) of the Regulations provide that:

An adult ('P') who lacks capacity to consent…is deemed to have consented to the activity where—

(a) the activity is done for a purpose specified in paragraph 4 or 7 [7 is transplantation] by a person who is acting in what he reasonably believes to be P's best interests.

Under section 2(3) of the Act, children who have sufficient maturity to consent to such a serious operation (see Chapter 5) might be able to make their own decision to donate an organ:

Human Tissue Act 2004 section 2

2(3) Where—

(a) the child concerned is alive,

(b) neither a decision of his to consent to the activity, nor a decision of his not to consent to it, is in force, and

(c) either he is not competent to deal with the issue of consent in relation to the activity or, though he is competent to deal with that issue, he fails to do so,

'appropriate consent' means the consent of a person who has parental responsibility for him.

Where the child lacks capacity or does not wish to make a decision, anyone with parental responsibility could give consent, but this alone would not be sufficient for the transplant to go ahead, and court approval should be sought. The HTA's Code of Practice suggests that living donation from children should be extremely rare, and that it is good practice to consult the parents even if the child is competent.

---

[120] Human Tissue Act 2004 (Persons who lack capacity to consent and transplants) Regulations 2006.

HTA Code of Practice paras 28, 30, and 33[121]

> 28 The removal of an organ, part organ or tissue continues to be governed by the common law and before the removal of a solid organ from a child, whether competent or not, it is good practice for court approval to be obtained…
>
> 30 Children can be considered as living organ donors only in extremely rare circumstances, and donation under the Act should go ahead only with the approval of a panel of no fewer than three members of the HTA (after court approval to the removal has been obtained)….
>
> 33 Even if the child is competent, it is good practice to consult the person with parental responsibility for the child and to involve him and/or her in the child's decision-making process regarding storage and use of transplantable material for transplantation. However, it must be emphasised that, if the child is competent, the decision to consent (under the Act) must be the child's.

(b) Restrictions on live donation

Independent Assessors (IAs) must assess all living solid organ donor-recipient pairs and make a recommendation to the HTA. The HTA will then decide whether the donation can go ahead. IAs should be NHS consultants, or of equivalent standing, should not be working in the field of organ transplantation, and should have been trained and accredited by the HTA.[122] These Independent Assessors consider all living organ donations for transplantation that fall into the following categories:
Directed:

- Genetically related
- Emotionally related
- paired and pooled

Non-directed:

- domino
- altruistic (the decision in these cases should be made by the HTA until practice is established as routine).

Directed donation means that the donor's organs are to be donated to a specified individual, usually a partner or close family member. In non-directed donation, the recipient's identity is not known to the donor. Paired donation takes place when someone volunteers to donate to someone they know, but they turn out to be a poor tissue match. In such circumstances, donor and donee may be paired with another similar couple so that each recipient can receive a well-matched organ. Pooled donation is similar, but involves a larger 'pool' of willing but unmatched emotionally related donors.

Non-directed donations include 'domino' transplants, where the primary purpose of the donation is the medical treatment of the donor. Because it is more straightforward to carry out heart and lung transplants than to transplant lungs alone, someone who is in need of a lung transplant might receive the heart and lungs from a cadaveric donor. In such

---

[121] Code of Practice 2 (Donation of Solid Organs for Tranplantation), available at <www.hta.gov.uk>.
[122] Paras 55 and 56.

circumstances, the recipient's own heart might then become available for transplant into another person. This would, of course, be a living unrelated transplant, but, unlike most living donation, the donor is undergoing the operation *for her own benefit*, and so fewer ethical difficulties arise.

The Independent Assessor must interview donor and recipient and certify that the statutory and all other requirements are satisfied. This report will be valid for 6 months, after which a further report will become necessary, in case the circumstances have changed.

Entirely altruistic living donation, where donor and recipient are strangers, is now possible, and there have been a small number of cases since the Act came into force in 2006. It is clear that the HTA will take extra care to ensure that an altruistic non-directed donation is made voluntarily. Walter Glannon and Lainie Friedman Ross argue that suspicion of the motives of non-directed altruistic donation is not necessarily justified, since a potential organ donor who has *no* emotional ties to a potential recipient may be better able to make an entirely free and uncoerced decision to donate.

Walter Glannon and Lainie Friedman Ross[123]

An altruistic donor has no obligation to donate. The decision to donate goes beyond the obligatory and permissible to the supererogatory, and a decision not to donate does not invite or warrant moral criticism because there is no moral basis on which to criticize not performing an act that would have been beyond the call of duty. In contrast, the family member who is a potential donor has a prima facie obligation to donate because of the nature of relationships within the family.

(c) Payment

Under section 32 of the Human Tissue Act, payment for human organs is prohibited.

Human Tissue Act 2004 section 32

Prohibition of commercial dealings in human material for transplantation

32(1) A person commits an offence if he—

(a) gives or receives a reward for the supply of, or for an offer to supply, any controlled material;

(b) seeks to find a person willing to supply any controlled material for reward;

(c) offers to supply any controlled material for reward;

(d) initiates or negotiates any arrangement involving the giving of a reward for the supply of, or for an offer to supply, any controlled material;

(e) takes part in the management or control of a body of persons corporate or unincorporate whose activities consist of or include the initiation or negotiation of such arrangements.

[123] 'Do Genetic Relationships Create Moral Obligations in Organ Transplantation?' (2002) 11 Cambridge Quarterly of Healthcare Ethics 153–9.

Under sections 32(8) and (10), the prohibition covers both cadaveric and living organ donation. Notice that it is not just organ traffickers who would commit an offence under section 32(1). Recipients of organs too could face prosecution, as could anyone involved in arranging an organ sale. The maximum penalty for offences under section 32(1) is three years' imprisonment. Under section 32(2), it is also an offence to publish or distribute an advertisement for the sale of an organ, and the maximum penalty is 51 weeks' imprisonment.

Under section 32(6)(a) payment to the holder of a licence (that is, the hospital) in money or money's worth is not to be considered a reward if it 'is in consideration for transporting, removing, preparing, preserving, or storing controlled material'. This means that covering the costs associated with the transplantation process is not to be treated in the same way as a payment *for* an organ. Similarly, under section 32(7)(a), 'any expenses incurred in, or in connection with, transporting, removing, preparing, preserving or storing the material' are not to be treated as a reward.

Section 32(7)(c) permits payments to living organ donors to cover 'any expenses or loss of earnings incurred by the person from whose body the material comes so far as reasonably and directly attributable to his supplying the material from his body'. So, a living organ donor could reasonably expect to receive compensation for time that she has to take off work during the organ donation process, and for associated expenses, such as travel costs. The reference to expenses or loss of earnings makes it clear that any such payments are not to be seen as payment for the organ itself, or even compensation for the inconvenience of donation, but rather must simply cover financial costs which are directly attributable to the donation.

(d) WHAT, IF ANYTHING, WOULD BE WRONG WITH A MARKET IN ORGANS?

A number of reasons are commonly put forward for maintaining a prohibition on the sale of organs. First, it is argued that there is something intrinsically wrong with commodifying the human body, and that it would be either impossible or degrading to put a value on human body parts. Secondly, commercialization of organ transplantation is believed to undermine the principle that donation should be altruistic. In the next extract, for example, Barbro Bjorkman adopts a virtue ethics approach (see Chapter 1), and suggests that selling an organ is not something a virtuous person would do.

Barbro Bjorkman[124]

Virtue ethics rejects commodification of organs because it fails to make us flourish, not because it has bad consequences or breaks some rule... Virtuous persons would not sell their organs but rather donate them because they wish to help their less fortunate fellow man, they 'see' that this is fine, noble, and worthwhile. The fact that this is not the current practice in society today only shows that people in general are not virtuous. The way to redeem the problems of organ shortage in a given society is not to create a market but rather to increase the sense of virtue.

---

[124] 'Why We Are Not Allowed to Sell That Which We Are Encouraged to Donate' (2006) 15 Cambridge Quarterly of Healthcare Ethics 60–70.

Thirdly, a black market in organs already exists in some parts of the world. Wealthy patients have travelled to countries such as India, Estonia, Moldova, Turkey, and Ukraine for transplant surgery, which depends upon the payment of relatively modest sums to local volunteers: in India, payments of £360–£610 have been reported.[125] In the next extracts, the existence of a flourishing market in organs in developing countries is cited as evidence that it is only poor and marginalized people who would agree to donate their organs for money.

G Berlinguer[126]

The truth of the matter is that, as far as human organs are concerned, the traffic always takes place between the South and the North of the world, or between the poor who sell and the rich who buy … [I]n the twenty-first century, the North could attempt to treat its more seriously ill by importing and using organs from members of the poorer classes, in particular from the underdeveloped countries. Supplies would be more than sufficient, as bodies are the only goods that these countries produce in abundance.

Madhav Goyal, Ravindra L Mehta, Lawrence J Schneiderman, and Ashwini R Sehgal[127]

Our quantitative findings, along with those of previous qualitative studies, undercut 5 key assumptions made by supporters of the sale of kidneys. First, although paying people to donate may have increased the supply of organs for transplantation, the financial incentive did not supplement underlying altruistic motivations. Only 5% of participants said wanting to help a sick person was a major factor in their decision to sell. Second, selling a kidney did not help poor donors overcome poverty. Family income actually declined by one third, and most participants were still in debt and living below the poverty line at the time of the survey. Third, regardless of these poor economic outcomes, sellers arguably have a right to make informed decisions about their own bodies. However, most participants would not recommend that others sell a kidney, which suggests that potential donors would be unlikely to sell a kidney if they were better informed of the likely outcomes. Fourth, safeguards such as eliminating middlemen or having an authorization committee did not appear to be effective. Middlemen and clinics paid less than they promised, and the authorization committees did not ensure that donations were motivated by altruism alone. Fifth, nephrectomy was associated with a decline in health status. Previous qualitative reports suggest that a diminished ability to perform physical labor may explain the observed worsening of economic status.…

A majority of donors were women. Given the often weak position of women in Indian society, the voluntary nature of some donations is questionable. In fact, 2 participants said that their husbands forced them to donate.

---

[125] Ganapati Mudur, 'Kidney Trade Arrest Exposes Loopholes in India's Transplant Laws' (2004) 328 British Medical Journal 246.

[126] *Everyday Bioethics: Reflections on Bioethical Choices in Daily Life* (Baywood Publishing: New York, 2003) 101.

[127] 'Economic and Health Consequences of Selling a Kidney in India' (2002) 288 Journal of the American Medical Association 1589–93.

Fourthly, it has been argued that financial incentives may overbear a person's will, and thus cast doubt upon the voluntariness of their consent.

EB Brody[128]

In countries without legal prohibition of organ selling, recruitment campaigns have used selling techniques which effectively negate informed consent among the poorest citizens for whom the possibility of a one-time financial gain of previously unimaginable proportions is so irresistible as to obviate rational judgement. Financial incentives in these circumstances are tantamount to coercion.

Fifthly, donation does involve some pain, discomfort, and risk, and there are those who are troubled by the prospect of people assuming some risk to health in return for financial reward. Finally, a free market in organs would mean that only rich people would be able to afford to buy them, thus disrupting the principle that scarce health care resources should be distributed according to need rather than ability to pay.

Not all of these arguments withstand logical analysis. For example, it is not strictly true that it would be impossible to put a value on a human organ, nor that doing so is inevitably degrading. Tort law routinely quantifies the loss of various body parts. Victims of criminal injuries are paid damages, without any assumption that such damages undermine the intrinsic value of the human body.

Secondly, even if poor people do find the offer of money in return for a kidney especially attractive, this must also be true of many other sources of income which may pose some risk to a person's health (often much greater than the small risk of living with one kidney). Yet few people would argue that we should pay soldiers extremely modest wages in order to ensure that they have not signed up for a career in the army because of the lure of the salary. Indeed, such a suggestion would seem self-evidently both paternalistic and unfair.

Thirdly, it is clear that a black market in human organs already exists, and Radcliffe-Richards *et al.* argue that it is this, rather than a regulated market, which poses the greatest risk to organ donors.

J Radcliffe-Richards, AS Daar, RD Guttmann, R Hoffenberg, I Kennedy, M Lock, RA Sells, N Tilney[129]

The first claim is that the vendors are not competent to make a genuine choice within a given range of options. The second, by contrast, is that poverty has so restricted the range of options that organ selling has become the best, and therefore, in effect, that the range is too small....

If our ground for concern is that the range of choices is too small, we cannot improve matters by removing the best option that poverty has left, and making the range smaller still.... The only way to improve matters is to lessen the poverty until organ selling no longer seems the best option; and if that could be achieved, prohibition would be irrelevant because nobody would want to sell.

---

[128] *Biomedical Technology and Human Rights* (Unesco, 1993) 100.

[129] 'The Case for Allowing Kidney Sales' International Forum for Transplant Ethics (1998) 351 The Lancet 1950–2.

The other line of argument may seem more promising, since ignorance does preclude informed consent. However, the likely ignorance of the subjects is not a reason for banning altogether a procedure for which consent is required. In other contexts, the value we place on autonomy leads us to insist on information and counselling, and that is what it should suggest in the case of organ selling as well....

[A]ll the evidence we have shows that there is much more scope for exploitation and abuse when a supply of desperately wanted goods is made illegal. It is, furthermore, not clear why it should be thought harder to police a legal trade than the present complete ban.

Fourthly, as we saw in Chapter 5, the principle of patient autonomy means that we let people assume considerable risks to their own health by refusing life-sustaining treatment, and that they are entitled to exercise this choice for irrational reasons or even for no reason at all. Is it then unduly paternalistic to prevent someone from incurring a less serious risk to health which might save someone's life?

Fifthly, nor is it clear that paid organ donation is necessarily incompatible with altruism. We would permit a mother to donate a kidney to her son if he has kidney failure, but what if the son's condition is instead a rare form of cancer, and optimum treatment is expensive and only available abroad? We would forbid this mother from selling a kidney in order to pay for her son's life-saving treatment, even though her motivation is just as altruistic as the mother whose son happens to have renal failure.

Sixthly, as Stephen Wilkinson points out, there is something wrong with the argument that we should not allow paid organ donation because it is risky. If this is true, then unpaid organ donation is equally risky, and presumably should also be prohibited.

Stephen Wilkinson[130]

No matter how dangerous paid donation is, it needn't... be any more risky than unpaid donation, since the mere fact of payment doesn't *add* any danger. So if paid donation is wrong because of the danger to which the donor is subjected, then free donation must also be wrong on the very same grounds. Free donation, though, is not wrong; on the contrary, we tend to regard it as commendable, heroic even. Therefore paid donation isn't wrong either—or, if it is wrong, it's wrong because of something other than the danger to which the donor is subjected.

Seventhly, allowing payments for organs does not necessarily mean embracing a completely free market. Instead, it would be possible for payments to be made by the NHS rather than individual recipients, and for the organs to then be distributed according to need. Because the cost savings of transplantation are so enormous—recall that the average kidney transplant will save the NHS £251,000—payments to donors could still be cost-effective. In the next extract, Charles Erin and John Harris suggest that it is possible to contemplate an 'ethical market' in organs.

---

130 *Bodies for Sale: Ethics and Exploitation in the Human Body Trade* (Routledge: London, 2003) 108.

Charles A Erin and John Harris[131]

There is a lot of hypocrisy about the ethics of buying and selling organs and indeed other body products and services…What it usually means is that everyone is paid but the donor. The surgeons and medical team are paid, the transplant coordinator does not go unremunerated, and the recipient receives an important benefit in kind. Only the unfortunate and heroic donor is supposed to put up with the insult of no reward, to add to the insult of the operation…

The bare bones of an ethical market would look like this: the market would be confined to a self-governing geopolitical area such as a nation state or indeed the European Union. Only citizens resident within the union or state could sell into the system and they and their families would be equally eligible to receive organs. Thus organ vendors would know they were contributing to a system which would benefit them and their families and friends since their chances of receiving an organ in case of need would be increased by the existence of the market…There would be only one purchaser, an agency like the National Health Service (NHS), which would buy all organs and distribute according to some fair conception of medical priority. There would be no direct sales or purchases, no exploitation of low income countries and their populations (no buying in Turkey or India to sell in Harley Street). The organs would be tested for HIV, etc, their provenance known, and there would be strict controls and penalties to prevent abuse.

Sellers of organs would know they had saved a life and would be reasonably compensated for their risk, time, and altruism, which would be undiminished by sale. We do not after all regard medicine as any the less a caring profession because doctors are paid.

Finally, insofar as the offer of money might persuade someone to volunteer to be a live organ donor, we should, as J Harvey explains, perhaps be equally or even more concerned about non-financial pressure, such as that exerted within families. If a person's consent can only be considered voluntary if they could realistically have said 'no', it is not obvious that payment is any more coercive than familial obligations.

J Harvey[132]

Now I think there is financial pressure when the potential donor is in poverty. And perhaps it may be argued that this alone is sufficient for banning all paid-for donations. But then, in consistency, the same reasoning should be applied to related donors: since *some* of them are open to heavy psychological and emotional pressure (for example, perhaps by being the submissive and 'guilt'-ridden offspring of an extremely domineering and now ailing parent), then all donations from relatives should be forbidden. This course is not advocated in connection with related donors. Rather, the difficult task of distinguishing between truly vulnerable relatives and those not vulnerable is undertaken. This would point to our attempting the analogous task in the case of paid for donations, namely the task of distinguishing between the truly financially vulnerable and those not so.

---

[131] 'An Ethical Market in Human Organs' (2003) 29 Journal of Medical Ethics 137–8.
[132] 'Paying Organ Donors' (1990) 16 Journal of Medical Ethics 117–19.

4 XENOTRANSPLANTATION

Although whole organ transplants from animals to humans are still at the experimental stage, other sorts of animal tissues have been used in human medicine for some time. Pig heart valves, for example, can be processed so that they act like inert material rather than living tissue, and they have been inserted into human patients for more than thirty years.

There have also been examples of animal-to-human whole organ transplants, but none has been successful, with maximum survival times of a few months. In the most infamous case, a baboon heart was transplanted into a 14-day-old neonate, known as 'Baby Fae', and she died within three weeks. Her parents were poor and uneducated, and the consent form they signed appeared to overstate the likely benefits from the transplant. It suggested that: 'Long-term survival with appropriate growth and development may be possible following heart transplantation...this research is an effort to provide your baby with some hope of immediate and long term survival.'[133]

In the next extract, Jeffrey Barker and Lauren Polcrack explain that the history of experimentation in xenotransplantation is not 'ethically promising'.

Jeffrey H Barker and Lauren Polcrack[134]

Many early xenotransplant recipients were unconscious and therefore never consented to the procedure; many were poor and uneducated. Some were prisoners, some were children. The first cardiac xenotransplantation subject (in 1964) was a deaf-mute who never consented to the procedure, and the consent form signed by his step-sister did not mention a non-human organ. Throughout the history of xenotransplantation, the medically, ethically and socially vulnerable have been used as experimental subjects.

The first documented xenotransplantation involving a human host occurred in 1902, when a pig kidney was used in the case of a young woman suffering from end-stage renal failure. Early in the twentieth century, kidneys were transplanted into humans from rabbits, pigs, lambs, goats, macaques, chimpanzees, marmosets and baboons. In each case, however, the transplant failed, and in most cases the patient died as a result.

The principal reason for pursuing research into xenotransplantation is that it would enable many more patients to receive organs, which might save their lives. If we could breed animals for their organs, in the same way as we breed them for food, the organ shortage might disappear. Not only would this benefit the thousands of patients currently on the organ waiting list, but it could potentially eliminate the risks to health incurred by living organ donors.

The question of *which* animal species should be chosen as the source of organs for transplant is also controversial. For a number of reasons, primates have been rejected and pigs appear to be the most promising source. First, chimpanzees and other primates, such as orang-utans, are endangered species. Secondly, primates are much 'closer' to humans: they look more like us and we do not eat them. Although note that Marie Fox suggests such reasoning is morally arbitrary.

---

[133] Jeffrey H Barker and Lauren Polcrack, 'Respect for Persons, Informed Consent and the Assessment of Infectious Disease Risks in Xenotransplantation' (2001) 4 Medicine, Health Care and Philosophy 53–70, 59.

[134] 'Respect for Persons, Informed Consent and the Assessment of Infectious Disease Risks in Xenotransplantation' (2001) 4 Medicine, Health Care and Philosophy 53–70.

Marie Fox[135]

> Certainly, given that pigs and primates are alike in the morally relevant respects, since both species are sentient, intelligent and sociable, the real reason to distinguish them seems not to rest on mental ability or capacity for suffering but on practical or emotional grounds.... [B]y permitting use of certain animals, but not others, as research tools and potential organ donors, law reflects the moral arbitrariness in our response to them.

Thirdly, the chance of zoonosis, that is cross-species disease transmission, seems to be more likely between more closely related species. Fourthly, pigs breed much more quickly than primates, and the organ supply could therefore be replenished more quickly. Finally, pig organs are about the same size as human organs.

Despite the obvious advantages in locating a potentially unlimited supply of transplantable organs, there are several reasons why xenotransplantation continues to be extremely controversial. These can be categorized as either practical problems, such as the risk of rejection and disease transmission, or ethical problems, such as animal welfare considerations. We consider these in turn, before looking at the current regulation of xenotransplantation in the UK.

(a) PRACTICAL PROBLEMS

(1) Rejection

The first major obstacle to successful xenotransplantation is the likelihood that the animal's organ will be rejected immediately. Although immunosuppressant therapy can now largely counterbalance the risk of rejection in human-to-human transplants, much larger doses might be necessary in animal-to-human transplants, and if given in sufficient quantities these drugs will destroy a person's immune system, and themselves cause death.

The use of animal organs will often prompt what is known as a hyper-acute rejection reaction within minutes or hours of the transplant, and this cannot be adequately controlled by existing immunosuppressant drugs. A more promising solution to the problem of rejection is to introduce human genes into the animal's genome, thus suppressing the gene that causes hyper-acute rejection. Such animals might then be cloned in order to increase the supply of suitable organs. There has been some success in creating transgenic pigs, and experiments involving primates appear to indicate that the rejection of organs from transgenic pigs can be controlled using drugs. Survival times of five and eight weeks have been reported in baboons that have received hearts from transgenic pigs.[136]

(2) Risk of Infection

Progress in minimizing the risk of hyper-acute rejection means that the most pressing danger currently presented by xenotransplantation is the possibility of cross-species

---

[135] 'Re-thinking Kinship: Law's Construction of the Animal Body' (2004) 57 Current Legal Problems 469–93.

[136] CGA McGregor, GW Byrne, WR Davies, K Oi, VP Rao, HD Tazelaar, RC Walker, CJ Gostout, and JS Logan, 'Cardiac Xenotransplantation: Early Success in the Orthotopic Position' (2005) 24 The Journal of Heart and Lung Transplantation, S95.

infection. Variant Creutzfeldt-Jakob disease (vCJD), the human form of bovine spongiform encephalitis (BSE) or 'mad cow' disease, is a dramatic example of cross-species disease transmission. Some people also believe that HIV/AIDS originated in primates. The risk of infection from transplantation would be particularly acute since placing an animal organ *inside a human body* provides a perfect 'platform' for cross-species infection.

It is thought that some viruses, such as the porcine endogenous retrovirus (PERV), which is harmless to pigs, and incorporated into the pig genome, would be impossible to eliminate from transgenic pigs, and might be able to cross the species barrier and cause cancer, or irreversible damage to the human immune system. Any risk of cross-species infection would, of course, be exacerbated if the recipient is taking immunosuppressive drugs which reduce her ability to fight a new virus.

It is important to remember that if a disease crosses the species barrier, the risk of infection is faced not only by the recipient herself, but also by her close contacts and the rest of society, which as we can see in the next sections, raises a number of complicated ethical issues.

(a) Impact upon the recipient and her close contacts

Could someone give a valid consent to receiving an animal's organ in the light of the risk of cross-species infection? The first problem here is whether their consent could ever be adequately informed. Insofar as the risks of cross-species infection cannot be known with any certainty before trials in humans have begun, and perhaps for some considerable time afterwards, it would be impossible to give a potential recipient *full* disclosure of the risks associated with xenotransplantation.

Nuffield Council on Bioethics[137]

It is not possible to predict or quantify the risk that xenotransplantation will result in the emergence of new human diseases. But in the worst case, the consequences could be far-reaching and difficult to control.... Put bluntly, it may be possible to identify any infectious organism transmitted by xenografting only if it causes disease in human beings, and after it has started to do so.

Since the first patients to receive xenografts will be doing so as part of a clinical trial, the more stringent duties of disclosure that apply when obtaining a subject's consent to participation in a research trial apply (see further Chapter 9). If there is an unknown and unquantifiable risk to the recipients' health, it is arguable that they could never give sufficiently informed consent to xenotransplantation.

A second problem comes from the principle that participants in therapeutic research trials should be assured of receiving, at the very least, the best current treatment (see Chapter 9). Initially at least, allografts (human-to-human transplants) will continue to be the best treatment for individuals with acute organ failure. It might be argued that xenotransplantation trials should therefore only recruit patients who would, for some reason, not be eligible for a human organ transplant. Patients who are not on the organ donor waiting list might be offered a xenograft on the grounds that this could have a greater chance of success than the treatment—ie, nothing—which would otherwise be available to them.

---

[137] Nuffield Council on Bioethics, *Animal-to-Human Transplants: The Ethics of Xenotransplantation* (Nuffield Council on Bioethics: London, 1996) paras 10.25, 6.14.

Related to this, if the first participants in clinical trials are asked to choose between immediate death or the unknown risks associated with xenotransplantation, it is of course readily understandable that they would opt to receive an animal organ. But being faced with such an invidious choice leads Sheila McLean and Laura Williamson to suggest that 'there must be questions about whether or not the vulnerability of the patients likely to be involved in early trials would cast doubt upon their competence or capacity to consent'.[138]

Of course, if trials were confined to potential organ recipients who are unable to wait for a human organ, or too sick to be placed upon the organ donor register, success rates of xenografts are likely to be lower than might be the case if comparatively healthy and robust patients were also included.

A further issue is the restrictions that would have to be placed on xenograft recipients. It would be necessary to monitor their health for the rest of their lives. Recipients would not be allowed to give blood or themselves donate organs. They might have to agree to autopsy after death, and if infection occurred, very serious restrictions might have to be placed upon their liberty. It is also possible that their present and future sexual partners would have to be monitored, and that, at least at first, their freedom to have children might be restricted, and they would be told to use barrier methods of contraception. Recipients could be asked to consent in advance to these limitations, and if the alternative is death, it is understandable that a person might be willing to give up some civil liberties in order to obtain a potentially life-saving transplant. In the next extract, however, Jeffrey Barker and Lauren Polcrack question whether it would, in fact, be possible to give fully informed consent to such serious curtailment of one's future liberty.

Jeffrey H Barker and Lauren Polcrack[139]

[T]here are significant concerns with regard to the individual informed consent of the potential xenograft recipient. The recipient must understand as completely as possible the risks to him or herself, to his or [her] contacts, and the risks to society at large, and must be willing to move forward despite those risks. The immediate contacts of the potential recipient must also consent to the probable risks. Any clinical trials of xenotransplantation would require long-term—and probably lifetime—monitoring and surveillance of recipients and their contacts, with the possibility of lifetime quarantine should serious xenosis occur. All recipients would need to be registered and monitored in order to protect public health. Truly informed consent to these types of radical changes in personal freedom would be difficult to obtain.

If third parties, such as sexual partners, might be subject to surveillance and restrictions upon their liberty, should their consent also be necessary? Informing them about the recipient's medical treatment would not only represent a breach of confidentiality, but also, as Sheila McLean and Laura Williamson points out in the next extract, it would be most unusual to give a third party a right of veto over another's medical treatment. McLean and Williamson further highlight the difficulties in enforcing the sort of surveillance regime which many people think would be necessary following the first xenografts.

---

[138] 'Xenotransplantation: A Pig in a Poke?' (2004) 57 Current Legal Problems 443–68, 464.
[139] 'Respect for Persons, Informed Consent and the Assessment of Infectious Disease Risks in Xenotransplantation' (2001) 4 Medicine, Health Care and Philosophy 53–70, 66.

Sheila McLean and Laura Williamson[140]

> If the consent of third parties is an essential prerequisite to a xenograft, then they are placed in the unusual position of being able, by refusal, to prevent the potential recipient from accepting a therapy which may be of benefit. Secondly, it is unclear just how such agreements [to restrict liberty] could be policed; agreement pre-transplant does not guarantee compliance post-transplant, yet compliance is presumably of the highest order of significance otherwise it would not be required in the first place. What, for example, would be done if a recipient decided not to use barrier contraception? It must be doubted whether or not the state could effectively enter the bedroom and prevent this from happening…
>
> To continue with this example, it must be asked what would be the state's authority should an individual xenotransplant recipient or the partner of one become pregnant. Could the state compel a pregnancy termination, and if so on what grounds—ethical or legal? In other words, if the surveillance regime is necessary—as seems to be generally agreed—then there are serious concerns about its enforceability. Indeed the…working party which drafted the surveillance document noted that any attempt to require rather than invite patients to agree to the limitations to be imposed on their future life would be likely to run contrary to the terms of the Human Rights legislation, in particular Article 8.

(b) Impact upon society

Although it is clearly the recipient of an animal organ who is most immediately at risk from cross-species infection, transmission of disease to others may be possible, and hence xenotransplantation also poses as yet unquantifiable risks to public health. Since it will never be possible to conclusively determine that no such risk exists, we instead have to determine whether the degree of risk is acceptable.

Interestingly, xenotransplantation reverses the usual risk/benefit calculation of participation in a research trial. Generally, as we saw in Chapter 9, the research subject assumes some risk to her own health and wellbeing for the benefit of scientific knowledge. Although the subject may hold out some hope of obtaining a health benefit from the trial, this is not the principal purpose of the research, which is instead to benefit society through the development of effective treatments. In xenotransplantation, the benefit may be to the individual recipient, since it is likely that she would die soon without a transplant. The risk, however, may be to society as a whole through the introduction of animal viruses into the human population. Unlike the individual research subject, it would be impossible to obtain the *public's* informed consent before a clinical trial began. Instead, Jeffrey Barker and Lauren Polcrack advocate greater public participation in the decision to go ahead with clinical trials.

Jeffrey H Barker and Lauren Polcrack[141]

> Xenografts put at risk not only the recipient but those directly associated with the recipient, including caregivers and family members. They also put at risk the public at large by creating the distinct possibility of introducing new or modified pathogens into the human species,

---

[140] 'Xenotransplantation: A Pig in a Poke?' (2004) 57 Current Legal Problems 443–68, 459.

[141] 'Respect for Persons, Informed Consent and the Assessment of Infectious Disease Risks in Xenotransplantation' (2001) 4 Medicine, Health Care and Philosophy 53–70, 65.

pathogens whose virulence, infectivity and mode of retransmission, and potential for treatment are all highly uncertain...

Where there is a significant risk to the public, as we believe there is in xenotransplantation, there must be a public process for informing and educating the public, and for ascertaining the willingness of the public to encounter, to consent to these risks. This process of 'collective informed consent' requires not merely public education but active public participation in the decision-making process.

A further problem, as Megan Sykes *et al.* explain in the next extract, is that 'xenotourism' is likely to mean that it will be very difficult for any country to successfully eliminate the risks posed by xenotransplantion.

Megan Sykes, Anthony d'Apice and Mauro Sandrin[142]

The potential risks of xenotransplantation will not be confined to the country in which the transplant is performed. Even the most assiduous safety efforts of any nation or group of nations may be ineffective in the absence of internationally agreed regulations and monitoring procedures for xenotransplantation. This problem arises because patients are mobile and could receive a xenograft in one country, which may or may not have appropriate regulatory and monitoring processes, and later leave that country and enter another without ever having to state that they are the recipient of a xenograft....

The scale of such 'casual' xenotourism is likely to be small. However, there is a risk that entrepreneurial xenotransplanters may deliberately set up business in countries with minimal or no regulation and set about attracting foreigners with organ failure to come to be transplanted and then return home. The absence of questioning about xenotransplantation upon re-entry, and the absence of a mechanism for bringing such patients into surveillance programs in their home countries almost guarantee that such patients will avoid surveillance when they return home.

(b) ETHICAL PROBLEMS

(1) Revulsion

Many people are repelled by the idea of transplanting animal organs into human beings. For some, this will be prompted by their religious beliefs. In Judaism, for example, the pig is not considered fit for human consumption, and the use of pig organs for transplantation might be similarly unacceptable. In order to accommodate these strongly held views, in any future regulation of xenotransplantation there would undoubtedly be a conscientious objection clause, similar to that in the Abortion Act, so that doctors did not have to participate in xenotransplantation; and patients too would be reassured their refusal to accept an animal organ would not mean that they would be taken off the transplant waiting list. Provided that no-one is compelled to take part in xenotransplantation against their wishes, it would seem inappropriate for some people's instinctive revulsion to be allowed to determine whether xenotransplantation goes ahead, especially since potential recipients' lives may be at stake.

---

[142] 'Position Paper of the Ethics Committee of the International Xenotransplantation Association' (2003) 10 Xenotransplantation 194–203.

There have also been suggestions that introducing human genes into pigs, and animal organs into humans threatens to blur the barriers between the species.

Jason Scott Robert and Françoise Baylis[143]

[S]cientifically, there might be no such thing as fixed species identities or boundaries. Morally, however, we rely on the notion of fixed species identities and boundaries in the way we live our lives and treat other creatures . . .

All things considered, the engineering of creatures that are part human and part nonhuman animal is objectionable because the existence of such beings would introduce inexorable moral confusion in our existing relationships with nonhuman animals and in our future relationships with part-human hybrids.[144]

Of course, barriers between the species are constantly evolving, albeit slowly. We share about 96 per cent of our DNA with chimpanzees, and so basing moral status upon biology is fraught with difficulty. Moreover, pig heart valves have been used to treat humans for many years, and there would seem to be no doubt that patients who have received them continue to be members of the human species. Perhaps, as Henry T Greely suggests in the following extract, it is a question of degree.

Henry T Greely[145]

[A]fter a few early reports of patient qualms, the use of pig heart valves for medical procedures now raises little concern. Apart from pragmatic fear of the passage of disease and some animal rights concerns that are quite distinct from issues of chimerism . . . other plausible single organ xenotransplants into human beings seem unlikely to be heavily controversial. On the other hand, if it were feasible to transplant a chimpanzee brain into a human, or if a human were given a large number of organs from nonhuman sources, people might worry whether the resulting organism was really human . . .

Chimeras made by moving human parts into nonhuman beings would raise concerns when they are significant enough to raise the question of the possible humanity of the recipient. In both cases the 'importance' of the parts—brains and gametes are more important than heart valves or skin—and the number of parts moved—transplanting five visceral organs would be more troubling than transplanting one—seems significant.

(2) Animal Rights

It is often said that if we are prepared to breed and kill animals for food, we should logically also accept xenotransplantation, especially since the purpose of breeding animals for their organs (saving lives) would seem to be more valuable and of more immediate benefit than the production of meat. This simple analogy between meat-eating and xenotransplantation has, however, been challenged for a number of reasons.

143 'Crossing Species Boundaries' (2003) 3 American Journal of Bioethics 1–13.   144 Ibid 9.
145 'Defining Chimeras . . . and Chimeric Concerns' (2003) 3 American Journal of Bioethics 17–20, 19.

Robin Downie[146]

[W]hereas the eating of animal flesh may or may not be ethically right, it is 'natural' in the sense that many other animal species in fact do it and (as has been claimed by some) human beings are biologically carnivorous or at least omnivorous. On the other hand, the transplant of animal tissue into human beings is 'unnatural'.

Of course, as Downie himself admits, all medical interventions, including most obviously human-to-human organ transplants, are also 'unnatural'. Downie therefore goes on to suggest that the insertion of human genes into animals and then transplanting their organs into humans is 'profoundly different from previous medical interventions'. This is, of course, a subjective judgement, and it is not clear why xenotransplantation is necessarily any more 'profoundly unnatural' than, say, in vitro fertilization.

Secondly, donor animals would have to be bred and raised in isolation in completely barren and sterile surroundings, and genetic modification might further impair their quality of life. Would this represent a more substantial interference with their welfare than happens when they are bred for meat? Possibly, although it should be remembered that the conditions in 'battery farms', and the techniques used to produce veal and foie gras are hardly conducive to animals' wellbeing. Of course, the inhumane treatment of animals by the food industry does not necessarily justify inhumane treatment in pursuit of organ transplantation. But insofar as the goal of xenotransplantation would be to save the lives of people who would otherwise die, there would seem to be no reason to be more squeamish about animal welfare where the goal is transplant retrieval than where the goal is to produce cheap chicken or foie gras.

A better analogy might be with the use of animals in research, when it is common for animals to be specially bred to take part in experiments, and to subsequently be killed. In animal experiments, we are using animals in order to further scientific knowledge and to improve the medical treatments that are available to humans. The benefits to individuals may be less direct and immediate than they would be if xenotransplantation were to be successful, but the ethical issues are similar.

Just like experiments on animals and non-vegetarianism, xenotransplantation rests upon the assumption that it is ethically acceptable to kill other species in order to save human lives. This is, according to commentators such as Peter Singer, an example of speciesism (that is, favouring one's own species and devaluing other species), which is said to be as morally objectionable as racism or sexism.

Peter Singer[147]

What kind of ethic can tell us that it is all right to rear sentient animals in barren cages that give them no decent life at all, and then kill them to take their organs, while refusing to permit us to take the organ of a human being who is not, and never can be, even minimally conscious? Obviously a speciesist ethic... My objection is to the fact that we disregard the interests of nonhuman animals by ranking them as less worthy of our concern and respect than *any* member of our species, no matter how limited in capacities and potential....

In a world that needlessly rears several billion animals in factory farms each year and then kills them to satisfy a mere preference of taste, it is difficult to argue persuasively against

---

[146] 'Xenotransplantation' (1997) 23 Journal of Medical Ethics 205–6, 206.
[147] 'Xenotransplantation and Speciesism' (1992) 24 Transplantation Proceedings 728–32.

the rearing and slaughter of a few thousand animals so that their organs can be used to save people's lives. That, however, is not a reason for using animals: it is, rather, a reason for changing our views about animals. In a better world, a world that cared properly for the interests of animals, we would do our utmost to avoid choices that pit the essential interests of animals against our own... This might involve more effective ways of obtaining organs from humans who are brain dead, or cortically dead. It might involve the development of artificial organs. Or it might involve using our limited medical resources to educate people in looking after the organs with which they were born.

Why do we think that human beings' lives are more valuable and important than animals' lives? Often some appeal is made to distinctively human qualities, such as sentience, consciousness, and the capacity for reason. But, as Singer explains, the problem here is that not all human beings possess these characteristics—patients in a permanent vegetative state or anencephalic infants, for example, do not—whereas they are possessed to some degree by animals such as chimpanzees and dolphins. If it is these qualities, and not species membership per se, that count morally, then as Jonathan Hughes points out, two possible consequences follow. Either we should refuse to contemplate using animals which possess the relevant characteristics as xenograft sources. Or we should also be prepared to take organs from human beings who have irrevocably lost the capacities in question.[148]

Jonathan Hughes[149]

Imposing harms on animals in order to benefit humans is acceptable, it is argued, because the harms and benefits that humans are capable of experiencing are greater than those that can be experienced by other animals. The physical pains suffered by animals, according to this argument, are less significant than those suffered by humans, because animals are less sensitive, or because they lack the capacity for fearful anticipation or distressing memory which amplify the effects of physical pain in humans. And death matters less for animals, it is argued, because animals have less to lose than humans in the form of potential for future pleasures and satisfactions, or because the loss of these things matters less to creatures who lack our capacity to foresee, desire and plan for them....

[T]his kind of argument is vulnerable to a well-known objection. The problem is that capacities for pleasure and pain, fulfilment and suffering vary not only between but within species, including humans. So while it is true that the capacities of a normal adult exceed those of a pig, the same cannot be said for all humans. There are many whose mental capacities are severely and tragically impaired, and it follows that if we are prepared to take organs from animals on the grounds of their limited capacities we should also be prepared to take the organs of those humans whose capacities are similarly restricted. Or conversely, if we insist that we should *not* take organs from such humans, then consistency demands that we refrain also from taking the organs of animals with similar or greater capacities.

Against this, AL Caplan argues that humans matter more morally because of their *relationships* with others.

---

[148] See also, RG Frey, 'Medicine, Animal Experimentation, and the Moral Problem of Unfortunate Humans' (1996) 12 Social Philosophy and Policy 181–211.
[149] 'Xenografting: Ethical Issues' (1998) 24 Journal of Medical Ethics 18–24, 23.

AL Caplan[150]

> Severely retarded children and those born with devastating conditions such as anencephaly have never had the capacities and abilities that confer a greater moral standing on humans as compared with animals. Should they be used as the first donors and recipients in xenografting research instead of primates?
>
> The reason they should not has nothing to do with the properties, capacities and abilities of children or infants who lack and have always lacked significant degrees of intellectual and cognitive function. The reason they should not be used is because of the impact using them would have upon other human beings, especially their parents and relatives. A severely retarded child can still be the object of much love, attention, and devotion from his or her parents. These feelings and the abilities and capacities that generate them are deserving of moral respect. Animals do not appear to be capable of such feelings.
>
> If a human mother were to learn that her severely retarded son had been used in lethal xenografting research, she would mourn this fact for the rest of her days. A baboon, monkey, dog or pig would not.

Of course, this argument might lead to the unedifying conclusion that where a profoundly incapacitated individual has no family or friends, then they could legitimately be used for research purposes or organ retrieval, since no-one stands to be harmed by learning that they were used as a means to an end. If we want to argue that friendless people's membership of our species determines that we should treat them differently from animals, are we necessarily grounding this differential treatment in a speciesist ethic?

It might also be argued that we should not address the question of xenotransplantation's ethical legitimacy in isolation from other possible solutions to the shortage of organs, especially since human organs are, at least for the foreseeable future, likely to offer recipients better health prospects than animal organs. We could massively increase the availability of organs if we moved away from a consent model for cadaveric donation, and instead treated the organs of the recently dead as a public resource. This would, admittedly, offend some people's desire to control what happens to their bodies after death, and it could cause distress to their relatives. But animal rights advocates might argue that these harms are relatively trivial when compared with the harm endured by a sentient animal, which is bred in an entirely sterile environment and then killed for its organs.

(c) XENOTRANSPLANTATION IN THE UK

In 1997, the UK Xenotransplantation Interim Regulatory Authority (UKXIRA) was set up, in order to add an additional layer of review to applications to carry out clinical trials involving xenotransplantation. UKXIRA was then disbanded in 2006, partly because no trials were, in fact, taking place, and partly because the system of research ethics governance, considered in Chapter 9, was assumed to offer sufficient safeguards. In announcing the abolition of UKXIRA, the Department of Health issued guidance on the research governance arrangements for xenograft trials.

---

[150] *Am I my Brother's Keeper? The Ethical Frontiers of Biomedicine* (Indiana UP: Bloomington and Indianapolis, 1997) 111.

Department of Health[151]

> The Government believes that it is right to explore the potential of xenotransplantation in a cautious, stepwise fashion. It is extremely important to carry out a xenotransplant procedure in a controlled research context. Clearly, the well-being of the individuals concerned, and the safety of the public in general, must be foremost in the consideration of any proposal to undertake a xenotransplantation procedure. No xenotransplantation procedures involving humans will be allowed to take place unless the approving body is fully satisfied that the evidence put forward is sufficient to justify the particular procedure proposed.
>
> Any proposal for a *clinical trial* of a xenogenic medicinal product requires approval from MHRA, who will assess safety, quality and efficacy. Such proposals must also go for ethical review. Under the Clinical Trials Regulations, ethical review takes place by a recognised ethics committee (REC)....
>
> If the xenogeneic product is genetically modified, investigators should apply to the Gene Therapy Advisory Committee (GTAC) for ethical approval...
>
> Research involving NHS patients that falls outside the Clinical Trials Regulations is also subject to an ethical review by a Research Ethics Committee.

Research involving animals will, as we saw in Chapter 9, also require Home Office authorization.

Williamson *et al.* are critical of the decision to disband UKXIRA. In addition to the concerns expressed in the next extract, they note that, unless the organs are modified in some way after removal from the animal's body, they are very unlikely to amount to 'medicinal products', and hence are unlikely to be subject to the Clinical Trials Regulations and to regulation by the MHRA. They are also concerned that the first uses of xenografts may not come through organized trials, with REC approval, but through clinicians' freedom to use innovative therapies, which have not been properly tested, when the person's condition is extremely grave and there are no other available treatments. As we saw in Chapter 9, this happened in relation to vCJD, with the approval of a court, in the case of *Simms v Simms*.[152]

Laura Williamson, Marie Fox, and Sheila McLean[153]

> While, as we have stressed, updating governance arrangements is to be welcomed in the face of developments in medicine and science, it is important that the drive for modernization does not result in a relaxation of safeguards necessary to protect the individual and the public. Elsewhere in healthcare law the normalization of certain biotechnologies, such as embryo research and IVF, has prompted calls for less state intervention, and a drive toward liberalization may well be a factor in the current review of the law in this area. However, the history of xenotransplantation to date, particularly difficulties in calculating the safety risks that it poses and its potential to transcend regulatory and national borders, should make us wary of acceding to attempts to normalize this technology as simply another form of research. The recent emphasis on promoting the United Kingdom as a centre for biotech research, coupled

---

[151] Xenotransplantation Guidance (DH: London, 2006), available at <www.dh.gov.uk>.

[152] [2002] EWHC 2734 (Fam).

[153] 'The Regulation of Xenotransplantation in the United Kingdom After UKXIRA: Legal and Ethical Issues' (2007) 34 Journal of Law and Society 441–64.

with what Woods has called the 'xenotransplantation imperative' lend weight to the argument that we should hesitate before abolishing an oversight body which, for all its flaws, had positioned the United Kingdom as a leader in this regulatory field.

5 CONCLUSION

As life expectancy increases, the number of people experiencing organ failure will rise, and the shortage of organs available for transplantation looks set to continue. Persuading more people to expressly consent to the use of their organs after death, and increasing the number of living donors will save some lives, but will not eliminate the ever-widening gap between supply and demand.

How could this problem be solved? It is not yet clear whether the ethical and clinical difficulties raised by xenotransplantation can be satisfactorily addressed. In the next chapter, we will encounter another possible 'solution' to the organ shortage, namely the possibilities opened up by stem cell research. Again, it is as yet unclear whether some of the claims made for the clinical application of stem cell research are realistic. In the short-to-medium term then, it is inevitable that people will die while waiting for organs that could save their lives.

It could plausibly be argued that it is extraordinary that we routinely burn or bury organs which could be used to save lives. Of course, taking organs without the consent of the deceased person, or in the face of their relatives' objections, might cause offence and distress, but it is worth remembering that the cost of avoiding this offence and distress is the certain death of identifiable individuals with acute organ failure.

Perhaps regrettably, the emphasis upon patient autonomy and the need for consent has spilled over into the treatment of our bodies after death. I do not mean to suggest that there is no value in respecting an individual's wishes after her death. For many people, exercising control over what happens to their resources and their bodies after they have died is of critical importance. But, in relation to testamentary freedom, the deceased's wishes are not always decisive. If I choose to leave all of my assets to a donkey sanctuary, when this will leave my dependants destitute, my choice can be overridden. In relation to organ donation, could it be argued that the decision to have one's organs burned or buried, when they could be used to save lives, is similarly unfair or immoral? Here we have another interesting example of the difference between legal and moral duties. It would be difficult (though perhaps not impossible) to argue that I have a *legal* duty to donate my organs after death, but the *moral* duty of easy rescue—that is the duty to save a life when to do so would be virtually costless—seems to me to be unarguable.

FURTHER READING

Emson, HE, 'It is Immoral to Require Consent for Cadaver Organ Donation' (2003) 29 Journal of Medical Ethics 125–7.

English, V and Sommerville, A, 'Presumed Consent for Transplantation: A Dead Issue after Alder Hey?' (2003) 29 Journal of Medical Ethics 147–52.

Erin, Charles A and Harris, John, 'An Ethical Market in Human Organs' (2003) 29 Journal of Medical Ethics 137–8.

Haddow, G 'Because You're Worth It? The Taking and Selling of Transplantable Organs' (2006) 32 Journal of Medical Ethics 324–8.

Harris, John, 'Organ Procurement: Dead Interests, Living Needs' (2003) 29 Journal of Medical Ethics 130–4.

Hughes, Jonathan, 'Xenografting: Ethical Issues' (1998) 24 Journal of Medical Ethics 18–24.

Human Tissue Authority <http://www.hta.gov.uk>.

Jacob, Marie-Andrée, 'Another Look at the Presumed-versus-informed Consent Dichotomy in Postmortem Organ Procurement (2006) 20(6) Bioethics 293–300.

Kerridge, IH, Saul, P, Lowe, M, McPhee, J, and Williams, D, 'Death, Dying and Donation: Organ Transplantation and the Diagnosis of Death' (2002) 28 Journal of Medical Ethics 89–94.

Mcguinness, Sheelagh and Brazier, Margaret, 'Respecting the Living Means Respecting the Dead Too' (2008) 28 Oxford Journal of Legal Studies 297–316.

McLean, Sheila and Williamson, Laura, 'Xenotransplantation: A Pig in a Poke?' (2004) 57 Current Legal Problems 443–68.

Nuffield Council on Bioethics, *Animal-to-Human Transplants: The Ethics of Xenotransplantation* (Nuffield Council on Bioethics: London, 1996).

Potts, M and Evans, DW, 'Does it Matter that Organ Donors are Not Dead? Ethical and Policy Implications' (2005) 31 Journal of Medical Ethics 406–9.

Wilkinson, Stephen, *Bodies for Sale: Ethics and Exploitation in the Human Body Trade* (Routledge: London, 2003) ch 7.

Williamson, Laura, Fox, Marie and McLean, Sheila, 'Regulation of Xenotransplantation in the United Kingdom After UKXIRA: Legal and Ethical Issues' (2007) 34 Journal of Law and Society 441–64.

EMBRYO AND STEM
CELL RESEARCH

CENTRAL ISSUES

1. Some people believe that an embryo is a person from the moment of conception. More common is the view that its potential to become a person gives the embryo an intermediate moral status, sometimes described as the need to treat it with a degree of 'respect'.

2. In the UK, embryo research is regulated by the Human Fertilisation and Embryology Act 1990 (HFE Act), as amended, and by the licensing regime of the Human Fertilisation and Embryology Authority (HFEA).

3. The original HFE Act stood the test of time rather well, but between 1990 and 2008, there were a number of new scientific advances, including the birth of Dolly the sheep, the isolation of the first human embryonic stem cell line

and the possibility of creating animal/human hybrid embryos for research. The HFE Act has recently been updated by a substantial amending Act, which received Royal Assent in 2008. The updated Act is in force from October 2009.

4. The Act lays down a number of restrictions on the use of embryos for research: no research can be carried out on an embryo after 14 days; the research must be necessary or desirable for one of the statutory purposes, and the use of embryos must be necessary. This latter restriction means it would not be possible to obtain a licence if the research could be carried out on tissue taken from adults.

---

1 INTRODUCTION

Until relatively recently, it was not possible to create human embryos outside of a woman's body, and so the question of what protection, if any, should be afforded to the early stages of new human life were inextricably bound up with the issue of abortion, considered in the next chapter. Now that eggs can be fertilized *in vitro*, new and difficult questions arise about how the resulting embryos should be treated. In this chapter our focus is upon whether, and in what circumstances, research on human embryos might be acceptable. In order to answer these questions, the potential benefits that may flow from embryo research have to be weighed in the balance with the embryo's moral status, whatever that might be. Some people believe that the respect due to a human embryo will always be incompatible with carrying out experiments upon it, regardless of the potential health benefits, while others believe that properly regulated embryo research is a legitimate scientific endeavour.

Some of the terminology in this chapter may be unfamiliar to law students, so first a brief description of what happens when an embryo is created is given. When an egg (*oocyte*) is fertilized by a sperm, a single cell *zygote* is formed. This then begins the process of cell division. After approximately four to five days, a *blastocyst* is formed, which will contain 50 to 150 cells. At the blastocyst stage it is possible to distinguish between the outer shell or *trophoblast* and the *inner cell mass*. The trophoblast will become the placenta. The inner cell mass at this stage contains *stem cells*. These are *undifferentiated* cells which will subsequently differentiate in order to become skin, bones, brain, blood, organs, etc. As we will see later, scientists have been able to extract these stem cells, and they believe that it will be possible to control this process of *differentiation* in order to reprogramme stem cells to become specialized tissue. Initially, research on embryos was principally directed towards improving assisted conception techniques; however, it is now thought that stem cell research might result in treatments for a wide range of degenerative diseases.

In this chapter, we begin with a brief survey of the philosophical debates over the embryo's moral status. Next, we look at regulation in the UK, where embryo research is regulated by the Human Fertilisation and Embryology Act 1990, as amended, and by the Human Fertilisation and Embryology Authority's licensing regime.

2 WHAT IS THE MORAL STATUS OF THE EMBRYO?

Deciding upon the embryo's moral status is not just an abstract question of philosophy, theology, or morality. As Maureen Junker-Kenny explains, because the embryo's status determines how we should treat it, this is also a question of enormous *practical* importance.

Maureen Junker-Kenny[1]

Any definition of the beginning and end of human personhood is caught up in a hermeneutical circle. We define its starting point because we want to act in a certain way, and we act according to how we have defined it. If we consider the moment of implantation in the uterus, or the presence of brain activity, or the ability to communicate, as the starting-point for ascribing personhood, we are free to use the embryo prior to this stage in any way we consider useful.

Each definition has a practical intent. Once we ascribe human life and personhood to an entity, we want to protect it. If one wants to give maximum protection, one has to use a minimal definition, such as the new genetic unity created by egg and sperm. A maximal definition of human life, such as the ability to communicate, or to act independently, offers minimal protection to the stages prior to these competencies and after they have been lost.

[1] 'The Moral Status of the Embryo' in N Messer (ed.), *Theological Issues in Bioethics: An Introduction with Readings* (Darton, Longman and Todd: London, 2002) 8–75.

(a) IS THE EMBRYO A PERSON?

Because any embryo that is used in research will be destroyed or allowed to perish, if an embryo is a person, research would obviously be unacceptable. While the law is clear that a legal person only exists after a child has been born, some religions, most notably Roman Catholicism, believe that a person comes into being at conception.

Catechism of the Catholic Church

> 2270 Human life must be respected and protected absolutely from the moment of conception.
> 2274 Since it must be treated from conception as a person, the embryo must be defended in its integrity, cared for, and healed, as far as possible, like any other human being.
> 2275 It is immoral to produce human embryos intended for exploitation as disposable biological material.

Interestingly, Catholicism has not always advocated treating embryos as if they were people from the moment of conception. Until the nineteenth century, *ensoulment* was believed to be the point at which the developing fetus achieved humanity, and this took place some time after fertilization. Male fetuses were ensouled at 40 days, and female fetuses at 80 days.

Now, according to the Vatican at least, it is fertilization that is critical. It is, however, worth noting that fertilization does not happen instantly. In normal sexual reproduction, fertilization may not begin until sometime after sexual intercourse, and it can take up to 30 hours for a sperm to fertilize an egg. Implantation—which is when the fertilized egg attaches itself to the woman's body—will not start until about six or seven days later, and may again take several days.

Moreover, an embryo will not autonomously become a baby: rather, this collection of cells will perish unless subsequently implanted in a woman's uterus and carried for at least five months. These are substantial prerequisites: most fertilized eggs fail to implant or to complete their development, and the vast majority of this natural wastage goes unnoticed. Even if a fertilized egg does implant, some of its cells will divide to form the placenta and umbilical cord, which are discarded at birth: this material is obviously not a 'person'. And up to about 14 days after fertilization begins, an embryo may split and become two embryos (which will, if born, be identical twins), so the early human embryo is not necessarily one identifiable human being, but may become two different ones.

In 2008, an updated Papal *Encyclical on Bioethics* was issued, which restated the Church's opposition to all research on embryos.

Congregation for the Doctrine of the Faith[2]

> The obtaining of stem cells from a living human embryo, on the other hand, invariably causes the death of the embryo and is consequently gravely illicit: 'research, in such cases, irrespective of efficacious therapeutic results, is not truly at the service of humanity. In fact, this

---

[2] Instruction *Dignitas Personae* on Certain Bioethical Questions (Vatican, 2008).

research advances through the suppression of human lives that are equal in dignity to the lives of other human individuals and to the lives of the researchers themselves. History itself has condemned such a science in the past and will condemn it in the future, not only because it lacks the light of God but also because it lacks humanity' (Benedict XVI).

It should, however, be noted that not all Catholics disapprove of all research on embryos. In the next extract, Margaret Foley offers a different Catholic perspective.

Margaret Foley[3]

[A] case for human embryo stem cell research can be made on the basis of positions developed within the Roman Catholic tradition. Growing numbers of Catholic moral theologians, for example, do not consider the human embryo in its earliest stages (before development of the primitive streak or implantation) to constitute an individualized human entity with the settled inherent potential to become a human being. In this view the moral status of the embryo is therefore not that of a person, and its use for certain kinds of research can be justified. Since it is, however, a form of life, some respect is due to it; for example, it should not be bought and sold. Those who make this case prefer a return to the centuries-old Catholic position that a certain amount of development is necessary in order for a conceptus to warrant personal status. Embryologic studies now show that fertilization (conception) is itself a process (not a moment), and provide warrant for the opinion that in its earliest stages (including the blastocyst stage, when the inner cell mass is isolated to derive stem cells for purposes of research) the embryo is not sufficiently individualized to bear the moral weight of personhood.

Some adherents to other religions—perhaps most notably Anglicanism and Judaism—believe that, while it is important to treat the human embryo with respect, this is not always incompatible with research. According to the Chief Rabbi's evidence to the House of Lords Select Committee on Stem Cell Research, in certain circumstances Judaism would allow the respect due to the early human embryo to be trumped by the benefits which might flow from research:

In Jewish law neither the foetus nor the pre-implanted embryo is a person; it is, however, human life and must be accorded the respect due to human life. Personhood, with its attendant rights and responsibilities begins at birth. Prior to birth, we have duties to both the embryo and the foetus, but these may, in certain circumstances, be overridden by other duties, namely those we owe to persons.[4]

In particular, given Judaism's clear mandate to promote life and health, research into stem cell therapies, which hold out the hope of curing serious disease and disability, may be permitted.

---

[3] 'Roman Catholic Views on hES Cell Research' in S Holland, K Lebacqz, and Laurie Zoloth (eds), *The Human Embryonic Stem Cell Debate: Science, Ethics and Public Policy* (MIT Press: Cambridge, MA, 2001) 113–18.

[4] Stem Cell Research Report, Feb 2002, available at <www.parliament.the-stationery-office.co.uk/pa/ld200102/ldselect/ldstem/83/8305.htm> para 4.19.

Laurie Zoloth[5]

> The task of healing in Judaism is not only permitted, it is mandated; if stem cells can save a life, then not only can they be used, they must be used...Furthermore, it is mandated to use the best methods available as soon as they are proved efficacious and not dangerous to the patient. Paradoxically, it might violate rabbinic premises to *stop* research if such research is life saving.

In the next extract, however, Søren Holm suggests that the standard liberal claim that embryos lack the criteria we associate with personhood, and that research is therefore justified may prove too much. In particular, it could also be used to defend research on young babies or adults suffering from dementia, on the grounds that they too lack qualities such as consciousness or the capacity to reason.

Søren Holm[6]

> By far the most common pro-stem cell argument is that derivation of human embryonic stem cells is morally innocuous because human embryos have no moral status. By analyzing their characteristics, we can see that they are not persons and that it is not wrong to kill them...
>
> One main problem with this argument is that it proves far too much...First, and perhaps most important, it justifies the (nonpainful) killing and use of any prepersonal human entity from the fertilized egg to the prepersonal infant. Such a killing can be justified by any kind of net benefit to others. In the current context, it can therefore just as easily justify the killing of infants for their stem cells as it can the destruction of embryos for the same purpose. There is no in principle difference between the two killings.
>
> Second, it places no restrictions on the use of biological material from prepersonal human entities that can justify the destruction of these entities, as long as those uses are beneficial. The derivation of a new and effective antiwrinkle cream can therefore be a perfectly acceptable justification for the production and destruction of embryos.

(b) THE ARGUMENT FROM POTENTIAL

Even if we accept that an early human embryo is not a person, it could instead be argued that its special moral status derives from its *potential* to become a person.

John Marshall[7]

> Why then do I oppose experimentation of the kind that I have defined, namely experiments which lead to the destruction of the entity? It is because I regard the potential to become a

---

[5] 'The Ethics of the Eighth Day: Jewish Bioethics and Research on Human Embryonic Stem Cells' in S Holland, K Lebacqz, and Laurie Zoloth (eds), *The Human Embryonic Stem Cell Debate: Science, Ethics and Public Policy* (MIT Press: Cambridge, MA, 2001) 95–111.

[6] 'The Ethical Case Against Stem Cell Research' (2003) 12 Cambridge Quarterly of Healthcare Ethics 372–83.

[7] 'The Case Against Experimentation' in A Dyson and J Harris (eds), *Experiments on Embryos* (Routledge: London, 1990) 55–64.

> human person as of tremendous importance, particularly in our society where there is a cer-
> tain ambivalence about, and paradoxical attitude towards, life. In opposing experimentation
> I recognize and do not hide the fact that some advances in knowledge will be lost, but I do
> assert that those advances are not so great as the scientists would have us believe. I do not
> therefore hold that the gain is commensurate with the loss. This really is the basis of the
> argument...
>
> On this argument, because the entity has the potential to become a person, one affirms
> that it should *not* be interfered with, that *nothing* should be done that prevents it realizing
> that potential, and things *can* be done which will help it to attain that potential. Therefore one
> opposes experimentation.

In contrast, Dan Brock argues that while an entity's potential is relevant to how it should be
treated when it realizes that potential, it does not confer a right to be treated as if the potential were already realized.

D W Brock[8]

> Sam has the potential to run faster than all the other competitors in the race, then he has the
> potential to claim the prize, but he has no actual claim or right to the prize until this potential
> becomes actuality and he has in fact run faster than all the other competitors. Moral rights in
> general have this character—they are grounded in the actual, not just potential, properties of
> a being. So the embryo's potential to become a person is relevant to the moral status it will
> have if and when it does become a person, but it does not confer the moral status on it when
> still an embryo that it will have later when it has become a person.

It is also important to remember that it is factually incorrect to say that all embryos have
the potential to become babies. In IVF, as with natural conception, embryos are commonly
created that are chromosomally or morphologically so abnormal that they have absolutely
no chance of implanting in a woman's womb and developing to term. Does the potentiality
argument then mean that an embryo's moral status differs according to whether it could be
said to be *viable*?

In the next extract, John Harris explains another difficulty with the argument from
potential, namely that gametes (sperm and eggs) also have the potential to become a new
human life. If the embryo is special because it has the potential to become a human being,
then since egg and sperm have the potential to become an embryo, logically they must also
have the potential to become a human being.

John Harris[9]

> There are two sorts of objections to the 'potentiality argument' for the moral significance of
> the embryo. The first is simply that the fact that an entity can undergo changes that will make
> it significantly different does not constitute a reason for treating it as though it had already

---

[8] 'Is a Consensus Possible on Stem Cell Research? Moral and Political Obstacles' (2006) 32 Journal of Medical Ethics 36–42.

[9] 'On the Moral Status of the Embryo' in A Dyson and J Harris (eds), *Experiments on Embryos* (Routledge: London, 1990) 65–81.

undergone those changes. We are all potentially dead, but no-one supposes that this fact constitutes a reason for treating us as if we were already dead.

The second objection is simply that if the potentiality argument suggests that we have to regard as morally significant anything which has the potential to become a fully fledged human being and hence have some moral duty to protect and actualize all human potential, then we are in for a very exhausting time of it. For it is not only the fertilized egg, the embryo that is potentially a full fledged adult. The egg and the sperm taken together but as yet ununited have the same potential as the fertilized egg. For something, or some things, have the potential to become a fertilized egg and whatever has the potential to become an embryo has whatever potential the embryo has.

Of course, the embryo is clearly a significant step further on in the process of becoming a person than a spermatazoa or an unfertilized egg. The mixing of the DNA from the sperm and the egg give it an entirely new genome. It is also true that most human gametes have the potential to be a person only in a rather remote sense. But for the sperm and eggs in a petri dish immediately before fertilization occurs, there is, according to Peter Singer and Karen Dawson, little difference between their potential to become a baby and that of the newly fertilized egg.

Peter Singer and Karen Dawson[10]

IVF has reduced the difference between what can be said about the embryo and what can be said about the egg and sperm, considered jointly. Before IVF, any normal human embryo known to us had a far greater chance of becoming a child than any egg plus sperm prior to fertilization taking place. But with IVF, there is a much more modest difference in the probability of a child resulting from a two-cell embryo in a glass dish, and the probability of a child resulting from an egg and some sperm in a glass dish....

[L]urking in the background of discussions of the embryo's potential is the idea that there is a 'natural' course of events, governed by the 'inherent' potential of the embryo. We have seen, however, that this notion of 'natural' development, not requiring the assistance of a deliberate human act, has no application to the IVF embryo. Hence those who wish to use the potential of the IVF embryo as a ground for protecting it cannot appeal to this notion of natural development; and for this reason, they find themselves in difficulty in explaining why the embryo in the laboratory has a potential so different from that of the egg alone, or the egg and sperm considered jointly. Unless a woman agrees to have an embryo transferred to her uterus, and someone else agrees to perform this transfer, that embryo has no future.

A different sort of problem with the argument from potential is that if the early human embryo's potential to become a human being rules out its destruction, this would also cast doubt on the legitimacy of certain types of contraception, such as the intrauterine device (IUD) and the morning after pill, both of which prevent the implantation of newly fertilized eggs. Indeed, the ordinary oral contraceptive pill also sometimes works by preventing implantation, so if this is illegitimate, the only acceptable form of contraception would be the condom.

---

[10] 'IVF Technology and the Argument from Potential' in P Singer *et al.* (eds), *Embryo Experimentation* (CUP: Cambridge, 1990) 76–89.

In vitro fertilization (IVF) treatment commonly involves the creation of embryos that will never be implanted in a woman, and hence have no chance of becoming a baby. If we believe that postcoital contraceptive techniques and IVF treatment, both of which routinely result in the destruction of embryos, are permissible, it is hard to see why potentially life-saving research on identical embryos should be prohibited.

In the next extract, John Harris goes so far as to argue that anyone who accepts normal sexual reproduction, which inevitably involves the creation and destruction of embryos, should, as a matter of consistency, also accept research on human embryos.

John Harris[11]

We now know that for every successful pregnancy that results in a live birth many, perhaps as many as five, early embryos will be lost or will 'miscarry' (although these are not perhaps 'miscarriages' as the term is normally used because this sort of very early embryo loss is almost always entirely unnoticed). Many of these embryos will be lost because of genetic abnormalities, but some would have been viable.

How are we to think of the decision to attempt to have a child in the light of these facts? One obvious and inescapable conclusion is that God and/or nature has ordained that 'spare' embryos be produced for almost every pregnancy and that most of these will have to die in order that a sibling embryo can come to birth. Thus, the sacrifice of embryos seems to be an inescapable and inevitable part of the process of procreation. It may not be intentional sacrifice, and it may not attend every pregnancy, but the loss of many embryos is the inevitable consequence of the vast majority (perhaps all) pregnancies.

Given that decisions to attempt to have children using sexual reproduction as the method (or even decisions to have unprotected intercourse) inevitably create embryos that must die, those who believe having children or even running the risk of conception is legitimate cannot consistently object to the creation of embryos for comparably important moral reasons....

I am saying that we do as a matter of fact and of sound moral judgment accept the sacrifice of embryos in natural reproduction, because although we might rather not have to sacrifice embryos to achieve a live healthy birth, we judge it to be defensible to continue natural reproduction in the light of the balance between the moral costs and the benefits. And if we make this calculation in the case of normal sexual reproduction we should, for the same reasons, make a similar judgment in the case of the sacrifice of embryos in stem cell research.

Finally, the possibility of human cloning adds some interesting twists to the potentiality argument. We do not yet know whether it will be possible to create cloned human beings using cell nuclear replacement (the technique which was used to create Dolly the sheep). If reproductive cloning is possible, in theory at least, *any cell* could become a new human being. If my skin cell has the potential to become a new person, does this weaken the argument that potentiality confers special moral status?

If, on the other hand, human reproductive cloning is not scientifically possible, then embryos created in this way do not have the potential to become human beings, and hence would not receive special protection, if that protection is grounded in an entity's potentiality.

[11] 'Stem Cells, Sex, and Procreation' (2003) 12 Cambridge Quarterly of Healthcare Ethics 353–71.

(c) THE COMPROMISE POSITION

Most people believe that embryos are in some important sense 'special', but would fall short of according them the same status as people. An embryo is clearly a member of our species, but this does not necessarily require us to treat a four-cell embryo, which cannot be seen with the naked eye, as if it had the same rights and entitlements as a person. The 1984 Warnock Report, which we consider below, embodied this compromise position. It admitted that the instrumental use of the early human embryo will inevitably offend those who believe that a person comes into being immediately after fertilization, but that that offence has to be put into the balance with the benefits which may flow from embryo research. The Warnock Committee recommended that embryo research should be permitted provided that the embryo is not simply treated as a resource for scientists, but is instead accorded proper 'respect'. The compromise view embodied in the Warnock Report formed the basis of the Human Fertilisation and Embryology Act 1990, which is intended to safeguard scientific progress within restrictions, which are designed to indicate that the early human embryo has some intrinsic moral importance, and should not be used frivolously or unnecessarily.

Interestingly, however, Baroness Warnock has since suggested that the report's use of the word 'respect' to describe the treatment of embryos used in research was 'foolish'.

Baroness Warnock[12]

I regret that in the original report that led up to the 1990 legislation we used words such as 'respect for the embryo'. That seems to me to lead to certain absurdities. You cannot respectfully pour something down the sink—which is the fate of the embryo after it has been used for research, or if it is not going to be used for research or for anything else.

I think that what we meant by the rather foolish expression 'respect' was that the early embryo should never be used frivolously for research purposes. That is perfectly exemplified by the regulations that are brought in and the licensing provisions that are looked after by the HFEA. It is the non-frivolity of the research which is conveyed by such expressions as 'respect for' or 'protection for' the embryo.

In contrast, Karen Lebacqz argues that it is possible to treat an embryo that will be used in research with respect:

Karen Lebacqz[13]

I believe that one can indeed speak meaningfully of respecting embryos or embryonic tissue, and that criteria for such respect can be established. Specifically, the tissue must not be treated cavalierly, but as an entity with value . . . To approach something with awe or reverence means that we never become hardened to its intrinsic value, its value apart from us. I suggest that the embryo should not be used cavalierly.

An entity is treated cavalierly if it is demolished without any sense of violation or loss; if it is treated as only one of many and easily replaceable; if its existence is made the butt of jokes

---

[12] Hansard, 5 Dec 2002: col 1327.

[13] 'On the Elusive Nature of Respect' in S Holland, K Lebacqz, and Laurie Zoloth (eds), *The Human Embryonic Stem Cell Debate: Science, Ethics and Public Policy* (MIT Press: Cambridge, MA, 2001)149–62.

or disrespectful stereotyping. Thus, to require that a blastocyst not be treated cavalierly is to require that it be treated as an entity with incredible value; as something precious which cannot be replaced by any other blastocyst, whose existence is to be celebrated and whose loss is to be grieved.

Regardless of whether the word 'respect' is useful or foolish in the context of embryo research, as John Robertson explains in the next extract, the compromise position is not concerned to protect individual human embryos, since these will ultimately be destroyed, but is instead directing towards protecting the *symbolic* value of early human life.

John A Robertson[14]

Many people, for example, reject the view that the embryo is a person but believe that the embryo is different from ordinary human tissue because of the unique potential it has to develop into a new human being. Sometimes described as 'special respect', this attitude towards human embryos shows or symbolizes our respect for human life generally...

In the context of *in vitro* fertilization (IVF) treatment, for example, the generation of more embryos than can be safely transferred to the uterus is widely accepted as not being unduly disrespectful of human life, because it enables children to be born to infertile couples. Similarly, destroying embryos that are left over from IVF procedures to develop cell-replacement therapies should also be ethically acceptable, for the goal of treating disease and saving life justifies the symbolic loss that arises from destroying embryos in the process. By contrast, selling human embryos or using them in cosmetic-toxicology testing seems to be disrespectful of the symbolic meaning that many people attach to embryos because those uses fulfil no life-affirming or other important purpose.

An analogy might helpfully be drawn with research on non-human primates. While not human persons, there is no doubt that primates are regarded as, in some sense, deserving of special consideration. Aside from the great apes, as we saw in Chapter 9, it is possible to use non-human primates in medical research, provided that the research serves an important scientific purpose and could not be done on creatures with lower neurophysiological sensitivity. Dan Brock has suggested that primates, like embryos, have an intermediate moral status: they need not be treated in the same way as human persons, but at the same time it would be unacceptable to use and destroy them for trivial purposes.[15]

One important dimension of the compromise position is that alternatives should always be pursued in preference to embryo research. The destruction of human embryos is therefore permissible only where there are no other ways of carrying out the research. This limiting criterion has become especially significant given scientists' recent progress in inducing pluripotency in adult cells.[16] We consider this further below.

[14] 'Human Embryonic Stem Cell Research: Ethical and Legal Issues' (2001) 2 Nature Reviews Genetics 74–8.

[15] 'Is a Consensus Possible on Stem Cell Research? Moral and Political Obstacles' (2006) 32 Journal of Medical Ethics 36–42.

[16] K Takahashi *et al.*, 'Induction of Pluripotent Stem Cells from Adult Human Fibroblasts by Defined Factors' (2007) 31 Cell 861–72; G Vogel and C Holden, 'Developmental Biology. Field Leaps Forward with New Stem Cell Advances' (2007) 318 Science 1224–5; J Yu *et al.*, 'Induced Pluripotent Stem Cell Lines Derived

(d) MORE ROBUST ARGUMENTS IN FAVOUR OF EMBRYO RESEARCH

The compromise position is based upon a utilitarian calculation: do the good consequences from permitting research outweigh the symbolic harm of disposing of early human life? There are, however, those who believe that any reverence for early human embryos makes little sense. In the next extract Helga Kuhse and Peter Singer argue that embryos do not possess the qualities which ground our respect for persons—such as consciousness and sentience—and that it would therefore be legitimate to use them as a resource for experimentation up to the point at which they can feel pain, which would be several months later than the current fourteen-day limit.

Helga Kuhse and Peter Singer[17]

We believe the minimal characteristic need to give the embryo a claim to consideration is sentience, or the capacity to feel pleasure or pain. Until that point is reached, the embryo does not have any interests and, like other non-sentient organisms (a human egg, for example), cannot be harmed—in a morally relevant way—by anything we do. We can, of course, damage the embryo in such a way as to cause harm to the sentient being it will become, if it lives, but if it never becomes a sentient being, the embryo has not been harmed, because its total lack of awareness means that it never has had any interests at all....

Finally, we point to a curious consequence of restrictive legislation on embryo research. In sharp contrast to the human embryo at this early stage of its existence, non-human animals such as primates, dogs, rabbits, guinea pigs, rats and mice clearly can feel pain, and thus often are harmed by what is done to them in the course of scientific research....Why, then, is it considered acceptable to poison conscious rabbits in order to test the safety of drugs and household chemicals, but not considered acceptable to carry out tests on totally non-sentient human embryos?

In the next extract, Julian Savulescu defends stem cell research on human embryos from an alternative perspective. Even if the embryo *is* a person, Savulescu argues that stem cell research is likely to be of such overwhelming benefit that it would justify killing a few innocent 'persons' for the greater good of everyone.

Julian Savulescu[18]

To employ the Rawlsian veil of ignorance again, I would prefer a world in which I have some chance of being snuffed out as an embryo but a much higher chance of having my fatal diseases successfully treated as an embryo, foetus, child or adult...

from Human Somatic Cells' (2007) 318 Science 1917–20; In-Hyun Park *et al.* 'Reprogramming of Human Somatic Cells to Pluripotency with Defined Factors' (2008) 451 Nature 141.

[17] 'Individuals, Humans and Persons: The Issue of Moral Status' in P Singer *et al.* (eds), *Embryo Experimentation* (CUP: Cambridge, 1990) 65–75.

[18] 'The Embryonic Stem Cell Lottery and the Cannibalization of Human Beings' (2002) 16 Bioethics 508–29.

We are all at risk of death and serious disability. ES cell technology stands to benefit every-one: embryos, children and adults. It is this property which makes it reasonable to kill some embryos to conduct ES cell research even if the embryo is a person…

Opponents of ES cell research will likely remain unconvinced. They will argue that what-ever the benefits, intentionally killing embryos is failing to 'respect human dignity'…

Is it respecting of human dignity to allow people to wither in nursing homes, unable to swallow, speak or move while all the time embryos are destroyed? What more twisted ver-sion of respect for human dignity could there be? It is ES cell research, like organ transplant-ation, that is respectful of human dignity in its reverence for the lives of the living.

Against this, Søren Holm argues that the promise of stem cell therapy may not be as great as is often claimed.

Søren Holm[19]

The benefits that are put into the balance to justify the sacrifice are mainly the therapeutic potential promised by stem cell therapy. The public presentation of the benefits of stem cell research has often been characterized by the promise of huge and immediate benefits. As with many other scientific breakthroughs, the public has been promised real benefits within five to ten years (i.e., in this case, significant stem cell therapies in routine clinical use). Several of the five to ten years have now elapsed, and the promised therapies are still not anywhere close to routine clinical use.…It is likely that many of the current sufferers from some of the conditions for which stem cell therapies have been promised will be long dead before the therapies actually arrive.

3 REGULATION IN THE UK

(a) THE BACKGROUND TO THE HUMAN FERTILISATION AND EMBRYOLOGY ACT 1990

Research into the possibility of *in vitro* fertilization started in the first half of the twentieth century. In 1969, Bob Edwards, Barry Bavister, and Patrick Steptoe published a ground-breaking paper in *Nature*, in which they reported that they had successfully fertilized human oocytes *in vitro*.[20] With hindsight, the paper's tentative suggestion that 'There may be certain clinical and scientific uses for human eggs fertilized by this procedure' seems an example of breathtaking understatement.

Nine years later, in July 1978, the first IVF baby, Louise Brown, was born in Oldham. Her birth prompted the government to assemble a committee, chaired by Mary Warnock, to consider how both embryo research and fertility treatment should be regulated. The Committee started its deliberations in 1982, and issued its final report in 1984. On the question of embryo research, the Committee was divided, and the minority issued a formal expression of dissent.

[19] 'The Ethical Case Against Stem Cell Research' (2003) 12 Cambridge Quarterly of Healthcare Ethics 372–83.

[20] 'Early Stages of Fertilization In Vitro in Human Oocytes Matured In Vitro' (1969) 221 Nature 632–35.

A year after the publication of the Warnock report, a private member's Bill, the Unborn Children (Protection) Bill, which would have banned all embryo research, attracted considerable parliamentary support. On its second reading 238 MPs voted in favour, and 66 against. Only lack of parliamentary time prevented it from becoming law. The following year, the Unborn Children (Protection) Bill was re-introduced, and despite again commanding a significant parliamentary majority, it too failed for lack of parliamentary time.

By the end of the 1980s, public and parliamentary attitudes to embryo research had changed. In part, this was a result of greater understanding of exactly what embryo research involves. A six-cell embryo is invisible to the naked eye, and even by the two-hundred cell stage, it is still no bigger than a pin head. The Act itself embodied the Warnock Report's compromise position, restricting the circumstances in which embryo research is permissible. In 2004, when the government announced its intention to introduce new legislation to update the 1990 Act, it was made clear that it did not intend to reopen the question of whether embryo research is legitimate. The existing regulatory regime would simply be updated in order to accommodate scientific developments since 1990.

(b) THE DEFINITION OF AN EMBRYO

Section 1(1)(a) of the original version of the Human Fertilisation and Embryology Act 1990 appeared to contain a statutory definition of the word 'embryo'. It stated that, 'in this Act, except where otherwise stated, embryo means a live human embryo where fertilisation is complete'. This wording has come under particular scrutiny in relation to two new ways of creating embryos: cloning and the creation of animal/human hybrids.

(1) Cloned Embryos

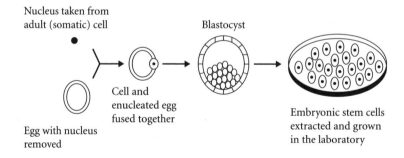

The statutory wording in section 1(1)(a) first came under pressure after the birth of Dolly the sheep was reported in 1997. Dolly had been created through a technique known as cell nuclear replacement (CNR). This involves removing the nucleus from an egg, and inserting a cell taken from an adult into the denucleated egg. An electric current is used to trick it into beginning the process of cell division. As we see later, CNR may have particular significance for stem cell research. This process undoubtedly leads to the creation of embryos, but it does not involve fertilization, and so would not appear to fall within section 1(1)(a)'s statutory 'definition'.

This apparent gap between the statutory wording and the procedure involved in Dolly's creation was the subject of a judicial review action brought by Bruno Quintavalle, on behalf of the Pro-life Alliance. He claimed that the definition of 'embryo' in the 1990 Act did not cover embryos created by CNR. If he was right about this, then creating embryos in this way would fall outside the statutory regime, and be entirely unregulated. This was not, of course, Bruno Quintavalle's preferred outcome. Rather, he wanted Parliament to revisit the regulation of embryo research, with the hope that this would result in a more restrictive piece of legislation.

At first instance, Bruno Quintavalle succeeded. The government had argued that the subsection should be read as if it read: 'a live human embryo where [if it is produced by fertilisation] fertilisation is complete', but Crane J held that the words were not sufficiently ambiguous to allow him to ignore their clear meaning. Following his judgment, emergency legislation was immediately passed to ban reproductive cloning, but the question of the legality of cloning for research purposes remained. The government appealed successfully to the Court of Appeal, and, in *R (on the application of Quintavalle) v Secretary of State for Health*, the House of Lords dismissed Bruno Quintavalle's appeal.

R (on the application of Quintavalle) v Secretary of State for Health[21]

Lord Bingham

Does the creation of live human embryos by CNR fall within the same genus of facts as those to which the expressed policy of Parliament has been formulated? In my opinion, it plainly does. An embryo created by in vitro fertilisation and one created by CNR are very similar organisms. The difference between them as organisms is that the CNR embryo, if allowed to develop, will grow into a clone of the donor of the replacement nucleus which the embryo produced by fertilisation will not. But this is a difference which plainly points towards the need for regulation, not against it....

Is the embryo created by CNR different in kind or dimension from that for which the Act was passed? Plainly not: as already pointed out, the organisms in question are, as organisms, very similar. While it is impermissible to ask what Parliament would have done if the facts had been before it, there is one important question which may permissibly be asked: it is whether Parliament, faced with the taxing task of enacting a legislative solution to the difficult religious, moral and scientific issues mentioned above, could rationally have intended to leave live human embryos created by CNR outside the scope of regulation had it known of them as a scientific possibility. There is only one possible answer to this question and it is negative.

Lord Steyn

The long title of the 1990 Act makes clear, and it is in any event self-evident, that Parliament intended the protective regulatory system in connection with human embryos to be comprehensive. This protective purpose was plainly not intended to be tied to the particular way in which an embryo might be created. The overriding ethical case for protection was general.... For my part I am fully satisfied that cell nuclear replacement falls within the scope of the carefully balanced and crafted 1990 Act.

---

[21] [2003] UKHL 13.

Lord Millett

The definition in para (a) is in part circular, since it contains the very term to be defined. It assumes that the reader knows what an embryo is. The purpose of the opening words of the paragraph is not to define the word 'embryo' but rather to limit it to an embryo which is (i) live and (ii) human. These are the essential characteristics which an embryo must possess if it is to be given statutory protection. The important point is that these characteristics are concerned with what an embryo is, not how it is produced....

 This construction does not require words to be written into the section. There is no gap to be filled by implication. Nor is it a matter of updating the meaning of the word embryo by reference to subsequent developments. It is simply a matter of giving the opening words of para (a) their natural meaning...Once it is accepted that the embryo is defined by reference to what it is and not by reference to the process by which it is created, all need for updating falls away. The result is to bring within the regulatory scope of the Act embryos produced by a process which was unknown to Parliament when the Act was passed. But such embryos are in all respects save the method of their creation indistinguishable from other embryos. They are alive and human, and accordingly possess all the features which Parliament evidently considered make it desirable to regulate their use for treatment or research. A construction which allowed for the regulation of embryos produced by fertilisation and not of embryos produced without fertilisation would not only defeat the evident purpose of Parliament to make comprehensive provision for the creation and use of human embryos but would produce an incoherent and irrational regulatory code. While this could be the inevitable result of legislation enacted at a time of rapid technological development, a construction which leads to this result should not be adopted where it can be avoided.

The House of Lords did not admit to having had to strain the language in the statute. Instead, it took the view that section 1(1)(a) was not intended to offer a special statutory redefinition of the word 'embryo'. Rather, the 'ordinary language' meaning of the word embryo (which would undoubtedly include embryos created through CNR) must have been taken for granted by the statutory draftsman because the definition is 'a live human *embryo* where fertilisation is complete', which itself contains the word it is supposed to define, with no further elaboration. The important words in this phrase, according to Lord Millett, are 'live' and 'human'—this is the *sort* of embryo that is regulated by the statute—so dead and/ or animal embryos are plainly not covered.

 Unsurprisingly, the 2008 amendments to the 1990 Act remove the reference to fertilization. Section 1(1) now reads: 'In this Act...embryo means a live human embryo and does not include a human admixed embryo.' As with the previous legislation, embryos that are in the process of creation, whether by fertilization or otherwise, are brought within regulation as well by section 1(1)(b).

(2) Hybrid Embryos

Notice the reference in the amended Act to 'human admixed embryos'. These are not covered by section 1(1)(a), but can be created for research purposes, under section 4A. 'Admixed' is the term the legislature has chosen to use to refer to animal/human hybrid embryos. At the moment, the only type of admixed embryos that scientists are interested in creating are ones created through cell nuclear replacement (CNR), using denucleated animal eggs and human nuclear DNA (these have also been referred to as cytoplasmic hybrid embryos).

These embryos contain only mitochondrial animal DNA (this is the DNA in the outer 'shell' of the denucleated egg). The embryos themselves will be 99.9 per cent human, and any stem cell lines extracted from them will be 100 per cent human.

The reason for wanting to use animal eggs in this way is that human eggs are in short supply. The process of egg donation is intrusive and women are not paid. It is therefore unsurprising that very few women are likely to want to donate their eggs for research. Moreover, the process of deriving stem cell lines from embryos is currently extremely inefficient—it has been estimated that there is a success rate of 0.7 per cent in primates.[22] Some scientists have argued that it would be foolish, or even unethical, to use scarce human eggs to perfect these techniques, and hence that it is sensible to pursue this sort of basic research on animal eggs, retrieved from abattoirs, which can readily be obtained in large numbers.

The HFEA had already determined, in September 2007, following an intensive public consultation exercise, that licensing the creation of this sort of hybrid embryo lay within its statutory powers under the original legislation. Because such embryos contain a full nuclear human genome, it was determined that they too were both live and human, and hence covered by regulation. Drawing upon the House of Lords judgment in *Quintavalle*, the HFEA decided that these embryos are within the same 'genus of fact' as other embryos covered by the 1990 Act, in particular that embryos created in this way have a full human nuclear genome and are live.

The HFEA also took into account that Parliament's intention was for the regulatory scheme to be comprehensive. In Lord Bingham's words, 'there was to be no free for all'. If human admixed embryos were *not* covered by the 1990 Act, then there could be no restrictions upon their creation. They would not be subject to Home Office regulation, since this would not be seen as research on animals. As a result, if not covered by the 1990 Act, scientists could mix animal and human material in this way in their garden sheds, if they so wished, and then do whatever they liked to them.

The HFEA's research licence committee issued the first two licences for research projects which intended to use animal eggs to create admixed embryos in January 2008, and a third one was licensed a few months later. Scientists announced in April 2008 that they had successfully created the first animal/human hybrid embryo.

The decision to grant the first licences to carry out research using animal eggs was then challenged in the courts. Comment on Reproductive Ethics (CORE)—whose chair is Bruno Quintavalle's mother Josephine—and the Christian Legal Centre sought judicial review of the research licence committee's decision on the grounds that the HFEA had acted outside of its powers. Their claim was that these sorts of embryos cannot be described as 'human' and therefore the 1990 Act did not apply.

Before the case came before the court, Parliament had enacted the 2008 amendments to the 1990 Act, although they were not yet in force. The creation of admixed embryos was one of the most controversial provisions in the amending legislation, and MPs were given a free vote on the issue. A majority voted in favour, and so the amended Act specifically permits the creation of human admixed embryos for research purposes, subject to all of the ordinary restrictions discussed below, such as not keeping embryos for longer than 14 days.

The fact that Parliament had expressed its intention to permit the creation of human admixed embryos made it difficult for the applicants to argue that what the HFEA had done went against Parliament's intention. In December 2008, in *R (on the application of*

---

[22] S Minger, 'Interspecies SCNT-derived Human Embryos—A New Way Forward for Regenerative Medicine' (2007) 2 Regenerative Medicine 103–6.

Quintavalle and CLC) v HFEA, Dobbs J refused to grant permission for leave to apply for judicial review of the decision to grant the first two licences, describing the application as 'entirely without merit'.

The 1990 Act did not define 'human', and Dobbs LJ thought that the HFEA's legal advice—namely that it should take a cautious approach and treat such embryos as human to ensure that they are regulated—was in accordance with the spirit and purpose of the 1990 Act. She also noted that Parliament had made its intention in relation to hybrid embryos clear, and that the scientists who had received the first two licences to carry out this research would, even if the original licence committee decision was struck down, be able to re-apply for their licences when the new Act came into force in October 2009.

R (on the application of Quintavalle and CLC) v HFEA[23]

Dobbs J

The Act did not seek to define 'human embryo'. What is 'human' will be dependent on the particular facts of any case and informed by scientific knowledge at the time. I do not accept the claimants' submission, that the fact that this technique is in a separate category under the new Act, means that Parliament did not intend it to fall within the definition of 'human embryo' under section 1 of the 1990 Act. The technique was unknown and not envisaged at the time. What is clear, as I have already found, is that regulation of these activities was important. The approach advocated by the defendant's lawyers in the advice of November 2007—namely to take a cautious approach by treating the technique as coming within regulation—is, in my judgment, in accordance with the spirit and purpose of the 1990 Act...

It would be futile to suggest that the licence be revoked for what might be a matter of months, with the attendant disruption to the third parties, whilst knowing full well that Parliament intends such work to be subject to regulation by the defendant, who has the power to grant licences in appropriate cases. To be expending the court's time and resources, as well as those of the defendants and the interested parties, bodies relying to some degree on public funding, in debating what Parliament intended, is not in the interests of good administration, in my judgment; the more so, when it is now known what Parliament intends in this regard.

(c) THE UK'S RESTRICTIONS ON EMBRYO RESEARCH

The restrictions placed upon embryo research, discussed in the following sections, are intended to embody the compromise position embodied in the Warnock report, namely to ensure that valuable scientific research can take place within limits which are designed to show some 'respect' for the early human embryo, or to ensure its non-frivolous treatment.

Responsibility for ensuring that research on embryos only takes place within these limits lies with the HFEA's research licence committee. This is a committee made up of HFEA members whose role is to determine whether a licence application fits within the limits set out in the legislation. They receive legal advice, reports from peer reviewers and information gathered by the HFEA's inspectors. Licences are normally granted for three years, although for novel projects, twelve-month licences are the norm so that the licence committee has a greater opportunity to monitor the researchers' progress.

---

[23] [2008] EWHC 3395 (Admin).

(1) The 14-day Limit

Under the Act, no research can be carried out on an embryo after 14 days. This time limit was chosen because it is at about 14 days that what is known as the 'primitive streak' first appears. The primitive streak is a heaping up of cells which will eventually become the spinal column, and the Warnock report described it as 'one reference point in the development of the human individual'.[24] Fourteen days is also the last point at which twinning can occur, so before this time it is not clear whether the embryo will become one individual or two (though of course, the embryo used in research has no chance of becoming an individual).

Mary Warnock[25]

Fourteen days was decided on as the limit because of the great change in the development of the embryo heralded by the development of the primitive streak. It is only after that that an individual exists with its own now quickly developing central nervous system, its own limbs, its own brain. Even though before that an embryo has a genetic individuality, it has no pattern of human identity, any more than human tissue has. The history of each person who is born can be traced back to the development of the primitive streak and not before. Before that there could have been two or three people formed of the same material. It is because of the enormous change that comes at this stage of development that scientists generally prefer to think of the embryos as actually beginning to exist at this stage. Before that there is the egg and the sperm, and the *conceptus*, that which comes from their conjunction. All these, egg sperm and conceptus are human (that is, they differ from the eggs, sperm and conceptus of other animals) and are of course alive, but are not yet distinct embryos.

Others would contest the idea that something special happens to the embryo at 14 days. Bernard Williams, for example, suggests that the 14-day limit does not reflect a relevant characteristic in the embryo itself, but is instead simply a reasonable regulatory response to a slippery slope argument against embryo research. The limit could equally well, Williams implies, have been drawn a bit earlier or later, but that does not undermine the value of choosing to draw a line somewhere.

Bernard Williams[26]

Is drawing a line in this way reasonable? Can it be effective? The answer to both these questions seems to me to be 'yes, sometimes', and, as that unexciting reply suggests, there is not a great deal to be brought to deciding them beyond good sense and relevant information. It may be said that a line of this kind cannot possibly be reasonable since it has to be drawn between two adjacent cases in the range, that is to say, between two cases that are not

---

[24] The Warnock Report (1984): Report of the Committee of Enquiry into Human Fertilisation and Embryology (London: HMSO, 1984) para 11.22.
[25] 'Experimentation on Human Embryos and Fetuses' in H Kuhse and P Singer, *A Companion to Bioethics* (Blackwell: Oxford, 1998) 390–6.
[26] 'Types of Moral Argument Against Embryo Research' in The Ciba Foundation, *Human Embryo Research: Yes or No?* (Tavistock: London, 1986) 184–94.

different enough to distinguish. The answer is that they are indeed not different enough to distinguish if that means that their characteristics, unsupported by anything else, would have led one to draw a line there. But though the line is not, in this sense, uniquely reasonable, it is nevertheless reasonable to draw a line there. This follows from the conjunction of three things. First, it is reasonable to distinguish in some way unacceptable cases from acceptable cases; second, the only way of doing that in these circumstances is to draw a sharp line; third, it cannot be an objection to drawing the line just here that it would have been no worse to draw it somewhere else—if that were an objection, then one could conclude that one had no reason to draw it anywhere.

Dan Brock makes a similar point, drawing an analogy between the 14-day limit on research and setting the voting age at 18.[27] Both lines are inevitably arbitrary. There is no essential moral difference in the status of the embryo at 13 days and at 15. Likewise, a person does not miraculously acquire the capacity to exercise sound political judgement on their 18th birthday. However, in both cases drawing a line somewhere is desirable, and, in the context of embryo research, 14 days is judged a reasonable time limit.

Many other countries, such as Australia, Japan, and Singapore, have also adopted a 14-day limit. Currently, there is little pressure from scientists to extend this limit because it has proved impossible to keep an embryo alive *in vitro* beyond about nine days. If, or perhaps when, this becomes feasible, scientists may argue more vigorously that the 14-day limit is an arbitrary cut-off point, capable of stifling valuable research.

(2) The Sources of Embryos

There are two possible sources of embryos for use in research. First, research might be carried out on embryos that are left over after a couple have had fertility treatment. This happens in one of two ways. During an ordinary IVF cycle, it is common for couples to produce more embryos than the one or two (or in rare circumstances, three) which will be transferred in one treatment cycle. Spare embryos which are suitable for use in future cycles will usually be frozen. Often there will also be embryos which are of poor quality, and unsuitable for use or freezing. Unless they are donated to research, these will have to be discarded.

After their family is complete, or perhaps after they have separated, a couple may decide that they no longer wish to store their frozen embryos for their own treatment. At that point, they can be destroyed, donated for the treatment of others, or again donated for research. Most embryo research in the UK is carried out on these two sorts of 'spare' IVF embryos, donated by couples who have undergone fertility treatment.

In the next extract, Sarah Franklin explains that these spare embryos have what she describes as a dual reproductive identity. They were created in order to become children, but once they become 'spare' or 'leftover' they have a different sort of potential. Because the existence of IVF treatment is dependent upon embryo research, many couples feel that donating their leftover embryos to research is a way of 'giving something back'.

---

[27] 'Is a Consensus Possible on Stem Cell Research? Moral and Political Obstacles' (2006) 32 Journal of Medical Ethics 36–42.

Sarah Franklin[28]

> [T]he embryos that form the basis for hES [human embryonic stem cell] derivation and banking have a *dual reproductive identity*: their reproductive past, or pedigree, is determined by their production in the context of the highly emotive and labour-intensive process of IVF—a procedure that usually fails. Their reproductive future, or potential, lies in the capacity of science to transform the vital power of individual cells into colonies of regenerative cells...
>
> The factors that influence couples' decisions to donate embryos to stem cell research, or not to, vary and are not well understood. Some couples may be particularly keen to donate their embryos to stem cell research as a result of the publicity and excitement surrounding this field, whereas for others such publicity may arouse suspicion....
>
> Embryo donation rates in the UK are high, and this is often correlated in studies of donor motivations to a sense of obligation to 'give something back'. A research project undertaken at the Guy's and St Thomas' Centre for PGD to find out more about factors affecting patient perceptions of embryo donation to stem cell research which ran from 2002 to 2005 identified a 67% rate of willingness to donate, of whom more than 80% expressed a desire to 'give something back'.

Secondly, embryos could be specifically created for use in research. This might be necessary, first, if scientists want to create embryos with particular characteristics, such as a specific genetic disease. It will not be possible to control the characteristics of embryos which are left over from IVF treatment, but by using cells taken from people with particular genetic conditions to create embryos, it will be possible to carry out disease-specific research, most commonly on stem cell lines, extracted from these embryos. Secondly, if scientists wish to create embryos using cell nuclear replacement, or cloning, there will obviously not be any embryos left over after fertility treatment, since reproductive cloning is a criminal offence, and so it would be necessary to create embryos specifically for this sort of research.

Is there a moral difference between conducting research on spare IVF embryos and creating embryos with the express purpose of carrying out experiments upon them? Clearly, many people believe so, but why? The House of Lords Stem Cell Research Committee suggested that where the initial intention is to create a baby, the embryo is less instrumentalized than where the sole intention is to create an embryo in order to use it in research.

House of Lords Stem Cell Research Committee[29]

> 4.27 The creation of embryos (whether by IVF or CNR) for research purposes raises difficult issues. Some argue that, if an embryo is destined for destruction, it is more honest to create it specifically for the purpose of research than to use one created for reproductive purposes. But most of those who commented on this issue regarded it as preferable to use surplus embryos than to create them specifically for research. They took the view that an embryo created for research was quite clearly being used as a means to an end, with no prospect of implantation, whereas at the time of creation the surplus embryo had a prospect of implantation, even if, once not selected for implantation (or freezing), it would have to be

---

[28] 'Embryonic Economies: The Double Reproductive Value of Stem Cells' (2006) 1 BioSocieties 71–90.

[29] Stem Cell Research Report, Feb 2002, available at <www.parliament.the-stationery-office.co.uk/pa/ld200102/ldselect/ldstem/83/8305.htm>.

> destroyed. We agree that for this reason it is preferable to use surplus embryos for research purposes if the same results can be achieved with them. It is currently unavoidable that there should be some surplus embryos from IVF treatment, although desirable that the numbers should be reduced as more effective techniques are developed.

In contrast, Erik Parens argues that it is unusual to base an entity's moral status upon the intention of its creator.

Erik Parens[30]

> One ethical intuition that seems to motivate the discarded-created distinction is that whereas the act of creating an embryo for reproduction is respectful in a way that is commensurate with the moral status of embryos, the act of creating an embryo for research is not... In this view, the moral status of the embryo (and thus the moral status of research on it) is a function of the intention of its maker. The problem with this intuition is that it is difficult to see what the intention of the maker of something has to do with the moral status of that thing once it has come into being. We do not think, for example, that the moral status of children is a function of their parents' intentions at the time of conception. If what something is obliges us to treat it some ways and not others, how it came to being is usually thought to be morally irrelevant.

Unlike many other countries, in the UK the use of spare IVF embryos *and the creation of research embryos* are both permissible. Under Schedule 2(3)(1)(a) of the 1990 Act, as amended, a research licence may authorize 'bringing about the creation of embryos in vitro... for the purposes of a project of research'. But, this does not mean that scientists in the UK are free to create as many research embryos as they like. There is no numerical limit upon the creation of embryos for research purposes in the Act, but in deciding whether to grant a licence, the HFEA's licence committee must be satisfied that the creation of embryos is *necessary*.

Human Fertilisation and Embryology Authority[31]

2005–7	Number used
Fresh eggs	368
Frozen eggs	64
Failed to fertilise eggs	2,432
Fresh embryos (not suitable for use in treatment or for freezing)	5,994
Frozen embryos (which a couple decide not to use themselves)	2,146
Created embryos	429

[30] 'On the Ethics and Politics of Embryonic Stem Cell Research' in S Holland, K Lebacqz, and Laurie Zoloth (eds), *The Human Embryonic Stem Cell Debate: Science, Ethics and Public Policy* (MIT Press: Cambridge, MA, 2001) 37–50.

[31] *Human Embryo Research in the UK 2006–7* (HFEA, 2007), available at <www.hfea.gov.uk>.

As is evident from the table above, the vast majority of research on embryos in the UK is carried out on embryos that are donated by couples either because they are not suitable for use in treatment, or because the couple has decided that they no longer wish to use their frozen embryos in future treatment cycles. Likewise, the majority of eggs used in research are donated because they are not suitable for use in treatment.

(3) The Purposes of Research: Stem Cell Research and Therapeutic Cloning

A further restriction on the use of embryos in research is that they can be used only for certain purposes. The restrictions are contained in Schedule 2 of the Act, as amended:

The Human Fertilisation and Embryology Act 1990 Schedule 2

2(3A) (1) A licence under paragraph 3 cannot authorise any activity unless the activity appears to the Authority—

(a) to be necessary or desirable for any of the purposes specified in sub-paragraph (2) ("the principal purposes")

(b) to be necessary or desirable for the purpose of providing knowledge that, in the view of the Authority, may be capable of being applied for the purposes specified in sub-paragraph (2)(a) or (b), or

(c) to be necessary or desirable for such other purposes as may be specified in regulations.

(2) The principal purposes are -

(a) increasing knowledge about serious disease or other serious medical conditions,

(b) developing treatments for serious disease or other serious medical conditions,

(c) increasing knowledge about the causes of any congenital disease or congenital medical condition that does not fall within paragraph (a),

(d) promoting advances in the treatment of infertility,

(e) increasing knowledge about the causes of miscarriage,

(f) developing more effective techniques of contraception,

(g) developing methods for detecting the presence of gene, chromosome or mitochondrion abnormalities in embryos before implantation, or

(h) increasing knowledge about the development of embryos.

(a) The 'necessity' principle

It is important to remember that scientists are not entitled to a licence just because they want to do research that falls within one of the specified purposes. Licences can be granted only if the licence committee is satisfied that the research is 'necessary or desirable' for one of these purposes, *and* that the proposed use of embryos is 'necessary' (sometimes referred to as the necessity principle). All research licence applications are peer-reviewed, and the reviewers are asked to confirm both that the research is necessary or desirable for one of the specified purposes, and that the use of embryos is necessary.

The licence committee must be satisfied that the research could not be done *without* using human embryos, and the peer reviewers are asked to confirm whether this is the case. This means that if it were possible to conduct the research on animals or on tissue taken from adults, the licence committee could not be satisfied that the use of embryos was *necessary*, and no licence could be granted.

The 'necessity principle' is fairly easily satisfied where the research is directed towards improving IVF techniques. Research into new freezing methods or new techniques for pre-implantation genetic diagnosis can only discover their impact upon the human embryo if human embryos are used in the research.

Until relatively recently, research scientists who wanted to carry out human embryonic stem cell (hES) research could also satisfy the necessity principle comparatively easily. Recently, however, scientists have had remarkable success in inducing adult cells to act in the same way as embryonic stem cells. If a proposed stem cell research project could be carried out on these induced pluripotent stem cells (iPS), rather than embryonic stem cells, then it would not be possible to establish that the use of embryos is *necessary*. So far, pluripotency can only be induced in adult cells with the help of viral factors, which mean that cells derived in this way would not be suitable for clinical use. It has been estimated that around 20 per cent of such cells are carcinogenic.

Many scientists believe that hES research and research on iPS cells should continue in parallel, since iPS cells have not yet obviated the need to understand more about embryonic stem cell lines. Nevertheless, it is clear that the development of iPS cells has intensified the debate between opponents and defenders of research on embryos, since opponents now have a further source of opposition to this sort of research. In the past, their arguments were largely limited to the claim that embryo research is unethical. Now they further argue that such research may be *unnecessary*.

An interesting twist to the triumphant claims made for iPS cells by opponents of embryo research is described in the next extract. With appropriate reprogramming iPS cells might themselves be able to *become embryos* which, far from solving the debates over the instrumental use of human embryos, might create new dilemmas.

R M Green[32]

Nor is it clear that this technology really solves the ethical problem of embryo destruction that has generated the opposition to hES cell research. iPS cell technology brings an adult cell back to its pluripotent embryonic state. As the work of Nagy and others has shown, with appropriate technical manipulations and sufficient support, such a cell might have the potential to develop into a human being. Since opponents of stem cell research and therapeutic cloning research usually base their arguments for the sanctity of fertilised or nuclear transfer embryos on precisely this kind of developmental capacity, it is not clear why they have not voiced similar concerns about iPS cell technology....

The opponents of hES cell research—now enthusiasts for iPS cell research—appear less concerned about the lives of the entities that could become people than with declaring victory in a cultural war.

---

[32] 'Embryo as Epiphenomenon: Some Cultural, Social and Economic Forces Driving the Stem Cell Debate' (2008) 34 Journal of Medical Ethics 840–44.

(b) Extending the research purposes

Notice that the Schedule builds in the possibility of the statute's revision by regulations that can extend the purposes for which embryo research may be carried out. This is an attempt to 'future-proof' the legislation, in case unanticipated research purposes subsequently emerge. The original legislation contained a similar provision, which was used in 2001 to extend the research purposes—which initially only covered advances in reproduction—to include the goals of hES research.

As we have seen, embryonic stem cells are undifferentiated cells that are capable of becoming all the specialized cells in the body. The inner cell mass of the early human embryo contains stem cells of remarkable plasticity. The first embryonic stem cells are totipotent, which means that they can become *every* cell in the human body, and even a whole new human organism. Later on, embryonic stem cells become pluripotent, which means they are capable of differentiating into several different types of cell. Stem cells are also immortal: they can continue to divide indefinitely without losing their genetic structure. In 1998, researchers at the University of Wisconsin published a paper explaining how they had, for the first time, derived and cultured a human embryonic stem cell line.[33]

Scientists think that it may become possible to trick these stem cell lines into differentiating into different types of tissue, which could then be used to repair damaged tissues or organs. When coupled with cell nuclear replacement (CNR), considered above, the possibilities become more remarkable still. Therapeutic cloning would involve the extraction of embryonic stem cells from cloned embryos. If the embryo from which embryonic stem cells are removed was cloned from the person with a damaged organ, the replacement tissue would be a perfect genetic match, and there would be no possibility of rejection.

For example, imagine that I need some replacement tissue—perhaps because I have a degenerative brain disease such as Parkinson's. If a cloned embryo is created from my skin cell, the stem cells, and any brain tissue grown as a result, will be genetically identical to me. This removes the problem of rejection, and the need to suppress the recipient's immune systems with immuno-suppressant drugs. If this process were to become relatively straightforward, it potentially offers a solution to the organ shortage we considered in the previous chapter: anyone whose organs had failed could simply use therapeutic cloning in order to produce genetically compatible replacement tissue.

(c) Artificial gametes?

Of course, if it is possible to create any human cell type from a stem cell line, it will also be possible to create reproductive cells, or gametes, from stem cell lines.[34] Experiments on mice have shown that it is possible to derive functioning artificial gametes from both embryonic and bone marrow stem cell lines,[35] and scientists are currently attempting to create the first artificial human sperm and ova.[36] In 2008, the Hinxton Group, an international

---

[33] JA Thomson *et al.*, 'Embryonic Stem Cell Lines Derived from Human Blastocysts' (1998) 282 Science 1145–7.

[34] See further G Testa and J Harris, 'Ethics and Synthetic Gametes' (2005) 19 Bioethics 146.

[35] K Hübner *et al.*, 'Derivation of Oocytes from Mouse Embryonic Stem Cells' (2003) 300 Science 1251–6.

[36] Nayernia *et al.*, 'Derivation of Male Germ Cells from Bone Marrow Stem Cells' (2006) 86 Laboratory Investigation 654–63; Nayernia *et al.*, 'In Vitro-differentiate Embryonic Stem Cells Give Rise to Male Gametes that can Generate Offspring Mice' (2006) 11 Developmental Cell 125–32; Steve O'Connor, 'The Prospect of All-female Conception' The Independent, 13 April 2007.

consortium interested in the interface between stem cell research, ethics, and law, made some predictions about the timescale for the development of gametes from pluripotent stem cells (PSCs):

Hinxton Group[37]

> Based on published data and theoretical considerations, it is probable that human eggs and sperm will be derived partly or entirely in vitro from PSCs. The pace of scientific progress is difficult to predict. Unanticipated findings can either accelerate or slow the pace of progress. With this caveat, the derivation of human eggs and sperm in vitro from PSCs, in whole or at least in part, is anticipated within 5 to 15 years.

Given this timescale, it is therefore likely that human eggs and sperm will be generated from stem cell lines during the lifetime of the amended 1990 Act. The 2008 amendments specifically allows artificial gametes to be created for research purposes, but not for use in treatment. They achieve this by allowing o nly 'permitted embryos' and 'permitted eggs and sperm' to be used in treatment services.

Human Fertilisation and Embryology Act 1990 sections 3 and 3ZA

> Section 3(2) No person shall place in a woman—
>
> (a) an embryo other than a permitted embryo (as defined by section 3ZA), or
>
> (b) any gametes other than permitted eggs or permitted sperm (as so defined).....
>
> Section 3ZA
> (2) A permitted egg is one—
>
> (a) which has been produced by or extracted from the ovaries of a woman, and
>
> (b) whose nuclear or mitochondrial DNA has not been altered.
>
> (3) Permitted sperm are sperm—
>
> (a) which have been produced by or extracted from the testes of a man, and
>
> (b) whose nuclear or mitochondrial DNA has not been altered.
>
> (4) An embryo is a permitted embryo if—
>
> (a) it has been created by the fertilisation of a permitted egg by permitted sperm.
>
> (b) no nuclear or mitochondrial DNA of any cell of the embryo has been altered, and
>
> (c) no cell has been added to it other than by division of the embryo's own cells.

Artificial gametes will be extremely useful for research purposes. They could be used to create a ready supply of eggs for stem cell research, and understanding more about gametes could lead to dramatic improvements in treatments for infertility.

Equally clearly, it is obvious that artificial gametes could have considerable benefits in the provision of treatment services. Given the Hinxton Group's time predictions, it is

[37] Consensus Statement: The Science, Ethics and Policy Challenges of Pluripotent Stem Cell-Derived Gametes, April 2008, available at <www.hinxtongroup.org/>.

interesting that the government chose not to 'future-proof' this aspect of the legislation by including regulation-making powers, which could enable the law to be changed fairly quickly to permit the use of artificial gametes in treatment services, if research establishes that this would be safe. There is, as we shall see in the next chapter, a shortage of donated gametes for use in treatment by those who do not have functioning eggs or sperm of their own. For now, the important point is that new primary legislation will be needed to over-turn the current ban on the use of artificial gametes in treatment. This may have significance for researchers who want to investigate the future clinical application of artificial gametes. Funding bodies may be reluctant to fund research projects into a clinical use which, for the foreseeable future, will be a criminal offence.

(d) The need for eggs

As we have seen, CNR is impossible without a supply of eggs, from which the nucleus can be removed in order to insert a cell, commonly a skin cell, taken from an adult. For research purposes, adult cells taken from people suffering from particular conditions, such as motor neurone disease, might be used in order to extract stem cells which can help scientists under-stand more about the disease in question. If therapeutic cloning becomes possible, a skin cell would be taken from a patient in need of replacement tissue and stem cells extracted from the resulting embryo in order to grow new patient-specific tissue.

Some feminists, have drawn attention to the emphasis placed upon the scientific and therapeutic potential of stem cell lines extracted from CNR embryos, and the correspond-ing lack of attention paid to the need for a plentiful supply of eggs. Renate Klein, for example, is concerned about 'the biotech industry's voracious appetite for eggs',[38] and argues that 'women's lives and bodies should not be invaded for the so-called public good'. Beeson and Lippman argue that women may come under pressure to consent to egg donation.[39] They argue that 'the apparently purposeful use of misleading language to describe this research has the potential to be coercive'.[40] Their proposed solution, however, is not to insist that women are given clear and frank information: instead they propose 'a moratorium on egg harvesting for cloning purposes'.

It is, of course, true that there are risks associated with ovarian stimulation, but proper monitoring should be able to minimize the chance of a woman suffering from ovarian hyper-stimulation syndrome (OHSS). In clinical trials, subjects not uncommonly expose themselves to unknowable risks.[41] In relation to egg donation, the risks are at least well known, and the donor can be properly informed in advance.

There is also the possibility that women may volunteer to donate eggs because they are under the mistaken impression that the research project is likely to result in an immediately available cure for a disease from which someone they love suffers. This is a variation of the 'therapeutic misconception' which we considered in relation to clinical research in chapter 9, whereby participants misunderstand the benefits that are likely to flow from their partici-pation. The solution normally adopted to this problem is not, however, to prevent patients from participating in research at all, but rather to ensure that information sheets and con-sent forms are as honest and comprehensive as possible.

---

[38] Rhetoric of Choice Clouds Dangers of Harvesting Women's Eggs for Cloning, available at <www. onlineopinion.com.au/view.asp?article=5229>.

[39] 'Egg Harvesting for Stem Cell Research: Medical Risks and Ethical Problems' (2007) Reproductive Biomedicine Online, available at <www.keinpatent.de/doc/RBM.pdf>.

[40] Ibid.   [41] See, for example, the TGN1412 trial discussed in chapter 9.

The issue of egg donation for research purposes came to the fore following the revelations that Professor Woo Suk Hwang—a Korean scientist who claimed to have cloned the first human embryo and extracted the first patient-specific stem cell line[42]—had falsified research results and obtained eggs, in very large quantities, by paying donors and recruiting them from his junior technicians and PhD students. Because Hwang himself was deeply involved in the consent process, this almost certainly amounted to a breach of Article 26 of the Helsinki Declaration:

> When seeking informed consent for participation in a research study the physician should be particularly cautious if the potential subject is in a dependent relationship with the physician or may consent under duress. In such situations the informed consent should be sought by an appropriately qualified individual who is completely independent of this relationship.[43]

In 2005, the HFEA carried out a public consultation on whether egg donation or egg sharing (where women receive reduced-price or free IVF in return for donating some of their eggs) for research purposes raised different issues from egg donation and egg sharing, where the eggs are used for the treatment of others. Following this, it issued guidance on the protections which should be in place to ensure that women who donate eggs to research, either entirely altruistically or via an egg sharing programme, receive proper information and the opportunity to receive counselling. Direct payment is prohibited, though women can be compensated for expenses which are directly attributable to the donation, such as travel costs and loss of earnings.

For women who are egg sharers, the Code of Practice sets out that the eggs must be divided by someone independent of the research project, and that there should be no difference in the benefits provided to women sharing their eggs for research compared with those sharing their eggs for the treatment of others.

HFEA 8th Code of Practice paras 12.31 and 12.32

> 12.31 If eggs are being donated to research through an egg sharing agreement, the centre must ensure that the eggs are divided between the egg donor and the recipient (the research project) by someone not directly involved in the research project.
>
> 12.32 If a centre offers egg sharing for treatment and research, equal benefits-in-kind should be available for both. This ensures that there is no advantage in donating to one recipient rather than the other.

One centre in the UK is currently permitted to invite women to altruistically donate eggs for research, and to offer reduced-price IVF in return for donation. Unsurprisingly, very few women have volunteered for entirely altruistic egg donation for research purposes.

---

[42] See further E Jackson, 'Fraudulent Stem Cell Research and Respect for the Embryo' (2006) 1 *Biosocieties* 349–56.

[43] World Medical Association, Declaration of Helsinki: Ethical Principles for Medical Research Involving Human Subjects (6th version adopted at the 59th WMA General Assembly, Seoul, South Korea Oct 2008), available at <www.wma.net>.

Radhika Rao has pointed out some contradictions in the preference for unpaid egg donors. In addition to the tension highlighted in the next extract, she also draws attention to the fact that everyone else involved in stem cell research *is* paid. If the researchers and the regulators are paid for their services, why should women be the only ones expected to provide their services for free?

Radhika Rao[44]

On the one hand, payment to egg donors is criticized as 'coercive' because the market value may be 'too high', enticing women to consent to a painful and risky procedure with the prospect of financial gain.... At the same time, payment to egg donors is condemned as a form of 'exploitation' because the market value may be 'too low', providing a level of compensation that is inadequate to attract anyone to undergo such a procedure except for those who are desperate to make money....

Such inconsistent attitudes toward payment appear to embody an assumption that egg donations should result from 'pure' altruism, rather than self-interest. To the extent that such assumptions are invoked when women are providing material that is intertwined with reproduction, they may stem from deep-seated stereotypes regarding the natural role of women as altruistic and the natural sphere of woman as the family, which should be kept separate from the market.

If it is impossible (or, in the views of some) undesirable to recruit women to donate eggs for stem cell research, what alternatives might there be? While in the future, the creation of artificial gametes might offer a solution, in the shorter term, animal eggs have, as we have seen, been used as an alternative source of eggs for basic stem cell research. It is probably unlikely that animal eggs would be suitable for the creation of what might be called 'clinical grade' stem cell lines, for use in the creation of stem cell therapies, and so once research reaches the point at which stem cell therapies might have clinical application, the problem of the need for eggs will remain, unless, by then, artificial gametes have offered a solution.

(e) Regenerative medicine

It has been suggested that therapeutic cloning, if successful, will lead to a new sort of regenerative medicine. Most people in the West now die as a result of degenerative diseases, such as heart disease and cancer. If it became possible to replace new tissue when required, these techniques might substantially interfere with the human body's natural degeneration. This prompts John Harris to consider a world in which ageing, and even death, might no longer be inevitable. If cloned human embryonic stem cells, appropriately reprogrammed, could be used for the constant regeneration of organs and tissue, might we significantly extend the life span?

---

[44] 'Coercion, Commercialization and Commodification: The Ethics of Compensation for Egg Donors in Stem Cell Research' (2006) Berkeley Technology Law Journal 1055.

John Harris[45]

> This brings us to the central issue: would substantially increased life expectancy or even immortality be in fact a benefit or a good? There are people who regard the prospect of immortality with distaste or even horror; there are others who desire it above all else. In that most people fear death and want to postpone it as long as possible, there is some reason to suppose that the prospect of personal immortality would be widely welcomed. But it is one thing to contemplate our own personal immortality, quite another to contemplate a world in which increasing numbers of people were immortal, and in which we and all or any future children would have to compete indefinitely with previous generations for jobs, space and everything else...
>
> To come down to earth, there is no doubt that immortality would be a mixed blessing, but we should be slow to reject cures for terrible diseases even if the price we have to pay for those cures is increasing life expectancy and even creating immortals. Better surely to accompany the scientific race to achieve immortality with commensurate work in ethics and social policy to ensure that we know how to cope with the transition to parallel populations of mortals and immortals.

On the one hand, the possibility of producing replacement tissue for people whose bodies are degenerating might appear to give rise to some complex ethical issues. For example, these techniques are likely to be expensive, and so significantly increased life expectancy might initially be available only to a small minority of very rich people, raising important questions of distributive justice. If in time, regenerative medicine became more widely available, what impact would significantly increased lifespans have for the world and its resources?

On the other hand, it could be argued that finding cures for diseases such as cancer and heart disease is self-evidently desirable. Just as the discovery of cures for infectious diseases increased life-spans dramatically during the twentieth century, so we should not be surprised if average life-spans continue to increase as medical knowledge becomes more sophisticated. It could also be argued that there is already an enormous difference between rich and poor people's life spans. In the UK, average life expectancy is now around 80 years, but for homeless people it is closer to 45 years. In some African countries, the average life span has been dropping as a result of the AIDS pandemic, and in some countries is now as low as 35. Regenerative medicine would not then pose uniquely difficult questions about distributive justice.

(4) Consent

One important prerequisite to the use of embryos in research is that, with three strictly limited exceptions, described below, the gamete or tissue providers must have specifically donated them to research. Without consent, even if the gamete providers do not want the embryos to be stored for use in their own treatment or donated to others, embryos must be allowed to perish. Under Schedule 3(2) of the 1990 Act, consent to an embryo's use in any project of research must be in writing. Consent can be withdrawn under Schedule 3(4) at any time until the embryo has been used in the project of research. Schedule 3(3) specifies

---

[45] 'The Ethics and Justice of Life-extending Therapies' (2002) 55 Current Legal Problems 65–95.

that the person giving consent must have been given a suitable opportunity to receive counselling, and must be provided 'with such relevant information as is proper'. Guidance on the information which should be provided is contained in the HFEA's Code of Practice.

HFEA 8th Code of Practice para 22.7

22.7 For any research project, the centre should ensure that before donors give their consent to their gametes or embryos, or cells used to create embryos, being used in research, they are given oral information, supported by relevant written material, that confirms:

- the specific research project and its aims
- details of the research project, including likely outcomes and how any individual donation will impact on the overall project
- whether the embryos will be reversibly or irreversibly anonymised, and the implications of this
- whether donors will be given any information that is obtained during the research and is relevant to their health and welfare
- that donors are expected to have an opportunity to ask questions and discuss the research project
- that donating gametes or embryos to research in the course of treatment services will not affect the patient's treatment in any way
- that patients are under no obligation to donate gametes and embryos for research and that their decision whether to do so will have no repercussions for any treatment they may receive
- that only fresh or frozen gametes and embryos not required for treatment can be used for research
- that research is experimental, and so any gametes and embryos used and created for any research project must not be used in treatment
- that donors may specify conditions for the use of the gametes or embryos
- that after the research has been completed, all donated gametes and embryos will be allowed to perish, and
- that, for any individual who donates cells for creating embryos for research, consent to use these cells includes consent to do so after the individual's death, unless stated otherwise.

New consent issues are raised by the possibility of extracting stem cell lines from embryos, since these lines are potentially immortal and might be useful to scientists (and in the future, pharmaceutical companies and clinicians) for many years to come. Again, it must be made clear to potential donors 'that any stem cell lines created may continue indefinitely and be used in many different research projects'.

The HFEA and the Medical Research Council have jointly contributed towards a standard consent form for the use of embryos for stem cell research. This stresses, among other things, that the couple will not benefit, medically or financially, from any discoveries made during research on their cells. The UK stem cell bank, set up in 2002, receives a sample of every stem cell line recovered by researchers, and the HFEA will not grant licences for stem cell research unless the researchers have made a commitment to deposit each stem cell line with the bank.[46] People donating embryos for stem cell research must be informed of the intention to bank any stem cell lines derived from their embryos.

Centralized banking of stem cell lines is important because their immortality means that they can continue to be made freely available to researchers throughout the world. It is possible that there will come a time when the worldwide stem cell banks contain sufficient high-quality embryonic stem cell lines to meet researchers' needs, and it will no longer be necessary to create more. Two issues arise from this. First, the possibility of openly sharing stem cell lines with researchers throughout the world means that it would be highly desirable, albeit perhaps impractical, to have greater regulatory harmonization. If scientists in California, say, are only permitted to carry out research on stem cell lines where the gamete/embryo donors received no direct or indirect compensation, a high-quality stem cell line deposited in the UK bank, derived from eggs provided by a woman who received reduced-price IVF in return, may be unavailable to them. While a global consensus on the regulation of embryonic stem cell research would have many practical advantages, it is unlikely to ever become a reality. There is certainly no global consensus on the moral status of the embryo, and, in the future, countries may effectively be in competition with each other as attractive locations for lucrative stem cell therapy research centres.

Secondly, if it does prove to be the case that there will, in the future, be enough embryonic stem cell lines in the banks to obviate the need to create further lines, it would be impossible to satisfy the Act's criterion that the use of embryos must be *necessary* for the project's research purposes. If scientists could carry out exactly the same research on an existing stem cell line, it would not be possible to establish that the use of further embryos was necessary.

(5) Creating Embryos without Consent

The 2008 reforms to the 1990 Act create three important exceptions to the need to obtain consent to the use of an embryo in a research project. Scientists and clinicians had argued that there might be certain diseases, for which stem cell research might offer the possibility of a cure, where it would be impossible to obtain consent from someone with the condition for the use of their tissue to create an embryo through cell nuclear replacement. An obvious example would be a disease like Tay Sachs disease, which leads to a child's death, normally by the age of four, but in any event, always long before a child would be competent to make the decision to consent to tissue donation for themselves. As a result, Schedule 3 now provides that, provided the 'parental consent conditions' are met, someone with parental responsibility can give consent to the use of their child's cells to create an embryo for research purposes.

Human Fertilisation and Embryology Act 1990 schedule 3

Parental consent conditions

15(2) Condition A is that C [the child] suffers from, or is likely to develop, a serious disease, a serious physical or mental disability or any other serious medical condition.

---

[46] See further <www.ukstemcellbank.org.uk/>.

(3) Condition B is that either—

(a) C is not competent to deal with the issue of consent to the use of C's human cells to bring about the creation in vitro of an embryo or human admixed embryo for use for the purposes of a project of research, or

(b) C has attained the age of 16 years but lacks capacity to consent to such use of C's human cells.

(4) Condition C is that any embryo or human admixed embryo to be created in vitro is to be used for the purposes of a project of research which is intended to increase knowledge about—

(a) the disease, disability or medical condition mentioned in sub-paragraph (2) or any similar disease, disability or medical condition, or

(b) the treatment of, or care of persons affected by, that disease, disability or medical condition or any similar disease, disability or medical condition.

(5) Condition D is that there are reasonable grounds for believing that research of comparable effectiveness cannot be carried out if the only human cells that can be used to bring about the creation in vitro of embryos or human admixed embryos for use for the purposes of the project are the human cells of persons who—

(a) have attained the age of 18 years and have capacity to consent to the use of their human cells to bring about the creation in vitro of an embryo or human admixed embryo for use for the purposes of the project, or

(b) have not attained that age but are competent to deal with the issue of consent to such use of their human cells.

In short, parents can consent to the child's cells being used for stem cell research if it would not be possible to do research into the child's condition by using cells from someone else who can give consent.

A similar provision applies to adults who lack capacity. Again, provided it would not be possible to carry out the research on cells taken from people who can give consent, it may be possible to use cells from an adult who lacks capacity in stem cell research involving the creation of embryos.

Human Fertilisation and Embryology Act 1990 schedule 3

Consent to use of human cells etc. not required: adult lacking capacity

17(2) Condition A is that P suffers from, or is likely to develop, a serious disease, a serious physical or mental disability or any other serious medical condition.

(3) Condition B is that P lacks capacity to consent to the use of P's human cells to bring about the creation in vitro of an embryo or human admixed embryo for use for the purposes of a project of research.

(4) Condition C is that the person responsible under the licence has no reason to believe that P had refused such consent at a time when P had that capacity.

(5) Condition D is that it appears unlikely that P will at some time have that capacity.

(6) Condition E is that any embryo or human admixed embryo to be created in vitro is to be used for the purposes of a project of research which is intended to increase knowledge about—

> (a) the disease, disability or medical condition mentioned in sub-paragraph (2) or any similar disease, disability or medical condition, or
>
> (b) the treatment of, or care of persons affected by, that disease, disability or medical condition or any similar disease, disability or medical condition.
>
> (7) Condition F is that there are reasonable grounds for believing that research of comparable effectiveness cannot be carried out if the only human cells that can be used to bring about the creation in vitro of embryos or human admixed embryos for use for the purposes of the project are the human cells of persons who—
>
> (a) have attained the age of 18 years and have capacity to consent to the use of their human cells to bring about the creation in vitro of an embryo or human admixed embryo for use for the purposes of the project, or
>
> (b) have not attained that age but are competent to deal with the issue of consent to such use of their human cells.

Paragraph 18 goes on to provide that the person responsible under the licence (here referred to as R) must identify someone (F) who is able and willing to be consulted as to whether, if they had capacity, P would have agreed to letting their cells be used in this sort of research.

Human Fertilisation and Embryology Act 1990 schedule 3

> 18(4) R must provide the person identified F…with information about the proposed use of human cells to bring about the creation in vitro of embryos or human admixed embryos for use for the purposes of the project and ask F what, in F's opinion, P's wishes and feelings about the use of P's human cells for that purpose would be likely to be if P had capacity in relation to the matter.

The final way in which the need for consent can be dispensed with is if the person's cells were stored before the Act came into force, and they have since died. For these stored cells to be used to create an embryo, there must be no evidence that the person would have objected to the use of their cells in this sort of research, and there is agreement from someone who stands in a qualifying relationship with them (this is from the Human Tissue Act 2004, and refers to a list of relatives, described in the previous chapter).

It will be difficult to establish that it is necessary to use cells from deceased people who have not given consent because paragraph 21 provides that there must be 'reasonable grounds for believing that scientific research will be adversely affected to a significant extent' if the only human cells that can be used are ones for which there is effective consent or ones covered by the first two exceptions. This provision exists to ensure that existing tissue banks can be used for stem cell research, but this condition is not easily satisfied.

4 CONCLUSION

Regulating a fast-moving area of science is inevitably a difficult task. The 1990 Act proved to be remarkably resilient in the face of developments, such as the possibility of CNR and stem cell research, which were not in the minds of legislators in 1990. Nevertheless, its updating in 2008 is to be welcomed, and it will be interesting to see how long it takes for the new legislation to come under pressure by as yet unforeseen developments.

In conclusion, it is also worth thinking about the existence of tensions between abortion law, considered in the next chapter, and the rules governing embryo research. For example, anti-abortion campaigners might argue that if embryos are protected when they are 14 days old, it is illogical to permit the destruction of fetuses at 23 weeks for 'social' reasons. Others might say that if a woman can abort a fetus during the first 24 weeks of pregnancy because termination promotes her best interests, it makes little sense to prohibit potentially life-saving research on 16-day-old embryos.

Certainly the House of Lords Science and Technology Committee suggested that given the legality of abortion, a ban on embryo research would be rather odd: 'It would be difficult to justify an absolute prohibition on the destruction of early embryos while permitting abortion in a relatively wide range of circumstances post-implantation—indeed well after the emergence of the primitive streak and into the foetal stage of development.'

Finally, it is worth noting that when the original 1990 Act was passed, fertility treatment and embryo research were equally novel and controversial, and there were good reasons to subject both to a special licensing regime. Now the reality is rather different. IVF treatment has become a routine medical procedure, whereas public confidence in embryo research continues to depend upon the drawing of strict lines, a rigorous licensing procedure and the ongoing monitoring of individual research projects.

FURTHER READING

Brock, D, 'Is a Consensus Possible on Stem Cell Research? Moral and Political Obstacles' (2006) 32 Journal of Medical Ethics 36–42.

Green, RM, 'Embryo as Epiphenomenon: Some Cultural, Social and Economic Forces Driving the Stem Cell Debate' (2008) 34 Journal of Medical Ethics 840–44.

Halliday, Samantha, 'A Comparative Approach to the Regulation of Human Embryonic Stem Cell Research in Europe' (2004) 12 Medical Law Review 40–69.

Harris, John, 'The Ethics and Justice of Life-extending Therapies' (2002) 55 Current Legal Problems 65–95.

Harris, John, 'Stem Cells, Sex, and Procreation' (2003) 12 Cambridge Quarterly of Healthcare 353–71.

Holm, Søren, 'The Ethical Case Against Stem Cell Research' (2003) 12 Cambridge Quarterly of Healthcare Ethics 372–83.

House of Lords Stem Cell Research Committee, Stem Cell Research Report, Feb 2002, available at <http://www.parliament.the-stationery-office.co.uk/pa/ld200102/ldselect/ldstem/83/8305.htm>.

Human Fertilisation and Embryology Authority, available at <http://www.hfea.gov.uk/Research>.

Jackson, Emily, 'Fraudulent Stem Cell Research and Respect for the Embryo' (2006) 1 BioSocieties 349–56.

Mulkay, Michael, The Embryo Research Debate: Science and the Politics of Reproduction (CUP: Cambridge, 1997).

Savulescu, Julian, 'The Embryonic Stem Cell Lottery and the Cannibalization of Human Beings' (2002) 16 Bioethics 508–29.

13

ABORTION

CENTRAL ISSUES

1. Underlying the question of abortion's legality are two intertwined issues. First, what is the fetus's moral status, and, secondly, should a pregnant woman's right to autonomy include the right to terminate an unwanted pregnancy?

2. When the Abortion Act was passed in 1967, its principal purpose was to enable doctors to act lawfully by terminating their patients' unwanted pregnancies. As a result, the Act gives the medical profession considerable discretion over the question of whether a woman should be permitted to terminate an unwanted pregnancy.

3. The most commonly used 'ground' for abortion is that continuing the pregnancy poses a greater risk to the woman's physical or mental health than termination. Abortions carried out for this reason are subject to a twenty-four-week time limit. Improvements both in fetal imaging techniques and in neonatal survival rates have led some to argue that the twenty-four-week time limit should be lowered.

4. Abortion on the grounds of serious fetal abnormality is lawful until birth. Doctors have considerable discretion in determining what counts as a sufficiently serious handicap.

1 INTRODUCTION

In this chapter we consider a contentious but common medical procedure: the termination of pregnancy. In 1969—the first full year in which the Abortion Act was in operation—49,829 abortions were notified to the Department of Health. By 2007, 198,700 abortions were performed on women resident in the UK, and 7,100 on non-residents.[1] Twenty years ago, access to abortion within the NHS was patchy, and approximately half of

---

[1] Abortion Statistics 2007 (DH: London, 2008), available at <www.dh.gov.uk>.

all abortions took place in the private sector.[2] In 2007, 89 per cent of abortions were funded by the NHS, over half of which (57 per cent) took place in the independent sector under NHS contract.

We begin this chapter with a necessarily brief survey of the ongoing debate over abortion's moral legitimacy. Should pregnant women have the right to terminate their unwanted pregnancies, or do fetuses have a right to life which should 'trump' women's reproductive freedom? As will be obvious, there is never likely to be agreement on the morality of abortion. Nevertheless, despite the absence of anything remotely resembling consensus, abortion has been legal in (most of) the UK for almost 40 years. We then examine the current legal position, and consider how the Abortion Act 1967, as amended, works in practice. Obviously, the conflict between the interests of the fetus and those of the pregnant woman could be framed in terms of 'rights', and so we also consider the impact of the Human Rights Act 1998.

In certain circumstances, the legality of abortion has proved to be especially controversial, and we investigate these cases separately. In particular, in recent years there has been considerable interest first, in whether abortion on the grounds of fetal abnormality amounts to a species of eugenic selection, and secondly, whether technological developments which enable very premature babies to survive mean that we should rethink the time limits within which abortion is legal. Finally, we highlight some differences between the regulation of abortion in the UK and in other countries.

At the outset, a brief note about terminology: in this chapter, I will not describe pregnant women as 'mothers', and nor will I use the term 'unborn child' to refer to a fetus. This is because, in legal terms, motherhood and childhood only begin after a child has been born. In the context of abortion, it is obvious that the fetus may never become a child and the pregnant woman may not become a mother.

2 THE ETHICS OF ABORTION

In what circumstances, if any, is it legitimate for a woman to terminate an unwanted pregnancy? Instinctive responses to this question will lie somewhere upon a spectrum which has 'never' at one end, and 'whenever she likes' at the other, with most people falling somewhere in between, believing that abortion is *sometimes*, but *not always* justifiable. Towards the restrictive end of the spectrum, it might be argued that abortion is legitimate where the woman's life is in danger, or when she is pregnant as a result of an act of rape and/or incest. At the more permissive end, it might be contended that abortion should be available upon request, at least during the first few months of pregnancy.

But while an instinctive response to the legitimacy of abortion may be a useful starting point, as we saw in Chapter 1, the requirement to give reasons, or to justify one's moral views is an important feature of ethical reasoning. Fortunately, in relation to abortion, there is a rich philosophical literature from which to draw. At the risk of drastic oversimplification, three different strands of analysis are worth identifying:

- an emphasis on the moral status of the fetus, and in particular upon its personhood, or potential personhood;

---

[2] Emily Jackson, *Regulating Reproduction* (Hart, Oxford, 2001).

- an emphasis upon the physical invasiveness of pregnancy, and upon the degree of self-sacrifice which would be forced upon women if they were compelled to continue their unwanted pregnancies;
- a compromise position in which abortion is permitted, but only in certain restricted circumstances which are designed to offer the fetus some protection.

Let us consider each of these positions in turn.

(a) THE MORAL STATUS OF THE FETUS

Opponents of abortion, such as John Finnis, have tended to concentrate on the fetus's moral status. Here he argues that conception is the moment at which a new individual comes into being, and that this should be the point at which it should acquire all the rights of personhood.

John Finnis[3]

> I have been assuming that the unborn child is, from conception, a person and hence is not to be discriminated against on account of age, appearance or other such factors insofar as such factors are reasonably considered irrelevant where respect for basic human values is in question...
>
> [At conception] two sex cells, each with only twenty-three chromosomes, unite and more or less immediately fuse to become a new cell with forty-six chromosomes providing a unique genetic constitution... which thenceforth throughout its life, however long, will substantially determine the new individual's makeup. This new cell is the first stage in a dynamic integrated system that has nothing much in common with the individual male and female sex cells, save that it sprang from a pair of them and will in time produce new sets of them. To say that *this* is when a person's life began is not to work backwards from maturity, sophistically asking at each point 'How can one draw the line *here?*' Rather it is to point to a perfectly clear-cut beginning to which each one of us can look back.

This sort of argument has been disputed by others, such as Mary Ann Warren, who contend that while the fetus may be human, it is not yet a person, and that its potential to become a person cannot justify giving it primacy over the rights of an actual person, namely the pregnant woman.

Mary Ann Warren[4]

> What characteristics entitle an entity to be considered a person?...I suggest that the traits which are most central to the concept of personhood..., are, very roughly, the following:
>
> (1) Consciousness..., and in particular the capacity to feel pain.
>
> (2) Reasoning (the *developed* capacity to solve new and relatively complex problems);

---

[3] 'The Rights and Wrongs of Abortion: A Reply to Judith Thomson' (1973) 2 Philosophy and Public Affairs, 117–45.

[4] 'On the Moral and Legal Status of Abortion' (1973) 1 The Monist 43–61.

(3) Self-motivated activity...

(4) The capacity to communicate...

(5) The presence of self-concepts, and self-awareness...

We needn't suppose that an entity must have *all* these attributes to be properly considered a person...Neither do we need to insist that any one of these criteria is necessary for personhood...

All we need to claim, to demonstrate that a fetus is not a person, is that any being which satisfies *none* of (1)–(5) is certainly not a person. I consider this claim to be so obvious that I think anyone who denied it, and claimed that a being which satisfied none of (1)–(5) was a person all the same, would thereby demonstrate that he had no notion at all of what a person is—perhaps because he had confused the concept of personhood with that of genetic humanity....

[A] fetus is a human being which is not yet a person, and which therefore cannot coherently be said to have full moral rights...But even if a potential person does have some prima facie right to life, such a right could not possibly outweigh the right of a woman to obtain an abortion, since the rights of any actual person invariably outweigh those of any potential person, whenever the two conflict.

Warren's criteria for personhood are themselves controversial. Philip Abbott, for example, points out that this sort of test for 'personhood' would exclude not only fetuses, but also some seriously disabled children and adults.

Philip Abbott[5]

What makes one a person (or human in the moral sense)? Warren suggests five 'traits'...Note how deftly Warren plies her trade. A fetus *might* be able to feel pain, but surely he or she is unable to reason, especially with *developed* capacity. What is shocking about this criterion (2) is that a two-year old may fail to meet it. What this means..., and let us be direct about this, is that we must restrain our emotions and come to regard an infant as not a person at all but a mere clump of genetic humanity. Are not then the comatose patient, the schizophrenic, the catatonic, the unaided mute, the paraplegic in danger of slipping into that awful category 'genetic human'.

While in legal terms at least, it is clear that a person with rights exists after birth but not before, in the next extract, Ranaan Gillon argues that it is not evident that a newborn baby is a morally different entity to a fetus immediately prior to birth.

Raanan Gillon[6]

UK law, like that of many other jurisdictions, is explicit that a fetus is not legally speaking a person and does not have the legal rights of persons including the right to life enjoyed by (natural) persons, whereas a born child is a person and does have a right to life. While in practical terms the simple criterion of birth is generally easy to apply and corresponds to a stage

5 'Philosophers and the Abortion Question' (1978) 6 Political Theory 313–35.
6 'Is There a "New Ethics of Abortion"?' (2001) 26 suppl II Journal of Medical Ethics ii5–ii9, ii8.

when what was previously hidden and private inside another human being is now a revealed, public, and clearly separate social entity, as a criterion for moral differentiation of a human being's intrinsic moral status it seems highly implausible. Essentially it is a criterion of what might be dubbed biological geography, asserting that a human being does not have a right to life if it lies north of a vaginal introitus but has a right to life once it has passed south and has (entirely) emerged from the vagina. What morally relevant changes can there have been in the fetus in its passage from inside to outside its mother's body to underpin such a momentous change in its intrinsic moral status?

Don Marquis avoids the person/not a person debate, and instead claims that abortion is wrong because it is relevantly similar to killing an adult human being. According to Marquis, what makes killing adult human beings wrong is that it deprives them of everything they might value in the future. Since the killing of a fetus will also deprive it of everything it might value in the future, by analogy, he argues that abortion is just as wrong as killing an adult human being.

Don Marquis[7]

When I am killed, I am deprived both of what I now value which would have been part of my future personal life, but also what I would come to value. Therefore, when I die, I am deprived of all of the value of my future. Inflicting this loss on me is ultimately what makes killing me wrong. This being the case, it would seem that what makes killing *any* adult human being prima facie seriously wrong is the loss of his or her future...

The claim that the primary wrong-making feature of a killing is the loss to the victim of the value of its future has obvious consequences for the ethics of abortion. The future of a standard fetus includes a set of experiences, projects, activities, and such which are identical with the futures of adult human beings and are identical with the futures of young children. Since the reason that is sufficient to explain why it is wrong to kill human beings after the time of birth is a reason that also applies to fetuses, it follows that abortion is prima facie seriously morally wrong.

Julian Savluescu accepts that Marquis has identified one reason not to have an abortion, but he argues that he has not thereby demonstrated that abortion would be wrong. Using contraception or deciding not to have sexual intercourse on a particular day may also deprive a possible future person of a future of value, but that does not mean that either is the wrong thing to do.

Julian Savulescu[8]

Even granting there is a reason to realise futures of value, however, generally the strength of the reason to bring a new life into the world is not sufficient to create an obligation to carry a particular pregnancy or conceive a particular child. The reason for this is that having an unwanted child can have a massively detrimental effect on the lives of its parents. This is a

---

[7] 'Why Abortion is Immoral' (1989) 86 Journal of Philosophy 183–202, 192.
[8] 'Abortion, Embryo Destruction and the Future of Value Argument' (2002) 28 Journal of Medical Ethics 133–5.

significant moral consideration.... In sum, Marquis establishes an argument that there are reasons against having an abortion (and by extension to contraception and embryo research). But that argument is *defeasible*. It is an argument that identifies one important property associated with killing fetuses or embryos. But it does not establish that either abortion or embryo destruction is wrong, all things considered. There are other important considerations that outweigh our obligation not to destroy embryos or fetuses.

A different criticism of Marquis comes from Mark T Brown, who argues that people are deprived of futures they might value whenever they die prematurely. Someone who needs a heart transplant, but does not get one in time, has been deprived of a future of value, but that does not mean that their *right* to that future has been violated, nor that they had any rights over someone else's heart. To give fetuses the right not to be killed would, according to Brown, be to give them:

[A] right to satisfy their needs at the expense of the autonomy, bodily integrity and wellbeing of another person. If I need a bone marrow transplant in order to realise my potential future of value, I do not thereby gain a right to your bone marrow.[9]

This line of argument is developed in the next section.

(b) THE PREGNANT WOMAN'S RIGHT TO SELF-DETERMINATION

This approach to abortion (exemplified below by Judith Jarvis Thomson and Eileen McDonagh) emphasizes the physical invasiveness of carrying a pregnancy to term, and argues that restrictions on women's access to abortion effectively compel them to exercise a wholly unprecedented degree of self-sacrifice. Margaret Olivia Little explains the starting point for this argument particularly well:

To be pregnant is to be *inhabited*. It is to be *occupied*. It is to be in a state of physical intimacy of a particularly thorough-going nature. The fetus intrudes on the body massively; whatever medical risks one faces or avoids, the brute fact remains that the fetus shifts and alters the very physical boundaries of the woman's self.[10]

Of course, the fetus is not a malicious intruder; it is occupying the woman's body through no fault of its own. However, the claim being made is that the state does not have the right to force the woman to continue in this relationship of unparalleled intimacy without her consent.

Eileen L McDonagh[11]

Pregnancy is a condition constituting massive transformations of a woman's body and liberty, and, thus, constitutes serious harm without her consent.

---

[9] 'The Morality of Abortion and the Deprivation of Futures' (2000) 26 Journal of Medical Ethics 103–7.
[10] 'Abortion, Intimacy, and the Duty to Gestate' (1999) 2 Ethical Theory and Moral Practice 295–312.
[11] 'My Body, My Consent: Securing the Constitutional Right to Abortion Funding' (1999) 62 Albany Law Review 1057.

The massive effects of a fetus on a woman's body correspond to the level of injury justifying the use of deadly force, if a woman does not consent to those effects. If a born person were to affect another born person's body in even a fraction of the ways a fetus affects a woman's body, the magnitude of the injury would be easy to recognize. Imagine a born person who injected into another's body, without consent, hormones 400 times their normal level, or someone who, without consent, took over the blood system of another to meet her own personal use, or someone who, without consent, grew a new organ in that person's body....

Some may object that if a woman consents to sexual intercourse (action X), then by extension she has consented to pregnancy (condition Y) as a foreseeable consequence of sexual intercourse....

Generally, when a person creates a risk, it does not follow that the person consents to injuries occurring subsequent to the risk. Thus, if a person consensually creates a risk that she will be mugged by walking down an alley alone, late at night, responsibility for causing the risk does not constitute consent to the injury of mugging that may be subsequent to that risk...In addition, even if a woman is contributorily negligent in creating the risk that a fetus will harm her, she nevertheless retains the right to self-defense to stop the fetus from harming her.

The woman's right to an abortion is not, on this view, necessarily dependent upon proving that the fetus is not a person. Rather, as Judith Jarvis Thomson argues in the next extract, even if we assume that the fetus *is* a person, it might be argued that pregnant women have the right to use self-defence in order to protect themselves from the physical invasion of an unwanted pregnancy.

Judith Jarvis Thomson[12]

[S]urely a person's right to life is stronger and more stringent than the mother's right to decide what happens in and to her body, and so outweighs it......

It sounds plausible. But now let me ask you to imagine this. You wake up in the morning and find yourself back to back in bed with an unconscious violinist. A famous unconscious violinist. He has been found to have a fatal kidney ailment, and the Society of Music Lovers has canvassed all the available medical records and found that you alone have the right blood type to help. They have therefore kidnapped you, and last night the violinist's circulatory system was plugged into yours, so that your kidneys can be used to extract poisons from his blood as well as your own. The director of the hospital now tells you, 'Look, we're sorry the Society of Music Lovers did this to you—we would never have permitted it if we had known. But still, they did it, and the violinist is now plugged into you. To unplug you would be to kill him. But never mind, its only for nine months. By then he will have recovered from his ailment, and can safely be unplugged from you.' Is it morally incumbent on you to accede to this situation? No doubt it would be very nice of you if you did, a great kindness. But do you *have* to accede to it? What if it were not nine months, but nine years? Or longer still? What if the director of the hospital says, 'Tough luck, I agree, but you've now got to stay in bed, with the violinist plugged into you, for the rest of your life. Because remember this. All persons have a right to life, and violinists are persons. Granted you have a right to decide what happens in and to your body, but a person's right to life outweighs your right to decide what happens in and

12 'A Defence of Abortion' (1971) 1 Philosophy and Public Affairs 47.

to your body. So you cannot ever be unplugged from him.' I imagine you would regard this as outrageous, which suggests that something really is wrong with that plausible-sounding argument I mentioned a moment ago.

A related argument draws attention to the common assumption that deciding to have an abortion is a more difficult and serious moral choice than deciding to carry a pregnancy to term, even though motherhood undoubtedly involves an extraordinarily demanding and longlasting commitment. Through the presumptions that women seeking abortion need counselling, and conversely, that women who are about to become mothers do not, motherhood is assumed to be an easy and natural choice for women, whereas, as Reva Siegel explains, rejecting motherhood is perceived to be unnatural and selfish.

Reva Siegel[13]

Legislators may condemn abortion because they assume that any pregnant woman who does not wish to be pregnant has committed some sexual indiscretion properly punishable by compelling pregnancy itself. Popular support for excusing women who are victims of rape or incest from the proscriptions of criminal abortion laws demonstrates that attitudes about abortion do indeed rest on normative judgments about women's sexual conduct....

If legislators assume that women are 'child-rearers', they will take for granted the work women give to motherhood and ignore what it takes from them, and so will view women's efforts to avoid some two decades of life-consuming work as an act of casual expedience or unseemly egoism. Thus, they will condemn women for seeking abortion 'on demand', or as a mere 'convenience', judging women to be unnaturally egocentric because they do not give their lives over to the work of bearing and nurturing children—that is, because they fail to act like mothers, like normal women should.

The idea that women should always have the right to decide for themselves whether they want to become mothers is disputed by Rosalind Hursthouse, who contends that motherhood is intrinsically good. Hursthouse analyses abortion from the perspective of 'virtue ethics' (considered in Chapter 1), and argues that a woman who rejects motherhood without a compelling or 'virtuous' reason for doing so, is acting wrongly.

Rosalind Hursthouse[14]

The fact that the premature termination of a pregnancy is, in some sense, the cutting off of a new human life, connects with all our thoughts about human life and death, parenthood and family relationship, must make it a serious matter. To disregard this fact about it, to think of abortion as nothing but the killing of something that does not matter, or as nothing but the exercise of some right or some rights one has, or as the incidental means to some desirable state of affairs, is to do something callous and light-minded, the sort of thing that no virtuous and wise person would do...

[13] 'Reasoning from the Body: A Historical Perspective on Abortion Regulation and Questions of Equal Protection' (1992) Stanford Law Review 261.

[14] 'Virtue Theory and Abortion' in Daniel Statman (ed.), *Virtue Ethics* (Edinburgh University Press Edinburgh, 1997) 227–44.

The familiar facts support the view that parenthood in general, and motherhood and child-bearing in particular, are intrinsically worthwhile, are among the things that can be correctly thought to be partially constitutive of a flourishing human life. If this is right, then a woman who opts for not being a mother (at all, or again, or now) by opting for abortion may thereby be manifesting a flawed grasp of what her life should be, and be about—a grasp that is childish, or grossly materialistic, or shortsighted, or shallow.

I say 'may thereby': this need not be so. Consider, for instance, a woman who has already had several children and fears that to have another will seriously affect her capacity to be a good mother to the ones she has—she does not show a lack of appreciation of the intrinsic value of being a parent by opting for abortion. Nor does a woman who has been a good mother and is approaching the age at which she may be looking forward to being a good grandmother. Nor does a woman who discovers that her pregnancy may well kill her, and opts for abortion and adoption. Nor, necessarily, does a woman who has decided to lead a life centred around some other worthwhile activity or activities with which motherhood would compete...

But some women who choose abortion rather than have their first child, and some men who encourage their partners to choose abortion, are not avoiding parenthood for the sake of other worthwhile pursuits, but for the worthless one of 'having a good time', or for the pursuit of some false vision of the ideals of freedom or self-realisation.

(c) A COMPROMISE POSITION?

Thirdly, as with the question of embryo research we considered in the previous chapter, a middle ground exists which acknowledges both that the fetus' potential personhood is a good reason to afford it some protection, and that the pregnant woman has a legitimate interest in self-determination. This 'third way' would protect the woman's right to terminate her pregnancy, but only in certain circumstances. This is consistent with almost every country's regulation of abortion: abortion is permitted within parameters—such as time limits—which are supposed to indicate the seriousness of fetal destruction.

Ronald Dworkin, for example, argues that most people share a deep belief in the sanctity of human life, and therefore regard abortion as a morally serious matter, but that they also do not believe that the fetus has exactly the same status as a person, otherwise it would be impossible to justify any exceptions to the prohibition of abortion—such as that it might be legitimate if the pregnant woman's life is in danger, or if she is pregnant as a result of rape.

Ronald Dworkin[15]

[D]iscussions of abortion almost all presume that people disagree about abortion because they disagree about whether a fetus is a person with a right to life from the moment of its conception, or becomes a person at some point in pregnancy, or does not become one until birth. And about whether, if a fetus is a person, its right to life must yield in the fact of some stronger right held by pregnant women....

[T]his account of the abortion debate, in spite of its great popularity, is fatally misleading....[E]ven those conservatives who believe that the law should prohibit abortion recognize

---

[15] *Life's Dominion* (Harper Collins, London) 1993.

exceptions. It is a very common view, for example, that abortion should be permitted when necessary to save the mother's life. Yet this exception is...inconsistent with any belief that a fetus is a person with a right to live. Some people say that in this case a mother is justified in aborting a fetus as a matter of self-defense; but any safe abortion is carried out by some-one else—a doctor—and very few people believe that it is morally justifiable for a third party, even a doctor, to kill one innocent person to save another.

Abortion conservatives often allow further exceptions. Some of them believe that abor-tion is morally permissible...when pregnancy is the result of rape or incest. The more such exceptions are allowed, the clearer it becomes that conservative opposition to abortion does not presume that the fetus is a person with a right to life. It would be contradictory to insist that a fetus has a right to life...that ceases to exist when the pregnancy is the result of a sex-ual crime of which the fetus is, of course, wholly innocent.

On the other side, a parallel story emerges....A paradigm liberal position on abor-tion...rejects the extreme opinion that abortion is morally unproblematic, and insists, on the contrary, that abortion is always a grave moral decision.

3 THE LAW

(a) THE CRIMINAL LAW

Until 1803, abortion was governed by the common law. It was a criminal offence only after 'quickening', the moment when the woman can first feel the fetus moving inside her, which is normally about 16–18 weeks into the pregnancy.

Bracton[16]

If one strikes a pregnant woman or gives her poison in order to procure an abortion, if the foetus is already formed or quickened, especially if it is, he commits homicide.

Coke[17]

If a woman be quick with childe, and by a potion or otherwise killeth it in her wombe; or if a man beat here, whereby the child dieth in her body, and she is delivered of a dead child, this is a great misprision, and no murder.

Blackstone[18]

Life...begins in contemplation of law as soon as an infant is able to stir in the mother's womb. For if a woman is quick with child, and by a potion, or otherwise, killeth it in her womb; or if any one beat her, whereby the child dieth in her body, and she is delivered of a dead child; this, though not murder, was by the ancient law homicide or manslaughter. But at present it is not looked upon in quite so atrocious a light, though it remains a very heinous misdemeanor.

---

[16] *De Legibus et Consuetudinibus Angliae* (On the Laws and Customs of England), thirteenth century.
[17] *Institutes of the Laws of England*, seventeenth century.
[18] *Commentaries on the Laws of England*, vol 1 (1765).

Since Lord Ellenborough's Act of 1803, abortion has been regulated by statute. Under the 1803 Act abortion became a felony throughout pregnancy, and the death penalty was introduced for abortion after quickening, though this was abolished thirty-four years later, as was the distinction between abortions before and after 'quickening'.

It is a nineteenth-century statute that continues to apply to abortion today. Statutory defences do now exist, but under sections 58 and 59 of the Offences Against the Person Act 1861, the maximum sentence for a woman who intentionally procures her own miscarriage is life imprisonment, and anyone who assists her could be imprisoned for up to five years.

Offences Against the Person Act 1861 sections 58 and 59

(58) Every woman, being with child, who, with intent to procure her own miscarriage, shall unlawfully administer to herself any poison or other noxious thing, or shall unlawfully use any instrument or other means whatsoever with the like intent, and whosoever, with intent to procure the miscarriage of any woman, whether she be or not with child, shall unlawfully administer to her or cause to be taken by her any poison or other noxious thing, or shall unlawfully use any instrument or other means whatsoever with the like intent, shall be guilty of felony.

(59) Whosoever shall unlawfully supply or procure any poison or other noxious thing, or any instrument or thing whatsoever knowing that the same is intended to be unlawfully used or employed with intent to procure the miscarriage of any woman, whether she be or not be with child, shall be guilty of a misdemeanor.

The critical ingredients of the offences under sections 58 and 59 are, first, that someone must *do* something with a poison or instrument or other noxious thing, and, secondly, that they must *intend* to procure a miscarriage. Notice also that the first limb of section 58 applies only to women who are in fact 'with child'. A woman could not be convicted of the full offence under section 58 unless she was actually pregnant. A woman who mistakenly believed that she was pregnant could, nevertheless, be guilty of *conspiring* to procure an abortion, as was the case in *R v Whitchurch*.[19] Other people can be guilty 'whether she be or not with child', provided that they believe her to be pregnant, and intend to cause her to miscarry.

It is also important to note that sections 58 and 59 refer to poison or instruments being used *unlawfully*. On one interpretation, the word 'unlawfully' is wholly redundant here: since the purpose of these sections is to create a criminal offence, it goes without saying that the act described is *unlawful*. A more plausible explanation is that the offence is only committed where the abortion is carried out *unlawfully*, meaning, of course, that it might be possible to lawfully procure an abortion. Because it has never been doubted that doctors are entitled to carry out life-saving surgery, even if its consequence would be the termination of pregnancy, it is likely that the word 'unlawfully' is intended to create an exception—akin to the one contained in the Infant Life Preservation Act 1929 (considered below)—for terminations performed to preserve the pregnant woman's life.

This was certainly the interpretation preferred by Macnaughten J in his summing up to the jury in *R v Bourne*, a case in which a distinguished obstetric surgeon, Aleck Bourne, had

---

[19] (1890) LR 24 QBD 420.

carried out an abortion on a fourteen-year-old girl, who was pregnant following a violent rape. His defence was that, in the circumstances of the case, the operation was not unlawful, because in his opinion the continuance of the pregnancy posed a serious risk to the girl's mental health. In his direction to the jury, Macnaughten J agreed that it would be possible for an abortion to be carried out lawfully not only where the pregnant woman was in imminent danger of death, but also where the effect of carrying the pregnancy to term might be to 'make the woman a physical or mental wreck'.

R v Bourne[20]

Macnaughten J

A man of the highest skill, openly, in one of our great hospitals, performs the operation. Whether it was legal or illegal you will have to determine, but he performs the operation as an act of charity, without fee or reward, and unquestionably believing that he was doing the right thing, and that he ought, in the performance of his duty as a member of a profession devoted to the alleviation of human suffering, to do it....

[I]n my view the proviso that it is necessary for the Crown to prove that the act was not done in good faith for the purpose only of preserving the life of the mother is in accordance with what has always been the common law of England with regard to the killing of an unborn child. No such proviso is in fact set out in s. 58 of the Offences Against the Person Act, 1861; but the words of that section are that any person who 'unlawfully' uses an instrument with intent to procure miscarriage shall be guilty of felony. In my opinion the word 'unlawfully' is not, in that section, a meaningless word. I think it imports the meaning expressed by the proviso in s. 1, sub-s. 1, of the Infant Life (Preservation) Act, 1929 [that 'no person shall be found guilty of an offence under this section unless it is proved that the act which caused the death of the child was not done in good faith for the purpose only of preserving the life of the mother'.] and that s. 58 of the Offences Against the Person Act, 1861, must be read as if the words making it an offence to use an instrument with intent to procure a miscarriage were qualified by a similar proviso.

What then is the meaning to be given to the words 'for the purpose of preserving the life of the mother'...I think those words ought to be construed in a reasonable sense, and, if the doctor is of opinion, on reasonable grounds and with adequate knowledge, that the probable consequence of the continuance of the pregnancy will be to make the woman a physical or mental wreck, the jury are quite entitled to take the view that the doctor who, under those circumstances and in that honest belief, operates, is operating for the purpose of preserving the life of the mother....

It is an observation that appeals to one's common sense that it must be injurious to a girl that she should go through the state of pregnancy and finally of labour when she is of tender years. Then, too, you must consider the evidence about the effect of rape, especially on a child, as this girl was...You are the judges of the facts and it is for you to say what weight should be given to the testimony of the witnesses; but no doubt you will think it is only common sense that a girl who for nine months has to carry in her body the reminder of the dreadful scene and then go through the pangs of childbirth must suffer great mental anguish, unless indeed she be feeble-minded or belongs to the class described as 'the prostitute

---

[20] [1939] 1 KB 697.

> class'... But in the case of a normal, decent girl brought up in a normal, decent way you may well think that Dr. Rees [a clinical psychologist] was not overstating the effect of the continuance of the pregnancy when he said that it would be likely to make her a mental wreck, with all the disastrous consequences that would follow from that.

Following Aleck Bourne's acquittal, it was apparent that an abortion could lawfully be performed if the pregnant woman's mental health was endangered by her unwanted pregnancy. Some doctors were evidently prepared to interpret this 'mental wreck' exception quite broadly, and terminate the pregnancies of women who were distressed, rather than mentally ill. Because such doctors were risking prosecution, their fees tended to be high, and these safe, 'legal' abortions were therefore inaccessible to the majority of women, who continued to rely on the services of illegal abortionists. Although exact figures are unavailable, it is thought that there were probably at least 100,000 illegal abortions each year prior to abortion's partial decriminalization in 1967. Some of these 'backstreet' abortionists' practices were extremely dangerous, and mortality rates were high.

Although it is now of minimal practical relevance, brief mention should be made of the Infant Life (Preservation) Act 1929, under which it is an offence to destroy the life of a child capable of being born alive, unless the act is done in good faith for the purpose only of preserving the life of the mother. The purpose of this Act was to close a legal loophole. In 1929, it was unlawful to kill a fetus *in utero*, and it was murder to kill a child which had been fully born and was living without any connection with its mother. However, no protection was afforded to the child while it was in the process of being born, before it had been completely separated from its mother. In order to fill this gap, the Infant Life (Preservation) Act provided that killing the child during childbirth would also be an offence.

Infant Life (Preservation) Act 1929 section 1

> 1(1) [A]ny person who, with intent to destroy the life of a child capable of being born alive, by any wilful act causes a child to die before it has an existence independent of its mother, shall be guilty of felony, to wit, of child destruction, and shall be liable on conviction thereof on indictment to penal servitude for life:
>
> Provided that no person shall be found guilty of an offence under this section unless it is proved that the act which caused the death of the child was not done in good faith for the purpose only of preserving the life of the mother.

Although not intended to apply to abortion, which was, of course, unlawful in 1929, once the Abortion Act 1967 came into force, the 1929 Act had the effect of setting a time limit for lawful abortion, since it provided that it is an offence to destroy the life of a fetus which is 'capable of being born alive'. In 1929, this was assumed to be the case at around 28 weeks. Before a time limit was specifically added to the Abortion Act in 1990, the age at which a fetus was capable of being born alive had dropped steadily, and was assumed to be around 24 weeks. For example, in *Rance v Mid-Downs Health Authority*,[21] Mr and Mrs Rance brought an action in negligence after Mrs Rance gave birth to a boy with spina bifida. They

---

[21] [1991] 1 QB 587.

argued that Mrs Rance should have been given the opportunity to terminate the pregnancy. Brooke J held that since the diagnosis was only possible at 26 weeks—at which point the fetus would be capable of being born alive—an abortion would have been unlawful under the 1929 Act.

The 1929 Act is no longer relevant in determining whether a proposed abortion is lawful. The Abortion Act 1967 was amended in 1990 to provide that no offence under the Infant Life (Preservation) Act is committed provided that the pregnancy is terminated in accordance with the provisions in the 1967 Act, and to set a 24-week time limit for abortions carried out under the 'social ground' (see below).

(b) THE ABORTION ACT 1967

(1) The Background to Legalization

In order to understand the form that abortion's legalization took in 1967, it is important to realize that the Abortion Act 1967, which provides limited statutory defences to the criminal offences described above, was not enacted in order to provide women with the *right* to terminate their unwanted pregnancies. Rather, the principal factor behind public and parliamentary support for legalization was concern about high mortality rates resulting from illegal abortions, especially among the poor. Inadequate contraception—the pill only became widely available during the 1960s—meant that unwanted pregnancies were common. Poor women were therefore faced with an invidious choice between giving birth to a child for whom they would be unable to provide adequate care, or resorting to an illegal and often hazardous abortion. In *R v Scrimaglia*,[22] a case in which a 'backstreet' abortion took place *after* legalization, the then Lord Chief Justice commented that 'one of the objects, as everyone knows, of the new Act was to try to get rid of the back-street insanitary operations'.

By the mid-1960s, it was clear that the law was not preventing women from terminating their unwanted pregnancies; instead it was ensuring that large numbers of abortions were performed in unhygienic surroundings, using dangerous techniques. Successful prosecutions were rare: women who had had abortions would seldom be prepared to give evidence against illegal abortionists, and the police were often reluctant to prosecute. The law was, in short, utterly ineffective.

Although, as we have seen, some doctors were prepared to perform abortions, the possibility of prosecution served as a powerful deterrent, even if the woman's circumstances were truly desperate. Despite the alarmingly high numbers of avoidable deaths caused each year by botched illegal abortions, the procedure's dubious legality inhibited most doctors from offering women safe legal abortions. Unsurprisingly, the medical profession resented the criminal law's interference with their freedom to act in the best interests of their patients. Abortion, then, was not legalized in order to enhance women's reproductive autonomy: rather, the Abortion Act's principal purpose was to enable doctors to act lawfully in assisting women who were driven to distraction by the prospect of yet another mouth to feed.

In the next extract, Sally Sheldon argues that supporters of David Steel's Abortion Bill appeared to share their opponents' belief that women could not be trusted to make the decision to terminate their pregnancies for themselves.

---

[22] (1971) 55 Cr App R 280.

Sally Sheldon[23]

> [In] the parliamentary debates preceding the introduction of the Abortion Act…[t]he doctor is talked of as a 'highly skilled and dedicated', 'sensitive, sympathetic' member of a 'high and proud profession' which acts 'with its own ethical and medical standards' displaying 'skill, judgement and knowledge'. The woman who experiences an unwanted pregnancy, on the other hand, is portrayed as someone who is fundamentally incapable of taking such an important decision for herself—either because she is downtrodden and driven to desperation (in the language of the reformers) or, for the opponents of reform, because she is selfish and morally immature. The first of these two images is summed up in the following quotation taken from the parliamentary debates:
>
> > There is the woman who already has a large family, perhaps six or seven children…There is the question of the woman who loses her husband during pregnancy and has to go out to work, and obviously cannot bear the strain of doing a full day's work, and looking after a child. There is the woman whose husband is a drunkard or a ne'er-do-well, or is in prison serving a long term, and she has to go to work.
>
> On the other side of the debate, the opponents of reform portrayed the woman as selfish, feckless and irresponsible. Jill Knight, a Conservative MP, was one of the leading opponents of reform…She reveals an image of women seeking abortion as selfish, treating babies 'like bad teeth to be jerked out just because they cause suffering…simply because it may be inconvenient for a year or so to its mother'. She later adds that a 'mother might want an abortion so that a planned holiday is not postponed or other arrangements interfered with'. The ability and willingness of the woman to make a serious decision regarding abortion, considering all factors and all parties, is dismissed. Rather, she will make a snap decision for her own convenience. The task of the law is thus perceived essentially as one of responsibilization: if the woman seeks to evade the consequences of her carelessness, the law should stand as a barrier.

Given this background, the form that legalization took is not surprising. Abortion is not available upon request. Rather, abortion continues to be proscribed by the Offences Against the Person Act 1861 (and in Scotland by the common law), but the Abortion Act 1967 provides that abortion will be lawful (in England, Scotland, and Wales—the Act does not apply in Northern Ireland), and no offence will have been committed, if the criteria laid out in the Act are met. We consider these in more detail below, but they are, in short, that two doctors agree that the woman's circumstances satisfy one of the four statutory 'grounds' for abortion; that the abortion is carried out by a registered medical practitioner in an approved place; and that it is notified within seven days to the Chief Medical Officer. Although the basic substance of the legislation remains unaltered since 1967, the Abortion Act was amended in 1990 by the Human Fertilisation and Embryology Act. Further amendments to the Act were tabled during Parliamentary debates on the Human Fertilisation and Embryology Act 2008, but none was successful.

(2) The Grounds for Abortion

The statutory defences to the criminal offences in the Offences Against the Person Act are contained in section 1 of the Abortion Act 1967, as amended:

---

[23] 'The Abortion Act 1967: A Critical Perspective' in Ellie Lee (ed), *Abortion Law and Politics Today* (Macmillan: London, 1998) 43–58.

Abortion Act 1967 section 1

1(1) Subject to the provisions of this section a person shall not be guilty of an offence under the law relating to abortion when a pregnancy is terminated by a registered medical practitioner if two registered medical practitioners are of the opinion, formed in good faith:

  (a) that the pregnancy has not exceeded its twenty fourth week and that the continuation of the pregnancy would involve risk, greater than if the pregnancy were terminated, of injury to the physical or mental health of the pregnant woman or any existing children of her family; or

  (b) that the termination is necessary to prevent grave permanent injury to the physical or mental health of the pregnant woman; or

  (c) that the continuance of the pregnancy would involve risk to the life of the pregnant woman, greater than if the pregnancy were terminated; or

  (d) that there is a substantial risk that if the child were born it would suffer from physical or mental abnormalities as to be seriously handicapped.

(2) In determining whether the continuance of a pregnancy would involve such risk of injury to health as is mentioned in paragraph (a) or (b) of subsection (1) of this section, account may be taken of the woman's actual or reasonably foreseeable environment.

Let us investigate the meaning of this section in more detail.

(a) Unsuccessful terminations

There is an unfortunate ambiguity in the first sentence of section 1. It appears to suggest that the defence only exists 'when a pregnancy is terminated'. Does this mean that the defence does not exist where the pregnancy is *not* terminated? Because the 1861 Act criminalizes anything done with the *intention* to procure a miscarriage, a literal interpretation of section 1 might leave unsuccessful terminations in an awkward lacuna: a person can be guilty of an offence under the 1861 Act even if the woman's pregnancy is not terminated, but the defence only exists if the pregnancy *is* terminated. A similar problem arises if the woman having the abortion turns out not to have been pregnant. The doctor could still be charged under the 1861 Act for *attempting* to procure a miscarriage, but no defence would exist if there had not in fact been a pregnancy to terminate.

The issue was considered by the House of Lords in *Royal College of Nursing v Department of Health and Social Security* (discussed in more detail below). A majority held that it would be 'absurd' and 'cannot have been the intention of Parliament' that anyone taking part in an unsuccessful termination would be unable to rely upon the defences contained in the Abortion Act and would therefore be guilty of an offence under the Offences Against the Person Act 1861. As Lord Edmund-Davies explained:

Were it otherwise the unavoidable conclusion is that doctors and nurses could in such cases be convicted of what in essence would be the extraordinary crime of attempting to do a lawful act.[24]

He then quoted with approval from Smith and Hogan's *Criminal Law*:

24 [1981] AC 800.

> [T]he legalisation of an abortion must include the steps which are taken towards it. Are we really to say that these are criminal until the operation is complete, when they are retrospectively authorised, or alternatively that they are lawful until the operation is discontinued or the woman is discovered not to be pregnant when, retrospectively, they become unlawful? When the conditions of the Act are otherwise satisfied, it is submitted that [the doctor] is not unlawfully administering, etc., and that this is so whether the pregnancy be actually terminated or not.

Hence, it seems likely that a doctor who unsuccessfully attempted to terminate a pregnancy within the terms of the Abortion Act 1967 would have a defence to the criminal offence contained in section 59 of the Offences Against the Person Act.

(b) The need for medical approval

Notice that the Act does not entitle a woman to decide to terminate an unwanted pregnancy, even if her circumstances clearly fit within the statutory grounds. Instead, what matters is the two doctors' opinions that an abortion would be lawful. It is also worth noting that the statute does not even specify that the section 1(1) conditions have to actually be satisfied. The legality of an abortion rests wholly upon whether the doctors have formed the *opinion*, in good faith, that the woman's case fits within the statutory grounds, not upon whether those grounds in fact *exist*. So, an abortion would be legal even if the woman's circumstances did not satisfy the statutory grounds, provided that the two doctors who authorized her termination had acted in good faith. Doctors performing abortions will therefore only fail to be protected by the defence in section 1(1) if there is evidence that they did not act in good faith.

There has been one successful prosecution since the Act came into force. In *R v Smith*, the evidence indicated that the doctor had failed to carry out an internal examination; had made no inquiries into the pregnant woman's personal situation, and had not sought a second doctor's opinion. He was convicted on the grounds that he had not, in good faith, attempted to balance the risks of pregnancy and termination. The Court of Appeal appeared to indicate that a doctor will have acted in good faith if he complies with accepted medical practice: 'good faith' thus seems to be synonymous with the *Bolam* test (discussed in Chapter 3).

R v Smith[25]

Scarman LJ

The [Abortion] Act (though it renders lawful abortions that before its enactment would have been unlawful), does not depart from the basic principle of the common law as declared in *R. v Bourne*, namely, that the legality of an abortion depends upon the opinion of the doctor. It has introduced the safeguard of two opinions: but, if they are formed in good faith by the time when the operation is undertaken, the abortion is lawful. Thus a great social responsibility is firmly placed by the law upon the shoulders of the medical profession....

The sequence of events was such as to call for very careful consideration as to whether it was possible to believe that Dr. Smith had formed in good faith, or at all, the opinion necessary to give him the protection of the Abortion Act. Had he, or had he not, abused the trust

25 [1974] 1 All ER 376.

reposed in him by the Act of Parliament? The burden was on the prosecution to prove beyond reasonable doubt that he had. All this was faithfully explained to the jury by the recorder. We quote only one passage towards the end of the summing up:

> ...If two doctors genuinely form an opinion in each case that they deal with that the risk of continuance is more than the risk of termination, it does not matter whether they are right or wrong in that view. If they form that opinion genuinely and in good faith, that in fact comes within the Act, and there is no guilt attached to it. You have to wonder in the case of Dr. Smith whether such a view could genuinely be held by a medical man.... The only indication on the case notes about any danger to her mental or physical health was the word 'depressed', 'not willing to marry and depressed'. Those are the only words about it on the case notes. You have to ask yourselves, was there any balancing of the risks involved in allowing the pregnancy to continue and allowing the pregnancy to be terminated, or was this a mere routine abortion for cash? That is what you have to consider. Was a second opinion even contemplated as a necessity in this case of Miss Rodgers? If, on the very first interview when the girl was seen by Dr. Smith, the very first interview he had with her, he offered to operate on her the next morning, was there any real contemplation or thought that a second opinion was necessary?

Further evidence that the statute's purpose is to protect medical discretion rather than women's rights comes from the inherent vagueness of the statutory grounds. The Act does not, for example, specify that abortion is legal where the pregnancy has resulted from an act of rape or incest. This ambiguity was deliberate. David Steel's Abortion Bill did initially contain more specific clauses, such as one which permitted abortion where the woman was pregnant as a result of rape, but these were opposed by both the British Medical Association and the Royal College of Obstetricians and Gynaecologists. While doctors will invariably allow rape victims to terminate their pregnancies, a definitive list of situations in which abortion is lawful was rejected in part because it would erode medical discretion, and might give women the impression that in certain circumstances abortion would be an entitlement. In *Paton v British Pregnancy Advisory Service Trustees*, a case in which a man wanted to stop his wife from terminating her pregnancy, Sir George Baker P explained very clearly that, under the 1967 Act, it is doctors rather than pregnant women who bear principal responsibility for deciding whether a pregnancy should be terminated.

Paton v British Pregnancy Advisory Service Trustees[26]

Sir George Baker P

My own view is that it would be quite impossible for the courts in any event to supervise the operation of the Abortion Act 1967. The great social responsibility is firmly placed by the law upon the shoulders of the medical profession...The two doctors have given a certificate. It is not and cannot be suggested that the certificate was given in other than good faith and it seems to me that there is the end of the matter in English law....

This certificate is clear, and not only would it be a bold and brave judge...who would seek to interfere with the discretion of doctors acting under the Abortion Act 1967, but I think he would really be a foolish judge who would try to do any such thing, unless, possibly, where there is clear bad faith and an obvious attempt to perpetrate a criminal offence.

---

[26] [1979] QB 276.

In the next extract, Sally Sheldon criticizes the Abortion Act's delegation of abortion decision-making to doctors, arguing that the decision *whether* to terminate a pregnancy is not necessarily a question that requires *clinical* expertise.

Sally Sheldon[27]

The granting of such power to doctors in the field of abortion is often justified by the argument that abortion is essentially a medical matter. However, the actual decision whether or not a given pregnancy should be terminated is not normally one that requires expert medical advice, or the balancing of medical criteria. Further, the doctors' decision-making power is not, according to the terms of the Abortion Act, contained within a narrow, limited medical field. In judging whether or not abortion could be detrimental to the mental or physical health of the pregnant woman, under s. 1(2) of the Act, 'account may be taken of the pregnant woman's actual or reasonably foreseeable environment'. The woman's whole lifestyle, her home, finances and relationships are opened up to the doctor's scrutiny, so that he may judge whether or not the patient is a deserving case for relief. The power given to doctors here far exceeds that which would accrue merely on the basis of a technical expertise.

In their 2007 Report on scientific issues relating to abortion, the House of Commons Science and Technology Committee were especially critical of the 'two doctors' requirement, suggesting that it served no useful purpose and delayed women's access to early abortions (it should be noted that the final Report represents a majority view, and a minority of the Committee publicly distanced themselves from its conclusions).

House of Commons Science and Technology Select Committee[28]

The Department of Health has ruled that both doctors are able to sign the HSA forms without seeing the patient, so long as they believe, in good faith, that the woman meets the legal grounds for abortion on the basis of the clinical notes. We have heard that the process of certifying abortions has become, in the words of the Christian Medical Fellowship, a "sham". Dr Vincent Argent...claims to have witnessed HSA1 signing practices that include:

- Signing batches of forms before patients are even seen for consultation;
- Signing the forms with no knowledge of the particular patient and without reading the notes;
- Signing forms without seeing or examining the patients;
- Signing forms after the abortion has been performed;
- Faxing the forms to other locations for signature;
- Use of signature stamps without consultation with the doctor.

If requests for abortions are being 'rubber stamped' by doctors, either the requirement for two signatures does not play a meaningful role in abortion practice or the law is not being properly applied....

[27] *Beyond Control: Medical Power and Abortion Law* (Pluto: London, 1997).
[28] Scientific Developments Relating to the Abortion Act 1967, Twelfth Report of Session 2006–07, available at <www.publications.parliament.uk>.

> We were not presented with any good evidence that, at least in the first trimester, the requirement for two doctors' signatures serves to safeguard women or doctors in any meaningful way, or serves any other useful purpose. We are concerned that the requirement for two signatures may be causing delays in access to abortion services. If a goal of public policy is to encourage early as opposed to later abortion, we believe there is a strong case for removing the requirement for two doctors' signatures. We would like to see the requirement for two doctors' signatures removed.

In the following sections we look at the four different grounds for abortion contained in section 1(1) in more detail.

(c) The 'social' ground

Abortion Act 1967 section 1

> 1(1)(a) that the pregnancy has not exceeded its twenty fourth week and that the continuation of the pregnancy would involve risk, greater than if the pregnancy were terminated, of injury to the physical or mental health of the pregnant woman or any existing children of her family;

(i) The time limit

Section 1(1)(a), often referred to as the 'social ground', is the only one which imposes a time limit. As we saw earlier, following the 1990 amendment to the Abortion Act 1967 the Infant Life (Preservation) Act no longer applies, and so the other three grounds for abortion are—in theory at least—available until birth. Obviously, the existence of a time limit means that it is important to know the moment at which a pregnancy begins. When calculating the length of a pregnancy that is being carried to term, the convention is to treat the first day of the pregnant woman's previous period as the relevant start date, even though conception would usually have occurred about two weeks later. The reason for this is that fertilization and implantation are processes that take place imperceptibly over several days. Fertilization may not begin until a few days after sexual intercourse, and will usually take several hours; implantation again takes several days and will not usually start until at least six to seven days after fertilization began. It is therefore impossible to detect the moment at which the fertilized ovum attaches itself to the wall of the uterus, and the woman can be considered pregnant. Dating the pregnancy from the woman's previous period allows doctors to calculate the length of gestation with greater precision.

For the purposes of the Abortion Act, however, using this convenient fictional 'start date' is more problematic. Insofar as section 1(1)(a) contains a defence to a criminal offence, any ambiguity must be construed in favour of the defendant: that is, the pregnant woman and/ or her doctor. It would seem unfair to deny a woman an abortion when she was, as a matter of fact, 22 weeks pregnant, but the date of her previous period fell outside the 24-week limit. Rather, the better interpretation is probably that the pregnancy began when, according to medical judgement, implantation is likely to have occurred. This undoubtedly introduces a margin of uncertainty, but again, if a borderline case were to arise, the ambiguity would have to be construed in favour of the pregnant woman and her doctors.

In practice, 70 per cent of abortions take place during the first 10 weeks of pregnancy, and 90 per cent take place within the first 12 weeks.[29] Only a tiny minority (around 1 per cent)

---

[29] Abortion Statistics 2007 (DH: London, 2008), available at <www.dh.gov.uk/>.

takes place after the nineteenth week of pregnancy,[30] so the introduction of a 24-week time limit for what is known as the 'social' ground has had minimal practical impact, especially since the Infant Life Preservation Act had already been interpreted as imposing a 24-week time limit upon abortion. It is, however, important to remember that women do not have the *right* to an abortion up to 24 weeks: rather, doctors have the *power* to carry out terminations if they believe the grounds in the Act are satisfied. Very few obstetricians are, in practice, prepared to carry out abortions for 'social' reasons late into the second trimester. Medical discretion, therefore, generally leads to an earlier time limit than that specified in the statute, and woman may encounter difficulties in obtaining an abortion under this ground late into the second trimester.

Advances in neonatal medicine, which mean that premature babies born before 24 weeks' gestation are now capable of survival, coupled with developments in visualization techniques, such as 4D ultrasound, which can now show fetal movements in extraordinary detail, have given rise to renewed interest in the time limits for abortion. In the next extract, Deborah Kirklin discusses the role of medical imaging and illusion in the abortion debate.

D Kirklin[31]

The latest developments in fetal ultrasound technology, made public by a group called *Create*, and first introduced to the wider UK public by the *Evening Standard*..., have evoked a flood of responses from the public, pro-life and pro-choice campaigners, and politicians, re-igniting the debate about abortion in the UK and elsewhere. The focus of the *Evening Standard* articles, on the smiling, walking, and waving babies that the images purport to show, was echoed throughout the worldwide media coverage that followed. In July 2004, Sir David Steel, sponsor of the 1967 Abortion Act, publicly stated that the *Create* images led him to believe it was time to review the legal time limit for abortions....

What interests me here is the powerful role that biomedical imaging, and the human artifice it involves, can play in influencing the nature, timing, and tone of this debate. The ultrasound technology involved is without doubt impressive. A computer is used to simulate the 3D appearance of the fetus in the womb by combining a series of 2D images and then filling in any gaps; the 4D images are generated by using the simulated 3D images to produce a rapidly changing sequence of images, an illusion of fetal movement is thereby created....What is not immediately apparent when viewing the video clips is that these video clips are in fact video loops, with the same movement shown again and again. Thus the waving fetus is an illusion created by showing the movement of the fetus' arm, from left to right across its body, over and over again. The smiling fetus, who appears to coyly smile then relax its mouth before coyly smiling again, is also an illusion. We do indeed see the fetus draw back its lips but instead of seeing what happens next, the illusion of smiling is created by the loop presentation of the images.

John Wyatt argues that developments in neonatal medicine since 1967 have also affected attitudes towards late abortion.

---

[30] Ibid.
[31] 'The Role of Medical Imaging in the Abortion Debate' (2004) 30 Journal of Medical Ethics 426.

John Wyatt[32]

Medical practice in modern perinatal centres can have a paradoxical element. In one part of the hospital a huge concentration of resources, human expertise, parental concern and professional dedication is devoted to ensuring the survival of babies born as early as twenty-three to twenty-four weeks. In an adjacent part of the hospital agonised discussions about the possibility of feticide in a much more mature fetus are taking place. Hospital staff may feel deeply uneasy about raising the option of feticide when a major abnormality is detected in the third trimester...Although late feticide is performed relatively rarely, the juxtaposition of this practice with neonatal intensive care units inevitably poses ethical conflicts for health professionals.

The development of neonatal intensive care is predicated on the belief that even tiny, immature and uniquely vulnerable babies deserve the very best care and that profession-als have an ethical duty to act in each baby's own interests even at considerable cost to society. If there is no responsibility to consider fetal interests until delivery, then it must be explained why the moment of birth in itself leads to a transformation of our ethical responsibilities.

While the 24-week time limit is assumed to derive from an assessment of when a fetus might be viable, it is not self-evident that viability should determine the time limit within which abortion is legitimate, particularly since viability is an inherently unstable bound-ary. It will depend, for example, on the availability of sophisticated medical equipment. A baby born next door to a leading neonatal intensive care unit will be 'viable' at a much earlier stage than a baby delivered without medical assistance in a croft in the Outer Hebrides.

Furthermore, deciding that 23 or 24 weeks marks the point at which a baby is 'viable', and abortion thereby impermissible, assumes that we can accurately date the duration of a pregnancy. Most doctors would say that there is a margin of error of a week or more in their capacity to diagnose gestational age.

It is also important to be clear about what we mean by viability. Is a fetus viable if it is born alive but dies in the delivery room, or the intensive care unit? Or should we only consider a fetus to be viable, as the BMA have suggested, at the point 'at which the prema-ture infant has a reasonable chance of surviving, without a very serious or life-threatening abnormality'?[33]

Some countries, such as France, have chosen a lower cut-off point for the legality of abor-tion, and we should acknowledge that setting the limit at 12 weeks, 14 weeks, 20 weeks or 24 weeks is essentially a *political* decision, rather than a biologically determined fact. Indeed, in the UK it is possible to terminate a fetus until birth where the pregnant woman's life is at risk, or where abortion would prevent grave permanent injury, or where the fetus is likely to be seriously disabled. In these cases, the fact that the fetus might be viable is 'trumped' by other factors, such as the need to protect the woman's life.

In the next extract, Sally Sheldon argues that reliance on viability as the cut-off point for lawful abortion might have negative consequences for women's access to abortion services.

---

[32] 'Medical Paternalism and the Fetus' (2001) 27 Journal of Medical Ethics ii15–ii 20.
[33] Abortion Time Limit: Briefing Paper (BMA: London, 2008), available at <www.bma.org.uk>.

Sally Sheldon[34]

The adoption of viability as the cut-off point for abortions was heralded as a victory for pro-choice campaigners, as it currently ensures an upper limit which is high in comparison to other Western abortion laws. However, the effect of the 1990 debates has been to entrench in the public—and parliamentary—consciousness that abortion is permissible prior to viability, but should be forbidden after this point. This is a notion which future campaigns may find hard to dislodge.... While the present state of medical science makes it impossible to sustain neo-natal life at much less than twenty-four weeks of gestational development for reasons of lung development, it is surely not inconceivable that this limit will be gradually pushed downwards. If this happens, pro-choice groups will face a particularly bitter struggle to try and separate out the legitimacy of abortion from the notion of viability...

The other worrying trend, highlighted during the [1990] debates...is the use of medical knowledges to support the construction of the foetus as a separate individual...During the 1990 parliamentary debates, the Society for the Protection of Unborn Children (SPUC) sent each MP a plastic replica of a foetus at twenty weeks of gestation. Although various MPs expressed their distaste at this strategy..., not one commented on what I would see as the most worrying aspect of this tactic: that the foetus is represented in total abstraction from the body of the woman that carried it...[T]he foetus is not and cannot exist without the body of the pregnant woman which actively nourishes and supports it. Its representation as a free-floating and separate entity embodies a fundamental deceit.

Of course, it is true that the UK's adoption of a viability-related cut-off point means that abortion for essentially social reasons is lawful until later in pregnancy than in many European countries. Some, including the BMA, have argued that the law should be changed to permit abortion 'on request' during the first thirteen weeks, but that abortions after that date should either continue to be subject to the 'two doctors' requirement, or should be further restricted.

In contrast, some pro-choice campaigners argue that it is important that abortion continues to be available in the second trimester. While most women who decide to terminate an unwanted pregnancy will want to do so as quickly as possible, there may be good reasons why some women are not able to access abortion until after the first trimester. In Ingham *et al.*'s study into the reasons why women have abortions in the second trimester, they found a combination of 'women-related' reasons—such as not realizing one is pregnant or finding the decision difficult—and 'service-related' reasons, such as encountering delays in referral for termination.

Roger Ingham, Ellie Lee, Steve Clements and Nicole Stone[35]

A lack of early awareness of pregnancy is a significant factor in second-trimester abortions. Half of the respondents were more than seven and a half weeks' gestation when they first suspected they were pregnant, while one quarter were over 11 weeks 2 days' gestation. For women who were more than seven and a half week's gestation, the key factors for a delay in suspecting pregnancy included:

---

[34] 'The Law of Abortion and the Politics of Medicalisation' in J Bridgeman and S Millns (eds), *Law and Body Politics: Regulating the Female Body* (Dartmouth: Aldershot, 1995).

[35] Second Trimester Abortions in England and Wales, Centre for Sexual Health Research University of Southampton, 2007, available at <www.soton.ac.uk/lateabortionstudy/late_abortion.pdf>.

- irregular periods (49 percent)
- continuing periods (42 percent)
- they were using contraception (29 percent)....

Around half of the respondents took one week or less between taking their test and then making the decision to have an abortion. For those who took more than one week to make the decision, the most commonly cited reason (by 65 percent of respondents) was: 'I was not sure about having the abortion, and it took a while to make up my mind and ask for one.' Reasons for this indecision included:

- concerns about what was involved in having an abortion
- difficulties in agreeing a decision with their partner.

A relatively large proportion of the sample (60 percent) reported a delay between requesting an abortion and having the procedure. Forty-two percent of the respondents waited more than two weeks between requesting and having an abortion, and 23 percent waited more than three weeks—beyond the minimum standard recommended by the Royal College of Obstetricians and Gynaecologists (RCOG). Some of the reasons for delay at this stage were clearly service related, and included:

- the person I first asked for an abortion took a long time to sort out further appointments for me (30 percent)
- there were confusions about where I should go to have the abortion (24 percent).

(ii) The risk to health

For an abortion to be lawful under section 1(1)(a), continuing the pregnancy must pose a risk, greater than if the pregnancy were terminated, of injury to the physical or mental health of the pregnant woman or her children. Under section 1(2) the doctor is specifically directed to take account of the woman's actual or reasonably foreseeable environment. In 2007, 98 per cent of all abortions were authorized on the grounds that the pregnancy posed a risk to the pregnant woman's own health, and only 0.5 per cent of these were due to a risk to her physical health. One per cent were authorized under this ground because of a risk to her children's health.[36] Usually, of course, having another brother or sister does not pose a direct risk to a child's health. Rather, it could be argued that by overstretching the family's resources and diverting the mother's attention away from the care of her existing children, the arrival of a new baby may have an adverse effect upon their health.

For two reasons, this ground is very easily satisfied. First, the Royal College of Obstetricians and Gynaecologists suggest that its reference to health is normally assumed to refer to the World Health Organization's definition of 'health', as 'a state of physical and mental well-being, not merely an absence of disease or infirmity'. This means that the abortion only needs to be necessary in order to promote the woman's mental wellbeing, rather than to prevent her from suffering physical or psychiatric harm. The mental wellbeing of a woman who does not want to be pregnant is, almost by definition, promoted by allowing her to have an abortion. Secondly, given that pregnancy and childbirth are almost always more risky than termination, an abortion will usually also pose less risk to the woman's *physical* wellbeing.

---

[36] Abortion Statistics 2007 (DH: London, 2008), available at <www.dh.gov.uk/>.

(d) Prevent grave permanent injury

Abortion Act 1967 section 1

> 1(1)(b) that the termination is necessary to prevent grave permanent injury to the physical or mental health of the pregnant woman.

An abortion may be lawful under section 1(1)(b) if it is necessary to prevent grave permanent injury to the pregnant woman's physical or mental health, or to prevent a risk to her life. 'Grave permanent injury' is not defined in the statute, but there seems to be no doubt that this ground will only be satisfied if the woman's condition is extremely serious. In the House of Lords debates in 1990, Lord Mackay described this as 'a stiff legal test to cover special situations'. It is also worth noting that abortion is not necessarily lawful under this ground just because the pregnancy is exposing the pregnant woman to the risk of grave permanent injury. Instead, the abortion must be 'necessary' to prevent this injury materializing. If the injury could be prevented *without* aborting the fetus, then abortion would not be justified under this section.

(e) Risk to the pregnant woman's life

Abortion Act 1967 section 1

> 1(1)(c) that the continuance of the pregnancy would involve risk to the life of the pregnant woman, greater than if the pregnancy were terminated.

Under section 1(1)(c), doctors must judge that continuing the pregnancy poses a greater risk to the pregnant woman's life than abortion. It is not necessary that abortion should *remove* the risk to the pregnant woman's life: rather, abortion merely has to *reduce* the risk. An abortion may not save a terminally ill woman's life, but it might nevertheless pose less risk to her health than carrying a pregnancy to term and going through childbirth. Recall that in *R v Bourne*, risk to life was broadly interpreted to encompass situations in which the pregnancy would 'make the woman a physical or mental wreck'. For the purposes of section 1(1)(c), however, an elastic interpretation of 'risk to life' would not be appropriate because it would render this section synonymous with section 1(1)(a), and therefore redundant as a separate ground.

(f) The fetal abnormality ground

Abortion Act 1967 section 1

> 1(1)(d) that there is a substantial risk that if the child were born it would suffer from physical or mental abnormalities as to be seriously handicapped.

Approximately one per cent of all abortions in England and Wales are carried out solely under section 1(1)(d), which permits abortion until birth where there is a substantial risk that the resulting child would be born seriously handicapped.[37] Access to abortion under

[37] Ibid.

this ground depends upon two doctors agreeing that a particular handicap is 'serious', and that the risk of it materializing is 'substantial'. Again, notice the doctors' wide discretion to decide whether a particular abnormality meets the threshold level of seriousness, and whether the risk of it materializing is substantial. This flexibility means that doctors might, for example, refuse to perform very late abortions unless the disability is so grave that the fetus would be likely to die shortly after birth.

In deciding whether a fetus's abnormality is sufficiently serious, the Royal College of Obstetricians and Gynaecologists have recommended that doctors take into account the probability that effective treatment will be available; the probable degree of self-awareness and ability to communicate with others; the suffering that would be experienced; and the extent to which the person might be dependent upon others. There is no definitive list of conditions which justify abortion, or of conditions which do not, and so there are inevitably discrepancies between different doctors' definitions of 'serious handicap'.

The question of what might count as a serious handicap was raised in an application for judicial review by Joanna Jepson in 2003 following her discovery that an abortion had been carried out on a fetus with a cleft palate after 24 weeks gestation.[38] Her argument was that when Parliament debated the 1990 amendments to the Abortion Act, which enabled abortion until birth for serious abnormalities, its intention had been that third-trimester abortions would be justifiable only for extremely serious conditions, and not for fairly minor abnormalities like cleft palate. West Mercia police launched an investigation following her complaint, but no prosecution was instigated. It was this failure to prosecute which prompted Joanna Jepson's legal action. In *Jepson v The Chief Constable of West Mercia Police Constabulary*, Jackson J initially granted her leave to apply for judicial review, on the grounds that the case raised an issue of public importance, but admitted that she would face considerable obstacles at the full hearing.

Jepson v The Chief Constable of West Mercia Police Constabulary[39]

Jackson J

For my part, having listened to the competing submissions of counsel, it does seem to me that the claimant in these proceedings faces substantial evidential hurdles and substantial legal hurdles. There will be arguments about standing and there will be considerable legal debate about whether, in the light of the advice received from the Royal College of Obstetricians and Gynaecologists, the decision not to prosecute can be challenged...Nevertheless, I am persuaded, having listened to the submissions of counsel, that this case does raise serious issues of law and issues of public importance which cannot be properly or fully argued in the context of a permission application.

West Mercia police then conceded that their initial investigation may not have been sufficiently thorough, and the case was reopened under a different team of officers, who referred it to the Crown Prosecution Service (CPS). In 2005, the CPS determined that the doctors who authorized the abortion had acted in good faith.

---

[38] *Jepson v The Chief Constable of West Mercia Police Constabulary* [2003] EWHC 3318.
[39] Ibid.

Chief Crown Prosecutor[40]

This complaint has been investigated most thoroughly by the police and the CPS has considered a great deal of evidence before reaching its decision. The issue is whether the two doctors who had authorised the termination were of the opinion, formed in good faith, that there was a substantial risk that if the child were born it would suffer from such physical and mental abnormalities as to be seriously handicapped. I consider that both doctors concluded that there was a substantial risk of abnormalities that would amount to the child being seriously handicapped. The evidence shows that these two doctors did form this opinion and formed it in good faith. In these circumstances I decided there was insufficient evidence for a realistic prospect of conviction and that there should be no charges against either of the doctors.

Under section 1(1)(d) there only need be a substantial *risk* of handicap, so an abortion could be justified under this section even if the fetus turns out not to suffer from any disability, provided that the doctor is of the opinion that there was a substantial risk that it might have done.

How might section 1(1)(d) apply to genetic tests which are increasingly able to predict *future* susceptibility to disease? Is a fetus, which has the gene that causes Huntington's disease (a degenerative adult-onset condition), at *substantial risk* of suffering from such abnormalities as to be *seriously handicapped*? If the child must be seriously handicapped from birth, many genetic diagnoses will not satisfy section 1(1)(d), and abortion would instead only be lawful within the first 24 weeks of pregnancy under section 1(1)(a). Where, as with Huntington's, possessing the abnormal gene will mean that, in adulthood, the child will develop an incurable degenerative disease, resulting in premature death, arguing that the child is at risk of 'serious handicap' would seem fairly straightforward. More difficult questions arise in relation to tests for genes which increase the susceptibility to adult-onset diseases, and we consider these questions in more detail in the context of pre-implantation genetic diagnosis in Chapter 15.

For some commentators, the fetal abnormality ground is especially controversial. In the next extract, Simo Vehmas argues that once a woman has decided to have a baby, it is not legitimate for her to reject a particular fetus on the grounds that it does not have the characteristics she requires.

Simo Vehmas[41]

When considering the parenting of a child with a cognitive impairment, people seem to forget the fact that *every* child is more or less a burden to her parents. Children without impairments may cause stress to their parents due to problems (e.g., drug and alcohol abuse and eating disorders) which children with cognitive impairments usually do not get involved in. Families of children with cognitive impairments do not necessarily experience any more difficulties than families with so-called normal children—their problems are just different...

Often...social and cultural factors contribute more to the well-being or ill-being of families than the child's impairment in itself. Families which receive support from their societies and

---

[40] 'CPS Decides Not to Prosecute Doctors Following Complaint by Rev Joanna Jepson' CPS Press Release, 16 Mar 2005 <www.cps.gov.uk/news/pressreleases/117_05.html>.

[41] 'Parental Responsibility and the Morality of Selective Abortion' (2002) 5 Ethical Theory and Moral Practice 463–84.

communities are, despite a child's impairment, likely to cope better than families which are emotionally and financially on their own...

The reason why parents view a disabled child as a problem is often a result of the fact that they generally tend to anticipate 'the birth of a usual perfect baby'.... It is true that parents generally wish their future child to conform more or less to some culturally formed ideal. This means that parents characteristically prefer having a good-looking, healthy and intellectually average (or, preferably, above average) child instead of an ugly, sickly and intellectually sub-average child. But to perform parental tasks well, the parents' commitment to care for their child has to be unconditional, which means that the commitment holds even if the child turns out to be ugly, sickly and intellectually subaverage.

Sally Sheldon and Stephen Wilkinson criticize the fetal abnormality ground from a different perspective, arguing that it is difficult to find a defensible reason for treating abortion on the grounds of fetal abnormality differently from other sorts of abortion. They consider three possible justifications for maintaining section (1)(1)(d) as a separate ground: first, the interests of the child-to-be; secondly, allowing the pregnant woman to conceive a non-disabled child instead; and, thirdly, protecting the pregnant woman's interests. The only logical justification for allowing women to terminate pregnancies where the fetus is disabled is—they suggest—to protect the woman's *own* interests, in which case this ground for abortion is functionally indistinguishable from section (1)(1)(a).

Sally Sheldon and Stephen Wilkinson[42]

The 'Foetal Interests Argument' attempts to justify s.(1)(1)(d) by claiming that termination actually benefits the disabled foetus, by saving it from a life of suffering. It claims that termination in these circumstances can thus be thought of as a kind of foetal euthanasia.... The first [objection] is that it only applies to a very narrow range of cases. These are cases where the likely alternative to termination is a resultant child whose quality of life is not merely low, but negative: that is, she would, quite literally, be better off dead, or better off never having been born. Whilst we are happy to grant, for the sake of argument, that there are cases where any resultant child will have a negative quality of life (for example, a child suffering from Tay-Sachs disease) many actual foetal impairments are indisputably not like this. For in most cases, the resultant child will have a quality of life which, although arguably less good than it would have been without impairment, is still positive overall and therefore a 'life worth living'....

The second argument for s.(1)(1)(d) is the 'Replacement Argument'... On this view, it is acceptable to 'trade off' the life of one foetus against that of another in a utilitarian way, their status being such that killing one solely in order to generate an increase in the general good is permissible....

The first [objection]... is that it assumes something which cannot simply be assumed: that the woman in question will at least try to become pregnant again... Admittedly, we cannot guarantee that each particular aborted foetus will be 'replaced' by another non-disabled foetus from the very same mother. However, viewing the situation holistically, it is likely that, if we allow abortion for reason of foetal disability, a *group* of mostly non-disabled fetuses will come to exist which would not otherwise exist... A second... more serious objection [is that] if the fetuses in question really do have very low status, such that they can be killed

[42] 'Termination of Pregnancy for Reason of Foetal Disability: Are There Grounds for a Special Exception in Law?' (2001) 9 Medical Law Review 85–109.

for purely utilitarian reasons, then it is not clear why *special* provisions covering disability are required.... We have a justification not for having a special exception for disabled fetuses but rather for a much more permissive policy across the board.

Even if section (1)(1)(a) more accurately describes the *reason* for aborting an abnormal fetus, a time limit is attached to the so-called 'social ground'. Maintaining fetal abnormality as a separate ground might therefore be desirable in order to allow for the tiny number of abortions carried out in the third trimester of pregnancy following the discovery of a grave fetal abnormality, without provoking the vigorous opposition which would be likely to defeat any proposal to remove the time limit from section (1)(1)(a).

(3) Other Restrictions upon Access to Abortion

(a) Personnel

Section 1 of the Abortion Act specifies that abortion will only be lawful if it is carried out *by* a medical practitioner. Terminations carried out by nurses or by the woman herself would therefore be unlawful. This restriction has particular significance for medical (as opposed to surgical) abortions, where the 'abortion pill', Mifepristone (known as RU486), is used to dislodge the embryo from the lining of the uterus. Medical abortions are increasingly common, and approximately 35 per cent of all abortions are now carried out in this way.[43]

If the woman herself takes the abortion pill, and—as happens in approximately 3 per cent of cases—miscarries before she returns to hospital for the insertion of a prostaglandin pessary, has she terminated the pregnancy herself? We would normally say that a person who takes a pill is the principal cause of that pill's consequences. In relation to euthanasia, a doctor who hands a patient a lethal drug has not killed her: rather, this would be a case of assisted suicide. Analogously, if a woman takes a pill, which causes her to miscarry, has she terminated her own pregnancy, and hence committed an offence under the Offences Against the Person Act 1861, to which the Abortion Act could not offer a defence?

The question of whether women who take the abortion pill might be terminating their own pregnancies has never been considered by a court. Nurses' involvement in non-surgical abortions has, however, been approved by a majority of the House of Lords in *Royal College of Nursing v Department of Health and Social Security*. Nurses, according to the majority, could actively participate in terminating pregnancies, provided that a registered medical practitioner is supervising the entire procedure.

Royal College of Nursing v Department of Health and Social Security[44]

Lord Diplock

What limitation... is imposed by the qualifying phrase: 'when a pregnancy is terminated by a registered medical practitioner'? In my opinion in the context of the Act, what it requires is that a registered medical practitioner, whom I will refer to as a doctor, should accept responsibility for all stages of the treatment for the termination of the pregnancy. The particular method to be used should be decided by the doctor in charge of the treatment for

---

[43] Abortion Statistics 2007 (DH: London, 2008), available at <www.dh.gov.uk/>.
[44] [1981] AC 800.

termination of the pregnancy, he should carry out any physical acts, forming part of the treatment, that in accordance with accepted medical practice are done only by qualified medical practitioners, and should give specific instructions as to the carrying out of such parts of the treatment as in accordance with accepted medical practice are carried out by nurses or other members of the hospital staff without medical qualifications. To each of them, the doctor, or his substitute, should be available to be consulted or called on for assistance from beginning to end of the treatment. In other words, the doctor need not do everything with his own hands; the requirements of the subsection are satisfied when the treatment for termination of a pregnancy is one prescribed by a registered medical practitioner carried out in accordance with his directions and of which a registered medical practitioner remains in charge throughout.

Women's own involvement in medical terminations might be justified on similar grounds provided that they are supervised by a medical practitioner, who retains responsibility throughout the process.

(b) Conscientious objection

Under section 4 of the Act, medical personnel have a right of conscientious objection to participation in the provision of abortion services, unless the abortion is necessary to prevent grave permanent injury to the physical or mental health of a pregnant woman, or to save her life.

Abortion Act section 4

4(1) [N]o person shall be under any duty, whether by contract or by any statutory or other legal requirement, to participate in any treatment authorised by this Act to which he has a conscientious objection.

Section 4 not only protects doctors who believe abortion is always wrong, but could also be used by doctors who are willing to perform abortions in the early stages of pregnancy, but who 'conscientiously object' to late abortions.

While the right is not limited to doctors, and nurses could undoubtedly refuse to assist during surgery, administrative staff are unlikely to be able to claim exemption. In *Janaway v Salford Heath Authority*[45] the House of Lords rejected a medical receptionist's claim that she had been unlawfully dismissed for refusing to type a letter of referral for an abortion. Lord Keith held that participation 'in its ordinary and natural meaning referred to actually taking part in treatment administered in a hospital or other approved place in accordance with section 1(3), for the purpose of terminating a pregnancy'.

'Taking part in treatment' is, however, still rather vague. Does a doctor who certifies that the woman's circumstances satisfy the statutory grounds (on what is now known as the 'blue form') 'participate' in her treatment? In *Janaway v Salford Heath Authority*, the House of Lords specifically declined to express an opinion, and left open the question of whether a GP's right of conscientious objection could extend to refusing to sign what was then the 'green form'. Lord Keith said:

---

[45] [1989] AC 537.

> It does not appear whether or not there are any circumstances under which a doctor might be under any legal duty to sign a green form, so as to place in difficulties one who had a conscientious objection to doing so. The fact that during the 20 years that the Act of 1967 has been in force no problem seems to have surfaced in this connection may indicate that in practice none exists. So I do not think it appropriate to express any opinion on the matter.[46]

Although the statute itself is unclear, referring a pregnant woman to another doctor is probably not 'participating' in her treatment. Certainly, in *Barr v Matthews*[47] Alliott J suggested that 'once a termination of pregnancy is recognized as an option the doctor invoking the conscientious objection clause should refer the patient to a colleague at once'. The Royal College of Obstetricians and Gynaecologist's most recent guidelines advise doctors with a conscientious objection to abortion that they should refer a patient who requests abortion to another doctor:

> Practitioners cannot claim exemption from giving advice or performing the preparatory steps to arrange an abortion where the request meets the legal requirements. Such steps include referral to another doctor, as appropriate.

Doctors are not legally obliged to publicize their conscientious objections to abortion, so women will not usually know in advance whether or not their doctor is a conscientious objector. As a result, it is possible that some women mistake their GP's lack of cooperation as an indication of their ineligibility for termination, rather than an expression of his moral convictions. In *Saxby v Morgan*,[48] for example, although the claimant's action in negligence ultimately failed, she had been told by her doctor that her pregnancy was too far advanced for him to refer her for a termination, despite being between 18 and 19 weeks pregnant, and so clearly within the time limits in the Abortion Act.

The GMC's latest guidance on doctors' personal beliefs suggests that doctors must tell women that they have a right to see another doctor, and that they should take steps prospectively to inform their patients about their unwillingness to refer for abortion. It also suggests that if the woman cannot easily make arrangements herself to see another doctor, the doctor is under a duty to assist her.

General Medical Council[49]

> 21. Patients may ask you to perform, advise on, or refer them for a treatment or procedure which is not prohibited by law or statutory code of practice in the country where you work, but to which you have a conscientious objection. In such cases you must tell patients of their right to see another doctor with whom they can discuss their situation and ensure that they have sufficient information to exercise that right. In deciding whether the patient has sufficient information, you must explore with the patient what information they might already have, or need.
>
> 22. In the circumstances described in paragraph 21, if the patient cannot readily make their own arrangements to see another doctor you must ensure that arrangements are made,

---

[46] [1989] AC 537.
[47] (2000) 52 BMLR 217.   [48] [1997] 8 Med LR 293.
[49] *Personal Beliefs and Medical Practice* (GMC: London, 2008).

without delay, for another doctor to take over their care. You must not obstruct patients from accessing services or leave them with nowhere to turn. Whatever your personal beliefs may be about the procedure in question, you must be respectful of the patient's dignity and views.

23. You must be open with patients—both in person and in printed materials such as practice leaflets—about any treatments or procedures which you choose not to provide or arrange because of a conscientious objection, but which are not otherwise prohibited.

While a woman whose GP has a conscientious objection to abortion clearly has the right to seek another doctor's assistance, her need to find another doctor may delay her abortion. Some women, such as those living in rural areas where there is only one local practitioner, may not easily be able to find a second doctor. Of course, doctors who work in private abortion clinics will not have conscientious objections to abortion, so any delays caused by the conscience clause will primarily affect women who are dependent upon NHS funding.

Because there is no need for doctors to formally record their conscientious objections to abortion, it is impossible to tell exactly how many doctors do conscientiously object, though it has been estimated to be between 18 and 24 per cent.[50] Significantly, there seems to be some evidence—highlighted in the next extract—that conscientious objection is becoming more common among medical students, which may have implications for abortion provision in the future.

R Gleeson, E Forde, E Bates, S Powell, E Eadon-Jones, and H Draper[51]

The majority of medical students rated themselves as pro-choice (62%), versus pro-life (33%)…One of the most striking results was that only half of all students thought they would sign paperwork and only 36% would perform an abortion in cases where the child was unwanted.…If there were a risk to the mother's health or life, 80% and 84% of students, respectively, would sign paperwork, and even most pro-life students would sign in these circumstances. Therefore, even though the students in our study would be willing to provide abortion services in these more extreme situations, their views might well prevent them from providing services in the vast majority of cases where abortion is requested…. Given that a study in 2000 found that 82% of general practitioners were pro-abortion, compared with 18% anti-abortion, it is possible that a shift in attitudes towards abortion is occurring that may affect future abortion provision.

(c) Places

Under section 1(3) of the 1967 Act, except in an emergency, 'any treatment for the termination of pregnancy' must be carried out in a National Health Service Hospital, or in a place approved for the purposes of the Act by the Department of Health. There are currently approximately 70 approved abortion clinics in the UK. Regulations provide that special approval is necessary to perform an abortion after 20 weeks in an abortion clinic, and that pregnancies of 24 weeks or more can only be terminated in NHS Hospitals.

---

[50] *General Practitioners: Attitudes to Abortion*, Marie Stopes International, London 1999.
[51] 'Medical Students' Attitudes Towards Abortion: A UK Study' (2008) 34 Journal of Medical Ethics 783–7.

The development of the abortion pill, RU486, raises two obvious difficulties here. First, if taking the pill is 'treatment for the termination of pregnancy', it must happen in an NHS Hospital or an approved place. There is no *clinical* reason why medical abortions should have to take place in hospital. Could women therefore be prescribed RU486 in their GP's surgeries? Section 1(3A) of the 1967 Act was added in 1990 to allow the Secretary of State for Health to approve classes of places where the treatment consists 'primarily in the use of such medicines as may be specified'. In theory, then, it would be possible for all GPs' surgeries and family planning clinics to be approved for the purposes of medical abortion. However, this has not yet happened and the abortion pill must be dispensed and taken in an NHS hospital or other approved place. It would also, of course, be *possible* for women to take the pill in their own homes, but clearly, this would be prohibited by section 1(3).

Secondly, after the woman takes the abortion pill, she must wait between 36 and 48 hours (during which time she may miscarry) before returning to the hospital, where a prosta-glandin pessary will normally be inserted in order to ensure that the pregnancy has been terminated. For up to two days, then, the drug is acting to terminate her pregnancy and may in fact do so. If 'treatment for the termination of pregnancy' is occurring throughout this period, the woman would have to remain in hospital. In practice, women are routinely sent home after being observed for a couple of hours, so it is only the taking of the pill which is classified as 'treatment'.

(d) Emergencies

Abortion Act 1967 section 1

> 1(4) Subsection (3) of this section, and so much of subsection (1) as relates to the opinion of two registered medical practitioners, shall not apply to the termination of pregnancy by a registered medical practitioner in a case where he is of this opinion formed in good faith that the termination is immediately necessary to save the life or to prevent grave permanent injury to the physical or mental health of the pregnant woman.

Under this provision, emergency abortions do not have to be performed in an NHS Hospital or other approved place, and may be carried out without seeking a second doctor's opinion. A similarly worded provision in section 4 means that doctors cannot invoke the conscientious objection clause where the abortion is necessary to save the woman's life or prevent grave permanent injury.

(e) Reporting

All terminations must be notified to the Chief Medical Officer of the relevant devolved nation within 14 days. In addition to notifying the Department of Health of the grounds on which the abortion has been authorized, and the length of gestation, the notification form also records information such as the woman's age and marital status, her place of usual residence, and the outcome of any previous pregnancies. This data allows detailed Abortion Statistics to be produced each year.[52]

---

[52] Available at <www.dh.gov.uk>.

(4) Third Parties' Rights (Or Lack of Them)

(a) Men

As we have seen, final authority over whether a pregnancy may lawfully be terminated rests with the two medical practitioners who have, in good faith, decided that the woman's circumstances fit within the statutory grounds. Given that the decision is constructed as a *medical* one, taken by doctors in their patients' best interests, it is unsurprising that the pregnant woman's sexual partner has no right to obstruct medical discretion and prevent her from obtaining an abortion. In *Paton v Trustees of the British Pregnancy Advisory Service*, a husband sought an injunction to restrain the defendants from terminating his estranged wife's pregnancy. Sir George Baker P rejected his application.

Paton v Trustees of the British Pregnancy Advisory Service [53]

Sir George Baker P

The first question is whether this plaintiff has a right at all. The foetus cannot, in English law, in my view, have a right of its own at least until it is born and has a separate existence from its mother…[T]here can be no doubt, in my view, that in England and Wales the foetus has no right of action, no right at all, until birth….

The father's case must therefore depend upon a right which he has himself….[T]his plaintiff must, in my opinion, bring his case, if he can, squarely within the framework of the fact that he is a husband…The two doctors have given a certificate. It is not and cannot be suggested that the certificate was given in other than good faith and it seems to me that there is the end of the matter in English law. The Abortion Act 1967 gives no right to a father to be consulted in respect of a termination of a pregnancy. True, it gives no right to the mother either, but obviously the mother is going to be right at the heart of the matter consulting with the doctors if they are to arrive at a decision in good faith…The husband, therefore, in my view, has no legal right enforceable in law or in equity to stop his wife having this abortion or to stop the doctors from carrying out the abortion….

Today the only way [counsel for Mr Paton] can put the case is that the husband has a right to have a say in the destiny of the child he has conceived. The law of England gives him no such right; the Abortion Act 1967 contains no such provision. It follows, therefore, that in my opinion this claim for an injunction is completely misconceived and must be dismissed.

Mr Paton then took his case to the European Commission of Human Rights,[54] where his submission that he had standing to protect his unborn child's right to life was dismissed. The European Commission also rejected his claim that his right to respect for his private and family life, guaranteed by Article 8 of the European Convention on Human Rights, had been violated. Instead, the Commission found that the pregnant woman's right to respect for *her* private life prevailed, and Mr Paton's claim was described as 'manifestly ill-founded'.

In *C v S*,[55] Robert Carver applied for an injunction to restrain Oxfordshire Health Authority and his former girlfriend, who was between 18 and 21 weeks pregnant, from terminating her pregnancy, on the ground that the foetus was a 'child capable of being born

[53] [1979] QB 276.   [54] *Paton v United Kingdom* [1980] 3 EHRR 408.   [55] [1988] QB 135.

alive' within the meaning of section 1(1) of the Infant Life (Preservation) Act 1929. His claim was rejected on the basis of evidence that this foetus was not capable of being born alive, but Lord Donaldson MR nevertheless suggested that if the question of his right to be heard had arisen, 'we should have had to have given very considerable thought to the words of Sir George Baker P in *Paton v British Pregnancy Advisory Service Trustees*'. Despite the failure of his legal action, Mr Carver did manage to persuade his former girlfriend to continue the pregnancy and to hand the baby over to him after the birth.

In 1997 a Scottish man attempted to prevent his wife from having an abortion. Initially, after an *ex parte* hearing, Mr Kelly was granted an interim interdict (injunction) preventing the abortion from taking place, which was subsequently withdrawn by a higher court.[56] Just before it was to be decided whether Mr Kelly should be granted leave to appeal to the House of Lords, he abandoned his case, and Mrs Kelly had an abortion in England.

It would be possible for the woman's sexual partner to notify the police if he believed that there had not been compliance with the Abortion Act 1967. However, because the statute gives doctors very broad discretion to determine the legitimacy of abortion, this strategy would be unlikely to succeed.

(b) Other interested parties

Aside from the putative father, other third parties might be interested in trying to prevent a woman from having an abortion, an obvious example being anti-abortion pressure groups, such as the Society for the Protection of the Unborn Child (SPUC). Usually, such groups attempt to influence women's abortion decisions by distributing anti-abortion literature, or dispensing anti-abortion advice to pregnant women. On one occasion, however, an anti-abortion pressure group sought a court injunction in order to try to prevent an abortion taking place. The case arose after an obstetrician, Professor Philip Bennett, had revealed in a press interview that a woman who was expecting twins had asked him to terminate one twin. Considerable media interest was generated by this story, and—on the assumption that the woman's request had been prompted by her straitened financial circumstances—SPUC approached the hospital where Professor Bennett worked, wishing to offer the pregnant woman a substantial sum of money so that she would be able to continue with the pregnancy. The Hospital refused to pass on their offer, and SPUC applied to the High Court, where they were initially granted an interlocutory injunction preventing the Hospital from carrying out an abortion until after the full hearing, which was due to take place the following morning. Later that day, it was revealed that the abortion had already taken place, and SPUC's application for judicial review was withdrawn.

SPUC's claim had been that the Hospital was under a duty to inform the pregnant woman about their offer of financial assistance, since—they argued—this was a relevant factor when considering the woman's 'actual or reasonably foreseeable circumstances' under section 1(2) of the Abortion Act. Although this argument was never fully considered, it is unlikely that it would have succeeded given that, first, under the Act it is the *doctors*, rather than the pregnant woman herself, who are entitled to take into account the woman's circumstances, and, second, that doctors have considerable clinical discretion in deciding whether abortion is appropriate. As Sally Sheldon points out in the next extract, the emphasis upon medical discretion within British abortion law has at times worked to protect the freedom of women seeking abortions.

---

[56] *Kelly v Kelly* [1997] SLT 896.

Sally Sheldon[57]

> If SPUC had succeeded in restraining this termination pending the giving of certain informa-
> tion to [the pregnant woman], it would have set a very dangerous precedent. The idea that
> it is the anti-choice groups who should dictate what information should be given to women
> considering abortion cannot fail to alarm. The spectre is raised of the kinds of measures
> deployed in the United States where, in some states, women have been subjected to dis-
> suasive counselling or forced to watch anti-choice material before deciding on termination
> in the name of the right to make an informed choice. However, this spectre seems unlikely
> to haunt British women. In this country, the approach taken by the courts has been one of
> protecting a broad space for medical discretion and refusing to second-guess the decisions
> made within it.

(5) The Human Rights Act 1998

It would, of course, be possible to frame the abortion issue in terms of rights, and in the
context of the Human Rights Act, to pit the woman's right to respect for her private and
family life under Article 8 against any right to life, which the fetus might have under
Article 2. The fetus is not a legal person and so it seems likely that it is not protected by
Article 2. In *Vo v France*,[58] a case that did not involve abortion, but negligence which led to a
fetus's death, the ECtHR decided that, at the European level, there was no consensus on the
moral status of the fetus. The only common ground was that the fetus was a member of the
human race. Its capacity to become a person meant that it should be protected as a matter of
human dignity, but did not make it a person with a right to life, which would be protected
by Article 2.

More recently, the Council of Europe has suggested that member states' 'margin of
appreciation' on the moral status of the fetus should not be sufficiently wide to permit some
states to make abortion unlawful. Rather, while member states have the right to restrict
access to abortion beyond a 'reasonable gestational limit', they should ensure that all women
have access to safe and legal abortion. A number of countries, including Northern Ireland
and the Republic of Ireland, do not meet this condition.

Council of Europe[59]

> 7. The Assembly invites the member states of the Council of Europe to:
>
>   7.1. decriminalise abortion within reasonable gestational limits, if they have not already
>   done so;
>   7.2. guarantee women's effective exercise of their right of access to a safe and legal
>   abortion;
>   7.3. allow women freedom of choice and offer the conditions for a free and enlightened
>   choice without specifically promoting abortion;

---

[57] 'Multiple Pregnancy and Re(pro)ductive Choice' (1997) 5 Feminist Legal Studies 99–106.
[58] (2005) 40 EHRR 12.   [59] *Access to Safe and Legal Abortion in Europe* Resolution 1607 (2008).

> 7.4. lift restrictions which hinder, *de jure* or de facto, access to safe abortion, and, in particular, take the necessary steps to create the appropriate conditions for health, medical and psychological care and offer suitable financial cover.

A further human rights' dimension to the abortion issue is the freedom of expression of those who are opposed to abortion. This was an issue in *Connolly v Director of Public Prosecutions*, in which the defendant, Mrs Connolly, had sent close-up colour photographs of dead 21-week-old foetuses to pharmacists who stocked the morning after pill. Dyson J held that Article 10 was engaged, but that interference was justified under 10(2), in order to protect the rights of others, namely the pharmacists' employees right to be protected from offensive material.

Connolly v Director of Public Prosecutions[60]

Dyson J

The sending of the photographs was an exercise of the right to freedom of expression. It was not the mere sending of an offensive article: the article contained a message, namely that abortion involves the destruction of life and should be prohibited. Since it related to political issues, it was an expression of the kind that is regarded as particularly entitled to protection by art 10....

In my judgment, the persons who worked in the three pharmacies which were targeted by Mrs Connolly had the right not to have sent to them material of the kind that she sent when it was her purpose, or one of her purposes, to cause distress or anxiety to the recipient. Just as members of the public have the right to be protected from such material (sent for such a purpose) in the privacy of their homes, so too, in general terms, do people in the workplace. But it must depend on the circumstances. The more offensive the material, the greater the likelihood that such persons have the right to be protected from receiving it. But the recipient may not be a person who needs such protection. Thus, for example, the position of a doctor who routinely performs abortions who receives photographs similar to those that were sent by Mrs Connolly in this case may well be materially different from that of employees in a pharmacy which happens to sell the "morning after pill". It seems to me that such a doctor would be less likely to find the photographs grossly offensive than the pharmacist's employees.... Although I respect Mrs Connolly's opinion that the effect of the morning after pill is not different in kind from that of an abortion after, say, 21 weeks, I believe that most people would say that they are fundamentally different.

4 SPECIAL SITUATIONS

(a) PATIENTS WHO LACK CAPACITY

As we saw in Chapter 4, patients who lack the capacity to consent to their medical treatment can be given treatment that is in their best interests. Accordingly, it is possible for minors or women who are mentally incapacitated to have their pregnancies terminated, if this is judged to be in their best interests.

---

[60] [2007] EWHC 237 (Admin).

(1) Adults

Unlike sterilization or organ donation, abortion is not a 'special case' for which court approval is necessary.[61] Rather, the Mental Capacity Act 2005 applies, and once it has been determined that a woman lacks capacity, the question will be whether abortion is in her best interests, bearing in mind the emphasis the Act places on taking account of the woman's own values, beliefs, and feelings. At the time of writing, no post-MCA cases on the application of the best interests test to abortion have come before the courts, so it remains to be seen whether the court's decision in *Re SS (An Adult: Medical Treatment)* should now be considered an historical oddity. In this case, S, a thirty-four-year-old schizophrenic woman, had her preference for a termination ignored on the grounds that an abortion at this advanced stage of pregnancy (24 weeks) would be traumatic, and hence not in her best interests. This was particularly troubling because Wall J admitted that his decision would almost certainly have been different if the hearing had taken place as soon as the hospital became aware of S's desire to have an abortion.

Re SS (An Adult: Medical Treatment)[62]

Wall J

If the pregnancy is not terminated, the applicant will be obliged to carry a child (which she does not want) to term, and it is very likely that the child will be removed at birth. There is also a risk of harm to the foetus during the pre-birth period, coupled with the stress of the events which are likely to follow the birth....

[W]hilst the risk of deliberate self-harm or harm to the foetus cannot be ruled out (a) there is no obvious evidence of self-harm (as opposed to self-neglect) in the applicant's medical history, and (b) medical and nursing supervision should reduce the risk of it occurring. The applicant has previously had a child removed from her care either at birth or shortly afterwards, and placed for adoption. I do not underestimate the stress of that process. However, there is no evidence that it caused a radical deterioration in her mental or physical health. It is for these reasons...that I came to the conclusion that, on a fine balance, the continuation of the pregnancy carried the lesser detriment to the applicant, and that, accordingly, a termination of pregnancy in these circumstances was not in her best interests.

(2) Children

As we saw in Chapter 5, 16- and 17-year old girls' consent to medical treatment, which would clearly include abortion, is as valid as it would be if they were adults. Where a girl is under sixteen, but *Gillick*-competent (see Chapter 5), the case of *R (on the application of Axon) v Secretary of State for Health*[63] makes it clear that she could give a valid consent to abortion, and that the termination could take place without her parent's consent or knowledge.

What about girls who are not yet *Gillick*-competent? Decisions about their medical treatment would normally be taken by their parents, subject to the possibility of being overridden by the courts if their decision is judged not to be in the child's best interests. The

---

[61] Mental Capacity Act 2005 Code of Practice. This was also the case at common law, *Re SG (Adult Mental Patient: Abortion)* [1991] 2 FLR 329.

[62] [2002] 1 FLR 445.   [63] [2006] EWHC 37 (Admin).

child's wishes are clearly highly relevant, although not necessarily decisive. In *Re B (wardship: abortion)*, B, who was twelve years old and had normal intelligence and understanding for her age, wanted to have her pregnancy terminated. She lived with her grandparents, who supported her decision, as did her boyfriend, who was sixteen years old. Her mother, however, did not want the termination to go ahead, because she disapproved of abortion. The local authority made B a ward of court, and applied for leave to have her pregnancy terminated.

Re B (wardship: abortion)[64]

Hollis J

The court, in its wardship jurisdiction, has been called in in this case to make the decision on the principle that the interests of the ward are first and paramount. Thus, it seems to me that the ward's wishes are not decisive but are, in my view, a part of the evidence which it is important to take into consideration. The mother's wishes, as the natural parent, are also of importance.... If the mother's view is to prevail, it means that this girl will be forced to continue with her pregnancy against her own expressed wishes. One can easily imagine what a mental turmoil she may thus suffer. She may have to leave school for an extended period, not least to avoid adverse comment there, she may reject the baby when born, she will have to face the traumatic considerations as to what should happen to the baby after birth.

There is, of course, the possibility that having felt the baby in her arms she will want to keep it, which the mother herself agrees would be impractical. There, thus, might follow a traumatic period for the ward when a decision is come to, possibly through the courts, as to whether the **baby** should be adopted or cared for by other members of the extended family...

In the end, I came to the clear conclusion that it would be in the ward's best interests to have her pregnancy terminated and that, having balanced all the risks, a continuance of the pregnancy would involve risk to the ward greater than if the pregnancy were terminated, of injury to her physical and mental health.

(b) THE BOUNDARY BETWEEN CONTRACEPTION AND ABORTION

Postcoital contraception, such as the morning-after pill, works by preventing the implantation of a fertilized egg. If a woman is considered to be pregnant as soon as fertilization occurs, then preventing a fertilized egg from implanting would trigger an extremely early abortion, and this could be lawful only if the conditions set out in the Abortion Act have been satisfied. Two doctors would have to certify that, in their opinion, one of the statutory grounds exists; the pill would have to be administered by a doctor, in an approved place, and the procedure reported to the CMO. Plainly this would make the use of postcoital contraception extremely time-consuming and inconvenient.

As we saw earlier, the Offences Against the Person Act 1861 defines abortion as 'procuring a miscarriage', so an offence would only be committed if the morning-after pill causes a woman to 'miscarry'. Miscarriage must be the antonym of 'carriage', a word that seems to

---

[64] [1991] 2 FLR 426.

imply that the fertilized egg must have attached itself to the pregnant woman's body. The legislation itself is silent on the meaning of miscarriage, leading Glanville Williams to suggest that 'there is, therefore, nothing to prevent the courts interpreting the word "miscarriage" in a way that takes account of customary and approved birth control practices'.[65] In a written answer to Parliament when the morning-after pill was first licensed for use in 1983, the Attorney General explained that the words in the 1861 statute should be presumed to have been used 'in their popular, ordinary or natural sense':

[I]t is clear that, used in its ordinary sense, the word 'miscarriage' is not apt to describe a failure to implant... Likewise, the phrase 'procure a miscarriage' cannot be construed to include the prevention of implantation.[66]

It seems to be settled medical opinion that pregnancy occurs when the fertilized egg implants in the woman's uterus (which, as we saw earlier, will normally be between six and seven days after fertilization began), rather than when the sperm starts to fertilize the egg. Pregnancy tests reveal the presence of the hormone human chorionic gonadotropin (hCG), which is released only once implantation has begun. It is therefore impossible to tell whether or not an egg has been fertilized unless and until it implants itself. Approximately 75 per cent of all naturally fertilized eggs will be lost before the woman's next period, and it would be counterintuitive to describe these losses as miscarriages. Rather, until a pregnancy test reveals that a fertilized egg has attached itself to her uterus, we would not consider a woman to be pregnant.

Adopting implantation as the defining feature of pregnancy is also consistent with the rules governing assisted reproduction. If eggs have been fertilized in a petri dish, common sense clearly dictates that implantation and not fertilization has to be the test for pregnancy. This is spelled out by section 2(3) of the Human Fertilisation and Embryology Act 1990 which states that:

For the purposes of this Act, a woman is not to be treated as carrying a child until the embryo has become implanted.

Despite the widespread belief that the use of postcoital contraception does not constitute an offence under the Offences Against the Person Act 1861, the matter has come before the courts on two occasions. First, in *R v Dhingra*,[67] a doctor was charged under section 58 of the 1861 Act after fitting a woman with an IUD eleven days after he had had sexual intercourse with her. Wright J held that there could not have been a miscarriage, and hence no offence had been committed under section 58.

Secondly, when regulations (which we considered in Chapter 10) were introduced allowing the morning-after pill to be dispensed by pharmacists without the need for a prescription, in *R (on the application of Smeaton) v Secretary of State for Health*, the Society for the Protection of the Unborn Child (SPUC) sought to challenge them. They argued that the morning-after pill is an abortifacient, and so women and pharmacists would be committing offences under the Offences Against the Person Act. In a long and wide-ranging judgment, Munby J dismissed their claim. His reasons can be summarized as follows. First, because miscarriage is not defined in the 1861 Act, it should be used in its ordinary sense, which is

---

[65] *Textbook on Criminal Law* (Stevens and Son: London, 1983) 294.
[66] Ibid.   [67] Unreported, 25 Jan 1991.

the termination of an established pregnancy. Before implantation, there is no pregnancy, and there can therefore be no miscarriage. Secondly, because other contraceptives, such as the pill and intra-uterine devices (IUDs) may also work by inhibiting the implantation of a fertilized egg, if SPUC's arguments were to be accepted, every method of contraception, except the condom, might involve the commission of a criminal offence. This would mean that 34 per cent of all women between the ages of 16 and 49 (approximately 4.5 million women) might be guilty of criminal offences. Thirdly, complying with the conditions set out in the Abortion Act would delay the use of the morning-after pill, which would mean that it was less effective, and would, in practice, lead to an increase in the number of abortions.

R (on the application of Smeaton) v Secretary of State for Health[68]

Munby J

I have made it clear that the court cannot concern itself with moral or religious issues. But that does not mean that I can blind myself to the social realities, which underlie this case, nor to the social implications were I to find in favour of SPUC....Here I merely outline two of the salient features of this aspect of the case. The first is this....On the logic of its own case SPUC's challenge, and the allegations of serious criminality *inter alia* by the woman concerned, are not simply to the morning-after pill. They extend to *any* chemical or device which operates, or may operate, by impeding, discouraging or preventing the natural process at any time after fertilisation has started, alternatively has completed. They extend to *any* drug or device which may operate in that way, even if it may also operate in a way which impedes, discourages or prevents the process of fertilisation. The medical profession and female members of the public have for years been operating on the basis that the use, prescription and supply of such chemicals and devices is legal and involves no potential criminality. The pill has been available since the 1960s and the morning-after pill since the early 1980s. That position has remained unchallenged until sought to be reopened in these proceedings. The other is this. Making Levonelle available from pharmacists without a prescription means that it can be obtained more quickly following intercourse when a woman knows or suspects that her regular method of contraception has failed, particularly during weekends and public holidays. If SPUC were to succeed in this challenge, the result would be, as I have said, that Levonelle could be prescribed only by doctors who had complied with the requirements of the Abortion Act 1967. This in turn would mean that:

- Levonelle would tend to be administered either not at all or at a later stage, when the expert evidence is that it is less effective and more likely to operate post-fertilisation.

- There would inevitably be an increase in the number of abortions as conventionally understood, a result which...SPUC would presumably not welcome.

[T]he correct approach can be set out in the form of four propositions:

  (i)   the 1861 Act is an 'always speaking' Act;

  (ii) the word 'miscarriage' is an ordinary English word of flexible meaning which Parliament in 1861 chose to leave undefined;

  (iii) it should accordingly be interpreted as it would be *currently* understood;

  (iv) it should be interpreted in the light of the best current scientific and medical knowledge that is available to the court...

---

[68] [2002] Criminal Law Review 664.

[T]here is in truth no substantial dispute as to the current meaning of the word 'miscarriage'…miscarriage is the termination of…a post-implantation pregnancy. Current medical—and, indeed, I would add, current lay and popular—understanding of what is meant by 'miscarriage' plainly excludes results brought about by IUDs, the pill, the mini-pill and the morning-after pill….

Finally, it is not irrelevant to note that my decision accords with social realities. I am declaring licit—not criminal—that which has in fact been the daily practice of countless people in this country for many, many years.

There would in my judgment be something very seriously wrong, indeed grievously wrong with our system—by which I mean not just our legal system but the entire system by which our polity is governed—if a judge in 2002 were to be compelled by a statute 141 years old to hold that what thousands, hundreds of thousands, indeed millions, of ordinary honest, decent, law abiding citizens have been doing day in day out for so many years is and always has been criminal. I am glad to be spared so unattractive a duty…

I have to say that I cannot see that it is any part of the responsibilities of public authorities—let alone of the criminal law—to be telling adult people whether they can or cannot use contraceptive devices of the kind which I have been considering….

Government's responsibility is to ensure the medical and pharmaceutical safety of products offered in the market place and the appropriate provision of suitable guidance and advice. Beyond that, as it seems to me, in this as in other areas of medical ethics, respect for the personal autonomy which our law has now come to recognise demands that the choice be left to the individual.

In the next extract, John Keown criticizes the *Smeaton* decision on two grounds. First, he disputes the existence of a medical consensus as to when pregnancy begins, and when a 'miscarriage' could therefore be procured, and, secondly, he suggests that Munby J placed too much emphasis upon the social consequences of a finding that the morning-after pill (MAP) is an abortifacient.

John Keown[69]

Tunkel advanced inter alia the telling argument that to hold that s 58 did not bite until implantation: 'would, in effect, give a sort of free-for-all moratorium of a week or more after intercourse during which every sort of abortionist could ply his craft with impunity…'

[T]o assert that 'carriage' requires implantation seems the merest invention. The judge cited not a single dictionary of English to ground his assertions about the popular meaning of the word or that there cannot be 'carriage' without 'attachment'. The dictionary meaning of 'carry' is simply 'To transport…' There is no requirement here of physical attachment….

There can surely be little doubt that…the 'great object' of s 58 was the protection of the unborn child from fertilisation….Any suggestion that the legislature which enacted s 58 intended its prohibition on attempted abortion to apply only after implantation is unsustainable.

Early in his judgment Munby J correctly observed that the issue for his decision was whether the use of the MAP may constitute an offence under the 1861 Act. It was not whether the MAP was either morally right or socially desirable…In view of this it may be thought surprising that significant portions of the judgment in *Smeaton* were devoted to

[69] 'Morning After' Pills, "Miscarriage" and Muddle' (2005) 25 Legal Studies 296–319.

the social implications of the case and disclosed the judge's opinion that the social consequences of finding for the claimant would have been highly undesirable.

(c) SELECTIVE REDUCTION

Fetal reduction, or the selective termination of one or more fetuses, is a much more complex procedure than complete termination, and it has only become possible in the past twenty years as a result of advances in ultrasonography. In practice, selective reduction of multiple pregnancies is rare, and the Human Fertilisation and Embryology Authority (HFEA)'s policy of reducing the number of embryos which can be put back in an IVF cycle means that the number of higher-order multiple pregnancies resulting from fertility treatment has reduced in recent years. In 2007, 47 selective terminations took place.

Initially it was unclear how the Offences Against the Person Act 1861 and the Abortion Act 1967 would apply to a procedure in which one or more fetuses are destroyed but the woman continues to be pregnant. This confusion was addressed by a further amendment to the Abortion Act effected by The Human Fertilisation and Embryology Act 1990.

Abortion Act 1967 section 5

5(2) For the purposes of the law relating to abortion, anything done with intent to procure a woman's miscarriage (or, in the case of a woman carrying more than one foetus, her miscarriage of any foetus) is unlawfully done unless authorised by section 1 of this Act and, in the case of a woman carrying more than one foetus, anything done with intent to procure her miscarriage of any foetus is authorised by that section if—

(a) the ground for termination of the pregnancy specified in subsection (1)(d) of that section applies in relation to any foetus and the thing is done for the purpose of procuring the miscarriage of that foetus, or

(b) any of the other grounds for termination of the pregnancy specified in that section applies.

Since section 5(2) specifies that the ordinary Abortion Act grounds apply equally to selective reduction, one or more fetuses can be destroyed if, for example, there is a risk to the woman's mental or physical health, or if there is a substantial risk that a child would be born seriously handicapped.

The application of section 1(1)(a), the so-called 'social' ground, to selective reduction is unproblematic given the considerable difficulties commonly encountered in caring for twins, triplets, and higher-order multiple births. But another indication for selective reduction, namely improving the chances of survival of the remaining fetuses, is not covered by a literal interpretation of section 1 of the Abortion Act. Such abortions would only be lawful if a slightly more elastic interpretation were accepted, and improving the chances that one or more babies will survive were taken to be necessary to avert a risk to their mother's mental wellbeing, or alternatively to reducing the risk that the child, if born, would be at substantial risk of suffering from a serious handicap.

(d) THE LIVING ABORTUS

The vast majority of abortions are performed when the fetus is not capable of surviving outside of the pregnant woman's body. Hence, removing the fetus from the woman's uterus inevitably leads to its death. Although abortion and fetal destruction are normally indistinguishable, they are not necessarily so. If the fetus happens to be born alive, following an abortion, it will have an existence separate from its mother, and she could not then insist upon its destruction. Where the fetus might be viable, abortion normally involves killing the fetus while it is still inside the woman's body, prior to its removal. In practice, a tiny number of abortions involve deliberate feticide, and in most of these, the fetus has an abnormality so serious that it would be likely to die shortly after birth. An example might be anencephalus, where the fetus is born with virtually no brain. The question of whether it is right for doctors to deliberately kill such a fetus prior to its delivery has not been especially controversial because the baby will in any event die during or very soon after birth. More complicated ethical dilemmas will be raised if 'artificial wombs' are developed which enable babies to develop outside of their mothers' bodies much earlier in pregnancy.

During the second half of the twentieth century, dramatic progress in neonatal medicine steadily reduced the age at which a fetus became viable. Babies have survived after as little as 22 weeks' gestation, but this is very unusual,[70] and the risk that the baby will be seriously disabled is extremely high. In one of the largest studies of extremely premature babies, EPICure 1, of all those born at 22 weeks' gestation, 84 per cent died in the delivery room, 14 per cent died in the neonatal intensive care unit, and 1 per cent survived to discharge.[71] Of the two children who survived to discharge, one had severe disability and one had mild disability at 6 years of age.[72]

At the time of writing, the results of EPICure 2 are not available, but early indications of their findings were presented to the House of Commons Science and Technology Select Committee, and quoted in their final report.

British Association of Perinatal Medicine[73]

[E]arly indications are that, for infants below 24 weeks of gestation, the survival to discharge home was very similar between the cohort of 1995 and that of 2006. Headline figures of approximately 10–15% survival were found. This is important for those working in perinatal care, who in general, do not believe that the survival for babies born below 24 weeks of gestation has improved to such an extent that they would see any value in redefining the lower limit of viability. Naturally a small number of these infants below 24 weeks of gestation do survive but BAPM would be concerned that a lowering of the legal definition of viability would imply that quality survival has improved for infants below the present limit of 24 weeks. The evidence for the UK population, to date does not support this.

---

[70] EPICure, available at <www.epicure.ac.uk>.

[71] Kate Costeloe, Enid Hennessy, Alan T Gibson, Neil Marlow, Andrew R Wilkinson, and for the EPICure Study Group 'The EPICure Study: Outcomes to Discharge From Hospital for Infants Born at the Threshold of Viability' (2000) 106 Pediatrics 659–71. For the most up-to-date analysis of EPICure 2, go to <www.epicure.ac.uk>.

[72] Ibid.   [73] Quoted in HoC Science and Technology Select Committee (2007).

It is not clear whether there is some absolute limit to the age at which a premature baby is capable of surviving independently. Before about 21 weeks, the fetus's lungs are solid and breathing would be impossible. A fetus that could not breathe could only survive outside of the pregnant woman's body if scientists were able to develop some sort of 'artificial womb' which could simulate the uterine environment until the baby became capable of independent life.

If this becomes possible, it will clearly raise some very complicated questions for abortion law. If a fetus at 12 weeks' gestation could be transferred to an artificial womb to continue its development, does abortion cease to be synonymous with fetal destruction? Could we say that a woman has the right to the fetus's removal from her body, but not the right to its death? Artificial wombs might enable the partners of pregnant women to both respect their partner's decision not to continue with the pregnancy *and* to bring up the child, which is gestated artificially. Given that the conflict between fetal life and women's self-determination has proved so intractable, the prospect of artificial wombs might seem superficially appealing. Because a woman could end her unwanted pregnancy without also ending the fetus's life, it might be possible simultaneously to protect both the woman's reproductive autonomy *and* fetal life.[74] By extending her famous 'violinist analogy', Judith Jarvis Thomson argues that there is no right to 'secure the death of the unborn child':

> I have argued that you are not morally required to spend nine months in bed, sustaining the life of that violinist; but to say this is by no means to say that if, when you unplug yourself, there is a miracle and he survives, you then have a right to turn round and slit his throat. You may detach yourself even if this costs him his life; you have no right to be guaranteed his death, by some other means, if unplugging yourself does not kill him.[75]

In practice, however, it is unlikely that artificial wombs, and the possibility of ectogenesis (gestation outside of the woman's body) would satisfy either pro-choice or anti-abortion advocates. According to Leslie Cannold's empirical research, those who are against abortion would also reject ectogenesis on the grounds that it represents an abdication of the woman's duty to gestate and raise every fetus she conceives.[76] Cannold also encountered opposition among women who are pro-choice, who argued that women want abortions not just to avoid pregnancy and childbirth, but because they do not want to be responsible for bringing an unwanted child into the world.[77] It is the unwanted prospect of motherhood and its responsibilities which lies behind the overwhelming majority of abortion decisions. Very few women seek abortions solely to avoid pregnancy and childbirth.

In addition, carrying out a fetal extraction rather than a termination would impose an additional physical burden on the woman. Medical abortions would not be possible, and a woman would have to undergo a type of caesarean section in order to remove the living fetus from her body. This would be a much more serious operation, and inevitably more risky and uncomfortable. In the next extract, I explore the implications ectogenesis might have for the meaning of viability.

---

[74] Peter Singer and Deane Wells, *The Reproduction Revolution: New Ways of Making Babies* (Oxford UP, 1984), 135.

[75] 'A Defence of Abortion' (1971) 1 Philosophy and Public Affairs 47.

[76] 'Women, Ectogenesis and Ethical Theory' (1995) 12 Journal of Applied Philosophy 55–64.

[77] Ibid.

Emily Jackson[78]

> Ectogenesis would reveal a degree of ambiguity in the meaning of viability. Does this represent the time at which a fetus is capable of having an existence separate from its mother, or a stage in fetal development? If it is the former, and a fetus could be removed to an artificial uterine environment at, say, twelve weeks, some might argue that this becomes the gestational period before which abortions are legitimate and after which they are not. More significantly, if a fetus can live independently of its 'mother' from the moment of fertilisation, viability in this sense ceases to represent a feasible cut-off point for abortions, unless they are unlawful throughout pregnancy....
>
> If instead we define viability as a stage in fetal development when it can survive with minimal assistance, we would have to acknowledge that hardly any babies born very prematurely can survive with minimal assistance. Neonatal intensive care units, where premature babies will spend the first weeks of life, are full of extremely high-tech equipment. While viability as independent existence would, with the advent of ectogenesis, mean that all fetuses were potentially viable, viability as unassisted survival would push the point of viability back to well over thirty weeks.[79]

5 ABORTION IN OTHER COUNTRIES

There is insufficient space to provide a detailed survey of abortion laws throughout the world. Instead, we briefly consider the law in Northern Ireland, Ireland, and the United States. It is, however, worth noting that there is enormous cross-national variation in the regulation of abortion. Despite European harmonization across many legal issues, there is no consistency in the regulation of abortion in Europe. Moreover, within different countries abortion laws have changed dramatically in order to reflect shifts in political and religious affiliations. For example, the liberal abortion regime that existed in Poland prior to the break-up of the Soviet bloc was replaced by a much more restrictive system, in part as a result of the power the Catholic Church acquired through its role in the anti-Soviet *Solidarity* movement.

In countries that prohibit or severely restrict access to abortion, women who can afford it may travel abroad to terminate their unwanted pregnancies. Irish and Northern Irish women travel to Scotland, England, and Wales, for example. If abortion 'tourism' is impracticable, women may resort to illegal and often unsafe abortions. In Nigeria, for example, the prohibition of abortion results in hundreds of thousands of unsafe abortions, with correspondingly high levels of maternal mortality. It is now possible for women who live in countries where safe abortion is illegal to access abortion pills through the internet, and while some internet providers may be reliable and relatively safe, others are not.

(a) NORTHERN IRELAND

The legal status of abortion in Northern Ireland is unclear. The Abortion Act 1967 does not apply, and so there are no *statutory* defences to sections 58 and 59 of the Offences Against

---

[78] 'Degendering Reproduction' (2008) 16 Medical Law Review 346–68.

[79] Hyun Jee Son, 'Artificial Wombs, Frozen Embryos and Abortion: Reconciling Viability's Doctrinal Ambiguity' (2005) 14 UCLA Women's Law Journal 213.

the Person Act 1861. However, as we saw earlier, *R v Bourne* indicates that a defence may nevertheless exist if the pregnancy is endangering the pregnant woman's life, and for this purpose, it is sufficient if the consequence of carrying the pregnancy to term would be to leave her a 'mental wreck'. Thus individual doctors must decide, on a case-by-case basis, and with the potential threat of criminal prosecution, whether a woman's circumstances are such that continuing with the pregnancy would leave her a 'physical or mental wreck'.

Court rulings in Northern Ireland have confirmed that there are circumstances in which abortion will not be a criminal offence, but because there is no specific statutory defence, the parameters within which abortion may lawfully be performed remain unclear.[80] The only cases that have come before the courts have involved girls and women who have either lacked capacity or been threatening suicide. In all these cases, the authorities caring for them have sought the court's approval for the termination of pregnancy, and medical opinion has been unanimous that abortion was in the girl or woman's best interests.

The first case to consider the lawfulness of abortion in the abstract was *Re Family Planning Association of Northern Ireland*.[81] This was a case brought by the Family Planning Association of Northern Ireland, which had asked the Department of Health for Northern Ireland for guidance on when abortion could be lawfully performed. Initially, Kerr J rejected their application on the grounds that the medical profession was not unclear about the law, which was governed by the *Bourne* exception—restrictively interpreted—to the Offences Against the Person Act 1861. This was, however, overturned on appeal. The Court of Appeal held that the Department of Health, Social Services and Public Safety could not be compelled to issue guidelines on abortion, but suggested it would be prudent to do so.

Draft guidelines were eventually prepared, and issued for consultation in July 2008. They summarize the law on abortion in Northern Ireland as follows:

Department of Health, Social Services and Public Safety[82]

2.3 In summary, it is lawful to perform an operation in Northern Ireland for the termination of a pregnancy, where there is:

- a threat to the life of the woman, or
- a risk of real and serious adverse effect on her health, which is either long term or permanent.

In any other circumstance it would be unlawful to perform such an operation.

2.4 Fetal abnormality is not recognised as grounds for termination of pregnancy in Northern Ireland. It will only be lawful to terminate a pregnancy in the case of actual or possible fetal abnormality if the continuance of the pregnancy threatens the life of the woman, or would adversely affect her physical or mental health. As in other cases, the adverse effect on the woman's physical or mental health must be a real and serious one, and must also be permanent or long term.

---

[80] *Northern Health and Social Services Board v F & G* [1993] NILR 268; *Northern Health and Social Services Board v A* [1994] NIJB 1; *Western Health and Social Services Board v CMB*, 29 Sept 1995, unreported; *Down Lisburn Health and Social Services Board v CH & LAH*, 18 Oct 1995, unreported.

[81] [2003] NIQB 48.

[82] *Guidance on the Termination of Pregnancy: The Law and Clinical Practice in Northern Ireland* (DHSSP, 2008).

> 2.5 In keeping with the law in Northern Ireland, it will always be for the medical practitioner responsible for the care of the woman to decide, as a matter of professional clinical judgment, whether the perceived effect of non-termination is sufficiently grave to warrant terminating the pregnancy. As with any exercise of clinical judgment, there will be occasions where this will be a difficult decision....
>
> 2.7 It is important for practitioners to appreciate that anyone who unlawfully performs a termination of pregnancy is liable to criminal prosecution with a maximum penalty of life imprisonment.

The draft guidelines go on to advocate rigorous assessment, including the need for a specialist second opinion of the risk to the woman's health. They also state that 'It is rare for pregnancy to cause adverse effects on mental health which are real and serious, long-term or permanent.'

Given the uncertainty over whether a risk to the mother's mental health could justify abortion in Northern Ireland, and the grave consequences for doctors who break the law, it is not surprising that abortion is largely unavailable in Northern Ireland. Women who wish to terminate unwanted pregnancies will generally travel to England, Scotland, or Wales. Officially, 1,400 women do so each year,[83] though because this figure only includes those women who give a Northern Irish address to the abortion provider, it is almost certainly an underestimate.

In addition to being extremely inconvenient, having to travel to the mainland will inevitably delay Northern Irish women's abortions. Women from Northern Ireland are three times more likely than other British women to have abortions after 20 weeks. Moreover, since Northern Irish women are not entitled to NHS abortions, they will have to pay for a private abortion, in addition to covering the costs of travel. This may be unaffordable for some women. One study has suggested that more than 10 per cent of Northern Irish GPs had encountered the consequences of amateur abortions.[84]

(b) IRELAND

Abortion is illegal in Ireland, except where the pregnancy poses a real and substantial risk to the pregnant woman's life. Ireland's abortion law consists in both constitutional and legislative provisions. Not only does the Offences Against the Person Act 1861 apply, but also the Irish Constitution was amended in 1983 by Article 40.3.3, which provides that the 'unborn' and the pregnant woman have an equal right to life. Hence, unless the pregnant woman's life is in danger, the fetus's right to life must take priority.

As in Northern Ireland, women from the Republic of Ireland will commonly travel to English (or Welsh or Scottish) clinics in order to terminate their unwanted pregnancies, and nearly 4,700 women do so each year.[85] The question of whether it is acceptable to offer advice on arranging abortions in England, Wales, or Scotland came before the European Court of Human Rights in *Open Door Counselling Ltd v Ireland*.[86] By a majority the ECtHR

[83] DH Abortion Statistics 2007.

[84] Polly Toynbee, 'Labour Stitch-Up will Deny Women Fundamental Rights', The Guardian, October 21 2008.

[85] Available at <www.dh.gov.uk>. At the time of writing the most recent statistics are Abortion Statistics 2007 (DH: London, 2008).

[86] The Times, 5 Nov 1992 (ECHR).

held that the restriction on the provision of information was disproportionate since non-directive counselling did not necessarily lead to the termination of fetal life, the information was in any event available elsewhere, and there was some evidence that the absence of information might pose a risk to women's health.

The Regulation of Information (Services outside the State for Termination of Pregnancies) Act 1995 defines the conditions under which Irish women can be given information about abortion services lawfully available in another state. Section 5 of the Act provides that it is not lawful to advocate or promote the termination of pregnancy to a woman, but that information can be given, provided that it is truthful and objective, fully informs the woman of all the courses of action that are open to her, and does not advocate or promote the termination of pregnancy.

The legality of travelling to England to avoid Irish abortion law was called into question in the case of *Attorney General v X*, in which a fourteen-year-old girl had become pregnant after being raped by a schoolfriend's father. The Irish Attorney General sought, and was initially granted an injunction to restrain X from travelling abroad to England to obtain an abortion. This was overturned on appeal, when the Irish Supreme Court held that the risk to X's life was great and outweighed the destruction of the unborn life; hence the abortion would, in fact, have been lawful in Ireland.

Attorney General v X[87]

O'Flaherty J

I believe that the law in this State is that surgical intervention which has the effect of terminating pregnancy bona fide undertaken to save the life of the mother where she is in danger of death is permissible under the Constitution and the law. The danger has to represent a substantial risk to her life though this does not necessarily have to be an imminent danger of instant death. The law does not require the doctors to wait until the mother is in peril of immediate death. I believe the instant case to come within this principle.

Egan J

In my opinion the true test should be that a pregnancy may be terminated if its continuance as a matter of probability involves a real and substantial risk to the life of the mother. The risk must be to her life but it is irrelevant, in my view, that it should be a risk of self-destruction rather than a risk to life for any other reason. The evidence establishes that such a risk exists in the present case.

There were obiter dicta from the majority in the Supreme Court which suggested that the right to travel *could* be restrained to prevent an abortion taking place in circumstances where the abortion would have been unlawful in Ireland, because there was no threat to the life of the mother: the right to travel did not trump the right to life.

In response to the X case, a referendum in 1992 led to a constitutional amendment which limits the State's ability to stop a woman from travelling abroad for an abortion. In the same referendum, voters decided that there should be a limited right to receive information on abortion services in England, and a proposal that suicide risk should be excluded as a

---

[87] [1992] 2 CMLR 277.

ground for life-saving abortion was rejected. A further referendum was held in 2002, and by a very narrow margin, voters again rejected the Government's proposal that the risk of suicide should cease to offer a justification for the termination of pregnancy.

The question of whether Irish women should be able to terminate pregnancies where the fetus suffers from an abnormality which is incompatible with life arose in *D v Ireland*. D was pregnant with twins and at fourteen weeks, following a routine scan, she discovered that one twin had died in utero and the other was diagnosed with a lethal chromosomal anomaly, known as Edward's syndrome, where the median survival age is 6 days. She could not face a further five months of pregnancy, knowing that one fetus was dead and the other would die almost immediately after birth, and so she travelled to England, where her pregnancy was terminated.

The applicant then complained to the ECtHR about the need to travel abroad to have an abortion in the case of a fetal anomaly which was incompatible with life. She submitted that having to travel abroad, to be treated by unknown medical personnel in an unknown hospital, and being deprived of follow-up care, such as counselling, autopsy, counselling for bereavement, and medical follow-up amounted to 'inhuman and degrading treatment', and was a disproportionate interference with her Article 8 right to private life. She further complained that her right to receive information, protected by Article 10, had been violated, and that, under Article 14, she was discriminated against as a pregnant woman with a lethal fetal anomaly because a non-pregnant person with a serious medical problem would not have encountered these difficulties in obtaining medical care and advice.

The ECtHR ruled that D's case was inadmissible, because she had not exhausted local remedies first. Nevertheless, the Court indicated that Ireland may now have to provide termination of pregnancy to women whose fetuses are diagnosed with a lethal anomaly. It held that:

> The presumption in the *X* case was that the foetus had a normal life expectancy and there is, in the Court's view, a feasible argument to be made that the constitutionally enshrined balance between the right to life of the mother and of the foetus could have shifted in favour of the mother when the 'unborn' suffered from a abnormality incompatible with life.[88]

In early 2009, the European Court of Human Rights will hear a claim from three women who had to travel to the UK mainland to obtain abortions, on the grounds that being forced to travel to terminate their pregnancies was incompatible with their human rights. In *A, B, & C v Ireland*, one woman had an ectopic pregnancy, while another was undergoing chemotherapy for cancer at the time of her pregnancy, and all three argue that Irish law interfered with their right to privacy, under Article 8 and amounted to inhuman and degrading treatment.

(c) THE UNITED STATES

In *Roe v Wade*,[89] the US Supreme Court recognized for the first time that a woman's freedom to choose whether to bear a child was a fundamental constitutionally protected liberty, which the state could restrict only in order to promote a compelling state interest. The right to privacy, the Supreme Court held, 'is broad enough to encompass a woman's decision

---

[88] Application no. 26499/02 (2005).   [89] 410 US 113 (1973).

whether or not to terminate her pregnancy'. Prior to viability, the state did not have a compelling interest in fetal life, and hence restrictions on a woman's right to decide to terminate her pregnancy would be unconstitutional. The decision in *Roe v Wade* has never been explicitly overturned, and yet its scope has been significantly narrowed by subsequent decisions of the Supreme Court. Anti-abortion campaigners have had some success in persuading state legislatures to pass regulations which in practice restrict women's access to abortion, and the constitutionality of these has been tested by the Supreme Court on a number of occasions.

In *Webster v Reproductive Health Services*,[90] the Supreme Court weakened the notion of a constitutionally protected right to choose abortion. It held that restrictions on women's right to choose abortion would be unconstitutional only if they imposed an 'undue burden', and even then, they might be justified by important state interests. Three years later, in *Planned Parenthood v Casey*, the Supreme Court upheld all but one of the restrictions that a Pennsylvania statute had imposed upon women's access to abortion. A mandatory 24-hour waiting period and a parental consent requirement for minors were held to be constitutional; only the spousal notification requirement was rejected on the grounds that, given the proportion of women who may fear assault at the hands of their sexual partner, it did represent an 'undue burden' on women's right to choose abortion. The State, it was argued in *Casey*, had a 'profound interest in potential life', and was therefore entitled, throughout pregnancy, to:

> take measures to ensure that the woman's choice is informed, and measures designed to advance this interest will not be invalidated as long as their purpose is to persuade the woman to choose childbirth over abortion, provided that they do not impose an 'undue burden on the right'.[91]

In the following extract, Sylvia Law argues that by permitting states to place obstacles in the path of women choosing abortion, the Supreme Court in *Casey* effectively overturned *Roe v Wade*.

Sylvia A Law[92]

> Many times over the past few months I have been puzzled when sophisticated people...ask me whether the Supreme Court will overrule *Roe v Wade*. This surprises me because, like Justices Blackmun and Scalia, I believe that the Supreme Court effectively overruled Roe in 1989....
>
> From a pro-choice point of view, one plausible assessment of the Casey decision is that it represents the worst of all possible worlds. The joint opinion affirmed a woman's 'fundamental constitutional right' to abortion, but simultaneously allowed the state to adopt measures that effectively curtail many women's exercise of the abortion right. This curtailment hits hardest those women who are most vulnerable, i.e. the poor, the unsophisticated, the young, and women who live in rural areas.

---

[90] 492 US 490 (1989).   [91] 112 S Ct 2791 (1992).
[92] 'Abortion Compromise: Inevitable and Impossible' (1992) University of Illinois Law Review 921.

The twenty-four-hour waiting requirement sends a powerful message that is degrading, condescending, and paternalistic to all women. It assumes that women make rash decisions, and reinforces negative stereotypes about women. It imputes women's competence as moral and practical decision-makers. Just as seriously, the impact of the twenty-four-hour waiting requirement will be sharply differentiated on lines of class, age, sophistication, and geography....

A compromise that says the rich and sophisticated can have abortions but the poor and naïve cannot should be rejected as hostile to our most fundamental commitments to equal treatment. Regulatory programs such as that adopted in Pennsylvania sabotage widely shared values. They make abortion more costly, more dangerous, and later in the pregnancy term.

States have further sought to restrict access to abortion by banning certain abortion procedures, particularly those used in abortions carried out later in pregnancy. As we have seen, terminations carried out in the final trimester of pregnancy may involve the fetus being killed *in utero* before being delivered in the normal way. While not a medical term, these late abortions have been emotively described as 'partial birth' abortions. In 2000, by a narrow (5–4) majority, in *Stenberg v Carhart*, the US Supreme Court struck down Nebraska's 'partial birth' abortion law on two grounds: first, the law was insufficiently clear and, secondly, it did not contain an exception where this type of abortion was necessary to preserve the woman's health.[93]

Following the retirement of a pro-choice Justice, the balance in the Supreme Court had shifted when it decided *Gonzales v Carhart* in 2007. In *Gonzales*, by a 5–4 majority, the Supreme Court decided that a state law which banned a certain type of abortion procedure, used late in pregnancy, called intact D&X, did not impose an 'undue burden' on women's access to abortion, and hence was constitutional. The majority opinion, written by Justice Kennedy, claimed that women would be protected by a rule which prevents them from consenting to a particular sort of abortion. While admitting that there was no evidence to this effect, the majority assumed that women who have abortions later regret their decisions, and that this regret was bound to be exacerbated when they realized how the abortion had been carried out:

While we find no reliable data to measure the phenomenon, it seems unexceptionable to conclude some women come to regret their choice to abort the infant life they once created and sustained. Severe depression and loss of esteem can follow.[94]

Because intact D&X is, in Kennedy's words, 'gruesome', the majority thought it likely that many doctors would not tell their patients precisely what it involves. This would therefore compromise the woman's ability to give informed consent and, as a result, the state was justified in banning the procedure. In the next extract, Graham Gee explains why this reasoning is problematic.

---

[93] *Stenberg v Carhart* US 120 S Ct 2597, 147 L.Ed.2d 743 (2000).   [94] No. 05–380.

Graham Gee[95]

Because of the woman's purported psychological fragility, physicians—the Court specu-
lates—withhold details about the abortion procedure to be used, confining themselves
instead to discussing the risks that the procedure entails.... What the Court seems to be
suggesting is that the pregnant woman—if only she knew what D&X entailed—would refuse to consent, and would instead carry the pregnancy to term. There is, however, a poor fit
between the problem that the Court identifies (ensuring informed choice) and the solution
the Court approves (banning D&X). The solution to the problem of informed consent—*if*
such a problem exists—would be to require physicians to inform women, accurately and
adequately, about what is involved in the different abortion procedures and their attendant
risks. Yet this is not the solution the Court approves. Instead, the Court approves a ban on a
specific abortion procedure, D&X. It seems, then, that the Court purports to protect a woman
from (what it takes to be) the problem of ensuring that her consent to D&X is informed by
depriving her of the right to elect to undergo that procedure in the first place....

In short, the woman is cast as too weak to decide for herself whether to have an abortion,
and so the State must decide for her. Under the Act, the State does so by deciding that D&X
is a procedure that no (well-informed) woman would decide to undergo. The State reduces
the woman's reproductive choice under the pretext of protecting her.

One of the most interesting features of the decision in *Gonzales* is the Supreme Court's
apparent endorsement of the anti-abortion movement's claims that abortion hurts women,
both psychologically and physically. These claims are not backed up by the evidence. In one
eight-year study of 5,295 women, it was evident that the most important predictor of emotional wellbeing in women who have terminated unwanted pregnancies was their well-being
before the abortion took place.[96] Russo and Dabul conclude that 'the experience of having
an abortion plays a negligible, if any, independent role in women's well-being over time,
regardless of race or religion'.[97]

In another study, Schmiege and Russo found 'no evidence of an association between
abortion and depression'.[98] They compared women who carried an initially unwanted pregnancy to term with those that had chosen termination, and 'found no evidence that terminating compared with delivering an unwanted first pregnancy changes risk for subsequent
depression'. Gilchrist *et al.* carried out a similar study in which the health of 13,261 British
women who had either continued or aborted unintended pregnancies was tracked for 11
years. They found that rates of reported psychiatric disorders were no higher after termination of pregnancy than after childbirth. Women who had a previous history of psychiatric
illness were most at risk of suffering from a mental disorder after the end of their pregnancy,
regardless of whether they had given birth or had a termination.[99]

---

[95] 'Regulating Abortion in the United States after *Gonzales v Carhart*' (2007) 70 Modern Law Review
979–92.

[96] NF Russo and KL Zierk, 'Abortion, Childbearing, and Women's Well-being.' (1992) 23 Professional
Psychology 269–80.

[97] NF Russo and AJ Dabul, 'The Relationship of Abortion to Well-being: Do Race and Religion Make a
Difference?' (1997) 28 Professional Psychology 1–9.

[98] S Schmiege and NF Russo, 'Depression and Unwanted First Pregnancy: Longitudinal Cohort Study'
(2005) 330 British Medical Journal 1136.

[99] 'Termination of Pregnancy and Psychiatric Morbidity' (1995) 167 The British Journal of Psychiatry
243–8.

Nevertheless, despite the lack of evidence, the anti-abortion movement has been remarkably successful in promulgating the claim that Post-Abortion Syndrome (PAS) exists and that abortion is bad for women. As Reva Siegel explains, this tactic is regarded as more likely to persuade a larger section of the population that access to abortion should be restricted.

Reva B. Siegel[100]

Growing numbers of movement leaders came to appreciate that woman-focused anti-abortion discourse might have strategic utility in persuading segments of the electorate the movement had heretofore been unable to reach: it might reassure those who hesitated to prohibit abortion because they were concerned about women's welfare that legal restrictions on abortion might instead be in women's interest. And so in the early 1990s, leaders of the antiabortion movement began to use PAS for new purposes and for a new audience...

In Making Abortion Rare, [David] Reardon is quite clear that empirical research on the psychological consequences of abortion is a useful way of talking about the moral evil of abortion in terms that have authority for audiences not moved by direct appeals to divine authority....

[O]f course to make this claim about women's interest persuasive, Reardon needed some explanation for the large numbers of women seeking abortions.... Reardon's response was to insist that women who have abortions do not in fact want them; they are coerced into the procedure or do not grasp its implications...

In Making Abortion Rare, Reardon urged antiabortion politicians to 'take back the terms "freedom of choice" and "reproductive freedom"' and 'emphasize the fact that we are the ones who are really defending the right of women to make an informed choice; we are the ones who are defending the freedom of women to reproduce without fear of being coerced into unwanted abortions'.

Since 1973, there has been an exceptionally acrimonious battle in the US over the legitimacy of abortion. Unlike in Britain, a candidate's views on abortion are often a crucial electoral issue, and nominations to the Supreme Court have been decided on the basis of a judge's track record on abortion. A hard-core minority of anti-abortion campaigners has murdered doctors and set fire to clinics. Fear of reprisals for carrying out abortions has led to a marked unwillingness among gynaecologists to provide abortion services. In the next extract Marlene Gerber Fried describes how abortion in the US may be legal but also substantially unavailable, particularly to poorer women, teenagers, and women living in rural areas.

Marlene Gerber Fried[101]

Public funding, an absolute necessity if all women are to have access to abortion rights, was lost in 1976, just three years after *Roe v Wade*...

Publicity surrounding the murders of doctors and clinic workers has made the public at large sharply aware of the extreme vulnerability of abortion providers. In fact, clinics and

---

[100] 'Dignity and the Politics of Protection: Abortion Restrictions under Casey/Carhart' (2008) 117 Yale Law Journal 1694.

[101] 'Abortion in the United States—Legal but Inaccessible' in R Solinger (ed.), *Abortion Wars: A Half Century of Struggle, 1950–2000* (University of California Press Berkeley, 1998) 208–26.

providers have been targets of violence since the early 1980s...These acts included death threats, stalking, attacks with chemicals, arson, bomb threats, invasions and blockades. While federal legislation such as the Freedom of Access to Clinic Entrances Act will certainly help, anti-abortionists are increasingly turning to harassment of individual doctors and their families, picketing their homes, following them, circulating 'Wanted' posters.

The provider shortage has only recently come to public attention, although it represents a major threat to abortion rights...While the overall numbers are themselves very disturbing, of even greater concern is the very uneven distribution of services. Nine out of ten abortion providers are now located in metropolitan areas...Ninety-four per cent of nonmetropolitan counties have no services....

Anti-abortion activists aim also to cut off the supply of potential future providers. They have targeted medical students, generating understandable concerns about taking up practice in such a dangerous and marginalized field...Few medical students are being trained in abortion techniques, despite the fact that abortion is the most common obstetrics surgical procedure. Almost half of graduating obstetrics and gynecology residents have never performed a first-trimester abortion.

6 CONCLUSION

It is often claimed that English law's medicalization of abortion has effectively depoliticized the issue. If the decision to terminate a pregnancy is taken by a woman's *doctor*, on the grounds that pregnancy poses *a risk to health*, it becomes very difficult to challenge both individual abortion decisions, and the rules governing access to abortion. Partly, this is because of the confidentiality that attaches to the doctor/patient relationship and partly because of the trust and confidence that most people have in the medical profession. In recent years, however, there has been increasing political and media interest in the question of access to abortion.

One of the principal areas of concern has been the time limit in section 1(1)(d) of the Abortion Act. If babies can survive at 22 weeks, it has been suggested that permitting abortion for 'social' reasons up until 24 weeks is anomalous. The reality is that fewer than 1 per cent of all abortions take place between 20 and 24 weeks, and most of these would probably fit within the fetal abnormality ground, and so be unaffected by any reduction of the time limit in section 1(1)(a). Reducing the time limit would, in practice, have virtually no impact upon the *number* of abortions carried out each year in the UK.

It is also important to think about *why* women have late abortions. There are three main reasons. First, the results from prenatal tests, such as the 18–20 week anomaly scan, may not be available until around the twentieth week of pregnancy. Secondly, a woman's circumstances may have changed drastically since she became pregnant. Her partner may have left her, or died, and she may feel unable to bring his child into the world. Thirdly, a woman may not realize she is pregnant until relatively late in pregnancy. This may be because she is close to the menopause, very young, or leads a chaotic life, perhaps because of drug use, and does not recognize the symptoms of pregnancy; or it may be because she is using a form of contraceptive, such as the progesterone-only pill, which can result in her periods stopping altogether. Reducing the time limit for abortion might mean that women who fall into these categories would be forced to continue their unwanted pregnancies to term.

It is also worth pointing out that there is currently a vast gap between the theory and the practice of abortion law. Students studying abortion law for the first time are often surprised to learn both that women do not have the right to terminate their unwanted pregnancies, and that abortion is still, prima facie, a criminal offence. This surprise is understandable, given that, in practice, abortion is available upon request in England, Scotland, and Wales within at least the first 13 weeks of pregnancy, and perhaps up to about 16 weeks. So while academic criticism of abortion law based upon its excessive medicalization is, in my view, persuasive and important, the reality is that women *do* make their own abortion decisions, and that the medical profession will very seldom interfere with their 'right' to do so.

A further possible reform of abortion law would therefore be to bring UK legislation into line with the reality of abortion provision. In many other European countries, the right to abortion on request tends to be confined to the first 12 or 14 weeks of pregnancy. In practice then, conformity with the European norm might make it *more difficult* for women who need access to abortion after 13 weeks, since they would have to fit within a special medical exception (such as that the pregnancy poses a grave risk to their health), rather than, at present, simply having to shop around for a provider who is willing to help them. Oddly then, the status quo, despite being peculiarly paternalistic and outdated, may in practice serve women's needs rather better than some plausible legislative alternatives.

Nevertheless, it is surely time to recognize that it no longer makes any sense for the regulation of what is now a straightforward and common medical procedure to consist in a set of defences to the criminal offence of terminating pregnancy. For women seeking abortion to have to persuade two doctors that their health is at risk if they continue their pregnancies is radically out of step with the principle of patient autonomy, which, as we have seen, now dominates medical law. Rather than making a decision which she is uniquely well placed to make for herself, about whether she wants to become a mother (again) at this point, or with this partner, the law suggests that abortion-seeking women should instead adopt the role of a supplicant, portraying themselves as mentally fragile and unable to cope. One-third of all women in the UK will have at least one abortion during their lives, and the vast majority regard the question of whether this is the right thing to do as a decision for them, and perhaps their partners, rather than a choice which is best made by two registered medical practitioners.

In 2008, amendments to the Human Fertilisation and Embryology Act were tabled which would have enabled Parliament to revisit some of the most outdated aspects of the 1967 Act. The need for two doctors' signatures, the ban on nurse-led treatment, and abortion's continued illegality in Northern Ireland were the subject of a number of liberalizing amendments supported by, among others, the Royal College of Obstetricians and Gynaecologists. For reasons which it is hard to understand, the government ensured that these amendments were effectively 'guillotined', and lack of parliamentary time meant that there was no chance of them being voted upon, let alone becoming law. Sally Sheldon points out that this happened shortly before MPs took the longest Christmas break since records began, making the lack of time explanation unsatisfactory. In the final extract, she explains why losing this opportunity to update the 1967 Act was regrettable.

Sally Sheldon[102]

[T]he fact that abortion decisions are serious, with potentially far-reaching implications is all the more reason for believing that it is pregnant women themselves who must make them.

[102] 'A Missed Opportunity to Reform an Outdated Law' (2009) 4 Clinical Ethics 3–5.

The women concerned are more likely to agonise over abortion decisions and they are better placed than doctors to be able to understand the implications of the decision for their own lives and the lives of those closest to them....

Further, any perception of a need to convince the doctor of the merits of one's case is hardly conducive to the medical encounter functioning as an occasion where one can discuss frankly one's concerns, doubts and options. Finally, it should be noted that the majority of doctors agree that the legal right to make these decisions would best be taken from them and given to the women concerned...

Ann Furedi, Chief Executive of the UK's largest abortion service provider, reports that:

Ministers and officials at the Department of Health have repeatedly said to us that they see no need to change the law because it is possible to 'work around' its deficiencies. This is not good enough. The law as it stands undermines the delivery of safe, evidence-based abortion services.

If this is the real explanation... the Government is not concerned by the point of principle: that the regulatory framework established in the Abortion Act is grounded in tired, inaccurate and sexist stereotypes of female irrationality, selfishness and moral immaturity.

FURTHER READING

BMA, Abortion Time Limits: A Briefing Paper from the BMA (BMA: London, 2005), available at <http://www.bma.org.uk/ap.nsf/Content/AbortionTimeLimits>.

Gee, Graham, 'Regulating Abortion in the United States after Gonzales v Carhart' (2007) 70 Modern Law Review 979–99.

Jackson, Emily, 'Abortion, Autonomy and Prenatal Diagnosis' (2000) 9 Social and Legal Studies 467–94.

Kirklin, D, 'The Role of Medical Imaging in the Abortion Debate' (2004) 30 Journal of Medical Ethics 426.

Lee, Ellie, Abortion, Motherhood and Mental Health (Aldine: New York, 2004).

Sheldon, Sally, Beyond Control: Medical Power and Abortion Law (Pluto, London: 1997).

Sheldon, Sally and Wilkinson, Stephen, 'Termination of Pregnancy for Reason of Foetal Disability: Are There Grounds for a Special Exception in Law?' (2001) 9(2) Medical Law Review 85–109.

Sheldon, Sally, 'Unwilling Fathers and Abortion: Terminating Men's Child Support Obligations?' (2003) 66 Modern Law Review 175–94.

Special issue of the Journal of Medical Ethics (2001) 26 suppl II.

14

LIABILITY FOR OCCURRENCES BEFORE BIRTH

CENTRAL ISSUES

1. Under English law, it is generally assumed that children cannot have an action for 'wrongful life', where their claim is that, but for the defendant's negligence, they would not have been born.

2. At common law, the fetus cannot be owed a duty of care, but a child's action for prenatal injuries crystallized at birth when the child 'inherited' her damaged body. This is also the position under the Congenital Disabilities (Civil Liability) Act 1976 With the exception of injuries sustained in road traffic accidents, a mother cannot be held liable for injuring her child *in utero*.

3. Parents can bring an action for 'wrongful pregnancy', usually following negligent sterilization or negligent post-sterilization advice. While recovery of costs directly associated with pregnancy is straightforward, the question of whether parents should be entitled to damages to cover the child's maintenance costs has proved extremely controversial.

4. In a series of cases, the courts have held that the maintenance costs of a healthy child are unrecoverable, but that parents are entitled to recover for the additional costs associated with caring for a disabled child. In its most recent judgment, the House of Lords, by a majority, awarded the mother a 'conventional sum' of £15,000, which was intended to acknowledge that there had been a wrongful interference with her reproductive autonomy.

1 INTRODUCTION

In this chapter, we consider the possibility of liability, either to the child herself or to her parents, for events that occur before birth.

If a child is born suffering from an abnormality, and this is attributable to another person's negligence, she might want to claim damages. If the reason for the child being born disabled is that her mother was deprived of the option of termination, the claim is referred to as a 'wrongful life' action because the disabled child is claiming that if the defendant had not been negligent, her disabled life would have been avoided.

Much more straightforward are cases where the child is injured because of something that happens before she is born. Before a child is even conceived, it is possible that her parents' capacity to give birth to a healthy baby might be impaired: an example might be exposure to toxic substances, which damage sperm or egg cells. Negligence during IVF treatment, before the embryo is transferred to the woman's body, might also result in the birth of a disabled child. And, of course, the child might have sustained injuries while *in utero*. All of these actions will usually be brought under the Congenital Disabilities (Civil Liability) Act 1976, but we also briefly consider the possibility of an action at common law for prenatal injuries because it is still theoretically possible (if unlikely) that a child born before the 1976 Act came into force could have an action for an injury caused prenatally.

Turning to actions which the parents might bring, we can divide these into 'wrongful pregnancy' claims and claims for 'wrongful birth'. A 'wrongful pregnancy' action might lie if the parents want to claim that the defendant's negligence led them to become pregnant with an unwanted child: examples include carrying out a sterilization operation negligently, or offering the patient misleading information about its success. In such cases, the mother might want to claim for the pain and discomfort of pregnancy and childbirth, and expenses such as maternity clothes. Much more difficult and controversial is the question of whether the parents should also be able to claim for the costs of the child's upbringing.

A 'wrongful birth' action involves the claim that the child's *birth* (as opposed to her conception) was the result of the defendant's negligence. The facts in these cases are often indistinguishable from those in 'wrongful life' claims, aside from the identity of the claimant. A woman might bring a wrongful birth action if negligent prenatal testing deprived her of the option of termination.

The terminology of wrongful life, pregnancy, and birth is in such common usage that it will, at times, be used in this chapter, but it is worth noting Harvey Teff's criticism of these labels. As we shall see later in this chapter, their implication that the claimant is 'impugning life itself' may be one of the reasons why these cases have proved to be so problematic.

Harvey Teff[1]

These labels are unfortunate not least in their bizarre, even macabre, overtones. One is not instinctively attracted to the cause of someone who appears to be impugning life itself. This aside, the terms are neither immediately intelligible nor readily distinguishable from each other. Though both signify claims for damages when negligent conduct has resulted in a child being born, they conceal a host of different legal and social implications, depending both on the circumstances leading up to the birth and on its consequences. Thus 'wrongful life', 'wrongful birth' and other expressions canvassed by courts and commentators are potentially a source of considerable confusion.

It would, perhaps, be preferable to refer to all the scenarios described in this chapter as 'reproductive torts', 'pregnancy-related torts', or 'prenatal torts'. However, these generic

---

[1] 'The Action for "Wrongful Life" in England and the United States' (1985) 34 International & Comparative Law Quarterly 423–41, 425.

terms do not capture the existence of important differences between cases that depend upon whether the defendant's negligence caused the child's *injuries*, or her *conception*, or her *birth*.

2 ACTIONS BY THE CHILD

In this section, we consider two ways in which a child might claim that they were harmed before they were born. First, we look at the controversial question of whether life itself could ever amount to a compensatable harm and, secondly, we examine claims for injuries suffered prenatally.

(a) 'WRONGFUL LIFE'

The essence of a wrongful life claim is that the child alleges that, but for the defendant's negligence, she would not have been born and the damage—ie, her wrongful life—would have been avoided. In these cases, it is not claimed that the defendant's action caused the child's disability, but rather that her parents were negligently deprived of the choice not to give birth to this particular child.

A wrongful life action might arise in a number of different situations. First, before conception, the child's parents might be negligently advised that they are not at risk of passing on a genetic disorder. Secondly, negligence during IVF treatment might result in an embryo, which is likely to be born disabled, being transferred to the woman's uterus. Third, negligent prenatal testing might mean that the fetus's abnormality is not detected, and the pregnant woman is not given the option of termination.

The issue has arisen in only one English case—*McKay v Essex Area Health Authority*—and the Court of Appeal rejected the possibility that life itself could be compensatable damage. Mrs McKay had come into contact with rubella when she was less than two months pregnant. She sought medical advice, but her blood samples were mislaid, and she was wrongly informed that she had not been affected by rubella, and that she need not consider a termination. Mary McKay was born seriously disabled as a result of rubella infection during pregnancy.

McKay v Essex Area Health Authority[2]

Stephenson LJ

In this case we are unanimously of the opinion that the infant plaintiff's claim for what has been called 'wrongful life' discloses no reasonable cause of action....

[T]his child has not been injured by either defendant, but by the rubella which has infected the mother without fault on anybody's part...The only right on which she can rely as having been infringed is a right not to be born deformed or disabled, which means, for a child deformed or disabled before birth by nature or disease, a right to be aborted or killed; or, if that last plain word is thought dangerously emotive, deprived of the opportunity to live after being delivered from the body of her mother. The only duty which either defendant can owe

---

[2] [1982] QB 1166.

to the unborn child infected with disabling rubella is a duty to abort or kill her or deprive her of that opportunity...

This analysis leads inexorably on to the question: how can there be a duty to take away life?...

To impose such a duty towards the child would, in my opinion, make a further inroad on the sanctity of human life which would be contrary to public policy. It would mean regarding the life of a handicapped child as not only less valuable than the life of a normal child, but so much less valuable that it was not worth preserving...

Added to that objection must be the opening of the courts to claims by children born handicapped against their mothers for not having an abortion...

The only loss for which those who have not injured the child can be held liable to compensate the child is the difference between its condition as a result of their allowing it to be born alive and injured and its condition if its embryonic life had been ended before its life in the world had begun. But how can a court of law evaluate that second condition and so measure the loss to the child? Even if a court were competent to decide between the conflicting views of theologians and philosophers and to assume an 'after life' or non-existence as the basis for the comparison, how can a judge put a value on the one or the other, compare either alternative with the injured child's life in this world and determine that the child has lost anything, without the means of knowing what, if anything, it has gained?...

To measure loss of expectation of death would require a value judgment where a crucial factor lies altogether outside the range of human knowledge and could only be achieved, if at all, by resorting to the personal beliefs of the judge who has the misfortune to attempt the task. If difficulty in assessing damages is a bad reason for refusing the task, impossibility of assessing them is a good one.

Ackner LJ

I cannot accept that the common law duty of care to a person can involve, without specific legislation to achieve this end, the legal obligation to that person, whether or not in utero, to terminate his existence. Such a proposition runs wholly contrary to the concept of the sanctity of human life...

The disabilities were caused by the rubella and not by the doctor... What then are her injuries, which the doctor's negligence has caused? The answer must be that there are none in any accepted sense. Her complaint is that she was allowed to be born at all, given the existence of her pre-natal injuries. How then are her damages to be assessed? Not by awarding compensation for her pain, suffering and loss of amenities attributable to the disabilities, since these were already in existence before the doctor was consulted. She cannot say that, but for his negligence, she would have been born without her disabilities. What the doctor is blamed for is causing or permitting her to be born at all. Thus, the compensation must be based on a comparison between the value of non-existence (the doctor's alleged negligence having deprived her of this) and the value of her existence in a disabled state.

But how can a court begin to evaluate non-existence, 'the undiscovered country from whose bourn no traveller returns?' No comparison is possible and therefore no damage can be established which a court could recognise.

Griffiths LJ

To my mind, the most compelling reason to reject this cause of action is the intolerable and insoluble problem it would create in the assessment of damage. The basis of damages for personal injury is the comparison between the state of the plaintiff before he was injured and his condition after he was injured. . . . In a claim for wrongful life how does the court begin to make an assessment? The plaintiff does not say, 'But for your negligence I would have been born uninjured.' The plaintiff says, 'But for your negligence I would never have been born.' The court then has to compare the state of the plaintiff with non-existence, of which the court can know nothing; this I regard as an impossible task.

The Court of Appeal gave a number of reasons for their 'firm conclusion that our law cannot recognize a claim for 'wrongful life'.[3] First, it would be contrary to public policy for a doctor to owe a child a duty of care to ensure that she did not exist, since this would undermine the sanctity of human life. Secondly, if such actions succeeded, doctors might be under a duty to try to persuade pregnant women to terminate their pregnancies. Thirdly, the law did not recognize being born as damage: life, however gravely disabled, had to be better than the alternative. Fourthly, assessing the quantum of damages in such a case would be impossible. Tort damages are intended to put the claimant in the position she would have been in if the tort had not been committed. This could not be done because it would require the court to judge the relative value of existence and non-existence.

There are some tensions at the heart of this reasoning. On the one hand, the Court of Appeal was anxious to stress that being born could not constitute damage because the law always treats life as beneficial. But on the other hand, all three judges argued that it is simply impossible to compare existence and non-existence. Surely we can only reach the first conclusion if we *have* compared the two outcomes, and decided that life is generally better than 'non-life'?[4] It is also perhaps a little misleading to suggest, first, that the law is incapable of comparing existence and non-existence, and, secondly, that if such a comparison is made, existence must always be preferred. When decisions about withholding and withdrawing life-prolonging treatment are taken (see further Chapter 17), the courts have sometimes undoubtedly decided that prolonging life is not in the patient's best interests. For example, in *Re J (A Minor) (Wardship: Medical Treatment)*, Taylor LJ said: 'Despite the court's inability to compare a life afflicted by the most severe disability with death, the unknown, I am of the view that there must be extreme cases in which the court is entitled to say: The life which this treatment would prolong would be so cruel as to be intolerable.'[5]

While, as Stephenson LJ admits, difficulty in assessing damages is not usually a good reason for denying a remedy at all in the law of tort, the Court of Appeal thought that assessing damages in this case would be *impossible*. Logically, there is some merit in this argument. If the tort had not occurred, the claimant would not have existed, and so to put her in this position, we would have to put a monetary value on non-existence.

It is, however, worth bearing in mind that *on exactly the same facts*, the courts would find themselves able to assess the damages payable to Mary McKay's *mother* for negligent antenatal care. As we see later, in wrongful birth actions the courts are much less troubled by the prospect of compensating a parent for the costs associated with bringing up a disabled child, who would not have been born 'but for' the defendant's negligence. Given that the costs associated with Mary McKay's disabilities would be compensatable if her mother was the claimant, is it overly legalistic to say that it is impossible to assess *exactly the same costs* where the claimant is Mary herself?

---

[3] Per Griffiths LJ.

[4] Harvey Teff 'The Action for "Wrongful Life" in England and the United States' (1985) 34 International & Comparative Law Quarterly 423–41, 433.

[5] [1991] Fam 33.

If the mother can claim damages for the 'wrongful birth' of a disabled child, why would it be contrary to public policy to allow the child herself—who is, after all, the one who suffers *physical harm* as a result of the doctor's negligence—to bring an action for her own injuries? This point has been made forcefully by Tony Weir:

> To assert that one cannot owe a duty to a foetus to kill it is plausible enough, but the plausibility fades a bit when one has to admit that a duty to kill the foetus may well be owed to the mother: if a duty is owed to one of the affected parties, why not to the other?[6]

Usually, of course, the existence of the mother's claim will mean the courts' rejection of wrongful life claims will make little practical difference, since the family as a whole will benefit from any damages received by the mother. If the mother is dead, however, the absence of the child's freestanding action might cause problems, since the child's needs undoubtedly survive her mother's death. Similarly, if the child has been adopted, or taken into care, she may not benefit from her mother's right to seek compensation.

In the following extract, JK Mason argues that the phrase 'wrongful life' may have been partly to blame for judicial hostility to Mary McKay's action.

JK Mason[7]

> [I]t is difficult to decide where and when the phrase 'wrongful life' originated—if it ever did as such.... Whoever is responsible, he or she certainly did the later plaintiffs no service as the implication that 'life' can, of itself, be wrongful, or a type of harm, has always been something that the courts—and perhaps even the general public—have found hard to accept. What the infant plaintiff finds 'wrong' is not that he or she is alive, but, rather, that he or she is *alive and suffering* as a result of another's negligence.

Harvey Teff makes a similar point about the judges' use of language, arguing that framing the issue as one of 'wrongful life' may explain the court's brisk dismissal of a claim that might have been dealt with more sympathetically if it had been described differently.

Harvey Teff[8]

> It is scarcely surprising that the characterization of 'birth' and 'life' as 'wrongful' has often prompted judicial hostility, if not sheer incredulity.... The widespread condemnation of 'wrongful life' actions thus affords a striking example of symbolic affirmation. Yet in such actions the child is manifestly not decrying birth or life *as such*. Rather he is making an undeniably powerful appeal to our sense of justice. He is asserting that he has been subjected to some particular disabling condition, typically because of the negligent conduct of a professionally qualified defendant, whose potential liability for inflicting comparable injuries on a live person would be beyond dispute.

---

[6] 'Wrongful Life—Nipped in the Bud' (1982) 41 Cambridge Law Journal 225, 227.

[7] *The Troubled Pregnancy: Legal Rights and Wrongs in Reproduction* (CUP: Cambridge, 2007) 189.

[8] 'The Action for "Wrongful Life" in England and the United States' (1985) 34 International & Comparative Law Quarterly 423–41.

The Court of Appeal in *McKay* assumed that there could also be no action for wrongful life under the Congenital Disabilities (Civil Liability) Act 1976, and this was certainly the Law Commission's intention. Their report claimed that:

> Such a cause of action, if it existed, could place an almost intolerable burden on medical advisers in their socially and morally exacting role. The danger that doctors would be under subconscious pressure to advise abortions in doubtful cases through fear of an action for damages is, we think, a real one.[9]

However, as we see later, while the 1976 Act would not permit someone in Mary McKay's position to bring an action, it does appear to inadvertently carve out a 'wrongful life' action where the child is born disabled as a result of negligent selection of embryos during fertility treatment.

In some other countries, wrongful life actions have had more success. In 2005, the Dutch Supreme Court awarded damages to both the parents *and the child*, after a midwife decided no further investigation was necessary when told that two members of the father's family suffered from a serious chromosomal abnormality.[10] Kelly Molenaar was born suffering from severe mental and physical disabilities. The Hoge Raad considered whether awarding damages would violate the principle of 'the dignity of human life', but decided that it would, in fact, support that dignity by enabling Kelly to lead a more bearable life.

When wrongful life actions have succeeded, the courts have concentrated on the fact that the claimant's disabled existence is attributable to the defendant's negligence, and have downplayed the existential problem, which dominated the judgments in *McKay*, namely that the child's claim is that they should not have been born. A wrongful life action, also brought following the failure to diagnose rubella during pregnancy, succeeded in France in 2000 in the controversial *Perruche* case,[11] discussed in the next extract, but legislation passed shortly afterwards (known as the *loi anti Perruche*) means that the case is now only of historical interest.

In the *Perruche* decision, as Anne Morris and Severine Saintier explain, the *Cour de Cassation* was adamant that it was compensating Nicolas for his disabilities, and not for his birth. And it could plausibly be argued that the child is not seeking damages for her very existence, but rather for the disabilities, which inevitably, as a result of the defendant's negligence, accompany it.

The child in a wrongful life action is not necessarily claiming that she would have been better off if she had never existed. Even if life itself must always be deemed to be a benefit, it is perfectly possible for that benefit to co-exist with the costs that flow from being born disabled. As the California Supreme Court observed in *Curlender v Bio-Science Laboratories*[12]—a US case in which a child recovered damages after negligent pre-natal testing failed to detect that she had Tay-Sachs disease—someone can be both benefited and harmed at the same time: 'The reality of the "wrongful life" concept is that such a plaintiff both *exists* and *suffers* due to the negligence of others.'[13]

---

[9] Report no 60 Report on Injuries to Unborn Children (1974) Cmnd 5709 para 89.
[10] *Leids Universitair Medisch Centrum v Kelly Molenaar*, no. C03/206, RvdW 2005, 42 (March 18, 2005).
[11] *Cass Ass Plen* 17.11.00 JCP G2000, II-10438, 2309.   [12] 106 Cal App 3d 811 (1980).
[13] Ibid. 830.

Anne Morris and Severine Saintier[14]

To condemn the Court for compensating Nicolas [Perruche] for being born is, however, to misconstrue the basis of the decision. Sargos, adviser to the court, . . . insisted that it is *not* for being born that the child seeks compensation, but for his disabilities and their consequences. The *Cour de Cassation* accepted that argument: since the child exists, the issue is not his birth but his disabilities. Some have argued that to accept that disabilities constitute 'harm' places a negative value on the life of a disabled child and is contrary to the principle of human dignity. For Sargos, refusing to compensate the child is equally contrary to human dignity. Compensation gives him the means to protect his dignity, and enhances that dignity by giving him, personally, the right to claim. It would be worse to allow only the parents to claim because that defines the child purely as a loss (or burden) to them and denies him the right, as any other legal person, to claim compensation for his injury . . .

Leaving aside the metaphysical considerations, the problems in wrongful life claims are not that different from other cases. In many cases of physical injury compensation cannot put the victim in the position he was in prior to the damage, rather it aims to give the victim, as far as money can, a 'normal' life or at least to ameliorate the effects of the tort. Similarly, compensation in a wrongful life claim could be aimed at ameliorating the consequences of the tort (living an impaired life) and providing the child with an improved quality of life.

The courts' rejection of wrongful life actions can also be contrasted with the acceptance of a child's action for prenatal injury, discussed in the next section. In both cases, the defendant's negligence leads to the birth of a disabled child, but in the latter case recovery is straightforward because the defendant *caused* the injury itself. Although there is clearly an important factual difference between the two claims, it does not necessarily seem fair that children whose injuries result from negligent prenatal testing should have to bear all of the financial costs associated with their disabilities, whereas children who are injured *in utero* can receive full compensation.

It is also possible that the difference between these two claims may become increasingly blurred once it becomes possible to offer *treatment* following prenatal diagnosis. If negligent prenatal testing deprived a fetus of the opportunity of an effective cure for their condition, it might be possible to argue that 'but for' the defendant's negligent, the child would have been born *healthy*, and so to put her in the position she would have been in if the tort had not occurred, the additional costs associated with her disability should be recoverable.

So far, we have assumed that the defendant in a wrongful life action will be a doctor who gave negligent advice about the likelihood that this child would be born disabled, and in this context, as we have seen, a number of commentators have questioned the courts' refusal to entertain such claims. But. of course, if it were to be accepted that an action should lie when a child claims that her birth ought to have been avoided, should children also be able to sue their parents for bringing them into the world in an impaired or less than ideal state? Could a child sue her mother for choosing not to undergo prenatal tests, for example, or for not having an abortion if an abnormality is detected?

Certainly, in *McKay* Stephenson LJ appeared to assume that actions against mothers for not aborting disabled fetuses would be the logical corollary of permitting children to bring 'wrongful life' actions against doctors: 'Added to [the sanctity of life] objection must be the

---

[14] 'To Be or Not to Be: Is That the Question? Wrongful Life and Misconceptions' (2003) 11 Medical Law Review 167–93.

opening of the courts to claims by children born handicapped against their mothers for not having an abortion.' And the point was conceded by Counsel for the plaintiffs who had: 'accepted that if the duty of care to the foetus involved a duty on the doctor, albeit indirectly, to prevent its birth, the child would have a cause of action against its mother, who had unreasonably refused to have an abortion'.

With respect, this seems doubtful. As we see below, the Congenital Disabilities (Civil Liability) Act 1976, with one exception, which is not relevant here, prevents children from suing their mothers for prenatal injuries. It therefore seems improbable that the courts would allow an action at common law against a mother who elected to bring up a disabled child, especially since the reality would generally be that she would be paying damages to *herself*.

(b) PRENATAL INJURY

Since 1976, recovery for injuries sustained before birth has been covered by statute. It is, however, still theoretically possible that a child born before the Congenital Disabilities (Civil Liability) Act came into force could bring an action for prenatal injury, which has not manifested itself until much later in life. We therefore first briefly consider the possibility of liability at common law in three situations: (a) where injuries were sustained *in utero*; (b) where a child is harmed as a result of something that happened to her parents before she was conceived; and (c) where the child is stillborn.

(1) At Common Law

(a) *Occurrences* in utero

A fetus is not a legal person, which means that it cannot be owed a duty of care. In *Paton v BPAS*, a case we considered in the previous chapter, the President of the Family Division was emphatic on this point.

Paton v BPAS[15]

Sir George Baker P

The foetus cannot, in English law, in my view, have any right of its own at least until it is born and has a separate existence from the mother. That permeates the whole of the civil law of this country...

[I]t was universally accepted, and has since been accepted, that in order to have a right the foetus must be born and be a child...[T]here can be no doubt, in my view, that in England and Wales, the foetus has no right of action, no right at all, until birth.

On the other hand, applying the 'neighbour' principle,[16] it is plainly foreseeable that negligent conduct might cause injuries to a developing fetus, and result in a child being born disabled.

At common law, the courts' solution has been to say that the *child* only suffers damage when she is born, and acquires legal personality. In *Burton v Islington Health Authority* the

---

[15] [1979] QB 276.   [16] *Donoghue v Stevenson* [1932] AC 562.

duty of care was said to 'crystallize' at birth when the child acquires legal personhood, and inherits her damaged body.

Burton v Islington Health Authority[17]

Dillon LJ

In law and in logic no damage can have been caused to the plaintiff before the plaintiff existed. The damage was suffered by the plaintiff at the moment that, in law, the plaintiff achieved personality and inherited the damaged body for which the health authority (on the assumed facts) was responsible. The events prior to birth were mere links in the chain of causation between the health authority's assumed lack of skill and care and the consequential damage to the plaintiff.

A similar approach is evident in other areas of the law. For example, child protection laws do not apply to fetuses, and so no steps to protect a child can be taken until she is born alive. This issue arose in *Re F (in utero)*, in which a local authority was concerned that a pregnant woman, who was mentally disturbed and led a nomadic existence, would not seek appropriate medical attention during childbirth. The Court of Appeal held that the local authority could not take steps to protect the fetus while it was still *in utero*, but that it acquired the power to take the child into care as soon as it was born.

Re F (in utero)[18]

May LJ

Even though this is a case in which, on its facts, I would exercise the jurisdiction if I had it, in the absence of authority I am driven to the conclusion that the court does not have the jurisdiction contended for...

I think that there would be insuperable difficulties if one sought to enforce any order in respect of an unborn child against its mother, if that mother failed to comply with the order. I cannot contemplate the court ordering that this should be done by force, nor indeed is it possible to consider with any equanimity that the court should seek to enforce an order by committal.

In relation to inheritance too, a fetus cannot inherit property, and yet if a child beneficiary is *en ventre sa mère* when a testator dies, the gift will materialize at birth.

Similarly, it is possible for criminal responsibility for acts which took place before a child's birth to 'crystallize' once the child is born alive. Homicide is the killing of a person, so the killing of a fetus cannot be either manslaughter or murder. But what if the child is born alive, and injuries which were sustained *in utero* subsequently cause her death? In *Attorney-General's Reference No. 3 of 1994*, the House of Lords held that there is no need for the person who died to have been a legal person at the time when the injuries which caused death were sustained, and hence a conviction for manslaughter would be possible.

---

[17] [1993] QB 204.   [18] [1988] Fam 122.

Attorney-General's Reference No. 3 of 1994[19]

Lord Hope

For the foetus, life lies in the future, not the past. It is not sensible to say that it cannot ever be harmed, or that nothing can be done to it which can ever be dangerous. Once it is born it is exposed, like all other living persons, to the risk of injury. It may also carry with it the effects of things done to it before birth which, after birth, may prove to be harmful. It would seem not to be unreasonable therefore, on public policy grounds, to regard the child in this case, when she became a living person, as within the scope of the mens rea which B had when he stabbed her mother before she was born.

(b) Occurrences pre-conception

Negligence before a child is conceived might also lead to the birth of a disabled child. An example might be if one of her parents was exposed to toxic chemicals or radiation, which impaired their capacity to have a healthy baby. No such case has been brought before the English courts, but it is possible that the same approach would be adopted, and the child would be said to sustain the injuries in question when she is subsequently born alive. Of course, if the child who suffers damage has not yet been conceived, she is undoubtedly a less foreseeable claimant than if she is *in utero* when she sustains her injuries, and so it may be harder to establish that the defendant owed her a duty of care.

Particularly difficult factual issues arise when the conduct which caused the injuries happened a very long time before the claimant was conceived. An example of this would be the drug diethylstilbestrol, which was taken by pregnant women in the 1950s in order to prevent miscarriage. In fact, it caused a variety of injuries, both to the pregnant woman and the fetus she was carrying at the time, but importantly it also affected any female fetuses' reproductive organs, thereby injuring *their* future children. Thus, children might be born disabled as a result of a drug taken by their *grandmothers*. In practice, identifying the defendant and proving causation would be exceptionally difficult where the alleged negligence took place several decades before the claimant's birth. And there might also be policy reasons for restricting liability to subsequent generations, in order to avoid the possibility of unquantifiable and indefinite future liability. Certainly, the Law Commission had reservations about liability in such circumstances, and under the Congenital Disabilities (Civil Liability) Act 1976, discussed below, a duty is owed only to the children of the person who was affected by the occurrence, and so there cannot be liability to future generations.[20]

(c) When the child is stillborn

There can be no action on behalf of a stillborn child. Any claim for a negligently caused stillbirth would be by the mother, who might—depending on the circumstances—have an action for personal or psychiatric injury, and by the father, if he could be said to have suffered psychiatric injury, perhaps as a result of witnessing the stillbirth, or its immediate aftermath.[21]

---

[19] [1998] AC 245.   [20] Report no. 60 Report on Injuries to Unborn Children (1974) Cmnd 5709.
[21] *Alcock v Chief Constable of South Yorkshire* [1992] 1 AC 310 and *White v Chief Constable of South Yorkshire* [1999] 2 AC 455. See further Chapter 3.

(2) Congenital Disabilities (Civil Liability) Act 1976

The Congenital Disabilities (Civil Liability) Act 1976 replaces any common law action for prenatal injuries for all births from 22 July 1976. It was amended by the Consumer Protection Act 1987 so that it also applies to children whose injuries are caused by defective products (see further Chapter 10).

Congenital Disabilities (Civil Liability) Act 1976, sections 1 and 4

1(1) If a child is born disabled as the result of such an occurrence before its birth as is mentioned in subsection (2) below, and a person (other than the child's own mother) is under this section answerable to the child in respect of the occurrence, the child's disabilities are to be regarded as damage resulting from the wrongful act of that person and actionable accordingly at the suit of the child.

(2) An occurrence to which this section applies is one which—

(a) affected either parent of the child in his or her ability to have a normal, healthy child; or

(b) affected the mother during her pregnancy, or affected her or the child in the course of its birth, so that the child is born with disabilities which would not otherwise have been present.

(3) Subject to the following subsections, a person (here referred to as 'the defendant') is answerable to the child if he was liable in tort to the parent or would, if sued in due time, have been so; and it is no answer that there could not have been such liability because the parent suffered no actionable injury, if there was a breach of legal duty which, accompanied by injury, would have given rise to the liability.

(4) In the case of an occurrence preceding the time of conception, the defendant is not answerable to the child if at that time either or both of the parents knew the risk of their child being born disabled (that is to say, the particular risk created by the occurrence); but should it be the child's father who is the defendant, this subsection does not apply if he knew of the risk and the mother did not...

(7) If in the child's action under this section it is shown that the parent affected shared the responsibility for the child being born disabled, the damages are to be reduced to such extent as the court thinks just and equitable having regard to the extent of the parent's responsibility.

4(3) Liability to a child under section 1 [1A] or 2 of this Act is to be regarded...as liability for personal injuries sustained by the child immediately after its birth.

Notice that under section 4(3) the Act adopts the common law 'fiction' that the injuries are sustained immediately after birth, when the child becomes a legal person, and the duty of care 'crystallizes'. The Act also confirms the common law position that there can be no liability to a child who is stillborn. Under section 1(1), the action only arises if the child is born, and 'born' is defined in section 4(2) as being 'born alive (the moment of a child's birth being when it first has a life separate from its mother)'.

Under section 1(2)(a) and 1(2)(b) the Act applies both to pre-conception occurrences which affect either parent's ability to have a healthy child, and to injuries sustained during pregnancy and childbirth. Section 1(4) provides that there is no liability for pre-conception risks if the parent knew of the risk of the child being born disabled, although this does not apply if the father is the defendant and he knew of the risk but the mother did not. This scenario might arise if the child's father had a disease, such as syphilis, which would be likely to cause his child to be born disabled. If, in such circumstances, he knew of the risk of infection but did not inform the child's mother, the child could have an action against her father.

Under section 1(3) the duty owed to a child under the Act is a derivative one, and exists only when a duty is owed to one of the child's parents. The parent does not actually have to have suffered actionable damage him or herself, but the defendant must have been in breach of a duty of care owed to one of the child's parents. This has a number of consequences. First, where the child suffers injuries because of a decision taken by the pregnant woman, for example to refuse caesarean delivery, the child could have no claim under the Congenital Disabilities Act 1976. Any claim is contingent upon establishing that there was a breach of a duty owed to the mother, and a doctor who respects his patient's refusal of medical intervention is clearly not in breach of his duty of care.

Secondly, the defences of *volenti non fit injuria* and contributory negligence apply.[22] If the parent's claim would have been defeated by the defence of *volenti*, then the child can have no action for her injuries. And if the child's injuries are partly attributable to the defendant's fault, and partly attributable to her parent's behaviour, then under section 1(7) any damages must be reduced according to the extent to which the parent is responsible for the child being born disabled.

Thirdly, because the child's action arises through the duty owed to her parents, the problem of liability to second- or third-generation claimants is resolved. It is only possible to recover for prenatal injuries if the defendant owed a duty of care to the claimant's parents, and this would obviously not be the case when the claimant's parent was *in utero* when the injuries which eventually led to the claimant's disabilities occurred.

Fourthly, it is worth noting that under section 1(2)(b), liability for prenatal injuries will exist only when the occurrence *affected the mother* during her pregnancy. Much turns on what is meant here by 'affected'. For example, an X-ray during pregnancy may have no effect at all on the pregnant woman, but could injure the developing fetus. Inadequate use of monitoring equipment will also not generally affect the pregnant woman, but could cause the child to be born disabled. Nevertheless, Adrian Whitfield argues that provided the defendant owed a duty of care to the pregnant woman in relation to the act which injured the fetus, regardless of whether it, in fact, affects her in any way, the child will have a cause of action.[23]

Finally, the Act confines liability to cases where the child is disabled as a result of an 'occurrence'. In *Multiple Claimants v Sanifo-Synthelabo*[24] the claimants had suffered injuries as a result of the epilepsy medication their mothers had taken during pregnancy. The court was asked to determine certain preliminary issues, one of which was whether there could have been an 'occurrence' for the purposes of the 1976 Act. The problem was, as Andrew Smith J pointed out, that the wording of the Act 'does not allow for the possibility that the occurrence was by way of an accumulation of the drug within the mother'. Expert evidence would be needed, he concluded, to determine whether the alleged 'transplacental spread' could properly be described as an 'occurrence'.

---

[22] See further Chapter 3.

[23] 'Actions Arising from Birth' in A Grubb with J Laing (eds) *Principles of Medical Law*, 2nd edn (OUP: Oxford, 2004) 789–851, 807.

[24] [2007] EWHC 1860.

The 1976 Act was amended in 1990 by the Human Fertilisation and Embryology Act, which added section 1A and section 4(4)(A):

Congenital Disabilities (Civil Liability) Act 1976 sections 1A and 4

1A(1) In any case where—

(a) a child carried by a woman as the result of the placing in her of an embryo or of sperm and eggs or her artificial insemination is born disabled,

(b) the disability results from an act or omission in the course of the selection, or the keeping or use outside the body, of the embryo carried by her or of the gametes used to bring about the creation of the embryo, and

(c) a person is under this section answerable to the child in respect of the act or omission, the child's disabilities are to be regarded as damage resulting from the wrongful act of that person and actionable accordingly at the suit of the child....

(3) The defendant is not under this section answerable to the child if at the time the embryo, or the sperm and eggs, are placed in the woman or the time of her insemination (as the case may be) either or both of the parents knew the risk of their child being born disabled (that is to say, the particular risk created by the act or omission).

4(4A) In any case where a child carried by a woman as the result of the placing in her of an embryo or of sperm and eggs or her artificial insemination is born disabled, any reference in section 1 of this Act to a parent includes a reference to a person who would be a parent but for sections 27 to 29 of the Human Fertilisation and Embryology Act 1990.

Section 1A extends liability under the Act to occurrences during assisted conception. A child whose disability results from the negligent selection or storage of embryos will have an action under the Act. If the parents knew of the risk that their child would be born disabled, there is no liability. An example might be if the parents are informed of an incident which may have damaged their stored embryos but they nevertheless choose to have these potentially damaged embryos implanted, perhaps because these embryos represent their last opportunity to have a genetically related child.

The application of the 1976 Act to cases where the child is born disabled as a result of the negligent selection of embryos raises the question of whether this might amount to a 'wrongful life' claim. In these cases, the negligent selection did not *cause* the child's disabilities. Rather, the negligent selection caused *this child to exist*, and the child's claim must be that if the doctors had exercised proper care and skill, *she would never have existed*. It is not clear that the legislature intended to create a statutory wrongful life action for children born following negligent embryo selection, and yet they appear to have done so. No cases under this section have come before the courts, but if they do, it will be interesting to see whether the courts would be as troubled as they were in *McKay* by the fact that the child would be claiming that, if the embryo selection had been carried out non-negligently, she would not have existed.

The purpose of section 4(4)(A) is to ensure that a child will still have an action where it is the sperm or egg donor (who will not be the child's legal parent) whose capacity to conceive a healthy child was affected.

(3) 'Maternal' Liability/Immunity

Under section 1(1) of the Congenital Disabilities (Civil Liability) Act 1976, liability under the Act is confined to people 'other than the child's own mother', so a child cannot bring an action against her mother for injuries sustained *in utero*. Allowing a child to sue her mother would, the Law Commission argued, create additional stress within the family.[25] Mothers of disabled children are often unable to work full-time, and will therefore rarely have sufficient funds to pay compensation to their children. And since a mother is normally already responsible for her child's care, any damages she might be ordered to pay would in practice usually be paid to herself.

An exception is, however, created in section 2 if the child's injuries were caused by her mother's negligent driving.

Congenital Disabilities (Civil Liability) Act 1976, section 2

2 A woman driving a motor vehicle when she knows (or ought reasonably to know) herself to be pregnant is to be regarded as being under the same duty to take care for the safety of her unborn child as the law imposes on her with respect to the safety of other people; and if in consequence of her breach of that duty her child is born with disabilities which would not otherwise have been present, those disabilities are to be regarded as damage resulting from her wrongful act and actionable accordingly at the suit of the child.

The reason for the driving exception to maternal immunity is that compulsory road traffic insurance means that the pregnant woman will *benefit* from her own liability. Damages would be paid *by her insurance company* to her child which will, in practice, assist *her* in caring for her disabled child.

Fathers are not exempt. The Law Commission had argued that there were fewer ways in which a father's conduct might injure the developing fetus, with one of the most likely possibilities being a serious assault on the mother. It concluded that there were no good policy reasons to exclude liability in such circumstances.

Now we know a great deal more about how a fetus might be injured prenatally as a result of a father's behaviour.[26] Smoking, drugs, and even excessive mobile phone use have been said to increase the chance of birth defects. However, a child could only sue her father under the 1976 Act if *he* owed a duty of care *to her mother* in relation to his exposure to toxic agents, and this is very unlikely to be the case.

In the next extract, Sally Sheldon comments on the historically specific and now rather outdated gender assumptions, evident both in the Law Commission report and in the parliamentary debates in 1976, which underpin the distinction the Act draws between mothers and fathers. Sheldon also notes an interesting difference between the UK, where, aside from road traffic accidents, mothers are exempt from liability for prenatal harm, and the US, where women have been imprisoned for taking drugs during pregnancy.

Sally Sheldon[27]

In this conceptualization of risks, the dangers posed by male bodies tend to be seen as occupational and this serves to generalize responsibility. Where female occupational risks are envisaged, these are those which result from housework, such as the use of air freshener

---

[25] Report no. 60 Report on Injuries to Unborn Children (1974) Cmnd 5709.

[26] Sally Sheldon, 'ReConceiving Masculinity: Imagining Men's Reproductive Bodies in Law' (1999) 26 Journal of Law and Society 129–49.

[27] Ibid.

and wood polish. However, more often, the dangers posed by female bodies result from the frivolous recreational behaviour of individual women who amuse themselves by drinking gin, smoking, going on rides at fun fairs, or by doing those other unspecified 'extraordinary things that women do to themselves'....

In the United States criminal cases, the defendant is typically a black 'welfare mom' on crack cocaine. The woman who seems to have informed the deliberations of the Law Commission seems to be a middle class housewife who, if she is to be criticized is guilty primarily of frivolity.

3 ACTIONS BY THE PARENTS

There are two sorts of action that parents might have when their child is born injured as a result of another's negligence. First, we consider actions when negligence led to the child's *conception*, usually because one of the parents had undergone a sterilization operation that, for some reason, failed to achieve sterility. While it is the child's *conception* which is caused by the defendant's negligence, as JK Mason has pointed out, there will only be a plausible cause of action if the conception results in a pregnancy, and so it may be more appropriate to refer to these as 'wrongful pregnancy' cases.[28] Secondly, we consider claims for wrongful *birth*, which arise where the defendant's negligence meant the mother was unable to avoid the child's birth.

(a) 'WRONGFUL PREGNANCY'

If a woman becomes pregnant following a negligently performed sterilization operation, or is given negligent advice about her or her partner's sterility, there are three possible outcomes. First, she might miscarry or the baby might be stillborn, in which case an action for her pain and suffering would be uncontroversial, although the sum would be relatively modest. Secondly, she could decide to terminate the pregnancy. Again, a claim for the costs of an abortion, and any associated pain and suffering or loss of income would be straightforward, and again the award is likely to be fairly small.

The third possibility is that the woman carries the pregnancy to term and gives birth to a live baby. In this third scenario, if the patient can establish that their sterilization operation was negligently performed, or that they were given negligent pre- or post-operative advice, their claim will be for damages to compensate them for costs associated with giving birth to a child that they did not want.

(1) Can there be Recovery for Wrongful Pregnancy?

Although in practice there is little difference between the claims, it is worth noting that an action for wrongful pregnancy might be brought in contract or in tort.

(a) Contract

If a sterilization operation is carried out in the private sector, the patient will have a contract with the clinic or hospital in which they are treated. If the sterilization is unsuccessful, and the patient (or his partner) subsequently becomes pregnant, an action in contract is possible.

---

[28] *The Troubled Pregnancy: Legal Wrongs and Rights in Reproduction* (CUP: Cambridge, 2007).

In practice, however, as we saw in Chapter 3, the courts will only imply into the contract a duty to exercise reasonable care in carrying out the sterilization, and in giving advice about sterility. There will certainly not be an implied warranty that sterility will be achieved. As a result, cases brought in contract law will generally be indistinguishable from the negligence actions we consider in the next section

In *Eyre v Measday*[29], the Court of Appeal rejected the argument that the doctor's statements that vasectomy and female sterilization were 'irreversible' amounted to guarantees of sterility.

Slade LJ

[I]n my opinion, in the absence of any express warranty, the court should be slow to imply against a medical man an unqualified warranty as to the results of an intended operation, for the very simple reason that, objectively speaking, it is most unlikely that a responsible medical man would intend to give a warranty of this nature.

This was followed in *Thake v Maurice*. The doctor had not warned Mr and Mrs Thake that there was a small risk that the operation, even if successful, might spontaneously reverse itself in the future. The Court of Appeal (Kerr LJ dissenting) rejected the Thake's claim for breach of warranty, but nevertheless found that the failure to warn of spontaneous reversal had been negligent.

Thake v Maurice[30]

Neill LJ

Both the plaintiffs and the defendant expected that sterility would be the result of the operation and the defendant appreciated that that was the plaintiffs' expectation. This does not mean, however, that a reasonable person would have understood the defendant to be giving a binding promise that the operation would achieve its purpose or that the defendant was going further than to give an assurance that he expected and believed that it would have the desired result. Furthermore, I do not consider that a reasonable person would have expected a responsible medical man to be intending to give a guarantee. Medicine, though a highly skilled profession, is not, and is not generally regarded as being, an exact science. The reasonable man would have expected the defendant to exercise all the proper skill and care of a surgeon in that speciality; he would not in my view have expected the defendant to give a guarantee of 100 per cent success.

Accordingly, though I am satisfied that a reasonable person would have left the consulting room thinking that Mr. Thake would be sterilised by the vasectomy operation, such a person would not have left thinking that the defendant had given a guarantee that Mr. Thake would be absolutely sterile.

(b) Tort

As we saw in Chapter 3, there are several stages to an action in tort. The defendant must owe the claimant a duty of care; the duty must be breached; and the breach must cause foreseeable damage.

[29] [1986] 1 All ER 488.   [30] [1986] QB 644.

(i) The existence of a duty of care

A person who is sterilized is unquestionably owed a duty of care. Whether a duty is owed to their partner is slightly more complicated. If a woman's sterilization goes wrong, her partner's loss will be purely economic. In such cases, it would be necessary to establish that there was a proximate relationship between him and the doctor who carried out his sexual partner's sterilization. This would generally only be possible if he was within the doctor's contemplation at the time of the operation because he was already the patient's husband or partner.

If it is the man's vasectomy that does not work, his partner might be said to suffer physical injury as well as financial losses. Although the physical injury element of her claim is not governed by the restrictive rules which cover pure economic loss, it is clear that the courts will not find that a doctor owes a duty to all future sexual partners of a patient undergoing sterilization, but only to women who are within the doctor's contemplation when the operation is carried out.

In *Goodwill v British Pregnancy Advisory Service*, Mr MacKinlay had had a vasectomy, arranged by the defendants, four years before he began having a sexual relationship with Mrs Goodwill. Although initially successful, the vasectomy had spontaneously reversed itself. Mrs Goodwill became pregnant, and sued the defendants for loss of income, and for the costs of bringing up her daughter. She argued that the defendants had owed *her* a duty of care to give Mr McKinlay proper advice about the permanency of sterility. The Court of Appeal struck out her claim as an abuse of process:

Goodwill v British Pregnancy Advisory Service[31]

Peter Gibson LJ

[T]he defendants were not in a sufficient or any special relationship with the plaintiff such as gives rise to a duty of care. I cannot see that it can properly be said of the defendants that they voluntarily assumed responsibility to the plaintiff when giving advice to Mr MacKinlay. At that time they had no knowledge of her, she was not an existing sexual partner of Mr MacKinlay but was merely, like any other woman in the world, a potential future sexual partner of his, that is to say a member of an indeterminately large class of females who might have sexual relations with Mr MacKinlay during his lifetime. I find it impossible to believe that the policy of the law is or should be to treat so tenuous a relationship between the adviser and the advisee as giving rise to a duty of care.

(ii) Breach of duty

Once a duty of care has been established, it is necessary to work out whether the duty has been breached. This might be the case where the operation was *performed* negligently, or where a doctor offered negligent *advice* about the operation's success, perhaps because post-vasectomy sperm samples were not properly tested.

It is now extremely unlikely that any case would be brought in which a doctor failed to warn either a male or a female patient of the risk that the operation may not succeed. Since the 1980s, it has been known that there is a small chance that a vasectomy might spontaneously reverse itself several years later, even when initial sperm samples indicate that the

---

[31] [1996] 1 WLR 1397.

operation has been successful. In *Newell v Goldenberg*[32] the court held that, in 1985 when Mr Newell underwent a vasectomy, no competent body of medical opinion would have failed to inform a patient of the small risk of vasectomy reversal, and Dr Goldenberg's failure to give an appropriate warning was therefore negligent.

Similarly, there is a small risk that the most common type of female sterilization (tubal occlusion) will fail to achieve sterility. The Royal College of Obstetricians and Gynaecologists' evidence-based clinical guideline[33] on male and female sterilization now recommends full and frank disclosure of both these risks.

Royal College of Obstetricians and Gynaecologists[34]

People requesting sterilisation should be informed that tubal occlusion and vasectomy are associated with failure rates and that pregnancies can occur several years after the procedure. They should be told of the lifetime risk of failure in general for tubal occlusion, which is estimated at one in 200. . . . The failure rate for vasectomy should be quoted as approximately one in 2000 after clearance has been given.

Given that it would clearly now be unreasonable not to warn patients undergoing sterilization of these risks, any future cases are overwhelmingly likely to be settled out of court. The only remaining scenario in which a statement about sterility might lead to litigation is where the parents were given inaccurate test results (as happened in *Mcfarlane*, below), either as a result of negligent testing, or negligent interpretation of the results.

(iii) Causation

While it is sexual intercourse, rather than the failed sterilization operation that actually *causes* a pregnancy, having unprotected sex will not amount to a *novus actus interveniens* (an act which breaks the chain of causation), unless the patient knows that the sterilization has failed. This was the case in *Sabri-Tabrizi v Lothian Health Board*.[35] The court found that S's decision to nevertheless expose herself to the risk of pregnancy was unreasonable, and constituted a *novus actus interveniens*.

It is also clear that the pregnant woman has no duty to mitigate her loss by having an abortion, or by having the child adopted, and that her decision to continue the pregnancy and bring up the child herself will not break the chain of causation.

Lord Steyn[36]

I cannot conceive of any circumstances in which the autonomous decision of the parents not to resort to even a lawful abortion could be questioned. For similar reasons the parents' decision not to have the child adopted was plainly natural and commendable. It is difficult to envisage any circumstances in which it would be right to challenge such a decision of the parents.

---

[32] [1995] 6 Med LR.
[33] *Male and Female Sterilisation* (RCOG: London, 2004).
[34] Ibid.   [35] [1998] BMLR 190.
[36] *McFarlane v Tayside Health Board* [2000] 2 AC 59.

A further reason not to treat the decision not to abort as a *novus actus* is that this would imply that the pregnant woman has a *right* to an abortion, which she would be free to exercise simply because an unwanted child has been conceived. While this may, in practice, be the case in the early stages of pregnancy, it is contrary to the letter of the Abortion Act 1967 (see further Chapter 13).

(iv) What losses can be compensated?   Once the existence of a duty of care towards a patient undergoing sterilization (and perhaps their partner) has been established, it is undoubtedly foreseeable that any breach of that duty might lead to pregnancy, and the birth of an unwanted child. Could this amount to compensatable damage? Pregnancy and childbirth are natural processes, which would not normally be described as 'injuries'. But, because they can be painful and risky, it has not proved difficult to persuade the courts that an unwanted pregnancy and delivery is a personal injury for which compensation can be sought. The question arose in *Walkin v South Manchester Health Authority*.

Walkin v South Manchester Health Authority[37]

Auld LJ

[T]he failure of the attempt to sterilise the patient was not itself a personal injury. It did her no harm; it left her as before. . . . However, it seems to me that the unwanted conception, whether as a result of negligent advice or negligent surgery, was a personal injury in the sense of an 'impairment'. . . . The resultant physical change in her body resulting from conception was an unwanted condition which she had sought to avoid by undergoing the sterilisation operation. It seems to me that the unwanted conception, whether as a result of negligent advice or negligent surgery, was a personal injury in the sense of an 'impairment'.

In *McFarlane* the House of Lords confirmed that pregnancy and childbirth could qualify as personal injuries for the purposes of an action in negligence.

McFarlane v Tayside Health Board[38]

Lord Steyn

Counsel for the health authority argued as his primary submission that the whole claim should fail because the natural processes of conception and childbirth cannot in law amount to personal injury...[E]very pregnancy involves substantial discomfort and pain. I would therefore reject the argument of the health authority on this point.

Lord Clyde

[N]atural as the mechanism may have been, the reality of the pain, discomfort and inconvenience of the experience cannot be ignored. It seems to me to be a clear example of pain and suffering such as could qualify as a potential head of damages.

There are also certain costs associated with pregnancy, such as maternity clothes, and these too have been recoverable on the grounds that they are consequential economic losses. The

---

[37] [1995] 1 WLR 1543.   [38] [2000] 2 AC 59.

costs of the child's upbringing are also, of course, foreseeable, but as we see below, their recovery in tort has proved to be much more controversial.

The issue was first raised in *Udale v Bloombsury AHA*[39] and it was decided that the maintenance costs of a healthy child were not recoverable for public policy reasons. Children, according to Jupp J, were a 'blessing', and their birth should be an occasion for joy not litigation. It would also, he reasoned, be undesirable for a child to learn that her birth had been a mistake.

The Court of Appeal took a different view in *Emeh v Kensington and Chelsea AHA*.[40] This was a case involving the birth of a disabled child, and it was held that public policy did not justify a blanket prohibition on the recovery of maintenance costs. The Court of Appeal did not specify that their judgment applied only to disabled children, and so from the mid-1980s, it was assumed that the costs of a child's upbringing were, in principle, recoverable.

A number of judges expressed regret or surprise that a doctor who made a mistake during the treatment of a patient undergoing sterilization might be liable for the full costs of any resulting child's upbringing, but until 1999, this appeared to be the law.[41] And, of course, awards could be very high indeed. In *Benarr v Kettering*,[42] for example, following a negligently performed vasectomy, damages were awarded to cover the child's future private education.

Then in 1999 in *McFarlane v Tayside Health Board* the House of Lords considered the issue for the first time, and decided that the maintenance costs of a healthy child were not recoverable. It is an important and complicated case, and it has been followed by a number of other cases that have tested its application to slightly different sets of facts, one of which also reached the House of Lords.

Six months after Mr McFarlane had undergone a vasectomy operation, the surgeon negligently informed him that his sperm counts were negative and that he and Mrs McFarlane no longer needed to use contraception. A year-and-a-half later, Mrs McFarlane became pregnant and gave birth to their fifth child, Catherine. A majority of the House of Lords (Lord Millett dissenting) found that she was entitled to general damages for the pain, suffering, and inconvenience of pregnancy and childbirth, but the Lords were unanimous that the McFarlanes were not entitled to be compensated for the costs associated with Catherine's upbringing.

McFarlane v Tayside Health Board[43]

Lord Steyn

It is possible to view the case simply from the perspective of corrective justice. It requires somebody who has harmed another without justification to indemnify the other. On this approach the parents' claim for the cost of bringing up Catherine must succeed. But one may also approach the case from the vantage point of distributive justice. It requires a focus on the just distribution of burdens and losses among members of a society. If the matter

---

[39] [1983] 1 WLR 1098.   [40] [1985] 2 WLR 233.

[41] *Allen v Bloomsbury Health Authority* [1993] 1 All ER 651, per Brooke J; *Jones v Berkshire Health Authority* (2 July 1986) (unreported) per Ognall J.

[42] (1988) 138 NLJ 179.

[43] [2000] 2 AC 59.

is approached in this way, it may become relevant to ask commuters on the Underground the following question: Should the parents of an unwanted but healthy child be able to sue the doctor or hospital for compensation equivalent to the cost of bringing up the child for the years of his or her minority, i.e. until about 18 years? My Lords, I am firmly of the view that an overwhelming number of ordinary men and women would answer the question with an emphatic 'No'. And the reason for such a response would be an inarticulate premise as to what is morally acceptable and what is not. . . . Instinctively, the traveller on the Underground would consider that the law of tort has no business to provide legal remedies consequent upon the birth of a healthy child, which all of us regard as a valuable and good thing.

My Lords, to explain decisions denying a remedy for the cost of bringing up an unwanted child by saying that there is no loss, no foreseeable loss, no causative link or no ground for reasonable restitution is to resort to unrealistic and formalistic propositions which mask the real reasons for the decisions. And judges ought to strive to give the real reasons for their decision. It is my firm conviction that where courts of law have denied a remedy for the cost of bringing up an unwanted child the real reasons have been grounds of distributive justice. That is, of course, a moral theory. It may be objected that the House must act like a court of law and not like a court of morals. That would only be partly right. The court must apply positive law. But judges' sense of the moral answer to a question, or the justice of the case, has been one of the great shaping forces of the common law. What may count in a situation of difficulty and uncertainty is not the subjective view of the judge but what he reasonably believes that the ordinary citizen would regard as right . . .

Relying on principles of distributive justice I am persuaded that our tort law does not permit parents of a healthy unwanted child to claim the costs of bringing up the child from a health authority or a doctor. If it were necessary to do so, I would say that the claim does not satisfy the requirement of being fair, just and reasonable.

Lord Hope

It is not difficult to see that in such cases a very substantial award of damages might have to be made for the child's upbringing. Awards on that scale would be bound to raise questions as to whether it was right for the negligent performance of a voluntary and comparatively minor operation, undertaken for the perfectly proper and understandable purpose of enabling couples to dispense with contraceptive measures and to have unprotected intercourse without having children, to expose the doctors, and on their behalf the relevant health authority, to a liability on that scale in damages. It might well be thought that the extent of the liability was disproportionate to the duties which were undertaken and, consequently, to the extent of the negligence.

As to the law, it has not been suggested that the costs of rearing the child are too remote, in the sense that they were not a reasonably foreseeable consequence of the defender's negligence. For my part, I would regard these costs as reasonably foreseeable by the wrongdoer. But in the field of economic loss foreseeability is not the only criterion that must be satisfied. There must be a relationship of proximity between the negligence and the loss which is said to have been caused by it and the attachment of liability for the harm must be fair, just and reasonable . . .

There are benefits in this arrangement as well as costs. In the short term there is the pleasure which a child gives in return for the love and care which she receives during infancy. In the longer term there is the mutual relationship of support and affection which will continue well beyond the ending of the period of her childhood.

In my opinion it would not be fair, just or reasonable, in any assessment of the loss caused by the birth of the child, to leave these benefits out of account. Otherwise the pursuers would be paid far too much. They would be relieved of the cost of rearing the child. They would not be giving anything back to the wrongdoer for the benefits. But the value which is to be attached to these benefits is incalculable. The costs can be calculated but the benefits, which in fairness must be set against them, cannot. The logical conclusion, as a matter of law, is that the costs to the pursuers of meeting their obligations to the child during her child-hood are not recoverable as damages.

Lord Clyde

But in attempting to offset the benefit of parenthood against the costs of parenthood one is attempting to set off factors of quite a different character against themselves and that does not seem to me to accord with principle. At least in the context of the compensation of one debt against another, like requires to be offset against like....A parent's claim for the death of a child is not offset by the saving in maintenance costs which the parent will enjoy....Furthermore, in order to pursue such a claim against the risk of such a set-off, a parent is called upon in effect to prove that the child is more trouble than he or she is worth in order to claim. That seems to me an undesirable requirement to impose upon a parent and further militates against such an approach. Indeed, the very uncertainty of the extent of the benefit which the child may constitute makes the idea of a set-off difficult or even impracticable....

But that the pursuers end up with an addition to their family, originally unintended but now, although unexpected, welcome, and are enabled to have the child maintained while in their custody free of any cost does not seem to accord with the idea of restitution or with an award of damages which does justice between both parties....

In the present case we are concerned critically with a claim for an economic loss following upon allegedly negligent advice. In such a context I would consider it appropriate to have regard to the extent of the liability which the defenders could reasonably have thought they were undertaking. It seems to me that even if a sufficient causal connection exists the cost of maintaining the child goes far beyond any liability which in the circumstances of the present case the defenders could reasonably have thought they were undertaking.

Furthermore, reasonableness includes a consideration of the proportionality between the wrongdoing and the loss suffered thereby....Counsel for the respondents sought to stress the modesty of the likely level of award in the present case. But once it is accepted that the cost of private education may be included in appropriate cases, a relatively much more sub-stantial award could be justified.

Lord Millett

I do not consider that the present question should depend on whether the economic loss is characterised as pure or consequential. The distinction is technical and artificial if not actually suspect in the circumstances of the present case, and is to my mind made irrelevant by the act that Catherine's conception and birth are the very things that the defenders' professional services were called upon to prevent....

I am also not persuaded by the argument that the remedy is disproportionate to the wrong. True, a vasectomy is a minor operation, while the costs of bringing up a child may be very large indeed, especially if they extend to the costs of a private education. But it is a common-place that the harm caused by a botched operation may be out of all proportion to the serious-ness of the operation or the condition of the patient which it was designed to alleviate...

There is something distasteful, if not morally offensive, in treating the birth of a normal, healthy child as a matter for compensation...In my opinion the law must take the birth of a normal, healthy baby to be a blessing, not a detriment. In truth it is a mixed blessing. It brings

joy and sorrow, blessing and responsibility. The advantages and the disadvantages are insep-
arable. Individuals may choose to regard the balance as unfavourable and take steps to forgo
the pleasures as well as the responsibilities of parenthood. They are entitled to decide for
themselves where their own interests lie. But society itself must regard the balance as beneficial. It would be repugnant to its own sense of values to do otherwise. It is morally offensive
to regard a normal, healthy baby as more trouble and expense than it is worth...

It does not, however, follow that Mr and Mrs McFarlane should be sent away empty
handed....They have suffered both injury and loss. They have lost the freedom to limit the
size of their family. They have been denied an important aspect of their personal autonomy.
Their decision to have no more children is one the law should respect and protect. They are
entitled to general damages to reflect the true nature of the wrong done to them. This should
be a conventional sum which should be left to the trial judge to assess, but which I would not
expect to exceed £5000 in a straightforward case like the present.

Although their conclusion on the non-recovery of maintenance costs was unanimous, as
Brooke LJ in pointed out in the Court of Appeal judgment in *Parkinson* (considered below),
the Law Lords certainly did not speak with one voice: 'Our task has been made more difficult
because the five members of the House of Lords spoke with five different voices.' And in a
subsequent case, one of them, Lord Steyn, revealingly described the task of discussing the
judgments in *McFarlane* as 'gruesome'.[44]

A majority of the House of Lords allowed Mrs McFarlane's claim for the pain and
suffering associated with pregnancy and childbirth, and for consequential financial losses,
such as clothing and loss of earnings. The costs of Catherine McFarlane's upbringing were,
according to the majority, pure economic loss. (Lord Millett dissented on this point, arguing that the distinction between consequential and pure economic losses was 'technical and
artificial'.) Readers who are familiar with tort law may remember that special rules cover the
recovery of pure economic loss. In short, the three-stage *Caparo v Dickman*[45] test applies:

(1) The loss should be foreseeable.

(2) There must be a relationship of sufficient proximity between the doctor and their
patient.

(3) It should be fair, just, and reasonable to impose a duty of care in these circumstances.

The House of Lords accepted that the birth of a child, and the costs of her upbringing, were
foreseeable consequences of negligently advising Mr and Mrs McFarlane that sterility had
been achieved. It is equally axiomatic that there was a relationship of sufficient proximity between the doctor who gave this advice and Mr McFarlane. Although Mrs McFarlane
was not herself being treated, she was undoubtedly identifiable as someone who would be
likely to suffer loss if she was negligently informed that Mr McFarlane's operation had been
successful. A majority of the House of Lords rejected the McFarlane's claim on the third
limb of this test, namely that imposing liability on the health authority for the costs of their
healthy child's upbringing would not be fair, just, and reasonable.

A number of different reasons were given for this conclusion:

(a) *The 'offset' calculation*

First, some of the Law Lords suggested that it would be unfair to compensate the parents for
the costs of rearing a child, unless these could be reduced in order to take into account the

[44] *Rees v Darlington Memorial Hospital NHS Trust* [2003] UKHL 52.   [45] [1990] 2 AC 651.

pleasure that the child would bring to her parents. However, they refused to embark upon this sort of balancing exercise on the grounds that it would be impossible and/or unseemly. Lord Hope, for example, argued that while the costs of a child's upbringing can be calculated, 'the benefits, which in fairness must be set against them, cannot'. For Lord Millett, the crucial point was not that it was impossible to weigh the advantages of raising children against the costs, but that society must always regard the balance as beneficial because it would be 'morally offensive' to do otherwise.

The Lords thus appeared to assume that this sort of offset calculation was necessary but either impossible or offensive. But is it really true that damages would have to be reduced in order to reflect the benefits the child brings to her parents? Two analogies, while imperfect, are instructive here. First, and this point was specifically acknowledged by Lord Clyde, when parents bring an action for the death of their child, their damages are not reduced in order to reflect the money that they will save by *not* having to pay for the child's upkeep. Secondly, the child support which an absent parent must pay to the caring parent in order to contribute towards a child's upbringing is not reduced in order to reflect the benefits the principal carer gains from the child's company. Again, an offset calculation would be unthinkable. Why then, given that in other contexts the law will not engage in a cost/benefit calculation in order to reduce sums payable to a child's parents, is such an exercise essential, but impossible, following negligent sterilization?

Further, as Lord Clyde again points out, an offset rule is normally dependent upon comparing like with like. Hence, financial damages might be reduced in order to take account of any financial benefit the claimant received. But in relation to wrongful pregnancy, the House of Lords assumes that damages for the *economic* costs of bringing up a child would have to be reduced in order to take account of the *emotional* benefits of the child's companionship. A trade-off between incommensurate goods is unusual. We would not normally say that an injured employee's damages for being unable to work should be reduced in order to reflect the benefits he enjoys from being able to spend more time with his family. Lord Clyde gave the example of a mineworker rendered unfit for work underground. If he claims damages for loss of earnings, the defendant is not entitled to offset 'the pleasure and benefit which he may enjoy in the air of a public park'.

Even if it were accepted that an offset calculation is necessary, it might also be argued that the question of whether an unplanned child's existence represents a net 'gain' for a family is a question of fact. It may be true that most people, most of the time, consider that the advantages of having a child, even if she was initially unwanted, outweigh the disadvantages. But this will not always be the case. For some families, the birth of another child might be a disaster.

In his dissenting judgment in the Court of Appeal in *Rees v Darlington Memorial Hospital NHS Trust*[46] (see below), Waller LJ gave the example of an impoverished single mother with four children, who knows that having a fifth child will lead to her mental breakdown, and who has no support from her family. If the birth of an unwanted child provokes the mother's physical or mental collapse, and leads to all of her children being taken into care, she may be able to *prove* that the advantages of having another child have not, in fact, outweighed the disadvantages. Yet the law will not allow her to bring forward such evidence, because it has already decided that, in Lord Millett's words, 'society itself must regard the balance as beneficial'.

Given that the claimants in 'wrongful pregnancy cases have attempted to remove the possibility of conception permanently through invasive surgery', it is plain that, at the time

---

[46] [2002] EWCA Civ 88.

of the operation at least, they believed that the disadvantages of having another baby out-weighed any joy that an additional child might bring. People are sterilized precisely in order to *avoid* the 'benefits' of parenthood. It is perhaps odd that the law insists that such people should view the failure of their surgery as a 'blessing' and an occasion for joy. If the benefits of parenthood always outweigh its disadvantages, it is unclear why anyone would want to be sterilized in the first place.

(b) *Proportionality*

Secondly, both Lord Hope and Lord Clyde were concerned that the size of any claim in dam-ages for a child's upbringing would be disproportionate to the degree of fault. It is clear from *Benarr v Kettering* that a child's maintenance costs will sometimes be very high indeed, and if recoverable, an NHS trust might have to pay vast damages for a doctor's relatively minor lapse of judgment. Moreover, not only would compensating parents for the costs of private education for the whole of a child's life lead to some extremely high awards, but it would also result in invidious distinctions between different families, since wealthy parents would receive much more money for their unwanted children than poor parents.

Lord Millett, rightly in my view, objected to this argument on the grounds that damages in tort are not intended to correspond to the *gravity* of fault, but rather to put the claimant in the position they would have been if the negligent act had not occurred. A minor and very com-mon lapse of judgement while driving—such as momentarily taking one's eyes off the road in order to admire the view—might have catastrophic consequences, and it would not be open to the driver to argue that the level of damages would be disproportionate to the degree of fault.

(c) *Distributive justice*

Thirdly, Lord Steyn based his judgment upon considerations of distributive justice. If chil-dren cannot claim for 'wrongful life', he reasoned that it would be unfair to allow parents to claim for 'wrongful pregnancy'. Lord Steyn was reluctant to attempt to squeeze his rejection of the McFarlane's claim into existing principles of tort law. Instead, he admitted that his was principally a moral judgment, and he specifically appealed to public opinion, or more precisely to commuters on the London Underground. For Lord Steyn, then, it is the *instincts* of the public which should determine the question, although if forced to fit this moral judg-ment within existing tort law rules, he said he would argue that 'the claim does not satisfy the requirement of being fair, just and reasonable'.

A final underlying reason for the Lords' rejection of the McFarlane's claim, may have been the concern that scarce NHS resources should not be diverted to the parents of healthy chil-dren. In recent years, as we saw in Chapter 2, there has been increasing judicial recognition that the NHS is financially overstretched. Given that the rationing of life-saving medical treatment is now inevitable, the House of Lords might have been alarmed at the prospect that the NHS might have to pay potentially very large sums of money for the private edu-cation and maintenance costs of a healthy child. This was certainly Tony Weir's principal objection to the post-*Emeh* case law: 'For the fourteen years since *Emeh* the National Health Service, short of resources for curing the sick, has been disbursing large sums of money for the maintenance of children who have nothing wrong with them.'[47]

In their more recent judgment in *Rees v Darlington Memorial Hospital NHS Trust*,[48] considered below, the House of Lords explicitly discussed the question of whether compen-sating parents for the birth of a healthy child is an appropriate use of NHS resources. But

---

[47] 'The Unwanted Child' (2000) 59 Cambridge Law Journal 238–41, 238.
[48] [2003] UKHL 52.

while it is undoubtedly true that Tayside Health Board has more pressing demands upon its budget than Catherine McFarlane's upkeep, it is not normally open to a court to deny a claimant damages because the defendant could deploy the money more usefully elsewhere.

In *McFarlane*, Lord Millett made an interesting suggestion, which was not taken up by any of the other judges, namely that the McFarlanes should be entitled to a 'conventional sum' of £5,000 to compensate for the wrongful interference with their freedom to limit the size of their family. In part, this proposal may have been prompted by the concern that full damages in a case such as this would not be a sensible use of scarce NHS resources. As we see below, Lord Millett's novel compensatory award was greeted with much more enthusiasm by a majority of the House of Lords in *Rees*.

Of course, it was inevitable that issues that were not directly dealt with by the judgements in *McFarlane* would rear their heads in subsequent litigation. On a comparatively minor point, in *Greenfield v Irwin*, the mother had been in full-time employment and sought to recover loss of earnings not just around the time of the birth, but during the subsequent years when she would be caring for the baby at home. While *McFarlane* had not directly addressed future loss of earnings, the Court of Appeal decided that these costs were in fact part of the costs of raising the child, and, since *McFarlane* applied, they were not recoverable.

Greenfield v Irwin[49]

May LJ

[T]here seems to me to be no material distinction between the costs of caring for and bringing up a child held to be irrecoverable in McFarlane and the mother's claim for loss of earnings in this appeal.

Laws LJ

It is to be noted that if this lady were to obtain the damages she seeks, she would happily be in a position whereby she would look after her much loved child at home, yet at the same time in effect would receive the income she would have earned had she stayed at work. In my judgment that is not just compensation; it is the conferment of a financial privilege, which has nothing to do with just compensation.

Of more importance, in *McFarlane* the House of Lords did not decide whether their judgment would have been the same if Catherine McFarlane had been born disabled. Lord Steyn did, however, suggest that 'in the case of an unwanted child, who was born seriously disabled the rule may have to be different', and Lord Clyde pointed out that 'it has to be noted in the present case we are dealing with a normal birth and a healthy child'.

Unsurprisingly, it was not long before the question of whether *McFarlane* applied to disabled children came before the courts in *Parkinson v St James and Seacroft University Hospital NHS Trust*. Angela Parkinson already had four children and did not think she could cope with a fifth. She was sterilized, but the operation was performed negligently, and she subsequently became pregnant. During the pregnancy, Mrs Parkinson was advised that the child might be born disabled, but she chose not to have an abortion. The Parkinson's fifth child, Scott, suffered from a serious behavioural disorder. It was accepted that his disability

49 [2001] EWCA Civ 113.

was not caused by the defendant's breach of duty. The family's resources were severely over-stretched: they were living in a cramped two-bedroomed house, and Scott's birth meant that Mrs Parkinson was unable to return to paid employment. The pregnancy placed an intolerable strain on the Parkinson's marriage, and they separated before Scott was born. At first instance Longmore J held that Mrs Parkinson could recover the costs of providing for Scott's special needs, and his judgment was upheld by the Court of Appeal.

Parkinson v St James and Seacroft University Hospital NHS Trust [50]

Brooke LJ

(i) the birth of a child with congenital abnormalities was a foreseeable consequence of the surgeon's careless failure to clip a fallopian tube effectively;

(ii) there was a very limited group of people who might be affected by this negligence, viz Mrs Parkinson and her husband (and, in theory, any other man with whom she had sexual intercourse before she realised that she had not been effectively sterilised);

(iii) there is no difficulty in principle in accepting the proposition that the surgeon should be deemed to have assumed responsibility for the foreseeable and disastrous economic consequences of performing his services negligently;

(iv) the purpose of the operation was to prevent Mrs Parkinson from conceiving any more children, including children with congenital abnormalities, and the surgeon's duty of care is strictly related to the proper fulfilment of that purpose;

(v) parents in Mrs Parkinson's position were entitled to recover damages in these circumstances for 15 years between the decisions in Emeh's case and McFarlane's case, so that this is not a radical step forward into the unknown;

(vi) for the reasons set out in (i) and (ii) above, Lord Bridge of Harwich's tests of foreseeability and proximity are satisfied, and...an award of compensation which is limited to the special upbringing costs associated with rearing a child with a serious disability would be fair, just and reasonable;

(vii) if principles of distributive justice are called in aid, I believe that ordinary people would consider that it would be fair for the law to make an award in such a case, provided that it is limited to the extra expenses associated with the child's disability.

I can see nothing in any majority reasoning in McFarlane's case to deflect this court from adopting this course, which in my judgment both logic and justice demand. . . . [I]n my judgment it would not be fair, just and reasonable to award compensation which went further than the extra expenses associated with bringing up a child with a significant disability.

What constitutes a significant disability for this purpose will have to be decided by judges, if necessary, on a case by case basis. The expression would certainly stretch to include disabilities of the mind (including severe behavioural disabilities) as well as physical disabilities. It would not include minor defects or inconveniences, such as are the lot of many children who do not suffer from significant disabilities.

Hale LJ

Not surprisingly, their Lordships [in *McFarlane*] did not go into detail about what is entailed in the invasion of bodily integrity caused by conception, pregnancy and childbirth. But it is worth while spelling out the more obvious features. Some will sound in damages and some

---

[50] [2001] EWCA Civ 530.

may not, but they are all the consequence of that fundamental invasion. They are none the less an invasion because they are the result of natural processes. They stem from something which should never have happened. And they last for a great deal longer than the pregnancy itself. Whatever the outcome, happy or sad, a woman never gets over it. I do not, of course, forget the serious consequences for many fathers, and will return to these later, but there are undoubted and inescapable differences between the sexes here...

From the moment a woman conceives, profound physical changes take place in her body and continue to take place not only for the duration of the pregnancy but for some time thereafter. Those physical changes bring with them a risk to life and health greater than in her non-pregnant state...Along with those physical changes go psychological changes. Again these vary from woman to woman. Some may amount to a recognised psychiatric disorder, while others may be regarded as beneficial, and many are somewhere in between....

Along with these physical and psychological consequences goes a severe curtailment of personal autonomy. Literally, one's life is no longer just one's own but also someone else's. One cannot simply rid oneself of that responsibility. The availability of legal abortion depends upon the opinions of others. Even if favourable opinions can readily be found by those who know how, there is still a profound moral dilemma and potential psychological harm if that route is taken. Late abortion brings with it particular problems, and these are more likely to arise in failed sterilisation cases where the woman does not expect to become pregnant....

Continuing the pregnancy brings a host of lesser infringements of autonomy related to the physical changes in the body or responsibility towards the growing child. The responsible pregnant woman forgoes or moderates the pleasures of alcohol and tobacco. She changes her diet. She submits to regular and intrusive medical examinations and tests. She takes certain sorts of exercise and forgoes others. She can no longer wear her favourite clothes. She is unlikely to be able to continue in paid employment throughout the pregnancy or to return to it immediately thereafter.

The process of giving birth is rightly termed 'labour'. It is hard work, often painful and sometimes dangerous. It brings the pregnancy to an end but it does not bring to an end the changes brought about by the pregnancy. It takes some time for the body to return to its pre-pregnancy state, if it ever does, especially if the child is breast fed. There are well known psychiatric illnesses associated with childbirth and the baby blues are very common...

Quite clearly, however, the invasion of the mother's personal autonomy does not stop once her body and mind have returned to their pre-pregnancy state....Parental responsibility is not simply or even primarily a financial responsibility...The primary responsibility is to care for the child. The labour does not stop when the child is born. Bringing up children is hard work....The obligation to provide or make acceptable and safe arrangements for the child's care and supervision lasts for 24 hours a day, seven days a week, all year round, until the child becomes old enough to take care of himself....

Of course, most pregnancies are not caused wrongfully. But this case proceeds on the basis that this one was. The whole object of the service offered to the claimant by the defendants was to prevent her becoming pregnant again. They had a duty to perform that service with reasonable care. They did not do so. She became pregnant as a result. On normal principles of tortious liability, once it was established that the pregnancy had been wrongfully caused, compensation would be payable for all those consequences, whether physical or financial, which are capable of sounding in damages....

A majority of their Lordships in McFarlane's case clearly recognised that on normal principles the claim would be allowable...[but] at the heart of it all is the feeling that to compensate for the financial costs of bringing up a healthy child is a step too far. A child brings benefits as well as costs; it is impossible accurately to calculate those benefits so as to give a proper discount; the only sensible course is to assume that they balance one another out....

A disabled child needs extra care and extra expenditure. He is deemed, on this analysis, to bring as much pleasure and as many advantages as does a normal healthy child. Frankly, in many cases, of which this may be one, this is much less likely. The additional stresses and strains can have seriously adverse effects upon the whole family, and not infrequently lead, as here, to the break-up of the parents' relationship and detriment to the other children. But we all know of cases where the whole family has been enriched by the presence of a disabled member and would not have things any other way. This analysis treats a disabled child as having exactly the same worth as a non-disabled child. It affords him the same dignity and status. It simply acknowledges that he costs more...

Whatever the commuter on the Underground might think of the claim for Catherine McFarlane, it might reasonably be thought that he or she would not consider it unfair, unjust or disproportionate that the person who had undertaken to prevent conception, pregnancy and birth and negligently failed to do so were held responsible for the extra costs of caring for and bringing up a disabled child.

It is of critical importance to remember that *Parkinson* is not a case in which the child's disability was *caused by* the defendant's negligence. If a botched sterilization operation not only failed to achieve sterility, but also damaged the patient's reproductive organs and impaired her ability to give birth to a healthy child, then the child would have a straightforward action under the Congenital Disabilities (Civil Liability) Act 1976.

In *Parkinson*, the defendant's negligence did not cause Scott's behavioural disorder: rather, it caused Scott, who just happened to be disabled, to be conceived. Because there is always a small risk—in *Parkinson* it was put at between one in 200 and one in 400—that a child might be born suffering from a congenital abnormality, the birth of a disabled child is a foreseeable consequence of any negligent sterilization operation.

It should, however, be noted that the maintenance costs of a healthy child are obviously much more foreseeable than the statistically less likely possibility that a child will be born disabled, and extra costs thereby incurred.[51] It is also true that the maintenance costs of a disabled child are likely to be higher than those of a normal healthy baby, and since crucially we are not concerned with cases in which the defendant *caused* the disability, the concern expressed by Lords Clyde and Hope in *McFarlane* about the level of damages being disproportionate to the degree of fault would be more compelling on the facts in *Parkinson*.

Furthermore, recall that several of the judgments in *McFarlane* argued that the benefits of the child's existence had to be put into the balance with the costs, but that this calculation was either unseemly or impossible. Surely, as Alasdair Maclean points out in the next extract, the same must be true when the child is born disabled.

Alasdair Maclean[52]

Unless one is prepared to argue that having a disabled child is not—as a matter of policy—a blessing, which might be interpreted as devaluing the disabled, then the [offset] calculation is no more possible for the birth of a disabled child than it is for the birth of a healthy child.

---

[51] Laura CH Hoyano, 'Misconceptions about Wrongful Conception' (2002) 65 Modern Law Review 883–906, 891.

[52] 'An Alexandrian Approach to the Knotty Problem of Wrongful Pregnancy: *Rees v Darlington Memorial Hospital NHS Trust* in the House of Lords', [2004] 3 Web JCLI <http://webjcli.ncl.ac.uk/2004/issue3/maclean3.html>.

> The costs arising from the disability are simply additional maintenance costs and, if the detriments cannot be weighed against the benefits then simply increasing the detriments cannot change that: if x cannot be balanced against y then nor can x be balanced against y + z.

At times, it must be admitted, the Court of Appeal appeared less than enthusiastic about the judgment in *McFarlane*. In particular, Hale LJ's impassioned description of the physical and psychological invasions of pregnancy and motherhood was not specifically directed to the burdens of being a mother of a disabled child, but applies to motherhood in general. Nevertheless, *McFarlane* was binding upon them, and so the important question was whether Scott's disabilities meant that Angela Parkinson's case could be distinguished. The Court of Appeal decided that the cases were different, and the extra costs incurred as a result of the child's disability were recoverable. This was not, the Court of Appeal insisted, because the birth of a disabled child is not a 'blessing': rather, it simply acknowledges that disabled children cost more.

Three problems of interpretation remained after the Court of Appeal's decision in *Parkinson*. First, what counts as a disability for these purposes? The Court of Appeal suggested that the disability must be 'significant', and Hale LJ argued that the test should be the same as that in the Children Act 1989.

Hale LJ

[H]ow disabled does the child have to be for the parents to be able to make a claim? The answer is that the law has for some time distinguished between the ordinary needs of ordinary children and the special needs of a disabled child. Thus, for the purposes of the services to be provided under Part III of the Children Act 1989,...'a child is disabled if he is blind, deaf or dumb or suffers from mental disorder of any kind or is substantially and permanently handicapped by illness, injury or congenital deformity or such other disability as may be prescribed'...I see no difficulty in using the same definition here.[53]

The child's disability must therefore meet some threshold level of seriousness before the extra costs associated with it are recoverable. But while we can be certain that parents are not entitled to recover the additional costs incurred as a result of a relatively minor abnormality, such as shortsightedness, future courts may have to address precisely what counts as a significant disability for these purposes.

Secondly, for there to be recovery, the Court of Appeal stressed that the child's disability must be a foreseeable consequence of the defendant's negligence. In *Parkinson*, they reasoned that it was foreseeable that a proportion of children will suffer from congenital abnormalities, and hence Scott's disabilities were a foreseeable result of the negligent sterilization. The Court of Appeal did not confine recovery to disabilities that were present from conception onwards.

Hale LJ

I conclude that any disability arising from genetic causes or foreseeable events during pregnancy (such as rubella, spina bifida, or oxygen deprivation during pregnancy or childbirth) up until the child is born alive, and which are not novus actus interveniens, will suffice to found a claim.

---

[53] *Parkinson v St James and Seacroft University Hospital NHS Trust* [2001] EWCA Civ 530.

But what if the child *subsequently* becomes disabled; are her extra needs also a forseeable consequence of the defendant's negligence? This question arose in *Groom v Selby*. Ms Groom had undergone a sterilization operation following the birth of her second child, and after having suffered two miscarriages. When the operation was performed, Ms Groom was in fact in the very early stages of another pregnancy. When she subsequently went to her doctor complaining of abdominal pains, and having missed a period, the doctor failed to test for pregnancy, and simply prescribed antibiotics. Pregnancy was eventually diagnosed when Ms Groom was 12 weeks pregnant, but by this stage, she did not feel able to have an abortion. It was admitted that the doctor's failure to carry out a pregnancy test was negligent, and that this had deprived Ms Groom of the opportunity to terminate the pregnancy. Ms Groom's daughter, Megan, was born prematurely, and subsequently developed meningitis complicated by brain abscesses.

Although strictly speaking this was a 'wrongful birth' rather than a 'wrongful pregnancy' claim, the question for the court was when the disability must have been caused in order to fit within the *Parkinson* exception to *McFarlane*. The doctor contended that Megan was a healthy child at birth, and hence *McFarlane* and not *Parkinson* applied, thus ruling out recovery for the additional costs associated with Megan's disabilities. However, the Court of Appeal held that Megan could not properly be described as a 'healthy child' at birth because the bacteria, which was responsible for her meningitis, was already present on her skin.

Groom v Selby[54]

Brooke LJ

We are concerned in the present case with a child whose severe handicap arose from the normal incidents of conception, intra-uterine development and birth. Her prematurity (which made her particularly vulnerable) was not due to any new intervening event and her exposure to the bacterium which proved her downfall occurred during the process of birth.

Hale LJ

There will always be borderline cases in the application of any principle. In *Parkinson*, Brooke LJ and I were also agreed on the source of the disability: it must be genetic or arise from the processes of intra-uterine development and birth. That was what the doctor negligently failed to prevent. Megan's meningitis was 'bad luck', in the sense that many newborn babies do not succumb to such infections. But it arose from the process of her birth during which she was exposed to the bacterium in question.

Interestingly, when setting out which disabilities fit within the *Parkinson* exception, Hale LJ specifically gave the example of 'oxygen deprivation during childbirth'. It is therefore possible that a doctor who carried out a sterilization operation negligently might be liable to pay vast damages to a severely brain-damaged child, on the grounds that it is foreseeable that they will be deprived of oxygen during childbirth, and suffer catastrophic brain damage as a result. If the oxygen deprivation was due to negligent obstetric care, this would be likely to amount to a *novus actus*, but if negligence on the part of the obstetric team could not be proved, liability might be traced back to the surgeon who carried out the sterilization. Given that awards for brain damage caused by oxygen deprivation during birth are often very high

---

[54] [2001] EWCA Civ 1522.

indeed—awards of over £1million are not unusual—it is again worth noting a tension with Lords Hope and Clyde's concerns about proportionality.

Thirdly, what if it is not the child but the parent who is disabled? This scenario was not left open as a possible exception by the House of Lords in *McFarlane*, but it has arisen twice since the decision in *Parkinson*. We can deal with the first case, *AD v East Kent Community NHS Trust*,[55] fairly briefly. This case involved a mentally disabled woman, A, who had become pregnant while living on a mixed psychiatric ward, by a man who was also in the defendant's care. A gave birth to a healthy daughter, C, and A's mother, Mrs A, agreed to look after C for the foreseeable future. The Court of Appeal dismissed A's claim for the costs associated with C's upbringing. She herself had suffered no loss. Mrs A was providing her services voluntarily, which meant that she too could not have an action in her own right,[56] but even if she could have brought a claim, Judge LJ assumed that an offset calculation would be necessary, and argued that: 'it would be invidious to attempt to put a money value on the benefit that she will derive from the joy of having her healthy granddaughter living with her and growing up in her home'.

The second case, *Rees v Darlington Memorial Hospital NHS Trust*,[57] requires rather more scrutiny. Karina Rees was severely visually handicapped. She was sterilized because she was concerned that her blindness meant that would be unable to look after a child. The operation was carried out negligently, and two years later, she gave birth to a healthy child. She claimed damages not only for the pain and discomfort of pregnancy and childbirth, but also for the additional costs incurred as a result of her disability.

By a 2 to 1 majority, the Court of Appeal allowed recovery on the grounds that the claimant's case could be distinguished from *McFarlane* because *McFarlane* only applied to healthy parents.[58] It is, however, worth noting Waller LJ's powerful dissenting judgment, in which he argued that whether the birth of an unwanted child is a 'disaster' will often depend more upon the resources and support available to the mother than on whether she happens to be disabled:

Rees v Darlington Memorial Hospital NHS Trust[59]

Waller LJ (dissenting)

If one takes the facts to be that a woman already has four children and wishes not to have a fifth; and if one assumes that having the fifth will create a crisis in health terms, unless help in caring for the child was available, she cannot recover the costs of caring for the child which might alleviate the crisis, as I understand McFarlane's case. I would have thought that her need to avoid a breakdown in her health was no different from the need of someone already with a disability, and indeed her need might be greater depending on the degree of disability. Does she, or ordinary people, look favourably on the law not allowing her to recover but allowing someone who is disabled to recover?

If one were to add that the lady with four children was poor, but the lady with a disability was rich—what then? It would simply emphasise the perception that the rule was not operating fairly. One can add to the example by making comparisons between possible family circumstances of the different mothers. Assume the mother with four children had no support

55 [2002] EWCA Civ 1872.   56 *Hunt v Severs* [1994] 2 All ER 385.
57 [2003] UKHL 52.   58 [2002] EWCA Civ 88.
59 [2002] EWCA Civ 88.

from husband, mother or siblings, and then compare her with the person who is disabled, but who has a husband, siblings and a mother all willing to help. I think ordinary people would feel uncomfortable about the thought that it was simply the disability which made a difference.

On appeal, the House of Lords was specifically invited to reconsider its judgment in *McFarlane*. In the intervening years, the High Court of Australia had been faced with a case with very similar facts to *McFarlane*, in which a majority had declined to follow its reasoning, and accused the British courts of drifting too far from ordinary tort law principles.

Cattanach v Melchior[60]

Justice Callinan

The applicants were negligent. The respondents as a result have incurred and will continue to incur significant expense. That expense would not have been incurred had the first applicant not given negligent advice. All the various touchstones for, and none of the relevant disqualifying conditions against, an award of damages for economic loss are present here.

Kirby J

Least of all may they do so, in our secular society, on the footing of their personal religious beliefs, or 'moral' assessments concealed in an inarticulate premise dressed up, and described, as legal principle or legal policy....

Neither the invocation of scripture nor the invention of a fictitious oracle on the Underground...authorises a court of law to depart from the ordinary principles governing the recovery of damages for the tort of negligence.

Despite this trenchant criticism, the seven Law Lords who were assembled to hear *Rees* unanimously declined to revisit the judgment in *McFarlane*, in large part because only four years had elapsed and it would, in Lord Bingham's words, 'reflect no credit on the administration of the law if a line of English authority were to be disapproved in 1999 and reinstated in 2003 with no reason for the change beyond a change in the balance of legal opinion'. Lord Millett was also clear that, 'it requires much more than doubts as to the correctness of the previous decision to justify departing from it'. While JK Mason acknowledges that 'see-saw lawmaking' would be undesirable, he argues that 'the man in the street might well think that, if something is wrong, the sooner it is put right, the better'.[61]

Having upheld the decision in *McFarlane*, the Lords next had to consider whether an exception should be made where the mother was disabled. On this question, the House of Lords was divided. By a 4 to 3 majority it held that *Rees* could not be distinguished: the child was healthy, so *McFarlane* applied. The fact of the mother's disability did not take this case outside the general *McFarlane* principle, which meant that there could be no recovery for any of the costs associated with the child's upbringing. In contrast, the dissenting judges would have allowed Karina Rees to recover for the extra costs associated with her disability.

It should, however, be noted that the majority also added a very significant 'gloss'.

---

[60] [2003] HCA 38.   [61] *The Troubled Pregnancy*, 168–9.

Rees v Darlington Memorial Hospital NHS Trust[62]

Lord Bingham

The policy considerations underpinning the judgments of the House [in *McFarlane*] were, as I read them, an unwillingness to regard a child (even if unwanted) as a financial liability and nothing else, a recognition that the rewards which parenthood (even if involuntary) may or may not bring cannot be quantified and a sense that to award potentially very large sums of damages to the parents of a normal and healthy child against a National Health Service always in need of funds to meet pressing demands would rightly offend the community's sense of how public resources should be allocated....

Subject to one gloss, therefore, which I regard as important, I would affirm and adhere to the decision in *McFarlane*.

My concern is this. Even accepting that an unwanted child cannot be regarded as a financial liability and nothing else and that any attempt to weigh the costs of bringing up a child against the intangible rewards of parenthood is unacceptably speculative, the fact remains that the parent of a child born following a negligently performed vasectomy or sterilisation, or negligent advice on the effect of such a procedure, is the victim of a legal wrong....

I can accept and support a rule of legal policy which precludes recovery of the full cost of bringing up a child in the situation postulated, but I question the fairness of a rule which denies the victim of a legal wrong any recompense at all beyond an award immediately related to the unwanted pregnancy and birth....

To speak of losing the freedom to limit the size of one's family is to mask the real loss suffered in a situation of this kind. This is that a parent, particularly (even today) the mother, has been denied, through the negligence of another, the opportunity to live her life in the way that she wished and planned. I do not think that an award immediately relating to the unwanted pregnancy and birth gives adequate recognition of or does justice to that loss. I would accordingly support the suggestion favoured by Lord Millett in *McFarlane* that in all cases such as these there be a conventional award to mark the injury and loss, although I would favour a greater figure than the £5,000 he suggested (I have in mind a conventional figure of £15,000) and I would add this to the award for the pregnancy and birth. This solution is in my opinion consistent with the ruling and rationale of *McFarlane*. The conventional award would not be, and would not be intended to be, compensatory. It would not be the product of calculation. But it would not be a nominal, let alone a derisory, award. It would afford some measure of recognition of the wrong done. And it would afford a more ample measure of justice than the pure *McFarlane* rule.

Lord Nicholls

I have heard nothing in the submissions advanced on the present appeal to persuade me that this decision by the House [in *McFarlane*] was wrong and ought to be revisited. On the contrary, that the negligent doctor or, in most cases, the National Health Service should pay all the costs of bringing up the child seems to me a disproportionate response to the doctor's wrong. It would accord ill with the values society attaches to human life and to parenthood...

But this is not to say it is fair and reasonable there should be no award at all except in respect of stress and trauma and costs associated with the pregnancy and the birth itself. An award of some amount should be made to recognise that in respect of birth of the child the parent has suffered a legal wrong, a legal wrong having a far-reaching effect on the lives of the parent and any family she may already have. The amount of such an award will

---

[62] [2003] UKHL 52.

inevitably have an arbitrary character. I do not dissent from the sum of £15,000 suggested by my noble and learned friend Lord Bingham of Cornhill in this regard. To this limited extent I agree that your Lordships' House should add a gloss to the decision in *McFarlane v Tayside Health Board*.

Lord Millett

I still regard the proper outcome in all these cases is to award the parents a modest conventional sum by way of general damages, not for the birth of the child, but for the denial of an important aspect of their personal autonomy, viz the right to limit the size of their family. This is an important aspect of human dignity, which is increasingly being regarded as an important human right which should be protected by law. The loss of this right is not an abstract or theoretical one. As my noble and learned friend Lord Bingham of Cornhill has pointed out, the parents have lost the opportunity to live their lives in the way that they wished and planned to do. The loss of this opportunity, whether characterised as a right or a freedom, is a proper subject for compensation by way of damages.

The award of a modest sum would not, of course, go far towards the costs of bringing up a child. It would not reflect the financial consequences of the birth of a normal, healthy child; but it would not be meant to. They are not the proper subject of compensation for the reasons stated in McFarlane. A modest award would, however, adequately compensate for the very different injury to the parents' autonomy.

Lord Steyn (dissenting)

In the present case the idea of a conventional award was not raised at first instance or in the Court of Appeal. For my part it is a great disadvantage for the House to consider such a point without the benefit of the views of the Court of Appeal. And the disadvantage cannot be removed by calling the new rule a 'gloss'. It is a radical and most important development which should only be embarked on after rigorous examination of competing arguments . . .

No United Kingdom authority is cited for the proposition that judges have the power to create a remedy of awarding a conventional sum in cases such as the present. There is none. It is also noteworthy that in none of the decisions from many foreign jurisdictions, with varying results, is there any support for such a solution. This underlines the heterodox nature of the solution adopted.

Like Lord Hope I regard the idea of a conventional award in the present case as contrary to principle. It is a novel procedure for judges to create such a remedy. There are limits to permissible creativity for judges. In my view the majority have strayed into forbidden territory. It is also a backdoor evasion of the legal policy enunciated in McFarlane. If such a rule is to be created it must be done by Parliament. The fact is, however, that it would be a hugely controversial legislative measure. It may well be that the Law Commissions and Parliament ought in any event, to consider the impact of the creation of a power to make a conventional award in the cases under consideration for the coherence of the tort system.

I cannot support the proposal for creating such a new rule.

Lord Hope (dissenting)

One can say, as in the case of a seriously disabled child, that a seriously disabled parent who has special needs is likely to require help if her child is to have a normal upbringing and that this is likely to lead to extra expenditure. Here again I do not see any conflict between the policy which the law has adopted about discrimination on the ground of disability and awarding damages for the extra costs that have to be incurred to enable a parent who has special needs to provide her child with as normal a life as possible...

I am left with the uneasy feeling that the figure which is to be established by the new rule will in many cases, and especially in this one, fall well short of what would be needed to satisfy Lord Millett's aim, which Lord Scott adopts, of compensating the parents for the wrong that has been done to them. The issue is, as Lord Steyn says, hugely controversial and I agree with him that its creation—which would surely then have been the product of much more study and research than has been given to its creation in this case by the majority—ought to have been left, preferably with the benefit of a report by the Law Commissions, to Parliament.

A majority of the House of Lords recognized that non-recovery in *McFarlane* was itself an exception to the ordinary rules of tort law, and that carving out exceptions to exceptions should be avoided. On the normal principles of tort law, the claimant should be able to recover all of the reasonably foreseeable consequences of the doctor's negligence, including the costs associated with the child's upbringing. But for a number of reasons, the majority in *Rees* explained that the law has refused to countenance the prospect of giving damages for the costs of a healthy baby.

First, the birth of a healthy baby is said to be a blessing, and it has been held that it would be contrary to public morality to regard it as a loss compensatable by damages. Secondly, although parents in these circumstances have the detriment of additional costs, they also experience the benefit of bringing up a child. Fair compensation for the detriment associated with having a child should, it has been argued, take account of this benefit, and yet the courts have held that it is impossible or undesirable to calculate benefit and detriment in this way. As a result, the preferred solution has been not to allow the payment of any damages at all. The underlying fear seems to be that parents who are, in the end, delighted by the child's existence would be *unjustly enriched* if they were able to deflect *all* of her maintenance costs onto the NHS.

But the new gloss added by the majority in *Rees* is based on the view that, while full compensation in these circumstances is inappropriate and unaffordable, the parents in these cases have undoubtedly been wronged: they have been deprived of their freedom to control the size of their family. As a result, the majority of the House of Lords advocated what they described as a modest 'conventional award', which would not be intended to compensate for the actual loss suffered by the claimants, but rather to offer some recognition of the wrong done to them. In short, the majority in *Rees* decided that it did not want to compensate Karina Rees according to ordinary negligence principles because this would give her too much money. Instead, it preferred to compensate her according to its own novel scheme, which would acknowledge that she had been wronged, without giving her exorbitant damages.

As JK Mason puts it, 'it is hard to find a commentator who does not, at this point, start to scratch his or her head'.[63] One generous explanation is that the majority in *Rees* was attempting to find a judicial solution to some of the problems clinical negligence poses for the NHS. Patients who are treated negligently do deserve some recognition that they received inadequate care, which may have caused them harm, inconvenience, discomfort, or financial loss. But at the same time, giving them full compensation for all of their losses undermines

---

[63] Ibid 176.

the capacity of the NHS to provide adequate health care to the rest of the population. By giving a handful of negligently treated patients full compensation, it becomes more difficult to guarantee universal access to comprehensive health services, free at the point of use. In these circumstances, it could be argued that it would be more sensible for patients who are the victims of inadequate treatment to receive a standard notional award, which recognizes that a wrong has been done to them, but does not attempt to provide full compensation.

But while moving towards a standardized compensation scheme within the NHS would undoubtedly have many merits, it is not clear that a decision of a narrow majority in the House of Lords is the right way to bring about such a system. The introduction of a radical departure from the existing tort system would, as the caustic dissenting judgments suggest, normally be a matter for Parliament.

The purpose of the 'conventional award' is also rather opaque. It is there to compensate for 'a wrong comprised of an affront to autonomy',[64] which is itself a novel head of damages. It is not meant to be derisory, and yet, while better than nothing, it comes nowhere near the amount that would be payable according to normal tort law principles. In the end, JK Mason may be right that it looks rather like 'a form of conscience money or as a charity designed to offset the sense of injustice left by the original *McFarlane* decision'.[65]

Following *Rees*, the status of the Court of Appeal judgment in *Parkinson* is a little uncertain. Three of the Law Lords specifically approved of the Court of Appeal's decision in *Parkinson*. Lord Hutton, for example, said: 'In my opinion the decision of the Court of Appeal in *Parkinson* was right... in my opinion it is fair, just and reasonable to award damages for the extra costs of bringing up a disabled child.' Similarly, according to one of the dissenting judges, Lord Hope: 'A disabled child is likely to need extra care and the provision of this care is likely to mean extra expenditure... I consider that, as a matter of legal policy, the Court of Appeal were right to hold that in principle these extra costs are recoverable.' And finally Lord Steyn, who also dissented from the majority's conclusions, expressly confined *McFarlane* to the birth of a healthy child: 'The legal policy on which *McFarlane* was based is critically dependent on the birth of a healthy and normal child. That policy does not apply where the child is seriously disabled physically and/or mentally.'

In contrast, three of the other Law Lords were critical of the *Parkinson* decision, and would have also applied the conventional award in cases where the child was born disabled. Lord Bingham, with whom Lord Nicholls agreed, offered a number of criticisms of the Court of Appeal's judgment in *Parkinson*.

Rees v Darlington Memorial Hospital NHS Trust[66]

Lord Bingham

I would for my part apply this rule also, without differentiation, to cases in which either the child or the parent is (or claims to be) disabled:

(1) While I have every sympathy with the Court of Appeal's view that Mrs Parkinson should be compensated, it is arguably anomalous that the defendant's liability should be related to a disability which the doctor's negligence did not cause and not to the birth which it did.

(2) The rule favoured by the Court of Appeal majority in the present case inevitably gives rise to anomalies such as those highlighted by Waller LJ in his dissenting judgment.

---

[64] Ibid 179.   [65] Ibid 178.
[66] [2003] UKHL 52.

(3) It is undesirable that parents, in order to recover compensation, should be encouraged to portray either their children or themselves as disabled...

(4) In a state such as ours, which seeks to make public provision for the consequences of disability, the quantification of additional costs attributable to disability, whether of the parent or the child, is a task of acute difficulty.

Similarly, Lord Scott said that he had 'some doubts' about the Court of Appeal's conclusion on foreseeability in *Parkinson*.

Lord Scott

The possibility that a child may be born with a congenital abnormality is plainly present to some degree in the case of every pregnancy. But is that a sufficient reason for holding the negligent doctor liable for the extra costs, attributable to the abnormality, of rearing the child? In my opinion it is not. Foreseeability of a one in 200 to 400 chance does not seem to me, by itself, enough to make it reasonable to impose on the negligent doctor liability for these costs. It might be otherwise in a case where there had been particular reason to fear that if a child were conceived and born it might suffer from some inherited disability. And, particularly, it might be otherwise in a case where the very purpose of the sterilisation operation had been to protect against that fear. But on the facts of *Parkinson* I do not think the Court of Appeal's conclusion was consistent with *McFarlane*.

The seventh Law Lord, Lord Millett, did not express an opinion either way, on the grounds that 'it is not necessary for the disposal of the present appeal to reach any conclusion whether *Parkinson* was rightly decided, and I would wish to keep the point open'.

Given this equivocation, and the lack of consensus in the Lords, it remains unclear whether the parents of disabled children should now receive the conventional award, or, following *Parkinson*, damages to compensate for the additional costs associated with the child's disability.

A factual variation, which has yet to be considered post-*McFarlane*, is where the sterilization operation was carried out privately, and an action might therefore be brought in contract. It is not clear what difference, if any, this would make. Certainly, it has long been assumed that the choice of action is in practice immaterial, since the courts will simply imply into a contract a duty to take reasonable care in carrying out the operation and in providing appropriate and accurate information.[67] Lord Slynn in *McFarlane* did suggest that 'If a client wants to be able to recover such costs he or she must do so by an appropriate contract', but it would seem highly improbable that any clinician would enter into a contract which provided for the full recovery of maintenance costs if the operation did not succeed. Nevertheless, one of the reasons for refusing recovery cited in *Rees*—namely the scarcity of NHS resources—would clearly not apply if the operation took place in the private sector.

Finally, it is important to note that although most 'wrongful pregnancy' cases have involved negligent sterilizations, or the giving of negligent advice about a sterilization operation's success or permanency, it is also possible that the negligent provision of other sorts of contraceptive treatment might lead to an unwanted conception. This happened in *Richardson v LRC*,[68] a case we considered briefly in Chapter 10 when we looked at product liability. In

[67] CR Symmons, 'Policy Factors in Actions for Wrongful Birth' (1987) 50 Modern Law Review 269–306, 271.
[68] [2000] PIQR P164.

Richardson, the claimant had become pregnant after a condom burst inexplicably, and she brought an action under the Consumer Protection Act 1987, including a claim for the costs of maintaining her child. Her claim was rejected, in part because *McFarlane* had excluded the possibility of recovering the costs of a healthy child's upbringing.

Ian Kennedy J

It is the policy of the law, albeit subject to the precise terms of any contract, to exclude from a claimant's claim the costs of the upbringing of an uncovenanted child. That is equally applicable whether the claim is laid in negligence or a breach of a statutory duty.

An interesting aspect of the decision in *Richardson* is Kennedy J's assertion that Mrs Richardson would, in any event, have been barred from claiming damages because she could have taken the morning-after pill in order to avoid pregnancy. This sits slightly uneasily with the established principle that a woman's claim for damages for wrongful pregnancy is unaffected by her decision not to have an abortion. Of course, there are differences between taking a pill and terminating a pregnancy, but JK Mason argues that: 'It is possible to argue that, in terms of a woman exercising her reproductive choice, the difference is merely one of degree—and particularly so when one remembers that at least some women would regard the destruction of an embryo as being morally equivalent to the destruction of a fetus.'[69]

(2) Should there be Recovery for Wrongful Pregnancy?

If the ordinary principles of tort law are applied to these cases, the costs of the child's upbringing would be recoverable. The type of loss is foreseeable, and full recovery of maintenance costs would be necessary to put the claimant in the position they would have been in if the tort had not been performed. Moreover, in the next extract Alasdair Mullis argues that the considerations which commonly inform the courts' decisions in negligence actions, such as the possibility of the 'floodgates' opening and the availability of insurance, would also point in favour of allowing recovery.

Alastair Mullis[70]

Where the doctor fails to exercise the required level of skill the patient should be entitled to recover damages to put him in the position he was in prior to the operation, so far as that is possible. The patient ordered his affairs in a particular way relying on the skill of the doctor, the doctor should, therefore, compensate him for any loss he suffers as a result of that reasonable reliance...

Secondly, there is the 'floodgates question'. Traditionally, the courts have been concerned to avoid imposing liability where to do so would involve making the defendant liable to an indeterminate number of people, in an indeterminate amount, for an indeterminate period of time. It is argued that generally, at least, there is no such risk here. First, the number of potential plaintiffs is in the usual case limited to two and they can recover once only. Secondly, in most of these cases the woman will become pregnant fairly soon, usually within a year,

---

[69] *The Troubled Pregnancy*, 142.
[70] 'Wrongful Conception Unravelled' (1993) 1 Medical Law Review 320–35.

after the operation. Finally, the amounts awarded have not usually been excessive and will of course be limited to the first child.

Thirdly, the courts have in a number of cases considered the insurance position. In wrongful conception cases, as in other cases of medical negligence, the loss will not be borne by the doctor himself... The parents, however, will not only be unlikely to insure against the risk of pregnancy but they may well be unable to do so. It is surely better, given this background, that the loss should fall on the health authority.

Despite the fact that all foreseeable damage caused by the defendant's negligence would normally be compensated, an exception has been carved out in *McFarlane*. *Parkinson* offers a limited exception to that exception. *Rees* now complicates matters further by permitting a novel non-compensatory award, and it is not clear whether this applies in *all* 'wrongful pregnancy' cases.

Is this situation satisfactory? As we can see from the following extracts, the general consensus among academic critics would appear to be 'no'. Even a commentator like Tony Weir who supports the result in *McFarlane*, questions the coherence of its reasoning:

Tony Weir[71]

For the fourteen years since *Emeh* the National Health Service, short of resources for curing the sick, has been disbursing large sums of money for the maintenance of children who have nothing wrong with them. To give but a single example out of very many: in 1993 the Lambeth Health Authority had to pay Mrs Cort no less than £140,679 ('James might not have been planned, but I wouldn't give him up for the world'). The House of Lords has now put an end to that...

The result in *McFarlane* is quite right, and we should not be surprised if the reasoning is uneasy: whenever it enters the family home the law of obligations—not just tort, but contract and restitution as well—has a marked tendency to go pear-shaped.

We saw earlier that the Australian Supreme Court have been critical of Lord Steyn's appeal to the 'inarticulate premises' of London commuters, and they are not alone. First, some have wondered whether the appeal to public morality is a way of lending objectivity to a judge's reliance upon his *own* instincts. This was the view of Lord Morison in the Scottish case of *McLelland v Greater Glasgow Health Board*:[72] 'I must confess that my perception of what "the traveller on the Underground" would think fair does not differ from that which I myself think and that therefore the test appears to me to be no less subjective if expressed in this way.'

Secondly, Robin Oppenheim questions whether Lord Steyn's commuters would, in fact, come up with a single view on the fairness or otherwise of recovery.

Robin Oppenheim[73]

The law's primary concern should be corrective justice. The courts are ill-equipped to start making judgments, at very least without evidence, as to what the hypothetical person would

---

[71] 'The Unwanted Child' (2000) 59 Cambridge Law Journal 238–41.   [72] [2001] SLT 446.
[73] 'The "Mosaic" of Tort Law: The Duty of Care Question' (2003) Journal of Personal Injury Law 151–71.

regard as an ideal solution of distributive justice. It assumes a hypothetical person who is, in truth a judicial cipher, in order to create a uniformity of view where perhaps none exists (as perhaps signified by the continuing legal debate as to the rights and wrongs of...McFarlane).

Thirdly, Laura Hoyano argues that appeals to commuters represent an abdication of judicial responsibility for producing coherent principled decisions.

Laura Hoyano[74]

Distributive justice has become yet another label, without pretending to intellectual rigour. The transmogrification of the man on the Clapham omnibus is not limited to a change of public transport, as he is no longer just a convenient measure for the standard of care expected on non-experts, but also the gatekeeper for negligence law itself.... Appeals to commuters on the Underground to decide duty of care issues allow the courts to avoid confronting the sharp edges of tort policy—deterrence, external scrutiny of professional standards of competence, cheapest cost avoidance of the risk, insurability against loss, other modes of loss-spreading—and whether carving out *ad hoc* exceptions to well-established legal principles is a matter for parliamentary rather than judicial action. Ultimately, it is Parliament, and not the courts, who are accountable to the commuters on the Underground.....

How much time is there between stops on the London Underground, to allow those passengers to assimilate the evidence, weigh up all the factors, and look down the track to future implications of their decision—as is the duty of the judiciary? Not only might London commuters not represent public opinion in the country as a whole, but they might not produce a clear majority, particularly in a complex case. With the utmost respect to Lord Steyn, it is not satisfactory for tort law to be based upon an 'inarticulate premise as to what is morally acceptable and what is not'...

Distributive justice...permits the judiciary to abdicate its responsibility to identify and explain intellectually rigorous and coherent principles as the basis for decisions, in favour of an empirically untested appeal to public opinion, yielding unpredictable results which invite reversal at every level of appeal, depending on each judge's subjective and avowedly instinctive notions of what justice requires. Thus distributive justice is no more illuminating—and arguably less—than the public policy which the Law Lords were anxious to eschew...

The 'wrongful conception' cases demonstrate that distributive justice can be just as unruly a horse as public policy for the courts to ride.

Fourthly, Samantha Singer suggests that, in *Rees*, considerations of distributive justice would in fact point in favour of recovery rather than non-recovery.

Samantha Singer[75]

[T]he conclusion of the majority, that distributive justice leads to a finding of no recovery, does not stand up in the circumstances of Ms Rees' case. In reality, most individuals placed in Ms Rees situation would be more than likely to require the State to financially provide for their children and support them in their upbringing.... This was indeed the case for Karina Rees, whose blindness grew worse and finally led her to cease employment...

---

[74] 'Misconceptions about Wrongful Conception' (2002) 65 Modern Law Review 883–906.
[75] 'Casenote: *Rees v Darlington*' (2004) 26 *Journal of Social Welfare and Family Law* 403–15.

> The House of Lords' decision that the entire financial costs of raising children like Ms Rees' son should lie with the individual, disabled parent is wholly shortsighted... By denying disabled parents damages for negligence—whether for the full expenses of bringing up the child or the additional costs—the risks that children in Ms Rees' son's situation will face being placed in care must increase. In turn, the fear of having their children removed often breeds reluctance in disabled parents to seek help in caring for their children. If this devastating end is avoided, the children of disabled parents often find themselves acting as carers for their parents. Indeed, Lord Millett used this fact as a reason for Ms Rees to be grateful for her surgeon's negligence:
>
> > Once the child is able to go to school alone and be of some help around the house, his or her presence will to a greater or lesser extent help to alleviate the disadvantages of the parent's disability. And once the child has grown to adulthood, he or she can provide immeasurable help to an ageing and disabled parent.
>
> It is surprising that such a naïve and unhelpful passage found its way into a speech in the House of Lords. What parent would wish this existence upon their child? Certainly not Karina Rees—this was part of her reason for being sterilised.

The gloss in *Rees* has also been subject to criticism. In the next extract, Nicky Priaulx suggests that it undermines the decision in *McFarlane*, and is derisory.

Nicky Priaulx[76]

> Quite simply, *McFarlane* no longer stands as good law in the light of *Rees*. If healthy children constitute a benefit serving to outweigh all of the detriments of parenthood, then surely a conventional award overcompensates parents?...
>
> But, one might ask, what of this conventional award?...While some might welcome this type of development and regard it as curative of the *McFarlane* legacy, it is argued that this scheme of 'compensation' pays nothing more than lip service to the principle of reproductive autonomy. On reflection, the award *is* best described as a gloss on *McFarlane*. Not only is the award derisory in a financial sense, certain to leave women for the greater part reliant upon their own resources in caring for the products of negligence, but so too must their Lordships' 'respect for autonomy' be seen in a similar light. How does the assumption that *all* parents are identically situated, with the same impact on their lives through the birth of an unplanned child illustrate respect for the notion *of individual* autonomy?

While Alasdair Maclean supports the 'gloss' in *Rees*, he admits that it may 'end up pleasing no one'.

Alasdair Maclean[77]

> The beauty of [the conventional] award is that it makes no unjustly arbitrary distinction between the claimants, all of whom will receive the same award. It will also make it consider-

---

[76] 'That's One Heck of an "Unruly Horse"! Riding Roughshod over Autonomy in Wrongful Conception' (2004) 12 *Feminist Legal Studies* 317–31.

[77] 'An Alexandrian Approach to the Knotty Problem of Wrongful Pregnancy: *Rees v Darlington Memorial Hospital NHS Trust* in the House of Lords', [2004] 3 Web JCLI <http://webjcli.ncl.ac.uk/2004/issue3/maclean3.html>.

ably easier to come to an out of court settlement since there will be no need to haggle over the projected expenses of raising a child or the impact of a disability on those costs. It is, however, a bold but risky strategy. It is bold because, with one stroke, it destroys the knotty tangle weaved by the courts' ill-considered use of distributive justice. It is risky because it may end up pleasing no one, except perhaps the NHS. Given the potential costs involved in raising a child, the parents of a healthy child may still feel hard done by. Disabled parents may feel aggrieved because the comparatively small award is unlikely to meet the additional costs incurred because of their disability. Those in favour of a full award in line with corrective justice principles may feel that the solution fails to do justice and those who believe *McFarlane* was a wholly just decision may feel that the judgment has been undermined.

Peter Cane suggests that the triad of cases—*McFarlane*, *Parkinson*, and *Rees*—illustrate the dangers of dealing with individual cases in isolation. It was, he argues, inevitable that *McFarlane* left the way open for an action in relation to a disabled child, and that in turn the question of whether the mother's disability makes a difference would also arise.

Peter Cane[78]

The real problem here is not the majority's solution [in *Rees*]—about the wisdom and fairness of which people might disagree—but the fact that the court in *McFarlane* apparently did not see *Parkinson* or *Rees* coming. What this sequence of cases shows is that if the Law Lords (and their successors on the UK Supreme Court) are to take their law-making function seriously—as they seem (to their credit) inclined to do—they must, at least, be prepared to contemplate the possibility that it may be dangerous to consider individual cases too much in isolation and on their precise facts. If the increasingly popular notion of 'distributive justice' is to earn its keep, it must force judges beyond the mantra of treating like cases alike to thinking hard about the criteria of likeness—which involves, at least, comparing and contrasting the case before the court with cases not before the court. Stumbling from one set of facts to the next is, as *Rees* shows, a formula for confusion and instability in the law.

Finally, Robin Oppenheim suggests that an alternative route for deciding these cases would be under the Human Rights Act 1998. If the 'limited recovery rule' in *McFarlane* interferes with a person's legitimate family planning decision, and therefore violates Article 8 (respect for private and family life), it could be justified only if it was proved to be both proportionate and *necessary* under Article 8(2).

Robin Oppenheim[79]

The point of departure should be as Hale LJ suggests in *Parkinson*, that a wrongful conception or birth claim involves an invasion of bodily integrity. This raises issues that can be addressed under Article 8 of the Convention, which provide respectively for the right to respect for a person's private and family life and home. . . .

It is eminently arguable that the ability to regulate one's own fertility and plan the size of one's family, in the context of loss of autonomy and bodily integrity that unwanted pregnancy entails, falls within the ambit of this bundle of rights and where negligent advice has the

---

[78] 'Another Failed Sterilisation' (2004) 120 Law Quarterly Review 189–93.
[79] 'The "Mosaic" of Tort Law: The Duty of Care Question' (2003) Journal of Personal Injury Law 151–71.

consequence of disrupting that ability when conception takes place there is an infringement of Article 8(1)....

If the limited recovery rule laid down by McFarlane is treated on the facts of a given case as an infringement of Article 8(1), the court must then go on to consider whether it fits within any of the restrictions under Article 8(2) that are necessary in a democratic society, namely whether it is a legitimate aim answering a pressing social need and applied proportionately. The only relevant exception is probably Article 8(2) on the basis that it was necessary 'for the protection of health or morals'.... It is difficult to see how non-recognition of a claim for economic loss could be said to be necessary for the protection of health or morals, as required by Article 8(2). There is no pressing social need for the restriction.

(b) 'WRONGFUL BIRTH'

In a wrongful birth action, the parents' claim is that the defendant's negligence led not to their child's *conception*, but to her *birth*. This might happen in a number of different ways. First, before conception, there might have been negligent genetic counselling which wrongly suggested to the parents that they were not at risk of passing on a genetic disease. If they had been properly advised, they would have been able to avoid the birth of their disabled child, perhaps by deciding not to have children, or by using a sperm or egg donor, or employing pre-implantation or prenatal genetic testing.

Secondly, negligence during IVF treatment—perhaps when a couple are undergoing preimplantation genetic diagnosis[80]—might lead to the birth of a disabled child who would not have existed if the embryos had been properly screened. Thirdly, where there has been negligence in offering prenatal tests, or in interpreting or communicating their results, the mother might argue that she was deprived of the option of termination.

When the claim is that, as a result of the defendant's negligence, the pregnant woman was not given the option of termination, an action will only lie if termination would, in fact, have been lawful.[81] If the abortion would have had to take place after 24 weeks, for example, it would be lawful only if the disability met the threshold level of seriousness (see Chapter 13).

The facts, which give rise to a wrongful birth action on the part of the parents, will often be indistinguishable from those that might prompt the child to bring a 'wrongful life' action. As we saw earlier, wrongful life actions are unlikely to succeed, whereas the assumption has been that 'wrongful birth' actions are less problematic, and it is therefore the child's mother, and not the child herself, who will normally sue when the claim is that proper care would have avoided the birth of a disabled child.

It is, however, worth noting Lord Steyn's obiter comments on this point in *McFarlane*.

McFarlane v Tayside Health Board[82]

Lord Steyn

There is no support in Scotland and England for a claim by a disadvantaged child for damage to him arising from his birth: see *McKay v Essex AHA*. Given this position, which also prevails in Australia, Trindade and Cane, The Law of Torts in Australia, 3rd ed. (1999) observe:

'it might seem inconsistent to allow a claim by the parents while that of the child, whether healthy or disabled, is rejected. Surely the parents' claim is equally repugnant to ideas of the

---

[80] See further Chapter 15. [81] *Rance v Mid-Downs HA* [1991] 1 QB 587.
[82] [2000] 2 ACS 9.

> sanctity and value of human life and rests, like that of the child, on a comparison between a situation where a human being exists and one where it does not.'
>
> In my view this reasoning is sound. Coherence and rationality demand that the claim by the parents should also be rejected.

As with all negligence actions, the claimant must establish the existence of a duty of care, its breach, and the causation of damage. Usually, establishing a duty of care will be unproblematic: a person who carries out genetic counselling, PGD, or prenatal screening unquestionably owes a duty of care to their patient.

Sometimes, however, it may be less clear whether there is a close enough relationship between the person who is negligent and the mother. This question arose in *Farraj v Kings Healthcare NHS Trust and Cytogenetic DNA Services*. Mr and Mrs Farraj were both healthy carriers of the Beta Thalassaemia Major (BTM) gene, and Mrs Farraj underwent prenatal testing at Kings College Hospital in order to establish whether her fetus had BTM. Kings sent the tissue sample to the second defendants, CSL, to be cultured. They argued that they were not in a sufficient relationship of proximity to owe a duty to Mrs Farraj, and so could not be liable for the fact that Mrs Farraj had been wrongly told that her fetus did not have BTM. This was rejected by Swift J.

Farraj v Kings Healthcare NHS Trust and Cytogenetic DNA Services[83]

Swift J

Those at CSL were aware that the cultured cells were to be used for testing for BTM. They knew that the tests were to be carried out on behalf of putative parents....In my view, parents in the Claimants' position who received a favourable report of DNA testing would have inferred (in the absence of information to the contrary) that the sample used for testing had been of appropriate quality to yield a reliable result and would have relied on the fact that that was so when making any decision based upon the results. Thus, in my view, CSL should have been aware that parents in the Claimants' position would rely, whether directly or indirectly, on their skill and care....

Adopting the test set out in Caparo, I find that there was, in all the circumstances, a sufficient relationship of proximity between the Claimants and CSL to satisfy the requirement for the existence of a duty of care....Furthermore, it is in my judgment fair, just and reasonable that such a duty should be imposed.

Once a duty of care has been established, the next question is whether that duty has been breached. This was an issue in *Lillywhite v University College London Hospitals' NHS Trust*.[84] Mrs Lillywhite had had an abnormal routine ultrasound scan and was referred to an eminent expert in fetal medicine, Professor Rodeck. He was found to have fallen below the standard of care which could be expected of a consultant sonologist who had specifically been asked to look for brain structures, which the first sonographer had been unable to find. The absence of these brain structures would mean that the fetus was very seriously disabled. The relevant brain structures were not in fact there, but Professor Rodeck wrongly

---

[83] [2006] EWHC 1228.   [84] [2005] EWCA Civ 1466.

concluded that they were. By a two to one majority, the Court of Appeal found that 'there was no plausible explanation for how he could have done so in the exercise of reasonable care and skill'.

Having established a breach of duty, the next step is to prove that the breach caused the damage for which the claimant seeks compensation. The damage which is caused when the mother is not given the option of termination is the birth of a disabled child, and, according to ordinary tort law principles, damages should attempt to put the mother in the position she would have been if the tort had not been committed. Two important issues arise. First, the mother must prove that, if she had known that her child was likely to be born disabled, she would have taken steps to avoid its birth. In the case of negligent prenatal screening, she must establish that, if she had been told about her fetus's disability, she would have had an abortion. This will always be difficult to prove because the woman is necessarily *speculating* about how she would have reacted to the diagnosis, with the benefit of hindsight, and with her claim for damages depending upon her assertion that she would have had a termination.

In *Lillywhite*, above, it was relatively straightforward for the mother to prove, on the balance of probabilities, that she would have terminated the pregnancy if Professor Rodeck had alerted her to the fetus's abnormalities. Following the original abnormal scan, Mrs Lillywhite sought two further second opinions: she was evidently very concerned about the prospect that her child would be born disabled, and the judge accepted her claim that she would have sought a termination if Professor Rodeck had identified the fetus's abnormal brain structure.

In contrast, in *Deriche v Ealing Hospital NHS Trust*[85] Mrs Deriche contracted chicken pox during pregnancy. Because her reaction to having been told of the possibility of a 'congenital malformation' was not to investigate the possibility of a termination, Buckley J was not persuaded by her assertion that she would have terminated the pregnancy if the fetal anomaly scan had identified her son Gabriel's disabilities: 'her assertion that any problem would have caused her to have a termination is, I am afraid, a product of the tragedy that subsequently occurred and I cannot accept it as an accurate statement of her state of mind in 1996'.

In addition to the factual difficulty of proving that, if she had known about her fetus's disability, she would have terminated the pregnancy, it might also be argued that this requirement puts the mother in an invidious position. By the time the case gets to court, the child may be a much loved addition to the family. The only way a mother can seek access to damages to help cope with her child's needs is to prove that, if she had known about her disabilities, she would have prevented her birth by having an abortion.

In the next extract, Wendy Hensel takes this point even further and argues that 'wrongful birth' actions send a 'regrettable message' to disabled people in general.

Wendy F Hensel[86]

No matter how compelling the need, or how gross the negligence involved, no assistance will be extended to the family who would have chosen to embrace or simply accept the

---

85 [2003] EWHC 3104.
86 'The Disabling Impact of Wrongful Birth and Wrongful Life Actions' (2005) 40 Harvard Civil Rights-Civil Liberties Law Review 141.

impaired child prior to his birth. Although the lost choice identified as the injury in wrongful birth claims is identical between the mother who would have aborted and the mother who would have decided to carry the impaired child to term, recovery is all or nothing. Against this background, the desperate parent is placed in an untenable position—either she must deny needing medical care for her child or disavow his very existence in open court in order to secure financial assistance....

Because wrongful birth...actions extend compensation only to those parents who would have chosen to abort an impaired child, these torts strengthen and reinforce the message that abortion is the preferred means of 'curing' disability in society.

Secondly, what would it mean to put the mother in the position she would have been in if the tort had not been committed? Should damages cover *all* of the costs of the child's upbringing, or only those associated with the disability? On the one hand, the defendant's negligence caused this child to be born, and if the child had not been born, then *none* of the costs associated with their upbringing would have been incurred. On the other hand, if the child had been healthy, the pregnancy would not have been terminated, and the parents would, in any event, have incurred the costs of caring for a healthy child. It might therefore be argued that it is only the *additional* costs associated with the disability that were caused by the defendant's negligence. In *Lee v Taunton and Somerset*[87] Toulson J appeared to endorse this latter approach: 'If, following a termination of her pregnancy with George, she had continued with her attempts and had been successful, she would have incurred the costs of bringing up a healthy child in any event.'

Wrongful birth cases clearly differ from wrongful pregnancy cases—JK Mason describes them as 'distinct legal entities'. A 'wrongful birth' case involves a claim for recovery of pure economic loss: there is no plausible physical injury because the negligence did not cause the woman to become pregnant. In a 'wrongful birth' case, the mother would have suffered the same pain and discomfort if the child had been healthy. In contrast, in 'wrongful pregnancy' cases, the physical discomfort of pregnancy and childbirth are caused by the defendant's negligence.

On the other hand, because both actions involve a claim for damages in respect of a child who would not have been born 'but for' the defendant's negligence, it is probably not surprising that in the wrongful birth cases which immediately followed *McFarlane*, we can see the lower courts grappling with what relevance, if any, *McFarlane* might have.

In *R and v East Dorset HA*,[88] the first wrongful birth action to be decided post-*McFarlane*, negligent prenatal screening had failed to detect that the fetus had Down's Syndrome. Newman J concluded that the House of Lords judgment in *McFarlane* had not ruled out compensation for the extra costs associated with a child's serious disability.

Henriques J in *Hardman v Amin* also held that *McFarlane* did not affect recovery for the wrongful birth of a disabled child. This was a case in which a GP had negligently failed to diagnose his pregnant patient's rubella infection, leading to the birth of her severely handicapped son. Despite distinguishing 'wrongful birth' from 'wrongful pregnancy', Henriques J was reassured that commuters on the Underground would accept the premise that the defendant should be responsible for the costs of a child's disability where it was his fault that the child was born disabled.

---

[87] [2001] 1 FLR 419.   [88] (2000) 56 BMLR 39.

Henriques J[89]

If the commuters on the underground were asked whether the costs of bringing up Daniel (which are attributable to his disability) should fall on the claimant or the rest of the family, or the state, or the defendant, I am satisfied that the very substantial majority, having regard to the particular circumstances of this case, would say that the expense should fall on the wrongdoer.

A similar approach was adopted in *Lee v Taunton and Somerset NHS Trust*. The couple believed themselves to be at risk of having a disabled child as a result of their epilepsy medication. A high resolution ultrasound was performed during pregnancy, but it failed to detect the fetus's spina bifida. Toulson J again suggested that commuters on the Underground would not regard the birth of a disabled child as a blessing, and nor would they regard it as unjust that a negligent doctor should be required to compensate the parents for failing to give them the option of preventing the child's birth.

Lee v Taunton and Somerset NHS Trust[90]

Toulson J

I do not believe that it would be right for the law to deem the birth of a disabled child to be a blessing, in all circumstances and regardless of the extent of the child's disabilities; or to regard the responsibility for the care of such a child as so enriching in the ordinary nature of things that it would be unjust for a parent to recover the cost from a negligent doctor on whose skill that parent had properly relied to prevent the situation.

If the matter were put to an opinion poll among passengers on the Underground, I would be surprised if a majority would support such a view....

The fact remains that in all the cited cases, before and after McFarlane, of birth of a disabled child after alleged negligence in failing to detect foetal abnormalities which would have led to a termination of the pregnancy, the courts have recognised the claimant's right to claim damages for the cost of meeting the child's special needs....I have considered whether the decision in McFarlane should lead to a different conclusion in this type of case, and I do not believe so.

4 CONCLUSION

The uncertainties that remained after the House of Lords' judgment in *McFarlane* made it inevitable that cases such as *Parkinson* and *Rees* would follow, in order to test whether slight variations to the facts would enable claimants to recover the maintenance costs of children conceived as a result of another's negligence. Interestingly, neither *Parkinson* nor *Rees* has in fact clarified the scope of *McFarlane*, which continues to be opaque, to say the least. Following the decision in *Rees*, two critical questions remain unanswered. First, the status of the exception to *McFarlane* in *Parkinson* is uncertain. The House of Lords was split over whether *Parkinson* had been rightly decided, and so until a further definitive judgment, a question mark inevitably hangs over that decision.

---

[89] *Hardman v Amin* (2000) 59 BMLR 58.   [90] [2001] 1 FLR 419.

Secondly, what is the scope of the conventional award in *Rees*? The justifications given for it are certainly not confined to *disabled* parents: in Lord Millett's words there had been a 'denial of an important aspect of... personal autonomy, viz the right to limit the size of their family'. Similarly, Lord Bingham held that 'the real loss suffered in a situation of this kind... is that a parent, particularly (even today) the mother, has been denied through the negligence of another, the opportunity to live her life in the way that she wished and planned'.

It is difficult to predict how future cases will be decided. Should another wrongful conception case reach the House of Lords, it would, however, be interesting if Baroness Hale was on the panel. In her judgments in the Court of Appeal in both *Parkinson* and *Rees*, her dissatisfaction with the decision in *McFarlane* is evident. Recall her extraordinarily detailed description of the physical and emotional invasiveness of pregnancy, childbirth, and motherhood. In *Rees*, a number of their Lordships admitted that the principal loss in these cases is an interference with the woman's reproductive autonomy, but none went quite so far as Hale LJ, as she then was, did in *Parkinson*.

Importantly too, the modest conventional award, and the possibility that it might have universal application provides a substantial disincentive towards further litigation. The costs of bringing a claim will often exceed the modest conventional award, and so both prospective claimants and their legal advisers may decide that it is not worth engaging in expensive and time-consuming litigation if the best that one could hope for might be an award of £15,000.

In relation to 'wrongful life' actions, it is often assumed that the door closed on them many years ago in *McKay*. Yet, for two reasons, I think this assumption may be premature. First, the judgments placed considerable emphasis upon the sanctity of human life, and while this would undoubtedly still be a relevant factor, it may exert less pull over the judiciary now than it did in 1982. Since then, as we see in Chapter 17, many cases have explored the question of when life-prolonging treatment might become futile, or not in the patient's best interests, and it is evident that the 'sanctity principle', while still important, does not always trump other considerations.

Secondly, there has not been very much litigation under the Congenital Disabilities (Civil Liability) Act 1976, but if or when a claimant brings an action under section 1A(2)(b), the court may be forced to address an inconsistency between the 1976 Act and the Court of Appeal's judgment in *McKay*. In such a case the claimant would be claiming that negligence in the process of embryo selection resulted in a genetically abnormal embryo being transferred to the woman's body. The disabled child would have to argue that non-negligence would have prevented her birth, and the courts would have to grapple with what would appear to be a statutory action for wrongful life.

FURTHER READING

Cane, Peter, 'Another Failed Sterilisation' (2004) 120 Law Quarterly Review 189–93.

Hoyano, Laura, 'Misconceptions about Wrongful Conception' (2002) 65 Modern Law Review 883–906.

Maclean, Alasdair, 'An Alexandrian Approach to the Knotty Problem of Wrongful-Pregnancy: *Rees v Darlington Memorial Hospital NHS Trust* in the House of Lords' [2004] 3 Web JCLI <http://webjcli.ncl.ac.uk/2004/issue3/maclean3.html>.

Mason, JK, *The Troubled Pregnancy: Legal Wrongs and Rights in Reproduction* (CUP: Cambridge, 2007) chapters 3–6.

Morris, Anne and Saintier, Severine, 'To Be or Not to Be: Is That the Question? Wrongful Life and Misconceptions' (2003) 11 Medical Law Review 167–93.

Priaulx, Nicolette, *The Harm Paradox: Tort Law and the Unwanted Child in an Era of Choice* (UCL Press: London, 2006).

Singer, Samantha, 'Casenote: *Rees v Darlington*' (2004) Journal of Social Welfare and Family Law 26, 403–15.

15

ASSISTED CONCEPTION

CENTRAL ISSUES

1. The provision of assisted conception services is regulated by the Human Fertilisation and Embryology Act 1990, as amended, and clinics must be licensed by the Human Fertilisation and Embryology Authority (HFEA). In addition to the rules set out in the Act itself, the HFEA maintains a more detailed and regularly updated Code of Practice. The Act contains strict rules relating to both consent and confidentiality. It also insists that clinicians must not provide a woman with treatment services unless they have first considered the welfare of any child that might be born as a result.

2. Anonymity used to be the norm when donated gametes (sperm and eggs) were used, but since 2005, donors must be identifiable. Donors cannot be paid, although they can receive compensation for their expenses. Egg-sharing schemes are permitted, and these represent substantial indirect payment.

3. Preimplantation genetic diagnosis (PGD) is generally used to prevent the birth of a child who would be born with a very serious illness. PGD can also, in certain circumstances, be used to find out if the child would be a compatible tissue donor for a sick older sibling, or to discover whether the child might be likely to develop a serious disease later in life.

4. Reproductive cloning is illegal in the UK. In part, this is because it is currently insufficiently safe to attempt in humans, though many people also believe that it would be unethical to clone human beings.

1 INTRODUCTION

In this chapter, we tackle a vast and potentially unwieldy subject: the regulation of assisted conception techniques. The birth of Louise Brown, the first baby created by *in vitro* fertilization (IVF) in Oldham on 25 July 1978 was undoubtedly one of the most important scientific breakthroughs of the twentieth century. Of course, assisted conception did not 'begin' in 1978. Donor insemination, for example, has a much longer history: the first reported case took place towards the end of the nineteenth century. Nevertheless, the possibility of creating and storing embryos *in vitro* has been particularly significant, not least because it has facilitated the subsequent development of a wide variety of other techniques, such as preimplantation genetic diagnosis.

Initially, the possibility of 'test-tube' babies, as they were then known, was greeted with scepticism, and even hostility. But because infertility is a common problem—about one in seven couples will experience some difficulty in conceiving[1]—it was not long before the public recognized that these new techniques had the potential to alleviate the considerable suffering experienced by couples who discover that they cannot have children naturally. It should, however, be remembered that not everyone who receives fertility treatment will become pregnant. The average success rate for IVF treatment in women under the age of 35 is 31 per cent, falling to 18.6 per cent for women aged 38–39; and 11.1 per cent for women aged 40–42. But even though fertility treatment offers no guarantee of success, now approximately 1.5 per cent of children born in the UK are conceived *in vitro*,[2] and most people know at least one family that has been created with medical assistance.

Anxiety about the propriety of interfering with human reproduction has now largely subsided, and there is broad public acceptance of most uses of reproductive technologies. It is, however, worth noting that there are still those who oppose assisted conception on grounds of principle. In 2008, a Papal Encyclical reaffirmed the Catholic Church's opposition to IVF, on the grounds that the only licit way to reproduce is through the 'conjugal act'.

Congregation for the Doctrine of the Faith[3]

[A]ll techniques of heterologous artificial fertilization, as well as those techniques of homologous artificial fertilization which substitute for the conjugal act, are to be excluded.... The Church moreover holds that it is ethically unacceptable to *dissociate procreation from the integrally personal context of the conjugal act*: human procreation is a personal act of a husband and wife, which is not capable of substitution....

Cryopreservation is *incompatible with the respect owed to human embryos*; it presupposes their production *in vitro*; it exposes them to the serious risk of death or physical harm, since a high percentage does not survive the process of freezing and thawing; it deprives them at least temporarily of maternal reception and gestation; it places them in a situation in which they are susceptible to further offense and manipulation.

Perhaps paradoxically, as Laura Purdy explains, opposition to the use of reproductive technologies has also come from feminists.

Laura Purdy[4]

Feminist objections can be traced to the fear that assisted reproduction will help men to subjugate women. Feminists emphasize that social pronatalism leads many women to undertake

---

[1] HFEA Guide to Infertility (HFEA: London, 2008), available at <www.hfea.gov.uk>.
[2] Ibid.   [3] *Instruction Dignitas Personae on Certain Bioethical Questions* (Vatican, 2008).
[4] 'Assisted Reproduction' in H Kuhse and P Singer (eds), *A Companion to Bioethics* (Blackwell: Oxford, 1998) 163–72.

costly and potentially risky procedures to remedy infertility that would not otherwise trouble them. Furthermore, since men still run society, and are especially prominent in science and medicine, women's quest for help with reproduction adds to men's power over them. A few feminists have claimed that if additional techniques, such as ectogenesis or cloning, were perfected, men might seek to eliminate women from society altogether . . .

Women's consent might also be questioned on feminist grounds. Pronatalism is pervasive in human society, as is the attitude that women who do not have children are necessarily unfulfilled, or even worthless. . . . The onus of barrenness is so great that some women will even undertake IVF when it is their husbands who suffer from a reproductive problem. Although these points suggest that women considering IVF should have lengthy counselling, they do not support a ban on the practice. Doing so 'to protect women against themselves' would treat women as legal incompetents, damaging women more than unwise reproductive treatments.

In this chapter, we begin by looking at the regulation of assisted conception in the UK, which involves a detailed look at the legislation—the Human Fertilisation and Embryology Act 1990, which was substantially amended in 2008—and at the work of the Human Fertilisation and Embryology Authority (HFEA). We break this down into analysis of the licensing procedures, through which clinics are inspected and authorized to perform certain procedures; access to treatment; consent to the use of gametes (sperm and eggs); gamete donation; rules governing the parentage of children; and preimplantation genetic diagnosis. We briefly examine the as-yet unrealized possibility of human reproductive cloning, which is currently illegal in the UK. In the next chapter we consider the regulation of surrogacy.

2 REGULATION OF ASSISTED CONCEPTION

In 1982, four years after the birth of Louise Brown, the Committee of Inquiry into Human Fertilisation and Embryology, chaired by Mary Warnock, an academic philosopher, was commissioned to make recommendations on the regulation of fertility treatment and embryo research.[5] Its report was published in 1984, and although it was debated in the House of Commons shortly afterwards, the Human Fertilisation and Embryology Bill, which was based upon the Warnock Committee's recommendations, was not introduced to Parliament until 1989.

In the meantime, a number of private members' bills were put forward which would have prohibited embryo disposal, and thereby effectively prohibited all IVF treatment and research. In the mid-1980s, the Unborn Children (Protection) Bill, for example, initially commanded a parliamentary majority of 172, and only failed to become law because of effective delaying tactics deployed by the Bill's opponents.

By the time the first Human Fertilisation and Embryology Bill finally came before Parliament, hostility towards embryo destruction appeared to have softened, and there was greater acceptance of both infertility treatment and embryo research. The announcement, towards the end of the 1980s, of the first successful cycles of preimplantation genetic diagnosis (PGD)—used to enable people at risk of having children with fatal diseases to give birth to healthy children—contributed to public sympathy for assisted conception techniques.

---

[5] *Report of the Committee of Enquiry into Human Fertilisation and Embryology* (HMSO, 1984).

The Human Fertilisation and Embryology Act was passed in 1990, and came into force the following year.

There were a number of factors behind the government's decision to substantially reform the 1990 Act in 2008. As we saw in Chapter 12 when we considered embryo research, new scientific developments had put pressure upon the statute's flexibility. This was also true in relation to treatment services: new uses for PGD, such as tissue typing, had emerged since the Act was passed. The government's initial intention was to merge the HFEA with the then newly formed Human Tissue Authority. After sustained opposition, perhaps most notably from clinicians themselves, this part of the reform agenda was dropped, and the Bill, which was introduced to Parliament in 2007, was directed only towards amending the 1990 Act. It leaves much of the regulatory framework intact, although it does make some significant changes to the attribution of parenthood and to the licensing process, and it contains much more detailed guidance on certain types of treatment—most notably PGD—than the original legislation.

(a) THE HUMAN FERTILISATION AND EMBRYOLOGY AUTHORITY

Section 5 of the Human Fertilisation and Embryology Act sets up the Human Fertilisation and Embryology Authority (HFEA). At the time of writing, the HFEA has twenty-two Members, more than half of whom must be 'lay' members: that is, they must not be clinicians or scientists.[6]

The HFEA has a number of different functions. It regulates the provision of fertility treatment and the carrying out of embryo research (see further Chapter 12) by inspecting clinics and granting licences, and by maintaining a register of information about the provision of treatment and its outcomes. The HFEA also has a role in the formation of policy. Under section 25, it must maintain a Code of Practice (at the time of writing in its eighth edition), which gives guidance to clinics about the proper conduct of licensable activities. The Code also sets out the general principles which should be followed in the carrying on of activities governed by the legislation, and in the carrying out of the Authority's functions. Section 8(cb) provides that the HFEA is under a duty to promote compliance with the Code. In addition to the Code, which is updated periodically, the HFEA also has the power to issue directions on specific issues, with which clinics must comply.

There are obvious advantages in using a regularly updated Code of Practice, rather than primary legislation, to regulate such a fast-moving area of clinical practice and research. A good example of the sort of flexibility offered by this model of regulation is the changes in the rules governing the number of embryos that may be transferred in each cycle of IVF. The health risks associated with multiple pregnancies are serious, both for the babies and for the mother. Twins and triplets are much more likely to be born prematurely, and the risk of death around the time of birth is 3–6 times higher for twins and 9 times higher for triplets. As a result of these risks, successive versions of HFEA policy—set out in the Code of Practice—have been directing towards trying to reduce the number of embryos that are transferred in any one cycle, in order to reduce multiple pregnancy rates. According to the latest version of this guidance, all clinics must have a 'multiple birth reduction strategy':

---

[6] See further <www.hfea.gov.uk/>.

HFEA Code of Practice 8th Edition

The strategy must set out:

(a) how the centre aims to reduce the multiple birth rate following treatment at that centre in any calendar year, and to ensure the rate does not exceed the maximum specified by the Authority as set out in Directions [at the time of writing, this is 24%, but it is expected to be reduced with the ultimate aim of a multiple birth rate of no more than 10%]

(b) the circumstances in which the person responsible would consider it appropriate to recommend Single Embryo Transfer (SET) to a patient.

The Code thus has the advantage of being able to respond fairly promptly to a continually shifting evidence base. The legal status of the Code of Practice is, however, a little unclear. A breach of the Code is not a criminal offence, unlike many breaches of the Act itself. Nevertheless, breaches of the Code can be taken into account by a licence committee when deciding whether to vary or revoke a licence.

The HFEA is also responsible for advising the Secretary of State for Health on, among other things, the need for new primary legislation. Under section 7 of the Act, it must produce an Annual Report to the Secretary of State for Health, describing the activities it has undertaken in the past twelve months, and setting out its work programme for the following year. These Reports are laid before Parliament by the Minister.

The full Authority meets about seven times each year; currently, two of these meetings are held in public. It also has a number of sub-committees, such as the Ethics and Law Advisory Committee and the Scientific and Clinical Advances Advisory Committee, which advise the main Authority on policy decisions, and in the case of the Compliance Committee, exercise certain delegated powers in relation to import and export of gametes and embryos and the issuing of directions. In recent years, the HFEA has increasingly engaged in public consultation exercises, using a wide variety of different techniques.

(b) LICENSING

One of the HFEA's most important purposes is to control the activities of licensed clinics and research centres. Sections 3 and 4 of the Human Fertilisation and Embryology Act 1990 provide that the creation, use, and storage of embryos, and the storage and use of gametes, can only be carried out under a licence granted by the HFEA. Carrying out any of these activities without a licence is a criminal offence.[7] It is also a criminal offence to procure, test, process, or distribute gametes without a licence.

It is perhaps worth asking why fertility treatment is subject to this special regulatory regime. A number of reasons might be put forward, not all of which are wholly convincing. First, it is true that there are some health risks associated with treatments like IVF, such as the risk of ovarian hyperstimulation syndrome (OHSS), but other potentially risky medical treatments are not subjected to this sort of special regulatory framework. In any event, some of the risks associated with IVF— such as OHSS or multiple births— also exist for *unlicensed* treatments, such as the prescription of fertility drugs.

A second possible explanation is the special *moral* concern for embryos created outside of the female body. But, of course, this justification does not apply to some licensed

[7] Section 41.

treatments, such as donor insemination. Thirdly, it might be argued that the creation of children through artificial means itself raises ethical dilemmas, such as who should be permitted to have access to treatment. Fourthly, because most treatment takes place in the private sector, regulation might be directed towards restraining the excesses of a completely free market in fertility treatment.

The final and most persuasive explanation is that the form regulation takes in the UK reflects the historical context of the 1990 Act. In 1989, when the original Bill was drafted, professional bodies, such as the Royal College of Obstetricians and Gynaecologists, had not yet produced their own guidance on the proper conduct of fertility services. Given the novelty and ethical controversy involved, it seemed sensible to consolidate the rules on best practice within a licensing regime. Now, of course, there is also a rich body of professional guidance, in addition to the HFEA's Code of Practice. Indeed, the HFEA increasingly relies upon professional bodies to develop guidance: an example would be the British Andrology Society's involvement in setting appropriate age limits for sperm donors.

Under section 11 of the Act, the HFEA can grant four different types of licence: for treatment services; non-medical fertility services;[8] storage of gametes and embryos; and research on embryos (see Chapter 12). Once an application for a licence has been received by the HFEA, an inspection team will visit the premises and prepare a report. Licences are granted by a Panel of HFEA staff, or in more controversial cases, by a Committee of HFEA members. Licences for treatment and storage can be granted for a maximum of five years,[9] although shorter licences are used to ensure more regular oversight where this is thought desirable. In addition to the regular programme of renewal and interim inspections, a programme of unannounced inspections is in place, some of which are random, and some targeted at clinics which give cause for concern.

Centres are under a duty to report incidents and 'near misses' to the HFEA. These are monitored and where the HFEA believes that there is a risk of reoccurrence, an anonymized 'Alert' will be issued to all licensed centres notifying them of the risk in question. Centres are not penalized for reporting incidents. On the contrary, the HFEA encourages them to do so as part of the trend towards learning from mistakes, which we explored in detail in Chapter 3. In the light of the HFEA's well-established system of recording and learning from mistakes, it is interesting to note that the rate of incidents, or adverse events (approximately one per cent) is lower in the assisted conception sector than in other areas of the health service, where it has been estimated that approximately 10 per cent of treatments result in some sort of adverse event.

Sections 12–15 of the Act specify a number of standard licensing conditions, which will automatically be attached to each licence. We look at some of these in detail below, but they include, under section 12(c), that the consent provisions contained in Schedule 3 are complied with; under section 13(5), that account has been taken of the welfare of any child that might be born; and under section 14(3) and (4), that the statutory storage periods for gametes and embryos are not exceeded. In addition, the licence committee may attach specific conditions to an individual centre's licence (perhaps in response to past breaches of the Act or the Code).

Under section 16(2) each licence application must designate a Person Responsible (PR), whom the licence committee must consider a suitable person to supervise the activities

---

[8] Defined in section 2 as any services that are provided, in the course of a business, for the purpose of assisting women to carry children, but are not medical, surgical, or obstetric services.

[9] Paragraphs 1(5) and 2(3) of Schedule 2.

authorized by the licence, and in particular, under section 17, to ensure that suitable practices are used, and the conditions of the licence complied with. Until the *Attorney General's
Reference (2 of 2003)*,[10] it was not clear whether the person responsible (PR) might be vicariously criminally liable for offences committed by his staff. In this case, the senior embryologist had been guilty of extremely serious misconduct, but the Court of Appeal decided that
the PR had not vicariously committed an offence.

Section 18 deals with the revocation and variation of licences. A licence can be revoked
or varied for a number of reasons, including if misleading information was provided for the
purpose of the licence application; or if the premises are no longer suitable; or if the PR has
failed to discharge his responsibilities or comply with directions; or if there has been any
other material change in circumstances. Revocation and variation are also possible if the
licence committee is not satisfied that the PR is a suitable person to discharge their duties, or
if the PR dies or is convicted of an offence under the Act. Section 19 sets out the procedure
for refusing, varying or revoking a licence. Notice must be given to the PR, who then has
an opportunity to make representations to the Licence Committee within 28 days, with a
further appeal possible to the Authority's separate Appeal Committee, which is now made
up of non-members.

As a public body, decisions of the Authority and its licence committees must comply with
the Human Rights Act and are judicially reviewable. Licensing decisions must therefore be
proportionate, lawful (that is, licence committees must act within their statutory powers)
and rational (that is, they must not be *Wednesbury*[11] unreasonable). Committees must take
into account relevant factors, and disregard irrelevant considerations.

There have been a number of applications for judicial review of decisions of the HFEA. In
one of the first, *R (on the application of Assisted Reproduction and Gynaecology Centre) and
Another v Human Fertilisation and Embryology Authority*, the Court of Appeal spelled out
that, provided the Authority's decision was rational and that it had not exceeded its powers,
the courts should have no role.

R (on the application of Assisted Reproduction and Gynaecology Centre) and Another v Human Fertilisation and Embryology Authority[12]

Wall J

The members thought that future treatment for Mrs H was likely to fail but that, if she did
succeed in becoming pregnant, there would be a higher risk of multiple pregnancy if five
embryos had been transplanted rather than three. The Authority therefore considered that
the possible marginal improvement in the chances of pregnancy were outweighed by the
albeit small risk of multiple pregnancy. Two scientists may disagree over that proposition, but
in our judgment it is impossible to describe it as irrational. . . .

Disagreements between doctors and scientific bodies in this pioneering field are inevitable. The United Kingdom, through the Act, has opted for a system of licensing and regulation. The Authority is the body which is empowered by parliament to regulate. Like any
public authority, it is open to challenge by way of judicial review, if it exceeds or abuses the

---

[10] [2004] EWCA Crim 785.

[11] The test is whether no reasonable body could have come to the same decision: *Associated Provincial
Picture Houses v Wednesbury Corporation* [1948] 1 KB 223.

[12] [2002] EWCA Civ 20.

powers and responsibilities given to it by parliament; but where, as is manifest here from an examination of the facts, it considers requests for advice carefully and thoroughly, and produces opinions which are plainly rational, the court, in our judgment, has no part to play in the debate, and certainly no power to intervene to strike down any such decision. The fact that the appellants may disagree with the Authority's advice is neither here nor there.

It is worth noting that the HFEA's ability to regulate fertility services is by no means comprehensive. The prescription of super-ovulatory hormones, for example, does not require a licence from the HFEA. More significantly, perhaps, as Margaret Brazier points out in the following extract, the HFEA exercises little control over the market in fertility services: the prices charged for treatment are outside of its regulatory ambit. Nor, of course, can the HFEA control the provision of treatment services in other countries.

Margaret Brazier[13]

The most profound change in regulating reproductive medicine since Warnock is, I would argue, the dramatically increased role of commerce. Warnock based its recommendations in relation both to fertility treatment and research on the supposition that fertility services would be integrated into the NHS... The enormous commercial potential of developments in reproductive medicine was hardly foreseen... Yet debate on commodification and commercialisation is at the forefront of debate today. A fertility 'industry' has developed to provide treatment on a profit making basis both to British citizens and 'procreative tourists' escaping more prohibitive regimes elsewhere in Europe. Pressure to pay gamete donors and surrogates continues.

The reproduction business, even in the United Kingdom, is set to spawn two rather different sorts of market. The first, which effectively exists today, is the market in fertility services. The private sector, involving both private licensed fertility clinics and the companies who will seek to develop both new fertility treatments and therapeutic cloning, necessarily operates on a profit-making basis. They have a vested interest in the expansion of their business. The more treatment cycles a woman undergoes, the more people who seek treatment, the greater the profit to a clinic....

Another nightmare awaits the HFEA and its counterparts in Continental Europe. Each national jurisdiction has sought to fashion a scheme of regulation acceptable to its own culture and community. However those wealthy enough to participate in reproduction markets can readily evade their domestic constraints. If I can order sperm on the internet, or hire a surrogate mother from Bolivia, are British regulators wasting their time? The international ramifications of the reproductive business may prove to be a more stringent test of the strength of British law than all of the difficult ethical dilemmas that have gone before.

This latter issue is sometimes described as 'reproductive tourism'. Although it is impossible to give exact numbers, it seems clear that British citizens are going abroad in increasing numbers to access services that they cannot obtain easily in the UK. There are three principal reasons why people might seek assisted conception services abroad: cost (IVF is cheaper in India); avoiding long waiting lists (there are more egg donors available in Spain because they receive some compensation); or avoiding legal restrictions in the UK (such as the bans on sex selection and anonymous sperm donation).

[13] 'Regulating the Reproduction Business?' (1999) 7 Medical Law Review 166–93.

While the treatment available overseas will often be of a very high quality, there can be dangers for patients. In some countries, there are no restrictions upon the number of embryos transferred in any one cycle. In 2009, for example, it was reported that a woman in the US had given birth to octuplets after a doctor replaced six embryos. While this is an extreme example, British women have returned from undergoing IVF treatment in India pregnant with triplets and quads. In addition to the health risks for the pregnant women and their children, higher order multiple births impose significant additional costs on NHS neonatal services. As we see in the next chapter, going abroad for surrogacy treatment can also cause problems, such as the child not being allowed entry into the UK because she is not a British citizen.

In the next extract Hunter and Oultram suggest that 'sperm ships'—the brainchild of a Danish entrepreneur who wanted to provide anonymous sperm donation in ships moored in UK waters[14]—make a mockery of national regulations.

D Hunter and S Oultram[15]

One of the more worrisome issues raised by sperm ships is the challenge that they pose to governments in the effective management and governance of their citizens....The key concern here is that sperm ships would allow someone to live in one country, but live by the rules of another country. Insofar as we value countries having sovereignty or at least the effective ability to regulate the availability of medical technology we ought to resist the introduction of sperm ships...While sperm ships don't technically challenge a nation's sovereignty they do challenge its ability to effectively regulate the healthcare technologies available to its citizens. And this challenge makes a mockery of the notion that states can regulate these technologies.

(c) RECORDING AND DISCLOSING INFORMATION

Section 31 of the Human Fertilisation and Embryology Act requires the HFEA to keep a register of information collected from licensed centres about the provision of treatment. Through directions, the HFEA can require licence holders to collect information about donors, recipients, treatment services, and the children born as a result. Special rules governing the disclosure of this information, and of any other information obtained in confidence by the HFEA, are contained in section 33.

Until the 2008 reforms, the confidentiality provisions under the Act were so strict that it was impossible to use the information in the HFEA's register for research purposes. This meant that it was not possible to carry out longitudinal epidemiological research into the health consequences of IVF, or newer techniques like ICSI (intra-cytoplasmic sperm injection—a treatment for male infertility in which a single sperm is injected into an egg), by linking the HFEA's register with other databases, such as cancer registries. Now, section 33D(1) provides that regulations can require 'the processing of protected information for the purposes of medical research' where this is 'necessary or expedient in the public interest or in the interests of improving patient care'.

---

[14] Ships are governed by the laws of the country whose flag they fly.
[15] 'The Challenge of "Sperm Ships": The Need for the Global Regulation of Medical Technology' (2008) 34 Journal of Medical Ethics 552–6.

(d) THE CONSCIENCE CLAUSE

As with the Abortion Act 1967, section 38(1) of the Human Fertilisation and Embryology Act 1990 provides that doctors with a conscientious objection to treatment or research can refuse to participate in its provision: 'No person who has a conscientious objection to participating in any activity governed by this Act shall be under any duty, however arising, to do so.'

The burden of proof of conscientious objection lies with the person claiming to rely upon it.[16] It seems likely that nursing staff too have a right to exclude themselves from the provision of fertility treatment. Whether or not administrative staff, such as receptionists, are entitled to conscientiously object to activities governed by the Act is unclear, and would depend upon whether they could be said to be 'participating' in any of the activities governed by the Act.

A person can invoke section 38 to exclude themselves from *any* activity governed by the Act, they do not have to object to everything covered by the Act. Would it be possible, therefore, for a clinician to 'conscientiously object' to the treatment of lesbians or single women? Michael Freeman has argued that this does not amount to a conscientious objection, but is instead 'rooted in prejudice', and that, in such circumstances, the clinician is not objecting to the *activity* in question, and hence could not claim statutory protection for their refusal to treat.[17]

Of course, such a refusal might also be incompatible with equality legislation or unlawful on human rights grounds. Certainly, the HFEA's Code of Practice stresses that persons responsible (PRs) are under a duty to familiarize themselves with relevant equality legislation and to ensure that their staff members do not discriminate against patients.

HFEA Code of Practice 8th Edition paras 29.9 and 29.11

29.9 A staff member's views about the lifestyle, beliefs, race, gender, age, sexuality, disability or other perceived status of a patient, patient's partner or donor should not affect that individual's treatment or care....

29.11 The person responsible should satisfy themselves that the staff member has a conscientious objection to providing a particular activity, and is not unlawfully discriminating against a patient on the basis of their race, disability, gender, religion or belief, sexual orientation or age.

(e) REGULATING ACCESS TO TREATMENT

In the UK there are two ways in which access to fertility treatment is restricted. First, the Act provides that treatment services must not be provided unless account has been taken of the welfare of any child who may be born as a result. This oddly worded provision amounts in theory, if not in practice, to a child-welfare filter upon access to treatment. Secondly, despite NICE guidance, NHS funding for fertility treatment is patchy and often inadequate,

---

[16] Section 38(2).
[17] 'Medically Assisted Reproduction' in A Grubb with J Laing (eds), *Principles of Medical Law*, 2nd edn (OUP: Oxford, 2004) 639–738, 687.

and private treatment is expensive. As a result, access to treatment is often contingent upon a person or couple's ability to fund their own treatment.

(1) Section 13(5)

The Human Fertilisation and Embryology Act contains no formal restrictions upon access to treatment, so any individual, regardless of their age, sexual orientation, or marital status, can legally receive fertility treatment in the UK. When the Bill was initially debated in 1990, an amendment that would have restricted access to treatment services to married couples was defeated by only one vote. As a result, in order to shore up support for the Bill, an amendment was introduced which instructed clinicians to take account of the welfare of any child to be born 'including the need of that child for a father'.

When the 2007 Bill came before Parliament, the government had assumed that deleting the 'need for a father' clause would straightforwardly bring the 1990 Act into line with post-1990 family law reforms and with equality legislation. Single women and lesbian couples can adopt children,[18] and same-sex couples can enter into civil partnerships and thereby acquire the same legal rights as married couples.[19] In the light of this, and of the prohibition of discrimination on the grounds of sexual orientation,[20] it seemed anomalous for the statute governing fertility treatment to contain a statutory clause which, on the face of it, looks like an *invitation to discriminate* against women without male partners.

Nor is a presumption against treating women without male partners, on welfare grounds, supported by the evidence. While there are numerous studies which appear to show some correlation between single motherhood and poor outcomes for children, these reflect the poverty and greater mobility that often accompany divorce, separation, or unplanned single motherhood. Women who seek treatment without men in licensed clinics are a very different cohort to those who have single motherhood thrust upon them, and this is reflected in the evidence, which in fact suggests that children conceived using donor insemination by women without male partners are, if anything, doing better than similarly conceived children who are being brought up by married couples.[21]

Single or lesbian women who want to have children are usually fertile, so if they cannot access treatment services in a licensed clinic, they could instead engage in casual, unprotected sex. Not only would this be less safe, but also it might mean that the resulting child would have no information about her genetic father. For reasons of safety and to ensure that offspring have access to information from the register (see below), there may be good reasons for *encouraging* women without male partners to make use of licensed services, rather than leaving them to try to find alternative ways to conceive.

It is also, of course, true that the existence of a potential father-figure, when assisted conception services are sought, offers no guarantee of his presence, either when the child is born, or throughout her childhood.

Despite this, the removal of the 'need for a father' clause proved to be hugely controversial, with peers and MPs from all parties suggesting that removing it was tantamount to

---

[18] Adoption and Children Act 2002.   [19] Civil Partnership Act 2004.
[20] Equality Act (Sexual Orientation) Regulations 2007.
[21] C Murray and S Golombok, 'Solo Mothers and their Donor Insemination Infants: Follow-up at Age 2 Years' (2005) 20 Human Reproduction 1655–60.

impugning the role of men in modern family life. In the end, the government's concession in the Lords was supported by a majority in the Commons, and section 13(5) now reads:

> A woman shall not be provided with treatment services unless account has been taken of the welfare of any child who may be born as a result of the treatment (including the need of that child for supportive parenting), and of any other child who may be affected by the birth.

The Code of Practice sets out how this is to be interpreted. Since 2005, the welfare of the child assessment has been regarded as a welfare of the child *risk* assessment. Rather than trying to ensure that would-be patients will be *good* or *ideal* parents, which would be an extraordinarily difficult task for fertility doctors, clinicians are instead instructed to consider whether there are any specific risk factors which indicate that the child's welfare might be jeopardized in the future.

HFEA Code of Practice 8th edition paras 8.3, 8.7, and 8.10

8.3 The centre should assess each patient and their partner (if they have one) before providing any treatment, and should use this assessment to decide whether there is a risk of significant harm or neglect to any child...

8.7 Those seeking treatment are entitled to a fair assessment. The centre is expected to consider the wishes of all those involved, and the assessment must be done in a non-discriminatory way. In particular, patients should not be discriminated against on grounds of gender, race, disability, sexual orientation, religious belief or age.

8.10 The centre should consider factors that are likely to cause a risk of significant harm or neglect to any child who may be born or to any existing child of the family. These factors include any aspects of the patient's or (if they have one) their partner's:

(a) past or current circumstances that may lead to any child mentioned above experiencing serious physical or psychological harm or neglect, for example:

    (i) previous convictions relating to harming children

    (ii) child protection measures taken regarding existing children, or

    (iii) violence or serious discord in the family environment

(b) past or current circumstances that are likely to lead to an inability to care throughout childhood for any child who may be born, or that are already seriously impairing the care of any existing child of the family, for example:

    (i) mental or physical conditions

    (ii) drug or alcohol abuse

    (iii) medical history, where the medical history indicates that any child who may be born is likely to suffer from a serious medical condition, or

    (iv) circumstances that the centre considers likely to cause serious harm to any child mentioned above.

The 2008 amendment means that the clinician must take account of the child's 'need for supportive parenting'. The Code of Practice gives guidance on how this should be interpreted, and the focus continues to be upon a risk assessment, with the assumption that, in the absence of specific risk factors, all parents should be assumed to be supportive.

HFEA Code of Practice 8th edition para 8.11

8.11 When considering a child's need for supportive parenting, centres should consider the following definition: Supportive parenting is a commitment to the health, well being and development of the child. It is presumed that all prospective parents will be supportive parents, in the absence of any reasonable cause for concern that either the child to be born, or any other child, may be at risk of significant harm or neglect.

Section 13(5) has been the subject of much academic debate. Certainly if interpreted literally, it is rather puzzling because it instructs a clinician to base his decision as to whether to attempt to bring a child into the world in part upon a consideration of that child's welfare. Given that, as we saw when we looked at 'wrongful life' actions in the previous chapter, the law tends to assume that existence must be preferable to non-existence, it is difficult to see how a clinician could decide that a child would be benefited by not being born. In practice, the section has not been interpreted literally, and is instead used to check whether there is any reason to believe that prospective patients would be inadequate parents. But this interpretation too is not without difficulty.

It must, for example, be admitted that clinicians do not have access to all the information which might be relevant in attempting to judge prospective patients' parenting abilities. Unlike adoption agencies, infertility clinicians will not make home visits, and nor do they undergo any specialist training in evaluating the capacity to be a good parent.

Policing section 13(5) is also difficult. It is a standard licensing condition that account must be taken of the welfare of any child that might be born, and in practice, clinics must have a protocol in place that sets out how this is done. It would, however, be very difficult to prove that the clinic had erred in this assessment. If account was not properly taken of the welfare of any child, and a future child's welfare suffered as a result, it is not clear that anybody would be able to sue the clinic for non-compliance with section 13(5). If the child were to bring an action, this would amount to a 'wrongful life' claim: the child would have to argue that the clinic failed to prevent her from being born into a life which is full of hardship. As we saw in the previous chapter, the courts have given very short shrift to the idea that life itself, however difficult, could amount to compensatable damage.

Section 13(5) has also been criticized for placing an unfair burden upon infertile individuals who are, it must be admitted, not necessarily any more likely to pose a risk to their children than fertile people, who can reproduce without anyone scrutinizing their parenting ability.[22] Indeed, the evidence suggests that children born following fertility treatment are, if anything, doing better than children conceived naturally.[23] This should not be surprising since the pool of individuals who use assisted conception services are clearly very committed to having children and, due to restrictions on NHS treatment, will additionally

---

[22] See, for example, Emily Jackson 'Conception and the Irrelevance of the Welfare Principle' (2002) 65 Modern Law Review 176–203.

[23] See, eg, S Golombok, R Cook, A Bish, and C Murray, 'Families Created by the New Reproductive Tecnologies: Quality of Parenting and Social and Emotional Development of the Children' (1995) 66 Child Development 285–98; S Golombok, A Brewaeys, MT Giavassi, D Guerra, F MacCallum, and J Rust, 'The European Study of Assisted Reproduction Families: The Transition to Adolescence' (2002) 17 Human Reproduction 830–40; C Murray and S Golombok, 'Solo Mothers and their Donor Insemination Infants: Follow-up at Age 2 Years' (2005) 20 Human Reproduction 1655–60.

often be fairly well off. In contrast, the pool of people who conceive naturally will include individuals who may find parenting difficult, such as children and drug addicts.

Of course, there is a difference between refraining from interfering with a fertile couple's right to conceive a child naturally and an infertile couple's need for assistance. But if we think that pre-conception assessment of parenting ability is necessary whenever positive steps are taken to help a couple conceive, we may need to draw a line between procedures that *do* require preconception parental assessment and procedures that *do not*. Surely we would not want to suggest that a doctor should not carry out investigations into the causes of infertility, or even try to repair a woman's fallopian tubes, without first assessing the couple's fitness to parent? Nor would it seem sensible to refuse to supply ovulation testing kits, which might help couples to conceive, unless consideration has first been given to the welfare of any child who might be born. If we think we need to judge parental fitness when doctors do *some* things which help women to become pregnant, but not others, we need to be able to explain why. For example, we could say that assessment is necessary only when doctors create a new life *in vitro*, but, of course, this would rule out the application of section 13(5) prior to donor insemination, when the creation of any new life will happen naturally *in vivo*.

The House of Commons Science and Technology Committee's 2005 report robustly criticized section 13(5) and recommended its abolition in future legislation, but the governement did not take up this suggestion.

House of Commons Science and Technology Committee[24]

The welfare of the child provision discriminates against the infertile and some sections of society, is impossible to implement and is of questionable practical value in protecting the interests of children born as a result of assisted reproduction. We recognise that there will be difficult cases but these should be resolved by recourse to local clinical ethics committees. The welfare of the child provision has enabled the HFEA and clinics to make judgements that are more properly made by patients in consultation with their doctor. It should be abolished in its current form. The minimum threshold principle should apply but should specify that this threshold should be the risk of unpreventable and significant harm. Doctors should minimise the risks to any child conceived from treatment within the constraints of available knowledge but this should be encouraged through the promotion of good medical practice not legislation.

It would be possible for a disgruntled would-be patient to apply for judicial review of a decision to refuse treatment in an NHS hospital. In a case which preceded the 1990 Act, *R v Ethical Committee of St Mary's Hospital (Manchester), ex parte Harriott*,[25] an application for judicial review of a consultant's decision to remove a woman from the waiting list for IVF treatment—after discovering that she had been turned down for adoption on the grounds of previous convictions for prostitution—was rejected on the grounds that 'it is not, and could not be, suggested that no reasonable consultant could have come to the decision to refuse treatment to the applicant'.[26]

---

[24] Human Reproductive Technologies and the Law Fifth Report (2005), paras 101, 107, available at <www.publications.parliament.uk/>.

[25] [1988] 1 FLR 512.   [26] Ibid at 519.

Now, of course, rejected would-be patients might also be able to turn to the Human Rights Act 1998, and in particular Article 8 (right to respect for private and family life); Article 12 (the right to found a family); and Article 14 (the right not to be discriminated against in exercising one's convention rights). There have, in recent years, been two such claims, both from prisoners who wanted to be able to artificially inseminate their wives while still in prison.

In the first case, *R v Secretary of State for the Home Department, ex parte Mellor*, the Court of Appeal found that the restrictions on prisoners' right to found a family and their right to family life were justifiable and proportionate under Article 8(2). The Secretary of State's policy was that the grant of facilities for artificial insemination to prisoners was made only in exceptional circumstances. Mrs Mellor would be 31 years old at the time of Mr Mellor's release, so depriving them of access to artificial insemination (AI) facilities would be likely to delay rather than prevent parenthood.

R v Secretary of State for the Home Department, ex parte Mellor[27]

Lord Phillips MR

Imprisonment is incompatible with the exercise of conjugal rights and consequently involves an interference with the right to respect for family life under article 8 and with the right to found a family under article 12. This restriction is ordinarily justifiable under the provisions of article 8(2)....

Exceptional circumstances may require the normal consequences of imprisonment to yield, because the effect of its interference with a particular human right is disproportionate....

By imprisoning the husband the state creates the situation where, if the wife is to have a child, that child will, until the husband's release, be brought up in a single parent family. I consider it legitimate, and indeed desirable, that the state should consider the implications of children being brought up in those circumstances when deciding whether or not to have a general policy of facilitating the artificial insemination of the wives of prisoners or of wives who are themselves prisoners...

I would simply observe that it seems to me rational that the normal starting point should be a need to demonstrate that, if facilities for artificial insemination are not provided, the founding of a family may not merely be delayed, but prevented altogether.

The issue surfaced again, with slightly different facts, in *Dickson v UK*.[28] Here Mrs Dickson would be fifty-one years old at Kirk Dickson's earliest possible release date: there was therefore virtually no chance that the couple would be able to conceive naturally. Without access to AI, then, their capacity to have a child together would not just be delayed, but eliminated. The Court of Appeal decided that, despite this, the Secretary of State had acted lawfully by deciding that their need for AI was trumped by other factors, such as that their relationship had not been tested in the normal environment of daily life; there was insufficient provision for the child's material welfare; and that there would be legitimate public concern that the punitive and deterrent elements of Kirk Dickson's sentence had been circumvented.

At first, this decision was upheld by the ECtHR, but the Dicksons successfully appealed to the Grand Chamber of the ECtHR. By a majority, the Grand Chamber held that prisoners retained their human rights on incarceration, and so any interference with the prisoner's Article 8 rights had to be justified, and it was not sufficient justification that providing AI

---

[27] [2001] EWCA Civ 472. [28] (App. No. 44362/04) (2007).

facilities to prisoners would offend public opinion. Because the Secretary of State's policy set an 'inordinately high exceptionality burden', it amounted to a disproportionate interference with their Article 8 rights.

Dickson v UK[29]

> **Decision of the Grand Chamber**
>
> [T]he court considers that the policy as structured effectively excluded any real weighing of the competing individual and public interests, and prevented the required assessment of the proportionality of a restriction, in any individual case.
>
> In particular,...the policy placed an inordinately high 'exceptionality' burden on the applicants when requesting artificial insemination facilities. They had to demonstrate, in the first place, as a condition precedent to the application of the policy, that the deprivation of artificial insemination facilities might prevent conception altogether (the starting point). Secondly, and of even greater significance, they had to go on to demonstrate that the circumstances of their case were 'exceptional' within the meaning of the remaining criteria of the policy (the finishing point)....
>
> [T]he court does not consider that the statistics provided by the government undermine the above finding that the policy did not permit the required proportionality assessment in an individual case....The court therefore finds that the absence of such an assessment as regards a matter of significant importance for the applicants must be seen as falling outside any acceptable margin of appreciation so that a fair balance was not struck between the competing public and private interests involved. There has, accordingly, been a violation of art 8 of the convention.

In the wake of the Grand Chamber's decision, in 2009 it was reported that six further prisoners had made applications for access to AI.[30]

(2) Financial Restrictions on Access

Infertility treatment is expensive—one cycle of IVF costs in the region of £4,000—and its availability within the National Health Service is patchy. In 2003, a clinical guideline issued by the National Institute for Clinical Excellence (NICE), whose role we considered in detail in Chapter 2, recommended that each infertile couple should be entitled to up to three cycles of IVF at public expense.[31] The government decided that this was unaffordable, but agreed that NHS funding should be available for one cycle per couple. Even this more modest recommendation has not been fully implemented. A Department of Health survey of IVF provision, carried out in 2007, found considerable variation in the number of cycles PCTs would fund, from three to zero. It also found that most PCTs impose additional eligibility criteria; such as that neither partner smokes or has a child from a previous relationship. Some PCTs impose lower age limits than the NICE guideline's upper limit of 40.[32] Even if a couple is eligible for one free cycle, given that, on average, the success rate of IVF is 23.1%, for the

---

[29] Ibid.   [30] Jamie Doward, 'Prisoners Demand Right to be Fathers' The Observer, 8 February 2009.
[31] Fertility: Assessment and Treatment for People with Fertility Problems (2004), available at <www.nice.org.uk/>.
[32] Primary Care Trust Survey—Provision of IVF in England 2007 (DH: London, 2008), available at <www.dh.gov.uk>.

majority of couples, this will not lead to the birth of a baby, let alone the family of at least two children which many parents hope for.

It is also important to note that the NICE guideline restricts access to free treatment to *infertile* couples. Lesbians and single women, whose inability to conceive without assistance is not the result of biological dysfunction, will often have to pay the full costs of treatment themselves. In the next extract, JR McMillan argues, first, that providing fertility treatment to single and lesbian women may in fact be *more* cost-effective (a criterion which is usually important to NICE) than treating infertile women, since the chances of achieving a successful pregnancy may be higher. And, secondly, that by confining NHS-funded treatment to heterosexual couples, NICE has made a social judgement about who *deserves* to have access to publicly funded fertility treatment.

JR McMillan[33]

> If pregnancy is the outcome that matters for cost effectiveness then there is no obvious reason why publicly funded fertility treatment should not be provided to lesbians and single women.…In fact it might be that lesbians and single women are more cost effective to treat than infertile heterosexual couples because they are less likely to have a physiological cause for their unwanted childlessness…
>
> [B]y recommending that publicly funded fertility treatment should be available to heterosexual couples and not, by implication, to single women and lesbians, the guideline does make social judgments. The guideline says that 'for the purposes of investigation, infertility should be defined as failure to conceive after regular unprotected sexual intercourse for two years in the absence of any reproductive pathology'. This definition rules the majority of lesbians and single women out of consideration.

(3) Counselling

A further standard licensing condition, under section 13(6) of the Act is that all patients, and where relevant their partners, should not be provided with certain treatments—involving the use of donated gametes or of embryos created outside of the body—unless they have been given 'a suitable opportunity to receive counselling'. Counselling is not mandatory, however, and nor is there any duty upon clinics to make it available free of charge.

The Code of Practice specifies that counselling must be clearly separated from other forms of 'information giving', and from the welfare of the child assessment process. It must be confidential.

HFEA Code of Practice 8th Edition para 3.7

> 3.7 The provision of counselling should be clearly distinguished from (a) the clinical assessment of a person's suitability to receive treatment, or to store or donate their gametes or embryos; (b) the provision of information before obtaining consent or providing treatment; and (c) the normal relationship between clinical staff and patients or donors.

---

[33] 'NICE, the Draft Fertility Guideline and Dodging the Big Question' (2003) 29 Journal of Medical Ethics 313–14.

(f) REGULATING THE USE OF GAMETES AND EMBRYOS

(1) Consent to the Use of Gametes

Consent to the storage and use of one's gametes must be voluntary and fully informed. Under Schedule 3 of the 1990 Act, unlike other much more invasive medical procedures, consent to the creation of an embryo, or to the use of one's gametes in the treatment of others *must* be in writing, and counselling must have been offered.

Consent must state what is to be done with the gametes in the event of the donor's death or incapacity, and must specify the maximum period of storage, if this is to be less than the statutory storage period of ten years. This ten-year limit can be extended for individuals whose fertility has or is likely to become significantly impaired, for example because they are about to undergo treatment for cancer which will leave them infertile.

The strictness of the rules governing consent to the use of gametes first came before the Court of Appeal in *R v Human Fertilisation and Embryology Authority, ex parte Blood*. Mrs Blood wanted to be inseminated with her deceased husband's sperm. The problem was that although Mrs Blood claimed that she and her husband had discussed the posthumous use of his sperm, Mr Blood had not given written consent. Sperm samples had been extracted at Mrs Blood's request while her husband was in a coma. Not only was there no effective consent for the purposes of Schedule 3, but the doctors who extracted the sperm had probably acted unlawfully. As we saw in Chapter 5, adults who lack capacity must be treated in their best interests. Since Mr Blood was not going to recover, the surgical retrieval of sperm was certainly not in his best *medical* interests; and it is hard to see how having genetic offspring after one's death could be said to be in a patient's best emotional or welfare interests.

Without an effective consent, it would have been unlawful for Mrs Blood to use the sperm samples for treatment in the UK, and the Court of Appeal admitted that their continued storage was also 'technically' an offence, although they said that there could be 'no question of any prosecution being brought in the circumstances'. Mrs Blood applied for permission to export the sperm to Belgium, where treatment without the gamete provider's consent would be lawful. The HFEA refused, and she applied for judicial review of this decision.

At first instance, despite expressing considerable sympathy for Mrs Blood, Sir Stephen Brown decided that the HFEA had acted within their discretion. On appeal, Mrs Blood succeeded. The Court of Appeal took the view that despite the unlawfulness of the sperm retrieval, in exercising their discretion the HFEA had not taken adequate account of Mrs Blood's right under European law to receive treatment in another Member State.[34]

R v Human Fertilisation and Embryology Authority, ex parte Blood[35]

Lord Woolf MR

Because this judgment makes it clear that the sperm of Mr Blood has been preserved and stored when it should not have been, this case raises issues as to the lawfulness of the use and export of sperm which should never arise again. . . .

The absence of the necessary written consent means that both the treatment of Mrs Blood and the storage of Mr Blood's sperm would be prohibited by the 1990 Act. The authority has

---

[34] EC Treaty, Art 59.   [35] [1997] 2 WLR 806 (CA).

no discretion to authorise treatment in the United Kingdom . . . Parliament by the 1990 Act had left issues of public policy as to export to be determined by the authority. . . . .

The first reason given by the authority is a correct statement that in this case there has not been compliance with the 1990 Act in relation to storage or use in the United Kingdom. This is the starting point for the subsequent reasoning which is the essence for the explanation why the authority was not prepared to exercise its undoubted discretion to permit export in Mrs Blood's favour. It was a permissible and proper starting point: in giving a particular direction, the authority is using delegated powers, which should be used to serve and promote the objects of the legislation, which clearly attach great importance to consent, the quality of that consent, and the certainty of it.

The authority must balance that against Mrs Blood's cross-border rights as a Community citizen . . .

Parliament has delegated to the authority the responsibility for making decisions in this difficult and delicate area, and the court should be slow to interfere with its decisions. However, the reasons given by the authority, while not deeply flawed, confirm that the authority did not take into account two important considerations. The first being the effect of article 59 of the [EC] Treaty. The second being that there should be, after this judgment has been given, no further cases where sperm is preserved without consent.

Although the Court of Appeal agreed that the HFEA was entitled to place restrictions upon the export of sperm, any restrictions had to be justified on grounds of public policy,[36] and the Court of Appeal was not satisfied that the public interest was served by refusing Mrs Blood permission to export her husband's sperm for treatment elsewhere in Europe. Following the Court of Appeal's judgment, the HFEA changed its mind, taking into account Mrs Blood's Treaty rights, and the fact that this would not set an undesirable precedent because sperm should never again be taken without consent. Mrs Blood was therefore allowed to export her deceased husband's sperm, and following treatment in Belgium, she has subsequently had two children.

In 2008, the Court of Appeal's prediction that there would be no further cases in which there was no effective consent to the use of gametes was proved wrong. L's husband H had died suddenly following routine surgery. L and H already had one child and were keen to have a second. An out-of-hours application was made to the court, and Macur J declared that it would be lawful to remove and store sperm from H's body. This declaration was made on the basis of misinformation, provided to Macur J, about the scope of the Human Tissue Act 2004. She was told that the Human Tissue Act permitted posthumous sperm retrieval, with the consent of a qualifying relative. In fact, the Human Tissue Act does not apply to gametes.

Because there was no written consent, H's sperm could not be used in the UK. An application to the HFEA for the sperm to be exported to a country where use without H's consent would be lawful was postponed pending L's application to the court to determine the lawfulness of the storage, use, and export of the sperm.

In *L v Human Fertilisation and Embryology Authority*,[37] Charles J found that the evidence that H would have wanted his sperm used posthumously by L was 'at least as compelling as that advanced by Mrs Blood': L and H already had a child together and six days before H's death they had enquired about the possibility of using IVF, due to L's age. He also found that the law was clear, and both storage and use of H's sperm in the UK would be unlawful,

---

[36] EC Treaty, Arts 56(1) and 66.   [37] [2008] EWHC 2149 (Fam).

but that the HFEA had a wide discretion to permit export. Following Charles J's judgment, and taking into account the decision in the *Blood* case, and the fact that L could (unlike Mrs Blood) rely not only on European Treaty rights but also on convention rights (especially Articles 8 and 12) as incorporated by the Human Rights Act, the HFEA decided to permit export to a clinic in the US, where the sperm could lawfully be used.

Charles J stated that he was 'not satisfied that it is possible to lawfully remove, or authorize the removal of, gametes from a dead person (who has not given an effective advanced consent to this)'. He also doubted whether it was possible for the Court to substitute its consent. Hence, notwithstanding the fact that a similar prediction in the *Blood* case turned out to be mistaken, no further cases should arise.

Until the 2008 reforms, the consent provisions in Schedule 3 presented difficulties for children or other patients unable to give effective consent for the storage of their gametes. Certain medical treatments for cancer, such as orchidectomy (the removal of testicles) and chemotherapy, may leave the patient permanently sterile. In such circumstances, it is routine to retrieve sperm for storage prior to treatment, on the grounds that the preservation of fertility will almost always be in a child's best interests. An exception might be if the child will not live long enough to benefit from having sperm in storage.

While retrieval would easily be justified at common law, the original legislation did not permit storage without the gamete provider's consent. This was remedied in the 2008 reforms, which provide that storage too can be lawful without consent. In the case of children, the consent of someone with parental responsibility is treated as the child's own 'effective consent',[38] until the child is old enough to make his own decision about continued storage.

(2) The Posthumous Use of Gametes

In the UK, sperm and embryos can be used posthumously, but only where the gamete provider explicitly consented to posthumous use. The 2008 amendments mean that, under section 39 of the 2008 Act it will be possible, provided the man consented, for him to be treated as the father of a child conceived after his death with his frozen sperm, but only for the purposes of birth registration. Other normal incidents of fatherhood, such as a child's inheritance rights in the event of intestacy, do not apply.

It is also possible under section 40 for a man who was married or a woman who was in a civil partnership at the time of an embryo's creation with donated gametes to be treated as the father or the second legal parent if that embryo is subsequently used after their death, again only for the purposes of birth registration and only if they have specifically consented both to the embryo's posthumous use and the posthumous acquisition of parenthood, for registration purposes.

(3) Consent to the Use of Embryos

When embryos are created *in vitro* they will be graded by an embryologist in order to determine which embryos are suitable either for immediate use or for freezing for use in future cycles. Unsuitable embryos will be disposed of, or donated to research. Of the remaining embryos, one or two (or exceptionally three) fresh embryos may be transferred to the woman's uterus, and the rest will be frozen for future use. These embryos can be stored

---

[38] Schedule 3, para 8 (2ZA).

for up to 10 years. This limit can be extended in exceptional cases, such as when a young woman is about to undergo treatment for ovarian cancer, which will leave her without any more eggs.

Of course, it is possible that the gamete contributors will subsequently disagree about the use of their frozen embryos. How should such disputes be resolved? As we saw in Chapter 13, when an embryo is *in utero*, men have no say over the pregnant woman's decision to have an abortion. But if an embryo has been frozen and is being stored *in vitro*, the practical justifications for giving women sole decision-making authority are less compelling. To some extent, cryopreservation reduces the asymmetry that normally exists between men and women's interest in their fertilized gametes.

Some differences do remain, however. First, it is possible for the embryos to be transferred to the woman's body and carried to term without involving a third party. In contrast, if the male partner wishes to use the embryos in treatment, he must find a woman willing to be implanted with them and carry the pregnancy to term.

Secondly, the use of frozen sperm is now well established, in contrast egg freezing is in its infancy and success rates are low. This means that a woman who is about to lose her eggs as a result of treatment for cancer may still be advised to freeze *embryos* created with her partner's sperm, rather than her eggs. If the couple subsequently split up, and the male partner withdraws his consent to their continued storage and use, the woman will be in a much worse position than a man in a similar situation, whose frozen sperm will be available for use with any future partner.

In the United Kingdom the position is relatively straightforward. The Human Fertilisation and Embryology Act 1990 allows for the variation or withdrawal of consent to the use or storage of an embryo.[39] Once either gamete provider has withdrawn their consent to their use or continued storage, stored embryos must be destroyed or allowed to perish. Hence, whichever partner does not want their embryos to be used in treatment effectively has a right of veto.

This provision was challenged in the UK courts, in *Evans v Amicus Healthcare*,[40] and in the Grand Chamber of the ECtHR in *Evans v UK*.[41] Following the discovery that Natallie Evans had ovarian cancer, she and her then partner, Howard Johnston, underwent a cycle of IVF treatment resulting in the storage of six embryos. Ms Evans was then successfully treated for cancer. She could carry a child, but had no more eggs, and so the stored embryos represented her last opportunity to have a baby that was genetically related to her. The couple then separated, and Mr Johnston wrote to the clinic to notify it of their separation, and to state that the embryos could be destroyed. Ms Evans sought a declaration that the relevant provisions of the 1990 Act were incompatible with her rights under Article 8 of the European Convention on Human Rights. She failed at first instance, and before the Court of Appeal, and her appeal to the ECtHR and finally to the Grand Chamber were also unsuccessful.

Evans v UK[42]

Decision of the Grand Chamber

It is not disputed between the parties that art 8 is applicable and that the case concerns the applicant's right to respect for her private life....

---

[39] Schedule 3, para 4.　　[40] [2004] EWCA (Civ) 727.
[41] (App. No. 6339/05) (2007).　　[42] Ibid.

> The dilemma central to the present case is that it involves a conflict between the art 8 rights of two private individuals: the applicant and J. Moreover, each person's interest is entirely irreconcilable with the other's, since if the applicant is permitted to use the embryos, J will be forced to become a father, whereas if J's refusal or withdrawal of consent is upheld, the applicant will be denied the opportunity of becoming a genetic parent. In the difficult circumstances of this case, whatever solution the national authorities might adopt would result in the interests of one or the other parties to the IVF treatment being wholly frustrated...
>
> While the applicant contends that her greater physical and emotional expenditure during the IVF process, and her subsequent infertility, entail that her art 8 rights should take precedence over J's, it does not appear to the court that there is any clear consensus on this point either.
>
> As regards the balance struck between the conflicting art 8 rights of the parties to the IVF treatment, the Grand Chamber, in common with every other court which has examined this case, has great sympathy for the applicant, who clearly desires a genetically related child above all else. However, given the above considerations, including the lack of any European consensus on this point, it does not consider that the applicant's right to respect for the decision to become a parent in the genetic sense should be accorded greater weight than J's right to respect for his decision not to have a genetically-related child with her.

In both the Chamber and the Grand Chamber, the ECtHR affirmed that the 'bright line' rule which the UK government had opted for—namely the continuing need for both partners' consent to an embryo's use and storage—was acceptable, notwithstanding the fact that it did not allow any variation in order to accommodate the particular circumstances of the individual. There were, in the courts' view, strong public policy justifications for this inflexibility—namely the promotion of certainty and the avoidance of arbitrariness and inconsistency.

The dissenting judges in both courts took a different view, and argued that the UK's 'bright line' rule had a disproptionate impact upon Natallie Evans' Article 8 rights. Rosy Thornton agrees, and argues that the courts were wrong to treat Ms Evans and Mr Johnston as though they were similarly situated.

Rosy Thornton[43]

> Domestic legislation that seeks to balance the article 8 rights of male and female gamete providers on the basis of formal equality, by means of an immutable rule that allows for no exceptions—given the overwhelming imbalance of impact on the woman and the man—must be necessarily problematic. To treat as like two such unlike situations does not produce true equality in terms of the law's effects.... It is, therefore, difficult to disagree with the dissenting judges at both levels of the ECtHR. A blanket rule, insensitive to the realities of profoundly unequal situations, must amount to a disproportionate infringement of the female partner's right to respect for her private life....
>
> The bright-line rule itself, though rooted in formal equality, in fact operates inconsistently and arbitrarily in terms of its real, differential impact on the female and male gamete providers in cases such as *Evans*. Second, if a bright-line rule is desirable at all, then why should it be fixed, as it is under the 1990 Act, at the time of implantation rather than allowing male

---

[43] 'European Court of Human Rights: Consent to IVF Treatment' (2008) 6 International Journal of Constitutional Law 317–30.

> consent to be withdrawn only up to the point of fertilization (as, for instance, in Austria and Estonia)? The latter threshold would both recognize the greater impact of the decision on the female partner and mirror more closely the situation of natural conception.

Craig Lind draws attention to the sharp contrast between the law's unsympathetic attitude to men who are 'careless' with their sperm, in the context of sexual intercourse, and the overriding priority given in the *Evans* case to Mr Johnston's desire not to become a father.

Craig Lind[44]

> It is, therefore, deeply ironic that, in the context of assisted reproduction, men are given such complete control over their procreative capacity. Mr Johnson is said to have had a fundamental objection to there being a child of his in the world which he was not actively raising with the child's mother. Yet, if he had fathered a child accidentally during sexual intercourse, he would have been denied the level of control over his procreation that the statute gives him. He would have had to support any child born as a result of that activity (even if it were of the briefest, most meaningless kind). His involvement in a clinical infertility venture is, however, a much more deliberate move to procreate than a casual sexual encounter is. However, only the latter can lead to substantial support obligations....
>
> After this series of decisions I am left with the abiding question: do we really believe that a greater injustice would have been done to Mr Johnson in 'foisting' an unwanted child on him than is done by preventing Ms Evans from ever have a child of her own?

Sally Sheldon has criticized the *Evans* case from a different perspective. If Natallie Evans had instead created embryos with donated sperm, and had these frozen, they would almost certainly have been available for use in the future, if her relationship with Mr Johnston broke down. Of course, given Natallie Evans' cancer diagnosis, the need to make rapid decisions about IVF was thrust upon Ms Evans and Mr Johnston, with much less time for discussion than would normally be the case. Nevertheless, given the potentially devastating implications for a woman in Ms Evans's situation, it would be sensible to give a couple some time to talk through the implications together, and some time for each of them to discuss their options separately with a member of the clinic's staff.

Sally Sheldon[45]

> On the facts of this case, the robustness of the consent obtained from each party is surely open to question. The lack of space for confidential, private discussions between each party and clinic staff on the one hand, and between the two parties themselves, on the other, makes for rather less than the quality of consent which might be thought desirable. While the courts seem cognisant of the necessity of a 'bright line rule' to offer certainty to clinics, the consenting procedures in this case were such as potentially to leave Ms Evans

---

[44] 'Evans v United Kingdom—Judgments of Solomon: Power, Gender and Procreation' (2006) 18 Child and Family Law Quarterly 576.

[45] 'Case Commentary: Revealing Cracks in the 'Twin Pillars'?' (2004) 16 Child and Family Law Quarterly 437.

and Mr Johnston in a position of considerable uncertainty about the implications of their treatment.

When reforming the 1990 Act, the government chose to retain the consent provisions, so under the amended Act, both partners continue to have the right to veto the use of embryos. There is, however, one small change, which is intended to apply in cases of dispute. Under Schedule 3(4A), if one party withdraws his or her consent to the use of embryos, the Act now provides for a twelve-month 'cooling off period', during which the embryos cannot be used or disposed of without both parties' consent. The hope is that this will enable couples in a similar situation to Natallie Evans and Howard Johnston to come to an agreement about the embryos' use or disposal.

(4) Status of Gametes

In *Yearworth v North Bristol NHS Trust*, for the first time, the court was faced with the question of whether or not stored gametes, in this case sperm, were property for the purposes of a claim in negligence. The containers which are used to store 'straws' of sperm are called dewars. They are filled with liquid nitrogen, and all dewars now have 'low nitrogen alarms' which alert clinic staff so that the nitrogen can be topped up before the samples are compromised.

In *Yearworth* following a reduction in nitrogen levels, the sperm samples were thawed, and no longer suitable for use in treatment. The claimants were all men who had undergone treatment for cancer, and they brought an action in neligence, seeking damages for the loss of their samples, and for psychiatric disorders which had been caused as a result. There were some factual complications: for some of the men, natural fertility had, in fact, been restored, and for one man, the stored sample did not contain sufficient sperm to give a reasonable chance of pregnancy. These questions went to the issue of what *loss* these men had suffered. For our purposes, the important point is that the Court of Appeal grounded a decision that the sperm samples were property, for these purposes, in the 1990 Act's consent provisions. Given the emphasis put upon consent, and the freedom people have to determine what should happen to their gametes, the Court of Appeal found that the rights they had in relation to their stored sperm were equivalent to *property* rights.

Yearworth v North Bristol NHS Trust[46]

Lord Judge CJ

In our judgment, for the purposes of their claims in negligence, the men had ownership of the sperm which they ejaculated:...

- The sole object of their ejaculation of the sperm was that, in certain events, it might later be used for their benefit....It is true that, by confining all storage of sperm and all use of stored sperm to licence-holders, the Act has effected a compulsory interposition of professional judgment between the wishes of the men and the use of the sperm....For two reasons, however, the absence of their ability to "direct" its use does not in our view

---

[46] [2009] EWCA Civ 37.

> derogate from their ownership. First, there are numerous statutes which limit a person's ability to use his property—for example a land-owner's ability to build on his land or to evict his tenant at the end of the tenancy or a pharmacist's ability to sell his medicines—without eliminating his ownership of it. Second, by its provisions for consent, the Act assiduously preserves the ability of the men to direct that the sperm be *not* used in a certain way: their negative control over its use remains absolute.
>
> - .... Thus the Act recognises in the men a fundamental feature of ownership, namely that at any time they can require the destruction of the sperm.
>
> - ...while the licence-holder has *duties* which may conflict with the wishes of the men, for example in relation to destruction of the sperm upon expiry of the maximum storage period, no person, whether human or corporate, other than each man has any *rights* in relation to the sperm which he has produced.

(5) Gamete Donation

Most people undergoing fertility treatment in the UK use their own gametes, but in some circumstances, treatment with donated sperm or eggs will be necessary. A number of distinctive questions are raised by gamete donation, such as whether donors should be anonymous, and whether they should be paid. It is also worth considering whether the same rules should apply to sperm and egg donors, given that the experience of sperm donation is much less intrusive and risky than the process of egg donation.

(a) Anonymity

Until April 2005, most gamete donation was anonymous. Children born following anonymous donation could be given access to non-identifying information, such as the donor's ethnic origin or occupation, and, once they reach the age of 16, they can ask the HFEA whether they were born following fertility treatment, and if they are related to a prospective spouse, civil partner, or 'person with whom the applicant is in an intimate physical relationship or with whom the applicant proposes to enter into an intimate physical relationship'.[47] The 1990 Act did not specify that donors *had* to be anonymous, and some patients chose to use a known donor. This was particularly common for egg donation, where the discomfort and inconvenience of donation means that a woman might be willing to donate her eggs to an infertile friend or sister, but not to a stranger.

For a long time, anonymity was believed to be in the interests of donors, recipients, and children. It shielded donors from unwanted contact with their offspring, and protected the privacy and security of the recipient family. It also undoubtedly helped to persuade young men, often medical students, to donate sperm safe in the knowledge that the consequences of their donations would not come back to haunt them in middle age.

These justifications have been challenged in recent years. In particular, it has been argued that the needs and interests of donor-conceived offspring should take priority over the interests of parents and donors. A belief that children have a psychological need to know about their genetic origins has been bolstered by a greater understanding of the importance of knowing about inherited genetic conditions. Children born following anonymous gamete donation are unable to give an accurate family medical history to their doctors, and this might compromise their ability to receive optimum health care.

---

[47] Section 31ZB(2).

It has also been argued that a child's right to information about her genetic parentage might be protected by Article 8 of the Human Rights Act 1998. In *R (on the application of Rose) v Secretary of State for Health*, it was accepted that Article 8 was engaged, although the full hearing to determine whether the failure to supply such information was a breach of Article 8 was superseded by the government's decision to implement regulations abolishing anonymity.

R (on the application of Rose) v Secretary of State for Health[48]

Scott Baker J

Everyone should be able to establish details of his identity as a human being. That, to my mind, plainly includes the right to obtain information about a biological parent who will inevitably have contributed to the identity of his child… The evidence before the court satisfies me that article 8 of the Convention is engaged in the circumstances of these claimants. Whether or not there has been a breach of it is, I emphasise again, an entirely different matter and does not fall for consideration by the court at this stage.

Regulations passed in 2004, which came into force in April 2005, removed anonymity for donations after that date. Stocks of anonymously donated sperm could continue to be used until April 2006, but after that date no gametes could be used in treatment unless the donor is prepared to be identifiable. Children born following non-anonymous donation will have access to identifying information about the donor once they reach the age of 18.

Anonymity was not removed retrospectively, although it is possible for pre-2005 donors to register their willingness to be identified. This means that some children may be able to access identifying information before 2023, when the first children conceived after anonymity was abolished reach the age of 18. At the time of writing, it has been estimated that 90 people who donated gametes between 1991 and 2005 have re-registered as identifiable donors.[49]

One potential problem with the shift towards identifiable donors is that a child will obviously only be able to apply to the HFEA for identifying information if she knows, or suspects, that she was conceived using donated gametes. If her parents have not told her about the circumstances of her conception, she will assume that she was conceived naturally, and will not have any reason to make an application to receive identifying information about her genetic parent.

Evidence appears to indicate that the majority of parents do *not* tell their children that they were conceived using donated gametes. A European study of families where the children were conceived using donated sperm found that, by the time children reached the age of 12, only 5 per cent of British parents had told their children about their origins. Some were yet to tell them or yet to decide, but 78 per cent of parents had decided never to tell their children, usually because they thought that the information would be difficult for them, and that it might complicate the child's relationship with their non-genetic parent.[50] Given

---

[48] [2002] EWHC 1593 (Admin).

[49] Clare Dyer, 'More Than 100 Sperm and Egg Donors Prove Ready to Reveal Identity to Offspring' (2008) 337 British Medical Journal a2110.

[50] S Golombok, A Brewaeys, MT Giavassi, D Guerra, F MacCallum, and J Rust, 'The European Study of Assisted Reproduction Families: The Transition to Adolescence' (2002) 17 Human Reproduction 830–50.

such high levels of non-disclosure, the right to identifying information about the gamete donor may make little difference to the majority of children conceived using donated gametes.

All possible solutions to this problem are themselves undesirable. The use of donated gametes could be recorded on the child's birth certificate, or the child could be informed by letter when she reaches the age of 18. While there was some support in Parliament for the first option during the 2008 debates, it is hard to see how this could be in a child's best interests. All the evidence suggests that donor-conceived children who are told about the circumstances of their conception from an early age cope well, but that it is much harder for children who find out later in life, or inadvertently. Not only would endorsing birth certificates unnecessarily stigmatize children, it might lead to them finding out about their donor-conceived status in a shocking and unhelpful way. Many people only see their birth certificate when they need it to obtain a passport, to get married or because a new employer demands to see it. Sometimes people find their birth certificates only when going through their parents' personal effects after their deaths.

Instead, it is hoped that the removal of anonymity will promote a culture of openness. The Code of Practice suggests patients should be strongly advised of the merits of being frank with their offspring from early childhood.

HFEA Code of Practice 8th edition paras 20.7 and 20.8

20.7 The centre should tell people who seek treatment with donated gametes or embryos that it is best for any resulting child to be told about their origin early in childhood. There is evidence that finding out suddenly, later in life, about donor origins can be emotionally damaging to children and to forming relations.

20.8 The centre should encourage and prepare patients to be open with their children from an early age about how they were conceived. The centre should give patients information about how counselling may allow them to explore the implications of treatment, in particular how information may be shared with any resultant children.

Evidence from Sweden, where anonymity was abolished in 1985, is not especially encouraging. Gottlieb *et al.* found that 89 per cent of Swedish parents of children created using donated gametes had not told their children about the circumstances of their conception.[51] Interestingly, in the same study 59 per cent of parents had told *someone else* about their use of donated gametes, increasing the chance that the child might find out inadvertently from someone other than their parents.

Ironically, as Andrew Bainham describes in the next extract, children born to lesbian couples or to single women, will be 'put on notice' that a third party played a role in their conception. For them, access to identifying information will therefore be a real right, which they will all be able to exercise once they reach adulthood. Bainham suggests that permitting children born to heterosexual couples to remain in ignorance means that are effectively discriminated against in their access to information.

---

[51] Claes Gottlieb, Othon Lalos, and Frank Lindblak, 'Disclosure of Donor Insemination to the Child: The Impact of Swedish Legislation on Couples' Attitudes' (2000) 15 Human Reproduction 2052–6, 2053.

> Given that the children of same-sex legal parents will be aware that the biological and legal positions diverge and can effectively exercise their rights in due course to obtain information about the donor, the question needs to be asked whether the much larger group of children of opposite-sex legal parents should not be given the legal right to be told of their conception so that they too may meaningfully exercise their rights to information when the time comes.[52]

In the following extract, Lucy Frith describes a different option, namely a two-track system in which both anonymous and non-anonymous donation is possible. This option was rejected in the UK, in part because it would lead to unfair differences between donor offsprings' access to information. As Frith points out, however, such a difference will exist *de facto* between parents who tell their children about their donor conception and parents who do not.

Lucy Frith[53]

> [Guido] Pennings has suggested a policy that would allow participants to choose between an anonymous or a non-anonymous donation programme. Donors would be able to choose whether they want to be identified and couples would be able to choose between an anonymous or a non-anonymous donor. In Iceland, where such a system already operates, donors can choose to give anonymously or non-anonymously and couples can choose what type of donor to use. This policy also operates at the Sperm Bank of California, for example, where donors can choose whether they want to be 'an identity release donor'.
>
> This type of donation programme would have the advantage of giving parents a greater choice over what they told their children and also of maintaining donor numbers. Such a programme would, though, while widening parental choice, still leave the provision of information at the discretion of the parents. However, as we have seen, unless a non-anonymous programme incorporates a formal mechanism to inform the children this too leaves the decision to the discretion of the parents.

(b) Payment

In the UK, neither sperm nor egg donors can be paid. Under section 41, paying donors in contravention of this standard licence condition is a criminal offence, unless authorized by directions. It is possible to receive compensation for expenses due to the donation, such as travel or child-care costs and time off work, although the latter compensation is subject to a ceiling of £61.28 per day (in line with the rules on compensation for loss of earnings for jury service), up to a maximum upper ceiling of £250.

Egg-sharing schemes are, however, permitted. These involve a woman who needs IVF treatment agreeing to donate half of the eggs retrieved during one cycle in return for free or much cheaper treatment for herself. Given inadequate NHS funding, these schemes are clearly very attractive to women who need treatment, but cannot afford the costs of around £4,000 per cycle. There cannot be any doubt that egg-sharing schemes involve substantial, albeit

---

[52] Andrew Bainham, 'Arguments about Parentage' (2008) 67 Cambridge Law Journal 322–51.
[53] 'Gamete Donation and Anonymity: The Legal and Ethical Debate' (2001) 16 Human Reproduction 818–24, 823.

indirect, payment for egg donation. The absolute prohibition on direct payment therefore coexists, perhaps oddly, with legitimate 'payment in kind' of several thousands of pounds.

Egg-sharing schemes carry no extra clinical risk, since the donor would be having the egg retrieval in any event. It has, however, been suggested that there may be psychological issues for women who share their eggs but whose own treatment fails. Knowing that another women might have been successfully treated with her eggs may be disconcerting, especially since the children will now have a right to find out her identity, and perhaps make contact, when they reach adulthood.

In the United States, egg donors are paid substantial sums of money: reimbursement for expenses, time, risk, and discomfort is typically between $2,000 and $5,000 per donation. Much higher sums—as much as $50,000—have reportedly been paid to models and Ivy League students and graduates. In the next extract, David Resnik defends paid egg donation.

David Resnik[54]

Some ethicists have pointed out that allowing the commodification of human tissues could destroy or threaten the gift relationship that currently exists between donors and recipients, which is an important moral value. If human tissues are assigned an economic value, they will no longer be considered gifts and people will sell tissues instead of giving them...

The mere fact that an object can be bought or sold need not destroy our ability to transfer that object as a gift. Many commodities that are routinely bought and sold are also given as gifts...People have reasons and motives for giving gifts, even when those gifts have commercial value. Of course, commodification may have some impact on the gift relationship: the ability to legally commodify something may encourage people to sell that thing instead of giving it as a gift. But once again, this is a speculative claim for which we have little evidence.

(c) Screening

There are certain limits upon who may donate their gametes. The HFEA imposes an upper age limit of 55 for male donors and 35 for female donors, and a lower age limit of 18 for both sexes. These restrictions are relaxed for the storage of an individual's gametes for their own treatment, so a 16-year-old who is about to undergo treatment for cancer could legitimately have his sperm stored for his own future use.

All donated sperm must be frozen to enable the HIV status of the donor to be conclusively established by a further HIV test six months after the donation was made. Egg donors too must be tested for HIV, but because eggs are used immediately, rather than being frozen for future use, nothing can be done to eliminate the risk that the donor was in the pre-seroconversion 'window' between infection and its detectability. Clinics are also expected to give careful consideration to the suitability of donors, taking into account their personal and family medical history, their potential fertility, including whether they have children of their own, and their attitude towards donation. It is, however, impossible to guarantee that the donor's medical history is accurate. Nor is it possible to screen gametes for all hereditary diseases.

As the number of identifiable genetic conditions increases, and the costs of screening decrease, there will inevitably be pressure upon clinics to carry out more extensive tests on

[54] 'Regulating the Market in Human Eggs' (2001) 15 Bioethics 1–25.

donated gametes. If a child is born suffering from a condition passed on by the gamete donor, it is also possible that the parents and the child herself could argue that failure to screen for the particular disease was a breach of the clinic's duty of care. Such actions would be similar to the 'wrongful birth' and 'wrongful life' claims that we considered in the previous chapter. As we saw in the previous chapter, the courts have been hostile to a child's claim that the defendant should have prevented her birth, and so in practice the parents would have to argue that, had they been told of the risk of a particular genetic condition, they would have rejected the gametes that were used in their treatment, and the harm—that is the child's birth—would have been avoided. It might also be possible to sue the gamete donor under the Congenital Disabilities (Civil Liability) Act 1976 (which we also considered in the previous chapter) for intentional or negligent failure to disclose an inherited condition, but as yet no such claims have been made.

(d) Number of offspring

There is a limit on the number of children that may be produced from the gametes of one donor, which is expressed as 'up to ten families'. Clearly, this is less specific than an upper limit of, say, ten children, but since under the previous 'ten live birth event' limit, it was always possible to extend this for sibling use, it was thought clearer to tell donors how many *families* could be created using their sperm. It is very unlikely that an egg donor would donate sufficient eggs to come anywhere near this upper limit.

Donors are entitled to set a lower limit, if they choose. Usually this is done where the donor is known to the recipient. A man might decide to donate sperm to his infertile brother's wife, but not be willing for it to be used by anyone else. He would therefore set a limit of one (named) family. Some people thought that the abolition of anonymity would lead more donors to set lower limits, in order to limit the number of potential children who might make contact eighteen years later, but there does not seem to be any evidence that this has happened.

The British Fertility Society has suggested—in the light of the shortage of donated sperm in the UK—that it would make sense to set a higher number than ten families, drawing attention to the fact that in the Netherlands, which has a much smaller and less geographically dispersed population, the upper limit is 25.[55] Others argue that it may be challenging for children to come to terms with the prospect of having a very large number of half-siblings.

(g) PARENTAGE

A further special feature of treatment with donated gametes is the separation of genetic and social parenthood. In such circumstances, how do we determine the identity of a child's legal parents? While the rules covering the identity of the child's mother are clear and unambiguous, for fathers and 'second legal parents' (in the case of same-sex couples), the law is a little more complicated.

An added complexity is the way in which the changes to the rules on parenthood, effected by the 2008 reforms, have been brought into force. Sections 27 and 28 of the 1990 Act remain on the face of the statute, because these provisions describe the ascription of parenthood for children born before the new law came into force in 2009. For children whose mothers were treated using donated sperm before April 2009, fatherhood is governed by section 28 of the 1990 Act.

The new parenthood provisions apply only to children whose mothers were treated with donated sperm after April 2009, and they have not been incorporated into the 1990 Act

---

[55] British Fertility Society, 'Working Party on Sperm Donation Services in the UK' (2008) 11 Human Fertility 147–58.

like the other 2008 amendments. Instead, they are to be found in the self-standing Human Fertilisation and Embryology Act 2008.

(1) Maternity

At common law,[56] and under both the 1990 Act (section 27) and the 2008 Act, the woman who gives birth to a child is her mother.

Human Fertilisation and Embryology Act 2008 section 33

> 33(1) The woman who is carrying or has carried a child as a result of the placing in her of an embryo or of sperm and eggs, and no other woman, is to be treated as the mother of the child.

Hence, the woman who gives birth is always the child's legal mother, regardless of whether they are genetically related. Indeed, section 47 of the 2008 Act spells out that a woman cannot be treated as the child's other parent merely because of egg donation. In some ways, this is redundant. Given the clarity of the rule that the woman who gives birth is *always* the child's mother, an egg donor could never be treated as the mother of any child born following egg donation. The reason for this provision is probably so that lesbian couples are clear that, for both of them to acquire parenthood, they need to fulfil the parenthood conditions or be civil partners. An arrangement whereby the egg of one partner was used but the other carried the pregnancy would not automatically result in both women being parents.

It is also irrelevant that the egg donation procedure itself took place in a country with different rules about parenthood. If a woman gives birth to a child in the UK, she is the child's mother.

(2) Paternity

(a) Married couples

If the woman receiving treatment is married, both the 1990 Act (section 28 (5)) and the 2008 Act (section 38(2)) provide for two routes that allow her husband to be recognized as the child's father. First, under section 28(5) of the 1990 Act and 38(2) of the 2008 Act, the presumption of paternity within marriage remains intact. In sperm donor cases, this presumption of paternity could be rebutted by DNA tests which would establish that the husband is not the biological father of the child.

Second, the presumption in section 35 of the 2008 Act (section 28(2) of the 1990 Act) applies, and provides that the mother's husband will be the father unless he did not consent to her treatment.

Human Fertilisation and Embryology Act 2008 section 35

> 35(1) If—
>
> (a) at the time of the placing in her of the embryo or of the sperm and eggs or of her artificial insemination, W was a party to a marriage, and

---

[56] *The Ampthill Peerage Case* [1977] AC 547.

(b) the creation of the embryo carried by her was not brought about with the sperm of the other party to the marriage, then, subject to section 38(2) to (4), the other party to the marriage is to be treated as the father of the child unless it is shown that he did not consent to the placing in her of the embryo or the sperm and eggs or to her artificial insemination (as the case may be).

In *Re CH (Contact: Parentage)*,[57] the husband had given written consent to his wife's treatment with donor insemination, and he had been registered as the child's father. The couple subsequently divorced, and the mother sought to prevent her former husband from obtaining a contact order on the grounds that he was not the child's biological father, and so did not benefit from the presumption in favour of contact. Callman J found that this father fitted squarely within the terms of the legislation, and that it would therefore be contrary to the intentions of Parliament to deny that he was the child's legal father.

(b) Unmarried fathers before April 2009

Where a child's mother was treated with donated sperm before April 2009, and the mother is not married, under section 28(3) of the 1990 Act, her male partner will be the child's father if they were provided with treatment services together.

On a literal interpretation, the wording of this section is puzzling because it is not clear in what sense the partner of a woman undergoing donor insemination is actually being *treated* by the clinic. This question has been considered by the courts, and it has been decided that a man will acquire fatherhood under this section if he and his partner jointly requested treatment 'as a couple'.[58]

(c) Agreed fatherhood conditions after April 2009

Where the woman having treatment is not married or in a civil partnership (see below), and wishes a man to be the father of a child conceived using donated sperm, the agreed father-hood conditions apply:

Human Fertilisation and Embryology Act 2008 section 37

The agreed fatherhood conditions

37(1) The agreed fatherhood conditions referred to in section 36(b) are met in relation to a man ("M") in relation to treatment provided to W under a licence if, but only if,—

(a) M has given the person responsible a notice stating that he consents to being treated as the father of any child resulting from treatment provided to W under the licence,

(b) W has given the person responsible a notice stating that she consents to M being so treated,

(c) neither M nor W has, since giving notice under paragraph (a) or (b), given the person responsible notice of the withdrawal of M's or W's consent to M being so treated,

(d) W has not, since the giving of the notice under paragraph (b), given the person responsible—

---

[57] *U v W (Attorney General Intervening)* [1996] 1 FLR 569.   [58] Ibid.

> (a) a further notice under that paragraph stating that she consents to another man being treated as the father of any resulting child, or
>
> (b) a notice under section 44(1)(b) stating that she consents to a woman being treated as a parent of any resulting child, and
>
> (e) W and M are not within prohibited degrees of relationship in relation to each other.

Thus under the new legislation, fatherhood can be acquired essentially by virtue of the consent of both mother and father. It is interesting that the government did not choose to confine access to 'agreed fatherhood' to the mother's unmarried partner. Other legislation, such as the Human Tissue Act, contain statutory definitions of partner ('living together in an enduring family relationship'), but no such restriction applies here. The only limit upon who may become a father under these provisions is that he cannot be within the prohibited degrees of relationship (for the purposes of incest) with the woman. This means that, with his consent, a woman can agree to a male friend becoming her child's father, but she could not agree to her brother being the father of her child.

(d) Same-sex couples

Under the 1990 Act, the female partner of a woman undergoing treatment with donated sperm could not acquire parenthood from birth, as was possible for male partners, both married and unmarried. The woman's female partner would be a legal stranger to the child at birth, but could subsequently apply for a parental responsibility order or could become the child's second parent via adoption. The 2008 Act changes this, and, with the exception of a difference in terminology, equalizes the position of civil partners and husbands, and treats unmarried same-sex and heterosexual partners in the same way.

The terminological difference is that while a mother's male partner can become the child's father from birth, the woman's same-sex partner cannot become the child's mother. If a child has two female parents, the one who gives birth will be the mother, and the other one is described as a second legal parent.

(i) Civil partners
Same-sex civil partners are in the same position as husbands in relation to the acquisition of parenthood.

Human Fertilisation and Embryology Act 2008 section 42

Woman in civil partnership at time of treatment

42(1) If at the time of the placing in her of the embryo or the sperm and eggs or of her artificial insemination, W was a party to a civil partnership, then subject to section 45(2) to (4), the other party to the civil partnership is to be treated as a parent of the child unless it is shown that she did not consent to the placing in W of the embryo or the sperm and eggs or to her artificial insemination (as the case may be).

(ii) Agreed female parenthood conditions
For non-civilly partnered same-sex couples, the agreed female parenthood conditions mirror the agreed fatherhood conditions for unmarried heterosexual couples. Once again, the only restriction on who may become a second legal parent in this way is that she must not

lie within the prohibited degrees of relationship, so a woman's sister could not become her child's second female parent.

Human Fertilisation and Embryology Act 2008 section 44

The agreed female parenthood conditions

44(1) The agreed female parenthood conditions referred to in section 43(b) are met in relation to another woman ("P") in relation to treatment provided to W under a licence if, but only if,—

(a) P has given the person responsible a notice stating that P consents to P being treated as a parent of any child resulting from treatment provided to W under the licence,

(b) W has given the person responsible a notice stating that W agrees to P being so treated,

(c) neither W nor P has, since giving notice under paragraph (a) or (b), given the person responsible notice of the withdrawal of P's or W's consent to P being so treated,

(d) W has not, since the giving of the notice under paragraph (b), given the person responsible—

(i) a further notice under that paragraph stating that W consents to a woman other than P being treated as a parent of any resulting child, or

(ii) a notice under section 37(1)(b) stating that W consents to a man being treated as the father of any resulting child, and

(e) W and P are not within prohibited degrees of relationship in relation to each other.

It is perhaps noteworthy that the outcry in Parliament and in the press over the move to delete the largely symbolic reference to the child's 'need for a father' was not mirrored by similar criticism of these radical changes to the parenthood provisions, which permit a child to have, in law, two female parents.

In the next extract, Andrew Bainham suggests that the move to recognize the mother's partner (female or male), as the child's 'parent', rather than someone exercising parental responsibility, are regrettable. Parentage, according to Bainham, is a biological kinship relationship, not a social one.

Andrew Bainham[59]

The argument, therefore, is that while it may be appropriate to give to the lesbian partner and other social parents parental responsibility (depending on the extent to which the individual actually performs parenting functions), it is *inappropriate* to make that person the legal parent because this is to distort and misrepresent kinship. The lesbian partner's mother and father, for example, would become the child's grandparents and her brothers and sisters the child's uncles and aunts....

The concept of parentage should rather be confined, to reflect as far as possible the unique position of biological parents and, through the child's filiation with them, the wider kinship links to the extended maternal and paternal families.

---

[59] 'Arguments about Parentage' (2008) 67 Cambridge Law Journal 322–51.

Privileging the genetic tie as the hallmark of familial relationships in this way is, however, controversial. Many would argue that we should recognize as a child's parents the individuals who do the exhausting and sometimes thankless work of parenting, rather than someone who simply shares some of her DNA.

(e) Single women

The final category of patients envisaged by the Act is women who do not wish anyone to be their child's second parent. Women whose husbands or civil partners do not consent to their treatment will also fall within this group. In these situations, the child has no legal father.

(f) What about transsexual parents?

The statutory scheme does not specifically address the possibility of transsexual parenthood. While normally couples who use their own gametes in treatment are self-evidently the child's parents, and not subject to any special rules, this may not be true for transsexual parents. People who store gametes or embryos created using their gametes before they undergo gender reassignment may find that their stored genetic material has to be treated as that of a third-party donor, rather than as their own.

If a male-to-female transsexual wants her female partner to be inseminated using sperm she stored before she became a woman, she could become the child's second legal parent, via the 'agreed parenthood conditions', rather than being the parent because her own gametes were used in treatment.

Similarly, if a female-to-male transsexual had eggs, or embryos created with her eggs. stored before gender reassignment, these could be used in the treatment of his female partner, but the transsexual man could again only acquire fatherhood through the agreed parenthood conditions, rather than because he is the child's genetic 'mother'.

Not only are both the statutory provisions and the HFEA's Code of Practice silent about the possibility of transsexual parenthood, but also, as Sheelagh McGuinness and Amel Alghrani point out, it is interesting that the preservation of fertility is not a routine aspect of preparation for gender reassignment surgery, in the same way as it is for patients undergoing treatment for cancer.

Sheelagh McGuinness and Amel Alghrani[60]

There is some evidence which suggests that transsexuals are not being counselled about their reproductive options pre-operatively. This may be due to the fact that in the past, infertility was seen as a 'price to pay' for transitioning—being a transsexual and being a parent were seen as mutually exclusive. We reject the notion that transsexuals have in some way chosen to be infertile and that this negates their rights to access artificial reproductive technologies. It is, correctly we believe, no longer accepted that same sex couples have somehow waived any options to parent by the mere fact they have elected to be in a relationship where natural reproduction is not possible. Nor do patients who elect treatment that may affect their fertility waive their reproductive interests; it is recognised that patients undergoing cancer treatment should be counselled about fertility preservation techniques. Transsexuals should not be deemed to have chosen to be infertile by opting for a treatment that results in infertility.

[60] 'Gender and Parenthood: The Case for Realignment' (2008) 16 Medical Law Review 261–83.

In addition to preserving fertility through sperm or egg/embryo freezing, a more dramatic way to become a transsexual parent arose in the US when a female-to-male transsexual, Thomas Beatie, became pregnant. He had not had his female reproductive organs removed, but had relied upon testosterone therapy and reconstructive surgery to change gender. Beatie was now married to a woman who had had a hysterectomy. In order to start a family, they decided that he would stop taking testosterone in order to become pregnant. He gave birth to a healthy girl in 2008, and became pregnant again soon afterwards.[61]

(g) Disputes about paternity/second parenthood

In practice, a patient's partner will be asked to sign consent forms that specify his or her agreement to being treated as the child's legal father or second legal parent prior to the provision of infertility treatment. Disputes are therefore uncommon, although not unprecedented.

In *Re D (A Child)*,[62] the House of Lords confirmed that whether an unmarried couple were being 'treated together' for the purposes of section 28 of the 1990 Act should be judged at the time of embryo transfer or insemination, and not when the couple were first accepted for treatment.

This case involved a woman, who had previously received unsuccessful treatment with donated gametes together with her partner, returning to the clinic after their relationship had ended. However, she did not tell the clinic that she was no longer being treated together with her ex-partner, and the clinic relied upon the consent forms signed previously by her and her ex-partner. After she gave birth to a child, her ex-partner applied for parental responsibility and contact orders, but the House of Lords held that they had not been treated together at the relevant time and so he could not be the child's father.

A different sort of dispute arose in *Leeds Teaching Hospital NHS Trust v A*, where Mr and Mrs A (who were white) were having treatment at the same time as Mr and Mrs B (who were black). Mr B's sperm was used to fertilize Mrs A's eggs by mistake, and Mrs A subsequently gave birth to mixed-race twins. Dame Elizabeth Butler-Sloss agreed that Mr A should be able to acquire fatherhood via adoption, but since Mr A had not consented to the treatment which his wife actually received, he was unable to acquire paternity under section 28(2).

Leeds Teaching Hospital NHS Trust v A[63]

Dame Elizabeth Butler-Sloss P

Looking superficially at s 28(2), it might appear that Mr A could be the legal father of the twins, since, at the time of the placing in Mrs A of the embryo, Mrs A was a party to the marriage with Mr A and the creation of the embryo carried by her was not brought about with the sperm of Mr A. The application of sub-s (2), however, is subject to two provisos. The first is contained in s 28(5) and provides for the common law presumption of legitimacy of a child born to a mother during her marriage. In the present case, that presumption is displaced by the DNA tests which established that Mr B is the biological father of the twins.

The second proviso, contained in sub-s (2) itself, is the requirement of the husband's consent. Subsection (2) applies unless it is shown that Mr A 'did not consent to...her

---

[61] James Bone, 'Pregnant Man, Thomas Beatie Gives Birth to Baby Girl', The Times, July 4, 2008.
[62] [2005] UKHL 33.   [63] [2003] EWHC 259.

insemination'....The question is whether Mr A consented to the insemination of Mrs A by a third person...

On the clear evidence provided in the consent forms Mr A plainly did not consent to the sperm of a named or anonymous donor being mixed with his wife's eggs. This was clearly an embryo created without the consent of Mr and Mrs A....I am satisfied that, on the proper interpretation of s 28(2)...Mr A did not consent to the placing in his wife of the embryo which was actually placed. Accordingly, s 28(2) does not apply.

In my judgment the twins' rights to respect for their family life with their mother and Mr A can be met by appropriate family or adoption orders...Although they lose the immediate certainty of the irrebuttable presumption that Mr A is their legal father, they will remain within a loving, stable and secure home. They also retain the great advantage of preserving the reality of their paternal identity...

I...am certain that the truth in this case is more important to the rights of the twins and their welfare than a fictional certainty. This is not a sperm donor case and should not be treated as such when considering the position of the twins. To refuse to recognise Mr B as their biological father is to distort the truth about which some day the twins will have to learn through knowledge of their paternal identity.

(h) OPENING THE REGISTER

While the HFEA register contains information on all types of treatment, it is particularly significant in the case of treatment involving donated gametes, because it is in these cases that the register will be 'opened' in order to provide information to donor-conceived people, and, in the future, to donors too. The first requests for information under the 1990 Act became possible in 2007 when the first children born since the Act came into force in 1991 reached the age of 16, and could ask if they were related to a potential spouse. In 2009, the first children became 18, and could ask for futher non-identifying information. Whether or not many requests will be made, and at what age people are likely to seek access to information is not yet known, though we do know that most children do not know that they are donor-conceived, and so the numbers coming forward are likely to be relatively low. For donor-conceived people who do know that the register holds information about them, it is anticipated that they may be more likely to seek information about the circumstances of their conception when they are contemplating marriage or starting a family themselves.

More requests for information are likely in the future when children conceived using an identifiable donor become old enough to access information. When this happens, offspring will be told of the donor's:

(a) full names (and any previous names);

(b) date of birth and town or district where born;

(c) last known postal address.

Section 31ZA (3) of the Act provides that before information about donor conception is given, the recipient of the information must have had an opportunity to receive counselling.

The 2008 reforms mean that it is now possible for donor-conceived offspring to find out non-identifying information about the number, age, and sex of any half-siblings, and, if they and the other siblings consent, to find out identifying information about each other. Donors can be told the number, age, and sex of children born following donation, but not the children's identity. Where relevant, donors can also be warned that a person conceived using their gametes has made a request for identifying information, though, of course, it will only be possible to inform them if they have kept the clinic or the HFEA informed of any change of address.

(i) PREIMPLANTATION GENETIC DIAGNOSIS (PGD)

(1) What is PGD?

When a newly fertilized egg has started the process of cell division, it is possible to remove one or two of its cells without compromising its capacity for normal development. The removed cell(s) can then be tested in order to detect certain genetic abnormalities. Affected embryos are discarded and only unaffected embryos will be transferred to the woman's uterus or frozen for use in future treatment. It is also possible to discover the embryo's sex, and hence avoid the transmission of X-linked conditions, such as haemophilia, which only affect boys. Because females have two X-chromosomes, they will invariably have a 'normal' gene that can correct a defective gene on the other X-chromosome. Males, on the other hand, have only one X-chromosome, so if they inherit a defective gene on the X-chromosome, they will usually develop the disease in question.

Preimplantation genetic diagnosis (PGD) is used by couples who are at risk of passing on a genetic disorder, and who will often have already had affected children or pregnancies. PGD, if successful, enables such couples to start a pregnancy in the knowledge that the resulting child will not have a particular abnormality, and enables them to avoid prenatal diagnosis and abortion. Because PGD inevitably means that fewer embryos are available for transfer than in a normal IVF cycle, live birth rates are lower.

Removing one cell from a four-cell embryo, and testing it is an extremely complex and time-consuming process, requiring considerable technical expertise, and costing much more than regular IVF. Because it is used to prevent the birth of children who will suffer from serious diseases (which may be very expensive to treat), many couples receive at least some financial contribution from their PCT. It is by no means a common procedure: since the first reported PGD births in 1990, fewer than 10,000 cycles have been performed worldwide.

(2) How is PGD Regulated?

So when will the use of PGD be authorized? Until the 2008 amendments, the 1990 Act did not mention the circumstances in which PGD would be legitimate, and these were instead developed by the HFEA and set out in its Code of Practice. Now, however, the statute contains detailed provisions about the circumstances in which PGD is, and is not, acceptable.

Human Fertilisation and Embryology Act 1990 schedule 2

Activities for which licences may be granted

Licences for treatment: embryo testing

1ZA (1) A licence . . . cannot authorise the testing of an embryo, except for one or more of the following purposes—

(a) establishing whether the embryo has a gene, chromosome or mitochondrial abnormality that may affect its capacity to result in a live birth.

(b) in a case where there is a particular risk that the embryo may have any gene, chromosome or mitochondrion abnormality, establishing whether it has that abnormality or any other gene, chromosome or mitochondrion abnormality,

(c) in a case where there is a particular risk that any resulting child will have or develop—

(i) a gender-related serious physical or mental disability,

(ii) a gender-related serious illness, or

(iii) any other gender-related serious medical condition,

establishing the sex of the embryo,

(2) A licence...cannot authorise the testing of embryos for the purpose mentioned in sub-paragraph (1)(b) unless the Authority is satisfied—

(a) in relation to the abnormality of which there is a particular risk, and

(b) in relation to any other abnormality for which testing is to be authorised under sub-paragraph (1)(b), that there is a significant risk that a person with the abnormality will have or develop a serious physical or mental disability, a serious illness or any other serious medical condition.

(3) For the purposes of sub-paragraph (1)(c), a physical or mental disability, illness or other medical condition is gender-related if the Authority is satisfied that—

(a) it affects only one sex, or

(b) it affects one sex significantly more than the other.

In many ways, the detail in Schedule 2 simply reproduces the rules that the HFEA had already developed. Embryo testing is acceptable where there is a significant risk that the child to be born will have or develop a serious illness, disability, or other condition.

It is possible to choose the sex of a child, but only where there is a risk that the child would have a serious gender-related condition. This sort of medical sex selection is likely to become less common as more sophisticated tests are developed so that it is possible to exclude only embryos that have, in fact, inherited the sex-linked condition, rather than the cruder technique of excluding all male embryos. If male embryos that are free from the sex-linked condition can also be used in treatment, the couple will have more embryos available for transfer, and thus a greater chance of achieving a successful pregnancy. It is not possible to choose the child's sex for social reasons, such as 'family balancing'.

(a) What is a serious disease?

Many genetic conditions self-evidently meet this threshold level of seriousness. If a child is born with Tay-Sachs disease, for example, her nervous system will start to degenerate during her first year of life, and she will die within three or four years. In the next extract, Søren Holm suggests that it will, at other times, be difficult to draw a line between severe and non-severe conditions.

Søren Holm[64]

[I]t is very difficult to produce a non-arbitrary dividing line between severe and non-severe conditions...It is disabling to be blind and deaf at the same time, and no amount of re-description can change that...

There are, however, many conditions where the situation is not nearly as clear. Many conditions are not universally disabling but only disabling in specific circumstances. Severe myopia (near-sightedness) is only marginally disabling in our society, whereas it was a severe disability before the invention of glasses...A more serious problem is that severity varises not only historically but according to the precise social context of each affected person. Even if we assume that the physical and psychological manifestations of a given condition are constant, there will be many conditions where the impact on the person with the condition will vary quite markedly. The degree to which for instance a severe case of club foot will affect a person will depend on the kind of family he or she is born into—whether physical or more sedate pursuits are the centre of family life—and the kind of other abilities which the person has. The severity in the global sense of a severe case of club foot is thus not determined by the medical severity of the condition. Two persons with the same medical severity might end up being widely separated on the global severity scale.

The statute appears to assume that an objective assessment of seriousness is possible, whereas many have argued that different people will judge seriousness differently. The Code of Practice acknowledges this, and instead suggests that when deciding whether to offer PGD, the family's particular circumstances and their subjective views of the condition in question are relevant.

HFEA Code of Practice 8th edition paras 10.4, 10.5, and 10.6

10.4 When deciding if it is appropriate to provide PGD in particular cases, the centre should consider the circumstances of those seeking treatment, rather than the particular heritable condition.

10.5 ...The perception of the level of risk for those seeking treatment will also be an important factor in the decision-making process.

10.6 The centre should consider the following factors when deciding if PGD is appropriate in particular cases:

(a) the views of the people seeking treatment in relation to the condition to be avoided, including their previous reproductive experience

(b) the likely degree of suffering associated with the condition

(c) the availability of effective therapy, now and in the future

(d) the speed of degeneration in progressive disorders

(e) the extent of any intellectual impairment

(f) the social support available, and

(g) the family circumstances of the people seeking treatment.

---

[64] 'Ethical Issues in Preimplantation Diagnosis' in J Harris and S Holm (eds), *The Future of Human Reproduction* (Clarendon Press: Oxford, 1998).

In Rosamund Scott *et al.*'s empirical research into the views of scientists and health care professionals, it was clear that the couple's previous experience—commonly of having an existing child with the condition—meant that their perception of the condition's seriousness was a very weighty factor. In addition, they found that some couples with an existing child had a further reason to prefer PGD to termination of pregnancy.

Rosamund Scott, Clare Williams, Kathryn Ehrich, and Bobbie Farsides[65]

Doctor 20 recalls an interesting couple:

I saw a couple last week who came for Cystic Fibrosis, a fertile, intelligent couple, who have a Cystic Fibrosis child. And I said, 'What are you doing this for? Why don't you just have another pregnancy?' And they couldn't consider terminating a Cystic child because, firstly they said, 'we do not want to have another child that we have to watch die or be very ill. But on the other hand, if we kind of [terminate the] pregnancy it's like terminating [our existing child]...And we feel we can't do that. And we want some other way of approaching this.'

In this case, the testing seems very much in the interests of the parents: although PGD is not 100% accurate, these parents clearly saw the possibility of a pregnancy achieved through PGD as a way of avoiding the potentially very painful issues they might face if a foetus tested positive for Cystic Fibrosis. The question of trying to avoid the dilemmas around termination is extremely important in PGD...

[W]hen people approach a clinic about the possibility of PGD for something they have experienced in some way, they must think that it is important enough to try to 'do something about it'. As one member of staff put this, 'of course it must be serious for them to come here'.

More fundamental than the difficulty in drawing a line between serious and non-serious conditions is the idea that some disabilities are social rather than medical problems. Until relatively recently, it was thought that disabilities were the result of physiological malfunction, and were a purely medical phenomenon. Now it is increasingly recognized that many people whom we think of as disabled are disabled more by society's attitude towards them, and failure to adapt to their needs, than they are by the condition itself. In the next extract, Jonathan Glover argues that only disabilities which limit functioning and human flourishing should properly be described as disabilities.

Jonathan Glover[66]

Belonging to a minority that suffers discrimination is not a disability. One consequence may be the need to reclassify some conditions now thought of as disabilities. For instance, achondroplasia, severely restricted height resulting from a genetic mutation, is normally classified as a disability. But the purely functional impairments are trivial, such as needing a stool to boost height when speaking in public. Provided that there are no associated medical complications, the only serious disadvantages result from the reactions of other people. This makes

---

[65] 'The Appropriate Extent of Preimplantation Genetic Diagnosis: Health Professionals' and Scientists' View on the Requirement for a Significant Risk of a Serious Genetic Condition' (2007) 15 Medical Law Review 320–56.

[66] *Choosing Children: Genes, Disability and Design* (Clarendon Press,: Oxford, 2006) 10.

it the same as being Jewish in an anti-Semitic society or gay in a homophobic society. This could push us towards saying that sometimes ethnic or religious membership, or sexual orientation, can count as a disability. Or, with less offence to our linguistic and moral intu‐itions, we can say that achondroplasia is not a disability.

(b) Adult-onset conditions

It is possible to carry out PGD for some adult-onset genetic conditions, such as Huntington's disease, and for an increased *susceptibility* to late-onset diseases, such as breast cancer. The child would be born healthy, but would be at risk of developing a serious disease in adult-hood. As we saw in Chapter 8, the gene responsible for Huntington's disease has a pene-trance of 100 per cent, which means that if you inherit the gene, then unless you die first from an unrelated cause, you will develop Huntington's disease.

In 2006, the HFEA carried out a public consultation on the use of PGD for lower pene-trance late-onset genetic conditions, such as breast, bowel, and ovarian cancer. Most cancers are not genetic, but there are some genes, like BRCA1 and 2, which are responsible for fewer than 5 per cent of all cases of breast cancer, but which greatly increase the risk of developing the condition, usually at a much younger age than normal. Someone with a faulty BRCA1 or BRCA2 gene may have an 80 per cent chance of developing breast cancer and a 60 per cent chance of developing ovarian cancer.

Following this public consultation,[67] the HFEA decided that, in principle, it would be acceptable to use PGD to detect these lower penetrance late-onset conditions. Since then, it has licensed PGD for a number of different cancer susceptibility genes. At the beginning of 2009 it was announced that the first child had been born following preimplantation testing for the BRCA1 mutation.

Of course, unless PGD is permitted for all susceptibility genes, it may become necessary to draw a line between penetrance which *does* justify PGD and penetrance which *does not*. Yet locating the tipping point on the scale between an 85 per cent risk—which clearly is substantial—and a one per cent risk, which is not, is going to be difficult, not least because a range of other factors, such as the risk of mortality, age of onset, and availability of treatment options may affect our judgement about whether PGD would be appropriate.

(c) Carrier embryos

It is possible to detect whether embryos are carriers of recessive disorders. These are dis-eases, like cystic fibrosis, where the defective gene must be inherited from both parents for the disease to manifest itself. Someone who has only one copy of the defective gene will be a carrier of the disease, but will not develop it herself. If she reproduces with another carrier, her offspring will have a one in four chance of receiving a double dose and inheriting the disease, and a fifty-fifty chance of inheriting one gene, and again being a carrier.

If a carrier embryo implants and is successfully carried to term, the resulting child will be free from the particular condition, but might go on to have a sick child or face diffi-cult reproductive choices in the future. Testing for carrier status alone would not fit within the statutory criteria. In practice, however, carrier embryos may be identified during PGD cycles carried out where *both* parents are carriers, and are undergoing PGD in order to avoid the birth of a child with a recessive condition. In such circumstances, if there are embryos

---

[67] Choices and Boundaries (HFEA, 2006), available at <www.hfea.gov.uk>.

which are neither affected nor carriers, it may make sense to transfer those embryos to the woman's womb.

(d) Testing for disability

The 2008 Act amendments prohibit a further possible use of PGD, namely where would-be patients want to positively select embryos which are affected by a particular condition, such as congenital deafness. No such cases had arisen under the previous law, but it had been anticipated that clinicians might be likely to invoke section 13(5)—the need to take the future child's welfare into account—in order to refuse to provide such services. Now the positive selection of embryos or donors known to have a particular abnormality is specifically prohibited.

Human Fertilisation and Embryology Act 1990 section 13

13(9) Persons or embryos that are known to have a gene, chromosome or mitochondrion abnormality involving a significant risk that a person with the abnormality will have or develop—

(a) a serious physical or mental disability,

(b) a serious illness, or

(c) any other serious medical condition,

must not be preferred to those that are not known to have such an abnormality.

The Act does not ban the transfer of affected embryos: rather, it does not allow them to be 'preferred'. This means that it is not possible to select embryos known to suffer from congenital deafness, where unaffected embryos are available. But if the *only* embryos suitable for transfer happen to be affected, then they would not be being preferred to embryos known not to suffer from the condition, and it would therefore be acceptable to transfer them to the woman's womb. The reason this scenario is very unlikely to arise is that in order to be in a position to choose embryos known to be affected by a genetic abnormality, the couple must have undergone PGD in order to *avoid* the birth of an affected child. Couples who wish to have affected children are very unlikely to be in this position, and much more likely to reproduce naturally, when there is a one in four chance of having an affected child.

One possible scenario when section 13(9) might come into play is if a woman stored embryos before undergoing treatment for ovarian cancer, which has left her infertile. If her cancer has a genetic origin—BRCA1, for example—she may wish to have those stored embryos screened for this mutation. Let us imagine that, following screening, there are no embryos suitable for transfer which do not have the BRCA1 mutation. In that scenario, she may take the view that she would rather have a child who was at risk of developing cancer in later life, rather than not having a genetically related child. She would not then be *preferring* an embryo with an abnormality. Before providing such treatment, however, the clinician would be under a duty to take account of the welfare of any child who may be born.

Section 13(9) also provides that a couple must not prefer a gamete donor *because* they suffer from a condition like congenital deafness. However, if a couple 'prefer' to use a relative—say, the infertile man's brother—as a donor, and he *happens* to be deaf, it could be argued that they would not be preferring him *because of his deafness*, but rather because of his genetic relatedness. Of course, it is almost impossible to legislate for people's preferences, and so a couple might prefer to use a deaf donor, but as long as they have other grounds for preferring the deaf man, it would be hard to *prove* that deafness was the principal reason for his selection.

During the legislative process, this provision was heavily criticized by disability groups, and perhaps most vociferously by the deaf community, who argued that it sent a negative message about living with disability. A deaf couple, who already had a deaf child but were contemplating using IVF in order to have a second child, became a focus of media attention. They did not want to positively select a deaf embryo, and would be equally happy to have a hearing child, but they did not want to be compelled to reject an embryo on the grounds of its deafness.[68]

In the next extract, Julian Savulescu criticizes the prohibition on selecting for deafness from another direction, sometimes described as the non-identity problem. He argues that, unless the child's life would be so impaired as to be not worth living, it will always be better to be born rather than not born, and hence positively selecting for disability should be allowed.

Julian Savulescu[69]

> What if a couple has in vitro fertilisation and preimplantation genetic diagnosis and they select a deaf embryo? Have they harmed that child? Is that child worse off than it would otherwise have been (that is, if they had selected a different embryo)? No—another (different) child would have existed. The deaf child is harmed by being selected to exist only if his or her life is so bad it is not worth living. Deafness is not that bad. Because reproductive choices to have a disabled child do not harm the child, couples who select disabled rather than non-disabled offspring should be allowed to make those choices, even though they may be having a child with worse life prospects....
>
> Reproduction should be about having children who have the best prospects. But to discover what are the best prospects, we must give individual couples the freedom to act on their own value judgment of what constitutes a life of prospect.

(3) Is PGD Acceptable?

The use of PGD has been fiercely criticized by commentators such as David King, who argue that it amounts to a new form of free-market eugenics.

David King[70]

> In PGD, parents adopt a far more pro-active, directing role, choosing their children in a way which is not so far removed from their experience as consumers, choosing amongst different products.

---

[68] Robin McKie and Gaby Hinsliff, 'This Couple Want a Deaf Child. Should We Try to Stop Them?' *The Observer*, 9 March 2008.

[69] 'Deaf Lesbians, "Designer Disability", and the Future of Medicine' (2002) 325 British Medical Journal 771–3.

[70] 'Preimplantation Genetic Diagnosis and the "New" Eugenics' (1999) 25 Journal of Medical Ethics 176–81.

There are a number of reasons why unrestricted free-market eugenics would be highly undesirable. Firstly, selecting the 'best' amongst multiple embryos sets up a new relationship between parents and offspring...They are no longer a gift from God, or the random forces of nature, but selected products, expressing, in part, their parents' aspirations, desires and whims...

At a social level there are further undesirable consequences. Opening the human gene pool to the winds of social market forces on a large scale might have a number of effects. Clearly, there is likely to be a tendency for parents to select offspring which conform best to social norms, with regard to health and physical ability, appearance and aptitudes. Disabled people have often expressed fears that an expanded free-market eugenics would correspondingly lessen society's tolerance for those with congenital and genetic disorders...It is also possible to imagine selection on grounds of IQ, skin colour, physical build and facial features, etc. It does not seem desirable to allow such forces to operate at the level of selection of who is permitted to be born. Rather, we should combat the social forces which lead us to disvalue some individuals and idealise others....

[A] logical consequence of a system of free-market eugenics in societies where large disparities of wealth and social class continue to exist is a gradual polarisation of society into a genetically privileged ruling elite and an underclass.

King is making a slippery slope claim about PGD: namely that allowing people to test for a handful of serious and often fatal diseases makes it more likely that one day parents will pre-select embryos on the basis of much more trivial characteristics, such as sporting ability or intelligence. But, one problem with this argument is that complex characteristics such as these are not purely genetic. Identical twin studies show that there may be some correlation between a person's genetic make-up and characteristics such as intelligence. But if the sole cause were genetic, the correlation would be 100 per cent, which it is not. It is, in any event, far too simplistic to say that there is a single gene *for* these traits, and hence PGD—which is capable only of testing for single gene mutations—could not be used to choose tall or sporty children.

A second problem with King's argument is that it presupposes that PGD is a relatively straightforward and generally successful technique, whereas nothing could be further from the truth. In their ethnographic study of couples who had undergone PGD, Sarah Franklin and Celia Roberts describe how gruelling the process is, and how seldom it succeeds.

Sarah Franklin and Celia Roberts[71]

The question of how patients had 'arrived' at PGD was the first thing couples were asked during interviews—and was always met with lengthy and upsetting replies. These 'how we got to PGD' stories could begin far back in time, with an initial miscarriage, an affected birth, or a chance occurrence, such as reading a newspaper article about PGD. In discussing their 'route' to PGD, couples often provided epic tales of hardship and struggle, in which a characteristic determination featured prominently. 'Getting to PGD' had often involved going through numerous painful experiences—not only of tragic events such as the deaths of children or repeated miscarriages—but also of previous failed forms of treatment, complicated family situations, and challenges to the couple's relationship....

[71] *Born and Made: An Ethnography of Preimplantation Genetic Diagnosis* (Princeton UP, 2006).

> In casual conversations, and also formal interviews with clinicians, nurses, PGD coordin-
> ators and genetic counsellors, a constant and consistent theme is that although PGD is a valid
> and necessary choice, it is not for everyone, is very difficult and often fails....
>
> Coming to terms with ending treatment means, for most couples, coming to terms with its
> failure, and facing the challenge of how to make sense of experiences that will remain with
> them for the rest of their lives.

Colin Gavaghan turns King's argument about the 'message' PGD sends to disabled people on its head. He argues in order to avoid sending a 'message' about the sort of lives that are and are not of value, it would be preferable for PGD to be made freely available, and for the state to play no role in deciding when it is, and is not legitimate.

Colin Gavaghan[72]

> When law and policy restrict the use of PGD to the avoidance of children with genetic
> defects, denying it to those with other values and priorities, it becomes at least arguable that
> our approach to this technology, far from being driven by an agenda of promoting individual
> choice and respecting diversity, is underpinned by judgments about the value of those lives
> that are avoided. It is scarcely surprising if those affected by genetic illnesses or disabilities,
> or those who care about or for such people, look with some offense and suspicion at those
> laws and policies.
>
> It is my contention, though, that their concerns could better be addressed by loosening
> the regulations applicable to PGD, thereby allowing...any other prospective parents to utilize
> this technology to implement their own values and preferences. In so doing, we might avoid
> the imposition by the state of a single, simplistic view of what constitutes "normality" and
> "disability," a view that is clearly not universally shared. The appropriate response—from
> the state, from the public, and from the Authority itself—to the HFEA 's question about the
> desirability of testing for cancer genes should be: "We hold no view on this, other than that
> prospective parents should be permitted to make informed choices for themselves, free
> from coercion, and safe in the knowledge that whatever choice they make will be respected
> and supported." Nothing, I submit, could be further removed from the pernicious taint of
> eugenics.

While fears of 'designer babies', pre-selected for intelligence, beauty, and sporting ability, are grounded in a complete misunderstanding of genetics, there is no doubt that rapid progress in understanding the genetic basis of diseases is going to throw up new issues for the regulation of PGD. Gavaghan's proposal that we should abandon the attempt to draw lines between conditions which do justify the use of PGD and those which do not would remove the need to make difficult decisions in the future, but given the 2008 reforms' much greater specificity about the legitimate uses of PGD, it can be predicted that in the future there is likely to be more rather than less debate over whether conditions meet the threshold level of seriousness.

In the field of genetics there has been especially rapid progress in identifying genes that may play a part in increasing susceptibility to a range of common diseases. If a cell from an

---

[72] 'Right Problem Wrong Solution: A Pro-Choice Response to "Expressivist" Concerns about Preimplantation Genetic Diagnosis' (2007) 16 Cambridge Quarterly of Healthcare Ethics 20–34.

embryo could be tested for a wide range of susceptibility genes, it becomes plausible to offer PGD to people who do not already know that they have a particular genetic disease in their family. Currently, PGD is only available if the clinicians know exactly what genetic mutation they are testing for. People with these sorts of genetic conditions in their family are the exception. In contrast, all of us almost certainly possess increased susceptibility to a range of conditions. When this sort of testing becomes possible, anyone potentially becomes a possible candidate for PGD. In late 2008, it was reported that a London clinic was developing what was referred to as a Genetic MOT for embryos, which could test for multiple conditions.[73]

While very few people are likely to be able to afford to pay thousands of pounds for this sort of testing, people who are *already undergoing IVF* might find paying £1500 for an additional test an attractive possibility.[74]

(4) Tissue Typing

A new use for PGD emerged at the start of the twentieth century. Tissue or HLA (Human Leukocyte Antigen) typing involves taking a cell from an early embryo, in the same way as for PGD, and testing it to see if the resulting child would be a good tissue match for a sick sibling in need of, say, a bone marrow transplant. If the selected embryo is a good tissue match, when the baby is born, blood can be taken from her umbilical cord, and can be used to treat her brother or sister.

When it first considered the issue in 2001, the HFEA initially decided tissue typing could be legitimate in certain circumstances, most notably, the child to be born had to be at risk of suffering from the same genetic disease as their sick older sibling. This meant a distinction was drawn between two couples, the Hashmis, whose son Zain had beta-thalassaemia major, and the Whittakers, whose son Charlie had Diamond Blackfan Anaemia. Each couple wanted to use PGD and tissue typing in order to select an embryo that would be a good tissue match for their sick child. Because Zain Hashmi's condition was genetic, and any future child might also have this disorder, the Hashmis fitted within the HFEA criteria, and so tissue typing could go ahead. In contrast, because Charlie Whittaker's condition was not inherited, the Whittakers were denied access to tissue typing in the UK. They subsequently had treatment in Chicago, and gave birth to a son who proved to be a good tissue match for Charlie.

Following the HFEA's 2001 decision, Josephine Quintavalle, on behalf of a pressure group called CORE (Comment on Reproductive Ethics), brought an application for judicial review. In *Quintavalle (Comment on Reproductive Ethics) v Human Fertilisation and Embryology Authority*, CORE argued that tissue typing was prohibited by the Act, which then defined 'treatment services' as services provided 'for the purpose of assisting women to carry children', including 'practices designed to secure that embryos are in a suitable condition to be placed in a woman or to determine whether embryos are suitable for that purpose'.

At first instance, Maurice Kay J interpreted the definition of 'treatment services' narrowly and literally. Since HLA typing was not *necessary* in order to help a woman to bear a child, it did not fall within this definition, and could not therefore be licensed by the HFEA. His

---

[73] Mark Henderson, 'Genetic MoT will Detect Disease in Unborn Child', The Times, October 24 2008.
[74] See also Z O Merhi and L Pal, 'Gender "Tailored" Conceptions: Should the Option of Embryo Gender Selection be Available to Infertile Couples Undergoing Assisted Reproductive Technology?' (2008) 34 Journal of Medical Ethics 590–93.

decision would not just have prevented the HFEA from licensing HLA typing, however, but would also have made it impossible to license PGD. On appeal, the Court of Appeal unanimously reversed his decision, taking a much more purposive interpretative approach. The House of Lords upheld this, again unanimously.

Quintavalle (Comment on Reproductive Ethics) v Human Fertilisation and Embryology Authority[75]

Lord Hoffmann

[T]he licensing power of the authority is defined in broad terms. Paragraph 1(1) of Sch 2 enables it to authorise a variety of activities (with the possibility of others being added by regulation) provided only that they are done 'in the course of' providing IVF services to the public and appear to the authority 'necessary or desirable' for the purpose of providing those services. Thus, if the concept of suitability in sub-paragraph (d) of 1(1) is broad enough to include suitability for the purposes of the particular mother, it seems to me clear enough that the activity of determining the genetic characteristics of the embryo by way of PGD or HLA typing would be 'in the course of' providing the mother with IVF services and that the authority would be entitled to take the view that it was necessary or desirable for the purpose of providing such services...

I would therefore...hold that both PGD and HLA typing could lawfully be authorised by the authority as activities to determine the suitability of the embryo for implantation within the meaning of para 1(1)(d).

Lord Brown

The fact is that once the concession is made (as necessarily it had to be) that PGD itself is licensable to produce not just a viable foetus but a genetically healthy child, there can be no logical basis for construing the authority's power to end at that point. PGD with a view to producing a healthy child assists a woman to carry a child only in the sense that it helps her decide whether the embryo is 'suitable' and whether she will bear the child. Whereas, however, suitability is for the woman, the limits of permissible embryo selection are for the authority.

Prior to the House of Lords' decision, in 2004 the HFEA reviewed the evidence and changed its policy. There was, the HFEA found, no evidence that embryo biopsy posed a risk to the future health of children. This was not because evidence had proved conclusively that the procedure was safe. Rather there have been too few children born following embryo biopsy for any definitive conclusions to be drawn about the procedure's safety, although there is no evidence that it is *not* safe.

The 2004 guidance replaced the 2001 guidance with a new set of criteria to be taken into account by a licence committee faced with an application for PGD and HLA typing. Most importantly, it is no longer necessary for the recipient child's condition to be inherited, and subsequently, the Fletchers, whose son had the same condition as Charlie Whittaker, were permitted to use tissue typing in the UK, and Mrs Fletcher gave birth to a tissue-matched daughter in 2005.

[75] [2005] UKHL 28.

In 2004, the HFEA also removed the requirement that the intention should be to take cord blood only. Evidence from haemotologists suggested both that there might be circumstances in which a bone marrow transplant might subsequently become necessary, and that extracting bone marrow from a very young child is much less intrusive and painful than adult bone marrow donation. Obviously, the HFEA cannot control subsequent decisions about the medical treatment of children born following licensed treatment and so the previous criterion could not, in practice, prevent a bone marrow transplant from taking place if the cord blood transplant did not work.

The 2008 reforms put the criteria for tissue typing on a statutory footing, and essentially reproduce the HFEA's 2004 policy.

Human Fertilisation and Embryology Act 1990 schedule 2

Activities for which licences may be granted

Embryo testing

1ZA (1) A licence...cannot authorise the testing of an embryo, except for one or more of the following purposes—....

(d) in a case where a person ("the sibling") who is the child of the persons whose gametes are used to bring about the creation of the embryo (or of either of those persons) suffers from a serious medical condition which could be treated by umbilical cord blood stem cells, bone marrow or other tissue of any resulting child, establishing whether the tissue of any resulting child would be compatible with that of the sibling...

1ZA (4) In sub-paragraph (1)(d) the reference to "other tissue" of the resulting child does not include a reference to any whole organ of the child.

Tissue typing can therefore only be done to select a tissue donor for an older sibling, and not for any other family member. It would not, therefore, be possible for a mother who herself needed a bone marrow transplant to undergo tissue typing to select a child who would be a good match. Why not? At first sight, it might seem that the mother in such a case would be contemplating tissue typing for *self-interested* reasons, though, of course, a woman who does not want to leave her existing children without a mother would also be acting out of concern for their welfare. This restriction is not, however, directed at the *intention* behind the request for tissue typing: rather, it reflects the practical reality that while the chance of producing an embryo that is a good tissue match for an existing sibling is 1 in 4, for parents or more distant relatives, the chance of producing a good tissue match is much more remote. For siblings, there is a realistic chance that one IVF cycle will produce at least one compatible embryo, but this is not the case for other relatives.

The Act also confirms that it could be legitimate to use tissue typing where the intention is to take bone marrow or other tissue, provided there is no intention to take a solid organ. This means that it would be possible for parents who have a child with leukaemia, which is currently in remission, to undergo tissue typing so that there would be a tissue-matched sibling, should their leukaemia return and a bone marrow transplant become immediately necessary.

The restriction upon taking a solid organ was inserted during the debates in the Lords. While it undoubtedly means that a clinic could not carry out preimplantation tissue typing *in order to* select a child who would be an organ donor in the future, it could not operate as a lifetime ban on the child who is born ever becoming an organ donor. As we saw in Chapter 11, the Human Tissue Act 2004 does not rule out childhood organ donation, although cases are expected to be very rare, and would require court approval. It is more likely that a child born as a result of tissue typing might choose, when she reaches adulthood, to become a live organ donor for her sick sibling. The Human Fertilisation and Embryology Act could not prevent this happening.

When the 2008 reforms were debated, the creation of what have been called 'saviour siblings' was one of the issues that sparked the greatest controversy and debate. In addition to the arguments against PGD considered in the previous section, tissue typing raises some additional concerns, set out here by Wolf *et al.*

Susan M Wolf, Jeffrey P Kahn, and John E Wagner[76]

[W]e know almost nothing about the psychological impact of being conceived to serve as an HLA-matched donor and save a sibling's life. The effects on the donor child are potentially profound. Indeed, if the cord blood transplant fails or the donor child is otherwise repeatedly considered for harvest over a prolonged period of time, there may be a potential for serious effects. The potential may be all the greater if the donor child comes to resist or refuse further procedures...

Moreover, even if one debates whether using PGD solely to conceive an HLA-matched donor may be said to harm the donor child, this use of PGD exclusively to create an opportunity for later harvesting may be wrong on other grounds, such as violating the ethical injunction to respect each individual and avoid using persons as mere means...

When PGD is used solely to create a donor and the sibling's disorder is non-heritable, then, the only possible benefit to the child-to-be will be the psychological benefit of saving the sibling....

The donor child is at lifelong risk of exploitation, of being told that he or she exists as an insurance policy and tissue source for the sibling, of being repeatedly subjected to testing and harvesting procedures, of being used this way no matter how severe the psychological and physical burden, and of being pressured, manipulated, or even forced over protest.

Wolf *et al.* argue that the child conceived in order to save an older sibling's life is being used solely as a means, and not as an end in herself, thus offending the Kantian imperative (see Chapter 1). Of course, this would be equally true of attempts to have another child naturally who might be a good tissue match, and yet few people would argue that couples like the Hashmis should be prevented from having further children in the hope that they would be a good tissue match for Zain. In any event, a child born following HLA typing is not used *solely* as a means, since she is not abandoned after the donation, but rather is overwhelmingly likely to be loved in her own right as a new and welcome member of the family.

People have children for a wide range of instrumental, and sometimes unedifying reasons, such as trying to save a failing relationship or having an heir to take over the family business. Having a second child in order to provide an only child with a companion is not uncommon. Unless the parents planned to abandon the new child at birth, it is hard to

[76] 'Using Preimplantation Genetic Diagnosis to Create a Stem Cell Donor: Issues, Guidelines and Limits' (2003) 31 Journal of Law, Medicine and Ethics 327.

understand why having a child whose umbilical cord might be able to save their sibling's life should be singled out as an unacceptable parental motivation.

It could also plausibly be argued that although the psychological risks associated with being conceived in order to be a donor are speculative, we *know* that the impact of bereavement in childhood is overwhelmingly negative. Children conceived naturally in an attempt to find a good tissue match are likely to be born into families which either have or will soon experience the death of a child. In the next extract, Sally Sheldon and Stephen Wilkinson argue that child welfare arguments might be mobilized to *support* the use of HLA typing. The child born following tissue typing is benefited by being a good tissue match for an older sibling since this enables her to be born into a family which is not wracked by bereavement, and to benefit from a relationship with her older sibling, which she would not otherwise have had.

Sally Sheldon and Stephen Wilkinson[77]

Banning the use of PGD and tissue typing to select saviour siblings would lead to the avoidable deaths of existing children. As such, it seems appropriate to assume that the onus of proof rests with the prohibitionists who must demonstrate that these consequences are less terrible than the results of allowing this particular use of PGD...

The first prohibitionist argument is that a saviour sibling would be 'a commodity rather than a person' and would be wrongfully treated as a means rather than an end in itself...[T]his argument fails to say what is wrong with creating a child as a saviour sibling, when creating a child for a number of other 'instrumental' purposes is widely accepted. Given that (for example) attempting to conceive a child in order to provide a playmate for an existing child is seen as reasonable, how would we distinguish this from the reasons advanced by the Hashmis or Whitakers?...

We turn now to the idea that saviour siblings will be psychologically harmed...But even if we concede for the sake of argument that it would be hurtful or upsetting for a selected sibling (A) to discover that she had been conceived for the primary purpose of saving the life of an existing child (B), is it really plausible to suppose that A would be less happy than another, randomly selected sibling (C) who was unable to act as a tissue donor? For it could surely be argued that A would benefit from B's company and may well derive pleasure from knowing that she has saved B's life. In contrast, imagine the psychological impact on C, born into a bereaved family, later to discover that she was a huge disappointment to her parents because of her inability to save B's life....[W]e can at least say that it is far from obvious that child welfare considerations should count against, rather than for, the practice of saviour sibling selection.

(5) Non-medical Sex Selection

There are a variety of different ways in which parents might try to control the sex of their offspring. First, there are a number of ineffectual folk remedies, such as having sex at a particular time during the woman's menstrual cycle, or in a particular position. Secondly, pre-conception sex selection might be accomplished by sperm sorting, which involves separating

---

[77] 'Hashmi and Whitaker, "An Unjustifiable and Misguided Distinction"' (2004) 12 Medical Law Review 137–63.

X and Y sperm, and artificially inseminating the woman with the separated sperm. Until the EU Tissues and Cells Directive came into force, this could be done without a licence in the UK. Now a licence would be necessary, but since success rates are too low to justify the use sperm sorting for medical reasons, and sex selection for social reasons is prohibited, it would not be possible to obtain a licence.

Thirdly, and more successful, is preimplantation sex selection, using PGD. This needs a licence from the HFEA, and is only permitted for medical reasons.

Fourthly, women can undergo prenatal sex diagnosis during pregnancy, and abort the fetus if it is the 'wrong' sex. This would be lawful only if it could be established that the pregnant woman's mental or physical health was endangered by carrying the pregnancy to term (see Chapter 13 for a description of abortion law). It seems unlikely that a doctor would knowingly authorize an abortion requested purely on the grounds of the fetus's sex, but it is, of course, possible that a woman might discover her fetus's sex, and be prompted to seek an abortion, ostensibly for other reasons. It is impossible to tell how many sex-selective abortions are carried out in the UK, but in some parts of the world, such as India, despite being illegal, they are relatively common.

Finally, infanticide has been used in the past in some countries when a woman gives birth to a child of the 'wrong' sex.

The legitimacy of sex selection for social reasons was considered by the HFEA following a public consultation in 2003. As is clear from the following extract, the HFEA was heavily influenced by the weight of public opinion against sex selection.

Human Fertilisation and Embryology Authority[78]

139. In our view the most persuasive arguments for restricting access to sex selection technologies, beside the potential health risks involved, are related to the welfare of the children and families concerned. There was considerable alarm among consultation respondents that children selected for their sex alone may be in some way psychologically damaged by the knowledge that they had been selected in this way as embryos. Some consultation respondents expressed concerns that such children would be treated prejudicially by their parents and that parents would try to mould them to fulfil their (the parents') expectations. Others saw a potential for existing children in the family to be neglected by their parents at the expense of sex-selected children.

147. In reaching a decision we have been particularly influenced by the considerations set out above relating to the possible effects of sex selection for non-medical reasons on the welfare of children born as a result, and by the quantitative strength of views from the representative sample polled by MORI and the force of opinions expressed by respondents to our consultation. These show that there is very widespread hostility to the use of sex-selection for non-medical reasons. By itself this finding is not decisive; the fact that a proposed policy is widely held to be unacceptable does not show that it is wrong. But there would need to be substantial demonstrable benefits of such a policy if the state were to challenge the public consensus on this issue. In our view the likely benefits of permitting sex-selection for non-medical reasons in the UK are at best debatable and certainly not great enough to sustain a policy to which the great majority of the public are strongly opposed. Accordingly we advise that treatment services provided for the purpose of selecting the sex of children, by whatever

---

[78] Human Fertilisation and Embryology Authority *Sex Selection: options for regulation* (HFEA, 2003).

means this is to be achieved, should be restricted under licence to cases in which there is a clear and overriding medical justification.

Again, the 2008 reforms simply place previous HFEA policy on sex selection on a statutory footing:

Human Fertilisation and Embryology Act 1990 section 13.8

13.8 With respect to any PGD programme the following conditions apply:...

  (d) that Centres should not use any information derived from tests on an embryo, or any material removed from it or from the gametes that produced it, to select embryos of a particular sex for social reasons,

So what are the arguments against allowing sex selection for social reasons? First, it is again argued that sex selection embodies a consumerist attitude towards children. Instead of welcoming a child regardless of its gender, would-be parents who want to choose their child's sex are accused of seeking to ensure that their new baby meets their specifications. Secondly, it is thought that the use of sex selection for social reasons is sexist and discriminatory. Thirdly, it is argued that allowing people to select the sex of their offspring might also have devastating demographic consequences.

Jodi Danis[79]

Some predict that a population in which males significantly predominate, known as a 'high sex ratio society', would have devastating results for women. A high sex ratio society might value women for their reproductive capacities, but would also be likely to force women to return to traditional roles centered around the home and family. Demographic imbalances would exacerbate existing sex discrimination because women would not have the political power or economic resources to change the status quo. The underrepresentation of women in positions of power would be even more significant. Oppression and violence against women might increase in male-dominated societies, especially if men felt the need to possess a limited resource and to ensure fidelity....

Some commentators predict that the psychological consequences of sex selection would translate into exacerbated male privilege....Males, through their greater numbers, would also know that they were selected more often and were thus more desired, increasing their sense of self-worth and self-importance while diminishing the self-esteem of their younger sisters or other girls....

[B]ecause only those in the middle or upper class can afford sex selection technology, and only those in the upper class can afford the more accurate in vitro technology, a higher proportion of boys would be born to the wealthy. This trend might result in the future masculinization of wealth.

Of course, a couple with four sons are not necessarily guilty of discriminating against boys when they hope their fifth child will be a girl. But it is further argued that even this sort

[79] 'Sexism and "The Superfluous Female": Arguments for Regulating Pre-Implantation Sex Selection' (1995) 18 Harvard Women's Law Journal 219.

of preference depends upon sexist preconceptions about a child's gender-specific behaviour. A couple with four boys only want a girl, some would argue, because they think that she will be different from their sons. In the next extract, Jonathan Berkowitz and Jack Snyder argue that this expectation of difference arises from sexist attitudes.

Jonathan Berkowitz and Jack Snyder[80]

[T]o choose a boy or a girl, parents must have preconceived notions, however vague, about the ramifications of having a certain sexed child: notions which are fundamentally sexist as they are predicated upon anticipated gender based behaviour. Preconceptive sex selection is disturbing because it can be used as a vehicle for parents to express spoken or unspoken sexual prejudice...

Furthermore, by making a choice, parents must essentially prefer one sex over another. This emphasis upon sex is in direct conflict with larger societal goals directed against sexism and which urge individuals to be sex-blind. Pre-conceptive sex-selection represents sexism in its purest most blatant form as prior to conception, before parents can possibly know anything about their child, a child's worth is based in large part upon its sex.

Even if we accept that gender-stereotypical attitudes towards child-rearing are undesirable, these are plainly not *caused by* a technique like PGD. Rather, parents with sexist attitudes will also inflict them upon any child that they might have naturally.

The principal argument in favour of allowing sex selection for social reasons derives from John Stuart Mill's harm principle. Liberty, according to Mill, should be restricted only when its exercise might cause harm to others. *If*, and of course this is a contentious question, sex selection does not harm anyone, then there is insufficient justification for restricting people's reproductive freedom. Of course, critics of sex selection would argue that it does harm others, such as the child herself (see Jonathan Berkowitz and Jack Snyder) and society in general (see Jodi Danis).

Others, such as David McCarthy and John Harris, disagree and contend that these harms are far too speculative and fanciful to justify a restriction on freedom.

David McCarthy[81]

In a pluralistic democratic society built upon the ideals of free and equal citizenry, there is always a presumption in favour of liberty. The burden of proof is always on those who want to restrict the liberty of others. Defenders of the legality of sex selection are not seeking to restrict anyone's liberty, whereas opponents are. So the burden of proof is on the opponents to show that those whose liberties they propose to restrict cannot reasonably reject this restriction. It is never sufficient grounds for one group to restrict the liberty of others that it is clear, as they see it, that the behaviour they are trying to restrict is morally objectionable. What must be established is that the behaviour they are trying to restrict itself results in something like significant harm to others or infringement of their basic liberties or significant social costs. In the case of sex selection, I have argued that no such grounds have been established.

---

[80] 'Racism and Sexism in Medically Assisted Conception' (1998) 12 Bioethics 25–44.
[81] 'Why Sex Selection Should be Legal' (2001) 27 Journal of Medical Ethics 302–7.

John Harris[82]

> The HFEA in effect rely on the following very limited arguments against gender selection. The first is set out in paragraph 139 where they say 'in our view the most persuasive arguments for restricting access to sex selection technologies, beside the potential health risks involved, are related to the welfare of the children and families concerned'. The HFEA then glosses this concern for children by noting that, 'children selected for their sex alone may be in some way psychologically damaged by the knowledge that they had been selected in this way as embryos'. This is a very tendentious and unwarranted way of putting the point....
>
> The suggestion that sons or daughters would be so unloved and treated so unacceptably badly that it would cause psychological damage is a piece of reckless speculation. Suffice it to say that for these highly speculative and fanciful dangers to count against the powerful formulation of the liberal imperative would be effectively to deny that imperative any weight or role at all...
>
> The illiberalism of this conclusion and the poverty of the arguments produced to defend and sustain it make it imperative that this report is not only rejected but that it be recognised for what it is, an attempt to formalise the tyranny of the majority and to institutionalise contempt for the principles of liberal democracy.

The so-called non-identity problem poses a difficulty for those who argue against sex selection for social reasons: any harm caused by choosing a child's sex is unlikely to be so grave that it would be better if the sex-selected child did not exist. If I found out that my parents had selected me from a range of embryos because I am female, I might think that they were a bit weird, but I am very unlikely to think that it would have been preferable if I had never been born.

In the next extract, McDougall sidesteps this intractable debate between those who believe sex selection should be prevented because it harms the child to be born and those who believe that either it does not cause harm, or, even if it does, that harm is unlikely to be so great that it would be preferable for the child not to exist. Instead of arguing that sex selection *causes harm*, she advocates looking at sex selection from the point of view of virtue ethics (see Chapter 1). Because a virtuous parent *accepts* their children, regardless of their characteristics, a sex-selecting parent does not act virtuously, even if the child herself is not, in fact, harmed.

R McDougall[83]

> Because a child's characteristics are unpredictable, acceptance is a parental virtue....Accepting one's child, regardless of his or her particular current characteristics, is already perceived as a necessary characteristic of the good parent....
>
> In acting on a preference to parent only a child of a particular sex, the sex selecting agent fails to act in accordance with the parental virtue of acceptance....The wrong is the sex selecting agent's failure to act in accordance with a parental character trait, acceptance, which is intrinsically linked on a general conceptual level to the flourishing of children. Sex selection is wrong because it is not in accordance with the parental virtue of acceptance, regardless of the outcome for a specific child.

[82] 'Sex Selection and Regulated Hatred' (2005) 31 Journal of Medical Ethics 291–4.
[83] 'Acting Parentally: An Argument Against Sex Selection' (2005) 31 Journal of Medical Ethics 601–5.

Some people have argued in favour of *limited* access to sex selection for social reasons in order to facilitate 'family balancing'. The American Society for Reproductive Medicine, for example, has argued that it is ethical to help couples to choose the sex of their babies for reasons of 'gender variety'. Similarly, the House of Commons Science and Technology Committee found that there was 'no adequate justification for prohibiting the use of sex selection for family balancing'.[84] In Israel, one of the only countries to specifically lay out criteria in which, exceptionally, sex selection for social reasons may be permitted, one of the criteria is that the couple must have at least four children of one sex and none of the other.[85]

Why do some people regard sex selection for 'family balancing' as more innocuous than other sorts of social selection? One possible argument is that, where there is an uneven number of children of each sex in a family, the would-be family balancer is not *preferring* one sex to another: rather, they value *both sexes equally* and would like to see both represented among their children. A second argument might be that family balancing would be unlikely to skew the sex ratio, because it might be predicted that the number of parents with daughters who would also like a son is likely to be roughly the same as the number with sons who would also like to have a daughter. In the next extract, however, Stephen Wilkinson disputes the suggestion that family balancing is necessarily less 'sexist' than 'regular' social sex selection.

Stephen Wilkinson[86]

[W]hile 'regular' sex selection is not *necessarily* supremacist, 'family balancing' *can* be supremacist. For example, a father who believes females to be second-rate might suffer (what he sees as) the misfortune of numerous daughters and want to even things up, not because he desires balance, but because he believes that boys are better....

As with 'regular' sex selection, whether 'family balancing' involves stereotyping depends on what exactly it is that the parents are aiming at. If what they want is a 'balance' of plainly biological features (if they want half their children to be capable of beard growth and other half to develop breasts, for example), then...while we may think that this is weird or objectionable in other ways, it does not seem to involve sex-stereotyping, for the desired sex-linked characteristics really are biologically determined. If, on the other hand, the sort of 'balance' that they are after is less clearly related to biology and more to do with character traits that may or may not be determined by physical sex, then there is a significant risk that the parents are guilty of stereotyping. It seems then that such stereotyping is as likely in the case of 'family balancing' sex selection as it is in 'regular' sex selection.

(6) Preimplantation Gene Therapy

Currently, the only way in which genetic knowledge can be used before implantation is by discarding embryos discovered to have some genetic abnormality. Preimplantation gene

---

[84] Human Reproductive Technologies and the Law, Fifth Report (2005), para 142, available at <www.publications.parliament.uk/pa/cm200405/cmselect/cmsctech/7/7i.pdf>.

[85] R Landau,' Sex Selection for Social Purposes in Israel: Quest for the "Perfect Child" of a Particular Gender or Centuries Old Prejudice Against Women?' (2008) 34 Journal of Medical Ethics e10.

[86] 'Sexism, Sex Selection and "Family Balancing"' (2008) 16 Medical Law Review 369–89.

therapy is not yet possible, but at some point in the future scientists may be able to alter the genetic make-up of an early embryo. It is, however, unlikely that it would ever be possible to modify multifactorial characteristics such as height, beauty, or intelligence through preimplantation gene therapy. Rather, simple gene insertion, which could be used to treat a very limited number of recessive disorders, such as cystic fibrosis, is all that is likely to be possible in the foreseeable future.

It seems likely that preimplantation gene therapy would be subjected to similar regulation as PGD, so that therapeutic intervention to treat a serious and debilitating disease might be legitimate, while attempts to enhance a normal genotype in order to create a child with particular traits or characteristics would be prohibited. As we saw in relation to medicines in Chapter 10, the line between therapy and enhancement is not always clear. For example, what if it were possible to ensure that babies had a gene that offered immunity from a disease, such as malaria? Plainly, in some parts of the world this would radically improve the population's health, but since such a gene is not a normal part of the human genome, it would appear to be an enhancement.

3   HUMAN REPRODUCTIVE CLONING

(a) THE REGULATION OF CLONING IN THE UK

The first cloned mammal was born in the UK in 1996. The birth of Dolly the sheep (named after Dolly Parton because she had been cloned from an adult mammary cell) was announced the following year, and was immediately followed by demands for the complete prohibition of human reproductive cloning. The *Daily Mail*'s headline on 24 February 1997, the day after news of Dolly's birth broke, was 'Could We Now Raise the Dead?'[87]

In the UK, as we saw in Chapter 12 when we considered research on embryos, there was initially some confusion over whether cloning by cell nuclear replacement (CNR) was covered by the Human Fertilisation and Embryology Act 1990.[88] This apparent lacuna was the basis of an action brought by Bruno Quintavalle, on behalf of the Pro-Life Alliance. We considered the case in full in Chapter 12, but for our purposes, the important point was that, at first instance, Crane J agreed with his argument that cloning lay outside of the HFEA's powers. Until the Court of Appeal reversed his decision, the consequence of Crane J's judgment was that cloning was unregulated in the UK. In response, maverick doctors, such as Severino Antinori, announced their intention to come to the UK to recruit volunteers for their cloning experiments. Unsurprisingly, emergency legislation was immediately laid before Parliament, and the Human Reproductive Cloning Act 2001 created a new criminal offence, punishable by up to ten years' imprisonment.

Human Reproductive Cloning Act 2001 section 1

1(1) A person who places in a woman a human embryo which has been created otherwise than by fertilisation is guilty of an offence.

---

[87] AJ Klotzko, 'The Debate about Dolly' (2007) 11 *Bioethics* 427–38.
[88] See Chapter 13 for a description of what CNR involves.

Because the 2008 reforms introduce the concept of the 'permitted embryo', which is the only sort of embryo that can be transferred to a woman's body, reproductive cloning is thereby outlawed, and the Reproductive Cloning Act is no longer needed.

The House of Lords Select Committee, which considered the regulation of stem cell research in the UK (considered in Chapter 12), endorsed the complete prohibition of human reproductive cloning in the UK, and further suggested that international agreement to ban reproductive cloning would be beneficial.

House of Lords Stem Cell Research Committee paras 5.2 and 7.18[89]

> 5.2(a) given the high risk of abnormalities, the scientific objections to human reproductive cloning are currently overwhelming;
>
>   (b) there are further strong ethical objections in addition to those based on the risk of abnormalities, although not all the arguments deployed against reproductive cloning are equally valid. The most powerful are the unacceptability of experimenting on a human being and the familial and child welfare considerations arising from the ambiguity of the cloned child's relationships; and
>
> 7.18 Despite the difficulties, we believe that there would be advantage in seeking to secure international agreement on prohibiting reproductive cloning. It would send a powerful signal of international opposition to the practice; it would put moral pressure on countries not to permit facilities in their jurisdictions to be used for this purpose; and it would afford further reassurance to the public that there was protection against the use of CNR for research purposes becoming a slippery slope to reproductive cloning.

Notice that the Select Committee suggested that there are both scientific and ethical objections to reproductive cloning. In the next section, we consider these in turn.

(b) ARGUMENTS AGAINST REPRODUCTIVE CLONING

(1) Practical or Safety-based Arguments

The most compelling reason not to allow human reproductive cloning is that it would present an unacceptable risk to the health of the pregnant woman and any child that might be born. As we saw in Chapter 9, research involving human subjects is legitimate only once trials in animals have established that there is a reasonable prospect of success, and that it meets a threshold level of safety. The burden of proof lies with the researcher, and although an absolute guarantee that a procedure is risk-free would be impracticable, cloning in animals is not yet sufficiently safe or effective.

Dolly was the sole survivor following the successful transplantation of nuclei to 277 enucleated ewe's eggs.[90] Cloning in animals appears to cause high rates of spontaneous late

---

[89] Stem Cell Research Report, Feb 2002, available at <www.parliament.publications.uk>.

[90] I Wilmut *et al.*, 'Viable Offspring Derived from Fetal and Adult Mammalian Cells' (1997) 385 Nature 810–13.

abortion and early postnatal death.[91] There is also some evidence that successfully cloned animals suffer long-lasting deleterious effects—Dolly herself developed arthritis at an abnormally young age, and died prematurely of an unrelated condition. It is thought that when an adult cell is cloned, it is possible that its advanced age will create an increased risk of cancer and other degenerative diseases. Given this backdrop, it would clearly be unethical to clone human beings for reproductive purposes.

A controversial argument is, however, made by John Harris in the next extract. He argues that since sexual reproduction also involves high levels of wastage of embryos, there should be no necessary objection to reproductive cloning on safety grounds.

John Harris[92]

The one decent argument against cloning that does command respect is the claim that in the current state of the art cloning would be likely to result in a high failure rate in pregnancy and an unacceptably high rate of birth defects and genetic abnormalities...But embryo wastage *per se* cannot be an objection to reproductive cloning, at least for anyone who accepts natural reproduction. Approximately 80 per cent of embryos perish in natural reproduction. But not only is natural reproduction inefficient, it is also unsafe. Around 3–5 per cent of babies born have some abnormality. Natural reproduction not only involves the foreseeable and unavoidable creation of some embryos which will die, but also some embryos which will go on to become very disabled human beings...

It is clear that natural sexual reproduction is a method that has a significant risk of failure, death and abnormality. It is however not immediately ruled out as unacceptably unsafe or 'untested' on this account....

One very important conclusion follows from this discussion. It is that for those who accept natural reproduction, there is no objection in principle to reproductive cloning on grounds of inefficiency or lack of safety...Even if attempts at reproductive cloning involve the loss of many embryos which will perish in early embryonic development and also involve the creation of other embryos which will become grossly deformed human beings, this is no different from natural reproduction...

This is a striking conclusion. Acceptance of natural reproduction entails acceptance of reproductive cloning, at least from the perspective of the safety and efficiency of the practice.

It is, of course, true that miscarriage and abnormalities happen in nature, but a clinician who *chose* to use a reproductive technique which massively increased the risk of miscarriage might be in breach of her duty of care. It would be difficult to argue that it was acceptable to expose female patients to a hugely elevated risk of miscarriage. As a result, most scientists and clinicians are of the opinion that concerns about safety currently justify a moratorium on reproductive cloning.

What if scientific progress means that at some point in the future cloning experiments involving animals will demonstrate an acceptable level of safety and efficacy? Once the safety objection to cloning is removed, we will have to decide whether human reproductive cloning is ethically acceptable.

---

[91] Y Kato *et al.*, 'Eight Calves Cloned from Somatic Cells of a Single Adult' (1998) 282 Science 2095–8.
[92] *On Cloning* (Routledge: London, 2004).

(2) Ethical Arguments

A number of different objections to human reproductive cloning have been raised. At the outset, it is probably worth noting that some of these arguments were also deployed following the birth of Louise Brown in 1978 by people who believed that 'test tube babies' were similarly unnatural, would threaten family relationships, and would be the first step upon a very slippery slope. So perhaps the novelty of cloning, like the novelty of IVF in the late 1970s, inevitably prompts hostility, which may soften with familiarity. On the other hand, many would argue that there is in fact something uniquely disturbing about reproductive cloning. Why?

First, it has been argued that cloning violates the individual's right to her own unique identity. This argument is undermined by the natural existence of identical twins, who have identical DNA, but undoubtedly have separate identities. The human brain is extraordinarily complex and even genetically identical twins are born with different neural connections.[93] These differences increase as their experiences and environment shape their neural development. Having a unique genotype is not, therefore, an essential prerequisite of individual identity. It is also important to remember that the clone and her DNA source will be less alike than monozygotic twins because their uterine environments, childhood experiences, and upbringing will be completely different. As Anne McLaren explains in the next extract, given that genetically identical individuals already exist, it is difficult to base an argument against cloning upon the unacceptability of creating such individuals.

Anne McLaren[94]

It has been argued that the unique identity of human beings must be protected; but monozygotic twins are at least as identical genetically as any deliberately cloned human beings would be, while all the important influences of upbringing and environment that make monozygotic twins not identical would ensure that individuals produced by nuclear transfer were still more different from one another and from their donor. If we do not wish to impugn the unique identity of each monozygotic twin, it is hard to base a convincing argument against cloning on this concept.

Secondly, Alexander Morgan Capron argues that even if we acknowledge the likelihood of significant differences between a clone and her DNA source, the *expectation* of similarity will significantly impair the clone's capacity for individuality.

Alexander Morgan Capron[95]

Given the uniqueness of each individual's environmental experience, from the earliest embryonic moment onwards, it's true that if Mozart were cloned, you wouldn't get another Mozart. But, so long as the impulse to act otherwise exists, the failure of the Mozart clones

---

[93] G Johnson, 'Soul Searching' in M Nussbaum and C Sunstein (eds), *Clones and Clones: Facts and Fantasies about Human Cloning* (Norton: New York, 1998) 67–70.

[94] 'Commentary on Ethical Aspects of Cloning Techniques' (1998) 7 Cambridge Quarterly of Healthcare Ethics 192–3, 193.

[95] 'Placing a Moratorium on Research Cloning to Ensure Effective Control over Reproductive Cloning' (2002) Hastings Law Journal 1057.

to measure up to expectations is likely to be a source of harm rather than benefit for them, as their makers' expectations—and elaborate plans or fantasies—are disappointed....Were medicine to sanction cloning as a legitimate way of getting the child you want, it would exacerbate rather than reduce the drive to regard children as objects to fulfil parental wants rather than as individuals who are entitled to their own, self-directed lives.

In essence, it is argued that clones would be burdened by the anticipation of uncanny similarity between the lives of the 'parent' and her clone. They would not, as Hilary Putnam puts it, be a 'complete surprise' to their parents.

Hilary Putnam[96]

As things stand now..., the amazing thing about one's children is that they come into one's life as different—very different—people seemingly from the moment of birth. In any other relationship, one can choose to some extent the traits of one's associates, but with one's children (and one's parents) one can only accept what God gives one to accept. And, paradoxically, that is one of the most valuable things about the love between parent and child: that, at its best, it involves the capacity to love what is very different from one's self....

Our moral image of the family should reflect our tolerant and pluralistic values, not our narcissistic and xenophobic ones. And that means that we should welcome rather than deplore the fact that our children are not us and not designed by us, but radically Other....What I have been claiming is that the unpredictability and diversity of our progeny is an intrinsic value and that a moral image of the family that reflects it coheres with the moral images of society that underlay our democratic aspirations...[P]erhaps one novel human right is suggested by the present discussion: the 'right' of each newborn child to be a complete surprise to its parents.

Whether or not the expectations parents would have for a cloned child are wholly different from the interest many parents already have in their children's inherited characteristics is debatable. It can be difficult to grow up in the shadow of a successful parent or older sibling, and being burdened by parental expectations is by no means unusual.

Furthermore, as Julian Savulescu argues in the next extract, the argument that cloned individuals would be treated differently by their parents and by society as a whole does not necessarily mean that we should prohibit their creation. Rather, it might instead be argued that we should be concerned to prevent discrimination against clones.

Julian Savulescu[97]

[I]n my view, what would make clones' lives problematic is the way in which their parents, peers and society might treat them. Negative attitudes towards clones would be a new form of discrimination—clonism—against a group of humans who are different in a non-morally significant way. To say that creating a clone is an affront to human dignity is like saying that

---

[96] 'Cloning People' in J Burley (ed.), *The Genetic Revolution and Human Rights* (OUP: Oxford, 1999) 1–13.

[97] 'Equality, Cloning and Clonism: Why We Must Clone', Bionews 16 May 2005, available at <www.bionews.org.uk>.

deliberately creating a black person, or a woman, affronts human dignity. The statement itself affronts the dignity of cloned people. Misinformed bigotry is not a reason to prevent cloning, rather a reason to drop the attitudes....

As we speak up for those affected by racism, sexism, homophobia—so we should protect future clones in society. We have nothing to fear from cloning or biological modification of human beings except ourselves.

Thirdly, a cloned child would be produced by replicating one parent's DNA, and some people are concerned about the impact this might have upon family relationships. Would it be unacceptably disturbing to raise a child who shared the same DNA as one's spouse? As we have seen, the clone and the DNA source are unlikely to be identical, but the prospect is, as Ian Wilmut and Alexander Morgan Capron explain in the next extracts, unsettling.

Ian Wilmut[98]

Using cloning to treat infertility raises first and foremost in my mind concern about family relationships. If my wife and I are infertile, and we decided that I should be cloned, could I have an effective, healthy relationship with someone who is a copy of me? Could my wife? And, importantly, could the child have a good relationship with me? Although I think eminently possible for one's attitude towards an adopted child to be the same as it is to one's own offspring, I strongly doubt that the same parity of attitude could be achieved in a family in which there was a genetic replica of one of the parents.

Alexander Morgan Capron[99]

My wife and I have nothing but sons. If we wanted to have a daughter, probably our best method would be to clone my wife. Now, suppose we did that and then, tragically, my wife died. Would her clone, who has no biological relationship to me, be a suitable replacement for my now dead spouse (assuming the clone were by then old enough to marry)? She would be the embodiment of the woman I had married, which is exactly the kind of 'replacement' that people who want to use cloning to replace a dead child are talking about.

Fourthly, cloning would also make it possible for women to reproduce without men. Currently, although single and lesbian women can have children, they still need to use men's gametes. Cloning would enable women to reproduce entirely autonomously, prompting inevitable speculation about the future redundancy of men.

Fifthly, it is argued that the random redistribution of genetic material through natural reproduction leads to a healthy genetic diversity among the population, and that this would be compromised by cloning, which simply involves replicating an existing individual's DNA. Of course, the clone also inherits mitochondrial DNA from the denucleated egg, so her genotype is not completely identical to the DNA source. Moreover, most people will

---

[98] 'Dolly: The Age of Biological Control, Eugenics and Human Rights' in J Burley (ed.), *The Genetic Revolution and Human Rights* (OUP: Oxford, 1999) 119–28.

[99] 'Placing a Moratorium on Research Cloning to Ensure Effective Control over Reproductive Cloning' (2002) Hastings Law Journal 1057.

always continue to prefer to reproduce naturally, so cloning is never likely to be so popular that it poses a risk to the health of the human species.

Finally, while perhaps not insurmountable, cloning would pose challenges for law. As with identical twins, maintaining the confidentiality of genetic test results between the DNA source and the clone would be impossible. Cloning would also raise complex questions about the parentage of the resulting child. Cloning would involve an egg donor, a DNA source, and a gestational mother. These could, of course, all be the same woman, in which case, would the child have only one parent? Alternatively, they might be three different people: would all three be the child's parents? A further possibility is that the DNA source's *own* parents might claim to be the parents of their child's 'delayed twin'.

(c) ARGUMENTS IN FAVOUR OF REPRODUCTIVE CLONING

The principal argument in favour of reproductive cloning would be that it could expand the options available to alleviate involuntary childlessness. A secondary argument might be that it is easier to control a practice if it is brought within the UK's strict regulatory framework. If cloning (once it becomes safe and effective) is unavailable in the UK, wealthy British citizens who want to produce cloned children will simply travel abroad.

In the next extract, John Robertson challenges the 'harm to offspring' justification for banning human reproductive cloning.

John A Robertson[100]

Preventing existence as a way to prevent harm to the person who would exist makes sense for that person only if it reasonably appears that once born, the child's existence would be so full of pain and suffering that its interests would be best served by nonexistence. But it is rare that the techniques at issue—whether cloning or other genetic manipulations—would cause harm or suffering to such an extent...

When carefully analyzed, the alleged harms of cloning tend to be highly speculative, moralistic, or subjective judgments about the meaning of family and how reproduction should occur. Such choices are ordinarily reserved to individuals, free of governmental coercion or definition of what provides reproductive meaning.

John Harris suggests that the arguments against human reproductive cloning tend to consist of intuitive feelings of revulsion or uneasiness, but he argues that these do not, in themselves, offer sufficient justification for banning a practice.

John Harris[101]

In a long discussion entitled 'The Wisdom of Repugnance' [Leon] Kass tries hard and thoughtfully to make plausible the thesis that thoughtlessness is a virtue. 'We are repelled by the prospect of cloning human beings not because of the strangeness or novelty of the undertaking,

---

[100] 'Liberty, Identity and Human Cloning' I (1998) 76 Texas Law Review 1371.
[101] 'Clones, Genes and Human Rights' in J Burley (ed.), *The Genetic Revolution and Human Rights* (OUP: Oxford, 1999) 61–94.

but because we intuit and feel, immediately and without argument, the violation of things that we rightfully hold dear'. The difficulty is, of course, to know when one's sense of outrage is evidence of something morally disturbing and when it is simply an expression of bare prejudice or something even more shameful. The English novelist George Orwell once referred to this reliance on some innate sense of right and wrong as 'moral nose', as if one could simply sniff a situation and detect wickedness. The problem, as I have indicated, is that nasal reasoning is notoriously unreliable, and olfactory moral philosophy, its theoretical 'big brother', has done little to refine it or give it a respectable foundation. We should remember that in the recent past, among the many discreditable uses of so-called 'moral feelings', people have been disgusted by the sight of Jews, black people, and indeed women being treated as equals and mixing on terms of equality with others.

Some people have argued that the *reason* why cloning is sought might make a difference to its acceptability. Let us imagine, for example, a couple in which the male partner has received treatment for testicular cancer and now produces no sperm at all, and the female partner has been treated for ovarian cancer and has no more eggs. The only way in which they can currently have a child is to use donated sperm and eggs, or to receive an embryo that has been donated by another couple. In both cases, the child will be genetically unrelated to them. It seems possible that they might prefer to employ cloning, using the DNA from one or other partner, rather than have a genetically unrelated child. Duplication of one partner's DNA is then a *side-effect* of their desire to have a child who will have a genetic connection to at least one of her parents. In contrast, a fertile couple might opt for cloning because they specifically want to duplicate one partner's, or an existing child's DNA. Is this less deserving of respect than the former case? In the following extract, Dena Davis suggests that it is.[102]

Dena Davis[103]

The first motivation I will call *logistical*. For some reason, this couple is having a very difficult time procreating, and cloning offers some unique advantage to them.... I call these logistical motivations because the parents' goal here is simply to have a child. The duplicative element of cloning is a side effect, perhaps even one they would avoid if they could. The parents see cloning as the best option from an array of choices: adoption, childlessness, or reproduction with the use of a third party. If we would support the reproductive efforts of these would-be parents *without* cloning..., then the additional factor of cloning should not necessarily doom them in our eyes....

In contrast, with *duplicative* motivations it is the genetic replication itself that is the attraction. Some duplicative motivations will not survive exposure to the facts; parents who think they can guarantee a saintly child if they could only get hold of Mother Teresa's DNA are clearly mistaken. Other duplicative motivations are less obviously foolish but more obviously perilous to the child herself. When parents, for example, wish a new genetically identical child to 'replace' a dearly beloved child who has died young, the psychological pitfalls are clear. No child could possible live up to such glorified expectations, and the parents are likely to be frustrated and disappointed that the 'new' child is so different. After all, the second child's experience will be dramatically different from that of her dead sibling, if only because the second child is a younger sibling in a family that has sustained such a tragedy.

4 CONCLUSION

The 2008 reforms to the 1990 Act continue the UK's tradition of fairly liberal but none-theless rigorous regulation of assisted conception services. Access to parenthood has been widened by the reforms, so that lesbian second parents can be parents from birth. The statute now specifically addresses the criteria for PGD, and it remains to be seen whether having this level of detail on the face of the legislation will help promote certainty and public confidence, or whether it might create difficulties in the future, given the inevitability of new tests and new techniques for testing. For example, it is thought that it might become possible to learn about some of an embryo's characteristics by testing the culture medium in which it is stored, rather than carrying out an embryo biopsy. Would we want the rules governing PGD to apply to non-invasive analysis of changes in culture media, or should different principles apply?

In the lifetime of the 2008 reforms, there will undoubtedly be new challenges ahead. As we saw in Chapter 12, it is likely that scientists will be able to create artificial gametes from stem cells within the next 5–15 years. New, primary legislation would be needed to enable these to be used in treatment. The government did not opt for regulation-making powers to allow their use more speedily, on the grounds that such a development would fundamentally change the way people have children.[104] While this is undoubtedly true, enabling people without their own sperm and eggs to reproduce without recourse to donor gametes would, at a single stroke, eliminate the shortage of donated gametes and resolve difficulties about anonymity and secrecy.

While the UK's regulatory system was the first of its kind in the world, and has been widely copied, it is not without its critics. Clearly many pro-life groups are concerned about the routine destruction of embryos in techniques like IVF and PGD. Disability rights groups have expressed anxiety about increasing recourse to embryo testing. Criticism has also come from a completely different direction, namely from those, like Sheila McLean, who believe that any regulation in this area unnecessarily restricts reproductive liberty.

Sheila McLean[105]

The state's interventionist role in assisted reproduction is based not in principle but on a general presumption of legitimacy: a presumption which can—and in my view should—be challenged. Most importantly it allows the imposition of the values of one group on others. Our relatively recent history—if nothing else—should teach us how potentially dangerous it is to cede authority over reproduction and reproductive practices to the state. Even if regulation is relatively benign, its very existence attacks freedom of choice; if it did not do so, it would have no reason to exist...

---

[104] Dawn Primarolo MP, Hansard 3 June 2008.
[105] *Modern Dilemmas: Choosing Children* (Capercaillie Books, 2006).

Certainly we will want to ensure that choices are taken in full knowledge of the risks, benefits and possible consequences of the decision, but this is a matter for the law on consent. It
is not an argument against reproductive liberty....

De-regulating the provision of assisted reproductive services is the only option that
adequately respects the liberties of citizens in this area, and the only one which reflects an
appropriate role for the state in our intimate, private lives.

FURTHER READING

Brazier, Margaret, 'Regulating the Reproduction Business?' (1999) 7 Medical Law
Review 166–93.

Gavaghan, Colin, 'Right Problem Wrong Solution: A Pro-Choice Response to
Expressivist Concerns about Preimplantation Genetic Diagnosis' (2007) Cambridge
Quarterly of Healthcare Ethics 20–34.

Glover, Jonathan, *Choosing Children: Genes, Disability and Design* (Clarendon Press:
Oxford, 2006).

Harris, John, 'Sex Selection and Regulated Hatred' (2005) 31 Journal of Medical Ethics
291–4.

Horsey, K and Biggs, H (eds), *Human Reproduction and Embryology: Reproducing
Regulation* (UCL Press: London, 2006).

Jackson, Emily, 'Conception and the Irrelevance of the Welfare Principle' (2002) 65
Modern Law Review 176–203.

Mcdougall, R, 'Acting Parentally: An Argument Against Sex Selection' (2005) 31 Journal
of Medical Ethics 601–5.

Mclean, Sheila, *Modern Dilemmas: Choosing Children* (Capercaillie Books: Edinburgh,
2006).

McMillan JR, 'NICE, the Draft Fertility Guideline and Dodging the Big Question' (2003)
29 Journal of Medical Ethics 313–14.

Sheldon, Sally, 'Fragmenting Fatherhood: The Regulation of Reproductive Technologies'
(2005) 68 Modern Law Review 523–53.

Sheldon, Sally and Wilkinson, Stephen, 'Hashmi and Whitaker: An Unjustifiable and
Misguided Distinction' (2004) 12 Medical Law Review 137–63.

Thornton, Rosy, 'European Court of Human Rights: Consent to IVF Treatment' (2008)
6 International Journal of Constitutional Law 317–30.

Wilkinson, Stephen, 'Sexism, Sex Selection and Family Balancing' (2008) 16 Medical
Law Review 369–89.

16

SURROGACY

CENTRAL ISSUES

1. Surrogacy agreements are not unlawful in the UK, but they are unenforceable.

2. In theory, surrogate mothers cannot be paid and commercial involvement in surrogacy is banned. In practice, payments to surrogate mothers can be authorized retrospectively by the courts.

3. The surrogate mother is always the legal mother of the child from birth. Identifying the legal father is rather more complicated.

4. There are two ways in which legal parenthood can be formally transferred to the commissioning couple: through parental orders and adoption. There

is, however, evidence that some commissioning couples do not formally acquire legal parenthood.

5. Over 10 years ago, the government commissioned the Brazier Committee to review the law relating to surrogacy. Its proposals were never implemented. While the Human Fertilisation and Embryology Act 2008 introduced a few relatively minor changes, many would argue that wholesale reform of the law on surrogacy is needed.

6. The question of whether it is acceptable to pay a woman to bear a child continues to be extremely controversial.

1 WHAT IS SURROGACY?

Surrogacy is the practice whereby one woman (the surrogate mother) becomes pregnant with the intention that the child should be han ded over to the commissioning couple (or individual) after birth. Surrogacy can simply involve the surrogate mother inseminating herself with the commissioning father's sperm. This is known as 'partial' surrogacy. Alternatively, in 'full' surrogacy an embryo is created *in vitro*, usually using the commissioning couple's egg and sperm, and is transferred to the surrogate mother's uterus. Because *in vitro* fertilization is involved, pregnancy can only be achieved following treatment in a centre licensed under the Human Fertilisation and Embryology Act and regulated by the

Human Fertilisation and Embryology Authority (HFEA). In contrast, self-insemination with fresh sperm can be accomplished without professional assistance, and so in practice, it is difficult to exercise much control over these arrangements, and there is little information about their outcomes.

Surrogacy is not a common way to have children. The Brazier Report, which we examine later, estimated that between 100 and 180 surrogacy arrangements are made in the UK each year, resulting in 50 to 80 births.[1] Approximately half of all surrogate mothers are initially unknown to the commissioning couple, while friends, sisters, and sisters-in-law are the most common known surrogates.[2] Disputes between surrogate mothers and commissioning couples are unusual. The Brazier Committee estimated that disputes occur in 4–5 per cent of cases, which given the small number of births, means that there will seldom be more than one or two disputes each year.

In this short chapter, we begin by describing the regulation of surrogacy, before turning to the controversial questions of whether surrogacy is an acceptable way to have children, and whether the contracts themselves should be enforceable.

2 REGULATION OF SURROGACY

There have been two major reports into the regulation of surrogacy in the UK. Although the principal focus of the Warnock Report, published in 1984, was the regulation of embryo research and fertility treatment, it also considered the practice of surrogacy. While not recommending its complete prohibition, the majority of the Warnock committee was clearly of the view that regulation should be designed to discourage people from entering into surrogacy arrangements. Its recommendations were never fully implemented.

Thirteen years later, the government commissioned a report from the Brazier Committee. While undoubtedly less hostile to surrogacy than the Warnock Report, the Brazier Committee was nevertheless again concerned that regulation should not appear to either endorse or encourage the practice of surrogacy.

Over the past thirty years, there has been a marked shift in the courts' attitudes towards surrogacy. In 1978, in *A v C*, one of the first cases involving a surrogacy arrangement to come before the courts, all three judges in the Court of Appeal were unanimous in their condemnation of surrogacy.

A v C[3]

Ormrod LJ

It is a simple, logical, but totally inhuman proceeding, and shows, in my view, very grave defects in his character and, indeed, in the characters of all three participants, because the lady with whom he was living was definitely involved in the plan, no doubt now to her great

---

[1] Margaret Brazier, Alastair Campbell, and Susan Golombok, *Surrogacy: Review for Health Ministers of Current Arrangements for Payments and Regulation* (HMSO: London, 1998) Cm 4068 para 6.22.

[2] Tim Appleton, 'Emotional Aspects of Surrogacy: A Case for Effective Counselling and Support' in R Cook, SD Sclater, with F Kaganas (eds), *Surrogate Motherhood: International Perspectives* (Hart Publishing: Oxford, 2003) 199–207, 200.

[3] Note that the case was decided in 1978 but not reported until 1985, [1985] FLR 445.

regret. One can feel very sorry for her in that she must feel that it was her fault in a sense that the father was in the position in which he was, so that she felt obliged to help him and take part in this most extraordinary and irresponsible arrangement. It is unnecessary to make any more comment on the irresponsibility shown by all three of the adults in this case, which is perhaps only rivalled by the irresponsibility of the person who performed the insemination on the mother....

In this case we have a situation where there is no bond between the father and the child except the mere biological one. There has never been any association, except of the most exiguous character, between the father and the mother. There has never been anything between them except a sordid commercial bargain....

This was a wholly artificial situation from the very beginning which should never have happened and which no responsible adult should ever have allowed to happen.

Cumming-Bruce LJ condemned the arrangement as 'a kind of baby-farming operation of a wholly distasteful and lamentable kind', and Stamp LJ described it as 'an ugly little drama'.

More recently, as we shall see later, the courts have refused to comment on the morality of surrogacy and have instead concerned themselves solely with protecting the resulting child's welfare. For example, in *Re C (A Minor) (Wardship: Surrogacy)*[4]—the Baby Cotton case—Latey J said that the 'difficult and delicate problems of ethics, morality and social desirability' raised by surrogacy were not relevant to his decision about what would be best for this child.

Latey J

The baby is here. All that matters is what is best for her now that she is here and not how she arrived. If it be said (though it has not been said during these hearings) that because the father and his wife entered into these arrangements it is some indication of their unsuitability as parents, I should reject any such suggestion.

(a) NON-ENFORCEABILITY

It is not an offence to enter into a surrogacy arrangement, but the agreement itself is not enforceable. Section 1B of the Surrogacy Arrangements Act 1985 was inserted by the Human Fertilisation and Embryology Act 1990.

Surrogacy Arrangements Act 1985 section 1B

1B. No surrogacy arrangement is enforceable by or against any of the persons making it.

Hence, the commissioning couple cannot sue the surrogate mother if she refuses to hand over the baby, and nor can she sue them if she does not receive any of the agreed payments, or if they refuse to take the baby after birth. So while it is lawful to enter into a surrogacy contract, none of the parties are bound by any of the obligations it purports to contain. Given that surrogacy agreements are so precarious, it is perhaps surprising that disputes are so rare.

---

[4] [1985] FLR 846.

(b) COMMERCIALIZATION

The Surrogacy Arrangements Act 1985 was passed in order to prohibit commercial involvement in the initiation and negotiation of surrogacy arrangements. It also makes the publication or distribution of advertisements indicating a willingness to take part in surrogacy arrangements a criminal offence. The Act was amended by the Human Fertilisation and Embryology Act 2008 to permit non-profit-making bodies to charge a reasonable fee in order to recoup their costs.

Surrogacy Arrangements Act 1985 section 2

2(1) No person shall on a commercial basis do any of the following acts in the United Kingdom, that is—

  (a) initiate or take part in any negotiations with a view to the making of a surrogacy arrangement,

  (b) offer or agree to negotiate the making of a surrogacy arrangement, or

  (c) compile any information with a view to its use in making, or negotiating the making of, surrogacy arrangements.

(2) A person who contravenes subsection (1) above is guilty of an offence; but it is not a contravention of that subsection—

  (a) for a woman, with a view to becoming a surrogate herself, to do any act mentioned in that subsection or to cause such an act to be done, or

  (b) for any person, with a view to a surrogate mother carrying a child for him, to do such an act or cause such an act to be done.

(2A) A non-profit making body does not contravene subsection (1) merely because—

  (a) (a) the body does an act falling within subsection (1)(a) or (c) in respect of which any reasonable payment is at any time received by it or another, or

  (b) it does an act falling within subsection (1)(a) or (c) with a view to any reasonable payment being received by it or another in respect of facilitating the making of any surrogacy arrangement....

(2C) Any reference in subsection (2A) or (2B) to a reasonable payment in respect of the doing of an act by a non-profit making body is a reference to a payment not exceeding the body's costs reasonably attributable to the doing of the act...

3(1) This section applies to any advertisement containing an indication (however expressed)—

  (a) that any person is or may be willing to enter into a surrogacy arrangement or to negotiate or facilitate the making of a surrogacy arrangement

  (b) that any person is looking for a woman willing to become a surrogate mother or for persons wanting a woman to carry a child as a surrogate

(2) where a newspaper or periodical containing an advertisement to which this section applies is published in the United Kingdom, the proprietor, editor or publisher of the newspaper or periodical is guilty of an offence

> (1A) This section does not apply to any advertisement placed by, or on behalf of, a non-profit making body if the advertisement relates only to the doing by the body of acts that would not contravene section 2(1).

While ostensibly surrogacy arrangements should not be made on a commercial basis, in practice things are rather different, and typically, unless they are acting as a surrogate for a close friend or relative, surrogate mothers receive around £10,000–£15,000 for their services. The reason for this gap between theory and practice is that the courts are entitled to authorize payments which have been made in contravention of the ban on commercial surrogacy. Where the court considers that it is in the child's best interests to remain with the commissioning couple, retrospective authorization of any illegal payments is, as we see later, relatively straightforward.

There is, of course, an important difference between the courts' willingness to retrospectively authorize illegal parents when to do so would be in the child's best interests, and *prospectively* condoning payments to surrogates. In *Briody v St Helens and Knowsley Area Health Authority*,[5] the Court of Appeal considered whether Mrs Briody's damages for negligent obstetric care, which had left her unable to carry a child, should include the costs of entering into a surrogacy arrangement. Initially, Mrs Briody had intended to employ a surrogate mother in California, and the illegality of the agreement led Ebsworth J to reject her claim. Before the Court of Appeal, Mrs Briody instead claimed for the costs of entering into a lawful surrogacy arrangement in the UK. However, Mrs Briody's case was again rejected, in part because the chance of success was 'vanishingly small' (less than 1 per cent), and the court did not think that it would be reasonable to fund a procedure with such a high chance of failure. Hale LJ concluded that 'expenditure on surrogacy in this case is not reasonable and the defendant should not be required to fund it'.

(c) THE DIFFERENCE BETWEEN PARTIAL AND IVF SURROGACY

When a surrogacy arrangement involves IVF, the IVF treatment must, as we saw in the previous chapter, take place in a clinic which has a licence from the HFEA, and which is under a duty to comply with the Human Fertilisation and Embryology Act 1990, as amended. Under section 13(5) of the Act, before providing a woman with treatment services, the clinician must take account of the welfare of any child who may be born, and any other children who may be affected by the birth. Hence, before providing treatment, a clinician should not only evaluate the impact of the surrogacy arrangement upon the resulting child, but must also take into account the welfare of the surrogate's existing children.

Treatment in an assisted conception clinic will often be subject to supervision by the clinic's independent ethics committee, which may impose its own restrictions upon access to surrogacy. For example, at Bourn Hall, surrogates must be under 40; have had at least one child, and preferably have completed their own family; they should be married, or in a stable relationship; and their partners must be involved in the counselling process.[6]

---

[5] [2001] EWCA Civ 1010.

[6] See further Peter Brinsden, 'Clinical Aspects of IVF Surrogacy in Britain' in R Cook, SD Sclater, with F Kaganas (eds), *Surrogate Motherhood: International Perspectives* (Hart Publishing: Oxford, 2003) 99–110.

In contrast, aside from the relatively ineffective prohibitions upon commercial surrogacy, partial surrogacy arrangements are largely unregulated. There are no rules governing access to treatment; the use of fresh sperm inevitably raises the possibility of HIV infection; and there is no formal data collection about the incidence and outcomes of surrogate births. There are no standard procedures for screening surrogate mothers and commissioning couples and there is no requirement that couples or surrogate mothers should have had an opportunity to receive counselling.

The ban on commercial involvement in surrogacy means that access to professional expertise, such as legal advice, is extremely limited. There are a number of non-profit-making organizations, such as COTS (Childlessness Overcome Through Surrogacy),[7] which help to put potential surrogate mothers in touch with would-be commissioning couples, but these operate within a regulatory vacuum. As we see later, this lack of professional advice, especially in relation to the legal consequences of surrogacy, can cause difficulties.

(d) STATUS

When a child is born as a result of a surrogacy arrangement, who are her legal parents? The rules governing the attribution of maternity and paternity are different and so we deal with each in turn.

(1) Maternity

There are three possible ways in which a child's mother could be identified, following a surrogacy arrangement. First, the legal mother could be the woman who gestates the pregnancy and gives birth; this, of course, would be the surrogate mother. Secondly, legal motherhood could be synonymous with genetic motherhood, so that the woman whose egg was fertilized would be the resulting child's mother. In full surrogacy, this would be the commissioning mother, and in partial surrogacy, the surrogate mother. Thirdly, legal motherhood could vest in the woman who intends to raise the child: that is, the commissioning mother.

As we saw in the previous chapter, the legal definition of 'mother' in the UK is clear and unequivocal: the woman who gives birth to a baby is its mother.

Human Fertilisation and Embroyology Act 2008 section 33

33 The woman who is carrying or has carried a child as a result of the placing in her of an embryo or of sperm and eggs, and no other woman, is to be treated as the mother of the child.

The law does not distinguish between different types of surrogacy and so the surrogate mother will *always* be the child's legal mother from birth, regardless of whether she is genetically related to the baby. Indeed, section 47 of the 2008 Act further spells out that a woman cannot be treated as a child's parent as a result of egg donation.

The principal merit of the British approach is that it unambiguously identifies the child's legal mother. A genetic test would also promote certainty, although it would obviously lead to different results, depending upon the type of arrangement. In partial surrogacy, a genetic test would vest motherhood in the surrogate mother, while in a full surrogacy

---

[7] <www.surrogacy.org.uk/>.

arrangement, the commissioning mother would (unless a donated egg was used) be the child's legal mother from birth.

A test based solely upon intention would, of course, be open to dispute, and might result in prolonged uncertainty about a child's parentage. It would, however, have certain advantages. If the commissioning couple decide that they do not want the child, perhaps because she is born with disabilities, a test based upon the pre-conception intentions of the parties would hold the commissioning couple to their agreement. The UK's approach instead puts the surrogate mother in the difficult position of having prima facie legal responsibility for a child that she never wanted, and leaves the commissioning couple with no legal responsibility for a child whose creation they brought about.

A number of other countries, such as France and Germany, also adopt a uniform gestational test for motherhood. In contrast, some courts in the United States have attempted to vary the definition of motherhood according to the circumstances of the child's conception. So, for example, in *Johnson v Calvert*, the California Supreme Court was faced with two possible mothers, each seeking a declaration of maternity. Following an IVF surrogacy arrangement, Anna Johnson had given birth to a child who had been conceived *in vitro* using Mr and Mrs Calvert's gametes. In the UK, Anna Johnson's gestational role would have been decisive. In contrast, in California Justice Panelli concluded that both women had 'presented acceptable proof of maternity',[8] and he chose to use intention as the factor which tipped the balance in favour of Crispina Calvert.[9]

Panelli J[10]

[B]y voluntarily contracting away any rights to the child, the gestator has, in effect, conceded that the best interest of the child is not with her..., a rule recognizing the intended parents as the child's legal, natural parents should best promote certainty and stability for the child.

---

(2) Paternity

Applying the rules governing the ascription of legal fatherhood to a surrogacy arrangement is rather complicated. At common law, the presumption of legitimacy within marriage would lead to the surrogate mother's husband (if she has one) being treated as the legal father of the child from birth. There is also a rebuttable presumption that the man who is registered as the father on the birth certificate is the child's father.[11] Evidence indicates that registrars in the UK give contradictory advice about who should be registered as the child's father.[12] Some suggest that no name should be recorded, others advise registering the surrogate's husband as the father, and others recommend registering the commissioning father's name.[13] If the surrogate mother registers her partner on the child's birth certificate, the presumption that he is the father could again be rebutted by DNA tests which will show that he is not. In the case of the commissioning father, however, DNA tests will usually confirm his paternity. Since section 111 of the Adoption and Children Act 2002 came into force in 2003,

---

[8] Ibid at 782.   [9] *Johnson v Calvert* 851 P 2d 776, 782 (Cal 1993).
[10] Ibid at 783.   [11] Births and Deaths Registration Act 1953, s 34(2).
[12] Gena Dodd, 'Surrogacy and the Law in Britain: Users Perspectives' in R Cook, SD Sclater, with F Kaganas (eds), *Surrogate Motherhood: International Perspectives* (Hart Publishing: Oxford, 2003) 113–20, 115.
[13] Ibid.

the man who is registered on the child's birth certificate automatically acquires parental responsibility for the child, regardless of whether he is married to the child's mother.

Common law rules governing the ascription of paternity are trumped by the rules in the Human Fertilisation and Embryology Acts 1990 and 2008, and yet these were designed to apply to conception using sperm donation, rather than surrogacy, and hence lead to some rather odd results (for a full description of these provisions, see Chapter 15). Section 28 of the 1990 Act and section 38 of the 2008 Act treat the surrogate mother's husband (if she has one) as the father of the child, unless it can be shown that he did not consent to her treatment. Where a married surrogate mother's husband knows of her decision to become a surrogate mother and does not object, he may be assumed to consent, and will, as a result, be the child's father. This raised particular difficulties in *Re G (Surrogacy: Foreign Domicile)*,[14] where it was initially thought that the surrogate mother's estranged husband was the child's father, because there was no evidence that he did not consent to her decision to become a surrogate, but his unwillingness to reply to any correspondence meant that it was impossible to obtain his consent to the granting of a parental order.

If the surrogate has an unmarried partner, under the old law, he would be treated as the father if the couple were being 'treated together', which seems unlikely. Since the 2008 Act came into force in 2009, he could acquire parenthood if he and the surrogate mother satisfy the 'agreed fatherhood' conditions; again this will be unlikely, unless they wish to keep the child. It will not usually be possible for a commissioning father to acquire legal paternity via the 'agreed fatherhood' route, because this only applies to men whose sperm was not used in conception. This would be possible but only if donated sperm had been used, and most surrogacy arrangements involve the use of the commissioning father's sperm.

(e) TRANSFERRING LEGAL PARENTHOOD

Because the surrogate mother will be the child's legal mother from birth, and the commissioning father might, but more usually will not be the child's legal father, if the commissioning couple want to become the child's legal parents they will either have to apply for a parental order under the Human Fertilisation and Embryology Act, or apply to adopt her. Before we consider each route in detail, it is worth noting that the law adopts what Julie Wallbank refers to as an 'either/or' approach to parenthood. Wallbank argues that the reality is that children conceived through surrogacy arrangements have two mothers, and that ideally the child should be able to have continued relationships with both of them.

Julie Wallbank[15]

It is my view that by continuing to forward the traditional two-parent family as the paradigmatic form for children's welfare and by denying the interested parties an input into the child's life, we merely reify the social standing of children born through surrogacy as somehow deviant. It way well be the time to institute into surrogacy law and social practice the idea that children can and should have knowledge of and contact with all interested parties whether we call them 'mother' 'father' or some other appropriate epithet....

[14] [2007] EWHC 2814 (Fam).
[15] 'Too Many Mothers? Surrogacy, Kinship and the Welfare of the Child' (2002) 10 Medical Law Review 271–94.

My own proposal is...that there should be no need to decide cases based on the either/or approach. The paramountcy principle is not inimical to child sharing, rather, it is the entrenchment of the ideology that children's interests are best served by the private nuclear family that continues to proscribe alternative ways of being a family...

We need to centralise the welfare of the child in these cases rather than subordinate it to the adults involved and ensure that the welfare principle encompasses a thorough consideration of the basic need for children to have knowledge of their birth origins and where possible their wider kinship network.

(1) Parental Orders

When a court makes a parental order, the Registrar General will re-register the child's birth. As with adoption, it will not be possible for the public to make a link between entries in the register of births and the parental order register, but once a child reaches adulthood, she will, after being offered counselling, have access to her original birth certificate. Here we reproduce an extract from the 2008 Act's provision governing access to parental orders, which comes into force in April 2010. With one important change—parental orders used to be available only when the commissioning couple were married—this reproduces the 1990 Act's section 30.

Human Fertilisation and Embryology Act 2008 section 54

Parental orders

54(1) On an application made by two people ("the applicants"), the court may make an order providing for a child to be treated in law as the child of the applicants if—

(a) the child has been carried by a woman who is not one of the applicants, as a result of the placing in her of an embryo or sperm and eggs or her artificial insemination,

(b) the gametes of at least one of the applicants were used to bring about the creation of the embryo, and

(c) the conditions in subsections (2) to (8) are satisfied.

(2) The applicants must be—

(a) husband and wife,

(b) civil partners of each other, or

(c) two persons who are living as partners in an enduring family relationship and are not within prohibited degrees of relationship in relation to each other.

(3) Except in a case falling within subsection (11), the applicants must apply for the order during the period of 6 months beginning with the day on which the child is born.

(4) At the time of the application and the making of the order—

(a) the child's home must be with the applicants, and

(b) either or both of the applicants must be domiciled in the United Kingdom or in the Channel Islands or the Isle of Man.

(5) At the time of the making of the order both the applicants must have attained the age of 18.

(6) The court must be satisfied that both—

(a) the woman who carried the child, and

(b) any other person who is a parent of the child but is not one of the applicants (including any man who is the father by virtue of section 35 or 36 or any woman who is a parent by virtue of section 42 or 43),

have freely, and with full understanding of what is involved, agreed unconditionally to the making of the order.

(7) Subsection (6) does not require the agreement of a person who cannot be found or is incapable of giving agreement; and the agreement of the woman who carried the child is ineffective for the purpose of that subsection if given by her less than six weeks after the child's birth.

(8) The court must be satisfied that no money or other benefit (other than for expenses reasonably incurred) has been given or received by either of the applicants for or in consideration of—

(a) the making of the order,

(b) any agreement required by subsection (6),

(c) the handing over of the child to the applicants, or

(d) the making of arrangements with a view to the making of the order,

unless authorised by the court....

(11) An application which—

(a) relates to a child born before the coming into force of this section, and

(b) is made by two persons who, throughout the period applicable under subsection (2) of section 30 of the 1990 Act, were not eligible to apply for an order under that section in relation to the child as husband and wife,

may be made within the period of six months beginning with the day on which this section comes into force.

Notice that a parental order can only be made where both the surrogate mother and any other person who is the child's parent (other than the commissioning father) has given free and informed consent. Unlike adoption, it is not possible to dispense with their consent on the grounds that it is being unreasonably withheld.

When a local authority is aware that a child has been, or is about to be born following a surrogacy arrangement, its social services department is required to make enquiries in order to satisfy itself that the child is not at risk of harm as a result of the arrangement.[16] Following the child's birth, if the local authority have reasonable grounds to believe that the child is suffering, or is likely to suffer significant harm, they would be entitled to seek a care order.[17]

Although a report from a Guardian *ad litem*[18] is needed before a parental order can be made,[19] this process effectively short-circuits some of the more cumbersome aspects of the adoption process. As a result, access to this fast-track procedure is limited. Under the old section 30 procedure, the applicants had be married to each other. The 2008 Act enables civil partners and cohabitees to apply. This will—for a period of six months—be capable of apply-

---

[16] Parental Orders (Human Fertilisation and Embryology) Regulations 1994.

[17] Children Act 1989, s 31(2).

[18] A person appointed by the court to represent the interests of a minor.

[19] Parental Orders (Human Fertilisation and Embryology) Regulations 1994.

ing retrospectively. Subsection 11 of the new Act enables people who were not previously eligible for parental orders to apply for them within six months of the new provision coming into force.

Other restrictions are that at least one of the applicants must be genetically related to the child; conception must not have been by natural intercourse; the child must be living with the applicants; and the court must be satisfied that no money or benefit, other than for expenses reasonably incurred, has been paid, unless authorized by the court.

In deciding whether to make a parental order, the court is directed to 'have regard to all the circumstances, first consideration being given to the need to safeguard and promote the welfare of the child'.[20] Since parental order applications are classified as 'family proceedings', the courts are entitled, if they see fit, to make an alternative order, such as a residence order, or an additional order, such as an order that the child should continue to have contact with the surrogate mother.[21]

An application for a parental order may be made in the Family Proceedings court. The guardian *ad litem* must first establish that the statutory criteria are satisfied, and second, must determine whether there is any reason why a parental order would not be in the best interests of the child. Guardians *ad litem* are therefore charged with policing the 'genetic link' and 'no payment' requirements, *and* with protecting the child's welfare. In carrying out their duties, they face two major problems. First, their powers are extremely limited, so in ensuring both that the child was created using the gametes of at least one of the applicants, and that there have been no unlawful payments, they only have access to information provided by the surrogate and the commissioning couple. Secondly, their two duties are not necessarily compatible with each other. Because the child must already be living with the commissioning parents before an application is made, her welfare will seldom be promoted by removing her from a settled home. So even if there has been a blatant contravention of the 'no payment' rule, the child's interests may still be best served by making a parental order.

Moreover, as we have already seen, the court has the power to authorize payments other than expenses reasonably incurred, and the Brazier Committee was unable to find any case in which an application for a parental order was refused on the grounds that an unacceptably large sum of money had changed hands.[22] In *Re C (Application by Mr and Mrs X under s 30 of the Human Fertilisation and Embryology Act 1990)*, for example, the couple had paid a woman who was in fact claiming benefits of £12,000 for 'loss of earnings'. Despite finding that the couple had made an unlawful payment, Wall LJ nevertheless judged that a parental order would be in the child's best interests.

Re C (Application by Mr and Mrs X under s 30 of the Human Fertilisation and Embryology Act 1990)[23]

Wall LJ

The questions which arise, accordingly, are: (1) can the court be satisfied that the sum of £12,000 paid by Mr and Mrs X to SM was for 'expenses reasonably incurred'? And (2) if the answer to that question is 'no', does the court have the power retrospectively to authorise the payment?

---

[20] Ibid 1(1)(a).   [21] Children Act 1989, s 8.   [22] Brazier, para 5.3.
[23] [2002] EWHC 157 (Fam).

The first question is a pure issue of fact, and it is reasonably clear that the answer to it is 'no'....

What is important, I think, is that on all the evidence it is clear that the memorandum was entered into by Mr and Mrs X in good faith, and without any corrupt intent. They were not paying £12,000 to buy a baby. They were paying a figure for expenses which they had been advised was on the high side, but which was not disproportionate.

None the less, it must follow that money other than for 'expenses reasonably incurred' has been given by Mr and Mrs X to SM as a consequence of the memorandum, and that the court cannot make a parental order unless the payments are 'authorised' by the court....

[T]he factors which seem to me to weigh in the scales when considering the degree to which Mr and Mrs X are tainted by the transaction are the following:

(1) The sum of £12,000 required of them was not disproportionate, given the usual figure quoted by COTS and Mr and Mrs X's wish to ensure that SM did not take employment during the pregnancy...

(2) Mr and Mrs X did not know that SM was claiming income support until after it was confirmed that SM was pregnant. At that point it was plainly too late for them to withdraw.

(3) Mr and Mrs X are plainly a genuine couple who have spent many years attempting to conceive a child; they entered into the memorandum in good faith and without any corrupt intent.

(4) If SM was defrauding the Department of Social Security by not disclosing the sums Mr and Mrs X were paying her, the responsibility for that behaviour is hers alone. There is no suggestion that Mr and Mrs X encouraged or aided and abetted her to do so in any way.

(5) It is very clear that C is a much loved and cherished child. It is manifestly in her interests that she should be treated in law as the child of Mr and Mrs X, and that both should have parental responsibility for her.

For all these reasons, I authorised the payment of £12,000 by Mr and Mrs X to SM and make a parental order under s 30 of the Act.

In *Re X & Y (Foreign Surrogacy)*, a case in which a British couple had employed a Ukranian surrogate mother, it had to be conceded that the payments of €235 per month to the surrogate mother during pregnancy and a lump sum of €25,000 on the live birth of the twins, to enable her to put down a deposit for the purchase of a flat, significantly exceeded 'expenses reasonably incurred'. Taking the twins' welfare into account, Hedley J agreed to authorize these payments in order to enable a parental order to be made, but he expressed considerable unease about doing so.

Re X & Y (Foreign Surrogacy)[24]

Hedley J

I feel bound to observe that I find this process of authorisation most uncomfortable. What the court is required to do is to balance two competing and potentially irreconcilably conflicting concepts. Parliament is clearly entitled to legislate against commercial surrogacy and is clearly entitled to expect that the courts should implement that policy consideration in its

---

24 [2008] EWHC 3030 (Fam).

decisions. Yet it is also recognised that as the full rigour of that policy consideration will bear on one wholly unequipped to comprehend it let alone deal with its consequences (i.e. the child concerned) that rigour must be mitigated by the application of a consideration of that child's welfare. That approach is both humane and intellectually coherent. The difficulty is that it is almost impossible to imagine a set of circumstances in which by the time the case comes to court, the welfare of any child (particularly a foreign child) would not be gravely compromised (at the very least) by a refusal to make an order.

Where the surrogate mother is happy to hand over the child, and the commissioning couple fulfil all the other criteria, an application for a parental order will be the simplest way for them to acquire legal parenthood. If the surrogate mother does not want the child, unless the commissioning couple would obviously be woefully inadequate parents, it would rarely be in the child's best interests for the parental order to be refused, and the child to be taken into the care of the local authority. Hence, provided that the statutory conditions are satisfied, obtaining a parental order will be relatively straightforward.

There are, however, several different reasons why a commissioning couple might not be able to apply for a parental order. If they do not apply within the six-month time limit, perhaps because of immigration delays, for example, or the surrogate mother refuses to consent to the making of an order, the only way in which the commissioning couple can acquire legal parenthood is through adoption.

(2) Adoption

The adoption process is onerous and time-consuming. In order to be eligible to adopt a child, the criteria in the Adoption and Children Act 2002 must be satisfied, and potential adopters must endure rigorous scrutiny by local authority social workers over a prolonged period of time. If the surrogate mother does not want the child, but for some other reason the couple are ineligible for a parental order, adoption will usually be in the best interests of the child. But where the surrogate mother has changed her mind and an adoption application is made, the situation is much less straightforward. Under section 52(1) of the Adoption and Children Act 2002, the parents must consent to a child's adoption, unless they cannot be found or are incapable of consenting, or the court is satisfied that 'the child's welfare requires that their consent should be dispensed with'.

So when should a surrogate mother's consent to adoption be dispensed with by the court? The answer will often depend upon where the child is living. If she is already settled with the commissioning couple, her interests in avoiding disruption may be decisive. On the other hand, if the child is still living with her mother, the courts would be slow to order her removal. Although decided under previous adoption legislation, the question of whether the mother's consent to adoption should be dispensed with arose in *Re MW (Adoption: Surrogacy)*.

Re MW (Adoption: Surrogacy)[25]

Callman J

I have had no evidence in this case, in any shape or form, of anything other than beneficial consequences flowing from the care lavished upon M. I think the mother now wants to undo what she did but the wish to undo this is for her benefit...

[25] [1995] 2 FLR 789.

To introduce uncertainty, to disturb the present position, is contrary to the welfare and interests of this small boy. . . . I have found that her withholding of consent under the circumstances of this case is not what a reasonably objective parent would want to do for her child. Under the circumstances I am prepared to dispense with the mother's consent in this case, bearing in mind that she had previously given her consent and plainly had entered into this arrangement from the beginning with the advice of a solicitor. . . . The reality is that sad as it is for the mother I must make an adoption order. . . .

This mother originally had a possible prospect of seeing her child by agreement, until there has been such a publicity campaign which has caused such anguish to the applicants and also brought M himself into the limelight. Through that very act she has undermined whatever prospects of contact she might have had. It is largely through her own actions. Accordingly I consider this to be one of those cases where there should be no contact during the minority of M to his mother or his half-sister. It is a sad case, but the mother in the last resort has mainly herself to blame about it. The reality is that I have to guard M's interests.

In contrast, in *Re P (Minors) (Wardship: Surrogacy)* the children had been living with the surrogate mother since birth, and Sir John Arnold held that this factor outweighed the material and other advantages of being brought up by the commissioning couple.

Re P (Minors) (Wardship: Surrogacy)[26]

Sir John Arnold P

These children have been, up to their present age of approximately five months, with, quite consistently, their mother and in those circumstances there must necessarily have been some bonding of those children with their mother and that is undoubtedly coupled with the fact that she is their mother, a matter which weighs predominantly in the balance in favour of leaving the children with their mother, but there are other factors which weigh in the opposite balance and which, as is said by Mr B through his counsel, outweigh the advantages of leaving the children with their mother and it is that balancing exercise which the court is required to perform. . . .

They are principally as follows. It is said, and said quite correctly, that the shape of the B family is the better shape of a family in which these children might be brought up, because it contains a father as well as a mother and that is undoubtedly true. Next, it is said that the material circumstances of the B family are such that they exhibit a far larger degree of affluence than can be demonstrated by Mrs P. That, also, is undoubtedly true. Then it is said that the intellectual quality of the environment of the B's home and the stimulus which would be afforded to these babies, if they were to grow up in that home, would be greater than the corresponding features in the home of Mrs P. That is not a matter which has been extensively investigated, but I suspect that that is probably true. Certainly, the combined effect of the lack of affluence on the part of Mrs P and some lack of resilience to the disadvantages which that implies has been testified in the correspondence to the extent that I find Mrs P saying that shortage of resources leads to her sitting at home with little E and overeating, because she has no ability from a financial point of view to undertake anything more resourceful than that. Then it is said that the religious comfort and support which the B's derive from their Church is greater than anything of that sort available to Mrs P. How far that is true, I simply do not know. I do know that the B's are practising Christians and do derive advantages from that circumstance, but nobody asked Mrs P about this and I am not disposed to assume that she lacks that sort of comfort and support in the absence of any investigation by way of cross-examination to lay the foundations for such a conclusion. Then it is said, and there is something in this, that the problems which might arise from the circumstance that these children who are, of course, congenitally derived from the semen of Mr B and bear traces of Mr B's Asiatic origin would be more easily understood and discussed and reconciled in the household of Mr and Mrs B, a household with an Asiatic ethnic background than they would be if they arose in relation to these children while they were situated in the home of Mrs P, which is in an English village and which has no non-English connections....

As regards the other factors, they are, in the aggregate, weighty, but I do not think, having given my very best effort to the evaluation of the case dispassionately on both sides, that they ought to be taken to outweigh the advantages to these children of preserving the link with the mother to whom they are bonded and who has, as is amply testified, exercised over them a satisfactory level of maternal care, and accordingly it is, I think, the duty of the court to award the care and control of these babies to their mother.

Under section 95 of the Adoption and Children Act 2002, any payment or reward made in consideration of the adoption of a child is a criminal offence. But if a child has settled with adopters following an adoption procedure tainted by illegality, removing the child from his or her home in order to 'punish' the wrongfulness of the circumstances in which the child was adopted would not necessarily be in the best interests of that child. As a result, illegal payments made in consideration of adoption can again be 'authorized' by the court.

The central problem, then, is that once a child has settled within a family, it will very rarely be in her best interests to force her to leave, and it would be unacceptable to attempt to 'punish' the parents by depriving the child of her settled home. The point is well made by Latey J in *Re C (A Minor)(Wardship: Surrogacy)*. This was the famous 'Baby Cotton' case in which a British woman, Kim Cotton, who went on to set up COTS, acted as a surrogate for an American couple.

Re C (A Minor) (Wardship: Surrogacy)[27]

Latey J

First and foremost, and at the heart of the prerogative jurisdiction in wardship, is what is best for the child or children concerned. That and nothing else. Plainly, the methods used to produce a child as this baby has been, and the commercial aspects of it, raise difficult and delicate problems of ethics, morality and social desirability. These problems are under active consideration elsewhere.

Are they relevant in arriving at a decision on what now and, so far as one can tell, in the future is best for this child? If they are relevant, it is incumbent on the court to do its best to evaluate and balance them.

In my judgment, however, they are not relevant. The baby is here. All that matters is what is best for her now that she is here and not how she arrived. If it be said (though it has not been said during these hearings) that because the father and his wife entered into these arrangements it is some indication of their unsuitability as parents, I should reject any such

---

[27] [1985] FLR 846.

suggestion. If what they did was wrong (and I am not saying that it was), they did it in total innocence.

It follows that the moral, ethical and social considerations are for others and not for this court in its wardship jurisdiction.

So, what is best for this baby? Her natural mother does not ask for her. Should she go into Mr and Mrs A's care and be brought up by them? Or should some other arrangement be made for her, such as long-term fostering with or without adoption as an end?

The factors can be briefly stated. Mr A is the baby's father and he wants her, as does his wife. The baby's mother does not want her. Mr and Mrs A are a couple in their 30s. They are devoted to each other. They are both professional people, highly qualified. They have a very nice home in the country and another in a town. Materially they can give the baby a very good upbringing. But, far more importantly, they are both excellently equipped to meet the baby's emotional needs. They are most warm, caring, sensible people, as well as highly intelligent. When the time comes to answer the child's questions, they will be able to do so with professional advice if they feel they need it. Looking at this child's well-being, physical and emotional, who better to have her care? No one.

Of course, it would be a mistake to assume that every illegal payment will automatically be authorized by the courts. In *Re C (A Minor) (Adoption Application)*, a couple made an arrangement with a pregnant woman that she would hand over the baby after birth and that, in order to bypass some of the restrictions of adoption law, the husband would pass himself off as the baby's father. The couple paid her various sums of money. Although there were other reasons for rejecting their application for an adoption order, Booth J also considered whether or not he should retrospectively authorize these payments.

Re C (A Minor) (Adoption Application)[28]

Booth J

But had I to consider whether or not I should authorise the payments that I find to have been made by Mr and Mrs S to the mother in regard to the adoption by them of C, I would have to take into consideration the purpose for which they were made and all the circumstances of the case. I have no doubt at all that they were payments made by Mr and Mrs S for the handing over to them of C, and that they were made with a view to ensuring that the mother would continue to adhere to the false story and to the deceit which would lead, in the end, to their adoption of the baby. To authorise such payments would be to sweep aside the protection given by the Act to children and it would, in effect, amount to ratifying the sale of a child for adoption. I would not, in the circumstances, have considered it right to authorise any of the payments which I find to have been made by Mr and Mrs S to the mother.

Re N (A Child)[29] is an unusual surrogacy case, in which despite the child, N, having lived with the surrogate mother, Mrs P, for his first 18 months, and despite evidence that Mr and Mrs P had given him high standards of care, a residence order was nevertheless awarded to Mr J, the commissioning father, who was also N's biological father. Usually the courts' concern to protect the child's best interests will mean that it will be very slow to remove a

---

[28] [1993] 1 FLR 87.   [29] [2007] EWCA Civ 1053.

child from a settled home, regardless of the circumstances of the child's conception. Here, however, the judge had found that 'the P's had deliberately embarked on a path of deception, driven by Mrs P's compulsive desire to bear a child or further children, and that she had never had any other objective than to obtain insemination by surrogacy, with the single purpose of acquiring for herself, and her family, another child'. In such circumstances, the Court of Appeal agreed with Coleridge J that it would be better for N if he were to live instead with the Js and to have no contact with Mr and Mrs P.

A particular difficulty arises in surrogacy arrangements made between British surrogate mothers and commissioning couples from abroad. Because the couple are not domiciled in the UK, they are ineligible for parental orders, but there are also restrictions upon foreigners adopting British children, which make adoption extremely problematic as well. This issue arose in *Re G (Surrogacy: Foreign Domicile)*. McFarlane J found a way to enable Mr and Mrs G to take M back to Turkey with them, but his judgment is notable for the criticism he makes of the absence of any 'regulatory umbrella', which leaves these exceptionally complex arrangements in the hands of 'well meaning amateurs'.

Re G (Surrogacy: Foreign Domicile)[30]

McFarlane J

The procedural history of this case, to which I am about to turn, is a cautionary tale which highlights the legal, emotional, and not least the financial consequences of surrogacy arrangements which are undertaken in this jurisdiction involving commissioning parents who are not domiciled in the UK....

It would be easy, but to a degree unjustified, to single COTS out as being responsible for bringing about this surrogacy in circumstances that it knew, or should have known, could not possibly result in a parental order and thereby creating the situation that has required substantial court intervention and the expenditure of some £35,000 of public money.

Of more concern is the understanding that the court now has as to the scale of COTS involvement in cases where the commissioning couple are domiciled overseas....

It is therefore a matter of significant concern that COTS has, albeit naïvely, been involved in the activities that I have described which are, and have long been, outside the law. For an agency working in the surrogacy field not to be aware of one of the basic requirements needed to obtain a parental order is a matter of some real concern...

The court's understanding is that surrogacy agencies such as COTS are not covered by any statutory or regulatory umbrella and are therefore not required to perform to any recognised standard of competence. I am sufficiently concerned by the information uncovered in these two cases to question whether some form of inspection or authorisation should be required in order to improve the quality of advice that is given to individuals who seek to achieve the birth of a child through surrogacy. Given the importance of the issues involved when the life of a child is created in this manner, it is questionable whether the role of facilitating surrogacy arrangements should be left to groups of well-meaning amateurs....

The one enormously positive feature in this case is that young M is said to be an absolute delight, who is well settled in the care of Mr and Mrs G who are turning out to be fine parents. The aim of the court has therefore been to identify and establish the most effective legal structure, short of a parental order, that can facilitate Mr and Mrs G in due course adopting M in their home country...

[30] [2007] EWHC 2814 (Fam).

By the Adoption and Children Act 2002 section 84(2) the High Court may, on an application by persons who the court is satisfied intend to adopt a child under the law of a country or territory outside the British Islands, make an order giving parental responsibility for the child to them. In addition to granting parental responsibility to the proposed adopters, an order under s 84 has the effect of terminating the parental responsibility of any other person (in this case, Mrs J).

Difficulties can also arise where the commissioning couple are British and the surrogate mother is a foreign national. Even if they are, in the end, eligible for a parental order, as was the case in *Re X & Y*, the child herself may face immigration difficulties. If the child's mother is the foreign surrogate, the child may be a foreign national from birth and hence may not be allowed entry to the UK. In *Re X & Y*, the child's legal position was worse still. Under Ukranian law, the commissioning couple are treated as the child's parents from birth, so the surrogate mother was not the child's mother. Under UK law, which applied to the commissioning couple, they could not be treated as the child's parents without a court order. The child was potentially then both stateless and parentless. This and other pitfalls are summarized here by Hedley J.

Re X & Y (Foreign Surrogacy)[31]

Hedley J

It will be readily apparent that many pitfalls confront the couple who consider commissioning a foreign surrogacy. First, the quality of the information currently available is variable and may, in what it omits, actually be misleading. Secondly, potentially difficult conflict of law issues arise which may (as in this case) have wholly unintended and unforeseen consequences as for example in payments made. Thirdly, serious immigration problems may arise having regard to the effect of Sections 27–29 of the 1990 Act, at least as understood by me. Children born to foreign surrogate mothers, especially to married women, may have no rights of entry nor may the law confer complementary rights on the commissioning couple....

Lastly, even if all other pitfalls are avoided, rights may depend both upon the unswerving commitment of the surrogate mother (and her husband if she has one) to supporting the surrogacy through to completion by Section 30 order and upon their honesty in not taking advantage of their absolute veto....

In any event part of the purpose of adjourning this case into open court was to illustrate the sort of difficulties that currently can and do appear. This relates to the obvious difficulties of nationality, control of the commercial element, the rules of consent and the question of legal parentage. Less obviously, but importantly, is the fact that the present law (at least as understood by this court) might encourage the less scrupulous to take advantage of the more vulnerable, unmarried surrogate mothers and to be less than frank in the arrangements that surround foreign surrogacy arrangements.

(3) Informal Transfers

While parental orders and adoption are the only ways in which the commissioning couple can become the legal parents of the child born following a surrogacy arrangement, this does not mean that every surrogate birth is followed by a formal application for legal parenthood.

---

[31] [2008] EWHC 3030 (Fam.).

A child may be handed over by the surrogate mother, and live with the commissioning couple without any legal formalities. For obvious reasons, it is impossible to tell how many unofficial transfers of children take place each year. Worryingly, however, the Brazier Report suggested that 'a substantial proportion of commissioning couples are failing to apply to the courts to become the legal parents of the child'.[32]

It is then possible that the parents will have no formal legal obligations towards 'their' child. Even if the child's parents have obtained a residence order,[33] which will give them parental responsibility, this would be shared with the surrogate mother, who will continue to have parental responsibility for the child, even if she has little or no contact with her. The potential for uncertainty and disputes is obvious.

(f) REFORM

There are a number of problems with the law governing surrogacy in the UK. First, the prohibition of commercialization has failed to prevent the routine payment of sums of £10,000–£15,000 to surrogate mothers. Secondly, the Human Fertilisation and Embryology Act's fatherhood provisions are intended to cover cases in which donated sperm is used, and they apply awkwardly and inappropriately to surrogacy arrangements. Thirdly, the complexity of the rules governing the transfer of legal parenthood undoubtedly deters some commissioning parents from acquiring a formal relationship with 'their' child, and this is clearly not in a child's best interests. Fourthly, as we can see from *Re G*, surrogacy arrangements are not properly regulated, and agreements are often made without legal advice, with potentially disastrous consequences for all concerned.

The government appeared to accept the need for reform some time ago when it appointed a committee, chaired by Margaret Brazier, to review aspects of the regulation of surrogacy in the UK. The Brazier Committee's report was published in 1998,[34] but none of its recommendations were implemented.

The Brazier Committee advocated the complete prohibition of any payments to surrogate mothers, other than compensation for specific expenses actually incurred as a result of the pregnancy. Surrogacy, it argued, should be 'a fully informed and free act of giving'.[35] A comparison was made with blood, tissue, and organ donation, all of which are, in the UK, legitimate only within a 'gift relationship'.[36] The Brazier Committee admitted that one consequence of eliminating payments for surrogacy could be that 'few women will be willing to undertake such a commitment, except for a relative or close friend',[37] but a drop in the number of surrogacy arrangements would not, according to the Brazier Committee, necessarily be a bad thing.

Interestingly, as Michael Freeman points out in the next extract, there may be a tension between the Committee's conclusion that a ban on surrogacy would be undesirable because it would push the practice underground, and their acknowledgement that a ban on payments will in reality mean that very few women come forward to act as surrogates. The

---

[32] Brazier, para 5.7.   [33] Children Act 1989, section 8.
[34] *Surrogacy: Review for Health Ministers of Current Arrangements for Payments and Regulation* (HMSO: London, 1998) Cm 4068.
[35] Brazier, para 4.37.
[36] Richard M Titmuss, *Gift Relationship: From Human Blood to Social Policy* (Allen & Unwin: London, 1971).
[37] Brazier, para 4.37.

unavailability of surrogate mothers, whether it results from an outright ban or a prohibition on payment, will in practice mean that people who need to employ surrogates in order to reproduce will 'go underground' or travel abroad.

Michael Freeman[38]

The [Brazier] Report fails to appreciate that withdrawing remuneration from surrogates will only drive potential surrogates away from regulated surrogacy into an invisible and socially uncontrolled world where the regulators will be more like pimps than adoption agencies. There is every reason to control surrogacy and to guard against perceived problems, but most women will expect to be rewarded. Brazier agrees and believes that surrogacy will rarely be undertaken by strangers once its recommendations are implemented. This prognosis is misplaced: surrogacy will continue; it will probably grow as infertility increases; it will go underground and the fees will become larger. We cannot stop women exercising their autonomy, nor can we persuade them that being paid aggravates their exploitation, when common sense tells them the reverse.

As we can see from the recent cases of *Re G and Re X & Y*, cross-national surrogacy arrangements can result in especially tricky legal problems for surrogate mothers, commissioning parents, and children. They also seem to be becoming more common. This is one of many factors prompting Natalie Gamble to call for a fresh review of surrogacy law.

Natalie Gamble[39]

Countries such as the Ukraine and India permit commercial arrangements under which the intended parents are registered as the legal parents at birth. Foreign clinics commonly advise patients that the legalities after the birth are very simple, and patients are unlikely to question this information, particularly given the absence of contrary advice available elsewhere.

What many patients do not realise, though, is that if they are domiciled in the UK, UK law applies to them regardless of where the conception occurs. This can result in the unfortunate situation where, at birth, neither the surrogate nor the intended parents are legal parents under their own home systems of law and the child is born an orphan. Any foreign birth certificate naming the English parents as the legal parents cannot be relied upon for UK legal purposes.

There is then no straightforward way for the English parents to apply for entry clearance to bring their child into the UK under the immigration rules, and in many cases the child will be 'stateless' which means he or she cannot even obtain a passport. If a commercial agreement has been made in the foreign jurisdiction, this will also prevent the English intended parents obtaining a parental order or an adoption order in the UK to become the legal parents. Commercial agreements are legal in the foreign jurisdictions I have mentioned, and UK patients may enter into them quite innocently. Ultimately, a biological child of two English parents may be left parentless and stateless in a foreign country, with the parents unable to secure a right to raise their own child or to bring him or her into the UK.

[38] 'Does Surrogacy Have a Future After Brazier?' (1999) 7 Medical Law Review 1–20.
[39] 'Why UK Surrogacy Law Needs an Urgent Review' Bionews 28 April 2008, available at <www.bionews.org.uk>.

3   IS SURROGACY ACCEPTABLE?

Some commentators have argued that surrogacy raises more difficult ethical issues than other assisted conception techniques. First, Elizabeth Anderson argues that it is not in the best interests of the child to discover that her gestational mother gave her away in return for money, shortly after her birth. Because of the small numbers of surrogate births, there is little evidence of the long-term impact of surrogacy arrangements upon children, so this sort of claim is necessarily speculative. In a related argument, Elizabeth Anderson maintains that the surrogate mother's own children's sense of security might be undermined by witnessing their mother giving away a child to whom she has just given birth. Again, there is little evidence to support or discount this claim.

Elizabeth Anderson[40]

Commercial surrogacy substitutes market norms for some of the norms of parental love... For in this practice the natural mother deliberately conceives a child with the intention of giving it up for material advantage. Her renunciation of parental responsibilities is not done for the child's sake, nor for the sake of fulfilling an interest she shares with the child, but typically for her own sake (and possibly, if 'altruism' is a motive, for the intended parents' sakes). She and the couple who pay her to give up her parental rights over her child thus treat her rights as a kind of property right. They thereby treat the child itself as a kind of commodity, which may be properly bought and sold...

The unsold children of surrogate mothers are also harmed by commercial surrogacy. The children of some surrogate mothers have reported their fears that they may be sold like their half-brother or half-sister, and express a sense of loss at being deprived of a sibling. Furthermore, the widespread acceptance of commercial surrogacy would psychologically threaten all children. For it would change the way children are valued by people (parents and surrogate brokers)—from being loved by their parents and respected by others, to being sometimes used as objects of commercial profit-making.

Secondly, it is often argued that surrogacy is exploitative. This claim has a number of different strands. It might, for example, be argued that the commissioning couple treat the surrogate mother as a means to an end, thus violating the Kantian imperative (which we considered in Chapter 1). Elizabeth Anderson again would subscribe to this view: 'The application of commercial norms to women's labor reduces the surrogate mothers from persons worthy of respect and consideration to objects of mere use.'[41]

Of course, as we have seen before in this book, the Kantian imperative just warns against treating another person *solely* as a means to an end. Provided that the surrogate mother is also treated as a person in her own right, employing her to carry a baby for nine months does not necessarily offend the Kantian imperative.

A different sense in which surrogacy is accused of being exploitative is the claim that the risk of actual exploitation, chiefly of the surrogate mother, is too great. On this line of argument, offering a woman money to bear a child creates the possibility of exploitation, especially since commissioning couples will usually be richer than surrogate mothers.

Richard Arneson disagrees, and claims that banning surrogacy in order to protect poor women from choosing surrogacy is both paternalistic and elitist.

---

[40] 'Is Women's Labor a Commodity?' (1990) 19 Philosophy and Public Affairs 71–92.   [41] Ibid.

Richard Arneson[42]

> Notice that the mere observation that the women who choose commercial surrogacy tend to be poor and to have few if any minimally attractive work options other than surrogacy is not a reason to ban commercial surrogacy unless one believes that these women are choosing incompetently. No matter how restricted one's life options, the idea that the narrow range of one's options unacceptably constrains one's choice is not a reason to limit further one's range of choice...
>
> My point is simply that a concern that some people are forced to choose their lives from an unfairly small menu of options is a reason to expand not restrict the range of options from which these people must choose....
>
> [T]he thought that commercial surrogacy should be banned because the poor working women who mostly choose it are too incompetent to be entrusted to make their own decisions in this sphere has an ugly, elitist sound.

Lori Andrews further points out that while money may influence a woman's decision to become a surrogate mother, it is seldom her only reason.

Lori Andrews[43]

> Studies have found that some surrogates have been affected by the plight of infertile family members and friends. Others enjoyed parenting and wanted to help infertile couples become parents. Many of the women I interviewed described the tremendous psychic benefits they received from the feeling that they were helping someone meet a joyous life goal. Many viewed themselves as feminists who were exercising reproductive choice and demonstrating an ethic of care. It seems crass not to try to understand the arrangement from the surrogate's vantage point, in which this type of employment is viewed as a higher calling, like being a health care professional or educator, and may consequently be preferable to working as a check-out clerk in a grocery store or at some other minimum wage job.

It is also sometimes argued that it is simply not possible for a woman's consent to bear a child for someone else to be fully informed and entirely voluntary, either because before conception it is difficult for a woman to know whether she will be able to hand over a child to whom she has given birth, or because she is unable to resist the offer of a substantial sum of money. Against this, Stephen Wilkinson argues that, provided a woman is given sufficient information, there is no reason to presume that she is necessarily incapable of agreeing to become a surrogate mother.

Stephen Wilkinson[44]

> [I]f (as is suggested) it's true that women's emotions are unpredictable, and that surrogates often have regrets, and that there's much that we don't know about surrogacy arrangements,

---

[42] 'Commodification and Commerical Surrogacy' (1992) 21 Philosophy and Public Affairs 132–64.

[43] 'Beyond Doctrinal Boundaries: A Legal Framework for Surrogate Motherhood' (1995) 81 Virginia Law Review 2343–75.

[44] *Bodies for Sale: Ethics and Exploitation in the Human Body Trade* (Routledge: London, 2003) 171–3.

and that direct experience changes women's attitudes to pregnancy and childbirth, then *simply by telling prospective surrogates in some detail about these facts* we go a long way towards making sure that their consents are adequately informed. Consequently, it seems to me that the general consent arguments considered here (most of which are to do with surrogates' consents being insufficiently informed) are weak and don't provide a justification for banning commercial surrogacy or even for morally condemning it.

It is interesting that the concern about surrogate mothers feeling pressurized into entering surrogacy arrangements appears to derive principally from the existence of a financial incentive. Social and emotional pressure to agree to bear a child for a distraught friend or family member is seldom presented as an equivalent obstacle to a potential surrogate's free and autonomous decision-making, although in practice it may be difficult to refuse a request from one's sister or best friend.

The third objection to surrogacy flows from the argument that reproduction should not be commodified. In the next extract, Margaret Jane Radin argues that converting procreation into an economic transaction would have a negative impact upon children, women, and society as a whole.

Margaret Jane Radin[45]

If a capitalist baby industry were to come into being, with all of its accompanying paraphernalia, how could any of us, even those who did not produce infants for sale, avoid subconsciously measuring the dollar value of our children? How could our children avoid being preoccupied with measuring their own dollar value? This makes our discourse about ourselves (when we are children) and about our children (when we are parents) like our discourse about cars.

Concerns about commodification of women and children...might counsel permitting only unpaid surrogacy (market-inalienability). Market-inalienability might be grounded in a judgment that commodification of women's reproductive capacity is harmful for the identity aspect of their personhood and in a judgment that the closeness of paid surrogacy to baby-selling harms our self-conception too deeply.

Janice Raymond also objects to surrogacy, but argues that altruistic surrogacy arrangements are just as demeaning for women as commercial exchanges.

Janice Raymond[46]

Surrogacy, situated within the larger context of women's inequality, is not simply about the commercialization of women and children. On a political level, it reinforces the perception and use of women as a breeder class and the gender inequality of women as a group. The practice of surrogacy strikes at the core of what a society allows women to be and become. Taking the commerce out of surrogacy but leaving the practice intact on a non-commercial

---

[45] 'Market-Inalienability' (1987) 100 Harvard Law Review 1849–937. This article formed the nucleus of a book, *Contested Commodities* (Harvard University Press: Cambroidge, MA, 1996).

[46] *Women as Wombs: Reproductive Technologies and the Battle over Women's Freedom* (HarperCollins: New York, 1993).

and contractual basis glosses over the essential violation—the social definition of women as breeders.

Others, such as Michael Freeman, dispute the idea that surrogate mothers need to be protected against entering surrogacy arrangements, and argue that women should have the right to make decisions about their own bodies.

Michael Freeman[47]

[I]t is worth asking what is entailed in the right to liberty. Central to that right, I would argue, is the right to do with your body as you please. On this analysis, the surrogate mother has a right to use her body to give birth to the baby of another. To deny her the decision to become a surrogate thus violates her right to liberty. We can take away liberty-rights. Very few of them are totally unqualified. But the onus rests on those who wish to restrict liberty to put forward sound moral arguments to support limitations on freedom. What arguments can they adduce? The arguments are phrased in various ways (motherhood or woman is dehumanized, children are commodified)...But as arguments preferred to buttress limitations on autonomy, they amount to little more than the enforcement of morality for morality's sake...

What of the child? Warnock, it will be remembered, thought a surrogacy agreement was 'degrading to the child who is to be the outcome of it since...the child will have been bought for money'. This is surely fallacious. The money is paid to the surrogate mother not to compensate her for giving up the child, nor to 'buy' the child. The money is payment for services, it is compensation for the burden of pregnancy. The child may have a right not to be sold, but that is a distortion of what is happening, even in cases of commercial surrogacy.

4 SHOULD SURROGACY CONTRACTS BE ENFORCEABLE?

As we have seen, in the UK surrogacy contracts are unenforceable. Those who are in favour of their unenforceability, such as Rosemarie Tong and Katherine Bartlett, argue that it would be unconscionable to force the surrogate mother to hand over 'her' child after birth.

Rosemarie Tong[48]

The value of a 'change of heart' period is very important from a feminist point of view. First, it acknowledges a parental relationship whose moral significance traditional philosophy has ignored—namely, the gestational relationship...A second advantage of the 'change of heart' period is that it challenges the notion that contracts must be honored no matter what—as if contracts were more important than people...

---

[47] 'Is Surrogacy Exploitative?' in Sheila McLean (ed.), *Legal Issues in Human Reproduction* (Gower: London, 1989) 164–84.

[48] 'Feminist Perspectives and Gestational Motherhood: The Search for a Unified Legal Focus' in J Callahan (ed.), *Reproduction, Ethics and the Law: Feminist Responses* (Indiana UP: Bloomington and Indianapolis, 1995) 55–79.

> The adoption approach, with its change of heart clause, replaces what strikes me as the *heartless* contract approach. A deal is not always a deal—at least not when one is trading in some of the deepest emotions human beings can ever feel. Any approach that *binds* women to reproductive decisions—as does the contract approach—must be regarded with deep suspicion.

Katharine T Bartlett[49]

> [It] would seem unwise either to criminalize surrogacy contracts or to allow specific enforcement of them. Declining the use of courts to enforce private surrogacy arrangements, even while allowing parties to make them, would retain, without coercing, the assumption (or ideology) of current law—that, ordinarily, parents will not give up their children. It would affirm that wanting to keep one's children, even where one has previously agreed otherwise, is not pathological or wrong, but rather understandable and defensible.

Arguments against the enforceability of surrogacy contracts often amount to the claim that an order for specific performance would be oppressive. Surrogacy arrangements are, however, akin to contracts *for services*, in which an individual agrees to surrender some portion of their liberty in return for something, such as an income, that may be more valuable to them. In a contract for services, if either party were to fail to fulfil their obligations under the agreement, the ordinary remedy would be damages, not specific performance.

There are many contracts where specific performance would be oppressive, and this is not generally regarded as grounds for their complete unenforceability. Just as contract law will not generally force an actor who refuses to go on stage to complete his performance, so a surrogate mother would not necessarily be compelled to hand the baby over after birth. A remedy in damages for breach of contract would protect the surrogate mother's 'right' to keep the child, while compensating the commissioning couple for at least some of their losses. It is perfectly plausible for a surrogate mother's right to renege upon her undertaking to hand over the child to coexist with the commissioning couple's right to compensation for losses resulting from their misplaced reliance upon the agreement.

There are, however, those who would argue that specific performance would be the appropriate remedy when surrogacy arrangements break down. Marjorie Shultz argues that in certain circumstances, the surrogate mother should be compelled to hand over the baby to the commissioning couple.

Marjorie Shultz[50]

> The mother–child bond is significant and fundamental; its disruption seems, to many, unthinkable. It is less frequently noted, however, that if specific performance is denied where a surrogate refuses to surrender the child, an analogous loss is sustained by the father and, indeed, by the adoptive couple. A reproductive agreement creates expectations regarding the opportunity to parent a child; those expectations have vital importance to those who

---

[49] 'Re-expressing Parenthood' (1998) 98 Yale Law Journal 293, 333.
[50] 'Reproductive Technology and Intention-based Parenthood: An Opportunity for Gender Neutrality' (1990) Wisconsin Law Review 297–398.

hold them...Even more emphatically, in a surrogacy example, a particular life actually comes into being because of such an agreement. Once conception has taken place, reliance on the promises made is about as intense and significant as could be imagined. If intentions and the expectations and reliance that result are taken seriously, the unfairness of denying the equitable remedy [specific performance] becomes comparable to the hardship of granting it.....

In holding that surrogates but not other parties to the arrangement must have an opportunity to change their minds after giving birth, the court reinforces stereotypes of women as unstable, as unable to make decisions and stick to them, and as necessarily vulnerable to their hormones and emotions...In particular, it exalts a woman's experience of pregnancy and childbirth over her formation of emotional, intellectual and interpersonal decisions and expectations, as well as over others' reliance on the commitments she has earlier made.

The law's failure to enforce surrogacy contracts inevitably contributes to their insecurity. It could even be argued that their complete unenforceability may persuade women to become surrogates even if they are not sure that they would want to give up the child after birth. Giving the surrogate mother complete freedom to withdraw from the contract and keep all of the money that she has been paid might also provide an opportunity for extortion. Once conception has occurred the commissioning couple may be vulnerable to threats from the surrogate mother that she intends to keep the baby, or have an abortion, unless she receives more money.

Unlike other domestic agreements that are outside the scope of contract law, surrogacy arrangements are often based upon an entirely illusory relationship of 'trust' or 'friendship' between strangers. And unlike ordinary contracts, surrogacy arrangements are seldom entered into as a result of the trust that results from reputation and/or a pre-existing relationship; or because effective sanctions exist should the other party fail to keep their promise. Clearly, people only enter into such patently risky arrangements because their desire for the best-case outcome is so overwhelming.

In Israel, one of the only countries to have introduced a regulatory regime to approve surrogacy arrangements, the surrogate mother is only permitted to renege on her agreement if there has been a change of circumstances, and the welfare of the child would not be damaged. In the next extract, Rhona Schulz points out that the rigorous approval process which precedes any surrogacy arrangement in Israel minimizes the chance that the surrogate mother will in fact change her mind.

Rhona Schulz[51]

The Approvals Committee's guidelines for drawing up the surrogate motherhood agreement start with a clear statement that it is necessary to ensure, so far as is possible, that the birth mother understands the nature of the commitments involved in the agreement and agrees thereto voluntarily and without coercion. A number of the Approvals Committee's requirements are designed to further this end.

First, the physician who examines the birth mother has to declare that s/he has explained to the birth mother the consequences and significance of acting as a surrogate...Secondly, the Approvals Committee will not consider any application until it is satisfied that the birth

---

[51] 'Surrogacy in Israel: An Analysis of the Law in Practice' in R Cook, SD Sclater, with F Kaganas (eds), *Surrogate Motherhood: International Perspectives* (Hart Publishing: Oxford, 2003) 35–53.

mother has obtained independent legal advice from a lawyer who is an expert in surrogate motherhood agreements... Thirdly, the birth mother is interviewed separately by the Approvals Committee and will be asked questions designed to test whether her consent is voluntary and informed. Finally, the Approvals Committee's practice is only to approve birth mothers who have previously given birth...

We are not aware of any cases where the birth mother has requested to keep the child. One reason for this may be the screening by the Approvals Committee. While, of course, we cannot be sure that there would have been problems if arrangements had gone ahead which the birth mother rejected as unsuitable, it seems likely that the Approvals Committee is in a better position than the intended parents to judge the suitability of the birth mother both because of the professional skills and experience of the Approvals Committee members and because they are more likely to be objective. Childless couples, with limited options open to them, perhaps need protecting against possible rashness and lack of judgement in choosing a birth mother.

5 CONCLUSION

It is important to keep the issue of surrogacy in perspective. Surrogacy arrangements are rare. Most would-be mothers want to give birth to their own children, and so surrogacy is always likely to be a last resort for women. Surrogacy may be the only option for men who do not want to reproduce with a female partner, but again, demand does not seem to be great.

Nevertheless, despite its rarity, surrogacy does raise some complicated legal questions, such as who should be considered the child's parents, and what should happen if the arrangement breaks down. Banning surrogacy altogether is not a realistic option, because partial surrogacy arrangements can be made without any third-party involvement. If we know that children are going to be born as a result of surrogacy agreements, we must have mechanisms to resolve important questions about their parentage.

In this chapter we have seen that surrogacy is currently regulated by a combination of surrogacy-specific rules, such as the largely ineffective prohibition of commercialization, and provisions, such as the rules governing the attribution of legal parentage, which apply incidentally and rather awkwardly to the practice of surrogacy. Furthermore, the combined effect of the various rules governing surrogacy is that arrangements remain largely unregulated, thus encouraging commissioning couples and surrogate mothers to make agreements without any formal guidance or professional advice. In short, and in sharp contrast to the intensive regulation of assisted conception services which we considered in the previous chapter, people who seek to have children through surrogacy do so within a regulatory vacuum.

As we can see from a number of recent cases, the courts commonly have to deal with the consequences of ill-advised arrangements, attempting to construct solutions to safeguard the interests of children from other family law provisions, since the law on surrogacy is inadequate to the task. While surrogacy may not be a common way to start a family, it is legally precarious, and this is not in the best interests of children or of the adults involved in these arrangements. Both McFarlane J in *Re G* and Hedley J in *Re X & Y* suggest that the law is in desperate need of review. Their sensitive and non-judgemental attempts to safeguard the interests of children and their parents with wholly inadequate legal tools should be required reading for ministers.

FURTHER READING

Brazier, Margaret, Campbell, Alastair, and Golombok, Susan, *Surrogacy: Review for Health Ministers of Current Arrangements for Payments and Regulation* (HMSO: London, 1998) Cm 4068.

Cook R, Sclater SD, with Kaganas, F (eds), *Surrogate Motherhood: International Perspectives* (Hart Publishing: Oxford, 2003).

Freeman, Michael, 'Does Surrogacy Have a Future After Brazier?' (1999) 7 Medical Law Review 1–20.

Radin, Margaret Jane, 'Market-Inalienability' (1987) 100 Harvard Law Review 1849–937.

Wallbank, Julie, 'Too Many Mothers? Surrogacy, Kinship and the Welfare of the Child' (2002) 10 Medical Law Review 271–94.

Wilkinson, Stephen, *Bodies for Sale: Ethics and Exploitation in the Human Body Trade* (Routledge: London, 2003) ch 8.

17

END-OF-LIFE DECISIONS

CENTRAL ISSUES

1. Euthanasia involves a doctor acting deliberately to end a patient's life. It is illegal in the UK, and a doctor who kills her patient could be found guilty of murder, which carries a mandatory life sentence.

2. Assisted suicide is also a criminal offence. Suicide itself is no longer a crime, but this does not mean that patients have a *right* to commit suicide.

3. It is, however, lawful to administer a dose of painkilling drugs which may shorten a patient's life, by virtue of the doctrine of double effect.

4. Competent adults have the right to refuse life-sustaining treatment, which in practice means a right to insist that doctors physically remove them from a mechanical ventilator or feeding tube which is keeping them alive.

5. The principal arguments in favour of legalizing euthanasia and/or assisted suicide are respect for patient autonomy; mercy; the inconsistency of the line the law currently draws between lawful and unlawful life-shortening practices; and the benefits of openly regulating a practice which would otherwise be shrouded in secrecy.

6. The arguments against legalization include respect for the sanctity of human life; the view that high-quality palliative care ought to make euthanasia unnecessary; the dangers of ensuring that requests for euthanasia are genuine; the negative impact legalization might have on the doctor–patient relationship; and the dangers of the slippery slope.

7. Some other countries have legalized euthanasia and/or assisted suicide, but opinion differs over whether this has improved matters for patients, or made things worse.

8. In relation to incompetent patients, the courts have had to decide whether withdrawing or withholding life-saving treatment could ever be in a patient's best interests. Where the incompetent patient's condition is extremely grave, and where medical opinion is that life-prolonging measures are futile, non-treatment will sometimes be lawful.

1 INTRODUCTION

(a) CONTROVERSY AT THE END OF LIFE

Although it will happen to all of us, nobody knows what it is like to die. We may have watched life slip away from another person, and some people's religious faith leads them to have certain expectations about what will happen after their body ceases to be alive. Despite its universal inevitability, the process of dying will always remain mysterious to us. As a result, when judging whether death could ever be preferable to continued life, we are all inevitably behind a 'veil of ignorance'.[1]

Interest in whether it might be legitimate to take steps that will speed up the process of dying is not new. A number of Greek and Roman philosophers, among them Seneca, believed that suicide was a rational response to extreme physical and mental deterioration:

> I shall not abandon old age, if old age preserves me intact as regards the better part of myself; but if old age begins to shatter my mind, and to pull its various faculties to pieces, if it leaves me, not life, but only the breath of life, I shall rush out of a house that is crumbling and tottering.[2]

For a number of reasons, the question of whether it could ever be legitimate for the medical profession to help patients to die has become more prominent in recent years. First, life support techniques are capable of significantly prolonging the dying process, leading some patients to fear a protracted and undignified death. Patients who would previously have died can now be kept alive using mechanical ventilators and artificially delivered nutrition and hydration. While these techniques were initially developed to enable potentially curable patients to survive, despite a temporary inability to breathe or swallow, they are now able to keep people who have no chance of regaining consciousness alive for many years. New technologies have therefore forced us to think about the circumstances in which it might be legitimate to discontinue life-prolonging medical treatment.

Secondly, although life expectancy has increased dramatically over the past few decades, medical progress has not been as successful in extending the period during which we are able to lead healthy, independent lives. If the population as a whole is living longer, a greater proportion of us—now around 70 per cent—will develop one or more of the diseases of old age, such as cancer or dementia, which are often characterized by late onset and extended decline.[3] As a result, a growing number of elderly people face the prospect of a protracted period of debilitating ill health. The fear of spending many years entirely dependent upon others, as one's bodily functions fail, has prompted an intensification of public interest in euthanasia and assisted suicide.

Thirdly, as we have seen in previous chapters, the principle of patient autonomy has become increasingly dominant within medical law, raising the question of whether a patient's right to make decisions about her medical treatment should extend to being able to exercise some control over when she dies. Fourthly, when we looked at religious bioethics in

---

[1] J. Rawls, *A Theory of Justice* (Harvard UP, 1971).

[2] Seneca, 58th *Letter to Lucilius* trans RM Gummere in TE Page *et al.* (eds), *Seneca: Ad Lucilium Epistulae Morales* vol I (Heinemann: London, 1961) 409.

[3] Agnes van der Heide, Luc Deliens, Karin Faisst, Tore Nilstun, Michael Norup, Eugenio Paci, Gerrit van der Wal, and Paul J van der Maas, 'End-of-life Decision-making in Six European Countries: Descriptive Study' (2003) 362 The Lancet 345–50.

Chapter 1, one common theme that seemed to cut across all of the major religions was the idea that life is not ours to dispose of as we please. As society becomes increasingly secular, the weight given to the proscription of suicide and euthanasia within religious teachings has correspondingly diminished.

Fifthly, a number of high-profile cases, such as those of Dianne Pretty and Debbie Purdy in the UK and Terri Schiavo in the US, have led to intense media interest in end-of-life decision-making. In the UK, since 2003 over 100 UK citizens have made the journey to Switzerland to die in one of Dignitas' suicide 'clinics', and some of their stories have received considerable press coverage.

(b) ORGANIZATION OF THIS CHAPTER

In this chapter, we are concerned with the legal status of practices that may result in life being shortened. We begin with the competent patient, and in order to avoid repetition, this chapter takes for granted that the reader already understands the concept of capacity (discussed in full in Chapter 5). First, we look at the current law, distinguishing between lawful and unlawful life-shortening practices. Secondly, the arguments for and against the legalization of voluntary euthanasia and assisted suicide are set out, with extracts from both sides of this emotional and acrimonious debate. Next, we examine some other countries' experience with decriminalization.

In the second half of this chapter, our focus is on patients who lack capacity (again, refer back to Chapter 5 for a definition). We start with children, discussing the status of non-treatment decisions both in the criminal law, and flowing from the courts' inherent jurisdiction, and we consider the extraordinary 'conjoined twins case', *Re A*.[4] In relation to adults, we begin with an analysis of the House of Lords' ground-breaking decision that life-sustaining treatment could be withheld from Tony Bland, a patient in a permanent vegetative state.[5] We then cover developments since the *Bland* case.

(c) TERMINOLOGY

The word 'euthanasia' comes from the Greek words *eu* (good) and *thanatos* (death). In modern usage, it has developed a different and more specific meaning. Although most of us would agree that someone who dies peacefully and suddenly in her sleep, after a long and healthy life, has had a 'good death', we would not say that this was a case of euthanasia. Rather, the *Oxford English Dictionary*'s definition is 'a gentle and easy death, the bringing about of this, especially in the case of incurable and painful disease'. We would also usually confine the term 'euthanasia' to cases in which *doctors* assist patients to die: if someone kills a relative in order to relieve their suffering, we would tend to say that this was a 'mercy killing', rather than an example of euthanasia.

In this chapter, I shall use the word 'euthanasia' to refer only to voluntary active euthanasia, that is where a doctor deliberately acts to kill a patient at her request. I will not employ the term 'passive euthanasia', which some commentators use to describe the withholding or withdrawal of life-prolonging medical treatment.

Euthanasia can also be contrasted with assisted suicide. In euthanasia, it is the doctor's conduct which causes the patient's death. In a case of assisted suicide, the patient causes her

---

[4] [2001] Fam 147 CA.   [5] *Airedale NHS Trust v Bland* [1993] AC 789 HL.

own death, but someone else (usually, but not always a doctor) has helped her, for example by prescribing a lethal dose of drugs.

Finally, it is worth noting that just as in everyday usage we often use elliptical or euphemistic phrases when talking about death (we might speak of someone having 'passed away' or 'passed on', rather than saying that they are dead), we find similar evasive language within the legal and medical communities. Doctors and judges may refer to 'letting nature take its course' or 'not prolonging the dying process', when discussing life-shortening practices, such as the removal of life support or the provision of life-threatening doses of painkillers.

2 THE COMPETENT PATIENT

(a) THE CURRENT LAW

(1) Euthanasia

A doctor who deliberately ends the life of her patient is subject to the ordinary criminal law, and would often satisfy both the *actus reus* (proof of conduct, and proof that the conduct caused death) and the *mens rea* (the intention to kill or to cause grievous bodily harm) for the crime of murder. The doctor's motive and the consent of the victim are irrelevant, as is the fact that the patient is likely to be terminally ill, and might have died soon without the doctor's intervention. Because murder carries a mandatory life sentence, the fact that the doctor acted for compassionate reasons cannot be taken into account in sentencing.

If someone in unbearable agony is killed by a friend or family member, it may be possible to reduce the charge to one of manslaughter on the grounds of diminished responsibility, thus allowing for some discretion, and hence leniency in sentencing. Whether or not mercy killers are actually suffering from an 'abnormality of mind', as opposed to making a rational decision, is open to question. There is some evidence that, in order to avoid the charge of murder, an inference is drawn that the defendant *must have* been suffering from a mental abnormality at the time of the offence, even though there is no sign of mental abnormality when the defendant is actually examined. Indeed, Dell goes so far as to say that mercy killers, in general, display a 'total lack of mental disorder'.[6]

Regardless of whether there is over-diagnosis, on compassionate grounds, of diminished responsibility among mercy killers, a health care professional who hastens a patient's death will seldom be able to claim that, 'he was suffering from such abnormality of mind . . . as substantially to impair his mental responsibility'.[7] Of course, when a doctor shortens the life of a patient who is terminally ill, there may be some evidential difficulty in establishing that it was the doctor's conduct rather than the pre-existing illness that caused the patient's death. To be guilty of murder, the defendant's conduct must have 'contributed significantly' or been 'a substantial cause' of death: it need not, therefore, be the sole reason for the patient's death. If causation cannot be established, the doctor who administered a potentially lethal injection could be charged with attempted murder, as happened to Dr Cox and Dr Moor (see below).

---

[6] S Dell, 'The Mandatory Sentence and Section 2' (1986) 12 Journal of Medical Ethics 28–31.
[7] Homicide Act 1957, s 2(1).

While there have been prosecutions, no doctor who has complied with a patient's request to end her life has ever been convicted of the full offence of murder. As we can see in the following cases, both juries and the judiciary have tended to be lenient towards doctors whom they judge to have acted for compassionate reasons.

In *R v Arthur*[8] (discussed below), Farquharson J instructed the jury to 'think long and hard before deciding that doctors of the eminence we have heard...have evolved standards which amount to committing crime'.

Eighteen years later, Dr Moor was arrested after taking part in a media debate about voluntary euthanasia, during which he admitted to having helped a number of his patients to die painlessly. In *R v Moor* he was prosecuted for the murder of George Liddell, an 85-year-old man who had been suffering from bowel cancer. Given the tone of Hooper J's direction to the jury, it is not surprising that the jury acquitted Dr Moor, reaching a unanimous verdict in less than an hour.

R v Moor[9]

Hooper J

You have heard that this defendant is a man of excellent character, not just in the sense that he has no previous convictions but how witnesses have spoken of his many admirable qualities. You may consider it a great irony that a doctor who goes out of his way to care for George Liddell ends up facing the charge that he does. You may also consider it another great irony that the doctor who takes time on his day off to tend to a dying patient ends up on this charge.

In *R v Carr*,[10] the patient had been suffering unbearable pain as a result of inoperable lung cancer, and had repeatedly asked Dr Carr to help him to die. Dr Carr gave him a massive dose of phenobarbitone, and the patient died two days later. Because natural causes could not be ruled out as the cause of death, it was impossible to prove that Dr Carr's actions had caused his patient's death, so Dr Carr was charged with attempted murder. Despite the considerable evidence against Dr Carr, and the judge's unfavourable summing-up, the jury acquitted him.

R v Cox is the only case to have resulted in a doctor's conviction, this time for attempted murder. Again, it was impossible to establish exactly what had killed Mrs Boyes because her body had been cremated, so only the lesser charge of attempted murder was possible. Dr Cox had given Mrs Boyes a dose of potassium chloride which was guaranteed to kill her, so it was difficult to avoid the conclusion that he had intended to end her life, especially since potassium chloride is not a painkiller. Mrs Boyes was 70 years old and terminally ill; she had rheumatoid arthritis and had developed gastric ulcers, gangrene, and body sores. She suffered extreme pain, which could not be controlled by pain-killing drugs. There was evidence that she had repeatedly asked Dr Cox, a consultant rheumatologist who had been treating her for the last 13 years, and others to kill her.

---

[8] (1981) 12 BMLR 1.
[9] C Dyer, 'British GP Cleared of Murder Charge' (1999) 318 British Medical Journal 1306.
[10] The Times, 30 Dec 1986.

R v Cox[11]

Ognall J

There can be no doubt that the use of drugs to reduce pain and suffering will often be fully justified notwithstanding that it will, in fact hasten the moment of death, but please understand this, ladies and gentleman, what can never be lawful is the use of drugs with the primary purpose of hastening the moment of death.... [I]n the context of this case potassium chloride has no curative properties...it is not an analgesic. It is not used by the medical profession to relieve pain..., injected into a vein it is a lethal substance. One ampoule would certainly kill...the injection here was therefore twice that necessary to cause certain death.

Despite being convicted of attempted murder, Dr Cox did not go to prison, but was given a 12-month suspended prison sentence. In a separate GMC hearing, he was not struck off the medical register, and, after a formal reprimand, he returned to practise within a year of his conviction.

(2) Assisted Suicide

At common law, suicide was regarded as self-murder, and was a criminal offence. In his Commentaries, William Blackstone stated that:

The suicide is guilty of a double offence; one spiritual, in invading the prerogative of the Almighty, and rushing into his immediate presence uncalled for; the other temporal, against the King, who hath an interest in the preservation of all his subjects.[12]

Obviously, it was only those who had *unsuccessfully* tried to commit suicide who could actually be prosecuted for their attempted suicide. If the suicide had been successful, it was the relatives of the deceased who would suffer, through the confiscation of property and restrictions upon burial rites. In 1961, suicide and attempted suicide were decriminalized by the Suicide Act.

Suicide Act 1961 sections 1 and 2

1 The rule of law whereby it is a crime for a person to commit suicide is hereby abrogated.
2(1) A person who aids, abets, counsels, or procures the suicide of another, or an attempt by another to commit suicide, shall be liable on conviction on indictment to imprisonment for a term not exceeding fourteen years....
    (4) No proceedings shall be instituted for an offence under this section except by or with the consent of the Director of Public Prosecutions.

---

[11] (1992) 12 BMLR 38.
[12] *Commentaries on the Laws of England*, vol. IV (1775).

The decriminalization of suicide means that even if a person's intention to commit suicide is known, the courts do not have the power to interfere with her decision. This issue arose in *Re Z (An Adult: Capacity)*. Mr Z had informed his local authority that arrangements had been made for Mrs Z to go to Switzerland so that she could be helped to die. The authority had initially obtained an injunction restraining Mr Z from taking his wife abroad, but this was discharged by Hedley J.

Re Z (An Adult: Capacity)[13]

Hedley J

Section 1 of the Suicide Act 1961 abrogated the rule that made suicide criminal. It did not make suicide lawful, much less did it encourage it; it simply removed suicide from being punishable as a criminal act. It follows inevitably that our law does not penalise the decision of a competent person to take their own life. Moreover nor does the law prohibit them from so doing. Human freedom, if it is to have real meaning, must involve the right to take what others may see as unwise or even bad decisions in respect of themselves; were that not so, freedom would be largely illusory. It follows that the court has no basis in law for exercising the jurisdiction so as to prohibit Mrs Z from taking her own life. The right and responsibility for such a decision belongs to Mrs Z alone…In the circumstances here, Mrs Z's best interests are no business of mine.…The court is simply not entitled to interfere whatever views it may have about the decision in question.

The fact that it is not now unlawful to commit, or attempt to commit suicide does not, however, mean that there is a *right* to do so. The criminal offences of suicide and attempted suicide were not abolished in order to *facilitate* ending one's life, but rather to protect already distressed relatives from the imposition of additional hardship, and to ensure that people who had unsuccessfully attempted suicide could seek medical help, without fearing prosecution.

Despite suicide's decriminalization, under section 2(1) of the Suicide Act 1961, assisting another person to commit suicide is a criminal offence punishable by up to 14 years' imprisonment. While it is unusual for assisting a non-crime to itself be a criminal offence, there are undoubtedly sound public policy reasons for proscribing suicide pacts (when one person persuades another to take their own life first in order to inherit their property), and for criminalizing the disgraceful 'egging on' of people with suicidal thoughts in internet chatrooms. Other examples of 'assistance with suicide'—such as helping a loved one make the journey to Switzerland—might be thought to be qualitatively different, but these are also captured by this provision, as are doctors who give advice on lethal doses of medication.

In *AG v Able*, Woolf J held that the supply of a booklet—*A Guide to Self-deliverance*—which contained one section setting out seven reasons 'Why you should think again', and another, which described five separate methods of suicide, would not necessarily amount to a criminal offence, but could do so if the supplier had the necessary intent that the advice should be used to assist another identifiable person to commit suicide.

---

[13] [2004] EWHC 2817 (Fam).

AG v Able[14]

Woolf J

I have no doubt that in the case at least of certain recipients of the booklet, its contents would encourage suicide. Ignorance as to how to commit suicide must by itself be a deterrent. Likewise, the risks inherent in an unsuccessful attempt must be a deterrent. The contents of the booklet provide information as to methods and methods which are less likely to result in an unsuccessful attempt. This assistance must encourage some readers to commit or attempt to commit suicide. This is clearly appreciated by the publishers, thus their care to control the persons to whom the booklet is to be sold and their advice as to the safe-keeping of the booklet...

I therefore conclude that to distribute the booklet can be an offence. But, before an offence can be established to have been committed, it must at least be proved: (a) that the alleged offender had the necessary intent, that is, he intended the booklet to be used by someone contemplating suicide and intended that person would be assisted by the booklet's contents, or otherwise encouraged to attempt to take or to take his own life; (b) that while he still had that intention he distributed the booklet to such a person who read it; and, (c) in addition, if an offence under section 2 is to be proved, that such a person was assisted or encouraged by so reading the booklet to attempt to take or to take his own life, otherwise the alleged offender cannot be guilty of more than an attempt.

Given that a person can commit suicide themselves without committing any criminal offence, what reason would there be for choosing to implicate someone else in one's suicide attempt, and thereby exposing them to potential criminal charges? There are, in short, two reasons why people might need assistance in committing suicide. First, they may be physically incapable of arranging their own suicide. Secondly, because patients lack expert knowledge, they may need advice on the combination and quantities of drugs needed to achieve a quick and painless death. Simply overdosing on readily available painkillers can lead to a prolonged and agonizing death.

In 2002 the impact of the Human Rights Act 1998 upon the proscription of assisted suicide came before the courts in the Dianne Pretty case.[15] Mrs Pretty suffered from motor neurone disease, a progressive and degenerative terminal illness, which often leads to a distressing and frightening death, during which the person's mental faculties remain sharp while their body fails. Mrs Pretty's husband was willing to help her commit suicide, but the couple were anxious that he might be prosecuted under section 2(1) of the Suicide Act 1961.

Mrs Pretty asked the Director of Public Prosecutions to give an undertaking that he would not consent to Mr Pretty's prosecution. She then sought judicial review of his refusal, on the grounds that it violated her Convention rights, as incorporated in the Human Rights Act 1998. While both the House of Lords and the European Court of Human Rights agreed that legalized assisted suicide would be compatible with the Human Rights Act, this did not amount to a right to assistance in committing suicide.

The House of Lords found that there had been no prima facie violations of any of Mrs Pretty's convention rights, whereas the ECtHR was prepared to admit that Article 8

---

[14] [1983] 3 WLR 845.
[15] *R (on the application of Pretty) v Director of Public Prosecutions* [2001] UKHL 61; *Pretty v UK* (2002) 35 EHRR 1.

was engaged, but that a complete prohibition of assisted suicide was not a disproportionate response to the state's concern to protect vulnerable members of society.

R (on the application of Pretty) v Director of Public Prosecutions[16]

Lord Steyn[17]

For [Mrs Pretty] to succeed it is not enough to show that the European Convention allows member states to legalise assisted suicide. She must establish that at least that part of section 2(1) of the 1961 Act which makes aiding or abetting suicide a crime is in conflict with her Convention rights. In other words, she must persuade the House that the European Convention compels member states of the Council of Europe to legalise assisted suicide...

The fact is that among the 41 member states—North, South, East and West—there are deep cultural and religious differences in regard to euthanasia and assisted suicide. The legalisation of euthanasia and assisted suicide as adopted in the Netherlands would be unacceptable to predominantly Roman Catholic countries in Europe. The idea that the European Convention *requires* states to render lawful euthanasia and assisted suicide (as opposed to allowing democratically elected legislatures to adopt measures to that effect) must therefore be approached with scepticism...[T]he fact is that an interpretation *requiring* states to legalise euthanasia and assisted suicide would not only be enormously controversial but profoundly unacceptable to the peoples of many member states.

If section 2 of the 1961 Act is held to be incompatible with the European Convention, a right to commit assisted suicide would not be doctor assisted and would not be subject to safeguards introduced in the Netherlands...In our parliamentary democracy, and I apprehend in many member states of the Council of Europe, such a fundamental change cannot be brought about by judicial creativity. If it is to be considered at all, it requires a detailed and effective regulatory proposal. In these circumstances it is difficult to see how a process of interpretation of Convention rights can yield a result with all the necessary inbuilt protections. Essentially, it must be a matter for democratic debate and decision making by legislatures...

The Director of Public Prosecutions may not under section 2(4) exercise his discretion to stop all prosecutions under section 2(1). It follows that he may only exercise his discretion, for or against a prosecution, in relation to the circumstances of a specific prosecution. His discretion can therefore only be exercised in respect of past events giving rise to a suspicion that a crime under section 2(1) has been committed. And then the exercise of this discretion will take into account whether there is a realistic prospect of securing a conviction and whether a prosecution would be in the public interest.

Lord Hope

I would be willing to give full weight to Mrs Pretty's assertion that she is not weak or vulnerable...But this does not meet the Director's argument. It is not unreasonable for him to think that, if he were to sanction one act of assisted suicide, this might lead to requests from others less well equipped to stand up to the unscrupulous. Separating out the good from the bad would be an impossible task for him, as he lacks the resources that would be needed to conduct the exercise. He is entitled to think that the public interest is best served by holding the line against granting undertakings of this kind. In the present uncertain climate of public

---

[16] [2001] UKHL 61; *Pretty v UK* (2002) 35 EHRR 1.
[17] *R (on the application of Pretty) v Director of Public Prosecutions* [2001] UKHL 61.

opinion, where there is no consensus in favour of assisted suicide and there are powerful religious and ethical arguments to the contrary, any change in the law which would make assisted suicide generally acceptable is best seen as a matter for Parliament.

I would hold therefore that the object which section 2(1) was designed to achieve struck the right balance between the interests of the individual and the public interest which seeks to protect the weak and vulnerable....I would also hold that, although the effect of the Director's decision that he had no power to give the undertaking is likely to be to expose Mrs Pretty to acute distress as she succumbs to her illness, his act cannot be said to be unfair or arbitrary or to have impaired her Convention right more than is reasonably necessary. It was not disproportionate.

Mrs Pretty then appealed to the European Court of Human Rights. Her claim was rejected on the 29 April 2002 and she died 12 days later.

Pretty v UK[18]

Judgment of the ECtHR

The Court is not persuaded that 'the right to life' guaranteed in Article 2 can be interpreted as involving a negative aspect...Article 2 of the Convention...is unconcerned with issues to do with the quality of living or what a person chooses to do with his or her life...Article 2 cannot, without a distortion of language, be interpreted as conferring the diametrically opposite right, namely a right to die; nor can it create a right to self-determination in the sense of conferring on an individual the entitlement to choose death rather than life.

Article 3...may be described in general terms as imposing a primarily negative obligation on States to refrain from inflicting serious harm on persons within their jurisdiction...A positive obligation on the State to provide protection against inhuman or degrading treatment has been found to arise in a number of cases...The suffering which flows from naturally occurring illness, physical or mental, may be covered by Article 3, where it is, or risks being, exacerbated by treatment...for which the authorities can be held responsible. In the present case, it is beyond dispute that the respondent Government has not, itself, inflicted any ill-treatment on the applicant. Nor is there any complaint that the applicant is not receiving adequate care from the State medical authorities...There is no...act or 'treatment' on the part of the United Kingdom in the present case.

The Court would observe that the ability to conduct one's life in a manner of one's own choosing may also include the opportunity to pursue activities perceived to be of a physically or morally harmful or dangerous nature for the individual concerned...The very essence of the Convention is respect for human dignity and freedom. Without in any way negating the principle of sanctity of life protected under the Convention, the Court considers that it is under Article 8 that notions of the quality of life take on significance. In an era of growing medical sophistication combined with longer life expectancies, many people are concerned that they should not be forced to linger on in old age or in states of advanced physical or mental decrepitude which conflict with strongly held ideas of self and personal identity...

The applicant in this case is prevented by law from exercising her choice to avoid what she considers will be an undignified and distressing end to her life. The Court is not prepared to exclude that this constitutes an interference with her right to respect for private life as guaranteed under Article 8(1) of the Convention.

---

[18] (2002) 35 EHRR 1.

The law in issue in this case, section 2 of the 1961 Act, was designed to safeguard life by protecting the weak and vulnerable and especially those who are not in a condition to take informed decisions against acts intended to end life or to assist in ending life. Doubtless the condition of terminally ill individuals will vary. But many will be vulnerable and it is the vulnerability of the class which provides the rationale for the law in question. It is primarily for States to assess the risk and the likely incidence of abuse if the general prohibition on assisted suicides were relaxed or if exceptions were to be created. Clear risks of abuse do exist, notwithstanding arguments as to the possibility of safeguards and protective procedures.

The Court does not consider therefore that the blanket nature of the ban on assisted suicide is disproportionate. The Government has stated that flexibility is provided for in individual cases by the fact that consent is needed from the DPP to bring a prosecution and by the fact that a maximum sentence is provided, allowing lesser penalties to be imposed as appropriate... It does not appear to be arbitrary to the Court for the law to reflect the importance of the right to life, by prohibiting assisted suicide while providing for a system of enforcement and adjudication which allows due regard to be given in each particular case to the public interest in bringing a prosecution, as well as to the fair and proper requirements of retribution and deterrence.

The Court does not doubt the firmness of the applicant's views concerning assisted suicide but would observe that not all opinions or convictions constitute beliefs in the sense protected by Article 9(1) of the Convention. Her claims do not involve a form of manifestation of a religion or belief, through worship, teaching, practice or observance... To the extent that the applicant's views reflect her commitment to the principle of personal autonomy, her claim is a restatement of the complaint raised under Article 8 of the Convention.

In addition to the possibility of discretion in sentencing, the ECtHR drew attention to the fact that under section 2(4) of the Suicide Act the Director of Public Prosecutions (DPP) is specifically charged with exercising discretion over whether or not to proceed with a prosecution. This is because, as Hedley J explained in *Re Z (An Adult: Capacity)*, it will not always be in the public interest to prosecute someone who has contravened section 2(1).

Re Z (An Adult: Capacity)[19]

Hedley J

[I]t seems to me inevitable that by making arrangements and escorting Mrs Z on the flight, Mr Z will have contravened Section 2(1) above. It follows that in order for Mrs Z actually to be able to carry out her decision, it will require the criminal conduct of another. That said I remind myself of sub-section (4). Although not unique, the provision is rare and is usually found where Parliament recognises that although an act may be criminal, it is not always in the public interest to prosecute in respect of it.

In the *Pretty* case, the DPP took the view that he could only exercise his discretion under section 2(4) once he had all the facts before him, *after* a police investigation. Similarly, in evidence to the House of Lords Select Committee on Assisted Dying, the Attorney General argued that to exercise this discretion *before* any suicide takes place would, in effect, amount to the DPP prospectively suspending a part of the criminal law.[20]

---

[19] [2004] EWHC 2817 (FAM).
[20] Assisted Dying for the Terminally Ill Committee, *Assisted Dying for the Terminally Ill Bill—First Report* (2005), 16.

On the other hand, in commenting on the Dianne Pretty case, Richard Tur persuasively argues that section 2(4)—which only allows the Attorney General to exercise his prosecutorial discretion *after* the assisted suicide has taken place—violates citizens' right to know in advance if a particular course of conduct will attract criminal sanctions.

Richard HS Tur[21]

[Th]ose responsible for the Suicide Act tried to ameliorate the potential injustice of a widely stated blanket rule criminalizing assisted suicide in a statute decriminalizing suicide itself by empowering the Director to prevent prosecution by withholding consent. This allocates to the Director the unenviable function of making the legal rule fit moral sensitivities at its margins. Though challenging, this seems preferable to the gross injustice and manifest absurdity of unqualified literalism, or the lottery of inscrutable post hoc dispensation.

Our imaginary couple are saying that they choose morally compelling assisted suicide but will implement their choice only if it is non-criminal… It is no answer to them to say that they must implement their choice in order to find out and indeed there is a peculiar cruelty or inhumanity in the law saying to them that because they respect the law so much they must endure their sad plight. It thus appears that those most respectful of the law are subjected to the greater distress which is counter intuitive. So the Pretty question…—whether the right to life includes a right to die—was entirely the wrong question and it obscured the fact that section 2 as drafted, interpreted, and applied is vulnerable to an argument that there is a right to know in advance what consequences the criminal law attributes to one's conduct…

There is something fundamentally wrong in saying to someone like Dianne Pretty, 'Well you have had a miserable time and morally we quite see that you should be allowed the assistance you seek in ending your own life, but you know, the greater good of society requires that you should continue to suffer for fear of being a bad example—hard cases make bad law.' Morally, society simply should not use someone like Dianne Pretty as a means only and not as an end in herself.

More recently, lawyers for Debbie Purdy, a woman in her 40s suffering from primary progressive multiple sclerosis, adopted a line of argument more akin to that proposed by Richard Tur, namely that people should be entitled to know, in advance, if they would be likely to face prosecution for taking a relative to Switzerland to die. Around 100 UK citizens have died in Switzerland, and most of them will have been assisted, in some way at least, by another person. Helping someone to book their flight, driving them to the airport, or accompanying them on their final journey could all be instances of 'aiding' a suicide. There have been a handful of police investigations—adding, inevitably, to the family's grief—but none has faced prosecution.

Ms Purdy's argument was that the DPP is plainly exercising his discretion not to prosecute such cases, and that the criteria which are being used to make these decisions should be open and transparent. If the criteria that the DPP used to make decisions about prosecution were published, Ms Purdy and her husband Omar Puente could consider them before deciding whether he would accompany her to Switzerland when her condition became unbearable. Ms Purdy said that unless she was able to weigh up the likelihood of prosecution in advance, she might have to go to Switzerland earlier than she would like, when she could still make the trip unaided.

---

[21] 'Legislative Technique and Human Rights: The Sad Case of Assisted Suicide' (2003) Criminal Law Review 3–12.

At first instance, the Divisional court held that it was bound by the decision in *Pretty*, and by the House of Lords' conclusion that none of Mrs Pretty's Convention rights were engaged.[22] Of course, the ECtHR had appeared to reach a different conclusion on this point, but Scott Baker LJ detected some equivocation and uncertainty, and, in any event, was not bound by their conclusion. The Court held that Ms Purdy's Article 8 rights were not engaged, and while this was sufficient to dispose of her claim, they further held that even if they had been, the interference with them would have been both proportionate and justifiable.

Ms Purdy was given leave to appeal, but before her case was heard by the Court of Appeal, the DPP, Keir Starmer QC, published a detailed explanation of the decision not to prosecute the parents of Daniel James, a 23-year-old man who had been very seriously injured in a rugby accident. Daniel James died at a Dignitas clinic in September 2008, accompanied by his parents. Although there was sufficient evidence to prosecute Daniel's parents, and a family friend who had booked the air ticket (who had, in fact, booked a return flight for Daniel in case he could be persuaded to change his mind), the DPP decided that the public interest would not be served by prosecution.

Director of Public Prosecutions Keir Starmer QC[23]

a. An offence under section 2(1) Suicide Act 1961 is serious. That points in favour of a prosecution.

b. Neither Mark and Julie James nor the family friend influenced Daniel James to commit suicide. On the contrary, his parents tried relentlessly to persuade him not to commit suicide. Daniel was a mature, intelligent and fiercely independent young man with full capacity to make decisions about his medical treatment. There is clear evidence that he had attempted to commit suicide on three occasions and that he would have made further attempts if and whenever an opportunity to do so arose. On the facts of this case, these are factors against prosecution.

c. Although the evidential test under the Code is met, a wide range of conduct of varying degrees of culpability is caught by section 2(1) Suicide Act 1961 and, although not truly minor acts, on the facts of this case the conduct of Mark James, Julie James and the family friend was…towards the less culpable end of the spectrum. That is a factor against prosecution.

d. Neither Daniel's parents nor the family friend stood to gain any advantage, financial or otherwise, by his death. On the contrary, for his parents, Daniel's suicide has caused them profound distress. That is a factor against prosecution….

I have decided that the factors against prosecution clearly outweigh those in favour. In the circumstances I have concluded that a prosecution is not needed in the public interest.

In February 2009, Debbie Purdy's appeal to the Court of Appeal was dismissed. In *R (on the Application of Debbie Purdy) v Director of Public Prosecutions*, the Court of Appeal agreed that it was bound by the House of Lords' decision that Dianne Pretty's Article 8 rights were not engaged. The Court of Appeal noted some important differences between Mrs Pretty's claim and that mounted by Debbie Purdy and her husband. Nevertheless, it decided that the DPP was not in dereliction of his duty, and that Ms Purdy's claim had to

---

[22] *R (on the Application of Debbie Purdy) v Director of Public Prosecutions* [2008] EWHC 2565.
[23] DPP Decision On Prosecution—The Death By Suicide Of Daniel James (2008), available at <www.cps.gov.uk>.

fail. Note, however, that the Court implies that there was ample evidence, not least from the DPP's decision in relation to Daniel James's parents, upon which Ms Pury's legal advisers might base advice to her about the likelihood of prosecution, but that she could not seek such advice, prospectively, from the DPP. While it did not say so explicitly, it was evident that the Court of Appeal believed that it was unlikely that Mr Puente would be prosecuted if he accompanied his wife to Switzerland.

R (on the Application of Debbie Purdy) v Director of Public Prosecutions[24]

Lord Judge CJ

But what in reality Ms Purdy is seeking, and we understand why she is seeking it, is the nearest thing possible to a guarantee that if the circumstances we have summarized come to pass, and her husband assists her suicide when she is no longer able to end her own life by her own unassisted actions, he would not be prosecuted. Without giving what in reality would amount either to immunity from prosecution or the promulgation of a policy which would effectively discount the risk of a prosecution in this particular case (which it is accepted cannot be provided) Ms Purdy cannot achieve her true objective....

In the course of argument, it was suggested by Ward L.J. that the combination of the general guidance, and with the example of the decision in the case of Daniel James available for analysis, there was ample material to enable Ms Purdy's legal advisers to address the likelihood of a prosecution if her husband assisted her suicide. And in truth, that is all that can be done. Ms Purdy must take legal advice, and no doubt she will, and she must then make her own decision. But she cannot do so on the basis that the DPP should either act as her legal adviser, or through the means of a crime-specific policy, offer the kind of case-specific indications which would provide her with the absolute security of mind she is seeking....

Like this Court the DPP cannot dispense with or suspend the operation of section 2(1) of the 1961 Act, and he cannot promulgate a case-specific policy in the kind of certain terms sought by Ms Purdy which would, in effect, recognise exceptional defences to this offence which Parliament has not chosen to enact...

Notwithstanding our sympathy for the dreadful predicament in which Ms Purdy and Mr Puente find themselves, this appeal must be dismissed.

(3) Palliative Care that May Hasten Death: The Doctrine of Double Effect

Recall that in his summing up to the jury in *R v Cox*,[25] Ognall J said that there 'can be no doubt' that doctors are entitled to administer painkilling drugs, notwithstanding the fact that they may simultaneously hasten the moment of death. And, as we can see from the following extracts, it does appear to be an accepted and well-established principle of law that it can be lawful to administer painkilling drugs which might also 'hasten death' or 'shorten life'.

R v Adams[26]

Devlin J

If the first purpose of medicine, the restoration of health, can no longer be achieved, there is still much for a doctor to do, and he is entitled to do all that is proper and necessary to relieve pain and suffering, even if the measures he takes may incidentally shorten life.

---

[24] [2009] EWCA Civ 92. [25] (1992) 12 BMLR 38.
[26] Unreported, 8 Apr 1957.

Re J (Wardship: Medical Treatment)[27]

Lord Donaldson

[T]he use of drugs to reduce pain will often be fully justified, notwithstanding that this will hasten the moment of death.

Airedale NHS Trust v Bland[28]

Lord Goff

The doctor who is caring for such a patient cannot, in my opinion, be under an absolute obligation to prolong his life by any means available to him, regardless of the quality of the patient's life.... It is this principle too which, in my opinion, underlies the established rule that a doctor may, when caring for a patient who is, for example, dying of cancer, lawfully administer pain-killing drugs despite the fact that he knows that an incidental effect of that application will be to abbreviate the patient's life.

This principle is often referred to as the doctrine of double effect, which has its origins in Roman Catholic moral theology, and distinguishes between results that are intended and results that are merely foreseen as likely, but unintended, consequences of one's actions. As a person's disease progresses, they may need steadily increasing doses of painkillers, often in the form of opoids like diamorphine (also known as heroin) and morphine, in order to alleviate their pain. When given in sufficient quantities, these drugs may cause respiratory depression and lead to the patient's death.

There is some debate over whether the use of opoids in pain relief would ever, in fact, shorten a patient's life. Some palliative care experts suggest that proper pain management should never have this consequence. Nevertheless, according to the doctrine of double effect, a doctor who intends a good consequence (relieving pain) is not guilty of murder just because she foresees, but does not intend, a bad consequence (death). But, while the doctrine of double effect may make sense when a procedure, such as surgery, carries a small risk to the patient's life, which is nevertheless worth taking in order to attempt to improve the patient's condition, in the context of palliative care, it has been used to excuse conduct where death is very likely indeed.

Despite its widespread acceptance, it is possible that the doctrine of double effect may be at odds with ordinary principles of criminal law. To be guilty of murder, the patient's death does not have to be the *sole* purpose of the defendant's action. Instead, as we can see from the following quote from Lord Steyn's judgment in *R v Woollin*,[29] the criminal law is clear that the jury may infer that a person has the requisite *mens rea* for murder if they engage in conduct which is virtually certain to cause death, even if this is not their primary purpose.

Lord Steyn

Where a man realises that it is for all practical purposes inevitable that his actions will result in death or serious harm, the inference may be irresistible that he intended that result, however little he may have desired or wished it to happen.

---

[27] [1991] 2 WLR 140.   [28] [1993] AC 789.   [29] [1999] 1 AC 82 HL.

In the next extract, Glanville Williams draws attention to the apparent discrepancy between the ordinary meaning of intention in the criminal law and the doctrine of double effect.

Glanville Williams[30]

There is no legal difference between desiring or intending a consequence as following from your conduct, and persisting in your conduct with a knowledge that the consequence will inevitably follow from it, though not desiring that consequence. When a result is foreseen as certain, it is the same as if it were desired or intended.

John Keown disagrees and argues that the interpretation of intention in *Woollin* should be resisted, on the grounds that it casts doubt upon the legality of much conventional palliative care:

John Keown[31]

In [*Woollin*], the Law Lords appeared to rule that a consequence foreseen as virtually certain is intended. The implications of this for doctors who foresee that their palliative care will shorten life are disturbing: are such doctors now *prima facie* liable for murder?...

Woollin is a retrograde step. First, it suggests that doctors engaged in proper palliative care...intend to kill—a gross misrepresentation of their state of mind...Secondly, *Woollin* raises wholly unnecessary doubts about the lawfulness of proper palliative care. It is hardly an answer to say that the courts would hopefully provide doctors with a defence such as necessity: doctors providing proper palliative care are, as all agree, doing nothing wrong in the first place; are entitled to work free from the fear of prosecution, and should not have to rely for acquittal on the chance of the judicial application of an ancient, vague and uncertain defence. Thirdly, because of the doubts it creates, *Woollin* may have a chilling effect on the provision of much-needed palliative care and leave patients dying in pain and distress. A ruling that hinders good medicine is clearly bad law.

It is, however, worth noting that Lord Steyn in *Woollin* does not go so far as to say that where death is inevitable, the inference *must* be irresistible that he intended that result: rather, he merely suggests that in such cases the inference *may* be irresistible. Plainly, although Lord Steyn envisages circumstances in which intention *may* be inferred from the inevitability of death, by implication there could also be times when this *may not* be the case, and an example might plausibly be the provision of palliative care.

Regardless of the precise meaning of intention within the criminal law, when a doctor foresees that the dose of analgesics that she is about to give to a particular patient may lead to her death, she must have reached the conclusion that death has become an acceptable outcome. If a doctor were to give a healthy patient with a mild headache a life-threatening injection of diamorphine, her conduct would not be excused by the doctrine of double effect. She could not claim that her intention was merely to relieve pain, and that the patient's death was a foreseen but unintended side-effect. Instead, while death may not be the *principal* purpose of a doctor who administers a potentially lethal dose of painkillers, she must have decided that the patient's interest in pain relief now outweighs her interest in continued life.

30 *Sanctity of Life and the Criminal Law* (Faber: London, 1957) 286.
31 *Euthanasia, Ethics and Public Policy: An Argument against Legalisation* (CUP: Cambridge, 2002) 28–9.

In the next extract, Glanville Williams suggests that it is artificial for doctors to think only about one consequence of their action (relieving pain), while ignoring another (causing death).

Glanville Williams[32]

It is altogether too artificial to say that a doctor who gives an overdose of a narcotic having in the forefront of his mind the aim of ending his patient's existence is guilty of sin, while a doctor who gives the same overdose in the same circumstances in order to relieve pain is not guilty of sin, provided that he keeps his mind steadily off the consequence which his professional training teaches him is inevitable, namely the death of his patient. When you know that your conduct will have two consequences, one in itself good and one in itself evil, you are compelled as a moral agent to choose between acting and not acting by making a judgement of value, that is to say by deciding whether the good is more to be desired than the evil is to be avoided.

Stephen Wilkinson points out a further difficulty with the doctrine of double effect, namely that it relies upon knowledge of the doctor's primary intention.

Stephen Wilkinson[33]

But *how do we know* what is intended and what is not? This question can arise from two different perspectives. First, from the 'first person' perspective, if a doctor administers dia-morphine to relieve pain, but at the same time would be glad if the patient's death was hastened..., she may not be sure herself which effects she intends and which she doesn't. Second, from the 'third person' perspective, how are other professionals, relatives and the public to know what was going on 'in the doctor's head' when she administered the drug? How are they to know what she intends? This problem may render the doctrine unworkable in practice. Furthermore, it also opens up the possibility of health carers abusing the doc-trine and using it as a way of 'smuggling in euthanasia by the back door'. In other words, the acceptance of the doctrine might make it possible to kill patients intentionally while *pretend-ing* that their death is an unintended side-effect.

On the other hand, in the next extract, Charles Douglas *et al.* draw upon their interviews with clinicians to suggest that a degree of ambiguity in relation to what is intended and what is not may be helpful for doctors.

Charles Douglas, Ian Kerridge, and Rachel Ankeny[34]

The most striking feature of these interviews is a sense of uncertainty and ambiguity with regard to intention.... As almost all the respondents stated in one way or another, there is

---

[32] *Sanctity of Life and the Criminal Law* (Faber: London, 1957) 286.
[33] 'Palliative Care and the Doctrine of Double Effect', in Donna Dickenson, Malcolm Johnson, and Jeanne Samson Katz (eds), *Death, Dying and Bereavement*, 2nd edn (Sage: London, 2000) 299–302.
[34] 'Managing Intentions: The End-of-Life Administration of Analgesics and Sedatives, and the Possibility of Slow Euthanasia' (2008) 22 Bioethics 388–96.

a 'grey area', where the intention is not explicitly to hasten death, but is no longer merely to palliate.... Instead of always expressing discomfort or even displaying equanimity about the dual effects of AS [analgesics and sedatives], there was often a sense that the possibility of a double effect was a good thing, that both outcomes (an expedited death and relief of suffering) were desirable, but that only one needed to be the apparent intention.

In a similar vein, Alexander McCall Smith argues that we should be slow to deny doctors the moral 'comfort' they may gain from framing their actions in terms of helping, rather than killing.

Alexander McCall Smith[35]

Doctors know full well what they are doing when they increase a dose of diamorphine, but they need not describe their act, to themselves or to others as an act of killing. This approach has been described as hypocritical, but if it accords with a moral distinction which is meaningful for doctors, then why should they be denied the comfort it affords them? The moral life is possibly more subtly nuanced than some of the proponents of euthanasia would have us believe. We live by moral metaphor, and the metaphor of helping rather than killing, may be a valuable one to those whose duty it is to look after the terminally ill.

Provided the drugs that caused a patient's death could plausibly be used as painkillers or sedatives, it would in practice be difficult to disprove a doctor's assertion that her principal aim was the relief of suffering. Hence, in *R v Adams*,[36] it was possible for the defence counsel to argue that Dr Adams had intended to relieve Mrs Morrell's pain by administering massive doses of morphine and diamorphine. Many years after Dr Adams's trial for murder, Patrick Devlin, the judge in the case, wrote a book about the issues it had raised. In *Easing the Passing*, he explained how fine the line will sometimes be between lawful palliative care and murder.

Patrick Devlin[37]

If he really had an honest belief in easing suffering, Dr. Adams was on the right side of the law; if his purpose was simply to finish life, he was not...A narrow distinction. But in the law, as in all matters of principle, cases can be so close to each other that the gap can only be perceived theoretically.

In contrast, in *R v Cox*,[38] Dr Cox's use of potassium chloride (which has no analgesic properties) effectively ruled out the application of the doctrine of double effect. If Dr Cox had used morphine rather than potassium chloride to kill Lillian Boyes, an assertion that his primary intention was to relieve her suffering would have been much harder to refute.

In addition to the administration of large, and potentially fatal, doses of analgesic drugs, palliative care may also involve what is sometimes described as terminal or palliative sedation. If someone is unable to breathe or swallow, they may experience intolerable distress that cannot be relieved by conventional painkilling drugs. In such cases, sedative drugs may

---

35 'Euthanasia: The Strengths of the Middle Ground' (1999) 7 Medical Law Review 194–207.
36 Unreported, 8 Apr 1957.
37 'Euthanasia: The Strengths of the Middle Ground' (1999) 7 Medical Law Review 194–207.
38 (1992) 12 BMLR 38.

be given in combination with analgesics in sufficient quantities that the patient is rendered unconscious. Once the patient is dependent upon artificial nutrition and hydration, as we see later, it can be removed, leading inevitably to the patient's death. Provided the principal purpose of giving the sedatives and painkillers is to relieve pain and suffering, despite the doctor's knowledge that the patient will become permanently unconscious and die shortly afterwards, according to the doctrine of double effect, this may be lawful palliative care.

From the patient's perspective, however, as Margaret Pabst Battin explains, terminal sedation will be indistinguishable from being given a lethal injection.

Margaret Pabst Battin[39]

Pain is not yet a 'thing of the past', nor are many associated kinds of physical distress. Some kinds of conditions, such as difficulty in swallowing, are still difficult to relieve without introducing other discomforting limitations.... Severe respiratory insufficiency may mean...'a singularly terrifying and agonizing final few hours'.

[O]f course, the patient can be sedated into unconsciousness; this does indeed end the pain. But in respect of the patient's experience, this is tantamount to causing death: the patient has no further conscious experience and thus can achieve no goods, experience no significant communication, satisfy no goals. Furthermore, adequate sedation, by depressing respiratory function, may hasten death. Thus, although it is always technically possible to achieve relief from pain, at least when the appropriate resources are available, the price may be functionally and practically equivalent, at least from the patient's point of view, to death.

(4) Refusal of Treatment

(a) Contemporaneous refusal

As we saw in Chapter 5, competent adult patients have the right to refuse medical treatment, even if their refusal will lead to their death. Although this right is not absolute, there are very few exceptions.[40] For the purposes of this chapter, and as the following quotes from the *Bland* case make clear, the important point is that doctors *must* comply with a competent adult's refusal of life-sustaining medical treatment.

Airedale NHS Trust v Bland[41]

Lord Goff

[I]t is established that the principle of self-determination requires that respect must be given to the wishes of the patient, so that if an adult patient of sound mind refuses, however unreasonably, to consent to treatment or care by which his life would or might be prolonged, the doctors responsible for his care must give effect to his wishes, even though they do not consider it to be in his best interests to do so...To this extent, the principle of the sanctity

---

[39] *The Least Worst Death: Essays in Bioethics on the End of Life* (OUP: Oxford, 1994).
[40] An example would be s 63 of the Mental Health Act 1983, see further Chapter 6.
[41] [1993] AC 789.

of human life must yield to the principle of self-determination...On this basis, it has been held that a patient of sound mind may, if properly informed, require that life support should be discontinued.

Lord Mustill

If the patient is capable of making a decision on whether to permit treatment and decides not to permit it his choice must be obeyed, even if on any objective view it is contrary to his best interests. A doctor has no right to proceed in the face of objection, even if it is plain to all, including the patient, that adverse consequences and even death will or may ensue.

Similarly, the British Medical Association's guidance to doctors explains that where a patient is competent, their right to refuse life-sustaining medical treatment must take priority over the doctors' duty to preserve life.

British Medical Association[42]

It is well established in law and ethics that competent adults have the right to refuse any medical treatment, even if that refusal results in their death. Patients are not obliged to justify their decisions but the health team usually wish to discuss the refusal with them in order to ensure that they have based their decisions on accurate information and to correct any misunderstandings. Where the health team considers that the treatment would provide a net benefit, that assessment should be sympathetically explained to the patient but patients should not be pressured to accept treatment...

Health professionals can find it very difficult when a patient with capacity refuses treatment that they believe would provide a reasonable degree of recovery. While they may discuss their concern with patients, they must not put pressure on them to accept treatment. Ultimately the decision of whether to accept or reject the treatment offered rests with the patient.

One of the clearest illustrations of the robustness of the law's protection of a competent patient's right to insist on the withdrawal of life-prolonging medical treatment is the case of *Re B (Adult: Refusal of Treatment)*. Ms B was tetraplegic, suffering complete paralysis from the neck down. She had respiratory problems, and was connected to a ventilator. She had repeatedly requested that she be removed from the ventilator, but the clinicians treating her were reluctant to comply. Ms B sought, and was granted, a declaration that she had mental capacity and that, as a result, the doctors working for the NHS Trust had been treating her unlawfully.

Re B (Adult: Refusal of Treatment)[43]

Dame Elizabeth Butler-Sloss P

I start with the presumption that Ms B has mental capacity...[T]he judicial approach to mental capacity must be largely dependent upon the assessments of the medical profession

---

[42] British Medical Association, *Withholding and Withdrawing Life-prolonging Medical Treatment: Guidance for Decision Making*, 3rd edn (BMA: London, 2007), para 25.5.
[43] [2002] EWHC 429 (Fam).

whose task it is on a regular basis to assess the competence of the patient to consent or refuse the medical/surgical treatment recommended to the patient. If, as in the present case, two experienced and distinguished consultant psychiatrists give evidence that Ms B has the mental capacity to make decisions, even grave decisions about her future medical treatment, that is cogent evidence upon which I can and should rely...

One must allow for those as severely disabled as Ms B, for some of whom life in that condition may be worse than death. It is a question of values and...we have to try inadequately to put ourselves into the position of the gravely disabled person and respect the subjective character of experience. Unless the gravity of the illness has affected the patient's capacity, a seriously disabled patient has the same rights as the fit person to respect for personal autonomy. There is a serious danger, exemplified in this case, of a benevolent paternalism which does not embrace recognition of the personal autonomy of the severely disabled patient. I do not consider that either the lack of experience in a spinal rehabilitation unit and thereafter in the community or the unusual situation of being in an ICU for a year has had the effect of eroding Ms B's mental capacity to any degree whatsoever.

I am therefore entirely satisfied that Ms B is competent to make all relevant decisions about her medical treatment including the decision whether to seek to withdraw from artificial ventilation. Her mental competence is commensurate with the gravity of the decision she may wish to make....I would like to add how impressed I am with her as a person, with the great courage, strength of will and determination she has shown in the last year, with her sense of humour, and her understanding of the dilemma she has posed to the Hospital. She is clearly a splendid person and it is tragic that someone of her ability has been struck down so cruelly. I hope she will forgive me for saying, diffidently, that if she did reconsider her decision, she would have a lot to offer the community at large.

In the light of my decision that the Claimant has mental capacity and has had such capacity since August 2001 I shall be prepared to grant the appropriate declarations. I also find that the Claimant has been treated unlawfully by the Trust since August.

It is worth noting that, despite the finding that they had been treating her unlawfully, the clinicians who had been caring for Ms B were not forced to participate in bringing about her death. Ms B was transferred to another hospital where she was removed from the artificial ventilator and died. I shall return to the significance of this below.

As we saw in Chapter 5, the competent patient's reasons for refusing treatment are irrelevant. As Lord Donaldson MR said in *Re T (Adult: Refusal of Treatment)*:[44] 'the patient's right of choice exists whether the reasons for making that choice are rational, irrational, unknown or even non-existent'. So, even if a patient refuses medical treatment *because* she wants to die, the doctor is still bound to comply with her wishes. But could a doctor who removes a feeding tube from a patient whose intention is to end her life, and provides her with assurances that she can be kept comfortable while she dies from lack of nutrition, be said to be assisting her suicide? Not according to Lord Goff in *Airedale NHS Trust v Bland*.

Airedale NHS Trust v Bland[45]

Lord Goff

In cases of this kind [a refusal of treatment], there is no question of the patient having committed suicide nor therefore of the doctor having aided or abetted him in doing so. It is simply that the patient has, as he is entitled to, declined to consent to treatment which might or

---

[44] [1993] Fam 95.   [45] [1993] AC 789.

would have the effect of prolonging his life, and the doctor has, in accordance with his duty, complied with the patient's wishes.

But why is there 'no question' of a patient whose intention is to take her own life, and who happens to be connected to a life-support system, committing suicide by refusing treatment? One possible explanation is that a patient who seeks to end her life through a refusal of life-sustaining treatment is not acting positively to bring about her death. Her 'suicide' is achieved by her failure to consent to treatment, and it would seem that it is not possible to commit suicide by omission. Certainly, the House of Lords Select Committee on Assisted Dying was of the view that suicide 'in law requires a "positive act"'.[46]

A different explanation for distinguishing between suicide and the refusal of life-sustaining treatment is offered by Margaret Otlowski, who suggests that we 'tailor our definition of suicide so as to exclude behaviour which is regarded as acceptable'.[47]

Margaret Otlowski[48]

It is difficult to deny that where a patient dies following the refusal of nutrition or hydration the patient's death is self-induced... [W]e need to recognize that refusal of treatment may amount to suicide, but must tailor our response to this particular form of suicide so as to take into account the special considerations applying in the medical context...

The most satisfactory way in which the legal principles regarding liability for assisted suicide and the refusal of treatment can be reconciled is for the courts to take a broad view of the patient's right to refuse treatment so that the withholding or withdrawal of treatment performed in recognition of that right is exempt from criminal liability even though the legal requirements for establishing liability for assisted suicide against the doctor may be present.

If a doctor withdraws life-sustaining treatment knowing that this will lead to the patient's death, might they additionally satisfy both the *actus reus* and the *mens rea* of murder? If the withdrawal of medical treatment is an act done with the knowledge that it will cause the patient's death, then the patient's consent to the doctor's action is irrelevant and the doctor may be guilty of murder. In order to avoid this conclusion, the withdrawal of medical treatment is commonly described as an omission rather than an action.

It is, nevertheless, possible to commit murder by omission. An omission will only constitute the *actus reus* of murder if the defendant was under a duty to act: an obvious example being a mother whose failure to feed her baby leads to his death. Doctors *are*, of course, under a duty to care for their patients, so in theory, if a doctor's failure to provide medical treatment to a patient results in her death, a charge of murder is possible. If the charge is murder, the patient's consent to the doctor's conduct is irrelevant. Does this mean that doctors who respect their patients' refusals of life-sustaining treatment are potentially subject to prosecution for murder?

Almost certainly not. Because the patient's right to refuse unwanted intervention suspends the doctor's duty to provide medical treatment, the doctor's omission can no longer constitute the *actus reus* of murder. So a doctor who maliciously unplugs the ventilator from

---

[46] Assisted Dying for the Terminally Ill Committee, *Assisted Dying for the Terminally Ill Bill—First Report* (2005), para 15.

[47] *Voluntary Euthanasia and the Common Law* (OUP: Oxford, 2000) 69.   [48] Ibid.

a patient who is temporarily unconscious, but expected to make a full recovery, may be guilty of murder because she had a duty to provide life-prolonging treatment. Whereas a doctor who respects a competent patient's refusal of further life-sustaining treatment no longer has a duty to provide that treatment—on the contrary, her duty is to comply with her patient's wishes—and she therefore acts lawfully by removing life support from the patient.

A further reason for treating the withdrawal of life support as an omission is that not starting life-sustaining treatment in the first place is plainly an omission, rather than an action. If doctors could be guilty of murder if they withdraw life-support, but not if they fail to initiate it, there would be a powerful incentive to withhold such treatment from patients altogether, which is self-evidently undesirable.

Some commentators have, however, questioned the description of the removal of mechanical ventilation or an artificial feeding tube as an omission.

Ian Kennedy[49]

[T]o describe turning off the machine as an omission does some considerable violence to the ordinary English usage. It represents an attempt to solve the problem by logic chopping. Such an approach may demonstrate to the satisfaction of some that no crime is involved, but it is surely most unsatisfactory to rest the response of the law to what is seen as a testing moral and philosophical issue on some semantic sleight of hand.

Further evidence that it may be inappropriate, albeit convenient, to describe the withdrawal of life-prolonging treatment as an omission comes from the suggestion that doctors' conscientious objections to treatment withdrawal should be respected. The British Medical Association's guidance to doctors, for example, states that: 'People who have a conscientious objection to withholding or withdrawing life-prolonging treatment should, wherever possible, be permitted to hand over care of the patient to a colleague'.[50]

As we saw earlier, the doctors who had been caring for Ms B were permitted to refuse to participate in the removal of the ventilator that was keeping her alive. Since it is hard to see how a doctor could have a conscientious objection to obeying the law by refraining from treating someone unlawfully, it is surely more plausible to admit that doctors whose consciences prompt them to refuse to participate in the withdrawal of life-prolonging treatment are unwilling to *act* deliberately to cause their patients' deaths. As Dame Elizabeth Butler-Sloss P explained, this was certainly the perspective of the treating clinicians in *Re B (Adult: Refusal of Medical Treatment)*.

Re B (Adult: Refusal of Medical Treatment)[51]

Dame Elizabeth Butler-Sloss P

[Dr C] had studied and spent her professional life trying to do her best to improve and preserve life. She did not feel able to agree with simply switching off Ms B's ventilation. She would not be able to do it. She felt she was being asked to kill Ms B. They had all been looking after Ms B for a long time on a very intimate level. She felt that a lot more needed to be done for these patients.

It was clear from their evidence that both the treating clinicians were deeply distressed by the dilemma which had faced them over the year that Ms B had spent in the ICU. They knew her well

---

[49] *Treat Me Right*, 351.
[50] *Withholding and Withdrawing Life-prolonging Medical Treatment: Guidance for Decision Making*, 3rd edn (2007), para 16.2.
[51] [2002] 1 FLR 1090.

and respected and liked her. They considered her to be competent to make decisions about her medical treatment. They could not, however, bring themselves to contemplate that they should be part of bringing Ms B's life to an end by the dramatic, (my word), step of turning off the ventilator. As I listened to the evidence of each of them I had the greatest possible sympathy for their position.

While lawyers may defend doctors' actions in withdrawing life support by pointing out the legal significance of the difference between acts and omissions, doctors themselves are more likely to justify their conduct by drawing a distinction between 'killing' and 'letting die'. So a doctor who withdraws life support does not kill, she merely lets the patient die. This explanation undoubtedly has intuitive appeal, perhaps because we instinctively feel that acting deliberately to end someone's life must be morally worse than letting them die.

In the next extract, Andrew McGee argues that there is also an important *causal* difference between euthanasia and treatment withdrawal.

Andrew McGee[52]

What is proposed in euthanasia is that we wrest from nature control of our ultimate fate: we decide when and how we should die, and we ensure thereby that we have the last word. In lawful withdrawal, by contrast, the very opposite is the case: we interfere with nature, not in killing the patient, but in keeping the patient alive, and the question of whether or not we should withdraw treatment is at bottom the question of whether we should restore to nature her dominion, allowing nature finally to take its course, with the patient dying a natural death....

This difference explains, I think, why, in the case of withdrawal, the principle of the inviolability of life remains undisturbed. In withdrawal, we are not taking control of death in the way we do in the practice of euthanasia, because the issue in withdrawal is when we should stop artificially prolonging life and allow nature to take its course—to stop deferring what, at some point, is inevitable. In euthanasia, by contrast, we anticipate nature and override it by bringing about the patient's death before its time.

In contrast, the authors of the following extracts argue that it is not in fact obvious that letting someone die is *necessarily* less blameworthy than killing them. Rather, as Jonathan Glover suggests, while killing (or acting positively) will *usually* be more reprehensible than letting someone die (or omitting to act), there may be circumstances in which this is not the case. Killing someone in self-defence, for example, is not a criminal offence, whereas a mother who lets her child die from starvation may be guilty of murder.

Jonathan Glover[53]

Sometimes when I do not do something, it would be entirely unreasonable to blame me for this. If someone I have never heard of killed himself last week in Brazil, without my knowing or doing anything about it, I cannot be blamed for it...But some omissions are at the other

---

[52] Finding a way through the Ethic and Legal Maze: Withdrawal of Medical Treatment and Euthanasia' (2005) 13 Medical Law Review 357–385.

[53] *Causing Death and Saving Lives* (Penguin: Harmondsworth, 1977) 95.

extreme of blameworthiness. A man who will inherit a fortune when his father dies, and, with this in mind, omits to give him medicine necessary for keeping him alive, is very culpable…It seems possible that some of the force of the acts and omissions doctrine derives from tacitly thinking of omissions in terms of examples drawn from the non-culpable end of the spectrum. The doctrine certainly seems less plausible where the omission is deliberate and results from a bad motive.

It is not the simple fact that a doctor lets someone die that makes their act excusable: rather, as Dan Brock explains, it is the surrounding circumstances—such as the patient's request and their intolerable distress—that justify the doctor's conduct.

Dan W Brock[54]

Consider the case of a patient terminally ill with ALS [Amyotrophic Lateral Sclerosis] disease. She is completely respirator dependent with no hope of ever being weaned. She is unquestionably competent and persistently requests to be removed from the respirator and allowed to die. Most people and physicians would agree that the patient's physician should respect the patient's wishes and remove her from the respirator, though this will certainly cause the patient's death. The common understanding is that the physician thereby allows the patient to die. But is that correct?

Suppose the patient has a greedy and hostile son…Afraid that his inheritance will be dissipated by a long and expensive hospitalization, he enters his mother's room while she is sedated, extubates her, and she dies. Shortly thereafter the medical staff discovers what he has done and confronts the son. He replies, 'I didn't kill her. I merely allowed her to die. It was her ALS disease that caused her death.' I think this would rightly be dismissed as transparent sophistry—the son went into his mother's room and deliberately killed her. But, of course, the son performed just the same physical actions, did just the same thing, that the physician would have done. If that is so, then doesn't the physician also kill the patient when he extubates her?

I underline immediately that there are important ethical differences between what the physician and the greedy son do. First, the physician acts with the patient's consent whereas the son does not. Second, the physician acts with a good motive—to respect the patient's wishes and self-determination—whereas the son acts with a bad motive—to protect his own inheritance. Third, the physician acts in a social role through which he is legally authorized to carry out the patient's wishes regarding treatment whereas the son has no such authorization. These and perhaps other ethically important differences show that what the physician did was morally justified whereas what the son did was morally wrong. What they do not show, however, is that the son killed while the physician allowed to die.…Both the physician and the greedy son act in a manner intended to cause death, do cause death, and so both kill.

The following example offers a further illustration of this point.

Emily Jackson[55]

Imagine a doctor who has two competent adult patients connected to the same artificial ventilator. Patient A wants to continue living, and patient B wants to die. The doctor switches

---

[54] 'Voluntary Active Euthanasia' (1992) Hastings Center Report 10–22.
[55] 'Whose Death is it Anyway? Euthanasia and the Medical Profession' (2004) 57 Current Legal Problems 415–42.

off the machine, and both patients die. In relation to patient A, because the doctor is under a duty to treat her, switching off the machine is characterised as an action, and the doctor might be guilty of murder. But in relation to patient B, switching off the machine is an omission. Exactly the same course of conduct is, in the eyes of the law, simultaneously both an act and an omission. But we cannot tell whether what the doctor did was an act, and hence culpable, or an omission, and hence blameless, unless we take into account extrinsic factors, such as, in this case, the competent patient's request for treatment withdrawal. Thus the morally relevant fact is not whether what the doctor does is an omission or an action, but rather whether the background against which the decision has been taken justifies the doctor's conclusion that life, in these circumstances, should not be artificially prolonged.

It is, however, worth noting that even if we accept that there is no *necessary* moral difference between killing and letting die, it does not follow that they are therefore morally *equivalent*. So, for example, because treating a patient in the face of a competent refusal is a battery, it might make sense to talk about a *right* to refuse unwanted medical treatment. Refusing to respect someone's request to be killed, in contrast, would not violate their bodily integrity.

So far, we have been assuming that the question of treatment withdrawal arises when the competent adult has been given the option of life-prolonging treatment, and exercises their right to refuse. But a different scenario is possible. What if the doctor recommends that life-prolonging treatment (such as cardiopulmonary resuscitation or CPR) should not be attempted if the patient suffers a respiratory or cardiac arrest? In 2002, in response to concern that hospitals were including DNR (Do Not Resuscitate) orders in the medical notes of competent elderly patients without prior discussion, the British Medical Association, the Resuscitation Council, and the Royal College of Nursing issued a joint statement on decisions relating to cardiopulmonary resuscitation. This guidance was updated in 2007. It uses the term, 'Do Not *Attempt* Resuscitation' (DNAR) in order to make clear that resuscitation is not always successful. The guidance emphasizes that it is good practice to discuss writing DNAR orders with competent adult patients, but stresses the need for sensitivity.

BMA, Resuscitation Council and the RCN[56]

When a patient with capacity is at foreseeable risk of cardiac or respiratory arrest, and the healthcare team has doubts about whether the benefits of CPR would outweigh the burdens, or whether the level of recovery expected would be acceptable to the patient, there should be sensitive exploration of the patient's wishes, feelings, beliefs and values. However, information should not be forced on unwilling recipients and if patients indicate that they do not wish to discuss CPR this should be respected. Patients with capacity should be given opportunities to talk about CPR, but should not be forced to discuss the subject if they do not want to. Any discussions with the patient about whether to attempt CPR and any anticipatory decisions should be documented, signed and dated in the patient's health record. If a DNAR decision is made and there has been no discussion with the patient because they have indicated a clear desire to avoid such discussion, this must be documented in the health record and the reasons must be recorded.

[56] Decisions Relating to Cardiopulmonary Resuscitation: A Joint Statement from the British Medical Association, the Resuscitation Council (UK) and the Royal College of Nursing (2007).

In practice, it is difficult to find a sensitive way to ask a patient who has just been admitted to hospital if she would wish to be resuscitated should she suffer a heart attack, and it seems clear that DNAR orders are not always discussed with patients. In the next extract, Sheila McLean notes the significance of this for debates about the legalization of assisted dying.

Sheila McLean[57]

[F]ar from respecting the sanctity of life, in fact decisions are sometimes taken, often without the involvement of the individual, that continued life is not preferable to death. Not only is this a challenge to the law's repeated claims to respect the sanctity of all life, it also denies people the respect to which they should be entitled....

It is necessary, therefore to conclude that, despite the rhetoric to the contrary, sometimes death is seen as the 'best' or the 'right' way out. It seems extraordinary that it is apparently permissible or accepted that *others* can decide on this, and even that I may initiate or be involved in the decision not to instigate CPR, yet I may not choose another route which would have the same result—a chosen, assisted death.

(b) Advance directives

As we saw in Chapter 5, advance directives or decisions (ADs) may involve a patient attempting to *prospectively* refuse life-prolonging treatment, once their condition reaches a certain point. In theory, according to the Mental Capacity Act (MCA) 2005, a valid and applicable advance refusal of medical treatment is as binding upon medical professionals as a contemporaneous refusal. In practice, however, while many people may have expressed a vague preference for 'not being a vegetable', it is comparatively unusual for patients to have drawn up advance directives which are precise enough to be legally binding.

In addition, for the need for the AD to be valid (ie still in force) and applicable (to the precise situation which has arisen), the MCA contains some additional criteria for ADs which consist in the refusal of life-sustaining treatment. The person (referred to as P) who has issued the advance refusal must specifically acknowledge that they intend to refuse treatment even if this puts their life at risk; the decision must be in writing and signed by P or a representative in P's presence, and the signature must be witnessed. This is more exacting than the common law, under which there was no requirement for an advance refusal to be in writing, regardless of the gravity of its consequences.

Where there is doubt about the validity or applicability of an AD, under section 26(4) an application can be made to the court of protection (again see further Chapter 5) for a declaration. While the court's advice is being sought, under section 26(5) nothing in the advance decision should prevent the provision of life-sustaining treatment or steps to prevent deterioration in the P's condition.

There have been cases where there was no ambiguity or doubt over the validity of an advance refusal of life-prolonging treatment. One such case was *Re AK (Medical Treatment: Consent)*. AK was 19 years old and had suffered from motor neurone disease for two-and-a half years. His physical condition had deteriorated, and he could communicate only through a tiny movement of one eyelid, through which he was able to answer 'yes' or 'no' to questions. At some point, he would lose this ability, and it would then be impossible to tell if he was in pain. Because motor neurone disease does not affect a person's intellectual capacity, AK

---

[57] *Assisted Dying: Reflections on the Need for Law Reform* (Routledge-Cavendish: Abingdon, 2007) 127,129.

would continue to be able to hear, see, feel, think, and understand. He asked that the doctors remove his ventilator two weeks after he lost his ability to communicate. The doctors treating him sought a declaration that it would be lawful to discontinue life-sustaining treatment in these circumstances, and Hughes J held that it would.

Re AK (Medical Treatment: Consent)[58]

Hughes J

In the present case the expressions of AK's decision are recent and are made not on any hypothetical basis but in the fullest possible knowledge of impending reality. I am satisfied that they genuinely represent his considered wishes and should be treated as such...Given that his express wishes are clear, the conclusion follows from what I have said that once the conditions which he has stipulated arise it will be unlawful to continue invasive ventilation.

Cases in which advance refusals are this precise, recent, and unambiguous are, perhaps, the exception rather than the norm. Because the patient is now incompetent, it is not necessarily easy to be certain that she was competent when she made the directive, or that she has not since had a change of heart. Doctors faced with an advance decision and some doubt about its validity and applicability are placed in a difficult position. If the patient with an AD had in fact had a change of heart before she became incapacitated, a doctor who withholds life-support will be failing to act in a situation in which she has a duty to act positively to save life. The patient will be dead, and, as we saw earlier, the doctor's conduct will satisfy the *actus reus* and *mens rea* for murder. If, on the other hand, the doctor ignores a refusal which turns out to have been valid, she will have committed the tort of battery. So where there is doubt about the validity of an AD, doctors may be faced with the choice between two evils—potentially committing the crime of murder or the tort of battery.

Perhaps unsurprisingly, doctors and the courts too, have tended to approach advance decisions with a presumption in favour of preserving life. The practical consequence of this that the normal burden of proof in relation to the presumption of competence is reversed: in effect, evidence has to be gathered to establish that the now incompetent patient was in fact competent when she executed the AD, rather than it being for others to prove that she lacked capacity.

Sabine Michalowski is critical of this approach, arguing that the existence of doubt should not lead a person's AD to be ignored in favour of the preservation of life, but, rather, that there should be an attempt to resolve any doubt by seeking further evidence. This is especially important because the very existence of the AD indicates that the P felt strongly about having their wishes respected after they lost capacity.

Sabine Michalowski[59]

Thus, it is submitted that instead of applying a presumption in favour of preserving life in all cases of a perceived ambiguity of an advance directive, an attempt should be made to interpret the existing living will by inferring from documentary or other evidence what the

---

[58] [2001] 1 FLR 129.
[59] 'Advance Refusals of Life Sustaining Treatment' (2005) Modern Law Review 958.

> patient's wishes were, without any bias in favour of or against the preservation of life. Given how difficult it is to make an entirely unambiguous advance directive and to make clear provision for all foreseeable contingencies, every other approach will undermine patient autonomy in favour of the views of the medical profession and/or society.

As well as the practical problem of working out whether the AD covers the circumstances which have arisen and reflects the P's wishes, some people have suggested that there may be more fundamental problems with respecting ADs made before a person really knew what it would be like to lack capacity. Rebecca Dresser and Allen Buchanan argue that profound incapacity may sever the 'psychological continuity' between the competent individual who issued the advance directive, and the incompetent person who now requires life support, meaning that the now incompetent person should not necessarily be bound by the competent person's wishes.

Rebecca Dresser[60]

> If little or no psychological connectedness and continuity exist between the individual at the two points in time, then there is no particular reason why the past person, as opposed to any other person, should determine the present person's fate.

Allen Buchanan[61]

> [The] very process that renders the individual incompetent and brings the advance directive into play can—and indeed often does—destroy the conditions necessary for her personal identity and thereby undercuts entirely the moral authority of the directive...
>
> So long as the degree of psychological continuity which we take to be necessary for the preservation of personal identity is present, the advance directive has full moral authority... [But] presumably a point is eventually reached at which the degree of psychological continuity between the author of the advance directive and the incompetent individual is so small that the advance directive of the former has no authority at all over the latter.

The idea that the incompetent adult may be so far removed from their previously competent self that they should not be bound by the latter's advance directive is, unsurprisingly, a controversial one. Ronald Dworkin, for example, has said that advance directives express values that we should continue to respect because the now incompetent patient is not just a collection of current interests, but rather is a person with a past.[62] Similarly, Nancy Rhoden has argued that the 'notion that a person is one person, and one person only, from birth through old age, despite whatever changes and vicissitudes she might undergo' is 'deeply embedded in our culture'.

---

[60] R Dresser, 'Life, Death, and Incompetent Patients: Conceptual Infirmities and Hidden Values in the Law' (1986) 28 Arizona Law Review 380–1, 373

[61] 'Advance Directives and the Personal Identity Problem' (1988) Philosophy and Public Affairs 131–54.

[62] Dworkin, 'Autonomy and the Demented Self' (1986) 64 Milbank Q 4, 14 (Supp. II).

Nancy K Rhoden[63]

> If we are to make decisions about them as persons, we must view them not only as they are in the present, but also as the persons they were—persons who had strong opinions about how their body, even when insensate, should be treated...We must see the person as she, when competent, would have imagined herself after incompetency, rather than viewing her from the outside and as she is now...
>
> [A]n entirely present-oriented view is a bad way to view even persons who left no living will; it is unlikely that they would want to be viewed just as a body that can experience only physical sensations...Considering the patient only in the immediate present divides the patient from her past, her history, her values, and her relationships—from all those things that make her human.

Let us imagine a practical example. As a healthy university teacher, I view the prospect of severe dementia with horror, and I might decide that should I become severely demented, and suffer a life-threatening infection, I would not want to be treated with antibiotics. I might then execute an unambiguous advance directive to this effect. But what if, once I am demented, it appears to my carers that I am able to gain pleasure (which may previously have seemed unimaginable) from my severely impaired existence. Perhaps I spend my days apparently enjoying watching the Teletubbies, as the philosopher and author Iris Murdoch was said to have done.[64] If I develop a serious, but easily treatable infection, should doctors withhold antibiotics, in accordance with my AD?

In the next extract, Inez de Beaufort explains why she would want her previously competent wishes to take priority.

Inez de Beaufort[65]

> For me, the thought of my children spending their precious time visiting me when I do not recognize them is very painful, as is the idea that I know that they would suffer from that situation. Their suffering would, in my view, not be compensated by any interest I have in continuing my life. They will be sad because they knew me as the person I was, and feel powerless in not being able to save me from this fate. The fact that I consider this, and take their future feelings at heart in viewing my possible future is an essential part of me, of who I am and what I value.
>
> When I am demented, I may enjoy the visit of my 'mother' or whomever I think is visiting me, and I may be genuinely pleased about that. But the purpose and point of my AED is precisely that I do not want to end up in the situation of someone who cannot be there for her loved ones anymore.... The argument that you will be another you, and you will experience things differently when you are demented, does not convince me. To the contrary, because what I want to prevent is precisely this fact that I will experience things differently. I do not want to become someone who does not recognize her children anymore even if the demented-me would not suffer from not recognizing them anymore.

---

[63] 'Litigating Life and Death' (1988) 102 Harvard Law Review 375, 414.
[64] John Bayley, *Iris: A Memoir of Iris Murdoch* (Abacus, 1999).
[65] 'The View from Before' (2007) 7 The American Journal of Bioethics 57–8.

It should also be admitted that if we were to subject all advance decisions to a 'present best interests' review, whereby the advance directive only had force if it happened to coincide with what the medical team believe to be in the incompetent person's immediate best interests, there would be little point in making an advance decision, since this medical decisions would be taken in the *absence* of an advance decision.

The difficulties advance decisions raise for doctors, confused as to whether the person's previous wishes should trump their present best interests, are even more acute in countries which have legalized euthanasia and permit advance euthanasia directives (AEDs).

Cees MPM Hertogh; Marike E de Boer; Rose-Marie Dröes and Jan A Eefsting[66]

AEDs of patients with advanced dementia create insuperable moral and practical dilemmas. They confront physicians and family members with the problem of a 'death wish in writing' while its author has long since forgotten completing such a document, so there is neither a possibility to communicate with the patient about formerly held ideas (and fears!) concerning a life with dementia, nor is there a way to explain to the patient what the execution of the AED will mean. Moreover, as the patient's current preferences and quality of life often appear to differ from the imagined suffering of the competent patient who completes the AED, physicians cannot but experience a profound reluctance to perform euthanasia.

(b) SHOULD EUTHANASIA AND/OR ASSISTED SUICIDE BE LEGALIZED?

As we have seen, the law draws a bright line between lawful practices which result in a patient's death (withholding/withdrawing life-prolonging medical treatment and providing palliative care which may, incidentally, shorten life), and unlawful practices which have the same effect (euthanasia and physician-assisted suicide). This means that doctors are allowed to help their patients to die provided that they *happen* to be connected to a ventilator or nasogastric feeding tube. They can also potentially shorten the lives of those who *happen* to require life-threatening doses of painkillers. Some commentators argue that access to medical assistance in dying should not depend upon a patient's fortuitous need for life support or substantial doses of diamorphine. Others believe that there is a fundamental difference between doctors letting their patients die and killing them, and that the integrity of the medical profession demands an absolute prohibition upon doctors acting deliberately to terminate their patients' lives. Who is right?

Before we review the arguments for and against legalizing euthanasia and physician-assisted suicide, it is worth pointing out one important difference between the positions adopted by proponents and opponents of assisted dying. Someone who argues in favour of access to assisted dying does not impose their views on others. Rather, they believe that assisted dying should be available to people who actively seek it in order to avoid a frightening or distressing death. In contrast, someone who argues that assisted dying should be prohibited is not just saying that *they themselves* would not want access to it—that position would be entirely consistent with legalization. Rather, opponents of euthanasia believe that

---

[66] 'Would We Rather Lose Our Life Than Lose Our Self? Lessons From the Dutch Debate on Euthanasia for Patients With Dementia' (2007) 7 The American Journal of Bioethics 48–56.

people whose values are different, and who believe that assisted dying would help reduce *their* pain or distress at the end of life, should be denied the assistance they require because of *other people's* beliefs about the undesirability of legalization.

(1) Arguments for

(a) Autonomy

It is often assumed that one of the strongest arguments in favour of legalizing euthanasia and assisted suicide is respect for patient autonomy. Throughout this book, we have seen that the principle of patient self-determination is increasingly dominant within medical law, and it has been argued that a patient's right to make decisions about her medical treatment should extend to deciding the time and the manner of her death. It is undoubtedly true that we all have a profound interest in how we die. To die quickly and painlessly, perhaps at home and surrounded by people we love, is obviously preferable to a lonely, protracted, and frightening death. As Sylvia Law suggests, giving patients some control over how they die might then appear to be an especially important aspect of respect for autonomous decision-making.

Sylvia A Law[67]

First, the core of this dilemma is the individual's desire to retain control over his or her body and life…

Second, the right to choice is valuable, however that choice is exercised. The dying patient has lost control of most significant aspects of his or her life. The assurance that assisted death is an option provides a measure of autonomy and control, however that autonomy is exercised. Indeed, evidence from medical practice suggests that frank recognition and discussion of the suicide option sometimes leads depressed patients to reject it. Third, prohibitions on physician-assisted dying enforce individual isolation and prevent individuals from seeking the help and companionship of others at a critical time. When suicide is allowed, but help in dying is prohibited, the state denies important associational interests.

Fourth, it is not easy to hasten death in a private, non-violent way. Bans on physician assistance, therefore, aggravate…suffering. It is, of course, possible to jump off a tall building or to leap in front of an oncoming train. But most terminally ill patients seek a death that is both more private and less violent.

In contrast, John Keown argues that a 'right to choose' is essentially meaningless and that an emphasis upon individualistic values such as autonomy marginalizes the impact our actions have upon others.

John Keown[68]

The 'right to choose x' often serves as a slogan with powerful emotional appeal. But crude slogans are no substitute for rational reflection, and one can hardly sensibly assert a right to choose 'x' until one has considered whether it is right to choose 'x'; to do otherwise is simply

---

[67] 'Physician-Assisted Death: An Essay on Constitutional Rights and Remedies' (1996) 55 Maryland Law Review 292.

[68] *Euthanasia, Ethics and Public Policy: An Argument against Legalisation* (CUP: Cambridge, 2002) 54.

to beg the question. Is there a 'right to choose...paedophilia'? Or a 'right to choose...cruelty to animals'? Does the mere fact that someone *wants* to blind ponies or to have sex with children carry any moral weight? The 'right to choose' only arguably makes any moral sense in the context of a moral framework which enables us to discern what it is *right* to choose and what choices will in fact promote human flourishing. And not only *our* flourishing, but that of others. For we do not live as atomised individuals, as much loose talk about absolute respect for personal autonomy appears to assume, but in community, where our choices can have profound effects not only on ourselves but on others.

There are a number of problems with relying exclusively upon the principle of autonomy when arguing for the legalization of euthanasia and assisted suicide. First, few advocates of legalization would allow unrestricted access to medical assistance in dying. On the contrary, it is generally accepted that a doctor should only be allowed to help a patient to die in certain, limited circumstances. The fact that a person wants to die is not, on its own, a sufficient reason for a doctor to give her a lethal injection. Although opinion differs over whether terminal illness should be a prerequisite, most people would agree that a doctor should only comply with a patient's request for euthanasia or assisted suicide if her pain or suffering has become intolerable. These sorts of restrictions are inconsistent with an important feature of respect for autonomous decision-making, namely that: 'A mentally competent patient has an absolute right to refuse to consent to medical treatment for any reason, rational or irrational, or for no reason at all, even where that decision may lead to his or her own death'.[69]

Secondly, as we saw in Chapter 5, a patient's right to make decisions about their medical treatment is usually confined to a right to *refuse* treatment. Patients do not have the right to demand that their doctor carry out a particular procedure. So while the principle of autonomy requires doctors to respect a competent patient's refusal of life-prolonging medical treatment, it could not require doctors to comply with a request for euthanasia or assisted suicide.

In response, advocates of legalization might accept that while patients have a virtually absolute right to refuse unwanted medical treatment, they would not be entitled to demand that their doctors perform euthanasia. Rather, their right would be to *ask* for assistance in dying, a request which a doctor could legitimately turn down, either because she has a conscientious objection or because it would be incompatible with her duty of care. The purpose of legalization, as explained in the following extracts, would simply be to *allow* doctors to act lawfully when they comply with a patient's request for assistance.

Ronald Dworkin, Thomas Nagel, Robert Nozick, John Rawls, Thomas Scanlon, and Judith Jarvis Thomson[70]

Certain decisions are momentous in their impact on the character of a person's life—decisions about religious faith, political and moral allegiance, marriage, procreation, and death, for

---

[69] *Re MB* (1997) 38 BMLR 175, per Butler-Sloss LJ.

[70] In two cases heard by the US Supreme Court at the same time [*Washington et al. v Glucksberg* 117 S Ct 2258 (1997) and *Vacco v Quill* 117 S Ct 2293 (1997)], these six distinguished philosophers presented an Amici Curiae Brief for Respondents—referred to as The Philosophers' Brief—to the Supreme Court.

example. Such deeply personal decisions pose controversial questions about how and why human life has value. In a free society, individuals must be allowed to make those decisions for themselves, out of their own faith, conscience, and convictions...Most of us see death—whatever we think will follow it—as the final act of life's drama, and we want that last act to reflect our own convictions, those we have tried to live by, not the convictions of others forced on us in our most vulnerable moment...

Since patients have a right not to have life-support machinery attached to their bodies, they have, in principle, a right to compel its removal. But that is not true in the case of assisted suicide: patients in certain circumstances have a right that the state not forbid doctors to assist in their deaths, but they have no right to compel a doctor to assist them. The right in question, that is, is only a right to the help of a willing doctor.

David Orentlicher[71]

Some commentators distinguish the withdrawal of treatment from euthanasia/assisted suicide on the ground that a right to refuse treatment is a negative right to be left alone while a right to euthanasia or assisted suicide would be a positive right to command aid. This argument mischaracterizes the nature of a right to euthanasia or assisted suicide. Such a right would not mean that patients could require physicians to assist suicides or perform euthanasia. Rather, the right would prevent the state from interfering when a patient and physician voluntarily agree on a course of euthanasia/assisted suicide. Physicians would participate in euthanasia/assisted suicide only if they were willing to do so.

(b) Mercy

A different sort of argument for legalization could be framed in terms of the principle of beneficence (see further Chapter 1). When curing a patient and restoring her to full health is no longer possible, the doctor's duty to 'do good' encompasses doing whatever she can to relieve the patient's suffering. If the only way that a patient's distress can be relieved is by ending her life, it could be argued that allowing doctors to take this step is compatible with their duty to act beneficently.

In addition to helping individual patients whose suffering has become intolerable, the legalization of euthanasia might also benefit a wider class of patients by reassuring them that their doctor will be allowed to help them to die if their condition becomes unbearable. It has been suggested that some patients are so fearful of a protracted and distressing death that they take their own lives prematurely while they are still capable of doing so. Other patients may go to Switzerland while they are still able to travel, whereas if they could have access to assisted dying at home, they could wait until they became more incapacitated. For such patients, the availability of legalized euthanasia would, in fact, prolong their lives. In *Purdy v DPP*, Lord Judge explained that this was the predicament in which Debbie Purdy found herself.

---

[71] 'The Alleged Distinction between Euthanasia and the Withdrawal of Life-sustaining Treatment: Conceptually Incoherent and Impossible to Maintain' (1998) University of Illinois Law Review 837.

Purdy v DPP[72]

Lord Judge CJ

[S]he wishes to live for as long as possible, and to end her life only when it becomes utterly unbearable. But the harsh reality is if she lives that long she will be unable to end her own life without assistance. By then, it will be beyond her capability to do so....

If Ms Purdy could achieve something practicable within the current legal structures to ensure that her husband would not be prosecuted after her death, then she will not need to bring her life to an end before she would otherwise be ready.

Using mercy or beneficence, rather than autonomy, as the justification for legalizing euthanasia and assisted suicide might explain the restrictions that most people believe should be placed upon its use. A doctor would only be acting beneficently in helping a patient to die if she has reasonable grounds for believing that the patient's life has ceased to be a benefit to her.

Philippa Foot analyses euthanasia from the perspective of virtue ethics (considered in Chapter 1). She does not rule out the possibility that voluntary euthanasia might, in certain circumstances, be 'compatible with both justice and charity', but this would be the case only where its 'pu rpose is to benefit the one who dies'.

Philippa Foot[73]

Disease too can so take over a man's life that the normal human goods disappear. When a patient is so overwhelmed by pain or nausea that he cannot eat with pleasure, if he can eat at all, and is out of the reach of even the most loving voice, he no longer has ordinary human life in the sense in which the words are used here...crippling depression can destroy the enjoyment of ordinary goods as effectively as external circumstances can remove them.

(c) Inconsistency of the status quo

Another reason commonly given for legalizing euthanasia and assisted suicide is that the line the law currently draws between lawful and unlawful life-shortening practices is incoherent and morally irrelevant.[74] On this view, if we are prepared to allow doctors to engage in some practices that will end their patients' lives (such as withdrawing life-prolonging medical treatment, or giving life-threatening doses of painkillers), there is no logical reason why we should not also allow doctors to give their patients lethal injections, particularly since dying from starvation or suffocation may be more protracted and distressing (both for the patient and for her carers) than the quick and painless death that would be induced by a single fatal injection. Paradoxically then, as James Rachels points out, the lawful means of hastening a patient's death will often result in a more prolonged and less peaceful death than the unlawful means.

---

[72] [2009] EWCA Civ 92.

[73] 'Euthanasia' (1977) 6 Philosophy & Public Affairs 85–112.

[74] See further E Jackson, 'Whose Death is it Anyway? Euthanasia and the Medical Profession' (2004) 57 Current Legal Problems 415–42.

James Rachels[75]

> Part of my point is that the process of being 'allowed to die' can be relatively slow and painful, whereas being given a lethal injection is relatively quick and painless…The doctrine that says that a baby may be allowed to dehydrate and wither, but may not be given an injection that would end its life without suffering, seems so patiently cruel as to require no further refutation.

The sort of death which most of us would prefer—quick, painless, at home, and holding the hand of someone we love—is not facilitated by any of the lawful means of hastening patients' deaths. On the contrary, the withdrawal of life-sustaining treatment will generally take place in hospital. Where artificial nutrition and hydration is withdrawn, the patient will slowly starve to death, albeit painlessly, over a period of about two weeks. The moment of death is unpredictable, and the patient's family may not be present.

If the patient is given life-threatening doses of painkilling drugs—justified by the doctrine of double effect—it will only be possible to ensure that her loved ones are present at the moment of her death if the doctor admits that which the doctrine of double effect forbids, namely that she is killing her patient rather than merely attempting to relieve her pain.

Voluntary euthanasia or assisted suicide, on the other hand, could be given to a patient in her home in the presence of the people she loves. In Oregon, 90 per cent of patients who die as a result of physician-assisted suicide die at home.[76] In the Netherlands, the figure is 80 per cent. Evidence from the Netherlands also appears to indicate that the bereaved relatives of patients who die as a result of euthanasia cope better with bereavement, and suffer fewer post-traumatic stress reactions than the bereaved of comparable patients who die naturally.[77] The opportunity to say goodbye; being prepared for the time and manner of the death; and having talked openly about dying all appear to have a positive impact upon a family's ability to come to terms with a person's death.

Moreover, as RG Frey argues in the next extract, making the lawfulness of medical assistance in dying contingent upon whether a patient *happens* to be connected to a ventilator or a morphine drip could be said to discriminate against certain patients whose suffering may be equally unbearable, but whose illnesses deprive them of access to the various lawful means of ending their lives.

RG Frey[78]

> It seems little short of incredible that the fact that a terminally ill patient is on a life-support system could so transform cases, morally, when both cases show quite clearly that patient and doctor are acting together to bring about the patient's death at the instigation of the patient…Withdrawing feeding tubes and starving the patient to death is permissible, supplying the patient with a pill that produces death is not. Yet both sorts of assistance assuredly produce death, and both sorts involve the patient and doctor acting together to produce that death.

[75] 'Active and Passive Euthanasia' (1975) 292 New England Journal of Medicine 79–80.
[76] Oregon Department of Human Services, Tenth Annual Report on Oregon's Death with Dignity Act (2007), available at <www.oregon.gov/DHS/ph/pas/docs/year10.pdf>.
[77] Nikkie B Swarte *et al.*, 'Effects of Euthanasia on the Bereaved Family and Friends: A Cross Sectional Study' (2003) 327 British Medical Journal 189.
[78] 'Distinctions in Death' 17–42 in Gerald Dworkin, RG Frey, and Sissela Bok, *Euthanasia and Physician-Assisted Suicide: For and Against* (CUP: Cambridge, 1998) 36, 38.

> To be prepared to see the patient dead; to take the step that will assuredly produce death; to know as a certainty that death will ensue or be hastened: is this not morally equivalent to intending the patient's death? If so, there is little difference here between the supply of pills and the withdrawal of feeding tubes, so far as intending the patient's death is concerned.

Sheila McLean agrees. In discussing the Ms B case, she says 'on all logic, Ms B's death was assisted';[79] people who happen to need artificial ventilation 'can orchestrate their deaths even when they need assistance in doing so'.[80]

A further argument from inconsistency is that, despite the illegality of assisted dying, prosecutions are rare, and convictions are rarer still. Despite the clarity of the definition of murder—which simply requires an act causing death and the intention to cause death or grievous bodily harm—acts carried out for compassionate reasons, whether by doctors or relatives, are not prosecuted or sentenced in the same way as other homicides. Sheila McLean asks 'what purpose is served by a law which technically criminalizes behaviour which it then effectively ignores and forgives?', and points out that this gap between the prohibition of assisted dying and its lenient treatment by the prosecutors and in the courts is 'an interesting indication of the law's actual rather than its theoretical approach to assisted dying'.[81]

(d) Benefits of regulation

Proponents of this argument for legalization tend to cite evidence which shows that, despite its illegality, doctors *do* help their patients to die. Obviously, because doctors who admit to practising euthanasia may be charged with murder, it is virtually impossible to gather accurate information about their participation in life-shortening practices. However, anonymous surveys consistently show that between 30 and 60 per cent of all doctors have been asked for assistance in dying, and that a significant minority has complied with such requests.[82] The House of Lords Select Committee concluded that between four and twelve per cent of doctors will admit to having assisted in bringing about a patient's death.[83]

Some commentators then suggest that if euthanasia is happening anyway, but being carried out in secret, legalization would enable it to be properly regulated. Not only are doctors currently very unlikely to report instances of euthanasia, but the threat of prosecution means that they are deterred from consulting other colleagues. As a result, euthanasia is being practised without safeguards, such as the requirement that a doctor seeks a second opinion, and without the monitoring that might be facilitated by the keeping of accurate records. In the next extract, Margaret Pabst Battin argues that the purpose of legalization

---

[79] *Assisted Dying: Reflections on the Need for Law Reform* (Routledge-Cavendish: Abingdon, 2007) 84.
[80] Ibid.
[81] Ibid 144.
[82] A survey published in the British Medical Journal (BMJ) in 1994 found that 45 per cent of doctors had been asked to take active steps to hasten death, and of these, 32 per cent had complied with such a request: BJ Ward and PA Tate, 'Attitudes Among NHS Doctors to Requests for Euthanasia' (1994) 308 British Medical Journal 1132. Three hundred GPs were interviewed by the Sunday Times in 1998, and 15 per cent admitted to having helped their patients die. Cherry Norton, 'Doctor Will You Help Me Die?' (1998) Sunday Times, 15 Nov 14. In an anonymous poll of 683 surgeons in New South Wales, Australia, 36 per cent admitted that they had administered high doses of painkillers to patients with the intent of bringing about their death. Five per cent said that they had given a patient a single lethal injection on their clear request (2001) 323 British Medical Journal 1268.
[83] House of Lords Select Committee (2005).

in the Netherlands was precisely to enable some control to be exercised over an otherwise secretive practice.

Margaret Pabst Battin[84]

[For] the Dutch...bringing euthanasia and related practices out into the open is a way of gaining control. For the Dutch, this is a way of identifying a practice that, in the Netherlands as in every other country, has been going on undercover and entirely at the discretion of the physician. It brings the practice into public view, where it can be regulated by guidelines, judicial scrutiny, and the collection of objective data. It is not that the Dutch or anyone else have only recently begun to practise euthanasia for the dying patient, nor is this a new phenomenon in the last decade or so; rather, the Dutch are the first to try to assert formal public control over a previously hidden practice and, hence, to regulate it effectively. Both open public discussion and the development of formal mechanisms such as guidelines, hospital protocols, and reporting requirements are seen as crucial in developing a social consensus, understood and accepted by both physicians and patients, about what can and cannot be permitted.

In the next extract, RS Magnusson draws upon his interviews with health care professionals to argue that we do not have a choice between legalized physician-assisted dying, where doctors help their patients to die, and illegal assisted dying, where it never happens. Rather, euthanasia's illegality instead means that it will inevitably be practised 'underground', which may be much more dangerous for patients.

RS Magnusson[85]

Despite the growing body of statistical evidence, remarkably little is known about the circumstances in which doctors provide covert assistance to die, whether these attempts result in what was perceived to be a good death for the patient, and the long term impact of involvement on health carers themselves. In *Angels of Death: Exploring the Euthanasia Underground*, I reported on 49 detailed, yet pseudonymous interviews with doctors, nurses, and therapists working in HIV/AIDS health care, principally in Sydney, Melbourne, and San Francisco....Despite their mostly good intentions, interviewees painted a troubling picture of covert PAS/AE...

For me, the most striking feature of these accounts was the way they betrayed the absence of norms or principles for deciding when it was appropriate to proceed. One doctor injected a young man on the first occasion they met, despite concerns from close friends that the patient was depressed...In another case, a patient brought his death forward by a week so as not to interfere with the doctor's holiday plans...

It is important to remember that our ability to castigate the Dutch about their rates of non-compliance comes courtesy of the relative transparency created by the Dutch policy of legalisation. If we wish to make ambit claims about slippery slopes, it is only fair to point out that the reporting rate for Britain, Australia, and most other countries, is zero. Nevertheless, even partial compliance with statutory safeguards may represent an improvement on the kinds of clinical decisions that currently occur in secret.

---

84 *The Least Worst Death: Essays in Bioethics on the End of Life* (OUP: Oxford, 1994) 141.
85 'Euthanasia: Above Ground, Below Ground' (2004) 30 Journal of Medical Ethics 441–6.

It might also be argued that legalization would facilitate the equal treatment of similarly situated patients. At present, as Charles Baron explains, a patient's access to euthanasia is contingent upon whether her doctor is willing to run the risk of life imprisonment. This inevitably means that it is only available to a small number of patients. It has further been suggested that the patients whose relationships with medical professionals are sufficiently close that they may be able to persuade them to act illegally are likely to be from the more privileged sections of society. Legalization would therefore enable access to euthanasia to depend upon need, rather than upon one's connections with members of the medical profession.

Charles Baron[86]

In March 1996, an Article in the Journal of the American Medical Association revealed that physicians in the State of Washington commit acts of physician-assisted suicide in percentages that rival those in Holland (where euthanasia and physician-assisted suicide are essentially legalized)...

It is an open secret that such technically illegal practices take place, but prosecutions and disciplinary actions involving them have thus far been almost non-existent... Potential abuses are left completely without internal or external checks, and such a regime encourages the view that medical personnel may safely consider themselves 'above the law'. Patients are also denied equal protection of the law. Only patients with 'connections' are able to find physicians to assist them in dying—much as only women with 'connections' were able to obtain professional help in terminating pregnancies before abortion was legalized.

(2) Arguments Against

(a) Sanctity of life

The legalization of euthanasia and assisted suicide would necessarily involve accepting that death can rationally be preferred to life. According to Luke Gormally, this contravenes the principle that all human life is intrinsically valuable.

Luke Gormally[87]

Euthanasiast killing, even when it is voluntary, involves denial of the ongoing worth of the lives of those reckoned to be candidates for euthanasia. It is a type of killing, therefore, which cannot be accommodated in a legal system for which belief in the worth and dignity of every human being is foundational... If the claim that a person lacks a worthwhile life is held to make killing lawful, then the state has ceased to recognize the innocent as having binding claims to protection.

The decriminalization of suicide (and attempted suicide, therefore) makes sense if we contemplate the plight of people having to face criminal proceedings after failed suicide attempts. Decriminalization motivated by the desire to ease the plight of such people does

---

[86] 'Physician Assisted Suicide should be Legalized and Regulated' (1997) 41 Boston Bar Journal 15.

[87] 'Euthanasia and Assisted Suicide: 7 reasons why they should not be legalized', in Donna Dickenson, Malcolm Johnson, and Jeanne Samson Katz (eds), *Death, Dying and Bereavement*, 2nd edn (Sage: London, 2000) 286–90.

not, however, imply that the law takes a neutral view of the choice to carry out suicide. Those who attempt suicide are clearly moved by the (at least transient) belief that their lives are no longer worthwhile. Since just legal arrangements rest on a belief in the ineliminable worth of every human life, the law must reject the reasonableness of a choice which is so motivated.

Hence the law must also refuse to accommodate the behaviour of those who effectively endorse the choice of the suicide: for they too are acting on the view that the person they are helping no longer has a worthwhile life.

This sort of argument against legalization often derives from the religious idea that life is not ours to dispose of as we please. For human beings to choose the moment of their death and to take active steps to bring it about is—on this view—to usurp God's monopoly upon the power to give and to take life.

In contrast, in the next extract Margaret Otlowski suggests that this sort of argument is effectively a matter of private faith, and that it should not be allowed to determine public policy.

Margaret Otlowski[88]

Religious arguments will naturally be convincing to those who accept the religious viewpoint but they clearly do not have universal relevance. Religion is a matter of personal commitment, and objections to active voluntary euthanasia based purely on religious views should not dominate the law nor impinge on the freedoms of others. Whilst the convictions of believers must obviously be respected, it must be recognized that in a pluralistic and largely secular society, the freedom of conviction of non-believers must also be upheld... Only if the legal prohibition on active voluntary euthanasia is removed will everyone be able to live according to their own convictions; those who oppose active voluntary euthanasia could reject it for themselves, and those who are in favour of the practice are not forced to live against their convictions.

(b) Legalization is unnecessary

For two different reasons, it is sometimes argued that the legalization of euthanasia is unnecessary. First, improvements in palliative care lead some opponents of legalization to contend that no patient should ever have to die in intolerable agony. On this view, the desire for euthanasia is evidence of our failure to provide sufficient hospice places and high-quality palliative treatment to terminally ill patients. If, so the argument goes, all patients were to be given optimum treatment at the end of life, none would request euthanasia, and the question of its legalization would become redundant. This is, to some extent, an empirical argument which depends upon evidence that all suffering at the end of life can be adequately relieved by palliative care.

While it is probably true that few patients now have to endure unbearable levels of pain, other distressing conditions, such as the inability to swallow or difficulties in breathing, cannot be relieved by conventional analgesics, and instead the only way to relieve suffering is

---

[88] *Voluntary Euthanasia and the Common Law*, 216.

to sedate the patient into a coma. As we saw earlier, from the patient's point of view, causing death and inducing permanent unconsciousness may be indistinguishable.

In any event, pain is seldom the principal or the only reason for patients' requests for euthanasia. On the contrary, patients more frequently cite fear of indignity, loss of control, and dependency as their reasons for wanting to be helped to die. The Remmelink study into euthanasia in the Netherlands, which we consider below, found that loss of dignity was a much more common reason for requesting euthanasia than unbearable pain. In Oregon in 2007, the principal reasons for requesting physician-assisted suicide were loss of autonomy (100 per cent); decreasing ability to participate in activities that made life enjoyable (86 per cent), and loss of dignity (86 per cent); inadequate pain control was much less commonly cited (33 per cent).[89] While optimum palliative care may be able to minimize physical pain, it is less clear that it can eradicate the helplessness and mental anguish that, as the House of Lords Select Committee acknowledged, many people experience as a result of their bodies' progressive deterioration.

House of Lords Select Committee on Assisted Dying

There was a general consensus among our witnesses as regards the limitations of palliative care in relieving patient suffering. The VES [Voluntary Euthanasia Society] took the view that 'no amount of palliative care can address some patients' concerns regarding their loss of autonomy, loss of control of bodily functions and loss of dignity'....The BMA echoed this view, observing that 'there are patients for whom even the best palliative care is not dealing with their pain', adding that 'in spite of excellent palliative care, the position is not necessarily one which those patients regard as beneficial to them'.[90]

The second reason for arguing that the legalization of euthanasia is unnecessary derives from the recognition that, in practice, doctors do help their patients to die. According to this line of argument, the status quo enables patients in desperate straits to have access to medical assistance in ending their lives, while simultaneously retaining the symbolically important prohibition upon doctors killing their patients.

Martha Minow[91]

For now, at least, it is better to live with the lie that prohibition prevents the practice than the lie that its approval would not cost all of us, deeply. It is better to live with the lie that prohibition works so that, at the margin, those who engage in it do so with trembling.

This sort of argument rests upon two different assumptions: first, that in individual cases euthanasia may be justifiable; and secondly, that openly legalizing euthanasia might have negative consequences for society as a whole. Of course, these assumptions initially appear to pull in entirely different directions, and so the argument that we should retain eutha-

---

[89] Oregon Department of Human Services, Tenth Annual Report on Oregon's Death with Dignity Act (2007), available at <www.oregon.gov/DHS/ph/pas/docs/year10.pdf>.

[90] Assisted Dying for the Terminally Ill Committee, *Assisted Dying for the Terminally Ill Bill—First Report* (2005), para 88.

[91] 'Which Question? Which Lie? Reflections on the Physician-Assisted Suicide Cases' (1997) 1 Supreme Court Review 30.

nasia's illegality while acknowledging that some doctors will be prepared to act unlawfully in order to help their patients to die is, as Yale Kamisar admits, an attempt to have it both ways.

Yale Kamisar[92]

I do not deny it is hard to defend an absolute prohibition when you not only expect the prohibition to be violated in certain situations, but you can visualize circumstances where you would understand and forgive the person who did so.

It could, of course, be argued that if we accept that euthanasia might be acceptable in some circumstances, retaining its absolute prohibition for 'symbolic reasons' is disingenuous. If we think that doctors sometimes act properly in helping their patients to die, it seems unreasonable to expect them to expose themselves to the risk of life imprisonment.

(c) Difficulties in ensuring that a request has been made voluntarily

Obviously, if it were to be legalized, it would be vitally important to ensure that patients' requests for euthanasia had been made voluntarily. For a number of reasons, some commentators have suggested that, in practice, this represents an insuperable obstacle to legalization. First, as Susan M Wolf explains, euthanasia is generally requested by patients whose judgement may be distorted by the depression that often accompanies the final stages of debilitating illness. It has therefore been argued that our inability to *guarantee* that a patient's desire to die is genuine—and not, for example, a symptom of treatable depression—should lead us to be extremely reluctant to comply with patients' requests for euthanasia.

Susan M Wolf[93]

[A]dvocates for legalizing assisted suicide...embrace a model that depicts patients as independent rights-bearers making decisions at the end of life free from undue pressure and coercion. Yet there are numerous problems with this vision. First, patients actually exercise little control over end-of-life care... In reality, patients are profoundly dependent on health professionals, with many patients reporting that they want their physician to make treatment decisions for them...The research shows...that depression is even more strongly correlated with requests for assisted suicide than pain is. Yet patients routinely face inadequate diagnosis and treatment of depression. Given these data, a patient requesting assisted suicide may actually be seeking relief from depression or pain...

Terminal patients are quite unlike independent rights-bearers freely negotiating in business transactions. Instead, they are profoundly dependent, often at the mercy of health professionals for everything from toileting to life-saving care, and may be experiencing too much pain, discomfort, or depression to make independent and truly voluntary decisions.

While it might be important to investigate the possibility of depression in patients requesting euthanasia, diagnosis of depression in terminally ill patients is difficult because many of

---

[92] 'Physician Assisted Suicide: The Problems Presented by the Compelling Heartwrenching Case' (1998) 88 Journal of Criminal Law and Criminology 1121, 1144.

[93] 'Pragmatism in the Face of Death: The Role of Facts in the Assisted Suicide Debate' (1998) 82 Minnesota Law Review 1063.

the symptoms of depression—such as weight loss, insomnia, loss of energy, and inability to concentrate—are also symptoms of conditions like cancer, or possible side-effects of medication. Nevertheless, there have been attempts to use standardized diagnostic tests to work out the frequency of depression among those requesting assistance in dying. A recent study in Oregon suggests that the overwhelming majority of people who have died as a result of assisted suicide did *not* suffer from any sort of depressive disorder.[94]

Secondly, because the consequence of euthanasia will be the patient's death, there is no scope for correcting mistaken decisions if it subsequently emerges that the patient had in fact lacked capacity when they made the decision to die. Nor is there room for the correction of decisions to die made following a mistaken diagnosis of terminal illness. Given the finality of euthanasia and this inevitable risk of error, opponents of legalization have suggested that we could never be sufficiently certain that a person's request for euthanasia had been properly informed and competently made.

Thirdly, as we saw in Chapter 7, consultations between patients and their doctors are protected by the principle of patient confidentiality. So while supporters of legalization often suggest that regulation would enable euthanasia to be scrutinized and monitored, in practice, as Daniel Callahan and Margot White argue in the next extract, it might be difficult to exercise much control over doctors' oral discussions with their patients.

Daniel Callahan and Margot White[95]

If it is true, as it indubitably is, that 'decisions about medical treatment are normally made in the privacy of the doctor–patient relationship', then an obvious question must be asked: how is it possible, or could it ever be possible, to monitor and regulate those decisions regarding physician-assisted suicide that occur within the ambit of that privacy? How can there be oversight of those discussions, decisions, and transactions which must remain secret, and the confidentiality of which is protected by [law]?

There are two possible ways to proceed here: either we can station a policeman in every doctor's office and next to every sickbed to monitor all conversations, or we can depend upon the individual physician to voluntarily reveal that he or she has been part of an agreement to pursue physician-assisted suicide. Since the former course would both violate doctor–patient confidentiality and be utterly impractical, only the latter option is available. But that course means, in effect, that any physician-assisted suicide regulation must, in the end, be physician self-regulated.

Of course, the obvious response to all three of these arguments is that we already allow patients to make decisions which will result in their deaths when we respect their refusals of life-prolonging medical treatment. Patients who are connected to mechanical ventilators may be depressed, and we may wrongly judge them to be competent, yet this inescapable risk of error does not persuade us that we should prevent patients from taking life-and-death decisions. Nor do we think that the principle of patient confidentiality represents an insurmountable obstacle to our ability to protect vulnerable patients from being coerced into agreeing to the withdrawal of life-prolonging treatment.

---

[94] L Ganzini *et al.*, 'Prevalence of Depression and Anxiety in Patients Requesting Physicians' Aid in Dying: Cross Sectional Survey' (2008) 337 British Medical Journal 1682.

[95] 'The Legalization of Physician-Assisted Suicide: Creating a Regulatory Potemkin Village' (1996) 30 University of Richmond Law Review 1, 8–11.

(d) Risk of abuse

In a related argument, some commentators are concerned that if euthanasia were readily available, elderly patients would be pressurized into electing a premature death. In some cases, pressure to opt for euthanasia might come overtly from unscrupulous or greedy relatives. But it is also common for elderly people to perceive themselves to be a burden to their family, and if death were an option, there is a danger that they might request euthanasia for altruistic reasons, despite their own desire to go on living. In the next extract, Hazel Biggs suggests that this desire to avoid becoming a burden to one's family is particularly acute for elderly women.

Hazel Biggs[96]

[M]any women feel vulnerable and concerned at the prospect of becoming the cared-for rather than the carer because society appears to no longer value them once they reach this state. Legal change to permit euthanasia could be perilous for women in these circumstances....

Yet if active euthanasia were to be permitted as a right, what is to prevent the endorsement of this *right* being translated into a duty? How long will it be before those who seek euthanasia in order to avoid being a burden lose the right to continue living until the natural end of their lives? The experiences of women in the Cheyenne and Inuit societies who were expected to withdraw from their communities once they had outlived their usefulness as carers, are indicative of the dangers which could flow from laws permitting euthanasia. The introduction of legal euthanasia could alter social and personal expectations of old age beyond recognition, changing it from a time for relaxation and quiet enjoyment of the twilight years to a time for resisting pressure and the expectations of those who perceive that all useful life is over.

There is, however, no evidence from places in which assisted dying has been legalized that women are more likely to request it than men. On the contrary, in Oregon 54 per cent of people receiving assistance in dying were men, and in the Netherlands too, men seek access to euthanasia slightly more frequently than women.[97]

Sheila McLean would also question the assumption that there is something wrong with requesting euthanasia because one would prefer not to be a burden. Rather, she suggests that 'being a burden—rather than simply perceiving oneself to be one—is arguably a morally acceptable and perfectly reasonable factor to take into account when planning for the future'.[98] McLean argues that a competent adult, contemplating a future in which the costs of their care will eat away the inheritance they hope to leave to their dependants, or one in which their family's lives will be taken over with caring duties, might reasonably take these factors into account when deciding whether to ask for assistance with dying.

[96] 'I Don't Want to be a Burden! A Feminist Reflects on Women's Experiences of Death and Dying' in S Sheldon and M Thomson (eds), *Feminist Perspectives on Health Care Law* (Cavendish: London, 1998) 279–95.

[97] Margaret P Battin, Agnes van der Heide, Linda Ganzini, Gerrit van der Wal, and Bregje D Onwuteaka-Philipsen 'Legal Physician-assisted Dying in Oregon and the Netherlands: Evidence Concerning the Impact on Patients in 'Vulnerable' Groups' (2007) 33 Journal of Medical Ethics 591–7.

[98] *Assisted Dying: Reflections on the Need for Law Reform* (Routledge-Cavendish: Abingdon, 2007) 54.

It is also possible that pressure to opt for an earlier death might come from the medical profession. Luke Gormally argues that because euthanasia would be cheaper than high-quality palliative care, it might seem like a cost-effective way to deal with the problems faced by the terminally ill.

Luke Gormally[99]

It is very important to bear in mind that a key element in the context of contemporary debates about legalizing euthanasia is the drive to reduce health care costs. One of the conspicuous dangers of legalization is that, before long, euthanasia would be seen as a convenient 'solution' to the heavy demands on care made by certain types of patient. Medicine would thereby be robbed of the incentive to find genuinely compassionate solutions to the difficulties presented by such patients. The kind of humane impulses which have sustained the development of hospice medicine and care would be undermined because too many would think euthanasia a cheaper and less personally demanding solution.

Of course, it would be unethical for doctors to try to persuade their patients to choose euthanasia, but Leon Kass and Nelson Lund argue that simply mentioning death as a treatment option might subtly influence patients' choices.

Leon R Kass and Nelson Lund[100]

With patients reduced—helpless in action and ambivalent about life—someone who will benefit from their death need not proceed by overt coercion. Rather, requests for assisted suicide can and will be subtly engineered. To alter and influence choices, physicians and families need not be driven entirely by base motives or even be consciously manipulative. Well-meaning and discreet suggestions, or even unconscious changes in expression, gesture, and tone of voice, can move a dependent and suggestible patient toward a choice for death....

When the physician presents a depressed or frightened patient with a horrible prognosis and includes among the options the offer of a 'gentle quick release', what will the patient likely choose, especially in the face of a spiralling hospital bill or resentful children?

Again, insofar as there is a risk that a patient might opt for a course of action that will result in her death out of a sense of obligation, or as a result of more direct pressure, this must be equally true when death is achieved by treatment withdrawal. If we think vulnerable patients need to be protected against choosing a premature death against their wishes, we should probably be *more* concerned about refusals of life-prolonging treatment, where the decision must be respected even if it is wholly irrational, than legalized euthanasia, which would only be available in certain tightly circumscribed circumstances.

---

[99] 'Euthanasia and Assisted Suicide: 7 Reasons Why They Should Not Be Legalized', 286–90 in Donna Dickenson, Malcolm Johnson, and Jeanne Samson Katz (eds), *Death, Dying and Bereavement*, 2nd edn (Sage: London, 2000) 285, 287.

[100] 'Physician-Assisted Suicide, Medical Ethics and the Future of the Medical Profession' (1996) 35 Duquesne Law Review 395.

David Orentlicher[101]

> The law does not limit withdrawals of treatment only to cases in which a patient is irreversibly ill. Patients whose lives could be saved and who could be restored to very good health with the brief use of a ventilator or the transfusion of blood can still refuse the treatment...Physicians are free to turn off ventilators not only when the patient will die without the ventilator, but also when the patient might still be restored to very good health...If the risks of...abuse are reason enough to condemn decisions to shorten a patient's life, they should lead a person to oppose treatment withdrawal as well as euthanasia and assisted suicide.

Even if we were to acknowledge the possibility that patients might feel pressurized into requesting assistance in dying, it does not necessarily follow that the only appropriate solution is a complete ban on assisted dying. Rather, unless we have concluded that there is no other feasible way of protecting vulnerable patients, it might be better to investigate the possibility of designing regulations which would confine assisted dying to cases where the request *does* reflect the patient's enduring and genuine desire to die. A blanket prohibition upon a practice is a peculiarly blunt and imprecise way to prevent its abuse, and may underestimate the law's ability to distinguish between real and coerced consent. Moreover, if we know that euthanasia is, in fact, currently practised covertly, any risk of abuse will be magnified by the secrecy and lack of transparency which are the inevitable consequence of its illegality.

(e) Effect on the doctor–patient relationship

A further argument against legalization is that it would have a profoundly deleterious impact upon the doctor–patient relationship, and would damage the integrity of the medical profession. There are two interrelated aspects to this argument. First, from the point of view of the patient, it might be argued that knowing their doctors could legally kill them would reduce patient trust. Brian Simpson, for example, has argued that 'for a doctor to kill his own patients involves a peculiarly alarming breach of trust, and one that is dramatically incompatible with the role of a doctor'.[102] Whether or not patients share this assumption that legalization would diminish their trust in the medical profession is, however, unclear. A 2004 opinion poll found that 70 per cent said that the legalization of assisted suicide would not affect their trust in their doctors, while 9 per cent would trust their doctors *more* and 9 per cent would trust their doctors less.[103]

Secondly, from the point of view of the doctor, if 'killing' were to become a treatment option, the ethical foundations of the medical profession would be undermined, and this in turn would reduce patients' willingness to trust their doctors. The GMC took this view in their evidence to the House of Lords Select Committee on Assisted Dying:

> [A] change in the law to allow physician-assisted dying would have profound implications for the role and responsibilities of doctors and their relationships with patients. Acting with the primary intention to hasten a patient's death would be difficult to reconcile with the medical ethical principles of beneficence and non-maleficence.[104]

---

[101] 'The Alleged Distinction between Euthanasia and the Withdrawal of Life-sustaining Treatment: Conceptually Incoherent and Impossible to Maintain' (1998) University of Illinois Law Review 837.

[102] 'Euthanasia for Sale?' (1986) 84 Michigan Law Review 807, 809.

[103] Assisted Dying for the Terminally Ill Committee, *Assisted Dying for the Terminally Ill Bill—First Report* (2005) 77.

[104] Ibid, 42.

In her evidence to the committee, Dr Vivienne Nathanson, head of science and ethics at the BMA, argued that it is difficult to imagine that many doctors would want to effectively specialize in death.

Vivienne Nathanson[105]

What doctors find it impossible to consider is who would want to provide that service. They find it almost impossible to conceive of a person who would want to spend their life administering lethal injections. Whether such a service could ever be set up, and who would be the people who took part in it, raises very serious questions.

In the next extract, Leon Kass and Nelson Lund suggest that an absolute 'taboo against medical killing' is necessary to preserve patient trust in the medical profession.

Leon R Kass and Nelson Lund[106]

Authorizing physician-assisted suicide would...overturn a centuries-old taboo against medical killing, a taboo understood by many to be one of the cornerstones of the medical ethic....

Just as patients necessarily divulge and reveal to the physician private and intimate details of their personal lives; just as patients necessarily expose their naked bodies to the physician's objectifying gaze and investigating hands; so patients necessarily expose and entrust the care of their very lives to the physician's skill, technique, judgment, and character. Mindful of the meaning of such exposure and vulnerability, and mindful too of their own human penchant for error and mischief, the Hippocratic physicians voluntarily set limits on their own conduct, pledging not to take advantage of or to violate the patient's intimacies, naked sexuality, or life itself.

Of course, as we have already seen, doctors do sometimes engage in practices that will 'hasten death' or 'shorten life', so this argument relies upon the existence of a sharp distinction between 'killing' and 'letting die'. For those who reject the idea that killing is always necessarily morally worse than letting die, this argument against legalization will be less persuasive.

(f) Slippery slope

It is important to remember that when someone invokes a slippery slope argument (see further Chapter 1), they are not arguing that there is something intrinsically wrong with doctors helping their patients to die. Of course, they may also believe this to be true, but this would not be a slippery slope argument. Rather, the slippery slope claim is that even if we were to accept that doctors might sometimes act reasonably when they comply with a patient's request for euthanasia, we should nevertheless continue to prohibit euthanasia because sanctioning some compassionate acts of killing would make it very difficult to prevent those with less benevolent motives from ending patients' lives.

Of course, proponents of slippery slope arguments must explain why allowing some cases of voluntary euthanasia would necessarily lead to other less acceptable practices. They might, for example, argue that it would be virtually impossible to adequately police the

---

[105] Ibid, 43.

[106] 'Physician-Assisted Suicide, Medical Ethics and the Future of the Medical Profession' (1996) 35 Duquesne Law Review 395, 402, 408–10, 418–19, 424.

boundary between acceptable and unacceptable medical killings. Some of the arguments we encountered earlier concerning the difficulty in distinguishing between voluntary and coerced choices might be relevant here.

Carl Schneider has argued that there is also 'a psychological aspect of slippery slopes', namely that 'they work partly by domesticating one idea and thus making its nearest neighbor [sic] down the slope seem less extreme and unthinkable'.[107] It is this latter type of slippery slope argument that is invoked in the next extract by Dieter Giesen, who argues that allowing doctors to kill their patients would weaken the absolute prohibition upon the taking of innocent life, and that we would all therefore become progressively desensitized to the horror of murder.

Dieter Giesen[108]

Recent history shows us that once firm constraints against killing are removed, a general moral decline will result. The German experience of the Nazi euthanasia programme, during which [about] 100,000 disabled persons were killed because they were classified as living 'lives not worth living', demonstrates the potential for perverse thinking and inhuman deeds once the first step upon the slippery slope is taken.

Experience in the Netherlands to date suggests that, in practice, no sharp distinction can be drawn between voluntary and non-voluntary euthanasia. Instead, commentators have documented a continuum of killing, from the (quite rare) paradigm case of informed and rational choice to frequent instances of familial and medical pressure, to the elimination of defenceless newborns, adjudged to be a burden upon society and to the purging of old people's homes.

In some ways, as Dan W Brock points out, a slippery slope argument is a straightforward empirical claim: does legalizing euthanasia make involuntary killing more likely?

Dan W Brock[109]

Slippery slope arguments . . . are the last refuge of conservative defenders of the status quo. When all the opponent's objections to the wrongness of euthanasia itself have been met, the opponent then shifts ground and acknowledges both that it is not in itself wrong and that a legal policy which resulted only in its being performed would not be bad. Nevertheless, the opponent maintains, it should still not be permitted because doing so would result in its being performed in other cases in which it is not voluntary and would be wrong. In this argument's most extreme form, permitting euthanasia is the first and fateful step down the slippery slope to Nazism. Once on the slope we will be unable to get off . . .

It must be relevant how likely it is that we will end with horrendous consequences and an unjustified practice of euthanasia. . . . Opponents of voluntary euthanasia on slippery slope grounds have not provided the data or evidence necessary to turn their speculative concerns into well-grounded likelihoods.

---

107 'Rights Discourse and Neonatal Euthanasia' (1988) 76 California Law Review 151, 168.
108 'Dilemmas at Life's End: A Comparative Legal Perspective' in John Keown (ed.), *Euthanasia Examined* (CUP: Cambridge, 1995) 204.
109 'Voluntary Active Euthanasia' (1992) Hastings Centre Report 10–22.

Given their empirical nature, we might attempt to evaluate whether legalizing euthanasia represents the first step on a slippery slope by examining data from the countries where legalization has taken place. But as we will see in the next section, the problem is that different (and often flatly contradictory) interpretations of the available data abound.

John Keown[110]

> [T]he Dutch experience lends weighty support to the slippery slope argument...Within a decade, the so-called strict safeguards against the slide have proved signally ineffectual; non-voluntary euthanasia is now widely practised and increasingly condoned in the Netherlands.

In contrast, Helga Kuhse *et al.*'s confidential survey of 3,000 Australian doctors found that non-voluntary euthanasia is five times more common in Australia, where euthanasia is illegal, than it is in the Netherlands.[111] Australian doctors were far less likely than their Dutch counterparts to discuss the decision to hasten a patient's death with the patient herself, or to seek her consent.

In their study of six European countries, Agnes van der Heide *et al.* found that non-voluntary euthanasia was more than twice as common in Denmark as it was in the Netherlands, and that: 'Ending of life without the patient's explicit request happened more frequently than euthanasia in all countries apart from the Netherlands.'[112]

If patients' lives are ended in the absence of an explicit request with similar or greater frequency in countries which have *not* legalized euthanasia, it is not clear that the legalization of euthanasia in the Netherlands has *caused* any propensity to engage in non-voluntary euthanasia. Moreover, all of the Dutch data cited by those who claim that it offers evidence of a slippery slope is data which has been gathered *since* legalization. Compelling empirical evidence of a slippery slope would need to compare data from before and after legalization in order to point to a possible link between legalization and undesirable practices. Otherwise, evidence (if indeed there is such evidence) that poor practices co-exist with legalization could simply suggest that poor practices existed anyway, and legalization has made no difference. Stephen Smith's analysis of Keown's slippery slope claims about the Netherlands further suggests that even if it could be established that non-voluntary euthanasia has increased in the years following legalization, this does not necessarily provide evidence of a causal connection.

Stephen Smith[113]

> The simple fact that something occurs after something else does not indicate, in any meaningful way, that the first action logically required the second to happen. Even if one can find a

[110] 'Euthanasia in the Netherlands: Sliding Down the Slippery Slope?' in J Keown (ed.), *Euthanasia Examined* (CUP: Cambridge, 1995) 261–96.

[111] H Kuhse *et al.*, 'End-of-life Decisions in Australian Medical Practice' (1997) 166 Medical Journal of Australia 191–6.

[112] Agnes van der Heide, Luc Deliens, Karin Faisst, Tore Nilstun, Michael Norup, Eugenio Paci, Gerrit van der Wal, and Paul J van der Maas, 'End-of-life Decision-making in Six European Countries: Descriptive Study' (2003) 362 The Lancet 345–50.

[113] 'Fallacies of the Logical Slippery Slope in the Debate on Physician-Assisted Suicide and Euthanasia' (2005) 13 *Medical Law Review* 224.

connection such that the first tends to precede the second, this will not provide evidence of a logical connection. Especially in the realm of human actions (as opposed to say the actions of physical laws), the preceding of an action by a first action does not indicate they must be connected in any logical way.

Moreover, even if we could establish that it would be difficult to draw or police the line between acceptable and unacceptable instances of euthanasia, it is, in my view, not obvious that an absolute prohibition is the optimum regulatory response.

Emily Jackson[114]

The slippery slope argument suggests that although we might be able to distinguish paradigm cases at the top of the moral slope from those at the bottom, it would be very difficult to locate or police the line between acceptable and unacceptable practices towards the middle of the slope. Yet this 'grey area' problem exists whenever we attempt to regulate *anything*. Let us apply slippery slope reasoning to a more mundane regulatory problem. Should I maintain an absolute prohibition on the late submission of essays on the grounds that giving an extension to student A who has a very compelling reason—say, the death of a close family member—might make it difficult for me to draw a line between her case and those of students B, C, D, and E who have progressively less persuasive grounds for late submission? An absolute prohibition would relieve me of the difficulty of drawing distinctions between borderline cases: perhaps student C's computer has stopped working, and student D left her essay on the bus. But I do a grave injustice to student A by preferring the simplicity of an absolute ban over the admittedly more time-consuming and complex task of drawing fine distinctions between serious and trivial excuses for late submission....

Nor is it obvious that a blanket ban is the optimum response to concerns about a practice's potential misapplication. If we can imagine circumstances in which euthanasia might be legitimate, prohibiting it completely in order to prevent it being employed in other less compelling situations is a peculiarly blunt approach to regulation, especially since the consequence for patients who do clearly merit access to euthanasia will be a protracted, painful or otherwise intolerable death. It would be more logical to advocate regulations which confine access to euthanasia to patients whose circumstances lie at the top of the moral slope (whatever those might be), and prohibit it in all other cases.

(3) A Third Way?

It would be a mistake to assume that there are only two options: legalization or continued criminalization. Rather, as Richard Huxtable explains in the next extract, a different solution would be to treat euthanasia as a particular *type of killing*, less grave than murder but not entirely non-criminal. Huxtable's point is that this way forward would be more honest than the status quo, in which the adverse effects of euthanasia's illegality tend to be softened by the leniency of judges and juries.

---

[114] 'Whose Death is it Anyway? Euthanasia and the Medical Profession' (2004) 57 Current Legal Problems 415–42, 430–2.

Richard Huxtable[115]

Open acceptance that euthanasia is a particular type of killing, subject to particular moral norms which are themselves the source of much conscientious competition, must be a move in the right direction...

The first, central reform is that the law ought explicitly to recognize mercy killing as an offence, which is also available as a partial defence to other homicide charges. In keeping this a crime, we can remain focused on the moral pause that should precede any attempt to kill; in making it a lesser crime, it is possible to admit that some deaths are not so bad, at least when the deceased was suffering and, in some cases, desperately wanted the escape that death can afford....

In moving from justification to excuse, by marking out euthanasia as a distinct (but reduced) crime, I believe that we begin to get there. We already have, and have long had, an unofficial defence of euthanasia; it now needs to be made official.... In short, the time has come to compromise.

(4) Is Legalization Likely?

In the early 1990s the House of Lords Select Committee on Medical Ethics investigated whether the law should be reformed. It concluded that there should be no change in the law on intentional killing. The committee was persuaded that 'it would be next to impossible to ensure that all acts of euthanasia were truly voluntary and that any liberalization of the law was not abused'. The committee was concerned about pressure being exerted on sick and elderly individuals to request euthanasia, and about the message legalization would send to vulnerable and disadvantaged people. Since the select committee's view was endorsed by most political parties, and by bodies such as the GMC and the BMA, the prospect of legalization looked very remote indeed.

Over a decade later, in 2004 Lord Joffe introduced a second version of his Assisted Dying for the Terminally Ill Bill into the House of Lords. It would have allowed competent adult patients who were terminally ill and experiencing unbearable suffering to request assistance in dying, either directly through euthanasia or by assisting their suicide, and would have provided doctors with a right of conscientious objection. The Bill had no chance of becoming law before the 2005 general election, but it was scrutinized by the House of Lords Select Committee on Assisted Dying, whose report was published in April 2005.

The select committee found that there had been a number of developments since the last select committee reported, most notably the legislation enacted in Oregon, the Netherlands, and Belgium. It therefore recommended that a new bill should be introduced, which would address the issues discussed in their report, but which should again be subjected to committee scrutiny before being put before Parliament. In particular, the select committee suggested that any new bill should distinguish between euthanasia and assisted suicide so that the issues could be addressed separately, and that it should provide for compulsory psychiatric assessment.

---

[115] *Euthanasia, Ethics and the Law: From Conflict to Compromise* (Routledge-Cavendish: Abingdon, 2007).

House of Lords Select Committee on Assisted Dying[116]

[W]here legislation is limited to assistance with suicide, the take-up rate is dramatically less than in places where voluntary euthanasia is also legalised.

[I]n the framing of any future bill consideration should be given to the inclusion of a requirement for any applicant for assistance with suicide or voluntary euthanasia to be given a psychiatric assessment in order both to confirm that the request is based on a reasoned decision and is free from external pressure and that the applicant is not suffering from a psychiatric or psychological disorder causing impaired judgement. In cases where such disorder was apparent, we would expect an applicant to be offered treatment.

A third version of Lord Joffe's Assisted Dying for the Terminally Ill Bill was then drawn up. This would have permitted assisted suicide only. For someone to qualify for assistance, they would have to sign a declaration asking for assisted suicide, witnessed by two people, one of whom must be a solicitor or public notary. The patient must have been asked to inform their next of kin, and must have had their capacity assessed by a doctor. If there is any doubt about capacity, the doctor should refer the patient to a consultant psychiatrist or psychologist.

The doctor would have to satisfy himself that the patient is terminally ill—defined as a progressive disease, which cannot be reversed, and is likely to result in the patient's death within six months. The patient must also be suffering unbearably as a result of the illness: defined as 'pain, distress or otherwise which the patient finds so severe as to be unacceptable'.

The patient must have been properly informed, both about assisted dying, and about the alternatives, including palliative and hospice care. A palliative care specialist must have attended the patient to inform them about the options. Fourteen days must elapse between the request and issuing the prescription. The patient must be asked to reiterate their request, and must be informed that they can revoke it any time. Again, health care professionals would have a right of conscientious objection. The Bill would also have set up a monitoring commission to maintain records of all instances of assisted dying.

One practical difficulty in legalizing assisted suicide, highlighted by Hazel Biggs in the next extract, is the role of informal carers. Lord Joffe's Bill would have protected members of the health care team who assisted a suicide, provided the above conditions were satisfied. This leaves the informal carer who might help the patient to obtain and take the medicine, unprotected.

Hazel Biggs[117]

Terminally-ill patients are not a homogenous group. They might, for instance, be cared for at home rather than in hospital, where some might simply need to be provided with a prescription for drugs, which they could collect and then administer themselves, Here the only assistance they would need would be the provision of a prescription and the dispensing of

---

[116] Assisted Dying for the Terminally Ill Committee, *Assisted Dying for the Terminally Ill Bill—First Report* (2005), 13, 86.

[117] 'Criminalising Carers: Death Desires and Assisted Dying Outlaws' in B Brooks Gordon *et al.* (eds), *Death Rites and Rights* (Hart, 2007) 57–73.

the drugs. Others, however, might be physically incapable of collecting a prescription from the chemist, even if well enough to be cared for at home. They may also not be able to ingest a drug orally or be too physically debilitated to put the cup to their mouth in order to drink it. Given that a great many terminally-ill people are primarily under the care of voluntary care-givers, it is at this level of application that it becomes apparent that legislation permitting assisted suicide would require precise drafting and meticulous attention to detail if such carers are to be adequately protected.

This version of the Assisted Dying for the Terminally Ill Bill was introduced to the House of Lords in 2006, and defeated by 148 to 100. Parliament's, or at least the House of Lord's, hostility to the legalization of assisted dying contrasts with the fairly stable and clear majority of the public, who say that they are in favour, in certain strictly limited circumstances. The 2007 British Social Attitudes Survey found that 80 per cent thought euthanasia should be available where a person is suffering from an incurable, painful, and terminal illness.[118] Support decreased considerably, however, where the person's condition was not terminal.

(c) EXPERIENCE IN OTHER COUNTRIES

A comprehensive analysis of the legal status of euthanasia and assisted suicide throughout the world is beyond the scope of this chapter. Nevertheless, as we have already seen, the experience of those countries where assisted dying has been legalized is often drawn upon in debates over the merits or otherwise of legalization.

Clearly, it would be a mistake to *ignore* evidence from the handful of countries where euthanasia and/or assisted suicide have been treated more leniently than in the UK: ranging from overt legalization in the Netherlands, to the de facto toleration of compassionately motivated assisted suicide in Switzerland. Yet on the other hand, what happens in other countries with different legal and health care systems and different cultural, religious, and social attitudes towards death, does not necessarily translate into compelling evidence of how legalized assisted dying might work, or not work in the UK.

Before we turn to examine the handful of countries which have experience of assisted dying taking place within, rather than outside the law, it is worth briefly mentioning two places where, at the time of writing, a change in the law is imminent. In Luxembourg, the question of the legalization of euthanasia provoked a constitutional crisis after the Parliament passed a law legalizing euthanasia, but its constitutional monarch, the Grand Duke, refused to sign it for reasons of conscience. In December 2008 he agreed to an amendment removing his power of veto.

In November 2008, the electorate in the US state of Washington voted in favour of permitting assisted suicide (58 per cent were in favour and 42 per cent were against). The Washington law is modelled on the Oregon statue considered below, and comes into force in 2009.

The issue of euthanasia has also received a great deal of attention in France. In 2008, Chantal Sébire—who suffered from a very rare form of cancer, which had eaten away much of her face—lost her court bid to have access to assisted dying. After the judge dismissed her

---

[118] 'Quickening Death: The Euthanasia Debate' by Elizabeth Clery, Sheila McLean, and Miranda Phillips, in *British Social Attitudes: The 23rd Report* (edited by Alison Park, John, Curtice, Katarina Thomson, Miranda Phillips, and Mark Johnson) (2007, London: Sage).

claim, Sébire made a public appeal to the president, Nicolas Sarkozy, claiming 'one would not allow an animal to go through what I have endured'. She killed herself two days later.

(1) The Netherlands

(a) The law

Although a statute specifically legalizing euthanasia was not introduced in the Netherlands until 2001, since 1973 the Dutch courts had gradually been developing exceptions to the express prohibitions on active voluntary euthanasia and assisted suicide that were contained in Articles 293 and 294 of the Dutch Penal Code. Through a series of court decisions, a set of guidelines had emerged which—if followed—served to protect doctors from criminal liability. To some extent, then, the 2001 Statute simply formalized existing practice in the Netherlands.

In 1973 a Dutch court indicated for the first time that euthanasia might be acceptable in certain circumstances. In the *Postma* case[119] a doctor was prosecuted for giving her mother a fatal dose of morphine. Dr Postma's mother had had a cerebral haemorrhage which had left her very seriously disabled. She had unsuccessfully attempted to commit suicide and had repeatedly expressed her desire to die. There was widespread public sympathy for Dr Postma, and although the Leeuwarden District Court convicted her under Article 293, it imposed a symbolic suspended sentence of a week's imprisonment. Furthermore, the Court took the opportunity to indicate that, despite Article 293, euthanasia could be acceptable if performed in certain circumstances: (1) the patient should be incurably ill; (2) the patient should be experiencing unbearable suffering; (3) the patient should have requested that his or her life be terminated; and (4) the termination is performed by the patient's own doctor, or in consultation with him or her.

Following this decision, a number of other cases were brought before the Dutch Courts that incrementally laid down a set of criteria, which served to exempt doctors who had helped their patients to die from punishment.[120] These guidelines were then adopted by the public prosecutor's office as the criteria which would determine whether or not cases of euthanasia or assisted suicide would be prosecuted.

The first case to come before the Dutch Supreme Court was brought in 1984. In the *Alkmaar* case,[121] Dr Schoonheim had given a lethal injection to a 95-year-old patient who had signed an advance declaration requesting euthanasia if her condition should deteriorate beyond a certain point, and who had more recently expressed a clear and unequivocal wish to die. Dr Schoonheim was initially convicted. On appeal, the Dutch Supreme Court ruled that there had been insufficient investigation of the possibility that the doctor had faced an irreconcilable conflict of duties. They invoked the *noodtoestand* or 'emergency' defence, which applies where the doctor's duty to abide by the law and preserve the life of his patient may be outweighed by his duty to relieve unbearable suffering. The case was referred back to the Court of Appeal in The Hague, and Dr Schoonheim was acquitted. Of course, the *noodtoestand* defence is only capable of absolving doctors of criminal liability where the patient's suffering is so extreme that it overrides the doctor's normal duty to preserve life.

---

[119] *Nederlandse Jurisprudentie* 1973 No. 183, District Court of Leeuwarden 21 Feb 1973.
[120] *Wertheim, Nederlandse Jurisprudentie* 1982 No. 63, Rotterdam Criminal Court.
[121] *Nederlandse Jurisprudentie* 1985 No. 106, Supreme Court 27 Nov 1984.

The next critically important case to come before the Dutch courts involved a patient whose suffering was mental rather than physical. In the *Chabot* case,[122] a psychiatrist complied with a woman's repeated requests for assistance in committing suicide after the death of both of her sons had left her overwhelmingly unhappy. The Supreme Court accepted that there might be circumstances in which the *noodtoestand* defence would apply despite the absence of physical suffering or terminal illness. The Court did, however, suggest that exceptional care would need to be taken when deciding that a person's mental suffering was both intolerable and incurable. Dr Chabot was convicted because there was insufficient independent evidence of the gravity of Mrs Boscher's condition, but no punishment was imposed.

More recently, in the *Sutorius* case, the Supreme court dismissed Dr Sutorius's appeal against his conviction for assisting the suicide of an 86-year-old man who was not suffering from any medically classifiable physical or psychiatric disorder.[123] The patient, Edward Brongersma, was obsessed with his physical decline and hopeless existence, he was 'tired of life' and had repeatedly expressed his wish to die. The Supreme Court decided that this was not grounds for assisted suicide, which would only be lawful if the patient's 'unbearable and hopeless suffering' was linked to a recognizable medical or psychiatric condition. However, no punishment was imposed on Dr Sutorius, because it was accepted that he had acted out of concern for his patient.

Prior to 1990, doctors were under a duty to report cases of euthanasia and assisted suicide to the police, who would then investigate whether the guidelines had been followed, and inform the public prosecutor. Now each case is considered by a regional review committee, usually consisting of a lawyer, a doctor, and an ethicist. If the committee is satisfied that the criteria have been fulfilled, the case is closed without informing the public prosecutor, who is notified only if the committee finds that the doctor did not fulfil the due care criteria. In about six per cent of cases each year, the regional review committee asks for more information, usually for further evidence that the patient's suffering was unbearable. In a handful of cases each year, it makes a finding of non-compliance with the 'due care' criteria (0.6 per cent in 2007).[124]

Initially, there was some concern that doctors were not reporting every instance of euthanasia. Reporting rates are now much higher, and it is thought that the remaining 'gap' between the number of euthanasia deaths calculated by national surveys and the number reported is not the result of doctors lying or concealing euthanasia deaths. Instead, there is some confusion over whether deaths which are preceded by palliative sedation or pain relief should be reported as euthanasia. It seems that many doctors do not consider these to be cases of euthanasia, whereas these are sometimes counted as euthanasia by researchers calculating its frequency by examining death certificates.[125] The reporting rate for 2005 was calculated as 80 per cent, but when cases involving opoids (where this difference of opinion exists) were excluded, the reporting rate was 99 per cent.[126]

The Termination of Life on Request and Assisted Suicide (Review Procedures) Act 2001 amended Articles 293 and 294 of the Criminal Code, and came into force on 1 April 2002.

---

[122] Ibid, 1994 No. 656, Supreme Court.

[123] T Sheldon, 'Being 'Tired of Life' is Not Grounds for Euthanasia' (2003) 326 British Medical Journal 71.

[124] Ministry of Health, Welfare and Sport, Evaluation Termination of Life on Request and Assisted Suicide (Review Procedures) Act (2007), available at <www.minvws.nl/en/themes/euthanasia/default.asp>.

[125] J Griffiths, H Weyers, and M Adams, *Euthanasia and Law in Europe* (Oxford, Hart Publishing, 2008) 203.

[126] Ibid, 204.

Euthanasia and assisted suicide continue to be criminal offences under Articles 293(1) and 294(1). But exceptions are introduced in Article 293(2) and 294(2), which both now read:

> The act referred to in the first subsection shall not be an offence if it is committed by a physician who fulfils the due care criteria set out in Section 2 of the Termination of Life on Request and Assisted Suicde (Review Procedures) Act, and if the physician notifies the municipal pathologist of this act in accordance with the provisions of section 7, subsection 2 of the Burial and Cremation Act.

Under section 2, the requirements of due care are that the physician:

(a) holds the conviction that the request by the patient was voluntary and well-considered;

(b) holds the conviction that the patient's suffering was lasting and unbearable;

(c) has informed the patient about the situation he was in and about his prospects;

(d) and the patient holds the conviction that there was no other reasonable solution for the situation he was in;

(e) has consulted at least one other, independent physician who has seen the patient and has given his written opinion on the requirements of due care referred to in parts (a)–(d); and

(f) has terminated a life or assisted in a suicide with due care.

As the Ministry of Foreign Affairs makes clear, the doctor who carries out euthanasia must be the patient's own doctor—hence excluding the possibility of euthanasia 'tourism'—and he must obtain a second opinion from an entirely independent doctor.

Ministry of Foreign Affairs[127]

> An important, basic principle established in case law is the existence of a close doctor–patient relationship. A doctor may only perform euthanasia on a patient in his care. He must know the patient well enough to be able to assess whether the request for euthanasia is both voluntary and well-considered, and whether his suffering is unbearable and without prospect of improvement…
>
> Before the attending physician complies with a request for euthanasia, he must first consult a colleague who is neither connected with him nor involved in treating the patient. The independent physician must see the patient for himself, review the progression of the illness, establish whether the request for euthanasia is both voluntary and well-considered, and communicate his findings to the attending physician in writing.

This point was stressed by Dr Kimsma, who sits on one of the five regional assessment committees, in his evidence to the House of Lords Select Committee:

---

[127] Q&A Euthanasia, available at <www.minbuza.nl> (2008).

[T]here is an absolute condition that [euthanasia] can only be done by the treating physician. It cannot be any other physician. We do not want to advertise 'euthanasia tourism'. What we insist on is that it only takes place within a meaningful medical relationship. That is an absolute condition.[128]

Two especially controversial aspects of the law are worth noting. First, the Act specifically allows for advance requests for euthanasia, with section 2(2) providing that doctors may comply with a request in a written declaration provided that the patient was capable of making a reasonable appraisal of his own interests when the request was made. Evidence indicates that compliance with advance euthanasia directives is rare.[129] Secondly, children over the age of 12 may be entitled to request euthanasia or assisted suicide. A doctor is only allowed to comply with a request from a minor between the ages of 12 and 15 with parental consent. For children aged 16 and 17, parents should be consulted, but they do not have a right of veto. Of all child deaths, fewer than 1 per cent are the result of euthanasia, and none result from assisted suicide.[130]

While the law specifically addresses the possibility of euthanasia for children over the age of 12, it is silent on the question of euthanasia for very severely disabled newborns. In the next extract Eduard Verhagen and Pieter Sauer suggest that provided certain requirements are met, euthanasia in severely disabled neonates can be acceptable. The Groningen Protocol, named after the Dutch hospital which developed these guidelines, lays out five factors which should be satisfied before doctors should proceed with euthanasia in newborn babies. It was accepted by the Dutch Association of Pediatrics[131] as a national guideline in 2005.

- The diagnosis and prognosis must be certain.
- Hopeless and unbearable suffering must be present.
- The diagnosis, prognosis, and unbearable suffering must be confirmed by at least one independent physician.
- Both parents must give informed consent.
- The procedure must be performed in accordance with the accepted medical standard.

Eduard Verhagen and Pieter Sauer[132]

When both the parents and the physicians are convinced that there is an extremely poor prognosis, they may concur that death would be more humane than continued life. Under similar conditions, a person in the Netherlands who is older than sixteen years of age can ask for euthanasia. Newborns, however, cannot ask for euthanasia, and such a request by

[128] House of Lords Assisted Dying for the Terminally Ill Committee, 2005, 175.

[129] ML Rurup *et al.*, 'Physicians' Experiences with Demented Patients with Advance Euthanasia Directives in the Netherlands' (2005) 53 Journal of the American Geriatric Society 1138–44.

[130] Margaret P Battin, Agnes van der Heide, Linda Ganzini, Gerrit van der Wal, and Bregje D Onwuteaka-Philipsen, 'Legal Physician-assisted Dying in Oregon and the Netherlands: Evidence Concerning the Impact on Patients in "Vulnerable Groups"' (2007) 33 Journal of Medical Ethics 591–7.

[131] NVK, Nederlandse Vereniging voor Kindergeneeskunde.

[132] 'The Groningen Protocol—Euthanasia in Severely Ill Newborns' (2005) 352 New England Journal of Medicine 959–62.

parents, acting as the representatives of their child, is invalid under Dutch law. Does this mean that euthanasia in a newborn is always prohibited? We are convinced that life-ending measures can be acceptable in these cases under very strict conditions: the parents must agree fully, on the basis of a thorough explanation of the condition and prognosis; a team of physicians, including at least one who is not directly involved in the care of the patient, must agree; and the condition and prognosis must be very well defined. After the decision has been made and the child has died, an outside legal body should determine whether the decision was justified and all necessary procedures have been followed.

Alexander Kon disagrees. He argues that it is impossible to tell whether a baby's suffering is unbearable, and that neonatal euthanasia is therefore unacceptable.

Alexander A Kon[133]

The judgment of whether a person's condition is so unbearable that death is preferable to life is a singularly personal choice.... Therefore, it is unreasonable to believe that either a physician or parent can accurately judge whether the burdens of an infant's life outweigh the benefits of living for that child. Even if one could accurately judge the amount of suffering that would be required to consider death as a favorable alternative, such a calculation would require precise quantification of an infant's suffering. Suffering, however, is wholly subjective and therefore can be gauged only by the individual..... The experience of pain, the experience of nausea, and all other aspects of the experience of suffering, however, are purely subjective....

Therefore, any quantification of an individual's suffering that is not based on the personal report of that individual is unreliable. Certainly, parents and physicians may be very poor judges of the subjective experiences of infants.... Because we cannot accurately judge the subjective suffering of an infant, we cannot accurately determine if the burdens of living outweigh the benefits and therefore can never judge with certainty whether death is in the infant's best interest....

The Groningen Protocol could only be viable if physicians were able to accurately determine the subjective suffering of infants and were unbiased in their judgment of the quality of life of persons with special needs. Given that the former is impossible and the latter is currently untrue, the practice of neonatal euthanasia cannot be supported.

(b) Euthanasia in practice

There have been a number of national studies of euthanasia in practice in the Netherlands, the first in 1991, with follow up studies in 1995, 2001, and 2005. These studies have looked at the frequency of other potentially life-shortening practices alongside euthanasia and assisted suicide. As is obvious from the abbreviated table reproduced below, euthanasia is not a common way to die in the Netherlands. There was a marked drop in the number of cases of assisted dying in 2005. Some physicians put this down to improvements in palliative care,[134] while other commentators argue that there has been a corresponding *rise* in

---

[133] 'Neonatal Euthanasia Is Unsupportable: The Groningen Protocol Should Be Abandoned' (2007) 28 Theoretical Medicine and Bioethics 453.

[134] Ministry of Health, Welfare and Sport, Evaluation Termination of Life on Request and Assisted Suicide (Review Procedures) Act (2007), available at <www.minvws.nl/en/themes/euthanasia/default.asp>.

the use of palliative sedation, perhaps because it is thought to involve less 'red tape' than euthanasia.[135]

Estimated frequencies of medical behaviour potentially shortening life in the Netherlands (percentage of all deaths)[136]

	1990	1995	2001	2005
Termination of life on request:	1.9	2.6	2.8	1.8
• Euthanasia	(1.7)	(2.4)	(2.6)	(1.7)
• PAS	(0.2)	(0.2)	(0.2)	(0.1)
Termination of life without request	0.8	0.7	0.7	0.4
Pain relief with life-shortening effect	19	19	21	25
Withholding or withdrawing life-prolonging treatment	18	20	20	16

It is also worth noting that, as with lawful life-shortening practices, euthanasia and assisted suicide are usually sought when the patient has very little time left to live:[137]

Estimated shortening of life	Euthanasia and PAS	Termination of life without request	Pain relief	Withholding or withdrawing treatment
Less than 1 week	46	88	81	73
Less than 1 month	46	7	2	8
More than 1 month	8	6	1	6
Unknown	0	0	16	13

The reported cases of euthanasia/PAS for each year from 1998 to 2006 show a fairly consistent pattern of euthanasia being much more common than PAS (in 2006, 91.8 per cent of cases involved euthanasia, 6.9 per cent involved assisted suicide, with 1.3 per cent involving a combination of both). Cancer is by far the most common medical condition among those requesting euthanasia (88 per cent in 2006). Most euthanasia/PAS is carried out by GPs

---

[135] Tony Sheldon, 'Incidence of Euthanasia in the Netherlands Falls as That of Palliative Sedation Rises' (2007) 334 British Medical Journal 1075.

[136] Onweatuka-Philipsen *et al., Evalutie Wet toetsing levensbeeindiging op verzoek en hulp bij zelfdoding (Evaluation of the Termination of Life on Request and Assisted Suicide (Review Procedure) Act of 2002)* (The Hague, Zon Mw, 2007); A Van der Heide *et al.* 'End of Life Practices in the Netherlands Under the Euthanasia Act' (2007) 356 New England Journal of Medicine 1957–65.

[137] Ibid.

(88 per cent in 2006), rather than specialist consultants, and most deaths take place in the patient's own home (79.5 per cent).[138]

It is also worth noting that not all requests for euthanasia are complied with. On the contrary, in 2005, only 25 per cent of concrete requests for assistance in dying resulted in the patient's death.[139] This is most commonly because the patient dies of her underlying condition first, rather than because requests are routinely turned down.

(c) Commentary

Unsurprisingly, there is intense international interest in how legalized euthanasia has worked in practice in the Netherlands. The problem is that commentators cannot agree on the lessons we should learn from the Dutch experience. John Keown has persistently warned that there is clear evidence of abuse, and that the Dutch are currently sliding down the slippery slope.

John Keown[140]

[T]he evidence points to the following three conclusions. First, voluntary active euthanasia is far from a rarity and is increasingly performed. Rather than being truly a 'last resort', it has quickly become an established part of mainstream Dutch medical practice to which doctors have resorted even when palliative care could have offered an alternative...

Secondly, despite the insistent claims by proponents of voluntary active euthanasia, inside and outside the Netherlands, that allowing it subject to 'safeguards' brings it from the shadows and 'into the open' where it can be controlled, the evidence indicates that such claims merit scepticism. The reality is that most cases of voluntary active euthanasia, until recently a substantial majority, have gone unreported and unchecked. In view of the intractable fact that in a clear majority of cases there has not even been an *opportunity* for official scrutiny, Dutch reassurances of effective regulation ring hollow.

In contrast, others argue that legalization has worked well, and in the next extract John Griffiths suggests that the Netherlands offers us an example of the benefits that flow from openly regulating euthanasia.

John Griffiths[141]

The Dutch data on medical practices which shorten life, in the cases of non-competent or of competent but not-consulted patients, are indeed a matter of concern. However, some differentiation is in order. Almost all of the behaviour concerned involves abstaining from or terminating life-prolonging treatment, or administration of heavy doses of painkillers, in circumstances in which remaining life expectancy was (very) short and the doctor's behaviour may, as far as we know, have been entirely appropriate. There is really not a shred of evidence that the frequency of this sort of behaviour is higher in the Netherlands than, for

---

[138] Annual Reports, Regional Review Committees, reproduced in J Griffiths, H Weyers, and M Adams, *Euthanasia and Law in Europe* (Oxford, Hart Publishing, 2008) 157.

[139] Ibid.

[140] *Euthanasia, Ethics and Public Policy: An Argument against Legalisation* (CUP: Cambridge, 2002).

[141] 'Assisted Suicide in the Netherlands: The Chabot Case' (1995) 58 Modern Law Review 232–48, 247–8.

example, in the United States; the only thing that is clear is that more is known about it in the Netherlands....[Those] who invoke the metaphor to criticise Dutch legal developments seem quite confused about the direction in which the 'slippery slope' is tilting...[T]he Dutch are busy trying to bring a number of socially dangerous medical practices which exist everywhere under a regime of effective societal control.

A different argument, expressed here by John Griffiths *et al.* is that distinctive features of Dutch society and, in particular, of the Dutch health care system reduce the international relevance of euthansia's legalization in the Netherlands.

John Griffiths, Alex Bood, and Heleen Weyers[142]

A[n] important characteristic of Dutch society concerns the level of confidence in public institutions and in professions. It seems no accident that legalization of euthanasia is conceived in the United States, for example, in terms of the rights of *patients* (with doctors' organizations often prominent in opposition) whereas in the Netherlands the public discussion concerns the scope of the professional discretion of *doctors* (doctors have from the beginning been prominent in the movement for legalization). On the whole, the Dutch seem comfortable with the idea that doctors can be trusted with the discretion to perform euthanasia, so that the public debate largely concerns the boundaries of this professional discretion and the sorts of procedural controls to which it should be subjected.

Interestingly, the House of Lords Select Committee on Assisted Dying drew attention to a survey, which found that out of eleven European countries, including the UK, the Dutch had the highest regard for and trust in their doctors.[143]

(2) Oregon

In the United States, a distinction has been drawn between euthanasia—which is illegal throughout the US—and physician-assisted suicide, which is a matter for individual states. A decision of the Supreme Court in 1997 confirmed that there is no constitutional right to assisted suicide, but that legalization is not unconstitutional.[144] Oregon was the first state to vote in favour of the legalization of assisted suicide. The Death with Dignity Act 1994 was the result, but its introduction was delayed as a result of a number of legal challenges, all of which were ultimately unsuccessful.[145] It came into force in 1998, and in its first year there were fifteen assisted suicides in Oregon (0.05 per cent of all deaths). Since then, the number of assisted suicides has increased, though the numbers remain small. In 2007, there were forty-nine assisted suicides (0.15 per cent of all deaths).[146]

The Death with Dignity Act provides that a physician may comply with a competent, terminally ill, adult patient's voluntary request for a prescription of drugs, which will allow her

---

[142] *Euthanasia and Law in the Netherlands* (Amsterdam UP: Amsterdam, 1998) 304.

[143] Assisted Dying for the Terminally Ill Committee, *Assisted Dying for the Terminally Ill Bill—First Report* (2005) 41.

[144] *Washington et al. v Glucksberg* 117 SCt 2258 (1997) and *Vacco v Quill* 117 SCt 2293 (1997).

[145] *Gonzales v Oregon* 546 US 243 (2006).

[146] Oregon Department of Human Services, Tenth Annual Report on Oregon's Death with Dignity Act (2007), available at <www.oregon.gov/DHS/ph/pas/docs/year10.pdf>.

to end her life in a humane and dignified manner. The Act only applies to residents of the state of Oregon. The patient must make an initial oral request, followed by a formal written request. At least 15 days after the written request, the patient must repeat their request orally, and a further 48 hours must elapse before the prescription can be filled. The patient's request must be witnessed by two people other than the doctor, at least one of whom must not be a relative, an heir or an employee of the institution in which the patient is receiving care. The patient must be asked to notify her family. A second doctor must confirm the patient's diagnosis and that the patient is competent and acting voluntarily. The patient must have received complete information about her diagnosis, prognosis, and alternative treatments, such as hospice care and pain control. If there is any suggestion that the patient is depressed or has a psychiatric disorder, she must be referred to a psychiatrist or psychologist.

In Oregon there were fears that PAS would be chosen by patients who did not have health insurance and could not afford high-quality palliative care, but the evidence does not bear this out. The overwhelming majority of patients who have sought PAS are middle class, well educated, and have access to health insurance.[147] One study found that 92 per cent of the patients who sought PAS were already enrolled in hospice care.[148] The patients who request PAS in Oregon are, on average, younger than most terminally ill patients.[149] They do not choose PAS because of any lack of access to medical care and social support mechanisms, or from any sense that they have become a burden, either emotionally or financially.[150]

In Oregon, it also seems that since legalization of PAS the quality of palliative care which is available to patients has actually improved.[151] Since legalization, death from physician-assisted suicide has been rare and there are now higher standards of care for terminally ill patients. In a study of all the physicians eligible to prescribe drugs under the Act, 30 per cent had increased their referrals to hospice care and 76 per cent reported that they made efforts to improve their knowledge of pain medication for the terminally ill. Sixty-nine per cent reported that they had sought to improve their recognition of psychiatric disorders, such as depression.[152]

As with the Netherlands, supporters and opponents of legalization offer different interpretations of the evidence from Oregon. In the next extract, Dan W Brock argues that there has been no evidence of abuse in Oregon since the statute came into force.

Dan W Brock[153]

Both the report of Coombs Lee and Werth and the report of the Health Division of the State of Oregon on the first year of operation of the Death with Dignity Act in Oregon that has made physician-assisted suicide legal under strict guidelines should be reassuring to supporters

---

[147] E Dahl and N Levy, 'The Case for Physician Assisted Suicide: How can it Possibly be Proven?' (2006) 32 Journal of Medical Ethics 335–8.

[148] Ibid.

[149] Oregon Department of Human Services, *Tenth Annual Report on Oregon's Death with Dignity Act* (2007).

[150] LL Miller *et al.*, 'Attitudes and Experiences of Oregon Hospice Nurses and Social Workers Regarding Assisted Suicide' (2004) 18 Palliative Medicine 685–91.

[151] E Dahl and N Levy, 'The Case for Physician Assisted Suicide: How can it Possibly be Proven?' (2006) 32 Journal of Medical Ethics 335–8.

[152] L Ganzini *et al.*, 'Oregon Physician Attitudes About and Experiences with End of Life Care Since the Passage of the Death With Dignity Act. (2001) 285 Journal of the American Medical Association 2363–9.

[153] 'Misconceived Sources of Opposition to Physician-Assisted Suicide' (2000) 6 Psychology, Public Policy, and Law 305.

of the Act as well as to many of its opponents. There is no evidence that any of the abuses feared by opponents of the Act have materialized in the first year of its operation. It has not led to unsuccessful suicide attempts; to assisted deaths accompanied by distress to the patient; to any influx of out-of-state residents seeking assisted death; to public deaths; to use of assisted death to avoid dealing with difficult symptoms or to reduce the financial costs of end-of-life care; to disproportionate use of assisted death for weak, vulnerable, or disabled patients or for women; or to increased suicide rates in the general population and especially among the young. On the contrary, the authors suggest several good consequences from the Act, including improvements in end-of-life care such as increased use of hospice…and several averted suicides or homicides.

Against this, Margot White and Daniel Callahan suggest that the lack of any reporting requirements casts doubt upon the reliability of the available evidence.

Margot White and Daniel Callahan[154]

The Oregon law does not require physicians or anyone else to report cases at all whether they follow the guidelines or depart from them. As a result, the probability of generating accurate and complete data about nonvoluntary or involuntary cases would appear to be virtually nil…The fact that no evidence is publicly available at this stage suggesting that the feared 'slippery slope' is at hand in Oregon does not alter the overall concern. It makes little sense to note that the abuse doesn't seem to have materialized if there is no mechanism in place for bringing it to anyone's attention or investigating it. If there is lack of clarity about abusive practices, responsibility for correcting this lies not with PAS opponents, but with the drafters of Oregon's Death with Dignity Act who chose to omit any obligations for health care professionals to report unlawful practices and to omit any sanctions for physicians who fail to report PAS cases in the first place.

(3) Belgium

Belgium formally decriminalized euthanasia in 2002.[155] The Belgian Euthanasia Act does not apply to assisted suicide; only euthanasia has been legalized, provided certain conditions are met. To be eligible, patients must be over the age of 18, competent, and conscious, and their requests for euthanasia must be explicit, unambiguous, repeated, and durable. The patient must be in a hopeless situation, suffering from persistent and unbearable pain or distress that cannot be alleviated, and must be suffering from a serious and incurable mental or physical disorder. It is the patient who determines whether her suffering is persistent and unbearable, the physician is simply charged with certifying that the patient herself finds her suffering unbearable.

The physician must give the patient full information about her condition and the possibilities of palliative care. A second doctor must consult the patient's medical file, examine the patient, and confirm that the patient's suffering is unbearable, and that it cannot be alleviated. If the patient is not terminally ill, two additional requirements are imposed. First, the physician must consult two colleagues, one of whom must assess whether the request is

---

[154] 'Oregon's First Year: The Medicalization of Control' (2000) 6 Psychology, Public Policy, and Law 331.
[155] *Loi relative l'euthanasie* (The Act Concerning Euthanasia), 28 May 2002, in force 23 Sept 2002.

voluntary, considered, and repeated, and secondly, at least a month must elapse between the request and the performance of euthanasia.

Advance directives requesting euthanasia may also be respected, provided certain conditions are satisfied. The directive must be in writing, signed by the patient, and witnessed by two adults, at least one of whom must have no material interest in the patient's death. If the patient is permanently incapable of writing down her request, she can appoint a representative who must have no material interest in her death to do so. A medical certificate certifying that the patient is permanently incapable of writing must be attached.

Doctors are not under a duty to comply with a patient's request for euthanasia; on the contrary, they are entitled to refuse on grounds of conscience or for medical reasons. There is, however, a duty to inform the patient or the patient's representative and explain the reasons for their refusal.

The physician must fill in a registration form and deliver it within four working days of the death to a national commission, consisting of sixteen members: eight of whom are doctors, four are lawyers, and four 'from groups charged with the problem of incurably ill patients'. If the commission is satisfied that any of the criteria were not satisfied, the file will be sent to the public prosecutor. The commission reports to Parliament on the implementation of the legislation. The Second Report into the operation of the law found that in 2004 and 2005, there were a total of 742 legal euthanasia cases, or an average of 31 per month.

It is also important to bear in mind, as Gastmans *et al.* explain, that the legalization of euthanasia in Belgium took place within a context in which there is a strong emphasis upon the provision of palliative care, and where the first response to a request for euthanasia will always be prompt extensive investigation of other palliative options.

C Gastmans, F Van Neste, and P Schotsmans[156]

[I]f euthanasia can ever be justified, it is necessary to provide good palliative care for all and to include in the euthanasia law a palliative filter—that is, a compulsory prior consultation with a specialised palliative care team...

The starting point of this clinical practice guideline is the principle that everything possible should be done to provide support and assistance to the competent, terminally ill person who asks for euthanasia, and his or her relatives. The aim is that such an active and integral palliative care approach can in many cases displace the request and allow the patient to die in a dignified manner without euthanasia.... In Belgium, the development of palliative care preceded the euthanasia debate. As a result, Belgian palliative care (for example, the Flemish Palliative Care Federation) played a very active role in the Belgian euthanasia debate. The Belgian euthanasia debate itself functioned as a lever that facilitated the further development of palliative care, as is illustrated by the new law on palliative care that was approved at the same time as the euthanasia law.

The legalization of euthanasia in Belgium rests upon the assumption that high-quality palliative care may be able to obviate many but not all requests for euthanasia. Euthanasia is very definitely a 'last resort', and the comprehensive palliative care framework means that euthanasia will be used only when all other options have been exhausted.

[156] 'Facing Requests for Euthanasia: A Clinical Practice Guideline' (2004) 30 Journal of Medical Ethics 212–17.

The decision-making process in Belgium does not just involve the patient and their doctor. On the contrary, nurses and the patient's family also play an important role. The legislation specifies that where a nursing team has had regular contact with the patient who has requested euthanasia, the physician must discuss the patient's request with them.[157] Even where a nursing team is not already involved, following a patient's request for euthanasia, a palliative care nurse will spend time with her in order identify the reasons for her request.[158] Finding out why a patient wants their life to be brought to an end helps the nurse to work out what palliative response might be able to alleviate the suffering that underlies the patient's request for euthanasia.

(4) Switzerland

Euthanasia—or 'murder upon request by the victim'—is illegal under Article 114 of the Swiss Penal Code. It is not considered as grave an offence as murder *without* the victim's request, and the actor's motive will be taken into account in sentencing. Assisting suicide is a criminal offence under Article 115 of the Code, but only if the defendant's motive is 'selfish'. Article 115 of the Swiss Penal Code does not specify that the suicide must be assisted by a doctor, nor does the patient have to be terminally ill or in intolerable pain. The only precondition for the act's legality is that the motive must be unselfish. Thus, provided that the person's motive for assisting the suicide is compassionate, no offence is committed.

There have been prosecutions in cases where the motive has been judged to be selfish. This is not necessarily confined to suicides assisted for material gain, but has extended to one case in which a psychiatrist permitted a TV camera team to be present during an assisted suicide. The desire for publicity was judged to be selfish, and the psychiatrist was convicted.[159]

A number of organizations offer assistance to patients who want to commit suicide, and these may impose some additional requirements upon patients. EXIT, for example, has around 50,000 members and helps 100–120 patients to die each year. Patients must be over the age of 18; mentally competent; and suffering from intolerable health problems. EXIT will only help Swiss nationals to commit suicide. Dignitas, a smaller organization set up in 1998, also assists non-Swiss residents to die. It has about 6,000 members in 57 countries. So far, over 800 people from 26 countries have used its services. Most had cancer, multiple sclerosis, or motor neurone disease, and the majority were from Germany. The prospect of Switzerland becoming the destination for 'suicide tourism' has led to a number of proposed bills that would prohibit foreigners from gaining access to assisted suicide, but none has so far become law.

It has been estimated that approximately 1,800 requests for assisted suicides are made each year. Two-thirds of these are turned down. Of the remaining 600 patients, half die from other causes. In total, about 300 suicides are assisted by the Swiss right-to-die organizations each year, representing around 0.45 per cent of all deaths.

---

[157] Euthanasia Act 2002, Art 3.

[158] B Dierckx de Casterl *et al.*, 'Nurses' Views on their Involvement in Euthanasia: A Qualitative Study in Flanders (Belgium)' (2006) 32 Journal of Medical Ethics 187–92.

[159] J Griffiths, H Weyers, and M Adams, *Euthanasia and Law in Europe* (Hart Publishing: Oxford, 2008) 476.

(d) EUTHANASIA OR ASSISTED SUICIDE OR BOTH?

As we have seen, some countries have only legalized euthanasia (Belgium), while other places have only legalized, specifically or de facto, assisted suicide (Oregon and Switzerland). In the Netherlands, while both may be performed, euthanasia is much more common. What reasons might there be for preferring one method of assisted dying to another?

Doctors can end patients' lives more effectively than patients themselves, who might, for example, fail to swallow the entire prescribed dose and be left both alive and severely damaged by partially ingesting a lethal substance. If assisted suicide is more likely to go wrong, preferring it to euthanasia is justifiable only if there is some residual fear that doctors might not be acting in accordance with the patient's wishes. In Oregon, the prevailing view is that legalizing assisted suicide is preferable to euthanasia because it provides an additional safeguard, or 'firewall'. Dr Nick Gideonse, a general practitioner in Oregon, told the House of Lords Select Committee that, 'The fact that the patient self-administers in a way that is not easy to do, drinking ounces of a bitter liquid, provides a final piece of clear evidence that this is completely volitional and self-administered.'[160] The importance of having this 'firewall' takes precedence over the fact that it imposes an additional unpleasant burden upon the patient.

It could, however, be argued that allowing *only* euthanasia provides a different sort of control over the practice. It is commonly said that one of the benefits of assisted suicide is that it enables a patient to obtain a prescription for a lethal dose of drugs as a sort of 'comfort blanket' or 'insurance policy', so that they know they will be able to end their suffering when it becomes unbearable. Many, perhaps even most patients will never actually take the drugs, but find it very reassuring to know that they have the means to end their lives if their quality of life deteriorates.

In Oregon, from 1997 until the end of 2003, 265 prescriptions had been written under the Death with Dignity Act, while only 117 people had chosen to take them. While some of these 148 people may have died before they had an opportunity to take the lethal dose, others will have decided not to go through with their decision to opt for an assisted suicide. This statistic could be read in two ways. First, the fact that few people who express an interest in PAS, and even a minority of those who obtain a prescription, in Oregon actually die as a result suggests that terminally ill patients do not, in practice, feel under pressure to complete their assisted suicide against their wishes.

Secondly, 148 prescriptions were issued which were never used for their intended purpose, and while most of these were probably never obtained from the pharmacy, it is of course possible that a prescription could be filled but not used by the patient. Only legalizing euthanasia rules out the possibility that lethal drugs could be given to a patient but not used by them, which would raise the concern that they might fall into the hands of someone else who has not gone through the rigorous assessment procedure. That this latter concern does not outweigh the importance of the 'firewall' provided by assisted suicide suggests that in places like Oregon (and perhaps the UK too), doctors may be trusted *less* than patients themselves.

3 THE INCOMPETENT PATIENT

In this chapter, because our interest is in practices which may result in an individual's life being shortened we are necessarily concerned with a very small subset of incompetent patients. As we saw in Chapter 5, patients who lack capacity must be treated in their best

---

[160] House of Lords, Assisted Dying for the Terminally Ill Committee, 2005, p146.

interests, and usually it is obvious that prolonging someone's life will be in her best interests. There are, however, a number of cases in which the courts have been faced with the question of whether it could ever be in an incompetent patient's best interests to withdraw or withhold life-prolonging treatment.

(a) CHILDREN

(1) The Criminal Law

As we saw earlier, failing to provide a patient with life-sustaining treatment could satisfy both the *actus reus* and the *mens rea* for murder. An omission can only constitute the *actus reus* of murder if the defendant was under a duty to act. So if a child dies because their doctor has withheld or withdrawn treatment that they were under a duty to provide, criminal charges are possible. If doctors were always under a duty to prolong children's lives, then the non-treatment of severely handicapped neonates would be murder. It is, however, widely agreed that doctors are not obliged to strive to maintain life at all costs. If treatment is futile (that is, it is not going to lead to any improvement in the patient's condition), doctors are generally assumed to be entitled to withhold or discontinue it. As a result, there have been hardly any prosecutions for murder, or attempted murder, following the decision to withhold life-prolonging treatment from a child.

In *R v Arthur*, a baby with Down's syndrome who had developed pneumonia died shortly after Dr Arthur had prescribed a powerful analgesic and 'nursing care only'. The baby's mother had told Dr Arthur that she did not want the baby to survive. Following Farquaharson J's controversial direction to the jury, Dr Arthur was acquitted.

R v Arthur[161]

Farquharson J

If a child is born with a serious handicap—for example, where a mongol [sic] has an ill-formed intestine whereby that child will die of the ailment if he is not operated on—a surgeon may say: 'as this child is a mongol I do not propose to operate; I shall allow nature to take its course'. No one could say that that surgeon was committing an act of murder by declining to take a course which would save the child...

Where a child gets pneumonia and is a child with an irreversible handicap whose mother has rejected him, if the doctor said: 'I am not going to give it antibiotics', and by a merciful dispensation of providence he dies, ... it would be very unlikely, I would suggest, that you (or any other jury) would say that the doctor was committing murder.

While in 1981, it might still have been possible for a judge to hold that a mother's rejection of a Down's syndrome child was a good reason to sanction her non-treatment, Ian Kennedy and Andrew Grubb have rightly suggested that, in the light of the Court of Appeal judgments in *Re B* and *Re J* (see below) 'the *Arthur* case can be consigned to legal history for the oddity it is'.[162]

---

[161] (1981) 12 BMLR 1.
[162] Ian Kennedy and Andrew Grubb, *Medical Law*, 3rd edn (Butterworths: London, 2000) 2167.

A case that came very close to neonatal euthanasia arose in the context of a fitness to practise hearing of a Scottish neonatologist, Michael Munro. He was cleared of malpractice by a GMC Fitness to Practise panel after he had given large doses of a muscle relaxant, pancuronium, to two dying babies. Just before death, each baby had suffered from 'agonal gasping', which was extremely distressing to the parents, though it was not clear whether the babies had by this time lost consciousness. He told the hearing that the parents,

> [W]ere utterly distraught. If you put yourself in their shoes, they have already said their last goodbyes to their baby, then suddenly there are these massive, racking agonal gasps that appeared to build up—they were utterly, utterly distraught. The parents were in tears, saying things like 'I can't take any more.' I took the decision then to administer pancuronium. I explained to the parents that this drug was to be used to ease the suffering but that one of the consequences of its use may be to hasten death. They were happy with that.[163]

Pancuronium would stop agonal gasping, but only because it would stop the babies from breathing, and hence could mean that they died sooner than they otherwise would. Because pancuronium is not an analgesic or a sedative (it is, in fact, used as part of the lethal injection given to executed prisoners in the US), its use as a palliative agent is doubtful, unless stopping the patient from breathing is classed as palliation. In the next extract, Anne Morris suggests that the GMC's Fitness to Practise panel (FTPP) were effectively condoning what may have been unlawful behaviour.

Anne Morris[164]

> There is a good argument for saying that a doctor who cares about his patients as much as Dr Munro should not be punished. It is also arguable that he poses no threat to patients or public. Nevertheless, he admitted doing something which, on the face of it, could have led to criminal charges. Of course, a jury faced with the desperately sad facts in these cases might not have convicted. But that is evidence of the public attitude to what is acceptable treatment at the end of life. Sympathy for the doctor, parents and patients does not alter the law.... [T]he failure of the GMC even to warn Dr Munro as to his future practice seems to invite the criticism that the profession is condoning (legally) questionable practice. The FTPP is not a court of law, let alone a criminal court, but it is worth asking to what extent a professional regulatory body should be bound to take account of the law, albeit that the law may be described as unsatisfactory.

(2) The Best Interests Test

It would be a mistake to imagine that all cases involving decisions about withholding or withdrawing treatment come before the courts. On the contrary, decisions about withdrawing life-prolonging measures are made routinely in the care of terminally ill children. In neonatal intensive care units, it has been estimated that up to 70 per cent of deaths are

---

163 Owen Dyer 'Doctor Cleared of Act 'Tantamount to Euthanasia'' (2007) 335 British Medical Journal 67.
164 'Fitness to Practise and the Ethics of Decision-making at the End of Life: Dr Michael Munro' (2007) Professional Negligence 228.

preceded by discussions about limiting or withholding treatment.[165] In later childhood too, in paediatric intensive care wards, between 43 per cent and 72 per cent of deaths result from decisions about treatment withdrawal.[166]

The Royal College of Paediatrics and Child Health have issued guidance about the circumstances when decisions to withhold or withdraw life-prolonging treatment are justifiable.

Royal College of Paediatrics and Child Health[167]

There are five situations where it may be ethical and legal to consider withholding or withdrawal of lifesustaining medical treatment:

1. *The 'Brain Dead' Child*. In the older child where criteria of brain-stem death are agreed by two practitioners in the usual way it may still be technically feasible to provide basal cardio-respiratory support by means of ventilation and intensive care. It is agreed within the profession that treatment in such circumstances is futile and the withdrawal of current medical treatment is appropriate.

2. *The 'Permanent Vegetative' State'*. The child who develops a permanent vegetative state following insults, such as trauma or hypoxia, is reliant on others for all care and does not react or relate with the outside world. It may be appropriate to withdraw or withhold life-sustaining treatment.

3. *The 'No Chance' Situation*. The child has such severe disease that life-sustaining treatment simply delays death without significant alleviation of suffering. Treatment to sustain life is inappropriate.

4. *The 'No purpose' Situation*. Although the patient may be able to survive with treatment, the degree of physical or mental impairment will be so great that it is unreasonable to expect them to bear it.

5. *The 'Unbearable' Situation*. The child and/or family feel that in the face of progressive and irreversible illness further treatment is more than can be borne. They wish to have a particular treatment withdrawn or to refuse further treatment irrespective of the medical opinion that it may be of some benefit.

The cases that have come before the courts principally involve the last three scenarios, and generally the courts will only become involved if there is some disagreement over whether the child's situation is unbearable or their treatment futile.

One sort of dispute might arise when the doctors believe that life support should be withheld while the parents want treatment to continue. In *Re C (A Minor) (Medical Treatment)*, C was 16 months old and gravely ill. She had been in intensive care on a ventilator for the past month, and medical opinion was unanimous that to continuing to ventilate her was likely to cause her increasing distress. The doctors proposed to remove C from the ventilator, and not to engage in resuscitation or reventilation if she were to suffer a further respiratory collapse. As a result of their orthodox Jewish faith, C's parents could not agree to a course of action that would indirectly shorten her life, and the doctors sought a court order that non-treatment would be lawful.

---

[165] Royal College of Paediatrics and Child Health *Witholding or Withdrawing Life Sustaining Treatment in Children: A Framework for Practice*, 2nd edn (2004).
[166] Ibid.   [167] Ibid.

Re C (A Minor) (Medical Treatment)[168]

Sir Stephen Brown P

The medical evidence is not in dispute. There is no issue in this case that this is a fatal disease and that in real terms this little child is approaching death. She has a desperately tragic existence. She is emaciated. Although she is conscious there is the prospect of increasing suffering as the days go by. The doctors are all of the view that it would be in her best interests that she be removed from ventilation and that in the event of what they believe to be an inevitable respiratory arrest it would follow that she should not be replaced on ventilation which would of itself give rise to increased suffering and distress...

In this case I have no doubt on the evidence before me, including the evidence of the parents themselves, that in this desperate situation it is in the best interests of C that she should now be taken off the ventilation presently being administered and that it should not be reimposed or restored if she should suffer a further respiratory arrest. It is a desperately sad situation for all concerned. The anxiety of the doctors as well as the parents can be well understood. Their objective in their profession is to save and to preserve life but, as has been said in earlier cases that whilst the sanctity of life is vitally important, it is not the paramount consideration. The paramount consideration is the best interests of little C...what the court is being asked to do in this case is to exercise its inherent jurisdiction to approve the course of treatment which is now proposed by the doctors and for which they cannot gain the consent of the parents. In other words to seek the court's consent in the absence of the consent of the parents...I believe that in this case I should assent to the course which is proposed by the Hospital Trust. I do so with a feeling of grave solemnity because I realise that the parents themselves will be greatly disappointed. It is a sad feature of this matter that there is, in fact, no hope for C, and what has to be considered is her best interests to prevent her from suffering as would be inevitable if this course were not to be taken.

A different sort of dispute might arise if the parents refuse to consent to a procedure that is necessary to save a child's life. As we saw in Chapter 5, the doctors might then apply to have the child made a ward of court, and if the court decides that treatment is in the child's best interests, the parent's refusal will be overridden. This occurred in *Re B (A Minor) (Wardship: Medical Treatment)*. B suffered from Down's syndrome and had an intestinal blockage, which required an immediate operation. If the operation were performed, it was probable that B's life expectancy would be 20 to 30 years. Her parents, having decided that it would be kinder to allow her to die rather than live as a physically and mentally handicapped person, refused to consent to the operation. The local authority made the child a ward of court and sought an order authorizing the operation to be performed. At first instance, the judge decided that the parents' wishes should be respected and refused to make the order, but this was overturned by the Court of Appeal.

Re B (A Minor) (Wardship: Medical Treatment)[169]

Templeman LJ

Fortunately or unfortunately, in this particular case the decision no longer lies with the parents or with the doctors, but lies with the court. It is a decision which of course must be made

---

[168] [1998] Lloyd's Rep Med 1 Fam Div.
[169] [1981] 1 WLR 1421 CA.

in the light of the evidence and views expressed by the parents and the doctors, but at the end of the day it devolves on this court in this particular instance to decide whether the life of this child is demonstrably going to be so awful that in effect the child must be condemned to die, or whether the life of this child is still so imponderable that it would be wrong for her to be condemned to die. There may be cases, I know not, of severe proved damage where the future is so certain and where the life of the child is so bound to be full of pain and suffering that the court might be driven to a different conclusion, but in the present case the choice which lies before the court is this: whether to allow an operation to take place which may result in the child living for 20 or 30 years as a mongoloid [sic] or whether (and I think this must be brutally the result) to terminate the life of a mongoloid child because she also has an intestinal complaint. Faced with that choice I have no doubt that it is the duty of this court to decide that the child must live. The judge was much affected by the reasons given by the parents and came to the conclusion that their wishes ought to be respected. In my judgment he erred in that the duty of the court is to decide whether it is in the interests of the child that an operation should take place. The evidence in this case only goes to show that if the operation takes place and is successful then the child may live the normal span of a mongoloid child with the handicaps and defects and life of a mongol child, and it is not for this court to say that life of that description ought to be extinguished.

Cases where there is no disagreement between parents and doctors may come before the court where the doctors simply want reassurance that non-treatment would be lawful, in order to avoid the possibility of criminal charges at a later date.

In *Re J (A Minor) (Wardship: Medical Treatment)*, the most optimistic prognosis suggested that J had a considerably shortened life expectancy, that he would become a serious spastic quadriplegic, probably without sight, speech, or hearing, but he would be able to feel pain. There was a possibility that he might at any time suffer respiratory collapse requiring further resuscitation. The consultant neonatologist recommended that, in the event of further convulsions requiring resuscitation, J should not be revived by means of mechanical ventilation unless it seemed appropriate to those involved in his care. This recommendation had been accepted by the trial judge. The Court of Appeal dismissed the Official Solicitor's appeal.

Re J (A Minor) (Wardship: Medical Treatment)[170]

Taylor LJ

Despite the court's inability to compare a life afflicted by the most severe disability with death, the unknown, I am of the view that there must be extreme cases in which the court is entitled to say: 'The life which this treatment would prolong would be so cruel as to be intolerable.' If, for example, a child was so damaged as to have negligible use of its faculties and the only way of preserving its life was by the continuous administration of extremely painful treatment such that the child either would be in continuous agony or would have to be so sedated continuously as to have no conscious life at all ... In those circumstances, without there being any question of deliberately ending the life or shortening it, I consider the court is entitled in the best interests of the child to say that deliberate steps should not be taken artificially to prolong its miserable life span ...

[170] [1991] Fam 33 CA.

> At what point in the scale of disability and suffering ought the court to hold that the best interests of the child do not require further endurance to be imposed by positive treatment to prolong its life? Clearly, to justify withholding treatment, the circumstances would have to be extreme...
>
> I consider the correct approach is for the court to judge the quality of life the child would have to endure if given the treatment and decide whether in all the circumstances such a life would be so afflicted as to be intolerable to that child. I say 'to that child' because the test should not be whether the life would be tolerable to the decider. The test must be whether the child in question, if capable of exercising sound judgment, would consider the life tolerable.

The test the courts apply when faced with all these applications is the 'welfare principle': that is, the child's best interests must be their paramount concern. So when will it be in a child's best interests to withhold or withdraw life-prolonging treatment? Because it will almost always be in a child's best interests to continue living, only children who are very gravely ill will be plausible candidates for non-treatment. But exactly how we tell whether a child's condition meets the threshold level of gravity is a difficult question, and a number of different approaches are evident in the caselaw.

First, some judges ask whether continued life would be intolerable to *this particular child*.[171] The purpose of this 'substituted judgment' test is to remind decision-makers that disabled people may be able to gain pleasure and satisfaction from a quality of life that might seem intolerable to an able-bodied member of the judiciary. Of course, this test is necessarily speculative because in these cases it will generally be impossible to discover what this particular child would think of their likely quality of life.

Secondly, Templeman LJ in *Re B* suggested that the child's life must be 'demonstrably awful' before non-treatment can be contemplated. While this indicates that the child's condition should be extremely grave, as a test for when non-treatment is justified, it is rather vague. All that the cases reproduced above tell us is that Down's syndrome does not lead to a life that is 'demonstrably awful' (*Re B*), while profound brain damage accompanied by paralysis, blindness, and deafness does (*Re J*). Where the line should be drawn between these two points of certainty is unclear.

What seems evident, however, is that the courts will tend to be guided by medical evidence on whether life-prolonging treatment should be withdrawn or withheld from a child and will not order doctors to treat contrary to their clinical judgement. In *Re Wyatt (A Child) (Medical Treatment: Parents' Consent)*, for example, medical opinion was 'unanimous' that invasive medical treatment would not be in Charlotte's best interests, and Hedley J's conclusion was therefore unsurprising:

> I do not believe that any further aggressive treatment, even if necessary to prolong life, is in her best interests. I know that that may mean that she may die earlier than otherwise she might have done but in my judgment the moment of her death will only be slightly advanced.[172]

---

[171] See, for example, the comments of Taylor LJ in *Re J* [1991] Fam 33 CA.
[172] [2004] EWHC 2247 (Fam).

Charlotte Wyatt's parents returned to court in 2005,[173] citing evidence that Charlotte's condition had improved and asking for the declarations that non-treatment would be lawful to be set aside. The case was again heard by Hedley J, who continued to be persuaded by the majority of medical opinion, that intensive care measures should not be taken in the future when, as was likely, Charlotte suffered a serious respiratory collapse. This decision was appealed in *Re Wyatt (A Child) (Medical Treatment: Continuation of Order)*.[174] The Court of Appeal considered that there were many disadvantages in granting declaratory relief in relation to a situation which had not yet arisen. Following the Court of Appeal's judgment in *Burke* (see below), they said the court should not be used as a general advice centre, and they expressed reservations about judges making open-ended declarations which they may have to re-visit if circumstances change. In this case, however, Charlotte's underlying condition had not changed, and so the Court of Appeal decided that Hedley J had been entitled to continue the declarations. The Court of Appeal stressed that the declarations are permissive, not mandatory, and pointed out that the trust had written to Mr and Mrs Wyatt making it clear that the trust's current decision not to reventilate Charlotte was being kept under clinical review and would be discussed with her parents before it is implemented.

Although only a first-instance decision, Holman J's judgment in *An NHS Trust v B* is noteworthy for a number of reasons, not least his decision to go against unanimous medical opinion, and the views of the Guardian appointed to represent MB's interests, and order that certain types of life-prolonging treatment should be provided to MB, a terminally ill little boy. MB suffered from spinal muscular atrophy (SMA), a congenital condition which varies considerably in severity. MB was diagnosed with the most severe type of Type 1 SMA. He could barely move, could not breathe unaided, could not swallow and, additionally, suffered from epilepsy. The doctors treating him considered that MB's quality of life had become so low and that the burdens of living so great that it would be unethical to continue artificially to keep him alive, and that his endotracheal tube should be withdrawn. This would lead to his death within a few minutes. His parents disagreed, and wanted treatment to continue.

Unusually, Holman J sided with the parents, and decided treatment should continue, although he did also recognize that there were some treatments, such as CPR, which went beyond maintaining ventilation, and which required the positive infliction of pain. If they became necessary, Holman J thought this would mean that MB had moved naturally towards his death, and that it would then be in MB's best interests to withhold those treatments.

In applying the best interests test, Holman J drew up a 'balance sheet' with the benefits or advantages of treatment on one side, and the burdens or disadvantages of continuing or discontinuing treatment on the other side. Holman found that on the benefits side were MB's capacity to gain pleasure from DVDs, CDs and stories, and, more importantly, from his relationship with his parents and family. The burdens were the discomfort, distress, or pain which accompanied the procedures to which he was subject, coupled with his inability to communicate his suffering. Holman J concluded that because MB's life did still contain benefits, it should be enabled to continue, despite the routine discomfort, distress, and pain to which he was subject.

---

[173] *Re Wyatt (No 3) (A Child) (Medical Treatment: Continuation of Order)* [2005] EWHC 693 (Fam).
[174] [2005] EWCA Civ 1181.

An NHS Trust v B[175]

Holman J

I fully accept all the burdens of discomfort, distress and some pain to which M is daily subjected, but from which I would now specifically exclude, if the need arises, CPR and the other treatments I have just described. Even excluding these, I accept that there is almost relentless discomfort, periods of distress and relatively short episodes of pain (deep suctioning). It is indeed a helpless and sad life.

But that life does in my view include within it the benefits that I have tried to describe and will not repeat. Within those benefits, and central to them, is my view that on the available evidence I must proceed on the basis that M has age appropriate cognition, and does continue to have a relationship of value to him with his family, and does continue to gain other pleasures from touch, sight and sound....

It is impossible to put a mathematical or any other value on the benefits. But they are precious and real and they are the benefits, and only benefits, that M was destined to gain from his life. I do not consider that from one day to the next all the routine discomfort, distress and pain that the doctors describe (but not the ones I have now excluded) outweigh those benefits so that I can say that it is in his best interests that those benefits, and life itself, should immediately end. On the contrary, I positively consider that as his life does still have benefits, and is his life, it should be enabled to continue, subject to excluding the treatment I have identified.

A year later, in *Re K (A Minor)*, Sir Mark Potter P distinguished K's situation from that of MB. Her ability to gain any pleasure at all from life was almost completely absent, and in those circumstances, he decided that it would be in her best interests to cease to provide artificial feeding (known as total parenteral nutrition or TPN).

Re K (A Minor)[176]

Sir Mark Potter P

In this case K is less than 6 months old and has a developmental age of only 3 months. She has no accumulation of experiences and cognition comparable with that of MB. She is not, and with her short expectation of life is never likely to be, in a position to derive pleasure from DVDs or CDs and the only indication of real feelings of pleasure in her limited developmental state is enjoyment of a bath. On the evidence before me there is no realistic sense in which one can assign to her the simple pleasure of being alive or having other than a life dominated by regular pain, distress and discomfort and unrelieved by the pleasures of eating.

Her muscular function is already severely diminished and any pleasure which might otherwise develop through increased activity and stimulation of the senses is denied to her. She has no prospect of relief from this pitiful existence before an end which is regarded as virtually certain by the age of one year and likely to be appreciably less. If her line is not removed she will continue to suffer pain and distress from the invasive treatment which she already experiences and the prospect is of the likely necessity for removal of her line in the near

---

[175] [2006] EWHC 507 (Fam).
[176] [2006] EWHC 1007 (Fam).

> future which will merely add to her distress. If she were to have the necessary further surgical operation to replace the line, she would require mechanical ventilation which is also invasive and painful. There would be no improvement in her condition or improvement in her expectation of life. In these circumstances, I have no doubt that it would not only be a mercy, but it is in her best interests, to cease to provide TPN while she is still clinically stable, so that she may die in peace and over a comparatively short space of time, relieved by the palliative treatment contemplated, which will cause her neither pain nor discomfort and will enable her to live out her short life in relative peace in the close care of her parents who love her.

Taken together, these two cases suggest that the child's degree of cognitive development and awareness may lead the court to favour life-prolonging measures, even where these cause discomfort, but that where that discomfort co-exists with significantly impaired capacity to gain pleasure from everyday life, non-treatment will be in a child's best interests.

Glass v UK is a case largely decided upon its very unusual facts. The mother believed that the doctors were intending, through the provision of diamorphine and 'Do Not Resuscitate' Orders, with which she disagreed, to covertly 'euthanase' her son. Relations between the medical staff and the mother were extremely poor, but the hospital did not make an application to the court to resolve the question of the child's treatment. The case reached the European Court of Human Rights, which decided that treatment in defiance of the parent's objections, without the authorization of a court, gave rise to an interference with the child's right to respect for his private and family life, and amounted to a violation of Article 8. It should, however, be remembered that the breach of Article 8 in the *Glass* case would have been prevented if the doctors had made a timely application to the court. Of course, it is clearly possible, perhaps even probable, that the court would have granted the declaration authorizing non-treatment of this severely disabled child.

Glass v UK [177]

Judgment of the ECtHR

The court is not persuaded that an emergency High Court application could not have been made by the Trust when it became clear that the second applicant was firmly opposed to the administration of diamorphine to the first applicant. However, the doctors and officials used the limited time available to them in order to try to impose their views on the second applicant. It observes in this connection that the Trust was able to secure the presence of a police officer to oversee the negotiations with the second applicant but, surprisingly, did not give consideration to making a High Court application even though 'the best-interests procedure can be involved at short notice'...

The court considers that, having regard to the circumstances of the case, the decision of the authorities to override the second applicant's objection to the proposed treatment in the absence of authorisation by a court resulted in a breach of article 8 of the Convention.

As is evident from both the Charlotte Wyatt litigation—estimated to have cost the taxpayer around £500,000– and the *Glass* case, litigation in these cases, as well as being expensive,

---

[177] (Application No. 61827/00) European Court of Human Rights.

often sours the relationship between parents and clinicians, and makes an already stressful situation worse for all concerned. These problems, and the fact that whether a case receives external review depends almost entirely upon the existence of disagreement between parents and doctors, led the Nuffield Council on Bioethics to propose two different approaches. First, instead of court involvement, the Nuffield Council suggested that there could be routine review of non-treatment decisions by Clinical Ethics Committees (CECs). Secondly, it recommended that mediation between parents and doctors should be attempted before resort to litigation.

Nuffield Council on Bioethics[178]

> CECs could be charged to review all decisions made in relation to withdrawal of intensive care, whether such decisions are made by agreement between parents and professionals or not. Such a review would ensure an external and independent evaluation of a baby's interests. Evidence of the concurrence of the CEC would provide some protection for clinicians whose decisions are later questioned. Two particular challenges would need to be addressed. First, the CEC in its present form is primarily designed to provide ethics support for health professionals. . . . [I]n cases of conflict, the CEC may not be perceived as sufficiently independent from the health providers. Secondly, for the kinds of dilemma addressed in this Report, there are logistical problems. Rapid advice would sometimes be required and mechanisms would be needed to achieve this. Such provision may well not be possible in all circumstances, for example with regard to decisions about resuscitation; however, one basis for such a mechanism would be for some members of existing CECs, or other facilitors, to be available on call to hospital staff. . . .
>
> When disagreements arise about the care of a very ill baby, there is rarely a 'right' answer and therefore the potential benefits of mediation merit examination. In the UK, mediation is increasingly used to assist parties in disputes that might otherwise be adjudicated in the courts. Mediation empowers the parties to a dispute to seek to resolve their disagreement themselves. . . .
>
> Mediation thus seeks to bring together the parties who disagree. It identifies the parties and clarifies their interests. It offers opportunities to draw in the wider family (and religious advisers). It seeks to minimise disparities in power and to find common ground. . . .
>
> Mediation will not however provide an answer to every dilemma. It may, however, facilitate better communication, reduce acrimony and narrow down the issues requiring formal adjudication in the courts. Inevitably some parties may have reservations about the process or there may be fundamental disagreement prompted by ethical concerns. For example, parents of a baby with trisomy 18 (Edwards Syndrome) whose faith requires that every possible intervention to prolong the life of their child is required are unlikely to find accord with doctors who consider that ventilating that child is futile. However, mediation may be able to help the parties understand each other better and help to reinforce and restore trust.

(3) The 'Conjoined Twins Case' Re A

(a) Re A[179]

As we have seen, the reason why doctors who discontinue life-prolonging treatment are not routinely charged with murder is that treatment withdrawal is treated in law as an omission.

---

[178] Critical Care Decisions in Fetal and Neonatal Medicine: Ethical Issues (2006), available at <www.nuffieldbioethics.org>.

[179] [2001] 1 FLR 267.

When the courts were first asked to authorize the separation of conjoined twins, a new problem arose. In *Re A (Children) (Conjoined Twins: Surgical Separation)* the weaker twin (known as Mary) would die as a result of an operation to separate her from her twin sister (known as Jodie), who would have a good chance of leading a normal life. If the twins were not separated Jodie's heart would fail and both twins would die. The parents, who were devout Roman Catholics from the Mediterranean island of Gozo, refused to consent to an operation which would inevitably kill one of their daughters. The hospital applied for a declaration that it could lawfully carry out separation surgery.

At first instance, Johnson J attempted to justify the operation by describing it as an omission: the operation would, he said, interrupt or withdraw the blood supply which Mary was receiving from Jodie. This explanation was rejected by the Court of Appeal, who robustly admitted that invasive surgery is unquestionably an action, and that this meant the doctors carrying out the operation would be guilty of murdering Mary, unless they could avail themselves of a defence.

Each of the four judges who heard the case appeared to start from the utilitarian presumption that saving one life must be preferable to losing two lives. The problem, of course, was that Jodie's life could only be saved by doing something that would kill Mary. So the judgments can be read as different attempts to justify a course of action which, on the face of it, is impermissible in order to achieve 'the lesser of two evils', that is the death of one child rather than two.

Re A (Children) (Conjoined Twins: Surgical Separation)[180]

Ward LJ

Just as the parents hold firm views worthy of respect, so every instinct of the medical team has been to save life where it can be saved. Despite such a professional judgment it would, nevertheless, have been a perfectly acceptable response for the hospital to bow to the weight of the parental wish however fundamentally the medical team disagreed with it. Other medical teams may well have accepted the parents' decision. Had St Mary's done so, there could not have been the slightest criticism of them for letting nature take its course in accordance with the parents' wishes. Nor should there be any criticism of the hospital for not bowing to the parents' choice. The hospital have care of the children and...there can be no doubt whatever that the hospital are entitled...to seek the court's ruling...

Family Law

The question of Mary's best interests is one of the key and one of the difficult issues in the case and it calls for thorough exposition. That Mary's welfare is paramount is a trite observation for family lawyers...

The question is whether this proposed operation is in Mary's best interests. It cannot be. It will bring her life to an end before it has run its natural span. It denies her inherent right to life. There is no countervailing advantage for her at all. It is contrary to her best interests. Looking at her position in isolation and ignoring, therefore, the benefit to Jodie, the court should not sanction the operation on her...

If the duty of the court is to make a decision which puts Jodie's interests paramount and that decision would be contrary to the paramount interests of Mary, then, for my part,...

---

[180] Ibid.

[g]iven the conflict of duty, I can see no other way of dealing with it than by choosing the lesser of the two evils and so finding the least detrimental alternative...

Mary may have a right to life, but she has little right to be alive. She is alive because and only because, to put it bluntly, but none the less accurately, she sucks the lifeblood of Jodie and she sucks the lifeblood out of Jodie. She will survive only so long as Jodie survives. Jodie will not survive long because constitutionally she will not be able to cope. Mary's parasitic living will be the cause of Jodie's ceasing to live. If Jodie could speak, she would surely protest, 'Stop it, Mary, you're killing me.' Mary would have no answer to that. Into my scales of fairness and justice between the children goes the fact that nobody but the doctors can help Jodie. Mary is beyond help.

Hence I am in no doubt at all that the scales come down heavily in Jodie's favour. The best interests of the twins is to give the chance of life to the child whose actual bodily condition is capable of accepting the chance to her advantage even if that has to be at the cost of the sacrifice of the life which is so unnaturally supported. I am wholly satisfied that the least detrimental choice, balancing the interests of Mary against Jodie and Jodie against Mary, is to permit the operation to be performed.

Criminal Law

The test I have to set myself is that established by [R v Woollin]. I have to ask myself whether I am satisfied that the doctors recognise that death or serious harm will be virtually certain, barring some unforeseen intervention, to result from carrying out this operation. If so, the doctors intend to kill or to do that serious harm even though they may not have any desire to achieve that result. It is common ground that they appreciate that death to Mary would result from the severance of the common aorta. Unpalatable though it may be...to stigmatise the doctors with 'murderous intent', that is what in law they will have if they perform the operation and Mary dies as a result...

[T]he proposed operation would not in any event offend the sanctity of life principle...The reality here—harsh as it is to state it, and unnatural as it is that it should be happening—is that Mary is killing Jodie....Mary uses Jodie's heart and lungs to receive and use Jodie's oxygenated blood. This will cause Jodie's heart to fail and cause Jodie's death as surely as a slow drip of poison. How can it be just that Jodie should be required to tolerate that state of affairs?...I can see no difference in essence between...resort to legitimate self-defence and the doctors coming to Jodie's defence and removing the threat of fatal harm to her presented by Mary's draining her lifeblood. The availability of such a plea of quasi-self-defence, modified to meet the quite exceptional circumstances nature has inflicted on the twins, makes intervention by the doctors lawful...

Lest it be thought that this decision could become authority for wider propositions, such as that a doctor, once he has determined that a patient cannot survive, can kill the patient, it is important to restate the unique circumstances for which this case is authority. They are that it must be impossible to preserve the life of X without bringing about the death of Y, that Y by his or her very continued existence will inevitably bring about the death of X within a short period of time, and that X is capable of living an independent life but Y is incapable under any circumstances, including all forms of medical intervention, of viable independent existence.

Brooke LJ

[T]he doctrine of double effect can have no possible application in this case, as the judge rightly observed, because by no stretch of the imagination could it be said that the surgeons would be acting in good faith in Mary's best interests when they prepared an operation which would benefit Jodie but kill Mary...It follows from this analysis that the proposed operation would involve the murder of Mary unless some way can be found of determining that what was being proposed would not be unlawful...

Mary is, sadly, self-designated for a very early death. Nobody can extend her life beyond a very short span. Because her heart, brain and lungs are for all practical purposes useless, nobody would have even tried to extend her life artificially if she had not, fortuitously, been deriving oxygenated blood from her sister's bloodstream...

There are sound reasons for holding that the existence of an emergency in the normal sense of the word is not an essential prerequisite for the application of the doctrine of necessity. The principle is one of necessity, not emergency...There are also sound reasons for holding that the threat which constitutes the harm to be avoided does not have to be equated with 'unjust aggression'...

According to Sir James Stephen there are three necessary requirements for the application of the doctrine of necessity: (i) the act is needed to avoid inevitable and irreparable evil; (ii) no more should be done than is reasonably necessary for the purpose to be achieved; (iii) the evil inflicted must not be disproportionate to the evil avoided. Given that the principles of modern family law point irresistibly to the conclusion that the interests of Jodie must be preferred to the conflicting interests of Mary, I consider that all three of these requirements are satisfied in this case.

Finally, the doctrine of the sanctity of life respects the integrity of the human body. The proposed operation would give these children's bodies the integrity which nature denied them.

Robert Walker LJ

In truth there is no helpful analogy or parallel to the situation which the court has to consider in this case. It is unprecedented and paradoxical in that in law each twin has the right to life, but Mary's dependence on Jodie is severely detrimental to Jodie, and is expected to lead to the death of both twins within a few months. Each twin's right to life includes the right to physical integrity, that is the right to a whole body over which the individual will, on reaching an age of understanding, have autonomy and the right to self-determination...

The surgery would plainly be in Jodie's best interests, and in my judgment it would be in the best interests of Mary also, since for the twins to remain alive and conjoined in the way they are would be to deprive them of the bodily integrity and human dignity which is the right of each of them...

In this case the purpose of the operation would be to separate the twins and so give Jodie a reasonably good prospect of a long and reasonably normal life. Mary's death would not be the purpose of the operation, although it would be its inevitable consequence. The operation would give her, even in death, bodily integrity as a human being. She would die, not because she was intentionally killed, but because her own body cannot sustain her life...The proposed operation would not be unlawful. It would involve the positive act of invasive surgery and Mary's death would be foreseen as an inevitable consequence of an operation which is intended, and is necessary, to save Jodie's life. But Mary's death would not be the purpose or intention of the surgery, and she would die because tragically her body, on its own, is not and never has been viable.

In deciding whether the separation operation should take place despite the parents' objections, the test the court had to apply was, of course, the welfare principle: that is, the child's best interests had to be the court's paramount consideration. Here, however, there were two children whose best interests could not be reconciled. The operation was clearly in Jodie's best interests, because it was the only way in which she could survive. But—according to

Ward and Brooke LJJ—it was equally clearly *not* in Mary's best interests, because it would kill her. Robert Walker LJ tried to argue that the operation would in fact be in Mary's best interests as well, because it would restore her bodily integrity and allow her to die with the dignity of a separated body.

What should the court do when faced with two children whose interests are diametrically opposed? Ward and Brooke LJJ agreed that Jodie's interests should take priority because Mary was 'destined for death'. But while they believed that the operation would be consistent with family law principles, the problem that it might nevertheless be murder remained. Ward LJ's solution was to say that Mary was effectively killing Jodie, by 'draining her life-blood', and that the operation could be justified as quasi self-defence. Brooke LJ, on the other hand, attempted to invoke the defence of necessity: here, he said the doctors were entitled to operate because it was the lesser of two evils. Robert Walker LJ appeared to justify the operation through the doctrine of double effect: Mary's death is a foreseen but unintended consequence of saving Jodie's life.

Following the Court of Appeal's judgment, an appeal to the House of Lords was anticipated, and seven Law Lords (as opposed to the normal five) were convened to hear the appeal. The parents had, however, had enough, and decided to accept the Court of Appeal's decision. The operation went ahead, leading to Mary's death and Jodie's survival. Jodie—whose real name is Gracie Attard—appeared not to need any further surgery, and returned to Gozo with her parents the following year.

(b) Commentary on Re A

Unsurprisingly *Re A* has generated considerable academic controversy. In the next extract John Harris rejects the Court of Appeal's reasoning and instead argues that the operation could be justified because Mary was not yet, and never would be a 'person', and death would therefore not deprive her of a life that she would be capable of valuing.

John Harris[181]

The idea that Mary was 'dying anyway' and could not long survive is I believe tenacious…Where the individual with short life expectancy has a life to lead and wants to lead it for whatever time is left,…it would seem inconceivable that they would be killed against their will by a decision of the courts. It is not then life expectancy *per se* that makes a difference; but perhaps the *sort of life* that is available may be relevant?

If we say that Mary is going to 'die anyway' we may not be concentrating on the *duration* of the life expectancy but on some other feature of that life expectancy. I believe that there is something about Mary's life expectancy that makes plausible the decision in *Re A*…It is that the life expectancy of Mary between the time when the operation would take place and her inevitable death, would not have been expectancy of what might be called 'biographical life', not the life of a person. Indeed neither Mary nor Jodie had started living biographical lives, neither were persons properly so called at the time of the operation. On this analysis, the life Mary would lose by the performance of the operation which would kill her, would not have been life from which she could benefit significantly, not life that could ethically be distinguished from her life *in utero*.

---

[181] 'Human Beings, Persons and Conjoined Twins: An Ethical Analysis of the Judgment in *Re A*' (2001) 9 Medical Law Review 221–36.

In the light of Harris's comments, it is interesting to contemplate whether the Court of Appeal would have made the same decision in a scenario with identical facts aside from the children's ages. Let us imagine that Jodie and Mary were in fact 9-year-old twins, with separate personalities, who had lived quite happily together, but whose health had suddenly deteriorated because their one heart could no longer support two bodies. In those circumstances, is it possible that the Court might have given more weight to the parents' refusal to sanction an act that would kill one of their daughters?

If instead the conjoined twins whose heart had started to fail had in fact been adults who expressed a clear wish not to be separated, it is unimaginable that the defence of necessity would have been invoked to sanction the killing of one twin in order that the other one should live.

Even in the case of newborn babies, Raanan Gillon argues that the parents' view that it would be wrong to kill one daughter in order to save the other's life was not 'eccentric' and should have been accorded greater respect.

Raanan Gillon[182]

> It seems to this writer morally far preferable for the court, having spelled out the moral dilemma, to have ruled that there was no legal obligation—and perhaps no legal justification—in this case for removing the normal responsibility and right of parents to make health care decisions for their children. The parents were neither incompetent nor negligent—the standard justifications for depriving parents of such authority—and their reasoning was not eccentric or *merely* religious, but was widely acceptable moral reasoning—as was the contrary moral reasoning justifying an operation. The court should thus have declined to deprive the parents of their normal responsibilities and rights in order to impose its own preferred resolution of the moral dilemma, and should have allowed the parents to refuse medical intervention—while still ruling as it did, that such separation would not have been unlawful had the parents consented.

The Court of Appeal's preference for separation—articulated most strongly in Robert Walker's suggestion that an intact, albeit dead, body might be in Mary's best interests—is questioned from a different perspective by Bratton and Chetwynd. Drawing on evidence that suggests that conjoined twins who live long enough to express an opinion do not necessarily want to be separated, they question the Court of Appeal's presumption that separation is always necessarily in conjoined twins' best interests.

M Q Bratton and S B Chetwynd[183]

> The ethical and legal thinking that treats conjoined twins as if they were physically separate entities who have unfortunately become entangled and need to have their separate existence restored, seems to have things the wrong way round. Conjoined twins are not separate and never have been. If we separate them, we should at the very least recognise that we are

---

[182] 'Imposed Separation of Conjoined Twins—Moral Hubris by the English Courts?' (2001) 27 Journal of Medical Ethics 3–4.

[183] 'One into Two Will Not Go: Conceptualising Conjoined Twins' (2004) 30 Journal of Medical Ethics 279–85.

creating two new separate entities from two who were one, and that in doing so we are removing from each of them part of themselves. It may, of course, be a decision that we need to make for the benefit of both twins, but we should be wary of assuming that a physically separate existence is automatically in their best interests. If we are more comfortable faced by singletons, if they conform better to the hidden assumptions of our ethical, legal, and medical notions of what is normal and acceptable, that does not mean these are good enough reasons to change conjoined twins to fit. If medical decisions made on behalf of conjoined twins should be made in their best interests, then we had better be sure that they are, and that they are not made just because they make things easier for us to deal with.

Finally, Barbara Hewson draws attention to Ward LJ's comment that it would have been equally legitimate for the doctors to comply with the parents' wishes and let both children die. This comment may have been prompted by media interviews with paediatric surgeons from Great Ormond Street Hospital in London, who said that if the twins had been born there, the medical staff would have respected the parents' wishes. Hewson argues that Ward LJ's apparent willingness to condone an entirely different course of action undermines resort to the doctrine of necessity, since logically something cannot be both necessary and optional.

Barbara Hewson[184]

The most surprising aspect of [his] judgment is Ward LJ's assumption that it would have been appropriate for the hospital to do nothing. Thus the whole case turned on a contingency: the fact that the twins happened to be in Manchester, rather than London. On any view, this is arbitrary, and cannot but undermine the application of a doctrine of necessity. By definition, necessity cannot properly apply to a course of action which is entirely optional and which only comes into play if one happens to live in town A rather than in town B. Another striking aspect of Ward LJ's judgment is his use of pejorative langauge, both about Mary and her parents. Initially, he cites a consultant's evidence that 'Mary does very little and her twin does all the work'. Subliminally, this description creates an impression of unworthiness. Mary is also described as growing normally, while Jodie remained thinner. She was thought to be 'growing at Jodie's expense'. Ward LJ seizes on these medical metaphors: 'She lives on borrowed time, all of which is borrowed from Jodie. It is a debt she can never repay.' This makes Mary seem positively culpable, in terms of conventional legal morality. By the end, in a logical leap, he portrays Mary as a killer: 'she sucks the lifeblood out of Jodie'.... Mary emerges from this forensic denunciation as akin to Dracula: not only monstrous, but also evil. Buoyed up by his disturbing metaphors, Ward LJ readily concludes that Mary 'has little right to be alive'...

Anatomically, Ward LJ's description was inaccurate: Mary was not sucking anything from Jodie. Rather the reverse: Jodie's heart was responsible for circulating blood around both of them. This was not Mary's fault.

(b) ADULTS

In Chapter 5 we saw that the Mental Capacity Act (MCA) 2005 has confirmed the common law position that, when an adult patient lacks capacity, doctors can give her treatment that is in her best interests. Best interests is not confined to the patient's objective clinical interests,

---

[184] 'Killing Off Mary: Was the Court of Appeal Right?' (2001) 9 Medical Law Review 281–98.

but encompasses social and welfare interests, and a subjective assessment of what treatment accords with the patient's own values, beliefs, and preferences.[185]

Usually, of course, it will obviously be in the incompetent patient's best interests to receive life-prolonging medical treatment. But our ability to sustain life artificially means that patients who are permanently unconscious or insensate may now be able to 'live' for many years. Thus medical progress has presented us with a new dilemma. Are doctors *always* under a duty to sustain life for as long as possible, or could there ever be circumstances in which prolonging life ceases to be in a patient's best interests? Although decided before the MCA came into force, the critical case remains *Airedale NHS Trust v Bland*.

(1) *Airedale NHS Trust v Bland*[186]

(a) *The facts*

Tony Bland, then aged 17, was very seriously injured in the disaster which occurred at the Hillsborough football ground on 15 April 1989. The supply of oxygen to his brain was interrupted, causing catastrophic and irreversible damage to his higher brain. For the next three-and-a-half years, Tony Bland was in a permanent (then known as a persistent) vegetative state (PVS). Medical opinion was unanimous in this diagnosis and it was agreed that there was no hope of any improvement. Given that when he set out for the FA Cup Semi-Final at Hillsborough, Tony Bland was a healthy teenager, it is not surprising that he had not expressed a view about how he would want to be treated if he was in a PVS. His father was nevertheless convinced that his son would not 'want to be left like that'.

With the agreement of Tony Bland's family and the support of independent physicians, the trust responsible for the hospital where he was being treated sought declarations that they might (i) lawfully discontinue all life-sustaining treatment and medical support measures designed to keep him alive, including the termination of ventilation, nutrition, and hydration by artificial means; and (ii) lawfully discontinue and thereafter withhold medical treatment except for treatment which would enable him to die peacefully with the greatest dignity and the least pain, suffering, and distress. The trial judge granted the declarations sought, and his decision was upheld by the Court of Appeal. The Official Solicitor then appealed to the House of Lords.

(b) *The legal and ethical questions raised by Bland*

The *Bland* case raised a number of novel and extremely complex legal and ethical questions. First, as we saw earlier, a doctor who breaches his duty to provide life-prolonging treatment to a patient may be guilty of murder. Since the doctors were proposing to withhold artificial nutrition and hydration from Tony Bland, knowing that this would lead to his death, might they satisfy both the *actus reus* and *mens rea* for murder?

Secondly, even if we allow that doctors are sometimes entitled to withdraw futile medical treatment from patients, is artificial hydration and nutrition 'medical treatment', or is it more accurately described as basic care, which, by definition, cannot be futile? Thirdly, doctors must treat incompetent patients in their best interests, but since the result of the proposed course of action would be Tony Bland's death, could death be said to be in his best interests? Would withdrawing Tony Bland's feeding tube be tantamount to saying that his life has ceased to have any value, and is this incompatible with respect for the sanctity of human life?

---

[185] Mental Capacity Act 2005, section 4.   [186] [1993] AC 789 HL.

(c) The decision

The House of Lords unanimously rejected the Official Solicitor's appeal, and confirmed that Airedale NHS Trust was entitled to the declarations sought. Although there are some important differences between the judgments (Lord Mustill for example, was especially critical of the law which he was forced to apply), the points of agreement can be summarized as follows:

- First, the Lords were unanimous that the principle of the sanctity of life, while important, was not absolute.

- Secondly, artificial nutrition and hydration was agreed to be medical treatment and not basic care.

- Thirdly, the Lords—with some notable reservations—accepted that withdrawing artificial nutrition and hydration was an omission rather than an action.

- Fourthly, prolonging Tony Bland's life had ceased to be in his best interests.

- Fifthly, since treatment was no longer in his best interests, the doctor is no longer under a duty to prolong his life, and treatment withdrawal could not constitute the *actus reus* of murder. Indeed, Lord Browne-Wilkinson and Lord Lowry went further and suggested that if continued treatment was not in Tony Bland's best interests, the doctor might actually be under a duty to cease treatment.

Airedale NHS Trust v Bland[187]

Lord Keith

In the case of a permanently insensate being, who if continuing to live would never experience the slightest actual discomfort, it is difficult, if not impossible, to make any relevant comparison between continued existence and the absence of it. It is, however, perhaps permissible to say that to an individual with no cognitive capacity whatever, and no prospect of ever recovering any such capacity in this world, it must be a matter of complete indifference whether he lives or dies... Given that existence in the persistent vegetative state is not a benefit to the patient, it remains to consider whether the principle of the sanctity of life, which it is the concern of the state, and the judiciary as one of the arms of the state, to maintain, requires this House to hold that the judgment of the Court of Appeal was incorrect. In my opinion it does not. The principle is not an absolute one... In my judgment it does no violence to the principle to hold that it is lawful to cease to give medical treatment and care to a PVS patient who has been in that state for over three years, considering that to do so involves invasive manipulation of the patient's body to which he has not consented and which confers no benefit upon him.

Lord Goff

I start with the simple fact that, in law, Anthony is still alive. It is true that his condition is such that it can be described as a living death; but he is nevertheless still alive...

It is on this basis that I turn to the applicable principles of law. Here, the fundamental principle is the principle of the sanctity of human life—a principle long recognised not only in our own society but also in most, if not all, civilised societies throughout the modern world... But this principle, fundamental though it is, is not absolute....

---

[187] [1993] AC 789 HL.

I must however stress, at this point, that the law draws a crucial distinction between cases in which a doctor decides not to provide, or to continue to provide, for his patient treatment or care which could or might prolong his life, and those in which he decides, for example by administering a lethal drug, actively to bring his patient's life to an end. As I have already indicated, the former may be lawful... But it is not lawful for a doctor to administer a drug to his patient to bring about his death, even though that course is prompted by a humanitarian desire to end his suffering, however great that suffering may be... So to act is to cross the Rubicon which runs between on the one hand the care of the living patient and on the other hand euthanasia—actively causing his death to avoid or to end his suffering. Euthanasia is not lawful at common law. It is of course well known that there are many responsible members of our society who believe that euthanasia should be made lawful; but that result could, I believe, only be achieved by legislation which expresses the democratic will that so fundamental a change should be made in our law, and can, if enacted, ensure that such legalised killing can only be carried out subject to appropriate supervision and control. It is true that the drawing of this distinction may lead to a charge of hypocrisy; because it can be asked why, if the doctor, by discontinuing treatment, is entitled in consequence to let his patient die, it should not be lawful to put him out of his misery straight away, in a more humane manner, by a lethal injection, rather than let him linger on in pain until he dies. But the law does not feel able to authorise euthanasia, even in circumstances such as these; for once euthanasia is recognised as lawful in these circumstances, it is difficult to see any logical basis for excluding it in others...

I agree that the doctor's conduct in discontinuing life support can properly be categorised as an omission. It is true that it may be difficult to describe what the doctor actually does as an omission, for example where he takes some positive step to bring the life support to an end. But discontinuation of life support is, for present purposes, no different from not initiating life support in the first place. In each case, the doctor is simply allowing his patient to die in the sense that he is desisting from taking a step which might, in certain circumstances, prevent his patient from dying as a result of his pre-existing condition; and as a matter of general principle an omission such as this will not be unlawful unless it constitutes a breach of duty to the patient. I also agree that the doctor's conduct is to be differentiated from that of, for example, an interloper who maliciously switches off a life support machine because, although the interloper may perform exactly the same act as the doctor who discontinues life support, his doing so constitutes interference with the life-prolonging treatment then being administered by the doctor. Accordingly, whereas the doctor, in discontinuing life support, is simply allowing his patient to die of his pre-existing condition, the interloper is actively intervening to stop the doctor from prolonging the patient's life, and such conduct cannot possibly be categorised as an omission...

[F]or my part I cannot see that medical treatment is appropriate or requisite simply to prolong a patient's life, when such treatment has no therapeutic purpose of any kind, as where it is futile because the patient is unconscious and there is no prospect of any improvement in his condition. It is reasonable also that account should be taken of the invasiveness of the treatment and of the indignity to which, as the present case shows, a person has to be subjected if his life is prolonged by artificial means, which must cause considerable distress to his family—a distress which reflects not only their own feelings but their perception of the situation of their relative who is being kept alive. But in the end, in a case such as the present, it is the futility of the treatment which justifies its termination.

Lord Browne-Wilkinson

Where a case raises wholly new moral and social issues, in my judgment it is not for the judges to seek to develop new, all embracing, principles of law in a way which reflects the individual judges' moral stance when society as a whole is substantially divided on the relevant moral issues. Moreover, it is not legitimate for a judge in reaching a view as to what is for the benefit of the one individual whose life is in issue to take into account the wider practical issues as to allocation of limited financial resources or the impact on third parties of altering the time at which death occurs...

For these reasons, it seems to me imperative that the moral, social and legal issues raised by this case should be considered by Parliament. The judges' function in this area of the law should be to apply the principles which society, through the democratic process, adopts, not to impose their standards on society. If Parliament fails to act, then judge-made law will of necessity through a gradual and uncertain process provide a legal answer to each new question as it arises. But in my judgment that is not the best way to proceed...

Murder consists of causing the death of another with intent so to do. What is proposed in the present case is to adopt a course with the intention of bringing about Anthony Bland's death. As to the element of intention or mens rea, in my judgment there can be no real doubt that it is present in this case: the whole purpose of stopping artificial feeding is to bring about the death of Anthony Bland.

As to the guilty act, or actus reus, the criminal law draws a distinction between the commission of a positive act which causes death and the omission to do an act which would have prevented death....Apart from the act of removing the nasogastric tube, the mere failure to continue to do what you have previously done is not, in any ordinary sense, to do anything positive: on the contrary it is by definition an omission to do what you have previously done. The positive act of removing the nasogastric tube presents more difficulty. It is undoubtedly a positive act, similar to switching off a ventilator in the case of a patient whose life is being sustained by artificial ventilation. But in my judgment in neither case should the act be classified as positive, since to do so would be to introduce intolerably fine distinctions. If, instead of removing the nasogastric tube, it was left in place but no further nutrients were provided for the tube to convey to the patient's stomach, that would not be an act of commission. Again, as has been pointed out...if the switching off of a ventilator were to be classified as a positive act, exactly the same result can be achieved by installing a time-clock which requires to be reset every 12 hours: the failure to reset the machine could not be classified as a positive act. In my judgment, essentially what is being done is to omit to feed or to ventilate: the removal of the nasogastric tube or the switching off of a ventilator are merely incidents of that omission...

In my judgment, there is a further reason why the removal of the nasogastric tube in the present case could not be regarded as a positive act causing the death. The tube itself, without the food being supplied through it, does nothing. The removal of the tube by itself does not cause the death since by itself it did not sustain life...

Finally, the conclusion I have reached will appear to some to be almost irrational. How can it be lawful to allow a patient to die slowly, though painlessly, over a period of weeks from lack of food but unlawful to produce his immediate death by a lethal injection, thereby saving his family from yet another ordeal to add to the tragedy that has already struck them? I find it difficult to find a moral answer to that question. But it is undoubtedly the law.

Lord Mustill

The conclusion that the declarations can be upheld depends crucially on a distinction drawn by the criminal law between acts and omissions...The acute unease which I feel about adopting this way through the legal and ethical maze is I believe due in an important part to the sensation that however much the terminologies may differ the ethical status of the two courses of action is for all relevant purposes indistinguishable. By dismissing this appeal I fear that your Lordships' House may only emphasise the distortions of a legal structure which is already both morally and intellectually misshapen. Still, the law is there and we must take it as it stands...

The whole matter cries out for exploration in depth by Parliament and then for the establishment by legislation not only of a new set of ethically and intellectually consistent rules, distinct from the general criminal law, but also of a sound procedural framework within which the rules can be applied to individual cases. The rapid advance of medical technology makes this an ever more urgent task, and I venture to hope that Parliament will soon take it in hand...

Unlike the conscious patient [Anthony Bland] does not know what is happening to his body, and cannot be affronted by it; he does not know of his family's continuing sorrow. By ending his life the doctors will not relieve him of a burden become intolerable, for others carry the burden and he has none. What other considerations could make it better for him to die now rather than later? None that we can measure, for of death we know nothing. The distressing truth which must not be shirked is that the proposed conduct is not in the best interests of Anthony Bland, for he has no best interests of any kind...

Thus, although the termination of his life is not in the best interests of Anthony Bland, his best interests in being kept alive have also disappeared, taking with them the justification for the non-consensual regime and the co-relative duty to keep it in being...Since there is no longer a duty to provide nourishment and hydration a failure to do so cannot be a criminal offence...

I must recognise at once that this chain of reasoning makes an unpromising start by transferring the morally and intellectually dubious distinction between acts and omissions into a context where the ethical foundations of the law are already open to question. The opportunity for anomaly and excessively fine distinctions, often depending more on the way in which the problem happens to be stated than on any real distinguishing features, has been exposed by many commentators...All this being granted we are still forced to take the law as we find it and try to make it work.

(d) Commentary on the legal and ethical issues raised in Bland

(i) Best interests

The House of Lords had to base their decision upon how Tony Bland should be treated upon an assessment of his best interests. It could, however, be argued that the best interests test is not especially helpful when the patient has effectively ceased to have any interests at all.

Lord Mustill

The distressing truth which must not be shirked is that the proposed conduct is not in the best interests of Anthony Bland, for he has no best interests of any kind...Thus, although the termination of his life is not in the best interests of Anthony Bland, his best interests in being kept alive have also disappeared.

Treatment does not benefit a permanently insensate patient like Tony Bland, nor is it burdensome to him. If, from the patient's perspective, it is a matter of complete indifference whether treatment is continued or withdrawn, how could we base the decision to withdraw treatment upon his best interests?

One possibility is to argue that such individuals *do* retain an interest in the manner of their death, and in its impact upon their relatives. In the Court of Appeal judgment in *Bland*[188], for example, Hoffmann LJ was of the opinion that Tony Bland did have an interest in putting 'an end to the humiliation of his being and the distress of his family'.

Hoffman LJ

It is demeaning to the human spirit to say that, being unconscious, he can have no interest in his personal privacy and dignity, in how he lives or dies. Anthony Bland therefore has a recognisable interest in the manner of his life and death.

Regardless of whether we think the best interests test useful or not once a patient has irrevocably lost the capacity for consciousness, a decision about whether to continue the treatment of a PVS patient who has not made his own wishes known cannot be made without imposing *our* judgement about whether a permanently insensate life is worth living. This inescapably involves making a quality-of-life judgement. It is, as Rebecca Dresser has observed:

conceptually impossible to keep the best interests evaluation completely focused on the individual patient. The only way to decide what is best for a patient is by reference to broader definitions of what is good and bad for human beings.[189]

Coming to different conclusions, in the next extracts Jonathan Glover and Sanford H Kadish ask whether a permanently unconscious life is 'worth living'.

Jonathan Glover[190]

I have no way of refuting someone who holds that being alive, even though unconscious, is intrinsically valuable. But it is a view that will seem unattractive to those of us who, in our own case, see a life of permanent coma as in no way preferable to death. From the subjective point of view, there is nothing to choose between the two...Those of us who think that the direct objections to killing have to do with death considered from the standpoint of the person killed will find it natural to regard life as being of value only as a necessary condition of consciousness. For permanently comatose existence is subjectively indistinguishable from death, and unlikely often to be thought intrinsically preferable to it by people thinking of their own future.

Sanford H Kadish[191]

A fundamental objection [to the best interests standard] arises from what is implicit in the standard...that in certain circumstances the quality of a person's life may be so low that it is not worth living. This stands in stark opposition to the tradition that human life is always

---

[188] Ibid 829.

[189] Rebecca Dresser, 'Missing Persons: Legal Perceptions of Incompetent Patients' (1994) 46 Rutgers Law Review 609.

[190] *Causing Death and Saving Lives* (Penguin: Harmondsworth, 1977).

[191] 'Letting Patients Die: Legal and Moral Reflections' (1992) 80 California Law Review 857.

valuable. It is one thing for courts to defer to the patient's choice to die. This has proved difficult enough for some courts…, but at least the decision requires no judgment by the court or some other agent that the patient's life is no longer worth living—only that this is the choice of the patient whose life it is. It is quite different when the best-interests standard is applied independently of the patient's inferred preferences, because this requires the deciding authority itself—the court or some other agent—to make the substantive judgment of whether what is left of the patient's life is worth the candle.

Nevertheless, in *Bland*, it seems clear that the House of Lords had decided that continued life in a PVS was not in Tony Bland's best interests, and that it would be preferable to stop treating him. Having decided this, it is, as Lord Browne-Wilkinson pointed out in *Bland*, difficult to see why the law insists that such patients must die slowly from starvation, rather than permitting doctors to administer a single lethal injection.

(ii) Acts and omissions

A majority of the judges in the House of Lords explicitly accepted that the doctors' intention in withdrawing artificial nutrition and hydration was to 'bring about the death of Anthony Bland'.[192] Had withdrawing the nasogastric tube been an act rather than an omission, this would have been a straightforward case of murder. Given that the doctors' intention was to cause death, it was of critical importance that withdrawing the tube was characterized as an omission.

Despite the importance of their reliance on the acts/omissions distinction, some members of the House of Lords were less than enthusiastic about it. Lord Mustill, for example, described it as 'intellectually and morally dubious'.

(iii) Is artificial nutrition and hydration medical treatment?

The Lords' categorization of artificial nutrition and hydration (ANH) as medical treatment, as opposed to basic care, is also controversial. In the next extract, John Keown points out that the reason for categorizing ANH as treatment was so that it could legitimately be withdrawn.

John Keown[193]

Why was tube-feeding not basic care, which the hospital and its medical and nursing staff were under a duty to provide? The Law Lords held that tube-feeding was part of a regime of 'medical treatment and care'. The insertion of a gastrostomy tube into the stomach requires a minor operation, which is clearly a medical procedure. But it is not at all clear that the insertion of a nasogastric tube is medical intervention. And, even if it were, the intervention had already been carried out in Tony Bland's case. The question in such a case is why the pouring of food down the tube constitutes medical treatment. What is it supposed to be treating?…

Their Lordships placed great weight on the fact that the medical profession regards tube-feeding as medical treatment. But whether an intervention is medical is not a matter to be determined by medical opinion, nor by the mere fact that it is an intervention typically performed by doctors. A doctor does many things in the course of his practice, such as reassuring patients or fitting catheters, which are not distinctively medical in nature. And, if

---

[192] *Per* Lord Browne-Wilkinson; see also Lord Lowry: 'the intention to bring about the patient's death is there'; and Lord Mustill: 'the proposed conduct has the aim…of terminating the life of Anthony Bland'.

[193] 'Restoring Moral and Intellectual Shape to the Law after Bland' (1997) 113 Law Quarterly Review 482–503.

it is opinion that is crucial, the answer one gets may well depend on whom one asks. Tube-feeding may be regarded as medical treatment by many doctors, but many nurses regard it as ordinary care.... Dr Keith Andrews, ... a leading authority on pvs, recently wrote 'it is ironic that the only reason that tube feeding has been identified as "treatment" has been so that it can be withdrawn'.

Even if ANH was properly described as medical treatment, could it be said to be either 'futile' or 'burdensome'?

Sheila McLean[194]

The purpose of ANH arguably is to keep the patient alive. It is not directly related in PVS cases, or cases where the person is in the process of dying, to effecting a cure. However, irrespective of the quality or length of the life ANH can sustain, its provision is certainly not futile as it achieves precisely what it is intended to: that is, it keeps the patient alive. Equally, if it is not normally regarded as being unduly burdensome in other cases, it must be asked why it should be so regarded for the patient at the end of life.

(2) Developments since *Bland*

Applying the *Bland* judgment in subsequent cases, the courts have had to confront a number of important questions. First, is *Bland* compatible with the Human Rights Act 1998? Could the withdrawal of artificial nutrition and hydration violate a patient's right to life (Article 2), or, because the patient will die from starvation, could it amount to inhuman and degrading treatment (prohibited by Article 3)? In one of the first cases to be brought after the Human Rights Act came into force, *NHS Trust A v M, NHS Trust B v H*, a court determined that withdrawing artificial nutrition and hydration from a PVS patient was compatible with Convention rights.

NHS Trust A v M, NHS Trust B v H[195]

Dame Elizabeth Butler-Sloss, P

Although the intention in withdrawing artificial nutrition and hydration in PVS cases is to hasten death, in my judgment the phrase 'deprivation of life' must import a deliberate act, as opposed to an omission, by someone acting on behalf of the state, which results in death. A responsible decision by a medical team not to provide treatment at the initial stage could not amount to intentional deprivation of life by the state. Such a decision based on clinical judgment is an omission to act. The death of the patient is the result of the illness or injury from which he suffered and that cannot be described as a deprivation...I cannot see the difference between that situation and a decision to discontinue treatment which is no longer in the best interests of the patient..., even though that discontinuance will have the effect of shortening the life of the patient...

---

[194] 'From Bland to Burke: The Law and Politics of Assisted Nutrition and Hydration' in Sheila AM Mclean (ed.) *First Do No Harm* (Ashgate: Dartmouth, 2006) 431–46.
[195] [2001] Fam 348 Fam Div.

> Article 2 therefore imposes a positive obligation to give life-sustaining treatment in circumstances where, according to responsible medical opinion, such treatment is in the best interests of the patient but does not impose an absolute obligation to treat if such treatment would be futile. This approach is entirely in accord with the principles laid down in *Airedale NHS Trust v Bland*... In a case where a responsible clinical decision is made to withhold treatment, on the grounds that it is not in the patient's best interests, and that clinical decision is made in accordance with a respectable body of medical opinion, the state's positive obligation under article 2 is, in my view, discharged.
>
> I am, moreover, satisfied that article 3 requires the victim to be aware of the inhuman and degrading treatment which he or she is experiencing or at least to be in a state of physical or mental suffering. An insensate patient suffering from permanent vegetative state has no feelings and no comprehension of the treatment accorded to him or her. Article 3 does not in my judgment apply to these two cases.

Given that the sanctity of life had been a consideration in cases decided before the incorporation of the ECHR, Dame Elizabeth Butler-Sloss's conclusion that 'a reasonable clinical decision... to withhold treatment' could not violate Article 2 is not surprising. Her judgment that Article 3 can only be violated if the victim is aware of the inhuman and degrading treatment is more controversial. Many would argue that it *is* possible to treat permanently insensate patients in an inhuman and degrading way, perhaps by failing to provide them with clothing and hygiene measures. Despite the fact that they would know nothing about it, we would not allow PVS patients' bodies to be used by medical students learning how to conduct internal examinations; again, regardless of their lack of awareness, might this be described as 'inhuman or degrading' treatment?

Secondly, should *Bland* be confined to PVS cases, or might there be patients who are not in a PVS but whose condition nevertheless justifies the withdrawal of life-prolonging treatment? Following the *Bland* case, the House of Lords' Select Committee on Medical Ethics recommended that the permanent vegetative state should be defined and a code of practice developed. A working group of the Royal College of Physicians (RCP) produced a set of guidelines, *The Permanent Vegetative State*, in April 1996.

The status of these guidelines has been tested in subsequent cases in which the patient does not quite fit the standard definition. In *Re D*, for example, the courts authorized the withdrawal of artificial nutrition and hydration from a patient whose condition was judged to be functionally indistinguishable from PVS, albeit that one paragraph of the RCP's guidelines was not fulfilled.

Re D (Adult: Medical Treatment)[196]

Sir Stephen Brown P

> It seems to me that, for all practical purposes... that this patient is in fact in what would be, in Professor Jennet's terms, a permanent vegetative state. It is merely—and it is not lightly stated by me—the fact that one of the paragraphs [in the Royal College's guidelines] is not actually fulfilled. However, it must be recalled that every single witness [has] made it clear that this patient has no awareness whatsoever. She is, in the words of Lord Goff in *Bland*, suffering what he described as 'a living death'. I do not, therefore, believe that, if a declaration

[196] [1998] 1 FLR 411 Fam Div. See Also *Re H* [1998] 2 FLR 36 Fam Div.

> were to be granted in this case, it would be extending the range of cases in which a declara-
> tion might properly be considered....The court recognises that no declaration to permit or to
> sanction the taking of so extreme a step could possibly be granted where there was any real
> possibility of meaningful life continuing to exist.
>
> In this case, all the evidence establishes, to my satisfaction, that there is no evidence of
> any meaningful life whatsoever. This sad, tragic patient is suffering what is rightly termed
> 'a living death'. Accordingly, I am driven to the conclusion...that it is not in this patient's
> best interests artificially to keep her body alive and that the declaration sought should be
> granted.

The courts have also had to consider whether a complete and permanent lack of awareness
is a precondition, or whether it might be lawful to withhold life-prolonging treatment from
patients who have some level of awareness. In *Re R (Adult: Medical Treatment)*, R was not
in a permanent vegetative state, but he had only minimal awareness. R's psychiatrist was
concerned that another admission to hospital would not be in R's best interests, and signed a
'Do Not Resuscitate' order. The NHS trust sought a declaration that it was lawful to withhold
CPR and antibiotics in the event of R developing a potentially life-threatening condition.

Re R (Adult: Medical Treatment)[197]

Sir Stephen Brown P

The extensive medical evidence in this case is unanimous in concluding that it would not be
in the best interests of R to subject him to cardio-pulmonary resuscitation in the event of his
suffering a cardiac arrest...I agree that this declaration should be made.

The withholding in the future of the administration of antibiotics in the event of the patient
developing a potentially life-threatening infection which would otherwise call for the administration of antibiotics is a decision which can only be taken at the time by the patient's responsible medical practitioners in the light of the prevailing circumstances.

There are, of course, some critical differences between *withholding* life-prolonging treatment and *withdrawing* it, and it is not clear that someone in R's situation could also lawfully
be deprived of artificial nutrition and hydration. Do Not Resuscitate orders will only result
in the patient's death *if* she has suffered a life-threatening event, so it could more plausibly be
argued that the cause of death is the respiratory or cardiac arrest, as opposed to the decision
to withhold treatment. Moreover, because resuscitation is invasive and traumatic—broken
ribs, for example, are not uncommon—it would also be more straightforward to argue that
the decision to withhold CPR has been taken in the patient's best interests.

At first sight, *An NHS Trust v J* looked like a case which would involve a fairly routine
application of the principles developed in *Bland*. J was a 53-year-old woman who had been in
a PVS for three years, and the patient's doctors and her family agreed that it would be appropriate to cease giving ANH. But instead of granting the order, Sir Mark Potter P was swayed
by a startling research paper, published around the time of the first hearing, suggesting
that an insomnia drug might be able to temporarily 'wake-up' PVS patients. J's family were
against this course of action, on the grounds that it would be distressing for her: they had

---

[197] [1996] 2 FLR 99 Fam Div.

always gained comfort from the thought that she had no insight into her condition. One of the leading experts in PVS, Dr Keith Andrews, suspected that the patients who appeared to have regained consciousness were not, in fact, in PVS. Nevertheless, he supported a brief trial of zolpidem—on the grounds that it could not do any harm—as did the Official Solicitor. Sir Mark Potter P was therefore persuaded that J should be given a short course of zolpidem.

An NHS Trust v J [198]

Sir Mark Potter P

I think I have already made it clear that, subject only to the recent emergence of published literature relating to zolpidem, I would unhesitatingly have granted the relief claimed. However, in the light of the evidence I have heard from Professor Andrews, I have come to the conclusion that I should accede to the submission of the Official Solicitor, whose duty is to represent the patient's interests, and the view of Professor Andrews on whom the Trust rely, that a short trial of three days should take place. I have hesitated in coming to that conclusion because it is Dr Andrews' expert opinion that the treatment is unlikely to have any beneficial effect. I also bear anxiously in mind the fears of the family. The last thing I would wish to do would be to take a decision which might, despite the best of medical intentions, revive the patient, not to her benefit, but so as to cause her suffering or anxiety. The position is however that, as the leading expert in this country, Professor Andrews, on the basis of what he has read and the enquiries he has made, considers that there is an outside chance worthy of trial, which is unlikely to involve any kind of suffering or upset should consciousness be restored. Thus, he does not regard the fears of the family to be well founded and he makes the point that, should any apparent distress be caused on the patient regaining consciousness, then of course the treatment can be stopped.

In those circumstances, it seems to me that the appropriate course is to sanction a short course of zolpidem in the near future with a view to a speedy return to this court for final disposal should the trial produce no positive or beneficial effect on J.

Zolpidem had no positive effect upon J's condition, and she simply fell asleep. The case returned to court, where Sir Mark Potter granted a declaration that it would be lawful to withdraw ANH.

Both the BMA[199] and the General Medical Council have issued guidance on the withholding and withdrawing of artificial nutrition and hydration (ANH).

General Medical Council[200]

81. Where death is imminent, in judging the benefits, burdens or risks, it usually would not be appropriate to start either artificial hydration or nutrition, although artificial hydration provided by the less invasive measures may be appropriate where it is considered that this would be likely to provide symptom relief.

---

[198] [2006] All ER (D) 73 (Dec).

[199] *Withholding and Withdrawing Life-prolonging Medical Treatment: Guidance for Decision making*, 3rd edn (GMC: 2007).

[200] *Withholding and Withdrawing Life-prolonging Treatments: Good Practice in Decision-making* (GMC: London, Aug 2002).

> Where death is imminent and artificial hydration and/or nutrition are already in use, it may be appropriate to withdraw them if it is considered that the burdens outweigh the possible benefits to the patient.
>
> Where death is not imminent, it usually will be appropriate to provide artificial nutrition or hydration. However, circumstances may arise where you judge that a patient's condition is so severe, and the prognosis so poor that providing artificial nutrition or hydration may cause suffering, or be too burdensome in relation to the possible benefits. In these circumstances, as well as consulting the health care team and those close to the patient, you must seek a second or expert opinion from a senior clinician (who might be from another discipline such as nursing) who has experience of the patient's condition and who is not already directly involved in the patient's care. This will ensure that, in a decision of such sensitivity, the patient's interests have been thoroughly considered, and will provide necessary reassurance to those close to the patient and to the wider public. . .
>
> 83. Where you are considering withdrawing artificial nutrition and hydration from a patient in a permanent vegetative state (PVS), or condition closely resembling PVS, the courts in England, Wales and Northern Ireland currently require that you approach them for a ruling. The courts in Scotland have not specified such a requirement, but you should seek legal advice on whether a court declaration may be necessary in an individual case.

This GMC guidance was challenged in *R (on the application of Burke) v The General Medical Council* by a patient who believed that to withdraw ANH, once he became incompetent, against his express wishes would breach his rights under the Human Rights Act 1998. At first instance, Munby J decided that the GMC's guidance was incompatible with Mr Burke's right under Article 3 not to be subjected to inhuman and degrading treatment, and his right under Article 8, not to have his physical and psychological integrity and dignity infringed.

Controversially, Munby J appeared to suggest that there might be times when a patient would have the *right* to demand that his doctors gave him treatment, even when this was contrary to their clinical judgment. It is probably unsurprising that his judgment was overturned by the Court of Appeal.

R (on the application of Burke) v The General Medical Council[201]

Lord Phillips

There are great dangers in a court grappling with issues such as those that Munby J has addressed when these are divorced from a factual context that requires their determination. The court should not be used as a general advice centre. The danger is that the court will enunciate propositions of principle without full appreciation of the implications that these will have in practice, throwing into confusion those who feel obliged to attempt to apply those principles in practice. This danger is particularly acute where the issues raised involve ethical questions that any court should be reluctant to address, unless driven to do so by the need to resolve a practical problem that requires the court's intervention. . . .

We have come to the clear view that this appeal must be allowed, and the declarations made by the judge set aside. It is our view that Mr Burke's fears are addressed by the law as it currently stands and that declaratory relief, particularly in so far as it declares parts of the

---

[201] [2005] EWCA Civ 1003.

Guidance unlawful, is both unnecessary for Mr Burke's protection and inappropriate as far as the Guidance itself is concerned...

The proposition that the patient has a paramount right to refuse treatment is amply demonstrated by the authorities cited by Munby J. The corollary does not, however, follow, at least as a general proposition. Autonomy and the right of self-determination do not entitle the patient to insist on receiving a particular medical treatment regardless of the nature of the treatment. Insofar as a doctor has a legal obligation to provide treatment this cannot be founded simply upon the fact that the patient demands it.

We have indicated that, where a competent patient indicates his or her wish to be kept alive by the provision of ANH any doctor who deliberately brings that patient's life to an end by discontinuing the supply of ANH will not merely be in breach of duty but guilty of murder. Where life depends upon the continued provision of ANH there can be no question of the supply of ANH not being clinically indicated unless a clinical decision has been taken that the life in question should come to an end. That is not a decision that can lawfully be taken in the case of a competent patient who expresses the wish to remain alive.

The Court of Appeal was concerned that it would be inappropriate to offer an opinion on the withdrawal of ANH in the abstract, divorced from the facts which may or may not justify such a decision. They also held that the patient's concerns were adequately addressed by the GMC's guidance, and that where a competent patient expresses his wish to receive ANH, a doctor who nevertheless withheld it might be guilty of murder.

While the patient's wishes were always part of the 'best interests' assessment—recall that Tony Bland's parents were asked whether he had ever given any indication of how he would want to be treated—the 'best interests' checklist in the Mental Capacity Act places doctors under a clear duty to take account of the patient's previous values and beliefs. This means that a patient's desire, perhaps as a result of their religious beliefs, to have life-prolonging measures continued at all costs, even when their doctors have decided that such treatment is futile, must be taken into account, although, unlike a valid and applicable advance *refusal* of treatment, it is not determinative. BMA guidance to doctors states that: 'If, for example, the patient is known to have held the view that there is intrinsic value in being alive, then life-prolonging treatment would, in virtually all cases, provide a net benefit for that particular individual.'[202]

This issue arose in a pre-MCA case, *An NHS Trust v A*.[203] Mr A's children had argued that discontinuing ventilation would be contrary to Mr A's beliefs as a practising Muslim. Waller LJ insisted that these beliefs, while 'highly material', did not foreclose the possibility that discontinuing ventilation could nevertheless be judged to be in Mr A's best interests.

An NHS Trust v A[204]

Waller LJ

I can say straightaway that when one examines the law, one finds obviously that the views, if one can interpret them, of what the patient might be and the views of the family are highly

---

[202] *Withholding and Withdrawing Life-prolonging Medical Treatment: Guidance for Decision Making*, 3rd edn (2007) para 40.2.
[203] [2005] EWCA Civ 1145.
[204] [2005] EWCA Civ 1145.

material factors. At the end of the day they are not however the governing factors when considering best interests....

It should be remembered in particular that the treating doctors had themselves had very much in mind the religious concerns of the family, and indeed all the concerns of the family. He was clearly right to consider what was certainly the key question first, as to whether there was in his view any chance of recovery of any quality of life so as to make the discomfort to which Mr A was being put justified. Once he had formed that conclusion—that it was not justified—it was obviously going to be difficult for the religious views and the views of the family to overcome the obvious point that, since any decision to put Mr A through further suffering would produce no benefit to Mr A, it would be difficult to see that it could be in Mr A's best interests.

Finally, it is worth mentioning that when the Mental Capacity Act 2005 was being debated in Parliament, there was concern that, by placing advance refusals of life-prolonging treatment on a statutory footing, it would introduce 'euthanasia by the back door'. This concern was probably misplaced because the MCA did not change the law relating to refusing life-prolonging treatment, and in fact introduced additional safeguards. Nevertheless, the government's response to this anxiety was a rather curious amendment to section 4 (which specifies the matters to be taken into account by the person judging whether treatment is in an incapacitated person's best interests). Section 4(5) states that:

Where the determination relates to life-sustaining treatment he must not, in considering whether the treatment is in the best interests of the person concerned, be motivated by a desire to bring about his death.

What does this mean? The use of the word 'desire' is strange, since it would be extremely difficult to conclusively determine what anyone actually 'desires'. However, the intention here is clear. Section 4(5) effectively means that although the decision to withhold or withdraw life-sustaining treatment can be in a person's best interests, ending the patient's life must not be the doctor's sole intention.

Of course, if there are circumstances in which it is in a patient's best interests to have their life brought to an end by non-treatment, the doctor may in fact have two goals in mind: ending suffering *by* ensuring that the patient dies. But the Act requires doctors to be able to separate out these two outcomes, and insists that the doctor must 'desire' only the former.

Mental Capacity Act Code of Practice para 5.31 and 5.33[205]

5.31 All reasonable steps which are in the person's best interests should be taken to prolong their life. There will be a limited number of cases where treatment is futile, overly burdensome to the patient or where there is no prospect of recovery. In circumstances such as these, it may be that an assessment of best interests leads to the conclusion that it would be in the best interests of the patient to withdraw or withhold life-sustaining treatment, even if this may result in the person's death. The decision-maker must make a decision based on the best interests of the person who lacks capacity. They must not be motivated by a

---

[205] (2007), available at <www.dca.gov.uk/>.

desire to bring about the person's death for whatever reason, even if this is from a sense of compassion....

5.33 Importantly, section 4(5) cannot be interpreted to mean that doctors are under an obligation to provide, or to continue to provide, life-sustaining treatment where that treatment is not in the best interests of the person, even where the person's death is foreseen. Doctors must apply the best interests' checklist and use their professional skills to decide whether life-sustaining treatment is in the person's best interests.

4 CONCLUSION

As we have seen in this chapter, end-of-life decision-making raises some extraordinarily difficult and ethically contentious questions. In relation to competent adult patients, the most important question is whether the law should move towards allowing doctors to help their patients to die, through the explicit legalization and regulation of euthanasia and/or assisted suicide. In relation to patients who lack capacity, the law is, as we have seen, heavily swayed by medical opinion about when it is appropriate to discontinue the treatment of profoundly incapacitated adults and children. In general, if doctors judge treatment to be futile, there is little chance of a court demanding that such treatment should nevertheless be given.

It is, in my view, interesting to contrast concern about the possible abuse of vulnerable patients if euthanasia were to be legalized, with the relative lack of interest in the much more common and *lawful* ways in which doctors are routinely involved in end-of-life decision-making. The safeguards in place to protect patients from the removal of life support are fairly minimal, and certainly much less restrictive than the conditions which would apply if euthanasia were legalized. As we have seen 'Do Not Attempt Resuscitation' orders can be written in patients' notes without any prior discussion with the patient. If a doctor is contemplating giving a patient steadily increasing doses of diamorphine, in the knowledge that this may shorten her life, there is no need for the patient's agreement. A competent adult patient can refuse minimally invasive but life-saving treatment, such as an insulin injection, for irrational reasons or for no reasons at all. When ANH or ventilation is withdrawn, the patient dies slowly if painlessly from dehydration, starvation, or suffocation. It could, in my view, plausibly be argued that the lawful ways in which doctors may shorten their patients lives are not only more common but also might be more open to abuse and likely to lead to more protracted deaths than assisted dying.

FURTHER READING

Assisted Dying for the Terminally Ill Committee, *Assisted Dying for the Terminally Ill Bill—First Report* (2005), available at <http://www.publications.parliament.uk/pa/ld/ldasdy.htm>.

Battin, Margaret Pabst, *Ending Life: Ethics and the Way We Die* (OUP: Oxford, 2005).

Battin, Margaret *et al.*, 'Legal Physician-assisted Dying in Oregon and the Netherlands: Evidence Concerning the Impact on Patients in 'Vulnerable' Groups' (2007) 33 Journal of Medical Ethics 591–7.

Brooks Gordon, Belinda *et al.* (eds), *Death Rites and Rights* (Hart: Oxford, 2007).

De Beaufort, Inez, 'The View from Before' (2007) 7 The American Journal of Bioethics 57–8.

Dworkin, Gerald, Frey RG and Bok, Sissela, *Euthanasia and Physician-Assisted Suicide: For and Against* (CUP: Cambridge, 1998).

Glover, Jonathan, *Causing Death and Saving Lives* (Penguin: Harmondsworth, 1977).

Huxtable, Richard, *Euthanasia, Ethics and the Law: From Conflict to Compromise* (Routledge: Cavendish, 2007).

Jackson, Emily, 'Whose Death is it Anyway? Euthanasia and the Medical Profession' (2004) 57 Current Legal Problems 415–42.

Keown, John, *Euthanasia, Ethics and Public Policy: An Argument against Legalisation* (CUP: Cambridge, 2002).

Magnusson, RS, 'Euthanasia: Above Ground, Below Ground' (2004) 30 Journal of Medical Ethics 441–6.

McCall Smith, Alexander, 'Euthanasia: The Strengths of the Middle Ground' (1999) 7 Medical Law Review 194–207.

Mclean, Sheila, *Assisted Dying: Reflections on the Need for Law Reform* (Routledge: Cavendish, 2007).

Otlowski, Margaret, *Voluntary Euthanasia and the Common Law* (OUP: Oxford 2000).

Tur, Richard, 'Legislative Technique and Human Rights: The Sad Case of Assisted Suicide' (2003) Criminal Law Review 3–12.

INDEX